ENCYCLOPEDIA
OF
Multicultural
PSYCHOLOGY

ENCYCLOPEDIA
OF
Multicultural
PSYCHOLOGY

Edited by
Yo Jackson
University of Kansas

CLARKSTON CENTER

A SAGE Reference Publication

SAGE Publications
Thousand Oaks ▪ London ▪ New Delhi

For information:

Sage Publications, Inc.
2455 Teller Road
Thousand Oaks, California 91320
E-mail: order@sagepub.com

Sage Publications Ltd.
1 Oliver's Yard
55 City Road
London EC1Y 1SP
United Kingdom

Sage Publications India Pvt. Ltd.
B-42, Panchsheel Enclave
Post Box 4109
New Delhi 110 017 India

Printed in the United States of America on acid-free paper

Library of Congress Cataloging-in-Publication Data

Encyclopedia of multicultural psychology / Yo Jackson, editor.
   p. cm.
Includes bibliographical references and index.
ISBN 1-4129-0948-1 (cloth)
  1. Ethnospychology—Encyclopedias. 2. Ethnic groups—Psychology—Encyclopedias.
3. Minorities—Psychology—Encyclopedias. I. Jackson, Yolanda Kaye. II. Title.
GN502.E63 2006
155.8′2—dc22

                        2006004938

06 07 08 09 10 10 9 8 7 6 5 4 3 2 1

Publisher:	Rolf Janke
Acquiring Editor:	Jim Brace-Thompson
Developmental Editor:	Yvette Pollastrini
Project Editor:	Sanford Robinson
Reference Systems Coordinator:	Leticia Gutierrez
Typesetter:	C&M Digitals (P) Ltd.
Proofreader:	Scott Oney
Indexer:	Molly Hall
Cover Designer:	Candice Harman

Contents

List of Entries

Reader's Guide

Multicultural psychology is a broad field covering a great multitude of topics. The list is designed to assist the reader in finding articles on related topics. Headwords are organized into nine main categories, including Conceptual Issues, Cultural Concerns, Ethnic Groups, Indigenous Concerns, Measurement, Professional Organizations, Psychopathology, Sociological Issues, and Treatment. Because many topics cannot be easily categorized into one area, some headwords are listed under more than one category.

CONCEPTUAL ISSUES

Acculturation
Acculturative Stress
African/Black Psychology
Africentric
Attribution
Biracial Identity
Blaming the Victim
Collectivism
Community Psychology
Context Communication
Coping Mechanisms
Critical Race Theory
Cross-Cultural Psychology
Cultural Barriers
Culture
Emic Versus Etic Distinction
Ethnic and Racial Identity
Ethnic Gloss
Ethnic Identity Development
Ethnic Minority Elderly Individuals
Ethnic Minority Youth
Ethnic Research
Ethnicity
Ethnocentric Monoculturalism
Ethnocentrism
Eugenics
External-Internal Control
Individualism

Intelligence Tests
Intergroup Relations
John Henryism
Language Proficiency
Marginality
Mental Health
Minority Status
Model Minority Myth
Models of Mental Health
Models of Second-Culture Acquisition
Multicultural Counseling
Multicultural Counseling Competencies
Multicultural Personality
Multiculturalism
Neuropsychology
Organizational Diversity
Race
Race Psychology
Racial Identity Development
Racial Identity Models
Religion
Self-Esteem
Social Justice/Action
Somatization
Spirituality
Teaching Racial Identity
Tokenism/Psychology of Tokenism
Translation Methods
Uncle Tom Syndrome

Culture-Bound Syndromes: Mal de Ojo
Culture-Bound Syndromes: Nervios
Culture-Bound Syndromes: Qigong
    Psychotic Reaction
Culture-Bound Syndromes: Shenjing Shuairuo
Culture-Bound Syndromes: Shin-byung
Culture-Bound Syndromes: Susto
Culture-Bound Syndromes: Taijin Kyofusho
Culture-Bound Syndromes: Zar
Familismo
Filial Piety
Indigenous Treatments and Healers
Indigenous Treatments: Coining
Indigenous Treatments: Cuento Therapy
Indigenous Treatments: Cupping
Indigenous Treatments: Curanderismo
Indigenous Treatments: Dichos
Indigenous Treatments: Moxibustion
Indigenous Treatments: Shamans
Indigenous Treatments: Sobadores
Machismo
Religious/Spiritual Beliefs: Espiritismo
Religious/Spiritual Beliefs: Fatalismo
Religious/Spiritual Beliefs: Marianismo
Religious/Spiritual Beliefs: Personalismo
Religious/Spiritual Beliefs: Santería

MEASUREMENT

Acculturation Measures
Acculturation Scales: Acculturation Rating Scale
    for Mexican Americans–II
Acculturation Scales: African American
    Acculturation Scale
Acculturation Scales: Asian American
    Multidimensional Acculturation Scale
Acculturation Scales: Bidimensional
    Acculturation Scale for Hispanics
Acculturation Scales: East Asian Acculturation
    Measure
Acculturation Scales: Short Acculturation
    Scale for Hispanics
Acculturation Scales: Suinn-Lew Asian Self-Identity
    Acculturation Scale
Center for Epidemiologic Studies Depression Scale
Ethnic Identity Development Measures
Ethnic Identity Development Measures:
    Asian Values Scale
Ethnic Identity Development Measures:
    Bicultural Involvement Scale

Ethnic Identity Development Measures:
    Cross Racial Identity Scale
Ethnic Identity Development Measures:
    Multigroup Ethnic Identity Measure
Ethnic Identity Development Measures:
    Orthogonal Cultural Identification Scale
Ethnic Identity Development Measures:
    Racial Identity Attitude Scale
Ethnic Research
Instrument Development for Ethnic Minority Research
Measures of Racial Prejudice
Measures of Racial Prejudice: Modern
    Racism Scale
Projective Testing
Qualitative Methods
Scholastic Assessment Test

PROFESSIONAL ORGANIZATIONS

American Counseling Association
American Psychological Association
Asian American Psychological Association
Association of Black Psychologists
Bureau of Indian Affairs
Committee on Ethnic Minority Affairs
Council of National Psychological Associations for
    the Advancement of Ethnic Minority Interests
Indian Health Service
National Latina/o Psychological Association
Office of Ethnic Minority Affairs
Society for the Psychological Study of Ethnic
    Minority Issues
Society of Indian Psychologists

PSYCHOPATHOLOGY

Alcohol/Substance Use and Abuse
Anxiety Disorders in Ethnic Minorities
Attention-Deficit/Hyperactivity Disorder
Child Abuse: Overview
Child Abuse: Physical
Dementia
Depression
Disabilities
Domestic Violence
Drapetomania
Drug Abuse Prevention in Ethnic Minority Youth
DSM-IV
Eating Disorders
Mental Health

About the Editor

Yo Jackson is a licensed clinical child psychologist specializing in trauma, stress, abuse, resiliency, and diversity issues in children. She is an associate professor at the University of Kansas and a core faculty member of the Clinical Child Psychology Program, appointed in both the Psychology and Applied Behavioral Science Departments. Her research interests are multifaceted. She has published numerous articles and conducts several research projects on the factors that make children resilient after exposure to stress, the development of interventions for children exposed to major life events and trauma, the role of protective factors in promoting adaptive behavior in children, and developing models of competence in children exposed to multiple stressors. Her research involves investigating typical children as well as special populations, such as children in foster care. She also conducts research on multicultural issues and is currently involved in two projects investigating ethnic identity development in adolescence and the influence of culture on how parents perceive mental illness in children. She teaches upper-level courses on child psychology, developmental psychopathology, advanced child and family assessment, and diversity issues in clinical psychology, and supervises clinical practicums.

Contributors

Ana Abraido-Lanza
Columbia University

Ignacio Acevedo-Polakovich
University of Kentucky

James Allen
University of Alaska Fairbanks

Jeanette Altarriba
University at Albany, State University of New York

Julie Ancis
Georgia State University

D. J. Angelone
The College of New Jersey

Consuelo Arbona
University of Houston

Adria Armbrister
Columbia University

Eleanor Armour-Thomas
Queens College (CUNY)

Gonzalo Bacigalupe
University of Massachusetts

Pamela Balls Organista
University of San Francisco

Audrey Bangi
The Consultation Center

Christy Barongan
Washington and Lee University

Declan Barry
Yale University School of Medicine

Monica Baskin
University of Alabama at Birmingham

Lana Beasley
University of Kansas

F. Beauvais
Colorado State University

Jessica Belanger
California State University–Northridge

Fred Bemak
George Mason University

Gary Bennett
Dana-Farber Cancer Institute

Dolores Subia Big Foot
The University of Oklahoma Health Sciences Center

Gilbert Botvin
Weill Medical College of Cornell University

Jenifer Bratter
University of Houston

Nicole Buchanan
Michigan State University

Larisa Buhin
Loyola University Chicago

Alberto Bursztyn
Brooklyn College, City University of New York

Lisa Campbell
Duke University Medical Center

Esteban Cardemil
Clark University

Andrew Case
Indiana University

Carrie Castañeda
University of Utah

Jeanett Castellanos
University of California, Irvine

Doris Chang
New School University

Rita Chi-Ying Chung
George Mason University

Ruth Chung
University of Southern California

Y. Barry Chung
Georgia State University

Caroline Clauss-Ehlers
State University of New Jersey at Rutgers

Sara Corbin
University of Kansas

Rebecca Corona
Loyola University–Chicago

Deone Curling
University of Toronto

E. J. R. David
University of Illinois at Urbana-Champaign

Edward Delgado-Romero
University of Georgia

Angela DeSilva
Boston College

Gretchen Diefenbach
Hartford Hospital/Institute of Living

Khanh Dinh
University of Massachusetts Lowell

Mimi Doll
DePaul University

Christopher Edwards
Duke University Medical Center

Annel Esparza
Northern Arizona University

Jameca Falconer
Southern Illinois University–Edwardsville

Vern Farber
University of California, Irvine

Miriam Feliu
Duke University Medical Center

Leila Flores-Torres
University of Texas, Pan American

Rebecca Ford
DePaul University

M. French
*Family and Child Mental Health Services,
Lee's Summit, Missouri*

Peggy Gallaher
University of Southern California

Miguel Gallardo
Pepperdine University

Y. Evie Garcia
Northern Arizona University

Maria Garcia-Larrieu
Private Practice, Miami, FL

Rose Girgis
University of Southern California

Alberta Gloria
University of Wisconsin–Madison

Michael Gomez
The University of Kansas

Diana Gonzalez-Eastep
Boston College

Harvette Grey
DePaul University

Arpana Gupta
University of Tennessee

MaryAnna Ham
University of Massachusetts Boston

Karen Hansen
University of Utah

Gary Harper
DePaul University

Shelly Harrell
Pepperdine University

Zaje Harrell
Michigan State University

Puncky Heppner
University of Missouri–Columbia

Shihoko Hijioka
Graduate Faculty, New School University

Richard Hirschman
Kent State University

Bertha Holliday
American Psychological Association

George Hong
California State University–Los Angeles

Joseph Hovey
The University of Toledo

Heather Hunter
University of Kansas

Michael Illovsky
Western Illinois University

Colette Ingraham
San Diego State University

Gayle Iwamasa
DePaul University

Chizuko Izawa
Tulane University

Margo Jackson
Fordham University

Yo Jackson
University of Kansas

Rochelle James
University of Kansas

Ellen Junn
California State University, Fullerton

Shannon Kelly
Indiana University

Alvin Killough
North Carolina University

Kerri Kim
University of Kansas

Mary Kopala
Hunter College, CUNY

Catherine Koverola
University of Alaska Fairbanks

Seunghee Kwon
Indiana University

Robert Lanza
Sonnenschein, Nath & Rosenthal, LLP

Christine Larson
University of Toledo

Mark Leach
University of Southern Mississippi

Courtland Lee
University of Maryland

Matthew Lee
University of Illinois at Urbana-Champaign

Richard Lee
University of Minnesota

John-Paul Legerski
University of Kansas

Frederick Leong
University of Tennessee

Paul Leung
University of North Texas

Jacob Levy
University of Tennessee

Michael Lewin
California State University, San Bernardino

Doug Longshore
University of California, Los Angeles

Tica Lopez
Argosy University

Christopher MacDonald-Dennis
Bryn Mawr College

Gerardo Marín
University of San Francisco

Renata Martins
West Virginia University

Nausheen Masood
University of Illinois at Urbana–Champaign

Daniel McNeil
West Virginia University

Brian McNeill
Washington State University

Matthew Miller
University of Notre Dame

Jeffery Mio
California State Polytechnic University, Pomona

Damon Mitchell
Central Connecticut State University

Marie Miville
Teachers College, Columbia University

Ruth Montero
University of Wisconsin–Madison

Ana Montes de Vegas
University of Utah

Roy Moodley
OISE/ University of Toronto

Lori Morales
University of Toledo

Eduardo Morales
*California School of Professional
Psychology at San Francisco*

Melissa Morgan
Loyola University of Chicago

G. Susan Mosley-Howard
Miami University

Cheryl Munday
University of Detroit Mercy

Cristin Murtaugh
University of Maryland

Nina Nabors
Eastern Michigan University

Donna Nagata
University of Michigan

James Nelson
Valparaiso University

Chee Ng
University of Melbourne

George Nichols
University of Wisconsin

Guerda Nicolas
Boston College

Sandra Nuñez
Diamond Bar, California

Carlota Ocampo
Trinity University

Sumie Okazaki
University of Illinois, Urbana-Champaign

Keum Pang
*Howard University, College of Pharmacy,
Nursing and Allied Health Sciences*

Young-Joo Park
Korea University

Judy Patacsil
San Diego Miramar College

Jean Phinney
California State University, Los Angeles

Jacob Pickard
University of South Dakota

Nnamdi Pole
The University of Michigan

Joseph Ponterotto
Fordham University

Chebon Porter
Birmingham Veterans Affairs Medical Center

John Powell
The University of Kansas

Paul Priester
University of Wisconsin–Milwaukee

Stephen Quintana
University of Wisconsin

Kathleen Ragsdale
Fordham University

Sheikh Rahim
King Faisal University

Reece Rahman
University of Pittsburgh at Johnstown

Sylvia Ramirez
University of Texas–Pan American

Pamela Reid
Roosevelt University

Carla Reyes
University of Utah

Charles Ridley
Indiana University

Elwood Robinson
North Carolina Central University

Scott Roesch
San Diego State University

Kimberlee Roy
University of Kansas

Jens Rydgren
Stockholm University

Vetta Sanders-Thompson
Saint Louis University

Lewis Schlosser
Seton Hall University

Kristina Schmukler
University of California Santa Cruz

Radhika Seghal
Eastern Michigan University

Theresa Segura-Herrera
University of Wisconsin

Isis Settles
Michigan State University

Marie Simonsson
University of Texas—Pan American

Joshua Singh
DePaul University

Gemma Skillman
The University of South Dakota

Tracey Smith
University of Wisconsin

Sueyoung Song
University of Minnesota

Jessica Soto
University of Texas–Pan American

Elizabeth Sparks
Boston College

G. Scott Sparrow
University of Texas–Pan American

Suzette Speight
Loyola University, Chicago

Michael Steele
The University of Kansas

Edward Stephenson
Florida Memorial College

Michael Stevenson
Ball State University

Sunita Stewart
University of Texas Southwestern Medical Center

April Taylor
California State University, San Bernardino

Jennifer Taylor
Humboldt State University

Karen Taylor-Crawford
University of Illinois at Chicago

Thomas Teo
York University

Amy Tsai
University of Michigan

Jennifer Unger
University of Southern California

Jesse Valdez
University of Denver

Veronica Vasquez
Loyola University, Chicago

Elizabeth Vera
Loyola University, Chicago

Ngan Vuong
University of Kansas

W. David Wakefield
California State University, Northridge

Barbara Wallace
Teachers College, Columbia University

Tamara Warner
University of Florida

Robert Weisskirch
California State University, Monterey Bay

Kellee White
Columbia University

Rebecca Widoe
West Virginia University

Wendi Williams
Georgia State University

Diane Willis
University of Oklahoma Health Sciences Center

Kazue Yamaoka
National Institute of Public Health

Barbara Yee
University of Hawaii at Manoa

Albert Yeung
Massachusetts General Hospital

Introduction

The study of multicultural psychology has a long and multifaceted history. The field encompasses a wide range of subdisciplines within psychology and includes a multitude of populations both within and outside of the United States. Early efforts to examine issues relevant to people of color in psychology often attempted to describe differences among populations as a way to better understand the influence of culture on the human organism. Unfortunately, the results of the early research were often interpreted in terms of inferiority on the part of one group over another and were usually of little benefit to people of color or nations as a whole. Current efforts include a broad range of methodologies for research and training and a strong desire to produce useful results for understanding the role of culture in human behavior.

Debates continue over the appropriateness of modern psychological theories to capture the influences of culture. Generally, Western approaches advocate for the universality of human development and behavior and the field as a whole has yet to embrace or understand the complexities of cultural styles in modern research and practice. Evidence over the past 30 years, however, suggests that long-standing academic traditions are woefully inadequate and inflexible to accurately measure, interpret, or support a universal approach.

Culture is important, and the focus of the *Encyclopedia of Multicultural Psychology* is to provide an index to the terms, concepts, and issues in the mainstream of field. Professional organizations since the 1970s have advocated and demonstrated the need for more comprehensive ideas when it comes to human behavior that include cultural background when studying psychological constructs. And, since the 1970s, international and ethnic minority psychologists alike reflected growing concerns regarding the meaning of psychology for all peoples. The field of multicultural and cross-cultural psychology has a relatively short history and is making its way into the foundations for training new psychologists. To this end, national accrediting organizations in psychology and licensure boards across the country continue to refine mandates for training that include a focus on multicultural psychology. As more multicultural research is compiled and the findings disseminated, the need for comprehensive texts like the *Encyclopedia of Multicultural Psychology* become stronger.

The *Encyclopedia of Multicultural Psychology* is meant to be an authoritative guide to the field of multicultural psychology. The title is intentional and supports the notion that culture, not race, is the best way to understand differences among individuals. Because the field is expansive and expanding, no one volume can cover all of the important topics germane to the area. Therefore, although this text includes entries on a broad array of issues and topics, it is not meant to be comprehensive. It is designed to be of particular interest to laypersons, students, and professionals new to the field with an interest in the role of culture in psychology.

The text includes topics that are relevant to social psychology, cognitive psychology, environmental psychology, cross-cultural psychology, and clinical psychology. Because one of the recent concerns in clinical psychology is the application of culture-based findings to multicultural populations, the text includes a focus on treatment or applied issues in multicultural psychology. The text also includes a focus on psychopathology and the manner in which it is defined and measured from different cultural perspectives. Folk illnesses or indigenous pathologies are also included so that the reader may explore how mental illness or mental health is perceived from a traditional culture viewpoint.

Every effort was made to include all large ethnic groups and subgroups in the United States in this text; however, other cultural groups may not be included due to limited research and knowledge. Even within subgroups, knowledge may be limited as research publication is only beginning to catch up to the need for information on cultural groups with smaller numbers.

One of the objectives of this text was to address culture across a broad spectrum of psychological perspectives. To this end, the text also includes topics on sociological issues as well as conceptual issues relevant to the field of multicultural psychology. Moreover, the text also addresses how some psychological constructs are measured, as the available data are only as good as the measurement tools used to gather the information. Finally, cultural concerns are also addressed, including, among others, topics on traumatic events that are especially relevant for understanding the worldviews of people of color.

With the arrival of new journals and professional organizations, the field of multicultural psychology is growing. Clearly the field has a long way to go to meet current empirical and professional standards enjoyed by many other disciplines of psychology. Part of this growth is embodied in the need for the *Encyclopedia of Multicultural Psychology* in that new and more established psychologists alike will need information and understanding of how cultural issues are relevant to their work.

Culture is not a topic with relevance limited to psychology. The need for greater understanding of the role of culture is at the forefront of national and international relations. It is also not a topic limited in interest to people of color. Although the universal perspective in psychology may no longer be a reasonable position, there is a universal call for increased research, knowledge, and awareness of how culture affects our lives. Public debate on culture seeks to find commonality and insight both within and between people from all cultural backgrounds. It is to this end that this text may highlight the major issues and bring to bear the field's appreciation for the influence of culture. The *Encyclopedia of Multicultural Psychology* presents an introduction to the field for those interested in improving their awareness and comprehension of cultural practices prevalent among and between all people.

Completing a volume on a broad and sometimes controversial topic would not be possible without the assistance of many individuals. I would like to acknowledge the tireless efforts of the Assistant Editor, Kimberlee Roy, in making this text a reality. Also, the text would not be possible without the work and expertise of the distinguished list of authors and the members of the advisory board. Finally, I would like to thank my father, James Warren Jackson, and my mother, E. Katherine Eberhard, for their support, guidance, and instruction on how to be a living model for tolerance and cultural appreciation.

—*Yo Jackson*
Lawrence, Kansas

ACADEMIC ACHIEVEMENT AND MINORITY INDIVIDUALS

The academic achievement of some minority individuals and groups remains a ubiquitous and seemingly intractable problem in the United States. The problem is usually defined in terms of mean differences in standardized achievement test scores between certain racial or ethnic groups. There is good reason for concern because on virtually every measure of academic achievement, African American, Latino, and Native American students, as a group, score significantly lower that their peers from European backgrounds. Moreover, it appears that gaps first manifest early in school, broaden during the elementary school years, and remain relatively fixed during the secondary school years.

THE NATURE AND SCOPE OF THE PROBLEM OF MINORITY ACADEMIC ACHIEVEMENT

One source of information that has documented academic achievement trends among minorities for more than three decades is the National Assessment of Educational Progress testing program. If the term "minority" is defined as a racial or ethnic group within a larger population, then the lower performance in achievement is associated with students from certain minority populations defined as African American and Hispanic. If the term "majority" is used to define a racial or ethnic group that characterizes the larger population, then the higher performance in achievement is associated with students from European backgrounds. These data have consistently shown significant achievement gaps between certain racial or ethnic groups on standardized tests in different subject areas and across grade levels. Other measures of academic achievement, such as grades and class rankings, show similar differences in minority and majority achievement.

Beyond the consistency of the disparities in minority and majority achievement, it is by no means clear what these discrepant scores really mean. To characterize racial and ethnic differences as minority differences suggests that these groups have had similar experiences and that these experiences influence their behavior in a similar way. However, this is not the case. There is tremendous variability within and across racial and ethnic groups even though they are ascribed minority status in U.S. society. For example, native-born African Americans and immigrants of African ancestry are similar in terms of race and minority status, but they have had different culturally mediated socialization experiences that affect their achievement motivation and academic performance differently. However, because academic achievement is usually reported as a mean score for African Americans, it is difficult to differentiate the nature of the performance of either minority group. But it is important to know which minority groups are performing high or low because such information is critical for informing appropriate intervention for both groups.

FACTORS THAT INFLUENCE LOW MINORITY ACHIEVEMENT

Since the 1960s, numerous perspectives have been advanced about the differences in academic achievement among minority and majority students and groups. Reasons include unequal opportunities to

1

learn, limited access to educationally relevant resources, ethnic and racial stereotyping, and cultural incompatibility between the home and school culture. Each will be discussed briefly.

Limited Opportunities to Learn

In reviewing the literature on who gets access to rigorous curricula in schools, it appears that, on the basis of standardized test results, a disproportionate number of racial and ethnic minority individuals, particularly those from low-income backgrounds, are judged as "low ability" and assigned to low-track or remedial classes. In contrast, individuals of European descent, particularly those from high-income backgrounds, are more likely to be considered "gifted and talented" and placed in enriched or accelerated programs. Because track enrollment determines the level of courses students take and the quality of the curriculum and instruction to which they are exposed, this means that minority students, on average, are less likely than their majority peers to engage in high-caliber curricula. Diminished opportunity to learn high-level material results in low academic achievement.

Limited Access to Institutional and Other Resources

Well-equipped libraries, mentoring, tutoring, quality teaching, rigorous curricula, low counselor–student and teacher–student ratios, small class sizes, extracurricular experiences, and computer and other technologies are examples of key resources in education that may be viewed as preconditions for enabling high levels of academic achievement. Unfortunately, a disproportionate number of individuals from certain minority groups (e.g., African Americans, Latinos, and Native Americans), particularly those from low-income backgrounds, are likely to attend schools with limited access to these resources, thus minimizing their opportunity to do well academically. Moreover, many of these individuals live in economically distressed communities where they experience poor health and inadequate nutrition, factors that place them further at risk educationally.

The Effects of Racial Stereotyping

Racial stereotyping is a deeply held, stigmatizing belief in unalterable genetic or cultural inferiority that many members of a majority population hold about individuals and groups who have been assigned minority status in society. In the United States, the effects of racial stereotyping have a particularly devastating effect on the academic motivation and achievement of some individuals from racial and ethnic minority groups, particularly those who have been brought into society involuntarily through slavery and conquest (e.g., African Americans, Mexican Americans, and Native Americans). In the education sphere, some individuals from these ascribed caste-like minority groups have rejected this form of stereotyping by developing coping mechanisms to protect their identity. In so doing, these identity-protection strategies serve to dampen their achievement motivation, which, in turn, results in low academic achievement.

Cultural Incompatibility Between Home and School Culture

Schooling is ineffective for some children from racial and ethnic minority groups because classroom practices may be incompatible with their cultural background. Cultural incompatibilities include a lack of respect for children's conversational style and collaborative participation structures. Such misunderstandings can contribute to diminished commitment to academic engagement and academic underachievement.

RECOMMENDATIONS FOR IMPROVING MINORITY ACHIEVEMENT

Reducing or eliminating the minority achievement gap remains one of the most serious challenges in U.S. education today. Efforts to close the gap should take the following considerations into account.

Disaggregation of Data

Individuals from minority groups have different socialization experiences that have a differential impact on their academic motivation and performance. Disaggregation of achievement data is necessary to identify which minority individuals and groups are doing poorly and which are doing well. Such information on the variability in minority achievement may then be used to target appropriate instruction for different individuals and groups.

Adequate Exposure to Supplementary Education

School alone cannot ensure high academic achievement. Indeed, parents or significant others of high-achieving students recognize the importance of supplementary education and routinely make it available to their children over the course of their schooling. Examples of supplementary education include academic summer camps, after-school and weekend tutoring, use of libraries and museums as resources for learning, and access to mentors and models who are themselves high achievers. Low-achieving minority students must have adequate exposure to supplementary education.

Adequate Exposure to High-Quality Teaching

Low-achieving students must have adequate exposure to high-quality teaching that is responsive to their strengths, needs, and interests. This means not only that they must have opportunities to participate in curricula and instructional activities that are known to be conducive to high academic achievement, but also that these experiences must be accommodative to their learning strengths and needs.

Access to Educationally Relevant Resources

High-achieving students have access to educationally relevant resources in the schools they attend and through their families and communities. Such resources must be made available to low-achieving students as well.

—*Eleanor Armour Thomas*

See also *The Bell Curve*; Head Start; Intelligence Tests; Scholastic Assessment Test

FURTHER READING

Braswell, J. S., Lutkus, A. D., Grigg, W. S., Santapau, S. L., Tay-Lim, B., & Johnson, M. (2001). *The nation's report card: Mathematics 2000*. Washington, DC: National Center for Education Statistics. Retrieved July 27, 2004, from http://nces.ed.gov

Gordon, E. W., & Bridglall, B. L. (2005). The challenge, context and preconditions of academic development. In E. W. Gordon, B. L. Bridglall, & A. S. Meroe (Eds.), *Supplementary education: The hidden curriculum of high academic achievement* (pp. 10–34). New York: Rowman & Littlefield.

Miller, S. (1995). *An American imperative: Accelerating minority educational advancement*. New Haven, CT: Yale University Press.

Ogbu, J. N. (1987). Variability in minority responses to schooling: Nonimmigrant vs. immigrants. In G. Spindler & L. Spindler (Eds.), *Interpretative ethnography of education: At home and abroad* (pp. 255–278). Hillsdale, NJ: Lawrence Erlbaum.

O'Sullivan, C. Y., Lauko, M. A., Grigg, W. S., Qian, J., & Zhang, J. (2003). *The nation's report card: Reading 2002*. Washington, DC: National Center for Education Statistics. Retrieved July 27, 2004, from http://nces.ed.gov

Steele, C. M. (1997). A threat in the air: How stereotypes shape intellectual identity and performance. *American Psychologist, 52*(6), 613–629.

ACCESSIBILITY OF HEALTH CARE

DEFINITION AND SCOPE OF HEALTH CARE ACCESS

The health disparities and health care inequalities experienced by major American ethnic groups (compared with Caucasian Americans) have been well documented. Health disparities are defined as higher rates of chronic and disabling illness, infectious disease, and mortality experienced by members of ethnic minority groups compared with Caucasians. One of the most important factors contributing to health disparities is limited access to health care. Therefore, improving access to health care is considered one of the greatest opportunities for reducing health disparities in the United States.

Access to health care can be considered at two levels: primary access and secondary access. Primary access involves entry into the health care system and access to basic care. Secondary access involves the quality of care received by individuals with primary access. Primary and secondary health care access will be discussed with respect to four major cultural groups in the United States: African Americans, Hispanic Americans, Asian Americans and Pacific Islanders, and American Indians and Alaska Natives. Primary access issues include health insurance rates and the accessibility of health care facilities. Secondary access issues include quality of care, access to specialists, access to culturally similar health care personnel, language barriers, and discrimination.

AFRICAN AMERICANS

Lack of insurance is considered the most significant barrier to health care, and for a majority of Americans, health insurance provided by employers makes health care affordable. The uninsured rate for African Americans under age 65 is 19.9%. Unemployment is strongly tied to the lack of insurance among African Americans; however, a disproportionate number of African American workers whose employers do not provide health insurance are also counted among the uninsured. Among African Americans, poverty and unemployment rates are 24.4% and 11.6%, respectively, compared with 8.2% and 5.6%, respectively, for Caucasians.

Another primary health care access issue for African Americans is the availability of health care providers. In poor, ethnic communities, there is a limited supply of health resources, primarily because patients in these communities cannot afford to pay for the services provided. As a result, health care facilities cannot be maintained. This reality has driven the creation of community health centers and hospital-based providers. Reduced geographic proximity to health care providers has a particularly strong impact on urban African American communities that rely heavily on public transportation, which increases the time and cost of accessing care.

A major secondary access issue is the quality of care received by African Americans. Inequalities in medical care exist even when African Americans have insurance plans that are similar to majority group members. For example, African American patients with health maintenance organization (HMO) insurance report more difficulty seeing a specialist and obtaining tests and treatment, suggesting that barriers exist well beyond entry into the health care system.

Another secondary access issue is the lower number of physicians from ethnic minority groups. This decreases health care access for minority patients because prospective patients are often reluctant to visit health care providers who may be racially or ethnically different from them.

Language barriers also influence secondary access. Patient–physician communication has been reported to be more problematic for African American patients than for Caucasian patients, even though both patients and physicians may speak the same language. Finally, discrimination is a major barrier to secondary access, affecting physicians' perceptions of patients as well as treatment decisions. For example, a negative perception of African American patients is associated with a lower likelihood of recommending treatment.

HISPANICS

The majority of the 35 million individuals in the United States counted as Hispanic or Latino are of Mexican heritage, and the remainder are from Caribbean and South American backgrounds. The uninsured rate for Hispanics under 65 years old is 33%, the highest rate among the major ethnic groups in the United States. The high uninsured rate among Hispanic populations is largely tied to immigration status. An estimated 72% of foreign-born persons in this group are not American citizens, and public insurance programs such as Medicaid deny services to immigrants. Furthermore, immigrants are more likely to work in low-wage, low-benefit jobs that do not offer health insurance. Hispanic Americans also rely heavily on public transportation, which necessitates traveling greater distances and incurring greater costs for medical care.

With regard to secondary access, Hispanic patients experience barriers similar to those of African Americans, including a lower quality of care afforded by lower-end insurance plans and discrimination. The language barrier is a significant secondary access issue for Hispanic groups: Limited English proficiency on the part of Hispanic patients, combined with a lack of Spanish-speaking health care providers, can result in misdiagnosis and inappropriate treatment of symptoms.

ASIAN AMERICANS AND PACIFIC ISLANDERS

Asian Americans and Pacific Islanders (AAPIs) represent a diverse group with more than 60 different national and ethnic origins and more than 100 different languages. This group makes up about 5% of the total U.S. population (more than 12 million). According to the Institute of Medicine, the uninsured rate for AAPIs under age 65 is 22%. The rates vary significantly, however, among subgroups, and the highest rate is found among Korean Americans (34%), who experience higher rates of poverty. The rates are also higher for Southeast Asian and South Asian groups. In addition to poverty, immigrant status is a significant barrier to obtaining insurance. Of the AAPIs who are foreign born, 52.9% are not American citizens and therefore cannot access publicly funded insurance programs.

Even for AAPIs who have health insurance, poor perceived quality of care is a major secondary access issue. A large survey of individuals in a West Coast HMO revealed that AAPIs consistently had the worst access ratings across a variety of measures compared with other minorities. Limited English proficiency is also a significant secondary access issue for AAPIs. Census data from 1993 estimated that more than 1.5 million AAPIs live in "linguistically isolated" households, that is, those in which no person over age 14 speaks English "very well."

Finally, discrimination affects secondary health care access for AAPIs. Because of their achievements in the socioeconomic and educational spheres, AAPIs have been labeled the "model minority." This label is misleading because it fails to recognize the tremendous diversity within the AAPI group and because it can blind people to the real needs and problems of AAPI subgroups.

AMERICAN INDIANS AND ALASKA NATIVES

American Indians and Alaska Natives (AIANs) represent a variety of culturally diverse and distinctive groups who speak more than 300 languages and comprise 562 federally recognized tribes. According to the 2002 U.S. Census, 4.1 million people (1.5%) identify themselves as AIANs. The health care situation of AIANs is somewhat unique compared with other ethnic groups because the U.S. government is obligated by treaty and federal statutes to provide health care to members of federally recognized American Indian tribes. The federal Indian Health Service (IHS) was established in 1955 to meet this need. Those AIANs who can readily access IHS services can receive free primary care; limited specialty services are available free of charge through contracts with private providers. Unfortunately, the IHS faces a number of obstacles to providing health care access to those it was intended to help. These obstacles include limited funding and geographical limitations. The IHS has 34 urban Indian health programs, but these programs represent only 1% of the total IHS budget. As a result of the limited funding, many areas have no services. In addition, IHS facilities are located on or near reservations, although the majority of AIANs live in urban areas away from their home reservations.

The gap between the need for IHS services and access to these services was highlighted by a 2004 Kaiser Foundation study, which revealed that more than one-third (35%) of AIANs under age 65 are uninsured and only 19% have access to IHS services. The problem is worse among low-income AIANs, almost half of whom (48%) are uninsured. Only 23% of uninsured, low-income AIANs have access to IHS services.

Finally, communication difficulties are important secondary access issues for AIANs. Compared with Caucasians, AIANs report more dissatisfaction with the quality of care received and poorer communication with health care providers.

CONCLUSION

Ethnic minorities in the United States have poorer health status and less access to health care than Caucasians, largely as a result of lower rates of insurance coverage. Although health insurance coverage addresses the primary access issue, it does not address the myriad secondary access issues that minority Americans face after they get their foot in the door of the U.S. health care system. These secondary access issues include less accessible facilities, poorer quality of care, language and communication barriers, and discrimination. Greater attention to both primary and secondary health care access issues is needed to elucidate the processes that place minority group members at a disadvantage when they seek health care.

—*Lisa C. Campbell*
—*Tamara Duckworth Warner*

FURTHER READING

Collins, K. S., Hughes, D. L., Doty, M. M., Ives, B. L., Edwards, J. N., & Tenney, K. (2002). *Diverse communities, common concerns: Assessing health care quality for minority Americans.* New York: The Commonwealth Fund. Retrieved January 13, 2006, from http://www.cmwf.org

Lillie-Blanton, M., Rushing, O. E., & Ruiz, S. (2003). *Key facts: Race, ethnicity, and medical care.* Menlo Park, CA: Henry J. Kaiser Family Foundation. Retrieved January 28, 2006, from http://www.kff.org/minorityhealth/6069-index .cfm

Smedley, B. D., Stith, A. Y., & Nelson, A. R. (Eds.). (2002). *Unequal treatment: Confronting racial and ethnic disparities in health care.* Washington, DC: National Academies Press. Retrieved January 13, 2006, from http://www.nap.edu/ books/030908265X/html/

Sohler, N., Walmsley, P. J., Lubetkin, E., & Geiger, H. J. (2003). *The right to equal treatment: An annotated bibliography of studies on racial and ethnic disparities in healthcare, their causes, and related issues.* New York: Physicians for Human Rights. Retrieved January 13, 2006, from http://www.phrusa.org/research/domestic/race/race_ report/report.html

U.S. Census Bureau. (2003). *Income, poverty, and health coverage in the United States: 2003.* Retrieved January 28, 2006, from http://www.census.gov/hhes/www/poverty.html

ACCULTURATION

Early conceptualizations of acculturation described an interpersonal transformation that occurs when cultures come into sustained contact. Social scientists noted complex changes that can take place, including the conversion of values, the blending or separation of cultures, and personality and developmental growth.

Researchers attempted to use the acculturation process to examine the impact of modernization and industrialization on various communities and cultures during the 19th and 20th centuries. In the early part of the 20th century in the United States, acculturation became synonymous with *assimilation,* the loss of one's original culture and the adoption of a new host culture. This process was used to describe the experiences of immigrants from an array of places (e.g., Europe, China, Japan, and Mexico). The ultimate goal of American acculturation became the achievement of assimilation into a melting pot society.

Today, acculturation is considered a more dynamic process that occurs along various dimensions rather than a simple movement from a culture of origin toward assimilation. In addition, acculturation can occur on both the group and the individual levels, thus considering more of the consequent psychological adaptation and adjustment. Four acculturative stages have been described: contact, conflict, crisis, and adaptation. Furthermore, adaptation can include several strategies: (1) *assimilation*—the individual or group gives up (or is forced to give up) the cultural identity of origin and desires a positive relationship with the host culture; (2) *separation*—the individual or group retains the original culture (or is restricted from adopting the new culture through segregation) and desires no positive relationship with the host culture; (3) *integration*—the individual or group desires to retain the culture of origin as well as maintain a positive relationship with the host culture; and (4) *marginalization*—the individual or group no longer retains the original culture and has no desire (or is not allowed) to have a positive relationship with the host culture.

The dynamic quality of acculturation is further expressed by the gradual changes that occur in several areas (or dimensions) and affect the individual and potentially the cultural group as a whole (e.g., language, cognitive style, behavioral patterns, personality, identity, attitudes, and values).

One particular negative consequence of the acculturation process is the phenomenon of *acculturative stress.* Acculturative stress is defined as negative tension that can be directly related to threats, conflicts, or crises centered on one's cultural identity, values, or other emotional and behavioral patterns of living. Prolonged stress, especially of an extremely high level, can manifest itself in both psychological symptoms of distress (e.g., anxiety, depression) and physiological symptoms of distress (e.g., pain, fatigue, dizziness).

MEASUREMENT OF ACCULTURATION

One of the greatest challenges in understanding the role of acculturation in adjustment is the assessment of this construct. Despite the shift in the conceptualization of acculturation from a one-dimensional process to a multidimensional one, the measurement of acculturation has failed to reflect this reformulation. Indeed, most of the published acculturation scales require respondents to choose among terms that assess the unidirectional movement of individuals from traditional culture to majority culture, or they include scoring techniques that reflect this unidirectional movement. However, there are a very small number of measures developed recently to assess the various dimensions of acculturation by measuring two or more cultures independently of each other. This measurement approach is consistent with the concept of *biculturalism* (or bicultural competence), namely that adaptation to a host culture is possible without completely abandoning the culture of origin.

The most commonly measured aspect of acculturation is language, including spoken or written language, language preference, and language proficiency. Cultural preferences—such as the preference for engagement with people from one's culture of origin versus the host culture, a sense of acceptance by a particular cultural group, or cultural pride—are other popular indicators of acculturation. In addition, it is common for many scales to use demographic or proxy variables of acculturation (e.g., generation of respondent, place of birth, language of interview).

In a small number of acculturation scales, an assessment of adherence to cultural traditions, beliefs, and values is provided. Measures that focus on these cultural indexes may be particularly important for cultural groups such as African Americans or American Indians, for whom English-language issues, length of U.S. residency, and immigration status may be less pertinent.

Indeed, certain ethnic groups have been significantly underresearched in regard to acculturation. It has been suggested that greater attention be given to developing theories of acculturation that are specific to these groups' cultures to inform the development of sound and appropriate measures. Similarly, little attention has been focused on acculturation in children and youth; greater consideration to acculturation across the life span would increase our knowledge of the specific challenges and adaptations related to the age of the individual.

THE RELATIONSHIP OF ACCULTURATION TO ADJUSTMENT

Measures of acculturation are often used to predict psychological and physical distress symptomatology (e.g., depression, anxiety, substance abuse, physical pain, fatigue). Research conducted primarily with Latino and Asian American immigrants suggests that the relationship of acculturation to adjustment is a complex one. Some studies suggest that newly arrived immigrants are more vulnerable to symptoms because of a heightened level of acculturative stress. In particular, low English proficiency seems to be one of the most consistent predictors of psychological distress in these groups. However, in most of these studies, it is difficult to know whether preexisting stressors (e.g., experience of torture and persecution, loss of loved ones and material possessions) encountered in the country of origin may have predisposed these groups to experience the negative impact of acculturation to a new culture. Demographic variables such as age, sex, and socioeconomic status may lessen the effects of acculturative stress.

Other studies indicate a higher level of acculturation may be related to higher levels of psychological and physical distress. For example, an immigrant who has lived in the United States for a long period of time may be more vulnerable to psychological problems because of the loss of traditional cultural beliefs, values, or behaviors, which may offer protection from stress. In addition, long-term U.S. resident immigrants or U.S.-born members of cultural groups may be exposed to racial discrimination, social oppression, and new cultural standards, leading them to engage in risky behaviors (e.g., casual sexual encounters or increased consumption of alcohol). Some large studies have found this to be the case in certain Latino groups, such as Mexican Americans and Puerto Ricans. Alternatively, some theorists suggest that newer immigrants are particularly strong and resilient

and therefore have lower levels of psychiatric disorders than their U.S.-born counterparts. However, research support for this position is limited.

Despite varying speculations regarding the nature of the relationship between acculturation and adjustment, it is important to avoid attempts to simplify explanations. This relationship should be viewed as representative of complex interactions among historical, social, cultural, group, and individual factors. In addition, multiple measures of adjustment and stress may be required when examining the effects of acculturative stress due to emic (culture-specific) ways of thinking about and expressing distress.

—*Pamela Balls Organista*

See also Acculturation Measures; Acculturative Stress; Biculturalism

FURTHER READING

Berry, J. W. (1997). Immigration, acculturation and adaptation. *Applied Psychology, 46,* 5–68.

Chun, K. M., Balls Organista, P., & Marín, G. (Eds.). (2003). *Acculturation: Advances in theory, measurement, and applied research.* Washington, DC: American Psychological Association.

ACCULTURATION MEASURES

In light of the growing number of people of color represented in the 2000 U.S. Census, research in psychology is working to expand the field's understanding of the needs of ethnically and culturally diverse populations. Besides documenting differences in how people from diverse ethnic groups think, act, and believe, the most progressive research seeks not only to determine where important distinctions lie but also to demonstrate the meaning of group differences. Researchers have argued that the most meaningful difference, both between and within ethnic groups, is the value that an individual places on his or her culture. Recently, the measurement of that value has come in the form of acculturation measures. Designed to identify attachment to one's culture of origin, to a new culture, or to both, acculturation measures can be invaluable tools for understanding group differences.

The need for acculturation measures was created in part by the problems researchers had interpreting findings when people of color were included in study samples. When people of color were combined into one group (i.e., people of color versus Caucasian sub-samples), researchers struggled to determine what role, if any, cultural differences played in the results. Furthermore, when people of color were separated into different groups according to ethnic identification, researchers also had difficulty determining the role of culture within and between groups. That is, it was and is unclear what role culture plays in research findings because researchers did not have a method for controlling or testing the level of "culturalness" present in a given sample of people of color. Within-ethnic-group differences are often larger than between-group differences, and researchers needed a way to ensure that when sampling people of color from one ethnic group, the group represented a homogeneous representation of a specific level of cultural attachment. Acculturation measures were thought to be one step toward untangling the effects of culture by creating a method for assessing levels of cultural attachment, especially within ethnic groups.

Early models for acculturation measures suggested that acculturation was best conceptualized on a single continuum. Advocates of this perspective believed that acculturation is a process of moving from one's culture of origin to the other end of the spectrum, whereby a person becomes a member of a new or host culture. Some measures of acculturation in this system indicated only high or low involvement in one's host culture (unicultural), and some represented a true continuum from attachment to the culture of origin to the dominant culture (dual cultural). A central tenet of these approaches was that individuals cannot be equally immersed in two cultures at one time and likely have to give up some aspect of one culture to be a part of a different culture. Examples of measures from this approach include the African American Acculturation Scale, the Asian Values Scale, and the Acculturation Measure for Chicano Adolescents.

During the 1980s, several researchers began developing an extension to the previous notion that acculturation was best represented by a linear progression and instead suggested that a unicultural or dual-cultural perspective ignored individuals who were *bicultural*. Biculturalism, in this sense, represents individuals who maintain adherence to more than one culture at a time. Researchers proposed that acculturation is a bilinear process with one continuum representing a process whereby individuals can experience either marginality (adherence to no culture) or involvement and either

uniculturalism or biculturalism. Examples of measures representing this approach include the Acculturation Rating Scale for Mexican Americans and the Biculturalism Involvement Questionnaire.

The idea of acculturation was expanded even further in the 1980s and 1990s, when research began to address a multilinear or typology approach to acculturative status. That is, researchers put forth the idea that individuals could be classified according to their acculturation perspective along four basic constructs. Specifically, individuals could demonstrate *integration, assimilation, separation,* and *marginalization.* Individuals were thought to express attitudes of acculturation that combined levels of adherence to the host and indigenous cultures. Furthermore, the level of adherence could be measured and placed on a continuum.

Integration is thought to be expressed when a person is bicultural, or active in his or her culture of origin and in the dominant culture. Assimilation is thought to occur when a person is active in the dominant culture and has little interest in aspects of his or her native culture. Separation is manifested when a person remains integrated into his or her culture of origin and uninterested in learning about or participating in the dominant culture. Finally, marginalization occurs when a person is inactive in both the culture of origin and the dominant culture. Although these ideas are fairly new, efforts are under way to create measures that assess the four acculturation typologies. The main difference between the latter perspective and the biculturalism model is that the multilinear model includes measurements of acculturation across different settings and cultures. From their earliest inception, acculturation measures, whether unicultural, bicultural, or multicultural, have generally been designed with the culture of origin in mind. That is, most measures are created to capture one's attachment to the culture of origin of a particular group (i.e., African Americans, Asian Americans). Despite efforts to this point, the field is still in its infancy, with most measures of acculturation requiring greater research and stronger psychometric findings before widespread use is possible.

AFRICAN AMERICANS

Targeting traditional African American culture, two measures of dual culturalism represent the available tools for measuring acculturation in the African American population: the African American Acculturation Scale and the Scale to Assess African American Acculturation.

Both measures offer promise to the study of acculturation among African Americans; however, the psychometric properties of both measures are rather unclear, and greater study of their validity and reliability, especially their stability over time, is needed.

HISPANIC AMERICANS

The choices for measuring acculturation in Hispanic populations are more varied than for the African American population and include measures of both monocultural and bicultural acculturation. Furthermore, measures specific to the cultures of Cuban, Mexican, and Puerto Rican Americans are available. Several of the bicultural measures (e.g., Bicultural Involvement Questionnaire, Cultural Lifestyle Inventory, Bicultural Scale for Puerto Rican Americans, and Acculturation Rating Scale for Mexican Americans) allow for measurement of attachment to the culture of origin as well as the host culture, but they lack normative data to enhance interpretation for their use. These measures represent adequate psychometrics and some evidence of construct validity.

NATIVE AMERICANS

The Navajo Family Acculturation Scale, the Navajo Community Acculturation Scale, and the Rosebud Personal Opinion Survey represent the best tools available for measuring acculturation among Native American samples. Although there are more than 500 recognized tribes in the United States, each with its own unique culture, so far only the Rosebud Personal Opinion Survey is designed to be a general measure for Native populations. More research is needed to establish the psychometric properties of these measures.

ASIAN AMERICANS

Like the Native American measures, only three measures are commonly used with Asian American populations: the Acculturation Scale for Chinese Americans, the Suinn-Lew Asian Self-Identity Acculturation Scale, and the Asian Values Scale. The latter two measures are designed for use with all subgroups of Asian Americans (e.g., Japanese, Korean) and appear to have adequate psychometric properties.

Only one measure, the Multicultural Acculturation Scale, is designed for use with all cultural groups and based on the bilinear acculturation model. The scores on this measure give a general sense of attachment to an ethnic group versus attachment to American values. This measure represents the first step toward developing a cross-cultural measure of acculturation, but more research is needed to determine its psychometric properties.

CONCLUSION

Researchers recognize that people of color represent more than differences in ethnic groups and bring to bear their cultural influences on research findings. Measuring the role of culture is the direction of the field, and to this end, several measures of acculturation are available for use with different cultural groups. By including a measure of acculturation, researchers can be assured that their findings are the result of the study variables and not necessarily within-group differences among the sample. For these measures to be of real use, however, more research is needed to establish the psychometric properties of acculturation measures. Moreover, new measures or updates of older versions are needed to keep up with changes in acculturation theory. Research that addresses the construct validity and long-term stability of acculturation measures would advance the field and allow for more sophisticated research questions. For example, acculturation measures that address biculturalism and measure acculturation status across settings are needed. Finally, acculturation measures generally measure behaviors (e.g., eating habits, social preferences) associated with attachment to a particular culture or cultures, and this may not represent the true nature of the acculturation experience. Focusing on behaviors only, researchers may neglect the importance of an individual's values, beliefs, and knowledge, all important parts of cultural adherence.

—*Yo Jackson*

FURTHER READING

Berry, J. W. (1980). Acculturation as varieties of adaptation. In A. M. Padilla (Ed.), *Acculturation: Theory, models, and some new findings* (pp. 9–25). Boulder, CO: Westview Press.

Berry, J. W. (1990). Psychology of acculturation: Understanding individuals moving between cultures. In R. W. Brislin (Ed.), *Applied cross-cultural psychology* (pp. 232–253). Newbury Park, CA: Sage.

Cuéllar, I., Arnold, B., & Maldonado, R. (1995). Acculturation Rating Scale for Mexican Americans–II: A revision of the original ARSMA scale. *Hispanic Journal of Behavioral Sciences, 17*(3), 275–304.

Kim, B. S. K., & Abreu, J. M. (2005). Acculturation measurement. In J. G. Ponterotto, J. M. Casas, L. A. Suzuki, & C. M. Alexander (Eds.), *Handbook of multicultural counseling.* Thousand Oaks, CA: Sage.

Kim, B. S. K., Atkinson, D. R., & Yang, P. H. (1999). The Asian Values Scale: Development, factor analysis, validation, and reliability. *Journal of Counseling Psychology, 46,* 342–352.

Landrine, H., & Klonoff, E. A. (1994). The African American Acculturation Scale: Development, reliability, and validity. *Journal of Black Psychology, 20,* 104–127.

Olmedo, E. L., & Padilla, A. M. (1978). Empirical and construct validation of a measure of acculturation for Mexican Americans. *Journal of Social Psychology, 105,* 179–187.

Szapocznik, J., Kurtines, W. M., & Fernandez, T. (1980). Bicultural involvement and adjustment in Hispanic American youths. *International Journal of Intercultural Relations, 4,* 353–365.

ACCULTURATION SCALES: ACCULTURATION, HABITS, AND INTERESTS MULTICULTURAL SCALE FOR ADOLESCENTS

Acculturation—the interchange of cultural attitudes and behaviors—involves changes in styles of speech, social behaviors, attitudes, beliefs, customs, celebration of holidays, and choices of foods and entertainment. Immigrants generally follow one of four general acculturation patterns: (1) *integration*—combining aspects of the new culture with aspects of the native culture; (2) *assimilation*—replacing the native cultural orientation with the new cultural orientation; (3) *separation*—retaining the native cultural orientation while rejecting the new cultural orientation; or (4) *marginalization*—becoming alienated from both cultures.

Measuring adolescents' acculturation levels in large, population-based surveys is difficult. Most published acculturation scales for adults contain words or concepts that young adolescents cannot comprehend. Most brief acculturation scales assess only language usage, which is only one facet of the acculturation process.

The Acculturation, Habits, and Interests Multicultural Scale for Adolescents (AHIMSA) is a brief, multidimensional, multicultural acculturation measure for use in large-scale, classroom-based, paper-and-pencil

surveys of early adolescents from varying cultural backgrounds. The AHIMSA includes questions that are relevant to adolescents, including their choice of friends, favorite music and television shows, favorite holidays, foods eaten at home, and general ways of thinking.

The items include the following: "I am most comfortable being with people from . . . ," "My best friends are from . . . " "The people I fit in with best are from . . . ," "My favorite music is from . . . ," "My favorite TV shows are from . . . ," "The holidays I celebrate are from . . . ," "The food I eat at home is from . . . ," and "The way I do things and the way I think about things are from . . ." The response options are "the United States," "the country my family is from," "both," and "neither." The AHIMSA generates four subscores: United States Orientation (assimilation), Other Country Orientation (separation), Both Countries Orientation (integration), and Neither Country Orientation (marginalization). Subscale scores are calculated by summing the number of responses in each of the four categories. The score on each subscale can range from 0 to 8. Researchers might elect to use one or more of the four orientation scores depending on their research questions.

The AHIMSA was developed through multiple rounds of pilot testing and psychometric analysis. First, existing acculturation measures were examined to identify questions that could be simplified or modified for adolescents. This resulted in an initial set of 13 items. These 13 items were shown to middle school students in focus groups to assess their interpretation of the items. Items that were confusing were reworded. The set of 13 modified items was administered to a pilot sample of sixth-grade students. Items with low variance were eliminated from the scale. Item response-curve analyses were used to select a final set of items that differentiated students at all levels of the scale. The final set of items included eight questions.

In a study of 317 sixth-grade adolescents in Southern California, the means on the United States Orientation, Other Country Orientation, Both Countries Orientation, and Neither Country subscales were 3.93, 0.50, 3.25, and 0.26, respectively. The United States Orientation, Other Country Orientation, and Both Countries Orientation subscales were correlated with the subscales of a modified Acculturation Rating Scale for Mexican Americans–II (ARSMA-II), English-language usage, and generation in the United States, providing evidence for the validity of those three subscales. The Neither Country Orientation subscale did not appear to be a valid measure of marginalization, a construct that is difficult to operationalize and difficult for adolescents to conceptualize.

Inclusion of the AHIMSA scale in surveys of adolescents provides a more complete understanding of the role of acculturation in adolescents' behavioral choices, which could lead to the creation of more culturally appropriate educational programs for adolescents in a multicultural society.

—Jennifer B. Unger

See also Acculturation

FURTHER READING

Unger, J. B., Gallaher, P., Shakib, S., Ritt-Olson, A., Palmer, P. H., & Johnson, C. A. (2002). The AHIMSA acculturation scale: A new measure of acculturation for adolescents in a multicultural society. *Journal of Early Adolescence, 22,* 225–251.

ACCULTURATION SCALES: ACCULTURATION RATING SCALE FOR MEXICAN AMERICANS–II

The Acculturation Rating Scale for Mexican Americans (ARSMA) is a seminal bilingual acculturation measure designed for use with both clinical and nonclinical Mexican American populations. The development of the ARSMA was a timely response to the booming Mexican American population. According to the 2000 U.S. Census, the Latino population is now the largest ethnic minority group in the United States, and 58.5% of this group is composed of Mexican Americans. Since its creation, the ARSMA has served as the model for many acculturation measures used with other ethnocultural groups.

The original ARSMA was a linear measure of acculturation developed by Israel Cuéllar, Lorwen C. Harris, and Ricardo Jasso in 1980 to assess cultural preferences and behavioral tendencies. In response to criticism that their measure obliged respondents to choose between two cultures and did not accurately reflect acculturation adaptation styles, Israel Cuéllar, Bill Arnold, and Roberto Maldonado produced a revised version in 1995. The ARSMA-II was designed to use an orthogonal, multidimensional approach to acculturation assessment by capturing varying levels

of biculturalism and allowing individuals to rate their orientation to Mexican and U.S. mainstream culture independently. This was achieved by dividing the original ARSMA items into two sections, one for each cultural orientation. The ARSMA-II classifies respondents into one of four styles of acculturation: *assimilation* (highly identified with U.S. mainstream culture only), *integration* (highly identified with both cultures), *separation* (highly identified with Mexican culture only), and *marginalization* (low levels of identification with both cultures).

The ARSMA-II retains its original version's behavioral focus but also includes an affective (positive/negative) affirmation of ethnic identity. Scale 1 of the ARSMA-II contains two subscales: the Anglo Orientation Subscale (13 items) and the Mexican Orientation Subscale (17 items). An optional Scale 2 (18 items) was included to assess feelings of marginality and difficulty accepting Anglo, Mexican, and Mexican American ideas, beliefs, customs, and values. All items are scored on a five-point Likert scale ranging from 1 (not at all) to 5 (extremely often/almost always). Overall, the measure assesses three principal constructs: language, ethnic identity, and ethnic interaction or ethnic distance. The ARSMA-II demonstrates good internal consistency of subscales (alphas ranging from .68 to .91) and test-retest reliability (ranging from .72 to .96). Additionally, the validity of the ARSMA-II has been supported by significant associations with the ARSMA and generational status.

The strong psychometrics of the ARSMA-II have made it a very popular instrument, used in more than 75 publications since 1980. The bilingual format, availability of a software scoring program, ease and brevity of administration, variety of content areas assessed (moving away from relying exclusively on language), and success in differentiating between generational levels are additional advantages. On the other hand, the ARSMA-II has been criticized for its limited applicability to other Latino ethnic groups, absence of an assessment of cultural values (e.g., individualism, collectivism, familism), nonrepresentative sample (379 college students), lack of norms for children, and problems with classification (portions of samples that do not fall into categorical acculturation styles, insignificant differences between classifications).

A host of studies using the ARSMA and ARSMA-II have empirically linked Mexican American acculturation with a variety of constructs, including ethnic identity, socioeconomic status, mental health, academic attainment, gang involvement, relationship satisfaction, health risk behaviors, eating disorders, suicidal ideation, depression, clinical elevations on personality tests, self-esteem, coping, and counseling expectations. Experts in the field of acculturation underscore the need for longitudinal studies of the acculturation process to more accurately capture the developmental and dynamic nature of acculturation. Many urge that revisions to acculturation scales should include direct measures of contextual mediators or moderators of acculturation (e.g., reason for immigration, immigration policies, attitudes toward immigrants, political environment).

—*Rebecca E. Ford*
—*Yarí Colón*
—*Bernadette Sánchez*

See also Acculturation; Mexican Americans

FURTHER READING

Berry, J. W. (1980). Acculturation as varieties of adaptation. In A. M. Padilla (Ed.), *Acculturation: Theory, models, and some new findings* (pp. 9–25). Boulder, CO: Westview Press.

Cabassa, L. J. (2003). Measuring acculturation: Where we are and where we need to go. *Hispanic Journal of Behavioral Sciences, 25*(2), 127–146.

Cuéllar, I., Arnold, B., & Maldonado, R. (1995). Acculturation Rating Scale for Mexican Americans-II: A revision of the original ARSMA scale. *Hispanic Journal of Behavioral Sciences, 17*(3), 275–304.

ACCULTURATION SCALES: AFRICAN AMERICAN ACCULTURATION SCALE

Acculturation is defined as the extent to which an ethnic minority individual participates in the values and beliefs of the dominant ethnic-majority culture. Acculturation can be thought of as a continuum from traditional at one extreme, to bicultural in the middle, to acculturated at the other extreme. Traditional individuals retain almost exclusively the values and beliefs of their culture of origin and do not participate in the majority culture. Bicultural individuals are fluent in both their culture of origin and that of the majority. Bicultural individuals can further be classified as "blended," having melded aspects of both cultures, or "code-switchers," those who alternate between the two cultures. Acculturated individuals

participate almost exclusively in the majority culture and have rejected most aspects of their culture of origin.

In the United States, the concept of acculturation has generally been applied to immigrant ethnic groups. However, as the developers of the African American Acculturation Scale (AAAS), Hope Landrine and Elizabeth Klonoff, have demonstrated, the concept of acculturation can be meaningfully applied to African Americans. Despite the long residence of African Americans in the United States, individual African Americans, like individuals in other ethnic minority groups, may choose to participate in the majority culture to a greater or lesser extent.

The AAAS is designed to tap some of the cultural domains in which African Americans display relatively distinctive beliefs and practices, such as religion, health, and child rearing. Scores on the scale have been found to be independent of demographic variables such as education, income, and gender. Three versions of the scale have been published: The first version (AAAS), published in 1994, contained 72 items that were divided into eight sections; a shorter version (AAAS-33), published in 1995, contained 33 items on 10 empirically derived subscales; and a revised version (AAAS-R), published in 2000, contained 47 items on eight factors. The AAAS-R, like its predecessors, has been shown to be psychometrically sound, with internal consistency reliability of .93 and split-half reliability of .79. Discriminant validity of the AAAS-R was established by comparing African Americans with differing levels of segregation; African Americans with other ethnic groups; and African American drinkers (who tend to be less traditional) with abstainers.

The AAAS has been used in studies in several areas of psychology, including health psychology, mental health, and neuropsychology. In health psychology, scores on the AAAS have been linked to cigarette smoking and hypertension. In general, the research suggests that an individual's level of acculturation may be related to (1) how much racism he or she experiences (more traditional people experience more racism), which is related to how much the person smokes (more racism results in greater smoking), and (2) how stressful the racism is perceived as being (more traditional people experience racism as more stressful), which is related to hypertension (more stressful racism results in higher blood pressure levels).

In mental health research, AAAS scores have been shown to predict depression, stress levels, and coping styles. Additionally, the relationship between mental health and coping styles may be different for acculturated individuals than for traditional individuals. In neuropsychology, the AAAS has been helpful in understanding why African Americans, particularly elders, score significantly lower than European Americans on tests of cognitive ability. The AAAS has proven to be a valuable tool in elucidating the unique role that cultural factors play in the experiences and behaviors of African Americans in the United States.

—*Tamara D. Warner*

See also Acculturation; Mexican Americans

FURTHER READING

Klonoff, E. A., & Landrine, H. (2000). Revising and improving the African American Acculturation Scale. *Journal of Black Psychology, 26*(2), 235–261.

Landrine, H., & Klonoff, E. A. (1996). *African American acculturation: Deconstructing race and reviving culture.* Thousand Oaks, CA: Sage.

Manly, J. J., Byrd, D. A., Touradji, P., & Stern, Y. (2004). Acculturation, reading level, and neuropsychological test performance among African American elders. *Applied Neuropsychology, 11*(1), 37–46.

ACCULTURATION SCALES: ASIAN AMERICAN MULTIDIMENSIONAL ACCULTURATION SCALE

The Asian American Multidimensional Acculturation Scale (AAMAS) is a measure of acculturation based on orthogonal assessment of three different cultural dimensions, which comprise four specific acculturation domains. Advancements in acculturation theory have established the desirability of a bidimensional approach to the measurement of acculturation, one that takes into account orientation to both the culture of origin and the host culture, thereby challenging the zero-sum assumption of a unidimensional approach in which acculturation to one culture comes at the expense of the other. The AAMAS is based on a *multidimensional* approach that includes orthogonal assessments of acculturation to the Culture of Origin (AAMAS-CO) and to European American culture (AAMAS-EA). The AAMAS further extends acculturation theory with the addition of a third cultural dimension, a pan-ethnic Asian American cultural dimension (AAMAS-AA), which is unique to the AAMAS. This dimension assesses the formation of a

shared Asian American identity and culture, which is of increasing significance for Asian Americans.

The items on the AAMAS were adapted from the Suinn-Lew Asian Self-Identity Acculturation Scale (SL-ASIA) and converted to a multidimensional format by asking respondents to rate each item according to three referent groups: (1) their Asian culture of origin, (2) other Asian American cultures, and (3) mainstream European American culture. The primary strengths of the AAMAS include its ability to provide a more complex assessment of Asian American acculturation along cultural and domain-specific dimensions, as well as its ease of administration and use across different ethnicities. The primary weakness of the measure is that, like the SL-ASIA, the AAMAS is primarily a measure of behavioral acculturation. The AAMAS is intended primarily as a research measure, and to date, the predominant application has been for this purpose.

ACCULTURATION DOMAINS

In addition to the three cultural dimensions, exploratory and confirmatory factor analyses support four specific acculturation domains: language, food consumption, cultural knowledge, and cultural identity. Measures of internal consistency for each domain by cultural dimension range from .65 (food consumption in the AAMAS-CO) to .89 (cultural knowledge in the AAMAS-CO).

RELIABILITY AND VALIDITY

Results of three separate studies provide strong evidence of the instrument's reliability and validity. Estimates of internal consistency for each cultural dimension ranged from .87 to .91 for the AAMAS-CO, from .78 to .83 for the AAMAS-AA, and from .76 to .81 for the AAMAS-EA, and estimates of stability over time ranged from .75 to .89. Evidence of validity includes a significant negative correlation between the AAMAS-CO and generational status. Assessment of concurrent validity comparing the AAMAS subscales with the Asian Values Scale revealed expectedly modest correlations, whereas for divergent validity, there was little to no relationship with the Rosenberg Self-Esteem Scale.

ADMINISTRATION AND SCORING

The 15 items on the AAMAS are worded so as to facilitate administration across different ethnicities.

The instructions direct the respondents to rate each item according to their own Asian culture of origin, other Asian groups in the United States, and the mainstream host culture. The items are scored on a scale ranging from 1 (not very well) to 6 (very well). Only item 15 is to be reverse scored before adding up the responses for each cultural dimension for a total score, then dividing by 15 to obtain the scale score. Using this method, a separate score is obtained for each cultural dimension.

—*Ruth H. Gim Chung*

See also Asian/Pacific Islander

FURTHER READING

Chung, R. H. G., Kim, B. S. K., & Abreu, J. M. (2004). Asian American Multidimensional Acculturation Scale: Development, factor analysis, reliability and validity. *Cultural Diversity and Ethnic Minority Psychology, 10,* 66–80.

Suinn, R. M., Rickard-Figueroa, K., Lew, S., & Vigil, P. (1987). The Suinn-Lew Asian Self-Identity Acculturation Scale: An initial report. *Educational and Psychological Measurement, 47,* 401–407.

ACCULTURATION SCALES: BIDIMENSIONAL ACCULTURATION SCALE FOR HISPANICS

The Bidimensional Acculturation Scale for Hispanics (BAS) was developed in 1996 to provide researchers with a relatively short measure of acculturation that could address the conceptual and psychometric limitations of other acculturation scales. The BAS uses two dimensions to define acculturation, avoiding the faulty assumption that gains in learning a non-Hispanic culture imply losses in the individual's understanding of or preference for Latino culture. As such, the BAS measures respondents' behavioral characteristics in two cultural domains: Hispanic and non-Hispanic. Furthermore, the BAS is useful in research with individuals from all Latino backgrounds rather than with individuals from one subgroup (e.g., Cuban Americans, Mexican Americans).

The BAS was developed by analyzing a large number of items addressing a variety of acculturative areas (e.g., language use, preference for ethnic social events). A random sample of 254 adult Hispanics was asked to report preferences and abilities in 30 areas in which acculturation can have an impact on behavior. Exploratory principal components and factor analyses were conducted on the original responses (separately for language-related items and social behaviors) to identify factors that accounted for large proportions of the variance. The final scale includes items that had correlations greater than .45 with a given factor and did not load heavily in more than one factor.

The BAS includes 24 items measuring linguistic usage, language proficiency, and electronic media usage. Half of the items refer to English use or English-language proficiency, and the other half addresses the same areas as they refer to Spanish use or proficiency. Each of the items is scored on a four-point Likert-type scale with anchors of "almost never" (scored as 1) and "almost always" (scored as 4) for the usage-related questions and "very well" (scored as 4) or "very poorly" (scored as 1) for the linguistic-proficiency items. The scale produces two acculturation indexes, one for each cultural domain, which are obtained by averaging responses to the 12 items relevant to each cultural domain (range of 1 to 4). An average score close to 1 indicates a low level of cultural proficiency in a given cultural domain (e.g., Latino), whereas an average score close to 4 indicates a high level of cultural proficiency on that same cultural domain. An average score of 2.5 can be used to dichotomize respondents into low or high levels of adherence to the specific cultural domain.

The BAS has shown high levels of reliability and validity. In the original study, the scale showed an alpha coefficient of .87 for the items in the Hispanic domain and .94 for the items in the non-Hispanic domain. Validity was established using a number of approaches, including correlations with respondents' generational status ($r = .50$ for the non-Hispanic domain and $-.42$ for the Hispanic domain), length of residence in the United States ($r = .46$ for the non-Hispanic domain and $-.28$ for the Hispanic domain), age of arrival in the United States ($r = -.60$ for the non-Hispanic domain and .41 for the Hispanic domain), and respondents' own assessments of their acculturative status ($r = .47$ for the non-Hispanic domain and $-.38$ for the Hispanic domain). In addition, the scale correlated highly ($r = .79$ for the non-Hispanic domain and $-.64$ for the Hispanic domain) with the Short Acculturation Scale for Hispanics (SASH).

The BAS has been used with Latinos of all national backgrounds and all generations, and the validation study was conducted with Mexican and Central

Americans. The items that make up the scale in English and in Spanish and the scoring instructions are available in the original publication. The scale has been useful in providing a comprehensive understanding of Hispanic acculturation in areas as diverse as physical health, mental health, drug and tobacco use, educational achievement, employment, and criminal behavior.

—*Gerardo Marín*

See also Acculturation; Acculturation Scales: Short Acculturation Scale for Hispanics

FURTHER READING

Marín, G., & Gamba, R. J. (1987). A new measure of acculturation for Hispanics: The Bidimensional Acculturation Scale for Hispanics (BAS). *Hispanic Journal of Behavioral Sciences, 18,* 297–316.

ACCULTURATION SCALES: EAST ASIAN ACCULTURATION MEASURE

The East Asian Acculturation Measure (EAAM) is a 29-item self-report instrument designed to measure the social interaction and communication styles (both competency and ease and comfort in communicating) of East Asian (i.e., Chinese, Japanese, and Korean) immigrants in the United States.

MODELS OF ACCULTURATION

Researchers typically conceptualize the acculturation of Asian ethnic groups as a unidimensional construct that ranges from low acculturation, indicating a primary Asian identification, to high acculturation, indicating a Western identification, with an imputed midpoint representing a bicultural identification. This model has three key deficits: (1) Acculturation often does not occur in a neat linear or unidimensional manner; (2) the distinction between acculturation and ethnic identity is often obfuscated; and (3) identification with neither Asian nor Western cultures (i.e., marginalization) is not assessed.

In contrast, the EAAM is based on a multidimensional model of acculturation and examines four modes of social interaction and communication: (1) with ethnic group peers (separation), (2) with members of the host culture (assimilation), (3) with members of one's ethnic group and members of the host culture (integration), and (4) with neither one's own group peers nor members of the host culture (marginalization). The EAAM items do not assess ethnic identity (i.e., identity associated with belonging to a certain ethnic group). Instead, ethnic identity among East Asian immigrants may be assessed using the East Asian Ethnic Identity Scale.

NORMS, RELIABILITY, AND VALIDITY

The EAAM was originally studied with 150 East Asian immigrants (75 men, 75 women) with a mean age of 28.7 (SD = 6.40). The internal consistency (alpha) coefficients were .76, .77, .74, and .85 for separation, assimilation, integration, and marginalization, respectively. Significant negative correlations were found between separation and assimilation and between integration and marginalization. Length of stay in the United States was significantly and positively associated with assimilation and integration but significantly and negatively associated with marginalization. Normative data for the EAAM are currently being developed. Although the EAAM performed well psychometrically on the initial sample, its psychometric properties need to be established with other East Asian and non-Asian samples, including those with varying socioeconomic and educational backgrounds and English-language proficiency.

CLINICAL PRACTICE AND RESEARCH

Although many acculturation measures provide proxy measures of acculturation (e.g., generational status, English-language proficiency), the EAAM allows researchers to assess a pattern of attitudes and behaviors relevant to socialization and communication in various situations along multiple dimensions. Such information may be of clinical as well as social importance. The EAAM assimilation scale score significantly predicts increased willingness to use psychological services, whereas the EAAM marginalization scale score significantly predicts guarded self-disclosure, a potentially important impediment to engagement in traditional psychotherapy. In terms of social functioning, the EAAM integration scale score significantly predicts perceived egalitarian treatment from Americans, whereas the EAAM marginalization scale score significantly predicts perceived ethnic-group discrimination (i.e., "people from my ethnic group are discriminated against").

—*Declan T. Barry*

See also Asian Values Scale; Asian/Pacific Islander

FURTHER READING

Barry, D. T. (2001). Development of a new scale for measuring acculturation: The East Asian Acculturation Measure (EAAM). *Journal of Immigrant Health, 3,* 193–197.

Barry, D. T. (2002). An ethnic identity scale for East Asian immigrants. *Journal of Immigrant Health, 4,* 87–94.

Barry, D. T., & Grilo, C. M. (2003). Cultural, self-esteem, and demographic correlates of perception of personal and group discrimination among East Asian immigrants. *American Journal of Orthopsychiatry, 73*(2), 223–229.

ACCULTURATION SCALES: SHORT ACCULTURATION SCALE FOR HISPANICS

The Short Acculturation Scale for Hispanics (SASH) is one of the most frequently used acculturation scales in research with Latinos. The SASH was developed in 1987 after lengthy analysis of the responses of 363 Hispanics (e.g., Cubans, Mexican Americans, Puerto Ricans, and Central Americans) and 228 Caucasians to questions dealing with ethnic contact patterns, proficiency and preference of language use, preferred ethnicity in social relations, and characteristics of media use. Exploratory principal components factor analyses were conducted on the original responses to identify factors that accounted for large proportions of the variance. The final scale includes items that had correlations greater than .60 on a given factor and did not load heavily in more than one factor.

The SASH includes 12 items measuring linguistic usage and preferences and the ethnicity of friends, social gatherings, and play partners for respondents' children. Each of the items is scored on a five-point Likert-type scale with anchors of "only Spanish" (scored as 1) and "only English" (scored as 5) for the language-related items and "all Latinos/Hispanics" (scored as 1) and "all Americans" (scored as 5) for the ethnic-preference items. The acculturation index is obtained by averaging responses to the 12 items (range of 1 to 5). An average score close to 1 indicates a low level of acculturation, whereas an average score close to 5 indicates a high level of acculturation.

An average score of 2.99 can be used to dichotomize respondents into low acculturation (i.e., those with average scores lower than 2.99) and highly acculturated respondents (i.e., those with average scores greater than 2.99). Further research has shown that, when needed, the scale can be shortened to the first five language-related items.

The SASH has shown high levels of reliability and validity. In the original study, the scale showed an alpha coefficient of .92 for all 12 items and .90 for the first five language-related items. Validity was established using a number of approaches, including correlations with respondents' generational status ($r = .65$, $p < .001$), length of residence in the United States ($r = .70$, $p < .001$), age of arrival in the United States ($r = -.69$, $p < .001$), and respondents' own assessment of their acculturative status ($r = .76$, $p < .001$). In addition, the scale discriminates between first- and second-generation Hispanics.

The SASH has been used with Latinos of all national backgrounds and all generations, as well as with individuals of limited reading ability. The scale has also been adapted for use with other ethnic and national groups by changing the response categories to more accurately reflect the group being studied. The items that make up the scale in English and Spanish are available in the original publication. A version for children is also available.

A major limitation of the scale is that it measures acculturation as a unidimensional phenomenon anchored at one cultural pole by a Latino dimension and at the other by a non-Hispanic dimension. Nevertheless, the SASH has a long history of effectively identifying Latinos with low or high levels of acculturation in different contexts and under a variety of circumstances. The Short Acculturation Scale for Hispanics is particularly useful when a rapid measure of acculturation is needed because of time constraints or length of study. The scale is also useful when researchers need to dichotomize respondents in terms of high or low levels of acculturation.

—*Gerardo Marín*

See also Acculturation; Acculturation Scales: Bidimensional Acculturation Scale for Hispanics

FURTHER READING

Barona, A., & Miller, J. A. (1994). Short Acculturation Scale for Hispanic Youth (SASH-Y): A preliminary report. *Hispanic Journal of Behavioral Sciences, 16,* 155–162.

Marín, G., Sabogal, F., VanOss Marín, B., Otero-Sabogal, R., & Pérez-Stable, E. J. (1987). Development of a Short Acculturation Scale for Hispanics. *Hispanic Journal of Behavioral Sciences, 9,* 183–205.

ACCULTURATION SCALES: SUINN-LEW ASIAN SELF-IDENTITY ACCULTURATION SCALE

Developed to gauge acculturation in Asian Americans, the Suinn-Lew Asian Self-Identity Acculturation Scale (SL-ASIA) assesses the cognitive, behavioral, and attitudinal aspects of acculturation. The SL-ASIA is the most widely used measure of acculturation in Asian American populations. The SL-ASIA is based on a unilinear conceptualization of acculturation, which suggests that increased adherence to mainstream culture results in the reduction of adherence to the person's culture of origin.

The SL-ASIA is a paper-and-pencil self-report scale that consists of 21 multiple-choice items, each of which is rated on a five-point scale. Items assess language, identity, friendship choice, behaviors, generation and geographic history, and attitudes, and they are worded so as to be relevant to various Asian subgroups (e.g., Korean, Chinese, and Japanese). Scores are obtained by summing the answers for all 21 items and dividing the sum of scores by 21 to derive the final acculturation score. Acculturation scores can range from 1.00 (low acculturation) to 5.00 (high acculturation). An acculturation score of 3.00 represents a bicultural experience. Higher acculturation scores infer a greater degree of Western identification. In addition to total score analysis, one item allows the participant to rate himself or herself as either "very Asian," "bicultural," or "very anglicized."

PSYCHOMETRIC PROPERTIES

There is much evidence to suggest that the SL-ASIA is capable of producing reliable scores (e.g., see Ponterotto, Baluch, & Carielli, 1998). Scores on the SL-ASIA have generated internal consistency estimates ranging from .68 to .88 but typically fall in the mid .80s. In addition, there is much evidence that speaks to the construct validity of the SL-ASIA. For example, relationships have been found between SL-ASIA scores and generational status, residency in the United States, self-reported ethnic identity, attitudes toward counseling, willingness to see a counselor, and counselor ratings. Suinn and colleagues found the SL-ASIA items to be influenced by five underlying factors: (1) reading, writing, and cultural preference; (2) ethnic interaction; (3) affinity for ethnic identity and pride; (4) generational identity; and (5) food preference. This five-factor model of the SL-ASIA has been validated in both exploratory and confirmatory factor analytic investigations. Miller and colleagues also found evidence suggesting the SL-ASIA measures acculturation in an equivalent fashion for both women and men. Together, these pieces of evidence suggest the SL-ASIA produces reliable and valid scores of acculturation for Asian Americans.

UTILITY OF THE SL-ASIA

Because the SL-ASIA is a relatively brief, clear-cut instrument, it can be an effective piece of formal or informal assessment in clinical practice. As an assessment tool, the SL-ASIA supplies information about an individual's ethnic interaction, ethnic identity, language use, and social networks. By obtaining a deeper cultural and ethnic understanding of the individual, clinicians can begin to understand the phenomenological experience of the Asian American individual. In addition, because of the wording of the SL-ASIA items, the measure can be used with a wide range of Asian American subgroups.

LIMITATIONS

When using the SL-ASIA, it is important to recognize that the majority of items assess the behavioral dimension of acculturation (e.g., language preference). Recently, multidimensional conceptualizations of acculturation, which suggest that acculturation occurs on multiple dimensions (e.g., values and behavior), have been postulated. Therefore, it is helpful to understand that the SL-ASIA may not address other dimensions of the acculturation process.

—*Matthew J. Miller*
—*Suzette L. Speight*

See also Acculturation; Acculturation Measures

FURTHER READING

Miller, M. J., Abe-Kim, J., Li, J., & Bryant, F. B. (2006). *A multisample confirmatory analysis examining the equivalence of the SL-ASIA across sex.* Manuscript submitted for publication.

Ponterotto, J. G., Baluch, S., & Carielli, D. (1998). The Suinn-Lew Asian Self-Identity Acculturation Scale (SL-ASIA): Critique and research recommendations. *Measurement and Evaluation in Counseling and Development, 31,* 109–124.

Suinn, R. M., Ahuna, C., & Khoo G. (1992). The Suinn-Lew Asian Self-Identity Acculturation Scale: Concurrent and factorial validation. *Educational and Psychological Measurement, 52,* 1041–1046.

ACCULTURATIVE STRESS

Acculturation refers to a process of cultural change that occurs when two or more cultural groups come into contact for an extended time, particularly when individuals in minority groups move into a new culture or host society. This is a complex, dynamic change process whereby individuals continuously negotiate among accepting, adapting to, or denying the characteristics of a majority culture, as well as retaining, changing, or rejecting certain components of their own culture. Psychological acculturation involves an adaptation or change in attitudes, behaviors, values, and identity.

As people undergo the process of cultural change, they often encounter difficulties or challenges in adapting to a new set of cultural customs and behavioral rules in a nonnative society, where they may lack resources and support from their native culture. *Acculturative stress* is defined as stress related to moving from one's culture of origin to another culture. Although the traditional view held that acculturation inevitably brings tremendous stress, the contemporary view attempts to understand acculturative stress through a lens of a stress-coping model. This model postulates that (1) acculturative stress may occur when the external and internal demands of the acculturation process exceed the individual's coping ability or resources, and (2) the level of acculturative stress depends on multiple factors, such as the mode of acculturation, nature of the acculturating group, characteristics of the host culture, and demographic variables (e.g., age, gender).

For example, it has been found that among international students in the United States, acculturative stress is associated with English fluency, satisfaction with social support, social connectedness, the need for approval, and maladaptive perfectionism. For African

American college students, acculturative stress is associated with racial identity and racial socialization. For Latinos, acculturative stress is related to the efficacy of stress-coping resources, degree of acculturation, cohesion of the family, language use, and length of residence in the United States.

Not surprisingly, acculturative stress has been linked to academic performance and negative mental health consequences. For example, acculturative stress has been positively associated with lower academic performance, lower quality of life in general, excessive alcohol intake, body dissatisfaction and bulimia, identity confusion, anxiety, psychosomatic symptoms, depression, and suicidal ideation. Moreover, during the past five years, research related to acculturative stress has begun to identify variables that might mediate or moderate the relationship between acculturative stress and depression. For example, it has been found that maladaptive perfectionism moderates the relationship between acculturative stress and depression in international students. Similarly, perceived social support from friends has been shown to have a buffering effect between acculturative stress and depression for Korean adolescents from immigrant families in the United States. Likewise, family closeness, hopefulness for the future, and financial resources have been found to provide a buffer against the negative effects of acculturative stress experienced by Mexican immigrants. Thus, the relationship between acculturative stress and mental health in not necessarily a simple linear relationship but can be buffered by a range of personality variables, social support, and financial resources.

—*P. Paul Heppner*
—*Hyun-joo Park*
—*Mei-fen Wei*

See also Acculturation; Cultural Barriers

FURTHER READING

Berry, J. W. (1990). Psychology of acculturation: Understanding individuals moving between cultures. In R. W. Brislin (Ed.), *Applied cross-cultural psychology* (pp. 232–253). Newbury Park, CA: Sage.

Rodriquez, N., Meyers, H. F., Mira, C. B., Flores, T., & Garcia-Hernandez, L. (2002). Development of the Multidimensional Acculturative Stress Inventory for adults of Mexican origin. *Psychological Assessment, 14,* 451–461.

Williams, C. L., & Berry, J. W. (1991). Primary prevention of acculturative stress among refugees. *American Psychologist, 46,* 632–641.

AFFIRMATIVE ACTION

Few governmental policies have been as controversial as affirmative action. During the last several years, battles over affirmative action captured the public's attention as two cases—*Gratz v. Bollinger* and *Grutter v. Bollinger*—were heard by the Supreme Court. Generally heralded as successes for affirmative action, the two Supreme Court decisions, handed down in June 2003, have not stopped anti–affirmative efforts.

Part of the reason for the continued controversy is that affirmative action is not well understood. Often misrepresented as quotas or reverse discrimination, affirmative action is actually a system whose purpose is to detect and correct systematic institutionalized discrimination. Affirmative action aims to ensure, not to undercut, true equality of opportunity for all ethnicities and both genders.

WHAT IS AFFIRMATIVE ACTION?

The American Psychological Association defines affirmative action as occurring when an organization expends energy to make sure that there is no discrimination in employment or education and to ensure that equal opportunity exists. The United States received its first governmental mandate to initiate affirmative action by way of Executive Order 11246, issued by Lyndon Johnson in 1965. The order required all governmental agencies, as well as organizations that contract with the federal government, to enact proactive measures to ensure that the diversity within their organizations matches the diversity in the pool of qualified labor.

Ideally, hiring in the workplace and admissions in educational organizations would result in diversity within businesses and schools equal to that in society. Yet research shows that this is not the case. Regardless of the value of equal opportunity, it is clear that equal opportunity does not always exist in practice within organizations in the United States. Because of old habits of thought and behavior that create racial and gender insensitivity, as well as blatant and subtle racism and sexism, Caucasian men still enjoy unearned privileges in American society. They can find and keep employment more easily than others who are similarly qualified. They obtain better mortgage rates, car deals, housing, and health care than others.

Given the persistence of gender and racial discrimination, organizations have a choice: They can deal with discrimination retroactively after a complaint is made, or they can adopt an affirmative action policy to stave off complaints and to ensure that women and minorities are indeed receiving opportunities equal to those of Caucasian men. Many organizations voluntarily opt for affirmative action to minimize the chances of having to clean up a problem after the fact.

Affirmative action aims to assure true equality of opportunity. Yet affirmative action can also be distinguished from the ideal of equal opportunity. Affirmative action takes a proactive stance on ensuring fairness and diversity in employment and education. In other words, rather than assuming that equal opportunity exists, affirmative action takes into account that equal opportunity is flawed because of institutionalized racism and sexism.

AFFIRMATIVE ACTION IN EMPLOYMENT

All federal organizations are required to comply with the policy of affirmative action. Private organizations with more than 50 employees that contract with the federal government for amounts greater than $50,000 are also required to act as affirmative action employers. They are required, in other words, to develop and maintain an affirmative action plan in the workplace.

At the core of any affirmative action plan for federal contractors is a monitoring system. Organizations must make sure that the ratio of minorities and women to Caucasian men in their labor force is equal to that of the qualified labor pool. Similarly, federal contractors must monitor their promotions.

Sometimes the monitoring process reveals substantive differences—for example, that the proportion of women in the organization's labor force is lower than the proportion of qualified women in the available labor pool. When differences appear, corrective actions must be identified and undertaken.

The Office of Federal Contract Compliance Program (OFCCP) is the governmental agency charged with oversight of businesses that have contracts with the federal government. Although the majority of private organizations self-monitor their own hiring statistics, the OFCCP does run 3,000 to 5,000 compliance reviews on privately owned businesses per year. If an organization is found to be in noncompliance, the OFCCP helps the organization adhere to the rules. Organizations that are flagrant offenders of the rules can be disbarred from holding federal contracts for a period of time.

AFFIRMATIVE ACTION IN EDUCATION

Affirmative action in education functions much as it does in employment. Typically, universities compile records from the admissions office that track the ethnicity and gender of applicants and students. The university uses these records to compare the diversity of the applicant pool to that of the accepted students, as well as to track the retention of students to make sure that all ethnicities and genders are being treated equally. If a problem is detected, the university can examine why the discrepancy exists and move to remedy the problem.

The state of California has a master plan for higher education that guarantees admission to the University of California to the top 12.5% of high school graduates. By monitoring the ethnicity and gender of the top students, the university noted that there were more Latino students available for admission than were being admitted. The problem was found to be the result of some specific factors. Latino high school students were less likely than others to be counseled by guidance staff to take the core class requirements to gain admission. In addition, Latino students were less able to take advantage of advanced placement courses than Caucasian students. To address these problems, the university has exempted the top tier of applicants (those who graduated in the top 4%) from the course requirements, and it is in the process of making advanced placement courses available online. These changes represent alternative paths to increasing diversity that aim to increase the eligibility of underrepresented students rather then giving preference to minority applicants.

In 1996, the voters of California passed Proposition 209 by a very narrow majority. In addition, the Regents of the University of California, under the prodding of Regent Ward Connerly, enacted two resolutions that removed the consideration of race, religion, sex, color, ethnicity, or country of origin as criteria for admission to the university as well as faculty and staff hiring. As a result of this policy change, the percentage of underrepresented group members admitted to the university dropped considerably in the following years. In 2001, the Regents unanimously voted to repeal the 1995 ban on race-conscious admission; however, because of the passage of Proposition 209, the ban is still in effect at the state level.

In recent years, the University of Michigan has been more in the public's eye than the University of California. In 1997, Jennifer Gratz and Patrick Hamacher, two European American students, challenged the race-sensitive admissions program of the undergraduate college at the University of Michigan. They had been rejected, whereas applicants of color with lower scores and grades had been accepted. Two months after the *Gratz* case was filed in federal court, Barbara Grutter, another rejected European American applicant, brought suit against the University of Michigan Law School. On June 23, 2003, the Supreme Court announced its decisions. It declared that race could not be used in formulaic approaches to admissions, but the Court also recognized diversity in higher education as a compelling state interest. Race-sensitive policies, the Court concluded, are not ipso facto unconstitutional.

WHY DO WE NEED AFFIRMATIVE ACTION?

Affirmative action is only one method of correcting injustices. More reactive means, such as bringing a lawsuit, are sometimes thought to be more fair and effective than affirmative action. There are three main reasons why affirmative action may be a more effective and less costly way of assuring fairness and stability than the reactive (lawsuit) approach. First, copious research in the social sciences has shown that, many times, the victims of discrimination "have blinders on," refusing to acknowledge discrimination until the situation is dire. Second, even fair-minded outside observers who have not themselves been the victims of discrimination have a hard time detecting imbalances without the help of systematically arranged aggregate data. Most affirmative action plans provide observers with aggregated data and thus allow them to detect patterns of fairness or unfairness that they would otherwise miss. Third, lawsuits are extremely costly for individuals and for organizations. Proactive measures that allow organizations to monitor their situations and to correct minor problems before they engender a lawsuit usually prove to be excellent investments.

DOES AFFIRMATIVE ACTION WORK?

Affirmative action plans in education have been shown to increase the presence and the success of hitherto underrepresented minorities. Indeed, without race-sensitive admissions plans, imperfections in the admissions criteria would result in student bodies more Caucasian than at present. In our multiethnic society, the state has a compelling interest in achieving diverse student bodies, according to the U.S. Supreme Court.

In industry, affirmative action has also proven to be effective. Cost–benefit analyses have found that, in material terms, companies that use affirmative action benefit not only from avoiding costly lawsuits but also from the diversity in their workforce. Meanwhile, ethnic minority workers and Caucasian women benefit from the reduction in barriers that affirmative action brings.

Some opponents of affirmative action claim that the policy undermines the confidence of its intended beneficiaries. Certainly, people do not like to believe that they may have obtained positive outcomes as a result of special privilege. Notwithstanding stereotypes to the contrary, only a handful of ethnic minority individuals and Caucasian women mistake affirmative action for special privilege. Careful surveys show that the majority of direct beneficiaries see the policy not as one that gives them special privilege, but rather as one that reduces the previously unquestioned special privileges of Caucasian males.

In sum, affirmative action is a policy that attempts to make the ideal of equal opportunity an actuality. In employment and education, it entails careful monitoring of information so that subtle patterns of discrimination can be detected and imbalances can be corrected. Affirmative action promotes diversity. Rather than simply giving lip service to the values of fairness, justice, and diversity, affirmative action helps to ensure that these values are fulfilled in our society.

—*Kristina R. Schmukler*

See also Equal Opportunity Employment; Institutional Racism

FURTHER READING

American Psychological Association. (1996). *Affirmative action: Who benefits?* Washington, DC: Author.

Bowen, W. G., & Bok, D. C. (1998). *The shape of the river: Long-term consequences of considering race in college and university admissions.* Princeton, NJ: Princeton University Press.

Crosby, F. J. (2004). *Affirmative action is dead: Long live affirmative action.* New Haven, CT: Yale University Press.

Crosby, F. J., Iyer, A., Clayton, S., & Downing, R. (2003). Affirmative action: Psychological data and the policy debates. *American Psychologist, 58,* 93–115.

AFRICAN AMERICANS AND MENTAL HEALTH

PREVALENCE OF MENTAL ILLNESS AMONG AFRICAN AMERICANS

Mental disorders are highly prevalent across all populations, regardless of race or ethnicity. Within the United States, overall rates of mental disorders for most minority groups are largely similar to those for Caucasians. However, ethnic and racial minorities in the United States face a social and economic environment of inequality that includes greater exposure to racism and discrimination, violence, and poverty—all of which take a toll on mental health. In some surveys, African Americans have been found to have higher levels of lifetime (or current) mental disorders than Caucasians. However, when differences in age, gender, marital status, and socioeconomic status are taken into account, the racial difference is eliminated.

In most major epidemiological surveys, the overall rates of mental illness for African Americans living in a community appear to be similar to those of non-Hispanic Caucasians. However, differences do arise when assessing the prevalence of specific illnesses. For example, African Americans are less likely to suffer from major depression and more likely to suffer from phobias than Caucasians. Although somatization is more common among African Americans than among Caucasians, rates of suicide for young men in both ethnic groups are similar. Researchers have also found lower lifetime rates among African Americans for several other major mental disorders, including panic disorder, social phobia, and generalized anxiety disorder. In contrast, African Americans have higher rates of posttraumatic stress disorder and substance abuse than Afro-Caribbeans or Caucasian Americans.

The general conclusion regarding the lack of racial differences in rates of mental illness does not apply to vulnerable, high-need subgroups such as the homeless or the incarcerated, who have higher rates of mental illness and are often not captured in community surveys. African Americans are overrepresented in these high-need populations. Although they represent only 12% of the U.S. population, African Americans make up about 40% of the homeless. The ratio is similar for people who are incarcerated: Nearly half of all prisoners in state and federal jails and almost 40% of juveniles in legal custody are African American. One explanation for African Americans' higher rates of certain mental health problems is the stressful conditions created by racism, discrimination, and poverty. Whether racism and discrimination by themselves can cause these disorders is not clear, but there does appear to be a significant association between poverty and incidences of mental illness.

THE EFFECTS OF RACISM ON MENTAL HEALTH

There is no question that racism exists in the United States and that African Americans have been the primary recipients of negative stereotypes and discrimination. There are numerous definitions of racism present in the research literature. For the purposes of this discussion, the term *racism* is used to refer to any behavior or pattern of behavior that tends to systematically deny access to opportunities or privileges to members of one racial group while perpetuating access to opportunities and privileges to members of another racial group.

It has been argued that racism has a pervasive, adverse influence on the health and well-being of racial and ethnic minority populations in the United States. There are three general ways that racism may jeopardize the mental health of minorities: (1) Racial stereotypes and negative images may be internalized, denigrating individuals' self-worth and adversely affecting their social and psychological functioning; (2) racism and discrimination by societal institutions have resulted in minorities' lower socioeconomic status and poorer living conditions, in which poverty, crime, and violence are persistent stressors that can affect mental health; and (3) racism and discrimination are stressful events that can directly lead to psychological distress and physiological changes affecting mental health.

Racial attitudes toward African Americans have shifted over time. During the early 1940s, survey research found that most Caucasians supported policies and practices that limited interracial contact in schools, neighborhoods, and marriages. By the 1990s, these attitudes had shifted, and a majority of Caucasians endorsed such practices as integrated schools and interracial marriages. Although there have been changes in the attitudes of Caucasian Americans toward African Americans, negative stereotypes of African Americans persist. In general, Caucasians view African Americans more negatively than any

other ethnic minority group. As recently as 1990, 29% of Caucasians viewed most African Americans as unintelligent, 44% believed that most are lazy, 56% endorsed the view that most prefer to live on welfare, and 51% indicated that most are prone to violence. There seems to be broad support for egalitarian attitudes toward African Americans, but this coexists with a desire to maintain at least some social distance from African Americans and a limited commitment to policies to eradicate entrenched inequalities.

Racism exists on both an individual and an institutional level. Historically, beliefs about the inferiority of African Americans were translated into policies that restricted their access to education, employment, health care, and residential opportunities. These restrictions led to disparities in essential resources, resulting in significant residential segregation and poverty within African American communities. Today, institutional racism is evidenced by the fact that the median income for Caucasian American households is almost 1.7 times higher than that of African Americans. Nearly 40% of African American children under the age of 18 are growing up poor, compared with 11% of their Caucasian peers. Racism can also be seen in less obvious differences, such as the economic benefits of educational attainment. In 1998, the U.S. Census Bureau noted that a household with an African American male college graduate earned 80 cents for every dollar earned by a comparable Caucasian household. The difference is even more marked for African American households with a female college graduate, whose median income is 74% of that of comparable Caucasians.

These differences in socioeconomic status and educational attainment have important consequences for mental health. Research has found that persons in the lowest categories of both income and education (who are disproportionately African Americans) are twice as likely as those at the highest levels (who are disproportionately Caucasian Americans) to meet the criteria for one of the major psychiatric disorders.

Racism is also thought to adversely affect mental health status through the subjective experience of discrimination. However, there are inconsistent results regarding the connection between racial discrimination and psychological distress. Some studies have found that exposure to racial discrimination is positively related to physical risk factors such as elevated levels of blood pressure and elevated levels of psychological distress. Other studies have found the opposite or no racial differences in rates of psychological distress in African Americans compared with Caucasians. Some have hypothesized that this pattern may reflect the presence of coping strategies within the African American population that may mitigate some of the psychological consequences of exposure to racism. The link between perceived discrimination and mental health appears to be complex, and understanding the variables that moderate this relationship is a relatively new area of empirical research.

USE OF MENTAL HEALTH SERVICES

Disparities in access to and use of mental health services persist across racial and ethnic groups in the United States. These disparities vary, however, depending on geographical location, socioeconomic status, and type of service. In general, racial and ethnic minorities use fewer mental health services than do Caucasians with comparable distress and problems and have less access to mental health services than do non-Hispanic Caucasians. Considering that the incidence of mental illness is similar across racial and ethnic groups, minority individuals who require mental health services carry a greater burden from unmet mental health needs. Studies have shown that African Americans are less likely than Caucasians to seek help from therapists in private practice, mental health centers, and physicians. Yet African Americans prove no different from Caucasians in their use of public-sector therapists, and they are more likely than Caucasians to use inpatient services and the emergency room for mental health care. African Americans who have undergone treatment for mental health problems are also more likely than Caucasians to be confined to jails, prisons, and mental hospitals and more likely to become homeless at some point. These findings highlight the vulnerability of African Americans who are mentally ill and their high degree of social fragility.

African Americans, both those in the general population and those who have been diagnosed with a mental illness, display more positive attitudes toward seeking mental health care than Caucasians, yet they use fewer services. It is interesting to note that prior to their actual use of services, African Americans' attitudes toward seeking mental health services are comparable to—and in some instances more favorable than—those of Caucasians. Once they have used services, however, African Americans tend to hold more

negative attitudes about mental health services and report being less likely to use them in the future than are Caucasians with comparable needs and usage.

BARRIERS TO MENTAL HEALTH SERVICES

A number of variables have been suggested to explain the racial disparity in the use of mental health services. Barriers to mental health care occur at three levels: individual, environmental, and institutional. *Individual barriers* reflect factors that originate from within the individual, such as culture-specific beliefs and knowledge about mental illness that may influence help-seeking behavior.

Mistrust of mental health services is as a major barrier for ethnic minorities seeking treatment, and it is widely accepted as pervasive among African Americans. It arises from both historical persecution and present-day struggles with racism and discrimination. Mistrust also arises from documented abuses and perceived mistreatment, both in the past and more recently, by medical and mental health professionals. It has been found that 12% of African Americans and 15% of Latinos—compared with 1% of Caucasians—feel that a doctor or health provider judged them unfairly or treated them with disrespect because of their race or ethnic background.

Individuals who are more mistrustful of Caucasian providers are less willing to seek mental health treatment and expect less satisfaction from such therapeutic encounters. Given the low numbers of ethnic minorities trained to deliver mental health services, many systems are unable to deliver racially matched providers. African American clients who must rely on racially different providers may face clinicians who are culturally insensitive, and this experience may negatively influence their attitudes toward mental health services.

For some African Americans, limitations in understanding the problem and in their awareness of possible solutions, strategies, and resources are obstacles to seeking mental health services. When experiencing problems, many African Americans perceive that they are having a normal response to a difficult life situation and believe that they should keep trying to manage their difficulties on their own. As their problems increase or reoccur and begin to interfere with their ability to function, African Americans are more likely to rely on informal support from friends, family members, and clergy to try to deal with the situation rather than seek formalized mental health services. It has been noted that about 43% of African Americans rely exclusively on informal help, 44% use both informal and formal providers, and less than 5% turn exclusively to formal sources of help when they are experiencing personal difficulties. This approach to handling problems seems to be supported by family members, significant others, and influential African American community members.

Certain cultural beliefs, such as the need to resolve family concerns within the family and the expectation that African Americans should always demonstrate strength in the face of problems, inhibit individuals from seeking mental health services. There is a cultural expectation that life is difficult and that African Americans as a cultural group should be able to effectively cope with adversity. Another cultural factor that may influence the use of mental health services is one's beliefs about the causes of mental illness. Individuals who identify causes that are consistent with those espoused by mental health professionals (such as the importance of early experiences in families and the effect of trauma on development) are more likely to seek mental health services than those who endorse more discrepant views. Ethnic minority populations more strongly endorse folk beliefs—for example, that imbalances in natural forces cause illness or that supernatural, spiritual, or mystical forces cause illness. They also believe that a lack of moderation or willpower and weakness of character cause illness. It is unlikely that individuals who hold such beliefs about the causes of mental illness will seek formal approaches to mental health treatment.

Environmental barriers reflect factors that occur within the external environment and inhibit attempts or increase the difficulty of efforts to seek help. Mental illness and mental health treatment continue to be plagued by a stigma that adversely affects help-seeking behavior. *Stigma* refers to a cluster of negative attitudes and beliefs that motivate the general public to fear, reject, avoid, and discriminate against people with mental illness. Stigma is widespread in the United States and other Western nations. Research conducted during the 1980s found that African Americans held more negative views of mental illness than Caucasians. In more recent studies, however, it has been found that African Americans hold less stigmatized views of mental health services than in the past. But there continues to be a belief that mental health services are only for those who are seriously mentally ill.

Institutional barriers are factors related to the ability of the individual seeking services to actually access mental health care. The surgeon general's report on culture, race, and ethnicity identified access to care as a major issue involved in mental health service disparities among African Americans. The report identified numerous institutional barriers to mental health services, including a lack of or inadequate insurance coverage, disjointed services, and the location of culturally specific services. There are few high-quality mental health services located in low-income communities, where the majority of African Americans reside. Twenty years ago, many more services were provided in these communities through federal and private funding. These services are no longer available because of increasing budget cuts and shifts in priorities for government spending and private philanthropy. African Americans seeking mental health services must often travel relatively long distances to find available, affordable care. They often experience problems with transportation, inflexible job schedules, and limited resource knowledge, all of which serve as barriers to care.

The cost of mental health services has also been noted as a significant barrier to seeking mental health treatment. African Americans, the majority of whom live in poverty, frequently lack adequate insurance to cover mental health services. Hourly fees for treatment are perceived as excessive and are considered a luxury in the face of basic needs and ongoing financial challenges. Even for African Americans who receive Medicaid benefits, bias is experienced because medication is often the recommended treatment. More often than not, psychotherapy and counseling are not offered as treatment options. With the further marginalization of African Americans by managed care and other insurance companies, access to quality mental health services has become more difficult and costly. Although there is considerable evidence that mental health service needs are high within the African American community, the service shortfall that exists precludes access, thereby exacerbating the emotional strain on African Americans as individuals and as a cultural group.

Misdiagnosis is a further barrier to African Americans and other ethnic minorities receiving adequate mental health care. Minority patients are among those at greatest risk for nondetection of mental disorders in primary care. Missed or incorrect diagnoses carry severe consequences if individuals are given inappropriate or possibly harmful treatments, leaving their underlying mental disorder untreated. Institutional racism was evident over a century ago in the form of separate and often inadequate mental health services for African Americans. It continues today in the form of medical practices for diagnosis, treatment, prescription of medications, and referrals. There is ample evidence that African Americans are overdiagnosed for schizophrenia and underdiagnosed for bipolar disorder, depression, and anxiety as a result of providers' stereotypical attitudes and beliefs. To date, there has been limited research on the extent of bias and stereotyping of African Americans among mental health providers; therefore, the role that stereotyping plays in the racial disparities in mental health service utilization and effectiveness remains unclear.

CULTURE-SPECIFIC APPROACHES TO ASSESSMENT, DIAGNOSIS, AND INTERVENTION

African American psychologists recognize that traditional psychology is limited in its understanding of people of color and that much of the history of the field has reflected bias and discriminatory attitudes and beliefs about African American individuals, families, and communities. Today, many ethnic minority researchers and scholars are recommending that mental health providers become more culturally sensitive in an effort to enhance the effectiveness of their intervention efforts with African American clients. It has been suggested that providers should take a multifaceted therapeutic approach, one that (1) identifies the therapist's own attitudes and beliefs about the world based on developmental and sociocultural influences; (2) examines how the therapist's background and worldview may differ from the client's and may hinder the therapeutic process; (3) strikes a balance between the therapist's need to learn from the client about his or her experiences and the use of community and interagency resources to help understand the client's background; and (4) stresses a therapeutic approach that incorporates multicultural theories and practices.

Understanding African Americans from a multicultural perspective requires that mental health providers really listen to clients and try to understand clients from within their cultural context. Adopting this approach to working with African American clients will help providers become more adaptable in their theoretical orientation, flexible with their skills and strategies, and

sensitive to clients' cultural idiosyncrasies. The development of a therapeutic or conceptual orientation is an ongoing process, and mental health providers must be willing to continue this developmental process well beyond their graduate school education. To be most effective in their work with African Americans, mental health providers must accept that different worldviews can coexist and adapt their skills and abilities so they are applicable to other cultures.

An abundance of literature on African Americans and their culture is available to mental health providers who are committed to enhancing their cultural sensitivity and awareness of this ethnic minority group. It is not possible to review this literature in detail, but a brief discussion of some of the newer theoretical approaches to working with African Americans can provide examples of new trends in the field.

One new approach is the multicultural assessment-intervention process (MAIP) model. This model requires the mental health provider to employ a systematic approach to assessment and intervention that uses cultural information to inform service delivery and improve the quality of services provided to African Americans. Questions are addressed at various points in the assessment-intervention process to emphasize the relevance of assessment instruments, increase the reliability and accuracy of clinical diagnoses, and foster the use of more credible and beneficial intervention services. In the MAIP model, there is a recognition that cultural and racial differences are essential in the understanding of the self and important in the delivery of mental health services to ethnic minorities. It requires a willingness to address problems on the basis of these differences during assessment, diagnosis, and treatment and a commitment on the part of mental health providers to undergo the necessary training to become culturally competent.

A second approach that seems to hold promise for enhancing access to mental health services calls for collaboration between the field of psychology and the African American church. The African American church in general and the clergy in particular have traditionally played important roles in providing supportive resources to the African American community. Although there are a number of African-centered models of psychotherapy in which spiritual development is understood as central to human development, few mental health providers have actively collaborated with the African American church. There are several barriers that impede collaborative efforts between psychologists and the church: Few academic departments require training for mental health providers in religious or spiritual issues, and mental health providers have limited understanding of the traditions of the different denominations that make up the African American church. To overcome these barriers, providers need to examine their own beliefs regarding religion and spirituality and obtain additional training in religious or biblical counseling. Increasing the collaboration between the African American church and mental health providers will make it possible to provide culturally relevant mental health services to many African Americans who currently do not use traditional mental health delivery systems.

A third recommended treatment approach for working with African Americans focuses on cultural strengths within the African American community and factors that promote resilience. *Resilience* refers to the notion that some people are able to succeed in the face of adversity. It involves factors and processes that interrupt the trajectory from risk to problem behavior or psychopathy. A resilience perspective highlights the development of competencies, assets, and strengths in individuals' lives, and it includes the maintenance of healthy development despite the presence of a threat or recovery from trauma. These psychosocial resources and resilience factors can insulate the individual from such significant stressors as racism or provide coping mechanisms to reduce the negative effects of stress.

Well-established psychosocial resources, such as supportive social ties, perceptions of mastery or control, and self-esteem, have been shown to serve as protective factors for individuals coping with stress and adversity. In addition, research suggests that other culturally specific resources seem to enhance coping among African Americans. These include religious beliefs and behavior, ethnic-group identity and consciousness, and racial socialization experiences. The term *racial socialization* refers to the process of communicating behaviors and messages to children for the purpose of enhancing their sense of racial or ethnic identity, partially in preparation for racially hostile encounters. The association between African Americans' perceptions of racial discrimination and mental health is moderated by experiences with racial socialization in families and by levels of self-esteem.

These newer approaches to understanding and promoting mental health in African Americans hold promise for the development of mental health services that are culturally appropriate and effective. As they become the accepted standard of care in the field, there is hope that existing racial disparities will be significantly reduced or eliminated in the future.

CONCLUSIONS

The mental health needs of African Americans have been well documented in the psychological literature, and over the last decade, there has been a serious effort to incorporate race, ethnicity, and culture into our understanding of mental health and mental illness. Although gains have been made in developing more culturally sensitive treatment interventions, there continues to be evidence of bias in the assessment and diagnosis of mental disorders among African Americans. There are also multiple barriers that have a negative impact on African American clients' access to high-quality mental health services and effective utilization. There are a number of areas for future research, such as the need to better understand the help-seeking attitudes and behaviors of African Americans in the utilization of mental health services and the role that stigma plays in this process. A final question that will need to be examined more thoroughly in the future relates to the effects of cumulative stress on the emergence and progression of mental health problems experienced by African Americans.

Focusing on cultural strengths and resilience is clearly an important direction for the future; however, we should not lose sight of the fact that promoting individual (or collective) resilience is not a substitute for systemic, institutional change. There is compelling evidence that African Americans and other racial and ethnic minorities experience a disproportionately high disability burden from unmet mental health needs. The racism, discrimination, and economic deprivation that plague much of the African American community require system-level change. Ultimately, reducing disparities in the mental health treatment of African Americans will require a societal commitment to social justice and equity.

—Elizabeth E. Sparks

See also African/Black Psychology; Africentric; Association of Black Psychologists; Black Racial Identity Scale

FURTHER READING

Dana, R. H. (2002). Mental health services for African Americans: A cultural/racial perspective. *Cultural Diversity and Ethnic Minority Psychology, 8*(1), 3–18.

U.S. Department of Health and Human Services. (2001). *Mental health: Culture, race, and ethnicity* (Suppl. to *Mental health: A report of the surgeon general*). Rockville, MD: Author.

Williams, D. R., & Williams-Morris, R. (2000). Racism and mental health: The African American experience. *Ethnicity and Health, 5*(3/4), 243–268.

AFRICAN/BLACK PSYCHOLOGY

African/Black psychology is a system of knowledge grounded in the perspectives of African-descent persons and designed to describe their personalities, attitudes, emotions, and behaviors. This system of knowledge is based on an African cosmology and corresponds to African conceptions of the social universe. Essentially, it is a science of exploring the lives of African-descent persons from a perspective that is centered on their experiences.

Although African psychologists acknowledge the existence of an African/Black psychology derived from the development of early African civilizations in Egypt and Ethiopia, formal study and articulation of African psychological concepts, theories, and models have only recently begun to take shape. This formal development is marked by three pivotal moments in history: (1) the work of Francis Cecil Sumner, (2) the founding of the Association of Black Psychologists, and (3) Wade Nobles's publication on the philosophical basis of African psychology in 1986.

In 1992 and 1996, Chancellor Williams and Daudi Ajani ya Azibo, respectively, discussed how the destruction of Black African civilization, beginning as early as 4500 BCE and continuing through the present day, has arrested the development and ownership of African-centered conceptions of the human experience. Historically, Eurocentric psychological explanations have been the primary mode of understanding the behaviors of African/Black persons. In response to this approach, Dr. Francis Cecil Sumner, the first African American to receive a PhD in psychology in the United States (in 1920), began a program of investigation to refute racist and pejorative theory and research that argued for African/Black inferiority. Sumner was named the "father of Black American psychologists," and his work is considered an initial response to Eurocentric psychology, which has been used to validate the mistreatment of African-descent persons.

In response to discontent with the American Psychological Association, the Association of Black Psychologists (ABP) was established in 1968 with an agenda to address issues of race, culture, and oppression as they concern African/Black persons and to promote the refutation of cultural-deficit models and comparative studies that portray African/Black persons as deviant. The ABP is credited with three contributions to the field of African/Black psychology. The first is the reemergence of African psychology based on an African cosmology; second, the development of the *Journal of Black Psychology;* and finally, the Annual International ABP convention, at which African/Black psychologists throughout the diaspora collaborate and learn from one another while building an African/Black psychological community.

In 1972, Wade Nobles's literary contribution, *African Philosophy: Foundations for Black Psychology,* was the final development to clearly link ancient African philosophical thought to the psychology of African/Black people. Following the establishment of the ABP, three camps developed among African/Black psychologists: Eurocentric, Black, and African. Eurocentric psychologists are of African descent and employ Eurocentric theory and research in their work with African-descent persons. Black psychologists are described as reacting to White supremacist notions and racist formulations promoted by Eurocentric psychological theory and research. Finally, African psychologists are described as being proactive in the development of African/Black psychological research and theory, which is centered on the experiences of African/Black people and connected to an African system of knowledge (i.e., cosmology, ontology, axiology, worldview, ideology, and ethos). Nobles's essay was the first published work to articulate the African philosophical basis of African psychology—a seminal piece that initiated the propagation of proactive African/ Black psychological research orientation, theory, and practice.

AFRICAN/BLACK PSYCHOLOGICAL DEVELOPMENTS

African/Black psychological research orientation, theory development, and practice are significantly guided by the Afrocentric school of thought founded by Molefi Asante during the late 20th century. Asante coined the term *Africalogy*—the Afrocentric study of phenomena, events, ideas, and personalities related to Africa—to describe the generation of theory and practice across all disciplines (including psychology) centered on Africa and African descendants. A review of developments in African/Black research orientation, theory, and practice follows.

Research Orientation

There are four tenets of the Afrocentric method by which Africalogists (i.e., researchers of Africa and African-descent persons) are guided. First, researchers examine themselves in the process of examining the subject of study, thus maintaining a practice of introspection and retrospection throughout the course of study. Second, the Afrocentric research method requires cultural and social immersion and discourages traditional scientific distance in the study of African and African-descent persons. Third, the Afrocentric method requires the researcher to have familiarity with the history, language, philosophy, and myths of the people under study. Fourth, the Afrocentric method views research as a vehicle by which to humanize research participants and, ultimately, the world. Later theorists elaborated the Afrocentric research method, explicating and concretizing concepts offered by Asante's initial work.

Theory

African/Black psychological theory has been developed to explain the personalities, attitudes, emotions, and behaviors of African-descent persons from a perspective that is centered on their experiences. Personality and developmental psychological theories have experienced the most growth. Additionally, identity theory has witnessed further growth and development. In her groundbreaking work, Dr. Frances Cress Welsing (1970) presented the *Cress theory of color confrontation and racism,* which explains the hostile treatment of African-descent persons by those of European descent. Other personality theories that explain African-descent persons have been offered by African/Black psychologists such as Na'im Akbar, Daudi Ajani ya Azibo, and Linda Meyers.

Akbar's early conceptualizations of African/Black psychology sought to redefine normalcy for African-descent persons by considering their logical reactions to an oppressive social environment. He coined terms such as *misorientation* and *mentacide,* which describe African-descent persons' psychological response to a

racially hostile and oppressive environment. Continuing this work, Azibo developed an African-centered nosology of Black personality disorders that systematized 18 disorders of the African personality. Several studies have substantiated the integrity of Azibo's nosology. Like Akbar and Azibo, Linda Meyers presented the framework of optimal psychology to explain the manifestation of the African worldview in the psychology of African/Black persons.

Developmental psychological theory has focused on the redefinition of normative growth and development of African/Black children. The work of Amos Wilson is noteworthy. Wilson's work concentrated on the developmental psychology of African/Black children and the development of culturally responsive child-rearing and learning environments that would promote their optimal development. In this vein, Neferkare Abena Stewart focused her work on the early development of African/Black infants across the world to generate developmental milestone norms (e.g., average age for sitting up, walking, talking, etc.) for these children.

Racial identity theory has also witnessed tremendous growth over the last 30 years. In 1970, William Cross introduced formidable work on "Nigrescence" (i.e., the Negro-to-Black conversion) that investigated the process by which African/Black persons develop an integrated identity with regard to race. Cross's initial work influenced subsequent developments in gender and racial identity development theory.

Practice

The practice of African/Black psychology has only recently been formally presented as a cohesive system of treatment, although African-centered approaches to treatment in social services, educational, and mental health settings have been employed for some time. In 1990, Frederick Phillips presented an Afrocentric approach to psychotherapy. This approach is spiritually based, focusing on achieving balance and alignment within persons and systems. Basic principles of Afrocentric therapy—harmony, balance, interconnectedness, cultural awareness, and authenticity—are guided by the African worldview.

CONCLUSION

The field of African/Black psychology continues to develop, reclaiming and elaborating on the African historical and cultural legacy. As growth in the field persists, several developments are anticipated. The expansion of existing theories and the development of new theoretical conceptualizations and practical approaches are expected, as the existing theories and models are at least three decades old. Additionally, psychological studies grounded in Afrocentric theory that demonstrate the effectiveness of African/Black psychological interventions and their generalizability among African/Black persons in diverse settings and contexts are needed. Finally, as a concerted effort takes hold among African/Black psychologists to meet the mental health needs of African-descent persons throughout the diaspora, the development, implementation, and evaluation of theory and interventions for African-descent persons outside the United States will most likely be expanded.

—*Wendi S. Williams*
—*Julie R. Ancis*

See also Association of Black Psychologists

FURTHER READING

Azibo, D. A. (1996). *African psychology in historical perspective and related commentary.* Trenton, NJ: Africa World Press.

Helms, J. E. (1990). *Black and White racial identity: Theory, research, and practice.* Westport, CT: Greenwood Press.

Nobles, W. (1986). *African psychology: Toward its reclamation, reascension, and revitalization.* Oakland, CA: Black Family Institute.

AFRICENTRIC

The term *Africentric,* and the more commonly used term *Afrocentric,* describe a worldview in which African people and culture are the central unit of analysis, with a focus on social and historical context. There are two critical aims in the framework of Africentric scholarship: (1) the reclamation and revision of the history of African people, who share common ancestral origins but are spread throughout the world (this international population represents the *African diaspora*) and (2) the resistance of European cultural hegemony and oppression.

The first aim is to transform scholarship. In particular, Africentric scholars have studied the impact of Black African civilizations, such as the ancient civilizations of the Nile Valley. This revisionist view of world history and antiquity counters the dominant perspective of African people, which commences with European conquest.

The second aim focuses on how individuals make meaning of the world within an Africentric cultural context. Africentric scholars argue that because the Western framework represents African people as deviant from the European ideal, it is futile to attempt to understand the behaviors of African people within a Eurocentric framework.

AFRICENTRIC PSYCHOLOGY

Connectedness is a primary tenet of the Africentric worldview. Contrary to the Western or Eurocentric perspective, which vales objectivity, the Africentric worldview recognizes the interconnectedness of the affective (feeling), cognitive (knowing), and behavioral (acting) domains. The African Self-Consciousness Scale is a measure that encompasses dimensions related to an individual's awareness of a collective sense of relationship to African people and resistance to forces of oppression. African self-consciousness is related to cultural and racial socialization among African Americans.

In the Africentric paradigm, the consequences of oppression manifest in the psyche of African people and are evident in behavior. The Africentric psychologist views cultural orientation as related to well-being. When African people adopt a foreign or Eurocentric worldview, maladaptive behaviors and psychopathology result. Thus, an Africentric framework explains the often-cited disparities between European Americans and African Americans in educational, health, or mental health outcomes as a consequence of oppression and detachment from the cultural source. Africentric psychologists and educators have designed culturally relevant interventions, such as youth rites of passage programs, to help counter the impact of racial oppression.

CHALLENGES TO AFRICENTRIC THEORY

One major challenge to Africentric theory is that within this framework, race is constructed as an essential characteristic. Africentric scholars have been critiqued for focusing on racial classification as deterministic rather than acknowledging the dynamic aspects of culture and the diversity of individual expressions of ethnicity. Some scholars of European classicism have challenged the veracity of some of the claims made within the revised analysis of African people in ancient civilizations throughout the African diaspora. Other critiques address some Africentric scholarship that makes arguably sexist or homophobic assertions about interpersonal relationships in an authentic African cultural context.

CONCLUSIONS

This entry offers a brief review of Africentric perspectives on knowledge production, meaning making, and behavior. Although Africentric theory has gained more attention in recent years, this intellectual tradition is evident historically throughout Black scholarship in the diaspora. Africentric theory in psychology provides a framework for understanding the context of human behavior liberated from Western cultural biases regarding mental health. An Africentric paradigm transforms the analysis of how cultural worldview affects micro- and macro-level outcomes.

—*Zaje A. T. Harrell*

See also African/Black Psychology; Association of Black Psychologists; Culture

FURTHER READING

Ani, M. (1994). *Yurugu: An African-centered critique of European cultural thought and behavior.* Trenton, NJ: Africa World Press.

Asante, M. K. (1998). *The Afrocentric idea.* Philadelphia: Temple University Press.

Kambon, K. K. (1992). *The African personality in America: An African-centered framework.* Tallahassee, FL: Nubian National Publications.

ALASKA NATIVES

Mental health is important to an individual's general health, family relationships, and relationships within the community. A number of factors can contribute to mental health status, including biological, social, and psychological phenomena. Mental illness can have a significant negative impact on individuals, families, and communities. To effectively prevent or ameliorate mental health–related problems, current research and practice focus on these contributors to mental health. Specifically, the role of culture on mental health has become an important area of interest for researchers

and mental health professionals. Although the Alaska Native community constitutes a small percentage of the U.S. population, an incredible diversity exists among its people. For example, differences among Alaska Native peoples can be found in geographical location, language, customs, beliefs, religion, family structures, and social structures. The degree of diversity among the Alaska Native peoples has important implications for psychological research and mental health treatment.

GENERAL INFORMATION

Though there is no single definition of *Alaska Native,* this term is typically used to describe the indigenous people of what is now the state of Alaska. Specifically, Alaska Natives are generally thought to include Eskimo, Indian, and Aleutian peoples. Nearly half of all Alaska Natives are Eskimo, which includes the Inupiat, Yup'ik, and Cup'ik peoples. About one-third of Alaska Natives are Indians, which encompasses the Athabascan, Eyak, Tlingit, Tsimshian, and Haida peoples. Finally, the Aleut people constitute approximately 15% of Alaska Natives.

The Alaska Native population is geographically dispersed throughout the state of Alaska, which is approximately one-fifth the size of the continental United States. In general, the majority of Alaska Natives reside outside the larger Alaska cities in villages of 2,500 people or fewer. Anchorage, the most populated city in the state, is home to approximately 14,000 Alaska Natives. Altogether, Alaska Native groups compose approximately 16% of the state's population. Not only are there geographical differences; linguistic and cultural differences can also be found among the Alaska Native peoples. For example, Alaska Natives speak 20 different languages, live in all major areas of Alaska, and vary in degrees of acculturation.

The Inupiaq live in the northern and northwestern region of Alaska, where they still live a subsistence lifestyle. Two major dialects, which resemble the dialects of Canadian and Greenlandic Eskimos, are spoken by the Inupiaq. The Inupiaq believe in the reincarnation of both animal and human spirits. This belief is often expressed in the ceremonial treatment of animals that are killed during a hunt and the naming of children after deceased relatives.

Distinguishable by their different dialects, the Yup'ik and Cup'ik are concentrated in southwestern Alaska. Also hunters and gatherers, the Yup'ik and

Cup'ik were once a mobile people following the migration of the game they hunted. Historically, social hierarchies among the Yup'ik and Cup'ik were based on gender, and men and women often lived in separate dwellings. Elders played an important role in the socialization of younger members of the group and were responsible for passing on cultural beliefs through storytelling.

Historically, the Athabascan people were concentrated around river ways in the Alaskan interior (central Alaska), where they would hunt, fish, and trap. Today, Athabascans live throughout the state of Alaska. Eleven languages are spoken by the Athabascan people. Although there are exceptions, the majority of Athabascan clans follow a matrilineal social structure. In the past, this matrilineal system influenced hunting practices, living arrangements, and the socialization of children. Among the many values the Athabascan people hold, sharing and respect for all living things are especially important.

The Eyak, Tlingit, Tsimshian, and Haida peoples inhabit the southeastern portion of Alaska, known as the Alaska panhandle, and use a matrilineal system of moieties, phratries, and clans. A *moiety* includes two subdivisions that can be broken down into several clans. A *phratry* is similar to a moiety but has four divisions instead of two. Like moieties, phratries include a specific number of clans. The matrilineal social system determines family name, inheritance, hunting practices, and living arrangements. The Eyak once occupied the southeastern corner of south-central Alaska and included two moieties. Currently, the Eyak people are concentrated on the Copper River Delta in Alaska, where they continue to live a subsistence lifestyle. As with the Eyak, Tlingit subsistence comes primarily from fishing but also includes the gathering of plants and hunting of game. Considered one of the most complex cultures of the North American Natives, Tlingit culture uses a social classification system that defines social norms and strata. Although one common language is shared by the Tsimshian people, four separate dialects are spoken depending on geographical location. Currently, the Tsimshian people are concentrated on Annette Island off the southeastern coast of Alaska. The Haida originally lived among the Queen Charlotte Islands in Canada, eventually settling on Prince of Wales Island off the southeastern coast of Alaska. Unlike the Tlingit and Tsimshian peoples, the Haida speak a language that is unrelated to the other Alaska Native languages.

Finally, the Aleut and Alutiiq peoples live in southern and southwestern Alaska, including the chain of islands off the Alaskan coast known as the Aleutian Islands. The Aleutian Islands are known for having some of the harshest weather in the world. The three major groups of the Aleut and Alutiiq peoples speak two different languages. The Aleut and Alutiiq also incorporate the Russian language into their everyday speech. This reflects the early contact between Russian fur traders and the Aleut and Alutiiq peoples. Like many of the others Alaska Native groups, the Aleut and Alutiiq peoples place a strong emphasis on kinship and sharing.

The Russian discovery of Alaska in 1741 brought significant changes to the indigenous Alaska Native population. Russian fur traders concentrated hunting efforts on much of the Alaskan coast in search of sea otter pelts, often trading with the Alaska Natives. By 1772, a permanent Russian settlement had been established in Unalaska. In 1795, Russian missionaries established the first Russian Orthodox Church on Kodiak Island. Although not all Alaska Native groups were negatively affected by the Russian fur trade, the mistreatment of the Aleuts is well documented. In particular, the Aleut people were enslaved and forced to hunt sea otters for the Russia fur traders. Eventually, interest in Alaska subsided when sea otters had been hunted to near extinction. In 1867, the United States purchased Alaska from Russia for 7.2 million U.S. dollars.

Outside interest in Alaska was rekindled when gold was discovered near Juneau in 1880 and again in the Klondike region in 1897. When vast quantities of gold were found in the Nome region in 1898, the Alaska gold rush began. This brought the arrival of numerous non-Natives to Alaska in a very short period of time. A booming commercial fishing and canning industry, in addition to a growing population of military personnel, created a significant population increase during the early 1900s. By 1959, Alaska's population had grown enough to qualify for statehood. With the discovery of oil and natural gas reserves on Alaska's North Slope, the influx of people to the state has continued to increase.

CUSTOMS AND BELIEFS

The cultural values and ways of life of the different Alaska Native groups have been permanently affected by the introduction of Western society. For example, non-Native people brought diseases, racial discrimination, and modern industry to Alaska. These things have, in some cases, led to a loss of the traditional ways of the Alaska Native peoples. However, traditional beliefs still persist among Alaska Natives. Today, spirituality remains an important aspect of Alaska Native culture, and the traditional belief that humans, animals, and the earth share a relationship is fundamental to the modern belief system of Alaska Natives. With the introduction of organized religion to Alaska, some Alaska Natives have come to view their spirituality concurrently through traditional Native customs and non-Native religious perspectives (e.g., shamanism, Christianity).

In addition to beliefs about the relationship between animals, humans, and the earth, Alaska Native culture emphasizes harmony among an individual's mind, body, and soul. This is considered important to preserving overall health. Disharmony between mind, body, and soul, therefore, can result in mental and physical deterioration. In addition to its holistic view of life, Alaska Native culture places an emphasis on helping within the Native community. This can be seen in the continuance of the subsistence lifestyle of many of the modern Alaska Native groups. Each individual has a role in the daily functioning of the community. For example, elders among the clan are considered an important source of wisdom and advice among Alaska Native peoples.

Although not all Alaska Native cultures believe in shamanism, the idea that an individual can possess the power to see and influence spirits does exist in some Alaska Native groups. Among these groups, a shaman is sometimes considered the spiritual leader of the clan. In other instances, the shaman is seen strictly as a healer or an individual who influences the luck of the community.

In the case of mental or physical illness, the shaman's duties include determining the causes of the illness and deciding how to treat the underlying causes of that illness. For example, many physical or mental problems are considered to be the result of a broken taboo. A *taboo* is an inhibition or ban on specific behaviors or even thoughts based on Native customs and beliefs (e.g., not hunting the animal of your clan name). Many taboos are related to preventing illness or the promotion of a healthy lifestyle. A broken taboo disrupts the harmony between mind, body, and spirit, not only for the individual but also for the community as a whole. The shaman is responsible for identifying which taboo has been broken and advising the individual or the members of the community on methods for remedying the problem. This process typically involves the shaman entering a trance-like state to improve his or her ability to perceive supernatural phenomena that are important to the healing process. The reason for the illness or problem is then identified in an attempt to prevent future problems for the individual and the community.

Alaska Natives believe that the underlying cause of an illness can be either natural or supernatural; the source of the problem determines the method of intervention. The healing ceremonies that follow involve reestablishing community harmony. For example, prayers, songs, and other activities are used to create an atmosphere that facilitates a healing environment. During these ceremonies, participants sometimes wear masks or ornate costumes, dance, play musical instruments, and use images depicting the spirits they intend to attract.

HEALTH DISPARITIES

Because Alaska Natives and American Indians tend to be grouped together when it comes to health issues, it can be difficult to determine the specific mental and physical health problems Alaska Natives face. However, some information does exist about the mental and physical health problems of Alaska Natives. Some of the leading causes of death among Alaska Natives are cancer, unintentional injury, suicide, and homicide. Although cancer rates are decreasing among the general population in the United States, cancer rates among Alaska Natives are increasing. Compared with their non-Native counterparts, Alaska Natives are less likely to survive once they are diagnosed with cancer. The most common types of cancer among Alaska Natives are colorectal cancer and lung cancer. The high rates of lung cancer among Alaska Natives may be related to the high smoking rates among Alaska Native groups. Additionally, because tobacco sales to minors are common, Alaska Natives tend to start smoking at a younger age.

Death as a result of unintentional injury among Alaska Natives has been estimated to be almost four times that of the general population in the United States. Additionally, unintentional injury is the leading cause of death among Alaska Native children. Risk factors related to unintentional injury include poverty, substance abuse, poor housing, lack of access to adequate medical treatment, and geographic isolation.

Suicide rates among Alaska Natives have been estimated to be twice the national average. Suicide rates are particularly high among Alaska Native males in their late teens and early twenties who live in nonurban areas of Alaska (i.e., villages). Though no one can say for sure, suicide is often the result of a lack of treatment for depression and substance abuse. These risk factors appear to be more common among the Alaska Native population. Barriers related to the utilization of appropriate mental health services may be a secondary contributor to suicide among Alaska Natives who suffer from depression and addiction. Some estimates show that Alaska Natives are four times more likely to die from homicide than their non-Native counterparts. In fact, nearly half of all deaths among Alaska Natives are a result of suicide or homicide. Again, alcoholism is considered by many to play a significant role in the high homicide rates within the Alaska Native community.

Alaska Natives also have higher rates of incarceration, homelessness, poverty, and alcohol and drug problems. Statistics on homelessness and poverty can be difficult to interpret because of the extreme variation in living circumstances among Alaska Natives groups. Several theories exist to explain the high prevalence of alcohol abuse among Alaska Natives. Some believe that the altered state induced by alcohol consumption was initially considered a valued spiritual experience among the Alaska Native peoples. Others postulate that the binge drinking of early Russian and American fur traders and trappers led to a skewed socialization of appropriate alcohol consumption. Finally, some believe that the problems many Alaska Natives face are the result of negative events experienced by their ancestors (e.g., racism, discrimination). These stressors are consequently passed down to each successive generation. Regardless of the reason for the high rates of alcoholism among Alaska Natives, most agree that this problem is a significant one.

TREATMENT AND PREVENTION EFFORTS

Smoking Prevention

A number of prevention programs have been developed to address the high rates of tobacco use among Alaska Natives. For example, the Alaska Native Health

Board has developed tobacco-prevention programs to assist Alaska Native communities in reducing tobacco use. These prevention programs focus on discouraging tobacco use and preventing tobacco-related illnesses that ultimately lead to death. These programs are also intended to target Alaska Native youth to prevent early tobacco use.

Suicide

The Department of Health and Social Services Division of the Alcohol and Drug Abuse Community-Based Suicide Prevention Program provides support for Alaska Native communities to create prevention programs aimed at reducing suicide. This resource is particularly appealing because it allows communities to develop prevention programs to meet the specific needs of the community. In addition to these services, a number of agencies and organizations proactively initiate programs for the purpose of educating the Alaska Native community about suicide risk factors, preventing suicides, and providing a forum for discussing concerns related to suicide.

For example, the Western Athabascan Natural Helpers Program is a school-based program that targets at-risk schools for suicide prevention. Additionally, the Zuni Life-Skills Development Curriculum, the Wind River Behavioral Health Program, the Tohono O'odham Psychology Service, and the Indian Suicide Prevention Center are prevention programs developed for American Indian populations. Although these programs are not designed specifically for Alaska Natives, they may provide useful information about tailoring suicide-prevention programs to include Native customs and beliefs.

Unintentional Injury

The Alaska Injury Surveillance and Prevention Program (ISAPP) currently provides resources for preventing unintentional injuries among Alaska Native peoples. These programs work to improve environmental surroundings (e.g., by installing child car seats), encourage safety law compliance (e.g., child car seat use), and provide safety-related education (e.g., proper use of child car seats). The ISAPP uses a community-level approach that focuses on establishing specific programs that target the problems a particular community is facing (e.g., car seat–related accidents).

Homicide

In addition to programs designed to prevent unintentional injury, resources exist for the purpose of reducing and preventing intentional injury within Alaska Native communities (i.e., homicide). An example of such an organization is the Alaska Injury Prevention Center, which works to increase general community safety. The center works with Alaska law enforcement and community agencies to reduce the incidence of homicide through education, public service announcements, and community-based programs.

Alcoholism

Although a number of substance abuse programs are available in Alaska, few incorporate Native beliefs into treatment protocol. However, recent efforts have been made by such organizations as the Department of Health and Human Services to promote culturally sensitive treatment programs for Alaska Natives. Also, Internet resources have been used by this organization to overcome barriers that often result from the geographic dispersion of Native communities.

ALASKA NATIVE ORGANIZATIONS

In addition to prevention programs and organizations, a number of groups exist to provide services to Alaska Natives. For example, the Alaska Native Health Board provides a forum for discussing Alaska Native health issues. The purpose of this organization is to promote the overall well-being of the Alaska Native community.

The Alaska Native Knowledge Network is an organization that compiles and exchanges information related to Alaska Native culture. It was developed to provide federal agencies, private organizations, educators, and the public with insight into the Alaska Native way of life. Additionally, this network provides Alaska Natives with a method for preserving information about their customs and beliefs. The Alaska Native Knowledge Network also has resources for educators who are developing curricula for Alaska Native children and adolescents.

The Alaska Native Tribal Health Consortium is an organization that is owned by the Alaska Native tribal government and various Alaska Native health services organizations. The consortium is part of the Alaska Tribal Health System, which provides medical and mental health services to Alaska Natives. This system of health service providers aims to improve the physical and mental health of Alaska Natives.

The National Center for American Indian and Alaska Native Mental Health Research is a research organization affiliated with the University of Colorado's Department of Psychiatry. This program is sponsored by the National Institutes of Mental Health. The center focuses its research efforts exclusively on American Indian and Alaska Native peoples. This organization was developed to improve understanding of psychological issues among American Indian and Alaska Native populations.

The Center for Alaska Native Health Research is a research organization that conducts research among Alaska Native populations. Sponsored by grants from the National Institutes of Health and the National Center for Research Resources to the University of Alaska– Fairbanks, the center collects health-related information (e.g., nutritional information) among Alaska Native people. Utilizing both scientific and cultural approaches to examining health issues, the Center for Alaska Native Health Research looks to improve the health of Alaska Natives.

MENTAL HEALTH SERVICE UTILIZATION

It is common knowledge that ethnic and racial minorities in general are less likely to use mental health services. Although the specific rates of mental health service utilization among Alaska Natives have not been carefully examined thus far, the use of these resources appears to be particularly low in this population. Alaska Natives face barriers that are common to other ethnic groups, but they also face obstacles that are unique to the cultural, social, and geographic characteristics of their way of life. Negative past experiences with non-Native peoples (i.e., racism, discrimination, segregation) may result in a general mistrust of mental health professionals. This, coupled with a relative lack of mental health professionals of Alaska Native descent, may help explain the underutilization of psychological services. Another barrier to the use of mental health services is cost. Fortunately, the Indian Health Service (IHS) is a federally funded agency that provides affordable health care, including mental health services, to Native populations. However, geographic isolation can make it difficult to access IHS-designated clinics that offer mental health services to Alaska Natives.

RECOMMENDATIONS FOR RESEARCH

There is still a great deal that is unknown about the mental health issues faced by Alaska Native peoples. In general, future research efforts that focus on conducting culture-centered research among Alaska Natives would help us better understand the psychological needs of this population. The influence of cultural beliefs on psychological phenomena may improve our understanding of the suicide, unintentional injury, homicide, and alcoholism rates in this population. Ethical research conducted among specific Alaska Native groups that highlights differences among these groups could be improved. For example, when reporting treatment research methods and design in an Alaska Native sample, researchers should include information related to the specific group assessed in the study (e.g., Tlingit, Aleut). This would improve our understanding of the generalizability of treatment results, which could, in turn, aid in the translation of research into effective treatments.

This is not to say that research has not been conducted among Alaska Native groups; however, additional research is necessary. Specifically, further research should focus on the effects of non-Native versus Native mental health professionals on the client–therapist relationship, different utilization rates of mental health services among specific Alaska Native groups, and the effectiveness of incorporating cultural values and beliefs into the treatment process. Research that answers these questions will enable mental health professionals to more effectively address the mental health needs of their Alaska Native clients.

RECOMMENDATIONS FOR PRACTICE

Assumptions should never be made about any individual based on his or her ethnicity or race. However, an understanding of specific cultural values and beliefs can be an important factor in establishing an effective therapeutic relationship. For example, some Alaska Native cultures display a reserved communication style, which is sometimes viewed as unfriendly by non-Natives. Additionally, in some Alaska Native cultures, sharing information related to personal problems or complaints is not encouraged by the Native community. In these circumstances, trust becomes crucial to the therapeutic relationship. A lack of trust in the context of cross-cultural mental health treatment and suspicion of mental health professionals may not be uncommon.

As in some American Native cultures, Alaska Natives speech may proceed at a slower rate than for other people. Silence, pauses, and a lack of eye contact may be common during conversations and should not be perceived as avoidance or disrespect. Additionally, extending mental health treatment to include family members, respected elders from the community, or other community members may help to facilitate the treatment process. Alaska Natives may have different perceptions of disability and illness. For example, Alaska Natives sometimes believe that mental illness stems from a spiritual rather than a psychological or biological cause. Inquiring about an individual's perceptions of the contributors to mental health can help improve the development of an effective treatment plan. For example, including traditional Alaska Native treatments in addition to more conventional psychological methods may improve treatment adherence. Improved adherence to treatment recommendations will therefore improve treatment outcomes. Again, the holistic view of health shared by many Alaska Native peoples should be considered when explaining and treating psychological issues.

In addition to client and patient factors, mental health professionals should be aware of their own beliefs and cultural background. Because mental health professionals are also products of their own culture, they should be aware of attitudes and beliefs that may influence their perceptions of Alaska Natives. Consistently monitoring one's own beliefs and preconceived notions about Alaska Native peoples can improve a mental health professional's ability to function effectively in cross-cultural situations.

—*Michael M. Steele*

See also Native Americans

FURTHER READING

Herring, R. D. (1999). *Counseling with Native American Indians and Alaska Natives: Strategies for helping professionals.* Thousand Oaks, CA: Sage.

U.S. Department of Health and Human Services. (1999). *Mental health: A report of the surgeon general.* Retrieved January 28, 2006, from http://www.mentalhealth.org/cmhs/surgeongeneral/surgeongeneralrpt.asp

ALCOHOL/SUBSTANCE USE AND ABUSE

Alcohol and illicit drug problems are not unique to the majority culture of the United States. They also exist throughout the many cultural groups that compose the nation's ethnic minority population. Within the ethnic minority population, alcohol and illicit drug problems span age, gender, educational background, occupation, and socioeconomic status. What follows is an overview of alcohol and illicit drug use and misuse as it pertains to the ethnic minority population of the United States. This overview is divided into discussions of (1) the distinction between substance use and forms of substance misuse, (2) the role of cultural norms and acculturation in substance use, (3) the prevalence of substance use and misuse among ethnic minority groups, (4) interventions for substance use and misuse in ethnic minority groups, and (5) the impact of drug-control policies on ethnic minority groups. This overview does not address alcohol and drug problems outside the United States, but it is important to note that substance problems are prominent in other nations and have a negative impact on cultural groups around the globe. Neither will this overview address nicotine and prescription drug problems, both of which are also prominent domestic and international concerns.

DISTINGUISHING BETWEEN SUBSTANCE USE AND SUBSTANCE MISUSE

Understanding the nature of alcohol and illicit drug use and misuse among ethnic minority groups must begin by distinguishing among *substance use, substance misuse, substance abuse,* and *substance dependence* (ordinarily referred to as addiction or chemical dependence). Clarification of the terminology is important because patients, researchers, policymakers, law enforcement, and the media often use these terms interchangeably, and the definitions may be at odds with those of the mental health and medical professionals who are responsible for diagnosing and treating alcohol and drug problems. For example, a man arrested for smoking marijuana at a concert may consider himself a *substance user,* but the criminal justice system may label him a *substance abuser* and him to drug treatment, where he may be diagnosed with a *substance dependence* disorder (such as a cannabis dependence) by a psychologist.

A person engaging in substance use can be described as using a substance without any identified problem associated with such use. For example, a teenager may experiment with marijuana, experience no adverse effects, and refrain from further use. The

term *substance misuse* is a general term that describes people who suffer from either a substance abuse or substance dependence disorder.

Colloquially, the term *substance abuse* is used to refer to any degree of substance use, ranging from one-time use of an illicit drug to severe addiction. Its definition among medical and mental health professionals, however, and its use here, refers to a *substance abuse disorder* marked by habitual use of a substance in a manner that is harmful to self or others but without strong signs of physical dependence or significant psychosocial negative consequences. For example, a man may drink heavily at bars on some weekends and then drive home in a state of intoxication. His behavior is dangerous because he is placing himself and others at risk of injury or death, but the role of alcohol in his life may not be so central as to reach the level of addiction.

Among medical and mental health professionals, a *substance dependence disorder* describes an addiction to a substance, marked signs of tolerance and withdrawal, and a number of negative consequences associated with the substance use, but continued use of the substance despite these consequences. Terms such as *alcoholic, junkie,* and *crackhead* are colloquialisms used to describe people who suffer from abuse of or dependence on alcohol, heroin, and crack cocaine.

THE ROLE OF CULTURAL NORMS AND ACCULTURATION IN SUBSTANCE USE

Each culture has a set of norms regarding the substance use of its members. Individuals within a given cultural group will vary in the extent to which their personal attitudes and behavior toward substances are consistent with these norms. Thus, the substance use of some individuals will closely follow their cultural norms, whereas the substance use of others will be at odds with their cultural norms. Despite these individual differences, cultural norms have been found to have a profound and multifaceted impact on the substance use of group members. They influence the particular drugs that are deemed acceptable for use, how and when drugs are used, and even the kinds of reactions that the drug produces in the user.

One facet of the relationship between cultural norms and substance use concerns the delineation between substances that are acceptable and unacceptable for use. The tolerance of some substances and the prohibition of others is a reflection of a cultural norm that varies from culture to culture. For example, in the United States, where drinking is a traditional part of many social customs and practices, alcohol use is legal for those above a certain age. In contrast, alcohol use is illegal in many Middle Eastern cultures, where alcohol use is regarded as sinful.

A second facet of the relationship between cultural norms and substance use concerns how a particular substance is used. A substance that is ingested in one form in one culture may be ingested very differently by another culture. For example, in parts of South America, indigenous cultures ingest cocaine by chewing coca leaves rather than by snorting or injecting powder cocaine or smoking crack cocaine. In contrast, cocaine users in the United States snort or inject powder cocaine or smoke crack cocaine but do not chew coca leaves.

A third facet of the relationship between cultural norms and substance use concerns the delineation of appropriate versus inappropriate contexts for substance use. The use of a substance may be tolerated in one context but prohibited in another. For example, members of the Native American church regard the use of peyote in the context of worship as a sacramental act, one that allows the believer communion with God. Peyote's use during Native American worship ceremonies has persisted for several centuries. However, the use of the drug outside the ceremonial context is not culturally proscribed.

Finally, cultural norms have a role in the kinds of effects a drug has on its user. For example, researchers investigating marijuana use in Jamaica during the 1970s found that marijuana users reported strength, endurance, and quickness from their drug use. These findings provide a sharp contrast to the amotivational syndrome marked by lowered drive, lack of ambition, and poor concentration that researchers have found among marijuana users in the United States.

Acculturation reflects the extent to which an individual has adapted to or acquired the beliefs of the majority culture. At first glance, the relationship between acculturation and substance use might appear straightforward. That is, the level of acculturation should yield predictable patterns of substance use, so that a minority group's substance use should come to closely resemble that of the majority culture as its degree of acculturation increases. This would intensify or lessen substance use depending on the culture's unique sanctions and prohibitions regarding substance use. For example, immigrants from a culture that

sanctions a high degree of alcohol use will likely decrease their alcohol use as they become more acculturated to an adopted culture that has strong prohibitions on alcohol use.

Research on the relationship between acculturation and substance use has not been so straightforward or consistent. In fact, the effects of acculturation on substance use have been found to vary by age, gender, and cultural group. For example, research has linked increased levels of acculturation with less drinking among middle-aged Mexican American men and more drinking with other groups of Hispanic men.

THE PREVALENCE OF SUBSTANCE USE, ABUSE, AND DEPENDENCE AMONG ETHNIC MINORITY GROUPS IN THE UNITED STATES

The measurement of substance use in the United States is constrained because of limitations in the research methodology. For example, researchers have used disparate measuring strategies in alcohol and drug use surveys. This inconsistency in measurement technique has led to difficulty comparing findings across studies. In addition, researchers attempting to measure alcohol and illicit drug use in the population are always faced with people's reluctance to admit to substance use. The measurement of substance abuse and substance dependence disorders is more complex than simply measuring substance use because of the added burden of assessing both the quantities of substance use and the negative consequences associated with such use. Therefore, estimating the prevalence of substance abuse and dependence disorders is imprecise. The best research available provides only a rough estimate of the percentage of Americans who drink, use drugs, and suffer from substance abuse or dependence disorders.

Estimates of alcohol and illicit drug use among ethnic minority groups are even more subject to error because of additional problems associated with ethnic minority research methodology. One such problem is that most of the research on ethnic minority substance use employs umbrella labels for disparate cultural groups. For example, labels such as *Hispanic, Asian,* and *American Indian/Alaska Native* are common ethnic minority categories in the research literature. These terms, though descriptively useful in many ways, mask an array of distinct cultural groups contained within these groups. The label *Hispanic* encompasses people with origins in Cuba, Puerto

Rico, Mexico, South America, and other Central American and Caribbean nations. The label *Asian* encompasses people with origins in China, Japan, Korea, Hawaii, and other Pacific Islands. The label *American Indian/Alaska Native* encompasses several hundred tribal groups, people who live on reservations, people who live off reservations, and people with varying degrees of tribal exposure.

The use of these labels would not be a problem if rates of substance use among the various cultural groups within the label were equivalent. Unfortunately, it has become apparent that there are significant differences among the various cultural groups contained within these umbrella labels. For example, rates of alcohol use differ significantly among Native American tribes. In addition, it has become apparent that substance use rates differ among ethnic minority members who were born in the United States versus those who have immigrated more recently. For example, rates of abstinence from alcohol are significantly higher among Mexican American immigrant women than among third-generation Mexican American women.

ALCOHOL USE

The results of the most recent large-scale government survey on alcohol use, the 2002 National Survey on Drug Use and Health conducted by the Substance Abuse and Mental Health Services Administration, found that 51% of Americans over the age of 12 reported current use of alcohol. Overall, the survey found differences in rates of alcohol use among the nation's largest cultural groups. For example, 55% of Caucasians reported consuming at least one drink in the 30 days prior to the survey. Respondents reporting heritage from two or more races had the second-highest rate of past-month alcohol use at 49.9%, followed by 44.7% among American Indian/Alaska Natives, 42.8% among Hispanics, 39.9% among African Americans, and 37.1% among Asians. The rate of past-month binge drinking (defined as consuming five or more drinks in one sitting during the past 30 days) was highest among American Indian/Alaska Natives at 27.9%, followed by 25.2% among Native Hawaiians and other Pacific Islanders, 24.8% among Hispanics, 23.4% among Caucasians, 21% among African Americans, and 12.4% among Asians.

Rates of alcohol use can vary significantly within the cultural groups that make up the umbrella labels commonly used in survey research. The extent of such

differences remains to be fully explored. However, research has thus far revealed differences among Hispanic cultural groups. For example, Mexican American men report a higher rate of frequent heavy drinking than do Puerto Rican and Cuban American men. Mexican American and Puerto Rican men are more likely to report a period of heavy drinking during their lifetime than Cuban American men. Cuban American women report less alcohol use than Mexican American and Puerto Rican women. In a similar vein, studies of drinking differences among Asian cultural groups have identified more alcohol abstainers than alcohol users in Filipino American and Korean American samples and more alcohol users than abstainers in Japanese American and Chinese American samples.

ILLICIT DRUG USE

The 2002 National Survey on Drug Use and Health found that 8.3% of the population 12 years and older had used an illicit drug during the month prior to the survey. Rates of drug use varied by cultural group. Respondents reporting heritage from two or more races had the highest rate of past-month drug use at 11.4%. American Indian/Alaska Natives had the second-highest rate of past month drug use at 10.1%, followed by African Americans at 9.7%, Caucasians at 8.5%, Hispanics at 7.2%, and Asian Americans at 3.5%. There were significantly different rates of drug use among those who fell under the umbrella label of *Hispanic*. Puerto Ricans had the highest prevalence rate at 10%, followed by Mexican Americans at 7.3%, Cuban Americans at 6.5%, and people of Central and South American origin at 5%. There were also significantly different rates of drug use among those who fell under the umbrella label of *Asian*. For example, past-month drug use among Korean Americans was 7%, whereas the rate was 5% among Japanese Americans and 1% among Chinese Americans.

SUBSTANCE ABUSE AND DEPENDENCE

The 2002 National Survey on Drug Use and Health estimated the prevalence rates of substance abuse and dependence disorders by asking respondents questions that reflect the criteria established by the American Psychiatric Association for the diagnosis of these disorders. For example, questions pertaining to substance abuse disorders probed for problems with the law, work, friends, family, or school as a result of alcohol or illicit drug use. Questions pertaining to substance dependence disorders probed for physiological signs of tolerance and withdrawal and continued use of the substance despite the negative consequences associated with its use.

In the sample, 4.5% of the population reported symptoms consistent with a diagnosis of a substance abuse disorder. The same percentage reported symptoms consistent with a diagnosis of a substance dependence disorder. Alcohol was the most commonly reported substance problem, followed by marijuana, cocaine, and prescription pain relievers. American Indians and Alaska Natives had the highest rate of abuse or dependence at 14.1%, followed by persons from two or more races at 13%, Hispanics at 10.4%, African Americans at 9.5%, Caucasians at 9.3%, and Asians at 4.2%.

The high rates of abuse and dependence among American Indians and Alaska Natives may explain the high rates of substance-related health and social problems in this ethnic minority group. The death rate related to alcohol misuse is higher among American Indians and Alaska Natives than among the general population. For example, death from chronic liver disease and cirrhosis (consequences of heavy drinking) is four times more common among American Indians and Alaska Natives than in the rest of the U.S. population. Fatal alcohol-related motor vehicle accidents are three times more common. Alcohol-related suicide and homicide are also more common among American Indians and Alaska Natives than in the general population.

Negative consequences associated with substance abuse and dependence are overrepresented among African Americans and Hispanics. African Americans compose 10% to 12% of the U.S. population, and Hispanics compose about 10% of the population. Yet recent estimates indicate that African Americans and Hispanics make up 50% of new AIDS diagnoses (often a consequence of injection drug use). African Americans represent 51% of marijuana-related emergency room visits and 34% of cocaine-related emergency room visits. Overall, African Americans make up 21% of drug-related emergency room visits. Hispanics represent 15% of methamphetamine-related emergency room visits and 11% of overall drug-related emergency room visits.

Cultural differences are also evident in drug-related deaths. Recent estimates place heroin and morphine as the most commonly implicated substances in drug-related deaths among Caucasians and Hispanics (mentioned in 41% of cases involving Caucasian decedents and 47% of Hispanic decedents). In contrast, cocaine is the most commonly implicated substance in drug-related deaths among African Americans, mentioned in 64% of cases.

INTERVENTION

Interventions in the area of substance use and misuse can be broadly grouped into prevention programs, screening and assessment techniques, and treatment programs. Prevention programs are typically targeted toward adolescents or other individuals at high risk for substance use and misuse. The aim of prevention programs is to prevent or prolong the initiation of substance use and to minimize the substance use of those who begin. Screening and assessment techniques are used to aid the identification and diagnosis of substance abuse and dependence disorders. Treatment programs are targeted toward individuals who have already been identified as having a substance abuse or substance dependence disorder, typically a population that is older than the audience of prevention programs. The aim of treatment programs is usually abstinence from substances; however, some programs seek moderation of substance use rather than abstinence. Traditionally, interventions have been provided to ethnic minority group members without considering the compatibility of the intervention with the values, beliefs, and practices of the ethnic minority group. Over the past few decades, awareness has grown in the field of clinical psychology and other helping professions that an individual's cultural values and beliefs about substances influence his or her response to substance use and misuse interventions.

This awareness has led to the modification of some existing prevention programs and the creation of new prevention programs to increase their sensitivity to the cultural backgrounds of the ethnic minority groups attending the programs. One example is Life Skills Training, a program developed to help adolescents successfully resist peer pressure to use alcohol, tobacco, and illicit drugs. Researchers modified the program to enhance its sensitivity to the cultural background of African American and Hispanic adolescents, and they found greater reduction in alcohol consumption among the Hispanic and African American adolescents who attended the culturally sensitive version of the program compared with those who attended the standard version.

Awareness of the relevance of cultural differences has also informed the practice of screening and assessment. Screening and assessment techniques in the field of addictions, and mental health in general, were often developed and standardized on Caucasian clients, with little regard for how the instrument or technique would perform with ethnic minority clients. Applying a screening or assessment instrument developed on one cultural group to a different cultural group without first testing its adequacy is problematic. For example, if a screening instrument inquires about a set of alcohol problem warning signs that are uniquely manifested in a particular cultural group, the successful screening of alcohol problems in a different cultural group will be questionable.

Attempts to improve the multicultural utility of screening and assessment instruments have occurred through several avenues. One avenue is exemplified by the development of the Alcohol Use Disorders Identification Test. This popular alcohol screening instrument was developed on clients from many cultures on several continents to ensure that the test items would be appropriate for different cultural groups. Other avenues to improve the multicultural utility of screening and assessment instruments have included translating instruments into foreign languages and collecting normative data on ethnic minority populations. Improvements in the assessment process have also been made by training counselors to be sensitive to the ethnic minority groups they serve and to assess an ethnic minority group member's language preference, degree of acculturation, and ethnic identity.

Awareness of the relevance of cultural differences has led to concerns about the adequacy of existing treatment programs for ethnic minority clients. The dominant modality of substance abuse treatment in the United States has been the "Minnesota model" of treatment, which was developed from the principles of Alcoholics Anonymous. Alternative forms of substance abuse treatment based on cognitive-behavioral therapy and motivational enhancement therapy have become popular as well. The utility of these treatments with ethnic minority clients has not been fully evaluated. Attempts to improve treatment outcomes among ethnic minority clients have led to the development of culturally sensitive and culturally specific treatments. Culturally sensitive treatments modify existing treatment programs to make them more compatible with the beliefs and values of the ethnic minority clients being served. Culturally specific treatments

use traditional cultural healing practices that fall outside mainstream psychological practices. For example, traditional cultural folktales have been incorporated into substance abuse treatment with Hispanic and Native Americans clients; peyote rituals and sweat lodges have been incorporated into treatment for Native American clients; and a public apology technique has been developed for Asian American clients. However, the use of such treatments is the exception rather than the norm with ethnic minority clients.

DRUG CONTROL POLICY

Historically, U.S. drug control policy has been associated with tension between majority group members and ethnic minority group members. Restrictions on alcohol, cocaine, opiates, and marijuana have all been linked with prejudices toward ethnic minority groups. For example, fear and intolerance of a new and growing immigrant group during the 19th century, the Irish, extended to their drinking habits and provided an impetus for the nation's first temperance movement. As a result of this movement, a third of American states were under alcohol prohibition by the end of the 1850s. Cocaine was a legal drug in the United States during the 19th century, used for a variety of recreational and medicinal purposes. Efforts to prohibit cocaine were prompted by claims that the drug provided African American men with superhuman strength and caused them to commit acts of violence against Caucasians, including raping Caucasian women.

Opiate drugs such as opium, morphine, and heroin also enjoyed widespread recreational and medicinal use during the 19th century. Opium smoking in particular was a common pastime of Chinese immigrants. Efforts to control opiates began as their addictive nature became more widely understood and were prompted by fear and intolerance toward the Chinese. Not surprisingly, prohibitions on smoking opium were enacted before prohibitions on morphine and heroin. Marijuana was used as a medicinal drug in the United States from the 19th century until the 1930s, and recreational marijuana smoking was a common pastime of Mexican immigrants. Similar to beliefs about African Americans and cocaine was the belief that marijuana could lead Mexicans to acts of violence and other forms of crime. These claims aided the establishment of legislation that ultimately led to the drug's prohibition.

Some have argued that contemporary drug control policy in the United States is discriminatory toward ethnic minority group members because they are more prone to the negative consequences of drug control policies than Caucasians. Compared with Caucasians, African Americans are more likely to be arrested for a drug-related offense, their drug-related arrests are more likely to result in conviction, they are more likely to be incarcerated after a drug-related conviction, and they serve longer prison terms for drug-related offenses.

The majority of individuals incarcerated for federal drug-related crimes are African American or Hispanic. Approximately 40% of incarcerated federal drug offenders are Hispanic, 30% are African American, and 25% are Caucasian. These numbers are well out of proportion to the percentage of each cultural group in the general population, and they are even more striking when one considers that rates of drug use among Hispanics, African Americans, and Caucasians are relatively similar.

Perhaps the most controversial topic concerning contemporary drug policy and ethnic minority groups concerns the federal mandatory minimum sentencing guidelines for crack and powder cocaine. The Anti–Drug Abuse Act of 1986 established vastly different mandatory minimum penalties for powder versus crack cocaine violations. For example, a first-time offender in possession of 5 grams of crack cocaine faces a mandatory minimum of five years' incarceration; however, a first-time powder cocaine offender would not face a five-year minimum penalty unless he or she were in possession of 500 grams of the drug. This discrepancy in the amount of crack versus powder cocaine required for a mandatory minimum has been called the "100:1 penalty." It has been argued that this sentencing guideline is especially discriminatory toward African Americans because approximately 85% of individuals convicted of crack cocaine offenses are African American.

In summary, cultural differences are a relevant variable in many aspects of psychoactive substance use. Cultural sanctions and prohibitions influence prevalence rates of substance use and misuse and explain differences in the rates of substance use among ethnic minority groups. The responses of ethnic minority group members to prevention and treatment programs is mediated by their cultural beliefs and values; positive and negative responses to programs may be related to the extent the intervention programs are congruent with culturally proscribed means of conceptualizing such problems. Finally, culture influences drug control policy to the extent that such policies reflect the formalization of the majority culture's views on legal and illicit substance use.

—*Damon Mitchell*
—*D. J. Angelone*

See also Drug Abuse Prevention in Ethnic Minority Youth

FURTHER READING

Aponte, J. F., & Wohl, J. (Eds.). (2000). *Psychological intervention and cultural diversity* (2nd ed.). Boston: Allyn & Bacon.

Kazarian, S. S., & Evans, D. R. (Eds.). (1998). *Cultural clinical psychology.* New York: Oxford University Press.

Straussner, S. L., & Ekrenkranz, S. M. (Eds.). (2001). *Ethnocultural factors in substance abuse treatment.* New York: Guilford Press.

AMERICAN COUNSELING ASSOCIATION

In 1952, four independent associations convened at a joint convention to form the American Personnel and Guidance Association. In 1983, this organization changed its name to the American Association of Counseling and Development, and 10 years later shortened its name to the American Counseling Association (ACA). Headquartered in Alexandria, Virginia, the ACA sees its role as promoting public confidence in the counseling profession. With members in the United States and 50 other countries, the ACA maintains a network of 56 branches and 18 divisions.

MISSION STATEMENT

The ACA's brief mission statement underscores its commitment to respecting human diversity: to enhance the quality of life in society by promoting the development of professional counselors, advancing the counseling profession, and using the profession and practice of counseling to promote respect for human dignity and diversity.

CODE OF ETHICS

Consistent with its mission statement, The ACA's code of ethics refers to the importance of respecting human diversity in virtually every major section of the code. Indeed, the preamble states that association members recognize societal diversity and support the individual's rights and development.

Under the section of the code titled "The Counseling Relationship," ACA members are expected to strive to understand the diverse cultural backgrounds of the clients with whom they work and to develop a clear understanding of how the counselor's own cultural, ethnic, and racial identity influences his or her values and beliefs about the counseling process.

An emphasis on cultural competency extends to other areas of the ACA's code of ethics. In the process of diagnosing their clients, for example, counselors are expected to recognize cultural influences on the definition of clients' problems and consider socioeconomic and cultural experiences before arriving at diagnoses.

When it comes to testing, the ACA code warns that counselors should be cautious in administering tests among culturally diverse populations, whose socialized behavioral and cognitive patterns may fall outside the range of the test's applicability and validity. Furthermore, counselors are advised to observe caution in interpreting the data of populations that differ from the norm group on which the test was standardized and to remain forever cognizant of the possible impact of a range of factors (age, color, culture, etc.) on test administration and interpretation.

Counselor educators are also expected to introduce material related to human diversity into all courses and workshops that are designed to promote the development of professional counselors.

MULTICULTURAL COMPETENCIES

One of the 18 divisions of the ACA is the Association for Multicultural Counseling and Development (AMCD). Chartered in 1972, the AMCD was originally called the Association of Non-White Concerns in Personnel and Guidance. The AMCD endeavors to advance cultural, ethnic, and racial understanding to improve and maintain personal development.

In 1992, an article was simultaneously published in the *Journal of Counseling and Development* and the AMCD's *Journal of Multicultural Counseling and Development*. The multicultural competencies that were outlined in that article have become part of the canon of the counseling literature. They are available from the ACA as three separate documents: "Cross-Cultural Competencies and Objectives," "Operationalization of

the Multicultural Counseling Competencies," and "Dimensions of Personal Identity."

—G. Scott Sparrow

See also Multicultural Counseling; Multicultural Counseling Competencies

AMERICAN PSYCHOLOGICAL ASSOCIATION

The American Psychological Association (APA), headquartered in Washington, D.C., is the largest scientific and professional organization representing psychology in the United States and the world's largest association of psychologists. The APA's membership includes more than 150,000 researchers, educators, clinicians, consultants, and students. Through its divisions in 53 subfields of psychology and affiliations with 60 state, territorial, and Canadian provincial associations, the APA works to advance psychology as a science, as a profession, and as a means of promoting health, education, and human welfare. The association's annual convention, held in late summer, is the world's largest meeting of psychologists.

The APA members sit on association boards, committees, and task forces and work with colleagues to shape policies for the association and to develop standards regarding psychological research, practice, education, and the application of psychology and psychological research to social issues.

The APA supports membership interests through its central offices and four directorates—Practice, Science, Education, and Public Interest—as well as through its meetings, journals (the APA publishes 46 journals), newsletters, books, e-products, continuing education programs, training, and accrediting activities. Members also benefit from the APA's federal legislative and regulatory advocacy and media relations, as well as an ethics education program.

The Science Directorate is the focal point of the APA's efforts to enhance psychological science and expand the recognition of its achievements. This directorate develops and manages programs serving APA members involved in academe and research and consolidates the APA's science activities.

The Practice Directorate promotes the practice of psychology and the availability and accessibility of psychological services for health care consumers through its national public education campaign, advocacy and legislative efforts, and work with state psychological associations.

The Public Interest Directorate promotes the science and practice of psychology by contributing to the improvement of the public's health and well-being. It works to inform social policies based on psychology's unique expertise in human behavior.

The Education Directorate works to advance the education and training of psychologists, the teaching of psychology, and the application of psychology to education and teaching.

Other functions of the association include the Research Office, the Office of Public Affairs, and the publication *Monitor on Psychology.* The primary mission of the Research Office is to collect, analyze, and disseminate information relevant to psychology's labor force and educational system. The Office of Public Affairs provides a link between the news media and the expertise of APA members. The *Monitor on Psychology,* the APA's official monthly magazine, informs readers of the latest advances in the field and the activities of the APA.

The APA is a nonprofit corporation chartered in Washington, D.C. In accordance with its bylaws and the association rules, the APA is governed by a council of representatives with elected representatives from its divisions and affiliated psychological associations. The APA's central office is guided by a board of directors and administered by a chief executive officer.

—Diane Willis

See also Committee/Office on Ethnic Minority Affairs, American Psychological Association; Council of National Psychological Associations for the Advancement of Ethnic Minority Interests

FURTHER READING

American Psychological Association. (2003). *Making APA work for you: A guide for members.* Washington, DC: Author.

AMERICANS WITH DISABILITIES ACT

The Americans With Disabilities Act (ADA) of 1990 is a civil rights act protecting persons with disabilities from discrimination. The ADA follows earlier civil rights legislation that provided similar protections against discrimination on the basis of race, gender, age, and national origin. The ADA is especially significant for ethnic and racial minorities with disabilities, whose experience has been described as a "double whammy" of having to cope with reactions to both race and disability.

The goal of the ADA is equal rights for persons with disabilities and their full inclusion and participation in society. The ADA brings a civil rights approach to persons with disabilities and moves away from seeing persons with disabilities as beneficiaries of charity.

The ADA specifically addresses employment discrimination, discriminatory access to local and state governments, public accommodations, access to establishments such as restaurants and supermarkets, and telecommunications availability (primarily for persons who are deaf and hard of hearing).

PRECURSORS OF THE ADA

The Architectural Barriers Act of 1968, which was concerned with access to federal and federally financed buildings for persons with disabilities, and Sections 501, 503, and 504 of the Rehabilitation Act Amendments of 1973, which mandated programmatic access of persons with disabilities to organizations receiving federal funds, were precursors of the ADA. The Education for All Handicapped Children Act of 1975 entitled children with disabilities to a free, appropriate education and reinforced inclusiveness by the U.S. government. The need for specific legislation protecting persons with disabilities from discrimination was bolstered by a report titled "Toward Independence," issued by the National Council on Disability in 1986.

The ADA's passage into law is significant because it involved many people working together to bring about change. The final passage of the ADA occurred because people with many different kinds of disabilities—from people who were blind to those with developmental disabilities, along with families and advocates—worked together in ways that were unprecedented in American disability history.

DISABILITY DEFINED

The ADA defines persons with disabilities as persons who have a physical or mental impairment that substantially limits one or more of their major life activities; who have a record of such impairment; or who are regarded as having such an impairment.

The ADA says that persons with disabilities may not be discriminated against in employment on the basis of their disability; however, they must be qualified for the job, with the requisite work, experience, education, and other requirements of the position, and must, with or without reasonable accommodation, be able to perform the essential functions of the position. At the same time, there is an inherent obligation of employers to remove barriers and to provide "reasonable accommodation."

The ADA also extends the antidiscrimination mandate to local and state governments and to organizations in the public arena, such as banks, supermarkets, retailers, and restaurants. Government and businesses must remove barriers that are "readily achievable" and are not an "undue hardship" for them.

—*Paul Leung*

See also Disabilities; Racism and Discrimination

FURTHER READING

Americans With Disabilities Act of 1990, 42 U.S.C.A. § 12101 *et seq.* Retrieved January 19, 2006, from http://www.usdoj .gov/crt/ada/pubs/ada.txt

Bruyere, S. M., & O'Keeffe, J. O. (1994). *Implications of the Americans With Disabilities Act for psychology.* Washington, DC: American Psychological Association.

Shapiro, J. P. (1993). *No pity.* New York: Random House.

ANTI-SEMITISM

Anti-Semitism refers to hostility toward Jews as a religious, ethnic, or racial group that is manifested on an individual, institutional, or societal level. This definition highlights one of the major difficulties of defining anti-Semitism accurately—that is, Jews often confound established notions of ethnic, racial, and religious identity. Unfortunately, many people see Judaism only as a religion, and others see Jews as Caucasian; the latter designation is particularly problematic for Jews of color. These categorizations are overly simplistic and do not fully describe the diversity of Jews. For example, there are Jewish ethnic differences (i.e., Ashkenazim, Sephardim, and Mizrachim) and different Jewish movements (i.e., Orthodox, Hasidic, Reform, Conservative, Reconstructionist, and Renewal). Hence, anti-Semitism is more than simple religious bias. It is important to note that many scholars no longer hyphenate the term *anti-Semitism* in order to cease the co-opting of this word for anything other than what it truly means: Jew hatred.

Anti-Semitism has been documented for more than 2,000 years and comes in many forms, including oppression, discrimination, segregation, pogroms, and

genocide. Scholars have outlined seven categories of anti-Semitism: (1) religious (e.g., Jews' "refusal" to embrace Jesus); (2) social (e.g., limiting Jews' occupational choices); (3) political (e.g., blaming Jews for communism); (4) economic (e.g., the myth that all Jews are rich); (5) psychological (e.g., the majority culture's desire to assimilate Jews is projected onto Jews so that they are seen as wanting to take over the world); (6) sexual (e.g., Jewish women are stereotyped as being both teases and prudes simultaneously); and (7) racial (e.g., Jews are seen as biologically inferior).

Other examples of anti-Semitism include questioning the Jewish identity of nonreligious Jews, violence against Jews at the individual and community levels, denying the occurrence of the Holocaust, and bashing the state of Israel.

Why does anti-Semitism persist? Three factors appear to be responsible. The first and foremost is Christian anti-Semitism. With the creation and maintenance of Christian state power, the deicide myth (i.e., the erroneous belief that the Jews killed Jesus), the blood libel myth (i.e., the belief that Jews killed Christian children for religious ceremonies), and the New Testament's depiction of Judaism (e.g., Christianity superseding the Hebrew covenant with God) became institutionalized. This made anti-Semitism a state- and church-sanctioned activity, lasting for hundreds of years. In the United States, this led to the creation of an invisible yet powerful anti-Semitic system that provides unearned privileges to Christians in a process parallel to the way racism benefits Caucasians. This Christian dominance is just beginning to be deconstructed.

Second, Jews historically served as a middle class whom those in power used as an intermediary between the oppressed and the oppressors. As a stateless people, Jews were permitted to enter countries in exchange for serving those in power; simultaneously, a continuous low-level, unofficial campaign of anti-Jewish propaganda was kept alive among the oppressed majority. In times of threatened revolt among the oppressed, violent, official anti-Jewish propaganda emerged. Pogroms, massacres, and expulsions were organized to turn the resentments of the oppressed majority, prepared to revolt against the oppressors, toward the Jews as scapegoats. This strategy has been used throughout the last 2,000 years, and scholars contend that Jews are difficult to categorize because this intermediary status has made them simultaneously part of both the dominant and subordinate groups.

The third factor is the invisibility of Jewish identity. The long history of oppression experienced by Jews, culminating in the *Shoah* (Holocaust), caused many Jews to hide or shed their Jewish identity in a desperate attempt to assimilate. Though many Caucasian Jews used their privileged skin color to "pass," the costs were severe (e.g., losing their Jewish culture). The success of Jewish American assimilation allowed anti-Semitism to persist because Jews became Caucasian and because their invisibility legitimized the denial of anti-Semitism.

—*Lewis Z. Schlosser*

See also Racism and Discrimination

FURTHER READING

Feldman, S. M. (1997). *Please don't wish me a merry Christmas: A critical history of the separation of church and state.* New York: New York University Press.

Langman, P. F. (1999). *Jewish issues in multiculturalism: A handbook for educators and clinicians.* Northvale, NJ: Jason Aronson.

Schlosser, L. Z. (2003). Christian privilege: Breaking a sacred taboo. *Journal of Multicultural Counseling and Development, 31,* 44–51.

ANXIETY DISORDERS IN ETHNIC MINORITIES

Of the major diagnostic groups of mental disorders, anxiety disorders have one of the highest—if not *the* highest—reported prevalence rates in the United States. Anxiety is the most common mental disorder among women and the second most common among men. This entry provides a brief overview of the current literature on anxiety disorders in racial and ethnic minority groups, particularly among the four principal racial and ethnic minority groups in the United States: African Americans, Asian Americans, Hispanic Americans, and American Indians/Alaska Natives. Although these descriptors are necessary for ease of reading, it is critical to bear in mind the diversity within each category. Racial and ethnic groups are multifaceted rather than unidimensional, with many cultures existing within each group. Furthermore, these distinctions are based on U.S. national boundaries, and

so they are somewhat arbitrary and do not entirely portray the cross-national status of some indigenous Hispanic and Native American groups. Given the scope of this entry, information concerning the assessment and treatment of anxiety disorders in ethnic minority groups is not included. Rather, attention is focused on known, unique aspects of anxiety disorders in ethnic minorities, as well as specific culture-bound disorders.

UNIQUE SYMPTOM EXPRESSION AMONG RACIAL AND ETHNIC GROUPS

The important role of culture in anxiety has been highlighted by developments in emotion theory. What constitutes anxiety varies by culture, and cultural variables may affect the way an individual describes his or her symptoms. For example, it may be more acceptable in certain cultures to express psychological distress through physical symptoms, such as a headache, as opposed to "feeling depressed." For further information on the somatization versus psychologization of descriptors for anxiety and depression, including idioms of distress, readers are referred to Laurence Kirmayer's review of differences in anxiety symptomatology by culture.

Thoughts, feelings, and bodily experiences are not necessarily seen as separate in many cultures. Therefore, in certain cultures, even serious anxiety symptomatology may not be brought to the attention of a health care professional. Additionally, the cultural expressions used to describe anxiety may overlap with traditional descriptors of affective, somatoform, and dissociative disorders, further complicating the clinical presentation. As a result, anxiety disorders in ethnic minorities may be misdiagnosed, perhaps more often than in the general population.

There are many examples of differences in the symptom expression of anxiety across cultures. In Hispanic cultures, for example, anxiety may present itself as *ataques de nervios,* a condition that involves attacks of anger, screaming, and other symptoms that may not be seen as panic or anxiety from other perspectives. Steven Friedman noted that, for men in some South Asian cultures, anxiety may be communicated as losing semen in urine. Qualitative ethnographic research has suggested that culture may affect the experience and presentation of anxiety among African Americans in a unique way, as described by Suzanne Heurtin-Roberts and collaborators. For example, African Americans may express anxiety through expressions such as "high-pertension," "high blood," "nerves," and "falling out" rather than traditional psychological nomenclature, and they may report somatic symptoms related to problems with their blood. In their review of ethnographic research, Heurtin-Roberts and colleagues concluded that many African Americans describe anxiety primarily through somatic terms.

RISK FACTORS

Risk factors for developing anxiety include discrimination and racism experienced both by the individual and vicariously through a legacy of historical trauma. Additional factors (noted by Gayle Iwamasa and Shilpa Pai) that may influence the development of anxiety and other psychological disorders are racial identity, ethnic identity, and acculturation level. These three culturally related aspects are unique to each individual; therefore, they may act as protective factors or as risk factors in the development and possible continuation of anxiety. Many ethnic minorities in the United States face increased social stressors when compared with the Caucasian majority. For example, minorities are more likely to live in substandard housing, be unemployed, and have no health insurance. For all ethnic minority groups, racism and poverty are risk factors for psychopathology.

EPIDEMIOLOGY AND PREVALENCE

Although relatively few cross-cultural studies have examined the epidemiology of anxiety disorders, those conducted thus far have reported similar rates of anxiety disorders across the world. Prevalence rates of anxiety disorders across racial and ethnic groups within the United States, however, are inconsistent. The Epidemiologic Catchment Area (ECA) studies, conducted by the National Institute of Mental Health from 1980 to 1985, determined the lifetime prevalence of specific phobias and agoraphobia to be higher in African Americans than in Caucasians and Hispanic Americans at every level of education. Research has also indicated that rates of phobias, panic disorder, and sleep paralysis are higher in African Americans than in the general population.

However, in a subsequent examination of anxiety disorder prevalence, the National Comorbidity Survey of 1989, no racial differences were found in the prevalence of any anxiety disorders. Furthermore, Charlotte Brown and collaborators found no differences in anxiety disorder prevalence, symptoms, or impairment between African American and Caucasian patients in a primary medical setting. Taken together, the disagreement in prevalence rate findings for anxiety disorders across racial and ethnic groups is not surprising, considering the wide range of anxiety symptomatology. Therefore, future epidemiological research on anxiety within ethnic minorities is needed.

UNIQUE MANIFESTATIONS OF ANXIETY DISORDERS AMONG RACIAL AND ETHNIC GROUPS

Variations in the expression and experience of anxiety symptoms exist across ethnic and racial minority groups. One important caveat to consider is the heterogeneity inherent within ethnic groups. For this reason, an idiographic approach is essential to understanding anxiety disorders. Aside from the culture-bound syndromes, there is an unfortunate dearth of information on unique manifestations of the major anxiety disorders among ethnic and racial minority groups. Currently, the African American experience of anxiety has the most literature, particularly on panic disorder, although the amount of research is still largely inadequate.

African Americans

Information regarding the epidemiology of anxiety disorders in African Americans currently is available for panic disorder and obsessive-compulsive disorder.

Panic Disorder

Although research is limited, studies have suggested several factors that may influence the presentation of panic disorder (PD) among African Americans and differentiate it from PD among Caucasians, particularly hypertension and isolated sleep paralysis. Isolated sleep paralysis (ISP) is a condition that occurs while one is falling asleep or awakening; the person cannot move and may experience hypnagogic or hypnopompic hallucinations, tachycardia, hyperventilation, and fear. Different from a nocturnal panic attack, ISP has been described by the phrase "the witch is riding you." In a study of Caucasian and African American anxiety patients from clinical and community samples, African Americans with PD had by far the greatest incidence of recurrent ISP (59.6%), leading Steven Friedman and colleagues to conclude that recurrent ISP may be a feature of PD that is unique to African Americans.

In an analysis of ECA data by Ewald Horwath and collaborators, African Americans and Caucasians had similar clinical features of panic disorder, although African Americans reported more tingling in the extremities and "hot and cold flashes" during panic attacks. African Americans with panic disorder described greater tingling and numbing of the extremities during panic attacks, as well as stronger fears of dying or going crazy, in studies by Steven Friedman and Cheryl Paradis and by Lisa Smith and collaborators.

Finally, in work by these same investigators, greater rates of comorbid posttraumatic stress and depression were noted among African Americans than among Caucasian panic disorder patients. These studies also revealed that the two groups employed different coping strategies; specifically, African Americans displayed less self-blame and used strategies involving religion, spirituality, and gratitude for one's good fortunes more than Caucasians.

Obsessive-Compulsive Disorder

The inclusion of African Americans in clinical research on obsessive-compulsive disorder (OCD) has been vastly inadequate despite the suggestion in the ECA data that the prevalence of OCD may be slightly higher in African Americans than in Caucasians. Current research has found little to distinguish the African American experience of OCD from that of other racial and ethnic groups. In a naturalistic treatment outcome study of African American, Caribbean American, and Caucasian OCD patients, Steven Friedman and colleagues found no differences in the type of OCD symptoms displayed, symptom severity, or treatment outcome across the three ethnic groups. Furthermore, no differences in religious symptomatology were found. Interestingly, although symptom severity was equivalent between Caucasians and African Americans, African Americans were less likely to report obsessive-compulsive symptoms initially and often revealed them only after the establishment of rapport. This hesitancy to disclose one's symptoms or distress may speak to the greater levels of shame found in African American compared with Caucasian OCD sufferers, as reported by Elaine Williams, Dianne Chambless, and Gail Steketee.

In case studies of African American women with OCD, Elaine Williams and colleagues described an unusually high amount of shame and a sense of being alone in the presentation of the disorder compared with Caucasian patients. Additional clinical issues for African American women with OCD included fears of going crazy (i.e., fear that their obsessions and compulsions indicated that they had "lost their mind") and, typical of OCD cases, obsessions that were influenced by their cultural belief systems. Specifically, one obsession involved a fear of being cast under a spell if the client touched a spot previously touched by another, which she explained could "put the root" on her. The authors noted the normalcy of a belief in root magic in some cultural groups, including those with Caribbean backgrounds. As noted by Peter Guarnaccia, clinicians should be cautioned against misdiagnosing patients' concerns about "root work," harmful magic, or supernatural forces as indicative of psychosis rather than anxiety.

Asian Americans

The Asian American population comprises a number of ethnic groups, including Asian Indians, Cambodians, Chinese, Filipinos, Japanese, Koreans, and Vietnamese, among others. Like other racial and ethnic groups, the extensive heterogeneity within this population proscribes broad assumptions concerning the cultural expressions of anxiety that are unique to Asian Americans. Research has indicated, however, a higher prevalence of certain anxiety disorders within subpopulations of Asian Americans. In particular, refugees of Southeast Asia are at increased risk for posttraumatic stress disorder (PTSD). This finding is consistent with the experience of brutal environmental strains such as habitation in refugee camps, combat, and torture. In addition, Asian American college students reported higher levels of social anxiety relative to Caucasians.

According to Derald Sue and David Sue, Asian Americans often express emotional and psychological stress through physical complaints, which are more culturally accepted. This tendency to communicate anxiety through somatic complaints was echoed by Dosheen Toarmino and Chi-Ah Chun in their guidelines for counseling Korean Americans; specifically, they noted that complaints about appetite, sleep disturbances, fatigue, headache, and restlessness often are expressed rather than descriptors such as "anxiety" or "depression." Sue and Sue noted that this emphasis on somatic complaints may result from a belief that emotional distress is caused by physical ailments and that it will cease upon proper medical treatment for the physical problem.

Hispanic Americans

In recent years, the Hispanic population in the United States has seen rapid growth and diversification, including individuals from Mexico, Puerto Rico, Cuba, and other Central and South American countries. Like other minority groups, Hispanic Americans often underutilize mental health care services for a variety of reasons, such as poor financial circumstances or preferences for family support. Although there is an unfortunate paucity of information concerning the experience of the major anxiety disorders among Hispanic Americans, information is available on unique idioms of distress that may be used to describe anxiety (e.g., ataques de nervios) and culture-bound syndromes (e.g., nervios). Peter Guarnaccia and others have suggested that culturally related anxiety disorders among Hispanic Americans, such as ataques de nervios, may be a culturally shaped response to extreme stress because they often elicit family or other social support and usually occur at family conflicts, funerals, or accidents.

One culture-bound syndrome among Hispanic Americans, *susto,* may be an expression of PTSD or acute stress disorder. Resulting from a distressing or frightening event, susto may involve complaints of sadness, troubled eating or sleeping, and reduced estimation of self-worth, as well as various physical ailments, such as stomachaches. Certain symptoms of susto, such as disturbing dreams, are consistent with the PTSD criterion related to the reexperiencing of a traumatic event. Although susto may also indicate depressive or somatoform disorders, its resemblance to PTSD and acute stress disorder merit its consideration as an anxiety disorder.

American Indians and Alaska Natives

Although psychological disorders such as depression and substance abuse are believed to be more common among American Indians and Alaska Natives, problems with anxiety are increasingly being recognized among these groups. There are also culturally specific anxieties and anxiety disorders that appear to uniquely affect Native Americans. As indigenous peoples of North America, American Indians and Alaska Natives have endured hundreds of years of onslaught by other dominating cultural groups. The cultural stressors involved in this forced acculturation are numerous and include the loss of ancestral lands and forcible relocation to inhospitable or culturally foreign areas, systematic attempts to eliminate religion and language, imposed outside governance, treaty violations, mandated education in boarding schools, exposure to non-Native diseases and practices with disastrous health consequences, and even genocide.

Given these historical and contemporary stressors, it is not surprising that many American Indians and Alaska Natives experience culturally specific anxieties. Such anxieties, spanning social involvement with Native Americans and cultural knowledge, economic issues, and social involvement with the majority culture, have been identified by Daniel McNeil and colleagues using the Native American Cultural Involvement and Detachment Anxiety Questionnaire. Consistent with this idea of unique historically and environmentally based influences on the anxiety of American Indians and Alaska Natives, J. Douglas McDonald, Thomas Jackson, and Arthur McDonald have suggested that Native American college students who leave home to pursue their education may experience greater generalized anxiety than both their non-Native counterparts and reservation-based Native American students who stay near home at a reservation-based college. In addition to such culturally specific anxieties, other disorders that are culturally bound (e.g., kayak angst) or culturally related (e.g., intergenerational PTSD) may affect the indigenous peoples of North America.

CULTURALLY SPECIFIC ANXIETY DISORDERS

The following disorders, listed alphabetically, are unique to various cultural groups. Many of them are described in greater detail in other entries in this volume. This list is not exhaustive. Furthermore, although culturally specific disorders with a strong anxiety component are included, the majority of the syndromes described here do not map exactly onto the diagnostic categories of the *Diagnostic and Statistical Manual of Mental Disorders,* 4th edition (DSM-IV-TR). Presentations may resemble adjustment, depressive, dissociative, somatic, or psychotic disorders. Many, but not all, of the disorders described here are included in the glossary of culture-bound disorders in the DSM-IV-TR.

Ataque de Nervios (Hispanic Americans)

Ataque de nervios (attack of nerves) is described in the DSM-IV-TR as an expression most closely related to panic attacks and commonly recognized among Latin American and Latin Mediterranean groups. Common symptoms include shaking, palpitations, numbness, and a sense of heat rising to the head. Peter Guarnaccia noted "screaming uncontrollably" as the most common symptom reported, followed by "attacks of crying."

Brain Fag (African Americans)

Brain fag is a phrase indicating fatigue or exhaustion from intense thinking in many cultures. Difficulty thinking and concentrating is a common symptom, and somatic complaints have also been reported. Brain fag syndrome is most prevalent in rural areas; it may be a form of anxiety or depression disparate from traditional North American psychological terms.

Dhat (Asian Americans)

Syndromes with presentations similar to *dhat* include *jiryan* in India, *sukra prameha* in Sri Lanka, and *shen-k'uei* in China. Inherent in these cultures is an ancient belief that a man's vital energy resides in his semen. Dhat refers to feelings of extreme anxiety related to a supposed discharge of semen, usually thought to be passed through the urine, and an accompanying whitish discoloration of the urine. Numerous somatic symptoms often accompany the complaint of semen loss; weakness and exhaustion are commonly associated with dhat.

Frigophobia (Asian Americans)

Frigophobia, also known as *pa-leng* and *wei han zheng,* is a condition characterized by a severe fear of cold and winds, which are believed to cause fatigue, impotence, or death. Frigophobia, a disorder that is well-known in Chinese mental health practice, often involves somatic complaints (e.g., headaches, numbness) and avoidance behaviors related to cold (e.g., compulsive wearing of heavy clothing, even in warm temperatures).

Intergenerational Posttraumatic Stress Disorder (Many Racial and Ethnic Minority Groups)

Posttraumatic stress disorder is an anxiety disorder that has unique considerations for ethnic minority members because of potential cumulative trauma and the possible transmission of traumatic events to individuals of subsequent generations. For example, work by Sandra Choney and colleagues has suggested that intergenerational PTSD may occur in Native Americans in response to historical trauma. Robert Robin and collaborators described the impact of community trauma on the psychological health of American Indian individuals, a consideration that is consistent with the collectivist, extended-family orientation and oral traditions within American Indian and Alaska Native cultures. Therefore, the development and presentation of PTSD in Native American individuals may involve additional clinical considerations. Similar ethnocultural historical effects may be risk factors for PTSD for a variety of racial and ethnic groups. For a comprehensive reference concerning PTSD among African Americans, American Indians, Asian Americans, and Hispanic Americans, the work of Anthony Marsella and colleagues is recommended.

Hwa-byung (Asian Americans)

Hwa-byung, or *wool-hwa-byung,* refers to "anger syndrome" in Korean folk culture. Presenting symptoms include panic, fear of imminent death, fatigue, and insomnia, as well as somatic symptoms of indigestion, anorexia, general aches, and feeling a lump in the front of the abdomen.

Kayak Angst (Native Americans)

Kayak angst, a condition that has been historically identified among the Inuit of Greenland, bears a striking resemblance to panic disorder. Kayak angst has been described as a discrete condition of severe anxiety that overcomes seal hunters while fishing in one-man boats. A loss of direction, helpless feelings, and psychophysiological responsivity are characteristic. An intense fear of drowning that decreases by returning to land or by the presence of other hunters has also been reported. Kayak angst shares many features of panic disorder, including unexpected onset and subsequent avoidance behavior (e.g., avoiding future hunting opportunities).

Koro (Asian Americans)

Koro, a diagnosis included in the Chinese Classification of Mental Disorders, is a syndrome known in Southeast Asia. Koro manifests as extreme anxiety that one's genitals will retract into the body, perhaps resulting in death, or that one's genitals have been stolen. Reports of koro have ranged from single cases to epidemics. Koro also is similar to *shen-k'uei,* or anxiety relating to a perceived loss of semen.

Nervios (Hispanic Americans)

Nervios is a frequently described expression of distress among Hispanic Americans. Nervios ranges from a small subset of symptoms to presentations resembling full disorders, and it includes broad categories of somatic symptoms, difficulty functioning, and emotional distress. Headaches, stomach problems, sleep disturbances, feelings of nervousness, dizziness, tearfulness, trembling, and tingling sensations are commonly reported symptoms.

Taijin-Kyofu-Sho (Japanese Americans)

Taijin-kyofu-sho, or *taijin kyofusho,* is often seen as a Japanese form of social phobia. Rather than intense fear of embarrassment or negative evaluation, as in the Western conceptualization of social anxiety disorder, this syndrome is characterized by anxiety resulting from a fear of offending others through one's body, appearance, odor, or movements.

CONCLUSIONS

Anxiety disorders are some of the most common psychological difficulties. As the population of the United States becomes increasingly more diverse, there is need for a greater understanding of anxiety disorders within ethnic and racial minority groups. Because one's expression and manifestation of anxiety may vary depending on one's cultural background, it is important for clinicians to understand each patient's conceptualization of his or her symptoms. In this vein, the ways in

which anxiety is communicated by ethnic and racial minority clients may vary according to the cultural acceptability of psychological descriptors of distress and the ways in which emotional states are described within the client's culture. An understanding of this cultural complexity is a step toward removing semantic and other barriers to valid assessment and treatment.

Despite the high prevalence of anxiety disorders in the population, limited epidemiological data are available for racial and ethnic minorities. Therefore, more systematic research is needed to identify idioms of distress and anxiety symptomatology that may characterize the experience of anxiety for different cultural groups. Recognition of the significant overlap of anxiety disorders with other clinical syndromes—particularly affective, somatoform, and dissociative disorders—is critical. Finally, guidelines for clinicians in regard to anxiety and its relationship to culture are required to move toward an understanding of anxiety across ethnic and racial groups.

—*Rebecca K. Widoe*
—*Renata K. Martins*
—*Daniel W. McNeil*

See also Cross-Cultural Psychology; Culture-Bound Syndromes: Ataque de Nervios; Culture-Bound Syndromes: Brain Fag; Culture-Bound Syndromes: Dhat; Culture-Bound Syndromes: Hwa-byung; Culture-Bound Syndromes: Koro; Culture-Bound Syndromes: Nervios; Culture-Bound Syndromes: Taijin Kyofusho; Posttraumatic Stress Disorder

FURTHER READING

Brown, C. B., Shear, M. K., Schulberg, H. C., & Madonia, M. J. (1999). Anxiety disorders among African-American and White primary medical care patients. *Psychiatric Services, 50,* 407–409.
Choney, S. K., Berryhill-Paapke, E., & Robbins, R. R. (1995). The acculturation of American Indians: Developing frameworks for research and practice. In J. G. Ponterotto, J. M. Casas, L. A. Suzuki, & C. M. Alexander (Eds.), *Handbook of multicultural counseling* (pp. 73–92). Thousand Oaks, CA: Sage.
Friedman, S. (Ed.). (1994). *Anxiety disorders in African Americans.* New York: Springer.
Friedman, S. (Ed.). (1997). *Cultural issues in the treatment of anxiety.* New York: Guilford Press.
Friedman, S., & Paradis, C. (2002). Panic disorder in African-Americans: Symptomatology and isolated sleep paralysis. *Culture, Medicine and Psychiatry, 26,* 179–198.
Friedman, S., Smith, L. C., Halpern, B., Levine, C., Paradis, C., Viswanathan, R., Trappler, B., & Ackerman, R. (2003). Obsessive-compulsive disorder in a multi-ethnic urban

outpatient clinic: Initial presentation and treatment outcome with exposure and ritual prevention. *Behavior Therapy, 34,* 397–410.

Guarnaccia, P. J. (1997). A cross-cultural perspective on anxiety disorders. In S. Friedman (Ed.), *Cultural issues in the treatment of anxiety* (pp. 3–20). New York: Guilford Press.

Guarnaccia, P. J., Rubio-Stipec, M., & Canino, G. J. (1989). Ataques de nervios in the Puerto Rican Diagnostic Interview Schedule: The impact of cultural categories on psychiatric epidemiology. *Culture, Medicine and Psychiatry, 13,* 275–295.

Heurtin-Roberts, S., Snowden, L., & Miller, L. (1997). Expressions of anxiety in African Americans: Ethnography and the Epidemiological Catchment Area studies. *Culture, Medicine and Psychiatry, 21,* 337–363.

Horwath, E., Johnson, J., & Hornig, C. D. (1993). Epidemiology of panic disorder in African-Americans. *American Journal of Psychiatry, 150,* 465–468.

Iwamasa, G. Y., & Pai, S. M. (2003). Anxiety disorders among ethnic minority groups. In G. Bernal, J. E. Trimble, A. K. Burlew, & F. T. L. Leong (Eds.), *Handbook of racial and ethnic minority psychology* (pp. 429–447). Thousand Oaks, CA: Sage.

Kirmayer, L. J. (2001). Cultural variations in the clinical presentation of depression and anxiety: Implications for diagnosis and treatment. *Journal of Clinical Psychiatry, 62*(Suppl. 13), 22–28.

Marsella, A. J., Friedman, M. J., Gerrity, E. T., & Scurfield, R. M. (Eds.). (1996). *Ethnocultural aspects of posttraumatic stress disorder.* Washington, DC: American Psychological Association.

McDonald, J. D., Jackson, T. L., & McDonald, A. L. (1991). Perceived anxiety differences among reservation and non-reservation Native American and majority culture students. *Journal of Indigenous Studies, 2,* 71–79.

McNeil, D. W., Porter, C. A., Zvolensky, M. J., Chaney, J. M., & Kee, M. (2000). Assessment of culturally related anxiety in American Indians and Alaska Natives. *Behavior Therapy, 31,* 301–325.

Robin, R. W., Chester, B., & Goldman, D. (1996). Cumulative trauma and PTSD in American Indian communities. In A. J. Marsella, M. J. Friedman, E. T. Gerrity, & R. M. Scurfield (Eds.), *Ethnocultural aspects of posttraumatic stress disorder* (pp. 239–253). Washington, DC: American Psychological Association.

Smith, L. C., Friedman, S., & Nevid, J. (1999). Clinical and sociocultural differences in African American and European American patients with panic disorder and agoraphobia. *Journal of Nervous and Mental Disease, 187,* 549–560.

Sue, D. W., & Sue, D. (2003). *Counseling the culturally diverse: Theory and practice* (4th ed.). New York: Wiley.

Toarmino, D., & Chun, C. A. (1997). The issues and strategies in counseling for Korean Americans. In C. C. Lee (Ed.), *Multicultural issues in counseling: New approaches to diversity* (pp. 368–394). Alexandria, VA: American Counseling Association.

Williams, K. E., Chambless, D. L., & Steketee, G. (1998). Behavioral treatment of obsessive-compulsive disorder in African Americans: Clinical issues. *Journal of Behavior Therapy and Experimental Psychiatry, 29,* 163–170.

ASIAN AMERICAN PSYCHOLOGICAL ASSOCIATION

The Asian American Psychological Association (AAPA) was founded in 1972 as a group effort spearheaded by a small but dedicated and influential handful of Asian American psychologists such as Derald Sue, Stanley Sue, Roger Lum, Marion Tin Loy, Reiko True, and Tina Yong Yee. What began as informal meetings to stay connected and offer an exchange of information and support among this select group in the San Francisco Bay Area has become a major ethnic minority psychological association with more than 400 members. The growth of the AAPA as an influential force within psychology reflects the growing needs and demands of the Asian American population, which is currently the fastest growing ethnic minority group in the United States.

Since its inception in the 1970s, the AAPA has grown and struggled to overcome many barriers to become a highly visible organization with many objectives, the focus of which are the mental and psychosocial health issues of Asian Americans. Some of these goals include advocating for Asian Americans and promoting Asian American psychology in the form of research, policies, and practices. Other key objectives of the organization include the training and education of Asian American mental health professionals. Important AAPA initiatives have included lobbying the U.S. Census Bureau to recognize and include Asian American subgroups in census data, presenting state-of-the-art information on Asian Americans to various presidential commissions and surgeon general's reports, and promoting Asian American perspectives within organized psychology.

Many journals, books, and newsletters focus on Asian American psychology and advocacy of service delivery to this population. From Stanley Sue's pioneering *Mental Health of Asian Americans* to the landmark *Handbook of Asian American Psychology,* each of these works have helped to lay the groundwork for development of the field of Asian American psychology.

The AAPA operates through an elected executive committee that serves a two-year term and consists of a board of directors, which includes a president, vice president, past president, membership and financial affairs officer, secretary/historian, and four board members. As the AAPA began to form an established identity, it began to publish an official newsletter, the *Asian American Psychologist,* which eventually evolved into a journal. Currently, the AAPA has returned to the newsletter format, which is published on a regular basis, three times annually. It consists of topics revolving around AAPA news, events, advertisements, accomplishments, and issues pertaining to Asian American psychology.

The AAPA holds a national annual convention the day before the American Psychological Association convention. The national convention features programs related to Asian American psychology, training, research, policies, and education. The convention is designed to optimize interactions between the presenters and the participants so that levels of intimacy, learning, mentoring, and comradeship are established. The AAPA also maintains a Web site (www.aapaonline.org) and an active Listserv for discussion. The current executive committee of the AAPA has initiated a Digital History Project for the association, and soon, digital copies of the historical record will be available on its Web site.

The future of the AAPA seems clear: to continue its efforts to promote the well-being of Asian Americans through training, research, and service and to serve as the primary professional organization for Asian American psychologists.

—*Frederick T. L. Leong*
—*Arpana Gupta*

See also Asian/Pacific Islanders

FURTHER READING

Leong, F. T. L. (1995). *History of Asian American psychology* (Asian American Psychological Association Monograph Series, Vol. 1). Phoenix, AZ: Asian American Psychological Association.

Leong, F. T. L., Inman, A., Elares, A., Yang, L., Kinoshita, L., & Fu, M (Eds.). (2006). *Handbook of Asian American Psychology* (2nd ed.).

ASIAN/PACIFIC ISLANDERS

Estimates suggest that, at the present time, just over 60% of the global population resides on the continent of Asia; however, this is an underestimate of the global population of Asian and Pacific Islanders (API) because numerous API reside outside Asia. In the United States alone, Asian and Pacific Islander Americans (APIA) represent one of the fastest-growing minority populations. Nonetheless, they remain overwhelmingly underrepresented in psychological research.

ASIAN AND PACIFIC ISLANDER AMERICANS IN THE UNITED STATES

The Chinese were among the first API immigrants to the United States. The increasing rate of Chinese immigration, initially fueled by the gold rush, was rapidly stifled with the passage of the Chinese Exclusion Act of 1882. As the number of immigrants from other API nations (e.g., Japan, Korea, and India) began to steadily increase, a number of parallel legislative acts were passed during the early 1900s to restrict their immigration as well. As a result, API immigration slowed to a trickle until the enactment of the 1965 Immigration Act, which eased restriction on immigration from API nations, catalyzing a resurgence of API immigration. Although the majority of APIA arrived after 1965, there are substantial numbers of APIA refugees and American-born APIA.

Current data suggest that there are more than 12.5 million APIA residing in the United States, representing nearly 4.5% of the nation's population. The majority of APIA have taken residence in the western United States (51%), and the remainder are spread throughout the South and Northeast (19% each), as well as the Midwest (12%). It is estimated that there are approximately 43 different ethnicities represented by API in the United States, displaying a tremendous diversity in terms of language, culture, religion, level of education, and socioeconomic status.

ISSUES IN THE RESEARCH CONCERNING ASIAN AND PACIFIC ISLANDER AMERICANS

Although significant advances have been made within the last 20 years in regard to ethnic minority research, research within the field of psychology using APIA participants remains sparse, and the literature that does exist is often inconclusive. There have been numerous attempts to illuminate the reasons for the paucity of research, as well as the inconsistencies within the existing literature, involving this group of people.

Some researchers argue that the discriminatory and exclusionary tactics aimed at APIA tend to be greater than those directed at other ethnic minority groups. These biases are believed to stem from the fact that API decided to immigrate to the United States, unlike other minorities, who had little choice. Thus, the sentiment suggests that APIA do not deserve to be studied until other groups have been given their due attention. Although some may consider this a rather extreme point of view, it should not be too quickly dismissed, regarded as an extremist position, or viewed as an impossibility. It is quite possible that at some level, these erroneous beliefs have the power to influence or even tarnish one's view of various ethnic groups, hence reducing interest in the conduction of research on those groups.

Additionally, many researchers have suggested that common (mis)perceptions of APIA as professionally and financially successful may lead to a lack of interest in research on this population. Such perceptions may contribute to a mistaken belief that these enhanced financial resources are accompanied by superior psychological resources, thus better equipping these individuals to combat the stresses typically associated with immigration and acculturation. Such unsubstantiated thinking may lead to the unfounded belief that APIA, because of their financial success, simply do not suffer from psychological distress, or if they do, they are in possession of superior coping resources that allow them to better deal with distress. Thus, their status as "worthwhile" and "important" subjects for research is further made subordinate.

One reason the research on APIA is so inconclusive may stem from the astonishing diversity of the people suggested for inclusion in this broadly defined group. The APIA represent one of the most diverse ethnic groups in the United States. However, the term *Asian* is ill defined and often leads to misunderstanding and ambiguity.

The definition of APIA currently used by the U.S. Census Bureau, though comprehensive, is not without its own complexities. Although it identifies several subcontinents and provides examples of the identified groups therein, its seeming "broad stroke" grouping of these minorities creates room for perceptions of cultural homogeneity among the distinct groups.

Within recent decades, social etiquette and political correctness have encouraged the discontinuation of the use of the term *Oriental*. Previously, this term was used primarily to describe individuals of East Asian descent, for example, those of Cambodian, Chinese, Japanese, Philippine, or Vietnamese background. However, when the term *Oriental* was deemed no longer appropriate for use in reference to individuals, it was replaced by the much broader and more nebulous term *Asian*. Thus, all the people of the vast Asian continent were grouped together under one umbrella term. No attention was given or attempt made to distinguish the vastly heterogeneous peoples of this immense continent. There are undoubtedly numerous significant differences among the cultures, customs, and fundamental beliefs of individuals originating from the different regions of Asia and the Pacific Islands, yet they are often treated as one group. Thus, the preponderance of research using "Asian" participants lacks a truly representative sample of APIA participants. Omissions in the literature become apparent as the Chinese and Japanese appear to be the predominantly addressed cultures.

This leads back to the question of defining the API population, both globally and within the United States. The importance of differentiating various API populations, such as South Asians from East Asians from Pacific Islanders, appears to stem naturally from the basic principles of scientific methodology and representative sampling. Psychological research has long been criticized for its overwhelming lack of sampling diversity and representativeness. The majority of our current psychological principles and theories are biased by research conducted primarily on middle-aged, Caucasian males or undergraduate psychology students. Such concerns have been echoed by a number of researchers within the psychological community.

The field of psychology, in its relentless pursuit of internal validity, has neglected the importance of external validity. It appears that this neglect has served as a fault in a good deal of the current literature. The balance between external and internal validity is a difficult matter for virtually all psychological research. Additionally, the lack of operational definitions to identify various groups has proven to be a disconcerting conundrum. At what point do we consider a people "a group" necessitating differentiation and separation as its own population? Many suggest that such a question opens up a never-ending Pandora's box. In fact, it appears that there is no definitive point at which a particular group of people is identified as a unique people, "deserving" of distinction and individuation from other groups. Such distinctions are potentially quite subjective, but they must be arrived at, operationally defined, and employed by the community of researchers in a way that is relevant to the research question under investigation and that allows the research to be more consistent and comparable across studies.

PSYCHOLOGICAL DISTRESS

Psychological distress is an expansive term that encompasses factors such as depression, anxiety, and other conditions. As our world continues to grow into a more unified and global community, constructs such as depression and anxiety require reevaluation and revision. Such constructs, as they currently exist, have been defined within a context of limited cultural and contextual variability. Cross-cultural variations in the manifestation of symptomatology associated with psychological disorders may render our current diagnostic and classificatory systems inadequate and inaccurate as we begin to consider such constructs in a cross-cultural context.

Numerous authors have commented on the role of culture in psychological illness, stressing the concerns of culturally specific perceptions of illness and the consequential responses. Thus, it may be posited that cultural context affects the ways in which biological changes within the body as well as psychological phenomena are manifested. An individual's manifestation of psychological distress is thus undoubtedly affected by his or her given culture's expectations, taboos, and beliefs regarding etiology.

It has been suggested that cultural influence on symptom manifestation affects the account of illness provided to the clinician. In other words, a construct such as depression may exist cross-culturally, yet its manifestations may vary in accordance with cultural variations and differences. Such disparity in the manifestations of psychological symptomatology may lead to difficulty in precise diagnoses. This may further result in the prescription of inappropriate, unsuitable, and thus ineffective treatments.

PSYCHOLOGICAL DISTRESS IN ASIAN AND PACIFIC ISLANDER AMERICAN POPULATIONS

A great deal of research has been conducted on distress manifestation in APIA populations; however, the findings have been equivocal. Some studies indicate a lower manifestation of depressive symptoms than in

Caucasian Americans, whereas others studies indicate no such trend. A few of these studies have gone so far as to hypothesize that many of the symptoms associated with depression—as it is currently conceptualized by the majority of the Western world—are rare and perhaps even nonexistent for individuals with backgrounds that are not rooted in Western societies. A number of factors may be implicated in the disparate findings within the literature. Given the array of distinct cultures that fall under the APIA umbrella, the confounding of classification may lead to erroneous results. Also, the measures used in the collection of data may not be appropriately normed or standardized for use within the various populations, effectively making the results uninterpretable or invalid. The age range of the participants may also play a role as an additional confound, as there is reasonable evidence suggesting that an individual's age may vary symptom presentation and manifestation.

Although it is important to bear in mind that these confounds have been obstacles to research on minorities in general, there are other factors that one must consider when attempting to integrate the contrasting research findings concerning APIA in particular.

From the lay perspective, many APIA are often referred to and viewed as the "model minority," based on perceptions and stereotypes of APIA as educationally, professionally, and financially successful. Therefore, one might then be tempted to explain research findings with hypotheses that are influenced by these stereotypical beliefs. For example, one might suggest that studies reporting elevated levels of symptomatology stem from the use of inappropriate assessment devices that have led to inaccurate and unsubstantiated elevations, or that observed elevations are the result of variations in culture. Another example is that studies suggesting lower levels of depression may be viewed as indicating a lack of depressive symptomatology in APIA populations and thus greater psychological adjustment and superior coping faculties. These hypotheses, which are potentially influenced by stereotypical beliefs regarding this population, are made to be consistent with popular belief.

FACTORS THAT SUGGEST INCREASED PSYCHOLOGICAL DISTRESS IN ASIAN AND PACIFIC ISLANDER AMERICAN POPULATIONS

In contrast to the mixed results of the APIA studies on depression, consistent results have been observed when one considers the concept of psychological distress from a much broader, and consequently more ill-defined, perspective. There are many indications that Asian Americans experience as much, if not more, emotional difficulty and psychological distress as Caucasians. The level of stress is attributed to increased experience of psychological stressors that are directly related to acculturative stress or to difficulties associated with the process of immigration. For example, immigrants are often faced with a variety of changes related to climate, the nature of their residence, and the characteristics of the community in which they reside. They also face changes in diet, perhaps because of the unavailability of foods and ingredients to which they are accustomed, and dangers associated with exposure to new and different diseases, which their immune systems may not be used to. Social changes also abound: Immigrants are often faced with the trauma of separation from family and friends, which is compounded by the lack of a social support system in their new environment. Finally—though quite significantly—changes associated with the general attitudes, values, and religious beliefs of the culture in which immigrants now find themselves may contribute to acculturative stress as well.

Immigrants face these challenges on a daily basis. They are continually inundated with aspects of their new culture, and although this process places pressure on both the immigrant and the host culture, the immigrant bears the brunt of the pressure to accommodate. Given these challenges and in light of the ingrained roles and values immigrants often arrive with, acculturation is often experienced as a difficult and at times a painful process. Some studies have proposed correlates associated with APIA immigrants' experience of acculturative stress. Some general trends in this research suggest that women exhibit greater acculturative stress than men and that immigrants who have chosen to migrate and plan to remain permanently express more positive attitudes about their new host culture and exhibit better overall mental health.

Furthermore, it has been suggested that APIA are seen as lacking a distinct position among the people and immigrants in the United States; they are often viewed simply as the "other" group, not quite fitting within other U.S. minorities. Many people of other ethnicities who have immigrated have a historical role that, to some extent, defines their place as an immigrant group. European Americans may be conceptualized as the conquerors from a historical perspective.

African Americans are perceived as being an oppressed people, having been brought to this continent under the chains of slavery, against their will. Latino Americans are viewed as the original inhabitants of this land or as a colonized people. Among this landscape of immigrants, APIA may be perceived as lacking a distinctive role in relation to other people who are here. This may adversely affect APIA ethnic identity formation during the process of acculturation, leading to even greater experience of psychological distress.

MANIFESTATION OF PSYCHOLOGICAL DISTRESS

One significant issue when studying ethnic minorities is that studies may use measures that do not focus on relevant manifestations of psychological distress in a given minority population. For example, a measure that assesses the social and emotional components of depression would be insensitive and inappropriate if a particular ethnic group manifests depression in a more somatic manner. Thus, attempting to assess depression with an inappropriate or insensitive device may lead to overlooked diagnoses. Conversely, the use of an inappropriate assessment device may lead to superfluous diagnosis or an overestimation of the severity of a disorder. For example, consistent elevations were found in Minnesota Multiphasic Personality Inventory scores on Scale 2 (Depression) and Scale 8 (Schizophrenia) in a sample of Hong Kong students. Such observations could lead one to believe that individuals from this population suffer from elevated levels of depression- and schizophrenia-related symptomatology. Furthermore, what is considered to be withdrawn behavior—and thus viewed as disturbed behavior among Caucasian Americans—may be the norm for Hong Kong Chinese. Similar problems with profile elevations have been observed in a variety of other ethnic minority groups.

It is difficult to make a global statement about the mental well-being of the APIA population because of the heterogeneity of the group. Although somatization has been indicated in groups such as South and East Asians, there is little evidence to suggest a similar trend within the Pacific Islander groups. Additional distinctions may be noted in the culture-specific disorders through which psychological distress is manifested. The Japanese, for example, conceptualize a disorder called *taijin kyofusho* as a multityped syndrome that encompasses some aspects of the Western personality, delusional, body dysmorphic, and anxiety disorders. The Korean *hwa-byung,* which may be grossly identified as a mixture of anxiety and depression, has distinct features (e.g., pain in the epigastrium) that are not found in depressive manifestations of other cultures. And *koro* and *dhat,* anxiety expressed through concern for genital function, are distinctly Asian Indian–bound disorders. This variance in symptom presentation, as well as the uniqueness of culture-bound disorders, creates an obstacle to generalization across the different groups.

Regarding the construct or theoretical identification of depression, it is quite possible that the manner in which it is conceptualized in the Western world is not culturally relevant to this population. Thus, it is possible that the construct of depression may be conceptualized and manifested in an entirely different manner. If this is the case, the instruments we currently use to assess that construct may not be valid with this population.

One consistent finding that lends support to this notion is the utilization of somatization as a means of expressing psychological distress among APIA. Somatization, or the physical manifestation of psychological stress, often includes the presentation of fatigue, dizziness, angina, and other body sensations. Though advances have been made in the battle against the negative stigmatization of mental illness and mental health concerns, these prejudices remain firmly seated within our society, as well as within many of the world's cultures. In this respect, API cultures are in no way exempt from these biases against mental illness. In fact, it may be argued that intolerance of mental illness is exaggerated in the eastern cultures of the API. These cultures adhere to a more collectivistic tradition rather than the individualistic tradition observed in Western cultures. As a result, the expression of emotion and mental illness is discouraged in these societies in an effort to maintain a given social status and to "save face" in their community. Thus, it is often more readily acceptable to display psychological distress through somatic manifestations, as has often been observed among individuals of API ancestry.

A number of researchers have suggested that APIA have different help-seeking preferences that result from this alternative expression of symptom manifestation. Studies suggest that APIA rarely present emotional or interpersonal problems on occasions when they do seek out professional treatment. Rather, they tend to focus on concerns regarding their occupation, somatic complaints, and educational concerns. In the

United States, Asian and Pacific Islander populations exhibit lower rates of both inpatient stays and employment of psychiatric services than any other cultural group.

One reason for the disparate rates may lie in the perception of the mind–body relationship. Western cultures tend to take a dualistic approach to the mind–body relationship, whereas Eastern cultures take a more holistic stance. This means that, although those of Western thought can make a distinction between somatic and psychological ailments, such a distinction can only be made with great difficulty and high inaccuracy for those of a holistic perspective. The implication of such variance has bearing on the language used in symptom description, as well as the cause attributed to their manifestation. Linguistic barriers, too, have been cited as a source of diagnostic problems, particularly in cases in which translation is used. Because translation is unable to coherently employ word-for-word equivalence between two languages, terms that are particular to a culture may fall by the wayside, effectively confounding the message's meaning. Perceptions of pain, for example, may be presented differently by those of the Asian culture, with psychological distress expressed as somatized pain. When faced with ambiguous symptom presentation, general practitioners and psychiatrists may be unable to classify the disorder. Research on the topic appears to support this conjecture and indicates that the Western construct of depression allows for only a subsyndrome in many evaluations of Asian individuals. This underdiagnosis and nontreatment effectively reinforces the tendency to seek aid from nontraditional medicine.

Another fact that might account for the low treatment rates is the perceived need for psychiatric assistance. Beyond the treatment efforts exerted for somatic symptoms, specific cultural views on the cause of the disorder often spur individuals to seek treatment from natural healers and other nontraditional medical personnel. Supernatural causes such as magic curses or the *Djinn* have been cited as reasons why such services have been employed.

When psychiatric disorders are diagnosed, the cultural barriers affecting the utilization of psychiatric services may also retard treatment progress. The patient's perception of his or her ailment and its cause has a great impact on the efforts of the psychologist. Because a good patient–clinician alliance is an integral part of any treatment, addressing culturally specific concerns (e.g., reporting style, spiritual beliefs, etc.), behavioral norms (e.g., direct eye contact), and therapeutic approaches has a great influence on the therapeutic outcome.

CONCLUSION

As the population of the United States grows and increases and its makeup becomes more diverse, greater understanding of cultural differences is a matter of increasing precedence. Though the body of literature on the APIA is increasing, the rate at which progress is being made is insufficient. Methodological and categorical issues impede the progress of research, and they are further complicated by erroneous "model minority" perceptions that often surround these groups. What may be abstracted from the literature is that the APIA are as vulnerable to psychological distress as any other culture. In fact, the process of acculturation may exacerbate this vulnerability through elevated stress levels. The manifestation of distress as a psychological disorder interacts with cultural background, affecting syndrome detection and inaccurately depicting these groups. If psychology is to disabuse itself of such misconceptualizations, misperceptions, miscalculations, and mistreatments, culturally specific manifestations and diagnostic criteria need to be addressed in the diagnosis, treatment, and research of individuals within these groups.

—*Reece O. Rahman*
—*Ilya Yaroslavsky*

See also Asian Values Scale; Chinese Americans; Filipino Americans; Japanese Americans; Korean Americans; Model Minority Myth

FURTHER READING

Cheung, F. (1985). *Cross-cultural consideration for the translation and adaptation of the Chinese MMPI in Hong Kong.* In J. N. Butcher & C. D. Spielberger (Eds.), *Advances in personality assessment* (Vol. 4, pp. 95–130). Hillsdale, NJ: Lawrence Erlbaum.

Doerfler, L. A., Felner, R. A., Rowlinson, R. T., Raley, P. A., & Evans, E. (1988). Depression in children and adolescents: A comparative analysis of the utility and construct validity of two assessment measures. *Journal of Consulting and Clinical Psychology, 56,* 769–772.

Durvasula, R. S., & Mylvaganam, G. A. (1994). Mental health of Asian Indians: Relevant issues and community implications. *Journal of Community Psychology, 22,* 97–108.

Furnham, A., & Malik, R. (1994). Cross-cultural beliefs about "depression." *International Journal of Social Psychiatry, 40,* 106–123.

Huang, L. N. (1994). An integrative approach to clinical assessment and intervention with Asian American adolescents. *Journal of Clinical Child Psychology, 23,* 21–31.

Ibrahim, F., Ohnishi, H., & Sandhu, D. S. (1997). Asian American identity development: A culture-specific model for South Asian Americans. *Journal of Multicultural Counseling and Development, 25,* 34–50.

Kaplan, G. A., Hong, G. K., & Weinhold, C. (1984). Epidemiology of depressive symptomatology in adolescents. *Journal of the American Academy of Child Psychiatry, 23,* 91–98.

Kim, W., & Rew, L. (1994). Ethnic identity, role integration, quality of life, and depression in Korean-American women. *Archives of Psychiatric Nursing, 6,* 348–356.

Krishnan, A., & Berry, J. W. (1992). Acculturative stress and acculturation attitudes among Indian immigrants to the United States. *Psychology and Developing Societies, 4*(2), 187–212.

Lee, S. M. (1998). Asian Americans: Diverse and growing. *Population Bulletin, 53*(2), 2–40.

Rahman, R. O., & Akamatsu, T. J. (2000, November). *Depressive symptomatology in Asian Indians.* Poster presentation at the Association for the Advancement of Behavior Therapy Annual Convention, New Orleans, LA.

Reeves, T., & Bennett, C. (2003). The Asian and Pacific Islander population in the United States: March 2002. *Current population reports* (Series P20, No. 540). Washington, DC: U.S. Census Bureau.

Sue, S. (1999). Science, ethnicity, and bias: Where have we gone wrong? *American Psychologist, 54,* 1070–1077.

United Nations Population Division. (2003). *World population prospects: The 2002 revision (highlights).* New York: United Nations.

U.S. Census Bureau. (2001). *The Asian and Pacific Islander population in the United States: March 2000 (update)* (PPL-146). Washington, DC: U.S. Census Bureau.

Zane, N. W. S., Sue, S., Hu, L., & Kwon, J. (1991). Asian-American assertion: A social learning analysis of cultural differences. *Journal of Counseling Psychology, 38,* 1–8.

ASSOCIATION OF BLACK PSYCHOLOGISTS

The Association of Black Psychologists (ABP) was founded in 1968 in San Francisco, California, by 28 psychologists of African descent. This was the first national organization to be established by and for psychologists of African descent. Its establishment was based on the unique history of African descent, especially enslavement and its social, economic, and psychological effects on people of African descent worldwide. These founding members called for specialized training and expertise in addressing the psychological well-being of the African community locally, nationally, and internationally.

The founding members also desired to develop an approach to psychology consistent with the experience of people of African descent. They envisioned that the newly formed organization would promote and advance the profession of African psychology, influence and affect social change, and develop programs whereby psychologists of African descent could help to solve the problems of people of African descent and other ethnic and racial groups.

FOUNDING MEMBERS

The 28 founding members of the ABP were Joseph Awkard, Aubrey Escoffery, Florence Farley, Wiley Bolden, Jane Fort, George Franklin, Alvis Caliman, Avlin Goings, Robert Green, Norman Chambers, Robert Guthrie, William Harvey, Harold Dent, Leslie Hicks, Thomas Hilliard, Anna Jackson, Walter Jacobs, Adelbert Jenkins, Reginald Jones, Melvin King, Lonnie Mitchell, Wade Nobles, David Terrell, Dalmas Taylor, Charles Thomas, Ernestine Thomas, Robert Williams, and Joseph White.

Members of this group represented a myriad of psychological disciplines, professions, and locations across the United States.

FIRST ACTIONS—RESPONSES

The formative group of founding members submitted seven petitions of concerns proposing that the American Psychological Association (1) officially endorse the Kerner Commission's Report of Civil Disorders; (2) develop or implement policies related to the African American community; (3) bring its resources to finding solutions to the problems of racism and poverty; (4) establish a committee to study the misuse of standardized psychological instruments; (5) reevaluate the adequacy of certified training programs in clinical and counseling training programs in terms of their relevance to social problems; (6) recommend to each psychology department steps to be taken to increase the number of African American students in their graduate program; and (7) implement and evaluate the progress of the foregoing recommendations in consultation with representatives from the ABP. The requests were received and reviewed by the American Psychological Association, but they were not fulfilled.

CURRENT ASSOCIATION GOALS

By examining approaches to research that had traditionally represented people of African descent as deviant, including but not limited to the inferiority, deficiency, or disadvantaged models, the goals of the association became not only to enhance the psychological well-being of people of African descent but also to promote constructive understanding through positive approaches to research. These research goals expanded to include the development of psychological concepts and standards consistent with African or African American culture, the development of support systems for psychology students, and the promotion of values that support well-being. Association members were also encouraged to foster relationships with local, state, national, and international policymakers to better influence the mental health and community needs of the African-descent community. Several annual awards are granted each year, including an award to support student research and an award for service, scholarship, and community service.

ORGANIZATIONAL STRUCTURE

The organization elects a president to a two-year term. The board of directors consists of a past president, president, and president-elect, along with a secretary, treasurer, four regional representatives, presiding elder, and parliamentarian.

COMMITTEE STRUCTURE

Committees are structured into three main clusters: advancing knowledge, community, and organizational maintenance. Located within the advancing knowledge cluster are professional development, the Committee to Advance African Psychology, the African Psychology Institute, Black Mental Health Month, and the Leadership Institute. The community cluster supports social action, testing and education, legislative education, health, and the African American Family Preservation and Revitalization committee. The final cluster comprises membership, the Committee on International Relations, chapter development, student affairs, and information technology. Additionally, there are seven standing committees: Ethics, Rules, National Convention, Personnel, Fiscal Affairs, Publications, and Reparations.

PUBLICATIONS

The Association of Black Psychologists has three regular publications: *PSYCHDiscourse; ABPsi*

NewsJournal, a monthly or bimonthly newsletter; and the *Journal of Black Psychology,* a professional quarterly journal of qualitative and quantitative research.

—*Harvette Armonda Grey*

See also African/Black Psychology; African Americans

FURTHER READING

Azibo, D. (2003). *African-centered psychology: Culture-focusing for multicultural competence.* Durham, NC: Carolina Academic Press.

Williams, B. (1997). *Coming together: The founding of the Association of Black Psychologists.* Unpublished doctoral dissertation, St. Louis University.

Williams, R. (1974). A history of the Association of Black Psychologists: Early formation and development. *Journal of Black Psychology, 1,* 9–24.

ATTENTION-DEFICIT/ HYPERACTIVITY DISORDER

Attention-deficit/hyperactivity disorder (ADHD) is one of the most frequently diagnosed disorders among children and adolescents. It is a lifelong condition that is estimated to affect 3% to 5% of school-age children. The disorder is characterized by core symptoms that include age-inappropriate levels of concentration, attention, distractibility, and impulsive behavior. For example, affected children seem unable to sit still, always appear to be daydreaming, or cannot focus on tasks long enough to finish. Children may exhibit a range of characteristics and varying levels of severity. Behaviors associated with ADHD are classified into three subtypes: predominantly inattentive, predominantly hyperactive-impulsive, and combined. Because ADHD often affects functioning in multiple settings, such as home, school, and peer relations, it may have a negative, long-term impact on academic and vocational performance and on social-emotional development.

A number of controversies surround ADHD: whether it exists as a distinct disorder, whether it can be accurately identified, and what the most effective treatments are. For people of color, there are also concerns about stigma associated with diagnostic labels, the rate at which ethnic groups are identified with ADHD, and access to appropriate treatment. Extant research focuses primarily on Caucasian, male, and middle-class populations, with limited consideration of gender, race, ethnicity, culture, and socioeconomic status.

CAUSES AND MAJOR CHARACTERISTICS

Comprehensive considerations of race, ethnicity, gender, and culture have generally been overlooked in the understanding of ADHD. Among individuals with ADHD, the core symptoms, such as distractibility or inattentiveness, are biologically influenced. There is no single known cause of ADHD. It occurs more frequently in individuals who have a family history of the disorder and more frequently in children who are exposed to prenatal insult, obstetrical complications, or high levels of lead. The disorder was once viewed as a neurological condition primarily involving attention, but it is now understood as a neurological condition primarily involving self-control and behavioral inhibition. Cultural environment is important because it determines how well or how poorly an individual functions, and it influences how behavior will be understood and treated. Parenting styles and educational methods do not cause ADHD, but they often play a role in effective treatment.

Studies examining the prevalence of ADHD or the proportion of individuals with ADHD in specific ethnic groups have reported conflicting results. The use of different assessment instruments and methods of diagnosis may account for the conflicting findings as much as any true differences in the rate of ADHD among ethnic groups. For example, rates of ADHD based on teacher ratings of children's behavior indicate higher rates among African American and Hispanic American children compared with European American and Asian American children. However, the observer's judgment about the quality of the child's behavior has been shown to be influenced by ethnicity, socioeconomic status, and student and teacher expectations.

Attention-deficit/hyperactivity disorder is a lifelong condition that is identified more often in boys. It is estimated that boys are three times more likely to be affected than girls, although ADHD may not be as easily recognized in girls. Boys are more likely to demonstrate disruptive and impulsive behavior that gets the attention of parents and teachers. Girls are more likely to demonstrate inattentiveness, depression, and academic problems that may be overlooked. Consequently, girls are more likely to be identified later than boys and less likely to receive treatment.

Until recently, ADHD was most often diagnosed during childhood. It is now known that ADHD continues into adulthood, although symptoms can change from childhood to adulthood. Hyperactivity, aggressiveness, impulsive behavior, and distractibility are more common among children. In older adolescents and adults, inattentiveness, impatience, and restlessness are more common with lessened hyperactivity, partly because of coping strategies that are learned with life experience.

Attention-deficit/hyperactivity disorder frequently coexists with other disorders, including disruptive behavioral disorders, specific learning disabilities, anxiety, depression, and tic disorders. A large proportion of adults with ADHD may also experience depression, anxiety, and major mood disorders. When ADHD goes untreated, substance abuse occurs in nearly half the people affected.

ASSESSMENT

Criteria for a diagnosis of ADHD includes the onset or beginning of symptoms before age seven, the presence of at least six inattentive or six hyperactive symptoms for at least six months, and significantly lowered performance in two or more areas of the child's life (e.g., difficulty at home and at school). Children may be mistakenly identified with ADHD because many of the key characteristics are typical for children of certain ages, and a diagnosis may be made based on poor information after a brief assessment. In addition, culture influences the expectations and behavioral norms of family, schools, and communities. What is acceptable and adaptive behavior from one cultural or ethnic group to another varies. People from different cultural and ethnic groups may also have different beliefs and attitudes about illness, helping professions, and trust in large institutions, as well as preferred community supports and healers.

There is no single psychological, educational, or medical test for ADHD. To accurately identify ADHD, a multisource (information obtained from multiple individuals) and multimethod (information obtained using many methods) process is necessary. Information from the child, parents, teachers, and others familiar with the child in different settings helps to assess the child's behavior compared with other children of the same developmental stage and cultural context.

Methods used in assessment may include interviews, behavior rating scales, and psychological testing. The use of rating scales and psychological tests is limited by how well the scales and tests have been designed for use with racial and ethnic groups and by possible rater or examiner bias. Rating scales that focus on specific core symptoms are helpful in identifying the child's behavior in different settings. Rating scales that focus on a wide range of behavior, attitudes, and feelings are helpful in making an accurate diagnosis and determining whether there are other coexisting problems. As a group, African American children are often rated with more ADHD behaviors and with more severe symptoms, which may be the result of bias or actual behavioral differences from other groups. Although psychological and educational tests are helpful in identifying academic and learning disabilities, their appropriate use with ethnic and racial groups requires an understanding of possible bias in test construction and interpretation.

TREATMENT

There are three basic types of treatment for ADHD: medication, behavioral intervention, and combined or multimodal intervention. Medications such as Ritalin are considered by medical professionals to be the most effective treatment for the core symptoms of ADHD. The use of medication is controversial because of concerns about the abuse and misuse of these drugs and because little is known about their long-term effect (i.e., longer than 14 months) on development. Possible racial and ethnic differences in how these medications are processed by the body have not been conclusively demonstrated.

Behavioral or psychosocial interventions include parent education, social skills training, structured positive reinforcement for appropriate behavior in school and at home, and counseling for organizational and socialization strategies. These treatments are more effective than medication in improving academic, vocational, and social functioning, but they are not as effective as medication in reducing the core ADHD symptoms. Ethnic groups may prefer psychosocial interventions over medication. Ethnicity and socioeconomic status may influence the motivation for various treatments.

Multimodal approaches combine medication and behavioral treatments to address ADHD symptoms and academic and social problems. Combined approaches work best when family, teachers, and other professionals coordinate their efforts to ensure consistency from one setting to another.

Although ADHD is not specifically designated under the Individuals With Disabilities Education Act, some children and adolescents may be eligible for special education services depending on the severity of their symptoms and the presence of specific learning disabilities. Many families of color are suspicious of in-school services because of stigma and because of the disproportionate representation of African American and Hispanic youth, especially males, in special education. Youth and adults may be eligible for school and workplace accommodations under Section 504 of the Rehabilitation Act and under the Americans With Disabilities Act.

—Cheryl C. Munday

FURTHER READING

Barkley, R. (1998). *Attention deficit hyperactivity disorder: A handbook for diagnosis and treatment* (2nd ed.). New York: Guilford Press.

Gingerich, K. J., Turnock, P., Litfin, J. K., & Rosen, L. A. (1998). Diversity and attention deficit hyperactivity disorder. *Journal of Clinical Psychology, 54*(4), 415–426.

LaRosse, M. (2004, November). *Ideas for accommodating individuals with ADD/ADHD in postsecondary training and college.* Retrieved from the Job Accommodation Network Web site: http://www.jan.wvu.edu

Livingston, R. (1999). Cultural issues in diagnosis and treatment of ADHD. *Journal of the American Academy of Child and Adolescent Psychiatry, 38*(12), 1591–1594.

U.S. Department of Education, Office of Special Education and Rehabilitative Services, Office of Special Education Programs. (2003). *Identifying and treating attention deficit hyperactivity disorder: A resource for home and school.* Washington, DC: Author.

Weiss, G., & Hechtman, L. (1993). *Hyperactive children grown up: ADHD in children, adolescents, and adults.* New York: Guilford Press.

ATTRIBUTION

Attributions involve making causal explanations for events or outcomes, particularly the behaviors that led to those events or outcomes. These explanations may be made by the individuals who experienced the events directly (self-attributions), or explanations may be given for why events or outcomes happened to other individuals (social attributions).

Individuals tend to take personal credit for successful outcomes by making attributions that reflect characteristics that are internal and stable to them (e.g., positive personality characteristics), whereas they tend to deflect blame for failure outcomes by making attributions that reflect external elements of the situation or context (e.g., the task was too hard). These self-serving attributions are important because they have been linked to psychological and physical health indexes such as self-esteem and immune functioning. Moreover, these self-serving attributions, though prevalent in all cultural groups, are typically stronger in Western (versus Eastern) cultures.

In explaining outcomes that happen to others, more pronounced cultural differences are found, particularly for failure outcomes. Individuals from Western cultures tend to make dispositional attributions to explain the unsuccessful outcomes of others (e.g., "She didn't get the job because she is not smart enough"), whereas individuals from Eastern cultures tend to make attributions that reflect situational constraints or pressures (e.g., "She was late for the meeting because she was caring for an ailing parent"). These social attributions are important because they can lead to stereotyping and discrimination when individuals, particularly those from Western cultures, make attributions within a multicultural society.

SELF-ATTRIBUTIONS

Self-attributions can be classified according to three dimensions: internality, stability, and globality. *Internality* is present when an outcome is an attribute of the self (e.g., ability, effort) rather than outside the self (e.g., difficulty of task, other people). *Stability* is present when an outcome is consistently present (e.g., an immutable personality trait) rather than temporary (e.g., effort). *Globality* is present when an outcome is cross-situational (i.e., occurs on many situations) rather than situation specific (i.e., occurs only in the target situation). Attributing negative or failure outcomes to internal, stable, and global causes (e.g., one's own personality) is referred to as a *depressive* or *pessimistic attributional style.*

Because the underlying attributions suggest the cause will be present in a multitude of situations in the future, individuals will experience feelings of helplessness, lowered self-esteem, and expectations that future failures are likely to reoccur. In contrast, attributing negative outcomes to internal, unstable, and specific causes (e.g., lack of effort) suggests that one's behavior can be altered to eliminate or reduce the negative outcome (e.g., if one just works harder). Conversely, attributing positive outcomes to internal, stable, and global causes (e.g., one's own personality) is referred to as an *optimistic* or *stress-buffering attributional style*. This attributional style (also referred to as having "positive illusions") is generally associated with heightened self-esteem and expectations that successful outcomes are likely to reoccur in the future.

Cross-cultural differences in attributional styles are explained by a cultural emphasis on individualism versus collectivism. Because individuals in Western cultures focus on the person as the source of negative and positive outcomes, one would expect these individuals to make more dispositional than situational attributions for their own behavior. Because individuals in Eastern cultures focus on the individual as rooted in the social environment, one would expect these individuals to make more situational than dispositional attributions for their own behavior. Research has shown that a self-serving attributional bias is relatively universal, though it is weaker in Eastern cultures.

There is a tendency, however, for some minority group members within the United States to experience attributional ambiguity for outcomes. This occurs when a minority group member is unsure whether an outcome is the result of his or her own personal characteristics or group membership. For successful outcomes, such as being hired for a job, individuals might wonder whether they were hired because of their perceived abilities (e.g., an internal, stable attribution) or because of perceived affirmative action policies (e.g., an external attribution). For unsuccessful outcomes, such as not being hired for a job, individuals might wonder whether they were not hired because they were unqualified (i.e., they did not have the abilities for the job) or because "they are African American." Thus, no clear self-serving attributions are made.

SOCIAL ATTRIBUTIONS

Similar cultural theories of individualism and collectivism can be used to explain cultural differences in the attributions that individuals make about the behavior of others. Differences in social attributions are largely a function of where individuals focus their attention. Individuals from Western cultures have a tendency to emphasize the traits and abilities of others at the expense of situational characteristics (e.g., how hard a task was) when making attributions for behavior, particularly for negative outcomes. Individuals

from Eastern cultures have a tendency to emphasize attributions as tempered by situational or contextual influences, such as the social-role obligations and social pressures that an individual is experiencing. Cultural differences in attributional thinking do not appear because there is an absence of dispositional thinking in Eastern cultures. However, Eastern cultures view dispositions as more malleable, and they are more sensitive to the fact that individuals behave differently under different circumstances.

Attributions that individuals make about the behavior of members from other groups (specifically, different cultural groups) are important because they can foster stereotypes and lead to discrimination. Attributions made by an individual (referred to as the *judge*) from a specific cultural group (referred to as the *in-group*) about the negative outcomes experienced by members (referred to as the *target*) of a different cultural group (referred to as the *out-group*) typically reflect negative personality characteristics and engender feelings of anger. For example, a Caucasian juror may attribute the criminal behavior of an African American defendant to the aggressive nature of the target individual. Conversely, attributions made for the behavior of a fellow in-group member are more likely to be situationally based and engender feelings of sympathy. For example, a Caucasian juror is more likely to attribute the criminal behavior (e.g., robbery) of a Caucasian defendant to extenuating circumstances, such as financial need. The implications of these attributions can be profound in the courtroom and beyond. The assignment of personality attributions for behavior is more strongly associated with judgments of guilt and retaliatory behaviors than the assignment of situationally based attributions for behavior.

Attributions provide an expectation about behavior. Behaviors leading to negative outcomes that are consistent with existing stereotypes are attributed to internal, stable, and global causes (e.g., negative personality traits). Behaviors leading to positive outcomes that are not consistent with existing stereotypes are attributed to external, unstable, and situation-specific causes (e.g., luck) or to internal, unstable, and situation-specific causes (e.g., "they [African Americans] happened to work hard in this one instance"). It has been found, for example, that the perceived successes of African Americans (and women, for that matter) are attributed more to luck and task ease than the perceived successes of Caucasians (particularly men).

A model of the effect of stereotypes on social judgments can be proposed to explain these social attributions. A target individual's behavior is first compared with a salient group stereotype that the judge (or the individual perceiving the behavior) has. Next, the target behavior is determined to be either consistent or inconsistent with the prevailing group stereotype. An observed behavior that is consistent with the group stereotype will lead to attributions that are ability or personality based. A behavior that is inconsistent with the group stereotype will lead to attributions that largely reflect luck or task ease.

For example, assume that a Caucasian high school student (the judge) has just learned that a fellow Hispanic classmate (the target) has been admitted to Harvard University (the target behavior or outcome). Further, assume that the Caucasian student holds the stereotype that Hispanics are lazy. Because the Hispanic student's target behavior is inconsistent with the Caucasian student's group stereotype, the latter will largely attribute the behavior to causes such as luck or affirmative action. However, if this Caucasian student holds the stereotype that Hispanics are hard-working, the same target behavior will be viewed as consistent with the stereotype and attributed to the ability of the target Hispanic. Thus, the attributions that individuals have—and ultimately, the discriminatory behaviors that individuals may engage in as a consequence of these attributions—begin with stereotypes. Nowhere is this more prominent than int the stereotypes that individuals hold about different cultural groups.

—Scott C. Roesch
—Allison A. Vaughn

FURTHER READING

Choi, I., Nisbett, R. E., & Norenzayan, A. (1999). Causal attribution across cultures: Variation and universality. *Psychological Bulletin, 125,* 47–63.

Mezulis, A. H., Abramson, L. Y., Hyde, J. S., & Hankin, B. L. (2004). Is there a universal positivity bias in attributions? A meta-analytic review of individual, developmental, and cultural differences in the self-serving attributional bias. *Psychological Bulletin, 130,* 711–747.

B

BELL CURVE, THE

The Bell Curve was published in 1994 by Richard J. Herrnstein and Charles Murray. This book reviewed the research on group differences in standardized intelligence tests and made some startling social policy recommendations. Given the persistent pattern of differential performance between minority groups and European Americans on intelligence tests, the authors concluded that social programs to increase the intelligence of minority group members are ineffective, that intelligence is genetically transferred and not amenable to intervention, and that we need to accept that our society has a cognitive elite (i.e., European Americans and a few representatives from minority groups) and a permanent working class (most minority members and a few representative European Americans). These conclusions led them to make social policy recommendations that included discontinuing all social programs designed to assist disenfranchised citizens from minority groups. These are not novel concepts, but *The Bell Curve* lent to them an unusual amount of visibility and seeming credibility. The attention paid to the book by both the political Right and Left marked an unprecedented politicization of the use and interpretation of intelligence tests and the validity of cross-racial comparison.

Many of the conclusions presented by Herrnstein and Murray have been present for a century. In the 1920s, the eugenics movement in the United States made similar claims about the inheritability of intelligence and the need to "clean up" the genetic pool through involuntary sterilization of individuals. The Third Reich explicitly based its scientific rationale for Aryan supremacy on the eugenics movement's arguments. Following World War II, the concepts received little attention, except as they related to individuals with disabilities.

One of the primary proponents of related concepts is J. Philippe Rushton. Rushton made the argument that the three main racial groups are at different stages of evolution. His conclusions were based on reviewing research on racial differences, on such divergent topics as size of cranium, age at which infants walk, age at first intercourse, aggressiveness, impulsivity, frequency of intercourse, and size of genitalia. According to Rushton, across these domains, there is a linear pattern: Asians > Caucasians > Negroid groups. He concluded that these patterns show that the three racial groups are at different evolutionary stages, with Asians having evolved to the highest degree, followed by Caucasians and the "Negroid" groups. Rushton's research is seen as being of questionable quality (relying on inadequate source data) and is widely ignored, if not ridiculed, by social scientists.

Herrnstein and Murray explicitly credited Rushton and cited his work in support of their contentions. The most significant aspect of *The Bell Curve* was its widespread acceptance among journalists and politicians of the political Right, as compared with Rushton's relative obscurity.

The conclusions and research approaches used by Herrnstein and Murray were widely criticized by many social scientists. The first criticism was the use of *g* as a global measure of intelligence. Advocates of intelligence research argue that it is possible to measure a single factor that is related to an individual's intelligence (*g*). Many researchers suggest that intelligence is a multifaceted construct and that there are multiple intelligences. A second criticism of the use of g is that it explains a small amount of variance in school or work success. Other criticisms attacked the authors' use of statistical techniques as inappropriate.

One of the most compelling criticisms against the research findings in *The Bell Curve* is that the authors viewed race as a biological rather than a social construction. They ignored the fact that within-racial-group differences are greater than between-group differences. Additionally, the argument for the genetic superiority of Asians is weakened by the inability to genetically differentiate members of racial groups.

—Paul E. Priester

See also Intelligence Tests; Scholastic Assessment Test

FURTHER READING

Brennecke, F. (1938). *The Nazi primer: Official handbook for schooling the Hitler Youth.* New York: Harper.

Herrnstein, R. J., & Murray, C. (1994). *The bell curve: Intelligence and class structure in American life.* New York: Free Press.

Kincheloe, J. L., Steinberg, S. R., & Gresson, A. D. (Eds.). (1996). *Measured lies:* The Bell Curve *examined.* New York: St. Martin's Press.

Rushton, J. P. (1999). *Race, evolution, and behavior.* New Brunswick, NJ: Transaction.

BICULTURALISM

Biculturalism describes the characteristics of persons whose psychological experiences have been shaped, to varying degrees, by two cultures. *Biculturalism* may also refer to the strategies that such individuals learn to use in response to cultural conflicts between two sets of cultural norms, values, or practices. Psychology's understanding of biculturalism is constantly evolving, and controversies regarding its conceptualization, assessment, and mental health implications abound. Nevertheless, the surge of psychological literature on biculturalism over the past decade indicates that this construct is of central importance not only for ethnic minority psychology, but also for the general field of psychology.

The current knowledge base regarding biculturalism can be traced to two major lines of research, one arising from acculturation research and the other reflecting the cognitive processes involved in being bicultural.

BICULTURALISM AS AN ACCULTURATION STRATEGY

When two or more intact cultures come into contact, as in cases of immigration and globalization, the involved individuals may experience change or conflict. How an individual deals with the contact and the subsequent changes and conflicts gives rise to the concept of *psychological acculturation.* Acculturation scholars have long debated which strategy for acculturating individuals results in optimal well-being and successful functioning. In this line of research, *biculturalism* has come to signify more than a state of being of two cultures. Within acculturation research, biculturalism *connotes* an optimal state of being able to function well in two cultural settings.

Early conceptualizations of acculturation have assumed that assimilation to the dominant society was the only psychologically healthy form of acculturation. This view contends that acculturating individuals need to shed their heritage cultures and completely adopt the new culture to eliminate acculturative stress and function well. Others, however, argued that preserving one's affiliation to one's heritage culture leads to better adaptation. Both of these views subscribe to the *unidimensional model* of acculturation, which holds that acculturating individuals can be placed on a continuum from being not at all assimilated to the second culture, to being highly assimilated to it. In this model, it is unclear how an individual who can be described as being at neither extreme of this continuum identifies or functions.

A more contemporary view of acculturation, however, has introduced the concept of *biculturalism—* an acculturation strategy in which an individual (or a group) identifies with and possesses the knowledge and skills to highly function within both cultural settings. This *bidimensional model* argues that processes of enculturation within one's heritage culture and acculturation to a second culture are independent of one another such that an individual may be highly functional in only one culture, in both cultures, or in neither culture. An example of this bidimensional model is John W. Berry's fourfold theory of acculturation strategies: assimilation (when an individual chooses not to value one's heritage culture and exclusively prefers the adopted culture instead), separation (when one seeks to operate within one's heritage culture almost exclusively and actively avoids interactions with the host culture), marginalization (isolation of an individual from both the heritage and host cultures), and integration (when one holds positive attitudes toward the host and heritage cultures).

The integration strategy is believed to lead to biculturalism. Researchers have empirically demonstrated that integration, and consequently biculturalism, is the most psychologically adaptive way for individuals to respond to the demands of acculturation. Studies show that the integration strategy is the least stressful among the four acculturation strategies. Furthermore, research suggests that relative to the separation and integration strategies of acculturation, marginalization and assimilation strategies are associated with more stress and psychological difficulties. Marginalization has been associated with dysfunctional behaviors such as delinquency and familial abuse, as well as increased depression levels. Assimilation has been associated with lower self-esteem.

The set of desirable characteristics of acculturating individuals has also been discussed as *bicultural competence*. Researchers have proposed that bicultural competence is composed of six dimensions: (1) *knowledge of cultural beliefs and values*—the degree to which one is aware of and knowledgeable about the history, institutions, rituals, and everyday practices of a culture; (2) *positive attitudes toward both groups*—the degree to which one regards both cultural groups positively; (3) *bicultural efficacy*—one's confidence to function effectively in both groups without compromising one's cultural identity; (4) *communication ability*—the ability to effectively communicate verbally or nonverbally in both cultural groups; (5) *role repertoire*—the range of culturally appropriate behaviors or roles a person possesses; and (6) *groundedness*—the degree to which one has established social networks in both cultural groups. It has also been argued that *biculturally competent* ethnic minority individuals have better physical and psychological health as well as academic and vocational success than those who lack bicultural competence.

A recent review of the psychological literature on biculturalism, however, suggests that there may not be consensus evidence supporting the notion that biculturalism is most adaptive. On the contrary, some scholars have argued that biculturalism is maladaptive because it is existentially inauthentic, inherently unstable, and thus may result in psychological conflict, distress, insecure self-identity, and alienation. Furthermore, the popular fourfold theory proposed by Berry and the associated constructs of integration and marginalization have been criticized by some scholars as lacking in explanatory and predictive powers. In summary, mental health implications of various acculturation strategies constitute an active area of scholarly inquiry.

THE BICULTURAL MIND

Another line of biculturalism research focuses less on its mental health implications and more on understanding the underlying cognitive processes of being bicultural. This line of research assumes that bicultural individuals will be able to behave in culturally appropriate ways depending on the context and that the cognitions behind such behaviors may operate without conscious awareness, intention, or control. Thus, studies investigating the automatic and unconscious cognitions associated with biculturalism typically use implicit methodologies.

One implicit method that researchers use to study the underlying cognitive processes involved in biculturalism is *implicit priming techniques*. Researchers employ implicit priming techniques to test whether individuals who live within a multicultural context (i.e., Chinese American and Hong Kong biculturals) have the ability to cognitively and behaviorally function in an appropriate way within each of the multiple cultural settings. Results show that the Chinese American and Hong Kong bicultural individuals exhibited thoughts and behaviors that are more characteristic of Chinese culture when primed with Chinese cultural icons, but exhibited thoughts and behaviors that are more consistent with American culture when primed with American cultural icons. These results demonstrate that bicultural individuals are capable of *cultural frame switching*—the ability to access multiple cultural meaning systems and switch between different culturally appropriate behaviors depending on the context.

The bicultural mind approach to the study of biculturalism has also empirically demonstrated that cultural frame switching is influenced by the extent to which bicultural individuals perceive their two cultural systems as oppositional or compatible, a concept researchers labeled as *bicultural identity integration*. Researchers argue that some bicultural individuals consider their two cultures to be conflicting and difficult to integrate. This perceived cultural conflict, in turn, may discourage the development of biculturalism. Other bicultural individuals, however, may perceive their two cultures as compatible and easily integrated. Thus, these individuals may be more adept at developing biculturalism. Using implicit priming methods, researchers have shown that bicultural individuals who perceived their two cultural systems as compatible were able to appropriately frame switch. For example, only those Chinese Americans or Hong Kong Chinese biculturals who perceive the two cultures as compatible behaved in a characteristically Chinese manner when presented with Chinese primes and characteristically American manner when presented with American primes. However, bicultural individuals who perceived their two cultural systems as conflicting or oppositional were not able to frame switch quite as easily.

CONCLUSION

Theoretical and empirical explorations about biculturalism continue to enhance psychology's understanding of this construct. However, there are still many critical questions left unanswered. For example, is the current manner in which biculturalism is conceptualized and measured the best way of doing so? Is biculturalism psychologically adaptive or maladaptive for which individuals under which contexts? These questions will continue to fuel the growth of the biculturalism literature and contribute to the ever-increasing vibrancy of multicultural psychology.

—*E. J. R. David*

See also Acculturation

FURTHER READING

Hong, Y. Y., Morris, M. W., Chiu, C. Y., & Benet-Martinez, V. (2000). Multicultural minds: A dynamic constructivist approach to culture and cognition. *American Psychologist, 55,* 709–720.

LaFramboise, T., Coleman, H. L. K., & Gerton, J. (1993). Psychological impact of biculturalism: Evidence and theory. *Psychological Bulletin, 114,* 395–412.

Rudmin, F. W. (2003). Critical history of the acculturation psychology of assimilation, separation, integration, and marginalization. *Review of General Psychology, 7,* 3–37.

BILINGUAL EDUCATION

Bilingual education has often been defined simply as the use of two languages as the medium of instruction within a school curriculum. One of the languages used is the students' native language, and the other is the language used to educate students in a particular country—that is, the majority language. The specific purpose of bilingual education is to teach academic content to nonmajority language students and, in some models, to majority language students. A multitude of bilingual education models have developed over time.

The development of numerous bilingual education models, and whether they have predominant components of intercultural or assimilationist orientations, has been a reflection of the historical, political, economic, and social issues under debate at the time, all of which influence an individual's attitudes toward immigrants or nonmajority language speakers.

BILINGUAL EDUCATION MODELS: INTERCULTURAL AND ASSIMILATION ORIENTATIONS

Bilingual education models have usually been developed to give support to children who are not speaking the majority language or language of instruction used in a school setting. Bilingual education models can be characterized as having an intercultural orientation or an assimilationist orientation. The micro-interactions that take place among students, teachers, and parents foster one of these orientations. An intercultural orientation leads to collaborative empowerment.

Intercultural Orientation

The intercultural orientation tends to empower students personally and academically. Teachers with an intercultural orientation see their role as assisting in adding a second language and culture while also maintaining the primary language and culture. This orientation leads to the creation of an atmosphere of collaborative empowerment. Teachers taking an intercultural orientation are more collaborative with parents, as they tend to encourage them to actively participate in their children's academic development at home and in school activities. Transformative instructional methodologies that are used by teachers involve the teaching of oral and written language through collaborative inquiry where social issues relevant to the students are included. Students use critical thinking as they describe, interpret, analyze, and use language creatively in the learning process. These instructional methods focus on student-centered rather than teacher-centered learning.

Assimilationist orientation

The assimilationist orientation tends to academically disable students. Teachers with an assimilationist orientation may see their role as assisting in subtracting the primary language and culture while assimilating students to the majority culture. An assimilationist orientation diminishes the possibility of creating an atmosphere of collaborative empowerment. Teachers taking an assimilationist orientation will be less collaborative with the parents as they fail to see the importance of parent involvement for students' academic success. The traditional instructional methodologies that are used by teachers involve the teaching of language through simple language components such as phonics, grammar, and vocabulary. Teaching moves sequentially in parts isolated from the whole. The lessons contain more emphasis on correct recall, drills, and isolated exercises. The social component students bring with them into the classroom is not drawn upon. These instructional methods focus on teacher-centered rather than student-centered learning.

MODELS CONSISTENT WITH THE INTERCULTURAL ORIENTATION

Enriched Immersion (Canadian Model)

The French immersion program in Canada is an example of an enriched immersion model. Students who are dominant in one language or are monolingual will study in both the majority and minority language from kindergarten to sixth grade. They are first immersed in the second language in the earlier grades and begin to develop literacy in their first language in second grade. For example, an English-speaking student will be immersed in French instruction until second grade, when English literacy is introduced.

Late-Exit Transitional Bilingual Education

Late-exit transitional bilingual education is also called *maintenance* or *developmental* bilingual education. In these classrooms, the students receive continued minority language support for an extended period of time, parallel with instruction in the majority language. In other words, the native language is maintained and

developed, and the second language is acquired and developed. All of the students in these classrooms are second language learners.

Dual Language/Dual Immersion/ Two-Way Bilingual Education

In dual language or dual immersion or two-way bilingual education, language minority and majority students are taught at the same time in the same classroom, with the goal for each group of students that of becoming fully bilingual. In these programs the students' knowledge of their native or first language is used as a foundation on which a second language is acquired. Students will become highly proficient in both languages.

MODELS CONSISTENT WITH THE ASSIMILATION ORIENTATION

English Immersion

Minority language students are immersed in the classroom where only the majority language is spoken. The approach is often referred to as the *sink-or-swim* approach to teaching nonnative speakers.

Structured Immersion

Minority language students are immersed in the classroom where only the majority language is spoken. However, the teachers have received training in sheltering techniques using visuals and carefully structured lessons to make the lesson content easier to understand for the minority student. The state of California uses this method since the passage of the English-only legislation under Proposition 227.

Traditional English-as-a- Second-Language (ESL) Pullout

Many different English-as-a-second-language (ESL) pullout methods are used. Some schools offer ESL on a daily basis whereas others offer ESL support a few times a week. The length of the ESL sessions may vary, as well. Also, students from different grade levels may or may not attend the same ESL sessions. In some schools, the ESL teacher is pulled into the classroom to work with students. Students who have a strong language foundation in their native or minority language may benefit more from ESL instruction than those who do not. The content of the traditional ESL pullout instruction consists of drilling language structure and memorizing vocabulary.

Content-Based English-as-a-Second-Language (ESL) Pullout

The content-based ESL pullout models use the themes of the content that is taught in the mainstream classroom while teaching the majority language. The students in these programs tend to perform better academically than those in the traditional ESL pullout programs.

Early-Exit or Transitional Bilingual Education

In early-exit programs, students are supported in some content areas in their first languages, although the amount of first-language support varies widely. When the student has acquired sufficient ability to demonstrate basic majority language proficiency, the student exits the program. The goal is that the child ends the bilingual education program in one to three years and transfers into a mainstream classroom.

—Marie Vanja Simonsson

See also Bilingualism; Academic Achievement; Education

FURTHER READING

Crawford, J. (2004). *Educating English learners: Language diversity in the classroom* (5th ed.). Los Angeles: Bilingual Education Services.

Cummins, J. (1996). *Negotiating identities: Education for empowerment in a diverse society*. Ontario, CA: California Association for Bilingual Education.

Freeman, Y. S., Freeman, D. E., & Mercuri, S. P. (2005). *Dual language essentials for teachers and administrators*. Portsmouth, NH: Heinemann.

BILINGUALISM

RELEVANCE

Bilingualism refers to the individual's ability to be fluent in two distinct languages. Bilingualism is becoming increasingly relevant to the work of clinical professionals, given the rapidly changing demographic makeup of the United States. The 1996 U.S. Census attributed much of this change to increased birthrates among Latino and American Indian, Eskimo, and Aleut populations, as well as a substantial increase in immigration rates. Consider, for example, that in the year 2000, ethnic minority youth constituted approximately 30% of the entire U.S. population. Some demographers estimate that almost 3,000 immigrants arrive in the United States each day, contributing approximately 1 million individuals to annual population figures. Because large numbers of immigrants in the United States speak their language of origin and subsequently acquire the ability to speak English, there is a vast need for bilingual clinical professionals.

Although not often a focus of psychological literature and clinical training, language is incredibly relevant to the enterprise of psychotherapy. Its relevance becomes especially apparent when we consider that what psychotherapists engage in is frequently referred to as "the talking cure." Thus, it is important that the clinical professional be conversant in the language through which the patient experiences his or her world. When working with the bilingual patient in psychotherapy, it is important not only to understand the verbal meaning of what the patient is saying, but also to understand the cultural representations that are communicated through the use of one or more languages. In this sense, language is representational of the cultural context in which psychotherapy occurs. Understanding the complexity of the cultural values associated with a language is critical for understanding the dual language systems of the bilingual patient.

HISTORY OF BILINGUALISM IN PSYCHOTHERAPY

Bilingualism was a part of early psychoanalytic work, as Sigmund Freud spoke German, a second language for many of his English-speaking United States patients. It was only in 1949, however, that bilingualism began to be written about in the psychoanalytic literature. This work involved the presentation of a case with a bilingual woman who spoke English and German. The woman's language of origin was German and she acquired English as a second language when she immigrated to the United States during her adolescence. Seeking psychotherapy as an adult, the patient refused to speak German and spoke only English in psychotherapy. Ultimately, it was only when the patient shared her anxieties in German, the language of her childhood, that she was able to share infantile sexual material. In this case, it was important to acknowledge how the context in which the patient's language capabilities were encoded had an influence on the language the patient chose to speak in psychotherapy. The author of the aforementioned case, for example, talked about how the patient came to the United States during World War II at a time in her life when survival was not taken for granted. Hence, to speak in German, her native language, would have called up the traumatic experiences associated with having to leave her homeland. The author concluded that recollections from a particular time period in one's life were accessed only when discussed in the language in which these experiences were encoded. The opposite was also thought to be true, meaning that the patient might choose to avoid speaking about an experience in the language in which it was encoded as a defense against experiencing painful material. Another early work, published in 1950, looked at psychotherapy processes when treatment occurred between a like-matched bilingual psychotherapist and patient. The focus of this writing was to examine defenses connected to switching languages in the psychotherapy session. The implication of this work was that different self-experiences were organized by language. More recent literature has discussed how language organizes one's sense of self and has explored the duality of the bilingual/bicultural person's world. Neurological research further supports this contention as it indicates that languages are stored in different areas of the cortex for bilinguals.

PSYCHOTHERAPY TOOLS WHEN WORKING WITH THE BILINGUAL PATIENT

There are several psychotherapy tools that clinical professionals may use if patients detach from emotional material through the use of the second language when emotional issues are raised. For like-matched bilingual clinical professionals and patients, one strategy is to analyze the process of code switching within the session. *Code switching* refers to how and when the individual shifts from using one language to another. For example, an analysis of code switching may explore whether the patient consistently shifts to the second language when threatening emotional issues are raised in treatment. Alternatively, the analysis may explore whether the patient is increasingly able to communicate emotional material in the language in which it was encoded, thus tapping into unexplored emotional experiences.

Additional psychotherapy tools in work with the bilingual patient are applicable to the clinical setting where patient and clinical professional are not like-matched bilinguals. Here the clinical professional may recognize that language-related phenomena can be incorporated into the psychotherapy process, despite the difference in language capabilities. One technique that the clinical professional may incorporate is to encourage bilingual patients to explore how they experience themselves in each language. In this sense, the duality of self will begin to get replicated and further understood within the context of treatment. A second strategy that incorporates the use of dual language systems is to have the monolingual clinical professional encourage the bilingual patient to express him- or herself in the language of origin and subsequently translate what has been said. This technique may be particularly useful if the patient has reached an impasse with regard to accessing emotional feelings while speaking in the second language. The patient and the clinical professional can subsequently explore the meaning and experience attached to the discussion of emotional content in the language of origin, as noted by C. S. Clauss in 1998.

A final cautionary note regarding tools that can be implemented in bilingual psychotherapy concerns the use of interpreters. Although psychotherapy through interpreters is not the best situation, it is possible. It is important to find an appropriate interpreter who is given a clearly defined role. It is not appropriate to put a bilingual child in the role of interpreter for the family. This approach can change the power structure of the family and risks having the child viewed as disrespectful to his or her parents and older relatives by being the messenger of delicate material.

—*Caroline S. Clauss-Ehlers*

See also Biculturalism; Bilingual Education; Language Proficiency; Models of Second Culture Acquisition

FURTHER READING

Clauss, C. S. (1998). Language: The unspoken variable in psychotherapy practice. *Journal of Psychotherapy, 35*(2), 188–196.

Clauss-Ehlers, C. S. (2003). Promoting ecological health resilience for minority youth: Enhancing health care access through the school health center. *Psychology in the Schools, 40*(3), 265–278.

Javier, R. A. (1995). Vicissitudes of autobiographical memories in a bilingual analysis. *Psychoanalytic Psychology, 12*(3), 429–438.

BIRACIAL

Biracial people are individuals who have parents or ancestors from two different socially defined racial heritages, such as African American, Asian American, European American, Latino, and Native American. Biracial people have lived in the United States since its inception but have not been officially recognized on the census until the year 2000. As of the 2000 Census, nearly 7 million Americans identified, or were identified as, members of more than one racial group. Today, many grassroots organizations and college student groups exist for the mutual support and enjoyment of interracial families and biracial individuals. The presence of a small yet significant biracial population challenges long-accepted ideas about the concept of race. Biracial persons face unique stressors that their monoracial counterparts do not, such as being forced to identify with, or pledge allegiance to, only one of their ethnic heritages, being told that they are not a true member of one of their racial or ethnic groups, being stared at by strangers, and exposure to racist jokes.

THE AMERICAN LEGACY OF HYPODESCENT

Miscegenation was a major force in pre–Revolutionary War America. *Miscegenation* refers to sexual relations between people of different races leading to the birth of children. During this time, miscegenation occurred most often between men of European descent and women of African or American Indian descent. Quite often, these sexual relations were not consensual; instead, they took the form of rape or concubinage.

Because European Americans held disproportionately more power than other racial groups in early America, they were able to establish the rules that determined the racial identity and social status of the offspring of interracial unions. For various reasons, European Americans forced individuals with multiple racial heritages to identify with and accept the social status of their heritage group that had less social power. This meant that people who had one European American parent and one African American parent were African American; they were not allowed to claim their European or Caucasian heritage. This classification system benefited European Americans in several ways. First, European Americans tended to view sexual relations across racial lines as immoral, illegal, and barbaric. As such, offspring of such unions were thought of as being biologically inferior, immoral, and barbaric. Hence, European American parents were able to distance themselves from their own behaviors and their biracial children by thrusting a non–European American identity onto them. Second, people with multiple racial heritages would serve as a cheaper source of labor if their status was non–European American. Third, and most important, forcing mixed-race individuals to accept a non–European American identity was a way for European Americans to continue to assert their dominance and clearly designate who was a member of their power group and who was not. Any individual with just a fraction of non–European American heritage was automatically excluded from holding the privileges of being European American, thereby clearly designating the lines between European American and non–European American.

This classification system is referred to as a system of *hypodescent,* or a system that forces all people, regardless of their racial heritage(s), to identify with only one race. Individuals with multiple racial heritages must identify with and accept the status of their racial heritage that has the least amount of social power. Therefore, hypodescent denies individuals with multiple racial heritages from having a socially accepted mixed-race identity or status and disallows them from choosing their own racial identity.

Both prior to and after the formation of the United States as a nation, laws were enacted to enforce this system. The One-Drop Law or One-Drop Rule was applied to individuals with less than 100% African ancestry. This law stated that any individual with so much as one drop of African American blood was to be considered African American and hold the social status of other African Americans. In several states, this law declared that an individual is African American if even one of his or her great-great-great-grandparents was classified as African American. The One-Drop Rule was an act of oppression against people of multiple racial ancestries. It limited the life choices of these individuals by assigning them to the lower-status racial group, thereby denying opportunities to vote, own land, advance educationally, secure high-paying jobs, and define the terms of their own existence.

People with multiple racial heritages were not only denied rights, but also were instilled with negative ideas about the meaning of racial mixing. For example, early research and theory pertaining to biracial people focused on their biological inferiority. Some scientists argued that biracial individuals were putting the human race at risk of extinction because of their inability to reproduce. This belief is demonstrated by the word *mulatto,* which is Spanish for "little mule" and refers to people of mixed European and African ancestry—mules being the infertile offspring between a horse and donkey.

To combat this oppression, some biracial individuals who were phenotypically Caucasian (i.e., having lighter skin and straight hair) publicly took on European American identities. This practice has been referred to as *passing.* Passing could range from drinking at a water fountain designated Caucasian-only, to attending all-Caucasian schools, to abandoning one's home, family, and community to pursue a life elsewhere as a European American person. Some biracial people chose this last option to secure better jobs, education, or housing. In general, the issue of passing was most relevant to individuals who had European American and African American parents and ancestors, as the racial divide between European Americans and African Americans has been most rigorously enforced in the United States.

Passing as European American to gain *legal* rights is no longer applicable, as the One-Drop Law has been revoked and individual rights such as the freedom to dine at particular restaurants or to attend certain schools are no longer based on one's race according to the law. Nevertheless, many individuals with multiple racial ancestries have single-race identities. Some of these individuals are assigned single-race identities by family members, peers, or society, whereas others choose a monoracial identity for themselves. Many factors influence how individuals with multiple racial backgrounds choose to identify racially. Such factors include, but are not limited to, one's phenotype, cultural preferences, socialization, political orientation, talents, and other social identities, and the context in which one chooses an identity (i.e., on a form, or being asked by a friend).

THE MULTIRACIAL MOVEMENT

Until the 1960s, a lack of trust, harsh treatment, contempt, and discrimination toward biracial people dominated in the United States. However, increased exposure between racial/ethnic groups due to the Civil Rights movement, the Vietnam War, and a landmark decision by the U.S. Supreme Court changed this dynamic. The biracial baby boom began with these changes, and attitudes toward interracial marriage and biracial people began to change.

According to Maria P. Root, a leading researcher of biracial people, the biracial baby boom began around 1967, occurring after the U.S. Supreme Court ruled in *Loving v. Virginia* that state laws declaring interracial marriage illegal were unconstitutional. At the time, 13 states, all of which were in the American South, had laws banning some form of interracial marriage. The state of Virginia had had such laws since 1662.

During the 1960s, racial dynamics in the United States were changing, as prolonged and meaningful interaction between members of different racial groups was occurring more than it had at any other point in U.S. history. Throughout the Civil Rights movement, European American sympathizers and supporters worked closely with African Americans who were fighting for their rights. During the Vietnam War, Americans from all ethnic/racial backgrounds fought together and, in so doing, decreased prejudice against one another and increased the likelihood of finding a mate from a different racial background after returning home. Many male soldiers stationed in Asia also married or had children with Asian women, thereby creating a sizable population of children born to American (usually European American or African American) fathers and Asian mothers. Offspring of such unions, who have been called *Amerasians,* have often spent some time growing up on military bases. Some of these children stayed in Asian nations such as Vietnam, Japan, and the Philippines, and others eventually immigrated to the United States, sometimes with their mothers, to live with their American fathers. Some Amerasian children growing up in Asia faced continuous racism and discrimination because of their mixed-race heritage. A small yet significant portion of this population were abandoned by their Asian mothers, who were constantly scorned and shamed for having children with non-Asian men.

Despite large numbers of interracial families and biracial individuals living within the United States, national organizations or local community groups that united such people did not become established until the late 1970s. At that time, families and individuals began meeting and organizing in several cities. Original organizations included I-Pride in San Francisco, Biracial Family Network in Chicago, Interracial

Family Alliance in Houston, and Interracial Family Circle in Washington, D.C. In November 1988, these organizations unified to develop the Association of MultiEthnic Americans (AMEA), which has served as an umbrella organization to unite the local groups.

Today, the multiracial movement continues to expand. For example, the MAVIN Foundation, a Seattle-based organization created by Matt Kelley in 2000, has organized national events such as Generation MIX and MatchMaker Bone Marrow Project. In Generation MIX, five biracial and multiracial young adults visited 16 cities across the United States to promote awareness of the biracial experience through workshops and speakers. In the MatchMaker Bone Marrow Project, the MAVIN Foundation has worked to register mixed-race bone marrow donors. People are most likely to find a life-saving match with donors of similar racial backgrounds. People of mixed heritage often have great difficulty in finding a match because of their unique genetic makeup. In addition to the MAVIN Foundation, there are national conferences focusing exclusively on biracial people, including an annual conference organized by and specifically geared for biracial college students.

THE 2000 CENSUS

During the 1990s, members of AMEA met with members of Congress and the House Subcommittee on the Census regarding the possibility of allowing biracial people to identify with all of their racial heritages on the 2000 U.S. Census. Prior to the 2000 Census, biracial U.S. citizens were forced to indicate their race by checking the box "Some Other Race," or to identify with only one of the racial groups available. If they checked "Some Other Race" and wrote in more than one race, they were counted as members of the first racial group listed. In large part because of the work of AMEA, the 2000 U.S. Census was modified to allow individuals the right to identify with more than one socially defined racial group.

More than 6.8 million Americans (2.4%) identified themselves or were identified by the head of their household as members of more than one race on the 2000 U.S. Census. The majority of these biracial (and multiracial) individuals included Caucasian as one of their races (80.1%), and almost half included Some Other Race (46.3%). Of those who identified as Some Other Race, 58.8% indicated they were also Spanish,

Hispanic or Latino in a separate question about ethnicity. The group Native Hawaiian and Other Pacific Islander had the highest percentage of its members identify with an additional racial group or groups (54.4%). The lowest was Caucasian; among people who identified as a member of this group, only 2.5% identified with a second racial group. Even so, the four largest biracial populations all included Caucasian as part of the combination.

According to this census, the four largest multiracial groups accounted for almost three-fourths of the multiracial American population: 32.3% of multiracial Americans identified as Caucasian and Some Other Race; 15.9% as Caucasian and Native American/Alaskan Native; 12.7% as Caucasian and Asian; and 11.5% as Caucasian and African American or African American. Although the European American and African American biracial population receives the most attention in the media and popular culture, this was only the fourth largest mixed-race group. It is possible that this is an underestimate of the European American–African American biracial population because more individuals in this group may identify solely as a member of one race (usually African American), owing to America's legacy of the One-Drop Rule, which was most forcefully applied to individuals with both European and African ancestry.

Multiracial Americans are disproportionately young; almost 42% are under the age of 18, compared with just 25% of monoracial Americans. The European American–African American biracial population is particularly young, with 71.7% of this group under the age of 18. Only 5% of multiracial Americans are over the age of 65, compared with 12% of those with one racial background. That the multiracial population is so young reflects the increase in miscegenation within the last few decades. Demographers predict that by the year 2050, between one-fifth and one-quarter of Americans will be biracial or multiracial.

CONTEMPORARY ISSUES

With the significant increase of the biracial population and an awareness of biracial people in the general public, there continues to be a fascination with people of multiple racial heritages. Biracial people whose physical appearance is racially ambiguous are frequently asked questions such as What are you? Where are you from? What language do you speak? What is your race, nationality, or ethnicity? Where are your parents from? These questions reflect contemporary society's adoption of the system of hypodescent, in which everyone must be a member of only one race. Although the One-Drop Law has been abolished and civil rights no longer depend on race, people continue to want to know the heritage of the people around them. Frequent questioning about their racial background can be overwhelming to biracial individuals.

A more insidious experience, similar to this line of questioning faced by biracial people, is hazing. *Hazing* is a process that mixed-race individuals endure to prove themselves full members of a racial/ethnic group. Multiracial people do not possess the full privileges that, for example, monoracial European Americans do, nor do they have the guaranteed sanctuary of immersion into a socially defined racial community of monoracial minorities. Instead, multiracial individuals are often forced to endure teasing or peer pressure to prove their conformity and belonging to a racial community. In hazing's most harmless forms, young multiracial people are pressured to say they prefer a certain type of music, dance, or clothing to gain acceptance. More disturbing forms may include being forced to modify one's speech or being teased for phenotypic features such as one's eyes, hair, skin color, body size, and bust size. The most sinister forms of hazing include being forced to say that you hate a particular race to be accepted into a peer group and even extend to physical beatings. When multiracial people are hazed, they are forced to choose between social isolation and compromising their well-being. Hazing can lead to a sacrifice of one's well-being and/or hatred toward one's own heritage group because of such painful incidents.

Other biracial people are never hazed nor asked about their physical appearance because they do not appear to be racially ambiguous. These individuals blend in physically with a monoracial group, usually one from which they have heritage, but occasionally with a group from which they have no heritage. For example, some European American–African American biracial people are mistaken as being Latino. These individuals may be less likely to be questioned about their ambiguous racial appearance, but they do face a different set of interpersonal challenges pertaining to race. They are forced to find a way to assert their racial identity to people in their heritage group whom they do not look like. The heritage group may also be less likely to accept them as part of the group.

As of yet, only a small percentage of the American population has chosen to embrace a biracial or multiracial identity, and relatively few organizations exist that are composed of all, or mostly, biracial people. With these racial dynamics, no natural situations exist in which a group is composed entirely of biracial people. If a biracial person wants to be surrounded by other people who are also biracial, that person must create the situation. Likewise, most biracial children do not have parents who can relate to being biracial from their own lived experience, as opposed to monoracial people, whose parents are the same racially.

For this reason, parallels have been drawn between the biracial experience and transracial adoption. Both biracial people and transracial adoptees challenge traditional notions of family and race; children are expected to look like other members of their family. In these families, however, children typically do not resemble their parents racially. Hence, when biracial children are with their biological parents and when transracially adopted children are with their parents, similar experiences occur. Both of these family types may be stared at and treated differently because of their nontraditional racial status. Biracial children may also be at greater risk for placement in adoptive homes when the biological family is not supportive of racial differences within the family.

PATHOLOGY AND TREATMENT

Because of the stress that can be associated with being biracial, several theorists have posited that biracial people may be at risk for developing psychopathology. For example, researchers have suggested that identity formation, social isolation, constant questioning about one's race, and family dynamics such as increased marital conflict may lead to emotional and behavioral problems within the multiracial population. Investigators, in testing whether biracial people are at risk for developing psychological symptoms, have demonstrated that biracial people are generally well adjusted but may be at risk for developing psychopathology. Fewer studies have examined the positive aspects of the biracial experience, such as growing up with exposure to two cultures.

The results of psychopathology within the biracial population are mixed. Some studies with biracial adolescents have shown that they are as well adjusted as their monoracial counterparts. Other studies have shown that biracial adolescents may be at higher health and behavior risks and experience more problems than their single-race peers. Conversely, a handful of studies have found some results that suggest that biracial adolescents are better adjusted than their single-race peers.

To date, no empirical evidence exists regarding exactly how having multiple racial heritages might be related to higher levels of pathology, although several links have been suggested. The most common explanation is that individuals with multiple racial heritages struggle to develop a consistent identity. The stress of navigating this process is thought to generate increased levels of psychopathology as well as health problems among biracial people.

Similar to their single-race counterparts, biracial people sometimes seek counseling. In the counseling setting, therapists should be aware of several factors when working with biracial clients as these factors may be related to the presenting problem(s). Issues counselors may want to address with their biracial clients include racial identity, acceptance by heritage groups, experiences with racism and discrimination, perception of one's physical appearance, and sexuality. The therapist should seek to understand how the client identifies racially both in private and in public. It is also important to understand how the biracial client is viewed and treated by his or her heritage groups and what types of experiences with racism he or she may have had, as these experiences may be related to the reason the client is seeking treatment. Because of myths that biracial people, particularly biracial females, are sexually promiscuous, the counselor may also want to ask about sexuality. Finally, the counselor should get an idea of how the biracial client is viewed by strangers in society and whether these perceptions match the client's perception of him- or herself.

The therapist should also be aware that biracial people are often identified as special or exotic and/or rejected by one or both of their heritage groups. If either of these possibilities has occurred, the therapist should know of potential effects. These experiences may produce a sense of uniqueness, which can manifest either positively (i.e., pride) or negatively (i.e., alienation). This feeling of uniqueness should not be pathologized or viewed as narcissistic by the therapist. Acceptance and belonging may also be issues to some biracial people who feel shunned by one or both heritage groups.

Therapists might also benefit from completing a genogram with biracial clients. Genograms are similar to family trees but also address patterns of communication, emotional cutoffs, significant family events, and assignment of roles. Creating a genogram with biracial clients can increase insight into the racial heritage of family members, how family members view and identify the client racially, and lifestyle choices related to ethnicity (e.g., child rearing, diet, stress and coping). The therapist can also take into account large social systems that affect the biracial client, such as work, medical services, social services, education, and peers.

—*Joshua A. Singh*
—*Gayle Y. Iwamasa*

See also Biracial Identity

FURTHER READING

Aldarondo, F. (2001). Racial and ethnic identity models and their application: Counseling biracial individuals. *Journal of Mental Health Counseling, 23,* 238–255.

Cooney, T. M., & Radina, M. E. (2000). Adjustment problems in adolescence: Are multiracial children at risk? *American Journal of Orthopsychiatry, 70*(4), 433–444.

Dalmage, H. M. (2000). *Tripping on the color line: Black–White multiracial families in a racially divided world.* Piscataway, NJ: Rutgers University Press.

Gaskins, P. F. (1999). *What are you? Voices of mixed-race young people.* New York: Henry Holt.

Harris, D. R., & Sim, J. J. (2002). Who is multiracial? Assessing the complexity of lived race. *American Sociological Review, 67,* 614–627.

Nakazawa, D. (2003). *Does anybody else look like me?* Cambridge, MA: Perseus.

Rockquemore, K. A., & Brunsma, D. L. (2002). Socially embedded identities: Theories, typologies, and processes of racial identity among Black/White biracials. *The Sociological Quarterly, 43,* 335–356.

Root, M. P. P. (Ed.). (1992). *Racially mixed people in America.* Newbury Park, CA: Sage.

Root, M. P. P. (Ed.). (1996). *The multiracial experience: Racial borders as the new frontier.* Thousand Oaks, CA: Sage.

Root, M. P. P., & Kelley, M. (Eds.). (2003). *Multiracial child resource book: Living complex identities.* Seattle, WA: Mavin Foundation.

U.S. Census Bureau. (2001, November). *Two or More Races Population: 2000.* Retrieved January 23, 2006, from http://www.census.gov/

Wijeyesinghe, C. L. (2001). Racial identity in multiracial people: An alternative paradigm. In C. L. Wijeyesinghe & B. W. Jackson (Eds.), *New perspectives on racial identity development* (pp. 129–152). New York: NYU Press.

Winters, L. I., & DuBose, H. L. (Eds.). (2003). *New faces in a changing America: Multiracial identity in the 21st century.* Thousand Oaks, CA: Sage.

BIRACIAL IDENTITY

Identity has been noted by psychologists and multicultural scholars alike to be a key psychological process in defining oneself, particularly in relation to other people. One area of identity that has received a great deal of attention in the multicultural literature is *racial identity,* the process of internalizing negative or positive images concerning one's racial group memberships. A number of racial identity development models have been proposed; a critical question has been the applicability of these models to biracial or multiracial people. As well, a number of conceptual models have been proposed describing the unique racial identity development of biracial and multiracial people.

RACIAL IDENTITY DEVELOPMENT MODELS—APPLICATIONS TO BIRACIAL IDENTITY

Racial identity development (RID) models identifying different themes regarding the quality of identification in one's racial group membership(s) have been applied to the racial identity development of multiracial people. In general, RID models propose that individuals do not react identically to conditions of discrimination or privilege, but develop various schemas or statuses for interpreting these experiences. For example, the person of color (POC) racial identity model describes racial identity development for people of color, according to their experiences with racial oppression and the capacity to relinquish external, generally negative views of people of color in favor of internal, more positive standards. Racial identity development models based on privilege also have been variously proposed by multicultural scholars, one of the better known being the White racial identity development (WRID) model. The WRID model describes cognitive strategies associated with relinquishing power as an aspect of internalized racial identity.

A current criticism of RID models is their applicability to multiracial people, given the monoracial emphases of these models. Thus far, few studies have been published providing empirical evidence concerning the relevance of RID models for multiracial people. However, although it is likely that RID models do not predict several important aspects of racial identity of biracial people, these models highlight critical commonalities of identity development for monoracial and biracial people. These commonalities center on experiences with overt racism and finding supportive others in the community with whom to identify. Common processes of RID models based on privilege also might be examined for their validity and relevance with biracial people. Finally, RID models do not necessarily preclude the development of more specific racial identity models for biracial people.

BIRACIAL AND MULTIRACIAL IDENTITY DEVELOPMENT MODELS

Beginning with W. S. Carlos Poston, multicultural scholars have proposed unique biracial identity models. For example, Poston proposed a five-stage model of biracial identity development, suggesting that all biracial individuals will experience some conflict and subsequent periods of maladjustment during the identity development process. The first stage of Poston's model, *personal identity,* usually occurs in childhood, when biracial individuals are not aware of their mixed-race heritage. During the second stage, *choice of group categorization,* numerous societal, communal, and parental influences compel individuals to choose one racial or ethnic group identity. The third stage, *enmeshment/denial,* is characterized by individuals' feelings of guilt and disloyalty about choosing one racial group over the other. Unable to resolve feelings of guilt and disloyalty, these individuals may deny racial differences and subsequently identify with both groups. In the fourth stage, *appreciation,* individuals may remain committed to one racial group, but might explore the previously ignored racial group as they experience increased awareness and knowledge of the ignored group. In the fifth stage of Poston's model, *integration,* individuals may still identify with one racial group but value the integration of their multiple racial identities.

Another model of biracial identity development, proposed by Christine Kerwin and Joseph Ponterotto, used age-based developmental markers to illustrate progression in racial awareness. However, unlike other models, Kerwin and Ponterotto's conceptualization incorporates variance in identity resolution styles (e.g., establishing a public racial identity that differs from a private one) that is influenced by personal, societal, and environmental factors. Their model also differed from the other models in that they acknowledged that biracial individuals might experience exclusion from groups of color as well as from the

European American community. In the *preschool* stage, which encompasses children up to 5 years of age, biracial children recognize similarities and differences in physical appearance, and this awareness might be a function of the degree of parental sensitivity to and addressing of race-related issues. In the *entry to school* stage, biracial children are in greater contact with social groups and may be asked to classify themselves according to a monoracial label. In the *preadolescence* stage, there is an increased awareness of social meanings ascribed to social groups as characterized by skin tone, physical appearance, ethnicity, and religion. Environmental factors, such as entry into a more diverse or more monocultural context, and direct or vicarious exposure to racism also may heighten these young adolescents' sensitivity to race. As biracial children enter *adolescence* stage, pressures to identify with one social group may be intensified by expectations of identification with the racial group of a parent of color. In the *college/young adulthood* stage, there may be a continued immersion in a monoracial group, accompanied by an acute awareness of the contexts in which race-related comments are made. The *adulthood* stage is characterized by a continued exploration and interest in race and culture, including self-definitions of racial and cultural identities and increased flexibility in adapting to various cultural settings.

A limitation of some biracial identity development models has been their assumption that a fully integrated biracial or multiracial identity is the desired end state. Maria Root, however, has suggested alternative resolutions of the biracial and multiracial identity development process. She proposed an ecological metamodel for understanding the potential influences of inherited influences (e.g., parents' identities, nativity, phenotype, and extended family), traits (e.g., temperament, coping skills, and social skills), and socialization agents (e.g., family, peer, and community) on resolution of racial identity for multiracial people. Different sources of experiential conflict lead to feelings of alienation and marginality, discrimination, and ambiguity that challenge the development of a healthy sense of self. Root also noted that multiracial individuals can negotiate identity development concerns through four possible "border crossings," or comfort in, across, and between racial categories: ability to carry multiple cultural perspectives simultaneously; situational identity, or shifting racial identity with regard to context or environment; claiming an independent multiracial reference point; and maintaining a monoracial identity when entering different cultural environments. Border identity, or identification with both or many racial groups, may be positive when personality and sense of self remain constant across racial contexts, although social validation of racial identity may be specific to regions of high concentrations of biracial and multiracial people.

RESEARCH ON BIRACIAL IDENTITY

Empirical evidence supporting variations of adaptive identity development resolutions for biracial and multiracial people is in its infancy. This research has grown substantially since 1990 and includes both quantitative and qualitative designs, each with a variety of strengths and limitations. The use of qualitative designs has been promoted by several scholars in the study of biracial identity because of the unique stories of biracial people. Generally, the themes described in such studies point to the fluidity, fluctuations, and variability in the race and racial identity development of biracial people. However, although the findings of many of these studies might be credible, a common problem with qualitative designs is their lack of generalizability (indeed, this is generally not the goal of qualitative studies). It is difficult to ascertain how themes found in one or another biracial participant group might help psychologists and other mental health professionals understand and assess identity development of biracial people in general. Thus, there is currently a need to incorporate designs that have potential for generalizing results (e.g., larger samples, use of control groups, use of standardized measures).

Research on biracial and multiracial people brings a unique set of challenges to overcome to present information that is accurate and applicable to others. Several problems have been common among research on biracial identity, including small, highly regional, and self-selected samples; lack of standardized instruments; lack of consistency in definitions of race identity variables; and lack of clarity or consistency regarding data analytic procedures (e.g., procedures of data analyses were not described). Much of the research has focused on adolescents and young adults, and thus little is known about biracial identity across the life span.

—*Marie L. Miville*

See also Multiracial Individuals; Racial Identity Development

FURTHER READING

Kerwin, C., & Ponterotto, J. G. (1995). Biracial identity development: Theory and research. In J. G. Ponterotto, J. M. Casas, L. A. Suzuki, & C. M. Alexander (Eds.), *Handbook of multicultural counseling* (1st ed., pp. 199–217). Thousand Oaks, CA: Sage.

Miville, M. L. (2005). Psychological functioning and identity development of biracial people: A review of current theory and research. In R. T. Carter (Ed.), *Handbook of racial-cultural psychology and counseling: Vol. 1. Theory and research* (pp. 295–319). New York: Wiley.

Root, M. P. P. (1992). *Racially mixed people in America.* Newbury Park, CA: Sage.

Root, M. P. P. (1996). *The multiracial experience: Racial borders as the new frontier.* Thousand Oaks, CA: Sage.

BLAMING THE VICTIM

Blaming the victim is an attributional error in which a person is seen as being primarily responsible for his or her own suffering. For example, regarding ethnic minority groups' lower scores on intelligence tests than those of European Americans, Richard J. Herrnstein and Charles Murray argue in *The Bell Curve* that European Americans are innately intellectually superior to minorities and that efforts to eradicate racial discrepancies, such as affirmative action, remedial programs, and welfare are of little use. Gays and lesbians who contract AIDS are accused of deserving their fate because of their "immoral" lifestyle. People with low socioeconomic status are perceived as lazy individuals who are on welfare because they are unwilling to work like the rest of us. Rape victims are blamed for their assault because of rape myths, such as the belief that women can cause rape by how they dress or behave, or because any respectable woman could prevent rape if she wanted to. Women were assumed to stay in abusive relationships because they suffer from battered woman syndrome or a masochistic personality. People with mental illnesses were assumed to be weak-willed, evil, or manipulative.

Blaming the victim can be internalized by the victim him- or herself, usually with negative consequences for the individual. Minorities who internalize the belief that they are less intelligent may not aspire to do well academically, or when they do they may be affected by stereotype threat: anxiety about poor performance may actually interfere with performance. For example, an African American student in an elite university in which there are few students of color may believe that African Americans are less capable than other students and less qualified because they are in the university only because of affirmative action. Thus, internalizing the blame for one's own suffering can become a self-fulfilling prophecy that can put the individual at risk for low self-esteem and other problems.

One reason people have a tendency to blame the victim is another attributional error, called the *just world theory,* which is based on the assumption that people get what they deserve. The just world theory occurs because it helps us to preserve the belief that the world is an orderly place and we can remain safe if we act appropriately. It follows from this assumption that if something bad happens to someone, she or he must have done something to deserve it. Unfortunately, this type of thinking often leads to blaming the victim, lack of empathy for those who are suffering, prejudice, and discrimination.

Another reason for blaming the victim is the tendency in individualistic cultures to locate the cause of behavior within the individual rather than in the situation, or what is called the *fundamental attribution error.* This bias is reflected in our theories of personality as well, in that we tend to think of personality as something that resides within us and is the cause of our behavior. If our behavior is caused by something that is within us, it follows that when something bad happens to us, it must be our fault.

—*Christy Barongan*

FURTHER READING

Aronson, J., Quinn, D. M., & Spencer, S. J. (1998). Stereotype threat and the academic underperformance of minorities and women. In J. K. Swim & C. Stangor (Eds.), *Prejudice: The target's perspective* (pp. 83–103). San Diego: Academic Press.

Lerner, M. J. (1980). *The belief in a just world: A fundamental delusion.* New York: Plenum.

Ross, L., & Nisbett, R. E. (1991). *The person and the situation: Perspectives of social psychology.* New York: McGraw-Hill.

BUREAU OF INDIAN AFFAIRS

Beginning in the late 1700s, the military arm of the U.S. government had to determine its response to American Indians recently relocated and contained in the western part of the United States. In 1824, the

U.S. War Department created the Bureau of Indian Affairs (BIA) after several years of trying to manage various aspects of different activities surrounding American Indian tribes. Initially, the BIA had jurisdiction over trade between American Indian tribes and non-Indians (trading companies that hired beaver and buffalo hunters who hunted on Indian land), removal and relocation from historical and traditional land bases to reservations and other containment (prisoners of war or crimes committed against non-Indians), and monitoring in an attempt to limit exploitation of natural resources (gold, water, and land). Unfortunately, the BIA was lacking in its efforts and possessed little power to counter the growing power of Congress, which demonstrated an increasing desire to acquire lands held by treaties between the federal government and the various tribes. In 1884, the BIA was transferred to the U.S. Department of the Interior (USDI), which had regulatory authority over lands and natural resources. Little consideration was given to the fact that, based on treaties, the health, education, and welfare of the American Indian people were majority responsibilities of the BIA, and these concerns ran counter to the purpose of the USDI. The Commission of Indian Affairs, as head of the BIA, quickly became the regulatory authority on marriages, orphans, lands, education, health, resolving disputes, clarifying language, and any other aspects of life involving the American Indians. Eventually, the BIA evolved into primarily a land-administration agency, a process speeded up by the Dawes Act of 1887, the Burke Act of 1906, and the Wheeler-Howard Act of 1934, which resulted in the BIA becoming the trustee over American Indian lands, funds, and resources (i.e., minerals, grazing, leases). It became apparent that increased monitoring and programmatic oversight was necessary within the BIA, leading to different departments being established to regulate housing, education, land, resources, leases, construction, banking, and especially trust issues. All activities involving enrolled American Indians and federally recognized tribes were regulated and controlled by the BIA. Once Alaska became a state, the BIA began to control and monitor programs for Alaska Natives. One effort to decrease the need for the BIA was the termination policy of the federal government in the 1950s. More than 100 tribes were terminated or lost their federal recognition status, and Congress passed Public Law 280, which allowed states to regulate tribes. It was not until the 1960s and the Self-Determination Act of 1975 that changes occurred, creating the climate for many but not all tribes to govern their own affairs without oversight by the BIA. (Certain PL-280 states still maintain control over some federally recognized tribes.) Since then, the BIA has assisted tribes in becoming more independent and moving toward self-governance. The BIA is no longer a regulatory agency for federally recognized tribes; however, it does monitor federal funds contracted by tribes for services, including police, courts, education, and social services. Many tribes have demonstrated their ability to conduct their own government systems and have managed to maintain independence from the BIA. The BIA continues to provide for several boarding schools both on and off reservations for American Indian and Alaska Native children. The U.S. government still has a trustee responsibility that is primarily managed within the Department of the Interior and by the BIA. The BIA remains the agency that receives applications from non–federally recognized tribes seeking federal recognition and determines whether the tribes in question achieve the status of being federally recognized. The BIA has come under increased scrutiny regarding the mismanagement of boarding schools and moneys involved in the Individual Indian Accounts.

—*Dolores Subia Big Foot*

See also Certificate of Degree of Indian Blood; Indian Health Service; Native Americans

FURTHER READING

Sipe, John L. (2005). *Carlisle Industrial School, Fort Marian Prisoners of War.* Retrieved January 23, 2006, from http://home.epix.net/~landis/ftmarion.html

CENSUS STATISTICS

Census statistics are population-level counts that report the composition of the population. Tabulations of race and ethnicity are crucial to the reporting of changes in the level of diversity in the U.S. population. Capturing recent and historical developments in the area of racial and ethnic diversity is wholly dependent on the consistent and accurate accounting of the ethnic and racial composition of the population. Methods of racial and ethnic enumeration and categorization have changed dramatically over the 200-year history of the U.S. Census.

EARLY DEFINITIONS OF RACE AND ETHNICITY IN THE CENSUS (1790–1960)

The history of Census racial classification can be divided into two eras. During the first era (before 1960), enumerators assigned race to respondents; during the second era (all Censuses since 1960), individuals were allowed to identify themselves on a mail-back form. The first Census in 1790 instructed enumerators to classify persons as either *free White males, free White females, all other free persons,* or *slaves.* Indians who embraced tribal rule, identified as *Indians not taxed,* were excluded from enumeration until the Census of 1880. The designation *free colored persons* was added in 1840 and 1850. From 1850 until 1920, enumerators were allowed to indicate that persons had both African and European American parentage by using the category *mulatto,* although enumerators were instructed that this was a generic term that applied to all types of mixed African and European heritage. This designation evolved to specify the extent of mixture, adding the categories *quadroon* and *octoroon* in 1890. All categories of racial mixture were dropped in 1930, and enumerators were instructed to list persons of mixed race as *Negro.*

Populations of Asian origin were first counted in 1870, when enumerators could choose to label persons as *Chinese,* and in 1890, *Japanese* was added. The categories *Korean, Filipino,* and *Hindu* were added in 1910. In addition, the 1910 Census was the first to provide the option of *Other,* giving enumerators the option to write in the respondent's race if none of the listed categories were appropriate. Pacific Islanders and Alaskans were identified for the first time in the 1960 Census under the categories *Part Hawaiian, Aleut,* and *Eskimo.*

Enumerating ethnic origins became a priority during this era, which saw several waves of immigration from Europe during the late 19th and early 20th centuries. Questions about respondents' place of birth, their parents' place of birth, nativity, and language use (called "mother tongue" and "father tongue") were added to the Census between 1850 and 1960. Hispanic origins were initially captured in the 1930 Census with a category on the race question despite the established presence of persons of Mexican origin in annexed territories of California and New Mexico. The category *Mexican* was dropped from the next Census because of opposition from Mexican Americans, who felt such a designation would label them *non-White.*

RACIAL CLASSIFICATION IN AN ERA OF INDIVIDUAL IDENTITY (POST-1960)

The 1970 Census allowed individuals to label themselves for the first time without the help of enumerators.

From this point on, the categories became more detailed, allowing greater room for self-expression. A variety of Asian and Pacific Islander categories are now listed, and Native Americans and Alaska Natives may write in their tribal affiliations. Ethnicity is also captured differently by questions on primary and secondary ancestry and by a Hispanic-origin question that allows respondents to specify Latin American countries as one's place of origin. All ethnic items are asked independently of racial questions. Therefore, persons of Hispanic origin may identified themselves as belonging to any race.

The importance of counting race has changed during this period. Beyond tabulating the characteristics of the population, counting race became an important element of enforcing antidiscrimination legislation established during the 1950s and 1960s. To ensure an accurate accounting of race, in 1977, the U.S. Office of Management and Budget (OMB) issued Statistical Directive No. 15, which provided guidelines for the measurement of race and ethnicity for all federal agencies. The directive instructed the enumeration of five distinctive racial and ethnic groups: White, Black, Asian/Pacific Islander, American Indian/Alaska Native, and Hispanic.

The standards were revised again in 1997, when the OMB recommended that respondents be allowed to choose multiple races. Approximately four million persons, or 2.4% of the U.S. population, identify themselves as more than one race. This marked a significant shift in the way the Census captures race and affected the size and distribution of racial and ethnic groups. It also raised some important questions about how to apply race-targeted policies that employ single-race definitions.

IMPLICATIONS FOR COUNTING AMERICAN RACIAL AND ETHNIC GROUPS

Providing a full and accurate count of the population through the Census has tremendous political and social significance. The clearest examples can be found in the early history of the Census. In the first Census, in 1790, the Great Compromise established that slaves would be counted as three-fifths of a person. This allayed the fears of northern colonists that the counting of southern slaves would result in undue representation of the South in Congress. American Indians, who were not taxed, were not counted until the 1880 Census because these individuals were not considered American citizens, and therefore would not be represented in Census figures.

Accurate counting was recently debated when the Census Bureau considered employing sampling, or counting a subset of a specific population and weighting the count to represent the full population. The race counts of the 1990 Census demonstrated a substantial undercounting of the number of African Americans, bringing the issue of sampling to the forefront. Sampling would compensate for the undercounting of certain hard-to-reach populations when enumerating the population for the 2000 Census. Ultimately, the Supreme Court declared sampling to be unconstitutional. Instead, the Census Bureau employed enumerators to follow up with those who did not return their Census forms.

How one's race or ethnicity is labeled may depend on the wording or ordering of Census questions. This influences the ultimate count of subgroups and observations of changes over time. Fluctuations in the size of the Native American population provide a clear example. Growth in the Census counts of Native Americans between 1960 and 1990 could not be accounted for by demographic changes (e.g., births, deaths, migration) and therefore was attributed to more persons choosing to identify themselves as Native American or American Indian than in prior Censuses. Some of this fluctuation can be attributed to differences in question wording. In the 1980 Census, more than four million people identified themselves as Native American in response to a question about ancestry, whereas a little more than one million people indicated Native American as their race.

The ordering of questions may also affect the reported size of groups. The number of people indicating Hispanic origin is greater when the Hispanic-origin question precedes the race question. If race is asked first, many Latinos indicate "other race" and write in Latino or Hispanic, leaving the Hispanic question blank. Results from surveys that provided the Hispanic and race questions in multiple formats strongly suggest that separate questions may confuse respondents who view the term *Hispanic* as a racial ascription. As a result, the 2000 Census allowed respondents to declare their Hispanic origin first and then assign themselves a racial label in the following question.

IMPLICATIONS OF APPLYING NEW DEFINITIONS: MULTIPLE-RACE RESPONSE

The newest revision to the Census race question, which allows respondents to choose more than one race, has raised important questions in the areas of law, politics, and social science analysis. Legally and politically, the implementation of antidiscrimination, civil rights, and voting rights laws requires a clear-cut count of the population by race. For antidiscrimination laws, the size and composition of racial and ethnic groups determines benchmarks for how the population should be represented within occupational or educational institutions. For voting rights cases, how and where district lines are drawn has to be weighed against the potential impact on the level of minority representation within that district.

The OMB has provided guidelines for reallocating multiracial persons to single-race categories. These allocations count multiracial persons as members of non-White single groups; however, specific guidelines exist for persons of multiple non-White origins. These guidelines do not serve to threaten the degree of minority representation, as some civil rights organizations feared when the multiracial enumeration was first proposed. However, the guidelines are problematic because they acknowledge only one aspect of a multiracial person's identity. The guidelines also provide people who partially identify with a racial group the same political representation and benefits from race-targeted policies (i.e., affirmative action policies) that single-race members have come to expect.

Social scientists who analyze Census data are faced with a similar difficulty: where and how to include multiracial individuals. There is some evidence that those who identify themselves as multiracial have different social-class profiles compared with their single-race groups. Applying the OMB's allocation strategy could under- or overestimate the degree of social and economic change occurring within a racial or ethnic population.

—*Jenifer Bratter*

See also Multiracial Individuals

FURTHER READING

Anderson, M. J., & Fineburg, S. E. (1999). *Who counts: The politics of census taking in contemporary America.* New York: Russell Sage Foundation.

Farley, R. (1991). The new Census question about ancestry: What did it tell us? *Demography, 28,* 411–429.

Nobles, M. (2000). *Shades of citizenship: Race and the Census in modern politics.* Stanford, CA: Stanford University Press.

Perlmann, J., & Waters, M. (2002). *The new race question: How the Census counts multiracial individuals.* New York: Russell Sage Foundation.

CENTER FOR EPIDEMIOLOGIC STUDIES DEPRESSION SCALE

The Center for Epidemiologic Studies Depression Scale (CES-D) is designed to study general patterns of the incidence and prevalence of depression among adults. Lenore S. Radloff published the original report on its development and suitability for use in the general population. The CES-D is frequently used to measure depressed mood and general psychological distress in research settings, and it is popular for screening for clinical levels of depression (such as major depressive disorder) in adult community populations where low levels of incidence are expected. It has been translated into several languages and used in cross-cultural samples. The CES-D was designed to be a self-report measure assessing current symptom levels of depression in the general population. Independently developed short versions with a reported predictive validity comparable to the original are also available.

The CES-D measures levels of depression on a continuous scale and is relatively easy to administer and score. However, it is not intended for use as a clinical diagnostic tool because high scores may also be a result of anxiety or other psychological distress. The CES-D is considered to be good (i.e., high on sensitivity) but relatively inefficient (i.e., low on specificity) at detecting possible cases of depression; its items emphasize a depressed mood state and do not evaluate other possible indicators of mood disorder, such as a loss of previous interest or pleasure in activities, suicide ideation, or duration of symptoms that make up the diagnostic criteria in the *Diagnostic and Statistical Manual of Mental Disorders,* 4th edition. The 20 items in the CES-D sample four domains, each weighted by frequency of occurrence (0–3) during the previous week: depressed affect (seven items; "I felt sad"), lack of positive affect (four items; "I enjoyed life"), somatic and retarded activity (seven items; "I felt that everything I did was an effort"), and interpersonal aspects of depression (two items; "People were unfriendly"). The summed score (after reverse scoring positively worded items) ranges from 0 to 60, with higher scores indicating endorsement of higher depressive symptoms. A cutoff score of 16 is generally accepted for screening purposes; those meeting the cutoff are to be followed up with a diagnostic interview.

Scores that are inflated because of systematically higher endorsements of somatic-domain items have been found in many study samples, such as East Asian and Spanish-speaking individuals, geriatric patients, and cancer patients; therefore, adjusted cutoff scores range from 20 to 34. A tendency to not highly endorse positively worded items may overestimate depression levels for East Asian and Asian American individuals. Moreover, higher endorsements of scale items in college samples also suggest that cutoff scores should be adjusted or used with caution. Omitting problematic items from the scale is another strategy that has been used to reduce the number of individuals falsely categorized as highly depressed.

Studies have explored the CES-D's suitability for diverse populations. Radloff's original report found comparable reliability, validity, and factor structures for different age, gender, racial (i.e., African American and European American), and education-level subgroups. A review of the literature shows inconsistent results for factor structures among diverse groups. Responses from some study samples replicate Radloff's four-structure model, whereas others suggest different factor structures and loadings for these and other groups. Most findings have consistently confirmed gender differences. The majority of studies, however, demonstrate the CES-D's reliability (internal consistency), a property that Radloff originally argued de-emphasizes the importance of its factor structure.

—Nausheen Masood
—Sumie Okazaki

See also Depression; DSM-IV

FURTHER READING

American Psychiatric Association. (2000). *Diagnostic and statistical manual of mental disorders* (4th ed., text rev.). Washington, DC: Author.
Radloff, L. (1977). The CES-D Scale: A self-report depression scale for research in the general population. *Applied Psychological Measurement, 1,* 385–401.

CERTIFICATE OF DEGREE OF INDIAN BLOOD

A Certificate of Degree of Indian Blood is a legal document issued by the U.S. Department of the Interior, Bureau of Indian Affairs, indicating status based on lineage or bloodlines and designating someone as American Indian, Alaska Native, Eskimo, Inuit, or otherwise federally recognized. Such individuals may be eligible for federally administrated programs or benefits from federally recognized tribes. In certain circumstances, an individual may be ineligible for enrollment in a federally recognized tribe but may be eligible for federal services based on a combined degree of Indian blood (CDIB) equaling one quarter. The CDIB is an arbitrary measure implemented by the U.S. government to account for American Indians when they were confined to select locations and before the Indian census began.

There is no true degree of Indian blood, as this term was originally based on English horse breeding. It was used by the commissioner of the Office of Indian Affairs during the 1800s so that the Department of War could track and provide an accounting of Indian men and their families by identifying intermarriages or children born of Indian females. The Indian agent provided a census to the Office of Indian Affairs that included head of household, occupation, name of wife or wives, and names and ages of children. The Indian agent, as an official representative of the federal government, made an arbitrary determination as to the degree of Indian blood. For example, if an individual was part of a tribe and both parents were of the same tribe, then that offspring was considered "full blood." If one parent was non-Indian, then the child was considered a "half-breed." The CDIB became an issue when tribes became eligible for federal funding and criteria were established.

Eligibility requirements were implemented for enrollment into federally recognized American Indian tribes and for villages in Alaska that were not American Indian but Alaska Native, Eskimo, and Inuit (who do not consider themselves to be American Indians culturally or linguistically). American Indian tribes established tribal constitutions beginning in 1934. Many tribes accepted the enrollment criteria based on guidelines from the Bureau of Indian Affairs. Politically and in federal regulations, Alaska Natives, Eskimo, and Inuit are listed under the labels *American Indian/Alaska Native* or *Native Americans.* However, the enrollment criteria are based on village status and their relationship to the regional organizations that were established as part of the Alaskan Settlement of 1973.

Some federally recognized tribes have restructured their constitutions to change the criteria for membership to the traditional matriarchal or patriarchal lineage that was determined by family names, kinships, or relationships. Some tribes use the original 1888–1898 Dawes Allotment Rolls from the Office of Indian Affairs. This permits tribes to select lineage as the determinate of eligibility for enrollment. Other tribes have changed their constitutions to be inclusive of all tribal heritage. Therefore, anyone eligible for tribal enrollment in a particular tribe would be considered 4/4 (100%) Indian or as much of any one tribe as the family line can document. There is also a federal process to become a federally recognized tribe. Texas, Louisiana, and South Carolina have state-recognized tribes.

The Certificate of Degree of Indian Blood was established prior to 1900 by the U.S. government as an accounting census, but it has evolved into a criterion for enrollment in federally recognized American Indian tribes and for eligibility for federal, state, or other funding opportunities. The U.S. Department of Education, the Indian Health Service, many universities, and even electric and phone companies require this document so that services can be offered.

—Dolores Subia Big Foot

See also Bureau of Indian Affairs; Indian Health Service; Native Americans

FURTHER READING

Meyer, M. (1999). Blood is thicker than family. In V. J. Matsumoto & B. Allmendiger (Eds.), *Over the edge: Remapping the American West.* Berkeley: University of California Press.

Sipe, J. L. (2005). *Fort Marian prisoners of war, 1875–1878.* Retrieved January 26, 2006, from the Carlisle Indian Industrial School Web site: http://home.epix.net/~landis/ftmarion.html

Wilkins, D. E. (2002). *American Indian politics and the American Indian political system.* Lanham, MD: Rowman & Littlefield.

Wilson, T. P. (1992). Blood quantum: Native American mixed bloods. In M. P. Root (Ed.), *Racially mixed people in America.* Newbury Park, CA: Sage.

CHICANAS/CHICANOS

According to the 2000 U.S. Census, Chicana/os represent roughly 67% of the 33.8 million Latina/os in the United States. Chicana/os are people of Mexican descent born in the United States, also known as Mexican Americans. Chicana/os are also called *la raza* (the race), *la raza de bronce* (the bronze or brown race), or *la raza cosmica* (the universal race). Given current and projected demographic changes for the Chicana/o community in the United States, it is necessary to develop a deeper understanding of the history, culture, and present-day status of Chicana/os.

CHICANA/OS: HISTORY AND TERM IDENTIFICATION

Traditionally, the United States has been a country with a majority population made up of Caucasian Americans, and U.S. values and beliefs have evolved around Western European cultural practices (this is called a *Eurocentric* perspective). In light of this Eurocentric perspective and an intent to preserve power among the majority, a history of oppressing ethnically and racially diverse individuals in the United States has been well noted. Chicana/os have not been excluded from the marginalization and discrimination projected in response to the "browning" of America. As an ethnic and racial group, Chicana/os have created a strong political and cultural presence in response to years of social oppression and discrimination. Within this social context, American society often categorizes minority status by physical appearance or race rather than by culture, values, and beliefs. Consequently, Chicana/os' physical appearance has become the most salient factor to those outside the community. The continued social and political influences of Western European society, a lack of understanding of the largest Latina/o group in the United States, and oppressive circumstances have provided a foundation for the manifestation of Chicana/o psychology.

Like most historically disenfranchised groups in the United States, some Mexican Americans have taken the term *Chicano,* previously considered a pejorative word, and used it to empower themselves. To fully understand the meaning of *Chicanismo,* the history of the term must first be examined.

Several theories address the root of the term Chicano. One presumption dates back to the 1930s and 1940s, when poor indigenous (Native Nahuatl) Mexicans came to America as seasonal migrant workers. The early Mexican farmworkers struggled to call themselves *Mexicanos* and instead referred to themselves in their own native tongue as *Mesheecanos.* The term Chicano was used by Caucasians in the fields to ridicule the laborers and their limited language proficiencies.

Another recognized cultural story that ties the term Chicano to Mexican Americans traces back to the Aztecs. During the Spanish invasion, an Aztec tribe referred to themselves as *Mexicas* (*Mesheekas*) or *Xicanos* (*Sheekanos*). The name of current-day Mexico was derived from the word *Mexica.* Until Spanish colonization in Mexico, the terms Mexicas and Xicanos were used with *orgullo* (pride) among the country's people. The Spanish, however, to maintain superiority over the Aztecs, used the terms Mexica and Xicano derogatorily. In particular, the Spanish created an inferior and inadequate mind-set among the Aztecs, ensuring the long-term effects of their conquest while reducing the likelihood of retaliation. Moreover, the Spanish reinforced a belief that Chicana/os were uneducated, lazy, and of a lower social class. Consequently, the Aztec community, which had such initial pride, internalized the inferior perception and rejected the foundation of their culture as beautiful and full of value.

Today, the term Xicano—currently transliterated as *Chicano*—is an essential component of the community's revitalization and renewed sense of hope and pride. Regaining and regenerating the term Chicano, and having Chicanismo (an identity embracing the political consciousness of the Mexicans' history in the United States), was the first step toward releasing the psychological barriers in the minds of many Mexican Americans. Initially, *Chicana/o* was used to refer to all people of Mexican origin. Currently, the term refers to people of Mexican descent born in the United States. The term *Chicana* has feminist (*feminista*) connotations resulting from its use by Mexican American female activists determined to raise the political awareness of those outside the Chicana/o community. In fact, during the Chicano Movement (*El Movimiento*) of the 1960s and 1970s, Chicanos established a strong political presence and agenda in the United States through the leadership of Corky Gonzales, Cesar Chavez, and Dolores Huerta. All three individuals gave strength to men and women in the community to fight for equality and demand social justice.

The Chicano Movement, political unrest, community disturbances, and a focus on ethnic conflict raised the consciousness of "Brown pride," "Chicano power," and Chicanismo. *Chicano power* signified that the community would no longer tolerate the injustices imposed by Caucasian society. Chicana/os demanded a change in the social and political climate in the United States and considered anything less inadequate. These ideologies became threatening to Caucasian society, but Chicana/os maintained momentum and encouraged others to regain what had been lost and to assert their civil liberties and rights as people who deserve social equality. A close analysis of today's social climate reflects the perceptions and attitudes of the Spanish conquerors. Specifically, Western European perspectives continue to influence the social infrastructure of the United States.

AMERICA'S ATTITUDES AND CHICANA/OS TODAY

Chicana/os represent a large percentage of the population in the states of California, Texas, Arizona, New Mexico, Nevada, and Colorado. Though the population continues to grow, many question the factors that hinder the social mobility of this group. After careful review of this group's social status, scholars have argued that Chicana/os continue to encounter similar problems to those faced before 1980. Today, Chicana/os continue to face discrimination in the schools, poverty, crime, violence, poor health care access, lack of health insurance, and underrepresentation in U.S. politics.

A group's success in society is highly dependent on its perceived social status. Hence, the way Chicana/os are perceived in the United States plays an important role in psychological and social factors within the community. Historically, the United States has compared Chicana/os to a Caucasian norm, immediately placing the group at a deficit, rather than examining their strengths. Without examining its cultural norms, the United States has assumed that Caucasian norms are the standard. Consequently, Eurocentric values and cultural norms have placed Chicana/os at a level in society where upward mobility has become extremely difficult and, at times, impossible. The limited social status caused by this social oppression, however, has been attributed to something inherent within Chicana/os (known as a *deficiency model*). Specifically, Caucasian Americans believe that Chicana/os have a biological makeup that allows them to exist within the boundaries of low-income *barrios* with poor health conditions and high educational attrition.

The social and cultural disconnection of Chicana/os from Caucasian American society reminds them of two distinct cultural experiences. In particular, Chicana/os or Mexican Americans live within what many have called "the space" or "the hyphen." The dual moniker *Mexican American* suggests that Chicana/os straddle two worlds—one experience is unique to being Mexican, whereas the process of

Americanization results in the loss of a place to call home. Further reinforcing their cultural incongruity, Chicana/os' experience of prejudice, racism, and mainstream attitudes remind them that although Mexico may not be their homeland, America is not home either. The irony, however, is that the Southwest region of the United States was once part of Mexico; the dominant sentiment in the community is that "we didn't cross the border, the border crossed us."

The questions of what constitutes an American and what role American culture has in a new group of *Nuevo Mexicanos*—Chicana/os—are important ones. Within this social framework, we can begin to understand the psychological and social impact these perspectives have on the community. In particular, the manifestations of acculturative distress, ethnic identity confusion, and marginalization begin to take shape.

ACCULTURATION AND ASSIMILATION

Investigating within-group comparisons of cultural identity and psychological concerns among the Chicana/o and Mexican communities reveals disparities between the two groups. Scholars have found that Chicana/os who maintain strong cultural ties to their Mexican heritage—those who are less acculturated—demonstrate lower rates of psychological distress. Mexican-born individuals living in the United States are healthier than more acculturated U.S.-born Mexican Americans. Recent immigrants from Mexico have more consistently positive attitudes toward doing well in school and graduating from college than more acculturated Chicana/os. Chicana/os who have lived most or all of their lives in the United States have the highest prevalence rates for depression, affective disorders, and psychiatric disorders compared with individuals of Mexican origin who were born in Mexico or lived most of their life in Mexico. This analysis reveals that acculturation and assimilation have multiple long-term effects on Chicana/os in the United States that are reflected in their psychological, social, and cultural adjustment.

CHICANA/O PSYCHOLOGY

The study of Chicana/o psychology includes but is not limited to the examination and understanding of acculturation and ethnic identity; health factors such as hypertension and diabetes; indigenous healing practices; and culturally appropriate testing, assessment, and therapy with Chicana/os. This culturally sensitive psychological framework incorporates the community's past, present, and future. Chicana/o psychology integrates a holistic strength-based cultural model rather than conceptualizing issues from a deficiency model that further demoralizes the community. The study of Chicana/o psychology provides cultural awareness, knowledge, and skills to adequately meet the needs of a growing community that is positioned to become the majority.

—*Miguel E. Gallardo*

See also Hispanic Americans; Mexican Americans

FURTHER READING

Cuéllar, I., Siles, R. I., & Bracamontes, E. (2004). Acculturation: A psychological construct of continuing relevance for Chicana/o psychology. In R. J. Velasquez, L. M. Arellano, & B. W. McNeill (Eds.), *The handbook of Chicana/o psychology and mental health* (pp. 23–42). Mahwah, NJ: Lawrence Erlbaum.

Meier, M., & Rivera, F. (1972). *The Chicanos: A history of Mexican Americans.* New York: Hill and Wang.

CHILD ABUSE: OVERVIEW

DEFINITION

The definition of child abuse comprises four types of abuse and neglect: physical abuse, sexual abuse, neglect, and emotional/psychological abuse. Despite the delineation of these four categories, there is little consensus about how to define abuse. This lack of universal definition makes it difficult to assess the prevalence of child abuse and point to its existence. Moreover, as a result of cultural differences in child care and socialization, certain behaviors may be identified as abusive in one cultural context but not in others.

These four forms of child abuse are difficult to define because parenting and disciplinary practices vary across cultures. For example, the practice of separating the infant from his or her parents by putting the child in a separate room or in a crib after birth is common for many parents in the United States. In contrast, this practice is seen as neglectful and hurtful among others who view the infant as totally dependent on the parents after birth. Thus, it is the parent's responsibility to be close to the infant in order to identify and respond to the infant's ongoing needs. Hence, in these cultures, the infant may stay in the same room as the parents or sleep in the same bed.

An Asian custom called *cao gio* involves rubbing a small, warm coin on the child's body. This practice is considered a common folk remedy for fever, but it may be seen as abusive by other cultures. Another example concerns the use of caretakers to watch young children. In some cultures, for example, the use of a full-time nanny or babysitter is considered neglectful because the child is deprived of seeing his or her parents and having the consistency of parental care. Yet in other cultures, the use of hired caretakers is a common practice. Similarly, although some cultures value extended family members who take on child-rearing and caretaker roles, other cultures view parents who engage in this practice as not fulfilling their parental responsibilities. These examples and the differing child care practices they illustrate highlight the complexity associated with any attempt to define child abuse in a cultural context. The complexity of attempts to define child abuse in a world of varying parenting practices sets the backdrop for the following general definitions of the four types of abuse (see the Safe Child Program Web site listed in Further Reading for additional information on child abuse).

Physical abuse is defined as a specific abusive behavior that involves the physical maltreatment of a child under the age of 18 by a caretaker. Physical abuse may be indicated by bite marks, unusual bruises, burns, lacerations, frequent injuries or "accidents," fractures in unusual places, discoloration of the skin, beatings, shaking, strangulation, brain damage, and swelling to the face and extremities.

Sexual abuse is defined as behavior that obligates or tries to obligate a child or adolescent to engage in a sexual relationship in which consent is not given or cannot be given. Sexual abuse is perhaps one of the most taboo forms of abuse, and therefore it is often underreported. It is important to consider sexual abuse on a continuum of behaviors. For example, sexual abuse may be equated with penetration, but this is only one type of abuse in this category. Sexually abusive behavior includes oral, vaginal, or anal penetration; fondling of the genitals or asking the child to fondle the genital area; exposing private parts to the child, including exposing private parts to a child with another child in the room who is aware of the behavior (even if he or she cannot see the exposure); asking a child to expose him- or herself; entering the vagina or anus with fingers or objects; and engaging in pornography, prostitution, and voyeurism.

Neglect is broadly defined as occurring when the caregiver of a child under the age of 18 has not provided him or her with the basic care necessary for adequate growth and development. This may include not providing medical and mental health care, food, shelter, or education. Neglect also refers to a caregiver failing to provide a child under the age of 18 with adequate supervision and proper safety, thus putting the child at risk for harm. This encompasses situations in which the caregiver is under the influence of alcohol or drugs, which leads to impaired judgment and inadequate supervision of the child.

Emotional/psychological abuse refers to any abuse that attempts to decrease the child's or adolescent's self-esteem or attempts to inflict fear through intimidation. Emotional/psychological abuse is directly aimed at undermining the child's or adolescent's emotional development. Emotional/psychological abuse includes aggressive, unrealistic demands on the child or adolescent in the form of impractical expectations and pressure. Emotional/psychological abuse also includes constantly putting down the child or adolescent; continually attacking the child's or adolescent's sense of self-worth; insulting or rejecting the child or adolescent; and acting inconsistently in terms of following through with verbal promises to the child or adolescent, fostering disappointment and a lack of trust and healthy dependence. Emotional/psychological abuse includes situations in which the caretaker does not provide a nurturing, loving, and supportive environment that offers healthy growth and development for the child or adolescent.

CULTURAL FACTORS TO CONSIDER IN DEFINITIONS OF ABUSE

There are few cross-cultural perspectives in the area of child abuse. Moreover, definitions of child abuse may differ among cultures and change over time. In the industrial world 30 years ago, for example, child abuse was thought to be uncommon. Research indicates that Western cultures have come to acknowledge the individual rights of the child. However, research on some non-Western cultures suggests these cultures see some Western child-rearing practices as neglectful and abusive; babysitting and toilet training are two such examples. In addition, some authors have talked about how support for mothers may be lost in cultures that are trying to adjust to external forces such as industrialization and war, among other larger contextual issues.

Other research discusses the role of culture in child-rearing practices and definitions of abuse. One study looked at ingredients of ethnicity that may influence child treatment, such as machismo, familism, and valuing children. This study found that fathers who held a belief in familism (placing value on the family) in low regard were more likely to physically punish their children in comparison with those fathers who held familism in high regard. In addition, familism was found to relate to a lower frequency of nurturing behaviors among all parents. Although these findings may seem contradictory, one explanation is that parents who value familism may live with their children and extended family members who help with child-rearing responsibilities.

The literature suggests that definitions of abuse consider three factors that promote sensitivity to cultural differences. The first is to consider cultural differences in child-rearing practices. The second is to consider idiosyncratic departures from what is defined as behaviorally appropriate and acceptable in one's culture. The third factor is to consider societal harm to children. If definitions of abuse consider these three factors, it is thought that the differences in parenting practices described previously, though they may be seen as abuse in one culture or society, may seem acceptable or appropriate in another culture.

PREVALENCE

Any discussion of the prevalence of the four forms of child abuse must begin with the caveat that all types of child abuse are greatly underreported and underestimated. It is difficult to accurately state the prevalence of the four types of abuse in the United States because of problems with the identification of abuse, the underreporting of abuse, and as mentioned earlier, the lack of an agreed-upon definition of abuse. Some studies provide a glimpse into the prevalence of underreporting. One report found that one state's vital records had underreported child deaths from abuse by almost 60%. In a study of hospital emergency rooms, it was found that child abuse had occurred in 10% of all blunt trauma patients under five years of age.

The underreporting of abuse is related to several factors. It is known that victims of child abuse often do not report the abuse. Children who are five years of age or older may know and care for the abuser, and therefore they find themselves trapped between the need for affection and loyalty and the sense that the

abuse is wrong. In the case of sexual abuse by a family member, loyalty and affection conflicts with the child's sense that the sexual activities initiated by the perpetrator are wrong. If a child tries to tell the truth and break away, he or she may be threatened with a loss of love or even violence. The child may be seen as a liar and a troublemaker and thus alienated by the family. Such responses only intensify the child's sense of self-blame and feelings of worthlessness.

Other literature states that, in addition to the victim's tendency to be silent about the abuse, observable behavioral indicators may not be noticed or reported by mandatory reporters. Mandatory reporters are professionals and institutions that all states require to report suspected abuse. Mandatory reporters include health care providers, mental health care providers, social workers, educators, school personnel, law enforcement professionals, and day care providers. Eighteen states require that any person who suspects child abuse must report it. Many states also require those who develop film to report suspected abuse. The literature indicates that failure to report abuse occurs because mandatory reporting laws are not enforced and because people do not think reporting the abuse will be helpful.

The National Child Abuse and Neglect Reporting System (NCANDS) is a federally funded annual collection of data on child abuse and neglect from state Child Protective Services (CPS) agencies across the country. The NCANDS data include cases in which children were investigated for probable child abuse, and the investigation determined that child abuse did occur. The NCANDS figures for 2000 identified 862,000 victims. Of those, 50.6% were Caucasian, 24.7% African American, 14.2% Latino, 1.6% Native American, and 1.4% Asian American/Pacific Islander. The 1999 figures found that 828,000 children had experienced abuse or neglect. This means that 11.8 out of every 1,000 children suffered from abuse or neglect. The figures showed that 1,100 children died from maltreatment and 2.1% died while they were in foster care. In terms of the prevalence of the different types of abuse, 58.4% of the cases involved neglect, 21.3% physical abuse, and 11.3% sexual abuse. In terms of gender, both males and females reported physical abuse and neglect at the same rate. However, females were more likely to experience sexual abuse than males: 1.6 for every 1,000 females in comparison with 0.4 for every 1,000 males. Younger children, those under the age of three, were most likely to be abused and neglected.

The National Incidence Study of Child Abuse and Neglect (NIS-3) is another national data set on incidences of child abuse. The NIS-3 found that 1,553,800 children in the United States were abused or neglected in 1993. The Children's Defense Fund has found that African American children are three times more likely to die from child abuse. Although the NIS-3 does not report on racial and ethnic differences, other research suggests that there may be racial and ethnic differences in the prevalence of abuse and neglect.

There is disagreement, however, about whether racial and ethnic differences in reporting are related to the prejudices of the reporter. For example, some researchers note that mandated reporters such as mental health professionals may apply Anglo-American standards of appropriate parenting practices when evaluating the behavior of parents from different cultural backgrounds. Moreover, others have argued that the NIS-3 data do not include a range of Caucasian families whose children may have experienced abuse in the data set. With regard to sexual abuse, data outside the NCANDS and NIS-3 data sets indicates that 10% of children who suffer from sexual abuse are preschoolers; 85% to 90% of children know the perpetrator; 35% of sexual abuse incidences involve a family member; and more than 50% of all assaults occur in the child's or the perpetrator's home.

CULTURAL COMPETENCE IN CHILD PROTECTIVE SERVICES

Disproportionality refers to instances in which the number of children from a particular racial or ethnic background who are either under investigation or have been investigated is much greater than their representation in the general population or in comparison with Caucasian children. Much research has examined the concern that children of color are disproportionately represented in the child welfare system, foster care, and CPS investigations and dispositions, and decisions about whether an alleged instance of abuse did indeed occur. Such research has found that African Americans are more likely to be investigated then their Caucasian counterparts when conditions include perpetrator use of alcohol or drugs, serious injury, emotional maltreatment, neglect, or fatalities. Research has also found that African Americans are more likely to be investigated when the report to CPS comes from a mental health or social service agency. In contrast, Caucasians are more likely to be reported when the alleged perpetrator is not a parent and when parents are unemployed.

CULTURALLY COMPETENT CHILD PROTECTION

Questions about how to define abuse, cultural variations in parenting practices, and disproportionality all lead to the concern that child protective services need to be implemented in a culturally competent fashion. Much of the current research has found that the experience of racial and ethnic minority children and the CPS system is characterized by differential access, differential assessment, differential treatment, and differential outcomes. African American children, for example, are less likely to be adopted, less likely to be given expensive treatment options such as placement in group homes, and more likely to stay in foster care for longer periods of time. Research has also found that African American children are less likely to be reunited with their family of origin and wait longer to be placed in foster care than their Caucasian counterparts.

Yet other research has found that a parent's income level is the deciding factor in whether children are placed in foster care. A limitation of child protective research cited in the literature indicates that much of the research on racial and ethnic differences focuses on differences between Caucasian and African American children. As a result, little information exists about the impact of child protective services on Latino American, Asian American, Native American, immigrant, and multiracial groups of children. There is also little information on the effectiveness of cross-racial assessment and intervention when racial and ethnic minority families are seen by Caucasian CPS workers.

The implications of the research findings indicate there is a need for culturally competent child protective services so that the needs and care of all children are adequately met. Authors have discussed how CPS agencies need to incorporate multicultural values to address these disparities. One step toward incorporating multicultural values is to provide training in cross-cultural competence for CPS workers.

One treatment approach that considers cultural context examines the ecology of the whole family. *Family ecology* refers to the family's cultural orientation, the way the family relates to the larger cultural community, and the family's involvement with the larger social community. Through this approach, intervention in potential cases of child maltreatment considers the family in interaction with the multiple systems involved in their lives. The literature also discusses how interventions may need to involve informal interaction to gain the trust and involvement of the family.

This requires that CPS professionals have the ability to understand cultural styles of engagement and relevant ways of interaction. Examples include knowing appropriate gestures when meeting someone in the family, sharing food in a social setting, recognizing different power structures in the family, and being aware of who should be present when significant information is discussed. For example, if the grandmother plays a powerful role in the family, it may be important to have her present when the assessment is conducted and the disposition discussed. Culturally appropriate engagement also includes the CPS worker's ability to know which family member to engage in conversation first when speaking with the family.

This is particularly important because the family may be overwhelmed and stressed in light of the reason (i.e., the allegation of abuse) that the CPS worker is visiting the home. For example, in some cultures, the mother may be the parent who is responsible for issues that concern the child. In other cultures, the father or male head of the household may be the parent who must be spoken with first. Styles of family interaction vary by cultural values. A mainstream U.S. family may view their social relations as individually oriented, and thus family cohesiveness is not as critical in initial discussions. Other families may be more hierarchical in their relationships and, as a result, feel that it is important for members at the top echelons of the hierarchy to be present at such family discussions. Finally, families that are group oriented may place a high value on having as many members of the family present as possible during meetings with the CPS worker.

Religion may be an important factor in the lives of families; therefore, it may be helpful to incorporate religious resources such as traditional healers, priests, ministers, and other religious leaders. This may prevent family members from feeling they have to choose between the services offered by the child welfare system and the spiritual guidance provided by their religion and religious leaders. The use of such stylistic approaches may build trust and rapport between the CPS professional and the family. These stylistic issues include using the native language; using proper terms for religious and medical beliefs; knowing whom to address and what is considered inappropriate to discuss with someone you do not know at initial meetings; using culturally appropriate greetings; understanding the appropriate uses of personal touch; understanding the appropriate uses of eye contact; knowing customs regarding the use of food; understanding where the intervention should take place; exploring traditional healing practices that may be used by the family; and investing the time needed to build trust and rapport before immediately jumping in to discuss treatment issues.

Culturally competent initial intervention and rapport building involves the use of the social ecological model as a framework for culturally competent intervention in child protective cases. The social ecological model takes a systemic perspective, examining how four contexts contribute to child abuse. These contexts include the individual (i.e., intrapsychic factors such as depression, sense of worthlessness), the family (i.e., type of family—single or dual career, support of extended family members), the larger environment (i.e., work, stress, unemployment, racism), and cultural factors (i.e., language, ideas about child rearing, immigration experience).

The idea behind this four-pronged approach is that families and their problems can be seen in their larger social and ecological contexts. The interaction of the family within each of the four contexts can be explored, with an emphasis on how the resulting interaction and its concomitant stresses have an impact on the child. According to this approach, all assessments, interventions, and treatments are provided in the real-life natural setting of these four contexts. Thus, intervention is not provided in a clinic or child protective agency but within the family's home, the child's school, day care, and in other settings. The objective of the social ecological approach is to further the professional's ability to incorporate cultural factors by seeing what the family does to guide the child, what the family values within the cultural context, and how interventions can incorporate the cultural factors that make up the fabric of family life.

Finally, cultural competence includes the recognition of within-group differences across racial and ethnic groups. Recognition of within-group differences means that the individual who is working with the family avoids stereotypes and realizes that there are significant differences within any one racial or ethnic group.

—*Caroline S. Clauss-Ehlers*

See also Child Abuse: Physical; Sexual Abuse

FURTHER READING

Kapitanoff, S. H., & Lutzker, J. R. (2000). Cultural issues in the relation between child disabilities and child abuse. *Aggression and Violent Behavior, 5*(3), 227–244.

Lu, Y. E., Landsverk, J., Ellis-Macleod, E., Newton, R., Ganger, W., & Johnson, I. (2004). Race, ethnicity, and case outcomes in child protective services. *Children and Youth Services Review, 26,* 447–461.

Safe Child Program. (n.d.). Retrieved December 11, 2004, from http://www.safechild.org/index.htm

CHILD ABUSE: PHYSICAL

Each week, state agencies designed to care for the needs of children receive more than 50,000 reports of child abuse and neglect. Of these reports, 19% involve potential physical abuse. Physical abuse is generally defined as any act of commission by an adult that leaves a mark on a child. Although the majority of the cases are not life threatening, all incidents of physical abuse leave lasting emotional and psychological scars on child victims.

CAUSES

Many theories have examined the causes behind acts of physical abuse. Since the 1970s, researchers have worked to develop models of the characteristics of acts physical abuse committed against children. Current perspectives agree that physical abuse is not caused by one or two factors but by a system of interconnected characteristics and events. The majority of causes can be organized into three broad categories: parent–child interactional variables; environmental and life stress variables; and social, cultural, and economic variables.

INTERACTIONAL PERSPECTIVE

Interactional perspectives generally view physical abuse as originating from a dysfunction in the relationship between the child and the perpetrator, most often the parent. The parent perceives the child as hard to manage, and he or she is significantly stressed by the child's behavior. Perpetrators tend to be young parents who lack experience managing child behavior. Without accurate information regarding appropriate developmental milestones, the parent comes to view even typical behavior (e.g., a toddler having a tantrum) as

pathological. The potential perpetrator has unrealistic expectations for the child's behavior, creating a cycle whereby the child is seen as misbehaving when he or she is acting normally. Often, these parents have few social supports or examples of child behavior for comparison, and subsequently they feel easily overwhelmed by the child's conduct. A negative bias toward the child is often present in the mind-set of parents who physically abuse children; therefore, they tend to interpret most of the child's behavior as disruptive or noncompliant. Indeed, perpetrators tend to have a high demand for compliance from their child, and this creates more opportunities for the child to get into trouble.

About one-third of parents who physically abuse children have a history of being victims of abuse in their own childhood, making it harder for them to know the characteristics of positive parenting firsthand. As a result, these parents often lack the requisite empathy necessary for positive parent–child relationships. Without empathy for the child's experience, the parent tends to interpret any act of misbehavior as a direct challenge to his or her authority. Perpetrators tend to have a limited repertoire of disciplinary skills and use aggressive methods to manage their child's behavior. Unfortunately, without alternatives to aggression, these parents find that they have to use harsher techniques each time the child disobeys because the child becomes habituated to the aggression of the parent. Perpetrators often respond to the child's behavior with an aggressive style and fail to adjust their response to the severity of the child's disobedience.

Parents who physically abuse children tend to exhibit low levels of positive or warm responses to their child's conduct, even when the child is compliant. Intrusiveness tends to be a hallmark of their interactions; little of what the child does escapes the parent's attention. Finally, parents who are at risk of physically abusing their children tend to use ambiguous commands when directing their child instead of specific commands that clearly let the child know what behavior is expected. Without a clear understanding of what the parent wants from the child, the child is at greater risk of failing to comply with the parent's demands.

Some characteristics of children place them at greater risk for physical abuse. For example, children who are born prematurely often place greater demands on parents than do full-term infants, increasing stress in the parent–child relationship and manifesting a greater likelihood of parental exhaustion. Children with disabilities or other mental and physical limitations are also at greater risk than their typically developing peers because of the greater care and support these children require. For example, children who are diagnosed with attention-deficit/hyperactivity disorder or oppositional defiant disorder tend to display behavior that is hard to manage, creating more interactional difficulties for overstressed parents.

ENVIRONMENTAL/LIFE STRESS PERSPECTIVE

Theories proposing the environmental or life stress approach tend to focus on the myriad of major life events present among families in which physical abuse is prevalent. For example, children who are physically abused are more likely to live in poverty than non–physically abused children. Although being poor does not cause parents to physically abuse their children, the experience of poverty tends to manifest significant emotional distress, and children may be an outlet for this distress. When parents have to move frequently and experience insufficient or inconsistent support systems in their neighborhood, they tend to feel more pressured by everyday life. Parents who are unemployed and who experience domestic violence and stressful family relationships are also at risk for physical abuse.

SOCIAL/CULTURAL/ ECONOMIC PERSPECTIVE

Social, cultural, and economic theories tend to indicate that different child-rearing patterns are found among people of color. Different cultures tend to have different definitions of what behavior is considered abuse and what behavior is considered appropriate discipline. For example, the cupping or coin-rubbing techniques practiced by some members of traditional Asian cultures may be misdiagnosed as physical abuse rather than a cultural method of alleviating a child's problems. Some cultures use techniques such as shame, folk medicine, and corporal punishment to manage the behavioral and emotional challenges of their children, whereas others do not and advocate using reasoning and logic to react to a child's behavioral concerns.

Viewed in comparison to each other, traditional cultural approaches (i.e., using an egg to remove negative energy to alleviate child misconduct) may be perceived as abusive by those who advocate a more reasoned approach to child rearing. This is especially problematic when those who are in a position to enforce child abuse laws ignore the significance of culture when making physical abuse reports. The child protection system has recently made strides to educate its staff about the importance of culture and the role that value systems play in the way parents of color manage their child's behavior and how they respond to state interference in child-management issues. State officials may run the risk of being perceived as racist by parents of color when they apply one general standard to all parenting practices. Furthermore, over the past decade, more cases of cultural disagreement have come to the forefront in the legal community as more parents are prosecuted for parenting practices that follow cultural mores (i.e., prayer instead of medical treatment) but may legally constitute physical abuse.

RISK FACTORS

Risk factors for physical abuse tend to vary among child, parent, and family system characteristics. As the number of factors present in a child's life increases, the child is at greater risk of being physically abused.

Child Risk Factors

Child risk factors begin with the child's age. So far, research has indicated that the younger the child, the greater the risk of physical abuse. Very young children (especially premature infants) are more demanding than older children and need their parents' attention the majority of the time. As a result, there is greater contact between child and parent and greater opportunity for problems to occur in managing the child's behavior and needs. Younger children also require less force for a caretaker to inflict serious harm. Hitting an infant or very young child is more likely to do greater physical damage to the child than hitting an older child. Although hurting an infant may seem inconceivable, according to statistics from the Children's Bureau for 2003, 28% of all cases of child physical abuse involved children under the age of three. Moreover, children who were under the age of seven years old represented more than half of all cases of child physical abuse. Finally, very young children are less able to get away from a violent parent; infants, in particular, have little to no recourse when a parent is responding abusively to their behavior.

Other child risk factors include the attachment the child and parent develop. Children who have not bonded successfully with their parents are at greater risk of becoming victims of physical abuse than children who demonstrate a secure attachment. If the parent perceives the child's temperament to be very different from his or her own—specifically, if he or she perceives that the child has a difficult temperament—the child may be at risk for physical abuse. Children who have physical or mental disabilities are also at risk for physical abuse because of their increased demands on a parent's time and energy. As children grow older, the presence of learning problems may place them at risk for abuse by parents who are unaware of the child's inability to understand interactions such as cause and effect. It is important to note that in any case of child physical abuse, even when child risk factors are present, the child is never responsible for the abuse. That is, physical abuse is never the child's fault because of the natural power differential between child and caretaker.

Parental Risk Factors

Parents who physically abuse their children tend to have few appropriate coping methods for everyday stressors. Problem-solving skills are especially limited in physically abusing parents, who tend to be rather rigid thinkers and easily overwhelmed. Feeling negatively toward their children may contribute to their ineffectiveness as parents, causing them to feel distressed with each new child-management concern. Although some research supports the notion that parents who are physically abusive are also mentally ill, the overall findings are mixed. For example, some studies have demonstrated that parents who physically abuse their children also tend to report experiencing clinical depression. Moreover, perpetrators are overrepresented in samples of adults engaged in substance abuse. Although depression and substance abuse may place a parent at risk of physically abusing his or her child, in the majority of cases, the perpetrator does not have a history of diagnosable mental problems.

Family-System Risk Factors

Families in which physical abuse is common are often isolated and have negative relationships with extended family members. Relationships within families tend to be strained and conflictual, and they are rarely seen as significant in the raising of the child. Links to support in the greater community also tend to be limited. Perpetrators report that they have few people whom they can turn to in times of distress and usually have few to no close confidants for support or information. It is common to find that poverty, illness, and significant life stressors affect family members who might otherwise be sources for support. It is not possible to predict which families will become physically abusive and which ones will not because the causes and risk factors are often interconnected and complex.

PHYSICAL SYMPTOMS

Children who are exposed to physical abuse can and do display a myriad of physical and psychological symptoms. The most common sign of physical abuse is bruises, especially when the child is not old enough to move around freely. Moreover, bruises on certain parts of the body and in certain shapes are more suspicious than others. For example, bruises on the backs of the legs and upper arms, especially those in the shape of a hand, hanger, or belt buckle, are often considered to be manifestations of abuse. The head and neck area are the most common targets for injury because these portions of the body are often closest in proximity to the perpetrator's hand. The result is often skull fractures or hematoma (i.e., pooling of blood in the brain) and cognitive delays. In addition to bruises, children exposed to physical abuse often suffer from brain injury resulting from shaking, bone fractures, and burns.

PSYCHOLOGICAL INDICATORS

Emotional and behavioral manifestations are often the most challenging and long-lasting consequences of physical abuse. The physical injuries are often easier to see and repair than the psychological damage done by physical abuse. Although there is no known, specific emotional and behavioral profile of children who are victims of physical abuse, several behavioral changes are generally consistent with physical abuse. For example, victims of physical abuse generally cry very little but become very upset when being examined by a physician. They tend to be avoidant or apprehensive around other children who are distressed. Because of the lack of empathy from their parents, these children tend to show no expectation of being comforted when they are upset and are generally slow to show empathy to others. Some research supports the notion that children who are victims of abuse develop a rather shrill cry that is not differentiated by their particular need (i.e., hunger versus cold). Victims tend to be slower than their nonabused peers in motor and social skill development and are often described by others as passive. They seem to show little interest in age-appropriate activities, unlike their nonabused peers, and show little reaction to loss.

Moreover, victims of physical abuse may display enuresis (i.e., inability to control the bladder) and temper tantrums beyond the preschool years. Not surprisingly, children who are exposed to physical abuse tend to display low self-esteem both at home and in the school environment. It is perhaps this lack of self-confidence that is also responsible for the withdrawn behavior often demonstrated by victims of physical abuse. Generally, victims use withdrawal as a defense to avoid further punishment, but they are also equally likely to display aggressive behavior. Mirroring the aggressive modeling of their parents, victims of abuse often become very angry about not having control over events in their lives and may take that anger out on others (i.e., pets, peers, other adults).

The capacity to form positive peer relations is often a challenge for victims of physical abuse because they have not experienced the appropriate give-and-take of healthy relationships. Moreover, victims are often as isolated from their peers as their parents, and they are often prohibited from engaging with others in activities. As a result, they may have fewer opportunities to learn and practice good social skills than their nonabused peers. Victims of physical abuse are also described in the literature as hypervigilant (i.e., overly watchful of their environment) and compulsive regarding their surroundings. They may develop a strong need to please others and avoid failure.

The characteristics of perpetrators and victims are complex and interrelated. Understanding the relations is more complicated when culture is considered. That is, research often reports that children of color are more likely to be victims of physical abuse than their Caucasian peers and that cultural differences among ethnic groups may influence how physical abuse is reported and understood. The measurement of abuse rates, however, may be hampered by cultural and socioeconomic differences among groups of color that are left unmeasured when only ethnicity is considered.

CULTURAL IMPLICATIONS

Recent research indicates ethnic differences in the prevalence and severity of child physical abuse. It may be, however, that bias exists in the way abuse is reported and defined by mandated reporters and other mental health personnel. Given the focus on Western values in most of modern psychology, reporters may apply an Anglo-American standard of quality parenting to parents of color and label benign behaviors as abusive. To better understand the influence of culture in parenting behaviors, the culture variable must be included in large-scale epidemiological research. Most of the available data, however, do not include a sampling of family, friends, and neighbors of Caucasian children, who are more likely to report abuse of Caucasian children. Other research shows that definitions of abuse differ depending on other variables such as socioeconomic status; people of color are often overrepresented in lower economic groups.

Given the complexities of child physical abuse, contextual factors that may promote or hinder a parent's likelihood of abusing his or her children must be considered. For example, cross-cultural research has demonstrated that child abuse is less likely in cultures in which children are valued for their economic contribution, role in perpetuating family heritage, or role as a source of parental emotional enjoyment. When ethnic or cultural differences are acknowledged in research, these efforts generally have only included samples of parents from different ethnic groups, with no actual measurement of cultural practices. Much to the contrary of the majority of research, studies on physical abuse generally assume that within-group differences are not present or influential in child outcomes.

For example, studies show that Samoan children are overrepresented and Japanese American children are underrepresented in prevalence research on physical abuse because of the Samoan cultural value placed on aggressiveness and physical punishment and the Japanese value on the power of shame as a parenting technique. Those studies that do address culture and cultural practices tend to show that values and beliefs are important in explaining the ethnic group differences in rates of child physical abuse. One study found that Hispanic American parents who strongly identify with the cultural value of *familismo* (i.e., the importance of the extended family system) are less likely to be abusive than those who place less importance on this value. Although familismo may be a more consistent value of traditional Hispanic American cultures, the construct was just as predictive of abuse among Caucasian parents as it was among Hispanic American parents.

Another study by Anne Ferrari found that levels of cultural practices such as familism, valuing children, and machismo are significant predicators of fathers' parenting behavior. Specifically, regardless of ethnic group, fathers who hold a low regard for familism are also more likely to use physical punishment with their children than fathers who value familism more highly. Strong machismo in fathers also predicts the use of physical punishment. Finally, fathers who value their children more also use more verbal punishment. The author suggested that children of color who receive verbal and physical punishment also tend to receive significant levels of positive nurturance. Although the study measured only a few cultural practices, it appears that when cultural practices are identified, they may help explain some of the within- and between-group differences among people of color and among physical discipline practices. The study showed that African American parents specifically use more physical discipline with their children than Caucasian or Hispanic American parents. Physical discipline is not he same thing as physical abuse, but the results do suggest that perhaps cultural differences play a role in how parents interact with their children. Because perpetrators of physical abuse tend to use harsh physical discipline, the results may provide some insight into how culture operates in the parent–child interaction.

Other studies suggest that children of color tend to display less behavioral and emotional maladjustment after harsh physical discipline than Caucasian children. When harsh physical discipline is present, it seems that Caucasian children are more likely to display aggression and other acting-out problems than children of color. It may be that when factors besides physical discipline are measured, factors such as warmth and positive regard are also prevalent. When physical disciple and warmth are both present, the negative consequences of physical discipline are not as severe for children, regardless of ethnicity or culture. The results of the research demonstrate that parents of color who use physical discipline only or harsh physical discipline only may be at greater risk for physical abuse, but not when this physical discipline is paired with positive support and warm parenting.

Finding cultural differences that can predict physically abusive parents is important, but the results need to be interpreted with caution. Like the construct of ethnicity, when it is applied broadly, the research on cultural differences can be used to aid the development of cultural competence when working with families of color, or it can be misused to further discriminate and prejudge the competence of families of color. Therefore, it is critical that both researchers and clinicians appreciate the tremendous within-group differences among people of color and be mindful of the wealth of individual differences.

—*Yo Jackson*

See also Child Abuse: Overview; Sexual Abuse

FURTHER READING

Caetano, R., Field, C. A., & Scott, N. (2003). Association between childhood physical abuse, exposure to parental violence, and alcohol problems in adulthood. *Journal of Interpersonal Violence, 18,* 240–257.

Collier, A., McClure, F. H., Collier, J., Otto, C., & Polloi, A. (1999). Culture-specific views of child maltreatment and parenting styles in a Pacific-Island community. *Child Abuse and Neglect, 23,* 229–244.

Crosson-Tower, C. (2005). *Understanding child abuse and neglect.* Boston: Pearson.

DeBruyn, L., Chino, M., Serna, P., & Fullerton-Gleason, L. (2001). Child maltreatment in American Indian and Alaska Native communities: Integrating culture, history, and public health for intervention and prevention. *Child Maltreatment, 6,* 89–102.

Egu, C. L., & Weiss, D. J. (2003). The role of race and severity of abuse in teacher's recognition or reporting of child abuse. *Journal of Child and Family Studies, 12,* 465–474.

Ferrari, A. M. (2002). The impact of culture upon child rearing practices and definitions of maltreatment. *Child Abuse and Neglect, 26,* 793–813.

Fontes, L. A. (2005). *Child abuse and culture: Working with diverse families.* New York: Guilford Press.

Korbin, J. E. (2002). Culture and child maltreatment: Cultural competence and beyond. *Child Abuse and Neglect, 26,* 637–644.

Logio, K. A. (2003). Gender, race, childhood abuse, and body image among adolescents. *Violence Against Women, 9,* 931–954.

Markward, M., Dozier, H., Hooks, K., & Markward, N. (2000). Culture and the intergenerational transmission of substance abuse, women abuse, and child abuse: A diathesis-stress perspective. *Children and Youth Services Review, 22,* 237–250.

Palusci, V. J., Smith, E. G., & Paneth, N. (2005). Predicting and responding to physical abuse in young children using NCANDS. *Child and Youth Services Review, 27,* 667–682.

Perez, D. M. (2000). The relationship between physical abuse, sexual victimization and adolescent illicit drug use. *Journal of Drug Issues, 30,* 641–661.

Terao, S. Y., Borrego, J., & Urquiza, A. J. (2001). A reporting and response model for culture and child maltreatment. *Child Maltreatment, 6,* 158–168.

Thompson, M. P., Kingree, J. B., & Desai, S. (2004). Gender differences in long-term health consequences of physical abuse of children: Data from a nationally representative survey. *American Journal of Public Health, 94,* 599–604.

Thompson, R., Briggs, E., English, D. J., Dubowitz, H., Lee, L., Brody, K., Everson, M. D., & Hunter, W. M. (2005).

Suicidal ideation among 8-year-olds who are maltreated and at-risk: Findings from the LONSCAN studies. *Child Maltreatment, 10,* 26–36.

CHILD ABUSE: SEXUAL

See Sexual Abuse

CHINESE AMERICANS

Chinese Americans are the largest group of Asian Americans. In the 2000 U.S. Census, 2.43 million people identified themselves as Chinese, and another 0.44 million identified themselves as Chinese in combination with another race or races. These numbers account for approximately 24% of the 10.24 million people who identified themselves as Asian alone and approximately 27% of the additional 1.66 million who reported themselves as Asian in combination with another race or races.

MIGRATION HISTORY

The Chinese were the first Asians to come to the United States in large numbers. During the 1800s, many of them came to work as laborers on the transcontinental railroad, in the gold mines of California, or on the plantations of Hawaii. However, when demand for labor decreased in the mainland United States, anti-Chinese sentiment developed and discriminatory state and federal legislation was enacted. Antimiscegenation laws were enacted in 14 states, prohibiting intermarriage between European Americans and Chinese or Mongolians, and the Chinese Exclusion Act was passed by Congress in 1882, restricting Chinese immigration and barring them from U.S. citizenship. Restrictions on Chinese immigration eased after World War II, and eventually the Immigration and Naturalization Act of 1965 (enacted in 1968) gave the Chinese equal status among immigrants from other nations. These policy changes led to a growth in the Chinese American population. In 1950, there were only 0.15 million Chinese Americans. By 1970, their number had tripled to 0.44 million and almost quadrupled to 1.65 million by 1990. Parallel with this growth was the development of a Chinese American middle class consisting of immigrants from white-collar and college-educated backgrounds and U.S.-born Chinese Americans who moved up the socioeconomic ladder.

PLACES OF ORIGIN

The majority of Chinese Americans came from mainland China, Taiwan (an island to which the Nationalist government retreated when the Communists took over the mainland in 1949), and Hong Kong (a former British colony that returned to Chinese sovereignty in 1997 as a special administrative region with a high degree of autonomy). Chinese Americans also came from other places, such as Macau (a former Portuguese colony that returned to Chinese sovereignty in 1999 as a special administrative region with a high degree of autonomy) and especially Southeast Asia. Among the Southeast Asian refugees who came to the United States in the aftermath of the Vietnam War were many ethnic Chinese, in particular, Vietnamese Chinese who were forced to flee by the new government there.

In recent years, some immigrants from Taiwan have begun to identify themselves as Taiwanese Americans. There are no definite rules for using this term, which has political and social roots and implications. It is used by people born in Taiwan or by people whose families were living in Taiwan before the Nationalist government moved there, as well as by people who have lived there for many generations. Yet others with the same family backgrounds may choose to call themselves Chinese Americans. In the 2000 U.S. Census, approximately 0.12 million people identified themselves as Taiwanese alone compared with approximately 2.31 million people who identified themselves as "Chinese not including Taiwanese."

CULTURAL ORIENTATION

The foundation of traditional Chinese culture is based on Confucianism, Taoism, and Buddhism, which are philosophies as well as religions. Their worldviews are deeply ingrained in Chinese culture and reflected in its norms and values, which include an emphasis on interpersonal harmony, moderation, compromise, mutual respect, modesty, nonassertiveness, nonaggression, respect for life and for nature, and acceptance of one's fate. Simply by following traditional Chinese culture, one would inadvertently be following the prescriptions of these philosophies or religions without consciously or overtly affiliating with them.

In terms of religious beliefs, besides the traditional religions, there are also folk religions or sects with local deities and worship rituals. Islam is practiced in certain minority regions in northwest China bordering central Asia. Christianity, both Protestant and Catholic, is observed by some, and it is particularly active in Hong Kong, where Christians operate many schools and other services. In Chinese American communities, Buddhism and Christianity are common religions. There are also many people, particularly those from mainland China, who do not subscribe to any religion.

CULTURAL VARIATIONS AND SUBCULTURES

China is a vast country with subcultural variations among its different regions, such as north and south, rural and urban. China has an area of about 3.70 million square miles and a population of about 1.28 billion (2002 estimate). In comparison, the United States has about the same area (3.68 million square miles, including the Great Lakes) but only about one-fourth the population (290 million, 2002 estimate). In addition to regional subcultural variations, the Chinese in metropolitan areas may be more influenced by Western cultures than those in rural or more insulated regions. These influences may be reflected in daily life, such as food, fashion, and entertainment, as well as in values and norms (e.g., more individualistic or less family or community oriented than traditional Chinese culture).

For Chinese in the United States, their orientation toward Chinese or Western culture may be influenced by many factors, such as upbringing, education, family environment, community environment, work environment, social network, reason for migration, age at migration, length of residence, and number of generations in the United States. Some people may be bicultural instead of identifying exclusively with one culture. Moreover, cultural identification is a process that may change over time with a person's life experiences and social environment. Thus, mental health clinicians must assess the cultural orientation of each Chinese American client rather than assuming that all Chinese Americans have the same cultural identification.

DIALECTS AND WRITTEN LANGUAGE

One of the most noticeable regional differences among the Chinese is the dozens of dialects spoken in different areas of China. Some dialects are phonetically similar, but others are practically incomprehensible to those who speak other dialects. Both mainland China and Taiwan use Mandarin (called *Putonghua* in mainland China and *Guo Yu* in Taiwan) as the official language or dialect,

and it is used in governmental affairs and in schools as the medium of instruction. However, the use of local dialects is widespread, and many people speak both Mandarin and their regional dialect. In Chinese American communities, the most common dialects are Cantonese, spoken by immigrants from Hong Kong, Macau, and Guangdong (Canton) Province; Toisanese, spoken by descendants of early immigrants, a large number of whom came from the Toisan area, and long-time residents of the Chinatowns; and Mandarin, spoken by more recent immigrants from mainland China and Taiwan. Recently, Taiwanese, Fujianese, and Sawtowese have become more common as the number immigrants speaking these dialects has increased. The different dialects are an obstacle to providing mental health services because it is often difficult to staff an agency with clinicians who are proficient in multiple dialects.

Unlike the spoken language, written Chinese is essentially unified. However, in recent decades, mainland China has adopted a simplified form of written Chinese, whereas Taiwan, Hong Kong, and Chinese communities in the United States continue to use the traditional form. Both forms follow the same grammatical rules. Traditional written Chinese is used by most Chinese newspapers published in the United States. It is also commonly used in Chinese American communities, evidenced in aspects of daily life such as signs for stores and restaurant menus.

MIGRATION ISSUES

According to the 2000 U.S. Census, about 1.52 million people reported China as their place of birth. This figure includes 0.99 million from mainland China, 0.20 million from Hong Kong, and 0.33 million from Taiwan. Based on these numbers, about 63% of the Chinese American population is foreign born. The percentage is higher if Chinese Americans born in other places (e.g., Southeast Asia) are included. It is even higher still when we consider immigrant families in which at least one parent is foreign born and the children are either foreign born or locally born.

Unlike the Chinese immigrants of the 19th century, who were mostly laborers, today's Chinese immigrants are generally more educated and financially secure. However, some do come from disadvantaged socioeconomic backgrounds. Overall, the Chinese immigrant population includes wealthy entrepreneurs and business owners who qualified for immigration visas by investing in the United States. Many Chinese immigrants have a college education or professional training. Some immigrants in this group obtained their degrees or training before coming to the United States. Many others came as students and applied for immigration when they obtained academic degrees or professional training that met immigration criteria. Other immigrants came through family reunification quotas to join their immediate family members living here or through marriage to U.S. citizens or permanent residents. The socioeconomic status of these immigrants varies according to their individual situations.

There are some immigrants who came from very destitute conditions, such as ethnic Chinese refugees from Southeast Asia. Some may even be undocumented immigrants who work in low-paying positions or exploitative situations. However, regardless of the differences in their backgrounds, Chinese immigrants often come to the United States seeking similar goals for themselves and for their children: social and political stability, freedom, and economic and educational opportunities.

Immigrants from higher socioeconomic backgrounds may have little or no immediate financial or material worries. However, foreign-trained professionals are often underemployed because of licensing obstacles, lack of English proficiency, lack of American sociocultural resources, or racism. Immigrants who are educated in the United States usually have greater upward mobility. Still, some of them face racial barriers in the form of glass ceilings. Overall, Chinese immigrants fill the entire spectrum of socioeconomic attainment. In general, immigrants who are more socioeconomically limited tend to settle in or near the traditional Chinatowns, whereas professional, white-collar, or middle-class groups tend to live in other urban areas and suburbs. Mental health providers must be cognizant of the socioeconomic makeup of the particular community they serve.

For most immigrants, psychoemotional adjustment to life in the United States is a major challenge. Many of them have to develop a new social support network of friends and confidants for emotional support, advice, or assistance with life problems. Even those who immigrated with their nuclear families may feel isolated because they no longer have members of the extended family to help with child care or to consult on family and personal matters. Adjustment also involves activities of daily life such as shopping, food, and entertainment. Overall, in spite of the migration stress, most immigrants succeed in adapting to life in the United States. Many Chinese immigrants choose to settle in areas where there are ethnic shops, restaurants, mass media, and other amenities that provide a semblance of their premigration lifestyle. In addition, community organizations, churches, and temples may play an important role in social networking and as sources of support. California and New York have the largest numbers of Chinese Americans, with concentrations in the Greater Los Angeles area, the San Francisco area, and the Greater New York Metropolitan area.

Because a large number of Chinese Americans are immigrants or from immigrant families, clinicians need to understand the impact of migration on their psychosocial well-being. The migration experience has effects on immigrants themselves, as well as on their offspring who are born and raised in the United States. The impact of migration can be particularly salient at transition points in one's life cycle stages. Adaptation to the cultural and social environment of the United States may be a lifelong process, and it is typically a transgenerational process for families.

CULTURAL GAPS WITHIN THE FAMILY

Members of Chinese American families—especially immigrant families in which one or both parents are immigrants and the children were born in the United States or came at a young age—often face a cultural gap on top of the generation gap. Parents who came to the United States as adults usually have more exposure and affinity to Chinese culture, whereas their children, who attend school here, are more socialized into mainstream American culture. This creates a gap between parents and children in their cultural identification, reflecting differences in values, behaviors, and expectations. For example, parents attuned to traditional Chinese culture tend to hold a hierarchical orientation, whereas their children may expect a more egalitarian relationship. Collectivism and familism versus individualism, as well as other differences in norms and values between the two cultures, are common sources of tension. In addition, parents from lower socioeconomic backgrounds often lack English proficiency, and they may eventually become dependent on their children to translate and take care of interactions with mainstream society. This situation threatens the family hierarchy and is particularly troublesome if the children are not on good terms with the parents.

On another level, children who were born in the United States or who came at a young age may have little or no affinity with their places of origin. They may find it hard to relate to or understand their parents' reminiscences about ethnic amenities in these places. Some may not appreciate the difficulties their parents have undergone or the sacrifices and risks their parents took in migrating to the United States. For example, U.S.-born children of Southeast Asian Chinese refugees may have no understanding of the trauma their parents experienced. Such differences in life experiences are barriers in the family relationship.

In the Chinese American community, *juk sing* is a slang term for American-born Chinese. Literally, it means a "bamboo pole closed at both ends"; figuratively, it describes how these children are between Chinese and mainstream United States cultures but not really connected with either side. Some of these children, especially teenagers, may actually feel marginalized or alienated from both cultures, feeling torn between both worlds but not belonging to either one. Because of the influence of schools and the mass media, many prefer mainstream culture to Chinese culture. However, over time, they may also realize that they are not accepted as fully mainstream by others. When they want to assert their Chinese heritage, they may recognize that they are not knowledgeable enough about Chinese culture. This struggle of cultural identification is a challenging experience for many young people in their developmental process.

SPLIT HOUSEHOLDS

Since the 1980s, two types of split households have emerged in the Chinese American community. In the first type, the father is the financial provider who, after escorting his family to the United States and settling down quickly, returns to his original job in the homeland while his wife stays on to care for the household and children. Usually these men have high-income positions or their own businesses in their places of origin and cannot find positions with equivalent income or status here. They are nicknamed "astronauts," "spacemen," or sometimes "acrobats" in the Chinese community because they fly frequently between their families in the United States and their work in their homeland. This situation is particularly common among immigrants from Hong Kong.

In the second type of split household, children, typically teenagers, are sent to attend grade school in the United States unaccompanied by their parents. They may be living in dormitories of private schools or in hostel-like arrangements in private homes. Some may live alone or with siblings in homes rented or bought by their parents or with relatives or family friends who act as legal guardians. These children are called *parachute kids* in the mass media because they are "dropped off from the plane" like paratroopers. Most are from Taiwan, though some are from Hong Kong and other places. They usually come from affluent families who can afford to send them abroad. Many of these children are concentrated in Southern California, but they are also found in other states, such as New York and Texas.

Although the family separation in both types of split households is voluntary and the families are often affluent, it is a stressful experience that affects the normative development of the family and its members, especially children. For the parachute kids, loneliness, depression, and risk of delinquency from lack of adult supervision are common problems. Though many of them are able to maintain good grades and go on to attend college, others require intervention. Youth activities and after-school programs offered by churches and other agencies in the community are useful resources for them. In working with members of both types of households, clinicians must empathize with their reasons for being in the United States rather than simplistically advise them to reunite with their family members by moving back to their premigration homes.

BILINGUAL SERVICES

According to the 2000 U.S. Census, about two million people speak Chinese at home. This translates into about 82% of the Chinese American population. Thus, bilingual mental health services are often required in the community. Even for Chinese Americans who are bilingual, there may be an issue of code-switching—that is, they may be proficient in English in a professional subject but still find it easier to express intimate feelings or thoughts in Chinese, their home language. Usually, clinicians can work with the locally born generations in English. With the exception of new immigrants, children and teenagers educated in the United States may prefer to receive services in English. In fact, some may consider it insulting if they are referred for services in Chinese because they feel they are being treated as nonmainstream or that their English proficiency is being questioned. However, even when children speak English in therapy, their parents may feel more comfortable speaking Chinese.

Thus, clinicians need to be sensitive to language preferences when working with different individuals or families.

COMMUNICATION STYLE AND SOCIAL ETIQUETTE

In traditional Chinese culture, subtlety is preferred over direct confrontation in social interactions. Clinicians should be careful about speaking in a confrontational manner, which may be seen as rude. Moreover, in general, clients oriented toward Chinese culture are more reserved in expressing their emotions than those who are acculturated into mainstream U.S. culture. Clinicians must be attuned to the polite or indirect ways in which these clients express themselves. For example, a client may not voice any disagreement with the clinician or may accept another appointment but have no intention of keeping it. Open disagreement or refusing an appointment would be socially awkward in the Chinese cultural context.

The Chinese saying, "Family shame should not be spread to the outside," reflects the cultural prohibition on disclosing family problems to outsiders. These sensitive topics may include intimate details of family problems, sexual behavior, family secrets, or sometimes even immigration details (for those with negative experiences or irregularities in their immigration or refugee process). Before discussing these topics, clinicians should prepare their clients by tactfully explaining the rationale for these inquiries and acknowledging the clients' privacy concerns.

In formal situations, children and others in subordinate positions may refrain from eye contact with their superiors as a sign of respect. This may also occur in the therapy setting. Chinese culture generally does not favor physical contact between individuals in social settings, especially between genders. Although even new immigrants may be familiar with the custom of handshakes, hugging or embracing can be problematic. Clinicians should keep this in mind when selecting activities for group sessions or family sessions.

ENGAGING CLIENTS IN THERAPY

Keeping in mind the differences in cultural identification among Chinese Americans, the adaptation of mainstream therapeutic techniques is necessary to make mental health services more amenable to clients who identify with Chinese culture. Many Chinese immigrants are unfamiliar with mental health services. In their homeland, these services are often equated with psychotropic medications for people with severe psychiatric disorders. They may know that guidance is available for children with school-related problems, but they are generally unfamiliar with the concept of psychotherapy or the "talking cure." When they seek mental health services, they often expect quick and direct relief, either in the form of medication, some concrete help (such as advice and instructions), or some type of social service. Thus, clinicians should be ready to assume the multiple roles of healer, doctor, expert, teacher, consultant, advocate, and resource person.

It is important to specify treatment goals that match the presenting problems that are perceived by the client or decision makers in the family. These often involve quick symptom relief or some direct advice, intervention, or advocacy by the clinician. Regardless of one's theoretical orientation, clinicians must be seen as actively addressing the presenting problems rather than waiting for the client to take the lead or probing too much into past events and family history without clearly relating them to the current problem or symptoms. After engaging the client in this manner, the clinician can gradually ease into modes of psychotherapy that are more appropriate to the client's actual problems, explaining and educating the client about the process along the way.

USE OF ALTERNATIVE HEALING PRACTICES

At times, clients who are more attuned to Chinese lifestyles may resort to traditional healing practices to alleviate their problems. These may involve spiritual or folk practices such as feng shui (geomancy) and fortune-telling; traditional Chinese medicine practices such as herbs, acupuncture, and other methods; or traditional health exercises such as *Tai Ji* (tai chi) or *Qi Qong* (qigong). Sometimes, the practices may simply involve eating certain types of food or soups in daily meals to restore the "balance of the forces" within the body. If a clinician overtly disapproves of these practices, he or she may be seen as culturally insensitive or ignorant and may lose the client's confidence. Instead, one can discuss these alternatives with the client and accommodate their use as adjuncts to therapy if there is no contraindication. If a clinician is unsure, consultation should be made with others who are knowledgeable about these practices.

SOMATIZATION

Chinese American clients who are oriented toward Chinese culture often have the tendency to somatize. Instead of complaining about depression or anxiety, they may report bodily symptoms such as insomnia, poor appetite, headaches, diffuse aches all over the body, or general feelings of weakness. Such somatization may be a product of Chinese medicine's conceptualization of the close interrelationship between the mind and the body. It may also be related to the sociocultural perception that physical aliments are less stigmatizing than psychoemotional problems. Furthermore, this mixture of somatic and emotional symptoms may reflect a culture-bound syndrome identified as *shenjing shuairuo* (neurasthenia) in the *Diagnostic and Statistical Manual of Mental Disorders,* 4th edition. Regardless of the reasons for somatization, in diagnostic interviews with Chinese American clients, clinicians need to look beyond the somatic symptoms and assess the emotional issues. Similarly, when providing therapy to Chinese American clients, especially those with depression or anxiety, clinicians must be attuned to their somatic complaints, if any, and visibly address these symptoms in the treatment plan.

TREATMENT APPROACHES

The literature indicates that all major psychotherapeutic approaches—psychodynamic, humanistic, and cognitive behavioral—can be used successfully with Chinese American and other Asian American clients. However, when using approaches that focus on early life experiences or family histories, clinicians need to familiarize themselves with the sociopolitical events that have occurred in their clients' places of origin. These may include unrest and civil war in pre–World War II China; the impact of World War II in Asia; conditions of life under the Communist government in mainland China and the Nationalist government in Taiwan; life under colonialism in Hong Kong and Macau and the psychosocial implications of their return to Chinese sovereignty; and other major sociopolitical events in these places, as well as in Southeast Asia.

These historical and sociopolitical events may have had a major impact on an individual's or a family's psychoemotional development and may have been the driving force behind their migration to the United States. In particular, clinicians must avoid the misinterpretation of events that took place in cultural and social environmental contexts that are different from those of the United States. For clinicians using other psychotherapeutic approaches, they also need to know about these sociopolitical events to empathize with the client. It is easier to develop therapeutic rapport if clients realize that the clinician knows about conditions in their homeland that had a major impact on their upbringing, education, career, or other important areas of their lives.

SERVICE-DELIVERY APPROACHES

Because many clients with Chinese cultural orientations are reluctant to seek mental health services, outreach efforts, networking agencies, and the establishment of socioculturally appropriate clinics are crucial in providing mental health services in Chinese American communities. Streamlining the intake and treatment process and minimizing the number of providers working with an individual or a family can help clients to overcome their inhibition about disclosing intimate matters to outsiders. Close liaison among agencies is essential to ensure that clients follow through with the referral.

One effective service-delivery model is for a clinic to work with schools in the community or even to send clinicians to provide services in the school setting to ensure a seamless referral process. Other models include the multiservice approach, in which a community center concurrently provides mental health, social, medical, and other related services, or at least a system in which these services are closely linked through close collaboration of service agencies. Considering the large percentage of immigrants and immigrant families in the Chinese American population, outreach, prevention, and early intervention services in schools and community agencies (e.g., addressing sociocultural issues faced by both children and adults) are very useful techniques for promoting healthy adjustment to life in the United States.

—*George K. Hong*

See also Asian/Pacific Islanders; Indigenous treatments: Coining; Indigenous treatments: Cupping

FURTHER READING

Chin, J. L., Liem, J. H., Ham, M. D., & Hong, G. K. (1993). *Transference and empathy in Asian American psychotherapy: Cultural values and treatment needs.* Westport, CT: Praeger.

Hong, G. K., & Ham, M. D. (2001). *Psychotherapy and counseling with Asian American clients: A practical guide.* Thousand Oaks, CA: Sage.

Hong, L. K. (2001a). China. In J. Ciment (Ed.), *Encyclopedia of American immigration* (Vol. 3, pp. 1157–1167). Armonk, NY: M. E. Sharpe.

Hong, L. K. (2001b). Hong Kong and Taiwan. In J. Ciment (Ed.), *Encyclopedia of American immigration* (Vol. 4, pp. 1229–1132). Armonk, NY: M. E. Sharpe.

Jung, M. (1998). *Chinese American family therapy: A new model for clinicians.* San Francisco: Jossey-Bass.

Lee, E. (1997). Chinese American families. In E. Lee (Ed.), *Working with Asian Americans: A guide for clinicians* (pp. 46–78). New York: Guilford Press.

Lin, J. C. H. (1998). *In pursuit of education: Young Asian students in the United States.* El Monte, CA: Pacific Asian Press.

Lyman, S. (1974). *Chinese Americans.* New York: Random House.

Ng, F. (1998). *The Taiwanese Americans.* Westport, CT: Greenwood Press.

Tong, B. (2000). *The Chinese Americans.* Westport, CT: Greenwood Press.

Wong, M. G. (1998). The Chinese American family. In C. H. Mindel, R. W. Habenstein, & R. Wright, Jr. (Eds.), *Ethnic families in America: Patterns and variations* (4th ed., pp. 284–310). Upper Saddle River, NJ: Prentice Hall.

CHOLO/CHOLA

The term *Cholo* (or the female *Chola*) is derived from early Spanish and Mexican usage and denotes racial or cultural marginalization. This Mexican American subculture originated in the *barrio* (neighborhood) street gangs of Southern California. Recently, some of its stylistic elements have been appropriated by pop stars and clothing manufacturers for consumption by the wider youth culture. Cholo style includes characteristic demeanor, clothing, makeup, speech patterns, hand signals, tattoos, and graffiti. Characteristics associated with choloization include low socioeconomic status, marginalized acculturation, problems in school, and the need for cultural support, protection, and a sense of belonging. Loyalty, honor, respect, and protection of territory are hallmark Cholo values that guide behavior and social organization. *Locura* (craziness), criminal activity, and fighting are accepted within the culture, and Cholos are at high risk for drug, alcohol, and tobacco use at an early age.

The forerunners of the Cholo tradition were the *Pachucos,* Mexican American adolescents who belonged to gangs between 1930 and 1950. Known as *zoot suiters* because of their style of dress—baggy, high-waisted trousers cuffed at the ankles; long, wide-shouldered sports coat; ducktail hairstyle; long decorative chains; and tattoos on the hands and arms—they are remembered for a 1943 confrontation in East Los Angeles known as the Zoot Suit Riots. Cholo slang, an amalgam of Spanish and English words, is called *Calo,* which was originally derived by Pachucos from the slang of Spanish gypsies.

Cholo gangs are loosely organized into age cohorts or cliques, called *klikas.* Most cliques are separated in age by two to three years, so that within a barrio there is a succession of cliques, which together make up a larger barrio unit of older and younger gang members. *Wannabes* are youngsters who emulate the gang style but are not yet members. As they prove their loyalty, they may be "jumped in" (initiated in) to a clique, usually between the ages of 10 and 14. Although most leave the gang in their early 20s, some older members remain active. *Veteranos* may serve as counselors and role models and are accorded considerable prestige.

A clique tends to have a unique behavioral and stylistic signature and may be known to specialize in particular activities, such as violence or drug use. Female cliques have become more prevalent in recent years and are structurally equivalent to male cliques. Cliques are a source of companionship, financial and emotional support, and physical protection.

Cholo culture finds myriad outlets for creative expression, including graffiti, tattoos, and customized "lowrider" cars. A prevalent form of Cholo graffiti is the *placa* or "hit-up." A symbol of territorial street boundaries usually executed in Old English lettering, the placa states a gang's name, the clique name, and the names of the writer and his or her closest friends. Cholo tattoos also employ this style of writing, often on the neck or face. Other common tattoos include praying hands, teardrops, and hand tattoos signifying specific criminal activities. Lowriders are of two basic types: immaculate restorations of 1930s- and 1940s-era family cars, and later-model cars that have been restyled with elegant upholstery, paint, chrome- and gold-plated undercarriage, elaborate sound systems, and hydraulic suspension that permits individual wheels to be raised from the ground while the car is in motion.

—Peggy Gallaher
—Rose Girgis

See also Mexican Americans

FURTHER READING

Harris, M. G. (1988). *Cholas: Latino girls and gangs.* New York: AMS Press.

Moore, J. W. (1991). *Going down to the barrio: Homeboys and homegirls in change*. Philadelphia: Temple University Press.

Phillips, S. A. (1999). *Wallbangin': Graffiti and gangs in L.A.* Chicago: University of Chicago Press.

Vigil, J. D. (1988). *Barrio gangs: Street life and identity in Southern California*. Austin: University of Texas Press.

COGNITIVE BEHAVIORAL THERAPY

The historical foundations of behavioral therapy (BT) and cognitive behavioral therapy (CBT) date back thousands of years to ancient philosophers who advocated the use of consequences to change behavior and the role of perception in mood. The modern history of CBT began with early learning theorists such as John B. Watson, the founder of behaviorism, who recommended focusing only on observable behaviors that can be reliably measured. Ivan Pavlov and B. F. Skinner laid the groundwork for classical and operant learning theories, which provide a framework for understanding the development and maintenance of emotions and behavior.

The 1950s marked the beginning of the modern era of contemporary CBT with the advent of behavioral treatments for the problematic anxiety reactions (e.g., systematic desensitization by Joseph Wolpe) seen in many of the returning World War II veterans. These early contemporary CBT theorists focused on the assessment of observable behavior and treatment changes to demonstrate the efficacy of the treatment plan. During the 1960s, Albert Bandura's social learning theory introduced the notion that we can learn through modeling; this required a role for cognition in learning and paved the way for CBT. At first, BT and CBT were met with skepticism by the clinical psychology field. Both theories proposed that current environmental and cognitive appraisals could be addressed in the here and now to produce lasting therapeutic change. These ideas were fought with vigor, and theories of symptom substitution—the notion that treatment without uncovering the intrapsychic source of symptoms could lead to the development of other symptoms—were presented but never empirically supported. Today, BT and CBT have been firmly established as mainstream treatments.

Cognitive behavioral therapy assumes that problems of thoughts, emotions, and behavior are developed, maintained, and changed through the process of learning (e.g., reinforcement, associative learning, modeling) unrealistic beliefs and expectations. It is based on the scientific method in that it involves a systematic assessment of problem thoughts, emotions, and behaviors and leads to specific interventions that are designed to target these problem areas, as well as the assessment and evaluation of treatment outcome. Behavioral assessment is characterized by multimodal (cognitions, emotions, physiology, and behaviors) and multimethod (interview, self- and other report, self-monitoring, observation of behavior) strategies. These procedures are designed to create measurable treatment goals that encapsulate the client's presenting problems and inform the treatment plan.

Cognitive behavioral therapy is a here-and-now treatment in that client problems are conceptualized on the basis of current maintaining factors (e.g., current environmental antecedents and reinforcement). The present focus of CBT is predicated on the notion that the factors and precipitants associated with the onset of symptoms are not necessarily responsible for the maintenance of these symptoms. For example, a 33-year-old client with a 10-year history of panic symptoms and behavioral avoidance that developed upon graduating college may respond better to the treatment of current unrealistic thought patterns and avoidance than to interventions focused on uncovering a presumed precipitating conflict.

Cognitive behavioral therapy takes an active approach in which the maintaining antecedents and consequences of behavior are treated through a collaborative therapy relationship. Clients actively engage in exercises jointly designed to learn new adaptive behavior (skill-building interventions) and develop alternative interpretations of life events (cognitive restructuring). In cognitive restructuring, clients learn that "thoughts are not facts." Collaborative analyses of specific problematic situations and their associated thoughts, emotions, and behaviors are often written on a *thought record*. The thought record is used to demonstrate how our thoughts lead to problematic emotional and behavioral responses and to develop evidence-based alternative interpretations and coping strategies. For example, an individual who expects that a request for a date will be met with a response of horror may be encouraged to engage in a behavioral experiment that is designed to collect information on whether that prediction is evidence based. It is important for the CBT therapist to remind the client that the experiment is designed to gather evidence about a belief (within the client's control), not to obtain a date (outside the client's control). Clients are encouraged to examine the evidence for negative or "hot" cognitions by retrospectively listing evidence for and against a particular belief.

Occasionally, behavioral assessment, role-playing, or experiments will identify a skill deficit that limits the client's range of behavior and sets the stage for problematic outcomes (thoughts, emotions, and behaviors). In the case of the client with social anxiety seeking a date, we may find out that during the role-play he or she displays limited eye gaze, frequent self-denigrating statements, and limited verbal output. In cases in which a skill deficit is identified, a specific skill-based intervention will be added to the CBT package to address prerequisite skill deficits. Likewise, CBT may include activities designed to develop effective skills in communication, parenting, relaxation, problem solving, anger management, or assertiveness. These skills are then practiced through in session modeling, role-play, and homework and later applied to specific problematic situations in real life.

Homework, or between-session therapy exercises, are a necessary component of CBT and help the client to transfer learned skills from the office to the real world. Typically, clients spend only one hour a week in session, leaving 167 hours per week for other activities. Scheduling a few hours of between-session exercises outside of therapy is critical for the transfer of in-session gains and enhanced treatment outcome.

Cognitive behavioral therapy is an individualized approach in that treatment is specifically tailored to the individual's learning history, culture, environmental contingencies, and cognitive appraisals. Although standardized CBT treatment manuals have been established based on the "average" client, they must be individually tailored to the needs of the particular client.

Interventions are designed to enhance successful changes in the way clients respond to thoughts, feelings, and behaviors. Often, the presenting problems have had a long learning history and are not easily changed. Therefore, CBT interventions often follow a stepwise sequence in which changes are accomplished in an incremental fashion from simple to complex, easy to difficult, less threatening to more threatening. This stepwise approach allows clients to achieve success and reinforcement as they make difficult behavioral changes.

Contemporary CBT is best described as a psychotherapy approach that consists of a package of specific treatment components that are tailored to the needs of a particular client. Many CBT approaches involve *psychoeducation,* in which clients are presented with pertinent information about their presenting problem (e.g., major depression, panic disorder, couples distress, anger) and the nature of CBT (e.g., here-and-now focus, use of homework, principles of reinforcement, view of connection of thoughts, emotions and behaviors) to help dispel myths and help clients become educated consumers of their therapy experience. The psychoeducation phase of treatment helps to form the foundation for a collaborative therapy relationship, as well as a realistic groundwork for future cognitive restructuring work.

A collaborative therapist–client relationship in CBT is critical for a successful outcome, as it is in most other therapies. A strong collaborative relationship with mutual respect, trust, and responsibilities leads to positive expectations, preservation of client autonomy, and better outcomes. The treatment package often includes relevant skill-based training depending on the nature of the problem. In the treatment of anxiety, for example, CBT often involves psychoeducation, relaxation-skills training, systematic graduated exposure to feared situations (a form of experiments), and cognitive restructuring.

Cognitive behavioral therapy has been applied and empirically supported for many different disorders and problems in children, adults, and couples. The American Psychological Association's Division 12, the Society for Clinical Psychology, has established research guidelines for the consideration of treatment efficacy. Although the merits of these guidelines have been debated, they have led to the publication of treatment manuals for specific disorders; when applied flexibly, these frameworks are excellent training tools and can enhance outcomes. This flexibility is especially relevant when working with clients of diverse cultural backgrounds.

Cognitive behavioral therapy and other mainstream therapies are based on middle-class, European American values that value individualism, self-control, and individual autonomy. Although these individualistic notions are often seen as reasonable goals in CBT and in the Anglo-American culture, they may not have the same relevance for other ethnic and cultural groups. Additionally, to the extent that clients are marginalized in a larger context, a focus on individual autonomy without an appreciation of the societal forces that perpetuate inequities may alienate the client. In these cases, it may be more appropriate to focus on addressing problems in the larger environmental context before addressing individual control and autonomy. Failure to adequately assess and address the worldviews of culturally different groups can invalidate the client's experience in therapy and interfere with the establishment of an effective collaborative relationship that is so central to treatment outcome.

—Michael R. Lewin

See also Multicultural Counseling; Multicultural Counseling Competencies

FURTHER READING

Barlow, D. H. (2001). *Clinical handbook of psychological disorders* (3rd ed.). New York: Guilford Press.

Beck, J. S. (1995). *Cognitive therapy: Basics and beyond.* New York: Guilford Press.

Spiegler, M. D., & Guervremont, D. C. (2002). *Contemporary behavior therapy* (4th ed.). Belmont, CA: Wadsworth/Thomson.

COLLECTIVISM

The term *collectivism* generally refers to cultures that give priority to group goals when those goals come into conflict with individual goals. A person's identity is defined in terms of group attributes and achievements as opposed to personal attributes and achievements. Collectivism is often equated with *interdependence.* Generally speaking, collectivism is associated with countries in Asia, Africa, Central and South America, and the Pacific Islands. Because collectivism is the norm in countries where psychology is not a dominant field of study, we will examine collectivism in more depth here than we have examined individualism elsewhere in this encyclopedia.

One of the most respected researchers in this area is Harry Triandis. His book *Individualism and Collectivism* is a seminal work that summarizes a great deal of research on individualism and collectivism. He suggests that collectivism should refer to a description of a society. In other words, a society identifies the importance of the pursuit of group goals and identities over individual goals. The degree to which an individual follows these values is referred to as *allocentrism.* An allocentric individual in a collectivistic society matches the value system. However, some allocentric individuals may live in individualistic societies, and this mismatch impedes the allocentric's pursuits. In these instances, others in the society may take advantage of the allocentric individual's worldview of sharing, and he or she may lose important resources to others who are pursuing idiocentric (individualistic) goals.

To illustrate how idiocentrics may take advantage of allocentrics, Jeffrey Mio, Suzanne Thompson, and Geoffrey Givens examined the "commons dilemma" (also known as the tragedy of the commons). The savings-and-loan system in the United States, for example, was set up to be a collective endeavor. People save money in a savings-and-loan institution in exchange for the ability to borrow money at a better interest rate than they can secure at a traditional bank. Each investor's or saver's account is insured for up to $100,000 by a federal system that was instituted in the aftermath of the Great Depression. The system works well as long as everyone acts allocentricly. However, some people may decide to act idiocentricly and profit from those who act in an allocentric manner.

Charles Keating is one famous example of an idiocentric: He made multimillion-dollar loans to his wife and children through his Lincoln Savings and Loan, then declared bankruptcy. Others like Keating did this across the country, destroying the entire savings-and-loan system. American taxpayers paid additional taxes to cover the insured amounts of money to investors in these savings-and-loan institutions while the families of the owners made millions of dollars. Thus, those acting in a collectivistic manner lost out, whereas those acting in an individualistic manner made money from the collective.

Over the years, many studies have examined the difference between individualistic and collectivistic societies. In his now-famous study of this dimension, Hofstede examined businesspeople in 50 countries across three regions of the world. In general, countries in Asia, Latin America, and the Pacific Islands were found to be the most collectivistic countries in the world. This collective worldview has definite implications for behavior in these countries. For example, V. L. Hamilton, P. C. Blumenfeld, H. Akoh, and K. Miura found that teachers from a collectivistic country (Japan) taught in a collectivistic manner even when children were working on individual projects.

Perhaps the most respected voice in the examination of individualism and collectivism is Harry Triandis. Triandis and his colleagues found that even the interpretation of some concepts differs between individualistic and collectivistic cultures. For example, self-reliance is associated with the freedom to do things on one's own in individualistic societies, whereas it is associated with not burdening others in collectivistic societies. Such differences in interpretation can have profound implications on what one chooses to study and how one attempts to generalize results across cultures. In fact, Triandis asserted that one *must* take collectivism into account when conducting research across cultures.

Triandis identified three key dimensions along which cultures may vary when asking questions about the self (private, public, and collective) that have an impact on the focus of the inquiry: (1) individualism–collectivism, (2) tightness–looseness, and (3) cultural complexity. If one is investigating an individualistic society that is complex and loose (such as the United States), one generally inquires about research participants' private self (e.g., personal opinions about a topic such as a political event or a social behavior). However, when one is investigating a collectivistic society, one generally inquires about the collective self, particularly in response to an external threat or competition with an out-group. Collectivistic societies emphasize group harmony, give greater social support to group members, and select conflict-resolution techniques that minimize animosity within the group.

Shinobu Kitayama and Hazel Markus examined issues of the self and the pursuit of happiness in a collectivistic society (Japan) and an individualistic society (United States). Interestingly, Japan was rated as the most individualistic society among the Asian societies measured by the Hofstede study, but it still scored far below the United States on the individualism–collectivism scale used in the study. Kitayama and Markus discussed the dynamic between two theoretical conversational partners in the United States and Japan. In the United States, as in other individualistic societies in Western Europe and North America, both conversational partners are expected to express high self-esteem to one another, and the interaction between the partners is marked by mutual approval, praise, and admiration. However, in Japan and other collectivistic East Asian countries, conversational partners are expected to express a self-critical attitude, and the interactional dynamic is one of mutual adjustment, sympathy, and compassion.

In examining how individuals feel about themselves, Kitayama and Markus suggested that good feelings exist within each individual in individualistic societies. Conversational partners possess good feelings, and their interactions affirm one another's good feelings.

In collectivistic societies, because people have a self-effacing tendency, conversational partners sympathize with one another. This creates an atmosphere of good feelings that exist in the *interaction* between these conversational partners rather than *within* each partner individually.

This finding seems to relate to Stella Ting-Toomey's discussion of "face giving" within Asian cultures. Because Asians feel it is bad manners to discuss one's own accomplishments, it is incumbent upon others in the collective to recognize these accomplishments publicly. For example, if I were to win a prestigious award, it would be rude and inappropriate to express, "I'm so happy! I just won this award." However, in order for others to know about the award—which will bring honor to the collective—another person is expected to announce the award to others. Even after this public recognition, the recipient is expected to be self-effacing and humble and attribute the award to the community support that he or she received.

Despite the wealth of evidence supporting a distinction between individualism and collectivism and the applicability of these terms to various countries, Daphne Oyserman, Heather Coon, and Markus Kemmelmeier challenged this distinction. In their large meta-analytic study, they concluded that although some differences seem to exist along this dimension, they may not be as profound as the literature suggests. The authors criticized the way that individualism and collectivism have been used; they believe these concepts have been defined overly broadly and that any cross-national differences can be seen as evidence of real differences in the dimension defined by these two constructs. Although the differences along this dimension may not be as great as some suggest, and one might examine other explanations for the differences observed, the Oyserman conclusions may be more providently taken as a caution as opposed to a firm conclusion. Certainly at an experiential level, researchers in the field have encountered striking differences between individualistic and collectivistic societies.

—*Jeffery Scott Mio*

See also Asian/Pacific Islander

FURTHER READING

Hofstede, G. (1980). *Culture's consequences: International differences in work-related values.* Beverly Hills, CA: Sage.
Oyserman, D., Coon, H. M., & Kemmelmeier, M. (2002). Rethinking individualism and collectivism: Evaluation of

theoretical assumptions and meta-analyses. *Psychological Bulletin, 128*, 3–72.

Triandis, H. C. (1995). *Individualism and collectivism.* Boulder, CO: Westview Press.

Triandis, H. C., McCusker, C., Betancourt, H., Iwao, S., Leung, K., Salazar, J. M., Setiadi, B., Sinha, J. B. P., Touzard, H., & Zaleski, Z. (1993). An etic-emic analysis of individualism and collectivism. *Journal of Cross-Cultural Psychology, 15*, 297–320.

COMMITTEE ON ETHNIC MINORITY AFFAIRS

G. S. Hall, the first president of the American Psychological Association (APA), inaugurated the association's meetings in Philadelphia in 1892 by announcing the goals of advancing psychology as a science and a profession and promoting human welfare. Today, the APA boasts 55 divisions that accommodate growing scientific, academic, and professional specializations, including current social, political, and environmental concerns.

At the same time, birthrates among ethnic minorities (e.g., Hispanics) and immigration (e.g., Vietnamese refugees) have continued to grow. The 2000 U.S. Census identified one out of four Americans as being a member of a minority group and projected that in a few decades, minorities will double in size and outstrip the Caucasian majority. As a consequence, academic and scientific interest and political reactions to ethnic minority issues have intensified.

Anticipating these trends, Asian Americans lost no time in forming the Asian American Psychological Association (AAPA). In 1972, it held its first convention under President Donald Sue and commenced publication of the *Asian American Psychologist.*

In 1979, the APA established the Office of Ethnic Minority Affairs (OEMA), incorporating the Committee on Ethnic Minority Affairs (CEMA) under its public interest agenda. The year 2004 marked the silver anniversary of OEMA and its support for diversity, inclusiveness, and the empowerment of psychologists of all colors. Both the CEMA and OEMA have promulgated lofty objectives designed to enhance psychology's competence in ethnically diverse and multicultural environments and to advance respect, better understanding of diverse ethnic values, community harmony, and multicultural psychology. Accordingly, the

CEMA involves a large number of representatives and includes divisional and state representatives from diverse ethnic groups.

The OEMA's role extends to many domains, including minority aging; AIDS; children, youth, and families; end-of-life issues; disability; lesbian, gay, and bisexual issues; violence against women; and work, stress, and health. The APA's minority fellowships and grants help to implement these goals. During 2004, health disparities and training among ethnic minorities were targeted for special attention.

The APA regularly promulgates a list of grants and opportunities to enhance ethnic minority recruitment, retention, and training in psychology. The OEMA administers federally funded projects on school and health, and it operates and supports the CEMA; the Psychology and Racism Project; a job bank; ethnic minority recruitment, retention, and training in psychology; textbook guideline initiatives; and the Council of the National Psychological Association for Advancement of Ethnic Minority Interests. In addition, the OEMA disburses and administers awards funded by individuals, such as the Jeffrey S. Tanaka Memorial Dissertation Award in Psychology and the APA's Suinn Minority Achievement Award. Scores of online and print publications, annual and semiannual reports, and newsletters, as well as booklets, brochures, and pamphlets on projects and topics may be obtained from the CEMA/OEMA offices. These publications include the *Directory of Ethnic Minority Professionals in Psychology* and the *Guidelines for Providers of Psychological Services to Ethnic, Linguistic, and Culturally Diverse Populations.* A recent issue of the newsletter *Communiqué* presented APA president Diane F. Halpern's remarks in celebration of the OEMA's 25th anniversary.

In 1986, seven years after the OEMA was established, the APA approved Division 45, the Society for the psychological Study of Ethnic Minority Issues. Shortly thereafter, the division began publishing *Focus,* a newsletter, and in 1999 its division journal, *Cultural Diversity and Ethnic Minority Psychology.* The CEMA and OEMA's achievements are truly remarkable. This encyclopedia is just one of many indicators of their zealous and effective commitment.

—*Chizuko Izawa*

See also Office of Ethnic Minority Affairs

COMMUNITY INTERVENTIONS

Many ethnic and racial minority groups in the United States experience disproportional rates of negative health and mental health outcomes. Given these health disparities, it is critical to develop interventions that address these populations' prevention and treatment needs. Community interventions are one effective way to reach a large number of individuals in their home communities with culturally specific health-promoting strategies and support.

Community interventions often involve improving people's well-being at the community level by altering factors that influence the targeted behavior or social situation. Thus, community interventions may create new neighborhood programs, bring about changes in public policy, or encourage the mass adoption of alternative behavioral practices.

Culturally appropriate community interventions involve components and strategies that are grounded in the values, norms, language, and customs of the targeted group. For community interventions to be culturally appropriate for racial and ethnic minorities, it is important to actively involve community members in all phases of intervention development, implementation, and evaluation. Using a participatory approach keeps all aspects of development and implementation transparent and alleviates concerns about the interventionists' motivations. This is especially important in light of the historical violation of ethnic minorities; one example is the Tuskegee syphilis study, in which the U.S. Public Health Service deceived 399 African American men with syphilis by making them believe they were receiving treatment when they were not.

By involving community members in all phases of the intervention process, the impact and sustainability of community interventions is often greater because communities (1) take ownership for and pride in the intervention, (2) are directly involved in intervention dissemination, (3) provide critical feedback regarding the appropriateness and success of intervention components, and (4) work to ensure that the intervention meets the cultural needs of the community. In addition, community interventions that involve the active participation of communities can build on existing strengths and resources, promote capacity building, and facilitate the development of new partnerships.

PLANNING AND IMPLEMENTING COMMUNITY INTERVENTIONS

Before implementing a community intervention with ethnic and racial minorities, it is critical to conduct an analysis of the targeted health or mental health outcome within the specific community. Even when utilizing an intervention that has been proven to be effective in one community, this initial work is critical because community-specific factors can influence outcomes. This analysis should work with members of the community to determine the conditions and behaviors that need to change in order to achieve the targeted outcome and to understand the level(s) at which the intervention must take place.

Once this preliminary work has been conducted, the intervention team needs to (1) set overall intervention goals and objectives, (2) investigate prior interventions with similar targeted outcomes, (3) gather intervention ideas from community members, (4) identify anticipated barriers and ways to overcome them, (5) develop a detailed action plan that clarifies who will be responsible for each component, (6) pilot test components, and (7) implement the intervention. Once the community intervention is in place, it is critical to continually monitor and evaluate the program and to make modifications as needed. These steps will increase the likelihood that the community intervention will meet the needs of the community and result in positive health or mental health outcomes.

—*Gary W. Harper*
—*Leah C. Neubauer*
—*Grisel Robles-Schrader*

See also Accessibility of Health Care; Community Psychology

FURTHER READING

Harper, G. W., Lardon, C., Rappaport, J., Bangi, A. K., Contreras, R., & Pedraza, A. (2003). Community narratives: The use of narrative ethnography in participatory community research. In L. Jason et al. (Eds.). *Participatory community research: Theories and methods in action* (pp. 199–218). Washington, DC: American Psychological Association.

Marin, G. (1993). Defining culturally appropriate community interventions: Hispanics as a case study. *Journal of Community Psychology, 21*(2), 149–161.

COMMUNITY PSYCHOLOGY

Community psychology is the study of human behavior in its multiple ecological, historical, cultural, and sociopolitical contexts. It is concerned with the interdependence of individuals and communities. Human behavior is understood as the result of interactions between persons, groups, and their environments. This understanding is applied to the creation of person–environment transactions that prevent dysfunction, facilitate empowerment and social justice, and promote wellness in individuals, groups, and communities. Community psychology is a shift away from psychology's internal, cognitive, and nuclear family emphases toward the incorporation of greater attention to the role of social systems and structures in human functioning.

Community psychology insists on multiple levels of analysis: *individual* (e.g., attitudes, cognitions, emotions), *microsystem* (e.g., family, classroom, team), *organizational* (e.g., a school, a church, an agency), *community* (e.g., geographic, identity, common experience communities), and *macrosystem* (e.g., ideologies, cultures, societal institutions). The broader field of psychology has focused almost exclusively on understanding human behavior at the individual or microsystem levels. Community psychology encourages simultaneous analysis at all levels.

Community psychology began to emerge during the 1950s, and its development was influenced by the sociopolitical climate of the 1960s and 1970s. Civil rights, peace activism, feminism, the antipoverty movement, and environmental awareness provided the context for defining the field. Fundamental to its development was the idea that psychology should not only focus on treating people once problems have emerged but also should play a significant role in addressing social conditions (e.g., poverty, racism) that increase the risk of disease and distress.

Community psychology has an identifiable set of principles that both define and guide the field. These principles include (1) wellness, strengths, and resources; (2) social justice and freedom from oppression; (3) a sense of community and connectedness; (4) multiple dimensions of diversity (e.g., gender, ethnicity, sexual orientation, disability); and (5) community collaboration, participation, self-determination, and empowerment.

Research in community psychology is grounded in a collaborative model in which the researcher works in partnership with the community to inform and meet community needs. Community psychology research should lead to action or have clear implications for action.

Intervention approaches based on community psychology include primary prevention programs, empowerment interventions, mutual support (self-help) groups, and social action strategies (e.g., community organizing and advocacy). The overarching goal of community psychology interventions is to address the root causes of disease and distress through strategies that target antecedent and facilitating factors. Examples of such interventions include a parenting program for teenage fathers, a conflict-resolution program for elementary students, a social support system for the elderly, and an organization of community members concerned about the proliferation of corner liquor stores.

Community psychology and multicultural psychology overlap in many areas. The emphasis on understanding people in their cultural, historical, and sociopolitical contexts provides a framework for examining acculturation, racial identity, and many other variables that are central to the psychological well-being of multicultural populations. Explicit attention to social asymmetries and resource disparities are closely connected to the study of racism and ethnocentrism in multicultural psychology. In addition, the emphasis on community strengths and connectedness is consistent with the cultural worldview of collectivism, which is critical to understanding many culturally diverse populations.

—*Shelly P. Harrell*

See also Blaming the Victim; Community Interventions; Social Justice/Action

FURTHER READING

Dalton, J. H., Elias, M. J., & Wandersman, A. (2000). *Community psychology: Linking individuals and communities.* Belmont, CA: Wadsworth/Thomson.

Rappaport, J., & Seidman, E. (Eds.). (2000). *Handbook of community psychology.* New York: Kluwer Academic/Plenum.

Trickett, E. J., Watts, R. J., & Birman, D. (Eds.). (1994). *Human diversity: Perspectives on people in context.* San Francisco: Jossey-Bass.

CONTEXT COMMUNICATION

Context communication refers to aspects of interpersonal communication that are influenced by two factors: culture-specific and situation-specific expectations. People's values, customs, and environment shape the cultural context; expectations for a specific situation in which the communication occurs shape the situational context. Cultural context creates a lens for perceiving, thinking, and behaving.

Edward T. Hall developed a way to classify and study context communication that refers to high-context (HC) and low-context (LC) messages and cultures. In LC messages, meaning is directly conveyed and requires little knowledge of the cultural context. Conversely, HC messages are subtle and indirect, relying on one's understanding of the culture, values, and patterns of discourse. In HC messages, meaning is embedded within nonverbal communication, gestures, and subtle, indirect oral discourse. These messages use specific code words, nuances, and forms of etiquette that express a person's emotions or intent, sometimes in indirect ways that are difficult to perceive by those who are unfamiliar with the culture and its norms for communicating meaning. For example, context communication occurs at a dinner party when the host asks his or her guests whether they would like a second serving of a dish. In some cultures, saying no to the host would be perceived as insulting, but in others, one would expect to say no a certain number of times before agreeing to accept more. Cultural context is what tells the guests how to respond in a polite and culturally appropriate way.

Cultures can be considered along a high- to low-context continuum. According to Hall, in HC cultures such as Japan and China, social norms are grounded in tradition and homogeneous cultural values. In contrast, LC cultures such as Sweden, Germany, and, to a lesser extent, the United States use more direct statements of meaning, are more culturally heterogeneous, and change more rapidly because communication is not embedded in traditional and stable ways of expression. Conflict may arise when members of LC and HC cultures interact because they are guided by different patterns of communication.

Hall noted that communication and cultures are very complex, and there is no simple distinction between HC and LC communication. Both types may occur within the same culture or between the same two people depending on the expectations of different situations. For example, a well-established couple will often use HC communication, giving just a glance or a comment as a cue for a much more complex set of thoughts and feelings. Because they know each other, they can correctly interpret that look or tone of voice. They may use LC communication when giving step-by-step instructions on how to fix something.

Low-context messages provide the details needed to attach meaning to new learning, whereas HC messages are confusing or frustrating to someone who does not know the unwritten assumptions necessary to decode their meaning.

The impact of HC and LC communication is evident when visiting a new culture. Without knowing the social norms for behavior in the new culture, a visitor may feel tenuous and unsure while trying to learn the appropriate ways to behave and communicate. A guide who uses LC communication to directly point out cultural differences and make expectations explicit helps the visitor learn to navigate in the new culture. In contrast, a guide who uses HC messages with many colloquial and symbolic expressions will frustrate the visitor who might be trying to translate these message literally.

—*Colette L. Ingraham*

See also Cultural Barriers; Culture; Language Proficiency

FURTHER READING

Gudykunst, W. B. (1994). *Bridging differences: Effective intergroup communication* (2nd ed.). Thousand Oaks, CA: Sage.

Hall, E. T. (1976). *Beyond culture.* Garden City, NY: Anchor Press/Doubleday.

COPING MECHANISMS

Coping mechanisms are the thoughts, emotions, and behaviors that an individual employs when encountering stress. Researchers have examined coping mechanisms at different levels, from specific individual coping strategies (e.g., making a plan of action) to broader, more global dimensions of coping (e.g., problem-focused coping). Researchers have also grouped these mechanisms into taxonomies; the two major mechanisms are approach/avoidance and problem-focused/emotion-focused. *Approach coping* refers to an active attempt to eliminate or alleviate the stressor (e.g., the suppression of competing activities), whereas *avoidance coping* refers an avoidance of the stressor altogether (e.g., denial). *Problem-focused coping* refers to the elimination of the source of the stressor (e.g., seeking informational support), whereas emotion-focused coping refers to the elimination of the feelings associated with the stressor (e.g., seeking emotional support). Finally, researchers have examined dispositional as well as contextual (situation-specific) coping mechanisms. *Dispositional coping* refers to the stable ways in which an individual handles stress. These are usually employed across situations. On the other hand, *contextual coping* mechanisms may change from situation to situation and are more transitory in nature.

Research on the stress and coping process has identified patterns of adaptive and maladaptive functioning. Certain coping mechanisms have been linked to stress resistance, psychological growth, and good physical health. Still others have been linked to psychological disorders, disease, and poor physical health. However, these patterns are not equivalent across all people. Gender and ethnic and racial differences have been identified in the literature, emphasizing that what works for one group may not work for another. Furthermore, many gender differences actually overlap with ethnic and racial differences, meaning that the man–woman distinction and the East–West distinction are not without a superordinate cultural context.

GENDER AND COPING MECHANISMS

Across age-groups, it has been noted that men tend to use more problem-focused coping mechanisms, whereas women tend to use more emotion-focused mechanisms. Situational contexts as well as socialization have been postulated to play a role in this finding. Men may have more control over their stressors, a situation in which problem-focused coping is more appropriate and advantageous. If women have less or no control over their stressors, emotion-focused coping is more appropriate and may be just as beneficial. Research on the use of support, both instrumentally and emotionally, has shown that men tend to use more instrumental support, whereas women tend to use more emotional support. In most cultural contexts, socialization teaches women to rely on others, especially for emotional support. On the other hand, men are taught to be independent, but if support is necessary, they should do so for informational purposes rather than for emotional ones.

ETHNICITY/RACE AND COPING MECHANISMS

Although the East–West distinction has been made in the literature and cross-cultural comparisons have included people from different countries, the majority of the research on coping mechanisms has been done in the United States and has used primarily European American or Caucasian participants. Furthermore, when culture is examined as a variable of interest, Caucasian comparison groups have been consistently used to show relative differences in coping between ethnic or racial groups. This weakness of the current literature has been noted many times in reviews; however, few studies have addressed it directly. The following sections highlight the findings of previous researchers with regard to specific ethnic and racial groups. But keep in mind, however, that most of these findings are *relative* and limited to the scope of the research from which they were retrieved. That is, many (if not most) of the studies examining coping mechanisms in ethnically diverse samples chose to include more negative variables, such as depression, anxiety, alcohol and substance use, and avoidance coping strategies.

African Americans

In many comparative studies, African American participants report using more religious coping compared with Caucasian Americans. There is some debate about whether the use of religious coping mechanisms is an adaptive or maladaptive strategy for dealing with stress. However, in studies with African Americans, the use of religious coping mechanisms has been associated with benefits (e.g., increased self-esteem, decreased levels of depression).

Much research on African Americans and coping has examined the role of avoidance coping, such as denial and disengagement. Once again, the literature suggests that the use of avoidance coping mechanisms is maladaptive. However, when we consider the role that socioeconomic status (SES) plays in the types of stressors that individuals encounter and the resources available to cope with those stressors, the picture is different for diverse groups. For example, many ethnic and racial groups, such as African Americans, have lower SES than Caucasian Americans. Urban African Americans may be dealing with uncontrollable stressors such as crime, poverty, poor education, and inadequate health care. Actively dealing with these uncontrollable stressors in an "adaptive" way may not be so adaptive. Therefore, using avoidance coping mechanisms (e.g., denial) may be beneficial in the short term until resources become available to better handle the stressor. Once again, we see that a coping mechanism may be adaptive for one group and maladaptive for another.

Hispanic and Latina/o Americans

The focus on religion and the family within Hispanic and Latina/o American cultures is very strong and engenders more use of religious coping and social support compared with Caucasian Americans. As with African Americans, the use of religious coping among Hispanic and Latina/o Americans has been shown to be an adaptive coping response to stress. Likewise, the more collective familial ties within the Hispanic and Latina/o American culture provide a network through which social support is not only available but also an encouraged form of coping. Unlike the Caucasian American family structure, Hispanic and Latina/o Americans' inclusion of extended family (i.e., grand-parents, aunts, uncles, and godparents) within a closer geographic location allows the beneficial use of social support to be a commonplace practice.

Hispanic and Latina/o Americans report using more self-distraction and venting coping mechanisms than do Caucasian Americans. But here we also see the interplay of gender and culture: Hispanic and Latino American men use more self-distraction strategies, whereas Hispanic and Latina American women use more venting. The cultural notion of *machismo* among Hispanic and Latino men refers to a belief that identity is strongly associated with strength, aggression, and virility. Therefore, when Hispanic and Latino American men are faced with stressors (especially uncontrollable stressors), cultural norms do not allow for the expression of feelings and emotions, making distraction a viable option. On the other hand, Hispanic and Latina American women are allowed and encouraged to vent their emotions as a way to cope with stressors. These two coping mechanisms do not always lead to adaptive outcomes, but they are nonetheless culturally appropriate ways to handle stress within the Hispanic and Latina/o American culture.

Asian Americans and Pacific Islanders

Asian Americans are quite possibly the most diverse of the many different ethnic groups identified in the research. They include Chinese, Japanese, Vietnamese, Koreans, Filipinos, and many other groups from the Pacific Islands (e.g., Samoa, Palau). These groups are typically aggregated into one group in the research—Asian Americans and Pacific Islanders.

Compared with Caucasian Americans, Asian Americans and Pacific Islanders use more acceptance, distancing, and escape-avoidance coping mechanisms. The East–West distinction is usually made between Caucasians or European Americans and Asian Americans. The more passive views of the East can be seen in acceptance forms of coping and distancing. Likewise, their emphasis on harmony may be accomplished through escape-avoidance forms of coping rather than through more approach-oriented forms of coping. However, not all coping strategies yield beneficial or adaptive outcomes. Escape-avoidance coping within Asian Americans and Pacific Islanders is also associated with higher levels of distress, highlighting the fact that not all culturally appropriate coping mechanisms are adaptive.

—*Scott Roesch*

FURTHER READING

Hobfall, S. E. (1998). Our coping as individuals within families and tribes. In S. E. Hobfall, *Stress, culture, and community: The psychology and philosophy of stress* (pp. 119–140). New York: Plenum Press.

Zeidner, M., & Endler, N. S. (Eds.). (1996). *Handbook of coping: Theory, research, and applications*. New York: Wiley.

COUNCIL OF NATIONAL PSYCHOLOGICAL ASSOCIATIONS FOR THE ADVANCEMENT OF ETHNIC MINORITY INTERESTS

The Council of National Psychological Associations for the Advancement of Ethnic Minority Interests (CNPAAEMI) comprises the presidents of the national minority psychological associations, including the Asian American Psychological Association, the Association of Black Psychologists, the National Latina/o Psychological Association, the Society of Indian Psychologists, and the Society for the Psychological Study of Ethnic Minority Issues (Division 45 of the American Psychological Association). The president of the American Psychological Association (APA) is an ex officio member. The past and ongoing history of the CNPAAEMI is a case study of the process of racial and ethnic reconciliation and the building of diversity within the context of national associations.

Before the 1960s, the growth and development of the discipline of psychology involved almost no significant participation by psychologists of color. However, the social justice concerns and economic incentives (e.g., National Student Defense Loans, generous GI education benefits, the establishment of minority scholarships and fellowships) of the 1960s and 1970s fostered the training of the first cadre of ethnic minority professionals in psychology. The participatory and challenging posture of this new cadre was visibly symbolized at the 1968 APA convention in San Francisco when representatives of the newly formed Association of Black Psychologists walked in on a meeting of the APA board of directors and presented their Petition of Concern. By 1975, independent national psychological associations had been formed by three major racial and ethnic minority groups, and these associations strategically challenged the APA, pressed for greater inclusion of people of color, and nurtured and promoted psychological theories and issues of special relevance to their communities. The racial and ethnic fault lines of U.S. psychology were marked.

It was not until 1988 that the APA's Policy and Planning Board and Board of Ethnic Minority Affairs proposed an initiative to begin the reconciliation: Presidents and representatives of the ethnic minority psychological associations were invited to a breakfast meeting with APA officials during the association's 1989 convention in New Orleans, where the APA's chief executive officer presented the idea of a President's Council whose meeting hosts and moderators would rotate among the associations. This suggestion was endorsed in principle.

The annual breakfast meetings, organized by the APA's Office of Ethnic Minority Affairs, increasingly focused on public and professional policy issues of mutual concern and continued until August 1992, when the presidents approved the CNPAAEMI's Governing Rules and began meeting twice a year, with the APA paying all expenses for the winter meeting. By 1994, CNPAAEMI had developed a federal advocacy agenda with an associated management strategy and reaffirmed the inclusion of Division 45 as a voting CNPAAEMI member. In 1995, the CNPAAEMI held a critical meeting with federal officials to discuss American Indian health care and violence prevention in communities of color. As a

result of that meeting, the CNPAAEMI launched its publication series. To date, two brochures have been published: *Guidelines for Research in Ethnic Minority Communities* and *Psychological Treatment of Ethnic Minority Populations*. The CNPAAEMI has also promoted its concerns through symposia at APA conventions and at the National Multicultural Conference. In 2001, the CNPAAEMI approved designs for its letterhead and Web site and began holding annual meetings at the convention of one of its members (on a rotating basis). In 2002, the CNPAAEMI's Governing Rules were revised to change APA participation from member to ex officio status and to encourage all representatives to serve two- to three-year terms.

In 2003, the CNPAAEMI initiated discussions about requesting seats on the APA's Council of Representatives. Subsequently, Division 45 representatives to the council submitted a new business item that called for establishing a seat for each of the ethnic minority psychological associations. In February 2005, in support of this proposal, the APA's president invited the minority association presidents to be introduced and briefly speak to the APA's Council of Representatives. All accepted the invitation and climbed onto the podium stage under the spotlights, where the council greeted them with two rounds of standing ovation.

—*Bertha G. Holliday*

See also Asian American Psychological Association; Association of Black Psychologists; Committee/Office on Ethnic Minority Affairs of the American Psychological Association; National Latino/a Psychological Association

FURTHER READING

Holliday, B. G., & Holmes, A. L. (2003). A tale of challenge and change: A history and chronology of ethnic minorities in psychology in the United States. In G. Bernal et al. (Eds.), *Handbook of racial and ethnic minority psychology* (pp. 15–64). Thousand Oaks, CA: Sage.

CRITICAL RACE THEORY

Critical race theory (CRT), which originated in the legal community, elucidates the relationship between social structure and White privilege by looking at how race and power intersect. According to CRT, the self-interest of Caucasians determines the allowance and retrenchment of civil rights. Therefore, CRT rejects the notion that racism can be abolished through the legal system because racism is deemed necessary for the maintenance of the socioeconomic structure in the United States. The central principles of CRT fall into six categories: racism as a norm, economic determinism, antiliberalism, interest convergence, revisionism, and experience-based narratives.

The central tenet of CRT is that *racism is normal,* as evidenced by the everyday experiences of raced groups (i.e., Native Americans, African Americans, Latinos, and Asians). The theory states that racism is a normative structural feature in the United States that serves as a means to delineate and uphold privilege. Accordingly, *economic determinism* is the driving force behind racism because racism is a mechanism used to justify the inequitable distribution of resources and the exploitation of raced groups. Therefore, attitudes and behaviors that support racial inferiority serve a practical purpose. Consequently, CRT rejects the belief that racism can be eradicated through antiracism education or civil rights programs because such appeals only alleviate overt forms of racism but leave the race-based socioeconomic caste system intact.

The CRT model challenges the effectiveness of incremental steps toward civil rights. It also questions liberalism, the belief that the United States was founded on principles of reason and rationality. Because liberalism attempts to uphold the idea that citizens are defined by their individual merit rather than by their group affiliation, race neutrality is considered a reasonable alternative to race consciousness. Liberalists believe that appealing to constitutional law and the moral fabric of U.S. citizens will force the collapse of racism. However, CRT confronts this belief in race neutrality and points out that, historically, White privilege has been and remains institutionalized through legal precedence. Therefore, CRT views the color-blind argument as inherently flawed; indeed, CRT argues that race neutrality promotes race-based structural inequality.

According to CRT, civil rights gains are a matter of interest convergence. The pioneering theorist Derrick Bell stated that interest convergence occurs when the needs of raced groups are aligned with the self-interests of Caucasian Americans. Therefore, any benefits awarded to raced groups are granted by default. Furthermore, such benefits are subject to retrenchment if Caucasians feel threatened. Advocates of CRT point to the 1954 *Brown v. Board of Education of Topeka, Kansas* decision as a key example of the ebb and flow of civil rights gains. Although it was championed as the pinnacle of civil rights jurisprudence, in actuality, the desegregation mandate faced fierce resistance, to the extent that segregated schools remain an impermeable feature in the United States. Some CRT advocates argue that the *Brown* decision served the purpose of maintaining a semblance of democratic social order and equality during an era of growing communist dominance. In essence, *Brown* protected the self-interests of Caucasian elites while appeasing African Americans seeking equality through integration.

Critical race theory's focus on the relationship between race and power and the perspective of raced groups is the central means by which it engages in revisionist history. In this respect, CRT challenges the interpretation of issues by looking at the relationship between race and access to resources. In questioning U.S. history, the lived experiences of marginalized groups are brought to the forefront through narratives, validating and making room for alternative perspectives.

—*Pamela Trotman Reid*

FURTHER READING

Crenshaw, K., Gotanda, N., Peller, G., & Thomas, K. (Eds.). (1995). *Critical race theory.* New York: New Press.

Delgado, R., & Stefancic, J. (2001). *Critical race theory.* New York: New York University Press.

CROSS-CULTURAL PSYCHOLOGY

Psychologists in the field of cross-cultural psychology study how an individual's behavioral, mental, and emotional functioning reflect the influence of prior experiences and development within a particular social, cultural, and environmental context. They also compare findings obtained in one social, cultural, or environmental context with data obtained in another culture or in many other cultures. In this manner, the field of cross-cultural psychology strives to bring the very best of the psychological research tradition to the task of studying the relationship between psychological and cultural factors.

The work of psychologists within the field of cross-cultural psychology was truly historic during the 1970s, and it helped to spur a general cultural movement in psychology, counseling, and other disciplines during the 1980s. By the 1990s, cross-cultural psychology had become truly multicultural, encompassing all dimensions of diversity. Thus, the field of cross-cultural psychology was a vital predecessor of multicultural psychology.

DEFINITION(S)

Cross-cultural psychology can be defined as a field that specializes in studying and conceptualizing the relationships between cultural factors and human behavioral, mental, and emotional functioning. Psychologists working in this field pay special attention to the changes in and complex relationships among cultural, biological, social, and environmental factors when studying the psychology (or behavioral, mental, and emotional functioning) of individuals from different cultural groups.

Other definitions suggest the diversity of the field. For example, cross-cultural psychology studies the nature and scope of human diversity at the level of the individual and the reasons for that diversity, yet it also studies that which is universal in the psychology of human beings. It is a field that values discovering the full and complete range of variation in human behavior; therefore, it seeks to engage in research on the wide variety of sociocultural and environmental contexts in which humans may be found and studied. It is a field of study in which culture is typically seen as the primary factor contributing to individual-level differences in behavior. The field also values comparisons of individual-level human behavior as they are manifest in one culture and then in another culture, making these comparisons either overtly or more subtly and using means of measuring differences that are seen as equivalent (using valid methods of taking measurements in the different cultures being compared). Finally, it is a field of study that seeks to develop a psychology that is much more universal in scope, focus, and application than prevailing mainstream psychology.

EXPLANATION: RATIONALE, GOALS, AND VALUES

Cross-cultural psychologists distinguish themselves by bringing to their work a tremendous sensitivity to and respect for the role of cultural factors in human life. They understand that cultural factors influence how they approach, conceptualize, analyze, and interpret the behavioral, mental, and emotional functioning of the human beings they study. Thus, the field is rooted in a specific rationale and has important goals and values.

Rationale for the Field

The rationale for the field of cross-cultural psychology can be found in the limitations of mainstream psychology. The psychologists who created the theories and produced the research findings that are at the heart of mainstream psychology failed to systematically attend to the influence of culture on the human beings they observed and studied. Psychologists within mainstream psychology brought to the process of observing and studying other human beings the powerful influence of their own Western culture, creating a bias.

Mainstream psychology's theories are ethnocentric. Ethnocentric people have unexamined assumptions reflecting how humans grow up in a specific culture and learn to believe that the standards, principles, and expectations acquired from that culture constitute the correct and proper way of viewing the world. Culture has a direct impact on the creation of the psychological theories that are presented as true.

Mainstream psychology, therefore, presents theories that reflect a consensus about what is true, but this consensus is a biased and false agreement. Cross-cultural psychology represents a way to correct the false perceptions about what is true; the field achieves this by comparing the results of research that follows from a theory that is in dominant Western culture with the results obtained in a different culture or in many different cultures.

The terms *culture-bound* and *culture-blind* have been used to describe the limitations in mainstream psychology. *Culture-bound* conveys the way culture has played a major role in shaping psychological theories; mainstream psychology may be considered culture-blind because it fails to see or acknowledge the influence of culture.

Psychologists who believe they are engaged in the objective (free of bias) pursuit of knowledge and that the science they engage in is value free or neutral may in fact be doing something else. They may be creating a psychology that is totally bound to or tied up with the cultural lenses that the psychologist brings to the task of observing and studying other human beings. Such psychologists, blind to the influence of culture, fail to see not only how culture operates on and influences them as psychologists but also how culture influences the humans they study.

Goals

One major goal of cross-cultural psychology involves testing the limits of mainstream psychology. Specifically, this involves exploring the extent to which mainstream psychology's theories and hypotheses may be extended to other cultures. The resulting research helps to determine the extent to which these theories and the hypotheses that arise from them generalize or apply to other cultures. This process has been referred to as the "transport and test" function, meaning that a theory or hypothesis is transported to a new cultural context (a non-Western culture) and tested to see whether it successfully applies to the new cultural group.

A second major goal involves going into a new cultural context and seeking to explore and discover some new variation in human behavioral, mental, or emotional functioning. This goal often follows from instances in which the transport and test function resulted in a failure to generalize a theory or hypothesis—that is, the theory did not apply in the new cultural context. Findings of some new variation in human behavior can inform how the theory or research hypotheses need to be expanded or modified.

A third major goal involves the integration function, which follows from the transport and test function and the exploration and discovery of some new variation in human behavior. The new variation in human behavior is effectively integrated into preexisting theory and hypotheses, which are then modified to take the new information into account. The theory and hypotheses expand to accommodate some new discovery, creating something new. This something new may be a more universal psychology. In this manner, an advantage of cross-cultural studies is the production of a more universal psychology. Thus, a new culture may provide a setting for a natural experiment that tests the extent to which a theory or hypothesis generalizes, applies to another culture, or contributes to a universal psychology.

Some emphasize that cross-cultural psychology still has much in common with mainstream psychology. For example, the field has an interest in studying individual differences and the sources of those differences; it believes in the important role of the environment or context in shaping human behavior; and it uses the research methodologies of the natural sciences, which follow from a specific theory or hypothesis.

Values

There are several guiding values that allow the field of cross-cultural psychology to maintain integrity and that hold the field together. These are beliefs that cross-cultural psychologists tend to hold that distinguish them and guide their work. First, the field of cross-cultural psychology acknowledges and studies the central influence of culture on human behavior. Second, cross-cultural psychology aspires to establish universal characteristics of human behavior and to identify which aspects of human behavior generalize or apply in diverse cultures and which general laws of human behavior may be documented through their field of study. Because mainstream psychology as it has developed and is practiced in the dominant Western world is a relatively young branch of science, mainstream psychology may benefit and mature from the global or international focus provided by cross-cultural psychology.

DEVELOPMENT OF THE FIELD

The development of the field of cross-cultural psychology is marked by key historical events. Its development reflects diversification among researchers in the field, the growth of subfields, and the use of diverse methods.

Historical Roots

Cross-cultural psychology emerged as a field of study during the late 1960s and early 1970s. However, the scientific study of the link between culture and psychology can be traced to the 19th century with the publication of Auguste Comte's *Cours de philosophie positive,* in six volumes, between 1830 and 1842. Other roots can be seen in the later work of Wilhelm Wundt, who conducted research in the first psychology laboratory at the University of Leipzig in Germany and founded European psychology in the 1870s; he was considered the founder of experimental psychology. Wundt focused on the development of *Volkerpsychologie*—a psychology of the peoples, or something akin to ethnopsychology—during the last 20 years of his life. Wundt investigated the products of culture such as languages, myths, and customs, but found that the experimental method did not apply to the study of complex cultural dynamics. The value placed on such investigations seemed to stop after Wundt's death, but his work is nonetheless viewed as a pioneering appreciation of the value of studying culture in relation to psychology, and it established a basis for the eventual birth of cross-cultural psychology.

W. H. R. Rivers, another experimental psychologist based at Oxford University and a contemporary of Wundt, was the first experimental psychological researcher to study human beings in a culture outside his own. Specifically, Rivers accompanied anthropologists to the Torres Straits and investigated the sensory functioning of Trobriand Islanders located near northern Australia. After the pioneering work of Wundt and Rivers, however, psychologists' efforts to study cross-cultural psychology were, at best, infrequent, remote, and sporadic until the 1960s.

The birth and growth of cross-cultural psychology has been traced to several institutions and publications that were introduced during the late 1960s and early 1970s. The *International Journal of Psychology* was founded in 1966, partly to promote the cross-cultural point of view. In 1967, a meeting of social psychologists concerned with cultural influences was held in Nigeria, leading to one important outgrowth: the initiation of the *Cross-Cultural Social Psychology Newsletter*, edited by Harry C. Triandis. Because of this and other acts of leadership, some view Triandis as one of the most important leaders and spokespersons for the field of cross-cultural psychology.

Another important historical development was the 1968 publication of the *Directory of Cross-Cultural Psychological Research* in the *International Journal of Psychology*. Walt J. Lonner provided important leadership by establishing the *Journal of Cross-Cultural Psychology* in 1970. In 1972, under the leadership of John Dawson, the field witnessed the creation of the International Association for Cross-Cultural Psychology at an inaugural meeting in Hong Kong; the association continued to hold meetings in various countries around the world every two years. What has evolved throughout the decades since the early 1970s crystallized and articulated the objectives, methods, responsibilities, and tasks of cross-cultural psychology.

DIVERSIFICATION

Diversification has come to characterize the evolution of the field of cross-cultural psychology. Some psychologists engage in the work of comparing data collected in one culture to data collected in another.

Other psychologists work intensively within one culture and are often members of that culture. Still other psychologists work in societies where a plurality of cultural and ethnic groups (or many) are available for study. Despite this diversity in approach, a shared value is the production of a body of knowledge that expands our understanding of the complex of relationships that exist between culture and human behavioral, mental, and emotional functioning.

Examples

Cross-cultural psychologists take the tests and research procedures used in mainstream psychology and use them with research participants in non-Western cultures to learn more about the relationship between culture and mental functioning. The work of psychologist Jean Piaget identified the nature of mental functioning (e.g., concrete operational thinking) in adults in major European and American cities such as Geneva, Paris, London, and New York; however, his results were not replicated with many adults in major cities in the third world.

When Piaget's work was not replicated, assumptions about the extent to which his stages of mental functioning applied to all human beings were questioned. Such findings of differences from the Western standard spurred the search for similarities, fostering evolution and diversification in the field.

Another example of research in the field of cross-cultural psychology involves the concepts of *individualism* and *collectivism*. Individualists place priority on personal goals and emphasis on possessions, personal experiences, personal accomplishments, self-actualization, and competition. The term *individualism* is used to characterize a culture or society with this predominant orientation; individuals with this tendency may also be called *idiocentric*. People within Western culture (e.g., Europeans, Americans) tend to have the predominant characteristics of individualism. Collectivists, on the other hand, either do not differentiate between personal and collective goals or place collective goals (concern for others, sharing, loyalty) above personal goals; individuals with these tendencies may be called *allocentric*. People from non-Western cultures (e.g., Africans, Asians) tend to be characterized by collectivism.

Increasing diversity and evolution in cross-cultural psychology have helped the field to clarify the conceptualization of the difference–similarity contrast as a kind of continuum or dimension that has *relativism* at one pole and *universalism* at the other end. Relative differences emerge as individuals from different cultures are compared; similarities suggest qualities that are universal or held in common by people from many different cultures. This clarification has been brought to bear on research on individualism and collectivism, for example. Critics note that individualism and collectivism are often treated as polar opposites, yet these characteristics may coexist in individuals and in groups in different situations. Thus, these concepts may need to be refined and better studied through research, suggesting a need for even more evolution in the field.

Researchers' Diverse Demographics

The field of cross-cultural psychology has also seen diversification in the demographics of psychologists working within it. The field of cross-cultural psychology now includes psychologists who were not born in Western cultures, even though those who were born in Western cultures may still dominate the field. Psychologists from distant non-Western cultures, who were once the focus of study (as the "other" or as "tribes," "subcultures," or "minorities"), now stand among the ranks of those working within the field of cross-cultural psychology, creating even greater diversity in the field.

Subfields

Another result of the diversification of the field of cross-cultural psychology has been the birth of a subfield, *ethnic psychology*. Ethnic psychology, is the study of different ethnic and cultural groups living in a common plural society (one with many cultural and ethnic groups), particularly how they influence each other and are influenced by common societal institutions. The French call it *psychologie interculturelle,* for example. Ethnic psychology is often led by psychologists having the same ethnic heritage as the group studied within a plural society.

Another subfield of cross-cultural psychology, called *indigenous psychology* or *ethnopsychology,* also studies those once considered "other" and provides vital leadership in studying and articulating the behavioral, mental, and emotional functioning of those from their own culture, using culturally rooted concepts in the process. Some view the emergence of indigenous psychologies as moving the discipline of

psychology toward a more inclusive or universal psychology that applies to all human beings. Indigenous psychology emphasizes culture-specific factors in human functioning and searches for characteristics that are native or rooted in a specific culture.

Within indigenous psychology, a culture's local points of view and frames of reference are given greater priority than concepts and theories imported from Western culture in the study of human behavioral, mental, and emotional functioning. Artificial and experimentally contrived situations are valued less, whereas the daily, mundane activities of indigenous people are valued more. Indigenous psychology effectively corrects the ethnocentric tendency of Western psychological research in the way it selects topics for research, chooses instruments and research procedures, creates items and stimuli on tests, and defines theoretical concepts.

Diverse Methods

The increasing diversification and evolution of the field also is responsible for the variety of methods that are now used to study human beings. Cross-cultural psychologists tend to (1) select a psychological principle, test, or model; (2) test it to see whether a prior finding can be generalized; and (3) in the process, discover what is unique to the new cultural environment. This work occurs within an overall search for the universal in human behavioral, mental, and emotional functioning.

The methods used are not very different from those used in mainstream psychology. Research in cross-cultural psychology typically involves three steps: (1) Research questions are explicitly stated; (2) a method (design, sampling, administration, and instrumentation for data analysis) is selected that is appropriate in light of the research questions; and (3) data analysis strategies are chosen that are appropriate to the research questions raised and method chosen.

There are three common types of comparative studies in this field: (1) *Generalizability studies* use hypothesis testing and seek to establish the extent to which a finding obtained in a Western culture generalizes or applies to a non-Western cultural group; (2) *theory-driven studies* use hypothesis testing to make predictions about what should be found in research with a new cultural group, within a process that seeks to validate a model or theory by extending it to and discovering whether it applies to the new group; and (3) *external validation studies* de-emphasize hypothesis testing and seek to produce evidence to support a particular interpretation of a cultural difference (already found in the Western standard) while investigating the possible causes and meanings of that difference by exploring the role of the environment or social context.

Some research uses data from at least two cultural groups. Other studies are monocultural and focus on one cultural or ethnic group yet use previous research findings to engage in meaningful comparisons. Such comparisons are only possible if the data from the new, different culture are comparable; this leads us to the important issue of equivalence.

Equivalence refers to the extent to which the scores or responses obtained in two or more cultures are actually comparable. Research may be fatally flawed if equivalence has not been considered. For example, the meaning of physically identical stimuli may not be equivalent across cultures, as in the case of a smiling face; in one culture, a smiling face may mean friendliness, whereas it may signify submissiveness in another and ridicule in yet another. A statement made about one's preference for being alone could be presented as a test item; in an individualistic culture (Western culture, such as European or American), such a statement may mean the person has an acceptable need for privacy, but in a collectivistic culture (non-Western or third-world culture, such as Africa or China), it may signal an unacceptable demonstration of social withdrawal. The goal of attaining equivalence—even when only approximated—has led to ingenious solutions. There are now many different types of equivalence.

Two other key concepts that are central to understanding methods in cross-cultural psychology are *emic* versus *etic*. The emic involves that which is culturally indigenous and unique, whereas the etic involves that which is potentially universal and comparable cross-culturally. Emic research describes the characteristics and unique qualities of an indigenous cultural group. Etic research involves comparisons across cultures. Ultimately, principles linking culture and behavior arise from both emic and etic research approaches.

PRACTICAL APPLICATIONS

Cross-cultural training is one practical application of findings from the field of cross-cultural psychology. Here, research findings are practically used to train others about cultural variations in attitudes, beliefs, expectations, and values. Cross-cultural training prepares people from different cultural backgrounds to live, work, and communicate with each other—whether in integrated schools and neighborhoods, business activity, diplomacy, international study, or international travel. Such training may be brief, even occurring over a few days, and takes place in varied settings. It can help people to cope with their prejudices and stereotypes. Cross-cultural training tends to increase knowledge, assists people in managing affective reactions, and can change behavior so that it is more appropriate to the nature of a culture or cultural group. Emphasis is placed on accepting diversity.

The work of applied cross-cultural psychologists also addresses intercultural relations. For example, it may explore difficult intercultural relations between groups such as Jews and Palestinian Arabs on the West Bank of the Jordan River, Catholics and Protestants in Northern Ireland, or factions within an African country such as Rwanda.

CONCLUSION

The impact of cross-cultural psychology is evidenced by three realities: (1) the existence of a rich body of research findings on the links between culture and human behavioral, mental, and emotional functioning; (2) the contribution of cross-cultural training; and (3) applications that serve to improve global intercultural relations among diverse people. Finally, cross-cultural psychology is one dimension of efforts that contribute to what has been called the "fourth force" in psychology—a new valid area focusing on culture and serving as a predecessor to multicultural psychology.

—Barbara C. Wallace

See also Multicultural Counseling; Race Psychology

FURTHER READING

Adamopoulos, J., & Lonner, W. J. (2001). Culture and psychology at a crossroad: Historical perspective and theoretical analysis. In D. Matsumoto (Ed.), *The handbook of culture and psychology* (pp. 11–34). Oxford: Oxford University Press.

Berry, J. W. (1969). On cross-cultural comparability. *International Journal of Psychology, 5,* 119–128.

Berry, J. W. (1997). Preface. In J. W. Berry, Y. H. Poortinga, & J. Pandey (Eds.), *Handbook of cross-cultural psychology: Vol. 1. Theory and method* (2nd ed., pp. x–xv). Boston: Allyn & Bacon.

Berry, J. W., Poortinga, Y. H., Segall, M. H., & Dasen, P. (1992). *Cross-cultural psychology: Research and applications.* Cambridge, UK: Cambridge University Press.

Betancourt, H., & Lopez, S. R. (1997). The study of culture, ethnicity, and race in American psychology. In N. R. Goldberger & J. B. Veroff (Eds.), *The culture and psychology reader* (pp. 87–107). New York: New York University Press.

Carter, R. T. (2005). Uprooting inequity and disparities in counseling and psychology: An introduction. In R. T. Carter (Ed.), *Handbook of racial-cultural psychology and counseling: Vol. 1. Theory and research* (pp. xv–xxviii). New York: Wiley.

Draguns, J. G. (2005). Cultural psychology: Its early roots and present status. In R. T. Carter (Ed.), *Handbook of racial-cultural psychology and counseling: Vol. 1. Theory and research* (pp. 163–183). New York: Wiley.

Kagitçibasi, C. (1997). Individualism and collectivism. In J. W. Berry, M. H. Segall, & C. Kagitçibasi (Eds.), *Handbook of cross-cultural psychology: Vol. 3. Social behavior and applications* (2nd ed., pp. 1–49). Boston: Allyn & Bacon.

Lonner, W. J., & Adamopoulos, J. (1997). Culture as antecedent to behavior. In J. W. Berry, Y. H. Poortinga, & J. Pandey (Eds.), *Handbook of cross-cultural psychology: Vol. 1. Theory and method* (2nd ed., pp. 43–83). Boston: Allyn & Bacon.

Pedersen, P. (2005). The importance of cultural psychology theory for multicultural counselors. In R. T. Carter (Ed.), *Handbook of racial-cultural psychology and counseling: Vol. 1. Theory and research* (pp. 3–16). New York: Wiley.

Shweder, R. (1995). Cultural psychology: What is it? In N. R. Goldberger & J. B. Veroff (Eds.), *The culture and psychology reader* (pp. 41–86). New York: New York University Press.

Sinha, D. (1997). Indigenizing psychology. In J. W. Berry, Y. H. Poortinga, & J. Pandey (Eds.), *Handbook of cross-cultural psychology: Vol. 1. Theory and method* (2nd ed., pp. 129–169). Boston: Allyn & Bacon.

Triandis, H. C. (1995). The self and social behavior in differing cultural contexts. In N. R. Goldberger & J. B. Veroff (Eds.), *The culture and psychology reader* (pp. 326–365). New York: New York University Press.

Triandis, H. C. (1996). The psychological measurement of cultural syndromes. *American Psychologist, 51,* 407–415.

Triandis, H. C. (1997). Foreword. In J. W. Berry, Y. H. Poortinga, & J. Pandey (Eds.), *Handbook of cross-cultural psychology: Vol. 1. Theory and method* (2nd ed., pp. viii–ix). Boston: Allyn & Bacon.

CUBAN AMERICANS

Cuban Americans share many of the core values that are often attributed to Hispanic populations. Each group, however, is distinctive in its history. Cuban Americans have had unique experiences during the past 40 years, and these experiences have affected the way they have adapted and become acculturated to the United States. The issues presented here are merely broad brushstrokes offered to assist in the understanding of a diverse group.

CUBAN IMMIGRATION TO THE UNITED STATES

Before Fidel Castro's takeover of the Cuban government, upper- and upper-middle-class Cubans traveled to U.S. cities to shop and vacation. Cuba's geographic proximity to the United States allowed for easy exchange between the countries. Americans were landowners and business owners on the island as well as frequent vacationers. These Cubans were bilingual, watched American movies, and listened to American songs. Young men attended colleges and prep schools in the United States. This familiarity and the island's geographic proximity made the United States, and specifically Florida, a natural destination for those who left the island.

The greatest influx of Cubans to the United States began after Castro's takeover. Since then, Cubans have left their country and settled throughout the world in great numbers. A majority, however, have settled in the Dade County area in Florida and along the East Coast of the United States. Although some researchers have identified up to 10 distinct migrations of Cubans to the United States, four major groups will be discussed here.

The first wave of Cubans arrived in the United States during 1959 and the early 1960s. Most were highly educated Caucasian professionals of the upper and upper middle class who fled because of safety concerns and their refusal to live under communism. The Castro regime identified some of these Cubans as threats and took over their properties. Many Cuban children and adolescents, who later became known as "Peter Pan children," were sent to the United States by their parents after the Cuban government declared that all children were wards of the state and that parents had no legal rights over them. During this time, many changes were made in the schools, and Communist ideology became prominent in the curriculum. Private schools and prep schools were closed down.

The second wave of Cubans came to the United States during the mid-1960s and 1970s; these immigrants were mostly middle-class professionals. These individuals and families left Cuba because they did not wish to live under communism and had suffered the loss of jobs and properties.

These two groups of Cuban Americans prefer to call themselves *exiles* rather than immigrants. Their migration was based on ideology rather than economic concerns, and for many years they believed that their stay in the United States would be temporary. "Next year in Cuba!" became a standard toast during Christmas and New Year celebrations.

The socioeconomic level of the first two waves of Cuban immigrants and their bilingual status helped them to become rapidly established in the United States. They were well accepted by the population here, obtained employment, opened their own businesses, and acquired licenses to practice their professions (e.g., as doctors or attorneys). They are considered one of the most successful immigrant groups in the United States.

The success of these early Cuban immigrants and the importance they placed on their traditions and culture helped to solidify the Cuban community in the Miami area and establish the *Cuban enclave* that sociologists have identified. This community later served as a source of employment and support for subsequent Cuban immigrants to the area.

The third wave of Cubans (Marielitos) arrived in the United States through the Mariel boatlift in 1980, and reportedly, 124,000 people came to the United States during that time. The Cubans who migrated during this period included all races and socioeconomic classes but were a more representative racial sample of the general Cuban population (i.e., Caucasian, African, and biracial). The group included mostly working-class and unemployed Cubans, who were less likely to be bilingual.

Along with the thousands of well-functioning Cubans who arrived during this time, Castro sent approximately 2,000 individuals whom the government considered "undesirables." These included career criminals, prostitutes, homosexuals, and the chronically mentally ill.

These new Cuban Americans became established and successful members of the communities in which they settled, because there were opportunities for employment in Cuban American–owned businesses such as restaurants and markets, where the ability to speak English was not a requirement. Again, they soon established their own businesses and revalidated their professional credentials.

The fourth wave of immigrants are known as the Cuban rafters or *balseros*. Their name comes from their mode of transportation—rafts. This migration is still ongoing but reached its peak during the mid-1990s. Balseros have demonstrated great courage and ingenuity in their efforts to reach freedom. They have attempted many methods, from tying four inner tubes together to retrofitting cars and pickup trucks as boats. They sail these vessels to the Florida coast, hoping they will not be intercepted by the U.S. Coast Guard. Many have perished during this dangerous crossing.

Like the Marielitos of the 1980s, the balseros represent the racial composition of the island. Many consider them true economic immigrants because their exodus from Cuba was not politically motivated, unlike their predecessors.

These Cubans are also becoming established in the United States and show promise of success, like their predecessors. They express little interest in returning to their homeland and wish to pursue a successful life in the United States.

DEMOGRAPHICS

The 2000 U.S. Census identified more than 1.2 million individuals of Cuban origin living in the United States, the third largest Hispanic group in the United States. About two-thirds of these immigrants were born in Cuba, and the majority arrived during the 1960s, making this group a young immigrant population.

Immigrants in the United States tend to congregate in cities and states where they are most likely to receive the support of already established immigrants and feel the comfort of familiar languages, foods, and customs (e.g., Irish and Italian immigrants created their own neighborhoods in New York). These areas attract a large number of new immigrants and provide an "adjustment cushion" for them. Similarly, Cubans mostly settled in four states—Florida, New Jersey, California, and New York. Within these states, they tend to be concentrated in metropolitan areas such as Miami and Fort Lauderdale (where 56% of Cuban Americans live); New York, northern New Jersey, and Long Island; Los Angeles, Riverside, and Orange County; and Tampa, St. Petersburg, and Clearwater.

Cuban Americans have higher levels of educational achievement than other Hispanic groups. During the 1990s, the percentage of Cuban Americans over age 25 who graduated from college increased from about 16% to more than 22%, compared with 25% among the entire U.S. population. The income level of this group is also higher than that of other Hispanic groups. In fact, within Hispanic groups, more Cuban Americans are employed in managerial and professional capacities. On average, those living outside the Miami–Dade County area have noticeably higher education levels and higher incomes. However, this difference may be partly explained by the large number of newly arrived immigrants living in South Florida, which skews the statistics downward.

Second-generation Cuban Americans have a level of education that is not only far higher than that of Cuban Americans as a whole but also higher than that of the entire U.S. population. Among second-generation Cuban Americans over the age of 25, 95% have completed high school (versus 83% of the total U.S. population) and 43% have completed college (compared with 25% of the total U.S. population). The average income of second-generation Cuban Americans ages 25 through 44 has been shown to be "at least comparable" to that of the U.S. labor force.

Almost 57% of Cuban Americans are U.S. citizens. About half report that they are able to speak English "very well," and 21% state that they speak it "well." However, English is the only language spoken in only 10% of Cuban American homes. About 56% report having an intact family, a number that is comparable to non-Hispanic Caucasians.

Studies indicate that Hispanics and Caucasians in the United States have similar rates of mental illness, and the surgeon general's report states there is no evidence that Cuban Americans have lower rates than other Hispanics. There is evidence that the incidence of mental illness is more likely to be affected by socioeconomic status, acculturation stress, and trauma caused by mode of migration than by membership in a specific ethnic group.

ACCULTURATION, VALUES, AND BELIEF SYSTEMS

The level of acculturation to the dominant culture, command of the English language, and viewpoint and openness about issues of individuality, gender roles, and the family will dictate how comfortable an individual or family feels in the counseling setting.

The Cubans who came to the United States more than 40 years ago challenge the commonsense idea that length of stay in a country increases the level of acculturation. Perhaps because they had attained a high socioeconomic level in their own country, these exiles were empowered and proud and did not feel forced or inclined to accept values and customs that directly conflicted with their own. Class and socioeconomic level are important in their social activities. Families tend to congregate with others of similar background, and their children tend to marry other Cuban Americans of similar background. They have maintained Spanish as the primary language in the home and encourage their children to carry on their culture and customs.

The Cuban enclave allowed later arrivals to maintain these same customs and ideals. Families of the second wave of migration—mostly middle-class professionals—prefer to socialize within the same socioeconomic level, whereas immigrants of the third and fourth waves do not appear to have the same concerns. However, like most ethnic groups, all Cubans are most comfortable and feel a kinship with other Cubans, especially those who had similar experiences in their homeland.

Second-generation Cuban Americans and Cubans who came to the United States as young children (called "one-and-a-halfers" by some) show a higher level of biculturation, as do Cuban Americans who settled away from the enclave. Those who are bicultural maintain many of the cultural values and customs of their parents but incorporate many American ideals and traditions. For example, these families are more likely to allow their children to go out with fewer restrictions, and these children are increasingly finding spouses of other nationalities. At family celebrations such as Thanksgiving, they may cook the customary American turkey meal, but accompany it with *arroz con frijoles,* the traditional black beans and rice.

These more highly biculturated Cuban Americans are fully bilingual. They speak Spanish well, although their language skills in Spanish may be somewhat immature. They were educated in U.S. schools and have a full command of the English language. One interesting phenomenon has been the development of *Spanglish,* a combination of Spanish and English used easily by this group, who may make up new words or mix both languages in one conversation.

Cuban Americans have a strong sense of family unity and believe that the welfare of the family supersedes the needs of the individual. The family provides safety and protection for its members.

Children are brought up within the family group, and their first playmates are siblings and cousins. Language accentuates the closeness of these relationships. For example, first cousins are called "brother-cousin" or "sister-cousin," and the cousin designation is retained throughout extended family members to the third and fourth degree. A young child might ask his parents on meeting a new playmate, "Is he our cousin?" because in his short life, most of the children he has met are related.

Grandparents, aunts, uncles, and godparents maintain close and special bonds within the family unit. The relationship between a parent and the godparent of his or her child is called *compadre* or *comadre,* which literally translate as "co-father" and "co-mother." The "immediate family" in the United States means solely the parents and their children. In the Cuban American family, it includes grandparents, aunts and uncles, and first cousins. Many grandparents take care of the children while their parents work. This is accepted, expected, and wished for by all generations involved. In turn, elders are respected and cared for. Traditionally, the elderly are taken care of at home whenever possible, although this is becoming difficult as both spouses often work outside the home.

Cuban American families are child centered. The safety and care of the children are of paramount importance. Children are taught the values of dignity, respect for elders, love for family, and honesty. They are trained to behave with "appropriate breeding" outside the home. Many parents are gratified to hear from other parents, "He is so well behaved!" although the child may be quite the opposite at home. Children are shown tenderness, and hugs and kisses are customary in these families, even between a father and a son.

Cubans have always valued education and emphasize the importance of education to their children. Earlier waves of immigrants tended to have more traditional ideas about education and emphasized higher education for their male children. Girls may have gone to college, but it was expected that they would be homemakers or that careers would not be primary in the family. In addition to helping maintain the culture and heritage, Cuban Americans strongly believe that bilingualism is an asset that will be valuable in the future careers of their children.

The Cuban Americans who arrived during the 1980s have many of the same traditional values. However, they are more likely to understand the need for women to be full team workers in the family finances and place greater emphasis on the education of their daughters. Many of these immigrants are young adults who grew up and were educated under the Communist system. However, their parents and grandparents did not, and they were taught traditional Cuban values and religion at home.

The Cuban exiles brought their families with them or brought the rest of their family members shortly after arriving in the United States. However, Cubans who came during later migrations often left parents, children, and siblings behind. One of their priorities has been to send U.S. dollars to their families in Cuba to help make ends meet and to visit them on the island whenever possible, bringing needed supplies.

Cuban immigrants arriving since the 1990s were born, raised, and educated under the Communist regime, as were most of their parents. Although Cuba has experienced decades of economic difficulties and lacks adequate housing, food, and other needs for its citizens, the last few years have been particularly difficult. During this period, Cubans have experienced severe shortages of food and medication, and this has forced individuals to become resourceful in obtaining the necessary articles for survival. This resourcefulness has not always followed ethical constraints, and Cubans on the island reportedly have developed a sense of "double morality." Under this double morality, they justify actions taken to acquire items that are necessary for the survival and well-being of their families. A recent study, however, showed that, overall, this group has a clear sense of moral values and, when faced with impossible situations, they will do what is necessary for their families but may experience internal conflicts in doing so.

Other findings have shown that these individuals' priority in life is to get ahead and to teach their children to prepare for the future. These values are consistent with those of capitalist societies. Although an important goal of communist governments is to discourage individuality and emphasize obedience to the government's dictates and ideals, these individuals tend to be self-reliant in making decisions. They prefer to make their own decisions or consult with family members and friends rather than appeal to a superior for direction.

Cuba is a traditional patriarchal society. The man is the head of the household and the main breadwinner. The woman often has to work, but her main roles are homemaking and tending to the children. The attitude expressed by the statement, "Poor Elena, she has to get a job to help with expenses," implies that women are not supposed to enjoy working outside the home, and they are definitely not to get farther ahead than their husbands. This is similar to the attitude of *marianismo,* a belief that Hispanic women are expected to focus only on their families and ensure that others around them are happy and taken care of, without asking for that themselves. Marianismo, however, is not immune to acculturation, and many Cuban American women are becoming professionals and pursuing careers. Of course, there is always a grandmother in the background who makes sure that the home and children are tended to.

Notwithstanding patriarchal attitudes, Cuban American women are not without power. In most cases, they are the ultimate authority regarding the moral values of the family and the final decision maker on issues that affect the children.

A double standard survives in traditional Cuban American families. Men may have sexual experiences, but women are supposed to be chaste and preferably virgins when they get married. The family honor may be damaged if a girl becomes pregnant out of wedlock. However, more acculturated young couples are increasingly living together, although this is still frowned on among traditional families and older family members. Later groups of immigrants do not hold this negative view, as cohabitation is commonplace in present-day Cuba. Homosexuality is generally considered deviant, especially among the more traditional families; many of these families choose not to acknowledge a child who is gay or lesbian.

Cuban citizens practice a variety of religions, including Roman Catholicism and other Christian denominations, Judaism, and Cuban Santeria. Although a majority of Cuban Americans were brought up Roman Catholic, many no longer practice or have joined other Christian congregations in their communities. Cuban Santeria is a religion developed by African slaves that incorporates Catholic and African Yoruba beliefs. Cubans go to priests, pastors, and *santeros* (Santeria priests or shamans) as important sources of support.

TREATMENT CONSIDERATIONS

Cuban Americans tend to be apprehensive toward mental health professionals in general, and they often feel that Anglo clinicians will not understand them. Clients often seek clinicians who have some similarity to their own background or a link to family or friends. In addition, clients often prefer clinicians who are proficient in Spanish because this facilitates the expression of feelings more effectively. Parents often need a bilingual clinician, although children usually prefer English.

Clients may resist recommendations or interventions that go against their values, especially with regard to gender roles and child rearing. However, Cuban Americans have a deep respect for all doctors and will be respectful during the sessions. Cuban Americans will call their doctor *usted* (the formal *you*), even if the doctor is much younger. Unfortunately, this deference sometimes results in clients who will sit respectfully in the office and cancel the next session.

Cuban Americans expect the mental health clinician to give advice and provide guidance, like a medical doctor. These clients may be bewildered by the customary practice of encouraging clients to explore their issues, gain insight, and come up with their own solutions to problems. Some researchers believe that a cognitive behavioral approach is the best modality to use when working with Cuban Americans.

Clinicians must explore the value systems and levels of acculturation of Cuban American clients at the beginning of the therapeutic relationship, guarding against making any assumptions. Asking questions about the client's experiences, upbringing, and expectations for himself or herself and family members is essential. The clinician can then "join" the client and show that he or she understands and accepts the client at the onset of therapy. Sometimes, a well-intentioned clinician will strive for particular changes in a client without understanding the repercussions of those changes in the client's life. Attempting to confront the client's value system directly will usually result in termination of treatment.

In the past, the mental health field in the United States believed that assimilation was always desirable. However, recent studies show that individuals who live in a bicultural environment do best when they also become bicultural—that is, they acculturate to the new culture but maintain characteristics of their own culture. Individuals who tend to underacculturate or overacculturate (e.g., those who reject their culture of origin) become maladaptive, and adolescents become increasingly at risk for drug abuse and delinquency. Clinically, self-acceptance and a clear understanding of the mores of one's group help individuals to increase self-esteem and improve resiliency. In fact, therapy models have been developed to help individuals achieve biculturation.

Cuban Americans have a deep-rooted belief that one who needs help from a mental health professional is "crazy" or "weak." An individual who is depressed or anxious is often described as weak by family members. Many, particularly women, show their distress by presenting with somatic complaints or symptoms of anxiety and depression, called "having nerves" or having a "nerve attack." It is taboo to discuss personal family issues outside the home, and many prefer to speak with a priest or a pastor or to visit a family physician before seeking counseling. Primary care physicians often prescribe antidepressants and refer patients to a mental health professional only when necessary. Many older Cuban Americans tend to self-medicate with prescription tranquilizers.

It is important to normalize symptoms and to offer psychoeducation to these clients. As with all clients, a careful assessment of symptoms is essential. However, because of the importance of showing "good breeding" to outsiders and having self-respect, Cuban Americans may present in the clinician's office well-groomed, well-dressed, and with their hair and nails impeccably done. These clients will sit, look at the therapist alertly, and sometimes minimize complaints. Thus, appearance, grooming, and affect, observations that are important parts of the diagnoses, must be interpreted with caution.

Several members of the family may present for an initial session with a child; very infrequently will the child simply be dropped off for subsequent sessions. Parents, particularly mothers, prefer to be an integral part their children's treatment, and establishing good rapport with the mother is essential in successful interventions. For example, it is helpful to meet with parents for a few minutes at the beginning of each therapy session before meeting with the child alone.

Losses

Grief and loss are important issues for Cuban Americans. Cuban immigrants have experienced a significant loss in leaving their country. Most lost all of their belongings and property, and many left close family members behind and lost their support systems overnight. Because of these safety concerns, many individuals left Cuba in secrecy and were not able to take leave of family members and friends. For example, children were separated from primary caretakers without warning.

Anxiety

Anxiety is another significant issue for immigrants who face unfamiliar surroundings, language, and customs. Mode of migration (e.g., on rafts) and separation from parents may have residual trauma and anxiety consequences. Children of all ages are placed in schools that have unfamiliar curricula and activities, and they often are not offered assistance in maneuvering and understanding new surroundings.

Most individuals, when faced with unfamiliar circumstances, strive to keep some control over their lives by holding on to familiar activities and routines. In Cuban American families, this may be manifested primarily in the way that parents deal with their children.

In Cuba, as in many other Hispanic cultures, children socialize mainly with family members and the children of their parents' friends. This can be a great source of anxiety for parents because children in the United States meet friends mostly in school. Often, parents do not know the families of their children's friends, and they are very reluctant to allow their children to visit unknown households or go out with teenagers they have never met. Working through these issues with parents, acknowledging and respecting their fears, and making recommendations that are consistent with their belief system will maximize the possibility of successful compromises in these areas.

Trust

Cubans on the island do not trust others. Family members, coworkers, or neighbors could be secret "Committee Members" whose role is to report to government officials any deviation from the strictures of the Communist state. It will take time for these immigrants to feel safe and trust others, especially those whom they view as part of the establishment. For example, one woman in therapy was fearful that her children would be taken away if someone from the state found out that she was depressed.

CONCLUSION

Cuban Americans present a particular challenge in counseling. There are many diverse subgroups within this population, a result of their varied backgrounds and experiences. As with all clients, it is imperative that clinicians acknowledge and value clients' histories and show understanding of how these factors affect their functioning and outlook on life. Experiences, customs, and values must be placed in perspective to avoid pathologizing cultural practices and significant adaptive defenses of clients. If mental health professionals are unable to do so, it will be nearly impossible to establish the rapport necessary to keep clients in therapy and offer the help they seek.

—*Maria Garcia-Larrieu*

FURTHER READING

American Psychological Association. (2001). *Guidelines for multicultural counseling proficiency for psychologists: Implications for education and training, research and clinical practice.* Washington, DC: Author.

Bernal, G., & Shapiro, E. (1996). Cuban families. In M. McGoldrick, J. Giordano, & J. K. Pearce (Eds.), *Ethnicity and family therapy* (2nd ed., pp. 155–168). New York: Guilford Press.

Boswell, T. D. (2002, September). *A demographic profile of Cuban Americans.* Retrieved from http://www.miami.edu/iccas./publications.htm

Gil, R. M., & Vazquez, C. I. (1996). *The Maria paradox: How Latinas can merge old world traditions with new world self-esteem.* New York: Putnam.

Gomez, A. S., & Rothe, E. M. (2004, August). *Value orientations and opinions of recently arrived Cubans in Miami.* Retrieved January 26, 2006, from http://www.miami.edu/iccas/publications.htm

Huddy, L., & Virtanen, S. (1995). Subgroup differentiation and subgroup bias among Latinos as a function of familiarity and positive distinctiveness. *Journal of Personality and Social Psychology, 68,* 97–108.

Mezzich, J. E., Ruiz, P., & Munoz, R. A. (1999). Mental health care for Hispanic Americans: A current perspective. *Cultural Diversity and Ethnic Minority Psychology, 5,* 91–102.

Pederson, N. G. (2000, August). *Cuban Americans: Family systemic processes in an immigrant population.* Unpublished master's thesis, Texas Women's University, Denton, TX.

Rothe, E. M., & Pumariega, A. (2005). Entre Hernán Cortes y la esposa de Lot: Adaptación y salud mental de los exilados Cubanos en los Estados Unidos [Between Hernan Cortes and Lot's wife: Adaptation and mental health of the Cuban Exiles in the United States]. *Journal of Hispanic American Psychiatry, 4,* 35–40.

Santiago-Rivera, A. L., Arredondo, P., & Gallardo-Cooper, M. (2002). *Counseling Latinos and la familia: A practical guide.* Thousand Oaks, CA: Sage.

Santisteban, D. A., Coatsworth, J. D., Perez-Vidal, A., Kurtines, W. M., Schwartz, S. J., LaPerriere, A., & Szapocznik, J. (2003). Efficacy of brief strategic family therapy in modifying Hispanic adolescent behavior problems and substance use. *Journal of Family Psychology, 17,* 121–133.

Santisteban, D. A., Szapocznik, J., Perez-Vidal, A., Kurtines, W. M., Murray, E. J., & LaPerriere, A. (1996). Efficacy of intervention for engaging youth and families into treatment and some variables that may contribute to differential effectiveness. *Journal of Family Psychology, 10,* 35–44.

U.S. Department of Health and Human Services, Substance Abuse and Mental Health Services Administration. (2005). *Surgeon general's report: Chapter 6, Mental health care for Hispanic Americans.* Retrieved January 26, 2006, from http://www.mentalhealth.org/cre/ch6_introduction.asp

CULTURAL BARRIERS

Cultural barriers are sources of bias that can play a significant role in the effectiveness of multicultural psychotherapy. Culture-related, class-related, and language-related barriers are three major (and overlapping) sources of potential bias identified in the seminal writings of Derald W. Sue and David Sue. Each source of bias can produce problems that may affect the initiation, continuation, and success of psychotherapy. Among the problems that may arise are the misinterpretation of a client's cultural norms as symptoms of a disorder; misunderstanding of culture-bound syndromes and sociopolitical reasons for client behavior; and the misuse of interpreters.

Culture comprises the values, beliefs, and norms that are shared by a group of people, such as a racial on ethnic minority. Culture influences how people think about, act on, and see the world. Traditional psychotherapy theories and the mainstream European American/Caucasian culture in the United States (referred to as "Caucasian culture") share common values and beliefs that can be barriers in multicultural psychotherapy. Examples of these commonalities are the emphasis placed on the use of standard English, direct verbal expression, and long-term goals; the distinction between physical and mental well-being; and the determination of cause–effect relationships.

CULTURE-RELATED BARRIERS

Culture-related barriers in psychotherapy stem from cultural differences between therapists (who are predominantly Caucasian in the United States) and their clients. Common differences arise in the areas of (1) the value of individualism versus collectivism; (2) verbal, emotional, and behavioral expressions; (3) preferred therapeutic approaches; and (4) views regarding the separation of the mind and body.

Individualism is associated with the Caucasian culture and collectivism with non-Caucasian cultures.

The Caucasian culture tends to stress the importance of having a single identity that is not defined by anything or anyone else, whereas in non-Caucasian cultures, a person's identity is often defined by his or her family or cultural group. Consequently, a Caucasian therapist may misinterpret a client's need to consider family needs ahead of his or her own as unhealthy, overly dependent, and lacking maturity.

Tied to views regarding individualism and collectivism are the verbal, emotional, and behavioral expressions of different cultures. In the Caucasian culture, for example, when someone engages in wrongful behavior, he or she often feels guilt, but in many non-Caucasian cultures, the person is more likely to feel shame. Guilt is seen as an individual emotion and shame as a group emotion. Additionally, the importance of verbalizing emotions and emotional reactions is stressed in the Caucasian culture. Self-revelation requires the client to communicate his or her feelings about any topic the therapist probes, even if it involves the most intimate details of the client's life. If a client is not forthcoming, he or she may be viewed as paranoid, guarded, or inhibited. Non-Caucasian cultures are more likely to view such verbal expressions as a sign of disrespect and immaturity and tend to value remaining quiet and listening. Furthermore, culture is reflected in behavioral expressions such as assertiveness, which is valued to a greater extent in the Caucasian culture than in many non-Caucasian cultures.

There are also cultural differences in preferred therapeutic approaches. Traditional psychotherapy theories are generally analytical, linear, and logical, with the primary goal of searching for a cause–effect relationship that is responsible for the individual's problem(s). This contrasts with the more holistic, creative, and nonlinear worldview of many cultures. Additionally, traditional psychotherapy relies on the scientific method and its method of asking and answering questions, including completing quantitative evaluations. Direct and sometimes confrontational techniques are evident in traditional psychotherapy, whereas some cultures (e.g., Asian) value indirectness and subtlety in communication. Many cultures prefer not to be so straightforward in questioning and responding, and this may lead the therapist to a negative interpretation of the client's behavior (e.g., the client is nonresponsive and withdrawn).

Distinctions between mental and physical health are generally more clearly marked for Caucasians than for non-Caucasians. Non-Caucasian cultures are less likely to separate the mind and body and may be confused by the distinction in traditional psychotherapy. These clients may expect to receive the kind of treatment typically provided by physicians and the clergy. This includes immediate and tangible solutions such as advice and medication. Traditional therapies are more ambiguous and long term and tend to be less consistent with the expectations of non-Caucasian cultures.

Culture-bound syndromes can also play a role in creating cultural barriers in therapy. Some syndromes seem to exist only in certain cultures, and they may be mistakenly viewed as indicative of pathology. For example, many Latinos believe in the *evil eye,* a syndrome of distress also known as *mal de ojo*). Patients with this syndrome believe that when a person is given the evil eye by another, he or she will experience misfortunes in his or her career, love, and family life. In this case, the therapist may incorrectly conclude that the client is paranoid because of the client's perceived preoccupation with people causing him or her harm. Moreover, therapists must understand that many people do not seek help for certain symptoms of distress because those symptoms may be considered normal in their culture.

CLASS-RELATED BARRIERS

Class-related barriers include socioeconomic status (SES) and how others perceive this status. Although therapists are largely members of the middle to upper class, ethnic minority groups are disproportionately represented in lower SES classes. These groups may see themselves and be seen as inferior to the upper classes. It may be difficult for therapists to understand and relate to these clients (and vice versa), and class-related characteristics may be wrongly attributed to an individual's cultural group.

In traditional psychotherapy theories, clients are expected to gain insight into the causes of their so-called abnormal behavior. Usually, when this insight is gained, clients take the time necessary to think about their motivations and behaviors. Gaining insight may not be valued by some cultures, and the process is likely to be time-consuming. Many low-SES clients do not have the luxury of this kind of time. They may only think of the here and now and do not perceive insight as an appropriate goal for their life situation. They may instead be concerned with immediate questions such as, "How can I take care of my family when my job pays minimum wage?" Transportation and funds to attend therapy sessions (especially when they take place over the long term) are additional concerns.

LANGUAGE-RELATED BARRIERS

In the United States, the language of therapy is usually monolingual, standard English. However, for culturally diverse clients, this can be a significant barrier. Clients may become frustrated during therapy when attempting to communicate in a second language. The effort required to speak grammatically correct English may come at the cost of expressing the content that the therapist is seeking. Speaking in a second language may also cause clients to express their emotions differently. Some emotion-related words that are learned in a first language may have a deeper level of meaning than the words learned in a second language. Therefore, if the expression of feelings is made in the second language, emotions associated with experiences may not be effectively expressed.

Lack of awareness of nonverbal language and its associated cultural meanings can be a barrier in psychotherapy. Nonverbal communication differences occur in the areas of proxemics (personal space), kinesics (bodily movements), paralanguage (vocal cues, e.g., vocal inflections), and high- and low-context communication. High-context communication relies heavily on nonverbal messages, whereas low-context communication relies more on verbal messages. Misunderstandings can result form differences in nonverbal messages—for example, a therapist may mistakenly assume that a Latino client's lack of eye contact is indicative of unassertiveness or depression, although the behavior may be a culturally related sign of respect.

When a therapist uses an interpreter, several problems may occur. For example, the interpreter may not translate accurately, especially when it comes to mental health concepts that vary in meaning across cultures, and there may be concerns about dual relationships and loss of confidentiality. When a family member is used as an interpreter, his or her own concerns may affect the information that is transmitted and thus the power balance. Ideally, the interpreter is trained professionally. The interpreter should be fluent in both languages and know and understand the terminology the therapist uses. Moreover, the therapist and interpreter should meet before and after a counseling session with a client to answer any questions the interpreter may have and to review the important aspects of the translation.

—*Sylvia Z. Ramirez*
—*Jessica Soto*

FURTHER READING

Atkinson, D. R. (2004). *Counseling American minorities* (6th ed.). Boston: McGraw-Hill.

Lynch, E. W., & Hanson, M. J. (2004). *Developing cross-cultural competence: A guide for working with children and their families* (3rd ed.). Baltimore: Paul H. Brookes.

Sue, D. W., & Sue, D. (1977). Barriers to effective cross-cultural counseling. *Journal of Counseling Psychology, 24*(5), 420–429.

Sue, D. W., & Sue, D. (2003). *Counseling the culturally diverse: Theory and practice* (4th ed.). New York: Wiley.

CULTURE

The term *culture* covers a wide spectrum of meanings, from physical elements in a society such as buildings and architecture to abstract and metaphorical elements such as myths, values, attitudes, and ideas about spirituality. The concept of culture is so indeterminate that it can easily be filled in with whatever preconceptions a theorist brings to it. For example, culture has been defined as knowledge, beliefs, art, morals, law, custom, and any other capabilities and habits that are acquired by individuals as members of society. Related terms such as *subculture, popular culture, counterculture, high culture, ethnic culture, organizational culture, mass culture, political culture, feminist culture,* and *deaf culture* indicate the complexity, dynamism, and evolving nature of the concept of culture within the disciplines of social scientific and humanistic study. This understanding suggests that the concept of culture, like race, is neither linear nor fixed. It must be seen as dynamic and continuously evolving, producing its own meaning in specific contexts.

Since its earliest meanings, which were derived from the Latin word *colere*—to till, cultivate, dwell, or inhabit—culture, and its close ally *colonize,* have been powerful organizing influences in producing and reproducing a dominant worldview among Europeans. In other words, the process of colonization was clearly linked to the production and reproduction of a particular culture. Its ethnological origin appears to describe a process of expressing European power through colonization, domination, subjugation, and diaspora. During this time, the noun *culture* became a verb—a doing word—through which Eurocentric ideologies were formulated to cultivate not just crops and animals, but other humans, too. This was culture representing itself as civilization.

Although there is very little agreement among cultural commentators about the meaning of culture, it is generally accepted that culture is a process that is not static but constantly changing in time and space within a society. Although individuals tend to express or display cultural traits, culture appears to be understood as a coherent or incoherent phenomenon in human society. Human beings belong to thousands of different ethnocultural groups, each of which, through the specific interaction of their biological, psychological, and cultural natures, shapes each human being in a unique way, and these interactions are transmitted from one generation to another to promote individual and group adjustments and adaptation. Therefore, all individuals are cultural beings and have a cultural, ethnic, and racial heritage that can be best described as the embodiment of a worldview learned and transmitted through beliefs, values, and practices, including religious and spiritual traditions.

However, at the same time, culture should not be treated as a global entity but should be disaggregated as far as possible into a number of discrete variables (values, ideologies, beliefs, preferences) to avoid vagueness, multiple meanings, and circular definitions.

According to Jenkins and Karnos, culture is thought to provide an orientation for a person's way of feeling, thinking, and being in the world—an unself-conscious medium of experience, interpretation, and action.

It is the universal and global characterization of culture that offers methodological difficulties when an attempt is made to link it causally to individual behavior. This latter point is particularly important in understanding cross-cultural psychology. A contemporary critique of psychiatry contends that psychiatric discourse tends to link culture with now-outdated pseudoscientific theories on race and the Western sociobiology of the culturally different client. These approaches have often resulted in particular treatments for visible minority clients, some of which are now recognized as racist.

Though culture may seem to be everything to everyone, for Helms and Cook, culture is *not* the following: (1) a person's socioracial classification; (2) skin color, which is generally used as a synonym for race; (3) nationality or citizenship status; (4) a synonym for racial identity; or (5) a necessarily conscious construct. On the other hand, Brislin has specified seven cultural criteria that are useful for making culture visible. Thus, a culture can be recognized when one can specify (1) aspects of a way of life made

by a group of people; (2) ideas transmitted from generation to generation; (3) group-related childhood experiences that result in internalized values; (4) group practices for socializing children into adulthood experiences that result in internalized values; (5) consistent group-related patterns of behavior or ways of conceptualizing events; (6) cultural patterns that are maintained despite mistakes and oversights in the system that generates them; and (7) feelings of helplessness and bewilderment among group members when cultural patterns are changed.

Finally, it is important to remember that in contemporary poststructuralist thinking or definitions of culture, the concept of multiple cultures—that is, the idea that an individual can belong to many cultures simultaneously in terms of gender, race, sexual orientation, disability, class, religion, and age—is key to the theory, research, and practice of cross-cultural psychology.

—*Roy Moodley*
—*Deone Curling*

FURTHER READING

Ahmad, W. I. U. (1996). Trouble with culture. In D. Kelleher & S. Hillier (Eds.), *Researching cultural differences in health* (pp. 190–219). London: Routledge.

American Psychological Association. (2003). *Guidelines on multicultural education training, research, practice and organizational change for psychologists: Implications for education and training, research and clinical practice.* Washington, DC: Author.

Brislin, R. W. (1990). *Applied cross-cultural psychology.* Newbury Park, CA: Sage.

Bulmer, M., and Solomos, J. (1996). Introduction: Race, ethnicity and the curriculum. *Ethnic and Racial Studies, 19,* 777–788.

Fernando, S. (1988). *Race and culture in psychiatry.* London: Croom Helm.

CULTURE-BOUND SYNDROMES

Researchers refer to *culture-bound syndromes,* also called *culture-related psychiatric disorders,* by a variety of terms, such as *ethnic psychoses, ethnic neurosis, rare, unclassifiable, collective, and exotic syndromes,* and *atypical culture-bound reactive syndromes.* More recently, culture-bound syndromes have been defined as the development of a unique psychopathology or a collection of signs and symptoms that are observed only in a certain cultural environment.

Culture-bound syndromes present a particular challenge to clinicians, particularly in the area of diagnosis. There is a long debate in the literature about the role of biology and culture in the development of culture-bound syndromes, whether such behavior is universal or locally unique, and whether episodes are "normal" culturally based behavior or examples of "authentic" diseases and disorders. Similar questions include whether culture-bound syndromes are stable over time, whether they are truly distinct entities with commonalties across certain cultures, and whether there are common denominators among the syndromes. Other questions concern whether culture-bound syndromes should be viewed as part of all diagnostic categories of psychiatric illness or as static, bound entities.

The last few decades have witnessed an increased interest in culture-bound syndromes. However, their treatment in diagnostic classification systems has gained attention only in the last several years. Despite the history of culture-bound syndromes in the literature, culture-bound syndromes were not included in the psychiatric diagnostic system of the *Diagnostic and Statistical Manual of Mental Disorders* until the fourth revision in 1994 (*DSM-IV*). The *DSM-IV* includes a list of 25 culture-bound syndromes in Appendix I of the text.

COMMON CULTURE-BOUND SYNDROMES

Common culture-bound syndromes include *ataque de nervios* and *koro*. Ataque de nervios is an expression of distress that is particularly prominent among Latinos from the Caribbean. Commonly reported symptoms include uncontrollable shouting, crying, trembling, heat in the chest rising into the head, and aggression. Ataque de nervios is typically understood as an expression of adult women and often occurs as a direct result of a stressful family-related event. There appear to be similarities between some conventional diagnoses and the culture-bound syndromes. For example, researchers have identified the comorbidity of ataque de nervios with a range of anxiety and affective disorders.

Koro is commonly reported in areas of South and East Asia and refers to an episode of sudden and intense anxiety that one's sexual organs will recede into the body. Epidemics have been reported in Singapore, Thailand, India, and China. Koro is more commonly reported in men, but it has also been recognized among women. This syndrome may be related to the traditional Chinese concepts of yin and yang (balance theory), which assert that losing harmony between yin and yang can lead to somatic or mental disorders or even death.

LIMITATIONS OF DIAGNOSTIC CLASSIFICATION SYSTEMS

Ontological, phenomenological, and categorical problems with the inclusion of culture-bound syndromes in diagnostic classification systems have been raised. It is not clear whether culture-bound syndromes are distinctly different from conventional syndromes or just semantically and categorically different. Similarly, some argue that culture-bound syndromes are not restricted to specific cultures but are widely distributed. Many syndromes that have been described as culture bound comprise combinations of symptoms that have been observed universally. Culture-bound syndromes lack diagnostic uniformity and validity, making it difficult to attain universal descriptive criteria to describe these illnesses because of problems in language.

DIRECTIONS FOR FUTURE CLASSIFICATION AND RESEARCH OF CULTURE-BOUND SYNDROMES

One major challenge to classification systems is that, at the sociocultural level, the same distress reactions may be expressed differently as a result of cultural cues, language differences, and variations in experience. Additionally, some have noted that all classifications, including Western classification systems (such as the *DSM*), are examples of a cultural structuring of human behavior and knowledge regarding illness. Thus, the attempt to classify culture-bound syndromes, whether as distinct syndromes or as part of already classified illnesses, is an activity that is inextricably tied to culture. Additionally, several authors have specified the ways that culture and social processes limit the development of an internationally valid system of diagnosis.

It has been suggested that examining the context and symbolic structure of cultural reactions may yield a better classification of culture-bound syndromes than merely recording symptoms. The full symptom profile of each disorder—rather than a few predominant symptoms—is necessary to understand culture-bound syndromes. In addition, more attention to social factors, intracultural heterogeneity, and the way culture and other socioidentities (such as gender) interact can provide even better explanations of how culture-bound syndromes fit into diagnostic systems. As such, the culture-bound syndromes illustrate a generic way to think about the relationship between psychiatric illness and cultural context rather than viewing them as separate, bounded entities.

—*Julie R. Ancis*

FURTHER READING

Guarnaccia, P., & Rogler, L. (1999). Research on culture-bound syndromes: New directions. *American Journal of Psychiatry, 156*(9), 1322–1327.
Kirmayer, L. J. (1998). The fate of culture in DSM-IV. *Transcultural Psychiatry, 35,* 339–342.
Mezzich, J. E., Berganza, C. E., & Ruiperez, M. A. (2001). Culture in DSM-IV, ICD-10, and evolving diagnostic systems: Cultural psychiatry; International perspectives. *Psychiatric Clinics of North America, 24,* 407–419.

CULTURE-BOUND SYNDROMES: AMOK

The West was first introduced to *amok* through the journals of Captain Cook, although the history of the disorder dates back much further as a Hindu war tactic. Amok is a Malaysian term that means "to engage furiously in battle." Amok occurs only in males. The disorder is usually precipitated by an event such as the loss of a companion, the loss of economic or social prestige, or a perceived or actual insult. A period of brooding follows, after which the person commits apparently purposeless homicidal attacks on individuals in close proximity until he is restrained, killed, or exhausted. Following the rampage, the person has complete amnesia of the events. Amok is qualitatively different from other forms of homicide in that a larger number of people are killed or injured; the attack often occurs in a more crowded location; the choice of weapons may be different; the individual has often experienced a recent loss (e.g., spouse or job); and the act is often committed at certain times of day (e.g., weekends and between 7:00 p.m. and midnight). Alcohol use before the event is also more prevalent. One final distinguishing factor that is particularly important is that suicide is more likely during or after the event.

This disorder was first identified in Malaysia and was thought to be indigenous to that area. It is so well established in the Malaysian culture that Malaysian police have an amok device (a two-pronged stick) that is used to pin the individual to a wall in order to avoid coming within striking distance of him, killing him, or being injured themselves. However, research suggests that amok can and does occur in other countries, such as Laos, the Philippines, Polynesia, Papua New Guinea, Puerto Rico, and even the United States. Certain acts of random violence (e.g., school shootings and office shootings) may actually be presentations of an American version of amok.

Although amok is a fairly well-known phenomenon in Malaysia, it appears to be fairly rare. For example, over 11 years (1958–1969), researchers identified 24 cases of amok. Furthermore, there is the possibility of misidentifying amok. There appears to be a significant amount of psychopathology comorbid with amok, specifically, schizophrenia, bipolar disorder, and depression. One survey of the literature showed that all had comorbid disorders such as schizophrenia or bipolar disorder. Yet no discernible pattern could be ascertained, and the researchers concluded that comorbidity does not preclude amok from being a genuine phenomenon.

The underlying causes of amok run the gamut from infectious disease to an increased psychological susceptibility to hurt others. One theory that has been posited is that Malaysian culture indirectly causes this manifestation. In the Malaysian culture, passivity, lack of confrontation, and obedience are heavily stressed. This theory proposes that such a social structure does not allow for the adequate expression of anger. In certain people, this may manifest as amok, which is socially explainable (in the same way that insanity is socially explainable). Amok incidents tend to increase during times of political and economic unrest. This suggests that during times of famine, recession, or other large-scale national problems, amok will increase in response to these stressors.

—*Michael Gomez*

FURTHER READING

Schmidt, K., Hill, L., & Guthrie, G. (1977). Running amok. *International Journal of Social Psychiatry, 23*(4), 264–274.
Tseung, W. S. (2003). *Clinician's guide to cultural psychiatry.* San Diego: Academic Press.
Westermeyer, J. (1973). On the epidemicity of amok violence. *Archives of General Psychiatry, 28*(6), 873–876.

CULTURE-BOUND SYNDROMES: ATAQUE DE NERVIOS

Ataque de nervios is a culture-bound syndrome that occurs most often in Latino cultures of the Caribbean, but it is also associated with other Latino cultures. Its literal translation is "attack of the nerves."

The symptoms of ataque de nervios are transient in nature and typically occur suddenly in response to a severe psychosocial stressor. Symptoms include impulsive, dramatic behaviors such as screaming uncontrollably, crying, trembling and nervousness, anger and violence, and breaking things. Less common symptoms include seizure-like behavior, fainting, suicidal behavior, and dissociative experiences such as localized amnesia of events. Finally, brief psychotic symptoms such as incoherence, auditory hallucinations, and visual hallucinations have been documented during ataque de nervios episodes.

The occurrence of ataque de nervios in Caribbean Latinos appears to be relatively common. For example, it has been estimated that 13.8% of adults in Puerto Rico have experienced an ataque de nervios.

A number of sociodemographic factors are associated with ataque de nervios. Ataque episodes are more prevalent among women, individuals over the age of 45, individuals from lower socioeconomic backgrounds, and individuals who are widowed, separated, or divorced. In addition, ataques are associated with the loss of family support related to migration, conflicts with a partner, and the death of a loved one.

Episodes of ataque de nervios are also linked to the presence of psychiatric disorders. For example, in one study of Puerto Rican adults with ataque, 63% of the individuals met the criteria for a psychiatric disorder. Individuals with ataque were 4.35 times more likely to have a psychiatric disorder than individuals without ataque. Specifically, individuals with ataque report higher levels of mood disorders, including major depression and dysthymic disorder, and higher levels of anxiety disorders, including panic disorder, generalized anxiety disorder, agoraphobia, and other phobic disorders.

The expression of ataque de nervios appears to be influenced by coexisting mental disorders. For example, individuals with mood disorders report more anger, screaming, aggression, and breaking things when experiencing an ataque. On the other hand, individuals with panic disorder report more feelings of suffocation, fear of dying, and increased fear during their ataques.

Finally, a higher frequency of ataques de nervios has been found in individuals who experienced childhood physical or sexual trauma than in individuals who did not experience childhood trauma.

Clinicians who have clients reporting symptoms of ataque de nervios should carefully explore these correlates to thoroughly understand their clients' difficulties and to derive appropriate treatment plans.

—*Joseph D. Hovey*

FURTHER READING

Guarnaccia, P. J., Lewis-Fernández, R., & Marano, M. R. (2003). Toward a Puerto Rican nosology: Nervios and ataque de nervios. *Culture, Medicine and Psychiatry, 27,* 339–366.

Lopez, S. R., & Guarnaccia, P. J. (2000). Cultural psychopathology: Uncovering the social world of mental illness. *Annual Review of Psychology, 51,* 571–598.

Schechter, D. S., Marshall, R., Salmán, E., Goetz, D., Davies, S., & Liebowitz, M. R. (2000). Ataque de nervios and history of childhood trauma. *Journal of Traumatic Stress, 13,* 529–534.

CULTURE-BOUND SYNDROMES: BILIS, COLERA

Bilis and *colera* refer literally to bile or gall, but also to a Latino culture-bound syndrome in which physical illness is brought on by suppressed emotions or an uncontrolled emotional outburst, such as *coraje* (anger). For individuals who are characterized by an angry personality, constant irritability generates excessive bile and produces phlegm in the stomach. *Un derrame de bilis* (a spillage of bile, producing a type of emotional shock), left untreated, can create digestive problems and physical, emotional, mental, and spiritual toxicity in the individual. Excessive bile that is released throughout the body causes dysentery, liver ailments (such as cirrhosis and hepatitis), digestive conditions, and nervous breakdown. Protection from illness comes to those who become physically and mentally strong and who are neutral with their emotions.

Though it is believed that most cases are caused by a strong, sudden outburst, a person may also contract *bilis* if he or she has an angry disposition that constantly produces excessive bile and fails to purge on a regular basis. Symptoms include loss of appetite, headache, heartburn, inflammation of the stomach, yellowish eyes and stool, nausea with a strong desire to vomit, a sour or bitter mouth, unclean tongue, and bad breath. Aroused bile, according to the indigenous medical system, is considered a "hot" illness that is treated with "cold" remedies (drinking bitter teas, such as *estafiate*), dietary modifications, and psychotherapeutic treatment. Retraining the patient to express his or her emotions is a vital therapeutic intervention that teaches the avoidance of aggression and irritability in emotional expression but allows the patient to remain in control.

Uncontrolled rage can cause yet another culture-bound syndrome, *susto* (soul loss), in someone who witnesses a violent fit of rage. Bilis can lead to incidences of domestic violence and abuse. It is not only a Latino or ethnic condition but is found in all parts of the world. It is a social condition that is emotionally and energetically based, not a crisis that is based in superstition, culture, or ethnicity. It is important to understand its social and health implications.

Although this ailment is not currently understood in the pathological or psychological paradigms of classic medicine, it is part of the medical repertoire of traditional medicine, which believes that the adequate functioning of bodily organs such as the heart, liver, and lungs is greatly influenced by one's emotional state. Negative emotions and perceptions such as anger, rage, envy, greed, sadness, resentment, hate, vanity, intolerance, bitterness, pride, hypocrisy, and fear— which are all definite forms of energy—play a fundamental role in the creation of blocked energies. A curse, bad thought, feeling, emotion, word, or action can be toxic to the individual soul, poisoning every atom of the soul and producing discordant and unharmonious tones in the individual. Negative feelings, which consume a great deal of vital energy through the process of energetic metabolism, create larger amounts of unhealthy, wasted energy. When the production of these negative energies exceeds the body's capacity for distribution and elimination, negativity accumulates in a corresponding organ, clogging vital energy in important energy centers and initiating the physical disease process. Emotional outbursts are transmuted to the physical body, creating fertile ground for the development of disease.

Ignoring important facts—for example, that individual emotions absorb and emit energy at all times through feelings, thoughts, words, and actions—has prevented classic medicine from considering this symbiotic aspect of human energy, thoughts, and emotions in the pathological disease process.

—*Sandra Nuñez*

FURTHER READING

Avila, E. (1999). *Woman who glows in the dark.* New York: Tarcher/Putman.

Garcia, H., Sierra, A., & Balam, G. (1996). *Medicina Maya tradicional: Confrontación con el sistema conceptual chino* [Maya medicine and Oriental medicine: A comparative review]. Campeche, Mexico: Educe.

CULTURE-BOUND SYNDROMES: BRAIN FAG

Brain fag syndrome (BFS), first identified by Raymond Prince in 1960, is described in the *Diagnostic and Statistical Manual of Mental Disorders,* 4th edition, as a culture-bound syndrome that is endemic to West Africa. It is an anxiety disorder in which somatic symptoms, primarily involving heat or crawling sensations in the head, are caused by excessive intellectual effort. Other symptoms include difficulty concentrating, appearing tense and unhappy, and sleep disturbances. Most symptoms are associated with or exacerbated by attempting to study or, in more severe cases, attempting to read any printed material. Specifically, the disorder is thought to occur when non-Westerners are educated in a Western system.

Since BFS was first identified, it has been found across sub-Saharan Africa from Nigeria to Uganda and South Africa. It has also been found among Africans studying in Britain and in Ethiopian immigrants to Israel.

Although one study indicated that BFS is correlated with borderline-level intelligence, several later studies have contradicted this result. Other possible correlates include coming from a poorer home, having a greater frequency of past serious illness, exhibiting greater anxiety about school success, and seeing parents as intolerant of failure. Some researchers have suggested that males experience higher rates of BFS than females, but others have argued that this result can be attributed to the greater number of male students pursuing higher education in Africa rather than to gender. Overall, there is a consensus that both study-related and psychosocial stressors influence the development and maintenance of BFS.

Prince has suggested two theories to explain the development of BFS. The first is the "forbidden knowledge theory," which holds that the person unconsciously believes that gaining Western knowledge is a betrayal of traditional African knowledge. The second theory is the psychophysiological theory, which argues that BFS is the result of learning in a second language and associated stressors such as lack of sleep and the use of stimulants to enable late nights of studying.

More recently, some have questioned the validity of BFS as a separate and unique disorder. Detractors cite the similarity of its root symptoms to anxiety disorders, sometimes with an additional component of depressive symptomatology. They also state that in most cases, similar medications are effective in treating both BFS and anxiety disorders. Finally, R. O. Jegede reported in 1983 that BFS symptoms can be found in those who are illiterate and are not primarily engaged in intellectual activity. Olufemi Morakinyo and Karl Peltzer found in 2002 that those in apprentice training experienced BFS, even though this is an African rather than a Western method of teaching.

However, those who support defining BFS as a separate disorder argue that its unique somatic symptoms accurately identify those with this manifestation of anxiety. Therefore, individuals with this symptomatology can receive appropriate treatment. Prince also suggested in 1985 that African culture may require physical symptoms before a person is permitted to be ill. Furthermore, the most common illnesses in Africa involve fever (e.g., malaria) and crawling sensations (e.g., worms), which may explain why the somatic symptoms of BFS involve heat or crawling sensations.

Relaxation training and group therapy, working in tandem, have been reported as effective treatments for BFS. The relaxation piece is considered the most important component of the therapeutic regimen, a logical finding as BFS is an anxiety disorder.

—*Sara Corbin*

FURTHER READING

Jegede, R. O. (1983). Psychiatric illness in African students: "Brain fag" syndrome revisited. *Canadian Journal of Psychiatry, 28,* 188–192.

Minde, K. K. (1974). Study problems in Ugandan secondary school students: A controlled evaluation. *British Journal of Psychiatry, 125,* 131–137.

Morakinyo, O., & Peltzer, K. (2002). "Brain fag" syndrome in apprentices in Nigeria. *Psychopathology, 35,* 362–366.

CULTURE-BOUND SYNDROMES: DHAT

Dhat syndrome, a term first introduced by N. Wig in 1960, is a culture-bound syndrome of India and its surrounding areas in which men believe they are physically or mentally ill because of the excessive loss of semen. This syndrome is most common among young men and is attributed to excessive masturbation, nocturnal emissions, or premarital or extramarital sexual activity.

The belief that semen is vital to both physical and spiritual health stems from the Hindu religion. Hindus believe that 40 meals create one drop of blood, 40 drops of blood create one drop of marrow, and 40 drops of marrow create one drop of semen. The implication of this process is that the loss of semen is detrimental to one's health. Although the idea that semen loss can be harmful is not unique to the Indian subcontinent, it seems particularly strong in that region.

Common symptoms of dhat syndrome include anxiety or depression, preoccupation, sleep difficulties, sexual dysfunction, exhaustion, headache, loss of appetite, and opaque urine, which the patient believes to contain semen. Other correlates include being a young male, being unmarried or recently married, coming from a rural background, and having a family with particularly conservative views concerning sexual activity.

It is unclear whether the somatic complaints or affective symptoms of dhat syndrome occur before or after the patient begins to believe that his sexual activity has become detrimental to his health or begins to feel guilt over his actions. One case study found that the patient's sexual activity was followed by warnings from friends and family that his actions would be harmful, and these warnings were followed by somatic complaints and anxiety. Regardless of this finding, the etiology of dhat syndrome remains unknown.

It has been suggested that dhat syndrome could be classified as an undifferentiated somatoform disorder according to the criteria listed in the *Diagnostic and Statistical Manual of Mental Disorders,* 4th edition. Dhat syndrome commonly occurs in patients from rural backgrounds and with less education. Therefore, it may be classified as an anxiety or depressive disorder, conditions that are often expressed somatically in non-Western societies.

Some descriptive reports indicate that dhat syndrome often remits within six months to a year. Others report that education to teach patients that semen loss is harmless or cognitive behavioral therapy are effective treatments. However, because these studies did not include a control group and because dhat syndrome has been shown to remit spontaneously, the efficacy of these treatments remains unclear.

One study looked at two groups of patients with dhat syndrome, one that received medication only and one that received both medication and supportive psychotherapy. Though both groups improved, the combination-treatment group saw greater improvement. However, this single study did not include a control group; therefore, further investigation into these treatment modalities is needed.

Finally, regardless of the treatment used, the therapist or physician is cautioned against immediately confronting the patient's inaccurate beliefs about semen loss. Such disregard for cultural beliefs is the primary cause of the high drop-out rates among dhat syndrome patients.

—Sara Corbin

FURTHER READING

Kulhara, P., & Avasthi, A. (1995). Sexual dysfunction on the Indian subcontinent. *International Review of Psychiatry, 7,* 231–240.

Paris, J. (1992). Dhat: The semen loss anxiety syndrome. *Transcultural Psychiatric Research Review, 29,* 109–116.

Shukla, P. R., & Singh, R. H. (2000). Supportive psychotherapy in dhat syndrome patients. *Journal of Personality and Clinical Studies, 16,* 49–52.

CULTURE-BOUND SYNDROMES: FALLING OUT, BLACKING OUT

The anthropological literature describes traditional ways that African Americans express psychiatric distress and other forms of emotions. Data gathered through clinical case reports, in-depth household interviews, and a review of emergency services records in the city of Miami all point to *falling out* as a culture-bound syndrome. *Falling out* is the general term used to describe variations of a syndrome that are believed to be functionally equivalent: falling out, blacking out, and indisposition. *Falling out* and *blacking out* are terms used most often in the southern United States, whereas *indisposition* is the term used in Haiti.

Falling out is conceptualized as a dissociative reaction that is associated with constricted consciousness and designed to cope with anxiety. The most common descriptions note a sudden collapse or fainting spell that may be preceded by dizziness or "swimming in the head." The syndrome may occur with or without warning. Individuals who report falling out indicate an awareness of their surroundings, although some report an inability to move. Some individuals claim they are unable to see, although their eyes are open and there is no indication of physical impairment. An analysis of emergency services data from Miami suggests that the syndrome is not the result of chronic organic illness (it can be differentiated from illnesses such as epilepsy) but a psychological reaction to specific stressors.

Falling out is not treated as an illness until or unless it becomes disabling. Falling out is viewed as a reasonable response when attending a funeral or receiving shocking news, and it has been described as common in stressful school situations and very hot weather. Episodes of such behavior have been noted during religious services and ceremonies. Falling out is reportedly tolerated in the context of intense anger, rage, or fear. Falling out episodes prevent the individual from completing an undesirable or harmful act in response to intense anger. In the context of trauma, episodes may become chronic and thus debilitating because they interfere with employment and life functioning. Finally, falling out has also been noted in the context of inner-city life, particularly when multiple stressors such as overcrowding, high crime, and financial concerns are present.

It is not known how widely this syndrome occurs among African Americans because the existing prevalence data are based on studies conducted during the 1970s. However, the data support the hypothesis that falling out is more prevalent among people of African descent living in the United States than among other ethnic groups. Estimates indicate a prevalence of 23% among Bahamian households and 10% among southern African American households in Miami. Studies also suggest that most Haitians report having known someone who has fallen out.

The relationship between help-seeking behavior and patterns of psychological and physical distress similar to falling out (anxiety and somatic symptoms) has been explored. An association between anxiety and somatic symptoms as a characteristic idiom of distress has been demonstrated; these symptoms have a stronger association with help-seeking behavior among African Americans than among European Americans. Efforts to initiate group and network therapy for cases of falling out conceptualized in this way have failed.

—Vetta L. Sanders Thompson

FURTHER READING

Lefley, H. P. (1979). Prevalence of potential falling-out cases among the Black, Latin and non-Latin White populations of the city of Miami. *Social Science and Medicine, 13B,* 113–114.

Snowden, L. R. (1999). African American folk idiom and mental health service use. *Cultural Diversity and Ethnic Minority Psychology, 5,* 364–370.

Weidman, H. H. (1979). Falling-out: A diagnostic and treatment problem viewed from a transcultural perspective. *Social Science and Medicine, 13B,* 95–112.

CULTURE-BOUND SYNDROMES: GHOST SICKNESS

Ghost sickness is an illness found in many Native American cultures and characterized by a preoccupation with death. Found in tribes from the Southwest and Southern Plains, it is characterized by an intense fear of ghosts and results in the development of elaborate rituals to defend against these spirits of death. These cultures believe that after death, a vital force or spirit containing good qualities and elements that control the individual's impulses exits the body. Upon death, this spirit is believed to move toward heaven or toward the sky, leaving behind its evil or rage to wander the earth. These cultures believe that the final destination of ghosts is an afterworld—but sometimes, the ghosts do not want to reach this destination because they feel the loneliness of those who are in mourning or experience loneliness themselves for the loss of family, home, or possessions. In some cultures, ghost sickness is believed to be very dangerous; the ghosts of the recently departed are believed to cause illness or even death among the living.

Although ghosts are believed to cause other illnesses, the most common is known as ghost sickness. Ghost sickness is thought to be caused by the touch of a ghost, who comes up behind an individual and tries to pull him or her back. The individual hears a sound as he or she feels the touch of the ghost and is immediately overwhelmed by terror. If the individual turns to look over his or her shoulder, it is believed that the right side of the body will be twisted into a spasmodic palsy or muscular spasm. Symptoms of ghost sickness include cannibalistic fantasies, epileptiform spells, and eating and psychological disturbances. Other symptoms may also include weakness, dizziness, hallucinations, feelings of danger, and anxiety.

To avoid ghost sickness, some cultures take measures to ensure that the recently deceased cannot find their way back to the home in which they lived. For individuals who are already suffering from the illness, treatment consists of gathering the family together to perform peyote ceremonies.

—Lana Beasley

FURTHER READING

Freeman, D. M., Foulks, E. F., & Freeman, P. A. (1976a). Ghost sickness and superego development in the Kiowa Apache male. *Psychoanalytic Study of Society, 71,* 123–171.

Freeman, D. M., Foulks, E. F., & Freeman, P. A. (1976b). Superego development and psychopathology. *Psychoanalytic Study of Society, 71,* 107–122.

CULTURE-BOUND SYNDROMES: HWA-BYUNG

Hwa-byung (from *hwa,* meaning fire, and *byung,* meaning disease) is a Korean folk illness precipitated by a situation that is beyond the power of one's control. Literally, the term means "an illness of fire." It is categorized as a Korean culture-bound syndrome and translates to anger syndrome in the *Diagnostic and Statistical Manual of Mental Disorders,* 4th edition, because its recurrent and specific symptom patterns and pathogenesis do not correspond to a particular diagnostic mental disorder category. The prevalence of hwa-byung is reported to be 4.2% in the general population of Korea and 4.95% among middle-aged Korean women.

DYNAMIC MECHANISMS OF HWA-BYUNG

The dynamic mechanisms of hwa-byung can be explained differently depending on one's perspective. In Western medicine, hwa-byung is defined as a chronic psychosomatic illness that results from the incomplete suppression of anger or the projection of anger into the body. The emotion of *hwa* is different from that of anger in terms of its duration. Though anger may be characterized as a one-time emotion, *hwa* is characterized by an accumulation over a long period of time. *Hwa* is a complex mix of emotions, including frustration, anxiety, mortification, anger, apprehension, and disappointment, that has physical manifestations.

In Eastern medicine, hwa-byung is defined as an illness related to disharmony between the vital energy (*ki*) and the *fire;* an illness with the patterns of *hwa;* an illness related to the *hwa* concept in Chinese medicine (neurosis and psychosomatism); or an illness caused by a disturbance in the balance between yin (negative force) and yang (positive force).

SYMPTOMS

The major psychological and emotional reactions etiologically related to hwa-byung are feelings of mortification, dissatisfaction, worry, anger, pessimism, depression, hatred, *hahn* (in Korean), anxiety, nervousness, regret, loneliness, fear, disgust, guilt, and shame. *Hahn,* a unique emotion among the Korean people, signifies a unique, depression-like affective state that results from chronic suppression and frustration. Major physical symptoms include feeling oppressed (stuffy in the chest), sighing, palpitations, sensations of heat, headache heaviness, feeling of pushing up in the chest, insomnia, localized or generalized pain, dry mouth, epigastric mass, indigestion, anorexia, dizziness, paresthesia, nausea, constipation, blurred vision, cold sensations, and cold sweats. Behavioral symptoms include talkativeness, loss of interest, impulsive need to leave, absent-mindedness, short-temperedness, paranoia, and suicidal ideas. In addition, patients with hwa-byung tend to use anger as a defense mechanism more frequently.

MEDICAL TREATMENTS

Medical treatments for hwa-byung are still under development. Antidepressive or antianxiety medications are used in Western medicine, and acupuncture for some meridian points, particularly Tanzhong (REN-17, directing the meridian point of the middle of the chest), are used in Eastern medicine. However, these treatments have transitory positive effects in the acute stage of hwa-byung and require repeated medical interventions. Many studies are ongoing to find a clear answer to the medical treatment of hwa-byung.

—*Young-Joo Park*

FURTHER READING

Kim, J. W. (2004). Hwabyung in oriental medicine. *Behavioral Science in Medicine, 3*(1), 103–107.

Min, S. K. (2004). Cultural relatedness of hwabyung and beyond. *Behavioral Science in Medicine, 3*(1), 97–102.

CULTURE-BOUND SYNDROMES: KORO

Koro is a Malay-Indonesian term meaning "turtle's head." It describes a psychiatric, nonpsychotic syndrome involving an acute, panic-like anxiety about the penis receding into the abdomen. This is accompanied by belief that total disappearance of the penis will cause death. In Chinese cultures, koro is also termed *Suoyang, Shuk Yang,* or *Shook Yong,* although numerous alternative terms exist within the Chinese language. Examples in other cultures include *Jinjinia Bemar* (Assam) and *Rok-Joo* (Thailand).

Symptoms of koro include considerable anxiety about the penis, particularly its size and shape, and substantial fears about impotence or impending death. The symptoms of koro have been compared to those of hypochondriasis and body dysmorphic disorder, as well as a range of anxiety and sexual disorders. Sufferers often express somatic complaints about the area around the genitals and abdomen. Typical koro patients are young single males from low educational backgrounds in Asian countries; however, koro (or at least symptoms of the syndrome) has also been reported in African, European, Middle Eastern, and North American countries. Females may experience symptoms of koro that concern the nipples, breasts, vulva, labia, or tongue receding into the body. Prepubertal males report fearing the nose or ears will recede into the body.

Because koro (or at least its symptoms) is a universal disorder, it has been termed *genital retraction syndrome,* indicating that it may not be culture bound but rather a culture-related psychiatric disorder. However, this classification is the subject of much debate. Consequently, researchers attempt to discriminate between koro syndrome, koro-like symptoms, and koro presentation during epidemics. Koro syndrome, in its classic form, is distinguished primarily by the panic-like fear of death, and the etiology involves Chinese medical views, traditional folk beliefs, and superstitions regarding human sexuality and evil spirits. Alternatively, koro-like symptoms usually include only fear of the genitals retracting or shrinking and may be caused by a number of factors, including guilt over perceived sexual transgression, fear after hearing of koro's occurrence, lack of self-esteem, dependent personality, psychotic features, inexperience in sexual relationships, and lack of masculinity. In addition, the use or abuse of illicit drugs or psychotropic medications and some tumors or strokes occurring in specific areas of the brain have elicited koro-like symptoms. Finally, koro epidemics, which have been reported in Singapore, India, China, Thailand, and Nigeria, are considered the result of panic that spreads following the occurrence of koro in one or more individuals within the same geographic area. However, investigators have noted a coincidence of widespread social tension during koro epidemics, implying that prevalent anxiety may be an underlying characteristic.

Folk treatments for koro involve drinking hot substances, creating noise to chase away spirits, and clamping weight cases to the genitals. Common psychiatric treatments include educational counseling and reassurance, behavioral therapies, cognitive therapies combined with religious instruction, and general attention to the sufferer's self-image, self-confidence, or perceived lack of masculinity. Reports indicate that electroconvulsive therapy, modified doses of insulin, and selective serotonin reuptake inhibitors also decrease symptoms. In many cases, treatment decisions are based on whether the patient is suffering from koro in its traditional form, koro-like symptoms, or koro during an epidemic. Outcomes are generally good, especially for those suffering only symptoms and those suffering koro during an epidemic. However, koro can be chronic, typically in cases in which the patient believes the syndrome is caused by culturally based folklore or superstition.

—*John L. Powell III*

FURTHER READING

Chowdhury, A. N. (1998). Hundred years of koro: The history of a culture-bound syndrome. *International Journal of Social Psychiatry, 44,* 181–188.

Kovacs, A., & Osvath, P. (1998). Koro (genital retraction syndrome): A symptom or a disease? *Psychiatria Danubina, 10,* 45–51.

CULTURE-BOUND SYNDROMES: LATAH

Latah is a condition in which, after experiencing a sudden shock or fright, a person suddenly displays an altered state of consciousness with abnormal levels of suggestibility. While in this state, individuals will follow the commands of people around them. They will often repeat the words (*echolalia*) and actions of others (*echopraxia*). In addition, they may display other socially inappropriate behaviors, such as singing out loud, saying sexually explicit words, and touching or hitting other people. A latah attack may last minutes or hours depending on the frequency of provoking stimuli. Afterward, the individual has no memory of the events that took place during the episode.

This syndrome is most prevalent among middle-aged Malaysian women. However, similar conditions have been found in Burma (*yaun*), Thailand (*bahtsche*), and the Philippines (*mali-mali*), among Siberian indigenous tribes (*myriachit*), and among the Ainu of Japan (*imo*). There is some debate as to whether this syndrome has been found in Western cultures as well (e.g., Jumping Frenchmen of Maine syndrome).

The etiology of the syndrome is unknown. Some individuals develop latah reactions with no identifiable preceding event. Conversely, others report developing the syndrome after a stressful event, such as the death of a loved one, in association with a startling stimulus that induces the initial dissociative state. In cases of severe latah, the reaction becomes habituated so that any startling stimulus, such as being surprised, tickled, or poked in the ribs, will trigger the dissociative response.

There is controversy as to whether latah is an actual illness or an unusual behavioral response. Field studies have shown that very few individuals with the disorder seek treatment. In addition, there are no documented traditional remedies for latah, suggesting that it is not viewed as an illness within Malay-Indonesian culture. Therefore, Western physicians may be responsible for pathologizing the behavior. Some theorists have suggested that latah may be a Malay-Indonesian idiom through which malingered symptoms are exploited for social purposes. They describe latah as a mechanism by which lower-status individuals can demonstrate socially inappropriate behavior in a culturally acceptable manner. This behavior may also be seen as an attention-seeking device.

The "malingering symptoms" hypothesis is supported by findings that indicate individuals who display latah symptoms seem to exhibit some restraint in their behavior. For example, there are no authenticated reports that latah attacks have ever resulted in murder, injury, or other dangerous acts. In addition, blasphemies against Islam are never uttered, which would be considered unacceptable in Malay culture. These findings suggest that latah behavior is consciously monitored on some level.

Opponents of this view propose a biopsychosocial model to explain latah, arguing that both biological and cultural elements have an etiological influence on its development. Researchers note that throughout the human population, some individuals can be identified as hypersensitive to being startled because of small neurophysiological discrepancies. Furthermore, social factors influence how these reactions are manifested. Therefore, latah is a culture-specific exploitation of a peculiar physiological response. This model resolves what is known as the *latah paradox:* If latah is an artifact of Malay-Indonesian culture, why can similar symptoms be found in many diverse and geographically distal cultures? Proponents of such theories argue that latah symptoms result from core features that can be found in a variety of cultures, each of which adds its own cultural elements.

—*John-Paul Legerski*

FURTHER READING

Bartholomew, R. E. (1994). Disease, disorder, or deception? Latah as habit in a Malay extended family. *Journal of Nervous and Mental Disease, 6,* 331–338.

Simons, R. C. (1994). The interminable debate on the nature of latah. *Journal of Nervous and Mental Disease, 6,* 339–341.

CULTURE-BOUND SYNDROMES: MAL DE OJO

Mal de ojo is a Spanish term for the *evil eye,* used most often in Spain and in Latin American countries of Hispanic descent. It is a folk belief, disease, or syndrome that is represented by an admiring look, a glance, or a voiced compliment and is believed to inflict injury or damage on the person, place, or thing that is the object of the gaze. Mal de ojo is one of the most widespread cultural beliefs and has many variations throughout the world.

The origins of this belief extend to the Old Testament, and it is found in Europe, the Mediterranean countries, India, and some parts of Asia. There is evidence of this belief in Hebrew writings, as well as in artifacts found in the south of Italy and in Sicily.

It is believed that most humans have the power to cast mal de ojo onto others and that the spell can be cast without one's knowledge. Some people may be more aware of their power and use it to protect or inflict damage. The most widespread uses of mal de ojo include envy, jealousy, greed, and retaliation.

Individuals who are most vulnerable to the consequences of mal de ojo include those of younger age, pregnant women, females, those with good health status, and the beautiful. Vulnerability lies in the propensity to attract the gaze from unsuspecting admirers or from malicious people in possession of the power. Based on these vulnerabilities, protection is gained from amulets, talismans, and rituals. For example, it is believed that when complimenting a child, phrases such as "God bless you" have a protective effect. In some Caribbean cultures, it is believed that the possession of a round black stone or the symbol of a pointing index finger is protective. These items are often given to newborn children as gifts to protect them from mal de ojo.

In other cultures, a talisman with an eye is considered protective. Particularly in some areas of the Mediterranean, possession of an amulet in the shape of horns or a hand with two extended fingers is considered protective. In still other parts of the world, the colors red and blue have traditional significance and serve as protection. Finally, on the islands of Malta and Gozo, the sign of the eye is drawn on the prow of boats for protection.

The range of symptoms associated with being cursed by mal de ojo include, but are not limited to, diarrhea, vomiting, crying, loss of appetite, and fever.

It is believed that once the mal de ojo is cast, the victim can only be treated by healers or by those with the knowledge, appropriate ritual training, and status to reverse its effects—often laypeople of Christian belief who invoke the power of the Holy Trinity. Tools for diagnosis and treatment include oils, anointed waters, and holy words. Rituals often include chanting and gestures in the sign of the holy cross.

—*Miriam Helen Feliu*
—*Christopher L. Edwards*

FURTHER READING

Franco, J. A., & Pecci, C. (2003). Physician-patient relationship, scientific medicine and alternative therapies. *Medicina, 63*(2), 111–118.

Lopez De Letona, C. (2000). On evil eye and its remedies. *Archivos de la Sociedad Española de Oftalmología, 75*(5), 359–360.

Weller, S. C., & Baer, R. D. (2001). Intra- and intercultural variation in the definition of five illnesses: AIDS, diabetes, the common cold, empacho and mal de ojo. *Cross-Cultural Research, 35*(2), 201–226.

CULTURE-BOUND SYNDROMES: NERVIOS

The way individuals interpret and express their emotions is influenced by culture. *Nervios* is a term used within Latino cultures to describe emotional responses to stressful life events. It is important to recognize that the meaning of the term *nervios* varies across Latino subcultures (e.g., Puerto Rican, Mexican, South American) and is influenced by each individual's unique cultural experience. However, this contribution summarizes some of the most consistent characteristics of nervios.

Nervios is loosely translated as describing someone who is vulnerable to stress and experiences intense emotional reactions to life stressors. For example, nervios may describe someone who worries excessively over daily events because he or she is unable to solve everyday problems. Nervios usually begins in childhood. Common cultural beliefs about the causes of nervios hold that it is inherited, results from traumatic experiences early in life, results from engaging in an unhealthy lifestyle (e.g., excessive alcohol consumption), or is caused by a "weak" constitution. Symptoms of nervios are emotional, physiological, and behavioral. Common symptoms include headache, stomachache, irritability, nervousness, depression, trembling, lack of concentration, chest pain, anger, crying, and sleep difficulties.

Estimates of the prevalence of nervios among Latinos suggests that this culture-bound syndrome affects 15.5% of the population. Nervios is more common among women. Gender differences in the prevalence of nervios tend to be greater in cultures with more traditional gender roles, among those living in poverty, and among those with limited social resources.

Nervios is generally chronic; however, this emotional state may worsen when many daily life stressors accumulate or during times of intense interpersonal loss (e.g., divorce, death of a family member). When nervios becomes more severe, the term *padecer de los nervios,* or "suffering from nerves," may be used. Although nervios is viewed as a state of mild emotional distress that can be dealt with informally (e.g., with family support, prayer, or over-the-counter medications), suffering from nerves is viewed as a more pathological state requiring professional help. Prescription medications or psychological counseling are common mainstream therapies; folk healing methods are less commonly used in the treatment of nervios.

Nervios is not a psychological disorder; however, those with nervios are at higher risk of developing mental health problems such as anxiety or depressive disorders. Those with nervios are also at increased risk of experiencing nervous attacks called *ataque de nervios.* Ataque is prominent in Latino cultures originating in the Caribbean, although this term is recognized as an idiom of distress in other Latino subcultures as well. Ataque may come on suddenly and intensify very quickly. It tends to occur in response to an extreme stressor, usually having to do with an interpersonal conflict or loss. Ataque is associated with extreme but short-lived emotional responses, often including crying, screaming, fainting, seizure-like experiences, dissociation, and violent behavior. Sometimes, individuals will not remember having the ataque. Because ataque is associated with a loss of control over one's emotions and behavior, this condition is generally viewed as more pathological than nervios.

—*Gretchen Diefenbach*

FURTHER READING

Baer, R. D., Weller, S. C., Garcia de Alba, J., Glazer, M., Trotter, R., Pachter, L., & Klein, R. E. (2003). A cross-cultural approach to the study of the folk illness nervios. *Culture, Medicine and Psychiatry, 27,* 315–337.

Guarnaccia, P. J., Lewis-Fernandez, R., & Marano, M. R. (2003). Toward a Puerto Rican popular nosology: Nervios and ataque de nervios. *Culture, Medicine and Psychiatry, 27,* 339–366.

Salgado de Snyder, V. N., Diaz-Perez, M. J., & Ojeda, V. D. (2000). The prevalence of nervios and associated symptomatology among inhabitants of Mexican rural communities. *Culture, Medicine and Psychiatry, 24,* 453–470.

CULTURE-BOUND SYNDROMES: QIGONG PSYCHOTIC REACTION

Qigong (pronounced *chee-gung*) is the ancient Chinese folk health-enhancing practice and exercise of vital energy, specifically, the movement of vital energy throughout the body. Qigong psychotic reactions result when individuals engage in erroneous or excessive practice of qigong. According to the *Diagnostic and Statistical Manual of Mental Disorders,* 4th edition, qigong psychotic reactions are "acute, time-limited episodes characterized by dissociative, paranoid, or other psychotic or nonpsychotic symptoms" occurring after participation in qigong.

INTRODUCTION

The exercise of vital energy has been an integral part of traditional Chinese medicine and martial arts since 500 BCE. Combining the exercise of body (*qi*) and mind, qigong is considered a form of psychotherapy in Eastern cultures, and it has become a widely accepted alternative form of psychotherapy in Western cultures. Similar practices include meditation, yoga, stretching, calisthenics, and self-massage.

Qigong is practiced to improve health and longevity; to achieve physical healing, spiritual growth, and enlightenment; and to attain strength and power. Qi can be inside or outside, flowing or still, quick or slow, patterned or spontaneous, hard or soft. Because qigong varies in method and purpose, some types of qigong may have negative mental and physical health consequences. Thus, it is important to engage in the proper practice of qigong by (1) choosing the proper qigong technique to accomplish a specific goal, (2) choosing the proper technique for one's age and health condition, and (3) receiving proper and competent guidance while practicing qigong.

MANIFESTATION

Qigong involves the circulation of energy through controlled breathing and the combined movement of body and mind. During qigong practice, biological, psychological, and physiological changes occur within the body, affecting one's mental and emotional state. Therefore, inappropriate or excessive practice can result in abnormal physiological or psychological symptoms resembling psychosis.

Most qigong psychotic reactions occur a few days following qigong practice and resemble symptoms of schizophreniform disorder. Symptoms can also resemble other neurotic disorders, such as affective or dissociative disorders. Specific psychological symptoms can include disorientation, paranoia, auditory and visual hallucinations, delusional thoughts, mood lability, hypochondriasis, suicidal ideation, obsessive thoughts, agitation, impulsiveness, mania, hysteria, depression, difficulty thinking, poor memory, generalized fear, disorganized speech, and insomnia. Physiological symptoms can include generalized body pain, dark and stagnant facial complexion, rapid and choppy pulse, dark red tongue, red eyes, reddish urine, profuse phlegm, chest oppression, headache, bitter taste in the mouth, dry mouth and throat, night sweats, hypertension, heart disease, and stroke. Symptoms usually persist for two to four weeks. At the first sign of a qigong psychotic reaction, qigong practice should be stopped immediately or monitored by an expert.

DIAGNOSIS

According to the *Chinese Classification of Mental Disorders,* 2nd edition (CCMD-2), there is a specific diagnostic category for this controversial culture-bound syndrome. According to the diagnostic criteria, the onset of the mental disorder occurs after qigong practice. Second, the syndrome is associated with some kind of qigong method found in a book or identified by a qigong instructor, with abnormal language and uncontrolled behavior that does not cease after qigong practice has stopped. Third, the mental disorder cannot be classified or the following conditions do not obtain: (1) the condition is a result of self-treatment or treatment by others for a physical or psychological aim; (2) the condition is aimed at cheating others; or (3) the condition can be self-induced or stopped at will. Finally, the mental disorder cannot otherwise be diagnosed according to the *CCMD-3.*

—Ngan Kim Vuong

FURTHER READING

Flaws, B. (2002). *Qigong disease: What it is and what to do about it.* Retrieved January 2, 2005, from http://www.kundalini.se/eng/qigong-disease.html

Shan, H. H. (2000). Culture-bound psychiatric disorders associated with qigong practice in China. *Hong Kong Journal of Psychiatry, 10,* 12–14.

CULTURE-BOUND SYNDROMES: SHENJING SHUAIRUO

Shenjing shuairuo is defined by the *Chinese Classification of Mental Disorders,* 3rd edition (CCMD-3), as a neurotic disorder associated with physical or mental fatigue, irritability, excitability, headaches or other pains, and sleep disturbances. Secondary symptoms include dizziness, concentration and memory difficulties, gastrointestinal problems, and sexual dysfunction.

ORIGINS OF SHENJING SHUAIRUO

Loosely translated as "weakness of nerves," shenjing shuairuo is often described as a Chinese culture-bound syndrome. However, it has roots in the Western disease construct of neurasthenia, which was introduced into China in the 1920s. The concepts of *shen* (spirit) and *jing* (channels that carry vital energy and blood) were combined into a single term, *shenjing,* meaning "nerve" or "nervous system." When *shenjing* becomes *shuai* (degenerate) and *ruo* (weak), a variety of symptoms may develop. However, a key feature of the disorder is that these symptoms cannot be traced to an organic cause.

CONCEPTUALIZATIONS AND CURRENT STATUS OF SHENJING SHUAIRUO

By 1980, shenjing shuairuo had become the most common disorder in China, diagnosed in nearly 80% of psychiatric outpatients. However, some questioned the diagnostic specificity of the category in light of the country's recent emergence from the Cultural Revolution (1966–1976). During the 1980s, ethnographic and psychodiagnostic studies of shenjing shuairuo led to its conceptualization as both a culturally meaningful diagnostic entity and an idiom of distress operating within local Chinese social worlds. A means of communicating profound experiences of loss and regret, shenjing shuairuo was interpreted as a bodily expression of the social disruptions and moral tragedies that had befallen the society at large.

Since the mid-1980s, the cultural significance of neurasthenia has gradually faded. Broad social and economic reforms have resulted in the greater assimilation of Western lifestyles, values, and ideas in all sectors, including psychiatry. The diagnostic concept of shenjing shuairuo has evolved to mirror the epistemological assumptions of the *Diagnostic and Statistical Manual of Mental Disorders,* 4th edition (*DSM-IV*), and the *International Classification of Diseases.* Today, the diagnosis of shenjing shuairuo requires the exclusion of affective and anxiety disorders, effectively discarding the traditional emphasis on the holistic integration of the mind and body. In urban areas, where Chinese are beginning to fashion themselves after the psychologically oriented West, depression and anxiety appear to be rapidly replacing shenjing shuairuo in local discourses. Elsewhere, however, shenjing shuairuo continues to be invoked in clinical interactions with traditional patients as a means of facilitating communication and bypassing the lingering stigma associated with mental illness.

Shenjing shuairuo is referenced as neurasthenia in the *DSM-IV*'s glossary of culture-bound syndromes. Neurasthenia is also mentioned under undifferentiated somatoform disorder as "a syndrome described frequently in many parts of the world and characterized by fatigue and weakness." However, the *DSM-IV*'s emphasis on fatigue and weakness does not correspond to the more heterogeneous symptom profiles reported in studies of shenjing shuairuo. Therefore, one must exercise caution when comparing shenjing shuairuo to undifferentiated somatoform disorder. Different cultural frameworks for conceptualizing illness require that diagnostic categories be interpreted within the contexts in which they were developed.

—*Doris F. Chang*

See also Somatization

FURTHER READING

Chang, D. F., Myers, H. F., Yeung, A., Zhang, Y., Zhao, J., & Yu, S. (in press). Shenjing shuairuo and the DSM-IV: Diagnosis, distress, and disability in a Chinese primary care setting. *Transcultural Psychiatry, 42*(2), 204–218.

Kleinman, A. (1982). Neurasthenia and depression: A study of somatization and culture in China. *Culture, Medicine and Psychiatry, 6*(2), 117–190.

Lee, S. (1998). Estranged bodies, simulated harmony, and misplaced cultures: Neurasthenia in contemporary Chinese society. *Culture, Medicine and Psychiatry, 60*(4), 448–457.

Rin, H., & Huang, M. G. (1989). Neurasthenia as nosological dilemma. *Culture, Medicine and Psychiatry, 13*(2), 215–226.

CULTURE-BOUND SYNDROMES: SHIN-BYUNG

Shin-byung is a culture-bound syndrome prevalent among Korean women. The initial stages of the syndrome involve anxiety and somatic complaints such as weakness, dizziness, fear, loss of appetite, insomnia, and gastrointestinal problems. These symptoms are followed by dissociative states in which the individual is believed to be possessed by ancestral spirits. Shin-byung is also referred to as the "divine illness" and literally means spirit (*shin*) possession (*byung*).

According to traditional Korean folklore, shin-byung is a shamanic initiatory process. While suffering from anxiety or somatic problems, individuals with shin-byung frequently report experiencing a *ki* (energy or spirit) enter the body. This is later identified as a *shin,* or ancestral god, which is believed to be the cause of the shin-byung symptoms. To alleviate symptoms, the individual must allow the shin to enter the body and become a shaman. There are no other known folk remedies for the syndrome. However, shamans are sometimes solicited to dissuade the shin from entering the body and remove the unwanted foreordained shamanistic obligations.

The syndrome is believed to have three phases. During the initial prodromal phase, the victim experiences anxiety and somatic symptoms. These symptoms, which may last weeks to decades, often warrant a visit to the physician, who is unable to identify the cause. During the trance phase, dissociative features become apparent. The individual may report dreams and hallucinations in which he or she is beckoned to permit spiritual beings to enter the body. These experiences are often very disturbing and ego dystonic to the individual and may cause him or her to seek counsel from a shaman, physician, or psychiatrist. During the final phase, possession, the individual may exhibit double or multiple personalities as the shin attempts to enter the body. This lasts until the shin personality dominates the individual's consciousness and behavior. Many Korean and Korean American psychiatrists believe that the transition from the trance phase to the possession phase is inevitable; however, this progression may take days to years.

According to Korean folk belief, women living in chronically stressful family situations are vulnerable to developing shin-byung. The victim's family is often stigmatized as being responsible for the development of the syndrome. In addition, shamans are viewed as social deviants in Korean society. Thus, considerable effort is made by the family and the victim to avoid the progression of shin-byung to shaman status. Conversely, there are thought to be grave consequences if the victim fails to acquiesce to the demands of spiritual possession. Individuals who deny shamanistic prompts are believed to be at great risk for "going crazy" through the incessant torments of their ancestral apparitions.

The cause of shin-byung is unknown. Though many Western researchers have noted similarities between shin-byung and schizophrenia, there is some debate as to whether the condition constitutes a mental illness. Some have even suggested ways this behavior may be adaptive. Individuals who develop the disorder are thought to come from stressful family situations; therefore, the disorder may be used as a technique to shift the focus of family members toward alleviating the needs of the victim. In addition, Korean women who make the transition to shaman often enjoy greater independence. The power structure in the home often changes because shamans are believed to possess greater authority over others. They also gain greater economic autonomy and professional identity through their role as a shaman in the community.

—John-Paul Legerski

FURTHER READING

Havery, Y. K. (1979). *Six Korean women: The socialization of shamans.* St. Paul, MN : West Publishing.

Yi, K. Y. (2000). Shin-byung (divine illness) in Korean women. *Culture, Medicine and Psychiatry, 24,* 471–486.

CULTURE-BOUND SYNDROMES: SUSTO

Susto, also known as "soul loss," is a prominent feature of many cultures, including the Latin American and other Spanish-speaking communities of the United States. It is considered a folk illness with extreme psychological overtones, also characterized as "fright sickness." Millions of people believe that frightening incidents such as witnessing a death, having an accidental fall or scare, losing something valuable, or being attacked or deserted by someone close can lead to susto. These incidents tend to have a common thread of helplessness and the inability to remove the cause of the fear. The biological responses that normally prepare the body for action against fear are absent, partially as a result of social norms or cultural inhibitions. The frightening event leads the soul to become dislodged, and subsequently it leaves the body.

The literature has identified both natural and supernatural susto. Natural susto may occur after a near miss or an accident; supernatural susto may occur after observing a supernatural phenomenon such as a ghost or spirit. This sudden natural fright afflicts individuals regardless of economic class, demographic location, age, or sex and regardless of the language that is spoken. There are also reported ethnic differences in the conception of susto within different subpopulations of the Latino community.

Susto results in illness that has highly variable symptoms. These symptoms can include nervousness, loss of appetite, restlessness, apathy, depression, involuntary muscle tics, inability to urinate, and diarrhea. Variations of these symptoms can include fever, muscle pains, nausea or other stomach pains, and dizziness. It is also widely believed that if the illness is not cured, it will culminate in death. Diagnosis of susto is made by considering the composite of symptoms and examining the history of the traumatic event believed to have caused the illness.

These cultures believe that remedies for susto include oral medication of teas with orange blossom, brazilwood, or marijuana. What is considered the most effective remedy is a ceremony characterized as the *barrida,* also known as "sweeping." This ceremony is to be performed immediately after the traumatic event and should be done in the home of a *curandero,* a healer or folk doctor. During the barrida ceremony, the patient recounts the traumatic event while lying on the ground at the axis of a crucifix. The term *sweeping* refers to the patient being swept with fresh herbs consisting of basil, purple sage, rosemary, or rue. In addition to the sweeping, the curandero and other individuals recite ritual prayers in groups of three. This ceremony is believed to return the frightened soul into the body. This ceremony is repeated every third day until the patient is healed.

—*Lana Olivo*

FURTHER READING

Glazer, M., Baer, R. D., Weller, S. C., De Alba, J. E., & Liebowitz, S. W. (2004). Susto and soul loss in Mexicans and Mexican Americans. *Cross-Cultural Research, 38,* 270–288.

Logan, M. H. (2004). New lines of inquiry on the illness of susto. *Medical Anthropology, 15,* 189–200.

CULTURE-BOUND SYNDROMES: TAIJIN KYOFUSHO

During the 1920s, the Japanese psychiatrist Shoma Morita first described the cluster of symptoms known as *taijin kyofusho* (TKS), which literally means the disorder (*sho*) of fear (*kyofu*) of interpersonal relations (*taijin*). The American diagnostic system for mental disorders lists TKS as a culture-bound syndrome that is similar to social phobia but unique to Japan. However, similar symptoms have also been reported in Korea, several European countries, and the United States. Nonetheless, TKS is most common among the Japanese people. In Japan, TKS is diagnosed in 7% to 46% of psychiatric patients, making it the third most common diagnosis. The traditional Japanese treatment for TKS is Morita therapy. Understanding TKS and its cultural influences is beneficial in adopting a culturally sensitive approach to the conceptualization and treatment of mental disorders.

Taijin kyofusho is an obsession with shame, manifested by intense fear of embarrassing or offending others by blushing, staring inappropriately, trembling, stuttering, emitting unpleasant odors, sweating, or displaying improper facial expressions or physical deformity. Fear of blushing is one of the most common symptoms.

There are two subtypes of TKS, one based on the particular fear and the other on severity. First, TKS can be categorized as (1) *sekimenkyofu,* the fear of blushing; (2) *shubo-kyofu,* the fear of a deformed body; (3) *jikoshisen-kyofu,* the fear of eye-to-eye contact; or (4) *jikoshu-kyofu,* the fear of one's own foul body odor. Second, TKS varies on a continuum of severity including (1) transient type, a typical social anxiety that is limited to adolescents; (2) phobic type, the most common type, which corresponds to the American concept of social phobia; (3) delusional type, which features an obsession with imagined or exaggerated physical defects or behaviors that offend others; and (4) phobic disorder accompanied by schizophrenia.

The onset of TKS symptoms typically occurs during adolescence and early adulthood. Symptoms rarely begin after age 40 and usually decrease after age 30. The disorder occurs more often in males than females, with a ratio of 5:4 to 3:2. Men in their 20s are the most frequent sufferers of TKS. Although there is a transient type of TKS, the course of TKS is typically chronic. The trigger is rarely an extreme outrageous event, but rather a minor incident occurring in particular social situations. The trigger provokes enduring anxiety that is heightened whenever the individual is in similar situations. To lessen their anxiety, TKS sufferers often attempt to cover up their appearance (e.g., by applying facial cream to hide blushing) or avoid social situations. The delusional type of TKS tends to focus predominately on one symptom in the individual. However, the focus may shift to another symptom throughout the course of the disorder.

Taijin kyofusho is influenced by the Japanese culture. Interdependence and responsibility for others are pillars of the Japanese value system, and Japanese society maintains a very specific and complex social etiquette. Japanese psychiatrists consider the delusions of TKS to be the result of excessive sensitivity and preoccupation with culturally dictated etiquette in social situations. Symptoms of TKS are displayed more often in individuals with low independence and high interdependence, characteristics that are associated with Japanese values. In addition, the more acculturated Japanese individuals are to American society, the less likely they are to experience symptoms of TKS.

—*Rochelle James*

FURTHER READING

Kirmayer, L. J. (1991). The place of culture in psychiatric nosology: Taijin kyofusho and DSM-III-R. *Journal of Nervous and Mental Disease, 179,* 19–28.

Takahashi, T. (1989). Social phobia syndrome in Japan. *Comprehensive Psychiatry, 30,* 45–52.

CULTURE-BOUND SYNDROMES: ZAR

Zar is an ancient healing practice based on a folk belief that possession by alien spirits can cause disease and that disease can be managed by the ceremonial placation of the possessing spirits. The word *zar* is used in reference to the type of possessing spirit, the illness it inflicts on humans, and the rituals performed to pacify it. Believed to have originated in Ethiopia, the cult currently prevails under different names (*sar, bori, tumbura, dastur, red wind, shaitani*), in many countries of Africa and the Middle East, including Sudan, Egypt, Ethiopia, Somalia, Algeria, Morocco, Nigeria, Kenya, Tanzania, Zambia, the Arabian Peninsula, and Iran. Although it has unmistakable pre-Christian and pre-Islamic features, contemporary zar is strongly influenced by these two religions.

Zar spirits constitute a broad spectrum of individually or collectively named entities, including holy saints, sect leaders, great monarchs, victorious generals, colonial officers, wealthy aristocrats, professional elites, nomadic warriors, savage bushmen, rebellious youth, flirtatious playgirls, and many others. By ethnicity, they include Ethiopians, Arabs, Southern Sudanese, Europeans, West Africans, Turks, Gypsies, and others. The reservoir of zar spirits continually expands to encompass ongoing sociodemographic and cultural changes.

Each spirit or group exhibits a distinctive pattern of behavior, personality traits, mood, attitudes, habits, mannerisms, idiosyncratic whims, and social interests. However, they share a common quality of being amoral, capricious, hedonistic, and intrusive.

Most clients resort to zar after unsuccessful treatment by Western physicians and traditional religious healers for complaints such as persistent headaches, palpitations, tightness of the chest, anorexia, gastrointestinal disturbances, generalized body aches, fatigue, dizziness, insomnia, anxiety, fear, sadness, and motor or sensory impairments. The formal "diagnosis" of zar is a faculty of the *zar shaykha* (leader), usually a woman who embarked on zar as a patient herself before apprenticing with a recognized shaykha and becoming formally recognized as a zar practitioner.

Once a novice is convinced that she has zar, she is to make an inception ceremony under the supervision of the shaykha and with the active participation of the shaykha's aides, musicians, and clientele.

Symbolically mimicking a wedding festivity, the inception celebration continues for seven days of fervent drumming, singing, dancing, and feasting in a large, jubilantly decorated room with a profusely incensed and perfumed background. During the heat of the activity, the novice, referred to as the "bride" of zar, is escorted by two bridesmaids into the room, gracefully swaying in her new clothing adorned with jewelry, henna, and fragrance to the participants' roaring applause. As the drumming, singing, and dancing grow progressively more vigorous, the shaykha begins summoning the spirits, each by its characteristic "thread" (chant), until the bride lapses into a trance, marking the entry of a particular spirit into her body and the displacement of her earthly self. A dialogue commences between the shaykha and the spirit to reach a negotiated appeasement. Thereafter, the client is to become symptom free, subject to her unwavering compliance with the spirit's demands, which are enjoyed through the senses of the host.

Field surveys have consistently reported the preponderance of zar among middle-aged women who are infertile, divorced or unhappily married, unemployed, of rural origin, or uneducated or who have a family history of zar or enduring interpersonal conflicts. Clinical studies have consistently reported higher prevalence of zar among patients who are diagnosed with dissociative, conversion, somatoform, or anxiety disorders.

Researchers attribute the beneficial effects of zar to social support, club membership, group therapy, milieu therapy, recreation therapy, psychodrama, catharsis, abreaction, and hypnotherapy.

Zar spirits never completely abandon their hosts, nor do the latter wish them to be exorcised. This culturally sanctioned state of ritually induced switching between a distressed host and an empathic spirit creates a picture that is phenomenologically indistinguishable from the putatively psychopathological state currently diagnosed as dissociative (multiple) identity disorder.

—Sheikh Idris Rahim

FURTHER READING

Boddy, J. (1989). *Wombs and alien spirits: Women, men, and the zar cult in Northern Sudan.* Madison: University of Wisconsin Press.

Lewis, I. M. (1986). *Religion in context: Cults and charisma.* New York: Cambridge University Press.

Rahim, S. I. A. (2001). Zar and female psychopathology in Sudan. *Arab Journal of Psychiatry, 12,* 20–32.

DEMENTIA

Dementia is a condition marked by generalized decline in memory and other cognitive functions, leading to impairment in social or occupational functioning. The behavioral and psychological symptoms associated with dementia can be found throughout the world and follow similar patterns in diverse cultural settings. However, cultural factors also influence the problem and its effects in many ways.

Dementia is an increasing multicultural problem because of shifts in demographics. Older adult populations are increasing internationally, thus increasing the number of people who are most at risk of developing a dementia. This is particularly a problem in countries with poor health care for the elderly or a high ratio of older to younger adults, but it poses a problem in other countries as well. In the United States, improved standards of living for non-Caucasian ethnic groups have increased life expectancies; as a result, these individuals have a greater chance of developing cognitive problems. The non-European portion of the U.S. age cohort that is most at risk for dementia is expected to be 25% by 2010 and 33% by 2050, leading to potentially large increases in dementia rates within those groups.

PREVALENCE AND CHARACTERISTICS

Although we lack knowledge of prevalence patterns for dementia in some areas of the world, it is clear that dementia does not affect all groups in the same way. Studies indicate a number of differences in dementia rates among ethnic and racial groups, both outside and within the United States. Rates for some East Asian (e.g., Chinese) and South Asian groups appear to be lower than those of European Americans. In the United States, dementia rates for African Americans and Latinos appear to be higher than those of Caucasians. The significance of these differences is not clear. Cognitive impairment is more common among those of low socioeconomic status and poor health status, characteristics that are found disproportionately among U.S. minority populations, but this does not appear to account for all of the difference. Health problems that are comorbid with dementia also vary. For example, African American patients with Alzheimer's disease tend to have fewer mood, anxiety, and sleep difficulties but higher rates of psychosis compared with other groups.

CAUSES

Although dementia affects individuals from all cultural and racial groups, there are differences in the patterns of disease that cause the problem. For example, in the United States and Europe, the most common cause of dementia is Alzheimer's disease, whereas in Russia and East Asian cultures, such as Japan or China, the most common cause is vascular dementia. People of Japanese ancestry living in Japan, Hawaii, and the U.S. mainland have different relative proportions of Alzheimer's and vascular dementia, suggesting that environment has an effect on dementia type and prevalence. In the United States, African Americans and Latinos have higher rates of stroke and associated risk factors (e.g., hypertension) than Caucasians. Therefore, it is not surprising that although Alzheimer's is still the leading cause of dementia in these groups, vascular dementia appears to account for a larger percentage of cases than among Caucasians.

Genetics plays a role in the development of dementia and may help to explain differences in prevalence and causal patterns among groups. Greater frequency of the e4 allele on the ApoE gene from the long arm of chromosome 19 has been connected with increased rates of Alzheimer's and vascular dementia, although the strength of the relationship may be weaker among Asians and African Americans. Internationally, substantial differences in e4 allele frequencies have been found, ranging from a low of 7% in East Asia (China, Japan), to 14% in the general U.S. population, to a high of 26% for African Americans and 31% in Nigeria. This suggests a possible genetic basis for some of the differences in dementia risk.

ASSESSMENT

Dementia assessment in multicultural settings is difficult. Because dementia is defined as a *relative* decline in functioning, it is essential to estimate an individual's lifetime level of cognitive ability, which may be difficult for patients who come from cultural backgrounds with constrained educational or occupational opportunities. Cognitive functioning is typically assessed through neuropsychological testing, but this is difficult in multicultural settings because of test bias. African Americans and other groups have been observed to perform more poorly than Caucasians on these tests, which were typically developed using Caucasian, English-speaking individuals. These performance discrepancies frequently disappear or diminish when differences in educational background, acculturation, and health status are taken into account. Some ethnic differences appear to persist, however, so care must be taken to use tests that have appropriate norms, have demonstrated cross-cultural reliability and validity, and have been screened for possible item bias.

REACTIONS TO ILLNESS AND CAREGIVING

Multiethnic issues in caregiving are just beginning to be understood through a combination of quantitative and qualitative studies that capture both the significance of factors and the richness of cultural and subjective experience. These studies show that the meaning that patients and their families attach to dementia is affected by their cultural views on aging, including the types of changes that are expected in the aging individual, the level at which dementia behaviors are viewed as problematic, the roles and valuation of older people in the community and family, the obligations of the family and community toward the older person, and the degree of perceived control over the problem—in other words, the moral and ethical stance of the culture toward aging, illness, and disability. These meanings affect responses to dementia, including how quickly the problem is recognized, how much and what type of support is provided to the patient, and whether outside assistance is sought. Differences in cultural outlook among the patient, family, and professionals can significantly increase stress for caregivers, and negative racial attitudes on the part of patients and families may cause problems for ethnically diverse staff.

Dementia caregiving patterns show definite cultural differences. Caucasian families tend to use spouses as caregivers, whereas other groups have broader models that include extended family, informal support, and less professional assistance. The burden of caregiving is high for all, but some groups—Chinese, African Americans, and to some extent, Latinos—appear to experience less burden and distress than Caucasians, whereas Koreans and Korean Americans appear to have higher levels of burden. Differences may be partly the result of differences in coping strategies; for example, the use of religious coping is more common among African American and Hispanic American caregivers. Though specific coping strategies may differ, the variables involved in the overall coping process and its outcome appear to work in similar ways. Depression in caregivers is typically a function of (1) illness attribution, (2) primary appraisal of stress, (3) coping strategies, and (4) secondary appraisal of resources such as social and family support. Social role also plays a part; for example, among Koreans, spousal caregivers exhibit higher levels of depression than daughters-in-law.

FUTURE DIRECTIONS

Dementia is difficult for both the patient and the family regardless of culture. The impending explosion of the world's older adult population is a call to develop culturally appropriate strategies for research, education, assistance, and care. Cultural and religious beliefs or practices are critical issues that should always be taken into account in patient care, along with the explanatory models and resources of patients and families. In the developing world, there is a relative lack of problem awareness, as well as special services and trained personnel to deal with dementia. For example, as recently as 2000, it was reported that there were only four trained psychogeriatricians in all of Mexico, a country of about 100 million people. In these situations, it is tempting for experts to develop and impose programs from the outside. However, the outcome literature clearly demonstrates that top-down initiatives are likely to be ineffective; instead, increased community involvement is essential. Cultural advisory groups and other partnerships are especially effective in designing community intervention and education programs for diverse populations. These types of collaborative programs allow the rich resources of the culture to be successfully directed toward social problems such as dementia.

—*James M. Nelson*

FURTHER READING

Ferraro, F. (Ed.). (2002). *Minority and cross-cultural aspects of neuropsychological assessment.* Lisse, The Netherlands: Swets & Zeitlinger.

Froehlich, T., Bogardus, S., & Inouye, S. (2001). Dementia and race: Are there differences between African Americans and Caucasians? *Journal of the American Geriatric Society, 49,* 477–484.

O'Brien, J., Ames, D., & Burns, A. (Eds.). (2000). *Dementia* (2nd ed.). London: Arnold.

Valle, R. (1997). *Caregiving across cultures: Working with dementing illness and ethnically diverse populations.* Philadelphia: Taylor & Francis.

DEPRESSION

Depression is a mental disorder that affects individuals of all racial, ethnic, and socioeconomic backgrounds. Symptoms that are generally associated with depression include feelings of sadness, hopelessness, diminished level of interest, dysregulation in appetite and sleep patterns, hopeless and guilty thoughts, and suicidal ideation. It has been estimated that up to 17% of the general population will meet the criteria for major depression at some point in their lives. These numbers are even higher for children and adolescents: Some studies have found that the proportion of children and adolescents who will experience a depressive episode by the end of high school is as high as 25%. The consequences of major depression are not insignificant, producing significant human suffering and even loss of life.

Despite considerable advances in our understanding of depression, researchers have only recently begun to examine depression in the complicated contexts of race, ethnicity, and culture. This emerging depression research has identified several key areas in which race, ethnicity, and culture may play an important role and should be explored further.

MANIFESTATION OF DEPRESSION

Although researchers have attempted to identify a set of core symptoms that can be reliably associated with depression, this task has proved difficult. For example, some researchers have noted that somatic symptoms are more commonly expressed in individuals from non-Western cultures, whereas feelings of guilt, self-depreciation, and suicidal ideation are more common among individuals from Western cultures. Some have suggested that there are fundamental racial, ethnic, and cultural differences in the experience and manifestation of depression. Others, however, have suggested that these symptom differences reflect racial, ethnic, and cultural differences in patients' willingness to report symptoms to mental health providers. For example, there is evidence that African American and Latino American men may be less willing to report depression and its associated symptoms because they fear appearing weak or unmasculine. At this point, it is unclear to what extent veritable racial, ethnic, or cultural differences exist in the expression of depressive symptoms.

In addition to the difficulties associated with determining the extent to which depressive symptoms are similar across cultural groups, researchers have only recently begun to explore the relationship between culture-bound syndromes and depression. For example, in some Latin American cultures, individuals report experiences that may be similar to depression (e.g., *pena, decaimientos,* or *nervios*). Though it is possible these syndromes are mental disorders that are categorically distinct from depression, the possibility remains that they represent culturally specific ways in which depression is diagnosed or expressed.

PREVALENCE OF DEPRESSION

Given the difficulty of diagnosing depression among racial and ethnic minorities, it has been difficult to establish accurate prevalence rates of depression in the United States. Nevertheless, some interesting patterns have emerged. For example, two national epidemiological studies found that depression is less prevalent in African Americans than in Caucasians or Latinos. Several smaller studies have documented higher rates of depression among Latinos, and in particular Latina women, than among individuals from other racial, ethnic, or cultural groups. Unfortunately, no large-scale epidemiological study has included sufficiently large Asian American and Native American samples to provide accurate prevalence rates of depression in these groups.

Moreover, there are inconsistencies in the literature concerning racial and ethnic differences in adolescent depression. For example, although African American adolescents appear to be at greater risk for certain behavioral and health problems than Caucasian adolescents, they seem to be at lower risk for depression. The research examining depression in Latino Americans has produced similarly equivocal findings. Some researchers have found that Latino American adolescents report fewer depressive symptoms than Caucasians, whereas others have found the opposite. It is unclear how these discrepant findings should be interpreted; one possibility is that differences in depression exist among Latino American subgroups. In support of this possibility, one study found that Puerto Rican American adolescents report more depressive symptoms than Mexican American and Cuban American adolescents. More research is needed, however, to fully explore these nonconverging data.

RISK FACTORS FOR DEPRESSION

Demographic risk factors that have been consistently associated with depression include a family history of depression, low socioeconomic status, and specific stressful life events (e.g., assault, robbery, serious marital problems, divorce, loss of employment, serious illness, and significant financial problems). Although extensive research focusing on risk factors among individuals from racial, ethnic, or cultural minority groups does not yet exist, converging evidence suggests that a myriad of social risk factors, such as socioeconomic status, acculturative stress, racism, and urban living, may contribute to depression in nonmajority individuals.

Interestingly, research that has focused on the immigration and acculturation experiences of certain racial and ethnic minority groups has produced conflicting findings. Some studies found that Latinos who had

recently immigrated from Latin America were less likely to experience depression than Latinos born and raised in the United States. Similarly, a study conducted with Vietnamese American students found that students who were less able to identify with their Vietnamese culture were more likely to manifest symptoms of depression. Some researchers have speculated that first-generation immigrants may possess certain protective factors (e.g., increased religiosity, more familial social support, a clearer sense of ethnic identity) that later-generation immigrants do not have.

At the same time, many researchers have noted that some experiences related to immigration are stressful and associated with exposure to violence, a decline in socioeconomic status, and separation from family and social support systems. Such experiences have been associated with a higher incidence of depression and other psychological problems.

ASSESSMENT AND TREATMENT OF DEPRESSION

Assessment and treatment of depression is a complicated issue, especially in light of the possibility that differences exist in the way individuals from different racial, ethnic, or cultural groups manifest depressive symptoms. Because clinicians often rely on assessment instruments that fail to consider possible differences in symptom expression, it is unclear how reliably depression is being diagnosed in racial and ethnic minority populations. Moreover, researchers have documented racial, ethnic, and cultural differences in willingness to report symptoms to mental health providers.

One significant issue related to the treatment of depression is the fact that individuals from racial and ethnic minority groups tend to underutilize and prematurely terminate formal mental health services. There are many reasons for this underutilization, including a lack of resources, a dearth of adequately trained professionals, and social stigmas associated with mental health and mental health treatment. Moreover, some individuals from racial and ethnic minority populations may first turn to alternative sources of support when experiencing depression, including family members, members of the clergy or other religious figures, or primary care physicians.

This underutilization of mental health services is unfortunate; some research has shown that racial and ethnic minority individuals who receive intensive outreach and subsequent treatment for depression significantly benefit from the treatment, not only with regard to their depressive symptoms but also with regard to higher psychosocial functioning. Therefore, there is a need to find creative ways to engage individuals from racial and ethnic minority backgrounds in treatment.

Researchers have begun to consider the possibility that prevention programs might offer a solution to this lack of engagement in formal mental health services. Well-designed prevention programs may be more appealing to racial and ethnic minority individuals because they can be advertised in nonstigmatizing ways (e.g., stress management programs), they can be delivered in nontraditional settings (e.g., schools, community centers), and they can be delivered by non–mental health professionals who have received less extensive training (e.g., teachers, caseworkers). Moreover, there is emerging research on the prevention of depression in Latinos that suggests these programs can be effective with racial and ethnic minorities. In general, however, there continues to be a need for the development of effective and culturally relevant forms of treatment.

FUTURE DIRECTIONS

As the United States continues to become increasingly more diverse, there is a critical need to better understand the important roles that race, ethnicity, and culture play in the development and maintenance of depression. This increased understanding of depression will help in the development of culturally appropriate assessment tools and intervention programs.

—*Esteban Cardemil*

See also Accessibility of Health Care; DSM-IV; Mental Health; Models of Mental Health

FURTHER READING

Allen, L., & Mitchell, C. (1998). Racial and ethnic differences in patterns of problematic and adaptive development: An epidemiological review. In V. C. McCloyd & L. Steinberg (Eds.), *Studying minority adolescents* (pp. 29–54). Mahwah, NJ: Lawrence Erlbaum.

Tsai, J. L., & Chentozova-Dutton, Y. (2002). Understanding depression across cultures. In I. Gotlib & L. Hammen (Eds.), *Handbook of depression* (pp. 467–491). New York: Guilford Press.

U.S. Department of Health and Human Services. (2001). *Mental health: Culture, race, and ethnicity* (Suppl. to *Mental health: A report of the surgeon general*). Rockville, MD: U.S. Department of Health and Human Services, Substance Abuse and Mental Health Services Administration, Center for Mental Health Services.

DISABILITIES

Persons with disabilities who come from diverse ethnic and racial populations in American society are not much different from those of Caucasian background, in that both often face the same physical and attitudinal barriers; however, they may be confronted with some unique barriers within their own ethnic and racial communities in addition to those faced in the larger society.

Persons with disabilities are defined by the Americans With Disabilities Act as those who have an impairment that affects their function in one or more major life activities, such as walking, seeing, hearing, speaking, learning, or working, or are regarded by others as having an impairment that limits their ability to perform these activities. Those who are regarded as having disabilities recognize they may be discriminated against because others assume they have limited function as a result of their impairment. For diverse ethnic and racial groups, the perception of disability is especially significant. Individuals who are members of a racial or ethnic minority group may not necessarily describe themselves as having a disability and may consider themselves as limited only in performing certain tasks. When individuals do not perceive themselves as having a disability, they may not use programs that are available to them. In addition, the prevalence of a disability may be underreported, leading to a perception within the community and within the larger society that disability is not a concern that needs to be addressed. Some ethnic and racial groups do not have a word in their language to describe the way that disability is conceived in American society.

INCREASED LIKELIHOOD OF DISABILITY

Disabilities occur at higher rates among ethnic and racial minority populations than in the majority population of the United States. Incidence and prevalence of disabling conditions among many ethnic and racial groups in the United States is higher than among Caucasians. The U.S. Census Bureau has reported that persons who are Caucasian and who are not Hispanic have low disability rates despite having a higher median age (often associated with disability) than other ethnic and racial groups. Asian Americans are the exception, although some Asian American subgroups, such as Southeast Asians from Vietnam or Cambodia, have higher rates of disability, possibly a result of refugee status, recent immigration patterns, lower education levels, and limited English facility.

The risk of disability is related to one's education, socioeconomic status, age, and occupation. Minority ethnic and racial groups in American society have generally lower education levels and, as a result, find themselves in lower socioeconomic status and working in jobs that have a higher risk of disability.

Health disparities also place members of these groups at higher risk of disabling complications. For example, diabetes is the leading cause of amputation among older Americans. Ethnic and racial minority populations are more likely to have diabetes, and thus a greater risk of amputation. Exposure to environmental pollutants, a result of living in low-income areas, may contribute to health problems and cause further disability.

For many persons of ethnic and racial backgrounds, having a disability directly affects their health status. An illness such as multiple sclerosis or cancer will directly affect one's health, and conditions associated with spinal injury and HIV/AIDS make people more vulnerable to infection. Health and disability are interrelated, although persons with disabilities do not like to foster the idea that disability equates with poor health.

DIFFERING REACTIONS TO DISABILITY

There are differences in the way that individuals and families from diverse ethnic and racial backgrounds react to disability. Reliance on the family for support is a traditional coping mechanism among groups that have historically lacked external support, because of either discrimination or self-defined roles and obligations. Minority ethnic and racial community organizations have not always supported individuals with disabilities, partly because of their beliefs and attitudes toward persons with disabilities. Civil rights organizations have focused on more pressing socioeconomic questions and survival rather than on disability, and they often have not included persons with disabilities in their agenda. In turn, disability advocacy has generally been an activity of Caucasian middle-class groups. However, relying on traditional family supports may strain relationships and confuse roles. Families may not have the resources or understand the requirements of persons with disabilities. Though they love their family member and are concerned about his or her well-being, much of the family's efforts may be directed toward protecting rather than allowing more participation in society.

DUAL IDENTITY

Persons with disabilities of diverse backgrounds must cope with dual-identity issues, that is, they have both an ethnic and racial minority identity and a disability identity. This is critical for children with congenital and developmental disabilities. Incorporating the messages of society, along with those of a specific ethnic or racial group, about oneself and how disability is regarded is a developmental task that is not well understood. Because of the wide differences in any given individual, this process is not a simplistic one, but it is one for which there is little empirical data.

CULTURE AND DISABILITY

Ethnic and racial groups have varying beliefs about the origin of disability. The perception of what constitutes a disability comes partly from one's culture. For example, in some ethnic and racial groups, disability is seen as a manifestation of behaviors from a previous life, punishment for wrongdoing, or exposure and reaction to trauma. One's beliefs about the etiology of disability may dictate one's attitudes as well as how one interacts with persons who have disabilities.

Programs that serve persons with disabilities are built on an individualistic Western philosophical perspective. The unique help-seeking behaviors of ethnic and racial populations may explain their reluctance to seek out disability and rehabilitation programs. Other barriers include concepts that are inherent to disability and rehabilitation that reflect Western philosophical values. Independence, a key rehabilitation value, is less likely to be understood in the context of a collectivistic perspective, which is characteristic of many ethnic and racial groups. Obligation and responsibility for disabled family members may also interfere with appropriate care. For example, if family members believe it is their responsibility to be caregivers, they may not allow an individual with a disability to perform tasks or participate in activities. However, the concern may have less to do with the abilities of the disabled family member than with whether the family is perceived by others as carrying out their defined roles and obligations.

ACCESS TO SERVICES

Access to and knowledge about the services that are available is a primary obstacle for persons with disabilities and their families. These include programs such as state and federal public vocational rehabilitation and private-sector insurance benefits as well as public benefit and entitlement programs such as Social Security.

Obstacles to participation in such programs include those that are internal to the programs, as well as those brought by persons with disabilities. Persons with disabilities from diverse populations may be confronted with unequal treatment and discrimination in disability and rehabilitation services. For clients who use English as a second language, programs often lack adequate and appropriate translators. Other obstacles to participation include a lack of knowledge and understanding of rehabilitation, suspicion of government-run programs, cultural mistrust, and feelings of uneasiness about disclosing and discussing disability.

There is a general lack of knowledge and awareness of the challenges faced by individuals with disabilities who are also members of an ethnic or racial population. Faced with indifference within their own communities and the traditional service model of many disability programs, persons with disabilities from ethnic and racial communities often must rely on themselves, with little outside support. Racial-identity issues, combined with disability identity (growing up with a disabling condition), presents unique challenges. Psychologists can help by understanding the dynamics of the interface of disability, ethnicity, and race and by developing effective interfaces for persons with disabilities from diverse communities.

Public policy needs to address the concern of dual discrimination. Counseling and education about disabling conditions, the use of assistive technology, and the availability of supports within a cultural context are all necessary if persons with disabilities from diverse ethnic and racial backgrounds are to participate in and contribute fully to American society.

—*Paul Leung*

See also Americans With Disabilities Act; Collectivism; Ethnic Identity Development; Help-Seeking Behavior

FURTHER READING

Leung, P. (2003). Multicultural competencies and rehabilitation counseling/psychology. In D. B. Pope-Davis, L. K. Coleman, W. M. Liu, & R. L. Toporek (Eds.), *Handbook of multicultural competencies in counseling and psychology.* Thousand Oaks, CA: Sage.
Stone, J. H. (Ed.). (2005). *Culture and disability: Providing culturally competent services.* Thousand Oaks, CA: Sage.

DOMESTIC VIOLENCE

WHAT IS DOMESTIC VIOLENCE?

Domestic violence is defined as intentional abuse or assault committed by a past or present spouse, intimate partner, family member, or household member, regardless of age or gender. Domestic violence may take the form of psychological abuse, physical battery, or sexual assault. In recent years, there has been a proliferation of research on domestic violence; however, relatively little attention has been paid to the influence of minority status and culture on the experience of domestic violence.

Domestic violence is most frequently perpetrated by a male partner against a female partner. Female-to-male domestic violence does occur, but estimates suggest that in only 5% of cases is the primary aggressor female, and in cases of mutual violence, women are seven times more likely to be seriously injured than men. Historically, domestic violence was considered a private family matter rather than a criminal matter; however, significant changes in the U.S. criminal justice system within the past 20 years have provided law enforcement officials with the capacity and mandate to intervene.

TYPES OF VIOLENCE

Psychological abuse involves the use of threats, coercion, intimidation, stalking, economic control, and isolation. Psychological abuse is distinct from discord that is reported in nonviolent marital relationships.

Physical battery refers to acts of physical aggression, such as kicking, punching, choking, slapping, stabbing, shooting, beating with fists, burning, biting, and throwing corrosive substances. Some cases of physical assault result in death.

Sexual assault involves rape and other forcible sexual acts, such as forced masturbation, fellatio, and oral coitus. Sexual assault also encompasses psychological abuse of a sexual nature, such as sexual humiliation.

PREVALENCE OF DOMESTIC VIOLENCE

U.S. population: Approximately 25% to 30% of women in America are victims of domestic violence during adulthood.

African Americans: Prevalence rates of domestic violence among African American women are 35% to 50%

higher than rates among European American women. African American women experience domestic violence at about two and a half times the rate of women of other minority races.

Latinas: The prevalence of domestic violence among Latina women is thought to be slightly higher than among European American/Anglo women. Studies of specific Latina ethnicities have estimated the prevalence of domestic violence to be nearly twice as high as the prevalence in the European American/Anglo population; however, rates depend on how women are classified.

Asians and Pacific Islanders: Rates of domestic violence among Asian Americans and Pacific Islanders are reported to be much lower than the average for European Americans and all other ethnic minority groups. However, it is believed this is a function of underreporting in this population.

Native Americans and Alaska Natives: The prevalence of domestic violence in Native American and Alaska Native populations is believed to be higher than in the European American population, and some experts believe it is the highest among all ethnic minority groups. These groups remain largely understudied, and there is little data to confirm these assertions.

The data suggest that domestic violence may be more prevalent among some ethnic minorities than among the majority population in the United States. However, studies that examined variables such as poverty and social class have identified these factors as better predictors of domestic violence prevalence than ethnicity. Poverty and social class appear to exacerbate the risk for domestic violence, particularly in minority groups.

IMPACT OF DOMESTIC VIOLENCE

Victims of domestic violence experience a host of physical, psychological, and social effects resulting from the abuse. Physical effects include a wide range of injuries, such as broken bones, hearing and vision loss, injuries to internal organs, severe burns, and, in the most serious cases, death. The psychological effects of domestic violence often result in disorders such as depression and anxiety, specifically, posttraumatic stress disorder (PTSD). Other psychological effects include low self-esteem, suicidal behavior, and dependence on alcohol or drugs. Social effects include being cut off from family and friends as well as social reprisals.

Batterers also experience physical and psychological consequences resulting from domestic violence. Batterers report increased levels of stress, depression, and substance abuse and lower self-esteem following incidents of violence. The physical effects of domestic violence on perpetrators are neither as severe nor as widespread as those experienced by their victims, with the exception of self-inflicted physical injuries.

Children who are exposed to domestic violence may exhibit a range of emotional difficulties, including depression, anxiety, PTSD, low self-esteem, and academic and cognitive difficulties. Domestic violence is believed to be harmful to children's development and psychological adjustment.

THEORIES ABOUT DOMESTIC VIOLENCE

Intraindividual theories emphasize the role of individual pathology as the root cause of domestic violence. There is a growing body of research that points to the importance of personality, neurological, and even physiological factors in models of relationship aggression. In contrast, sociopsychological theories argue that domestic violence is learned behavior that is acquired by exposure to and reinforcement of the acceptability of this behavior in the family unit.

Feminist theory asserts that domestic violence is a result of male domination of women and an imbalance of power that is sanctioned by society. The feminist movement is largely credited with significant improvements in the lives of domestic violence victims, which have been achieved by altering public perceptions of domestic violence, implementing public policy changes, increasing resources such as shelter and legal advocacy, and improving the response by the health care community. Although the efforts of the feminist movement have resulted in many improvements for victims of domestic violence, the movement has been criticized for inadequate advocacy on behalf of women of color.

ROLE OF CULTURE AND ETHNICITY IN DOMESTIC VIOLENCE

Ethnic minority victims of domestic violence experience a unique set of problems that are not necessarily experienced by European American women, and thus their social realities are significantly different, as are the needs of their children and the perpetrators of violence.

Attitudes about domestic violence vary tremendously among cultures. Culture and ethnicity influence domestic violence victims' help-seeking behavior, that is, the pattern of behavior followed when seeking treatment or legal advocacy. For example, in Asian cultures, there is an emphasis on "saving face" or honor. This value prohibits many victims from seeking help because of they are concerned with bringing shame on the family. Similarly, in Latino cultures, the concept of "cultural fatalism" may prevent many victims from seeking help. In many ethnic groups, there are religious and cultural values pertaining to "keeping the family together" at all costs; these values prohibit women from leaving violent relationships. Ethnic minority women often live with extended families. The extended family network may provide support and a wide range of resources for the woman, or conversely, it may keep the woman trapped in a system that supports and condones the abuse and prevents her from seeking help.

There are many pragmatic barriers for ethnic minority women who wish to leave a violent relationship. Many domestic violence victims are financially dependent on the perpetrator; this is particularly true for immigrant women, especially if they are not proficient in English or do not have work skills. Lack of affordable housing and shelter is often a significant deterrent to leaving a violent relationship, and this is especially problematic for ethnic minority women. Many of the resources available to victims of domestic violence are available exclusively to English speakers. Only recently have shelters begun to appreciate the importance of providing culturally appropriate accommodations, such as serving familiar food and having staff of the same cultural background. Ethnic minority women often report that services do not meet their needs. Recommendations to take legal action or to leave the relationship are often not perceived by ethnic minority women as viable because of their experience of racism and oppression in the legal system; this is particularly true for African American women. Furthermore, ethnic minority women are at a clear disadvantage with respect to navigating the complex legal system, which is daunting even to highly educated English speakers. Finally, the fear of deportation is very real for undocumented immigrants. Although there are provisions for women to file a petition if they are in this situation, many victims are unaware of this provision and lack the legal resources to take advantage of these new laws.

Like their mothers, ethnic minority children who are exposed to domestic violence experience unique challenges in coping with their situation, and there are inadequate resources to meet their needs. Finally, batterers who are ethnic minorities may face harsher sentencing and receive fewer intervention resources to address their needs.

—Catherine Koverola
—Cristin Murtaugh

FURTHER READING

Kasturirangan, A., Krishnan, S., & Riger, S. (2004). The impact of culture and minority status on women's experience of domestic violence. *Trauma, Violence, and Abuse*, 5(4), 318–332.

Koverola, C., & Panchanadeswaran, S. (2004). Domestic violence interventions with women of color: The intersection of victimization and cultural diversity. In K. A. Kendall-Tackett (Ed.), *Health consequences of abuse in the family: A clinical guide for evidence-based practice* (pp. 45–61). Washington, DC: American Psychological Association.

DOZENS

To limit the amount of information that slave traders in the antebellum slave market had to send, the traders often categorized slaves into packages, perhaps a dozen, that were distinguished by particular characteristics: extra men, number one men, second-rate or ordinary girls, tall field fellows, young and lively, and so forth. Out of this habit came the term and practice of "playing the dozens," denoting an individual as having less importance.

Playing the dozens is a game of verbal insult and display—an opportunity for sublimation and catharsis, providing training in verbal quickness and physical restraint in front of one's peers, where the risk of injury or death is minimal. This practice became popular at a time when the suspected infraction of any rule by an African American could provoke lynching or mob violence. This game of verbal insult—usually initiated by elders of the extended family, then played among equals—is a social ritual that teaches about social class system impositions and gender roles, especially masculinity. Being "man enough to bring it, as well as take it" was a central training function of playing the dozens. This function continues today, when African Americans are more likely to be subject to the American legal system than to acts of brutality by European American citizens or slave masters.

Moreover, for many African American children, the dozens is a ritual started in childhood to promote resiliency in the face of injustice and developmental threats. The training promotes verbal skills to express this strain but also the ability to manage challenge and threat—to become unaffected and undeterred by insult. Those who "get good" not only shield themselves from the verbal abuse of others, but they also raise their social status by their ability to attract and entertain an eager audience with their quick wit and sharp tongue.

1st person:	Yo' mama's so ugly that when she wakes up in the morning, the sun go down.
2nd person:	Yo' mama's so backwards that she sits on the TV watching the couch.
1st person:	When I get finish with you, you gonna reach in your pocket and give me yo' last dollar for the education you just got.
2nd person:	At least I got a dollar. You can't even pay attention.

In today's youth culture, the "best" rapper is the person who can string together comedic insults and inflammatory statements in a rhythmic rhyming pattern. This banter may reinforce the categorization of human beings based on stereotypes created centuries earlier. Even the more conscious and conscientious in hip-hop and rap music view the "battle rap," a glorified game of the dozens, as an integral part of the culture. These public feuds, played out in music, have brought critical acclaim to rap artists such as KRS-One, MC Shan, Kool Moe Dee, LL Cool J, Biggie Smalls, Tupac Shakur, Jay-Z, and Nas. In the opinion of some, though, playing the dozens has replaced the physical shackles of slavery with the mental bondage created by self-hate.

—*Karen D. Taylor-Crawford*

See also African Americans; Ethnic Minority Youth

FURTHER READING

Gilligan, J. (1996). *Violence: Reflections on a national epidemic.* New York: Vintage Books.
Horton, J. O. (1998). *In hope of liberty: Culture, community, and protest among northern free Blacks, 1700–1860.* New York: Oxford University Press.

DRAPETOMANIA

Drapetomania, from the Greek *drapetes* (runaway slave) and *mania* (mad or crazy), literally means "the disease causing slaves to run away." Dr. Samuel A. Cartwright, an eminent surgeon in the antebellum American South, coined the term to express the idea that runaway slaves exhibited symptoms of mental disorder. Cartwright's position—that sanity meant accepting the condition of enslavement, whereas fleeing slavery was insane—illustrates the role of prevailing sociocultural norms in the construction of psychiatric diagnoses.

Thomas S. Szasz, author of *The Myth of Mental Illness*, referenced drapetomania in describing the political function of psychiatry in his 1971 essay "The Sane Slave." Szasz asserted that psychiatric diagnoses emerge from normative standards of a given historical era as mechanisms of social control. The pathologizing of deviations from social norms continues today, Szasz argued, particularly for minorities and other oppressed groups (e.g., battered women's self-defense may be pathologized as battered women's syndrome). Thus, the prevalent diagnoses of a historical era reveal more about social pathology than about individual mental illness.

Cartwright's treatise on drapetomania was written in 1851, a time when abolitionist criticism of slavery threatened to undermine Southern economic and social stability. Cartwright attempted to counter abolitionists by claiming that enslavement engendered psychological health in African Americans, who required paternalistic care, whereas freedom engendered pathology. Cartwright opined that following proper medical advice prevented drapetomania and its symptom (running away): The recommended cure was to keep slaves in their "natural" position of submission while providing for their needs, along with whipping at the onset of the disorder.

The idea that freedom was pathological for African Americans was also presented in Cartwright's report on another diagnosis, dysaesthesia aethiopis, a disorder characterized by intellectual stupor, somatic lesions, "breaking, wasting and destroying" property, wandering at night, avoiding work, and general trouble making ("rascality"). Cartwright thought the disorder prevalent among "free negroes" who were not under supervision, of whom Cartwright stated that nearly all were afflicted. Dysaesthesia aethiopis and drapetomania medically justified the institution of slavery for the "good" of the enslaved while answering abolitionists' charges that slavery debased both the enslaved and the enslaver.

The term "drapetomania" first appeared in Cartwright's 1851 "Report on the Diseases and Physical Peculiarities of the Negro Race," published in the *New Orleans Medical and Surgical Journal* (since reprinted several times). The term appears periodically in medical and psychological literature as a critique of the politicization of psychiatry. Noted African American psychiatrist Alvin F. Poussaint, who has argued that racism, rather than reactions to it, should be pathologized, observed that the criteria for abnormality are continually shaped by societal values. Cultural psychologists have argued that these diagnoses represent ethical violations that still resonate in clinical practice. It was not unusual in the antebellum South for a European American doctor to describe disease in people of African descent; ample evidence of slaves put to medical use, including medical experimentation, exists. Psychologist Arthur L. Whaley proposed that the historical trauma incurred by abusive diagnoses such as drapetomania contributes to present-day cultural mistrust of European American mental health providers.

—Carlota Ocampo

See also Institutional Racism; Models of Mental Health

FURTHER READING

Savitt, T. L. (2003). The use of blacks for medical experimentation and demonstration in the old South. In S. Plous (Ed.), *Understanding prejudice and discrimination* (pp. 134–139). Boston: McGraw-Hill.

Szasz, T. (1971). The sane slave: An historical note on the use of medical diagnosis in justificatory rhetoric. *American Journal of Psychotherapy, 25,* 228–239.

Whaley, A. L. (2001). Cultural mistrust of white mental health clinicians among African Americans with severe mental illness. *American Journal of Orthopsychiatry, 71,* 252–256.

DRUG ABUSE PREVENTION IN ETHNIC MINORITY YOUTH

Although drug abuse affects all segments of society, the negative impact of drug abuse is most severe in minority communities, particularly among African American and Hispanic American adults in economically disadvantaged urban settings. Fortunately, significant advances have been made in preventing drug abuse in recent decades, and effective programs are available for school, family, and community settings. Many of these interventions focus on adolescents because it is during the teenage years that substance use typically begins. Prevention programs can be categorized into three major types. *Universal* programs focus on all youth in a particular setting. *Selective* programs target high-risk youth, such as those having academic problems in school. *Indicated* programs are designed for youth who are already experimenting with drugs or engaging in other high-risk behaviors.

Most of the research and development on youth drug abuse prevention programs has focused on universal programs designed to be implemented in schools. Of these, the most effective approaches either (1) teach youth how to recognize and resist social influences promoting drug use or (2) teach teens a variety of social and personal skills to increase their overall competence in handling life's challenges, as well as teach them to resist social influences to use drugs. However, these approaches were initially developed and tested primarily with European American, middle-class adolescents. Some efforts to develop prevention approaches that are appropriate for racial and ethnic minority youth have focused on the cultural, social, environmental, or historical factors believed to influence drug use or abuse in a particular racial or ethnic minority group. However, research evidence indicates that the most effective approaches for minority youth are the same as those used with European American youth. These prevention programs target social influences to use drugs and enhance general personal competence. Although they are effective with a broad range of adolescents, the effectiveness of these approaches can be increased by tailoring or adapting them to specific racial and ethnic groups in ways that make them more culturally sensitive and relevant to the target population.

CONTEMPORARY PREVENTION APPROACHES

The majority of prevention programs are universal school-based programs that focus on middle or junior high school students. The goal of these primary prevention programs is to prevent substance use before it begins by addressing the risk and protective factors associated with the early stages of drug use.

Preventing the onset of drug use during the early teenage years is presumed to reduce the prevalence of drug abuse during later adolescence and early adulthood. The most promising contemporary approaches are conceptualized within a theoretical framework that is based on the etiology of drug abuse and psychological theories of human behavior. Effective prevention approaches can be grouped into two general categories: (1) social-resistance approaches and (2) competence-enhancement approaches.

Social-Resistance Strategies

According to the social-resistance approach, adolescent drug use results from a variety of social influences, including the direct modeling of drug use behavior (particularly that of peers) and persuasive advertising and media portrayals that encourage alcohol, tobacco, and other drug use. Therefore, social-influence programs focus primarily on teaching youth how to recognize and resist pressures to use drugs using a variety of skills-training exercises. The goal of these exercises is to have students learn ways to avoid high-risk situations in which they are likely to experience pressure to smoke, drink, or use drugs, as well as to acquire the knowledge, confidence, and skills needed to handle social pressure. These programs frequently include a component that makes students aware of prodrug influences in the media, with an emphasis on the techniques that advertisers use to influence consumer behavior.

Competence-Enhancement Strategies

A limitation of the social-resistance approach is that it assumes that young people do not want to use drugs but lack the skills or confidence to refuse the social influences promoting their use. For some youth, however, using drugs may not simply be a matter of yielding to peer pressure but instead may have instrumental value; for example, drug use may help them deal with social anxiety or low self-esteem. According to the competence-enhancement approach, drug use is conceptualized as a socially learned and functional behavior that is influenced by an adolescent's prodrug cognitions, attitudes, and beliefs. These factors, in combination with poor personal and social skills, are believed to increase an adolescent's susceptibility to social influences that favor drug use. The most effective competence-enhancement approaches to drug abuse prevention emphasize the teaching of generic personal self-management skills and social-coping skills, including decision-making and problem-solving skills, cognitive skills for resisting interpersonal and media influences, skills for enhancing self-esteem (goal setting and self-directed behavior change techniques), adaptive coping strategies for dealing with stress and anxiety, general social skills (complimenting, conversational skills, and skills for forming new friendships), and general assertiveness skills.

For both social-resistance and competence-enhancement programs, the most effective way to teach these skills is to use a combination of methods, including instruction and demonstration, role-playing, group feedback and reinforcement, behavioral rehearsal (in-class practice), and extended (out-of-class) practice through behavioral homework assignments. Furthermore, because adolescents tend to overestimate the prevalence of drug use, prevention programs often attempt to correct normative expectations that nearly everybody smokes, drinks alcohol, or uses drugs, which is called *normative education*. Programs that combine social-resistance skills, competence-enhancement skills, and normative education appear to be the most effective.

PREVENTION PROGRAMS FOR ETHNIC MINORITY YOUTH

An important limitation of most research on the etiology and prevention of drug abuse is that, historically, it has focused mostly on European American, middle-class students. Fortunately, this is changing: An increasing number of preventive interventions are being developed or adapted to prevent alcohol, tobacco, and drug abuse among minority youth and multiethnic populations. Some research has tested prevention programs that target risk and protective factors that are unique to one or more racial or ethnic minority groups. Other research has tested the extent to which prevention approaches that have proved effective with European American youth are also effective with minority youth. Still other research has tested the effectiveness of tailoring those approaches to one or more minority groups.

Targeted Prevention Programs for a Specific Racial or Ethnic Group

One approach has been to develop targeted prevention programs that address the unique risk and protective factors for substance abuse in a particular racial or ethnic minority group. For example, a prevention program for African American youth may build on concepts from African culture and tradition to enhance cultural identity, ethnic pride, and self-esteem. An important advantage of targeted prevention programs is that they are more likely to be readily adopted by the target population. However, this approach assumes that differences in the etiology of substance use outweigh the similarities across racial and ethnic groups—in most cases, an untested assumption. The approach also assumes a high level of homogeneity within a particular racial or ethnic group—referred to as *ethnic glossing*—which, in some cases, may unintentionally mask important differences in national origin, socioeconomic status, norms, values, and traditions. For example, in the United States, Hispanics come from Cuba, Puerto Rico, the Dominican Republic, Mexico, and Central and South America, and each group has different histories and traditions regarding substance use. Furthermore, even if there are differences across populations that warrant different interventions, it would be logistically difficult to implement separate interventions for different racial and ethnic groups in school settings, which contain multiethnic student populations. Thus, on both a scientific and a practical level, current research does not support developing different prevention programs for different populations.

Tailoring Prevention Programs to Increase Cultural Sensitivity

The most effective drug abuse prevention approaches are those that target prodrug social influences and enhance personal and social competence. A limited but growing body of research indicates that these approaches are also effective with minority youth. In other words, prevention approaches that work with European American youth also appear to work with minority youth. However, some research suggests that the effectiveness of these approaches can be improved by tailoring or adapting them to increase cultural appropriateness and sensitivity for a particular racial or ethnic minority group. For example, a prevention program that has been found to be effective with European American youth could been tailored for urban minority youth by including relevant graphics or illustrations of minority youth, modifying the situations for behavioral rehearsal or role-play scenarios

so that they are more appropriate, and making sure that the language and reading level of intervention materials are appropriate for the target population. Such tailoring should be based on exploratory, qualitative research, such as focus group testing with the target population, review of intervention materials and methods by experts, and feedback from students and staff of the school and local community. Ideally, these adaptations should be built in to an intervention rather than made on an ad hoc basis by local implementers or teachers. Major changes to the program may inadvertently compromise the underlying prevention strategy or weaken the core components of an intervention. An advantage of adapting an effective prevention program to a specific population is that the tailoring process may enhance the relevance and acceptance of an already effective intervention.

—*Gilbert J. Botvin*

FURTHER READING

Hawkins, J. D., Catalano, R. F., & Miller, J. Y. (1992). Risk and protective factors for alcohol and other drug problems in adolescence and early adulthood: Implications for substance abuse prevention. *Psychological Bulletin, 112,* 64–105.

National Institute on Drug Abuse. (2003). *Preventing drug use among children and adolescents: A research-based guide for parents, educators, and community leaders* (2nd ed.). Bethesda, MD: U.S. Department of Health and Human Services. Retrieved February 1, 2006, from http://www.nida.nih.gov/Prevention/PREVOPEN.html

Resnicow, K., Soler, R., Braithwaite, R. L., Ahluwalia, J. S., & Butler, J. (2000). Cultural sensitivity in substance abuse prevention. *Journal of Community Psychology, 28,* 271–290.

Sloboda, Z., & Bukoski, W. J. (2003). *Handbook of drug abuse prevention: Theory, science, and practice.* New York: Kluwer Academic/Plenum.

DSM-IV

In 1952, the American Psychiatric Association (APA) published its first official listing of mental diseases. Titled the *Diagnostic and Statistical Manual of Mental Disorders* (*DSM*), it was conceived as a way to establish a common diagnostic language and to increase interclinician reliability, which ranged from just over 20% to about 42%, depending on the study. Largely ignored when it first appeared, the initial

DSM was a spiral-bound notebook with cursory descriptions of about 100 disorders, and it was sold primarily to mental institutions for a mere $3.50. The third edition, the *DSM-III* in 1980, and more recent updates—the *DSM-III-R* in 1987, *DSM-IV* in 1994, and *DSM-IV-TR* in 2000—have expanded to 900 pages in length and sold hundreds of thousands of copies at over $80 each.

THEORETICAL INFLUENCES

The first two versions of the manual—the *DSM* and *DSM-II*—were heavily influenced by the psychoanalytic model. Mental disease terms, such as neurosis and psychosis, derived from Freud's view that psychopathology resides within the person and can be traced to unconscious conflicts. From this standpoint, symptom profiles are comparatively worthless in understanding the etiology of a patient's intrapsychic conflicts and designing an effective treatment.

In contrast, the *DSM-III* was compiled by research-oriented psychiatrists who were intent on devising a scientifically supportable system that could be widely used by clinicians, regardless of their theoretical orientation. Unfortunately, adequate research was still lacking at the time the *DSM-III* was developed. In the absence of reliable data, it was not unusual for the editor of the *DSM-III*, psychiatrist Robert Spitzer, to formulate new diagnoses with the help of only a few committee members.

Carefully navigating a course away from psychoanalytic assumptions and terminology, Spitzer and his colleagues retained, in a few instances, the traditional psychoanalytic language while shifting to a method of diagnosis contingent on explicit symptoms. For the first time, each disorder was based on a list of operationally worded criteria, on which a final diagnosis could be determined. If a patient exhibited a certain number of symptoms out of the total list, the diagnostic threshold was crossed and the diagnosis was thus applied.

Critics have alleged that political and economic agendas, not science, account for the changes in the *DSM*'s emphasis over the last 50 years. When insurance companies began to reimburse patients for mental health treatment during the 1960s, they pressed for a comprehensive list of specific and treatable disorders. In response, the *DSM*'s formulators expanded the diagnostic categories in the *DSM-III* to more than 300 disorders. Such compliance was amply rewarded. Shortly after its publication, the *DSM-III* leapt into

prominence as insurers began to require *DSM-III* codes as a prerequisite for reimbursement. Alongside the proliferation of disorders, the influence of pharmaceutical companies may account, at least in part, for the *DSM*'s growing emphasis on the biological basis of mental disorders. By the time the *DSM-IV* was published in 1994, mental disorders had been largely recast as biologically based disorders that could be treated with medication. It was a convenient transformation, considering the rising influence of managed care and diminishing support for traditional long-term psychodynamic therapy.

MULTICULTURAL ISSUES

From the standpoint of culture and gender sensitivity, the *DSM* has been criticized for minimizing the impact of contextual factors on the development of psychological disorders. For example, the *DSM-IV* defines a personality disorder as an enduring pattern of behavior and experience that deviates significantly from the individual's culture, is stable over time, has an onset in adolescence or early adulthood, and leads to impairment. By implying that personality disorders originate within the individual and remain relatively stable over time, the *DSM* discounts the way that social norms can influence the way individuals behave. Consequently, the *DSM* effectively renders exaggerated compliance with gender and racial stereotypes a form of psychopathology. For example, women who have been taught to be more nurturing, more dependent on relationships, and more emotional than men may be diagnosed with dependent or histrionic personality disorders because they exhibit exaggerated compliance with prescribed gender roles. Similarly, African American men who show resistance to authority may qualify for a diagnosis of antisocial personality disorder if the clinician conducting the diagnostic interview fails to take into account the environmental stressors contributing to the patient's defiance or the effect of identifying with prevailing racial stereotypes. In contrast, the *DSM* does not render Anglo male stereotypical behavior, such as putting work above relationships and disregarding others' needs when making decisions, as a psychopathological disorder.

The influence of culture and gender bias in the formulation of *DSM* disorders is especially apparent in so-called mental disorders that have been revised, stricken from later editions, or effectively challenged prior to inclusion. For example, the *DSM-III* treated homosexuality as a personality disorder, but the *DSM-III-R* downgraded it to an ego-dystonic disorder. By the time the *DSM-IV* was published, homosexuality had been dropped as a mental disorder because of social and political pressure to treat homosexuality as a normal gender choice.

Two other controversial diagnoses would have been enshrined in the *DSM-III* if women had not objected. Under Spitzer's editorship, which lasted through the publication of the *DSM-III-R*, the diagnosis of masochistic personality disorder was briefly considered before women expressed concern that it would only serve to diagnose patients who had been abused—especially women—with this disorder. Another diagnosis that was considered would have made premenstrual syndrome a mental disorder, but again, outrage from women dissuaded Spitzer and his colleagues from including it.

Beyond the possible biases inherent in the *DSM*'s criteria, there is evidence that mental health professionals frequently misdiagnose on the basis of gender and race. For example, *DSM* field trials revealed that African American men are more likely to receive a diagnosis of schizophrenia than Anglo men, and Anglo males are more often diagnosed with affective disorders than their African American counterparts. Furthermore, African Americans are more likely to be described as "paranoid" and Hispanics as "histrionic." When a structured interview approach is used to minimize clinician subjectivity, the African American/ Anglo differences disappear, leading to the conclusion that misdiagnoses, not objective racial differences, account for the skewed results.

In recent years, the APA has called for increased cultural competency among its members. At an APA symposium in New Orleans in 1999, APA president Allan Tasman referred to cultural competency as one of the most important and often neglected issues in psychiatry. Speaking at the same conference, Francis Lou, a clinical professor of psychiatry at the University of California, San Francisco, said that psychiatry needs to be concerned with the whole person and to resist tendencies to reduce human experience to mere diagnostic labels.

To its credit, the *DSM-IV* reflects a growing sensitivity to the role of culture in influencing individual behavior and how cultural competency is essential in making accurate diagnoses. It contains a section at the back of the book on dimensions of culture's influence.

In it, clinicians are called on to consider the difficulties of applying *DSM-IV* criteria to members of different cultural or ethnic groups. A clinician who is ignorant of the subtle aspects of an individual's cultural background may unwittingly overdiagnose behaviors and beliefs that are considered normal in the individual's culture. In particular, the application of personality disorder criteria across cultural settings is especially susceptible to cultural bias because concepts of the self, coping styles, and communication patterns vary significantly across settings. To combat such misuses of the *DSM*, the chapter addresses the meaning of cultural or ethnic reference groups, the impact of culture on psychosocial environment and functioning, cultural explanations of illness, cultural elements influencing the patient–therapist relationship, and ways that an overall cultural assessment may affect diagnosis and care.

Despite its universal use by clinicians seeking third-party compensation and by the court system to determine the sanity of defendants, the *DSM* remains far from universally respected. Some critics argue that the *DSM* is an "emperor without clothes" and represents an unscientific system that enshrines the opinions of a few powerful psychiatrists. Detractors also point to the sobering fact that the initial premise on which the *DSM* was conceived—that it would increase interclinician diagnostic reliability—remains unsupported by research. Indeed, reliability studies indicate that interclinician reliability associated with the *DSM*'s use is no higher than the levels produced prior to its publication, and in some cases it is lower. Although clinicians may endeavor to improve their sensitivity to the influence of culture in the use of the *DSM*, the refinement of the user can never entirely compensate for the weakness of the tool itself.

—*G. Scott Sparrow*

See also Depression; Eating Disorders; Schizophrenia

FURTHER READING

American Psychiatric Association. (2000). *Diagnostic and statistical manual of mental disorders* (4th ed., text rev.). Washington, DC: Author.

Brown, L. S. (1994). *Subversive dialogues.* New York: Basic Books.

Caplan, P., & Cosgrove, L. (Eds.). (2004). *Bias in psychiatric diagnosis.* Lanham, MD: Jason Aronson.

E

EATING DISORDERS

Eating disorders are a phenomenon affecting millions of young women in Western societies. Eating disorders are a food-related dysfunction in which a person changes her eating habits in a way that is harmful to the mind and/or body. Cultural elements are at the root of eating disorders—primarily the expectation that beauty is defined by thinness. To begin a discussion of eating disorders, it is first necessary to identify the criteria for making diagnoses and to clarify distinctions among specific eating disorders. This section presents the *Diagnostic and Statistical Manual of Mental Disorders, Fourth Edition, Text Revision* (DSM-IV-TR) criteria for eating disorder diagnoses and introduces the prevalence rates for women.

THE DSM-IV-TR EATING DISORDER CRITERIA

The DSM-IV-TR defines the criteria for mental disorders and provides universal standards for mental health practitioners that will aid in their treatment.

Anorexia nervosa (anorexia) is defined as an eating disorder characterized by self-starvation and a weight of 15% or more below normal. The DSM-IV-TR criteria for anorexia nervosa include a relentless pursuit of thinness and a refusal to maintain normal weight, an intense fear of gaining weight, preoccupation with weight, and lack of menstruation (for females beyond puberty).

Bulimia nervosa (bulimia) is defined as an eating disorder in which a person has uncontrollable urges to eat excessively and then purge. The cycle of bingeing (e.g., eating an excessive amount of food accompanied with a feeling of lack of control) and purging (i.e., vomiting, use of diuretics, etc.) must occur twice a week for 3 months to warrant a psychiatric diagnosis.

In addition to anorexia and bulimia, the DSM-IV-TR includes the category of "eating disorder not otherwise specified" (EDNOS), defined as eating disturbances that don't meet the criteria for any specific eating disorder. Thus, this type of eating disorder is characterized by elements of anorexia and/or bulimia, but not enough of them to warrant a clinical diagnosis of either disorder. Individuals with this diagnosis are at higher risk for eventual diagnosis of anorexia or bulimia. Examples of this type of eating disorder are the regular use of compensatory behaviors by an individual of normal body weight after eating small amounts of food, or binge-eating disorder, which is characterized by recurrent episodes of binge eating without regular use of compensatory behaviors.

PREVALENCE ESTIMATES

It is estimated that anorexia affects from .5% to 1% of the population and bulimia from 1% to 3% of the population in the United States. However, these numbers can be even greater in college student populations. For example, one study at a midwestern university found that among introductory psychology and sorority-member participants, 2% met criteria for bulimia and 5% met criteria for an EDNOS diagnosis.

CONSEQUENCES OF EATING DISORDERS

Eating disorders often have serious psychological and medical consequences. Most bodily systems are affected by starvation, and cardiac, gastrointestinal, and electrolyte disturbances can result. Clinical depression and anxiety disorders commonly co-occur with eating disorders.

It has been estimated that 20% to 30% of overweight persons seeking help at weight-loss programs are classified as binge eaters. Because binge eating is highly associated with obesity, numerous health issues result among patients who engage in it. The consequences of eating disturbances need to be taken seriously, given that obesity increases one's risk of developing conditions such as high blood pressure, diabetes, heart disease, stroke, gall bladder disease, and cancer of the breast, prostate, and colon. Without treatment, up to 20% of people with serious eating disorders die, and with treatment, that number falls to 2% or 3%.

RACIAL/ETHNIC DIFFERENCES OF EATING DISORDERS

Undeniably, the stereotype exists that women who suffer from eating disorders are young middle- to upper-middle-class European Americans. However, evidence is now emerging that eating disorders in fact occur in a wide range of ethnic, cultural, and socioeconomic groups within the United States. The estimates of the prevalence of anorexia and bulimia in non–European Americans can range from 1% to 4%, depending on age, ethnicity, and location. The inferences drawn from earlier studies were that ethnic and racial differences in the prevalence of eating disorders were linked to socioeconomic status. In other words, as family or household income increases, so does the rate of diagnosable eating disorders. Nevertheless, the belief that non–European American women seldom suffer from eating disorders contributes to barriers to diagnosis, treatment, and prevention for women who fit this description.

Of the many different racial groups, African American women have probably been studied most often to understand the complexity of their body image and eating behavior. By and large, research on African American women indicates that they are more satisfied with their bodies than are their European American counterparts. Nonetheless, they still suffer from various types of disordered eating. Most disordered eating among African Americans has been found to be related to assimilation to European American culture, as measured by the

Racial Identity Attitude Scale for African Americans. Thus, as African Americans take on the values of the larger (European American) culture, their rates of eating disorders will increase. One large-scale investigation of eating disorders among African American women shed light on this phenomenon. *Essence* magazine conducted a survey asking readers about disordered eating behavior and attitudes. Results from the survey showed that more than half (53.5%) of African American women respondents evidenced some symptoms of eating disorders. Even though there was no way to distinguish between those with diagnosable eating disorders and symptoms of disordered eating, such findings highlight the eating-related struggles of African American women, an overlooked population.

Only a few studies have investigated the eating behaviors of Asian American women. Inconsistent results regarding binge eating, vomiting, and bulimia have been reported among Asian American populations. Some studies cite more vomiting and bulimia among Asian Americans, whereas others state that the rates are far lower among this group.

The Hispanic culture—similar to African American culture—has a different standard of beauty that often includes an acceptance of higher body weights. Thus, Hispanic women are able to maintain some level of body satisfaction despite their higher weights. The research on Hispanic American women and eating disorders, however, seems to be consistent. A small amount of the research states that Hispanic women have eating disorder rates similar to those of European American women, and most of the remaining research states that binge eating is more severe in this population. Obesity is another factor directly related to binge eating and has long been a major health issue in the Hispanic population.

Another American minority group that may be affected by the dominant European American culture's focus on weight and body size is Native Americans. One study has found that Native American adolescents received significantly higher dieting and restricting/ purging scores than their European American counterparts. A high percentage of individuals attempting to control their weight through controlled eating could suggest a higher prevalence of eating disorders among this group. Still, there has been such a deficiency of research on this population that no significant estimates of disordered eating can be declared.

The characteristic that all of the studies regarding minority women and eating disorders highlight is *acculturation*, defined as the process of assimilating new ideas into an existing cognitive structure. Thus, the more acculturated to American values—especially those regarding appearance—minority women are, the higher their risk for developing eating disorders.

It seems that there are no ethnic differences in the likelihood of obtaining treatment for eating disorders. However, there may be such forces at work as referral bias. In other words, clinicians might have a tendency to refer only patients who look like the stereotypical individual who suffers from an eating disorder. Other issues come into play, such as cultural values about seeking help and fears about being treated unfairly by health professionals, that also contribute to treatment seeking for eating disorders among minority women. Further research is needed to examine ways that we as a society can begin to diminish the numbers of women suffering from this condition. Despite the growing interest in and concern about the risks, consequences, and treatment of eating disorders, little is known about effective means of preventing these disorders. An understanding of prevention is urgently needed to combat this growing threat to the health of women in this country.

—*Jameca Falconer*

See also DSM-IV; Models of Mental Health

FURTHER READING

American Psychiatric Association. (2000). *Diagnostic and statistical manual of mental disorders, fourth edition, text revision* (DSM-IV-TR). Washington, DC: Author.

Brock, K. J. (1999). *Exploring evidence for a continuum of eating disturbances: Self-objectification, parental attachment, and sociotrophy-autonomy in college women.* Unpublished doctoral dissertation, University of Missouri– Columbia.

National Institute of Mental Health. (1996). *Mental health research in eating disorders* (NIMH Publication No. PA-96-064). Bethesda, MD: Author.

EDUCATION

Education is the formal process by which people learn, utilize, and analyze knowledge; it occurs at both the individual and institutional levels. *Multicultural education* refers to any education program that aims to improve the educational experiences of racial or ethnic minority (REM) students or students who may be considered a minority as a result of their gender, religious orientation, sexual orientation, or disability. Although the initial goal of multicultural education was to integrate diversity into American education systems, currently the majority of multicultural education programs are designed to improve the quality of education for REM students. Given public education's history of institutional oppression, the use of Eurocentric (European-oriented) values in curriculum, and the continuation of limited educational persistence for minority groups, multicultural education seeks to provide REM students with educational access, equal opportunity, and culturally sensitive curriculum.

The following entry provides a summary of the educational experiences of REM students in U.S public education. An overview of the history of REM students and education, educational inequities, REM educational challenges, multicultural efforts, and recommendations is presented.

OVERVIEW

The diversification of America has created a shift in the demographic composition of many social institutions, including education. Despite the growing number of REM students, the educational attainment and persistence of REM students does not parallel the attainment and persistence of European American students. Although REM enrollment has increased, persistence and graduation rates remain dismal for REMs in secondary- and higher-education institutions. The limited educational progress of REM students merits a detailed analysis for a better understanding of their educational journeys.

HISTORY OF MULTICULTURAL EDUCATION

United States public schools (K–16) have a long history of marginalization and assimilation efforts for REM students. After the abolishment of slavery in 1865, the United States established a legal plan for "separate-but-equal" institutions for African American and European American students. However, segregation only secured the racial caste system that provided unequal opportunities and inadequate resources for REM students. African Americans were denied a quality education based on the color of their skin for more than a century, and other REM groups encountered similar challenges in relation to equal access and resources.

Beginning as early as the late 1800s, the influx of immigrants to the United States created a question for public schools and their administrations: how would public schools teach such a wide variety of cultural/linguistic groups of all social classes? In response, public schools began to implement Americanization programs as early as the 1900s. Americanization programs actively *forced* immigrant students to learn "American" or Eurocentric values and de-emphasized the importance of their native cultures. For example, early Americanization efforts included the removal of Native American children from reservations to be placed in large boarding schools that denied the students the right to speak their native tongues, dress in their cultural attires, and practice Native cultural values (i.e., spirituality and collectivism). Americanization efforts not only reflected the racist and discriminatory perceptions of European Americans, but also reinforced the unequal power structure between European Americans and minority groups. Although most blatant Americanization programs ended in the 1940s, arguably, assimilation continued as a covert component of curriculum.

The civil rights movement of the 1960s created a new awareness of the lack of educational advancement of all minorities in U.S. schools. Schools all over the United States began to implement many different types of programs, efforts, measures, or policies to help improve the education of various groups, such as REMs, immigrants, and disabled, gifted, and religious minorities. For instance, policies such as Title IX and the Individuals With Disabilities Education Act were implemented to improve the educational access of women and students with disabilities. Thus, *multicultural education* has come to describe a wide range of programs designed to help any minority group; there is no specific curriculum or program that fully embodies multicultural education.

CURRENT EDUCATIONAL INEQUALITY

Public education in the United States is not a uniform system that offers equal resources and opportunities to each and every student. Underprivileged and REM youth are more likely to attend poorer-quality schools with subordinate forms of instruction, curriculum, programs, resources, and opportunities than their European American peers. Upper- and upper-middle-class schools provide spacious playgrounds, computer and science labs, various class selections ranging from honors to advanced placement (AP), certified teachers, and a college-preparatory curriculum. In comparison, urban schools (which the majority of REMs attend) offer various training tracks (e.g., academic, vocational, and general) and are limited in political and economic resources. The property tax base of public education results in considerable disparities between suburban and innter-city schools. Larger, urban schools become powerless and remain reliant on overextended state and local budgets to provide resources to an often REM-majority student body; the phenomenon supports the sentiment that the education system remains separate and unequal. Exacerbating the issue, the unequal system facilitates subordinate learning environments—further enlarging the achievement gap between REM students and their European American peers.

Quality of curriculum, instructional processes, and school environment also introduce significant influences on students' learning and academic achievement. In particular, research has noted the impact of curricular relevance and differentiation of teaching methods on student progress. Research supports REM students' interest in learning about their histories and communities, as well as the negative effects of Eurocentric curriculums on student motivation, involvement, and self-efficacy.

Other factors embedded in student–teacher interactions include preconceived perceptions of specific groups, cultural biases, stereotypes, and limited student expectations. Specific examples of such biases can be reflected in grades and direction from counselors in relation to educational planning and class placement (e.g., curricular tracking). The cultural values of REM students have also been noted to be incongruent with mainstream practices of individualism, competitiveness, and linear learning. As a result, REM students experience lower qualities of experiences, less advancement, less integration, and ultimately lower rates of graduation.

Beyond the educational infrastructure, additional factors contribute to educational experiences and academic progress of REMs. Specific background and environmental variables have been found to substantially affect REM educational persistence, including REM students' parental education, parental involvement, generational status, socioeconomic status, language proficiency, acculturation level (students' level of cultural adaptation to mainstream culture), gender, and social support from peers and the community environment. For example, Latino first-generation students have more negative perceptions of the educational system than their immigrant Latino student counterparts. Additionally, less acculturated (those preserving their native culture) students experience greater incongruity with their environment and a sense of marginalization from the majority culture.

MULTICULTURAL EFFORTS IN EDUCATION

The rise in diversity and the growing achievement gaps between REM groups have introduced a drastic rise in equal opportunity programs, including multicultural education. Multicultural education promotes a culturally inclusive perspective, while de-emphasizing Eurocentric curriculum and Eurocentric education systems. Traditionally, teachers have implemented culture by using the *contribution approach* (e.g., focusing on holidays) or *additive approach* (e.g., adding terms and content) without transforming the curriculum or their cultural frameworks. Conversely, the integration of a multicultural paradigm includes substantial change to the structure of the curriculum and the intervention of social problems and community solutions for social action. Examples of incorporating multicultural techniques include open discussion of racial conflict, writing and critical-thinking assignments on diversity, heritage exploration, cultural value/worldview comparisons, and community projects.

The implementation of multicultural education is essential not only for curriculum, but for school environment and student relations. The utilization of a multicultural paradigm allows administrators and teachers to create a school environment that is representative of various cultures, respectful of cultural differences, sensitive to diversity, and discouraging of assimilation. As teachers, administrators, and educational systems work toward becoming more culturally sensitive and competent, a multicultural approach will alleviate the educational disparities experienced by REM students.

CONCLUSION

The transformation of the makeup of U.S. schools demands a cultural evaluation and assessment of all educational institutions. For progress to occur, both structural and curriculum changes are required in America's educational system. Facilities and resources need to be more evenly distributed, and teachers and administrators must work at addressing issues in and out of the classroom. Personal reflection and inventories by staff of cultural biases and perceptions will assist in the development and implementation of culturally sensitive environments, and the practicing identification and appreciation of cultural differences will enhance cultural integration and student adaptation. The perspective that the education system is to serve as a melting pot for the development of American culture must be eliminated, and a more progressive, culturally integrative approach that embraces diversity must be implemented.

—*Jeanett Castellanos*
—*Vern Farber*

See also Academic Achievement and Minority Individuals; Bilingual Education; Head Start

FURTHER READING

American Psychiatric Association. (2000). *Diagnostic and statistical manual of mental disorders* (4th ed., text rev.). Washington, DC: Author.

Banks, J. A., & Banks, C. A. (Eds.). (2004). *Multicultural education: Issues and perspectives*. Hoboken, NJ: Wiley.

EMIC VERSUS ETIC DISTINCTION

The *emic* versus *etic* distinction suggests that some terms or concepts are specific to a culture (*emics*), whereas some terms or concepts are common across cultures (*etics*). For example, in the Japanese language, there is no distinction between the *l* and *r* sounds. The nearest equivalent sound is more like a quickly rolled *r* sound, so *l* is more foreign to the Japanese ear. Therefore, from a phonemic perspective, *r* is meaningful, whereas *l* is not. In English, Brislin cited the *ng* sound as being nonexistent to begin a word, whereas it is a common sound at the beginning of words in other languages.

On the other hand, from a phonetic perspective, *l, r,* and *ng* are all identifiable sounds. Linguists have compiled a list of sounds that are meaningful in at least one culture, and although a sound may be meaningful in one culture and not in another, all cultures can at least identify that the sound exists. In English, we do not have a trilled *r* sound in any of our words, but we can certainly identify this sound in many Spanish words.

In applying these linguistic roots to cross-cultural investigation, emics deals with terms and concepts that are meaningful within one culture, whereas etics deals with terms and concepts that can be generalized across cultures. Those who attempt to identify universal characteristics of people across all cultures (e.g., all cultures have something equivalent to "work" and equivalent to "play" and a way to distinguish between the two) are approaching human behavior from an etic perspective.

Harry Triandis has been among the leaders in examining emic and etic issues. As an example of how a term may have a different meaning within one culture, Triandis and other researchers have discussed the term *self-reliance*. In individualistic societies, *self-reliance* carries with it a sense that one can pursue one's own goals, and it has a tinge of competition in its definition. However, in collectivistic societies, *self-reliance* carries with it a sense that one does not want to burden those around them, and there is no sense of competition. Thus, whereas *self-reliance* does have meaning across cultures, it has different connotations within cultures.

Although etics may be an important pursuit, researchers can often impose their own culture-bound perspective on other cultures. John Berry calls this phenomenon *imposed etics*. For example, the famous Walter Mischel studies on delay of gratification have been cited as examples of imposed etics. Mischel sought to study delay of gratification and had a predictive model based on examination of European American children. When he applied this methodology to African American children in the inner city, he concluded that these children lacked the ability to delay gratification, which contributed to their continued existence in the inner city. However, upon further analysis, the children in his study seemed to actually be responding in an adaptive manner that eluded Mischel's detection. Thus, his conclusion of their lack of delay of gratification was an imposed etic based on his culturally encapsulated view.

Imposed etics may apply to the very topic under study. Although the Mischel studies can be criticized for misinterpreting the results, the criticism was that Mischel was using one interpretation instead of another. No one denies that the concept of delay of gratification is understood in both the European American and African American communities. However, because delay of gratification may be more appropriate to study in European American communities as opposed to inner-city African American communities, it may be inappropriate to even venture to study delay of gratification in communities where such a construct is irrelevant.

—*Jeffery Scott Mio*

FURTHER READING

Berry, J. W. (1969). On cross-cultural comparability. *International Journal of Psychology, 4,* 119–128.
Brislin, R. (2000). *Understanding culture's influence on behavior* (2nd ed.). Fort Worth, TX: Harcourt.
Pike, K. L. (1967). *Language in relation to a unified theory of the structure of human behavior.* The Hague, The Netherlands: Mouton.
Triandis, H. C., Bontempo, R., Betancourt, H., Bond, M., Leung, K., Brenes, A., et al. (1986). The measurement of etic aspects of individualism and collectivism across cultures. *Australian Journal of Psychology, 38,* 257–267.

EQUAL EMPLOYMENT OPPORTUNITY

Equal employment opportunity is a legal concept that suggests that employers should practice nondiscrimination in their labor practices. This concept became codified into law by President Lyndon Johnson in the form of Title VII of the Civil Rights Act of 1964. This law "prohibits employment discrimination based on race, color, religion, sex, or national origin." From this law, the Equal Employment Opportunity Commission (EEOC) was established. Other laws that fall under the EEOC jurisdiction are the Equal Pay Act of 1963, which protects both men and women from sex-based wage discrimination; the Age Discrimination in Employment Act of 1967, which protects older individuals (40 or more years old) from hiring discrimination; Title I and Title V of the Americans With Disabilities Act of 1990, which protects qualified individuals with disabilities from employment discrimination by the private sector and state and local governments; Sections 501 and 505 of the Rehabilitation Act of 1973, which protects individuals with disabilities from employment discrimination by the federal government; and the Civil Rights Act of 1991, which provides monetary compensation for intentional employment discrimination.

According to the EEOC, protections from discriminatory practices cover hiring and firing, recruitment, testing, fringe benefits, harassment, retaliation against individuals for filing claims of discriminatory practices, employment decisions based on stereotypes, and employment opportunities based on marriage to persons covered by the EEOC. Thus, the EEOC task has evolved from protecting individuals against discriminatory practices that were prevalent in employment to enforcing a host of civil rights laws that include affirmative action policies through which businesses were expected to actively seek out those who were historically shut out of hiring practices.

The evolution of equal employment to affirmative action was codified in 1972, when President Richard Nixon strengthened Title VII of the Civil Rights Act of 1964. The Johnson administration had assigned the Office of Federal Contract Compliance (OFCCP) the duty to monitor affirmative action efforts of federal contractors. The Nixon administration expanded this task by requesting that organizations have an affirmative action plan to identify underrepresented groups, conduct an analysis of these "protected groups" in the area, and develop a timetable of how the organizations will meet their goals of diversifying their workforce. The OFCCP developed an eight-factor computation method that is seen as the federal definition of affirmative action. The eight factors are the percentage of protected group members (1) in the immediate area around the facility, (2) who are unemployed in the immediate area, (3) in the total workforce in the immediate area, (4) in the immediate area who have relevant work-related skills, (5) in a reasonable recruitment area who have relevant work-related skills, (6) working within the organization who can be promoted or transferred to the specific facility, (7) who are at institutions that provide training in the required work-related skills, and (8) at the specific facility who could be trained in the required work-related skills. This definition has been used by the OFCCP to evaluate a company's affirmative action plan, which can determine if the company should continue as a federal contractor.

Because the federal government has the power to terminate federal contracts (or withhold funds, in the case of agencies receiving federal support, such as universities) of those organizations not in compliance with affirmative action regulations, there have been at least two reactions. First, some organizations have been eager to come into compliance with these regulations and have wholeheartedly embraced these objectives. On the other hand, a second reaction has been one of resistance, fighting against equal employment and affirmative action regulations. Besides resisting externally imposed hiring requirements, these programs also allow racist individuals to easily target and stigmatize protected group members. Moreover, many European American men who have felt victimized by so-called reverse discrimination

have used this legal concept to dismantle equitable treatment gained through equal opportunity/affirmative action policies.

Those who resisted affirmative action policies asserted that the EEOC moved from prohibiting race-based policies to imposing them when selecting workers or students. Moreover, some warned that affirmative action policies will lead to a form of civil war in the country. These conservative voices have used a variety of techniques to overturn the gains made by those who worked toward social justice. John Fobanjong observed that there has been a paradox in the ways in which these conservatives have gone about trying to overturn these advances, because the Fourteenth Amendment of the U.S. Constitution and the 1964 Civil Rights Act were considered to be ultra-liberal policies at the time of their passage and were opposed by social conservatives. However, Fobanjong went on to point out that these conservatives are now using these very laws to further their cause of resisting affirmative action policies.

As an example of how the Fourteenth Amendment and Title VII have been used to try to dismantle affirmative action programs, between 1990 and 1994, over 3,000 discrimination lawsuits were filed with the EEOC. Of these 3,000 cases, fewer than 100 (3%) involved reverse discrimination, and only 6 cases were deemed to have merit. The basis of these lawsuits was that European Americans, particularly males, claimed that their civil rights were being abridged because of a violation of equal protection under the law. Moreover, because Title VII sought to prevent discrimination based on race, the application of affirmative action principles necessarily discriminated against European Americans in favor of people of color or other protected groups.

Fred Pincus conducted a comprehensive analysis of more recent statistics involving discrimination cases. He examined 183,445 cases involving race and 153,579 cases involving sex examined by the EEOC between 1995 and 2000. Of the cases involving race, 166,724 were filed by African Americans (90.9%) and 16,721 were filed by European Americans (9.1%). However, because European Americans make up 83.8% of the workforce and African Americans make up only 11.4%, African American filing of discrimination cases is 55 times higher than European American filings. Moreover, only 38 of these reverse discrimination cases between 1998 and 2001 were deemed valid enough to make it to the federal appeals court level.

On the other hand, Pincus discovered that of the 153,579 cases involving sex discrimination, 125,578 were filed by women (81.8%) and 28,001 were filed by men (18.2%). In other words, over 11,000 more reverse discrimination cases involving sex than for race were filed between 1995 and 2001. Thus, despite the fact that when people discuss reverse discrimination they typically mean reverse racism, many more reverse discrimination cases are filed based on sex than on race. Although we are not attempting to pit women against people of color, such statistics need to be understood, because the EEOC and affirmative action programs have been developed within a context of race, given that the Fourteenth Amendment was passed in the aftermath of the Civil War of the 1860s and Title VII was passed in response to the civil rights movement of the 1960s.

—*Jeffery Scott Mio*

See also Academic Achievement and Minority Individuals; Bilingual Education; Head Start

FURTHER READING

Doverspike, D., Taylor, M. A., & Arthur, W., Jr. (2000). *Affirmative action: A psychological perspective.* Huntington, NY: Nova Science.

D'Souza, D. (1991). *Illiberal education: The politics of race and sex on campus.* New York: Free Press.

Equal Employment Opportunity Commission. (2004). *Federal equal employment opportunity (EEO) laws.* Retrieved December 15, 2004, from http://www.eeoc.gov

Fobanjong, J. (2001). *Understanding the backlash against affirmative action.* Huntington, NY: Nova Science.

Pincus, F. (2003). *Reverse discrimination: Dismantling the myth.* Boulder, CO: Rienner.

ETHNIC AND RACIAL IDENTITY

Social identity theory suggests that group identity development is a cognitive process that uses social categories to define self and establish a relationship with a reference group. These categories may be based on nationality, skin color, common history of oppression, ancestry, and so forth. Social identities are based on the emotional significance and importance of group memberships for self-definition and their relevance to worldview. Racial/ethnic group identity is only one of several possible social identities.

Historically, researchers have operated using either a narrow or a broad definition of *ethnicity*. The narrow definition focuses on national origin and/or unique cultural patterns. The broad definition has focused on cultural notions such as language, traditions, history, and other issues and attributes unique to a particular group, as well as physical characteristics. Using the broad notion of ethnicity, *race* and *ethnicity* are terms that may be and have been used interchangeably. Some researchers have argued that ethnicity is a value- neutral concept, whereas *race* inherently carries negative connotations. This argument and our increasing ability to call the notion of human races into question have resulted in an increasing preference for the use of the term *ethnicity*.

Racial/ethnic group identification specifically refers to a psychological attachment to one of several social categories available to individuals, when the category selected is based on "race" or skin color, common history, language, nationality, culture, ancestry, and so on. The importance of racial/ethnic group identity is rooted in its presumed influence on the ways that individuals conduct their lives and interact with others. Members are believed to share an implicit understanding of what it means to be a member of a designated racial group. Not all possible members of the group identify, nor do all members identify equally. Members may differ in their willingness to identify with specific group issues or aspects, exposing the complexity of racial/ethnic identification. Recent theorizing and empirical work have suggested the dynamic, fluid nature of racial/ethnic identity.

Numerous racial/ethnic identity models have been introduced, and various aspects of identity—including feelings of belonging and commitment, shared values and attitudes, and cultural variables such as language, behavior, and history—have been studied. Most models of racial/ethnic identity focus on racial minorities; however, the Janet Helms model of White racial identity is an exception. Factors that facilitate and inhibit the development of racially or ethnically based identities have also been addressed in this literature. It is clear that these identities are not merely reactions to racial oppression; the culture, history, and community of most ethnic/racial groups also contribute to the development and salience of an ethnic/racial identity.

RACIAL IDENTITY

In research and other literature pertaining to African American identity, ethnic identity is referred to as *racial identity,* the term being historical. Hope Landrine and Elizabeth Klonoff have noted that race is a social construction based on arbitrary physical criteria that change over time and culture and is typically used to justify oppression. Healthy African American identity formation must address the development of understanding and acceptance of the group in the face of lower status and prestige in society, stereotypes, and racism.

Researchers have always focused on varying aspects of racial identification. Early work focused on physical identification, partially because of initial and extensive work with children. Others have focused on the awareness aspects and acceptance of group identification. Four categories have been developed to organize and provide an overview of approaches to racial identification. These include (1) developmental approaches, (2) Afrocentric approaches, (3) group-based approaches, and (4) measures of racial stereotyping. The first three categories are relevant to this discussion of racial/ethnic identity.

Developmental Models

One of the most well-known developmental theories of racial identity is W. E. Cross's nigrescence model of African American identity. First developed in 1971, this model was based on the social context of the civil rights and Power or consciousness movements of the 1960s and early 1970s. This theory proposed that racial identification was developed in stages. Cross suggested that African Americans were socialized into the dominant culture, resulting in diminished racial identification. A process of exploration and discovery was necessary if the individual was to acquire a strong African American identity, essentially a resocialization experience from a non-Afrocentric identity to an Afrocentric identity.

According the nigrescence model, development of an African American identity proceeded through five stages. The first of these was called the *preencounter* and described the individual's original identity as accepting of a Eurocentric worldview. In stage two, *encounter,* an event occurred that threatened the original identity and worldview and caused the individual to question them. The third stage, *immersion,* involved the individual's attempt to destroy the preencounter identity and build a new identity by immersing him- or herself in African American culture, with African American associates and political ideologies, and by denigrating European culture. During the emersion phase of this stage, the individual developed less emotional involvement and the ability to be more open

and objective in assessing Blackness and other ethnic groups. The fourth stage, *internalization,* consisted of having confidence in the personal meanings of being African American. The individual was able to focus on systems of oppression rather than maintaining hostility toward European Americans as a group, and reintegrated African American identity into his or her other existing identities. The fifth stage, *internalization– commitment,* was an extension of the fourth stage and was characterized by long-term commitment to social justice for African American people and a sense of African American pride and communalism.

Thomas Parham introduced a lifespan approach to the nigrescence model. He asserted that true racial identity, distinct from parental attitudes, could not manifest itself until adolescence. Second, he introduced the idea that the initial identity state could be more advanced than preencounter, depending on educational and socialization experiences. Parham also asserted that the differing developmental demands and the nature of new challenges or encounters in the environment of adolescence/early adulthood, middle adulthood, and late life could precipitate a recycling through Cross's five stages.

Research, particularly early studies, found support for Cross's model. Individuals appeared to experience distinct changes in self-image and perceptions of other African Americans as they progressed through the stages. Organizational membership, ideologies concerning race, and racial preferences in help-seeking behavior changed in a manner consistent with Cross's stages.

There have been a number of critiques of developmental models of racial identity. One of the early critiques of nigrescence theory argued that developmental models of racial identity were based on the trends of the era of their development and discounted situational influences on identity. Some researchers have challenged the idea that racial identity development begins in adulthood and suggested the examination of racial identity at younger ages. In addition, it has been suggested that these models are narrow in their conceptualization of racial identity and that no empirical research has directly investigated the underlying assumptions and processes of nigrescence. Finally, there are critiques of the measure, called the Racial Identity Attitude Scale, associated with the original nigrescence model. Researchers noted problems with the reliability of the measure, and they failed to confirm the existence of the encounter stage.

Revised Nigrescence Model

In 1991, Cross substantially revised the original nigrescence model. The newer version of the theory suggested that self-concept is composed of two parts: first, personal identity, personality features, and traits; and second, reference group orientation and social group memberships. Personal identity plays only a small role in African American identity, which is a social identity. This revision weakens the historical association between the strength of the reference group orientation and self-esteem and positive mental health. The theory posits that five functions contribute to an African American identity profile. The functions are buffering, bonding, bridging, code-switching, and individualism. The buffering identity function is a psychological defense against discrimination; *bonding* refers to attachment to African American people and culture; and *bridging* addresses the individual's ability to participate in other cultural frames of reference while retaining his or her own culture. *Code-switching* addresses the ability to temporarily make use of the norms of another group with individualism serving as the expression of the individual's unique personality. The use of these racial identity functions depends on the salience of race in the overall identity.

In addition, four stages of African American racial identity are described instead of the original five. The names represent the theme or focus of the stages and are not identity elements. The four stages are *preencounter, encounter, immersion–emersion, and internalization.* Three of the stages are further characterized by identities. The preencounter stage consists of three potential identities: *assimilation, miseducation,* and *self-hatred.* The immersion–emersion stage consists of two identities: *intense involvement* and *anti-White,* and three identities represent acceptance associated with the internalization stage: *nationalist, biculturalist,* and *multiculturalist.* The encounter stage is not characterized by component identities. This revision and the measure associated with it may address the previous criticisms of this model, but additional research is required.

Afrocentric Models

Afrocentric models address the issue of a developmental progression in racial identity, but from a more explicitly Afrocentric perspective. The Asante model proposed several levels of awareness: skin recognition, environmental recognition, awareness, interest, concern, and Afrocentricity. These levels represented the developmental progression from physical acceptance of Blackness to complete psychological and sociopolitical commitment to an Afrocentric perspective. The critiques of stage models apply to Afrocentric approaches, as well as to the nigrescence models.

The African self-consciousness model is another Afrocentric approach to racial identity. African self-consciousness theoretically includes (1) the recognition of oneself as African (biologically, psychologically, and culturally) and what being African means; (2) the recognition of African survival and proactive development as one's first-priority value; (3) respect for and active perpetuation of all things African, African life, and African institutions; (4) having a standard of conduct toward all things non-African, and toward things, peoples, and so forth that are anti-African. African self-consciousness is directly influenced by the nurture or neglect of a proposed personality system.

Theoretically, African self-consciousness gives conscious direction and purpose to the spirituality inherent in the African American personality. This consciousness is of extreme importance to the effective and/or adaptive functioning of African American personality. The atrocities of slavery and the continued legacy of racial hostility directed toward African Americans are viewed as examples of societal pressures that influenced the differentiation of African self-consciousness.

Afrocentric theories have been critiqued because of their lack of empirical validation. In addition, many psychologists resist the notion of a biogenetic construction of African self-consciousness.

Group-Based Models

Contemporary models of racial identity are multidimensional and group-based. Among the best-known group-based model of racial identity is the multidimensional model of racial identity (MMRI). This model emphasizes both the meanings associated with membership in the racial group and the importance of racial identity in the individual's self-concept. The MMRI, unlike early stage models of racial identity, focuses on the significance and qualitative meaning of an individual's racial identity at one point in time. In addition, the individual's perception of his or her racial identity is emphasized over the behavioral manifestations of that identity.

In the MMRI, the importance of racial identity is reflected in two dimensions: the centrality and salience of identity. *Centrality* of racial identity is the extent to which an individual defines him- or herself in terms of race. *Salience* is the extent to which race is an important aspect of identity in a given situation. In addition to these dimensions, the MMRI addresses the individual's regard for and ideologies concerning his or her ethnic group. *Regard* addresses the individual's affective and evaluative stance as it relates to his or her racial group. Regard has two components: public, which is the extent to which the individual feels that others view African Americans positively or negatively; and private, which is the extent to which the individual feels positively or negatively toward the group and his or her membership in it.

The ideology dimension of the MMRI has four components: a nationalist philosophy that emphasizes the importance and uniqueness of African heritage and descent; an oppressed-minority ideology that addresses the commonalities among oppressed groups; an assimilationist philosophy that stresses the links between African Americans and the larger American society; and a humanist philosophy that emphasizes the relationships and similarities among all humans. The ideologies are assumed to affect behavior manifest across domains of functioning that include political, economic, cultural, social, and group relations. Preliminary evidence for the construct validity of the MMRI was found in an investigation of its corresponding measure, the Multidimensional Inventory of Black Identity. Other researchers have provided support for the validity of the model and the measure, with some cautionary notes related to the articulation of the nationalist ideology.

The African American identity attitude model was developed to permit a different conceptualization of African American behavior that has often been viewed as supporting a notion of self-hatred. The assumption made is that racial identification among African Americans is composed of varying aspects. The greater the consistency in these aspects or levels of identification on the parameters proposed, the less obvious these varied aspects or dimensions become, and the more the sense of peoplehood noted within the group increases. The more inconsistent the parameters, the less peoplehood and group unity one can expect.

Consistent with this approach, this model suggests four parameters of racial identification. The parameters are physical, cultural, sociopolitical, and psychological and were empirically demonstrated through factor analysis. The psychological parameter refers to a sense of belonging and commitment to the group. The sociopolitical parameter refers to an awareness of and a commitment to the resolution of social, economic, and political issues that affect African Americans. The physical dimension refers to the acceptance of physical characteristics often associated with African American heritage. Cultural racial identification is the final parameter and refers to the individual's awareness of African American contributions to society, as well as comfort with the language, art, literature, and social traditions of the African American community. The African American identity attitude scale provides a measure of these parameters. In addition, salience and centrality are measured.

Factors Influencing Racial Identity

Researchers interested in racial identity development have proposed that it occurs in response to transactions among a variety of factors, including parental, family, school, and institutional influences. Many of the factors theoretically associated with the development of racial identity have been examined empirically. The social experiences of the individual within the family and community affect aspects of racial identity, as does racial socialization, the process by which individuals are exposed to the messages and actions that provide information on group identity and race-related matters. Age, income, education, geographic location, religion, and neighborhood composition have been associated with racial identity attitudes, as well. Older, less educated African Americans living outside the western United States reported more positive racial identity attitudes. Interaction with other African Americans, experiences of discrimination, and political activism are noted as strong predictors of racial identity. Theoretically, these variables likely influence racial identity because of their impact on the ability to observe and interact with in-group and out-group members.

Research demonstrates an association between racial identity salience and racial identity attitudes. Racial identity salience has been found to correlate with racial socialization and interaction with other African Americans. A sense of disadvantaged status, group comparison and competition, and the racial composition of the environment have also been associated with racial identity salience.

ETHNIC IDENTITY

Scholars studying ethnic identity address the construct from two distinctive positions that focus on acculturation and developmental approaches. Within the acculturation framework, individuals are believed to adopt a bicultural, assimilated, traditional, or marginal orientation toward their own and the dominant culture. Ethnic identity is typically viewed as independent of identification with other groups, including the dominant culture.

Developmental Models

The most prominent models of ethnic identity are developmental. Research suggests that members of minority groups have very similar patterns of adjustment to oppression. Thus, it is not surprising that ethnic identity models have followed a development path similar to the one followed by racial identity models. One approach to ethnic identity proposes a five-stage model of minority identity development (MID). The model addresses the struggle that oppressed individuals engage in to understand themselves in the context of their own culture, as well as the nature of the oppressive relationship between the dominant culture and minority culture. Although this model posits stages, they are not meant to be distinct. The stages are believed to represent a continuous process. In addition, there is no assumption that all minority individuals transition through every stage or that stages are irreversible.

The stages of the model are *conformity, dissonance, resistance and immersion, introspection,* and *synergetic articulation and awareness.* Individuals in the conformity stage demonstrate a preference for dominant-culture values over those of their own culture. These preferences affect their beliefs about and views of self, other group members, and other minorities. During stage 2, dissonance, individuals begin to experience conflict between their depreciating attitudes toward their own group and culture and acceptance and appreciation of dominant-group individuals and culture. This is typically a gradual process but may be sudden depending on the event(s) that precipitate(s) it. In stage 3, resistance and immersion, the individual accepts and endorses minority views and culture and rejects the views, attitudes, and culture of the dominant group. This complete, rigid adherence to minority-group views is challenged and reexamined during stage 4, introspection. Stage 5, synergistic articulation and awareness, permits greater individual

control and flexibility. The individual accepts and rejects the views, values, and attitudes of minority groups and the dominant group based on experience.

As has been noted with each developmental model, this model lacks adequate empirical testing and validation. Although MID level has been associated with preference for counselor race, more work is needed. It should also be noted that as observed with the nigrescence and Afrocentric developmental approaches, there is an implicit assumption of an optimal level of identification associated with positive mental health. Failure to reach this optimal level of identification with one's own culture or overidentification with the dominant culture is believed to have negative psychological consequences. Such assumptions fail to consider the fluidity of ethnic identity, as well as the influence of situational factors on it. Cross's revised nigrescence model is an important exception to this criticism.

The multiethnic identity model examines the process of ethnic identity development and proposes that ethnic identity develops in a progression that involves three stages. In the first stage, which is similar to stage 1 of the MID model, the individual is largely unaware of ethnic identity and uncritically expresses a preference for the dominant culture. Stage 2 involves examination of the culture of origin and may involve rejection of the dominant cultural values and attitudes, similar to stages 2 and 3 of the MID model. The final stage in the model is characterized by the resolution of conflicts between one's own culture and the dominant culture, and the appreciation of one's ethnicity.

Ethnic identity researchers have asserted that there are aspects of ethnic identity common across groups: ethnic attitudes and sense of belonging, ethnic identity achievement, and ethnic behaviors and practices. The model of ethnic identity is based on Erikson's theory of ego identity. Ethnic identity attitudes and sense of belonging tap the personally meaningful aspect of ethnic identity and the value and emotional significance attached to membership in a group. This aspect is a sense of the extent to which membership in the group affects personal identity. Ethnic identity achievement addresses exploration and resolution of identity issues and concerns. The issue is commitment to a secure sense of ethnicity. Ethnic behaviors and practices reflect the extent to which group affiliation affects and/or is manifested in behavior.

The Multiethnic Identity Scale was developed to measure these components of ethnic identity. This multiethnic measure has been used successfully with

African Americans, Asian Americans, and Latino Americans, as well as Navajo Indians.

White Racial Identity

The Helms White racial identity model proposes that group identity development takes place among dominant group members, as well as among members of ethnic, racial, and oppressed groups. This model of White racial identity formation suggests the existence of two phases of this process. Phase 1 is the abandonment of racism. This phase begins in the *contact* stage. In this stage, individuals are unaware of their own racial identity, and there may be an assumption that ethnicity is relevant only for ethnic minorities. This stage is followed by a *disintegration* stage that involves the individual's acknowledgement of his or her White identity. The individual then moves into the *reintegration* stage. In this stage, the individual idealizes Whites and denigrates African Americans.

In phase 2, individuals define a positive White identity. There are three stages in this phase, as well. This phase begins with the *pseudo-independent* stage, which involves the questioning of African American inferiority to Whites and recognition of the advantages of being White. The questioning that takes place in this stage may result in guilt, discomfort, and denial. The *immersion/emersion* stage involves an examination of racism and what it means to be White and may involve an analysis of one's own contribution to racism. The final stage is *autonomy*. In this stage, the individual assumes nonracist attitudes and develops a multicultural identity. White individuals in this stage are able to relate to other ethnic minorities and are more open when interacting with members of other groups.

As with other developmental models of identity, this model is narrow in its conceptualization of White racial identity, and no empirical research has directly investigated the underlying assumptions and processes of White racial identity. Some researchers have noted the possibility that a large number of European Americans generally do not perceive any privileges of being a member of the dominant ethnic group, an issue the model fails to consider.

Variables Associated With Ethnic Identity

A major goal of ethnic identity research has been examining the relationship between ethnic identity and psychological well-being. Research thus far suggests relationships of high ethnic identity to high self-esteem, vocational maturity, psychological adjustment, and spiritual development. In addition, researchers have addressed group differences in ethnic identity, with African Americans scoring higher compared with other ethnic groups.

NEW DIRECTIONS

Theorizing and research on racial/ethnic identity continues to expand. New models reflect the growing recognition of the complexity of racial/ethnic identity and the increased diversity of our society. One example is the development of a theory to address the ethnic identity of Ethiopian immigrants, taking into account their status as African immigrants in the United States.

Models and measurement strategies are less linear and more complex and multifaceted. Increased attention has been paid to the development of psychometrically sound instruments. Existing measures have been adapted for new populations. In addition, models and measures specific to groups other than African Americans have been developed and studied. New research should explore the dynamic aspects of racial/ethnic identity. This research will need to explore which situations and social settings affect the salience and expression of racial/ethnic identity as well as when and how they do so.

—*Vetta L. Sanders Thompson*

See also Race; Ethnicity

FURTHER READING

Atkinson, D. R., Morten, G., & Sue, D. W. (1998). *Counseling American minorities* (5th ed., pp. 3–50). Boston: McGraw-Hill.

Cross, W. E., Jr. (1991). *Shades of Black: Diversity in African-American identity.* Philadelphia: Temple University Press.

Cross, W. E., Jr., Strauss, L., & Fhagan-Smith, P. (1999). African American identity development across the life span: Educational implications. In R. Hernandez Sleets & E. Hollins (Eds.), *Racial and ethnic identity in school practices: Aspects of human development* (pp. 29–47). Mahwah, NJ: Lawrence Erlbaum.

Helms, J. E. (1990). The beginnings of a diagnostic model of racial identity. In J. E. Helms (ed.), *Black and White racial identity: Theory, research, and practice.* Westport, CT: Greenwood.

Phinney, J. (1996). Understanding ethnic diversity: The role of ethnic identity. *American Behavioral Scientist, 40,* 143–152.

Sellers, R. M., Smith, M. A., Shelton, N., Rowley, S., & Chavous, T. (1998). Multidimensional model of racial identity: A reconceptualization of African American Identity. *Personality and Social Psychology Review, 2,* 18–39.

Utsey, S. O., Chae, M. H., Brown, C. F., & Kelly, D. (2002). Effect of ethnic group membership on ethnic identity, race-related stress, and quality of life. *Cultural Diversity and Ethnic Minority Psychology, 8,* 366–377.

ETHNIC GLOSS

Ethnic gloss is the practice of inferring that all members of an ethnic group tend to share a common set of culture-related characteristics, including, for example, ethnic identification, acculturation to the dominant or host society (if applicable), political opinions, interpersonal style, language, and music and food preferences. Such an inference is implicit in analyses testing group membership as a predictor of psychological or other outcomes. Alternative approaches to the study of ethnicity include refocusing on conceptually relevant aspects of ethnic identity and specifying explanatory models for each ethnic group separately.

Social scientists often classify persons by ethnic group when reporting vital statistics and describing study samples and populations. This usage is widely accepted if there is no inference regarding characteristics shared by persons so classified. The inference of shared characteristics is, however, subject to three criticisms. First, ethnic identity, acculturation, interpersonal style, and other culture-related characteristics vary within as well as across groups. Ethnic group membership is therefore uninformative as an explanatory factor and can be misleading (when, for example, variability within groups is greater than the difference between groups or when the distribution of a characteristic within a group is not bell-shaped). Second, the external validity is problematic because ethnic group membership per se has little or no meaning; study findings will therefore be difficult to generalize. Third, ethnic gloss perpetuates and may even foster stereotyping in social science and public discussion. Accordingly, social scientists are urged to avoid use of ethnic group membership as a simple proxy for unmeasured explanatory factors.

One alternative is to refocus on conceptually relevant aspects of ethnic identity. Multidimensional self-report measures can be employed to capture within-group variability in the salience of ethnic group membership, emotional ties to the group, political views, interethnic contact, language, and so on. These and other dimensions of ethnic identity, instead of group membership per se, can then be tested as predictors of psychological and other outcomes. Because ethnic identity is multidimensional, it is important to select a measure that captures the dimension(s) of interest. For example, measures of Afrocentrism typically focus on cultural values and social philosophy. Measures of cultural mistrust focus on a set of sociopolitical expectations. Measures of acculturation, biculturalism, and acculturation-related stress focus on aspects of the person's adaptation to a dominant or host society. Important distinctions also exist between personal aspects of ethnic identity on the one hand and collective or relational aspects on the other. Finally, stage measures capture differences in ethnic identity development within a person over time or across persons.

A second alternative to ethnic gloss is to specify explanatory models for ethnic groups in parallel. Differences in the relevance of predictors can be tested for statistical significance and may point to explanations for variation in outcomes across groups. In addition, implications for policy and practice may be derived by identifying ethnic differences in the direction or magnitude of the relationship between predictors and outcomes. The value of this second alternative depends on having a sufficiently large number of each ethnic group of interest in the study sample or population. Sample stratification is often required to ensure sufficient numbers of each group.

—*Douglas Longshore*

FURTHER READING

Trimble, J. (1995). Toward an understanding of ethnicity and ethnic identity, and their relationship with drug use research. In G. Botvin, S. Schinke, & M. A. Orlandi (Eds.), *Drug abuse prevention with multiethnic youth* (pp. 3–27). Thousand Oaks, CA: Sage.

Yee, A. H., Fairchild, H. H., Weizmann, F., & Wyatt, G. E. (1993). Addressing psychology's problems with race. *American Psychologist, 48*(11), 1132–1140.

ETHNIC IDENTITY DEVELOPMENT

Understanding identity is a major challenge for psychologists. The challenge is exacerbated by the need to understand how an individual's multidimensional identity develops. During everyday conversations, psychologists use myriad identity-related referents, such as *real versus ideal self, identity crisis, self-esteem,* and *self-schema.* These various terms imply that identity is not easily defined and that complexity is inherent in the construct. Theoretical guidance in conceptualizing identity and explaining its development is essential to psychological research, practice, and training.

THEORIES OF ETHNIC IDENTITY DEVELOPMENT

Understanding ethnic identity is of special interest, its importance having been brought into sharper focus by the increasing diversity within the United States. In particular, a number of theories of ethnic and racial identity have emerged. Each of these theories offers a unique perspective on how individuals develop.

Without question, the two most influential of the racial/ethnic identity development theories are those of William E. Cross and Janet Helms. The seminal writings of these scholars have left an indelible mark on the field, stimulating a significant body of research. Influenced by Cross and Helms, Jean S. Phinney, as well as Derald W. Sue and David Sue, developed two important theories that further enlighten the process of ethnic identity development.

Phinney's Model of Adolescent Ethnic Identity Development

According to Phinney et al., ethnic identity development occurs as members of minority groups work to resolve two primary issues or conflicts. The first issue is the existence of *stereotypes and prejudices* toward their group. The second issue entails the presence of *contrasting value systems.* As a result, minority group members must learn to (1) manage stereotypes and prejudice and (2) choose among available value systems and/or construct a value system of their own. The resolution of these two issues leads to the development of a secure ethnic identity.

Phinney's model consists of four coping strategies used to resolve the two central conflicts. The first coping strategy is *alienation/marginalization.* This strategy entails individuals accepting the negative self-image attached to their ethnic group. These individuals become alienated from their cultural group and do not adapt to the majority culture. The second

coping strategy is *assimilation.* These individuals become members of the majority culture and break ties with their assigned cultural group. The third coping strategy is *withdrawal/separation.* This strategy entails individuals who withdraw from the majority culture and solely associate with members of their ethnic group. The final coping strategy is *integration/ biculturalism.* These individuals retain their ethnic culture and also learn key skills and practices that are accepted by the dominant culture.

Sue and Sue's Racial/Cultural Identity Development (R/CID) Model

Sue and Sue have provided a five-stage model of what oppressed individuals encounter as they struggle to understand themselves. First is the *conformity stage.* In this stage, minority group members prefer the values, beliefs, and perspectives of the dominant culture. Second is the *dissonance stage.* In this stage, a specific event yields information that is inconsistent with the individual's beliefs and values. This event results in an increase in questioning and challenging of the values and beliefs held in the conformity stage. Third is the *resistance and immersion stage.* This stage is characterized by the individual immersing himself or herself in the minority culture and possessing negative attitudes toward the dominant culture. Fourth is the *introspection stage.* Here individuals focus on understanding themselves and their own cultural group. Additionally, individuals may experience some discontent with some group views held during the resistance and immersion stage. Fifth is the *integrative awareness stage.* In this stage, the individual exhibits an inner sense of stability while appreciating components of his or her own culture and other cultures.

IDENTITY DEFINED

Identity is the definition of self based on the context, salience, meaning, and attachment people give to their combined and interactive personal, social, intragroup, group, and human dimensions. The first component of this definition is a person's definition of *self.* A *self-definition* is the way in which people perceive themselves. The perception is influenced by context, salience, meaning, and attachment, but ultimately, the definition comes from the individual. *Context* includes the environmental factors that influence an individual's actions, thoughts, and feelings. For example, loud cheers, passionate emotions, and opinionated commentary on team strategies befit fans at a basketball game. *Salience* is the degree of prominence and awareness accorded to a specific dimension of identity at a given time. A person's identity as a parent may have little or no salience when he or she is single and has not had children. However, upon that person marrying and having twins, parenting will likely have high salience. *Meaning* is the value people place on themselves as a result of the process of organizing, interpreting, and integrating their experiences. Two students may value themselves differently even though they receive the same grade on a final examination. The difference in reaction is based on the meaning each individual makes out of the grade (i.e., "my intellect is declining" versus "time to celebrate"). *Attachment* is the degree to which individuals feel bonded to a specific aspect of their identity. At work, an individual may feel highly bonded to success and efficiency. At home, an individual may feel a stronger bond to other roles, such as mother and wife.

The second part of the definition enumerates the various dimensions of identity. The first dimension is *personal,* which consists of specific physical and personal characteristics. Physical characteristics include height, hair color, and eye color. Personal characteristics (personality) may include being shy, charming, or logical. The second dimension is *social,* which is based on group membership that is representative of an existing social system of categories. An example is a European American heterosexual male who is categorized based on his race, sexual orientation, and gender. The third dimension is *intragroup*—the position an individual occupies within specific groups. Within the African American community, an individual may be a mentor, role model, consultant, and churchgoer. The fourth dimension is *group,* which consists of the boundaries, values, history, and reputation of groups as a whole. Every group possesses a unique group identity, regardless of the characteristics of similar and dissimilar groups. Westminster Presbyterian Church has a group identity that sets it apart from rotary clubs, small colleges, and restaurants, as well as from other Presbyterian churches. The last dimension is *human.* Human identity stands in contrast to the identity of other species, such as animals and plants. The major differences lie in the multidimensionality of human identity, whereas in other species, identity is unidimensional. The combination and interaction of personal, social, intragroup, group, and human dimensions defines a person's *individual identity.* In addition, individual identity is subject to

change, depending on the context, salience, meaning, and attachment given to its various dimensions.

SUMMARY AND CONCLUSIONS

Identity is multidimensional, and ethnic identity is a particular instance of this construct. A number of theories of ethnic identity development have been proposed, further illustrating the challenge and opportunity to understand how people give themselves meaning as ethnic beings. Helping individuals develop healthy ethnic identity requires psychologists to embrace the multidimensionality of the construct and facilitate purposeful progression through the various stages of development. The ultimate goal of ethnic identity development is respecting oneself and respecting others regardless of variations in ethnicity.

—*Charles R. Ridley*
—*Andrew Case*

See also Ethnic Identity Development Measures; Ethnicity

FURTHER READING

Aponte, J., & Crouch, R. (1995). The changing ethnic profile of the United States. In J. F. Aponte, R. W. Rivers, & J. Wohl (Eds.), *Psychological interventions and cultural diversity* (pp. 1–18). Boston: Allyn & Bacon.

Atkinson, R., Morten, T., & Sue, D. (1998). *Counseling American minorities: A cross-cultural perspective* (5th ed.). New York: McGraw-Hill.

Cross, W. (1971). The Negro-to-Black conversion experience: Toward a psychology of liberation. *World, 20,* 13–27.

Cross, W. (1978). The Cross and Thomas psychological models of nigrescence. *Journal of Psychology, 5,* 13–19.

Cross, W. (1989). Nigrescence: A nondiaphanous phenomenon. *The Counseling Psychologist, 17,* 273–276.

Helms, J. (1990). *Black and White racial identity: Theory, research, and practice.* New York: Greenwood.

Kunnen, E., & Bosma, H. (2000). Development of meaning making: A dynamic systems approach. *New Ideas in Psychology, 18,* 57–82.

Phinney, J. S. (1990). Ethnic identity in adolescents and adults: Review of research. *Psychological Bulletin, 108,* 499–514.

Sue, D. W., & Sue, D. (1990). *Counseling the culturally different: Theory and practice.* New York: Wiley.

Tajfel, H., & Turner, J. C. (1979). An integrative theory of intergroup conflict. In W. G. Austin & S. Worchel (Eds.), *The social psychology of intergroup relations* (pp. 33–47). Monterey, CA: Brooks/Cole.

Turner, J. (1984). Social identification and psychological group formation. In H. Tajfel (Ed.), *The social dimension: European developments in social psychology* (Vol. 2, pp. 518–538). Cambridge, UK: Cambridge University Press.

Worchel, S., & Coutant, D. (2001). It takes two to tango: Relating group identity to individual identity within the framework of group development. In M. Hogg & S. Tindale (Eds.), *Black Group processes* (pp. 461–481). Malden, MA: Blackwell.

ETHNIC IDENTITY DEVELOPMENT MEASURES

A variety of psychometrically valid instruments have been developed to measure the construct of ethnic identity development, which is typically described as the developmental process of exploring the meaning and significance of one's ethnic group membership (see *ethnic identity development*). These instruments assess the extent to which individuals have explored and reflected on the significance and importance of their ethnic group membership and the role their ethnic group membership plays in their lives. Most measures are designed for use with monoethnic or monoracial individuals (i.e., people who self-identify with one ethnic or racial group). The majority of these measures are based on theories and principles of identity development and ethnic and racial socialization within the context of the United States. In the United States, part of the exploration of ethnic group membership for most minorities includes confronting the meaning of membership in an often oppressed and marginalized group (see *ethnic identity development*). One consequence of ethnic exploration is a heightened awareness of discrimination directed to in-group members. This heightened awareness becomes personally relevant when one commits to identifying with the ethnic in-group. Measuring ethnic identity development is often helpful for practitioners and researchers who hope to better understand the complex natures of ethnicity and race, and their impact at the individual and group level on personal and group identity.

Recently, considerable research has examined the construct of ethnic identity development; however, there is limited consensus about how *ethnic identity development* differs from or is related to the concepts of *racial identity* and *acculturation* (see *ethnic identity development, racial identity development,* and *acculturation*). Many of the current measures interchange the concepts of ethnic identity development and racial identity development. The name or title of the measure does not always accurately determine the construct being measured. Instruments that claim to measure ethnic identity may in fact be measuring the theoretical construct of racial identity. As a result, it is critical to understand the theoretical concept of interest before selecting an ethnic identity development instrument.

Currently, the majority of ethnic identity instruments and measurement literature focuses on African American ethnic and racial identity development. In contrast, only a relatively small body of research has been devoted to measuring ethnic identity development in other ethnic minority groups. Research in understanding ethnic identity development among a variety of ethnic groups is needed as communities become more ethnically and culturally diverse.

From an analysis of current research, three broad and qualitatively distinct conceptual models of measuring ethnic identity can be distinguished. First, there are *ethnicity-general measures,* which are typically based on group identity theory and social identity theory. Within this construct, *ethnic identity* is defined as one facet of a person's social identity and describes the degree to which a person is aware of, knowledgeable about, and committed to the ethnic and cultural heritage of his or her in-group. Some of the most widely used ethnicity-general measures broadly define *ethnic identity* as an individual's understanding of his or her ethnic group membership in the U.S. macroculture and are designed for use with multiple ethnic groups. Second, in contrast, *ethnicity-specific measures* are routinely based on specific facets, traits, and experiences shared by members of a particular ethnic group. Ethnicity-specific measures provide rich information regarding specific cultural aspects and features relevant to particular ethnic groups. These measures are useful when studying an ethnically homogeneous population or when trying to understand particular ethnic groups' experiences in relation to the dominant culture. Regarding both specific and general models of ethnicity, it is worthy to note that many researchers operationalize ethnic identity by conflating ethnicity (identity based on common culture and language) with race (a sociopolitical construct). Third, there are measures of *White identity,* which deal with European Americans' understanding of the connections among racism, power, and privilege, as well as interethnic and interracial relations.

ETHNICITY-GENERAL MEASURES OF ETHNIC IDENTITY

Ethnicity-general measures of ethnic identity development are grounded in the theoretical foundations of identity development (e.g., Erik Erikson, James Marcia), group identity (e.g., Gordon Allport), and social identity (e.g., Henri Tajfel). The measures also capture the significance and qualitative meaning of race, ethnicity, culture, and self-concept for members of a specific ethnic group.

One of the most widely used and well-known ethnicity-general measures of ethnic identity is the Multigroup Ethnic Identity Measure, developed by Jean Phinney. This measure assesses adolescents' ethnic identity development using a model comprising three distinct stages: *unexamined, exploration,* and *achieved.* An unexamined ethnic identity implies little or no understanding of issues related to ethnicity. One with an unexamined ethnic identity internalizes the beliefs and attitudes about the in-group that are most readily available in the broader cultural context. In contrast, individuals at the ethnic identity exploration stage are examining the meaning of their ethnic group membership in relation to the dominant culture. At this stage, group members are typically immersed within their ethnic group's history and cultural practices. Finally, individuals at an achieved stage of ethnic identity have a working knowledge of their ethnic heritage, a clear idea of the meaning of their ethnic group membership, and a commitment to their ethnicity and the role it plays in their lives.

Ethnicity-general measures often include subscales measuring various facets of ethnic identity. An ethnic identity development subscale is often one facet of the measure; however, dimensions such as self-identification, sense of belonging, attitudes toward one's ethnic group, and social participation in cultural practices are examples of other dimensions commonly measured by the subscales within ethnicity-general measures.

ETHNICITY-SPECIFIC MEASURES OF ETHNIC IDENTITY

Ethnicity-specific measures of ethnic identity generally assess the process of ethnic identity development within specific ethnic and racial groups. These measures are often grounded in counseling and clinical psychology literature and are connected to contextual features of a specific ethnic group's experience in the United States. These measures capture specific dynamics of racial and ethnic groups' experiences in the United States that are often untapped in ethnicity-general measures. The dynamics of specific ethnic and cultural groups are particularly meaningful for

understanding psychological processes related to particular ethnic groups' experiences in the United States.

The Multidimensional Inventory of Black Identity (MIBI), developed by Robert Sellers and colleagues, is one example of a widely known and used measure of ethnic identity development among African Americans. The MIBI is based on African American racial identity theory. This model posits four dimensions of African American identity: (1) the salience of race and ethnicity in a person's life, (2) the extent to which a person's race and ethnicity are central to self-definition, (3) a person's philosophy of self in relation to the dominant culture, and (4) the level of positive and negative feelings regarding one's own racial and ethnic group. The MIBI measures each of these dimensions except for *racial salience,* because this dimension tends to vary by context and situation. For example, the racial salience of an individual may differ within a school environment versus a church setting.

Ethnicity-specific measures of ethnic identity development tend *not* to be based in social identity and group identity theory and therefore are less likely to measure levels or stages of ethnic identity development. Instead, they focus on specific features and processes that are directly related to self-concept and self-definition within a particular ethnic group experience in the United States.

White Ethnic Identity Development Measures

A body of research also exists on measuring ethnic identity development among European Americans. These assessments, typically described as *White racial identity measures,* are based on the premise that European Americans undergo a developmental process exploring and understanding the significance, privileges, and numerous advantages of being European American in the United States. There is often a focus on European Americans' attitudes regarding members of minority groups, because being of the majority race is usually theoretically defined as *not* being a person of color. Ethnic identity development among European Americans is described as a developmental progression that is based on understanding the privileges of being White and movement toward adopting nonracist ideologies. The highest level of development in these models tends to be achieved by individuals who have a nonracist identity as White Americans. Two of the most well known of these measures are the White Racial Identity Attitudes Scale, developed by Janet Helms and Robert Carter, and the Oklahoma Racial Attitude Scale, developed by Sandra Choney and John Behrens.

—*W. David Wakefield*
—*Jessica H. Belanger*

See also Acculturation; Ethnic and Racial Identity; Ethnic Identity Development; Racial Identity Development

FURTHER READING

Fischer, A. R., & Moradi, B. (2001). Racial and ethnic identity: Recent developments and needed directions. In J. Ponterotto, J. M. Casas, L. A. Suzuki, and C. M. Alexander (Eds.), *Handbook of Multicultural Counseling* (pp. 341–370). Thousand Oaks, CA: Sage.

Helms, J. E., & Carter, R. T. (1996). Development of the White Racial Identity Inventory. In J. E. Helms (Ed.), *Black and White racial identity: Theory, research, and practice* (pp. 67–80). Westport, CT: Greenwood.

Phinney, J. S. (1990). Ethnic identity in adolescents and adults: Review of research. *Psychological Bulletin, 108,* 499–514.

Phinney, J. S. (1992). The multigroup ethnic identity measure: A new scale for use with adolescents and young adults from diverse groups. *Journal of Adolescent Research, 7,* 156–176.

Sellers, R. M., Smith, M. A., Shelton, J. N., Rowley, S. A. J., & Chavous, T. M. (1998). Multidimensional model of racial identity: A reconceptualization of African American racial identity. *Personality and Social Psychology Review, 2,* 18–39.

Sodowsky, G. R., & Impara, C. (1996). *Multicultural assessment in counseling and clinical psychology.* Lincoln, NE: Buros Institute of Mental Measurement.

Umaña-Taylor, A. J., Yazedjian, A., & Bamaca-Gomez, M. (2004). Developing the ethnic identity scale using Eriksonian and social identity perspectives. *Identity, 4,* 9–38.

ETHNIC IDENTITY DEVELOPMENT MEASURES: ASIAN VALUES SCALE

Developed to provide a more complete understanding of the acculturation process in Asian American populations, the Asian Values Scale (AVS) assesses the degree to which individuals adhere to traditional Asian values (e.g., deference to authority). Although a majority of acculturation scales currently used focus on behavioral aspects of the acculturation (e.g., language use), the AVS considers values in the acculturative process. Specifically, it explores the degree to which Asian Americans have maintained their (traditional) Asian cultural values while in the presence of Western culture and its value system (e.g., independence and autonomy). The AVS developers posited the necessity of assessing the value dimension of acculturation because they presupposed that the degree to which an individual espouses traditional Asian values changes at a slower rate than the degree to which the same individual engages in Asian behaviors (e.g., speaking an Asian language).

The AVS consists of 36 items that cover the following six-factor, analytically derived Asian cultural value dimensions: collectivism, conformity to norms, emotional self-control, family recognition through achievement, filial piety, and humility. These items were selected from an original pool of 112 by their ability to differentiate between first-generation Asian Americans and European Americans. Listed in random order, items are answered on a seven-point rating scale (1 = *strongly disagree;* 7 = *strongly agree*) in which the participant indicates the extent to which he or she agrees or disagrees with the item. For purposes of reliability, 18 of the 36 items are reverse scored. The AVS total score is obtained by adding the item scores together. The scaled score is obtained by dividing the total score by 36 and is used in determining the subject's adherence to Asian cultural values. Thus, scores on the AVS range from 1 to 7 (with 1 indicating the least adherence and 7 indicating the greatest adherence to Asian values).

PSYCHOMETRIC PROPERTIES

The AVS has been shown to produce reliable scores with coefficient alphas of .81 and .82 in two separate studies. The AVS has also provided evidence as to the stability of scores with a test–retest reliability estimate (two weeks) of .83. Content representativeness and relevance of the AVS were established by identifying a set of items that reflected cultural values espoused by Asian American ethnic groups. Concurrent evidence was shown in a confirmatory factor analysis in which the AVS was shown to be a reliable indicator of Asian values acculturation. Discriminant evidence was provided when a small correlation ($r = .15$) was found between AVS scores and behavioral acculturation scores as measured by the Suinn-Lew Asian Self-Identity Acculturation Scale (SL-ASIA). Also, the finding that AVS scores changed at a slower rate than SL-ASIA scores across generational status provides further discriminant evidence of the AVS.

UTILITY OF THE AVS

When used with behavioral measures of acculturation, the AVS can provide a more comprehensive representation and understanding of the acculturative process for Asian Americans. The more nuanced understanding one can gain from using the AVS may help researchers and clinicians tease out the relationship between acculturation and help-seeking behaviors and other salient psychological constructs. In addition, the AVS will allow mental health professionals to make more culturally sensitive assessment interventions.

LIMITATIONS OF THE AVS

The AVS is a measure that is intended to represent the value systems of more than 40 distinct Asian ethnic groups. It may be beneficial to take the unique cultural beliefs and values of the Asian ethnic group of interest when using the AVS.

—Matthew J. Miller
—Suzette L. Speight

See also Acculturation; Acculturation Measures

FURTHER READING

Kim, B. S. K., Atkinson, D. R., & Yang, P. H. (1999). The Asian Values Scale: Development, factor analysis, validation, and reliability. *Journal of Counseling Psychology, 46,* 342–352.

ETHNIC IDENTITY DEVELOPMENT MEASURES: BICULTURAL INVOLVEMENT SCALE

The bicultural involvement questionnaire (BIQ) is a 33-item self-report measure used to assess cultural orientation. The measure generates scores for individuals' independent association with each of the two cultures, their degree of biculturalism, and a rating of their total cultural involvement. Originally developed for use with Hispanic and American individuals, the measure has also been modified for use with individuals from other cultures, including Asia and Australia.

BACKGROUND

Adapted from the acculturation scale, the bicultural involvement questionnaire was developed by José Szapocznik, William M. Kurtines, and Tatjana Fernandez in 1980 as a multidimensional tool for measuring cultural orientation. Unlike the majority of acculturation measures that preceded it, the BIQ does not assume that involvement in one culture necessitates exclusion of association with another. Rather, the BIQ assesses individuals' degree of comfort with host-culture norms and the practices of their culture of origin, simultaneously.

MEASURE DESCRIPTION

The BIQ is structured on a five-point Likert-type scale. Respondents provide self-report ratings, ranging from "not at all comfortable" to "very comfortable," for 24 items and rate their preferences for the remaining 9 questions by marking whether they would prefer the items to be "completely" Hispanic or American, "mostly" Hispanic or American, or "both" Hispanic and American. Questions target individual preferences and practices related to language use, food, music, holiday celebration, and other traditions. Both Spanish and English copies are available.

SCORING

The measure consists of two subscales, each reflecting the degree of association reported by an individual to a specific culture (e.g., Americanism and Hispanicism). Subscale scores are computed by summing the items reflective of involvement in that particular culture. For example, Americanism scores consist of the sum of items associated with involvement in American culture (e.g., "How comfortable do you feel speaking English at home?" and "How much do you enjoy American music?"). Similarly, Hispanicism scores are computed by summing items reflective of Hispanic culture.

Scores are then computed for two conceptually independent, bipolar dimensions. The first dimension, the Biculturalism Scale, ranges from monoculturalism to biculturalism and is computed by subtracting one subscale from the other (e.g., Hispanicism minus Americanism). Scores approaching 0 on this dimension are reflective of biculturalism, and scores deviating from 0 reflect monoculturalism. Within the context of the aforementioned example, a large positive-difference score on the biculturalism dimension would indicate Hispanic monoculturalism, whereas a large difference score in the negative direction would indicate American monoculturalism. The second dimension within the BIQ, the Cultural Involvement Scale, ranges from cultural marginality to cultural involvement and is computed by summing the two scale scores (e.g., Hispanicism plus Americanism). Higher scores reflect a greater degree of overall cultural involvement, and lower scores reflect cultural marginality or a lack of involvement with either culture.

PSYCHOMETRICS

During instrument development, adequate internal consistency was demonstrated. Alpha coefficients for Hispanicism, Americanism, biculturalism, and cultural involvement were reported to be .93, .89, .94, and .79, respectively. Test–retest reliability, evaluated over 6-week intervals, ranged from .14 to .79. Criterion-related validity was examined using teacher-report ratings of biculturalism on a five-point scale. The measure was found to best predict biculturalism among children living in bicultural environments.

—*Heather L. Hunter*

See also Biculturalism; Bilingualism

FURTHER READING

Sonderegger, R., Barrett, P. M., & Creed, P. A. (2004). Models of cultural adjustment for child and adolescent migrants to Australia: Internal process and situational factors. *Journal of Child and Family Studies, 13,* 357–371.

Szapocznik, J., Kurtines, W. M., & Fernandez, T. (1980). Bicultural involvement and adjustment in Hispanic-American youths. *International Journal of Intercultural Relations, 4,* 353–365.

Szapocznik, J., Scopetta, M., Kurtines, W. M., & Arnalde, M. A. (1978). Theory and measurement of acculturation. *International Journal of Intercultural Relations, 12,* 113–130.

ETHNIC IDENTITY DEVELOPMENT MEASURES: CROSS RACIAL IDENTITY SCALE

The Cross Racial Identity Scale (CRIS) is a 40-item self-administered scale developed to measure racial identity attitudes of people in the United States. More specifically, each identity type measured in the CRIS reveals unique racial perspectives as to how people identify themselves in relation to their racial group. Cross first articulated nigrescence theory in 1971 and revised his original theory in 1991. The subsequent development of the CRIS yielded an expanded model of nigrescence. As a result of the connection of the scale to theory (and vice versa), the CRIS and the expanded nigrescence model are linked together (e.g., for interpretation) and not to previous versions of the model or prior scales. The development of the CRIS occurred over a 5-year period. The CRIS items were developed by the scale authors, rated by experts, and refined through rigorous phases of scale development. At each phase, the CRIS was administered to college students from two predominantly White universities. The current version of CRIS consists of 40 (30 CRIS and 10 filler) items answered on a seven-point scale ranging from 1 (strongly agree) to 7 (strongly disagree). Each of the six subscales of the CRIS, composed of five items, represents six of the nine nigrescence identities from the expanded nigrescence model. The subscales are examples of three different identity types: preencounter (assimilation, miseducation, self-hatred), immersion-emersion (anti-White), and internalization (Afrocentricity, multiculturalist inclusive).

According to the expanded nigrescence theory, racial identity is significantly shaped by reference group orientation (RGO), rather than personal identity (PI) based on personality features. As a function of a RGO, race is manifested differently among the six identities with a varying degree of race salience and affiliation to community. For example, race from the assimilation perspective is either invisible or deemed unimportant because of an RGO of being American. The RGO in the immersion-emersion stage changes to a pro-Black, anti-White perspective. A positive identity becomes more salient along different perspectives in the internalization stages, whereas anti-White attitudes fade away as a multicultural perspective emerges. For example, from the multicultural perspective, an RGO of being American is as important as an RGO of being Black. Because racial identity is conceptualized as dynamic and fluid, the CRIS was developed as a multidimensional scale in which a person's identity is interpreted with a profile comprising all six subscale scores (e.g., through cluster analysis). Subscale scores are obtained by summing items on a subscale and dividing by 5. If comparisons across subscores are desired, one may either use mean scores from each subscale or convert raw scores to standard or z scores. Vandiver and colleagues have documented estimated reliability and validity of the CRIS. All six subscale scores were shown to reach internal consistency on or above .78, while keeping subscale intercorrelations below the .30 range. Factor analyses tended to favor the current six-factor structure of the CRIS over other models. Also, preliminary evidence supports convergent validity and discriminant validity of the CRIS. Directions for future research with the CRIS include continued revision of nigrescence theory, research on populations other than college students, use of the CRIS in clinical practice, and long-term replications.

—*Edward A. Delgado-Romero*
—*Seunghee Kwon*

See also African Americans and Mental Health; Racial Identity Models

FURTHER READING

Cross, W. E., Jr., & Vandiver, B. J. (2001). Nigrescence theory and measurement: Introducing the Cross Racial Identity Scale (CRIS). In J. G. Ponterotto, J. M. Casas, L. M. Suzuki, & C. M. Alexander (Eds.), *Handbook of multicultural counseling* (2nd ed., pp. 371–393). Thousand Oaks, CA: Sage.

ETHNIC IDENTITY DEVELOPMENT MEASURES: MULTIGROUP ETHNIC IDENTITY MEASURE

The Multigroup Ethnic Identity Measure (MEIM) is a survey measure of ethnic identity. It was developed for use with adolescents and young adults. It can be used with adults, but it is not appropriate for children. The original measure, published in 1992, was based on the developmental theory of Erik Erikson and the social identity theory of Henri Tajfel. It has undergone revision to increase the clarity of the measure in relation to the concept. In the current version of the measure, ethnic identity is conceptualized in terms of two processes, *exploration* of the meaning and implications of one's ethnicity, and *commitment* to one's group. These processes parallel the exploration and commitment processes of ego identity formation described by James Marcia.

Ethnic identity exploration involves learning about one's ethnicity through studying or reading about it,

talking to people, visiting museums and exhibits, and taking part in ethnic events. The exploration subscale of the MEIM includes items such as, "I have spent time trying to find out more about my ethnic group" and "I have often talked to other people to learn more about my ethnic group." Research across ethnic and age groups has yielded high reliability coefficients, with Cronbach alphas between .65 and .83.

Ethnic identity commitment involves a strong sense of membership in one's ethnic group and positive feelings about being a group member. Typical items in the commitment subscale are, "I have a strong sense of belonging to my own ethnic group" and "I feel good about my cultural or ethnic background." Reliabilities have been consistently high across ethnic groups, with alphas between .81 and .92.

Factor analyses of the MEIM have demonstrated that *exploration* and *commitment* are distinct factors. Research has shown that they have different correlates; commitment is generally more strongly correlated with self-esteem than is exploration, whereas exploration appears more strongly related to the perception of discrimination. The commitment subscale corresponds closely with the common usage of the term *ethnic identity* and can be used alone to assess a sense of belonging to one's group.

The two subscales are related, with Pearson correlations ranging from .54 to .69 across studies. Therefore, the MEIM can be used as a single scale combining the two subscales. Reliabilities for the single scale are typically above .90. High scores on the single scale indicate an *achieved ethnic identity,* defined by the presence of both exploration and commitment. An individual with an achieved ethnic identity has a secure sense of self as an ethnic group member, based on a clear understanding of the meaning of his or her group membership. Low scores indicate a *diffuse ethnic identity,* defined by the lack of both exploration and commitment. This individual has a relatively weak sense of belonging and a lack of interest in, and understanding of, his or her group. Individuals high in exploration and low in commitment are considered in *moratorium;* those high in commitment and low in exploration are in *foreclosure.* Because of the correlation between exploration and commitment, moratorium and foreclosure statuses may overlap and may not be clearly identifiable using the MEIM.

Validity of the MEIM is indicated by correlations between the scale and variables expected to be related to ethnic identity on the basis of developmental or social identity theory. As would be expected theoretically, the MEIM is positively related to self-esteem and psychological well-being and negatively to depression. Norms have not been developed for the MEIM, because mean scores vary widely across ages and ethnic groups. The measure is most useful for examining the correlates of ethnic identity with other variables of interest or for making between-group or within-group comparisons in a single study.

—*Jean S. Phinney*

See also Ethnic Identity Development

FURTHER READING

Phinney, J. (1992). The Multigroup Ethnic Identity Measure: A new scale for use with diverse groups. *Journal of Adolescent Research, 7,* 156–176.

Roberts, R., Phinney, J., Masse, L., Chen, Y., Roberts, C., & Romero, A. (1999). The structure of ethnic identity in young adolescents from diverse ethnocultural groups. *Journal of Early Adolescence, 19,* 301–322.

ETHNIC IDENTITY DEVELOPMENT MEASURES: ORTHOGONAL CULTURAL IDENTIFICATION SCALE

The Orthogonal Cultural Identification Scale assesses identification with one or more cultures. The adolescent and young adult scale is supported by considerable research. The adult scale has high reliability, meaning that repeating the scale usually results in the same answers, but it has been used less in research than the adolescent and young adult scale. The scale is designed to be used cross-culturally. It does not, therefore, focus on specific culture-related behaviors but on general attitudes toward involvement in a culture. Identification with any culture can be assessed, as long as the culturally related items on the scale are carefully constructed so as to be familiar to those taking the test.

Some theories assume that as identification with one culture is gained (as in the acculturation to a new culture), identification with the original culture is lost. In contrast, orthogonal cultural identification theory proposes that identification with one culture is fundamentally independent of identification with another culture, thus raising the possibility that one can be simultaneously highly identified with more than one culture.

Orthogonal cultural identification is a *stake* theory. Cultural identification is developed through social learning—the reinforcement of attitudes, beliefs, and behaviors in the social environment provided by the culture. When the person is reinforced for behaviors within the culture, the person will tend to continue that behavior, will be likely to engage in related behaviors, will feel a sense of satisfaction, will maintain involvement with the culture, and will express higher levels of cultural identification. When the culture fails to reinforce behaviors that are perceived to be culture-related or when the rewards provided by the culture fail to meet the individual's needs, the person will avoid those and related behaviors, will feel dissatisfied, may seek reinforcement in other cultural contexts, and will express a lower level of cultural identification.

The primary sources for this reinforcement are the family, peers, and school. Others can play important roles, and, in some cultures, religious training may play a strong role. During early development, the family is the most important source of cultural identification, and the individual's perception of the family's cultural identification is likely to be indistinguishable from his or her own. Among adults, peers are likely to become an important source for cultural identification.

Identification with a specific culture, as measured by the scale, will be highly related to involvement in that culture and, therefore, involvement in culture-related activities. The researcher can therefore expect high correlations between cultural identification, satisfaction with that culture, and behaviors and activities that are clearly specific to the culture. In contrast, the correlations between cultural identification and other personal and social characteristics are likely to be much lower. There is a belief that cultural identification is a major source of personal and family strength, particularly identification with a minority culture that has many positive qualities. There is often a hope that identification with that culture is enough to protect the person from problems and assure success. Indeed, research has shown that the individual and family with high identification have been and are being reinforced and that reinforcement will produce satisfaction and a sense of well-being. These are valuable benefits, but they do not necessarily stretch to cover everything. Unless the behavior is very specific to the culture, many other variables are involved, and cultural identification can play only a partial role in determining that behavior. Simple relationships between cultural identification and complex problems and outcomes therefore are not likely. Careful study will probably find that cultural identification plays a partial, moderating, or mediating role in determining that behavior, and insights into the role played by cultural identification can produce a deeper understanding and, potentially, ideas for intervention.

—*Fred Beauvais*

See also Ethnic Identity Development; Models of Second Culture Acquisition

FURTHER READING

Beauvais, F., & Oetting, E. R. (1990). Orthogonal cultural identification theory: The cultural identification of minority adolescents. *International Journal of the Addictions, 25*(5A–6A), 655–685.
Oetting, E. R. (1997). Orthogonal cultural identification theory: Theoretical links between cultural identification and substance use. *Substance Use and Misuse, 32*(12–13), 1913–1918.

ETHNIC IDENTITY DEVELOPMENT MEASURES: RACIAL IDENTITY ATTITUDE SCALE

Racial identity measurement originated in nigrescence stage models developed in the early 1970s by William E. Cross and Charles W. Thomas. Thomas A. Parnham and Janet E. Helms developed the Racial Identity Attitude Scale–Black (RIAS-B) to measure four racial identity development sequences rooted in the Cross model.

DEVELOPMENTAL SEQUENCES OF RACIAL IDENTITY

The RIAS-B consists of four subscales, labeled *conformity, dissonance, immersion/emersion,* and *internalization.* The subscales measure a progression within African American identity development of movement from internalization of negative racial messages to deepening adoption of a positive racial identity. Racial identity is a dynamic maturational process through which African Americans understand themselves within the context of a race-based society.

During *conformity* (previously labeled *preencounter*), African Americans internalize negative racial stereotypes, perceiving elements of their racial background as a stigma out of socialization experience, a Eurocentric cultural orientation, or a victim–blame attitude within a context of individualistic values. *Dissonance* (previously labeled *encounter*) is an awareness that this previous identity is no longer viable. This awareness is typically initiated through a critical event, such as exposure to cultural/racial information or an experience with racism. The event provides impetus to seek an alternative racial identity. In the twin components of *immersion* and *emersion, immersion* refers to participation in an African American world of art, media, and people, and rejection of the White, or dominant culture, world. *Emersion* connotes a reduction in the intensity of this experience, enhanced feelings of control, and a movement toward internalization. *Internalization* describes a state of belongingness and a resolution of racial identity conflicts; a positive racial identity serves as a point of departure for transactions outside an African American world.

RIAS-B SUBSCALE PSYCHOMETRIC EVIDENCE

The RIAS-B is available in a long form and a more widely used short form. The 30-item short form has four subscales of 8-, 6-, 10-, and 6-item length. Several studies have established acceptable internal consistency coefficient alpha reliabilities for three of the four RIAS-B subscales. Reliability findings for the encounter subscale have been mixed, with some studies finding unacceptable levels. RIAS-B subscale intercorrelations are generally consistent with the Cross model. Support for the construct validity of three RIAS-B scales has emerged in the research literature; evidence for the validity of the encounter subscale is weaker.

RECENT RESEARCH WITH THE RIAS-B

A growing body of literature using the RIAS-B supports the theoretical assertion that greater internalization of a positive racial identity is related to better adjustment. A series of recent studies using the RIAS-B found positive racial identity is associated with enhanced adaptive functioning, increased ego identity, higher self-esteem, and reduced symptomatic distress. One recent study found immersion-emersion scores predicted increased MMPI psychopathology scores, suggesting a risk for counselors and clinicians to pathologize facets of normative racial identity development.

Recently, racial identity theory has been used with other groups that have also experienced historical and ongoing discrimination. The Visible Racial/Ethnic Identity Attitude Scale (VIAS) is an adaptation of the RIAS-B for Hispanic/Latino individuals. The VIAS has been used successfully to replicate a number of the RIAS-B findings with this group.

The RIAS-B is the primary instrument in the current literature for measuring racial identity in African Americans. A major contribution of the RIAS-B research has highlighted the influence of collective identity processes such as racial identity, in contrast to individual identity processes. Most significantly, the RIAS-B research has focused psychology's attention on the experience of racism's impact on self-concept, as well as the important role of positive racial identity in mental health and positive psychological adjustment.

—*James Allen*

See also African Americans and Mental Health; African/Black Psychology; Ethnic and Racial Identity; Racial Identity Development; Racial Identity Models

FURTHER READING

Cross, W. E., Jr. (1978). The Thomas and Cross models of psychological nigrescence: A review. *Journal of Psychology, 5,* 13–31.

Cross, W. E., Jr., Parham, T. A., & Helms, J. E. (1991). The stages of identity development: Nigrescence models. In R. Jones (Ed.), *Psychology* (3rd ed., pp. 319–338). Berkeley, CA: Cobb & Henry.

Helms, J. E. (Ed.). (1990). *Black and White racial identity: Theory, research, and practice.* New York: Greenwood Press.

Helms, J. E. (1995). An update of Helm's White and people of color racial identity models. In J. G. Ponterotto, M. J. Casas, L. A. Suzuki, & C. M. Alexander (Eds.), *Handbook of multicultural counseling* (1st ed., pp. 181–198). Thousand Oaks, CA: Sage.

Helms, J. E., & Parham, T. A. (1996). The Racial Identity Attitude Scale. In R. L. Jones (Ed.), *Handbook of tests and measurements for populations* (Vol. 2, pp. 167–174). Hampton, VA: Cobb & Henry.

Miville, M. L., Koonce, D., Darlington, P., & Whitlock, B. (2000). Exploring the relationships between racial/cultural identity and ego identity among African Americans and Mexican Americans. *Journal of Multicultural Counseling and Development, 28,* 208–224.

Whatley, J. P., Allen, J., & Dana, R. H. (2003). Racial identity and the MMPI in African American male college students. *Cultural Diversity and Ethnic Minority Psychology, 9,* 344–352.

ETHNICITY

The term *ethnic* is derived from the Greek word *ethnos,* which refers to a nation, and is closely related to *ethnikos,* meaning "heathen"; the term has strong references to ethnic minority groups. Members of ethnic groups are conscious of themselves as in some way united or at least related because of a common origin and a shared destiny. *Ethnicity* refers to the national, regional, or tribal origins of one's oldest remembered ancestors and the customs, traditions, and rituals handed down by these ancestors. Ethnic, as well as cultural and racial, variability exists among members of the same racial or ethnic groups. For example, Native American and African American people may speak Spanish, French, or English, and many Latinos self-identify as "Black," whereas others see themselves as "White."

In much of the writing on multiculturalism, there is a tendency to use the terms *race, culture,* and *ethnicity* interchangeably. Over time, the conflation of these terms has created much confusion for students and scholars alike. In the 1990s, the socioeconomic and geopolitical changes in the international arena, particularly in the West, summoned *ethnicity* out of the inner cities (from primarily immigrant and ethnic minority communities) to include many European White minority groups. This move has brought into consciousness the fact that the color "White," which is often forgotten in this category, is also a part of ethnicity. In the late 1990s, we began to see that *ethnicity* has become the term of the hour in political science and the practice of government in various places around the globe. The term's importance is clearly demonstrated in the violent domestic conflicts and international security breaches that are happening in this early part of the 21st century. Associated terms, such as *ethnic cleansing, Balkans' racism,* and *Rwandan genocide,* have come to grip our consciousness as historic events that marked the last century. Currently we are conscious of a similar process in Darfur in the Sudan. Clearly, ethnic cleansing is a metaphor for our time.

The concept of ethnicity found its way into political and academic discourse largely as a response to dissatisfaction with the idea of race and with the assimilationist assumptions of a focus on immigration. Race as a conceptual and empirical idea to locate difference was proving problematic because of its articulation within a political discourse, so the term *ethnicity* was more appealing and privileged because of its flexibility and its inclusiveness of all those minorities who appeared to be outside the fixed meanings of race—that is, South Asian, Chinese, and others.

The positioning and repositioning of individuals and groups in terms of race, racism, culture, and ethnicity have been seen as a cyclic process throughout the pre- and postwar periods. For example, the idea of ethnicity referred to the Irish, Italians, and Jews in the early part of the 20th century but took on a more sinister and racialized meaning for the Jewish community. In the latter half of the century, after the migration of West Indians, East Asians, Pakistanis, and Bangladeshis, the term revised itself to exclude, except for Jews, those White Europeans defined earlier and focused negatively on Africa, Asia, and the Caribbean.

The majority of ethnic minority people's analysis of a culture of difference appears to be compatible with their social and economic realities of an inner-city existence. Perceptions of racial inferiority, social injustice, and economic hardship have accompanied the term *ethnicity* in the West. However, as a result of ideas such as resilience, hope, and forgiveness, there appears to be a new sign of cultural and ethnic identity, within which the subjects speak from a particular ethnic cultural history but also from a specific individual experience.

These new cultural forms of ethnic identity (sometimes embracing notions of race) can often be seen as fragmentary, in a postmodern sense. This positioning may give the feeling of interrogating and opposing the unity (or the illusion of unity) offered by an ethnicity that is primarily fixed to multiculturalism. In other words, this new cultural politics of race and the experiences of racism seem to also articulate this newer conception of ethnicity. This is far from the position taken by Modood and others, who suggest that, where *Black* and *South Asian* have been used to describe ethnicity, such categories are heterogeneous, containing ethnic groups with different cultures, religions, migration histories, geographical locations, and socioeconomic statuses. Combining these categories leads to differences between them being ignored. However, one of the thorniest problems in theorizing about ethnicity is the question of how political identities are

shaped and constructed through the meanings attributed to race, ethnicity, and nation.

For psychologists, it seems that the key to understanding the concept of ethnicity is awareness that like the terms *race* and *culture, ethnicity* is constructed within changing sociopolitical and cultural ideologies that may have consequences for psychology and psychotherapy research as well as practice. Alvidrez and colleagues recommend that researchers ask simple questions when measuring self-identification, country of origin of participant or parents of participant, and geographic residence. The more dimensions that investigators can provide in their descriptions of the sample, the less the likelihood of glossing over the diversity and variety of subcultures within each ethnic group.

Adhering to a rigid understanding of ethnicity may offer psychologists cognitive, emotional, and professional security but may lead them to indulge in stereotyping clients negatively with dire consequences for a vulnerable client. The client, on the other hand, may from time to time alter the meaning of the concept of ethnicity during the conversations with the therapist and many times through his or her various stages of psychotherapy. Individuals are often torn between the need to experience themselves existentially in the here and now and the desire to be historically or psychically connected to a specific, but not too distant, past. These conflicting desires may be constructed in ethnic terms. In essence, the subjective self can manage both performances: the inner psychological world's needs, and the outer social, cultural, and political environment's demands, with ethnicity being the mediator of both these worlds.

—*Roy Moodley*
—*Deone Curling*

See also Culture; Ethnic and Racial Identity; Ethnic Identity Development

FURTHER READING

Ahmed, A. S. (1995). "Ethnic cleansing": A metaphor for our time? *Ethnic and Racial Studies, 18,* 1–25.

Alvidrez, J., Azocar, F., & Miranda, J. (1996). Demystifying the concept of ethnicity for psychotherapy researchers. *Journal of Consulting and Clinical Psychology, 64*(5), 903–908.

Cashmore, E. E., & Troyna, B. (1983). *Introduction to race relations.* London: Routledge & Kegan Paul.

Helms, J. E., & Cook, D. A. (1999). *Using race and culture in counseling and psychotherapy: Theory and process.* Boston: Allyn & Bacon.

ETHNIC MINORITY COUNSELORS

Counselor characteristics such as ethnicity, culture, race, language, and attitudes can influence the degree to which clients seek mental health care and remain in the care of a mental health professional. Consequently, factors such as these may influence the degree to which counselors are viewed as credible and trustworthy mental health providers.

COUNSELOR–CLIENT MATCH

In all mental health settings, but especially when the ethnicity of the counselor does not match that of the client, it is important to set aside any personal biases in favor of treatment modalities that may lead to favorable treatment outcomes.

For example, within some cultural groups, various complaints that are based in spirituality and religious practices may be legitimate and explored as part of the treatment process. Thus, similar symptoms may hold different meanings in different cultures. Counselors with a different worldview would need to be sensitive to the possibility that a treatment modality different from the one they would use with a patient from their own background might be most beneficial for the patient.

In addition, counselors need to be attuned to their own biases and beliefs toward their own ethnic group. Thus, counselors who possess an ethnocentric view of their own culture in relation to other cultures may try to impose their beliefs and stereotypes, consciously or unconsciously, on a client. Note that this behavior may have negative consequences regardless of the ethnic match between the counselor and the client.

DEGREE OF ACCULTURATION

Another factor that might bias the nature of the counseling environment for ethnic minority counselors is their own degree of acculturation. That is, counselors should examine the extent to which they have adopted or adapted aspects of the worldview, culture, and beliefs of their host culture and the degree to which those ideas influence their work in the counseling setting.

Ethnic minority counselors typically possess a number of advantages because of their experience in being acculturated to at least two different cultures—their own and that of the host. Thus, knowledge of both cultures can be applied in working with patients in the counseling setting.

In a situation in which ethnicity of the counselor and the client matches, it is important to note the degree of acculturation for both prior to making assumptions about perceptions, expectations, beliefs, needs, and so forth. Note that the acculturation process is not the same for everyone, and both the counselor and the patient need to assess the degree to which they have integrated a new set of value orientations into their own belief systems. Factors such as age, gender, and age of immigration all play a role in assessing level of acculturation for both ethnic minority counselors and their clients.

THE ROLE OF CULTURAL MATCH

To the extent that the cultural values of the counselor match those of the client, the counselor is better able to devise a treatment plan that is culturally responsive and informed by a clear knowledge of the expectations, knowledge, and beliefs of a member of a specific culture. Those values may be closely linked to ethnic background.

Cultural practices may include those that revolve around religion, family values, and socialization, beliefs surrounding personal relationships, and attitudes regarding education, work, and seeking help with mental health issues. The benefit of a treatment program that is culturally responsive to the client is that this approach fosters greater rapport between the counselor and the client, leading to more positive outcomes.

In cases in which cultural background or cultural knowledge does not match across the counselor and the client, it is important to have a good working knowledge of both belief systems and to understand their similarities and their differences. For example, with regard to family values, some cultures value stoicism and the ability to solve problems within the family, whereas other cultures support and encourage the seeking of mental health treatment outside the family unit.

Further, cultures are often divided into those that promote individualism versus those that value collectivism. This cultural nuance may influence the degree to which a suggested mode of treatment emphasizes the needs and beliefs of the individual or whether it is informed by common beliefs and values held collectively by members of a given cultural group.

RACE

Racial differences, in addition to differences in ethnicity, may affect the nature of the relationship between a counselor and a client. Although there is a long-standing debate regarding the definition of *race,* most people would agree that a general idea of the meaning of this term involves a description of an individual's physical characteristics.

Members of certain cultural groups who find it easier to discuss personal issues with someone they see as outside of their own ethnic group might seek an ethnic minority counselor whose racial features differ from those of the client. This is particularly the case with individuals for whom discussion of personal events with members of the same group could be perceived as shameful and inappropriate.

In other instances, individuals feel an instant bond or liking for a counselor of the same racial background because there is an underlying assumption that the counselor will understand the prejudices, biases, and stereotypes that are applied to members of that racial group.

Thus, the ways in which counselor–client match with regard to race lead to effective treatment outcomes depend on the specific characteristics of each individual and his or her cultural values and personal beliefs with regard to racial characteristics.

LANGUAGE MATCH

Client–therapist matches in language may encourage specific processes in communication that may result in effective treatment. Typically, ethnic matches also entail some degree of language match between the counselor and the patient. However, this might not always be the case.

Clearly, when there is a language match, the ability to communicate effectively is enhanced. Research indicates that minority clients may not return to therapy after the first session because they do not feel understood by a counselor who does not match their ethnicity or language background.

Differences in word use may occur across languages. It has been demonstrated, for example, that words that label one's emotions, such as *happy* or *sad,* may not be represented in memory the same way across different language groups. Moreover, certain words that describe emotional states might only exist in a single language and may not have a single-word counterpart in an alternate language. Because verbal communication is such an important part of the counseling setting, it is clear that language barriers may exist if there is a mismatch between the counselor and the client in this domain.

Further, if both the therapist and the client are bilingual, several advantages may be afforded, such as the ability to code switch or mix languages to better express concepts that are available only in a single language. Thus, the use of code-switching and language-mixing techniques in a strategic fashion might lead to more positive outcomes in therapy.

COUNSELOR BIASES

Although a good deal of research has indicated that overall there are positive benefits to creating a match between counselors and patients on the basis of ethnicity, culture, race, and language, caution should be applied when generalizing these conclusions across all members of a specific group. That is, there is heterogeneity among members of a specific group, and it may not be possible to use a single set of characteristics to describe all members of a given group.

In addition, it has been suggested that counselors whose ethnicity matches that of their clients may assign less severe ratings of psychopathology to those clients, at least for some ethnic groups. Whether these ratings are somewhat biased on occasion or driven by a stronger degree of client–patient understanding is a factor that should be examined in each specific case.

—*Jeanette Altarriba*

See also Multicultural Counseling Competencies; Multicultural Counselors

FURTHER READING

Altarriba, J., & Santiago-Rivera, A. L. (1994). Current perspectives on using linguistic and cultural factors in counseling the bilingual Spanish-speaking client. *Professional Psychology: Research and Practice, 25,* 388–397.

Atkinson, D. R., Thompson, C. E., & Grant, S. K. (1993). A three-dimensional model for counseling racial and ethnic minorities. *The Counseling Psychologist, 21,* 257–277.

Gamst, G., Dana, R. H., Der-Karabetian, A., Aragon, M., Arellano, L. M., & Kramer, T. (2002). Effects of Latino acculturation and ethnic identity on mental health outcomes. *Hispanic Journal of Behavioral Sciences, 24,* 479–504.

Gim, R. H., Atkinson, D. R., & Kim, S. J. (1991). Asian American acculturation, counselor ethnicity and cultural sensitivity, and ratings of counselors. *Journal of Counseling Psychology, 38,* 57–62.

Ridley, C. R. (1989). Racism in counseling as an adversive behavioral process. In P. B. Pedersen, J. G. Draguns, W. J. Lonner, & J. E. Trimble (Eds.), *Counseling across cultures* (3rd ed., pp. 55–77). Honolulu: University of Hawaii Press.

Yeh, M., Eastman, K., & Cheung, M. K. (1994). Children and adolescents in community health centers: Does the ethnicity or the language of the therapist match? *Journal of Community Psychology, 22,* 153–163.

ETHNIC MINORITY ELDERLY INDIVIDUALS

Ethnic minority elderly individuals include five ethnic populations in the United States: African Americans; Alaska Natives and American Indians; Asian Americans; Hispanics and Latinos; and Pacific Islander Americans. *Elderly* is defined as the age of eligibility for social security benefits (65, 66, or 67 in the future). Another way to define *elderly* may be by age norms (e.g., transition to grandparenthood) determined by society.

The number of ethnic minority elders is projected to grow rapidly over the next 50 years, from 12.3% in 2000, to 14.1% in 2020, to 18.3% of the elderly population in 2050 (or a change from 984,000 in 2000, to 5.8 million by 2050). Ethnic groups can differ in health and mental health status, culture, acculturation, immigration status and history, discrimination history and its ongoing negative legacy impacting socioeconomic status and educational and employment opportunities, and stressors that impinge on the quality of later life.

AFRICAN AMERICAN ELDERS

The number of African American elders in the United States is predicted to grow from 2.9 million in 2000 to 8.6 million in 2050. The slave health deficit and cumulative lifelong disadvantage remain for elderly African Americans and have not narrowed over the last 50 years. Life expectancy at birth is approximately 67.8 for African American males and 74.7 for females, and 74.0 for U.S. Virgin Islander males and 77.0 for females, in comparison to 74.6 for European American males and 79.9 for females. This may suggest that health and health care improvements benefit African Americans at a slower pace, or that health care innovations and services do not equally improve the health status of African Americans as compared with European Americans.

African Americans suffer from health disparities in disability and deaths from heart disease, stroke, cancers, and other chronic diseases. Poorer socioeconomic and social resources result in inadequate access to preventive and cutting-edge medical services, including hospitalization for a large group of middle-age and elderly African Americans, and accumulative health disparities in mortality and morbidity outcomes. Although several studies indicate higher utilization of certain preventive screening tests (e.g., mammography and Pap smears), they have not produced sufficient health benefits. African Americans still struggle with later diagnosis of illnesses and fewer options for follow-up care and timely treatments. Diagnosis and appropriate treatment are especially problematic for those without health insurance.

Significant mental health disparities exist, yet little is known specifically about the prevalence rates of mental disorders and cognitive impairment among African American elders. Severe cognitive impairment, depression, and other mental health disparities may exist over and above those which have been accounted for by socioeconomic status and educational differences. Research on African American elders should pursue the impact of health and other comorbid conditions, lifelong discriminatory experiences, and environmental exposures and stressors during important developmental time periods.

HISPANIC AND LATINO AMERICAN ELDERS

By the year 2030, Hispanic American elderly will be the largest minority elderly group in the United States. Of all races' elders segments, Hispanic American elders are projected to grow most rapidly, from 1.5 million in 2000 to 13.8 in 2050. Hispanic American elders consisted of 50% Mexican, American, 17% Cuban American, 11% Puerto Rican American, and 24% Other Hispanic Americans in 2002. Elders constitute a rather small percentage of the Hispanic and Latino population: 4% of Mexican Americans, 5% of Americans from South and Central America, and 6% of Puerto Ricans are elderly. The exception is Cuban Americans, of whom 21% are classified as elderly. The health status of Hispanics in the southwestern United States is comparable to the health status of non-Hispanic European Americans. Life expectancies at birth are 76.0 for Hispanic males and 83.0 for females in California, and 71.0 for Puerto Ricans in the commonwealth. A closer examination of this Hispanic paradox is warranted, because there are better mortality outcomes despite Hispanics being more socioeonomically disadvantaged in infancy and at older ages.

A few large-scale studies include Hispanic Americans adults over 60 years of age, but they show a 26% rate of major depression, with 20.5% of those individuals having a comorbid health problem or higher rates of somatic symptoms (difficulty sleeping and loss of appetite), high blood pressure, or other chronic diseases, such as diabetes. Hispanic American elderly may be at higher risk of developing Alzheimer's disease. Research should attempt to determine causal factors (e.g., link to diabetes) that contribute to the poorer mental health status among Hispanic elders.

ASIAN AMERICAN ELDERS

There are 861,725 Asian American elders, the fastest-growing group fueled by immigration. Asian American elders in the United States were composed of 29% Chinese, 21% Filipino, 20% Japanese, 9% Korean, 8% Vietnamese/Cambodian, 1% Hmong, and 12% other Asian ethnicities in 2002. National aggregated statistics indicate a physically healthy Asian and Pacific Islander elderly population, with some noted exceptions. Life expectancy at birth is 79.5 years for Japanese males and 84.5 for females, 79.8 for Chinese males and 86.1 for females, 77.6 for Filipino males and 81.5 for females in Hawaii. Although Japanese and Chinese immigrant elderly populations have excellent physical health, their more acculturated American counterparts, Hmong or Pacific Islander elders, have poorer health outcomes. There are high rates of preventable cancers such as cervical cancers among Vietnamese women and alarming rates of breast cancer among Japanese and Chinese American women. Native Hawaiian women have the second-highest prevalence of breast cancer among Asian Americans.

Although scarce, there is much more information about the physical health of Asian and Pacific Islander elderly than on their mental health status during the second half of life. Although there are no large prevalence studies of psychiatric disorders among Asian American elderly samples, several small studies indicate comparable depression, somatic psychiatric distress, and dementia rates between European American and Asian American (Chinese, Korean, Japanese) elderly samples. However, the high rate of suicide among Asian elderly women suggests poor mental health outcomes.

NATIVE HAWAIIAN AND PACIFIC ISLANDER ELDERS

There were 43,802 Native Hawaiian and Pacific Islander elders in the United States according to the 2000 Census. Native Hawaiians and Pacific Islanders are a relatively young population, with only 5% of the population being age 65 and older. Pacific Islanders consist of 45.9% Native Hawaiian, 15.2% Samoan, 10.6% Guamanians, 4.2% Tongans, 1.6% Fujians, and 20% other Pacific Islanders. Life expectancies for Hawaiian, Samoan, and Guamanian males are 71.5, 71.0, and 72.4 years, respectively, as compared with 73.2 for European Americans. Life expectancies at birth for Hawaiian, Samoan, and Guamanian females are 77.2, 74.9, and 76.1 years, respectively, as compared with 79.6 for European Americans. Data from Hawaii indicate that Native Hawaiian, Samoan, and Chamorro groups had significantly higher mortality rates for most causes of death. These higher rates may be because of advanced disease diagnosis; high rates of hypertension, heart disease, stroke, and diabetes; and poorer health behaviors, such as higher smoking rates and obesity, among Pacific Islanders.

The prevalence of psychiatric mental health status of Pacific Islanders is currently unknown; however, key indicators suggest poorer mental health status than for other ethnic groups in Hawaii. These few studies indicate higher rates of antisocial behavior, assaults, suicides, depression, anxiety, conduct disorder, and substance abuse, associated with lower educational attainment and poorer health behaviors, such as number of cigarettes smoked.

ALASKA NATIVE AND AMERICAN INDIAN ELDERS

In 2000, there were 259,663 Alaska Native and American Indian elders in the United States, and this group is expected to grow by a little over 1.5%. American Indian elders come from more than 550 federally recognized tribes who live on or near reservations and across U.S. urban areas. Life expectancy at birth is approximately 67.6 years for American Indian males and 74.7 for females, but similar to the situation for Asian, Hispanic, and Pacific Islander American populations, the quality of data is very poor. American Indians have the lowest rate of health insurance coverage, at 62%, with lack of health service access, especially in urban areas. Multiple chronic conditions contribute to health disparities, with 57% reporting three or more chronic conditions, 17% with a single chronic condition, and 26% without chronic conditions.

Large-scale studies of the prevalence of mental disorders among American Indian elders is lacking, but smaller studies indicate between 20% and 30% of elders suffer from dementia or alcohol-related dementia. Investigators have attributed poorer mental health status to a high rate of personal loss, such as family deaths, threats, and societal denigration for traditional American Indian identities and cultures.

MEASUREMENT AND CULTURALLY COMPETENT RESEARCH ISSUES

Culturally competent and responsive measures with validity research studies must be conducted on minority and limited-English-speaking populations. Important explanatory research variables include lifelong impact of discrimination and socioeconomic status, culture, immigration, and acculturation. We need to move beyond the science of ethnic minorities that is based on the experiences of college students and English-speaking research populations to ensure the validity of our scientific findings and resulting interventions.

—*Barbara W. K. Yee*

FURTHER READING

Anderson, N. B., Bulatao, R. A., & Cohen, B. (Eds.). (2004). *Critical perspectives on racial and ethnic differences in health in late life.* Washington, DC: National Research Council, the National Academies Press.

Skinner, J. H., Teresi, J. A., Holmes, D., Stahl, S. M., & Stewart, A. L. (2002). *Multicultural measurement in older populations.* New York: Springer.

Whitfield, K. E. (2004). *Closing the gap: Improving the health of minority elders in the new millennium.* Washington, DC: The Gerontological Society of America.

ETHNIC MINORITY YOUTH

DEFINING ETHNIC MINORITY YOUTH

The term *ethnic minority youth* is used to describe children or adolescents who are members of a U.S. racial or ethnic minority group. *Childhood* is defined as the time between birth and puberty when rapid physical and cognitive developments occur. *Adolescence* is the period of time between childhood and adulthood, typically around ages 11 to 19, characterized by the transition to physical, sexual, and psychological maturity, with an emphasis on the development of independence from family and a reliance on peers. *Youth* encompasses both terms and indicates a variety of developmental issues that differ from those of adults.

Ethnicity refers to a collective cultural heritage shared by a group of people who have a common ancestry. In the United States, the term *ethnic minority* typically refers to four major groups: African Americans, Hispanics, Asian/Pacific Islanders, and Native Americans. However, these classifications are also based on racial categories historically used to stratify people based on physical differences such as skin color, facial structure, and hair texture. Although *race* is often discussed as a biological category and *ethnicity* as a cultural one, both can be considered social constructions and are labels used to classify the roles and expectations of each group.

ETHNIC MINORITY YOUTH LITERATURE

The literature on ethnic minority youth is vast but has many methodological flaws. Most discussions are based on a European American, middle-class reference that neglects the experiences of minorities. When there is discussion of minority youth, it is often in comparison to European American youth, which does not allow for the formation of ideas and theories pertinent to these groups, but rather considers their development secondary to a dominant cultural experience. Furthermore, the literature often confounds the effects of ethnic categorization with that of socioeconomic status (SES). Minority youth from lower SES groups are often compared with European American youth with higher SES. Most studies do not record the SES of the children they study, and when they do, the comparisons between minority and European American youth are often unequal or uncontrolled. Study of minority youth also takes place almost exclusively in urban, low-income samples without comparison groups. It is difficult to conclude whether the outcomes presented in most studies stem from either ethnic or socioeconomic background, and this difficulty precludes generalizable conclusions about ethnic minority youth. Keeping this in mind, below are some important characteristics of each of the four minority youth populations.

AFRICAN AMERICAN YOUTH

Most African American youth come from families that have been in the United States for generations, as descendants of slaves. In the early and mid-20th century, this history created survival responses to discrimination that encouraged self-control and subjugation as a means of avoiding violent confrontations with European Americans. With recent structural changes, such as desegregation and anti-discrimination laws, the experiences of African American youth are changing and they are developing healthier senses of self. In more recent history, Blacks from Africa and the Caribbean have also immigrated to the United States. These groups also deal with the legacy of discrimination but additionally face issues relevant to immigrants. Although these groups have distinct experiences, rarely are they separated in the literature, and most studies treat African American youth as a homogeneous set.

For African American youth, contextual influences are the strongest in affecting adolescent adjustment, including peer relationships, school and neighborhood interactions, and parental influence and involvement. African American youth are well supported by their families, as indicated by strong bonds with extended family, favorable attitudes toward the elderly, adaptable familial roles, and a strong religious and spiritual orientation. Difficulties for African American youth arise in the context of acculturative stress and present themselves in higher arrest and incarceration rates than for other ethnic groups, increases in high school drop-out rates for inner-city youth, and recent increases in suicide rates. It is important to remember that many of these characteristics are related to SES and that African Americans living in poverty have very different life experiences than those with higher levels of education and financial means.

HISPANIC YOUTH

The category *Hispanic* is defined by the U.S. Census Bureau as those people who are of Cuban, Mexican, Puerto Rican, South or Central American, or other Spanish culture or origin regardless of race. Census data from 2002 show that Mexican Americans are the largest of the subgroups, constituting 65% of all Hispanics, followed by Puerto Ricans at 10% and then Cubans at 4%. Consequently, most literature on Hispanic youth focuses on one of these three groups. Generally, for Hispanic youth, level of acculturation has been shown to influence successful growth and development. As generational status increases, there is less of a buffering effect, likely because of increased interactions outside of their community and an increased likelihood of experiencing racism and conflict between familial value systems and mainstream culture. Success for Hispanic youth is built on a delicate balance between developing a healthy sense of ethnic identity and developing skills that help the youth to navigate the outside world.

Psychological functioning of Hispanic youth has been the topic of many researchers' work. Studies on resiliency have found that peer influence and ethnic pride are related to academic achievement. Drop-out and retention rates have also been examined in Latino youth. Although girls fare better than their male counterparts, drop-out rates among urban Latino youth can be as high as 50%. It is important that future research be aimed at increasing the school retention of Hispanic youth.

ASIAN/PACIFIC ISLANDER YOUTH

Asian American youth are similar to Hispanics in that they are exposed to issues of immigration and acculturation; however, their experiences are also very different. Asians as a group tend to be more diverse, coming from at least 15 countries of origin/descent and speaking as many if not more languages. Additionally, some groups of Asians have been in the United States for generations, whereas others have recently immigrated, often as refugees to escape political oppression. Asian youth also typically outperform all other ethnic and racial groups' educational attainment and eventual income levels, leading to a model minority myth that characterizes Asians as fitting into the mainstream and has been used as a false standard to live up to for members of minority groups.

Studies have shown that the success of Asian adolescents can be attributed to effort and use of time with regard to school activities, as well as to parental involvement and commitment to education. Asian family systems have also been shown to be the most "traditional" of all ethnic groups in the United States, with more than 80% of all Asian American children living with both biological parents. Although Asian students outperform other groups, this is likely because of a significant investment in education by both youth and their families, and does not buffer other experiences such as racism, acculturative stress, and language barriers.

NATIVE AMERICAN YOUTH

When compared with other minority youth, Native American adolescents are more likely to suffer a variety of health concerns (diabetes, suicide, tuberculosis, fetal alcohol syndrome) and are at higher risk for living in poverty, being unemployed, and earning low wages. Because there are between 400 and 500 differing tribal affiliations, it is difficult to make very many broad generalizations concerning Native American youth. Family structures are typically diffuse compared with other groups, with children sometimes being raised collectively and having an extensive tribal connection. Children may consider themselves to have many different parents (biological as well as those primarily responsible for their care) and may consider cousins and aunts and uncles of similar age to be siblings.

American Indian youth are similar to other minorities in that they have inherited a long-standing legacy of legalized discrimination. In addition to the relocation of Native Americans to reservations in the late 19th century, Indian children were historically removed from their homes and sent to boarding schools to be stripped of their language and cultural practices, which were outlawed from 1870 to 1930. This removal created a precedent for Native American children to be caught between two worlds, often struggling with an inability to identify with either their tribal heritage or the European American culture that surrounds them and often treats them with hostility. Many Native American cultures do not recognize an adolescent developmental stage, which may further contribute to these feelings of being caught between worlds. Youth may have responsibilities as adults in their tribal environment (such as caring for siblings or tending to livestock), although they may be treated as children by a contemporary school system.

CONCLUSION

Although this review of it has been brief, the literature on ethnic minority youth in the United States continues to grow. The majority of this literature tends to paint a rather disparaging picture of this population, but the resiliency and successes of many ethnic minority youth are becoming better documented. Improving educational achievement of ethnic minority youth and differentiating between ethnic and socioeconomic differences are critical topics for future research.

—Rufus R. Gonzales
—Elizabeth M. Vera
—Melissa L. Morgan

FURTHER READING

McLoyd, V. C., & Steinberg, L. (Eds.). (1998). *Studying minority adolescents: Conceptual, methodological, and theoretical issues.* Mahwah, NJ: Lawrence Erlbaum.

Montemayor, R., Adams, G. R., & Gullota, T. P. (Eds.). (2000). *Adolescent diversity in ethnic, economic, and cultural contexts.* Thousand Oaks, CA: Sage.

ETHNIC RESEARCH

The psychological study of ethnic behavior draws from many disciplines. The psychologist involved in ethnic research obtains information and data from such fields as ethnology, sociology, anthropology, social psychology, medicine, and social work. In their guidelines for research applicants, the federal government and research sponsors increasingly ask for more interdisciplinary collaboration. These guidelines fit well into the study of ethnic behavior, because important data outside the traditional realm of psychological research can be relevant.

Ethnic research can be found under many terms; for example, *interdisciplinary, cross-cultural, minorities, racial, ethnic, multicultural,* and *indigenous populations.* Those involved in these studies make distinctions among these terms. But for most people, some of these terms are frequently used in a synonymous manner. Ethnic research can also be found under groupings such as Arabs, Asians, African Americans, Gypsies, Hispanics, Native Americans, European-Americans, and tribes.

The researcher looking for ethnic studies done prior to the 1960s will need to be aware that terms have changed for ethnic groups. For example, the contemporary term *African Americans* was preceded by different terms to designate this group; *Indians* are now often referred to as *Native Americans; Oriental* is no longer acceptable; instead, *Asian* and more specific terms such as *Chinese* and *Japanese* are preferred.

As with the term *minority,* the term *ethnic* is difficult to define and there is controversy as to how to define it. Most definitions of *ethnic* refer to groupings of people classified according to common racial, national, tribal, religious, linguistic, or cultural background. By this definition, everyone belongs to an ethnic group. However, it is common practice for those who control a society to refer to those not in their group as ethnic. In the United States, the term *ethnic group* usually designates those who are not of European ancestry. In the research literature, those who are not of European ancestry are often contrasted with *Caucasians* and *European Americans.* These latter terms are also problematic because they engender many of the same problems as those encountered for designating ethnic groups. No matter which terms are used, there are issues as to whether the terms are accurate, and there are issues of how to measure and determine which people to include and exclude in the group.

Ethnic research draws from, and is applicable to, an enormous range of human activities. Wherever humans are studied, it is highly likely that there are people of different ethnic backgrounds. The studies of ethnic groups can apply to political science, international studies, marketing, education, the military, and many other areas of endeavor.

Just as there are many reasons for conducting research on ethnic group members, there are also many groups that engage in these activities. Many countries have governmental agencies and departments that study ethnic behavior, and these can serve many functions. Governmental agencies can engender the perception in the ethnic community that the government is interested in them and cares for them. Information that is gathered can provide a possible avenue for ethnic community members to express themselves. The data that are obtained can serve as a rationale for the government to channel resources. The data can also be used to obtain information on how to exploit and control a particular ethnic group.

Just as with governmental groups, nongovernmental groups can serve varied functions. Universities, charities, commercial enterprises, and political, social, and religious groups often have their own agendas when they conduct research on ethnic groups. Their functions can be benign or detrimental; often they are both.

Ethnic research can increase the understanding of the dimensions and robustness of human behavior. When approaches, techniques, tests, theories, and hypotheses are applied to different cultural groups, it is possible to obtain information on the strengths, weaknesses, and cultural biases involved. For example, studies in one culture can find that suicidal behavior is inversely correlated with socioeconomic status, and a generalization can then be made that this relationship is part of the human condition. If researchers do not find a similar correlation in another culture, their hypothesis would need to be examined under a different rubric— that is, suicide and socioeconomic status are not necessarily correlated for all peoples, and there can be different factors involved in different cultures. Most of the theorists in psychology assert that what they espouse is universal. However, very few of them actually test their approaches and techniques under cross-cultural conditions, and when they do, their analyses and conclusions are usually biased. Submitting our ideas and instruments to the crucible of cross-cultural examination can increase our understanding of human behavior.

Ethnic studies can help delineate universal and culture-specific behaviors. If a behavior is observed across cultures, then there is a greater likelihood that the behavior is universal. If a behavior is observed in only one culture, then cultural factors can be more cogent in the expression of that behavior. Being able to distinguish between the two can help determine more effective approaches and treatments. For example, schizophrenia is observed in all cultures, providing evidence that it is a universal condition. Therefore, treatment approaches used in one culture might be applicable across a wider range of cultures. In contrast, *ataque de nervios* is a condition more prominent in Latinos from the Caribbean who have experienced stress. Many of those with this condition are women over 45 years old from a lower socioeconomic background. In this case, there is likelihood that effective treatment would entail the consideration of cultural, social, and economic factors. This is not to say that culture-specific treatments are not also applicable in the treatment of schizophrenia. But one can say that cultural factors can be more involved in disorders such as ataque de nervios than in schizophrenia. Psychologists involved in ethnic research can help delineate which behaviors are more universal and which are more culture-specific. Such information can help teachers, salespersons, psychologists, military recruiters, and those who work with various ethnic group members obtain greater understanding of their particular culture and how to interact with them.

Ethnic research in psychology is not an endeavor that is relevant only to the group being investigated. Studies of people in one culture can help people in different cultures. Just as areas such as those in medicine have found that drugs (e.g., herbs) and approaches (e.g., acupuncture) from other cultures can benefit us, so, too, can ethnic studies enhance our understanding and options. For example, one culture can believe that the avoidance of eye contact is a sign of deviousness. Another culture can view the avoidance of eye contact as a sign of respect. Such awareness can lessen the likelihood of the person in the first culture from assuming that when someone in their own, or another, culture avoids eye contact that the person is devious, dishonest, or engaging in subterfuge. Such knowledge can aggrandize perspectives and ameliorate the negative connotation associated with some behaviors. Another example is from studies of eating disorders: as minorities become more acculturated into European American, middle-class values, their rates of bulimia and anorexia increase. Perhaps studies of ethnic groups that have lower incidences of eating disorders can provide values, perceptions, and attitudes that are healthier than those of the European American middle class that induce eating disorders. We can benefit from learning about the behaviors of other cultures. Their behaviors can expand our repertoire of ways to cope with our environment and enable us to look at behaviors from a less limiting ethnocentric perspective.

Ethnic research can have important consequences. It has been used in many different ways. For example, research into IQ scores has resulted in controversial interpretations of ethnic differences in intelligence among groups. Research into the utilization of services has resulted in determining where and how to provide services. Census surveys have resulted in determining which groups obtain resources. Marketing research has provided information on how to persuade ethnic members to buy products and how to obtain their votes. Developmental, neurological, linguistic, and educational research have helped schools determine whether they should provide bicultural education. The integration of African Americans and European Americans was facilitated by psychological studies (e.g., psychological research that indicated that attitudes can follow behavior, so that if European Americans were forced to integrate public swimming pools, their initial resistance would change—which is what happened). These and a host of other research studies in many fields have influenced politicians, the public, and society in general.

When one investigates, understands, and contends with the issues involved in ethnic research, the result is to obtain a good grasp of many of the key issues involved in psychological research and methodology. Among the usual problems that confront the ethnic researcher are the following:

1. *How to define ethnicity.* This is a multifaceted variable. For example, an individual's self-identification can change over time, or people in the person's environment can change their definition of the person's ethnic identity, or the various governmental agencies and the states can differ or change their definitions.

2. *How to choose a representative sample.* Sampling problems have been a recurrent feature in ethnic research. Samples in ethnic research are often small and drawn from local participants. This makes generalizations difficult. A sample from a Native American tribe in the Southwest of the United States raises the issue of which Native American groups the sample can be generalized to. To validly gauge Latino behaviors and perceptions, a sample would need to consider the enormous variations within the Latino community (e.g., there are Latinos from Argentina, Mexico, and Puerto Rico).

3. *How to classify those of multiple ethnicities.* There are an increasing number of people with more than one ethnicity. The question often arises as to how to categorize them. Should they be in a separate multiethnic category? Or should they be relegated to an ethnic group—and if so, which ethnic group should they be placed in?

4. *How to obtain accurate data.* When a researcher obtains information from individuals and institutions, political, economic, and social factors often influence the provision of ethnic data. For example, an institution can inflate its figures because funding is contingent on having a higher number of ethnic members, or the institution can inflate its figures out of concern that that they would be perceived as inhospitable to certain groups. There are many reasons why inaccurate information might be provided.

Because ethnicity is greatly influenced by political and social factors, it is difficult to develop a scientific definition and measure of it. For the most part, the American psychologist involved in ethnic research uses the terms and definitions of the lay culture—which change frequently, making any objective, relatively stable definition and measurement of *ethnicity* controversial and difficult.

Ethnic research is a broad term. Typing the term in a search engine resulted in 57,400,000 hits; *ethnic psychology research* resulted in 6,980,000 hits. To determine the areas the term *ethnic research* covered in psychology, a library search was conducted. The search covered 1,300 periodicals, books, book chapters, and dissertations, from 1887 to the present.

Unlike anthropology's Human Relations Area Files (HRAF) at Yale, which stem from an attempt to create a central point for gathering and facilitating worldwide comparative studies of human behavior, society, and culture, there has been no comprehensive undertaking in the United States to centralize and catalog ethnic research in psychology. However, there have been periodical reviews of material published in selected areas of psychology. Reviews of professional periodicals indicate that there has been an increase in ethnic minority articles. An analysis of the articles published in the *Journal of Counseling Psychology* indicated a 6% increase in ethnic minority articles between 1976 and 1986. A follow-up study found a 12% increase from 1988 to 1997. Reviews of the contents of the *Journal of Multicultural Counseling and Development* between 1985 and 1999 indicated that 21% of the articles dealt with multicultural competence/counseling; 14% with psychosocial adjustment/development; 10% with multicultural training/curriculum; and 9% with worldview; 8% were on women and 6% were on men. African Americans were written about the most. The elderly were written on the least (1%). About 3% of the articles were on religion, disability, sexual orientation, and forms of diversity; about 48% were expository or descriptive, 47% were quantitative, and 3% were original qualitative research; 4% were on identity development; 2% were on acculturation; and 2% were on racism, discrimination, and prejudice. Within each of the major ethnic groups, there was underrepresentation of articles dealing with such areas as career development, academic achievement, indigenous models of healing/alternative treatment, assessment, systemic influences, professional issues, religion, sexual orientation, disabilities,

the middle-aged, and the elderly. However, despite the increase in ethnic research, reviews of the literature indicated that there has been, and continues to be, an underrepresentation of ethnic views in the editing, reviews, selection, analysis, and publication of psychological literature.

There is an abundance of material on ethnic research that is conducted from a psychological perspective or that is relevant to ethnic psychology. There are journals that focus primarily on ethnic psychology research. There are handbooks, encyclopedias, Web sites, and books. These, along with many federal agencies, often provide guidelines on how to conduct ethnic research. The content and guidelines that they provide are often the same—this article summarizes much of what has been published.

The general quality of ethnic research is highly variable. There are many reasons for this. Part of the variability is because of the quality of the research, and part of it is because of the perceptions of ethnic research. The variability of the quality of the research can be the result of many factors, including the confounding factors entailed in ethnic research, poor scholarship, and the lack of support for such studies. Variability owing to perceptions can be attributed to the influence of personal values, biases, and misunderstanding. Although the consequences can be highly significant, the results of many studies, even if statistical terms and techniques are used, are basically anecdotal, in large part because of the approaches, statistics, and instruments that are used and because the research is often conducted in an ad hominem manner. Variability can also result from the manner in which the data are presented—poor studies that have surface validity and that are understood are more likely be read and valued, whereas good studies that are complicated and pedantic are not as likely to be read and are valued only by a cabal of the few. The latter phenomenon is not unique to the study of ethnic psychology; it is a common feature of much of psychological and scientific literature.

Ethnic studies are often undervalued. This perception can be influenced by those who view ethnic studies as of secondary or tertiary relevance compared with studies of the general U.S. population. The research is often valued less because it is viewed as partisan activity; that is, the research is the expression of the researcher's biased perspective, or the research is viewed as relevant only to the group being investigated.

A significant reason why measuring ethnicity can be a problem is that it is defined as a construct. In the area of assessment, it is usually easier to measure physical, overt phenomena than to measure social and cultural constructs. In studies using more obtrusive constructs, such as achievement and abilities, the reliability coefficient is about .90. The reliability coefficient for constructs such as personality, interests, and values, by contrast, is around .80. Ethnicity is in the latter category; therefore, lower reliability and validity can be expected in studies using it as a variable. Even using overt, physical criteria can produce spurious results. For example, if skin color were to be used, the results would be questionable because biological variations in skin color are in clines, which have characteristics that overlap between populations.

Perhaps one of the most salient features of ethnic research is that nothing can be taken for granted. The givens—the accepted methods, measures, approaches, concepts, and analyses—are questioned in ethnic research. The problems of doing psychological research in general are accentuated in ethnic research. The following are some examples of these problems:

1. The conceptual problems that start and guide the researcher can be problematic. The researcher is limited by the beliefs, mores, definitions, behaviors, perceptions, and paradigms of the larger, general U.S. population. There is often the assumption of the universality of these factors—in effect, that what is apropos for mainstream America is apropos for ethnic groups. This assumption has often been wrong.

2. There are often greater problems in getting ethnic group members to participate in research. There are a number of possible reasons for this problem with participation. The ethnic group member often does not value the research that is being conducted. The ethnic member can view the data to be collected as possibly harmful; for example, data on the number of illegal immigrants in an ethnic community could be used to bring in immigration officials. It is usually easier to sample European Americans. They are the largest group in the United States. They often feel less threatened by research—perhaps because they dominate the country and can control the misuse of the research—and they can have greater recourse if the research is used in a detrimental manner. Furthermore, perception of the possible exploitive nature of the research is lower in the dominant group, whereas ethnic communities often feel the research will promote gains for the researcher and the community will not garner any benefits.

3. The ethnic sample is often smaller compared with samples from the general U.S. population. This disparity can have enormous ramifications. For instance, a large sample will be more generalizable. The smaller sample decreases the credibility of the study. If a stratified sampling technique is used, the effects of the larger sample from the general U.S. population will statistically mitigate the effects of the ethnic group.

4. Another strident problem is that of equivalence—the constructs, terms, and test format can have different effects on different groups. For example, there can be differences in the perceived magnitude of a behavior. That is, if a person in one ethnic group responds that he or she is a *1* on a scale of depression, is that *1* equivalent to the response of a person in another ethnic group? In ethnic research, the problems of equivalence raise many issues—including issues of reliability and validly.

5. If the measurement depends on the observer to accurately measure the behavior, then there can be a problem of observer bias. This problem is illustrated in a study of European American and Chinese American therapists' perceptions of Chinese patients. The European American therapists were more likely to evaluate the Chinese patients as more depressed, more inhibited, less socially poised, and having greater social skills deficits. The Chinese American therapists rated the same clients as alert, ambitious, adaptable, honest, and friendly. There have also been studies that found that members of ethnic groups sometimes present themselves differently to therapists of different ethnicity.

Ethnic research provides an excellent training opportunity to learn the problems of conducting, evaluating, interpreting, and statistically analyzing research. It provides good training in questioning basic assumptions and evaluating all aspects of research.

ADAPTING MEASURES IN CROSS-CULTURAL RESEARCH

It is often the practice of psychological researchers to have some method to quantify what they are doing. With quantification, subsequent research can add, change, and correct the data. Questionnaires, inventories, and surveys are frequently used to obtain data. The researcher has to encode what is collected. To control for some of the problems entailed in the development, adaptation, administration, documentation, scoring, and interpretation of data, the

International Test Commission (ITC) has provided guidelines for adapting psychological and educational tests for different linguistic and cultural groups. The ITC consists of national psychological associations, test commissions, and publishers and organizations involved in the proper development, evaluation, and uses of educational and psychological instruments. Their guidelines are divided into four categories: context; test development and adaptation; administration; and documentation/score interpretations.

COMPUTERS, TECHNOLOGY, DATA GATHERING, AND RESEARCH

Computers and technology can serve many useful purposes in ethnic research. Computers can be programmed to interact in the language, idiom, dialect, and vernacular of the ethnic member. Computers can help overcome some of the barriers and biases entailed in face-to-face data gathering, such as the effects of the interviewer's ethnic characteristics.

Opportunities exist for members of ethnic communities to define their own problems and conduct their own research to educate themselves and those outside their communities. Many simple, user-friendly programs are capable of statistical work. Data can be obtained at such sites as religious gatherings, shopping facilities, schools, and eating establishments. The data that are gathered can be shared with ethnic members throughout the country, for example, through the Internet. Ethnic community members can use the information to provide mutual support and to gain more insight into their problems and solutions. They also can share their research with other ethnic communities in the world.

CONCLUDING REMARKS

The present definitions of *ethnicity* are based on what society defines it to be. Such approaches make it difficult to advance this area of research, because the definitions change and are often spurious. Areas such as ethnology and cultural anthropology have made remarkable contributions in analyzing and describing ethnic behaviors. However, their main approaches have been heavily influenced by qualitative studies. If psychology is to further advance ethnic studies, it needs to adhere to its traditional affiliation with the type of approach that is objective and based on sound science. Such an approach should enable data from studies to be accurately cataloged and systematically changed. The uses of neuroimaging and technological

advances in science appear to be some of the tools that can be used to facilitate this process. Just as biology, evolution, and chemistry have placed humans on common ground, so, too, can the examination of brain activity across cultures reveal commonalties in treatment, reactions to stress, mental illness, and the plethora of areas of interest to psychologists.

There are many reasons and opportunities to engage in ethnic research. As the United States interacts with the world, it will need to understand and communicate with people of different cultures, values, and perceptions. Within this country, we have had exponential growth in non-European immigrant groups. The groups that have been traditionally defined as ethnic will soon outnumber those of European ancestry. Their sheer numbers will constitute a rationale for increased ethnic studies. As the populations of ethnic members increase in this country and as those of European ancestry decrease in number and influence, there will be greater competition among ethnic groups for resources and power. There will be more interactions among them. These factors can engender hostility among the groups. We will need to study the factors that promote mutually beneficial conditions and interactions to alleviate and ameliorate antagonism.

On a global level, advances in travel and communication technology have increased tremendously throughout the world. There is contact among the peoples of the world on an unprecedented scale. The United States has the economic and political resources to be the main source to gather and disperse information on the cultures of the world. In addition, we are a live prototype: Our country is an experiment of how peoples of diverse backgrounds can live together. What we learn can benefit the entire world and ourselves.

—*Michael Edmond Illovsky*

FURTHER READING

Brislin, R. W., Lonner, W. J., & Thorndike, R. (1973). *Cross-cultural research methods.* New York: Wiley.

Burlew, K. A. (2003). Research with ethnic minorities: Conceptual, methodological, and analytical issues. In G. Bernal, J. E. Trimble, A. K. Burlew, & F. T. Leong (Eds.), *Handbook of racial and ethnic minority psychology* (pp. 179–197). Thousand Oaks, CA: Sage.

Campbell, D., & Stanley, J. (1966). *Experimental and quasi-experimental designs for research.* Chicago: Rand McNally.

Cook, T. D., & Campbell, D. T. (1979). *Quasi-experimentation: Design and analysis issues for field settings.* Chicago: Rand McNally.

Lonner, W. J., & Berry, J. W. (Eds.). (1986). *Field methods in cross-cultural research.* Newbury Park, CA: Sage.

Matsumoto, D. (Ed.). (2001). *The handbook of culture and psychology.* New York: Oxford University Press.

Triandis, H. C., & Berry, J. W. (Eds.). (1980). *Handbook of cross-cultural psychology: Methodology* (Vol. 2). Boston: Allyn & Bacon.

van de Vijver, F. J. R. (2001). The evolution of cross-cultural research methods. In D. Matsumoto (Ed.), *The handbook of cultural and psychology* (pp. 77–97). New York: Oxford University Press.

ETHNOCENTRIC MONOCULTURALISM

Ethnocentric (valuing of one's ethnic/cultural group over others) monoculturalism (belief in one "right" culture) is an unconscious or conscious overvaluation of one's own cultural beliefs and practices, and simultaneous invalidation of other cultural worldviews. In application, ethnocentric monoculturalism posits the individual's culture as normal and valid. Other cultures are viewed as abnormal, inferior, or pathological, with corresponding differential treatment. Psychology and counseling have a history of being both monocultural and ethnocentric, resulting in limited validity for many psychological theories and practices within the United States. Recognition of ethnocentric monoculturalism is meaningful to psychology and counseling, as multiculturalism not only is required for clinical competency by the ethical principles of psychologists and code of conduct guidelines of the American Psychological Association, but is also important to the interpersonal and personal development of consumers of psychology.

Ethnocentric monoculturalism is based on the concept of group power. When one group gains social power, it gains the capacity to define sociocultural norms. Group power manifests differently in different countries, with a particular ethnic/cultural group perhaps dominant in one country but oppressed in another. Ethnocentric monoculturalism, therefore, is not limited to any one country or ethnic/cultural group. Psychology generally recognizes that European American males hold the dominant group power in the United States and thus hold the ability to create social norms. Although some argue that social revolutions in the 1960s and 1970s have fostered change, the distribution of social power can be seen in the demographics of people holding powerful positions. In the United States, European American men currently hold an estimated 92% of Forbes 400 chief economic officer positions and 80% of tenured academic positions in higher education. European American men hold 80% of the seats in the U.S. House of Representatives and 84% in the United States Senate, and 100% of the U.S. presidents have been men, although European American men constitute only 33% of the general population. The statistical representation of European American males in these positions counters a random or fair distribution; uncontrolled distribution by gender alone would normally result in a 50% split between males and females. The concept of dominant group power offers clarification for this statistical discrepancy.

Ethnocentric monoculturalism explains the frequently espoused perspective of *colorblindness* in the United States, or the ideal of treating all cultural groups the same—a monoculture. In reality, people in the United States are treated differently, based on others' perception of their cultural validity or normalcy (a centric perspective). For example, the homeless are treated differently than those who live in a home, as living in a home is considered normal in the dominant U.S. culture. The ability of any dominant group to define social, economic, and political reality makes it difficult for that group to see how the centric reality is a constructed, versus natural, phenomenon. For example, race is important only in cultures valuing skin pigmentation differences and is meaningless in other cultures. Ethnocentric monoculturalism has been proposed to explain not only overt but covert or modern forms of group and individual discriminatory beliefs and practices.

In the United States, the European American ethnic/ cultural group holds the majority of social power and therefore determines the dominant cultural values. European American culture is considered the norm, and other cultures are considered deviant from the norm. When faced with the abnormal, many people react with distaste and want to remove the abnormal. Historically, this reaction can be seen in the active eradication of cultural differences within the United States, resulting in the frequent perception of a homogeneous American culture, or monoculturalism. Ethnocentric monoculturalism proposes cultural homogeneity to be a logical fallacy, as all cultural worldviews are valid for the individuals holding them.

—Jennifer F. Taylor

See also Ethnocentrism; Institutional Racism; Multicultural Counseling Competencies; White Privilege

FURTHER READING

Johnson, A. G. (2001). *Privilege, power, and difference.* Mountain View, CA: Mayfield.

Sue, D. W. (2004). Caucasianness and ethnocentric monoculturalism: Making the "invisible" visible. *American Psychologist, 59,* 761–769.

Takaki, R. (1993). *A different mirror: A history of multicultural America.* Boston: Little, Brown.

ETHNOCENTRISM

Ethnocentrism is broadly defined as an interpretive framework based on the perception that one's own ethnic or cultural group (in-group) is superior to other groups (out-groups). The concept of ethnocentrism was developed by sociologist W. G. Sumner in 1906 and expanded by Theodor Adorno et al. in 1950. Ethnocentrism is often linked to *cultural bias,* which is defined as judging behaviors and beliefs in terms of what is normative and appropriate to one's own culture. Although ethnocentrism and cultural bias can involve positive stereotyping, these concepts are more often used to frame outsiders as biologically or morally inferior. This entry includes a brief discussion of the sociopolitical roots of ethnocentrism within the context of European colonialist expansion; power relations and genocidal cleansing within sociopolitical contexts; ethnic markers; and the contemporary debate regarding ethnocentrism versus cultural relativism.

ETHNOCENTRISM'S ROOTS

Historically, ethnocentrism was associated with European expansion and colonization across the globe, and was often conflated with racism. Within the context of White European ethnocentrism, culturally based biases were often assumed to be grounded within the laws of nature or seen as supported by biologic or other scientific fact. For example, early Europeans conceptualized non-Europeans as natural slaves who were innately savage, imperfect, and subservient. Over time, this concept underwent a theological modification that conceptualized non-Europeans as natural children who could be uplifted from savagery through Christianity.

After the introduction of Darwinian theory, European proponents of scientific racism used questionable quantitative data on intelligence (such as cranial capacity) to establish the natural superiority of White European males over their female counterparts and over all peoples of color. These attitudes were used to justify the enslavement of subjugated peoples as well as to establish institutional barriers to sharing sociopolitical power with designated out-groups. Although the emergence of ethnic identity and ethnocentric bias has historically taken the form of Eurocentrism, in the late 20th century the political mobilization of groups such as African diaspora and Hispanic populations has resulted in the growth of, for example, Afrocentrism and the Chicano movement.

POWER RELATIONSHIPS

Social status and power relationships are continuously negotiated within every culture; however, those who hold more authority are able to maximize their status and advance a particular agenda. For example, by naturalizing socioeconomic and status differences and devaluing the cultural systems of the out-group, the in-group creates an environment that fosters individual and institutionalized prejudice against the out-group. Therefore, ethnocentrism is closely linked to differential social power, wherein the more dominant group can systematically inhibit, exclude, or deny access to privileges, resources, and opportunities to subordinate groups when competition for strategic interests ensues. Conflicts over scarce resources, such as arable land, potable water, or access to political or economic power, are often framed within ethnocentric terms as competition increases and hostilities escalate.

ETHNIC CLEANSING

Two of the most infamous ethnic conflicts of the 20th century took place in Rwanda in 1994 and Bosnia-Herzegovina between 1992 and 1995. In the Bosnian conflict, political leaders exploited religious, cultural, and linguistic differences to rally in-group support among Orthodox Christian Serbs and to divide them against Catholic Christian Croats and Serbo-Croat-speaking Muslims. In January 1992, Bosnian Muslims and Croats voted to seek recognition of the country's independence by the European Community (EC). At the request of the EC, a second vote confirmed that Muslims and Croats overwhelmingly favored independence. The Serbian population boycotted the referendum, and clashes over independence led to ethnic violence in several Bosnian cities. In April, the EC recognized Bosnia-Herzegovina's independence, and in May, the country became a member of the United Nations, which only increased ethnic conflicts among the Serbs, Croats, and Muslims.

Over the next months, ethnic violence escalated as Bosnian Serb forces declared almost two-thirds of the country an independent Bosnian state, and Croats declared an independent Croatian state in territory they held. Under the leadership of former Yugoslav president Slobodan Milosevic, genocidal atrocities were most often committed by Bosnian Serbs against Muslims and Croats, such as the Srebrenica massacre uncovered by journalist David Rohde in 1995. In addition to genocide, Serbian paramilitary and military forces instigated a policy of systematic rape of women held in rape/death camps as another means of promoting the ethnic cleansing of Muslims and Croats from Serb-held territory. It is estimated that this ethnic conflict left between 150,000 and 250,000 dead and resulted in more than 250,000 rape victims—many of whom had forced pregnancies.

In contrast to the military-led Bosnia-Herzegovina conflict, ethnic cleansing in Rwanda was primarily perpetrated by civilian Hutu against their Tutsi neighbors. Also in contrast to the Bosnian conflict, Tutsi and Hutu were largely integrated in terms of religion, culture, and language, and had lived and interacted socially for centuries. Although the Tutsi were a minority population, their tradition of cattle herding had given them economic and political domination over the Hutu, who practiced traditional farming. The Tutsi had also received privileged treatment by Belgian colonialists for more than a century, until Hutu revolutionaries took over political leadership in the early 1960s.

In 1990, the Tutsi-led Rwandan Patriotic Front (RPF) invaded Rwanda and a three-year civil war ensued. The 1993 Arusha Peace Accords created an uneasy cease-fire, as Hutu felt their newly acquired political power would be reduced. In 1994, Rwanda experienced an increase in mass killing and political assassinations as Hutu extremists began to issue anti-Tutsi propaganda in the media, drew up death lists, and imported tens of thousands of machetes. That same year, Rwandan president Juvénal Habyarimana was killed when his plane was shot down near the capital of Kigali. Immediately after the president's assassination, the Rwandan Armed Forces (FAR), Presidential Guard, and *Interahamwe* (Hutu youth militia) began a premeditated program of genocide targeting the Tutsi population and moderate Hutu political leaders. Fearing a replay of their failed Somali mission, the United Nations Security Council ordered all peacekeeping and diplomatic personnel to evacuate Rwanda. This power vacuum allowed Hutu extremists to step up the systematic extermination of civilian Tutsi and moderate Hutu, which resulted in the genocide of an estimated 800,000 Rwandans in just over 3 months.

ETHNIC MARKERS

How is ethnocentrism socially reproduced? In the case of the Rwandan massacres, media propaganda was instrumental in increasing ethnic tension between the Tutsi and Hutu. The social construction of in-group identification is also commonly reinforced through community rituals, holidays, education, religion, language, dress, and behavioral rewards and sanctions. These ethnic markers are often exaggerated to increase social cohesion and identification among group members. Within multicultural societies, in contrast, the dominant culture may seek the forced assimilation of an ethnic minority population by inhibiting (or even criminalizing) the use of traditional ethnic markers. In the United States, Canada, and Australia, for example, indigenous children were forcibly removed from their families to attend boarding schools where the use of native languages was punished. Among White colonialist powers, such governmental actions were justified on the grounds that "civilizing the savage" was a social good that preempted parental rights.

Associated with ethnocentrism is the assumption that the modes of living, norms, values, and behaviors of some members of a society are common to the experience of all members of a society. For example, within the United States there has been a historical tendency to identify the nuclear family system, in which a married, heterosexual couple lived with their children in a single dwelling, as normative. Within a normal nuclear family, the male head of household was the sole wage earner. The cultural bias for the male-headed nuclear family, which cast other family systems as deviant, predominated in the social sciences until relatively recently. However, in much of the non-Western world, there is a diversity of family systems.

Within the extended family system common in Asia, three or more generations of relatives live communally in a single building or compound, and members include grandparents, parents, uncles, aunts, and children. A female-headed family system occurring throughout the Caribbean is made up of a multigenerational, single-parent family, in which the grandmother or a senior female is the designated matriarch. In contrast, the practice of having more than one wife (polygamy) remains a normative way to display male status among many traditional Islamic and African societies. Within contemporary American society, the a priori assumption that the heterosexual nuclear family is the universal standard has become increasingly challenged by political activists and social scientists, even as structural social changes have increased the acceptability of nontraditional family systems, such as blended families and same-sex families.

CULTURAL RELATIVISM

Such examples of social change and cultural diversity demonstrate the need for cultural relativism, the concept that different groups are best understood within the social context of their own cultural expectations. A key factor associated with ethnocentrism is an inability among members of in-groups to acknowledge that cultural differences are not intrinsic markers of the social inferiority of others. However, extending cultural relativism beyond the social context into the political arena should be done with caution. For example, if cultural relativism is taken to a political extreme, Germans who facilitated Jewish persecution were acting according to social expectations, given that such abuse became an institutionalized norm in Nazi Germany.

CONCLUSION

In the modern world, postcolonial restructuring and globalization have facilitated the expansion of multicultural societies, even as indigenous activism has helped many native communities regain portions of ancestral lands and restore some cultural practices. Recognition of the intrinsic value of ethnic identity, language, and culture has increased the acceptance of cultural relativism at many levels. Yet there are bound to be points of friction when one cultural system is superimposed on or transplanted into another. For example, a contemporary debate on cultural relativism has immigrant African traditionalists at odds with the

French judicial system over the practice of female genital cutting (FGC), which was criminalized in France in 1984. Proponents frame FGC as an important religious tradition and claim that the ban is a form of cultural imperialism, whereas opponents frame FGC as a painful and abhorrent practice that violates international standards of human rights. Ethnocentrism and cultural relativism, which have probably existed since our human ancestors first differentiated between "us" and "them," will continue to have important roles within the global community. The understanding of difference and the acceptance of diversity at the individual and group level can help strangers to become friends within the ever-increasing global village of the world community.

—*Kathleen Ragsdale*

See also Ethnicity; Ethnocentric Monoculturalism

FURTHER READING

Adorno, T. W., Frenkel-Brunswik, E., Levinson, D. J., & Sanford, R. N. (1950). *The authoritarian personality.* New York: Harper.

Barker, G. (2004, April 1). Ghosts of Rwanda. *Frontline.* Retrieved November 5, 2004, from http://www.pbs.org/wgbh/pages/frontline/shows/ghosts/

Rohde, D. (1995, August 18). Evidence indicates Bosnia massacre. *Christian Science Monitor.* Retrieved November 5, 2004, from http://www.csmonitor.com/atcsmonitor/specials/bosnia/p-bosniaindex.html

Sumner, W. G. (1906). *Folkways: A study of the sociological importance of usages, manners, customs, mores, and morals.* Boston: Ginn.

EUGENICS

Eugenics, from Greek roots *eu-* (meaning "good") and *gen-* ("birth" or "family"), is often translated as "well-born." Eugenics is the application of genetic studies to the improvement of the human species—genetic manipulation to produce so-called better human beings. Applied eugenics, widely popular in the United States and northern Europe in the early 20th century, sought to control the heredity of individuals or groups carrying supposedly desirable and undesirable genes by evaluating their phenotypes, or expressed physical/ behavioral traits. Selective breeding methods included positive eugenics, such as providing marriage incentives and parenting rewards, and negative eugenics, such as mandatory sterilization, segregation, and genocide. Although the eugenics movement began as a progressive effort to eradicate social ills of feeble-mindedness, poverty, drunkenness, prostitution, criminality, epilepsy, and insanity in the mid- to late 19th century, desirable and undesirable quickly equated to superior and inferior and, in the racialized atmosphere of Western culture, attached to the concept of race. Eugenicists, concerned with racial purity, usually White (Nordic) or Aryan purity, believed that degeneracy, atavism (evolutionary regression), or mongrelization would result from procreation between undesirables or across racial lines. Eugenic ideologies contributed to anti-immigration, antimiscegenation (mixed marriage), and mandatory sterilization laws. Many then-prominent psychologists embraced eugenics and applied psychometric methods to help achieve "a more perfect human society." However, American eugenic social policies declined in popularity after the fall of Germany's Nazi regime, which exposed the Third Reich's "final solution" (eradication of Jewish people to maintain Aryan purity). Nevertheless, some eugenics practices continue in medicine and social policy today.

CONCEPTUAL BASIS OF EUGENICS

Genetics is the study of the structure and function of genes. Genes are sections of helically structured deoxyribonucleic acid (DNA), which makes up chromosomes. From within cellular nuclei, genes provide instructions for producing proteins essential to physiological growth and functioning. Genes are also thought of as units of inheritance, because specific forms (alleles) of genes inherited from one's parents in part determine one's expressed traits (phenotype). Thus, if one parent has brown eyes and passes that trait (allele) to its offspring, the probability of brown eyes in the offspring increases. Population alleles fluctuate as a function of natural selection and other processes; members of a species possessing features that enable environmental adaptation are most likely to survive, procreate, and increase the frequency of their alleles in subsequent generations.

For thousands of years, humans applied fundamentals of trait inheritance to animal husbandry, without understanding its precise mechanisms. The mid- to late-19th-century confluence of Darwin's evolutionary theories, rediscovery of Mendel's postulate of single-trait factors, and industrial-era interest in social reform

gave rise to eugenics. The amalgamation of these ideas into social Darwinism fueled early-20th-century eugenics movements in England and America. Social Darwinism argued that the fittest exemplars of humanity would—and should—survive ("survival of the fittest"): human endeavor could improve on natural selection and assist the evolutionary process. The tendency to attribute human failings to internal, not external causes (blaming the victim) contributed to the focus on eugenics over euthenics, or environmental engineering. Euthenics proposes environmental change as a method of social progress (i.e., welfare programs).

In addition to supporting social premises of eugenics, many psychologists used psychometric methods in eugenic research, including now discredited anthropometric measures comparing racial phenotypes and intelligence tests to distinguish fit from unfit. Unlike theories of natural selection and genetics, however, the premises of social Darwinism are now widely repudiated, and many of its methods—such as scientific racism (empiricism in support of theories of racial hierarchy)—are considered pseudoscience.

HISTORY OF EUGENICS

In *The Republic,* Plato described selective breeding of the ruling caste of a utopian state, a passage often cited as the first endorsement of eugenics. However, the term *eugenics* was not coined until 1869, when Sir Francis Galton published "Hereditary Genius," a study of traits in eminent families. An early statistician, Galton is generally credited as originator of the modern eugenics movement. After adopting his cousin Charles Darwin's evolutionary theories, Galton used basic correlation to examine inherited abilities and postulated the hereditary determination of traits. He proposed that human evolution could be accelerated by arranged marriages to produce gifted children. Galton wrote extensively on racial concepts, particularly "distinct racial character." Although Galton generally propounded positive eugenics, critics have noted that his advocacy provided a rationale for "race hygiene" (maintaining racial purity by eliminating undesirables), the ideology of genocide. Galton also initiated the anthropometric intelligence testing movement, superseded in the early 1900s by Alfred Binet and Theodor Simon's test to improve the French educational system (they were not eugenicists). This test, later known as an intelligence test, was exported to Stanford University, where it was revised in 1916 as the Stanford-Binet test by psychologist Lewis M. Terman, a eugenics proponent. Intelligence quotient (IQ) testing was widely adopted as a dependent measure in tests of mental ability to distinguish the fit from the unfit (although data collection methodologies were often suspect, as in the case of Sir Cyril Burt, a 20th-century British researcher who fabricated IQ data).

Other leading scientists of the American eugenics movement included Harvard-trained Charles B. Davenport, founder of the Eugenics Record Office in 1910; William McDougall, student of William James and 1920s chair of Harvard's Psychology Department; Raymond B. Cattell, a developer of factor analysis and personality trait theory; and Henry H. Goddard, who famously administered intelligence tests to immigrants at Ellis Island. Many prominent members of society joined the American Eugenics Society, formed in 1921. The society popularized eugenics through exhibitions at state fairs and other venues. Miscegenation (intermixing with Blacks and eastern/southern Europeans) was by now a major concern, and eugenicists' political agitation resulted in the Immigration Restriction Act of 1924. Sterilization laws represented another political initiative, the first a 1907 Indiana law requiring mandatory sterilization of the institutionalized mentally ill. By 1930, 24 states had adopted sterilization laws; in 1927, the Supreme Court upheld forced sterilization in *Buck v. Bell,* in which a "feeble-minded" European American woman, Carry Buck, failed to prevent her state-coerced sterilization. These political successes were noted internationally, and sterilization laws were passed in several northern European countries. Germany's Third Reich admired these initiatives and incorporated American eugenics thought in its race hygiene policies, which led to the Holocaust, a program of Jewish extermination resulting in the deaths of more than six million Jewish people as well as Catholics, homosexuals, the disabled, people diagnosed with mental illness, and others viewed as unfit by Nazi standards.

EUGENICS TODAY

Following World War II, Western scientists and leaders were faced with the atrocities of the Holocaust. Coupled with anti-Semitism and various social prejudices, eugenics' progressive goals had become ideological mechanisms of mass genocide. Many earlier eugenics sympathizers abandoned the field; the word *eugenics* was replaced with the word *genetics*. The

1960s saw the rise in psychology of cognitive behaviorism, which emphasized social/environmental explanations of behavior. However, basic premises of eugenics lingered on in medicine, aided by new birth control technologies, legalization of abortion, and development of tests to determine the probability that a fetus might develop a hereditary disorder.

The 1990s saw a resurgence of scientific interest in the genetic approach to disease control with the establishment of the National Human Genome Research Institute at the National Institutes of Health near Washington, D.C. The institute sought to map the full sequence of genes on chromosomes to enable researchers to establish which genes were implicated in diseases that ran in families. These included known autosomal-dominant (single gene) disorders such as Huntington's disease, as well as disorders for which no single gene has been found, including alcoholism, asthma, cancers, Parkinson's disease, and schizophrenia. Gene therapy, an approach in which a functional copy of a disease-producing gene is introduced into an organism, is one as-yet-experimental outcome. Currently, however, there is no way to repair disease-producing genes. Instead, the field of genetic counseling has seen rapid growth in the early 21st century. Genetic counselors assist prospective parents in determining their genetic risk by compiling family pedigrees and/or administering prenatal genetic testing. Parents can then choose whether to procreate or adopt or, in the case of an existing pregnancy, terminate the fetus.

This approach poses an ethical challenge to contemporary medicine and is widely debated by bioethicists, who often cite the historical and potential misuses of eugenics in their arguments. Another historical legacy of the earlier eugenics movement is the educational testing industry, whose roots can be traced to 20th-century intelligence tests. Some contemporary psychologists argue that although the tests have undergone revisions, they continue to serve the social function of promoting the "deserving" through allocation of greater social resources. Eugenics also contributed to present-day cultural mistrust of the field of medicine, particularly among minorities.

—Carlota Ocampo

See also Anti-Semitism; *Bell Curve, The;* Blaming the Victim; Intelligence Tests; Racism and Discrimination; Xenophobia

FURTHER READING

Gould, S. J. (1981). *The mismeasure of man.* New York: Norton.

Guthrie, R. V. (2003). *Even the rat was white: A historical view of psychology.* Boston: Allyn & Bacon.

University of Virginia Health System Center for Biomedical Ethics. (2004). *Eugenics bibliography.* Retrieved February 1, 2006, from http://www.healthsystem.virginia.edu/internet/bio-ethics/bibliographylombardo.cfm

EXTERNAL–INTERNAL CONTROL

J. B. Rotter's seminal work on external–internal control has stimulated much theoretical and empirical work in personality psychology, in general and multicultural psychology, in particular. Rotter described external-internal control as a general personality trait of attribution tendency. Persons with an external locus of control tend to attribute causes of events and future conditions to external forces such as other people, society, luck, or fate. On the other hand, persons with an internal locus of control tend to take responsibility for life conditions and believe in their ability to shape their future. Rotter developed the Internal–External Locus of Control Scale, a 29-item measure that uses a forced-choice format with two options (internal or external control) for each item.

Multicultural psychologists find the concept of external–internal control particularly relevant for studying the experience of racial and ethnic minorities and other oppressed groups (e.g., women). They theorize that discrimination, oppression, a lack of power, and cultural beliefs may contribute to minority persons' endorsement of external locus of control. Such control attributions may also influence a person's perceptions, motivation, behavior, and adjustment. For example, Rotter suggested that internal locus of control is associated with higher motivation for achievement, whereas external locus of control is associated with perceptions of limited opportunity.

Researchers have investigated racial and ethnic differences in external–internal control, as well as within-group differences in locus of control and its correlates. Racial and ethnic minorities (i.e., African, Asian, Hispanic, and Native Americans) often exhibit more external locus of control than European Americans. Because internal locus of control is deemed more desirable in mainstream American culture than external control, racial and ethnic minorities may be stereotyped as lacking self-confidence, personal responsibility, and achievement motivation. However, Derald Wing Sue and David Sue cautioned viewing external control as universally undesirable, because of cultural differences in worldview as well as minorities' experience with discrimination. In some cultures, an external locus of control is part of a worldview about the relationship of people to nature. Racial oppression and lack of power and opportunity may also contribute to an external locus of control.

Sue and Sue further defined external–internal control as having two dimensions: locus of responsibility and locus of control. In this framework, locus of responsibility refers to whether individuals attribute life conditions and consequences to external forces (external responsibility) or themselves (internal responsibility). *Locus of control* refers to whether individuals believe that their fate is determined by others (external control) or that they can control their future and take actions to affect outcomes (internal control). In other words, locus of responsibility is about beliefs in "who caused it?" whereas locus of control is about "who can change it?" This multidimensional model results in four worldviews: (1) internal responsibility, internal control; (2) internal responsibility, external control; (3) external responsibility, internal control; and (4) external responsibility, external control. Readers are referred to Sue and Sue's discussion of the characteristics of these four worldviews for multicultural groups and counseling implications.

—*Y. Barry Chung*

FURTHER READING

Rotter, J. B. (1966). Generalized expectancies for internal versus external control of reinforcement. *Psychological Monographs: General and Applied, 80,* 1–26.

Sue, D. W., & Sue, D. (2003). *Counseling the culturally diverse: Theory and practice* (4th ed.). New York: Wiley.

FAMILISMO

Among Latinos, family plays a central role and is a source of pride, identity, and support. *Familismo* is the term within the Latino culture that describes this family structure and the importance of family relationships. *Familismo* represents the beliefs and attitudes that operate within the family system. Intertwined with *familismo* are the values of respect (*respeto*) and trust (*confianza*). Family provides reciprocity or mutual support and is viewed as one of the foundational structures of the culture. Parents are highly valued and respected. The needs and concerns of the family supersede the needs of any individual family member; conversely, family members are expected to support each other when there is a problem and to resolve the situation as a family unit. The responsibility of the family is to care for all of the members of the family.

The concept of family refers to more than just the nuclear family. The nuclear family is most commonly defined as a household consisting of a husband and wife and their children. *Familismo* refers to the nuclear family, but also incorporates the extended family, which includes grandparents, aunts, uncles, and cousins. Non-blood-related individuals, such as godparents (*padrinos*), are also viewed as being part of the family system. It is not uncommon within Latino families for members of the extended family to share a household with the nuclear family. Members of the extended family may be involved in child rearing, economic decisions, and social activities. Respect and trust are the underlying ideals that support family relationships and lead to closeness and interconnectedness.

Traditionally, Latino families are characterized by a patriarchal hierarchy. Father is the head of the household and has the responsibility of providing safety and security for the family. Mother is considered the primary caregiver for the children, and her responsibilities revolve around the children. Both parents are involved in making important decisions regarding the overall well-being of the family. Older family members, such as grandparents, are viewed as authority and are to be respected and obeyed. As Latino families immigrate to the United States and younger generations acculturate to the dominant culture, changes begin to occur to the family structure and traditional gender roles. For example, more and more Latinas are working outside the home and are contributing financially to the family. Even with these changes in gender roles, it is common to see extended family members assisting with household activities and caring for the children. In summary, *familismo,* or the family network, provides the support and structure to meet the needs of each family member.

—*Tica Lopez*

See also Hispanic Americans; Machismo; Marianismo

FURTHER READING

McGoldrick, M., Pearce, J. K., & Giordano, J. (1996). *Ethnicity and family theory* (2nd ed.). New York: Guilford Press.
Sue, D. W., & Sue, D. (2003). *Counseling the culturally different: Theory and practice* (4th ed.). New York: Wiley.

FAMILY THERAPY

Over more than a half century, as the family therapy field has evolved into a viable model within mental health care, family therapy has based its theory and functionality on assumptions divergent from models used for individual mental health treatment. The prevailing mental health treatment frameworks have been rooted in a Western tradition based on a belief in linear causality and particular theories of individual motivation. From this Western tradition come certain assumptions: problems are solvable if we can identify their cause; reality is considered to be external to us, to exist outside our minds; the meaning of reality comes from external experience and we are the recipients; the world operates according to law-like principles that will reveal some absolute truths about reality. In contrast, family therapy has developed from assumptions drawn from systems theory and has sometimes been characterized as an epistemological revolution. In family therapy, a clinician's attention is drawn away from the individual and individual problems and toward relationships and relational issues, a noncausal process of mutual influence in which both participants are equally involved. Family therapy embraces multiple truths and theoretical explanations for human motivation and behavior. The relational epistemologies that inform family therapy assessment and interventions are especially significant in the development of multicultural and intercultural counseling models of practice and research.

PHILOSOPHICAL PERSPECTIVES

Universalist Perspective

Family therapists are commonly trained from a universalist perspective, the primary approach promoted by family therapy theorists and clinicians in the 1960s and 1970s. The universalist approach emphasizes the commonalities of different ethnicities, races, social classes, religions, genders, and sexual orientations and may elevate only those themes that are prevalent in the existing social order and context. The broad view of a universalist perspective has the potential of glossing over the sociopolitical sources of a family's problems and simply constructing problem-solving strategies that are compatible with the goals of the dominant culture. From a universalist perspective, culture may become merely another variable to influence family therapy rather than a contextual framework that qualitatively affects its total processes and outcomes. Critiques of the universalist perspective of families claim that a family therapist can limit one's

knowledge of families by categorizing the family engaged in mental health treatment into broad general stereotypes, which can suppress an authentic human reality.

Culture-Specific Perspective

Culture-specific approaches to family therapy affirm both the client's cultural identity and human worth by emphasizing simultaneously the characteristics of the individual and unique aspects of cultural group membership. The goal of the culture-specific approach to family therapy is to decrease negative stereotyping by generating a more complex rather than simplistic understanding of the family and therapeutic interventions useful to the family. The importance of human differences and recognizing cultures is acknowledged by recognizing that mental health and illness, and therapeutic interventions, are defined by a specific community and society.

In a culture-specific perspective, interpretations of family behaviors are not based solely on values and prevailing norms of industrialized Western Europe and the United States. These norms frequently ignore the political and historical realities of nondominant cultures. Instead, from a culture-specific perspective, important human conditions such as power, historical self-consciousness, and transformation are crucial elements to acknowledge and challenge in family therapy. In addition, family therapists recognize that therapeutic interventions are often used as tools to control and exert power. For example, questions asked by a family therapist can be a deceptive guise to acquire information for constructing an ethnocentric interpretation. Determining who asks and answers them, directly or indirectly, requires one person to exert control and power over another. Similarly, a culture-specific approach emphasizes some of the inequalities that persist across genders and sexual orientations.

Critiques of culture-specific family therapy emphasize the consequences of narrowing the perspective of clients. One possible consequence is that the family therapist may fail to see idiosyncratic aspects of clients and consequently may view families only as members of a cultural group. Another possible consequence is that the family therapist may overlook the transferability from one cultural-ethnic-racial group to another of concepts such as oppression and loyalty.

Postmodern Perspectives

More recent family therapy approaches, taken from postmodern theory, envision interpretations of family behaviors as a common text, a mutual interpretation wherein both the family therapist and the family conceive family behavior as a negotiated meaning. In postmodern family therapies (1990–2005), the therapeutic focus is on the processes by which people come to describe, explain, or otherwise account for the world (including themselves). Postmodern family therapists are interested in the construction of meaning as a narrative metaphor and in multiple realities, diversity, and pluralism. Because knowledge is actively built up by interacting communities rather than passively encountered and observed by isolated individuals, a family therapist participates with families in a transformative, collaborative therapeutic conversation. Thus, in family therapy each member of the family can be a contributor to the therapy by offering new knowledge through elaborations and descriptions of events. Neither the family therapist nor any single family member has the final word in the framing of the family narrative or in its synthesis.

EFFECTIVE FAMILY THERAPY INTERVENTIONS WITH DISENFRANCHISED FAMILIES

With families who are marginal and disenfranchised by the dominant culture, such as families of color, immigrant families, and families of mixed origin, the most effective family therapy interventions are those in which therapeutic interventions occur in flexible treatment contexts, the helpers are diverse and come from a broad spectrum of life experiences, and definitions and meanings of *client* and *family* are expansive and variable. The most current family therapies that meet these criteria are *integrative family therapy, collaborative postmodern therapy,* and *ecosystemic approaches.*

Integrative family therapy is a philosophy of treatment based on what is best for the family. The effective use of this therapy increases the complexity of the approach without sacrificing coherence in the treatment of a family and thus is a synthesis, not a haphazard snatching of inconsistent elements, of different family therapy theories and techniques. Emotion-focused therapy, narrative solutions, and problem-centered brief therapy are examples of therapies that concentrate on particular aspects of family life and provide for families a clear direction for using their own strengths and skills.

Collaborative postmodern therapy focuses on the attitude or stance therapists have in relation to clients. In collaborative therapy, therapists and clients are coparticipants, and the participants, in conversation, speak and listen. The family therapist, through respect for and curiosity about the family, opens up a discourse or conversation in which everyone is encouraged to share his or her own narrative. Together, in collaboration, all the participants have an opportunity to examine and reexamine their own narratives and one another's narratives, and then to construct in the collaborative conversation a new narrative. Because reconstructed narratives are negotiations between families and therapists, these therapeutic negotiations reflect societal politics. Thus, disenfranchised families and family therapists, together, develop a vision for developing family strengths.

Ecological approaches emphasize the interaction of multiple factors, both within the family and in larger social systems, that form an interdependent, relational, and large ecosystem. The therapeutic ecosystem includes everyone who is involved meaningfully in conversations about family issues brought to the therapy. These conversations are inherently collaborative, for meaningful conversations are co-constructed conversations. An ecological approach is also the basis of family group conferencing, a new direction in community-centered child and family therapeutic practice. The foundation of family group conferencing attempts to merge two systems of power relations: communications and worldviews. For disenfranchised families, conferencing as a therapeutic approach requires planning for family care as teamwork. The team is made up of people, having complementary knowledge and skills, who come together to plan, provide, monitor services, and support the team members. The family is part of the team and is empowered by interactions with their environment.

—*MaryAnna Domokos-Cheng Ham*
—*Gonzalo Bacigalupe*

FURTHER READING

Anderson, H. (1997). *Conversation, language, and possibilities: A postmodern approach to therapy.* New York: Basic Books.

Boyd-Franklyn, N., & Bry, B. H. (1999). *Reaching out in family therapy: Home-based, school, and community interventions.* New York: Guilford.

Burford, G., & Hudson, J. (Eds.). (2000). *Family group conferencing: New directions in community-centered child and family practice.* New York: Aldine de Gruyter.

Falicov, C. J. (2000). *Latino families in therapy: A guide to multicultural practice.* New York: Guilford.

Freedman, J., & Combs, G. (1996). *Narrative therapy: The social construction of preferred realities.* New York: Norton.

Hong, G. K., & Ham, M. D. (2001). *Psychotherapy and counseling with Asian American clients: A practical guide.* Thousand Oaks, CA: Sage.

Madsen, W. C. (1999). *Collaborative therapy with multistressed families: From old problems to new futures.* New York: Guilford.

McGoldrick, M. (Ed.). (1998). *Re-visioning family therapy: Race, culture, and gender in clinical practice.* New York: Guilford.

Mikesell, R. H., & Lusterman, D. D. (Eds.). (1995). *Integrating family therapy: Handbook of family psychology and systems theory.* Washington, DC: American Psychological Association.

FILIAL PIETY

In *Classic of Filial Piety,* Confucius (551–479 BCE) prescribed proper behavior in family relationships, such as the behavior of filial sons toward their parents in daily life, during sickness, and in the afterlife through ancestor worship. The Chinese ideograph *xiao* is composed of two characters; *lao* ("old") is positioned on top of the character *zi* ("son"), indicating that the older generation should be supported by the younger one. The fundamental instructions for practicing filial piety are found in the *Chu Li* (summary of the rules of filial piety) from the *Li Chi* (Book of Rites). Family elders and parents have a duty to instruct and correct their children to achieve proper values, behavior, and attitudes. Sons were encouraged to be obedient, reverent, and compliant in response to requests made by family elders, to support their parents' physical needs, and to honor and act in a respectful manner with family elders.

A closer examination of filial piety must be undertaken in psychology, because it has been identified as an important explanatory variable for Asian cultures, noted to influence socialization patterns and family and intergenerational relationships. Although filial piety is an important Asian concept, psychology has just begun to measure it and use it as an explanatory variable. An important barrier to making progress is inconsistency in how filial piety beliefs and behavior are defined and measured. Theoretical models of morality that have been used to study filial moral reasoning have been criticized for their limited ability to explain cross-cultural and cross-gender differences in their cultural norms for moral behavior. Another approach examined parent–child dyads, motivational factors, attributes of the social relationships, and goals of the filial actions. The wide differences in the measurement of filial piety may partly account for some conflicting empirical literature.

Traditional filial piety attitudes have been linked to lower socioeconomic status and, to a lesser extent, to females, elders, minorities, non-Westernized peoples, and those with non-Christian beliefs. Filial piety may have been idealized based on the assumption that it produced only positive outcomes. Filial piety has been associated with both beneficent outcomes (e.g., care of elderly family members; positive family relationships and family solidarity; positive societal and community outcomes) and negative outcomes (e.g., orientation to the past; fatalism and superstition; authoritarianism, dogmatism, and conformism; adoption of a passive, uncritical, and uncreative orientation toward learning).

Another caveat is that filial beliefs may not highly correspond to enactment of traditional filial behaviors. Enactment of absolute obedience, continuation of the family line, and living together with one's parents appear to be changing. Ancestor worship and repaying one's indebtedness to parents' beliefs appear to be retained; however, the manner in which one repays indebtedness to parents has changed through time, acculturation, and Westernization. Instead of living with their parents and providing for all the needs of their parents, adult children may provide financial support or provide coordination of care during the frail years. Elders with traditional beliefs about filial piety may experience dissatisfaction in the expressions of filial piety exhibited by their acculturated adult children. Future research must examine the relationship between filial attitudes and values, their corresponding behavioral expressions of filial behaviors, and the beneficial and harmful effects of holding filial piety beliefs.

—*Barbara W. K. Yee*

See also Chinese Americans; Japanese Americans; Korean Americans

FURTHER READING

Ikels, C. (2004). *Filial piety: Practice and discourse in contemporary East Asia.* Stanford, CA: Stanford University Press.

Yeh, K. H. (2003). The beneficial and harmful effects of filial piety: An integrative analysis. In K. S. Yang, K. K. Hwang, P. B. Peterson, & I. Daibo (Eds.), *Progress in Asian social psychology: Conceptual and empirical contributions* (pp. 67–82). Westport, CT: Greenwood.

FILIPINO AMERICANS

Filipino Americans are individuals of Filipino ancestry/heritage who reside primarily in the United States. A Filipino American is often a citizen of the United States by either birth or naturalization. However, Filipino Americans also include immigrants, permanent residents, mixed-heritage Filipinos, students, tourists, businesspeople on visas, *tago ng tago* (undocumenteds), temporary workers, and transnationals who decide to reside in or move between the United States and the Philippine Islands.

INTRODUCTION

Filipino Americans are one of the fastest-growing Asian American ethnic groups immigrating to the United States. According to the 1990 census, there were 1.4 million Filipino Americans nationwide. By the 2000 census, there were more than 2.4 million people with Filipino ancestry living in the United States, making Filipino Americans the second-largest Asian American group after Chinese Americans. Filipino Americans are a unique ethnic group representing diverse strengths and assets, as well as issues and problems that are not always manifested or shared with other Asian American individuals and communities.

In terms of assets, Filipino Americans have a long history of contributing to and being part of the historical fabric of the United States. Even in the early days of immigration, wherever Filipino Americans resided, the immigrants contributed significantly to the economy and to religious, community, political, and labor organizations. They were loyal to the various American institutions where they worked, despite the economic exploitation and racism they experienced. In recent years, Filipino Americans have contributed to the fields of government and politics, engineering and discovery, the military, and journalism and communications. Filipino Americans have been elected and appointed to positions in government, including a state governor. Likewise, Filipino Americans have contributed to the areas of education, business, medicine, the arts and entertainment, and sports.

FILIPINO AMERICAN HISTORY: ORIGINS AND IMMIGRATION

History helps to underscore the heterogeneity and differences among Asian Americans/Pacific Islanders, the group to which Filipino Americans are commonly assigned. To fully understand the Filipino American experience, it is first necessary to gain an awareness of Philippine history.

The Philippines, named after King Philip II of Spain, is a nation consisting of approximately 7,100 islands divided into three major regions: Luzon, Visayas, and Mindanao. The archipelago is situated in the southeast region of Asia. Over the centuries, various ethnic, cultural, and religious groups influenced the development of the Philippines as a nation. These groups included Indonesians, Malaysians, Chinese, Muslims, and Spaniards, as well as people of the United States. Early archeological records and narratives pointed to the islands maintaining relations with neighboring countries. Before the Spanish presence in the Philippines, Filipinos had their own culture, customs, arts, literature, religious beliefs, government, and social structures. The indigenous Filipino culture was shaped by the island environment and was also influenced by its neighbors, the Malays and Indonesians, the Chinese, and the Asian Indians. For example, Tagalog, a language commonly spoken in the Philippines and by Filipino Americans, has been identified as sharing linguistic roots with Sanskrit. In the late 1300s, Islam was introduced to Mindanao, the southernmost island of the Philippines. With the Spanish arrival in 1521, Filipino Muslims resisted Spanish colonization and fought against Catholic-Spanish conversion, and they maintain their Islamic culture and traditions today. However, for more than three centuries the Philippines was under Spanish colonial rule and was profoundly influenced by the Roman Catholic Church, producing the only predominately Catholic country in Asia. Catholicism shaped the political landscape and social development of Filipinos.

Spanish-Catholic Church governmental and religious policies in the Philippines included forced labor, unjust taxation, and political suppression. Filipinos resisted the conquerors from the beginning. Early in the Spanish colonization, Magellan was killed by a Filipino native, Lapu-Lapu. As the Filipinos became increasingly oppressed under Spanish rule, a movement toward reformation was lead by José Rizal, who was eventually executed by the Spaniards. It was not until 1896 that a national Filipino revolution arose, led initially by Andres Bonifacio. The result was the establishment of the first Philippine Republic on June 12, 1898, headed by Emilio Aguinaldo. However, Spain was reluctant to give up control of the Philippines, and with additional conflicts with the United States, Spain became engaged in the Spanish-American War. The independence of the first Philippine Republic was short-lived. Instead of recognizing and supporting Philippine independence from Spain, the United States decided to claim the islands as a territory. In 1898, after the Spanish-American War, Spain ceded the Philippines to the United States for $20 million. What ensued was the bloody and violent Philippine-American War, known to Americans as the Philippine Insurrection. Hundreds of thousands of Filipinos died under brutal and inhumane conditions. The Filipinos were unable to sustain their fight for freedom against the military might of the United States.

For nearly half a century, from 1898 to 1946, the Philippines was a protectorate of the United States. One of the most significant contributions of the United States throughout the Philippines was the establishment of an English-based system of public education. In addition, the Americans helped shape governmental structure, elections, and public health programs, and instituted improved sewage and road systems. In 1934, the United States promised to give independence to the Philippines. However, the Japanese bombing of Pearl Harbor and subsequent Japanese invasion of the Philippines led to the U.S. involvement in World War II. The Philippine Islands were too strategically located for the United States to relinquish all control. Japan's initial successful invasion of the Philippines drove General MacArthur out of the country. Many Filipinos and Americans lost their lives during the war with Japan, especially in the infamous Bataan Death March. Filipinos in the Philippines and Filipinos living in the United States joined forces to fight against the Japanese until the end of the war in 1945. Subsequently, in 1946, the Philippines became an independent nation. In recent years, the Philippines has severed ties with the United States (i.e., closure of U.S. military bases) and maintained others that have influenced Filipino American history and immigration.

FILIPINO AMERICAN HISTORY

Most of the literature available on Filipino Americans is historical in nature. Documentation of Filipino settlements in America dates back to 1763, even prior to the American Revolution. Filipinos escaped and jumped from Spanish galleon ships that had traveled from the Philippines and established settlements in the bayous of what is now known as Louisiana. By and large, Filipino immigration patterns have been described as occurring in four waves.

The first wave of Filipino immigration points to historical evidence of Filipinos arriving in present-day California dating back to October 18, 1587. Filipinos were used as shipbuilders, militiamen, navigators, sailors, and slave laborers onboard the Spanish galleon trade ships. Spanish explorer Pedro Unamuno recorded that Filipinos were part of an expedition to map the area now known as Morro Bay in the central coast of California. This documentation was the basis for the Filipino American National Historical Society (FANHS) designating October as Filipino American History Month, celebrated on college campuses and in communities. This period was designated by FANHS as the first wave of Filipino immigration, consisting of *Manila men* and *Luzones Indios* from the Spanish galleon trade of the 1500s, and including seafaring exiles, working sojourners, and others who arrived as stowaways, until 1906.

The second wave of immigration occurred between 1906 and 1934. Filipinos were referred to as *nationals,* 'neither American citizens nor aliens,' because the Philippines was considered a territory of the United States. These Filipino immigrants, primarily men, proudly called themselves *pinoys.* They were allowed to travel to the United States to work as inexpensive agricultural and manual laborers, and to seek out the American dream. However, they were not allowed to vote, own property, start businesses, or marry European Americans. Included in this group were *Pensionados, Sakadas, Alaskeros,* and *Manongs* primarily from the Ilocos and Visayas regions. The Filipinos in America during these times suffered tremendous discrimination, especially during the Great Depression.

The third wave occurred from 1945 to 1964 and included Filipinos who were enlisted and fought in World War II and their war brides. During World War II, numerous Filipinos residing in the United States and in the Philippines joined forces with the United States to fight against the Japanese, after Japan attacked the Philippines subsequent to the bombing of Pearl Harbor. Following the war, Congress passed the War Brides Act in 1945, allowing Filipinos who enlisted in the U.S. armed forces to become United States residents and, for those who were married during their service in the Pacific, to bring their brides from the Philippine Islands. The War Brides Act also encouraged dependents of those who had enlisted to immigrate. Filipinos who served in the armed forces as scouts in the Philippines were also allowed to enter the United States with their wives and children. The arrival of many more women and families helped in the development of Filipino American communities.

The fourth wave, from 1965 to the present, coincided with the passage of the Immigration and Nationality Act of 1965, which resulted in profound demographic changes. The act of 1965 eliminated national origin quotas and instituted a series of preferences for immigrants to relieve occupational shortages and to achieve family reunification. The immigrants of the fourth wave included professionals, reunified family members, and military, especially enlisted navy men.

CULTURAL VALUES

It is important to understand Filipino cultural values, customs, and traits. Various values and customs have been transported from the Philippines. Filipino values and customs serve multiple functions in the lives of Filipino Americans by simultaneously preserving, reinterpreting, and reinventing the various cultural elements that contribute to the Filipino American experience.

Importance of Family

Many Filipino cultural values, traits, and customs emphasize loyalty to and dependence or interdependence within the family. For Filipinos, family remains central throughout life. Cohesiveness and closeness are emphasized. Harmony and loyalty are taught at an early age. Members of the family depend on one another for emotional, psychological, and financial support. The structure of the Filipino family is built on cultural values that reflect a system of cooperation and mutual support that members depend on for a sense of belonging. The needs and welfare of the family come before those of the individual. The concept of self for the Filipino is strongly identified with the individual's nuclear and extended family. Kinship relations are highly valued and are regarded as familial whether defined by blood, marriage, or fictive kinship.

Respect is especially valued in Filipino families and kinship relations. Elders, parents, and authority figures are particularly esteemed. Younger generations are expected to not disagree with their elders or to talk back to their parents. When talking to an elder, it is customary and often expected for the younger individual to interject terms such as *po* as a sign of respect (*po* is a polite term similar in effect to *sir* or *ma'am*). Respect is also demonstrated in the form of deference, obedience, and sacrifice within family relationships.

Traditional Cultural Values

Family relationships are maintained primarily through four values or customs characteristic of Filipino culture. These are *utang na loob* ("reciprocal obligation"), *hiya* ("shame"), *amor propio* ("self-respect"; "self-esteem"), and *pakikisama* ("ability to get along with others").

Within the Filipino family, an internalized debt of gratitude called *utang na loob* is owed to one's mother (*nanay*) and father (*tatay*). Children are eternally indebted to their parents for giving them life. This debt can never be repaid. *Utang na loob* is a form of social control that works most strongly within the family unit. Failure to meet this debt or reciprocal obligation within the family results in feelings of shame (*hiya*).

Hiya is also a form of social control, especially within the family. *Hiya* is directly related to the importance of respect. If disrespect is shown to parents or family elders by neglecting the appropriate behaviors (referred to as *walang na hiya,* meaning "don't you have any shame or respect"), social or familial sanctions from other relatives or community members could result. The family or group comes before the self. Because of the need for approval, acceptance, and belonging, an individual avoids unacceptable actions that may cause shame and, thus, result in loss of self-respect or self-esteem (*amor propio*).

Pakikisama is also related to avoiding shame and maintaining self-respect in the family, as this value references the ability to get along with others. It can involve the sacrifice of an individual's interests or desires for the sake of the family or group. *Pakikisama* assures the maintenance of cooperation, positive feelings, and smooth interpersonal relationships among family and community members.

Decolonization Perspective

It is argued that these Filipino values, especially the value of *pakikisama,* as well as the values of *utang na loob* and *hiya,* have been misinterpreted in Western-oriented social science literature. The supposed "values" of *pakikisama, utang na loob,* and *hiya* perpetuate an accommodative and servile image of the Filipino. It is important to advocate Filipinos reclaiming a more indigenous and decolonized perspective, especially with regard to values within the culture. The core value of *kapwa,* which refers to a shared identity, is a basic root of all Filipino values. Understanding this value incorporates a decolonized perspective. From a decolonized perspective, traditional Filipino values include (1) interaction with others on an equal basis; (2) sensitivity to and regard for others; (3) respect and concern; (4) helping one another out; (5) understanding one another's limitations; and (6) rapport with and acceptance of others. Decolonization promotes the cultural connection to one's *kapwa,* making it possible to identify with one's people and history despite personal, generational, educational, social, or economical differences or other forms of difference. Through conscious decolonization, the colonized can become agents of their own destiny, uplifting the Filipino American community.

FILIPINO AMERICAN IDENTITY AND ACCULTURATION

Filipino American identity is a topic that often surfaces in the Filipino American community. Filipino American ethnic identity is a product of historical and cultural backgrounds related to Filipino ancestry and heritage, as well as the consequence of the process of negotiating and constructing a life within the context of the United States. The significance of Filipino American identity is founded on and nurtured by individuals and families who experience a sense of belonging to the Filipino American group. This affiliation and sense of belonging are an expression of the traditional culture and values that are so essential in family and community life, and they help enhance Filipino Americans' self-concept and self-esteem.

The complex experience of Filipino Americans is encapsulated in Nadal's Pilipino American identity model. According to this model, individuals of Filipino heritage progress through a six-stage, recursive, nonlinear model in which growth and development of self-identity are connected to attitudes and

beliefs toward self, other Filipino Americans, other Asian Americans, other minority groups, and the European American/dominant group. Depending on the positive, neutral, and/or negative valence toward self and others, Filipino Americans progress and move through the stages of (1) ethnic awareness, (2) assimilation to the dominant culture, (3) awakening to sociopolitical consciousness, (4) panethnic Asian American consciousness, (5) ethnocentric consciousness, and (6) incorporation. Reaching the sixth stage, incorporation, is the high point of identity development and maturation and requires a transformative process wherein Filipino Americans attain an enduring self-acceptance, satisfaction, and pride in being Filipino, along with acceptance by and full involvement in the Filipino American community. Attitudes toward others of Asian American and minority background, and the dominant European American culture, are founded on an appreciation for and acceptance of individual differences within these groups and the conviction that social justice belongs to everyone. Accordingly, interactions and interpersonal relations genuinely reflect these principles.

In considering the Pilipino identity model within the family setting, Filipino American families are similar to families across the United States in their beliefs in providing for family members and in creating opportunities for the next generations. Regardless of being United States–born or Philippine-born, Filipino American family members carry with them the historical legacy of Spanish–United States colonization and control, experiences of discrimination and racism based on physical appearance (i.e., being brown), perceptions of being "foreigners," and the acculturation process. These experiences, together with variations in level of Pilipino identity among family members and the normative challenges of family life, often unfold into family conflict in which marital and parent–child relationships are challenged and strong Filipino values of family cohesion and nonconfrontation are compromised. Differences in acculturation–assimilation levels among Filipino youth, parents, and grandparents can lead to questions and disagreements regarding loyalty and betrayal of the essence of being Filipino/Filipino American. Although conflict in some families is welcome and reflects the vibrancy of family life, for many Filipino American families, conflict can be experienced as profoundly painful.

There is a diverse range in the acculturation level experienced by Filipino Americans, from recent

Filipino immigrants who are in the process of becoming accustomed to the American way of life, to third- or fourth-generation United States–born Filipino Americans who are community and professional leaders. Although economic and educational opportunities have afforded many Filipino Americans freedom to pursue upward mobility and family recognition, there are also Filipinos who experience challenges and setbacks in the pursuit of success and prosperity. As an example, Filipino youth strive for educational advancement as they enroll in college, yet they lag behind other Asian Americans in terms of the number of young adults who seek postsecondary education. Moreover, there is a high drop-out rate for those who attend colleges and universities. For young adults pursuing advanced degrees, appropriate post-degree jobs are not always obtainable, and when jobs are available, many Filipino Americans are overqualified and underpaid in their positions. As such, even with higher educational attainment, Filipino Americans tend to earn less than Anglo Americans.

HEALTH AND MENTAL HEALTH CONCERNS

Although Filipino Americans are the second-fastest-growing minority group in the United States, second only to Latino Americans, and the second-largest Asian American/Pacific Islander group, limited published psychological, social science, and medical research are available that illustrate Filipino American experiences and challenges in health and mental health. It is essential that researchers examine issues related to Filipino Americans to better understand the Filipino American experience and to help inform more appropriate educational, psychological, and social programs for Filipino Americans.

When grouped with Asian Americans, Filipino American health and mental health concerns are often diminished, resulting in misperceptions of optimal health of Filipino Americans and the perpetuation of the model minority myth. What follows is a brief overview of research on health and mental health conditions that can pose significant concerns for Filipino Americans.

MEDICAL ILLNESS

Among Asian Americans and Pacific Islanders, cancer is the leading cause of death. For Filipina women, breast cancer is the most frequently diagnosed cancer

and is the leading cause of death, and prostate cancer is the most frequently diagnosed cancer for men. Additional health concerns experienced by Filipino Americans at rates disproportionate to those of other Asian American and Pacific Islanders are tuberculosis (TB) and HIV/AIDS. Associated with diet and nutrition, obesity and diabetes also pose significant health problems for Filipino Americans. Although there is limited research investigating the prevalence of cardiovascular disease in Filipino Americans, it has been identified as one of the leading causes of death in Asian Americans. In addition, Filipino Americans have been found to have high blood pressure levels, comparable to those of African Americans and higher than any other Asian American/Pacific Islander group.

Diet and nutritional acculturation have been identified as playing a role in the development of some of these health problems. Traditionally, Filipino diet contains steamed white rice as a staple, accompanied by vegetables and meat often high in fat (seafood, pork, beef, and chicken). In addition, dipping sauces high in sodium are regularly offered during meals: soy sauce, fish sauce, and vinegar. This traditional diet, combined with the availability of a deep-fried and fast-food lifestyle that is high in fat and sodium content, poses a challenge for many Filipino American families, for whom affordability is less of a concern, as it once was in the Philippines, so that finances do not limit food consumption. Furthermore, many communitywide religious and festive celebrations center on the availability, abundance, and sharing of traditional foods to encourage and strengthen community relationships among Filipino Americans. In these settings, community members may have difficulty in limiting food portions in efforts to maintain relationships and to not offend family members or others. Consequently, implementing health-related intervention that is culturally appropriate must involve the contributions of the family and, on a larger scale, the community. Health providers and community interventionists must be mindful of providing recommendations that preserve the Filipino American's family and community dignity.

Mental Health

Depression has been found to be a considerable concern in Filipino American community samples, as rates are higher than in the general population. In one survey, nearly 50% of San Diego public high school Filipino female students seriously contemplated attempting suicide. Within this sample, approximately 25% had attempted suicide during the same time frame. Filipino American male youth are also reportedly having difficulty with depressive symptoms, suicidal ideation, and engaging in suicide attempts.

Clearly, depression, suicide, and emotional suffering are of serious concern within the Filipino American community. These depressive symptoms and the emotional suffering experienced necessitate an understanding from a traditional Filipino cultural framework. Recall that Filipino Americans significantly value a sense of belonging and self-worth/dignity in the context of the family, the Filipino American community, and various multicultural settings including at work and at school. When acceptance and self-dignity are compromised, through the actions of the individual or through treatment by others, rejection and a sense of failure are intensely experienced. The rejection overwhelms the individual, further stimulating feelings of disappointment, despair, and frustration, eventually leading to dangerous self-isolation that is in considerable opposition to the Filipino American worldview, which is community-based. Alarmingly, Filipino American adolescents and adults have been engaging in alcohol and substance use and abuse, as a means to fit in and/or to cope the problems they are experiencing.

Barriers to Mental Health Care

Barriers exist for Filipino Americans seeking mental health care. Because of the perceived potential negative impact on the family and community, and to a certain extent the need for protecting the family/community, Filipino American youth and adults often conceal the emotional pain and suffering (i.e., depression and/or domestic violence) they are experiencing until they become of enormous severity or are life-threatening. Likewise, there is pervasive concern of burdening family members even in these urgent situations. Consequently, Filipino Americans often delay seeking mental health services. Stigma and how mental illness is perceived by the local Filipino community members can also impede a person in need of care. Filipino Americans may first rely on a trusted family friend, and then priests and spiritual healers, to help them through challenging times. Similarly, Filipino Americans may also share their mental health concerns and ailments with trusted family physicians prior to seeking specific mental health services or specialists. As such, trusted friends and community members, spiritual leaders, and physicians must have an awareness of and/or training in how to manage these potentially high-risk situations while considering the influence on the family and community. They then can serve as critical connections for appropriate services for many Filipino Americans.

—*Judy Patacsil*
—*Gemma Dolorosa Skillman*

See also Acculturation; Asian/Pacific Islanders; Model Minority Myth; Racism and Discrimination

FURTHER READING

Enriquez, V. (1990). Indigenous personality theory. In V. Enriquez (Ed.), *Indigenous psychology: A book of readings.* Quezon City, Philippines: Pima Press.

Nadal, K. L. (2004). Pilipino American identity development model. *Journal of Multicultural Counseling and Development, 32,* 45–62.

President's Advisory Committee on Asian Americans and Pacific Islanders. (2003). *Asian Americans and Pacific Islanders addressing health disparities: Opportunities for building a healthier America.* Retrieved January 27, 2006, from http://www.apiahf.org

Root, M. P. P. (1997). *Filipino Americans: Transformation and identity.* Thousand Oaks, CA: Sage.

Tolentino, C. P. (2004). Filipino children and families. In R. Fong (Ed.), *Culturally competent practice with immigrant and refugee children and families* (pp. 60–80). New York: Guilford.

H

HEAD START

Head Start was launched in 1965 as a comprehensive child development program for low-income and disadvantaged children ages three to five. President Lyndon B. Johnson's War on Poverty and its desire to improve intellectual capacity and school performance of poor children provided the impetus for the creation of Head Start. It has been one of the government's most successful programs, serving millions of poor children and ensuring, according to a set of performance standards developed for Head Start, that every child enrolled has a medical home (immunizations, health care, and dental care), social and psychological services, parental involvement in the program, and an educational program designed to meet his or her individual needs. Class size and space are closely monitored, and meals provided to the children are monitored for their nutritional value.

Each community in the United States applies for grant monies from the Head Start Bureau, which is housed in the Administration on Children, Youth and Families (ACYF) in the U.S. Department of Health and Human Services (DHHS) in Washington, D.C. Grants are awarded by DHHS regional offices, except for the American Indian and Migrant programs, which are administered in Washington, D.C. Programs that receive funding must follow the Performance Standards Regulations developed for Head Start. Federal monitors review programs every three years to see whether programs are in compliance with the regulations. Poor programs that are out of compliance with many of the performance standards are shut down because research has shown that poor Head Start programs, like poor day care, can harm children.

Research has demonstrated that Head Start not only raises the self-esteem and motivation of children but also improves their health. In addition, fewer of the children in Head Start require special education, and more low-income parents receive an education and become involved in Head Start as volunteers or employees.

EARLY HEAD START

Recognizing that earlier intervention is needed for low-income families and their children, Early Head Start was begun in 1994 under President Bill Clinton. Early Head Start (EHS) is a comprehensive, two-generation program that provides intensive services that begin with the pregnant mother and work with the family and child during the critical first three years of life. The EHS programs look for improved outcomes in four domains:

- Child development: health, secure attachments, social competence, and cognitive and language development
- Family development: parenting, home environment, family functioning, family health and mental health, economic sufficiency, and parent involvement
- Staff development: professional development and relationships with parents and children
- Community development: enhanced child care quality, community collaboration, and integration of services to support families with young children

221

Early Head Start programs, like Head Start programs, are guided by the Revised Head Start Performance Standards, which were published in 1996 and became effective in January 1998. Early Head Start programs, like Head Start programs, are monitored to ensure compliance with the federal regulations.

THE IMPACT OF EARLY HEAD START

A seven-year study requested by the chief of the ACYF to assess the impact of EHS followed 3,000 EHS and control group families. Results demonstrated that EHS had a positive impact on outcomes for low-income families with infants and toddlers. Although EHS children scored below national norms on language screening tests (mean score of 100), they still scored higher than children in the control group. The social and emotional development of EHS children showed positive gains: They were not as aggressive as children in the control group, they engaged their parents more, and they were more attentive to games and educational objects. Parenting outcomes were also favorable: The parents read more to their children than control group parents, and they were less negative and more supportive in their behavior toward their children. The parents also participated more in job training activities or working toward their GED diploma than control parents.

Other positive results occurred in the areas of fathering and father–child interactions. Fathers were less likely to spank their children and participated more in program-related child development activities. Researchers found that programs that adhered to Head Start performance standards had better outcomes for their populations but that EHS had a positive impact across demographic groups. Parents who were at risk for depression because of the stresses of job insecurity and poverty were significantly less depressed when engaged in the EHS program than the control parents. Teenage parents attended school more often than control parents who were not enrolled in EHS.

RESEARCH

Head Start and EHS have done more to focus attention on the importance of early intervention and early childhood development than any other governmental program. Researchers from many disciplines have worked together to develop a blueprint to help communities overcome the negative influences of poverty and disadvantage for the nation's low-income children

and families. Studies have demonstrated that Head Start children score higher than comparable non–Head Start children in preschool achievement tests; that the early enhanced relationships among child, parent, and EHS/Head Start teacher play a critical role in teaching literacy skills; and that children have a greater desire to learn. The needs of minorities and low-income families have been better addressed because of Head Start's emphasis on these populations and because of the number of volunteers and community organizations who have become involved with Head Start. Programs for migrant families and their children and for children residing on American Indian reservations have fared well with EHS and Head Start.

—*Diane J. Willis*

See also Education; Poverty

FURTHER READING

U.S. Department of Health and Human Services, Administration on Children, Youth, and Families, Head Start Bureau. (2002). *Making a difference in the lives of infants and toddlers and their families: The impacts of Early Head Start: Vol. 1. Final technical report.* Retrieved February 1, 2006, from http://www.acf.hhs.gov/programs/opre/ehs/ehs_resrch/index.html

Zigler, E., & Muenchow, S. (1992). *Head Start: The inside story of America's most successful educational experiment.* New York: Basic Books.

HELP-SEEKING BEHAVIOR

People think about seeking help almost daily. Questions about the need for assistance with a problem or a task are often perplexing. To understand help-seeking behavior, we can take a look at the research. We can also learn how help seeking is shaped by who we are, our beliefs, our traditions, and our experiences. Over the decades, our understanding of help seeking has grown in scope and depth. Here, we will provide (1) a definition of help-seeking behavior, (2) an overview of why people seek help, (3) a discussion of help seeking among ethnic groups, (4) a summary of cultural factors that influence help seeking, and finally, (5) an analysis of the cultural effect of help seeking.

DEFINITIONS OF HELP SEEKING

Research on help-seeking behavior offers numerous perspectives. First, help seeking can be viewed as a buffer, an act that keeps us from feeling the full negative effect of some stressful life event. Help seeking may be viewed as formal or informal. The use of institutions or professionals such as physicians or teachers to provide help and support represents formal help seeking. This formal system prescribes the mode of treatment, categorizes the cause for needing help, and monitors progress. The formal system also can dictate how to help those seeking assistance.

Help may also be sought from those who are not a part of common help-seeking professions (the informal system). Those in the informal network may be family, friends, or indigenous persons and systems. This informal system also prescribes ways for addressing the problems or needs of the help seeker. The informal system, however, often conceptualizes the problem differently than the formal system. Often, it is more acceptable to seek help from the informal system than the formal one. People may look down on those who seek help from mental health professionals, for example, yet find visiting a grandparent, aunt, "big mama," or pastor or using a home remedy to be acceptable.

INFLUENCES ON HELP SEEKING

Why do some people seek help and others do not? Again, studies can help us to understand the answer. Gender, prior help seeking, social support, and levels of distress all contribute to help-seeking behavior. Furthermore, researchers have reported that comfort with self-disclosure or revealing personal issues also influences help seeking. Often, these factors are categorized as *approach* factors or *avoidance* factors. For example, an approach factor might be a high level of distress (which may make someone seek help or move toward getting help), whereas an avoidance factor might be having a non-Western cultural belief system (which may dictate it is not right to discuss problems outside the family).

The drive to seek help is also connected with whether one is forced to seek help or chooses to do so oneself. Through studies, we have learned that almost half of the people who enter a mental health facility choose to do so, whereas 10% report some use of force and 34% report persuasion by others. Studies on elders or senior citizens suggest they are often influenced by many people to seek help. Not surprisingly, children are influenced by parents to seek help, and partners are reported to heavily influence men seeking

help. Finally, culture has been studied to determine its impact on help seeking.

IMPACT OF CULTURE ON HELP SEEKING

Although it is difficult to measure whether people live by their cultural beliefs and traditions, it has been suggested that ethnic and racial minorities underutilize help-seeking agencies because of cultural perspectives and acculturation. For example, barriers such as a lack of diverse staff to provide help may keep some people from accessing mental health services. More recent research suggests that other factors influence help-seeking behavior—for example, positive relationships between Mexican cultural values and positive views of counselors, inaccessibility, lack of transportation, or language barriers may have more influence on the prevalence of help seeking. An additional variable that shapes help-seeking behavior is the way the problems precipitating help seeking are perceived. For example, European American parents tend to view their children's behavior as more problematic than Thai parents. Chinese parents' perceptions of the severity of their child's problem shapes how they respond to it.

Cultural values are believed to decrease formal help seeking and the use of mental health services. African Americans, Asian Americans, Hispanic Americans, and immigrants generally exhibit patterns of low help-seeking behavior and mental health service use. In these groups, cultural resources such as family, friends, and clergy (healers, spiritualists) are used more extensively. African American and Latino American college students are sometimes hindered by the stigma of seeking help, mistrust European American counselors, and hold cultural values that prohibit help seeking.

Although research suggests that Asian Americans have high mental health needs (debunking the "model minority" view), mental health services are significantly underutilized among this group. Again, cultural perspectives are believed to play a role. The emphasis on talking about problems is perceived to be incompatible with many traditional Asian cultural beliefs or values. Though some of these views about cultural perspectives that affect help seeking among Asians have been challenged by recent research, the impact of shame is believed to remain an influential factor in these cultures.

Among African Americans, underutilization of mental health services has been consistently noted. There are many reasons for these help-seeking differences. Study results suggest that African American ethnic identity and levels of alienation influence help-seeking attitudes: the more one believes in a "traditional" African American identity, the lower the value placed on help seeking. In one of the most comprehensive examinations of help-seeking behavior among African Americans, the interaction of race, age, social support, socioeconomic status, proximity, and religion were considered in terms of help seeking. This research suggests that levels of help seeking depend on these demographic variables. Religious practices were found to be a major factor in the lives of African American elderly and women, who use prayer as a way to cope.

Although the cultural view is more complex than ever, years of research seem to say that acculturation, culture, demographic variables, high stress levels, and satisfaction with support all contribute to formal and informal help-seeking behavior in multicultural populations.

SUMMARY

Research suggests that cultural factors play a major role in help seeking. Furthermore, help seeking is often perceived as a way to prevent mental health problems and influences future help-seeking behavior. Our understanding of how and why cultural groups chose to seek mental health or health services is critical to addressing the needs of cultural groups. In this rapidly changing world, where minority groups are fast becoming the majority and cross-cultural relationships are growing, our capacity and ability to understand cultural dynamics is important. To effectively and ethically meet the needs of clients, professionals must not only understand culture but also be sensitive to the way others approach the helping relationship. Research findings and everyday observations suggest that culture partly shapes help-seeking views.

—*G. Susan Mosley-Howard*

FURTHER READING

Broman, C. L. (1987). Race difference in professional help seeking. *American Journal of Community Psychology, 15*(4), 473–489.

Cohen, B., Guttman, D., & Lazar, A. (1998). The willingness to seek help: A cross-national comparison, cross-cultural research. *Journal of Comparative Science, 32,* 381–387.

Leong, F. Y. L., Wagner, N. S., & Tata, S. P. (1995). Social and ethnic evaluations in help-seeking attitudes. In J. G. Ponterotto, J. M. Casas, L. A. Suzuki, & C. M. Alexander (Eds.), *Handbook of multicultural counseling* (pp. 415–438). Thousand Oaks, CA: Sage.

Neighbors, H. W., & Jackson, J. S. (1996). *Mental health in Black America.* Thousand Oaks, CA: Sage.

Vogel, D. L., & Wester, S. R. (2003). To seek help or not to seek help: The risks of self-disclosure. *Journal of Counseling Psychology, 50*(3), 351–361.

HISPANIC AMERICANS

Hispanic Americans (also known as Latinos/Latinas) are individuals whose ancestors came from Latin American countries, such as Mexico, Puerto Rico, Cuba, the Dominican Republic, and other South and Central American countries, such as Colombia, Nicaragua, and Costa Rica. Hispanic Americans are one of the fastest growing ethnic minority groups in the United States. According to the 2000 U.S. Census, Hispanic Americans are now the largest ethnic minority group in the United States, representing a total of 35,305,818 Americans or 12.5% of the total population. Hispanic Americans represent a very heterogeneous group of people in terms of race, ethnicity, region, and socioeconomic status. As a group, however, Hispanic Americans tend to be younger than other Americans (median age is 26 years), and the majority are located in metropolitan areas. Although Hispanic Americans live throughout the United States, the majority are concentrated in a number of regions and states, including the Southwest (e.g., California, Arizona), Texas, Florida, Illinois, and the Northeast (e.g., New York, New Jersey). For a variety of reasons, Hispanic Americans tend to be overrepresented in the areas of poverty and unemployment and underrepresented in the areas of education and high income.

HISTORICAL CONSIDERATIONS

Hispanic Americans have lived in the region that is now the United States for more than 500 years. The ancestors of today's Hispanic Americans were present when Christopher Columbus arrived in the New World on the island of Hispaniola, which today comprises Haiti and the Dominican Republic. From the start, European settlers and indigenous people intermarried, giving birth to the *mestizo* culture that is found among most Hispanic American ethnic groups. The European conquest involved oppressive forces of enslavement, persecution, religious conversion, and the overall disempowerment of the indigenous people of the Americas by the conquistadores. Part of the process involved the extensive destruction and extinction of several indigenous groups, such as the Taino Indians of Puerto Rico and the Dominican Island and many native tribes and nations in what is today the southwest United States. The enslavement of people of African descent was also a part of this process and led to the intermingling of African cultures with European and indigenous groups; these groups became known as *criollos* and *mulattos.*

During the early 1800s, many Latin American countries fought for and won independence from their European colonizers, and the newly established countries created constitutional democracies. However, during this same period, the United States began to practice a policy of expansion known as Manifest Destiny, annexing portions of Florida, Texas, and the Southwest. At times, U.S. expansionist policies led to overt hostilities and warfare with the new Latin American democracies. As a result of these events, many Hispanic Americans were forcibly reclassified as "aliens" in their own land (such as Mexican Americans in 1848) or recolonized as noncitizens in U.S. territories (Puerto Ricans in 1898, although they were later made citizens in 1917). Migration and immigration continue to play a major role today among Hispanic Americans; many came to the United States for a variety of reasons, including political asylum, better jobs, and education. Although the majority of Hispanic Americans are U.S. residents, nearly one-half are immigrants.

DEFINITION OF TERMS: WHAT'S IN A NAME?

Because of the unique and complex histories of Hispanic Americans, this large population has often clashed internally over the proper term by which they wish to be referred. According to Lillian Comas-Diaz, Hispanics are still "in search of a name."

The term *Hispanic* was created by the U.S. Census Bureau so that people of Spanish origin could designate themselves as such in the 1970 Census. This term is based on the Spanish historical and cultural origins of Hispanics. The term is considered controversial, even offensive, today because it represents only a part of the ethnic and racial heritages that have influenced the history and culture of Hispanic Americans. Further, the term is viewed as excluding Hispanic Americans who are of indigenous or African descent.

Latino/a is currently the preferred term to refer to people of Latin American heritage. The term is seen as more inclusive of the racial and ethnic diversity that make up Hispanic Americans. The term *Latino/a* represents the least common denominator among all peoples of Latin America and recognizes the romance languages (Spanish, Portuguese, French) that are the native languages of most Latin Americans. Today, the term has come to represent the common languages, values, and history that Hispanic Americans share while living in the United States. Because much of the Spanish language uses masculine and feminine connotations, the combined terms Latino/a or Latina/o are used to represent both genders (e.g., the National Latina/o Psychological Association).

Spanish people is a term that is sometimes used in the United States to indiscriminately refer to anyone who speaks Spanish. The term is both imprecise and inappropriate because it represents a group that is much larger than Hispanic Americans and includes people from other Latin American countries, the Caribbean, and Spain.

Americano/a is a Spanish term that is generally used to represent those who are not of Latin American heritage. However, the term has been used recently to represent Latinos/as living in the United States. The term, like *Latino/a,* also conveys a sense of commonality because it is based on language and traditions that bind Hispanic Americans together.

PRIMARY ETHNIC GROUPS

Hispanic Americans are a very heterogeneous group, coming from several different countries, though primarily from Mexico, Puerto Rico, and Cuba. A smaller percentage come from other South and Central American countries, such as Colombia, Costa Rica, and Panama and from the Caribbean, including the Dominican Republic.

Mexican Americans

Mexican Americans, also known as *Chicanos/as,* are the largest ethnic group of Hispanic Americans, representing more than 20 million individuals and approximately 64% of all Hispanic Americans. The majority of Mexican Americans live in Texas, California, New Mexico, Arizona, and Colorado and trace their ancestry to an area that was originally Mexican territory in the southwest United States. As a result of the Treaty of Guadalupe-Hidalgo, which ended the Mexican War in 1848, Mexican Americans came to hold a unique status, being both early settlers *and* the largest group of new arrivals ever. That is, overnight, Mexican Americans were deemed to be aliens in a land they had owned and lived on for many centuries; property and *ranchos* that had been in their families for generations were turned over to the United States.

Further military strife between the United States and Mexico continued into the 20th century. As a result of the defeat of the Mexican people during this time, poverty, disrespect, and economic oppression set in. Mexicans and descendant Mexican Americans were forced to take low-wage and temporary jobs on farms and in factories. Immigration across the United States–Mexico border continues today, as it has for many generations, affected by cycles of economic downturn on either side and the need for inexpensive labor and driven by the large, continuous border that the two countries shared.

Mexican Americans have deep roots in the region of the United States that was once Mexican territory. Recently arrived Mexican immigrants often already have long historical ties to the Southwest. Journalist Juan Gonzales, for example, recounted the migratory circuit between Mexico's Baja California and U.S. California, which was used by the same extended family of miners and farmers for nearly two hundred years. Issues of acculturation and immigration are made more complex by this circuitous generational migratory history.

Puerto Ricans

Puerto Ricans are the second largest ethnic group of Hispanic Americans, numbering more than 3 million and representing 11% of the Latino/a population. Puerto Ricans have a much shorter history of contact with the United States, though they share a similar history of conquest, extinction, and enslavement with other Hispanic Americans. Puerto Rico was a Spanish colony for nearly 400 years until the Spanish-American War of 1898, when the island became a U.S. territory. The political status of Puerto Ricans is one of ambiguity and contradiction. For example, Puerto Ricans were made U.S. citizens in 1917 and are eligible to be drafted for military service. However, Puerto Ricans do not pay federal taxes, nor do they vote; thus, they have neither taxation nor representation in the U.S. government. Puerto Ricans come and go from the mainland United States and Puerto Rico, often in search of better-paying jobs. A major migration of Puerto Ricans occurred shortly after the end of World War II until 1960, during which time more than 1 million Puerto Ricans moved to the United States. Many settled in the northeast United States. Today, nearly as many Puerto Ricans live in the United States (3 million) as in Puerto Rico (4 million). As U.S. citizens, however, Puerto Ricans have suffered none of the economic and psychological effects of immigration that stem from being an undocumented worker. Nevertheless, Puerto Ricans have had a tense relationship with the United States, stemming in part from Puerto Rico's use as a current military testing site. Another area of tension today is the island's unclear political relationship with the United States government. Puerto Ricans remain split regarding whether to move toward statehood and independence or to remain a commonwealth.

Cubans

Cubans are the third largest group of Hispanic Americans (1.5 million or 5% of Hispanic Americans) and the most recently immigrated of the three largest ethnic groups. Cuba shares a similar history with Puerto Rico. It was briefly a territory of the United States after the 1898 Spanish-American War until 1902, when it became an independent country. Beginning with the Cuban Revolution in 1959, several waves of Cuban immigrants made their way to the shores of the United States, most commonly settling in Florida (primarily Miami and Tampa). The early waves of Cuban refugees were typically wealthy and well-educated, of European descent, and from the middle to upper socioeconomic classes. Beginning with the *Marielito* boatlift in 1980, however, poorer Cubans of mixed racial backgrounds began immigrating as well. The most recent wave of Cuban refugees, the *balseros* of the mid-1990s, were made up of Cubans who floated on makeshift rafts and rowboats in an attempt to enter the United States illegally. Unlike previous waves of Cuban immigrants, who were embraced by the U.S. political system as political refugees of an enemy communist government, the *balseros* were viewed with hostility and suspicion. With the Cold War over by 1994, the United States began to view Cuban immigrants with the same feelings of dread and fear as other immigrants.

Because of the wealth and education of the first waves of Cuban immigrants, this ethnic group had the resources to establish one of the first bilingual education programs in the country. The area known as Little

Havana in Miami, Florida, became a major cultural and economic center for Cubans, developing a loyal market that often hired workers and purchased goods from their own community. Today, an entire generation of Cuban Americans has been raised in the United States; their only experiences of Cuba are the lively stories told to them at family gatherings. Returning to Cuba is a politically and financially difficult process to manage, as well as an emotionally evocative experience. Many Cuban Americans still have family members living in Cuba whom they have not seen for years, even decades. Although there is still much pride in Cuban heritage among the newer generations, acculturation into Cuban or Hispanic American culture is usually mixed with Anglo or mainstream American culture. One result has been the evolution of the Spanish language to reflect a mix of English and Spanish idioms, often referred to as *Spanglish.*

Dominicans

Dominicans immigrated to the United States more recently; they come from the Dominican Republic in the Caribbean, which shares an island with Haiti. Dominicans are typically racially mixed, sharing both African and European roots represented in a variety of phenotypes. Between 1961 and 1985, almost 500,000 Dominicans legally immigrated to the United States and Puerto Rico. Most have settled in the Northeast, particularly in New York City; Dominicans now make up the second largest ethnic group of Hispanic Americans in the Northeast. Many Dominicans came to the United States to search for jobs and a better living, but they also migrated in response to political unrest in their country. Though most Dominicans are generally better educated and more adept at business, many have experienced racism and discrimination in the United States, including discrimination by other Hispanic Americans. Today, Dominicans are among the most politically active Hispanic Americans.

Central Americans

Central Americans come from Belize, Guatemala, El Salvador, Honduras, Nicaragua, Panama, and Costa Rica. Although Central Americans have been immigrating to the United States for some time, during the 1980s, the number of Central American immigrants increased as a result of devastating civil wars and economic crises in the region. In addition to having low skills and little formal education, many *Centroamericanos* have suffered the traumatic effects of having survived a war. Central Americans are greatly influenced by their indigenous roots as well as their African and European heritages. Today, settlements of Central Americans in major U.S. cities rival those of many Central American cities, and they have helped to redraw the Hispanic American mosaic beyond the three main groups that are typically discussed.

South Americans

South Americans come from Argentina, Bolivia, Brazil, Chile, Colombia, Ecuador, Paraguay, Peru, Uruguay, and Venezuela. Because of its greater distance from the United Status, a different relationship has evolved between the United States and the South American countries. Much of their relations have been driven by economics, military training and agreements, and other forces; no South American country has ever been colonized by the United States. Although extreme poverty exists in South America, many of the South Americans who immigrate to the United States tend to be wealthy and educated, seeking greater resources or entrepreneurial opportunities.

CULTURAL VALUES

Despite the heterogeneous nature of both their history and culture, Hispanic Americans share a number of cultural values. The most important value is *familismo,* the belief in maintaining close connections with family. Hispanic Americans display a willingness to sacrifice at the individual level in service to the family, and there is a shared sense of responsibility within Hispanic American families that is marked by specific role responsibilities for the mother, father, son, daughter, and *abuelo/abuela* (grandparents). Even Hispanic American families who have lived in the United States for several generations and become acculturated into U.S. society exhibit fairly strong values of familismo. Though the customs surrounding familismo may have changed (e.g., young people may date without the presence of an older relative), new customs have arisen that continue to express this core value (e.g., siblings may live together or close to each other while attending college away from home and family).

As a result of the increased availability of jobs and education to all members of the family, along with recurring migratory cycles, changes can be seen in the structure of Hispanic American families, which have traditionally been headed by the father. Examples of these newer family structures include (1) single-parent *familias,* who may face issues of poverty; (2) bicultural *familias* who cross generations; and (3) immigrant *familias,* who may need to deal with acculturative stress and trauma.

Hispanic Americans typically have strong extended family networks, and they are often in close contact with uncles and aunts (*tios/tias*), cousins, and non-blood relatives, such as godparents (*padrinos* or *compadres/comadres*). Godparents may serve as substitute parents at times, and they are expected to be a part of major family activities.

Personalismo refers to the value of positive social skills and relationships, which is considered an integral part of the familistic framework of Hispanic Americans. It is common to have close relationships with most Hispanic American family members, friends, and other relations that are marked by warmth, humor, and friendliness. Agencies that serve large Latino/a populations should be aware of this essential core value, making sure that personnel are well-trained to greet clients in a personal manner (use of a personal names, brief small talk).

Spirituality is another core value that is central to Hispanic Americans. Although most Latinos/as follow the Roman Catholic religion, it is important to understand that regardless of their religion, spiritual beliefs are likely to dominate the worldview of Hispanic Americans. An outgrowth of these strong religious beliefs is *fatalismo,* the belief that what is fated to happen will occur despite individuals' efforts, and events must simply be endured. Part of the practice of spirituality among Hispanic Americans is the adoration of certain religious figures (e.g., the Virgin of Guadalupe among Mexican Americans), the observance of special days of recognition throughout the year, the presence of altars or religious figurines in the home, and daily prayer. Indigenous religions such as *Santeria* continue to be practiced by many in both overt and covert ways; many of these religions use indigenous healers, such as *curanderos.* The values of *marianismo* and *machismo* refer to women's spiritual orientation and gender role to endure the hardships of life and to men's duty to take care of their family and carry on the family name, respectively.

ACCULTURATION

As a result of generational and cyclical patterns of immigration and migration, Hispanic Americans must deal with the clash of cultural worldviews that stems from interactions with one's own ethnic group, other Hispanic Americans, and mainstream U.S. society. Hispanic Americans differ from one another in their degree of *acculturation.* A number of acculturation models have been proposed, but most describe a process of interaction between individuals and various cultural groups, particularly one's own cultural group and the dominant society.

Acculturation depends on several components, including the degree of identification with one's culture of origin, the importance of contact with other cultures, and the balance between U.S. culture and one's culture of origin. Acculturation is a dynamic process that changes over time and place in terms of beliefs, values, and behaviors. Factors that contribute to acculturation include age at migration and education. Aspects that are typically measured to gauge one's acculturation into the dominant culture and retention of the culture of origin include language usage, customs, family style, cognitive style, coping style, emotional and interpersonal behaviors, and political awareness. Typically, acculturation is conceived as a continuum ranging from overall assimilation to the dominant culture, to retention of the original culture, to the adoption of both or multiple cultural worldviews (i.e., bicultural). Although most scholars conceptualize acculturation as an all-or-nothing process, others believe that it is possible to be differentially acculturated across several domains. Typically, multicultural psychologists emphasize bicultural orientation as the most adaptive and link it with psychological health factors.

According to psychologists Julie and David Smart, variables that uniquely affect acculturation for Hispanic Americans include (1) discrimination on the basis of race and ethnicity, (2) emphasis on social and family ties, (3) illegal immigration, (4) geographic proximity, and (5) the legacy of war within one's own country and with the United States. Many instruments are available to assess acculturation among Hispanic Americans (some with ethnic group specificity), such as the Acculturation Scale for Mexican Americans–II, by Israel Cuéllar and colleagues, and the Behavioral Acculturation Scale for Cubans, by Jose Szapocznik and associates. Other measures are more generic, such as the Abbreviated Multidimensional Acculturation Scale by Maria Cecilia Zea and colleagues.

Integral to the acculturation process is the experience of *acculturative stress,* which arises from the movement from one cultural context to another. According to Julie and David Smart, acculturative stress is often characterized by three aspects: (1) life-long duration, (2) pervasiveness, and (3) intensity. Individuals may experience acculturative stress in stages. A common portrait of acculturative stress among Hispanic immigrants may go something like this: Initially, there is relief and joy about being in a new country and having new hope. However, multiple stressors associated with language barriers, finding a job, and other important resources may lead to post-decision regret. Perhaps the most significant aspect of acculturative stress for Hispanic Americans is the loss of social support in the form of family, which can lead to pervasive feelings of anxiety and loss of control, affecting their ability to cope with challenges. Treatment can help Hispanic Americans focus on finding new resources such as employment, church, job-skills training, and language skills, as well as others who speak their native language. Rebuilding a sense of community and family is essential to mitigate the effects of acculturative stress.

HISPANICS AND EDUCATION

Hispanic Americans face a number of challenges with regard to education: Only 54% graduate high school, and only 8.5% graduate college or university. At 50%, Hispanic Americans have the highest high school drop-out rate of any racial or ethnic group in the United States (70% of these drop out by the 10th grade). A history of racism and segregation of Hispanic Americans has played out in the school system. Hispanic Americans, like other racial and ethnic minorities, have often been steered away from college-oriented programs.

Psychological concerns that are related to these harsh educational realities include the misuse of high-stakes testing by psychologists, including the incorporation of standardized assessment protocols that are unvalidated on Hispanic American populations (alternatively, Latino/a educators and psychologists have proposed using nonstandardized assessments to mitigate the misuse of assessment); school system tracking; and the continued use of college entrance exams by admissions personnel, despite evidence that these exams have poor predictive ability for Hispanic Americans and other people of color. Acculturative stress and culture shock are issues for many Hispanic American students, as are depression and anxiety.

Given their lack of educational resources and role models, Hispanic American students may lack the motivation to succeed in school; the development of positive and realistic academic expectations is a critical need for many. As a result of oppressive historical forces, many Hispanic Americans may lack the self-esteem necessary for school achievement; there is evidence demonstrating that positive self-esteem and Latino/a identity can be a source of pride and motivation to succeed in education.

The identity struggles that characterize adolescent youth are more complex for Hispanic Americans because they must learn to adjust and develop cultural competency for a number of settings and cultural groups. Sex role socialization and conflicts may further complicate identity development and acculturation. To create effective counseling and educational interventions, it is important to examine programs and schools that have been effective in helping Hispanic students, such as the active involvement of parents, teachers, and administrators.

IMPLICATIONS FOR CLINICAL PRACTICE

Assessment

Historically, psychology has played a negative role in misdiagnosing Hispanic Americans. Culturally appropriate behaviors, such as those exhibited in a familistic orientation, for example, have been misdiagnosed as enmeshment by those who are unfamiliar with Hispanic American cultural values. Clinicians who are not trained in cultural awareness may miss important culture-bound syndromes such as *ataques de nervios,* a type of anxiety and anger response found among Hispanic American women. A culture-centered clinical interview, as well as culturally oriented assessment techniques (see next section), have been developed to build trust with clients and to deal with potential resistance to therapy.

With respect to Hispanic American students, the following alternative-assessment approach has been suggested by educators Ann del Vecchio, Cyndee Gustke, and Judith Wilde:

- Define the purpose clearly.
- Gather information over time.
- Assess broad progress in multiple skills, such as conceptual understanding, problem solving, and reflective thinking.

- Focus on the process, not just drills.
- Integrate diversity, such as language and learning styles (e.g., cooperative, rather than individualistic or competitive).
- Foster active student and parent involvement.
- Create a climate of trust.
- Use anecdotal records and observations, classroom products, and checklists.

Therapy

Counseling and therapy with Hispanic Americans should incorporate historical, cultural, and language considerations. Effective strategies for use with Hispanic Americans have been identified by psychologists Azara Santiago-Rivera, Patricia Arredondo, and Maritza Gallardo-Cooper. In the early stages, incorporating *personalismo* and related values, such as *respeto* (respect), *dignidad* (dignity), *simpatia* (pleasantness), *confianza* (trust and familiarity), and *cariño* (endearing qualities) is essential to building a trusting working relationship. Other strategies that might be incorporated include telephoning clients prior to the first appointment; engaging in small talk (*platicar*) as a way to engage the client; educating clients about the counseling process and structure and issues of confidentiality; utilizing apologetic terms prior to asking direct questions (e.g., "Excuse me, but I need to ask some difficult questions"); and accommodating language preferences, such as the use of translators.

The middle to late stages of therapy and counseling may incorporate microskills that are common to most psychology training programs, as well as a number of culture-centered techniques, such as the innovative storytelling *cuento* approach developed by Robert Malgady and his colleagues. Language switching (from English to Spanish and back to English) should also be observed, particularly for emotional content.

Group- or family-oriented methods have been found to be highly effective, particularly in light of the collectivistic orientation of most Hispanic Americans' cultural frameworks. Jose Szapocznik and his colleagues in Miami, Florida, pioneered an innovative family intervention technique, the bicultural effectiveness training model, which sought to minimize generational tensions arising from acculturative stress by externalizing them to the environment. Lillian Comas-Diaz and her colleagues in Washington, D.C., developed the Latino transactional model based on cultural values and the unique interpersonal style used by many Hispanic Americans, such as indirect problem resolution. Such models contextualize interventions within a cultural framework that is congruent with most Hispanic Americans, and thus they have a greater likelihood of effectiveness.

Group therapy has been used effectively with Hispanic Americans, for both men and women. However, given the strong gender role socialization of Hispanic Americans, maintaining groups that are men only or women only will go further toward increasing trust and easing communication, increasing the overall effectiveness of the group strategy.

—*Marie L. Miville*

See also Acculturation; Cuban Americans; Culture-Bound Syndromes; Familismo; Indigenous Treatments and Healers; Language Proficiency; Machismo; Mexican Americans; Puerto Rican Americans; Religion

FURTHER READING

Comas-Diaz, L. (2001). Hispanics, Latinos or Americanos: The evolution of identity. *Cultural Diversity and Ethnic Minority Psychology, 7,* 115–120.

Garcia, E. E. (2001). *Hispanic education in the United States: Raices y alas.* Lanham, MD: Rowman & Littlefield.

Garcia, J. G., & Zea, M. C. (1997). *Psychological interventions and research with Latino populations.* Boston: Allyn & Bacon.

Gonzalez, J. (2000). *A history of Latinos in America: Harvest of empire.* New York: Viking Press.

Gonzalez, M. L., Huerta-Macias, A., & Tinajero, J. V. (1998). *Educating Latino students: A guide to successful practice.* Lancaster, PA: Technomic.

Padilla, A. M. (1995). *Hispanic psychology: Critical issues in theory and practice.* Thousand Oaks, CA: Sage.

Santiago-Rivera, A., Arredondo, P., & Gallardo-Cooper, M. (2002). *Counseling Latinos y la familia: A practical guide.* Thousand Oaks, CA: Sage.

Slavin, R. E., & Calderon, M. (2001). *Effective programs for Latino students.* Mahwah, NJ: Lawrence Erlbaum.

Smart, J. F., & Smart, D. W. (1995). Acculturative stress: The experience of Hispanic immigrants. *Counseling Psychologist, 23,* 25–42.

HISTORICAL TRAUMA (NATIVE AMERICANS)

Historical trauma response is an intergenerationally transmitted cluster of trauma symptoms experienced by members of an ethnic group or community whose history includes severe and cataclysmic trauma, such as genocide. Symptoms of historical trauma response may include depression, anxiety, anger, low self-esteem, emotional numbing, substance abuse, suicidal ideation or suicide, and other self-harming behaviors. Maria Yellow Horse Brave Heart, a seminal originator of the theory, has defined historical trauma as the cumulative and pervasive "emotional wounding" of survivors of mass group trauma, occurring over the course of their lives and across generations. The construct of historical trauma was first articulated (largely by psychoanalytic thinkers) during case studies of children of Holocaust survivors, who exhibited trauma symptoms even though they had not lived through the Holocaust themselves.

The historical trauma model appears to fit the experiences of Native Americans, who have undergone nearly 400 years of catastrophic trauma: warfare, massacres, ethnic cleansing, epidemic disease, forced relocation, forced acculturation, boarding school abuse, and other genocidal consequences of European colonization. During the mid-1990s, historical trauma emerged as an explanatory framework for the high rates of suicide, family violence, psychophysiological disease, substance abuse, and other psychiatric disorders among Native Americans. As these conditions proved resistant to traditional psychological treatment, Native American and community psychologists formed a grassroots movement to conceptualize, identify, and use the historical trauma model in strengthening the mental health of indigenous peoples of North America.

Historical grief is an ancillary of historical trauma and refers to an unresolved, dysfunctional grieving of historical losses that interferes with an individual's well-being. Historical grief has also been explored among Native peoples, as the traumas to which they have been subjected have incurred multiple, catastrophic losses: loss of land, loss of sovereignty, loss of language, loss of cultural identity, loss of religion and spirituality, loss of extended family and social structure, loss of traditional livelihood and ways of life, and loss of trust in European Americans, who represent the dominant culture.

DEFINITION AND MECHANISMS OF TRAUMA

Psychological or emotional trauma is traditionally defined as occurring in the aftermath of an experience of intense fear, physical or mental stress or distress, or threat to one's life or livelihood, such as military combat, physical or sexual assault, terrorism, natural disaster, or even witnessing violence. Posttraumatic stress disorder, which has been recognized in the psychological literature, is characterized by intense physiological arousal, panic, flashbacks, intrusive thoughts and dreams, "reliving the trauma," and other anxiety symptoms with onset at least 30 days following a traumatic event. Generally, the trauma response is construed as something that happens *after* the event that is sudden, unexpected, and of limited duration; furthermore, it is characterized as an individual-level phenomenon. This definition has proved too limited to capture the full range of historical trauma.

Proponents of historical trauma theory broaden the definition to include ongoing reactions to cumulative historical events that have occurred over generations and may still be occurring (not of limited duration) and whose symptoms are expressed not only in anxiety but also in depression, substance abuse, and other self-harming behaviors. Historical trauma, which may also occur at the group or collective level, has been called a "soul wound" because it strikes at the very core of selfhood and group identity.

Parent–child transmission has been proposed as an intergenerational mechanism of historical trauma. Children may develop secondary trauma on hearing their parents or grandparents talk about past violence or genocide. However, traumas are often hidden and not discussed to avoid emotional pain. Therefore, another possible mechanism of parent–child transmission is impaired parenting. The maladaptive behaviors of parents or grandparents who have experienced trauma directly may be passed on to children through dysfunctional child rearing or the consequent erosion of the family social structure.

For example, in the early to mid-20th century, many Native Americans were forcibly removed from their families and tribes and brought up in boarding schools (often run by the Christian church) in order to be acculturated to the ways of the dominant culture. In these boarding schools, they were forbidden to speak their own languages and practice their own religions; taught a curriculum of subservience; corporally punished; and often belittled, beaten, and sexually abused. Once released, many of these psychologically scarred individuals began to abuse alcohol and other substances, possibly as a form of self-medication, and repeated the cycle of violence in their adult relationships. Children of boarding-school-raised parents have expressed trauma in qualitative studies of their memories of childhood: Their parents had no parental role models or roots in cultural traditions of child rearing, and therefore they were unable to be effective parents, increasing their children's risk of trauma exposure and self-destructive behavior. However, historical trauma persists in generations whose proximal relatives were not personally exposed to boarding school or other past genocidal abuses; the precise mechanisms of persistence across generations have yet to be elucidated.

Mechanisms of historical trauma are intimately intertwined with the constructs of loss and unresolved grief. Historical trauma posits that the past is not past; rather, it intrudes on one's present life in multiple ways, not only as a direct, sociopolitical cause of poverty, discrimination, lack of education, lack of health care, and marginalization but also as an acute, emotionally lived sense of loss. Like the feeling of reliving the event reported by clients with posttraumatic stress disorder, survivors of historical trauma reexperience the losses, often on a daily basis. Native Americans have undergone immense loss—deprived of culturally relevant venues for mourning, grief resolution has been hindered. Historical trauma theorists appreciate the challenge of parceling out the immediate effects of lived trauma from cumulative historical trauma. However, several promising avenues of research are generating data on the unique nature of the trauma response in historically traumatized populations.

HISTORICAL TRAUMA THEORY, RESEARCH, AND TREATMENT

Maria Yellow Horse Brave Heart introduced historical trauma theory in the late 1980s; within 10 years, it formed the core of a grassroots mental health intervention movement in Native American communities. Brave Heart, a social worker and founder of the Takini Network (Native American therapists who incorporate historical trauma into their practices), and her colleagues advanced the theory through workshops, conferences, and research initiatives. Brave Heart has explored empirical questions of gender differences and substance abuse in the context of historical trauma response. Historical trauma response may also mediate impaired physical health and the development of psychophysiological disease (such as diabetes, which has reached epidemic proportions in indigenous communities). Treatments piloted by Brave Heart include the *historical trauma and unresolved grief*

intervention, a therapeutic group psychoeducational and grief-resolution technique. As with all trauma, validation of the clients' reality and permission to express associated emotions—rage, grief, guilt, hopelessness, anxiety—are necessary parts of the healing process. In addition, the use of traditional, culturally relevant Native healing approaches, such as healing ceremonies and traditional medicine, have shown promise when combined with therapeutic approaches.

Although historical trauma theory has been intuitively embraced among Native American mental health workers, its research base is in its infancy, highlighting the different approaches of indigenous and Western psychology. Western psychology traditionally requires quantitative empiricism prior to the widespread acceptance of a psychological construct. Accordingly, researchers have begun to develop historical trauma measurement scales: The Historical Loss Scale and the Historical Loss Associated Symptoms Scale are two instruments developed to assess the response in Native communities. Preliminary testing has suggested that historical trauma response is indeed prevalent among indigenous peoples, evidenced by the amount of time they spend thinking about losses of the past and the extent to which they associate symptoms and emotions with historical losses. Two major factors or symptom clusters have emerged from this research: a depression/anxiety dimension and an anger/avoidance dimension. Future research questions will likely address specific mechanisms of historical versus proximal trauma, prevalence across Native American communities, and the ways in which historical trauma mediates and moderates the complex social issues of contemporary life for First Nations peoples.

Historical trauma is relevant not only to Native Americans and survivors of the Holocaust but also to other populations who have experienced mass trauma. Recently, the construct has gained currency among descendants of Japanese American survivors of World War II internment camps, Latino indigenous survivors of slavery and colonization (who have some of the highest rates of suicide in the world, often tied to the loss of land), and African American descendants of slaves, in whom the response has been called *posttraumatic slavery syndrome.* The concept of historical trauma may have international relevance wherever survivors of genocide are found.

—Carlota Ocampo

See also Bureau of Indian Affairs; Drug Abuse Prevention in Ethnic Minority Youth; Indian Health Service; Indigenous Treatments and Healers; Native Americans; Posttraumatic Stress Disorder

FURTHER READING

Brave Heart, M. Y. H. (2003). The historical trauma response among Natives and its relationship with substance abuse: A Lakota illustration. *Journal of Psychoactive Drugs, 35,* 7–13.

Duran, E., & Duran, B. (1995). *Native American post-colonial psychology.* Albany: State University of New York Press.

Sue, S. (1999). Science, ethnicity, and bias: Where have we gone wrong? *American Psychologist, 54,* 1070–1077.

Whitbeck, L. B., Adams, G. W., Hoyt, D. R., & Chen, X. (2004). Conceptualizing and measuring historical trauma among American Indian people. *American Journal of Community Psychology, 33,* 119–130.

HIV/AIDS PREVENTION

GENERAL EPIDEMIOLOGY OF HIV

Increasing numbers of people are living with the human immunodeficiency virus (HIV), which causes acquired immunodeficiency syndrome (AIDS). Worldwide, between 35.9 million and 44.3 million people are living with the virus, and in 2004 alone, between 4.3 million and 6.4 million people became infected with HIV. In the United States, an estimated 349,000 adults and adolescents were living with HIV/AIDS at the end of 2003.

Not all ethnic and racial groups in the United States have been affected by the HIV/AIDS epidemic equally. African Americans and Latino/as have been disproportionately affected by HIV/AIDS in comparison with their proportional distribution in the general U.S. population. This disparity is especially pronounced for women. In 2003, African American and Latina women together represented about 25% of the female population, yet they accounted for 83% of reported AIDS diagnoses. Although it is not possible to fully explain these ethnic and racial disparities in HIV/AIDS rates, most experts believe they are related to social and economic phenomena (e.g., poverty, inadequate access to preventive health services, discrimination, and increased rates of social violence and incarceration).

HIV PREVENTION: WHAT WORKS

A number of HIV prevention efforts in the United States have generally been able to slow rates of infection, and the effectiveness of several different HIV prevention programs has been proved scientifically. Research on HIV prevention programs has shown that in order for programs to be most effective, they must be targeted to a specific population and address the specific cultural, social, linguistic, and developmental needs of that population. Thus, a one-size-fits-all approach cannot be used for HIV prevention with different ethnic and racial groups, and programs that have been developed for one ethnic or racial group need to be culturally modified and tailored before use with another group.

In addition to being culturally specific, the most effective HIV prevention efforts reach people in a variety of settings with a range of health-promoting messages. They are intensive and long term, address the sometimes hidden social barriers to effective prevention, and provide populations at risk with the information, support, and skills needed to change high-risk behavior. Effective HIV prevention strategies teach people the skills they need to negotiate difficult social situations, continually reinforce behavioral-change techniques to enhance long-term behavior change, and promote safer practices by ensuring access to condoms and sterile needles. Once people decide to reduce or eliminate their risk, they also need familial and community support for sustained healthy decision making.

HIV PREVENTION: MULTIPLE LEVELS OF INTERVENTION

Although the ultimate goal of any HIV prevention program is to significantly decrease the likelihood that people will become infected with HIV, approaches used to bring about this outcome may vary. There are generally four levels at which interventions may work to lower rates of HIV infection: (1) individual (changes in personal risk behaviors), (2) romantic couple and family (changes in risk behaviors based on the relationships people share), (3) community (changes in group risk behaviors within a specified community), and (4) policy and legal level (changes in structural factors, such as those related to poverty and discrimination). The majority of scientifically tested interventions for ethnic and racial minority populations have focused on the individual level. Several literature reviews and meta-analyses of well-controlled behavioral interventions aimed at decreasing the spread of HIV among diverse samples of ethnic and racial minority adolescents and adults have shown that such programs can reduce HIV-risk-associated behavior and theory-based determinants of such behavior. Despite the benefits of the programs that have been investigated in these reviews, several limitations have been noted (e.g., lack of sustained behavioral change).

An examination of the factors that have been hypothesized to increase rates of HIV infection among ethnic and racial minorities in the United States suggests a need to move beyond the individual-level approach in HIV prevention. The behaviors that lead to infection (i.e., sexual behavior and substance use) are complex and influenced by a range of social, cultural, economic, and political forces. Thus, there has been a shift from individual HIV risk focus to a greater awareness of the role of social and ecological factors in fueling the HIV pandemic among ethnic and racial minorities. With this shift has come a greater realization that factors such as social injustice, inequality, discrimination, prejudice, oppression, disempowerment, and exploitation promote the continued risk of infection among populations that are already vulnerable in other respects. If HIV prevention efforts are to be both effective and sustainable, researchers and interventionists must continue to use integrated and multidisciplinary approaches.

HIV PREVENTION: MEETING THE NEEDS OF ETHNIC AND RACIAL MINORITIES

To help curb the threat of HIV/AIDS with effective prevention interventions, it is imperative to recognize the unique realities and needs of ethnic and racial minorities. A multitude of cultural and environmental issues present barriers to HIV prevention for many communities of color. Cultural issues related to the avoidance of discussing sexual behavior, illness, and death present challenges to engaging in safer sex practices and garnering community and familial support for those who are HIV positive. Religious and moral themes also affect access to and the content of messages about sexual and reproductive health.

Furthermore, cultural conceptualizations of female and male gender roles affect sexual decision-making practices and communication about sexual partners' risk for HIV infection. In some cultures, double standards exist for females, who are expected to remain virgins until they marry (and then monogamous after marriage), whereas males are pressured to prove their manhood through multiple sexual encounters and sexual aggressiveness. These gender roles are further complicated by cultural issues such as acculturation, migration, and urbanization. For immigrant populations, adapting to the norms and values of mainstream communities in the United States influences their HIV risk by altering attitudes and views about sexual and drug-related behaviors, as well as the nature of their relationships with sexual partners in the United States or their country of origin. Sexual inequality in heterosexual relationships is also a significant issue, particularly between ethnic minority female adolescents and older men, relationships in which sexual coercion and exploitation present challenges to negotiating condom use.

Racial and ethnic minorities' experiences of racism, discrimination, oppression, and poverty in the United States present additional barriers to HIV prevention. For example, obstacles to obtaining financially viable and sustainable employment affect one's involvement in activities that increase the individual risk of HIV infection (e.g., substance use, commercial sex, homelessness, and incarceration). The denial of public benefits, such as Medicaid and Social Security disability, for many immigrants and undocumented individuals under current welfare and immigration laws further complicates the use of preventive health care. Ethnic minorities living in poverty and those who experience severe health problems (e.g., alcoholism, diabetes) face a daily struggle for survival that may take precedence over concerns about HIV infection, the impact of which may not be recognized for several years. This is exacerbated by the underreporting and lack of detailed HIV surveillance for some racial and ethnic groups, which may contribute to continued denial that HIV is a problem. High rates of disease for other groups, on the other hand, may influence perceptions of distrust of government programs and health institutions, which, in turn, influence the development and implementation of community-based prevention programs.

Although communities of color confront a myriad of challenges in preventing HIV, it is imperative to acknowledge the strengths of these communities and their influence on the promotion of sexual health and well-being. These strengths are instrumental in developing viable and effective HIV prevention interventions and in challenging the social inequalities faced by racial and ethnic minorities that affect HIV risk. Family, community, and spirituality are fundamental to many communities of color and present strong support systems that can protect against HIV risk (e.g., destigmatize HIV, drug use, and sexuality). Strong group and collective norms that promote health behaviors can enhance self-esteem, communication between parents and youth about safer sex behaviors, and sexual health knowledge. Community-based organizations in communities of color may also provide leadership skills and job training that, in turn, can influence the likelihood of engaging in healthy behaviors.

—Gary W. Harper
—Audrey K. Bangi

FURTHER READING

Beatty, L. A., Wheeler, D., & Gaiter, J. (2004). HIV prevention research for African Americans: Current and future directions. *Journal of Black Psychology, 30,* 40–58.

Díaz, R. M. (1998). *Latino gay men and HIV: Culture, sexuality, and risk behavior.* New York: Routledge.

Duran, B., & Walters, K. L. (2004). HIV/AIDS prevention in "Indian Country": Current practice, indigenist etiology models, and postcolonial approaches to change. *AIDS Education and Prevention, 16*(3), 187–201.

Harper, G., Contreras, R., Bangi, A., & Pedraza, A. (2003). Collaborative process evaluation: Enhancing community relevance and cultural appropriateness in HIV prevention. In Y. Suarez-Balcazar & G. W. Harper (Eds.), *Empowerment and participatory evaluation in community intervention: Multiple benefits* (pp. 53–71). Binghamton, NY: Haworth.

Parker, R. G. (1996). Empowerment, community mobilization and social change in the face of HIV/AIDS. *AIDS, 10,* S27–S31.

Yoshikawa, H., Wilson, P., Hsueh, J. A., Rosman, E. A., Chin, J., & Kim, J. H. (2003). What front-line CBO staff can tell us about culturally anchored theories of behavior change in HIV prevention for Asian/Pacific Islanders. *American Journal of Community Psychology, 32*(1/2), 143–158.

I

IMMIGRANTS

Between 1990 and 2000, the foreign-born population in the United States grew by more than half. In 1990, there were 19.8 million foreign-born individuals in the United States, composing 7.9% of the total population. By 2000, the number of foreign-born residents had risen to 31.1 million, representing 11.1% of the U.S. population—the highest proportion since 1930. The share of the U.S. foreign-born population began to wane in 1910, falling from 14.8% to 11.1% between 1910 and 1930. By 1970, the foreign-born as a percentage of the total U.S. population had reached a low of 4.7%. The proportion only began to climb again during the 1980s.

The volume and nature of immigration to the United States are the results of legislative and social forces that influence the political, economic, physical and mental health, and life chances of immigrants and their families. Multicultural approaches to immigrant health must encompass an understanding of the spectrum of sociopolitical and historical factors that affect immigrants in the United States. To that end, this entry presents an overview of key historical policies and trends concerning immigration, including those that promote or "pull" immigration of specific groups to the United States, as well as factors that "push" groups to leave their countries of origin. Controversial issues and psychosocial contexts are highlighted to illustrate frameworks for adopting a multicultural approach to immigrant health.

A NOTE ON TERMINOLOGY

The term *foreign born* refers to persons who were not U.S. citizens at their time of birth, regardless of naturalization or legal status, and includes all immigrants and legal nonimmigrants (e.g., refugees). The term *immigrant* refers to persons who left their country of origin to reside in another country or state and who have not become naturalized citizens of that new country. Once naturalized, the immigrant becomes a foreign-born citizen. Popular parlance, however, applies the term *immigrant* to all persons of immigrant origin regardless of naturalization status. For this reason, this entry will employ the terms immigrant and foreign born interchangeably to describe both naturalized citizens and noncitizen foreign-born persons.

HISTORICAL OVERVIEW OF IMMIGRATION POLICY IN THE UNITED STATES

Debates about immigration policy date back to the colonial era, when an influx of German and Scotch Irish immigrants arrived during the early 1700s. During this period, concerns about the integration of immigrants and economic shortfalls fueled anti-immigrant sentiment; however, these concerns dissipated during the American Revolution, when immigration promoted the success of the nation. For more than 200 years, U.S. immigration policy followed a cyclical pattern of pull, promoting immigration during periods of national political or economic need, then opposing immigration when the influx of newcomers had reached a critical mass. This trend was most visible with regard to immigrants from so-called undesirable racial or ethnic groups. For example, during the 1860s, Chinese immigrants were recruited to work on the Central Pacific Railroad Company's transcontinental railroad. A period of economic decline following the completion of the project led Congress to pass the Chinese Exclusion Act of 1882, which prevented immigration of Chinese laborers for 10 years. Two years later, the law was revised to exclude all Chinese and remained in force until 1943.

Similarly, increasing numbers of immigrants from eastern and southern Europe, many of whom were labeled "mentally incompetent" and otherwise "racially inferior" based on the claims of the eugenics movement, prompted the Quota Law of 1921. A few years later, the National Origins Act of 1924, which was directed mainly at the Japanese, prevented the immigration of individuals who could not qualify for citizenship. In addition, during this period of economic decline, the repatriation campaign of the Great Depression forced large numbers of Mexican immigrants to leave the country. About two decades later, however, a labor shortage created by World War II led to the Bracero Agreement, which encouraged approximately 4 million Mexicans to migrate to work as laborers for U.S. agriculture between 1942 and 1964.

The U.S. race- and ethnicity-based exclusionary quota system remained unchallenged even in 1952, when the Immigration and Nationality Act was passed, shifting the rationale for the quotas from racial superiority to cultural balance. During the Cold War period, this act denied entry to individuals who were members of or sympathetic to the Communist Party. As in the past, individuals with certain health conditions (e.g., mental deficiencies) were also denied entry. Immigration policy did not undergo a radical reformation until 1965, as part of the larger society-wide push for civil rights. By substituting the national-origin quota system with a preference system based on hemispheres, amendments to the Immigration and Nationality Act, ratified in 1965, removed many of the barriers for immigrants from Latin America, Asia, and Africa. For the first time, nation-specific limits were set on countries in the Western hemisphere, and modifications were made to health-exclusion factors. Immigrants were to be admitted based on their skills rather than their country of origin. Since 1965, a variety of legislative acts have allowed increased international migration. These include the Immigration Reform and Control Act of 1986, which allowed some illegal aliens to obtain lawful permanent residence, and the Immigration Act of 1990, which increased the annual immigration cap.

IMMIGRANT INFLOWS, TYPES OF IMMIGRANTS, AND PUSH FACTORS

As a result of these social, political, economic, and historical factors, the vast majority of immigrants who arrived during the early 20th century came from western European nations. However, the 2000 U.S. Census indicated that European immigrants now compose only 15% of the total foreign-born population. Two regions in particular, Latin America and Southeast Asia, are currently contributing the largest numbers of immigrants to the United States.

Estimating the flow of immigrants is problematic, for a number of reasons. These include the difficulty of coordinating surveillance at myriad ports and points of entry and the administrative difficulty of estimating the number of immigrants who enter the country without documentation. However, estimates of immigrant inflows demonstrate that between 1986 and 2002 alone, immigration increased almost 80%—from 601,708 in 1986 to 1,063,732 in 2002, with significant fluctuations within that span of nearly 20 years. The patterns and causes for this rise in immigration are many and center on both political and economic causes.

Today, immigrant status in the United States comprises five categories: (1) naturalized citizenship, (2) permanent migration (green card acquisition), (3) temporary migration (usually labor related), (4) tourism, and (5) undocumented migration (also called illegal migration). Under current U.S. law, permanent migrants are eligible to become U.S. citizens after five years of legal permanent residence (three years if they are married to a U.S. citizen). Refugees and successful asylum seekers, permanent residents who have served in the armed forces, and beneficiaries of the 1986 amnesty law experience shorter wait times for citizenship eligibility. Refugees and asylum seekers may seek refuge from war, genocide, gender-related persecution and repression, political persecution, and torture. To be granted asylum in the United States, asylum seekers (those already within the borders of the country) and refugees (in protected camps abroad) must prove that they have a "well-founded fear" that returning to their country of origin will result in continued persecution or death.

Some legal permanent residents enter the country as temporary migrants and subsequently apply for permanent residence, whereas others are sponsored by U.S. citizen relatives. Avenues for temporary migration include labor-recruitment efforts, which supply work visas to skilled foreign labor; education visas for academic study or technical training; and diversity lottery and international adoption.

Although it is illegal to do so, many additional immigrants enter the United States as tourists and overstay the agreed-upon expiration date of their visas. These immigrants can become citizens by securing labor-related sponsorships, marrying a U.S. citizen, or receiving amnesty from the government. In the absence of these conditions, these immigrants remain undocumented. In 2002, about 26% of the 34.5 million foreign-born immigrants in the United States were believed to be undocumented. Estimates placed the total stock of undocumented persons in the United States at 9.3 million in 2004.

A number of push factors play an integral role in understanding immigrant psychology and range from mild to severe threats. For many migrants, economic considerations, including high unemployment rates in their home country or lack of educational opportunities, may drive emigration, whereas for others, political conflict is the primary impetus. These sociopolitical or economic factors work in conjunction with individual characteristics and family dynamics to create a unique mental health picture for every immigrant.

WHO ARE TODAY'S IMMIGRANTS?

According to the 2000 U.S. Census, slightly more than half (51.7%) of the total foreign-born population is composed of immigrants from Latin American nations. Immigrants from Asia constitute the next largest group, representing 26.4% of the U.S. foreign-born population.

Latin American Immigrants: Mexicans and Cubans

Mexicans represent the highest proportion (54%) of foreign-born Latin Americans and account for 29.5% of the total U.S. foreign-born population. Cubans constitute the next largest group (7%) of foreign-born Latinos and represent 2.8% of the U.S. foreign-born population. Mexicans and Cubans are heterogeneous populations with varying sociodemographic profiles. Most notably, these groups differ in their political and economic histories, a fact that accounts for some of the between-group and within-group variation in socioeconomic status and other indicators of well-being that are

often noted. For example, Cubans arrived in the United States in successive waves, in contrast to Mexicans, who immigrated at a steadier pace, at higher rates, and for reasons (civil war, temporary labor agreements with the United States, and economic instability) that evoked U.S. sympathies and passions much less than anti-Communist sentiments did during the early 1960s.

The first large-scale wave of Cubans immigrated to the United States after Fidel Castro announced that he would institute a socialist economy following his overthrow of dictator Fulgencio Batista in 1959. The Cubans who migrated during this wave (1959–1965) tended to be of European heritage and belonged to the upper and middle classes—the primary objects of Castro's wealth-redistribution campaign. Although the U.S. Migration and Refugee Assistance Act of 1962 was passed specifically to aid the settlement of these early refugees, subsequent waves of working-class and ethnically diverse Cubans received a much less hearty welcome from U.S. authorities as concerns about the financial strain on Florida's economy (the primary settlement site for Cuban immigrants) began to surface.

Altogether, these sociopolitical and selection processes contributed to different sociodemographic and health profiles between the groups in the United States. Compared with Mexicans, for example, Cubans are skewed toward higher socioeconomic status and greater social and political capital in the United States, especially on issues concerning domestic and foreign policy matters.

Asian Immigrants

According to the 2000 U.S. Census, the majority (61.4%) of the 12.5 million Asian and Pacific Islander population in the United States is foreign born (only 39% of all Latinos in the United States are foreign born). The largest groups of foreign-born Asians are Chinese and Filipino, who make up 4.9% and 4.4% of the total U.S. foreign-born population, respectively. Representing an array of countries with unique political and economic histories, Asian immigrants fall into two main categories: those for whom generations-old infrastructures were established by earlier immigrant waves, including Chinese, Japanese, and, to a lesser extent, South Korean, Filipino, and Indian immigrants; and newer refugee populations from Southeast Asia, including Hmong, Vietnamese, Laotians, and Cambodians. Push factors for each of these groups differ dramatically, and their well-being in the United

States is determined largely by conditions in their home countries and by their reception by the United States.

The Asian American population is split in terms of indicators of well-being, including educational attainment and employment. According to the U.S. Census Bureau, Asians and Pacific Islanders are both more likely than non-Hispanic Whites to have earned at least a college degree and more likely to have less than a ninth-grade education. This split can be attributed to the reasons for migration. East Asian migrants, especially those from China and Japan, immigrated in pursuit of higher educational opportunities, whereas other populations, such as recent refugees from Southeast Asia, were pushed from their countries by the threat of political persecution. For example, many Hmong refugees fled their adopted Laos when the Laotian government threatened them with persecution for joining U.S. armed forces in the fight against communism during the Vietnam War. Between 1979 and 1990, more than 100,000 Hmong were relocated from refugee camps in Thailand and Laos to the United States, namely, to states in the Midwest and West. Unlike the Chinese and Japanese population, the Hmong had no established networks when they arrived in the United States in the late 1970s; therefore, they represented a high proportion of the poor, unemployed, or public assistance recipients in some states.

IMMIGRANTS: CURRENT POLICY AND LEGISLATIVE CONTROVERSIES

One of the most heated debates regarding immigration policy concerns undocumented workers. The primary legislation governing undocumented workers is the Immigration Reform and Control Act of 1986 (IRCA). On March 31, 2003, the U.S. Department of Homeland Security assumed responsibility for administering the act from the Immigration and Naturalization Service. The purpose of the IRCA is to curtail the influx of immigrants to the United States by limiting potential employment. Under the IRCA, for the first time, employers became subject to penalties for hiring illegal workers and were required to verify an employee's right to work in the United States. The breadth of penalties for an employer who willfully employs an undocumented worker ranges from civil fines to criminal penalties.

Recently, the provision of labor rights for undocumented workers has become a hot-button topic because of concerns ranging from national security to economic growth. The primary argument is whether undocumented workers should be entitled to the same protections that citizens are granted by U.S. labor laws. Some argue that immigration laws may restrict the economic interests of citizens, whereas others argue that excluding undocumented workers from the laws' protections undermines the very purpose of the legislation.

Although an in-depth discussion of the impact of immigration law is beyond the scope of this entry, the interplay of the statutes governing workers was a key issue in the U.S. Supreme Court's 2002 decision in *Hoffman Plastics Compounds, Inc. v. National Labor Relations Board.* In that case, the Court held that under the National Labor Relations Act, one of the primary remedies for an employee who has been the victim of illegal conduct by an employer—back pay—is not available to undocumented workers. Although many commentators assert that this decision creates a significant problem for undocumented workers, it appears that because it is so narrowly crafted, the actual impact cannot be evaluated at this time.

Other attempts to curtail the number of undocumented immigrants entering the United States involve increasing border patrols. The past decade has seen a dramatic increase in the amount of funds allocated by the federal government to monitor the United States–Mexico border. One of the consequences of enforced border patrols has been an increase in the fees demanded by coyotes, or smugglers, to assist immigrants across the border. In Ciudad Juárez, Mexico, there are an estimated 20 active coyotes networks available to smuggle immigrants into El Paso, Texas. The border crossings are dangerous, and over the past several years, border deaths have averaged approximately one per day. In 2000, for example, 311 undocumented individuals died attempting to cross the border. By 2001, the number had increased to 491. Despite efforts to strengthen border patrols, the number of undocumented immigrants has not diminished.

Another source of political debate concerns access to health care for immigrants. Although some advocates argue that health care is a fundamental human right, recent legislation has created significant barriers to access. As a result of the Personal Responsibility and Work Opportunity Act of 1996, qualified immigrants who entered the country after August 22, 1996, are no longer eligible for immediate access to federal means-tested programs (i.e., welfare, Medicaid, and food stamps). In some cases, the eligibility proscription ends after five years (e.g., for food stamps), and in other cases, state governments make the decision as to immigrant eligibility (e.g., Temporary Aid for Needy Families). Other legislation, such as the Illegal Immigration Reform and Immigrant Responsibility Act of 1996, discourages immigrants from accessing health care. One criterion that is used to determine whether an immigrant will be allowed to enter or remain in the United States is the likelihood that he or she will become dependent on public benefits. Although recipients of Medicaid and CHIP (Children's Health Insurance Program) are not considered public charges, limited awareness of the eligibility requirements and fears concerning public-charge status prohibit many immigrants from applying for the health care benefits they need and to which they are entitled. Immigrant children and citizen children of immigrant parents are particularly at risk of being uninsured.

TOWARD A MULTICULTURAL PSYCHOLOGY OF IMMIGRANT HEALTH

A multicultural approach is clearly needed to develop theories and interventions that are relevant and appropriate to diverse populations in the United States. For psychology to remain relevant, it must be responsive to the demographic shifts that characterize the changing world. Concepts developed in predominantly European American populations may not be applicable to diverse immigrant populations in the United States. The need for culturally relevant theories that address the specific issues that immigrant groups face should not be understated. We cannot assume, for example, that constructs (such as locus of control) exist or have the same meaning across cultures.

Among the psychosocial issues that immigrants confront are profound changes in social networks, socioeconomic status, and culture. In addition, the conditions under which emigration occurs may also affect immigrants' adaptation to life circumstances in the United States. Immigrants differ in their level of exposure to stressors in their countries of origin, as in cases of trauma due to war-related atrocities or during the migration process (e.g., traveling through dangerous territory), or immediately upon arrival (e.g., being forced to live in crowded and unsafe refugee camps). In cases in which immigrants are seeking political asylum, the process of obtaining permanent, legal status presents many additional difficulties, as applicants may be

held in detention centers for prolonged periods. Moreover, the living conditions in these centers are often harsh and sometimes abusive, which may result in symptoms of posttraumatic stress disorder (PTSD), especially among immigrants who experienced violence or other adverse events in their home countries.

There is an expansive literature on the effects of stress on mental and physical health outcomes. Similarly, the stress of immigration has been found to affect mental health. For example, there is evidence of dose-response associations between traumatic events experienced prior to and during immigration and symptom severity of depression and PTSD. Furthermore, immigration-related stresses have cumulative effects that compound the impact of postmigration stressors on mental health. After settling in the United States, immigrants may face continued stressors and challenging circumstances. These may include racism (both structural and interpersonal), professional difficulties (e.g., credentialing, lack of jobs), and limited opportunities for advancement as a result of low education or vocational skills. In addition, a lack of or limited English language proficiency can be degrading, frustrating, and frightening, especially under stressful circumstances (e.g., instances in which immigrants require emergency medical care). Psychologists and other health professionals must recognize that broad structural factors such as societal, political, and economic forces impinge on individual behavior. Failure to take these oppressive factors into account may lead mental health professionals to blame the victim and misdiagnose the causes of psychological disorders among their clients.

With regard to health care, a number of surveys indicate that Latinos and Asian Americans use fewer outpatient services than do European Americans. Barriers to care may include limited language proficiency, lack of health insurance, cultural proscriptions against seeking help (especially for emotional difficulties), and cultural incompatibility with health care providers. As a result, Asians, Latinos, and other immigrant groups may seek help from indigenous providers. Further study is required to assess the health benefits of these sources of help, especially among recent immigrants.

The failure of health professionals to understand the cultural values of diverse patient groups may lead to misconceptions, misdiagnoses, incorrect treatments, and misguided intervention programs. For example, a lack of familiarity with the Asian belief that suffering is unavoidable may lead health educators to develop programs to increase rates of screening or adherence to treatment recommendations that are culturally inappropriate. Other traditional health behaviors, such as the Asian practice of rubbing a coin on a symptomatic area of the skin (i.e., coining), may be interpreted by health care providers as unnecessary and perhaps even dangerous. These values take on particular significance during clinical encounters in health care settings. The importance of understanding cultural beliefs and values has sparked a growing movement toward improving cultural competence education in the health professions.

THE PSYCHOSOCIAL CONTEXT OF IMMIGRATION: AREAS FOR FUTURE RESEARCH

There is a particular need to develop multicultural theoretical models that focus on the processes of adaptation, as well as the broader societal structures that pose barriers to the health and well-being of immigrant groups. An ecological paradigm that considers the individual, family, and group within a sociocultural context could be particularly useful in understanding the issues that immigrant populations face. The ecological approach would consider a number of interacting and interdependent contextual influences on health, including the interpersonal context (e.g., the relationship between two individuals), the sociocultural context (e.g., cultural values, age, gender, socioeconomic status), the situational context (e.g., neighborhood quality, community cohesion), and the temporal context (e.g., life or developmental stage at time of migration).

Theoretical models of immigrant health and well-being should also incorporate the transactional processes by which immigrant groups affect and are affected by their environments. It is often assumed that individuals are passive recipients of stressful events or adverse circumstances. In contrast, the contextual approach asserts that bidirectional relationships exist between individuals and their contexts. When faced with discrimination, for example, immigrants might mobilize support networks and other community resources, which, in turn, change the context of the negative event. There is also a need for longitudinal studies to examine whether particular behaviors, coping strategies, and other psychological and social processes that are adaptive at particular points in time (and contexts) are beneficial over longer periods as immigrants adapt to circumstances in the United States.

In particular, the research should address psychosocial issues among immigrant populations. Research attention could focus on cultural values, perhaps exploring how the orientation to community takes precedence over individual needs in some Asian cultures. These inquiries may lead to the development of strategies to minimize interpersonal conflict and to maintain family or community harmony. Additional questions need to be explored: How do values such as communality (versus individuality) help immigrants adjust to life circumstances in the United States? Might these cultural values buffer the impact of stress on immigrants' physical and mental health? How do these values change (if at all) over time, and what is the impact of these changes on health?

Strong family ties and expectations of support from family members (rather than from friends) are especially common among Latinos (expressed in the cultural value of familism) and Asians. The orientation toward family is considered a core feature of Latino value systems. Three-generation reciprocal family support systems that benefit younger as well as older family members are common among certain Latino and Asian American groups; this is reflected in observations that foreign-born households in the United States are larger, on average, than native households. These family networks are crucial sources of social support—a documented contributor to physical and psychological well-being. The need to reestablish social networks in a new country is a major source of psychological distress among immigrants. Research has yet to elucidate the psychosocial and other factors that help immigrants to rebuild family and social networks.

Emphasis should also be placed on understanding the coping resources and strategies that immigrants use to adjust to life in the United States. A large body of evidence attests to the importance of coping mechanisms as a psychological resource for dealing with stressful events. Despite an extensive literature on coping and adjustment, research focusing specifically on coping among ethnically diverse and immigrant populations is sparse. To date, there has been little research on whether Latino cultural nuances result in specific approaches to coping (e.g., reliance on spirituality) and the extent to which different forms of coping are associated with psychosocial adaptation among immigrant groups.

Finally, despite multiple hardships, Latinos have better health than their social-class profiles would predict—a finding that presents an epidemiologic paradox. Although the mechanisms underlying the paradox have not been adequately uncovered, the health differentials do not appear to be artifacts of migratory processes (e.g., the healthy migrant effect). Instead, they may reflect cultural protective factors, such as healthy behaviors or other beneficial psychosocial factors. If cultural resources serve as protective factors, then acculturation (e.g., espousing the values, beliefs, and behaviors of the host country) should have adverse effects on immigrants' well-being. Several studies, in fact, indicate that greater acculturation is related to poorer outcomes among Latinos and other immigrant groups, but the mechanisms accounting for this finding are not clear. The literature has only begun to identify the cultural, psychological, social, and behavioral processes that foster health and well-being among immigrants as they adapt to life in the United States.

In summary, a multicultural approach to research and practice with immigrant groups should encompass the myriad social, historical, political, and psychological factors that affect health. Ecological models may be especially useful for understanding immigrant health issues and for designing effective and culturally relevant interventions for this diverse and significant population of the United States.

—*Ana F. Abraído-Lanza*
—*Adria N. Armbrister*
—*Kellee White*
—*Robert J. Lanza*

See also Asian/Pacific Islanders; Hispanic Americans

FURTHER READING

Abraído-Lanza, A. F., Dohrenwend, B. P., Ng-Mak, D. S., & Turner, J. B. (1999). The Latino mortality paradox: A test of the "salmon bias" and healthy migrant hypotheses. *American Journal of Public Health, 89,* 1543–1548.

Chan, S. (1991). *Asian Americans: An interpretive history.* New York: Twayne.

Hall, C. C. I. (1997). Cultural malpractice: The growing obsolescence of psychology with the changing U.S. population. *American Psychologist, 52,* 642–651.

National Council of La Raza. (2004). *State of Hispanic America 2004: Latino perspectives on the American agenda.* Washington, DC: Author. Retrieved February 3, 2006, from www.nclr.org

Perez Foster, R. (2001). When immigration is trauma: Guidelines for the individual and family clinician. *American Journal of Orthopsychiatry, 71,* 153–170.

Rogler, L. H. (1994). International migrations: A framework for directing research. *American Psychologist, 49,* 701–708.

Schmidley, A. D. (2001). *Profile of the foreign-born population in the United States: 2000* (Current Population Reports, Series P23-206). Washington, DC: U.S. Census Bureau. Retrieved February 3, 2006, from http://www.census.gov/prod/2002pubs/p23-206.pdf

Therrien, M., & Ramirez, R. R. (2000). *The Hispanic population in the United States: Population characteristics* (Current Population Reports, P20-535). Washington, DC: U.S. Census Bureau. Retrieved February 3, 2006, from http://www.census.gov/population/socdemo/hispanic/p20-535.pdf

Waddell, B. (1998). United States immigration: A historical perspective. In S. Loue (Ed.), *Handbook of immigrant health* (pp. 1–17). New York: Plenum Press.

INDIAN HEALTH SERVICE

Since 1955, the Indian Health Service (IHS), an agency within the U.S. Department of Health and Human Services, has had the responsibility of providing federal health services to American Indian and Alaska Native peoples. The health services provided include medical, dental, and environmental health programs. The provision of health services to federally recognized Indians grew out of a special relationship between the federal government and Indian tribes. This government-to-government relationship is based on Article 1, Section 8 of the U.S. Constitution and has been given form and substance by a number of treaties, laws, Supreme Court decisions, and executive orders.

The IHS comprises 12 regional administrative units called area offices, which are located in areas of highest Indian concentration. The area offices consist of 155 service units, 92 of which are operated by tribes. The IHS operates 36 hospitals, 59 health clinics, two school health centers, and 49 health stations. Tribes have the option of exercising self-determination by taking over the operation of an IHS facility through a Title I contract (P.L. 93-638) or Title V self-governance compact (P.L. 93-638). The 1975 Indian Self-Determination Act built on IHS policy by giving tribes the option of staffing and managing IHS programs in their communities and providing funding for the improvement of tribal capacity to contract under the act.

In fiscal year 2001, the IHS user population, which counts American Indians and Alaska Natives who used IHS services at least once during the prior three years, was more than 1.3 million.

Indian people using IHS hospitals and clinics must be members of a federally recognized tribe and have a Certificate of Degree of Indian Blood (CDIB), which is issued by the tribe of which the person is a member. Medical services are limited to those with a CDIB. However, if a patient is married to a non-Indian, his or her spouse may be seen for counseling, but other medical services may be withheld from the non-Indian spouse.

CURRENT POPULATION SURVEY

The U.S. Census Bureau's 1997–1999 Current Population Survey (CPS) revealed that the Indian population has larger families, lacks health insurance, and has lower household median incomes than the general U.S. population. The CPS also revealed that Indians live in poverty at a level nearly three times the rate of the rest of the U.S. population. Thus, providing health care through the IHS, which is free of charge, is critical for American Indians and Alaska Natives. According to the IHS Web site (http://info.ihs.gov), between 1990 and 2001, the U.S. American Indian and Alaska Native population increased 22.4%, from 2.1 million to 2.5 million. The IHS service area population represents 61% of the U.S. Indian population and increases at a rate of approximately 2.5% per year. This further taxes a system that is already challenged to meet even 60% of the health needs of American Indians and Alaska Natives.

Although the Indian population served by IHS is living longer than it did 30 years or even 20 years ago, Indian people still lag behind all races in the United States in health status. Statistics on age at death show that from 1972 to 1974, life expectancy at birth for the Indian population was 63.5 years. Life expectancy has now increased to 73.2 years. Diseases of the heart, malignant neoplasms, accidents, diabetes mellitus, and chronic liver disease and cirrhosis are the leading causes of death among this population (1994–1996).

CHALLENGES FACING THE IHS

Health care for most Indian people is provided through the IHS, presenting a number of problems for American Indians and Alaska Natives. Sources of medical care are not available in many facilities (laboratories, x-ray machines, heart catheterizations, certain surgeries, EEGs, etc.). Facilities are severely overcrowded, with insufficient monies and resources to handle ongoing operations and maintenance needs.

The specialists required to treat complex medical conditions are nonexistent in most IHS facilities; therefore, patients must be referred to large county or state hospitals.

Because of financial constraints within the IHS, patients are often placed on a waiting list, and each week a determination is made as to who will be referred for complex medical care. This decision is often based on financial considerations as well as serious medical need, that is, how much money is available in the IHS budget to pay for referrals to state and county hospitals and specialists. As a result, American Indians and Alaska Natives have lower health status and lower life expectancy compared with other Americans. According to the IHS, the health disparities of American Indians and Alaska Natives are great: They die at higher rates than other Americans from alcoholism (517%), tuberculosis (533%), motor vehicle crashes (203%), diabetes (210%), unintentional injuries (150%), homicide (87%), and suicide (60%). (Rates are adjusted for misreporting of Indian race on state death certificates, 1999–2001.)

The reasons for these disparities are numerous. Lower life expectancy and the disproportionate disease burden may be the result of inadequate education, disproportionate poverty, discrimination in the delivery of health services, and cultural differences. These broad quality-of-life indicators are rooted in economic adversity and poor social conditions. Furthermore, because many IHS facilities are located in rural or isolated areas, it is difficult to find staff who are willing to move to these areas. Salaries to pay health professionals in rural areas are not competitive with those offered in the private sector.

Finally, looking at mental health issues among American Indians and Alaska Natives, we see that more than one-third of the demands made on IHS and tribal health facilities involve mental health and social service issues. The challenges of treating mental health concerns (the suicide rate is 60% higher than for the general population) include underutilization of services and high drop-out rates for therapy. Because the poverty rate is so high among American Indians and Alaska Natives, this population often faces greater economic stress, overcrowding in homes, greater health problems, and higher school drop-out rates, resulting in poor education.

Although the mission and goal of the IHS is admirable, it is underfunded by about $1 billion, making it very difficult to meet all of the health care needs of American Indians and Alaska Natives. The

IHS's goal is to ensure that comprehensive, culturally acceptable personal and public health services are available and accessible to all American Indian and Alaska Native people. The IHS's mission, in partnership with the American Indian and Alaska Native people, is to raise their physical, mental, social, and spiritual health to the highest level.

—*Diane Willis*

See also Bureau of Indian Affairs; Certificate of Degree of Indian Blood; Native Americans

FURTHER READING

Indian Health Service. (2004). *Trends in Indian health, 2000–2001.* Rockville, MD: Author.

INDIGENOUS TREATMENTS AND HEALERS

Indigenous treatments and healers are found in many ancient ethnomedical systems and draw their extensive knowledge and therapeutic techniques from ancient native wisdom and healing traditions. Most have little formal medical education but believe they have received a divine gift to heal from the greater realms of medicine. Today, many depend on indigenous healers and treatments for their health, just as others rely on biomedical practitioners, pharmacists, chiropractors, massage therapists, and psychoanalysts. Indigenous healers—also known as lay folk healers, traditional healers, *curanderos* (in Latin America), and medicine men and women (in indigenous cultures)—treat physical, mental, emotional, and spiritual health problems. In the Western world, indigenous treatments and healers have been shaped by a unique Native American worldview that equates good health with homeostasis and harmony and embraces knowledge gained from European, African, and Asian healing traditions.

Diagnostics in traditional medicine go beyond the parameters known to biomedicine, extending the classification of conditions beyond the biomedical model. Indigenous healers, who are knowledgeable in many folk conditions that are unknown to biomedicine, may, in fact, be able to more adequately treat illness by considering both the natural and supernatural elements of causation. In Latin America, conditions such as *empacho* (a blockage in the stomach or digestive tract), *bilis*

(overreactive bile), *susto* (fright or soul loss), *envidia* (envy), *celos* (jealousy), *mal de ojo* (evil eye), and *nervios* (emotional instability) are diagnosed and treated according to an ancient equilibrium model of health. Thus, restoring the patient's energy equilibrium (physical, emotional, mental, and spiritual) becomes the healer's primary objective. The healer's reputation depends on his or her ability to adequately classify, identify, and effectively treat disease.

The folk medicine classification of disease comprises three main categories: physical conditions, emotional diseases, and diseases of the spiritual realm. Diagnosing involves the careful interpretation of physical, mental, spiritual, and emotional signs and symptoms. Common treatment protocols (depending on the condition) include *limpias* (cleansing), purification rituals and enemas, sweat baths, herbal remedies, prayer, massage, bonesetting, personal and dietary modifications, and spiritual advice. Faith is an important modality in indigenous healing practices. Traditional therapeutic techniques (based on long-term observation and experimentation) are applied with the invocation of divine intervention.

There are parallels between patients and healers that allow the patient's own perceptions of illness to be considered in the diagnosis and treatment. In contrast to the emphasis on diagnostic equipment found among biomedical practitioners, in folk healing practices, there is more therapeutic touch to the afflicted areas between healer and patient. Indigenous treatments possess a unique mystical element that comes from the summoning of the healing spirit of God, angels, saints, and benevolent spirits and signals a holistic approach to the folk healing regimen.

A wide range of medical specializations and specialty practitioners exists in traditional medicine and in world healing traditions, each having its own particular cultural elements and linguistic terminology. In Latin America, these specialists include herbalists and leaf doctors (*yerberos/as* and *docte feys*), village healers and shamans (curanderos and *chamanes,* or medicine men and women), massage therapists (*sobadores*), lay bonesetters (*huesero/as*), channeling healing mediums or seers (*espiritistas—lloles* and *videntes*), midwives (*parteras*), healers who remove illness by sucking the afflicted area (*chupadores*), bush doctors (experts in jungle survival), and snake doctors (experts in snakebites).

Herbalists (yerberos, leaf doctors) treat diseases of physical and emotional origin. They possess extraordinary and sophisticated knowledge of plants. A legitimate yerbero knows the bioenergetic properties of plants, their botanical classification and divisions, and the effects that herbs have on the human body. Most important, herbalists provide a powerful spiritual element while working with the spirit energy of the plant. They know the general use and applications of medicinal plants—tinctures, syrups, and infusions—and have knowledge and understanding of acceptable strengths and dosages. A great deal of the advances made in pharmaceutical trials working in the research and development of new therapies for chronic illnesses (such as cancer and AIDS) are the result of ancient ethnobotanical lore and therapies.

Midwives (parteras) are common throughout the world, particularly in developing countries, where women who live in isolated rural villages depend on them for prenatal care, birthing, and postpartum care. Another type of healer, a chupador/a, is a healer who sucks on an afflicted area with his or her mouth to extract foreign objects (such as glass, dirt, mud, corn, chicken bones, twigs, and nails) that may be under the skin, causing illness or imbalance in the patient.

Village healers (curanderos) and shamans (chamanes) are well-respected community members who treat medical, mental, emotional, and spiritual health problems. Massage therapists (sobadores) treat physical ailments (folk conditions such as empacho, *mal aire,* and constipation) and emotional illnesses (such as bilis and nervios). Lay bonesetters (hueseros) are a type of folk chiropractor or sports therapist; they bind and reset bones and realign displaced joints.

Espiritistas (healing mediums, *cajas,* shamans, faith healers, videntes) heal with the help of spirit. Not to be confused with *espiritualistas* (spiritualists, spiritual healers who pray for divine intervention), espiritistas (spiritists) use mediumistic healing techniques that go beyond the sensorial aspect to incorporate a knowledgeable and benevolent healing spirit. Spiritist healers (mediums) are found in all world healing traditions and deal specifically with diseases of the supernatural realm. They are masters of spirits and posses a unique specialization as soul doctors. With the help of the spirit world, they serve as counter-witchcraft specialists in removing spells, conducting exorcisms, and removing negative energies from patients. Spiritists can repair the loss of the soul (caused by susto); reestablish the circulation of the body fluids within the body; identify, locate, and expel pathogenic agents sent by a sorcerer; and invoke supernatural powers and master the ritual orations.

Thus, a spiritual healer heals by performing rituals that reestablish the connection between the ill patient and the universe.

Spirit healers provide the patient with a spiritual consultation, examine the spiritual framework (spirit biography) of the ill patient, and identify the source of the ailment. They believe that the only way for the patient to achieve integral healing is by activating the patient's soul, which allows important spiritual, emotional, mental, and physiological processes to take place. Spiritual therapy, therefore, involves working with the patient's soul, mind, energy, and biological system and providing the patient with a multidimensional adjustment of spirit, mind, and body. A genuine healing medium teaches patients to act on internal direction and learn to discriminate between thoughts motivated by strength (faith) and those by fear and illusion (characteristic of human weakness). A patient's treated soul, mind, and emotions are then ready for optimal performance in the flow of healing energy between the patient and cosmos.

All traditional healers aim to maintain health through a particular focus on prevention, diagnosis, and improvement of physical and mental illness and through a variety of holistic therapeutic techniques. Traditional healers in the United States are not recognized by the government and do not interact with the health care system. This is not the case in some developing countries, where allopathic and alternative service providers work together to meet most (if not all) of the primary health care needs of their people. Although some view folk healers negatively or consider them dangerous because they are unregulated or unorthodox, folk healers may be more accessible and affordable than biomedicine, particularly among rural populations, for whom biomedical facilities and economic resources are limited.

Focusing on the patient rather than the disease, traditional healers understand the patient's unique mental constructs and thus may be more effective at treating illness that requires behavior modification. They are aware of culture-specific norms, values, symbols, and metaphors, which helps them to build trust and confidence with their patients, ultimately lowering the patient's psychosocial resistance to the healing process. The healer's unique cultural understanding of the patient's belief system (which, for Latinos, is rooted in Catholic, indigenous, and African beliefs) enhances his or her ability as a psychoanalyst and spiritual adviser. Folk healers employ important mediation principles with their patients, allowing greater flexibility and less control in the healer–patient relationship.

Specific Latino cultural norms that express the collective and unifying processes through which Latinos establish their identity, existence, and relationships (particularly the patient–healer relationship) include *personalismo* (personalism), *respeto* (respect), *confianza* (trust), *fatalismo* (fatalism), *humildad* (humility), and *familismo* (familism). Sharing similar cultural knowledge, norms, and lay beliefs with their patients helps traditional healers provide patients with bidirectional consultations and plans of treatment, which in most cases do not interfere with biomedical therapy and optimize the patient's treatment outcome.

—*Sandra Nuñez*

See also Immigrants; Refugees; Religion

FURTHER READING

Avila, E. (1999). *Woman who glows in the dark*. New York: Tarcher Putman.

Hayes-Bautista, D. E., & Chiprut, R. (1998). *Healing Latinos: Realidad y fantasia*. Los Angeles: Cedars-Sinai Health Systems.

INDIGENOUS TREATMENTS: COINING

Coining is an ancient Southeast Asian folk remedy used to treat common minor illnesses. It is still frequently practiced today, and cross-cultural understanding is enhanced by knowledge of the procedure. A special ointment is placed on the skin. The edge of a coin or other object is then rubbed on the skin in downward parallel lines until redness, welts, or a small amount of bleeding occurs (see Figure 1). Family members, friends, or traditional healers may perform this procedure as the first line of therapy for cough, headache, vomiting, diarrhea, dizziness, fever, and other symptoms. The part of the body that is coined depends on the symptom that is being treated—for example, the back and chest may be coined to treat respiratory symptoms, and the arms, neck, and forehead may be coined to treat headaches. Coining is practiced in Vietnam, where it is referred to as *cao gio* (pronounced *gow yaw*), meaning "scratch the wind." It is also practiced in Cambodia, China,

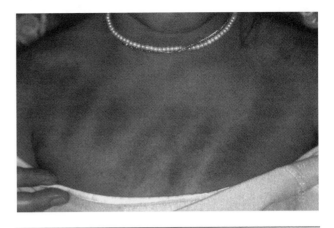

Figure 1   Typical marks from coining

Korea, Laos, and Thailand. Coining is also called *coin rubbing, coin rolling,* and *skin scraping.*

Southeast Asian folk practices reflect cultural beliefs about the causes of illness. Disease is seen as a state of imbalance. The four elements of the body—fire (heat), water (wetness), wind (cold), and earth (dryness)—must be in balance. Too much or too little wind is often related to disease states, and coining is believed to relieve the body of wind. The concept of wind does not refer literally to rapidly moving air but to a moving element of the human body that is associated with blood. The marks produced by the coining procedure affirm the presence of excess wind in the body and show that wind has left the body. The procedure aims to increase circulation, respiration, and warmth and stimulate trigger points.

Although the marks left by coining appear painful, many describe the process as pleasurable, similar to a massage. People who are unfamiliar with the practice may confuse coining with child abuse. Families are often devastated when this happens. The practice is otherwise benign and only rarely does the patient experience complications. Because the practice is so deeply embedded in Southeast Asian culture, attempts to dissuade people from practicing coining are unnecessary and ineffective.

Coining and other traditional healing practices can be beneficial. Patients may feel empowered by taking action to treat their symptoms and tend to believe that coining works. Their problems are recognized and attended to, which is comforting to them. Coining is well thought of and closely tied to family and culture, and patients remain connected with their traditions through its use. Coining can be detrimental if modern medical care is delayed for serious treatable conditions, but this is not the usual practice. Coining and other folk remedies remain prevalent among Southeast Asian immigrants, who are best served when both Western and traditional health care systems are recognized and accepted.

—*Karen Kirhofer Hansen*

See also Child Abuse: Overview; Indigenous Treatments: Cupping; Indigenous Treatments: Moxibustion

FURTHER READING

Aronson, L. (1987). Traditional Cambodian health beliefs and practices. *Rhode Island Medical Journal, 70,* 73–78.

Buchwald, D., Panwala, S., & Hooton, T. M. (1992). Use of traditional health practices by Southeast Asian refugees in a primary care clinic. *Western Journal of Medicine, 156,* 507–511.

Davis, R. E. (2000). Cultural health care or child abuse? *Journal of the American Academy of Nurse Practitioners, 12,* 89–95.

Hansen, K. K. (1997). Folk remedies and child abuse: A review with emphasis on caida de mollera and its relationship to shaken baby syndrome. *Child Abuse & Neglect, 22,* 117–127.

Look, K. M., & Look, R. M. (1997). Skin scraping, cupping, and moxibustion that may mimic physical abuse. *Journal of Forensic Sciences, 42,* 103–105.

Saulsbury, F. T., & Hayden, F. (1985). Skin conditions simulating child abuse. *Pediatric Emergency Medicine, 1,* 147–150.

INDIGENOUS TREATMENTS: CUENTO THERAPY

Cuento therapy is a group treatment modality that uses Spanish-language folktales (*cuentos*). Historically, storytelling has played an important role in the education of children by relaying social morals, values, rules, and customs, as well as by providing a functional means of coping. Storytelling, which has theoretical underpinnings in social learning theory, is used in cuento therapy to enhance emotional and behavioral outcomes by modeling appropriate thoughts, beliefs, and behaviors.

Giuseppe Costantino and his colleagues developed cuento therapy for use with Puerto Rican youth and conducted several studies to document its efficacy. In cuento therapy, the selected stories have ethnic themes and characters with whom children can identify. Because the children's difficulties are viewed as the result of acculturation stress, weak traditional cultural values, and loss of ethnic pride, a goal of the therapy is the transmission and reinforcement of traditional Puerto Rican culture.

In the first study of cuento therapy, participants included 208 kindergarten to third-grade students who were second-generation Puerto Rican children in New York City. The children were selected for inclusion based on a behavioral screening and were randomly assigned to one of four groups: original cuento therapy, adapted cuento therapy, art/play therapy, and a control group. The adapted cuento therapy group experienced modifications in the treatment protocol, particularly the adaptation of the original Spanish-language cuentos to the life experiences and coping skills needed by Puerto Rican children in New York City.

Bilingual therapists and the children's mothers were involved in the therapy, which included (1) reading Puerto Rican folktales (in English and Spanish) to groups of four to five children; (2) discussing the meaning of the tales; (3) role-playing the characters in the stories; and (4) discussing the relationship of the role-play to the children's personal lives. The therapy comprised 20 two-hour sessions over a six-month period. The results indicated that the adapted cuento group experienced a greater reduction in anxiety than the other three groups, and the original cuento therapy group experienced a greater reduction in anxiety than the control group only. Additionally, social judgment (measured by the Comprehension Subtest of the Wechsler Intelligence Scale for Children–Revised) increased to a greater degree for the two cuento therapy groups than for the other groups. After one year, the anxiety treatment effects remained stable, but the social judgment treatment effects were not maintained.

Cuento therapy has been adapted for use with Puerto Rican adolescents who face acculturation, ethnic identity, and other adjustment issues that are common to their group. In the therapy, termed "hero/heroine modeling," the adolescents are exposed to the biographies of adult Puerto Rican role models (in sports, politics, arts, and education) who have successfully coped with adversity, such as poverty or discrimination. In a study of hero/heroine modeling, treatment and control groups comprised 90 English-dominant Puerto Rican eighth- and ninth-grade adolescents who had been identified as at risk for behavioral problems. The therapy sessions were similar to cuento therapy. Compared with the control group, the hero/heroine therapy group had a significantly higher level of Puerto Rican ethnic identity, and a lower level of anxiety among eighth graders.

—*Sylvia Z. Ramirez*
—*Leila L. Flores-Torres*

See also Hispanic Americans; Puerto Rican Americans

FURTHER READING

Bandura, A. (1977). *Social learning theory*. Englewood Cliffs, NJ: Prentice Hall.

Costantino, G., Malgady, R. G., & Rogler, L. H. (1984). Cuentos folklóricos as a therapeutic modality with Puerto Rican children. *Hispanic Journal of Behavioral Sciences, 6*(2), 169–178.

Malgady, R. G., Rogler, L. H., & Costantino, G. (1990). Hero/heroine modeling for Puerto Rican adolescents: A preventive mental health intervention. *Journal of Consulting and Clinical Psychology, 58*, 469–474.

INDIGENOUS TREATMENTS: CUPPING

It is said that no other therapy can move the blood and vital energy faster than cupping in order to restore balance and harmony in the body. Cupping is a treatment in which warm vacuum cups are applied to acupuncture points. Cupping is performed as an alternative to or in combination with acupuncture and moxibustion (the practice of burning an herb on skin). Transparent glass cups are used so that the progress of the cupping procedure can be observed.

The cup is warmed by burning an alcohol-soaked cotton ball inside the cup for a short period of time. The cup is then quickly placed over the selected acupuncture point, affected skin, or painful area of the body. The heating of the cups creates suction that seals the skin around cup. The flame works to remove all of the oxygen from the cup; when placed on the skin, a vacuum is created, fixing the cup onto the skin and raising the skin into the glass. The cups are moved along the surface of the skin, maintaining the suction between the skin and the cup. The application of warm vegetable or herb oil to the skin helps the cup to move around smoothly.

Cupping is performed for about 5 to 15 minutes. The cup is unsealed by putting pressure on the skin along the rim of the cup. Sometimes, bloodletting is performed by pricking a vein and then applying the cup. Cupping promotes blood circulation and treats coldness, blood stagnation, pain, and swelling. The pressure created by the cupping encourages the flow of vital energy (*qi, ki,* or *chi*) and blood in the area beneath the cup, and the local stagnation begins to clear.

Cupping leaves redness with congestion of the blood on the skin. Cupping is commonly applied immediately after acupuncture or bloodletting. The cupping method combined with bloodletting is used to treat acute sprains accompanied by blood stasis. Cupping is performed to heal pain, gastrointestinal ailments, hypertension, cold, anemia, asthma, boils, carbuncles, cough, constipation, varicose veins, and lung disease. Cupping can also be used for tonification or reduction to bring holistic harmony. According to recent research, cupping can also be applied for the treatment of head pain, frozen shoulder, acne, acute trigeminal neuralgia, and lumbar sprain. Cupping is contraindicated for inflamed skin, high fever, convulsions, and bleeding, and should not be applied to the abdominal and lower sacral regions of pregnant women.

The cupping method functions to warm and promote the free flow of vital energy and blood in the meridians, dispel cold and dampness, and diminish swelling and pain. In clinics, the cupping method is used to treat disorders caused by wind dampness, such as pain of the low back, shoulders, and legs; gastrointestinal disorders such as stomachache, vomiting, and diarrhea; and lung diseases such as asthma. When cupping is combined with the bloodletting technique, the skin is first sterilized, a small vein is pricked with a sterile needle, and then the cupping is applied. Cupping can be practiced by laypeople.

—*Keum Young Chung Pang*

FURTHER READING

Chirali, I. Z. (1999). *Traditional Chinese medicine: Cupping therapy*. New York: Churchill Livingstone.

Pang, K. Y. (1989). The practice of traditional Korean medicine in Washington, D.C. *Social Science and Medicine, 28*(8), 875–884.

Pang, K. Y. (1991). *Korean elderly women in America: Everyday life, health, and illness*. New York: AMS Press.

INDIGENOUS TREATMENTS: CURANDERISMO

Curanderismo is a Mexican American folk healing tradition that represents a fusion of Judeo-Christian religious beliefs, symbols, and rituals, along with

Native American and indigenous herbal knowledge and health practices. The *curandero* or *curandera* is believed to have supernatural power or access to supernatural power; his or her abilities are perceived as *el don* (a gift) from God. Curandero/as treat a variety of physical ailments and social problems and can be found in most Mexican American communities.

The curandero/a is typically a well-known individual in the community who shares his or her clients' experiences, geographic location, socioeconomic status, class, language, religion, and beliefs about the causes of pathology. This shared worldview between the patient and the healer is the reason Mexican Americans seek help from curandero/as and find them effective. Curandero/as are respected for their role as healers, spiritual advisers, and counselors and for their lengthy training and education in indigenous and religious beliefs, practices, and rituals. Therefore, the curandero/a is often the first person to whom individuals turn in times of need, even before they seek treatment from a physician or psychologist or when a family's attempts at conventional treatment have failed.

Curandero/as have a holistic orientation that values good relations between the physical and social environment and the supernatural. Curative activities typically fall into four categories:

- Confession, atonement, and absolution to rid the body of sin and guilt, which can cause illness and maladjustment.
- Restoration of balance, wholeness, and harmony through self-control: Illness and maladjustment are believed to result from the lack of self-control, which allows feelings, emotions, or desires to run unchecked, or a lack of balance, which causes the spirit to fragment.
- Involvement of family and community in treatment: Family members and close friends may accompany the patient to the home of the curandero/a and make a commitment to support his or her reintegration into the family, community, and culture.
- Communication with the supernatural: This sets the curandero/a apart from others; he or she is believed to be able to communicate with the spirit world.

Curandero/as diagnose and treat within the realm of their expertise, referring patients to others (e.g., physicians) when necessary. There are many different types of curandero/as, including *parteras* (midwives), *sobadores* (healers who treat muscle sprains), and *yerberos* (herbalists). Spiritual healing, massage, tea, and prayer are prescribed by curandero/as for emotional conditions or cultural syndromes such as *susto* (extreme fright or fear), *mal puesto* (hexes), *mal de ojo* (evil eye), and *envidia* (envy or extreme jealousy). Professional curandero/as also address physical ailments (e.g., diabetes), social problems (e.g., marital conflicts, family disruptions), and psychological disturbances (e.g., depression); work to change people's fortunes in love, business, or home life; and help to remove or guard against misfortune and illness. In 1983, E. Fuller Torrey published *The Mind Game,* in which he suggested that the differences between psychiatrists and so-called witch doctors may not be so great. Recent research on factors associated with psychotherapy effectiveness supports the view that all healing traditions share common healing practices. Perhaps for these reasons, curanderismo continues to survive and serve a vital function in Mexican American communities.

—Brian McNeill

See also Mexican Americans

FURTHER READING

Harris, M., Velásquez, R. J., White, J., & Renteria, T. (2004). Folk healing and curanderismo within the contemporary Chicana/o community: Current status. In R. J. Velásquez, L. M. Arellano, & B. W. McNeill (Eds.), *The handbook of Chicana/o psychology and mental health.* Mahwah, NJ: Lawrence Erlbaum.

Torrey, E. F. (1983). *The mind game: Witchdoctors and psychiatrists.* New York: Jason Aronson.

Trotter, R. T., & Chavira, J. A. (1984). *Curanderismo: Mexican-American folk healing* (2nd ed.). Athens: University of Georgia Press.

INDIGENOUS TREATMENTS: DICHOS

Dichos, also known as *refranes,* are Spanish-language sayings that can be used as a psychotherapeutic tool when working with Latino clients. *Proverbs, aphorisms,* and *adages* are other English terms that are often used interchangeably to refer to the same concept. Dichos are brief, humorous, moralistic, and picturesque statements that express what many individuals from the same cultural group accept as representative of their perspective about the human condition. They are considered significant core beliefs in the development of moral standards, attitudes, and social conduct within a culture. Dichos address numerous and diverse subjects and may be philosophical, psychological, or religious in nature. They commonly fall into one or more of the following categories: food; love and marriage; work and monetary issues; and friendship, family, and human relations. Dichos are used frequently by Latinos to demonstrate or illustrate a point, reconcile a disagreement, give advice to a family member or friend, or merely entertain.

In psychotherapy, dichos can be an effective and culturally sensitive tool when used with Latino Spanish-speaking clients with varying levels of acculturation and bilingualism. Because dichos are important in Latino culture and spoken in the client's language, they can facilitate communication and participation in the therapeutic process. They may be used to develop rapport, decrease resistance, address critical and sensitive issues, enhance motivation and cultural identity, explore emotions and feelings, and reframe or gain insight into problems. It is important to note, however, that the examples provided here should be used with caution because of within-group diversity.

Latino clients relate easily to dichos and appreciate the therapist's efforts to recognize their cultural background; this, in turn, can reduce anxiety and resistance and enhance trust, especially with defensive patients. In particular, dichos are effective in building rapport, and essentially any dicho can be useful for this purpose. Examples of dichos include the following: *hablando se entiende la gente* (things become clear through communication) and *de médico, poeta, músico y loco, todos tenemos un poco* (of a doctor, poet, musician, and madman, we each have a trace).

The use of dichos is a nonthreatening way to approach the discussion of critical and sensitive issues. They can also enhance motivation—for example, *no hay mal que por bien no venga* (there is nothing bad from which good does not come) or *la esperanza es lo último que muere* (hope dies last of all). Some dichos can aid in the exploration of the Latino client's values and experiences by tapping the client's sense of self and cultural identity. For example, one dicho might say, *más vale un momento de pie que toda una vida de rodillas* (it is better to stand on your feet for a moment than to be an entire life on your knees).

Dichos are useful in the exploration of emotions and feelings, for example, *solo quien carga el morral sabe lo que lleva adentro* (only the person who carries the bag knows its contents). Feelings of belonging, hope, and empathy can be communicated through certain dichos, such as, *a cada capillita se le llega su fiestecita* (each person will have his/her day of reward). Finally, the utilization of dichos can help clients to gain insight and reframe problems—for example, *todo depende del cristal con que se mire* (everything is a reflection of the mirror from which it is seen).

—*Leila L. Flores-Torres*
—*Sylvia Z. Ramirez*

See also Bilingualism; Hispanic Americans

FURTHER READING

Aviera, A. (1996). "Dichos" therapy group: A therapeutic use of Spanish-language proverbs with hospitalized Spanish-speaking psychiatric patients. *Cultural Diversity and Mental Health, 2*(2), 73–87.

Zuniga, M. E. (1991). "Dichos" as metaphorical tools for resistant Latino clients. *Psychotherapy, 28*(3), 480–483.

INDIGENOUS TREATMENTS: MOXIBUSTION

Moxibustion is a treatment modality of traditional Chinese medicine in which the herb *moxa* (mugwort or *Artemlsia vulgaris*) is heated and applied directly or indirectly to particular sections of the body. Recipients report feeling localized internal warming in and around the treated area, resulting in generalized feelings of relaxation and overall increased energy (called *chi* or *qi*). Western cultural applications of moxibustion are generally practiced in conjunction with acupuncture (the insertion of fine needles into key body points or meridians). In the United States, acupuncture and moxibustion are largely viewed as alternative medical practices; however, both are gaining recognition and popularity. Acupuncture and moxibustion have long histories in the medical treatment of disorders such cold and flu, and recently they have been recognized as efficacious in the treatment of some psychological conditions.

Moxibustion was rarely practiced in the United States before President Richard M. Nixon's 1972 visit to China, which brought publicity and increased recognition to Eastern thought. Traditional Chinese medicine is reported to have originated as early as the first use of fire; it was first recorded as a medical practice in China around 475 BCE. Early applications involved the warming of sand or hot stones, which were then applied to the body; more formalized approaches developed as the healing arts progressed. Traditional Chinese medicine is practiced throughout Asia. Acupuncture and moxibustion have slightly different applications across cultures. Practitioners in Western cultures generally prefer indirect application, with the moxa preformed into a cigar-like shape and held over the body or applied directly to inserted acupuncture needles; some practitioners use specialized acupuncture needles to hold the burning moxa.

Although historical artifacts of stone and bone needles have been found, modern-day acupuncture uses sterilized, single-use stainless steel needles. A trained traditional Chinese medicine practitioner inserts fine needles into the body at key meridian points, where the chi energy is believed to flow. Theories of traditional Chinese medicine propose that the stimulation of meridian points through moxibustion corrects imbalances in energy flow, bringing increased quantities of energy heat (yang) to the body. Alternatively, acupuncture without moxibustion works to disperse the flow of chi in the body. Western medicine proposes that the heating of the body stimulates the capillaries, resulting in increased blood flow. Recent empirical research from both the United States and China indicates significant changes in dopamine and serotonin levels as a result of moxibustion; this research proposes that changes in neurotransmitter activity are the key treatment effect.

Moxibustion is most frequently used in medical treatment of pain, muscular or menstrual cramps, inadequate circulation, and generalized immune system deficiencies. Experimental research has also found that moxibustion increases the positive effects of cancer treatment and decreases the negative effects of chemotherapy. Studies of the psychological applications of moxibustion indicate efficacy in the treatment of stress, anxiety, and depression.

Though moxibustion is viewed positively in traditional Chinese and in a growing body of both Eastern and Western empirical research, it is not for everyone—specifically, those who have been diagnosed as having too much heat (yang) in their body energy, or those who find smoke and odor uncomfortable (some believe that moxa smoke smells similar to marijuana smoke).

—*Jennifer F. Taylor*

See also Chinese Americans

FURTHER READING

Beijing College of Traditional Chinese Medicine, Shanghai College of Traditional Chinese Medicine, Nanjing College of Traditional Chinese Medicine, & Acupuncture Institute of the Academy of Traditional Chinese Medicine. (1980). *Essentials of Chinese acupuncture.* Beijing: Foreign Language Press.
O'Connor, J., & Bensky, D. (1981). *Acupuncture: A comprehensive text.* Seattle, WA: Eastland Press.

INDIGENOUS TREATMENTS: SHAMANS

A *shaman* is a man or woman who enters an altered state of consciousness at will in order to contact and use an ordinarily hidden reality to acquire knowledge or power and to help people. Derived from the language of the Tungus people of Siberia, shaman is the term adopted by anthropologists to refer to people known as witches, witch doctors, medicine men and women, sorcerers, wizards, and magic men and women. Shamans have practiced for thousands of years in different cultures worldwide. Long recognized as healers, these individuals are believed to possess awareness, knowledge, and skills that grow out of a timeless wisdom. As keepers of this wisdom, they enlist it to help people solve problems or make decisions. The wisdom of the healers rests on intuition and spiritual belief.

These notions are grounded in basic principles that form the foundation of the credibility and effectiveness of the shaman. These principles can be summarized within the context of the *universal shamanic tradition.* Though substantive cultural distinctions exist in this tradition, three salient characteristics define indigenous helping methodologies: (1) a holistic approach, (2) a nonordinary reality, and (3) an emphasis on the psychospiritual realm of personality.

HOLISTIC APPROACH

Most traditional healers make little distinction between physical and mental well-being. Many shamans perceive human distress as an indication that a person has fallen out of harmony with both the internal and external environment. Therefore, shamans may be consulted for a wide range of physical and emotional issues, which are often treated in a holistic manner.

NONORDINARY REALITY

In many indigenous helping systems, shamans believe in multiple levels of human experience, which often include a spirit world, where it is believed that answers to human destiny can be discerned. Shamans will generally "journey" to these other levels of reality on behalf of others to find answers to their problems. During the journey, the shaman will enter an altered state of consciousness. Indigenous healers in some cultures induce this altered state with drugs, whereas others use a monotonous percussive sound, such as the steady beating of a drum.

EMPHASIS ON THE PSYCHOSPIRITUAL REALM OF PERSONALITY

Shamanic helping activities usually focus on the realm of personality that transcends thoughts, feelings, and actions to arrive at a spiritual domain of consciousness. Shamans consider this personality domain to be the seat of the soul. Helping or healing practices, therefore, often involve religious or spiritual rituals that invoke higher powers or forces for assistance with problem resolution or decision making.

The shamanic tradition can be observed in the ancient helping practices of individuals throughout the world who are acknowledged as healers within their communities. For example, in Korea, shamans called *mudangs* are traditional healers who use sorcery to chase out demons or evil spirits believed to be in possession of an individual. In many Islamic countries, *piris* and *fakirs* are religious leaders within the Muslim faith who use verses from the Koran to treat illness. Similarly, in Mexico, the shamanic tradition is carried on by *curandero/as,* healers who use herbalism to alleviate suffering.

—*Courtland C. Lee*

See also Immigrants; Mental Health

FURTHER READING

Harner, M. (1990). *The way of the shaman.* San Francisco: Harper & Row.

Lee, C. C. (1996). MCT theory and implications for indigenous healing. In D. W. Sue, A. E. Ivey, and P. B. Pedersen (Eds.), *A theory of multicultural counseling and therapy* (pp. 86–98). Pacific Grove, CA: Brooks/Cole.

Lee, C. C., & Armstrong, K. L. (1995). Indigenous models of mental health intervention: Lessons from traditional healers. In J. Ponterotto, J. M. Casas, L. A. Suzuki, & C. M. Alexander (Eds.), *Handbook of multicultural counseling* (pp. 441–456). Thousand Oaks, CA: Sage.

INDIGENOUS TREATMENTS: SOBADORES

A *sobador* is a traditional folk healer, masseuse, and therapist in Latino culture who treats common ailments such as constipation and diarrhea, as well as culture-bound syndromes such as *empacho* (a blockage of the stomach or digestive tract) and other digestive disorders by using therapeutic touch to relieve physical pain and by massaging the stomach and lower back to release blockages. The patient is counseled about proper diet and herbal remedies that will aid digestion. When treating emotional conditions such as *bilis* (overreactive bile) or *nervios* (nervous breakdown or mental crisis), a sobador draws from important ethnobotanical and psychotherapeutic knowledge and ancient healing wisdom to effectively and comprehensively treat patients. In the United States, these specialists do not interact with professionals of the biomedical system.

Sobadores, who possess a good understanding of the four bodily humors, acknowledge that disease is caused by an imbalance between hot and cold principles (referring to their quality or valence rather than temperature). For health maintenance, the avoidance of exposure to extreme temperatures is important. Vasoconstriction (constriction of the blood vessels) and a low metabolic rate signify cold diseases, whereas hot conditions are characterized by vasodilation (dilation of the blood vessels) and a high metabolic rate. The goal of treatment is to restore equilibrium by treating hot diseases with cold remedies, and vice versa, to withdraw excess heat or cold from the body.

Sobadores provide important physical, emotional, and mental healing benefits. Their therapeutic massage involves more than the skillful manipulation of muscles and nerves to relieve stress and pain. With prayer intercession and divine intervention, sobadores also help to relieve a patient's emotional and spiritual anxiety. They relax the physical body (particularly the joints and muscles), help to restore flexibility and movement, and soften muscles and nerves as if melting the pain with love (in Spanish, this is called *apapachando*).

A *huesero/a*, lay bonesetter, is a specialized type of sobador. He or she diagnoses and treats dislocated bones, sprains, tendons, muscles, and nerves using a combination of pressure, traction, and resistance to realign what has been displaced. This practice restores total movement, function, and energy to the afflicted area as well as to the patient's nervous and immune systems and overall health. Treating physical injuries related to accidental falls or sports injuries, hueseros treat a predominantly young male clientele, who are more susceptible to these types of injuries. Considered a lay chiropractor or sports therapist, the huesero is effective at resetting displaced joints and unblocking nerve blockages, offering significant results and improving patients' strength, agility, speed, and balance. Hueseros assess muscle strength or weakness and the range of spinal motion and joint mobility, and they identify and correct posture-related problems. They also provide heat therapy with their own healing energy, invoke divine intervention with their treatment, and offer nutritional counseling and appropriate exercises.

Most sobadores are not trained professionally; rather, theirs is a vocation, a call to heal using their hands to channel God's healing energy. Many come from a long family tradition of *curanderismo* and learn this important healing art through oral tradition. Most do not charge for their services, but some may accept donations. Legitimately skilled sobadores and hueseros who are accessible and affordable (particularly where Latinos are not covered by health plan coverage) offer a practical and effective solution to their patients' primary health concerns.

—Sandra Nuñez

See also Accessibility of Health Care; Hispanic Americans

FURTHER READING

Garcia, H., Sierra, A., & Balam, G. (1996). *Medicina Maya tradicional: Confrontación con el sistema conceptual chino* [Maya medicine and Oriental medicine: A comparative review]. Campeche, Mexico: Educe.

Paul, B. D., & McMahon, C. E. (2001). Mesoamerican bonesetters. In B. E. Huber & A. Sandstrom (Eds.), *Mesoamerican healers* (pp. 243–269). Austin: University of Texas Press.

INDIVIDUALISM

The term *individualism* is typically contrasted with collectivism. Individualism generally refers to cultures that give priority to individual goals when those goals come into conflict with group goals. A person's identity is defined in terms of personal attributes and achievements as opposed to group attributes and achievements. Individualism is often equated with independence. Generally speaking, individualism is associated with countries in North America and Western Europe, Australia, and New Zealand.

In his book *Individualism and Collectivism,* Harry Triandis summarized a great deal of research on individualism and collectivism. He suggested that individualism should refer to a description of a society. In other words, a society identifies the importance of the pursuit of individual goals and identities that are separate from the society itself. The degree to which an individual follows these values is referred to as *idiocentrism.* An idiocentric individual in an individualistic society matches the value system, and it is easier for the individual to pursue his or her own goals. However, some idiocentric individuals may live in collectivistic societies, and this mismatch impedes the idiocentric's pursuits. In these instances, society is seen as a constraint from which the individual desires to escape.

The original notion of individualism may have been negative, connoting anarchy. Individualism has been identified as an outgrowth of the French Revolution. Individualism was a perspective that resisted the more common community and collective social structures of the world. Paradoxically, though, the destruction of collective social structure often leads to the destruction of individualism because it is the community that protects one's individual rights.

An important dimension of individualism is *power distance.* Geert Hofstede called the endpoints of the power-distance dimension "masculine" and "feminine"; Triandis later renamed them "vertical" and "horizontal." Triandis's terms are more common in the literature. A society can be vertically individualistic or horizontally individualistic. Vertical individualistic goals result in hierarchy, in which some people are more successful than others; achievement orientation is a result of vertical individualism. In an academic context, students compete for grades in courses, and those with higher achievement orientations will receive higher grades than those with lower achievement orientations. In a business context, those who have higher drives might make more money than those with lower drives. Horizontal individualistic goals result in uniqueness. In these societies, one is not "more unique" than others because this would result in a hierarchy. Rather, each individual's uniqueness is valued equally. Triandis cites Sweden as a prototypical horizontally individualistic society. Although Swedes score highly on scales of individualism, they prefer to be unique without being conspicuous.

As Triandis indicated, vertical and horizontal individualism do not really represent endpoints on a continuum but dimensions that can be compared relative to one another. For example, Triandis identified the United States as a vertical individualistic society, with a horizontal individualism score of 40% and a vertical individualism score of 30%, whereas Sweden is a horizontal individualistic society, having scores of 50% and 20%, respectively. Thus, although the United States has a higher horizontal score than vertical score, it is considered a vertical society because its vertical individualism score is higher than other cultures (in this case, Sweden, whose vertical score is comparatively lower). According to Triandis's speculations, England and Germany actually have higher vertical individualism scores than the United States, although all would be considered vertical individualistic societies because their combined scores are higher than those of most other countries. However, Hofstede's empirical results examining business workers in international corporations found that the United States, Australia, and Great Britain were the most individualistic countries overall.

—Jeffery Scott Mio

See also European Americans; White Racial Identity

FURTHER READING

Hofstede, G. (1980). *Culture's consequences: International differences in work-related values.* Beverly Hills, CA: Sage.

Oyserman, D., Coon, H. M., & Kemmelmeier, M. (2002). Rethinking individualism and collectivism: Evaluation of theoretical assumptions and meta-analyses. *Psychological Bulletin, 128,* 3–72.

Triandis, H. C. (1995). *Individualism and collectivism.* Boulder, CO: Westview Press.

INSTITUTIONAL RACISM

After months of studying for the Law School Admissions Test, an African American man and a Puerto Rican woman arrive at their testing sites. At the African American man's site, the proctor directs all minority examinees to sit beside a noisy air conditioner. He lets Caucasian examinees sit on the room's quieter side. At the Puerto Rican woman's site, the proctor treats all examinees equally. Later, the man and woman are horrified to learn that their scores fell below the 145-point cutoff for admission to most law schools. Neither receives an offer from any school that year.

The proctor's individual racism at the first testing site is obvious because it conforms to the popular belief that racism entails the actions of a few bigots. However, another form of racism lurks within this story. The law school cutoff score prompts the rejection of nearly half of all African American and Puerto Rican applicants whose college grades otherwise would qualify them for admission, whereas only 20% of Caucasian students are rejected under these circumstances. Although law schools recognize standardized tests' limited ability to predict academic performance, they continue to weight test scores heavily in admissions decisions. Some schools justify the practice as an efficient processing method, but few acknowledge the real issue: institutional racism.

Institutional racism refers to the intentional or unintentional manipulation or toleration of institutional policies that unfairly restrict the opportunities of particular groups of people. Unlike individual racism, which involves the adverse behavior of one person or a small group of people, institutional racism comprises the adverse behavior of organizations or institutions. Aside from law school admissions, institutional racism appears in mental health care, the judicial system, business, politics, education, the media, and medicine. Given the insidiousness of institutional racism, individuals must understand how it permeates organizational structures, how it can be detected, and how it can be overcome. The historical background of institutional racism, its characteristics, and strategies for its elimination are outlined here.

HISTORICAL BACKGROUND

The arrival of the English colonists in North America marked the beginning of institutional racism in the United States. The colonists considered themselves superior to the Native Americans in the eyes of God and embraced a mission to "civilize" the continent's inhabitants. When Native Americans resisted these efforts, the settlers began conquering and killing them. To justify their actions, the colonists preached that the "savages" should not impede the God-willed progress of their superior civilization.

A similar rationale pervaded the country during slavery, perhaps the most blatant manifestation of institutional racism in the United States. Caucasians perceived Africans as heathens, and dominant religious, political, economic, and educational policies reinforced the ideology of Western superiority. Even after emancipation, an ideology of social Darwinism permeated Caucasians' mentality and seemed to justify oppression despite its contradiction of the values of freedom, equality, and justice, which were central to the Declaration of Independence. This philosophy dictated that stronger, more advanced civilizations would naturally prevail over weaker, inferior ones. Corollaries to social Darwinism included Manifest Destiny, which proposed that God's will mandated Anglo-Saxon control of North America, and the "White man's burden," which furthered the idea of White supremacy by suggesting that non-Caucasian populations could not function without Caucasians' care.

Today, social Darwinism continues to persist. For example, society often attributes racial inequality to minorities' supposed deficiencies rather than to the racism inherent in the Caucasian-dominated social structure. Furthermore, Caucasians often blame minorities for the disadvantages stemming from inequality, frequently denying or overlooking the racism that permeates this country's institutions.

CHARACTERISTICS OF INSTITUTIONAL RACISM

The definition of institutional racism alludes to one of the construct's most important features: its behavioral nature. Racism always comprises behaviors that result in the systematic denial of access and opportunities to members of minority groups, coupled with the perpetuation of access and opportunities to members of majority groups. Therefore, to identify institutional racism, we must pinpoint organizations' actions rather than their intentions. Indeed, institutional racism can be intentional or unintentional, overt or covert. Intentional institutional racism involves malicious intent, whereas unintentional institutional racism does not involve malfeasance. Overt or blatant institutional racism is always intentional; however, covert institutional racism is more subtle and can be either intentional or unintentional.

Unintentional institutional racism stems from organizational members' mind-sets, which stimulate their behavior. Although many people mistakenly assume that prejudice must precede racism, the real hallmark of an unintentional racist mind-set is the denial of racism. Denial allows organizations to avoid threats to their liberal self-image by refusing the possibility that

they are racist. Three factors reinforce this denial: (1) miseducation, which oversimplifies racism by dictating that prejudice must precede racist behavior; (2) dysconsciousness, which involves the uncritical acceptance and rationalization of the status quo, the avoidance of disruption to self-image, and the maintenance of White privilege; and (3) groupthink, which encourages members to preserve group harmony by viewing the group positively and uncritically. These factors operate when institutional racism is either individually meditated (i.e., stemming from the discriminatory practices of a single influential leader) or a standard of practice (i.e., encompassing long-entrenched institutional policies).

Regardless of its source, institutional racism imposes a variety of consequences on minority group members. From a temporal perspective, institutional racism may have proximal, immediate effects or distal, delayed effects. Institutional racism may inflict apparent consequences, which noticeably stem from racist behaviors, and unapparent consequences, which are harder to link to racism. Institutional racism that wreaks proximal, apparent consequences is easiest to recognize; institutional racism that triggers delayed, unapparent consequences is hardest to identify.

Although racism is behavioral, it encompasses not only what institutions do but also what they fail to do. Thus, institutional racism may fall into one of three categories: (1) no initiatives, (2) misguided initiatives, or (3) mismanaged initiatives to combat racism. The lack of organizational initiatives is the most overlooked and undocumented form of institutional racism; even if it is well-intended, inaction fuels the problem by allowing it to perpetuate. Misguided initiatives, which include measures such as inadequately funded special programs, fail because they emphasize surface problems rather than the complex structural patterns underlying racism. Finally, mismanaged initiatives are philosophically and structurally sound, but they fail because of poor management practices, including lack of commitment and inadequate delegation of tasks.

STRATEGIES FOR OVERCOMING INSTITUTIONAL RACISM

Identifying institutional racism can be challenging, but it is only half the battle. Indeed, simple knowledge of a problem falls far short of solving it. To eliminate institutional racism, organizations may employ macrosystem and microsystem interventions.

Macrosystem interventions address the way minorities should be treated and tackle problems in the social structure. One such intervention is researching minority experiences to gain a better understanding of the pertinent issues. Another macrosystem intervention is reforming an industry so that it strives for equitable service delivery, data-driven policy, well-targeted community assistance, cultural flexibility, and collaboration with other sectors. A final macrosystem intervention is providing multicultural training that accounts for trainees' learning and cultural differences, teaches skills step by step, states clear objectives, and relates to the achievement of those objectives.

Microsystem interventions address the way minorities are treated in individual settings. Institutions should develop a core ideology that embraces diversity and outlines the organization's central purpose and values. Other microsystem interventions include seeking consultation, which can yield useful advice, feedback, and instruction from an outside expert; action research, which generates local data that can help to improve service to surrounding minority communities; and affirmative action, which can help to ensure equality in the recruitment, selection, and mentoring of students and employees.

SUMMARY AND CONCLUSION

Institutional racism is a well-established feature of American society. It assumes many forms, it is always behavioral, and it can arise even when it is unintended. Although macrosystem and microsystem interventions can help to eradicate the problem, many people resist these measures because they believe that racism is no longer a problem and want to preserve the current structure of White privilege. Nevertheless, reformers must persevere in the face of this resistance by continuing the dialogue about institutional racism and working to eradicate it.

—Charles R. Ridley
—Shannon Kelly

See also Affirmative Action; Equal Opportunity Employment; Organizational Diversity

FURTHER READING

Dovidio, J. F., & Gaertner, S. L. (Eds.). (1986). *Prejudice, discrimination, and racism.* San Diego: Academic Press.

Jones, J. M. (1997). *Prejudice and racism* (2nd ed.). New York: McGraw-Hill.

Knowles, L. L., & Prewitt, K. (Eds.). (1969). *Institutional racism in America.* Englewood Cliffs, NJ: Prentice Hall.

Ridley, C. R. (2005). *Overcoming unintentional racism in counseling and therapy* (2nd ed.). Thousand Oaks, CA: Sage.

Wellman, D. T. (1977). *Portraits of White racism.* New York: Cambridge University Press.

INSTRUMENT DEVELOPMENT FOR ETHNIC MINORITY RESEARCH

Most psychological test instruments have been developed and validated only with majority group populations; therefore, their universal applicability cannot be assumed. When adapting or developing instruments for use with minority populations, construct bias must be avoided and linguistic and semantic relevance should be ensured in the preparatory phase. Psychometric properties should then be established and normative indicators derived for each group with which the instrument is to be used. Single-culture versus cross-cultural group comparisons require some different considerations.

A CONCEPTUAL MODEL TO GUIDE INSTRUMENT DEVELOPMENT

There has been a move away from the assumption that research questions and methods developed among majority groups are invariably relevant in research with ethnic minority groups. A parallel trend at the international level is reflected in the indigenous psychology movement, which offers a paradigm to guide new instrument development for use with minority groups. Indigenous psychology rejects the innocent ethnocentrism that underlies psychological research in non-Western nations. This movement questions the assumption of universal applicability of questions, constructs, and methods developed in the Western world. Instead, indigenous psychology emphasizes the development of new knowledge that is relevant to the sociocultural reality of the groups being examined. The movement was propelled by a belief that psychology is not externally imposed but develops from cultural traditions, a position that is consistent with ethnic minority research in North America. Because minority cultures are not isolated and may share many continuities with their larger culture, such an approach modifies and expands existing psychological constructs to better fit the ethnic minority cultural context.

ADOPTION, ADAPTATION, SUPPLEMENTATION, AND SUBSTITUTION

Instruments that are used with ethnic minority groups may be identical to those that already exist (adopted); they may be changed to include additional items and to exclude items that are not relevant (adapted or supplemented); or they may be created in their entirety to replace an existing test or establish a new instrument (substitution). When the constructs to be examined do not overlap at all with existing measures, new instruments must be developed. This is an uncommon situation. More often, concepts show some overlap with those in the majority culture.

For example, *guan,* a guiding structure for Chinese parenting derived from Confucian philosophy, combines some facets of parenting constructs that have been developed in work with Caucasian youth, but it is not entirely captured by the items developed to tap these constructs. Where parallels exist, careful qualitative work during the preparation stage can guide additions and accommodations to existing instruments. Such work is invaluable in the decision to adopt, adapt, substitute, or supplement existing instruments for use with ethnic minority groups.

PREPARATORY WORK

Qualitative methods in the early stages of instrument development are particularly important to protect against construct bias. Construct bias results when the items used to tap the construct are inappropriate for the group of interest. This bias is a particular danger in the adaptation of existing instruments, where manifestations of the construct to be assessed may not be equivalent in the minority and original groups. For example, parenting inventories developed with middle-class, majority-culture adolescents include the item "My parent offers to help me with my homework" as a measure of involvement. This item would not be an accurate measure of the construct of involvement in first-generation immigrant families, whose language and academic skills may not be conducive to such shared activity. Test-item composition should reflect culture-specific variations of the expression of the construct in the target group. Focus groups with participants from the culture of interest and expert panels may be more important sources of information about the culture-specific manifestation of the construct.

Preparatory work should also include consideration of administration procedures that might influence specific cultural groups differentially. For example, the use of majority-culture interviewers may influence responses to sensitive issues in minority groups. Paper-and-pencil measures that assess internal states require a certain degree of comfort and practice with introspection and self-report that cannot be assumed in some recent immigrants. Input from culturally knowledgeable informants is important to assess the appropriateness of the method planned to gather data.

Linguistic equivalence refers to the comparability of items in the original and adapted versions. Metaphors such as "feeling blue" in a depression scale, for example, may not translate well. *Forward/ backward* translation involves translation from the original into the target language, followed by an independent translation from the target into the original language. Similarity between the two versions indicates linguistic equivalence. A second procedure, the committee approach, involves a group endeavor that includes individuals with expertise relevant to different domains (e.g., linguistic and psychological) and arrives at a translation through discussion and consensus. Even when the instrument is administered in the native language, minority experts should be consulted for the comprehensibility (and relevance) of each item for the target group.

PSYCHOMETRIC PROPERTIES

Psychometric properties of adopted instruments may not match those of the original instrument. Individual items on a test—whether they are used in their original form, translated, or assembled based on face validity—may show weak loading on the intended factor in a cultural group in which they have not been previously validated. If sample size allows, structural equation modeling techniques offer more powerful methods than conventional confirmatory factor analysis techniques to examine measurement equivalence in different groups. Items may not separate as expected into the a priori factors assumed in test construction. Initial piloting of the instrument can guide the composition of the final scale. Items with low item-total correlation and weak loadings on the intended factor should be dropped because the noise they add may interfere with the sensitivity of the instrument. Therefore, it is important to generate a broad list of items that capture the construct to be assessed and to anticipate the dropping of weak items following a pilot test. In describing the psychometric properties with a new cultural group, factor loadings, the minimum loading used to retain items, and internal reliability for each subscale should be clearly reported.

When existing tests are adopted in their entirety for use with ethnic minority groups, equal meaning of specific scores in the original and target groups cannot be assumed. The use of cutoff scores in screening measures, for example, is inappropriate unless ROC (receiver operating characteristic) curves have been computed for the specific target group. Face and content validity can be ensured through the qualitative processes involving focus groups and expert consultation described previously. However, criterion and construct validity must also be demonstrated independently.

MULTIGROUP COMPARISONS

When cross-ethnic-group comparisons are of interest, the scale may have to be adapted for each group. Because the meaning of individual items and their statistical properties may be different in each different group, it can be difficult to develop forms that are equally rich but identical in their item composition for different cultural groups. Between-group comparisons require the same items for both groups. This requirement poses the dilemma that shared items with adequate loadings on a priori factors may be few, drastically reducing the length of the scale and resulting in construct underrepresentation (insufficient sampling of the different domains that contribute to a construct). However, careful preparatory work, together with the combination of culture-general items for both groups and culture-specific items for each group, can yield rich insights regarding shared and specific processes.

—*Sunita Mahtani Stewart*

See also Acculturation Scales; Ethnic Identity Development; Ethnic Identity Development Measures; Measures of Racial Prejudice; Qualitative Research

FURTHER READING

Byrne, B., Stewart, S. M., & Lee, P. W. H. Validating the Beck Depression Inventory–II for Hong Kong community adolescents. *International Journal of Testing, 4,* 199–216.

Greenfield, P. (1997). You can't take it with you: Why ability assessments don't cross cultures. *American Psychologist, 52,* 1115–1124.

Matías-Carrelo, L. E., Chávez, L. M., Negron, G., Canino, G., Aguilar-Gaixola, S., & Hoppe, S. (2003). The Spanish translation and cultural adaptation of five mental health outcome measures. *Culture, Medicine and Psychiatry, 27,* 291–313.

Sinha, D. (1997). Indigenizing psychology. In J. W. Berry, Y. H. Poortinga, & J. Pandey (Eds.), *Handbook of cross-cultural psychology: Vol. 1. Theory and method* (2nd ed., pp. 129–170). Boston: Allyn & Bacon.

Stewart, S. M., & Bond, M. H. (2002). A critical look at mainstream parenting research: Problems uncovered while adapting Western research to nonwestern cultures. *British Journal of Developmental Psychology, 20,* 379–392.

van de Vijver, F. (2001). The evolution of cross-cultural methods. In D. Matsumoto (Ed.), *The handbook of culture and psychology* (pp. 77–97). New York: Oxford University Press.

INTELLIGENCE TESTS

Tests of human intelligence are designed to provide an estimate of an individual's or a group's ability to perform cognitive tasks. Intelligence tests produce an intelligence quotient (IQ) score and are generally intended to measure several related cognitive functions. Intelligence tests are generally created using current definitions of intelligence, which tend to emphasize the ability to adjust to the environment, the ability to learn, and the ability to think abstractly. Over time, the definition of intelligence has expanded to include survey measures of skills such as adaptation to the environment, basic mental processes, and higher-order thinking (i.e., reasoning and problem solving). As the definition of intelligence has changed, so have the methods for measuring intelligence. Whereas early testing focused on comparisons between chronological age and mental age, current methods appreciate biological and environmental factors in the development and expression of intelligence and often include a norm-referenced comparison group for computing scores. When scores are computed, they are compared with a norming or standardization sample to determine how an individual compares with others in the same age-group.

Intelligence tests comprise multiple subtests that are combined to produce composite scores of various dimensions of intelligence. For example, tasks measuring one's fund of available information, verbal comprehension, and reasoning are combined with other tasks to create a composite score of verbal intelligence. The majority of IQ tests produce overall or composite scores indicating verbal and performance (nonverbal) intelligence. Composite scores are generated by converting the raw scores from the subtests into scaled scores (average range 7–13). Generally, a score of

85 to 100 on any composite score indicates intelligence in the average range. Composite scores are generally combined to create an overall IQ score. However, critics have argued against the use of standard intelligence tests with populations of color because of problems with the way the measures are created and used.

Early research documented that people of color tended to score significantly lower on IQ tests than Caucasian people; in the most controversial turn, this finding was interpreted as indicating inherited intellectual inferiority among people of color. However, researchers were quick to point out that the debilitating effects of unequal socialization experiences within and between people of color may account for the discrepancies in scores. As a result, critics have questioned the use of standard IQ tests to accurately measure the intellect or cognitive potential of people of color.

Another concern was the way the test scores of people of color were used—namely, to make educational and employment decisions. Fundamental to this concern was the notion that differences in test scores reflect fundamental differences in intelligence, and special placement was needed to meet these underlying differences. Critics, however, questioned the legitimacy of this assumption, noting that judgments about ability often parallel ethnic and economic differences. They argued that low-income children of color, for example, were more likely than their Caucasian peers to be judged as low in ability and therefore placed in remedial classes or special education programs. Research suggests that placement in special education may contribute to performance disparities.

In 1970, the Association for Black Psychologists summed up these arguments by stating that IQ tests label African American children as uneducable, provide them with potentially inferior education, deny them educational opportunities, and limit their intellectual growth and development. Over the past three decades, the creators of intelligence tests have strived to answer these criticisms and develop measures that best meet the needs of all people. Furthermore, training programs that teach IQ tests now mandate that all training include information on the limits of intervention and assessment in populations of color.

For example, to be more culturally consistent, recent updates to standard measures of intelligence have focused on including culture-free item content, placing fewer verbal demands on the respondent, and fewer timed tasks. Some of the more popular IQ tests have been developed in languages other than English for individuals who are not native speakers of English. Over the last few decades, efforts have been made to create a comparison sample with similar demographics to recent U.S. Census data. Although people of color remain the minority, the idea is to minimize comparisons to a Caucasian-only sample and instead include more people of color in the standardization group. Although the designers of IQ measures are careful to match their comparison samples to U.S. Census data, the authors do not suggest that IQ tests are necessarily sensitive to ethnic differences.

EXAMPLES OF COMMON IQ TESTS

Of the measures currently in use, the Wechsler Intelligence Scales are by far the most popular. The Wechsler system includes the Wechsler Preschool and Primary Scale of Intelligence, the Wechsler Intelligence Scale for Children, and the Wechsler Adult Intelligence Scale.

Wechsler Preschool and Primary Scale of Intelligence

In 1967, the Wechsler Preschool and Primary Scale of Intelligence (WPPSI) was published for use with children between the ages of 4 and 6½ years. It was designed as a comprehensive measure of cognitive ability for preschoolers. It is appropriate for assessment of general intellectual functioning and can be used as a part of an assessment to identify giftedness, delays, or mental retardation. The results are useful in guiding clinical or school-related placements.

Throughout the last several decades, the WPPSI has been revised twice; the WPPSI-III is the most recent version of this measure. The WPPSI-III includes an extended age range (2.6–7.3 years old), updated norms, new subtests, and composite scores and claims to have a developmentally appropriate structure that is based on contemporary intelligence and cognitive development theory. The WPPSI-III does not require reading or writing. Verbal subtests include oral questions without time limits. Performance subtests are nonverbal (both spatial and fluid reasoning) problems, several of which are timed. Research on the reliability and validity of the scores generated by the WPPSI-III suggest that this measure is psychometrically sound. The normative sample included 1,700 children in nine age-groups. The sample was representative of the U.S. population of children aged 2.6 to 7.3 years for gender, ethnicity, parental education level, and geographic region.

Wechsler Intelligence Scale for Children

The Wechsler Intelligence Scale for Children (WISC), now in its fourth edition, provides subtest and composite scores representing intellectual functioning in general and specific cognitive abilities for children ages 6.0 to 16.11 years. The changes in the WISC-IV reflect current research on cognitive development, intellectual assessment, and cognitive processes. The revisions also include updated norms and additional subtests and emphasize scores reflecting discrete areas of cognitive functioning.

Instead of verbal and performance IQ composite scores, the WISC-IV comprises the Verbal Comprehension Index, which is composed of three subtests that are mostly verbal; the Perceptual Reasoning Index, which includes three subtests that rely less on verbal skills; the Working Memory Index, which consists of items that require recall and repetition of letters and numbers; and the Processing Speed Index, which uses nonverbal, timed search and coding tests.

The reliability of subtest scores has improved compared with previous versions of this measure. Overall, the research on this measure shows that the composite scores or index scores demonstrate good reliability and validity. One of the goals of the newest version was to update the norms to be more representative of children in the United States. The normative sample included 2,200 children ages 6.0 to 16.11 years and additional samples from special groups. The sample was stratified on demographic variables of age, gender, ethnicity, parent education level, and geographic region based on U.S. Census data from 2000.

Like the WPPSI, the WISC-IV is an appropriate instrument for practitioners and clinical researchers to assess children's intelligence and general cognitive functioning. When used with other assessment tools, it is useful in identifying giftedness, mental retardation, and cognitive strengths and weaknesses. The test results are also useful in treatment planning, placement, and provision of clinical or educational services, and they can add important information to neuropsychological evaluations.

Wechsler Adult Intelligence Scale

The most recent version of the Wechsler Adult Intelligence Scale (WAIS), the third edition, can be used for understanding learning disabilities, identifying attention-deficit/hyperactivity disorder, assessing mental retardation, and interpreting age-related differences in ability, such as age trends in working memory and intelligence. The WAIS-III is a modern version of an earlier measure, the WAIS-Revised. The new version includes updated norms for individuals ages 16 to 89 years. Some items have been modified, and there is greater discrimination for individuals in the mild to moderate mental retardation range (new items were added to make these categories easier to detect). The artwork has been updated, but it has been criticized as being distracting, too detailed, and unfair to color-blind individuals. There is less emphasis on timed performance in the latest version, and the changes appear to strengthen the theoretical basis and statistical linkage to other measures of achievement and cognitive functioning.

Fourteen subtests make up the Verbal and Performance Scales (seven subtests each); however, three of the subtests are optional. Eleven subtests are used to compute the IQ scores. Like the WISC-IV, there are four index scores measuring verbal comprehension, perceptual organization, working memory, and processing speed. Like the other Wechsler tests, the research on the reliability and validity of this measure indicates that it is psychometrically sound. The normative sample was stratified for many key variables and found to be consistent with the latest Census data. Oversampling was done for research on educational level and cognitive abilities and to determine whether the items could be biased for African American and Hispanic American individuals.

Stanford-Binet

The Stanford-Binet (SB) test, now in its fifth edition, includes features of earlier editions with recent improvements in psychometric design. The SB5 can be used to determine mental retardation, learning disabilities, developmental cognitive delays in young children, and placement in gifted programs. The measure is intended for use with individuals ages 2 to 85 years and designed to measure behavior at every age. The items can be customized to cognitive level, resulting in greater precision in measurement. The fifth edition maintains many of the same subtests and items of previous editions, and includes a global *g* or intelligence factor. Some of the artwork and content has been updated in the most recent version. The SB5 now comprises five factors or composite scores measuring fluid reasoning, knowledge, quantitative reasoning, visual-spatial processing, and working memory (the previous version contained only four). Several of the subtests use toys in the administration and measurement of intelligence, a method that appears to be helpful with early childhood assessment. Unique to the SB5 is the use of a nonverbal mode of testing covering all five cognitive factors. The range of the scales has been extended to more accurately measure both higher and lower areas of functioning.

As in the Wechsler series tests, raw scores from the subtests are converted into scaled scores. The scaled scores are summed for nonverbal, verbal, and full-scale IQ and for the five factor index scores. Research on the reliability and validity of the SB5 indicates good, reliable performance of the scores and high correlations with other measures of intelligence. The norming sample consisted of 4,800 participants ages 2 to 85 years. The authors made efforts to ensure that the sample was representative of U.S. Census data from 2000 and stratified by age, ethnicity, geographic region, and socioeconomic level.

Kaufman Assessment Battery for Children

The Kaufman Assessment Battery for Children (K-ABC) is another clinical instrument for assessing cognitive development. Its construction incorporates several recent developments in psychological theory and statistical methodology. The K-ABC gives special attention to certain emerging testing needs, such as use with handicapped groups, application to learning disabilities, and appropriateness for cultural and linguistic minorities. The authors rightly caution, however, that success in meeting these special needs must be judged through practical use over time. They also point out that the K-ABC should be supplemented by other instruments, such as the Stanford-Binet or the Wechsler scales, to meet individual needs.

The 16 subtests are grouped into a mental processing set and an achievement set, which yield separate global scores. The mental processing set is then grouped into subtests requiring primarily sequential processing of information and those requiring simultaneous processing, with separate global scores for each. The validity and reliability of this measure is quite good. Norms for the battery are based on administration of the tests to representative samples of 100 children at each six-month age interval from 2.5 years to 12.5 years, a total

of 2,000 individuals. A variety of supplementary norms are provided, some requiring the testing of additional subjects. Sociocultural norms are provided based on a comparison by ethnicity (i.e., African American and Caucasian) and by parental education (i.e., less than high school education, high school graduate, and one or more years of college or technical school).

Kaufman Adolescent and Adult Intelligence Test

The Kaufman Adolescent and Adult Intelligence Test (KAIT) is considered an alternative to the Wechsler scales as a measure of general intellectual functioning for individuals ages 11 to 85 years. It has also demonstrated potential for making diagnoses of learning disabilities and other cognitive delays. The KAIT is an individually administered intelligence test battery composed of three intelligence scales measuring fluid, crystallized, and composite intelligence. The tests for the fluid scale include paired-associative learning, deductive reasoning, and a test of both inductive and deductive reasoning. The tests for the crystallized scale contain measures of lexical knowledge and listening ability. They require synthesis and integration and memory for meaningful material. In addition to the six core battery subtests, the expanded battery contains an alternate test for the fluid score that involves visual memory, analysis and synthesis and an alternate test for the crystallized score assessing general factual knowledge, long-term retrieval and integration of facts, and immediate and delayed memories.

All KAIT subtests were constructed following Piaget's stage of formal operations and Luria and Golden's conception of planning ability. The 10 items on the Mental Status Subtest are designed to assess attention and orientation in time and space, and performance is classified as average, below average, or lower extreme. The lower extreme category is subdivided into mild, moderate, and severe deficit; for individuals in this range, the Kaufmans suggest administration of the Famous Faces Subtest only.

Research has demonstrated adequate reliability and validity performance for the KAIT. The normative sample included 2,000 individuals ages 11 to 85 years, spanning 13 age levels with at least 125 individuals at each level. The sample was representative of the U.S. population for gender, socioeconomic status (examinee or parental education levels), and ethnic group.

Although this review has touched on some of the most commonly used IQ tests, many other instruments are available. Some alternative measures place less verbal demand on the examinee and can be used with individuals with physical handicaps (e.g., deafness, blindness). Moreover, several short IQ measures are available (e.g., Kaufman Brief Intelligence Test–II) that allow for a 10- to 15-minute administration and strong correlation of scores with the longer, standard versions of IQ tests (2 hours or more). Despite the abundance of IQ tests, critics of these measures apply their concern across the field of IQ testing, identifying no particular test as meeting the issues raised by their concerns. The range of arguments regarding the creation and use of IQ testing is as varied as the tests themselves.

INTELLIGENCE TESTING AND PEOPLE OF COLOR

Many arguments have been raised regarding the reasonable use of IQ tests with people of color. These concerns address both the design of the tests and the practical application of the tests with ethnic minority populations. That is, a test may be valid for a specific purpose, but if the test results are interpreted or used incorrectly, the decision based on the results may be biased. Researchers and scholars have asserted in both benign and controversial terms that IQ tests demonstrate bias because they tend to show that people of color score lower than Caucasian individuals and therefore are less intelligent than their Caucasian counterparts. Part of the concern lies in the fundamental criteria on which many IQ tests are created and used. That is, IQ tests tap cognitive processes and underlying intellectual behavior, the tests include tasks that measure these attributes, and the tasks reflect prior experience. When applied to people of color, these criteria produce potential problems regarding the validity and utility of comparisons between people of color and Caucasians in the United States.

Theorists have assumed that intelligence is made up of two constructs, a general g factor and a number of specific skills. Other researchers have suggested that intelligence is made up of multiple components. Without an agreement on what intelligence is, measuring the construct of intelligence and creating valid interpretations of the results are compromised when making comparisons between and within groups. The lack of theoretical consensus has led some to argue that IQ tests reflect the cultural orientation of the test creator, creating a bias when applied to people from other cultural groups.

The issue, then, is fairness, in addition to the long-standing concern that overall, IQ tests are culturally biased. For example, the creators of IQ tests tend to include item content that is not relevant to the life experiences of people of color and instead is written with attention to the common values and experiences of Caucasian individuals. Moreover, the content in the tests does not necessarily mean the same thing to individuals from different cultural groups, and items on IQ tests do not necessarily measure the same constructs or abilities.

Most of this concern rests on findings that children of color tend to display lower scores on common measures of intelligence than Caucasian children. When differences are found, factors such as educational opportunities and social disparities between groups are not considered. Most authors suggest that it is these environmental factors—not dispositional differences between Caucasian and ethnic minority children—that account for these differences. So far, research has yet to demonstrate any systematic or statistical bias in the content of recent IQ tests. However, research on how the tests are used demonstrates more support for the cultural bias contention. For example, when IQ tests are administered in English, individuals who are linguistically diverse or whose primary language is not English, tend to have lower IQ scores, especially lower verbal IQ scores, than those who are native English speakers. Generally, it is recommended that verbal tests of IQ should never be used alone to estimate a person's level of cognitive skill when English is not his or her primary language.

Another concern raised by critics is that IQ tests are based on norm samples that are inappropriate for people of color. The idea of pluralistic norms, whereby individuals are compared only with other members of their cultural or ethnic group (i.e., separate norms for Hispanic Americans, African Americans), is one alternative. It is possible, however, that the use of pluralistic norms may create bias between groups and lower expectations of culturally and linguistically diverse individuals. It also does not aid in the assessment of biracial or multicultural individuals. Although this idea has yet to gain wide-ranging support, test designers have made considerable efforts to create comparison samples that are consistent with the U.S. population in general.

The idea is that national norms allow for comparison of the examinee to the population as a whole. Examiners are encouraged to be mindful of the nature of the norming sample in any IQ test before making conclusions about the performance of a person of color. Furthermore, when IQ tests are based on the assumption that the scores reflect not only cognitive processes but also acquired knowledge from life experience, cultural differences between and within groups make the use of unequal standardization groups more troubling. That is, standardized tests assume that prior experience with given intellectual tasks is similar across cultural groups. However, research shows that life experience varies greatly among cultural groups. Moreover, inequity exists between people of color and Caucasian groups in the distribution of educational opportunities, especially for individuals from lower socioeconomic backgrounds. Therefore, grouping individuals by age (the practice for most IQ tests) for the purposes of comparison to peer groups may not be sufficient.

Critics also suggest that people of color and linguistically diverse individuals may feel uncomfortable taking traditional IQ tests because they may have little or no exposure to this kind of interaction and may have poorer test-taking skills than their Caucasian peers. For example, culturally and linguistically diverse individuals may differ in motivation, test practice, interpretation of the meaning of the results, and exposure to other cultures. Western culture tends to value achievement and problem solving, but culturally and linguistically diverse children may fail to appreciate the demand in the test situation for high achievement. Although there is research to support the notion that children of color may have limited test-taking skills, it is not clear what impact this has on their overall scores.

The next concern has to do with the rapport or relationship between the examinee and examiner. Having good rapport is crucial for producing accurate test results. Because the majority of psychologists are Caucasian, research suggests that there is a high probability that the examinee and examiner will have different cultural backgrounds. Cultural differences may cause the examiner to misinterpret the test behavior and response style of an examinee who is unfamiliar with the examiner's culture or customs. Although examiners want to get the best performance from the individuals they test, it is possible that cultural confusion or lack of knowledge of another culture may influence their rapport with the examinee, therefore hampering the examinee's performance. This is especially problematic when the examiner is a native English speaker and the examinee is not because the likelihood of miscommunication is heightened. Although research has not documented that Caucasian examiners working with examinees of color impair the test performance of the examinees, all examiners should be cognizant of the potential for misunderstanding and inaccurate conclusions when interpreting the behavior of someone from a different culture.

Finally, some are concerned because the results of IQ tests have a significant impact on the disproportional placement of children of color in special education classrooms. That is, the results of IQ tests are used to place children of color in classrooms that limit their ability and potential to achieve in school. Similarly, critics argue that IQ scores create lower expectations for children of color in the classroom; therefore, these children perform at a lower level, creating a self-fulfilling prophecy.

CONCLUSION

Intelligence tests are an important facet of psychological assessment and represent early efforts to quantify behavior. Research on IQ tests has improved, and many of the commonly used measures are being revised to improve their utility for people of color. It is important to consider, however, some guidelines in the applicability of these measures with culturally and linguistically diverse groups.

To ensure that IQ test results represent the individual's true cognitive abilities, test creators and users need to consider several factors. First, the acculturation level of the examinee has a significant influence on the accuracy of the interpretation of behavior and results. That is, people of color represent many different groups and many within-group differences; therefore, examiners and test creators should have a mechanism for assessing the degree to which the examinee is a more or less traditional member of his or her culture of origin.

Second, the primary language of the examinee is crucial in producing precise IQ test scores. When an alternative form of the test is not available (i.e., it is not produced in a language other than English), the examiner may refer the examinee to a native speaker of the examinee's language for assessment.

Third, the examinee's history of test taking should be evaluated and current test-taking skills assessed. Fourth, the examiner should address the client's culture (when it is different from his or her own) to determine how different cultural beliefs and values may influence test performance. The examiner must also ensure that proper rapport is established with the examinee to promote the examinee's best performance. The examiner should explore the examinee's needs and motivations during testing and his or her perspective on mental health and illness to establish his or her expectations for the assessment. Test developers and users need to remember to contextualize their assessment and evaluate the significance of environmental and social differences for people of color. It is important to see examinees as embedded in their family and culture—as diverse and complex beings—and to require the examinee to have bicultural competence. Examinees are encouraged to interpret test scores cautiously. That is, IQ test scores may tell how well examinees do but not why they perform as they do. Therefore, the test score information is incomplete. Because test scores and test creators are not perfect, there is always a degree of error in the IQ score; that is, the observed score may differ from the individual's true score. Many examiners, however, use test scores as though they were free from error, and this leads to misinterpretation.

It is important that examiners check the items of any IQ test for relevant content and possible misinterpretation. Examiners must be vigilant in checking the standardization sample and altering their conclusions to fit the group from which the scores are compared. If the examinee possesses different social and demographic characteristics than the comparison group, the examiner should include a relevant focus on the influence of education level differences and socioeconomic status in the IQ test results.

Finally, when the examinee demonstrates differences in test-taking skills, the examiner should assess his or her experience with testing and include a focus on the possible impact on scores in their interpretation of behavioral observations. Finally, examiners and test developers should be clear about their limitations regarding culture and consult with experts to increase their understanding of the impact of culture and language on test performance.

—*Yo Jackson*

See also *The Bell Curve*; Education; Scholastic Assessment Test

FURTHER READING

Aby, S. H. (1990). *The IQ debate: A selective guide to the literature.* New York: Greenwood Press.

Blackwell, T. L., & Madere, L. N. (2005). Test review of the Slosson Intelligence Test–Revised. *Rehabilitation Counseling Bulletin, 48,* 183–184.

Canivez, G. L., Neitel, R., & Martin, B. E. (2005). Construct validity of the Kaufman Brief Intelligence Test, Wechsler Intelligence Scale for Children–Third Edition and Adjustment Scales for Children and Adolescents. *Journal of Psychoeducational Assessment, 23,* 15–34.

Caruso, J. C., & Jacob-Timm, S. (2001). Confirmatory factor analysis of the Kaufman Adolescent and Adult Intelligence Test with young adolescents. *Assessment, 8,* 11–17.

Flanagan, D. P., & Kaufman, A. S. (2001). *Essentials of WISC-IV assessment.* Hoboken, NJ: Wiley.

Kaufman, A. S., & Lichtenberger, E. O. (1999). *Essentials of WAIS-III assessment.* New York: Wiley.

Lichtenberger, E. O., & Kaufman, A. S. (2003). *Essentials of WPPSI-III assessment.* Hoboken, NJ: New York.

MacKintosh, N. J. (1998). *IQ and human intelligence.* Oxford, UK: Oxford University Press.

McGrew, K. S., & Flanagan, D. P. (1998). *The intelligence test desk reference (ITDR): GF-GC cross assessment battery.* Boston: Allyn & Bacon.

Richardson, K. (2002). What IQ tests test. *Theory and Psychology, 12,* 283–314.

Sattler, J. M. (2001). *Assessment of children: Cognitive applications* (4th ed.). San Diego: Sattler.

Stenberg, R. J. (2000). *Handbook of intelligence.* Cambridge, UK: Cambridge University Press.

Te-Nijenhuis, J., Tolboom, E., Resing, W., & Bleichrodt, N. (2004). Does cultural background influence the intellectual performance of children from immigrant groups? The RAKIT Intelligence Test for immigrant children. *European Journal of Psychological Assessment, 20,* 10–26.

Valencia, R. R. (2000). *Intelligence testing and minority students: Foundation, performance factors, and assessment issues.* Thousand Oaks, CA: Sage.

INTERGROUP RELATIONS

Research on intergroup relations involves the study of two main topics: (1) social behaviors and processes such as conflict, cooperation, discrimination, inclusion, and exclusion, and (2) cognitions such as stereotyping and attitude formation. Understanding intergroup relations can reveal how biases, stereotypes, and group conflicts arise as well as how they can be reduced. This is important to ethnic minority psychology because disagreement, distancing, and aggression frequently occur between different ethnic groups. Applying our understanding of group relations and processes can help to foster social harmony and reduce racism and ethnocentrism.

DEFINITIONS

The term *intergroup relations* refers to conflicts and connections between two groups, whereas *intragroup relations* refers to conflicts and connections among people of the same social identity group. A person is considered part of an in-group when he or she is a member of a social identity group composed of people with similar characteristics and experiences. An out-group is a social group that is outside one's in-group and generally assumed to possess characteristics and experiences that are different from those of the in-group.

HISTORY OF THE STUDY OF INTERGROUP RELATIONS

The psychological study of intergroup relations flourished during the decades following World War II, when social scientists sought to advance the understanding of racism and segregation. This period was exceptionally rife with social discord, evidenced by anticommunist invectives in the United States (the Red Scare), anti-Japanese sentiment and Japanese American internment, Nazism and the Holocaust, and stifled race relations. Social psychologists in particular were interested in why ethnic group conflicts incite individuals to perform hostile and cruel acts toward members of out-groups; their efforts focused on understanding how in-group biases and negative attitudes toward out-groups are formed. Early studies on group dynamics considered the size and structure of groups, characteristics of group leaders, and the amount and quality of interaction among group members.

One significant theory to emerge from these attempts to understand intergroup conflicts was Gordon W. Allport's *contact hypothesis,* which posited that intergroup relations could be improved by increasing intergroup contact, encouraging cooperation and equal status of group members, and reducing the support of authority figures. Allport argued that all people have stereotypes about other groups, but people who maintain their prejudices tend to blame out-groups for social problems, use group differences to reject members of the out-group, and do not tolerate ambiguity.

Intergroup relations are often strained by the realities or perceptions of sociohistorical problems—for example, conflict over rights to existing resources, as in the case of the Arabs' and Jews' perspectives on Israel.

Research has shown, however, that even in the absence of an external threat to resources, the mere inclusion and identification with a group can foster hostility and bias toward an out-group. The landmark Robber's Cave study by Muzafer Sherif and others examined in-group formation and attitudes toward out-groups. In the experiment, boys from similar backgrounds were brought to a campsite and randomly assigned to two separate groups. As each group bonded and became aware of the other, in-group cohesion developed, which led to competitive feelings toward the out-group. The researchers noted an escalation in intergroup hostilities, such as name-calling, derogatory songs, and discriminative taunts and threats, as well as increased feelings of in-group favoritism, pride, and superiority. Later, the groups were told that vandals had prevented the camp water supply from being distributed properly. When this superordinate goal was presented, members from both groups cooperated to solve the problem, thus reducing intergroup conflict. Positive behaviors resulted, such as sharing the water supply and rejoicing over a deed well done. This experiment showed that group identity and cohesion can foster biased feelings toward one's in-group and negative attitudes and reactions toward members of the out-group; however, intergroup relations can be improved by facilitating goals and connectivity between members of different groups.

THEORIES OF INTERGROUP RELATIONS

The most popular model for understanding intergroup relations is *social identity theory.* Tajfel and Turner's model explains intergroup relations on the basis of four individual processes: (1) individuals categorize others to derive their own self-concept (social categorization); (2) individuals seek to achieve positive values related to their social identity (social identity); (3) individuals evaluate this identity by comparing themselves with members of other groups (social comparison); and (4) individuals desire uniqueness and higher status in comparison with other groups (positive distinctiveness). Studies in which participants categorized faces from different racial backgrounds yielded findings suggesting that people from a racial in-group assume higher status and favoritism for their group and lower status for members of a racial out-group. This theory may explain findings on out-group derogation and discrimination, perceptions of attractiveness, and the self-protective function of prejudice.

Realistic conflict theory has origins in William Sumner's sociological understanding of ethnocentrism and group competition. This theory assumes that individuals are motivated to obtain rewards for themselves and that intergroup conflict arises from incompatible group interests. This theory suggests that the resource or reward, such as equitable education, land, or water supply, causes groups to want to maintain their own economic interests. Proponents of this theory are interested in conflict resolution; for example, this theory has been used to develop United Nations strategies to prevent war between economic superpowers and to promote understanding of controversial topics such as war and segregation policies. This theory has also been used to understand conflicts between African American residents and Asian American business owners in low-income communities where few economic resources exist.

The *equity theory of intergroup relations,* put forth by Elaine Walster and colleagues, suggests that although individuals seek to maximize personal rewards, if the ratio of effort applied to achieve an outcome is perceived to be unjust or inequitable compared with the effort required of another group, poor relations may result. Equity theorists often strategize to achieve social justice by applying mathematical and economic models to predict, for example, how much money or how many votes are needed to effect social change. Other proponents of this theory draw on the experiences of the minority perspective, whereby individuals from disadvantaged and underrepresented groups feel that social resources are unequal or unjustly distributed. This theory has been used to explain why Asian Americans tend to vote in lesser numbers—there is a common perception in that community that voting does very little because of the history of anti-Asian politics in the United States—and why African Americans, many of whom have long suffered from classism, tend to vote for candidates whose policies redistribute wealth.

Social dominance theory, proposed by Jim Sidanius, draws from political science and sociology to suggest that specific forms of intergroup conflict (e.g., racism, classism, sexism) result from the formation of hierarchies within a society that develop from a basic human need to construct groups based on a particular social identity. This theory explains intergroup conflict as a result of disproportionate power in favor of men, adults, and what the authors call "arbitrary sets," or social constructions of group membership based on race, ethnicity, or region.

RESOLVING INTERGROUP CONFLICT

Efforts to reduce intergroup conflict are evident in person perception studies and training modules that encourage intergroup communication. Social cognition and person perception studies attend to attributions and stereotypes and the processes of interpersonal cues and characteristics; these studies recommend reevaluating group norms and values to reduce intergroup differences. Models of social justice often incorporate an understanding of individual and group-level privileges and oppression. These models stress collective action, community building, and greater consciousness of social identities and power relations, often achieved by applying the contact hypothesis in a structured setting. Educational programming on college campuses, such as intergroup dialogues, residence hall community sharing, faith- or morals-based discussions, studies on racial climate, and experiential learning and interpersonal sensitivity training, have been shown to effectively reduce stereotyping and bias and increase conditions for positive contact and behaviors. Workplace training on cultural sensitivity and norm setting also help to reduce intergroup conflict. Finally, public policy can be influenced by applying our understanding of intergroup relations. Psychologist Kenneth Clark, for example, provided testimony in the *Brown v. Board of Education of Topeka, Kansas* case to support the idea that segregation had negative effects on African American children, such as feelings of inferiority and in-group resentment. Psychologist Susan Fiske provided favorable testimony in the *Price Waterhouse v. Hopkins* case regarding the negative effects of intergroup stereotypes on gender-based experiences of workplace climate.

—*Matthew R. Lee*
—*Sumie Okazaki*

FURTHER READING

Allport, G. W. (1954). *The nature of prejudice.* Reading, MA: Addison-Wesley.

Billig, M. G. (1976). *Social psychology and intergroup relations.* London: Academic Press.

Sherif, M., Harvey, O. J., White, B. J., Hood, W. E., & Sherif, C. W. (1961). *Intergroup conflict and cooperation: The Robbers Cave experiment.* Norman, OK: Institute of Group Relations.

Sidanius, J., & Pratto, F. (1999). *Social dominance: An intergroup theory of social hierarchy and oppression.* New York: Cambridge University Press.

Tajfel, H., & Turner, J. (1986). The social identity theory of intergroup behavior. In S. Worchel & W. G. Austin (Eds.), *Psychology of intergroup relations* (2nd ed., pp. 7–24). Chicago: Nelson-Hall.

Walster, E., Walster, G. W., & Berscheid, E. (1978). *Equity: Theory and research.* Boston: Allyn & Bacon.

INTERNALIZED RACISM

Internalized racism has historically been described in reference to the African American experience. Over time, the term has developed a broader meaning that encompasses the experience of other oppressed persons of color. Current psychological literature describes internalized racism in reference to many groups, including Native Americans, Asian Americans, indigenous peoples of Mexico, and others who incorporate into their thoughts and behaviors the oppressors' views of them, including negative attitudes, prejudiced beliefs, stereotypes, values, perspectives, and notions of racial superiority.

Internalized racism results from insidious institutional and social presumptions that those of Western European origin—who often live in safer neighborhoods, attend better schools, enjoy more lucrative job opportunities, and earn higher incomes—are superior because of their inherited predisposition and personal effort, whereas people of color—who often live in unsafe neighborhoods, attend underachieving schools, have fewer educational opportunities, and work in lower-wage jobs—are inferior because of genetic predisposition and insufficient effort.

Persons of color who internalize these racist beliefs begin to accept negative stereotypes about their ability and worth. Limitations in aspirations, goals, and freedom to define the self are accepted, along with the belief that those benefiting from unearned privilege are, in fact, superior in fundamental biological ways. In the same way that racism permeates every aspect of our society, internalized racism works its way into the fabric of the self and manifests initially as a preference for light skin, straight hair, and Western values of individualism, competition, materialism, and youthfulness. Many people of color who espouse these preferences may be unaware that their preferences are the result of oppression. Denial and unawareness of the characteristics and etiology of internalized racism make exploration of this complicated issue difficult, painful, and sometimes shaming.

Devaluing of the self and others of the same racial group results in passive, inwardly directed symptoms of resignation, helplessness, and hopelessness and may progress to more active and outwardly directed behaviors, such as mocking one's ethnic group, adopting racial slurs to describe one's self and others, rejecting one's cultural heritage (foods, traditions, and values), and demonstrating hostility toward others of one's race (evidenced by high murder rates and other crimes in communities of color). In the process of devaluing one's self and others, internalized racism leads individuals to become isolated from communities of color. Isolation, in turn, thwarts collective action to rectify long-standing inequalities and discrimination that are deeply rooted in societal norms, beliefs, and behaviors.

Internalized racism may be transmitted from generation to generation through parents' belief in their own worthlessness and the worthlessness of their people relative to the dominant society. Even young children whose families attempt to inculcate them against the loss of self-worth are nonetheless able to perceive their unequal status compared with the light-skinned children of families of European origin whom they encounter in life and in the media. Thus, youth of color, despite their parents' efforts to the contrary, may develop a deep sense of worthlessness by virtue of belonging to a marginalized group that is clearly not valued by those in power.

Internalized racism is believed to contribute to a pervasive sense of alienation from the self (personal identity), others (family and group), other race groups, culture and history, and human potential and self-determination. For African Americans, internalized racism may be conceptualized as contributing to four types of conditions: (1) *alien-self disorder* involves the rejection of one's heritage, denial that racism exists, and attempts to take on the worldview of the dominant society; (2) *anti-self disorder* is a manifestation of alien-self disorder with additional hostility toward everything related to African culture; (3) *self-destructive disorder* results from the fruitless and inherently self-harming effects of trying to adjust oneself to living within an oppressive system; (4) *organic disorder* describes the physiological impact of living with inequality of opportunities, poor nutrition, substandard schooling and housing, and other oppressive conditions. The term *cultural misorientation* refers to alienation from natural African cultural realities and encompasses all of the symptoms of these four disorders of the self.

For healing to occur, internalized racism must be externalized and recognized as one of the most lethal effects of racism. Consistent with the views of liberation psychology, efforts to heal internalized racism must be directed at the causes of oppression, with the goal of collective liberty. Changing the oppressive society and changing the perceptions of self and culture that have been instilled by the dominant society takes place through community education about the effects of racial supremacy on the oppressed and on the oppressors. Psychoeducation must also include awareness training about how the consequences of living under oppression have been attributed to personal or racial weakness (blighted achievement, poverty, health problems, etc.). Members of oppressed groups must learn about historical perceptions of strengths and wellness valued by their traditional culture, and they must begin to live by healthy standards, values, spiritual rituals, and beliefs of their own rather than by Western European values. Support and resources must be directed toward community projects and businesses that reflect traditional values such as collectivism, reciprocity, rhythm, interdependence with nature, equilibrium, and respect for elders.

Other aids to the process of externalizing racism are individual, family, and group therapy. This can be done in a variety of ways that are consistent with liberation psychology's focus on collective action. For example, individuals can form small groups or "sanctuaries" where they feel safe to collectively discuss and address the internal and external effects of racism.

Narrative therapy, in particular, has been used to assist individuals in exploring personal stories (unexamined values, assumptions, and beliefs) in which unspoken aspects of internalized racism can be brought into awareness and evaluated by the individual. Experiences and patterns of thinking and behaving that are exceptions to the individual's experiences of negative social conditioning are highlighted. Problems are externalized in a way that allows the person to understand that his or her problems are based on racism rather than personal or culture-group deficiencies. The individual is then encouraged to reauthor his or her life story in a way that moves the locus of responsibility from internal causes (race, level of effort) to external causes (effects of oppression and racism). He or she is then able to use personal, familial, and group resources to challenge racism and to become empowered to work more effectively to solve problems and engage in collective action to achieve societal change.

—Y. Evie Garcia
—Annel Esparza

See also Model of Second Culture Acquisition; Racism

FURTHER READING

Comas-Diaz, L., Lykes, M. B., & Alarcon, R. D. (1998). Ethnic conflict and the psychology of liberation in Guatemala, Peru, and Puerto Rico. *American Psychologist, 53,* 778–792.

Jones, C. P. (2000). Levels of racism: A theoretic framework and a gardener's tale. *American Journal of Public Health, 90*(8), 1212–1215.

Semmler, P. L., & Williams, C. B. (2000). Narrative therapy: A storied context for multicultural counseling. *Journal of Multicultural Counseling and Development, 28*(1), 51–61.

Utsey, S. O., Bolden, M. A., & Brown, A. L. (2001). Visions of revolution from the spirit of Frantz Fanon. In J. G. Ponterotto, J. M. Casas, L. A. Suzuki, & C. M. Alexander (Eds.), *Handbook of multicultural counseling* (2nd ed., pp. 311–336). Thousand Oaks, CA: Sage.

Watts-Jones, D. (2002). Healing internalized racism: The role of a within-group sanctuary among people of African descent. *Family Process, 41*(4), 591–601.

INTERNMENT OF JAPANESE AMERICANS

The internment of Japanese Americans refers to the forced removal and confinement of approximately 120,000 Americans of Japanese heritage to one of 10 incarceration camps in desolate areas of California, Idaho, Utah, Arizona, Wyoming, Colorado, and Arkansas during World War II. The uprooting commenced after President Franklin D. Roosevelt signed Executive Order 9066 on February 19, 1942, shortly after Japan's military attacked Pearl Harbor. The order allowed for the exclusion of anyone of Japanese descent, citizen or alien, from western areas of the United States. Although military necessity was cited as the justification for the mass removal of Japanese Americans, a later government commission investigation revealed no evidence of this need and attributed the internment to racial prejudice, wartime hysteria, and the failure of political leaders. Germany and Italy also threatened the Allies, yet only Americans of Japanese heritage were forced en masse into camps and imprisoned for an average of two to three years. More than two thirds were U.S. citizens.

With little time or information to prepare for removal, families took only what they could carry. Most were moved to temporary assembly centers, where they were confined for several months at fairgrounds and racetracks before being transferred to internment camps. The permanent camps were situated in harsh desert or swamp areas of the interior, surrounded by barbed wire and armed guard towers. Privacy was rare. Entire families lived in a single room within a barrack without plumbing or electricity, and eating, bathing, and laundering took place in communal facilities. Camps eventually developed schools, hospitals, and newspapers, but they constantly faced insufficient supplies and a severe shortage of medical personnel. Japanese Americans tried to make the most of their situation, but fear and uncertainty bred tensions among themselves and with the camp administration. One critical conflict concerned a registration procedure that was devised to determine the loyalty of Japanese Americans. The registration required the incarcerated to indicate their willingness to serve in the armed forces of the United States and to swear unqualified allegiance to the United States and forswear allegiance to the Japanese emperor. The ambiguity of the questions and anxiety over how their responses would be used led to serious divisions among the incarcerated. Disagreement also arose about the role that interned Japanese Americans should take in the government's military and draft orders. Aspects of both conflicts persisted long after the end of the war.

Some of those who were U.S. citizens were permitted to leave the camps during the war, but the rapid release and resettlement of the others did not occur until 1944. All but one camp had closed by January 1946.

During the 1970s, Japanese Americans actively began pursuing an apology and reparations from the federal government for their wartime incarceration. The 1980 Commission on Wartime Relocation and Internment of Civilians thoroughly reviewed the facts and circumstances surrounding the internment. It concluded that there had been no military necessity for the internment and recommended that the government apologize and pay monetary redress to those who had been wrongfully incarcerated. The Civil Liberties Act of 1988 eventually provided $20,000 redress and an official apology for each of the 60,000 surviving internees. Letters and accompanying payments were sent beginning in 1990.

—*Amy H. Tsai*
—*Donna K. Nagata*

See also Japanese Americans

FURTHER READING

Commission on Wartime Relocation and Internment of Civilians. (1997). *Personal justice denied.* Washington, DC: Civil Liberties Public Education Fund.

Daniels, R. (1993). *Prisoners without trial: Japanese Americans in World War II.* New York: Hill and Wang.

INTERPRETERS

Increasing diversity in the United States has brought an increase in the number of languages spoken in communities. The 2000 U.S. Census indicated that nearly 18% of the population speaks a language other than English. In many communities, particularly immigrant communities, individuals lack proficiency in English to communicate successfully and conduct the business of their everyday lives. Consequently, interpreters are used to translate meaning from the native language into English and vice versa. These interpreters may be trained professionals, laypeople, friends, adult family members, or children and adolescents.

SELECTING AN INTERPRETER

In most circumstances, a professional interpreter can provide the best and most accurate interpretation of meaning in the two languages. Professionals know that their role is to translate neutrally, without adding to or subtracting from the communication. Caution is required to ensure that the interpreter speaks the same language and possibly the same dialect as the client. For example, a Spanish-speaking interpreter from Argentina may not use the same phrasing, vocabulary, or colloquial expressions that an individual from rural Mexico uses. The difference in dialect may create confusion and lead to a feeling of distance or lack of understanding.

LAYPEOPLE, FRIENDS, AND ADULT FAMILY MEMBERS

Using laypeople, friends, or adult family members as interpreters may create problematic situations. Although laypeople may speak the native language, they may not have the specialized vocabulary or skills to convey the information accurately. Clinicians and others should consider the impact of involving others in the communication process. Adult family members may introduce the power structure of family dynamics into the interpreting situation. The family member may insert or omit information based on the nature of the relationship, clouding communication and judgment. Certain cultural groups may restrict the type of communication between males and females and between people of different ages. Although a friend or family member might be willing to interpret, the client may feel uncomfortable divulging personal details in front of that individual. In addition, individuals from collectivist cultures (e.g., Asian groups) wish to avoid bringing shame or undue attention to the family; therefore, using a friend or family member as an interpreter may alter the communication. The use of laypeople as interpreters should be limited to minimal forms of communication (e.g., setting appointments).

CHILDREN AND ADOLESCENTS AS INTERPRETERS

Children learn new languages at a faster rate than adults and are often asked to interpret for adults. They may find the experience of interpreting stressful and uncomfortable because most lack sufficient linguistic and cognitive skills to provide adequate translation of concepts. They may filter communication based on the power relationships and lines of authority between adult and child, especially with a parent. Nevertheless, many parents and other relatives ask children and adolescents to translate because of the convenience of access. They interpret in a variety of settings and can translate a range of items from school notes to sophisticated tax forms. For some, as they become more adept at translating, they may act as the family representative, making decisions on behalf of the family, independently, or in consultation with the parents. They may feel a sense of pride and maturity at being able to interact proficiently with adults and convey information. Some studies have indicated that adolescents who have interpreted in the past report higher grade point averages and higher self-esteem. However, practitioners cannot know how accurately children or adolescents deliver communication, and therefore, it is unwise to rely on children or adolescents for important interpretation.

ENGAGING THE SERVICES OF AN INTERPRETER

Once an interpreter has been selected, the practitioner should arrange a presession meeting. During the presession meeting, the practitioner should review the expected agenda and sequence of events. The practitioner should review any specialized vocabulary and provide a copy of any documents or assessments that might be used so that the interpreter can familiarize himself or herself with the material. In addition, the practitioner should clarify the expectations of the interpreter. An experienced interpreter may rephrase communication in an expressive way in the native language and may attempt to draw out information based on the meaning behind the practitioner's communication. The extent of the interpreter's insertion of communication needs to be clarified in advance.

The practitioner should also discuss any cultural conflicts that may arise from the expected communication. For example, a female client may be reluctant to discuss sexual matters with a male interpreter, even if the practitioner is female. Some cultures delimit the kind of communication by age. A young male client may not feel comfortable discussing certain matters with an older male interpreter. Other cultural issues can be discussed in the presession meeting.

CONFIDENTIALITY

Certain relationships require confidentiality, which extends to the interpreter. For example, mental health professionals and their clients have a level of confidentiality that is protected by law. An interpreter is held to the same legal confidentiality as the practitioner in most circumstances. Clients must be informed that the interpreter is also bound to the same standard of confidentiality. Because the interpreter speaks the same language and may be part of the same cultural community as the client, clients may be reluctant to divulge sensitive information without an assurance of confidentiality. The interpreter may also need to be reminded of the protection of confidentiality for clients.

ESTABLISHING RAPPORT

Involving a third person in the interaction creates a challenge for the practitioner in establishing and maintaining rapport. Rapport building between practitioner and client is already challenging, but adding another culture and language magnifies the situation. In many cultures, titles and polite forms of speech indicate roles and responsibilities. A practitioner may need to explicitly provide a culturally appropriate title for the interpreter. For example, a practitioner who introduces himself as Dr. Vasquez may want to give his interpreter similar status by introducing her as Interpreter Chang or Ms. Chang. The practitioner may also need to direct the interpreter about the polite form of address until the client says otherwise. For example, in Spanish, the formal "you" (*usted*) is used to indicate higher status, respect, or unfamiliarity. The informal *tú* is used to address people with whom one is familiar. The shift in form of address may be something that the interpreter would want to note as a means of indicating a shift in the relationship.

AFTER THE INTERPRETING SESSION

After the interpreting session, the practitioner and interpreter should meet to discuss the session. The practitioner may ask the interpreter to provide feedback about his or her impressions of the client, the process, and the direction of the work together. The interpreter may also be a valuable resource in discussing cultural aspects of working with the particular cultural group.

It is highly recommended that the same interpreter be used in subsequent sessions with the client. Just as clients become comfortable with a practitioner, the same may occur with a specific interpreter, particularly when it comes to feelings of trust. Practitioners should engage in ongoing assessment of the interpreting service with the client to understand how well the work is functioning.

TERMINATING SERVICE

Termination of services, particularly for therapeutic services, is a process that must begin far in advance of the actual termination date and should involve the interpreter. In some communities, once a professional interpreter is identified, the client may want to contact the interpreter for other services, formal and informal. Practitioners may need to point out that if services are needed in the future, only he or she should be contacted, and that the interpreter may not be able to rejoin them in future work. Also, the practitioner and the interpreter should negotiate in advance about providing direct contact information to the client. Many interpreters are self-employed, contracted workers, or work through an agency, so they may be eager for more work. Clients may not fully understand the status of interpreting work and may want to contact the interpreter, given the established rapport. Depending on the circumstance, it may not be ethically appropriate for

the interpreter to communicate directly with the client without the practitioner involved.

CONCLUSION

Engaging the services of quality interpreters can extend the depth of understanding between practitioner and client. A trained interpreter will not only communicate effectively but also reflect the nuances of meaning accurately. Clients who are not proficient in English will be able to gain access to culturally competent services with the aid of an interpreter. Effective communication between clients and practitioners creates better service for all.

—*Robert S. Weisskirch*

See also Biculturalism; Cultural Barriers; Language Proficiency; Multicultural Counseling Competencies

FURTHER READING

Freed, A. O. (1988). Interviewing through an interpreter. *Social Work, 33,* 315–319.

Hwa-Froelich, D. A., & Westby, C. E. (2003). Considerations when working with interpreters. *Communication Disorders Quarterly, 24,* 78–85.

Nadler, L., & Nadler, Z. (1987). Overcoming the language barrier. *Training and Development Journal, 41,* 108–111.

Tribe, R., & Raval, H. (2003). *Working with interpreters in mental health.* Hove, UK: Brunner-Routledge.

INTRARACIAL VIOLENCE

Violence occurs among people of all ages, races, and socioeconomic brackets; no population is insulated from its effects. During the past decade, the nature of violence has changed, evidenced by an increase in domestic aggression, substance abuse, and gang and street violence and the growth of organized and well-funded groups whose primary purpose is violence and territorial control.

During the past two decades, we have also accumulated a small but convincing body of evidence demonstrating that violence is both intraracial and interracial in nature. Although some researchers have challenged this assertion, there is little scientific consensus on explanations for variations in racial violence. When race is strongly correlated with socioeconomic status (i.e., education, income, wealth, and prestige), opportunities for contact between members of different groups (intergroup conflict) are infrequent.

Recently, researchers have provided some insight into intraracial violence by examining models of homicide by race. Of the few empirical studies of race-specific violence, most focus solely on African American urban violence. An important finding of this research is that differences are likely the result of structural conditions within communities rather than the availability of a particular target group. However, such an explanation does not consider social and psychological processes. Psychological and social conditions in the context of race create a sense of powerlessness, anger, anxiety, and alienation and provoke physical aggression in conflict situations.

THEORETICAL EXPLANATIONS

The causes of intraracial violence are complex, often resulting from a variety of interacting social and individual factors. Therefore, intraracial violence takes many forms, from simple property crimes to more aggressive crimes such as rape and homicide between known, unknown, domestic, or otherwise relational others. Thus, explanations for violence within racial groups come from a number of perspectives.

One explanation found in the literature is the *macrostructural perspective*. According to this perspective, racial residential segregation, labor market factors, and the political economic factors within communities differentially coincide with competition. Violence within racial groups is conceptualized as a by-product of marginalizing economic conditions. As individuals experience strain and economic deprivation, criminal activity is presumed to be a reaction to unfulfilled expectations of justice and equity. Therefore, researchers have tried to more precisely identify which economic conditions create a context for violence. Racial groups that experience blocked opportunities in the economic sphere (i.e., discrimination, relative deprivation) are also likely to experience vast resource deprivation and social isolation (i.e., multiple disadvantages). One hypothesis is that severe material deprivation and absolute poverty intensify the struggle for survival. Therefore, local opportunity structures—measured by changing employment opportunities over time—are considered to play a role in mediating the potential for strain and violence.

A second explanation is *social disorganization theory*. According to this theory, deteriorating structural conditions lead to social disorganization, which, in turn, accounts for intraracial violence. From this perspective, violence results from the inability of racial groups to realize their common values and maintain effective social control. Instabilities among families, such as lack of congruency in shared values and attitudes, lack of emotional cohesion, deviant beliefs, and poor parenting practices, or among neighborhoods (a lack of social cohesion) impede the group's ability to develop and promote problem-solving strategies.

A third and more traditional explanation is the *microstructural* or *interpersonal perspective*. On the micro level, individual characteristics such as motivations, values, and social-demographic variables function as underlying causal dynamics that engender the unjust or unwarranted exertion of force or power. This encompasses a broad spectrum of behaviors (e.g., physical, emotional or psychological, verbal, sexual, social, and financial) and an equally wide range of consequences. However, this view is problematic because traditional methods of exploring pluralist behaviors do not capture the nature and scope of this order of distinction: (1) Many behaviors are substantively intercorrelated; (2) some experiences are mutually influenced among similar others; and (3) some sets of experiences are driven by underlying sociocultural conditions that exert both enabling and disabling influences on behavioral, psychological, and social outcomes between groups of individuals.

CHALLENGES AND FUTURE DIRECTIONS

The question remains, how do we conceptualize intraracial violence as a subpopulation-level experience? Whether in terms of causality, expression, or mediation, the behavior of larger units of analysis is presumed to extend beyond the individual level to reveal an underlying construct. If the desire is to have a firm scientific basis for making cross-comparisons, we must shift the meaning of what constitutes population membership from simple, descriptive, manifest variables to explanatory causal explications of the nature of underlying external forces over the range of the population.

To more appropriately investigate intraracial violence and make cross-racial group comparisons, we must first address the question, what causes variability within and between individuals in a subpopulation surrounded by an ascribed racial context that defines membership before the determination of the nature and scope of population boundaries? It is one conceptual framework to describe race differences, but quite another to proscribe the differences as racial. This resolution may be as much a theoretical issue as an applied one.

Second, the utility of race as an explanation for violent crime is limited unless we embrace both the nature and scope of variables that not only motivate and control individuals' behavior but also provide a medium for occurrence. This view holds that it is society's lack of willingness to acknowledge (and thereby effectively respond to) the web-fashioned context of scarcity and inequality that creates an environment conducive to violence, perpetuating the maladaptive and sociopathogenic structural mechanisms that undergird the lives of many racial groups. If the desire is to have a firm scientific basis for making cross-comparisons, the contemporary scientific literature on intraracial violence must acknowledge that both the causes and effects of violence are ecological.

In this framework, explanatory power is achieved by reconceptualizing the notion of race and conceding that patterns of societal-level factors for one racial group of individuals are functionally different from those of another racial group. For example, cultures of honor place importance on responding to insults and threats to property, persons, or reputations with violence. Because of a perceived sense of powerlessness, individuals often suffer from diminished capacity, reduced quality of life, and lower self-esteem, which signify the social and psychological dynamics of racial communities as manifestations of history and context. Conceptually, this framework necessitates a paradigmatic shift in scientific theory, training, and

practice. Methodologically, the inclusion of culture in targeting the conditions of identified subpopulations would require (1) alternative ways of viewing and measuring the relations among influences that affect behavior, and (2) a concomitant shift in assessment in terms of the level of analysis.

—*Alvin L. Killough*
—*Christopher L. Edwards*

FURTHER READING

Anderson, L. M. (2002, February 1). *Community interventions to promote healthy social environments: Early childhood development and family housing* (Mortality and Morbidity Weekly Rep. 51). Washington, DC: U.S. Department of Health and Human Services, Centers for Disease Control and Prevention.

Felson, R. B., Liska, A. E., South, S. J., & McNulty, T. L. (1994). The subculture of violence and delinquency: Individual vs. school context effects. *Social Forces, 73*(1), 155–173.

Killough, A. L. (2001). A cultural ecological model of academic performance: Schools as a necessary but insufficient condition. *Community Psychologist, 34*(3), 27–30.

Killough, A. L., Webster, W. L., Brown, V. B., Houck, E., & Edwards, C. L. (2003). African American violence exposure: An emerging health issue. In C. C. Yeakey & R. D. Henderson (Eds.), *Surmounting all odds: Education, opportunity, and society in the new millennium* (pp. 147–173). Greenwich, CT: Information Age.

Markowitz, F. E. (2001). Attitudes and family violence: Linking intergenerational and cultural theories. *Journal of Family Violence, 16*(2), 205–218.

Parker, K. F., & McCall, P. L. (1999). Structural conditions and racial homicide patterns: A look at the multiple disadvantages in urban areas. *Criminology Beverly Hills, 37*(3), 447–478.

J

JAPANESE AMERICANS

The majority of Japanese Americans are American-born descendants of Japanese immigrants who started migrating to Hawaii around 1870 and later to the continental United States. The Immigration Act of 1924, which essentially ended further Japanese immigration, caused American-born Japanese children born after 1924 to manifest distinct identities: Nisei (second-generation), Sansei (third), Yonsei (fourth), and so on. The Issei (immigrant first-generation), for reasons based in Japanese history, came with a strong middle-class orientation, and a majority established themselves as entrepreneurs: farm owners, business proprietors, and workers.

Japanese Americans have been perceptibly influenced by their Japanese background. The most significant bicultural influences appear in their interpersonal style, the way they relate to other people, so how the two cultures shaped the Japanese American interpersonal style is of interest. One major project that focused specifically on this question is the research of an eminent Japanese mathematical statistician and survey researcher, the late Chikio Hayashi, and his associates at the Institute of Statistical Mathematics (ISM) in Tokyo. Because Japanese interpersonal patterns are not well understood, a brief clarification of those features is first needed.

UNDERSTANDING JAPANESE PATTERNS OF SOCIAL RELATIONS

Hayashi emphasized that Japanese character has been profoundly influenced historically by a concern to maintain *wa* ("peace"; "harmony"). *Wa* in this context means primarily a concern for conflict avoidance. This idea is supported by American child psychologist Fred Rothbaum and colleagues in their extensive review of child socialization studies in Japan and the United States. They concluded that Japanese children are trained toward accommodative relations, whereas American children, trained for individualism, show a stronger potential for conflict.

The most distinctive characteristic of the Japanese interpersonal style is the exceptional amount of perceptual attention each person gives the other, especially the other's inner feelings and motives, and low attention to the ego-oriented self. Evidence indicates that these tendencies were influenced historically by the strong concern of the Japanese to minimize interpersonal conflict, for conflict avoidance requires that one apprehend the other's attitudes and carefully avoid actions that might provoke the other's opposition. G. H. Mead has shown that all meaningful interactions require each individual to "take the attitude of the other"—that is, see things from the other's perspective. Our view is that the Japanese not only devote a great amount of attention to "taking the attitude of the other" (TAO), but also seek to probe the other's subjective self to a degree uncommon in most cultures.

"Taking the attitude of the other" is very similar in meaning to *role taking* and to *empathy*, but *role taking* implies the existence of institutionally or customarily defined roles, and *empathy* implies a conscious effort to sense another's inner feelings. TAO is a more inclusive concept, for as Mead shows, it is a perception that is involved in all meaningful interaction. When I say to another, "Please shut the door," the statement would be meaningless if I did not anticipate that the other would respond in a specific way. Thus, TAO is a universal in all human interactions. The Japanese engage in the process in a special way, however.

There are three types of social interaction, and TAO functions in each type differently. First is *sensory interaction,* in which the other's intent is judged from sensory perceptions. Second is *institutional* or *customary interaction,* in which the other's intent is assumed to be guided by customary rules that apply in the situations. The third is *intersubjective interaction,* in which the other's intent is inferred from guessing the other's subjective state. All interactions tend to be affected by both sensory and intersubjective perceptions, and most interactions are also guided by customary rules, but societies differ in the amount of emphasis given to each type.

In an ancient civilization with strong traditions, such as China, institutional or customary interaction receives strong emphasis. By contrast, in a new society like America, with weak traditions, emphasis is often given to the belief that "actions speak louder than words"— that is, observed behavior is the best criterion of the other's intent. Japan, like China, is a traditionalist country, and customary rules receive a lot of attention, but because of its deeply embedded concern for minimizing conflict, the society has also established an unusually strong emphasis on *intersubjective interaction.*

One other component of the interpersonal process needs clarification. Social interaction requires perception of the other, but to control one's own actions, perception of the self is no less important. There are two ways in which the self may be perceived. First, by taking the attitude of the other, one perceives self from the standpoint of the other. This *socially oriented self* (social view of self) constitutes much of our self-conception. Second, the *ego-oriented self,* which is conceptually distinct from the first, is identified by perceptions of one's own sensory impulses, or by awareness of those thoughts and feelings that one feels are one's own, as in an argument or in creative discovery. The Japanese tend to be weak in self-definition in the latter sense.

To summarize the characteristics of the Japanese interpersonal style, the Japanese in their interpersonal relations tend not only to give more attention to the other than is typical among Americans, but also in so doing tend to seek genuinely to see things from the other's point of view. That is, Japanese interpersonal relations are *intersubjective* to an unusual degree, and because of the concern with apprehending the other's inner feelings, the style might appropriately be called *sympathetic interaction.* Sympathetic interaction has the effects of heightening identity with others, establishing strong group bonds among those who relate with one another over an extended time, inducing a preference for group versus individual decision making, and establishing a strong sense of obligation and responsibility to one's associates. Sympathetic interaction also has the effect of inducing egalitarian attitudes in social relations, for one can scarcely understand another sympathetically if one regards oneself as different from the other. Given the strong authoritarian structure that has pervaded Japanese society historically, sympathetic interaction has given Japanese society a subtle unforeseen democratic base that has played a significant role in Japan's modernization. For Japanese Americans, the Japanese hierarchical tradition has had little effect, but the egalitarian orientation has proved invaluable.

The tempo at which Japanese interaction episodes develop is noticeably slower than among Americans. American interactions are generally not only much more informal than Japanese, but also more spontaneously goal-oriented. The Japanese develop their relations more cautiously, not only for conflict avoidance but also because intersubjective understanding takes time. Once consensus has been achieved, action can be very decisive.

BICULTURAL INFLUENCES ON JAPANESE AMERICANS

This discussion draws mainly on the findings of the ISM in Tokyo, whose thirty years of survey studies on the comparative Japanese and American influences on Japanese Americans offer a singularly effective basis for examining cultural influences. For this entry, selected data are summarized in Table 1, taken from their survey research studies of random samples drawn in Japan and the United States in 1988, and of Japanese Americans in Hawaii and the mainland United States in 1998–2000, using identical questions. The table was created using Hayashi's cultural link analysis, a cluster analytic method for determining attitude clusters that reveal similarities and differences between cultures.

The table shows three clusters of attitude variables: the first cluster, in which Japanese Americans are similar to the Japanese (Jp-Type); a second, in which they are similar to Americans (Am-Type); and a third,

Table 1   Relationship of Japanese American Attitudes to Those of Japanese and Americans

Item	Jp	JA$_H$	JA$_M$	Am
Jp-Type: Japanese American attitudes related to Japanese				
Ninjo scale: sympathetic interaction tendency	37	22	28	23
Giri-ninjo scale: responsive to duty/obligation	92	72	76	66
Intermediate response scale: delayed response tendency	72	38	31	20
Consensus more important than principle	68	62	65	47
Am-Type: Japanese American attitudes similar to American				
Science leads to loss of human feelings	45	75	69	69
Mechanization reduces human feelings	31	11	10	19
Science permits understanding of human mind	14	71	54	58
Best to leave decisions to outstanding political leaders	13	5	8	7
JA-Type: Distinctive Japanese American attitudes				
Most people are helpful	31	67	66	54
Most people are trustworthy	39	56	61	42
Parents and relatives are important	58	74	75	62
Politics is important	33	13	7	25

Source: Author

Note: *Data are percentage agreeing with item or scale.*
Sample size, *n*: Jp = 2,265, JA$_H$ = 206, JA$_M$ = 344, Am = 1,563

unique to Japanese Americans (JA-Type). For each variable listed at the left, the percentage favorable is shown for the Japanese (Jp), Hawaiian Japanese Americans (JA$_H$), mainland Japanese Americans (JA$_M$), and Americans (Am). The variables listed are abbreviated statements of survey questionnaire items, except for the first three under the Jp-Type, which are scales constructed by combining items using Hayashi's scaling methodology. The reported findings are correlational rather than causal analytic, so the interpretation of "influence" is admittedly inferred, but their consistency with other research results supports the idea of influences.

The scores for the Hawaiian and mainland Japanese Americans could have been combined because of their similarity but are shown separately because the similarity suggests that Japanese Americans residing in different regions do not differ greatly, a conclusion supported by samples drawn separately in California and Washington whose differences were small. The attribution *mainland Japanese Americans* might be questioned because the substantial minority of Japanese Americans in the Midwest, East, and South have not been sampled, but the regional similarity noted above suggests that the latter groups likewise would not differ greatly on these

variables. One difference not reported here deserves mention: the Japanese influence declines for each successive generation (the Nisei, Sansei, and Yonsei).

Jp-Type Attitudes. In Table 1, the first set of attitudes, the Jp-Type, is a group in which Japanese American attitudes are similar to the Japanese. On the four variables listed, the Japanese and American percentages differ noticeably, and the Japanese Americans' scores generally fall in between. The first three variables listed are scales representing characteristics that Hayashi has shown are among the most basic enduring features of Japanese national character. All three are directly related to the basic Japanese psychological tendencies described earlier: emphasis on taking the attitude of the other and seeing things from the other's point of view, concern to apprehend the other's inner feelings and motives, and relating to others sympathetically.

The first scale, the *ninjo* scale, measured the Japanese tendency to relate to another sympathetically and warmly. The difference between Japanese and Americans on this scale is not large, for Americans are also a basically sympathetic and friendly people, but the Japanese inclination to probe others' inner feelings tends to yield a stronger sense of sympathetic relations.

The *ninjo* attitude is noticeably present among Japanese Americans, as other studies also reveal. The strong group bonds based on *ninjo* typically found among the Japanese may also be seen among Japanese Americans. However, the *ninjo* attitude is less apparent when Japanese Americans step outside their own group.

The second scale, *giri-ninjo,* is a measure of the combined effect of *giri* (sense of duty and obligation) and *ninjo,* the variable discussed above. In Japanese society, *giri,* the sense of duty and obligation, tends to be a frequently felt attitude. *Giri* often arises within institutional settings, where it may be dealt with in some customary fashion, but when *giri* arises in a *ninjo* relationship, in which sympathetic feelings are involved, it tends to acquire a forcefulness not felt in institutionalized obligations.

Kazue Yamaoka showed that when the *giri* and *ninjo* components are measured separately, *ninjo* by itself is a stronger attitude among Japanese Americans than *giri-ninjo,* which indicates that *giri* is relatively weak. Fugita and colleagues suggest that *giri* is an institutionalized concept in Japanese society and, lacking the institutional setting, Japanese Americans tend to be less responsive to the Japanese ideas of duty and obligation. However, *giri* is related to the more general concept of responsibility. Responsibility is a necessary psychological condition for strong organized relations, and, as we show below, Japanese Americans have a notable proclivity for forming organizations.

The *intermediate response scale* is a measure of the frequency with which "Don't Know" or "Undecided" responses were given on difficult survey questions, a tendency much more frequently observed among the Japanese than among Americans. Our interpretation of this Japanese tendency is that it reflects a *delayed response,* a tendency to move slowly and tentatively on an action until some consensus is apparent. Decisive responses are characteristic of people who are confident of their individualized opinions, and they are less prevalent among people who try to take account of the differing attitudes observed among their associates. Japanese Americans are more individualized than the Japanese and less habituated to seeing things from others' points of view, but it is noteworthy that Japanese Americans show some similarity with the Japanese on this measure.

Some may question the validity of using "Undecided" responses for such a global interpretation, but it should be noted that Hayashi, who was a close friend of Louis Guttman, devised scalability and reproducibility tests for all of these scales. Also, this interpretation of the Intermediate Response Scale is consistent with other findings on the Japanese.

The fourth variable, concerning consensus seeking, asked respondents to choose between a person who prefers consensus seeking over holding to his or her own principle, versus one stressing the opposite. Fugita and colleagues have shown that Japanese Americans appear to favor consensus seeking because they find it more comfortable as an interpersonal style than the more assertive, spontaneous, and individually aggressive style generally characteristic of Americans.

Am-Type Attitudes. This is a class of attitudes on which Japanese Americans show little similarity with the Japanese and appear to have been influenced mainly by their American training. Three of the items bear on the question of how science and technology may affect human feelings and the human mind, and the fourth on political decision making. The first two, regarding the effect of science and technology on human feelings, yield contradictory results for the Japanese. They will not be discussed, because the "Undecided" responses of the Japanese were very high, suggesting that the items were ambiguous to them. However, the third item, that science permits understanding of the human mind, on which the Japanese show a distinctly low level of agreement, is revealing. We noted above that the Japanese in their interpersonal relations depend heavily on trying to sense the inner feelings of the other. That is, a high degree of subjectivity is involved in their understanding of others, but subjectivism is contrary to the ultimate requirements of science. Americans, by contrast, depend much more on a behavioristic basis of understanding one another and in fact are inclined to distrust subjectivist assessments of the human mind. Japanese Americans understand and accept the American orientation. The latter actually employ a good deal of subjectivism in their social interactions, but intellectually they understand and appreciate the American view. It should be noted in this connection that the Am-Type attitudes were probably acquired through schooling and adult experiences, whereas the Jp-Type attitudes, which reflect Japanese influences, were probably acquired through infant and early childhood socialization. The last item, showing disagreement with "leaving decisions to outstanding political leaders," indicates the thoroughgoing way in which Japanese Americans have absorbed the American democratic philosophy.

JA-Type Attitudes. Observers have noted that a hybrid Japanese American culture exists that differs from either Japanese or American. The hybrid is a product of adapting the Japanese forms to the American scene, and also of adapting American attitudes to their ethnic minority status.

On the first two items, concerning the helpfulness and trustworthiness of people, we need to ask why the Japanese scores are lower than those of Americans. The Japanese are often said to be helpful and trusting, but these data belie that judgment. We believe the explanation is that the Japanese, in their initial contacts, tend to be cautious and tentative, and it is only after interaction that sympathetic understanding tends to emerge. By contrast, Japanese Americans approach interactions without the tentativeness of the Japanese, tend to adopt a sympathetic attitude toward others, and, in the benign American middle-class and ethnic communities in which much of their lives are spent, generally find little reason to distrust others.

On the third item, regarding the importance of parents and relatives, again the question arises as to why the Japanese percentage is low when that society is thought to emphasize strong family relations. The low score, however, is consistent with observations that in Japan, relations among adult blood-related family members are often distant, whereas relations in functional groups, such as work groups, in which they are regularly involved, are very strong. Japanese Americans, on the other hand, although they generally enjoy participating in group relations with other Japanese Americans, rarely are involved in them on an everyday basis. For them, therefore, family relations take on greater significance.

Finally, the low-percentage response of Japanese Americans on the question of the importance of politics, we believe, reflects the fact that Japanese Americans have felt excluded from the American political process, because of discrimination and their wartime incarceration, and their political experience has grown comparatively slowly.

SOME EXAMPLES OF THE ASSOCIATIONAL TENDENCIES OF JAPANESE AMERICANS

Japanese Americans may tend to choose fellow Japanese Americans for close friends, as do members of other racially and ethnically distinct minority groups. But Japanese Americans tend to be distinctive among ethnic minorities in America in the extent to which they establish their own ethnic voluntary organizations. Evidence indicates that the *ninjo*-based sympathetic interaction style among Japanese Americans, and also the *giri-ninjo*-based support of socially responsible behavior, has influenced this notable organizational tendency.

One significant example of this organizational proclivity among Japanese Americans is the Japanese American Citizens League (JACL). When first established in 1929, it was the largest Asian American political organization in the country, and it still is. At its height during the 1980s, it had a total membership of around 33,000. It currently has approximately 20,000 members in over 100 chapters throughout the United States.

Its policies during World War II were controversial, but in the decades thereafter the JACL became the most popular Japanese American organization. Ostensibly a civil rights and cultural group, the JACL has a heavily social character at its grassroots level. Typically, chapters host a wide range of social activities, such as community picnics, scholarship dinners, craft fairs, and bowling tournaments. Moreover, individuals in given local chapters have friendship or familial ties with many in chapters in other cities, such that the regional and biennial national conferences are quite intimate. These social ties proved critical in mobilizing Japanese Americans during the drive to pass redress legislation. More germane to this discussion, organizations such as the JACL provide a vehicle for Japanese Americans to interact with others who have a similar interpersonal style. Further, the activities of the organization serve to propagate the norms of the group among the younger generation.

Sports are another area in which the importance of the group orientation and interpersonal style of Japanese Americans can be seen. For example, Nisei baseball teams were a major fixture in the ethnic community by the 1920s and were highly organized into regional and statewide ethnic leagues by the 1930s. Virtually every town that had a significant Japanese American population fielded a team.

After World War II, basketball became the dominant youth team sport in the community. Many parents expend great effort to organize and administer the teams and leagues. The desire of youths from other ethnic groups to play on these teams has presented some difficult decisions, for some parent organizers object, arguing, for example, that Japanese American youths are smaller and thus need a league of their own. Frequently, elaborate rules were developed based on the percentage of Japanese heritage or the number of non-Japanese who could play on a team, a divisive issue when protests arose concerning the discriminatory implications of the rules.

One reason Japanese Americans have difficulty integrating non-Japanese Americans into such socially intimate group activities may be that their interpersonal style and norms differ enough from those of the mainstream that they are substantially more comfortable in the *ninjo*-oriented Japanese American groups. This is not to say that they cannot function in mainstream groups, as they clearly can. Moreover, ideologically, they strongly support the larger society's emphasis on multiculturalism and diversity. However, because relations with other groups often require an interpersonal style unlike their own, such as spontaneity and assertiveness, many Japanese Americans prefer personalized associations with members of their own group. The strength of this effect is substantially reduced in the later generations but is still visible.

Japanese American religious participation is another area that illustrates their group orientation and interpersonal style. Compared with Japan, where 1% of the population reported their religion as Christianity, mainland Japanese Americans self-identified as 30% Christian, 33% Buddhist, and 26% "No religion." Comparable figures are found among Hawaii's Japanese Americans. Remarkably, in a society in which the structural assimilation of the Japanese Americans is now little contested, most of those who go to Christian churches and Buddhist temples attend those where a majority (100% of the Buddhists, 63% Christians, 63% "Other") of the congregation is made up of other Japanese Americans. Another remarkable feature of Japanese American religiosity is the absence of vociferous interreligious conflicts. The maintenance and popularity of such segregated religious institutions, as well as a notable interpersonal harmony with regard to religious differences, may stem from their maintenance of the Japanese American interpersonal style and orientation.

THE LEGACY OF THE WORLD WAR II INCARCERATION

The defining event in the history of Japanese Americans is their mass removal from the Pacific Coast and incarceration during World War II. Forced from their homes, businesses, and farms in the spring of 1942, they were confined in temporary "assembly centers," usually ill-prepared former racetracks or fairgrounds, and subsequently sent to 10 permanent compounds in desolate areas of the country's interior.

Although the internees adapted outwardly to the harsh conditions in the camps, the experience produced painful and difficult-to-articulate feelings. Some felt shame because of their implied association with the enemy. Others experienced resentment about the government's unjust treatment. Some openly resisted the authorities. Substantial hostility was turned inward toward fellow internees who had different political interpretations of their circumstances. Other feelings were suppressed—perhaps the most efficacious way for them to deal with their sense of powerlessness.

Some 60 years have passed since the upheaval of the incarceration. Socioeconomically, Japanese Americans made a rapid recovery to middle-class status. However, the internees' psychological recovery appears to be on a slower path. They have gone from suppressing and not giving voice to their feelings about their World War II experiences to believing, in the twilight of their lives, that their wartime experiences need to be shared with the larger society so that a similar episode will not be repeated. Facilitating this transformation has been the larger society's move through the civil rights era and subsequent dramatic changes in racial attitudes and laws. More specifically, the Japanese Americans mounted a movement seeking an apology and redress from the federal government, and its success has proved cathartic. Nonetheless, the community memory of the incarceration will remain central to individuals' identity for many years to come. Even the Sansei (third generation) and Yonsei (fourth generation), most of whom never experienced the camps and have grown up in a vastly changed America with respect to racial and ethnic attitudes, still identify with the experiences of their parents and grandparents.

CONCLUSION

The psychology of Japanese Americans can, and has been, studied using various conceptual frameworks. This discussion emphasized a bicultural perspective that examined Japanese and American influences on this group's attitudes and behavior. With the use of a Meadian framework, a unique Japanese American interpersonal style was highlighted which can be traced to its Japanese cultural origins as well as the pressures to accommodate to the American context.

—*Kazue Yamaoka*

See also Internment of Japanese Americans

FURTHER READING

Fugita, S., Miyamoto, S., & Kashima, T. (2002). Interpersonal style and Japanese American organizational involvement. *Behaviormetrika, 29,* 185–202.

Fugita, S., & O'Brien, D. (1991). *Japanese American ethnicity: The persistence of community.* Seattle: University of Washington Press.

Hayashi, C., & Kuroda, Y. (1997). *Japanese culture in comparative perspective.* Westport, CT: Praeger.

Hayashi, C., & Suzuki, T. (Eds.). (1990). *Beyond Japanese social values: Trend and cross-national perspectives.* Tokyo: The Institute of Statistical Mathematics.

Hayashi, C., Suzuki, T., & Sasaki, M. (1992). *Data analysis for comparative social research: International perspectives.* Amsterdam: North-Holland.

Kashima, T., Miyamoto, S., & Fugita, S. (2002). Religious attitudes and beliefs among Japanese Americans. *Behaviormetrika, 29,* 203–229.

King, R. C. (2002). "Eligible to be Japanese American": Multiraciality in basketball leagues and beauty pageants. In L. Trinh Võ & R. Bonus (Eds.), *Contemporary Asian American communities: Intersections and divergences* (pp. 120–133). Philadelphia: Temple University Press.

Miyamoto, S., Fugita, S., & Kashima, T. (2002). A theory of interpersonal relations for cross-cultural studies. *Behaviormetrika, 29,* 149–183.

Okamura, J. Y. (2002). Baseball and beauty queens: The political context of ethnic boundary making in the Japanese American community in Hawai'i. *Social Process in Hawai'i, 41,* 122–146.

Rothbaum, F., Pott, M., Azuma, H., Miyake, K., & Weisz, J. (2000). The development of close relationships in Japan and the United States: Paths of symbiotic harmony and generative tension. *Child Development, 71,* 1121–1143.

Yamaoka, K., & Hayashi, C. (2003). Cultural link analysis of Japanese Americans. *Behaviormetrika, 30*(1), 7–19.

JOHN HENRYISM

A PREDISPOSITION FOR ACTIVE COPING

John Henryism (JH) is scientifically known as a strong behavioral predisposition to cope actively with psychosocial and environmental stressors. As a coping strategy, JH is based on the legend of an uneducated steel-driving African American laborer who possessed phenomenal strength and who in competition defeated the mechanical steam drill in a race to drive railroad spikes. Unfortunately, but key to the legend and current medical research, John Henry died immediately after his success, from mental and physical exhaustion, but certainly having completed his goal. Accordingly, the term *John Henryism* now symbolizes the coping strategy characterized by aggressive tenacity, determination, and hard work while unconsciously sacrificing health issues in reaching the goal of meeting an environmental demand.

John Henryism is most effectively thought of as a dominant personality trait that promotes active and determined coping in response to significant environmental stressors. Like most personality traits, JH is characterized as consistency in behavior, thinking, and emotional responses over time and across situations. The style of coping is likely to produce successful outcomes and significant achievement until environmental demands exceed the available interpersonal, intellectual, financial, and other situationally relevant resources. Above such a threshold, active, single-minded, and determined coping tends to yield the opposite of productivity and achievement, including negative health and other consequences.

John Henryism can be behaviorally indexed by (1) efficacious mental and physical vigor; (2) a strong commitment to hard work; and (3) a single-minded determination to succeed. These predispositions in the context of inadequate financial resources, for example, can yield significantly increased stress and negative health outcomes. Here, *inadequate* emphasizes the relative conceptualization of *resources* and implies that the absolute value of income, social support, and/or any other resources is not as important as the degree to which resources are capable of addressing the need. Consequently, an eight-figure income can yield negative health consequences in the context of high JH, particularly if a nine-figure income is needed to address the need. Similarly, a four-figure income in the context of high levels of JH can yield health and wellness if and when the need is less than four figures. The same principle applies to social support and other contributors to resources.

Several studies have explored JH as a predispositional and dispositional characteristic independent of its historical match with available resources. For example, in one recent study, working adult African American smokers were effectively discriminated from those who never smoked based on high levels of JH. Those who reported never smoking exhibited higher JH scores than those who used to smoke but quit and those who were current smokers.

In another study and in a sample of African American college students, higher JH was found to be associated with lower rates of smoking in the last 30 days, a reduced propensity to have started smoking before the age of 18, and a reduced likelihood of previously seeing a weapon carried by another student on campus. Students with higher levels of JH were also less likely to have carried a weapon as a mechanism to feel safer on campus. In terms of consequences, students with high JH were more likely to have been arrested for Driving While Impaired (DWI)/Driving Under the Influence (DUI), and to have missed a class due to alcohol use. The authors concluded that the consequences of substance use may be differentially problematic for African American college students based on the presence of high-effort coping.

INTERACTION OF PREDISPOSITION AND THE ENVIRONMENT

There is evidence that the disparity between environmental demands and available resources, as is indexed by education and income, may be particularly predictive of negative health outcomes in African Americans with high levels of JH. African Americans who exhibit high levels of JH and low levels of education exhibit increased cardiovascular reactivity and subsequently higher risk for hypertension. African Americans are more likely to be undercompensated for hard work and determination in the workplace and often work for only a fraction of the compensation received by their equally experienced and qualified European American counterparts. Their hard work and determination to succeed (high JH) in employment settings (high demand) are too frequently met by inequitable compensation and a sense of powerlessness to influence their outcomes (low resources). This disparity can breed high levels of stress and increased risks for negative health outcomes, including hypertension.

Recent studies have found that exposure to chronic workplace stressors may be associated with dysregulation of the hypothalamic-pituitary-adrenal axis (HPA-axis), the classical neuroendocrine system that responds to stress, particularly among individuals with high levels of JH and in African Americans. Consistently, scientists have interpreted these and similar findings as a physiological index of the significant stress that is associated with balancing occupational demands among individuals with high-effort coping. Other recent studies have found that individuals who display this predisposition toward high-effort coping, combined with psychosocial stressors associated with low educational attainment, are more susceptible to cardiovascular morbidity.

THE FUTURE OF JOHN HENRYISM

The future of JH research appears promising, with several new studies defining new uses for the coping construct. There is interest in evaluating the influence of JH on outcomes among African Americans with an increasingly diverse array of chronic illnesses. For example, there are emerging studies that evaluate the effects of the interaction of JH and self-efficacy (SE) on pain and psychiatric morbidity in adult patients with sickle-cell disease (SCD). These studies hypothesize that high-effort coping in the context of deficient or altered psychological resources is associated with increased reports of pain and pain-related morbidities in a manner consistent with the original JH hypotheses.

Other studies are designed to evaluate the influence of JH on nociceptive reflex flexion (NRF), an indicator of peripheral neurological functioning in African American and European American patients with osteoarthritis of the knee. Yet other studies are evaluating the role of JH as an index of active coping among females treated for metastatic breast cancer.

Some of the most interesting work in coping among African Americans is designed to answer the question of whether JH is a situational (i.e., a state) or a characterological (i.e., a trait) influence on health outcomes. Sherman James and his colleagues are beginning to ponder the range of environmental influences that may precipitate transient escalations of efficacious mental and physical vigor with a strong commitment to hard work and a single-minded determination to succeed. Further, there are attempts to better understand the complex neurological and neurohormonal processes that are likely activated and may sustain increased risk of negative health outcomes during unremitting environmental demands in individuals with high levels of JH. How these transient states interact with available resources to influence health outcomes is not yet understood, but such research may yield a better understanding of the complex process of coping among African Americans and in other populations. Better understanding of coping may also yield innovative tools for conceptualization and intervention among populations at risk.

—*Christopher L. Edwards*
—*Gary Bennett*

FURTHER READING

Bennett, G. G., Merritt, M. M., Edwards, C. L., Whitfield, K. E., Brandon, D. T., & Tucker, R. D. (2004). Stress, coping, and health outcomes among African Americans: A review of the John Henryism hypothesis. *Psychology and Health, 19*(3), 369–383.

K

KOREAN AMERICANS

According to the 2000 U.S. Census, Korean Americans are one of the fastest growing immigrant groups in the United States. More than a million Korean Americans live in the United States, representing the fourth largest Asian American ethnic group. The majority of Korean Americans live in California. As the number of Korean Americans in the United States grows, our modern psychological understanding of this population needs to grow as well. To better serve Korean Americans, researchers have begun to clarify what is known about traditional Korean values and how these values might be relevant to psychological research and practice.

Like other Asian American groups, Korean Americans are often described as part of the "model minority," having few personal or professional problems. Generally, researchers have neglected the study of Korean Americans because of a belief that the cultural values of Koreans protect them from psychological difficulties. For example, in the 1990s, research documented lower rates of mental illness, juvenile delinquency, and divorce among Korean Americans than among their Caucasian peers. It is now clear, however, that no ethnic or cultural minority group is immune to acculturation and adjustment problems. Korean Americans, like other Asian American groups, experience a variety of emotional, psychological, and social problems. It is believed that traditional Korean Americans are at risk for misdiagnosis and that their rates of mental illness are underestimated at best.

Knowing how to identify and measure the needs of Korean Americans has not come easily to the field. Language barriers and traditional prohibitions against sharing intimate information can make research with Korean Americans challenging. For example, traditional Korean values discourage self-disclosure and emotional expression, making it unlikely that this population would feel comfortable with the process of psychotherapy or with personal questions in research. Furthermore, traditionally oriented Korean Americans often underutilize modern mental health services, reducing their contact with professionals in the field. Those who do participate in Western therapy tend to have higher premature termination rates than do Caucasian clients.

HISTORY

Korea is a modern nation with a history of more than 5,000 years. According to Korean mythology, the Korean nation was born when a god named Hwanung left heaven and transformed a bear into a woman. Hwanung married the woman, and she gave birth to a son, Tangun. Tangun established the first capital of the Korean nation in 2333 BCE and called it *Joseon*, "land of the morning calm."

The Korean nation has a long history of war with China and Japan. In 1919, many Koreans were killed or put in prison nationwide as they protested Japanese colonial rule.

On August 15, 1945, Japan surrendered to the Allies, ending the war in the Pacific. Ten days later, Korea was divided into North and South Korea. The United States took control of surrendering Japanese soldiers south of the 38th parallel, and the Soviet Union took control of the North. The United Nations called for elections in 1947, but the North Koreans refused. A communist form of government came into power in North Korea (known as the Democratic People's Republic of Korea). The United States turned over its authority to South Korea (the Republic of Korea) in 1948, leaving behind a small group of military advisers. North Korea invaded South Korea on June 25, 1950, starting the Korean War. This war lasted three years and inflicted terrible damage on Korea before a cease-fire ended the conflict in 1953. The 4-kilometer-wide area along the military demarcation line that divides North and South Korea became known as the DMZ, or demilitarized zone. Since the end of the Korean War, conflicts have continued to arise along the DMZ. South Korea continues its efforts to unify North and South Korea.

Immigrants from Korea to the United States represent both North and South Korean heritage. Koreans immigrated in three distinct waves beginning in 1903–1924. From 1903 to 1905, some 7,000 Koreans migrated to Hawaii to labor on the sugar plantations; approximately 1,000 of them came to the continental United States. In 1905, Korea became a protectorate of Japan and was later annexed by that nation in 1910. Japan severely restricted further emigration to the United States to stop the exodus of skilled labor and to stem the Korean independence movement. In 1924, the Johnson-Reed Immigration Act limited Koreans entering the United States to 100 per year.

The period from the end of the Korean War in 1953 through 1965 marked the second immigration wave. It was facilitated by an earlier law, the War Brides Act of 1945, which allowed spouses and adopted children of U.S. military personnel to enter the United States. Today, it is estimated that one in four Korean immigrants can trace their lineage to the arrival of a Korean war bride. The end of the Korean War also marked the beginning of American families adopting Korean children.

The third immigration wave began with the Immigration Act of 1965, which removed "national origins" as the basis for American immigration policy. Until then, Koreans were a small minority with a population of around 10,000.

The 1992 riots in Los Angeles, which became known as *sa-i-gu* by Korean Americans, transformed the Korean American community across the nation. Nearly half of the city's $1 billion in damages was suffered by Korean Americans. Only the World War II incarceration of Japanese Americans hurt a large Asian American community so deeply. The extreme and disproportionate damage suffered by Korean

Americans suggested that sa-i-gu was a backlash against the model minority myth of Asian Americans in general.

CULTURAL VALUES

Perhaps no other ethnic group in the United States has retained so strong an attachment to the values and practices of their native culture as Korean Americans. Most Korean Americans can and do speak some Korean, eat mainly Korean food, and practice Korean cultural behaviors. In 1998, a study found that 90% of Korean immigrants in Chicago spoke mainly Korean at home, and 82% were affiliated with an ethnic organization.

The strong attachment to Korean values seen among Korean Americans is likely the result of several factors. First, Korea, especially South Korea, is a homogeneous country. Unlike China or Japan, where several dialects and languages are spoken, South Koreans have only one language. Second, Korean Americans tend to be affiliated with Korean churches. The church provides a place for meeting other Korean immigrants and maintaining social ties to Korean culture. Third, Korean American immigrants tend to work in Korean businesses and maintain interactions with other Koreans. Furthermore, working in small businesses increases ethnic solidarity as Korean store owners work to compete together in the mainstream marketplace. Attacks on Korean-owned businesses during the 1992 Los Angeles riots, though tragic, promoted more ethnic and cultural unity among Korean business owners and workers and provided an opportunity for the community as a whole to contemplate its future.

Many Korean Americans have been exposed to and have adopted the laws of Confucianism. The Confucian rules of conduct are clear in many of the cultural practices of Korean Americans. For example, Korean Americans tend to display a strong respect for educated people and emphasize their children's education. Social mobility is seen as possible mainly through education, and it is a focus for parents wanting to enhance their children's socialization. Most Korean immigrants with school-age children decide where to live based largely on the quality of the schools in the neighborhood. Assisting children in getting a good education often involves tutoring, private lessons, and private schools. Most traditional Korean American parents are willing to make personal sacrifices to make sure that their children are well educated. The results of their efforts seem to bear fruit: Two or three of the annual recipients of the presidential merit scholarships, given to the two best high school seniors from each state, are Korean American.

ISSUES TO CONSIDER

Stigma toward mental illness is a common finding among samples of people of color. Like most groups, traditional Korean Americans view the presence of mental illness to be a sign of weakness on the part of the individual. The effect is often a sense of shame, not only for the person but also for the family of the afflicted individual. Because they feel they will be dishonored or "lose face" if others outside a trusted minority are told of the mental illness, traditional Korean Americans are often reluctant to seek Western mental health services until all other resources have been exhausted. As a result, Korean American clients often present severe or more advanced stages of distress than were originally identified by the individual or family member. Keeping mental health problems hidden from professionals may avoid the feeling of shame but also may contribute to difficulty with treatment once the issue is shared with others. When Western mental health treatment is sought, traditional Korean Americans tend to report problems with educational and vocational goals. The causes to which traditional Korean Americans ascribe mental illness (e.g., spirits, bad energy) tend to be different from those of Western mental health literature.

Despite their success in school and in business, the traditional Korean American population has not escaped discrimination. Many Korean Americans felt a sense of resentment toward other ethnic groups after the riots in Los Angeles brought feelings of rejection and oppression and examples of racial discrimination to the forefront. Korean Americans, though less assimilated into mainstream U.S. values than other ethnic groups, have struggled to find a place in mainstream society. In a study of children living in New York City, 30% of Korean high school students reported feeling discriminated against by American students or teachers. Cultural differences often are responsible for misunderstandings between teachers and Korean children, and there are too few Korean teachers and counselors available to meet the needs of children and the larger community. Moreover, Korean American children are not immune to psychological maladjustment.

Conflicts resulting from differing levels of acculturation within the family are a source of stress for some Korean American families, as they are for members of many other ethnic groups. Because most immigrant parents speak Korean, whereas their U.S.-born children speak little Korean and mostly English, language barriers within the family also contribute to family conflicts. Value differences tend to increase family distress and individual psychopathology—for example, Korean parents may value hard work, education, social status, and family ties, but their children may adopt more mainstream U.S. values. Moreover, Korean parents often have to spend long hours at work, leaving little time to supervise and play at home with their children. At the same time, traditional Korean parents may put pressure on their children to be successful at school, a task the children may be less interested in when unsupervised and available to spend time with friends and enjoy other activities.

Participation in youth gangs is rising among Korean American children and threatens the unity and cultural boundaries of Korean American culture. Like Chinese youth gangs, Korean gangs tend to recruit immigrant children who have limited English skills and difficulties with academic performance. The first Korean youth gangs were identified in the 1970s, but they increased in number and severity in the 1990s. These gangs began as a form of recreation and self-defense but quickly evolved into criminal-enterprise organizations. Because language barriers, cultural differences, alienation, and discrimination are more common among immigrant children than among native-born Korean Americans, the youth gangs seem to be more of a problem within the immigrant Korean population.

GUIDELINES FOR WORKING WITH KOREAN AMERICAN FAMILIES

Despite significant within-group differences among Korean American families, researchers have identified several strategies that may enhance the cultural competence of professionals working with this population. It is important to remember that because of differences in acculturation levels, the following practices work best with Korean Americans who identify themselves as traditional or bicultural in their Korean cultural attachment.

Identifying the Support System

Research shows that Korean Americans are more likely to seek out personal friends and extended family members than mental health professionals in times of distress; therefore, knowing the extent of the personal supports available to the family is important. It may be the case that a traditionally oriented Korean American will only seek the help of a mental health professional when other family supports are absent. Supports may also include religious or spiritual connections; it is important for professionals to determine how relevant spiritual leaders are for the Korean American individual. If the individual is a recent immigrant or first or second generation, assessment of the individual's use of native healers may be helpful in determining the range of possible solutions. Asking about the family's use of herbal remedies, acupuncture, and other native approaches may assist the professional in understanding the family's beliefs about culturally specific practices that are unique to Korean Americans. Some research also suggests that personal contacts involved in helping family and friends tend to report a strong quality of life. Being a supporter within the Korean American family may protect individuals from the feelings of sadness and displacement that can accompany immigration or acculturation stress.

Gathering Data on History of Immigration

It is important to assess each culture's immigration history to better understand the unique issues that individuals face when moving to another country. Some immigrants have a history of trauma, stress, or violence associated with departure from their home country, and their needs will differ significantly from those of people who came to the United States out of choice. Asian Americans are fairly recent immigrants to the United States compared with other ethnic groups; therefore, the Korean American population in the United States is likely to represent a significant number of first- or second-generation individuals. The majority of Koreans arrived in the United States after the 1965 Immigration and Naturalization Act. Generally speaking, first- and second-generation individuals tend to be more enculturated than those of later generations and may exhibit more traditional Korean cultural values. Professionals will be more effective when they gather information on the gender, age, reasons for leaving Korea, and length of stay in the United States of each member of the family. Like other immigrants, acculturation differences within a family can be a source of distress, especially when children are exposed to more U.S. culture and the English language, creating greater opportunities for children to acculturate faster than their parents. When the English proficiency of children is greater than that of their parents, disruption in the family hierarchy can occur because parents may have to rely on their children to communicate with school officials and other authorities.

Establishing Professional Authority

Research suggests that traditionally oriented Korean Americans may interpret the professional's credibility based on traditionally held beliefs about authority (i.e., age, gender, education history). For example, the feedback of an older Caucasian professional with a doctoral degree may hold more weight than that of a young Asian woman with a master's degree. The professional's reputation in the community is also important because knowledge of the therapist's skills may justify returning to family therapy. Knowing the age of the professional may help traditional Korean Americans know how to address the professional; address in the Korean language is often based on the person's position with respect to another. Older Korean Americans may be addressed more formally, indicating a higher status. Professionals who wish to demonstrate cultural competence should be aware of the relative positions within the family and show deference to those in higher positions and greater informality and candidness with those who are in a lower position.

Explaining the Role of Therapy

Members of non-Western cultures may be unfamiliar with the process of psychological therapy and research, and it is the professional's role to clarify what Korean American families can expect from interventions. The benefits of therapy should be explained to the decision maker in the family (typically the oldest member), and the role of family members should be explained clearly. Traditionally oriented family members may be unclear as to why they are involved in the treatment of another person. Using the first session to explain the intervention and to point out that the results may not be immediate can aid the family in better understanding how psychological treatment differs from traditional Korean models of the treatment process. By explaining the role of the therapist and family members in treatment, traditional Korean Americans may develop rapport and appropriate expectations regarding the nature of treatment and the duration of the intervention.

Assisting in "Saving Face"

Common to most traditional Asian American cultures is the notion of shame, or feeling embarrassed in front of anther person because of inappropriate conduct. Many traditional Korean Americans feel reluctant to express negative feelings about another family member in treatment and may be reluctant to return if the professional requires a direct confrontation. Professionals must strive to protect the honor and dignity of family members, and they must express support for the client and for the actions his or her family members may have taken to relieve distress.

It may be beneficial for professionals to resist labeling behaviors in terms of diagnoses. Diagnosing a disorder may communicate to the individual that he or she is inferior to others and has brought shame to him- or herself and the family. Early in the treatment process, professionals are encouraged to help family members—especially male family members—to "save face," as a loss of honor may result in early termination. This is especially important if the traditional Korean American family has not freely chosen to contact a mental health professional and has instead been mandated to come to treatment. Just being seen entering or waiting in the office of a mental health professional may be shameful for family members.

Attention to the males in the family is especially salient. Men are often called upon to be the decision makers in the family, and they may feel shame for needing the assistance of others to solve family problems. The role of the patriarch is assumed to include strength and competence; therefore, men may be more sensitive to issues and events that create a "loss of face." Because Western cultures focus on more egalitarian positions, understanding the patriarchal role of men in families may require some adjustment on the part of the mental health professional. Professionals are encouraged not to challenge the power hierarchy in traditional Korean American families but instead to practice flexibility and care when discussing issues that touch on traditional family roles.

Understanding Somatic Complaints

Like immigrants from other traditional Asian cultures, traditional Korean Americans may relate their emotional distress in physical or somatic complaints. When presenting in therapy, a traditional Korean American might report headaches or stomachaches when family problems are present. Culturally competent professionals will accept these physical complaints as real and understand that the resolution of the physical symptoms is just as important to the success of the treatment as any other emotional or stress-related complaints. Referrals may be necessary to address somatic issues and to demonstrate to the client respect and careful consideration of his or her problem. Traditionally oriented Korean Americans may be more likely to develop trust in a mental health professional when their physical health complaints are attended to, allowing more comfort to discuss emotional issues at a later time. For traditional Korean Americans, openly discussing emotional distress is often interpreted as a sign of weakness; expressing distress in the form of physical pain may lessen the self-perceived stigma and shame.

Being Direct and Present Focused

Because traditional Korean Americans may be unfamiliar with the therapy process, they may be reluctant to discuss personal issues and information. Researchers agree that the best method of addressing this sensitivity is for the mental health professional to be goal directed and focused on symptom mitigation. The therapist will be more likely to be perceived by the traditional Korean American client as sensitive to his or her culture. Traditional Korean American culture does not advocate efforts directed at uncovering the underlying causes of a problem. For example, one traditional Korean American value emphasizes coping with fate rather than trying to find solutions to alter fate. Finding out why something has occurred is not as important as finding a quick solution to the problem. This approach encourages the therapist to find pragmatic solutions without trying to uncover the origin. Given that Western therapy is often a last resort for most traditional Korean families, they have often tried other methods to resolve the presenting issue. This approach also helps the therapist to shift the focus from the client's behavior to a problem that affects the entire family. As a result, the family is less likely to place blame on one family member. Methods that require a lot of introspection on the part of the traditional Korean American client are not likely to be effective. Traditional Korean families may also be unsure how to act in Western therapy and may take a passive role, relying more on the therapist. To be culturally competent, it is recommended that health professionals take an active role in conducting the therapy process. Displaying confidence and expertise with the presenting problem will reduce the traditional Korean American family's anxiety and avoid early termination.

Assisting in Nonconfrontational Interactions

Although mental health professionals are encouraged to be direct with traditional Korean Americans, confrontation of family members is not recommended. Research has demonstrated that Korean American families are more concerned with social approval than families with Western values, and as a result, they may be more receptive to the therapist as a mediator of family disputes. Nondirect confrontation and harmonious relations are favored over confrontational approaches, which may increase the likelihood of "losing face" during treatment. Mental health professionals should avoid asking family members to address one another and should ensure that the therapeutic relationship is strong before challenging or confronting family members. Using gentle appeals and negotiation is a good way for therapists to gain a better understanding of the role of traditional cultural values within Korean American families. For example, one researcher found that when wives appealed to their husbands to participate more in housework, traditional husbands were reluctant to share gender roles because of their culture's patriarchal framework. However, when wives framed their request in terms of feeling fatigued or expressed that certain things needed to be done for the family to survive, the husbands were more cooperative. In this example, the husbands saw their new role as a way to care for family members who are tired and as evidence that a greater level of participation was needed for the family's well-being.

Reconceptualizing Mental Illness

Expressing positive attributes and pointing out what is working well can be helpful for traditional Korean American families who are managing emotional and behavioral problems. For example, family members are less likely to experience shame and to feel pessimistic when a father's strictness is reinterpreted as love and concern. As in other Asian cultures, mental illness carries a stigma, and getting help for a mental health problem can produce shame on the part of family members. Reinterpreting mental health treatment as strength and concern for each other can be advantageous in helping a family to meet mental health challenges. Family conflicts can be explained

as acculturation problems that are common to most immigrants. The distress is normalized and shame is lessened when family members feel that their issues are not unique deficiencies within their family. Furthermore, solutions offered by the therapist can be seen as new ways of behaving now that they are living in a new country.

—Yo Jackson

See also Immigrants

FURTHER READING

Hyun, K. J. (2001). Sociocultural change and traditional values: Confucian values among Koreans and Korean Americans. *International Journal of Intercultural Relations, 25,* 203–229.

Ishii, K. M. (1997). Intergenerational relationships among Chinese, Japanese, and Korean Americans. *Family Relations: Interdisciplinary Journal of Applied Family Studies, 46,* 23–32.

Kim, Y. S. E. (2003). Understanding Asian American clients: Problems and possibilities for cross-cultural counseling with special reference to Korean Americans. *Journal of Ethnic and Cultural Diversity in Social Work, 121,* 91–114.

Lee, E. (1997). *Working with Asian Americans: A guide for clinicians.* New York: Guilford Press.

Lee, R. (2005). Resilience against discrimination: Ethnic identity and other-group orientation as protective factors for Korean Americans. *Journal of Counseling Psychology, 52,* 36–44.

Lee, S. K., Sobal, J., & Frongillo, E. A. (2003a). Acculturation and health in Korean Americans. *Social Science and Medicine, 51,* 159–173.

Lee, S. K., Sobal, J. & Frongillo, E. A. (2003b). Comparison of models of acculturation: The case for Korean Americans. *Journal of Cross-Cultural Psychology, 34,* 282–296.

Lim, I. S. (1999). Korean immigrant women's challenge to gender inequality at home: The interplay of economic resources, gender, and family. In L. A. Peplau, S. C. DeBro, & R. C. Veniegas (Eds.), *Gender, culture, and ethnicity: Current research about women and men* (pp. 127–140). Mountain View, CA: Mayfield.

Min, P. G. (1995). Korean Americans. In P. G. Min (Ed.), *Asian Americans: Contemporary trends and issues* (pp. 199–231). Thousand Oaks, CA: Sage.

Shin, H., Song, H., Kim, J., & Probst, J. C. (2005). Insurance, acculturation, and health service utilization among Korean Americans. *Journal of Immigrant Health, 7,* 65–74.

Sohn, L. (2004). The health and health status of older Korean Americans at the 100-year anniversary of Korean immigration. *Journal of Cross-Cultural Gerontology, 19,* 203–219.

Toarmino, D., & Chun, C. A. (1997). Issues and strategies in counseling Korean Americans. In C. C. Lee (Ed.), *Multicultural issues in counseling: New approaches to diversity* (pp. 233–254). Alexandria, VA: American Counseling Association.

L

LANGUAGE PROFICIENCY

More than 300 different languages are spoken in the United States. Among the 47 million U.S. residents who speak a language other than English, most speak Spanish. Yet many states have passed English-only laws so that public services and state forms are less accessible to individuals who have limited English proficiency. In addition, a politically active effort exists to make English the official language of the United States.

Language proficiency can be defined as the ability to say what you want to say in the manner you want to say it and to be comfortable that you said it appropriately. Language is not merely the expression of words; rather, it integrates reading comprehension, writing ability, verbal comprehension, expressive ability, and cultural knowledge.

Immigrant children enter the school system and are exposed to the English language daily. Typically, they learn English more quickly than the older adults in their families, thus placing the children in a position where they must translate and interpret for their family members. These "language brokers" often participate in an adult world because they have more familiarity with the language and are expected to know the culture better. Although the children may be willing to translate for their family members, the stress on these children is apparent. Some of the sensitive information the child brokers may present challenges to the family structure or oppose cultural norms.

Linguistically diverse children are at high risk for school failure and dropping out. Although English as a second language programs have been implemented, backed by research that demonstrates the benefit of instruction in the child's native language with a gradual increase in English, these bilingual programs continue to be under assault politically. There has been a strong push to assess children with limited English proficiency with the least biased language assessment available. However, alternatives such as renorming assessments or modifying existing standardized tests come with consequences.

Language is a salient marker of ethnic group membership as well as one's level of acculturation or assimilation. Because those who speak English in the educational system and in the social environment gain certain privileges, many families have adopted an English-only rule. This suppression of the native language shifts not only the interaction of the family but also the acculturation process, identity development, and passage of cultural knowledge from generation to generation as each is exposed to a different level and degree of language.

Language is a barrier to acquiring appropriate social services, including education, health, and mental health services. The process of acculturation and learning English as a second language is stressful and can prompt a person to incorporate negative or maladaptive coping strategies. In accordance with the American Psychological Association's 2002 Ethics Code, mental health treatment should be delivered in the client's primary language. In this way, interpreters, translators, and bilingual clinicians are able to deliver services to this underserved population. However, to date, there are no language-proficiency guidelines to monitor the quality of services to populations with limited English proficiency.

The advantages of becoming bilingual and bicultural have been documented. The dominant U.S. population will no longer be dominant in a few years. It is time that English speakers no longer fear limited English speakers' use of their native language or their voice.

—*Carla J. Reyes*
—*Carrie Castañeda*
—*Ana Montes de Vegas*

See also Bilingual Education, Bilingualism

FURTHER READING

Acevedo, M., Reyes, C. J., Annett, R., & Lopez, E. (2003). Assessing language competence: Guidelines for research and clinical settings assisting persons with limited English proficiency. *Journal of Multicultural Counseling and Development, 31*(3), 192–204.

McQuillen, J., & Tse, L. (1995). Child language brokering in linguistic minority communities: Effects of cultural interaction, cognition and literacy. *Language and Education, 9,* 195–215.

M

MACHISMO

The concept of *machismo* and other ideas that define masculinity among Latino men serve to perpetuate stereotypes about Latinos and legitimate a constricted psychological portrayal of Latinos in the United States. In the definition of Latino males and masculinity, machismo reflects the complex interaction of behavioral, social, and cultural dimensions in the constitution of gender relations, and as such, it is a proxy for a narrow, negative view of Latino men. Machismo is the leading research and clinical construct used to characterize Latino men. It locates Latinos as deficient individuals or embedded in contexts in which they oppress others. Despite its importance in the definition of male identity, the psychological study of machismo lacks systematic study in the nonheterosexual world. This world supports an accepted bias in communities of males as much as in those studying it: Being a man in the Latino world assumes heterosexuality as the norm.

During the last two decades, researchers have questioned the concept of machismo as the central descriptor of Latino males' identity in the United States. This one-sided view of machismo has been criticized, and research has described it within a gender-relational view without denying the oppressive aspects that characterize machismo ideology—that is, an entitlement that locates women and/or the feminine as inferior. Thus, more recent research has focused on family protection, loyalty, compassion, respect, and dignity as components of machismo. A nuanced understanding of machismo proposes the existence of different forms in which masculinity and machismo are expressed among Latinos. Such research challenges the notion of a homogeneous Latino male identity, suggesting that this identity exists in the intersection of race, color, social class, and immigration. Research that advances a continuum of masculinities reflects Latino males' heterogeneity and the ambivalent ascription of machismo values. Some men may express the stereotypical forms of benevolent or archetypical machismo. Other groups of Latino males may be more compassionate and conflicted about how they participate in its stereotypical forms. Furthermore, some may have adopted or been socialized to adopt a more collaborative way of relating in the social world. Finally, a group, such as others from various ethnic, national, and racial origins, may present the more deleterious forms of patriarchal values. According to research, the way masculinity is expressed is not correlated with acculturation. Research is needed to study the linkage between different forms of masculinity and intimate violence.

As an ideology, machismo affects men and women of all sexual orientations, races, and cultures. As anthropologists have found, machismo as an expression of gender power that provides benefits for one group over others is found in most cultures of the world. Machismo is comparable to racism and classism because it sustains inequality and violence—the power of some men over women. It is not, however, a manifestation of one specific ethnic group but of specific cultural and historical contexts.

—*Gonzalo Bacigalupe*

See also Hispanic Americans

FURTHER READING

Baca Zinn, M. (1995). Social science theorizing for Latino families in the age of diversity. In R. Zambrana (Ed.), *Understanding Latino families: Scholarship, policy and practice* (pp. 177–189). Thousand Oaks, CA: Sage.

Casas, J. M., Wagenheim, B. R., Banchero, R., & Mendoza-Romero, J. (1995). Hispanic masculinity: Myth or psychological schema meriting clinical consideration? In A. M. Padilla (Ed.), *Hispanic psychology: Critical issues in theory and research* (pp. 231–244). Thousand Oaks, CA: Sage.

Mirande, A. (1997). *Hombres y machos: Masculinity and Latino culture.* Boulder, CO: Westview Press.

Torres, J. B., Solberg, S. H., & Carlstrom, A. H. (2002). The myth of sameness among Latino men and their machismo. *American Journal of Orthopsychiatry, 72*(2), 163–181.

MARGINALITY

The dictionary definition of the word *marginal* generally relates to the placement of an object—that is, an object is considered marginal in relation to another more centrally located object. Throughout history, a central task in defining marginalization has been to determine the criteria for placing an object in a position of centrality or in the margin. Racial and language characteristics, values, and cultural perspectives, all of which can be embedded in constructs of power and dominance, have been identified as criteria for differentiating objects as central or marginal. In this context, marginalization is the categorization of persons of nondominant culture as inferior or lesser persons.

CENTRALITY: A MYTHICAL NORM

Centrality provides a normative position that is defined by the prevailing political and socially dominant culture. Any position of thought can be normative and, by virtue of its centrality, exert undeniable power over a general domain. At any time, the locus of power may appear certain and familiar, yet at the same time it may be illusive. Because power is defined and perpetuated by those whose interests it serves, the locus of power can be challenged and redefined. Centrality can only be maintained within the security of a political power that claims to represent a stable center and define the margins. In other words, the dominant culture maintains its dominance, and groups of people on the margins of society remain marginalized.

CULTURAL CHANGES IN CENTRALITY AND MARGINALIZATION

Since the repeal of laws against miscegenation in 1967, we have seen an increase in biracial births in the United States. The presence of racially mixed persons has begun to change our society's long-held notions about the biological, moral, and social meaning of race and the role of European Americans and their values as dominant and central in our culture. In the past, feelings evoked by color and cultural ghettoization and stirred up by differences in language, values, codes of living, and religion resulted in the creation of dominant and marginalized races. These systems may now be ready to be deconstructed and reconstructed by those formerly considered to be marginalized individuals.

—*MaryAnna Domokos-Cheng Ham*

See also Accessibility of Health Care; Minority Status; Poverty

FURTHER READING

Ferguson, R. (1990). Introduction: Invisible Center. In R. Ferguson, M. Gever, T. T. Minh-ha, & C. West (Eds.), *Out there: Marginalization and contemporary cultures* (pp. 9–14). Cambridge: MIT Press.

Nelson-Jones, R. (2002). Diverse goals for multicultural counseling and therapy. *Counseling Psychology Quarterly, 15*(2), 133–143.

Park, R. E. (1937). Introduction. In E. B. Stonequist, *The marginal man: A study in personality and culture conflict* (p. xvii). New York: Russell & Russell.

Root, M. P. P. (Ed.). (1992). *Racially mixed people in America.* Newbury Park, CA: Sage.

Spickard, P. R. (1989). The illogic of American racial categories. In M. P. P. Root (Ed.), *Racially mixed people in America* (pp. 12–23). Newbury Park, CA: Sage.

MEASURES OF RACIAL PREJUDICE

Racial prejudice is an aspect of human behavior that psychologists have tried to measure in a variety of ways. There is currently some debate about the best way to measure racial prejudice. Fueling this debate is the difficulty of measuring racial prejudice. In today's society, exhibiting racial prejudice is not socially acceptable; therefore, it is sometimes difficult to assess a behavior or feeling that people are unwilling to admit to others or are sometimes unwilling to admit to themselves.

TYPES OF RACIAL PREJUDICE

Researchers in the area of racial prejudice are careful to define the types of prejudice that they are attempting to measure. These include blatant, subtle, aversive, and symbolic forms of racism. *Blatant racism* is defined as the expression of overt disdain for people of another race. *Subtle racism* is defined as the expression of ideas of racial preference that are hidden behind more socially acceptable ideals, such as economic or political arguments. *Aversive racism* refers to unconscious racism in individuals who claim to have very liberal ideals but who will act in a prejudiced manner if given the opportunity. *Symbolic racism* refers to contexts in which individuals of the majority culture use their values to judge and discriminate against others of different races. Researchers do not agree on the types of racism and their measurement; therefore, there are several different theories about the proper way to measure racial prejudice.

RACIAL PREJUDICE SCALES

One of the ways that psychologists traditionally measure behavior is by administering rating scales to a group of people and comparing their scores to the scores of others on the same scale. Many researchers believe that the best way to gauge someone's attitude is simply to ask them about it. Paper-and-pencil measures are usually the fastest and cheapest method of gathering information on racial attitudes from a large group of people.

Scales such as the Modern Racism Scale, the Pro-Black and Anti-Black Scales, the Diversity and Discrimination Scales, and the Subtle and Blatant Prejudice Scales ask individuals to agree or disagree with sets of statements that assess the individual's level of racial prejudice. Some of these scales are very direct in their questions, whereas others are more circumspect in their manner of questioning. Whatever the method, the scales all yield a score indicating the degree to which an individual's views are racially prejudiced compared with the views of other people from a similar background. The Subtle and Blatant Prejudice Scales are examples of a more direct approach and a more understated approach to measuring racial prejudice. Recently, researchers have used the scales in conjunction with a social desirability scale to ascertain whether the scales really measure what they claim to measure. They found that individuals who

self-ascribed items on the Blatant Prejudice Scale had lower scores on the social desirability measure, and individuals who self-ascribed items on the Subtle Prejudice Scale had much higher scores on the social desirability measure. It seems that people who are more subtle in their racism may wish to be socially desirable, and therefore do not exhibit blatantly racist attitudes.

QUALITATIVE METHODS

Taking into account the phenomenon of social desirability, some researchers have suggested that qualitative interviews with individuals about their racial views allow the researcher to be more sure of the origin of those views. Kevin Durrheim and John Dixon proposed that if researchers really want to know how people think about other races and racial situations, they need to discuss their views with them. For example, these researchers discussed the desegregation of a beach in South Africa with both racially European and racially African citizens. They found that although most respondents initially claimed they were not prejudiced against racially different beachgoers, they qualified these statements almost immediately. The qualifying statements often affirmed racial stereotypes but indicated that the individuals would accept members of different races who did not exhibit those stereotypical behaviors. The researchers argued that such qualifying statements are data that cannot be captured in a survey format—these individuals simply would have replied that they had no problems with individuals of other races using the same beach.

Other researchers argue that a qualitative interview format does not preclude the interviewee from trying to hide his or her views in order to be more socially desirable to the interviewer. In some cases, people being interviewed may be even more guarded when making racially based statements because they are voicing these statements to another person who may immediately judge their views. The level of formality of the interview, the setting, and the characteristics of the interviewer all play a role in how the individual might respond to racially based questions.

COGNITIVE PROCESSES AND RACIAL PREJUDICE

Researchers in the field of cognitive psychology have a different take on the measurement of racial prejudice. Cognitive and experimental psychologists focus on the measurement of reaction times and the effects of priming to measure racial prejudice. Classically, such studies ask individuals to classify adjectives as good or bad after priming them with an almost unnoticeable word, such as *white* or *black,* or ask the participant to engage in a racial classification of photographs or names and then complete a seemingly unrelated word-categorization task, measuring the individual's reaction time to racially charged words. In theory, racial prejudice can be calculated in groups of people by measuring the delay in reaction time to racially charged words or by tracking positive and negative categorizations of adjectives. Researchers in this area have found that after individuals are primed with the word *white,* they are more likely to categorize words that are considered racial descriptions of European Americans, such as *industrious* and *ambitious,* as positive; when primed with the word *black,* they are more likely to categorize words that are considered racial descriptions of African Americans, such as *athletic* and *streetwise,* as negative.

These types of methods are seen as tapping into unconscious racism, and therefore they are considered more accurate than traditional paper-and-pencil or interview methods. It remains to be seen whether these group-level differences can be reliably measured on an individual level.

CONCLUSIONS

There are several different avenues for measuring racial prejudice, including paper-and-pencil measures, qualitative interviews, measurement of reaction times, and categorization of adjectives after racial priming. Paper-and-pencil measures are the most commonly used method of measuring racial prejudice, but they are influenced by the individual's need for social desirability. Qualitative interviews can give a more in-depth look at the reasoning behind racial attitudes, but they are time intensive and also influenced by the individual's need to be socially acceptable in his or her views. Reaction times and categorical methods are objective measures, but they are not as accepted in the field of measuring prejudice and have not been shown to be sensitive enough to measure racial prejudice on an individual level.

—*Kimberlee M. Roy*

See also Minority Status; Racism and Discrimination

FURTHER READING

Durrheim, K., & Dixon, J. (2004). Attitudes in the fiber of everyday life: The discourse of racial evaluation and the lived experience of desegregation. *American Psychologist, 59*(7), 626–636.

Rattazzi, A. M. M., & Volpato, C. (2003). Social desirability of Subtle and Blatant Prejudice Scales. *Psychological Reports, 92,* 241–250.

MEASURES OF RACIAL PREJUDICE: MODERN RACISM SCALE

The Modern Racism Scale (MRS) was developed to measure subtle forms of racism that are prevalent in the United States today and includes questions that indirectly relate to racial attitudes. This newer and subtler form of racism comprises subconscious attitudes and may present itself as an endorsement of exaggerated ethnic differences or a rejection of minorities for supposed nonracial reasons. Current measures of racism (e.g., the MRS) were developed because older scales used very blatant questions to gauge racism—for example, "Do you agree or disagree that African Americans are inferior to Caucasians?" or "Do you think that it is a bad idea for African Americans and Caucasians to intermarry?" Because we are concerned with political correctness in the United States, individuals who are administered the older scales would likely deny racist beliefs, and results would drastically downplay the existence of racism. Modern racism has become less overt and prejudice more hidden because they are no longer deemed appropriate by society.

The MRS is an explicit (i.e., it measures conscious attitudes and beliefs, whereas implicit scales measure unconscious or unidentified attitudes and beliefs) and group-specific measure of bias. Further, the MRS is reliable and commonly used to measure conscious, self-reported beliefs and attitudes toward African Americans. It is a brief seven-item scale that uses a Likert-style format (-2 = *strongly disagree,* -1 = *somewhat disagree,* 0 = *neither disagree nor agree,* 1 = *somewhat agree,* 2 = *strongly agree*); total scores range from -14 to 14. Lower scores on the measure represent pro-African American beliefs and attitudes, whereas higher scores represent anti-African American beliefs and attitudes. Questions that make up the MRS include "African Americans have more influence upon school desegregation plans than they ought to have" and "Discrimination against African Americans is no longer a problem in the United States."

The MRS is often used by experimental social psychologists to distinguish between high-prejudice and low-prejudice persons or to test the role of prejudice as a moderating variable (e.g., political attitudes, racial policy preferences). Findings suggest that scores on self-report measures of bias, such as the MRS, predict deliberate behaviors (e.g., verbal content of interracial interactions), whereas measures of implicit prejudice predict spontaneous, automatic behaviors (e.g., nonverbal cues). Some studies that used both explicit and implicit measures of bias found that individuals who score low on explicit measures may still score high on implicit measures, evidencing strong pro-Caucasian beliefs. Such discrepancies support the importance of using implicit measures.

Although the MRS has considerable research evidence supporting its value as a racial prejudice measure, it also has limitations. One such measurement problem of the MRS is that it was designed with data collected during the 1970s; therefore, some of the questions are antiquated. Furthermore, because the MRS is an explicit measure of prejudice, it is susceptible to acquiescence bias because respondents may be motivated to avoid appearing racist.

—*Kerri Lynn Kim*

See also Measures of Racial Prejudice

FURTHER READING

Henry, P. J., & Sears, D. O. (2002). The Symbolic Racism 2000 Scale. *Political Psychology, 23*(2), 253–283.

McConahay, J. B. (1986). Modern racism, ambivalence, and the modern racism scale. In J. F. Dovidio & S. L. Gaertner (Eds.), *Prejudice, discrimination, and racism* (pp. 91–125). Orlando, FL: Academic Press.

MENTAL HEALTH

The focus of this article is mental health and mental illness in racial and ethnic minorities. Mental health and mental illness are not polar opposites but points on a continuum. Somewhere in the middle lie mental health problems, which most people experience at some time in their life. At the far end of the continuum are disabling mental illnesses, such as schizophrenia, major depression, and bipolar disorder. The term "mental health" is often difficult to define because its essence is rooted in value judgments that vary across individuals and cultures. As this country undergoes a transformation in terms of race and culture, it is imperative that we understand mental health within the context of these changing cultural and social dynamics.

MINORITY MENTAL HEALTH ISSUES

Although words such as "depression" and "anxiety" do not exist in certain Native American languages, the suicide rate for American Indian and Alaska Native males between the ages of 15 and 24 is two to three times the national rate. The overall prevalence of mental health problems among Asian Americans and Pacific Islanders does not differ significantly from prevalence rates for other Americans, but this group has the lowest utilization rate for mental health services among ethnic populations. Mexican Americans born outside the United States have lower prevalence rates for many lifetime disorders than Mexican Americans born in the United States, and 25% of Mexican-born immigrants show signs of mental illness or substance abuse, compared with 48% of U.S.-born Mexican Americans. Somatic symptoms are almost twice as likely to be found among African Americans as among Caucasians.

The four most recognized racial and ethnic minority groups are themselves quite diverse. American Indians and Alaska Natives comprise more than 500 tribes with different cultural traditions, languages, and ancestry. Asian Americans and Pacific Islanders include at least 43 separate subgroups who speak more than 100 languages. Hispanic Americans are of Mexican, Puerto Rican, Cuban, and Central and South American heritage. Diversity has increased in the African American community as Black immigrants have arrived from the Caribbean, South America, and Africa. Some members of these subgroups have largely acculturated or assimilated into mainstream U.S. culture, whereas others speak English with difficulty and interact almost exclusively with members of their own ethnic group.

DIAGNOSIS AND CULTURE

Western medicine has become the cornerstone of health worldwide because it is based on scientific research. The hallmark of Western medicine is its reliance on accurate diagnosis, that is, the identification and classification of disease. The accurate diagnosis dictates the type of treatment and supportive care, and it sheds light on the prognosis and course of illness. The diagnosis of mental disorders is arguably more difficult than diagnoses in any other areas of medicine and health because there are no definitive lesions or, in most cases, laboratory tests. Rather, a diagnosis depends on a pattern or clustering of symptoms (i.e., subjective complaints), observable signs, and behavior associated with distress or disability.

The formal diagnosis of a mental disorder is made by a clinician, and it is based on three components: (1) the patient's description of the nature, intensity, and duration of symptoms; (2) signs from a mental status examination; and (3) the clinician's observation and interpretation of the patient's behavior, including functional impairment. The final diagnosis rests on the clinician's judgment about whether the patient's signs, symptom patterns, and impairment meet the criteria for a particular diagnosis. The American Psychiatric Association sets forth diagnostic criteria in a standard manual known as the *Diagnostic and Statistical Manual of Mental Disorders* (*DSM*). This is the most widely used classification system, both nationally and internationally, for teaching, research, and clinical practice.

Mental disorders are found worldwide. Schizophrenia, bipolar disorder, panic disorder, and depression have similar symptom profiles across several continents. Yet diagnosis can be extremely challenging even for the most gifted clinician because the manifestation of mental disorders and other physical disorders varies with age, gender, race, ethnicity, and culture. For example, the many symptoms of depression—sadness, hopelessness, helplessness, withdrawal, despair—are difficult to understand and interpret within a culture, and even more so from one culture to another. The challenge rests not only with the patient but also with the clinician, as well as with their dynamic interactions. Patients from one culture may manifest and communicate symptoms in a way that is poorly understood in the culture of the clinician. Consider that words such as "depressed" and "anxious" are absent from languages of some American Indians and Alaska Natives. However, this does not preclude them from having depression or anxiety.

To arrive at a diagnosis, the clinician must determine whether the patient's signs and symptoms significantly impair his or her functioning at home, school, and work and in the community. This judgment is based on deviation from social norms (cultural standards of acceptable behavior). For example, among some cultural groups, perceiving visions or voices of religious figures may be part of a normal religious experience on some occasions but may reflect aberrant social functioning on other occasions. The interaction between clinician and patient is rife with possibilities for miscommunication and misunderstanding when the two come from different cultures. A clinician who is unfamiliar with the nuances of an individual's cultural frame of reference may incorrectly judge as psychopathology the normal variations in behavior, beliefs, or experiences that are particular to that individual's culture.

RELIGION AND MENTAL HEALTH

It is becoming increasingly evident that understanding the mental health of minorities is deeply rooted in understanding their religion and spirituality. Moreover, spirituality and religion are gaining increased research attention because of their possible link to mental health promotion and mental illness prevention. Religiosity and spirituality have been studied as psychosocial constructs that are predictive of many physical and mental health outcomes. Although spirituality is related to religiosity, the two constructs are distinct. According to the John E. Fetzer Institute, spirituality is concerned with the transcendent or transpersonal, addressing ultimate questions about life's meaning, with the assumption that there is more to life than what we see or fully understand. Spirituality is understood at the level of the individual, and it is a fundamental aspect of the person; it does not rely on religious contexts but focuses on issues of meaning, belief, and character.

The scientific study of human religiousness or religiosity has traditionally focused on religious affiliation, which has typically been operationalized as self-reported religious group membership (e.g., Roman Catholic or Southern Baptist). Religious involvement has generally referred to the frequency of attendance at religious ceremonies. However, current definitions of religiousness, religiosity, and spirituality differ from conventional definitions of religious affiliation and religious involvement in that they attempt to more comprehensively include behavioral, social, and experiential components along with values and belief systems. Religiosity is a social phenomenon that is characterized by one's engagement in religious beliefs and practices and defined by doctrinal, behavioral, and denominational characteristics.

Some research suggests that aspects of religious practice, affiliation, and belief are beneficial for mental health. For example, researchers examined whether a mother's religious devotion is correlated with the development of depression in children. The study found that over a 10-year period, two factors were correlated with children *not* developing depression: the mother's religiosity and having the same religious denomination as her children.

The association between religious involvement and mental health has been studied directly in African Americans. Using data from five large national samples, researchers found that African Americans report significantly higher levels of subjective religiosity than Caucasians. Other studies have shown that religious factors are strong predictors of life satisfaction for African Americans. A growing body of research indicates that religious and spiritual coping are protective against alcohol consumption in African American college students.

Spirituality plays a prominent role in the lives of the majority of all Americans; however, the literature suggests that it has a more significant impact on the lives of racial and minority populations. Each of the major minority groups in the United States has specific and unique religious and spiritual practices that significantly affect their health. For example, many American Indian and Alaska Native communities participate in spiritual traditions, and in many of them, Christian and Native beliefs coexist. African Americans in rural areas of the South participate in spiritual practices known as *witchcraft, voodoo,* or *roots.* It is not unusual for clinicians in these areas to report that many of their mental health patients believe their illness is the result of having engaged in these practices. Less is known about how these traditions relate to mental health. To study the relationship, researchers may need to develop new approaches and different outcome measures.

SOCIAL SUPPORT, FAMILIES, AND COMMUNITIES

Social support has been examined as an important factor in promoting positive mental health in minority populations. In about 75% of studies with clinically depressed patients, social-support factors increased the initial success of treatment and helped patients to maintain their treatment gains. Similarly, studies of people with schizophrenia or alcoholism have revealed that higher levels of social support are correlated with fewer relapses, less frequent hospitalizations, and success and maintenance of treatment gains. These findings indicate that providing social support has considerable promise as a technique for preventing or ameliorating mental illness and maintaining positive mental health.

Recent research has examined when and how social support works. One line of study has explored how the structure of social networks (such as variations in access to social clubs or voluntary organizations and the presence of close relationships) affects mental and physical health. This research indicates that access to such networks aids the flow of information, material assistance, and other resources to individuals. These resources, in turn, shape people's behavior and make it more likely, for example, that they will consult a physician when disturbing symptoms develop.

Researchers have explored the role of the extended-family concept in minority populations and the role it plays in the development and prevention of mental illness. A literature review on resilient African American children raised in inner-city neighborhoods concluded that such children had at least one adequate significant adult who could serve as an identification figure. In turn, the achieving children seemed to hold more positive attitudes toward adults and authority figures in general. In another study, African American children of low-income, divorced or separated parents were less likely to drop out of school if they were influenced by grandparents who provided continuity and support. Similarly, for urban elementary students chronically exposed to violence, the support of teachers enhanced their social competence in the classroom, as did support from peers and family. Family support was also found to be critical in relieving the children's anxiety.

For racial and minority groups, supportive families and communities help arriving immigrants with practical assistance with housing, transportation, and employment. In addition, they offer enduring support and a haven against racism and discrimination. They also help to confirm cultural identity, which has been shown to affect positive mental health in minority populations. It seems that community and family support are essential to the mental health of minorities.

RACISM AND HEALTH

Americans have struggled with matters of race, ethnicity, and immigration for hundreds of years. Each of the minority groups in this country has dealt with racism and discrimination. The ancestors of many African Americans were brought to this country as slaves and endured centuries of mistreatment. The Indian Removal Act of 1830 forced American Indians off their land and onto reservations in remote areas that offered few resources for growth and development. The Chinese Exclusion Act of 1882 barred immigration from China to the United States and denied citizenship to Chinese Americans until it was repealed in 1952. More than 100,000 Japanese Americans were unconstitutionally incarcerated during World War II. Many Mexican Americans, Puerto Ricans, and Pacific Islanders became U.S. citizens through conquest rather than by choice. Research is now demonstrating that the effects of racism and discrimination can lead to negative mental health outcomes.

Racism and discrimination are umbrella terms referring to beliefs, attitudes, and practices that denigrate individuals or groups because of phenotypic characteristics (e.g., skin color and facial features) or ethnic group affiliation. Despite improvements over the past three decades, research continues to document racial discrimination in housing rentals and sales and in hiring practices. Racism and discrimination have also been documented in the administration of medical care. They are manifest, for example, in fewer diagnostic and treatment procedures for African Americans than for Caucasians. More generally, racism and discrimination range from demeaning daily insults to more severe events, such as hate crimes and other violent acts. Racism and discrimination are perpetrated by institutions and by individuals acting intentionally or unintentionally.

Public attitudes underlying discriminatory practices have been studied in national surveys conducted over many decades. One of the most respected and nationally representative surveys is the General Social Survey, which found in 1990 that a significant percentage of Caucasians held disparaging stereotypes of African Americans, Hispanics, and Asians. The most extreme findings indicated that 40% to 56% of Caucasians endorsed the view that African Americans and Hispanics prefer to live on welfare and are prone to violence.

Minority groups commonly report experiences with racism and discrimination, and they consider these experiences to be stressful. In a national probability sample of minority groups and Caucasians, African Americans and Hispanic Americans reported experiencing higher overall levels of global stress than did Caucasians. The differences were greatest for two specific types of stress: financial stress and stress from racial bias. Asian Americans also reported higher overall levels of stress and higher levels of stress from racial bias, but sampling methods did not permit statistical comparisons with other groups. American Indians and Alaska Natives were not studied.

Recent studies have linked the experience of racism to poorer mental and physical health. For example, racial inequalities may be the primary cause of differences in reported quality of life between African Americans and Caucasians. Experiences of racism have been linked with hypertension among African Americans. A study of African Americans found perceived discrimination to be associated with psychological distress, lower well-being, self-reported ill health, and the number of days confined to bed.

A recent nationally representative telephone survey looked more closely at two overall types of racism, their prevalence, and how they may differentially affect mental health. One type of racism was termed *major discrimination,* referring to dramatic events such as being hassled by police or fired from a job. This form of discrimination was reported with a lifetime prevalence of 50% for African Americans, in contrast to 31% for Caucasians. Major discrimination was associated with psychological distress and major depression in both groups. The other form of discrimination, termed *day-to-day perceived discrimination,* was reported to be experienced "often" by almost 25% of African Americans and only 3% of Caucasians. This form of discrimination relates to the development of distress and diagnoses of generalized anxiety and depression in African Americans and Caucasians. The magnitude of the association between these two forms of discrimination and poor mental health was found to be similar to other commonly studied stressful life events, such as the death of a loved one, divorce, or job loss.

Though this line of research largely focused on African Americans, there are a few studies of racism's impact on other racial and ethnic minorities. For example, perceived discrimination was linked to symptoms of depression in a large sample of 5,000 children of Asian, Latin American, and Caribbean immigrants. Two recent studies found that perceived discrimination is highly related to depressive symptoms among adults of Mexican origin and among Asians.

These findings indicate that racism and discrimination are stressful events: Racism and discrimination adversely affect physical and mental health, and they place minorities at risk for mental disorders such as depression and anxiety. Whether racism and discrimination by themselves cause these disorders is less clear, but the subject deserves research attention.

SUMMARY OF MENTAL HEALTH AMONG MINORITY POPULATIONS

The surgeon general's report provides specific analyses for each ethnic group and includes a wide range of findings, including those outlined here.

African Americans

- The stigma of mental illness prevents African Americans from seeking care. About 25% of African Americans are uninsured. Additionally, many African Americans with adequate private insurance coverage are less inclined to use mental health services.
- Only about one in three African Americans who need care receive it. African Americans are more likely than Caucasians to terminate treatment early.
- If African Americans do receive treatment, they are more likely to seek help through primary care than through specialist services. As a result, they are frequently overrepresented in emergency departments and psychiatric hospitals.
- For certain disorders (e.g., schizophrenia and mood disorders), errors in diagnosis are made more often for African Americans than for Caucasians.
- African Americans respond as well as Caucasians to some behavioral treatments, but they are less likely than Caucasians to receive appropriate care for depression.

American Indians and Alaska Natives

- American Indians and Alaska Natives are the most impoverished of today's minority groups; more than one-quarter live in poverty.
- Certain *DSM* diagnoses, such as major depressive disorder, do not correspond directly to the categories of illness recognized by some American Indians.
- Four out of five American Indians do not live on reservations, but the facilities run by the government's Indian Health Service are located on reservation lands.
- One study found higher rates of posttraumatic stress disorder and long-term alcohol abuse among American Indian veterans of the Vietnam War than among their Caucasian, African American, or Japanese American counterparts.
- Although many American Indians and Alaska Natives prefer ethnically matched providers, only about 100 American Indian and Alaska Native mental health care professionals are available per 100,000 members of this ethnic group, compared with 173 per 100,000 Caucasians. In 1996, only an estimated 29 psychiatrists in the United States were of American Indian or Alaska Native heritage.
- As many as two-thirds of American Indians and Alaska Natives continue to use traditional healers, sometimes in combination with mental health care providers.

Hispanic Americans

- In the 1990 Census, about 40% of Hispanic Americans reported that they do not speak English well. However, very few providers identify themselves as Hispanic or Spanish speaking, limiting the opportunities for Hispanic American patients to match with providers who are ethnically or linguistically similar.
- The suicide rate for Latinos is approximately half the rate for Caucasians, but a national survey of more than 16,000 high school students found that Hispanic Americans of both sexes reported more suicidal ideations and suicide attempts than did African Americans and Caucasians.
- Many immigrants from Central American countries exhibit symptoms of posttraumatic stress disorder. Overall, however, Latino immigrants have lower prevalence rates of mental illness than Hispanics born in the United States.

Asian Americans and Pacific Islanders

- There are no studies that have addressed the rates of mental disorders for Pacific Islander American ethnic groups.
- When symptom scales are used, Asian Americans show an elevated level of depressive symptoms compared with Caucasians, but these

studies focus primarily on Chinese Americans, Japanese Americans, and Southeast Asians. Additionally, relatively few studies have been conducted in the subjects' native language.

- Asian Americans have lower rates of some disorders than do Caucasians but higher rates of neurasthenia. Those who are less Westernized exhibit culture-bound syndromes more frequently.
- Asian Americans and Pacific Islanders have the lowest rates of utilization of mental health services of any ethnic population.

CONCLUSION

It is clear that we are just beginning to understand mental health and illness as it is manifested in minority populations. If we are to provide mental health care to all Americans, it is incumbent upon the clinical and scientific communities to help us understand how race, ethnicity, and culture influence mental illness in all U.S. populations. Some factors relating to mental illness appear to be common to most ethnic and racial minorities. In general, minorities face a social and economic environment of inequality that includes greater exposure to racism, discrimination, violence, and poverty. These variables have been shown to influence health care utilization. It is important to eliminate any obstacles that keep minority group members with mental health problems from seeking or receiving effective treatment. There is also a need to reduce variability in diagnostic and treatment procedures by encouraging the consistent use of evidence-based, state-of-the-art medications and psychotherapies throughout the mental health system. At the same time, research must continue to aid clinicians in understanding how to appropriately tailor interventions to the needs of individuals based on factors such as age, gender, race, culture, and ethnicity.

—*Elwood L. Robinson*

See also Accessibility of Health Care; African American Mental Health; Culture-Bound Syndromes; DSM-IV

FURTHER READING

Clark, R., Anderson, N. B., Clark, V. R., & Williams, D. R. (1999). Racism as a stressor for African Americans: A biopsychosocial model. *American Psychologist, 54,* 805–816.

Finch, B. K., Kolody, B., & Vega, W. A. (2000). Perceived discrimination and depression among Mexican-origin adults in California. *Journal of Health and Social Behavior, 41,* 295–313.

Garmezy, N., & Neuchterlein, K. (1972). Invulnerable children: The fact and fiction of competence and disadvantage. *American Journal of Orthopsychiatry, 42,* 328–329.

Green, M. R., Williams, V. S. L., & Robinson, E. L. (2003). College student drinking and religiosity and spirituality. *University Undergraduate Research Journal* (North Carolina Central University)*, 6,* 123–144.

Hughes, M., & Thomas, M. E. (1998). The continuing significance of race revisited: A study of race, class and quality of life in America, 1972–1996. *American Sociological Review, 63,* 785–795.

John E. Fetzer Institute. (1999). *Multidimensional measurement of religiousness/spirituality for use in health research.* Kalamazoo, MI: Author.

Kessler, R. C., Mickelson, K. D., & Williams, D. R. (1999). The prevalence, distribution, and mental health correlates of perceived discrimination in the United States. *Journal of Health and Social Behavior, 40,* 208–230.

U.S. Department of Health and Human Services. (2001). *Mental health: Culture, race, and ethnicity* (Suppl. to *Mental health: A report of the surgeon general*). Rockville, MD: U.S. Department of Health and Human Services, Substance Abuse and Mental Health Services Administration, Center for Mental Health Services.

MEXICAN AMERICANS

Individuals of Mexican descent, or Mexican Americans, are the largest ethnic group of Latino/as in the United States. Differences in language, immigration experience, generational status, and social and political concerns have created a vastly heterogeneous group. As a result of these different cultural, social, and psychological influences, Mexican Americans hold a mixture of attributes, attitudes, behaviors, and values.

Several working assumptions will be used to synthesize the literature and research that describes Mexican Americans and to provide an integrative perspective on the experiences of Mexican Americans. That is, we acknowledge the role that acculturation, ethnic identity, and other factors (e.g., environmental and social attitudes) have in the socialization of individuals as they understand and make sense of themselves as Mexican Americans. Doing so necessitates the examination of the historical interaction between Mexico and the United States. Because Mexican Americans have diverse attitudes and behavioral approaches to understanding who they are and how they identify themselves, this information is intended to be used as a lens for understanding the social, cultural, and psychological realities of different Mexican Americans—it is in no way intended to delineate or construct an essentialist paradigm for the "qualifications" of a Mexican American. For example, individuals may have been born in Mexico yet identify themselves as Mexican Americans, whereas others may have been born in the United States yet identify themselves as Mexican. Instead, the salience, adherence, or identification of issues and constructs for individuals of Mexican ancestry is unique to each individual. Ultimately, the dilemma of definition and the intricacies of identity make it difficult to fully define or address all of the different aspects of the Mexican American experience. Therefore, a working source of culturally contextualized information about Mexican Americans is presented.

A descriptive overview of Mexican Americans in the United States will be provided. Next, a working table of constructs, which addresses salient environmental, cultural, social, and psychological aspects for many Mexican Americans, will be presented and discussed.

MEXICAN AMERICANS IN CONTEXT

Terminology

Mexican Americans, as well as other Latino/a subgroups, use multiple self-identifiers, such as Hispanic or Latino/a, as well as subgroup-specific terms such as Chicano/a, Mexican, and Mexican American. The complexity underlying the terminology and individual preferences in connoting the ethnic identification of Mexican Americans (as distinct from other Latino/a subgroups) is rooted in dynamic historical and sociopolitical contexts. Historical events (e.g., the taking of land from Mexico), sociopolitical climate (e.g., anti-immigrant movements), situational contexts (e.g., support from members of diverse and/or same Latino/a subgroups), and personal agency (e.g., ascribing self-meaning) all influence the preference of self-identifiers and often capture the fluidity of individuals' ethnic identification.

Because of the shortcomings inherent in specific terminology, many Mexican Americans prefer the umbrella identifier *Latino/a* because it captures the diversity of pan-ethnic and sociopolitical unity among individuals with a geographic and pre-Hispanic cultural ancestry in Latin America (regardless of racial and linguistic differences). Furthermore, the terms *Latino* and *Latina* are gendered (i.e., *Latino* = male,

Latina = female) and thus more closely emulate the Spanish language. The terms, however, are not always readily accepted or applied by those who ascribe emphasis to their Spanish-European ancestral roots, which may vary by geography or length of time in the United States. For example, Mexican Americans who have lived in the Southwest for many years often use the self-referents *Hispanic* or *Spanish*.

The identifier *Mexican* is a nongendered, subgroup-specific term that describes Mexican nationals or citizens who visit, reside, or work in the United States. These individuals often maintain ties (e.g., by visiting, phoning, or wiring money) to loved ones in Mexico and plan to return to Mexico after becoming financially secure. The term *Mexican American* is a nongendered, subgroup-specific term used to describe U.S. citizens of Mexican ancestry. Preference for this term, however, may vary because of individual differences in identifying with the Spanish-European, Mexican, and American cultures.

Chicano/a is a gendered (i.e., *Chicano* = male, *Chicana* = female), subgroup-specific term used to describe Mexican Americans. Historically used as a derogatory term to describe Mexican immigrants and poor, rural, indigenous farmworkers at the turn of the 20th century, the connotation of the word evolved during the Civil Rights movement of the 1960s. During this time of activism, political and labor movements emerged (e.g., Cesar Chavez and Dolores Huerta's United Farm Workers and the *Movimiento Estudiantil Chicano de Atzlán*, or MEChA), and the process of reclaiming the meaning of *Chicano/a* began. Today, the term *Chicano/a* continues to have ideological, cultural, and political meaning that fuels a new cultural identity for many Mexican Americans. Individuals who identify themselves as Chicano/a often emphasize both their pre-Hispanic indigenous roots (e.g., Aztec and North American) and their experiences within the United States. As a result, a sociopolitical consciousness or awareness that fosters a sense of social justice to redress current and historical inequities experienced by the Mexican American or Chicano/a community is advanced.

Population

The U.S. Latino/a population has grown substantially over the past two decades, with a growth rate more than three times that of the total U.S. population. As a result, Latino/as are a formidable social, political, and cultural influence in the United States that is estimated to comprise almost 100 million individuals by 2050. Currently, Latino/as make up more than 13% of the U.S. population, or about 37 million individuals. Individuals of Mexican origin are the largest ethnic group, composing more than two-thirds of the Latino/a population.

Although Latino/as reside in every state in the United States, there are primary areas of the country in which they generally live. For example, over half of all Mexican-descent individuals live in the West, and about one-third live in the South, whereas Puerto Rican–descent individuals primarily reside in the Northeast, and individuals of Cuban descent reside in the South. Mexican Americans have the highest population concentrations in Chicago, Houston, Los Angeles, Phoenix, and San Antonio.

Age, Immigration, and Generational Status

Latino/as are a young population: More than a third of Latino/as are under the age of 18, and relatively fewer Latino/as are 65 or older as compared with non-Latino/a European Americans. In particular, Mexican Americans have the highest percentage of individuals under the age of 18. Mexican nationals make up 20% of the foreign-born population in the United States. Although they are considered voluntary immigrants, this group often faces abject poverty with limited educational and employment opportunities and progressive deterioration in living standards. Mexican immigrants, however, view migration to the United States as an opportunity for improvement or, at times, a necessity for survival. The risk of migration, either legal or illegal, is often an enticing option, as the wages earned in several weeks of work in Mexico may be earned in a single day of labor in the United States.

Gathering accurate estimates of illegal immigration to the United States is difficult because individuals understandably do not disclose their undocumented status for fear of deportation. It is estimated, however, that more than 3 million illegal immigrants (from all countries) currently reside in the United States. Contrary to the popular belief that most Mexican immigrants enter the United States illegally, many come to the United States with legal documentation but become illegal immigrants when their documentation expires. U.S. policy on Mexican immigration has historically been described as a "push–pull" phenomenon in which immigrants are pushed out of the United States while simultaneously being pulled back as a function of economic need. For example, public discontent with Mexican immigration has prompted deportation raids and other anti-immigrant movements (e.g., Operation Wetback, Proposition 187), but businesses continue to lobby the federal government to allow increased entry for an inexpensive labor force from Mexico.

Directly related to immigration is generational status, or length of U.S. residence. The generational status of Mexican Americans may range from a recently arrived Mexican immigrant (i.e., first generation) to a fifth-generation Mexican American with an ancestral lineage to Spanish colonists who lived in the Southwest before the United States land annexation of 1848 (Treaty of Guadalupe Hidalgo). Generational status is often closely related to ethnic identification and often used as a single, approximate (and often inaccurate) measure of adherence to values. Specifically, time spent in the United States is frequently applied as a measure of the degree to which individuals adhere to traditional values and practices. However, it is often forgotten that Mexican Americans are the only Latino/a subgroup comprising both new immigrants and descendants of early U.S. settlers.

Language

Although a variety of dialects and linguistic nuances (i.e., indigenous languages and dialects) distinguish Mexican Americans from other Latino/a subgroups, the historical and current use of the Spanish language binds Latino/as together. Although language is a salient commonality for many, only about 60% of Mexican Americans speak Spanish. *Spanglish,* a mixture of Spanish and English, is often used when language loss has occurred. Spanglish represents the ability of many Mexican Americans to "code-switch" or effectively traverse two cultures simultaneously. Of Latino/a immigrants in the United States, almost 75% have adequate English-language skills to complete daily activities (e.g., secure a job, carry out work responsibilities). At the same time, 70% of Latino/a immigrant children become English dominant or monolingual English speaking within several generations of coming to the United States.

Education

Mexican Americans are by far the least educated of the Latino/a subgroups in the United States at all educational levels. One out of every three Latino/as fails to complete high school, and 25% of Latino/as have less than a ninth-grade education. These statistics are alarming considering that Mexican Americans are a young and fast-growing population. The discrepancy in educational attainment compared with other racial and ethnic groups begins as early as prekindergarten: Latino/a children are often less prepared to begin school because they are less likely to visit the library, have adults read to them, or attend prekindergarten programming.

Researchers have questioned whether the cultural values of Mexican American families limit students' educational pursuits. Despite the common belief and stereotype that Mexican Americans and Latino/as do not value education, Latino/a families often have equal if not higher aspirations for their children's educational advancement than European Americans. Instead, the educational system itself may be the culprit. There is historical precedence for the miseducation of Mexican Americans in the United States, indicated by landmark legal cases during the 1930s and 1940s in which Mexican and Mexican American children were segregated educationally as a function of race. Today, Latino/a students are more frequently misplaced into special education classrooms and directed into non-college-bound tracks because teachers often have low achievement expectations for these students and are not trained to address the cultural needs of Latino/a students. Despite increasing high school and college graduation rates among Mexican Americans, their overall educational advancement remains among the lowest in the nation.

Religion and Spirituality

Although no single denomination entirely captures the diversity of religious and spiritual practices among Mexican Americans, Spain's conquest and forced conversion of indigenous peoples in Mexico and Latin America to Catholicism has made Roman Catholicism the predominant religious denomination among many Mexican Americans. However, increased disagreement with the Catholic Church's stance on social issues (e.g., abortion, divorce, homosexuality, premarital sex), differing adherence to and practice of the Catholic faith, and conversion to other religious denominations (e.g., Protestant, Baptist, Jewish) have resulted in a variety of religious and spiritual practices among Mexican Americans. For example, indigenous traditions and

ethnomedical healing systems (i.e., *curanderismo* for individuals of Mexican descent) are central to the spiritual beliefs and practices of many Latino/as.

Employment, Health, and Health Care

Because of their rapid rate of population growth, Latino/as are expected to make up one-quarter of the U.S. workforce within the next 20 to 50 years. Latino/as are often unemployed and underemployed, and they frequently work in hazardous service occupations (e.g., operators, laborers, fruit and vegetable pickers, meat packers, and sanitation workers at slaughterhouses). With a high likelihood of work exploitation, poor work conditions, and no medical insurance or other benefits (e.g., paid time off), particularly among undocumented individuals, Mexican Americans often have limited opportunities for financial security and social advancement.

The U.S. economy benefits greatly from Mexican American workers, who represent 15% of the agricultural workforce and almost half of the service sector. Scholars, journalists, and filmmakers have challenged the public to imagine the multimillion-dollar losses in U.S. revenue if Mexican Americans did not work for just one day. It is estimated that halting these venues (e.g., agricultural fields, supermarkets, hotels, restaurants, and the sewing industry) would have severe consequences for the U.S. economy. Within the U.S. workforce, only a limited number of Latino/as hold managerial positions or have professional occupations; Mexican Americans are less likely to have such careers than other Latino/as.

Physical conditions such as cardiovascular and respiratory diseases and cancers are the leading causes of death among Latino/as. Mexican Americans are three to five times more likely than the general population to develop diabetes. A health risk for many Mexican Americans with type 2 diabetes is obesity, a condition that is often augmented by family history of obesity and insufficient physical exercise. Estimates indicate that about 70% of Mexican American men and women are overweight. Coupled with poor work conditions—for example, one of every three meatpacking workers sustains substantial injury each year or acquires an occupational infection from animal waste, and agricultural workers are exposed to airborne hazards such as pesticides, disinfectants, and fertilizers—there is tremendous cause for concern for the physical safety and daily health of Mexican Americans.

Table 1   Intersection and Interrelationship of Influencing Factors for Mexican Americans

Environmental	⇔	Cultural	⇔	Social	⇔	Psychological
Geographical location		Traditionalism-modernism		Familial network and community		Worldview: mestizo consciousness
Historical influences		Acculturation		Code-switching		Ethnic and cultural identity
Education		Attitudes, values, and behaviors		Phenotype		Internalization of stereotypes
Media representation				Stereotypes		
Immigration law and policy						

Regardless of income level, age, insurance status, or condition, Mexican Americans, Latino/as, and other racial ethnic minorities receive substandard health care treatment. It has been speculated that lower quality of health care treatment stems from the cultural biases and stereotypes held by providers and ineffective communication resulting from cultural and language barriers between providers and patients. Furthermore, more than a third of Mexican Americans under the age of 65 and almost 13% of Mexican American children are without health care. Health care access and quality of care are necessary and important considerations for all Mexican Americans.

THE INTERSECTION AND INTERRELATIONSHIP OF INFLUENCING FACTORS

A dimensionalized and contextualized perspective is necessary to understand the environmental, cultural, social, and psychological aspects of any group or community of individuals. The dynamic and nonlinear dimensions presented here are salient considerations that form the realities and experiences of Mexican Americans. Table 1 provides an overview of some of the most important considerations; however, it is not intended to be comprehensive, nor could it realistically capture the entire experience of a changing and heterogeneous group of individuals. The factors identified here have overlapping aspects and are not intended to be exclusive to any one dimension.

The arrows within the table signify interaction among and between the different dimensions, though they are not intended to represent direct linear relationships. Importantly, the role of each dimension and the variables within each dimension vary as a function of the salience or importance given to them by each individual. Although stereotypes abound about how or who Mexican Americans are, the effects of immigration, generation, education, adherence to values, and ethnicity (to name a few) make the aggregation of experiences impossible and somewhat unrealistic. Therefore, an integrated discussion of the environmental, social, cultural, and psychological considerations is needed to better understand Mexican Americans and their experiences.

A construct as simple as geography vastly influences the life experiences of Mexican Americans. From mundane daily activities (e.g., access to commodities) to the complex (e.g., generations of resentment regarding treatment by the U.S. government when land was annexed from Mexico), where Mexican Americans live plays a role in their lived experiences. For example, not all U.S. cities have radio stations that broadcast in Spanish, stores or restaurants that sell culture-specific foods, or even bookstores that have literature (in Spanish or English) written by Mexican American or even Latino/a authors. Similarly, access to one's native homeland of Mexico (for immigrants) or even venues that are primarily Mexican or Mexican American influences daily living. That is, feelings of isolation or alienation may emerge when one is unable to access familiar foods or feels like a stranger in one's own homeland.

Funding spent on schools throughout the United States also varies by geography. Most Latino/as do not attend schools with high expenditures per student, and they are more likely to attend school in states that have inequitable distribution of funding for education. These realities shed light on the educational context in which Latino/a students are taught. States in which inequitable distribution of funds is most prevalent include Arizona, Texas, and California, all states with high Mexican American populations. Unfortunately, Latino/a students are more likely to attend schools that have inadequate resources (e.g., outdated books or not enough books for students) or settings (e.g., classrooms that evidence mice or rats). As a result of inability or unwillingness to learn in this context of unwelcoming school climate, it has been suggested that Latino/as and other racial and ethnic minority students drop out of school because they are "pushed out." The undereducation and miseducation of Mexican Americans is pervasive and has extensive social, economic, and political ramifications.

Another insidious environmental force that influences the perceptions of Mexican Americans is the manner in which Latino/as are portrayed in the media. When Latino/as are addressed in the news media, the focus is typically on illegal immigration, terrorism, and crime. On television and in popular movies, Latino/as are often depicted as gang members, as criminals, or as maids or service workers. Yet when they are represented in fashion magazines or other print outlets, Latinas are rendered as exotic, oversexed women, and Latinos are portrayed as dominant, overly aggressive men. Furthermore, when Mexican Americans are portrayed in the popular media, those of lighter phenotype (European physical features) are more likely to be featured than those of darker phenotypes, who may be considered less desirable (e.g., darker skin is associated with laborers, individuals who work all day in the sun, or who are from lower socioeconomic statuses). Media images of Mexican Americans can be harmful to Mexican Americans' sense of individual worth and collective value.

Mexican Americans are perhaps most alike (and simultaneously most different) in their cultural attitudes, values, beliefs, behaviors, and practices. The continuum from traditionalism to modernism must be considered when examining the extent to which cultural values and practices are adhered to (acculturation) and the sense of pride that Mexican Americans have in their cultural group (ethnic identity). The traditionalism–modernism continuum, developed in 1974 by Manuel Ramirez and Alfredo Castaneda, represents adherence to cultural values. Modernism emphasizes individuality (e.g., individual competition and achievement) and relies on science or observation to understand life events, whereas traditionalism

focuses on connection to family and community throughout the life span and the creation of meaning through spirituality. Within the continuum, domains include gender role definition (e.g., strict division versus fluid and flexible gender roles), family identity (e.g., identification with and devotion to family versus individual identity), time orientation (e.g., value of past and present versus emphasis on future), the importance of tradition (e.g., focus on history and the practice of traditional ceremonies and rituals versus a view of tradition as an obstruction toward progress), and subservience to convention and authority (e.g., following norms and deferring to authority versus questioning authority). The values themselves (traditional versus modern) and the degree to which they are observed (acculturation) change as a function of time, education, and socioeconomics; however, many Mexican Americans continue to manifest these interrelated cultural values.

The value of *familismo* (familism) is perhaps the most important cultural value for Mexican Americans. Emphasizing a collectivistic worldview in which the family's needs take precedence over individual members' needs, familismo is the primary basis of Mexican American and Latino/a cultures. Interdependence, honor, and affiliation to family are reflected in strong feelings of unity, constancy, commitment, and reciprocity and a priority on intimate collective relationships. For many Mexican Americans, family serves as a support system that safeguards members from external, physical, and emotional stressors and often facilitates emotional and psychological well-being.

Within the family, the interpersonal communication style of *personalismo* (personalism) is valued. This interaction style comprises the values of *respeto* (respect), *confianza* (trust), *dignidad* (dignity), and *cariño* (affection, tenderness) and fosters interdependency and closeness in interpersonal relationships. Specifically, personal warmth and authenticity are emphasized through respect, that is, sensitivity and deference to an individual's social position (e.g., age, socioeconomic status, or gender); through trust, the distinct intimacy and familiarity that comes with being in close interpersonal relationships; through dignity, that is, the actions and behaviors that demonstrate and augment a sense of pride (e.g., strong work ethic); and through affection and tenderness, an approach that emphasizes genuine and loving interactions. For many Mexican Americans, the manifestation of these values emphasizes relationships rather than tasks.

Within many Mexican American families and in relationships with others, cultural gender roles are common, although the roles have changed over time and are salient (traditional modernism) and adhered to (acculturation) with great variability. *Marianismo* and *machismo* are traditional gender roles that have prompted scholarly discussion and a host of pathologized stereotypes about Mexican Americans within larger society. For example, the male gender role of machismo, in its strictest adherence, has been equated with marked aggression and obstinacy, excessive drinking and holding one's liquor, and intensified sexual prowess and arrogance with women. The female gender role of marianismo, in its strictest adherence, has been described as a cult of the Virgin Mary in which Mexican American women are expected to be semidivine, morally superior, and passively submissive. Because these values are frequently pathologized, their positive aspects are often overlooked. For example, the gender roles of Mexican American men emphasize being hardworking, devoted, and responsible protectors and providers of the family. Strength, dependability, trustworthiness, and caretaking are positive aspects of marianismo.

The role of *comunidad* (community) is also a central component of many Mexican American families. In addition to family, it is the comunidad in which cultural values are manifested with fictive and nonfictive family networks. Given the importance of family and relationships, the integration of new individuals into the family is a common occurrence. For example, Mexican Americans follow a system of *compradzco* of *comadres* and *compadres* (godparents or coparents) and *madrinas* and *madrinos* (also coparents, literally "best woman" and "best man"). Caretaking for individuals who are both nonfictive (e.g., aunts, uncles, cousins, grandparents) and fictive family (e.g., longtime friends) underscores the importance of community and explains why Mexican Americans often have more individuals in their households than any other Latino/a subgroup.

As Mexican Americans make sense of who they are individually, collectively, socially, politically, and culturally, the developmental process of self-awareness and self-understanding of one's ethnic group (e.g., pride, affiliation, knowledge of history) and behaviors (e.g., preferences in dating, friendships, food) is paramount. *Mestizo consciousness* represents the foundation of these psychological, social, cultural, and environmental processes for many Mexican Americans. The concept of mestizo consciousness was introduced

by Manuel Ramirez as an explicit call to limit the use of psychology's Western European approach to research, theory, and practice with culturally diverse populations. Because the word *mestizo* in the Spanish language signifies an individual of a mixed indigenous and European ancestry, it connotes the multicultural nature of mixed or multiracial people (e.g., Mexican Americans).

As a worldview, mestizo consciousness provides a frame of reference for understanding individual and group psychological processes, and hence a psychology that is congruent with the realities of diverse populations, including Mexican Americans. The tenets of mestizo consciousness include a sense of holistic interrelationship between individuals and their multiple social environments; spiritualism, or connection between the individual and the supernatural forces that mediate the attainment of self-control and self-awareness; a responsibility to give back to one's community; an emphasis on well-being and mental health that is rooted in working toward social justice, freedom, and empowerment; an engagement with lived hardship and suffering to facilitate growth and strength; and self-understanding of identity and the meaning of life based on an intimate comprehension of dualities and seemingly polar opposites (e.g., life and death). To various degrees, these tenets shape the unique worldviews of Mexican Americans and provide a foundation for cultural identity, its expression, and its vast variability.

CONCLUSION

Differences in the salience of and adherence to traditional cultural values, as well as differences in contending with environmental and social influences of the larger society, reflect the heterogeneity of Mexican Americans. Although this entry has attempted to illustrate commonalities that explain the realities and daily life experiences of Mexican Americans, it has also strongly reinforced that a "typical" Mexican American does not exist. The contextualized and integrative approach allows for the simultaneous coexistence of commonalities and interconnecting environmental, cultural, social, and psychological factors that create a more comprehensive yet accurate understanding of the heterogeneous rubric of Mexican Americans in the United States.

—*Theresa A. Segura-Herrera*
—*Alberta M. Gloria*
—*George C. Nichols*

See also Hispanic Americans

FURTHER READING

Anzaldúa, G. (1999). *Borderlands/La frontera: The new mestiza.* San Francisco: Aunt Lute Books.

Comas-Díaz, L. (2001). Hispanics, Latinos, or Americanos: The evolution of identity. *Cultural Diversity and Ethnic Minority Psychology, 7,* 115–120.

Falicov, C. J. (1996). Mexican families. In M. McGlodrick, J. Giordano, & J. Pearce (Eds.), *Ethnicity and family therapy* (pp. 169–182). New York: Guilford Press.

Falicov, C. J. (1998). *Latino families in therapy: A guide to multicultural practice.* New York: Guilford Press.

Gil, R. M., & Vazquez, C. I. (1996). *The Maria paradox.* New York: Perigee.

Gloria, A. M., & Segura-Herrera, T. A. (2004). ¡Somos! Latinos and Latinas in the U.S. In D. Atkinson, G. Morton, & D. W. Sue (Eds.), *Counseling American minorities: A cross-cultural perspective* (6th ed., pp. 279–299). Boston: McGraw-Hill.

Gonzalez, J. (2000). *Harvest of an empire: A history of Latinos in America.* New York: Penguin Press.

Guzmán, B. (2001). *The Hispanic population* (Current Population Reports, C2KBR/01-3). Washington, DC: U.S. Census Bureau.

Marín, G., & Marín, B. V. (1991). *Research with Hispanic populations.* Thousand Oaks, CA: Sage.

Santiago-Rivera, A. L., Arredondo, P., & Gallardo-Cooper, M. (2002). *Counseling Latinos and la familia: A practical guide.* Thousand Oaks, CA: Sage.

MINORITY STATUS

In 1945, sociologist Louis Wirth defined a *minority group* as a group of people who collectively receive unequal, differential treatment by others in society. Generally, a minority group is one in which members have less power and hold a subordinate or devalued status in society; as a result, they are oppressed, discriminated against, and have fewer opportunities to fight these experiences. Minority status is commonly used to describe racial and ethnic groups (e.g., African Americans and Latinos); however, minority status may describe any socially oppressed group, such as women, homosexuals, religious minorities, and the poor.

In the United States, the designations of majority and minority group status correspond to population. According to the 2000 U.S. Census, Caucasian Americans, who are considered the majority group, compose 69.3% of the population. African Americans, Latinos, Asians, and Native Americans represent 12.3%, 13.2%, 4.3%, and 0.8% of the population, respectively. These groups are defined as minorities in terms of both their group size and their unequal access to power and resources (e.g., money, education, housing, employment, and political influence).

Although the designation of minority group status would seem to imply that a group is smaller in size relative to other groups in society, this is not necessarily the case. For example, in South Africa, Blacks are considered a minority group but make up 80% of the population. Nevertheless, White South Africans hold much of the wealth and power in that society despite being a numerical minority. Thus, the principal factor that characterizes a group as having minority status is limited social power relative to the majority group, which is presumed to have higher social status and greater power to discriminate against others.

Often, minority groups possess characteristics that are assumed to indicate their inferiority and are used to justify their devalued position. For example, in the United States, people with darker skin tones are often perceived more negatively (e.g., as less intelligent, less attractive, more aggressive, and lazier) than lighter-skinned people. However, it is important to emphasize that these are stereotypes, not valid notions. It is the social belief that these factors are important that facilitates their use in maintaining inequality between majority and minority groups. The characteristics that serve as the basis for such group distinctions are socially defined and vary across cultures and over time.

Holding minority group status has important psychological implications. For example, rates of mental illness are typically higher for minority groups than for majority groups. This is thought to be the result of minority group members' devalued social position, which leads to increased exposure to factors that contribute to mental illness, such as stress, discrimination, hostility, and prejudice. These factors may also make it difficult for minority group members to deal with both stressful daily hassles and more severe crises. For example, they may have limited access to health care, fewer available coping resources, and fewer advocates in the political, legal, and social realms. However, minority group members also report larger social support networks and increased resilience, which may buffer the effects of these difficulties.

—NiCole T. Buchanan
—Isis H. Settles

See also Acculturation; Model Minority Myth

FURTHER READING

Maddox, K. B., & Gray, S. A. (2002). Cognitive representations of Black Americans: Reexploring the role of skin tone. *Personality and Social Psychology Bulletin, 28,* 250–259.

Phinney, J. S. (1996). When we talk about American ethnic groups, what do we mean? *American Psychologist, 9,* 918–927.

Sanchez-Hucles, J. V. (1998). Racism: Emotional abusiveness and psychological trauma for ethnic minorities. *Journal of Emotional Abuse, 1,* 69–87.

MODEL MINORITY MYTH

Throughout American history, Asian immigrants, like most minorities of color, have been cast in negative terms (e.g., inassimilable, yellow peril, opium addicts, coolies) and faced discrimination. However, this trend began to change in 1960, when sociologist William Peterson coined the term *Asian model minority* in an article in the *New York Times Magazine.* Similar sentiments began to appear in other news magazines during the 1960s. To bolster this argument, Asian Americans were shown to have higher educational attainment, higher-status occupations, rising median incomes, and lower rates of family instability, mental illness, and community crime. Asian family values such as academic achievement, hard work, discipline, and respect for authority were touted as leading to this success.

This characterization is problematic for several reasons. First, Asians are not a monolithic group; indeed, they represent an extraordinarily diverse range of 29 different ethnicities separated by geography, with sharply distinct differences in language, culture, religion, and politics. For example, among Southeast Asians such as Vietnamese, Cambodians, Hmong, and Laotians, educational attainment is quite low.

Second, Asian Americans tend to live in larger households with more working adults contributing to household income than do Caucasian families; when adjusted, Asians' individual income is lower than that of Caucasians. Poverty rates for some groups are extremely high—for example, as many as 40% of Cambodian, Hmong, and Laotian families receive public assistance. In addition, more than half of all Asian Americans live in five major U.S. cities (including Los Angeles and New York City) with high costs of living.

Third, data that showed greater Asian movement into higher-status occupations have been discredited; new data show a glass ceiling effect that prevents many Asian Americans with equal education and experience from being promoted to higher executive or managerial positions.

This myth has spawned a number of negative outcomes. For example, some have alleged that highly selective colleges are now intentionally decreasing the admission of Asian American students. There have been reports of increased racial incidents targeting Asian American students on campuses. College student affairs officials report greater campus resistance to offering specialized counseling services for Asian American students. Special poverty support programs for Asians in some cities have been eliminated. Finally, invoking the Asian model minority has become a new political tool for showing that racism does not exist—that America is indeed a color-blind meritocracy. Indeed, the model minority myth has been used as an argument for eliminating affirmative action altogether.

More recent data and analyses of the origins of the Asian model minority concept reveal that it is inaccurate and exaggerated and leads to a false, monolithic perception of Asians in America. Unfortunately, the perpetuation of this myth still appears to be accepted uncritically by the mainstream public, resulting in continued misunderstanding.

—*Ellen N. Junn*

See also Asian/Pacific Islander; Chinese American; Japanese American; Korean American

FURTHER READING

Nagasawa, R., & Espinosa, D. J. (1992). Educational achievement and the adaptive strategy of Asian American college students: Fact, theory, and hypothesis. *Journal of College Student Development, 33,* 137–142.

Sue, S., & Okazaki, S. (1990). Asian-American educational experience. *American Psychologist, 45*(8), 913–920.

U.S. Commission on Civil Rights. (1980). *Success of Asian Americans: Fact or fiction?* Washington, DC: Clearinghouse Publications.

MODELS OF MENTAL HEALTH

Clinical professionals use many tools to make determinations about mental health. Psychological assessments are based on models that describe behavior that is considered abnormal and behavior that is considered typical. These models can be helpful, but they can have potentially racist implications when applied to people of color.

DEFICIT MODEL

The *deficit model* views people of color as inherently inferior. This model was historically used to ascribe low status to people from ethnic minority groups and to explain perceived pathologies in people of color.

For example, according to the deficit model, people of color are described as having a genetic deficit. Psychological problems or behavior that differs from expectations is attributed to a deficiency in the genetic makeup of the individual. In this view, people of color were thought to be born with inferior brains and therefore were considered genetically less competent.

The deficit model is also at work when behavior is attributed to a cultural deficit. Specifically, when people of color are described as having a culture that is inferior to the mainstream culture or no culture at all, the deficit model suggests that cultural practices are responsible for psychological problems. That is, when so-called aberrant behavior is thought to be the result of the lifestyle of people of color, culture is targeted as the source of deviant functioning. Using this model, some describe people of color as "disabled under the weight of oppression" and therefore unable to adjust to the demands of mainstream society.

Racist Implications of the Deficit Model

The deficit model is a clearly racist model. Clinical professionals who hold this view are likely to be intentional in their racism (i.e., they believe the genetic deficit hypothesis), but they may also practice unintentional racism. It is likely that clinicians who subscribe to the cultural deficit position are at risk for making one of two treatment errors: (1) lowering expectations, or (2) setting unrealistically high expectations for clients of color. By setting expectations too high, clients are set up for failure. Conversely, setting expectations too low may encourage clients to underachieve, and their failure in therapy only reinforces their feelings of inadequacy. The deficit model clearly does not empower ethnic minority clients.

MEDICAL MODEL

The medical model is based on the association between mental problems and physical problems, and psychological problems are viewed just like physical diseases (i.e., "suffering from depression, afflicted by phobias"). The implications of this model are that mental health is the absence of symptoms and that successful treatment is the diagnosis and removal of the disease.

The medical model emphasizes the classic doctor–patient relationship. The therapist is considered to be an expert, and he or she is expected to be highly trained. Clients, however, are seen as needy recipients of the doctor's help, and they are expected to accept the doctor's diagnosis and treatment recommendations without question. According to this view, treatment is a verbal process: Clients are expected to self-disclose, and to be successful, the client must be highly verbal and capable of discussing his or her thoughts and feelings.

Racist Implications of the Medical Model

Although it is less racist on the surface than the deficit model, the medical model is also problematic. First, the premise of the medical model tends to over-pathologize the client. This may be especially important for people of color who present with behavioral problems because the medical model's focus on illness allows for external explanations of behavior to be overlooked. As victims of racism, ethnic minorities are more likely to be blamed for their problems and given a pathological label.

Therapists who are committed to the medical model may tend to search for intrapsychic explanations for behavior. The possibility that the problem behavior is a reflection of social pathologies such as racism, discrimination, poverty, poor education, and lack of health care may be ignored. This practice is similar to singling out a child who is acting out in a family that is dysfunctional.

Second, the implementation of the medical model may be limited in its accessibility to people of color. Because the goal of treatment is in-depth, long-term change, the expense and time of therapy eliminates a large pool of potential clients, especially lower-income persons of color. Third, the medical model fails to teach coping skills. Its focus on the connection with intrapsychic demands and resolution of internal conflicts provides little help in managing the stressful demands of reality. Fourth, therapists using this model may demonstrate some role confusion with their clients. That is, the one-down position may actually contradict some of the real requirements needed for change. Many therapists do not understand different cultures and use the treatment sessions to gain more cultural diversity expertise. However, ethnic minority clients find treatment of little use when the majority of their time is spent educating the therapist about their culture.

CONFORMITY MODEL

The conformity model evolved out of the general scientific tradition, which assumes a normal distribution of characteristics and behaviors within a population. The interpretation of individual behavior is referenced to a norm group. A person's behavior is compared with the norm group: If the behavior occurs in high frequency, then it is considered good, whereas if the behavior occurs infrequently, it is likely to be judged as bad.

According to the conformity model, there exists an *etic*—a culturally universal view of mental health that defines behavior on a fixed adjusted–maladjusted continuum. That is, there is a model of behavior that crosses cultural and racial lines, and the criteria for interpreting behavior remains constant regardless of the cultural context of the person being judged.

However, the conformity model also says that deviance need not be judged by one set of rules—that is, people may be judged according to the rules of the group to which they belong. The idea is called an *emic*—a culturally sensitive or specific model of mental health norms and expectations that vary across cultures. Deviance is defined as divergent attitudes and behaviors that arise out of a specific culture, allowing overt behaviors to mean different things to different people. The only valid interpretation depends on individual indigenous cultural norms.

Racist Implications of the Conformity Model

The racist implications of the conformity model are seen in the imposition of majority group values on minority group members—for example, when a clinical professional ignores individual and group differences in the context of a person's behavior. In general, most therapists do not struggle with these questions (i.e., how deviant must a person be, number of behaviors). Professionals tend to acknowledge the etic and emic distinctions, but in practice, most therapists are actually more etic. That is, they are more comfortable with clients who agree with their values and beliefs about what are and are not reasonable goals and behaviors.

—Yo Jackson

FURTHER READING

Atkins, M. S., Graczyk, P. A., Frazier, S. L., & Abdul, A. J. (2003). Toward a new model for promoting urban children's mental health: Accessible, effective, and sustainable school-based mental health services. *School Psychology Review, 32,* 503–514.

Cocking, R. R. (1994). Ecologically valid frameworks of development: Accounting for continuities and discontinuities across contexts. In P. M. Greenfield & R. R. Cocking (Eds.), *Cross-cultural roots of minority child development* (pp. 393–409). Hillsdale, NJ: Lawrence Erlbaum.

Dana, R. H. (1993). *Multicultural assessment perspectives for professional psychology.* Boston: Allyn & Bacon.

Sue, D. W., & Sue, D. (2004). The superordinate nature of multicultural counseling/therapy. In D. W. Sue & D. Sue (Eds.), *Counseling the culturally diverse: Theory and practice* (4th ed., pp. 3–29). New York: Wiley.

Weeks, S. (2005). Social perspectives in mental health: Developing social models to understand and work with mental distress. *Journal of Mental Health, 14,* 419.

Wilson, M. N., Kohn, L. P., & Lee, T. S. (2000). Cultural relativistic approach toward ethnic minorities in family therapy. In J. F. Aponte & J. Wohl (Eds.), *Psychological intervention and cultural diversity* (pp. 92–109). Boston: Allyn & Bacon.

MODELS OF SECOND-CULTURE ACQUISITION

Teresa LaFromboise, Hardin Coleman, and Jennifer Gerton coined the phrase *second-culture acquisition* to denote the process by which an individual gains competence in a culture other than his or her culture of origin. Although the term *acculturation* has historically been the predominant term for describing the general psychological process by which an individual exists in two cultures, it has also been used to describe a specific way in which individuals adjust to two-culture existence. Specifically, acculturation refers to the process by which individuals internalize the second culture while losing their connection to their culture of origin. The term second-culture acquisition was developed to clarify the distinction between acculturation as a process (synonymous with second-culture acquisition) and acculturation as a directional relationship in which an individual adheres more strongly to the second culture while loosening ties with the culture of origin. LaFromboise, Coleman, and Gerton suggested that *second-culture acquisition* be used to denote the broad process of coping with second-culture contact and that *acculturation* be used to describe a specific way in which an individual copes with the contact.

Second-culture acquisition, or the way in which an individual strategically interacts with two cultures, occurs in six ways. Specifically, separation, assimilation, acculturation, alternation, multiculturalism, and fusion are strategic ways in which individuals deal with the experience of existing in two distinct cultures simultaneously.

Separation: Individuals who orient themselves to a separationist approach to second-culture contact remove themselves from persons outside their culture of origin.

Assimilation: The assimilationist strategy has the goal of becoming a full member of the second culture (typically the majority culture) and losing identification with the culture of origin. Over generations, assimilationists and their offspring become indistinguishable from other members of the majority culture.

Acculturation: Similar to the assimilationist strategy, the acculturation model holds that individuals desire to gain second-culture competency. However, unlike assimilationists, these individuals do so with the knowledge that becoming full, indistinguishable members of the second culture is not likely. Thus, over time and generations, these individuals are still identified as members of a minority culture.

Alternation: The alternation model suggests that an individual can achieve competency in two cultures simultaneously without detriment to her or his cultural identity. Furthermore, these individuals are able to strategically alternate their behavior or mindset according to the cultural and social context.

Multiculturalism: The multicultural model suggests the possibility that individuals from different cultural contexts can coexist without a concurrent loss or compromise of cultural identity. The multicultural model is a pluralistic conceptualization that envisions complex interaction and sharing between distinct cultures without detriment to either.

Fusion: The fusion model suggests that as two (or more) cultures come into contact over time, they will fuse together until they form a new culture (e.g., Asian American culture). This new culture ultimately becomes essential to the identity of the members of this group.

Separation, assimilation, acculturation, alternation, multiculturalism, and fusion models for coping with second-culture contact provide a framework for understanding the complex process that occurs for individuals and society as multiple cultures coexist. It is important to note that for some individuals, some strategies or models may not be viable options given their sociopolitical climate or race-related issues. Although individuals may indeed choose the manner in which they cope with second-culture contact, the reason for that choice may be vastly different. It may be important to understand the context in which the choice is made.

—*Matthew J. Miller*
—*Suzette L. Speight*

See also Acculturation

FURTHER READING

Coleman, H. L. K., Casali, S. B., & Wampold, B. E. (2001). Adolescent strategies for coping with cultural diversity. *Journal of Counseling and Development, 79,* 356–364.

LaFromboise, T., Coleman, H. L. K., & Gerton, J. (1993). Psychological impact of biculturalism: Evidence and theory. *Psychological Bulletin, 114,* 395–412.

MULTICULTURAL COUNSELING

DEFINITION

The term *multicultural counseling* refers to a philosophy, a set of guidelines and recommendations for conducting counseling with culturally different clients, and a group of distinct approaches to psychotherapy. In the narrowest definition of the term, multicultural counseling is an interaction between a counselor and a racially or ethnically different client. More broadly defined, this term includes differences in gender, sexual orientation, and physical ability. As a philosophy rather than a specific theory, multicultural counseling is often equated with a tripartite model that incorporates knowledge, awareness, and skills and derives from the work of Derald Wing Sue, Patricia Arredondo, and Roderick McDavis. *Multicultural counseling competencies,* an extension of this model, offer general suggestions for gaining knowledge, increasing awareness, and obtaining skills for effective and ethical work with culturally different clients. Other models of multicultural counseling exist as well. Finally, culture-specific approaches address the cultural norms and needs of particular racial or ethnic groups—for example, counseling with African American persons or South Asian families.

RELEVANT TERMS

Defining multicultural counseling can be a confusing task, as there are many different ideas about which aspects of culture are relevant and which should be the focus of multicultural counseling. Aspects of individual identity that are often mentioned in conjunction with multicultural counseling are race, ethnicity, and culture. To facilitate discussion of this issue, some basic concepts must first be defined.

Traditionally, the counseling literature has defined *race* as a set of biologically determined characteristics that separate one group of people from another. Some of these characteristics include physical traits such as body type, skin color, and hair texture. Multicultural specialists have long criticized this definition because people who self-identify as members of a particular group may not conform in appearance to stereotypical conceptions of their racial group. Furthermore, race is socially and politically constructed.

The term *ethnicity* refers to groups of people who share a country or nation of origin as well as nonbiological factors such as language, religion, and customs. In this sense, ethnicity may be considered more specific than race because it refers to smaller groups of people and acknowledges immense within-group differences that may be overlooked by focusing on race. For example, both Japanese Americans and Pakistani Americans (ethnicity) might be considered Asian (race), but their ethnic differences surpass assumed racial similarities.

Culture is a context that dictates the use of language, structures a hierarchy of values, organizes a belief system, offers a unique interpretation of historical and present realities, and defines social roles. Within this context, cultural insiders know what is expected of them and what they can expect of others. Cultural outsiders, meanwhile, may find themselves confused by unfamiliar structures, excluded and ostracized by insiders, and devalued and oppressed by social and political institutions and by individual cultural insiders.

Culture can be thought of as a veil over one's face, a metaphor that was first used by multicultural psychologists D. W. Sue and D. Sue. The eyes of the wearer become so accustomed to the patterns of the fabric that the fabric is no longer perceived. To notice the pattern, the veil has to be removed, or another person's veil may be observed or even tried on. Although the fabric and the pattern may not be consciously experienced as separate from the view, they still shade one's perceptions in a particular way. Often, members of a majority culture forget that they, too, wear a veil. Alternatively, they may believe that their own cultural veil is the one true, healthy, or desirable view, whereas other worldviews are somehow distorted, maladjusted, or unworthy. This monocultural worldview, coupled with the political and economic power of the European American majority culture in the United States, has resulted in the dismissal and oppression of minority cultures' worldviews.

The term *counseling* describes a professional relationship that is established between two or more individuals, one of whom is a trained professional who provides services that are designed to assist clients in meeting their counseling goals. Here, counseling is used interchangeably with the term *psychotherapy.* Similarly, the term *counselor* refers to a variety of helping professionals, such as community counselors, clinical social workers, therapists, and psychologists. These individuals have completed a course of professional training and are bound by the ethical rules and guidelines of their professional organizations.

The term *counselor* can also be applied to practitioners of indigenous healing practices. Indigenous healers typically undergo a training process that is sanctioned by their community. At the end of this process, they have knowledge of and are skilled in culturally specific practices that are designed to offer emotional, psychological, or physical aid to their followers. Indigenous healers are often known by titles designated by their cultural groups rather than the generic term *counselor*—for example, *shaman* in Native American nations or *kahuna* among Native Hawaiians. For the sake of clarity, the same distinction is made here. Furthermore, the more specific designation *multiculturally skilled counselor* is used to distinguish helping professionals who have undertaken the process of self-examination and knowledge and skill acquisition that is necessary to conduct culturally sensitive counseling. It should be noted, however, that the foregoing definitions have been influenced by the European American view of helping relationships and helping professionals, and therefore they are inherently biased.

Divergent views of what constitutes multicultural counseling originate in differing opinions on relevant cultural variables. Psychologists Suzette Speight, Linda Myers, Chikako Cox, and Pamela Highlen assert that all counseling is multicultural: Although individuals may share a number of attributes and experiences, every individual is unique. In other words, by virtue of being human, we all have a set of shared experiences (e.g., being born). We also have a set of experiences in common with a group of people who are similar to us (e.g., a particular national identity or religious faith). Finally, there are qualities and experiences that are unique to each individual. Therefore, in the counseling relationship, even a counselor and client who are culturally similar in some ways will be culturally different in other ways, making every counseling situation and human interaction multicultural.

An alternative view advocates a less inclusive definition of multicultural counseling, one that focuses narrowly on race and ethnicity. This definition differentiates between *multiculturalism,* which refers to ethnicity and race, and *diversity,* which refers to other dimensions of an individual's identity, such as gender, age, physical ability, and sexual orientation. For example, psychologists D. W. Sue and Patricia Arredondo worry that the inclusion of other variables, such as gender, physical ability, or sexual orientation, may dilute the focus of multicultural counseling. From this perspective, multicultural counseling is defined only as a counseling encounter or relationship in which the counselor and the client are from different racial or ethnic backgrounds.

RATIONALE FOR MULTICULTURAL COUNSELING

Multicultural counseling acknowledges that culture forms the basis of our cognitions, emotions, behaviors, assumptions, beliefs, and expectations of others. Culture influences every aspect of our daily lives: communications, social interactions, familial relationships, and perceptions of reality. Therefore, members of different cultures may have very different expectations and perceptions of interpersonal interactions and events in the physical world. These differences can cause communication to break down. Effective counseling relies on a high degree of mutual understanding between the counselor and the client. A lack of accurate cultural understanding on the counselor's part is likely one reason why a large percentage of clients who belong to American racial and ethnic minority groups do not

continue counseling after the initial session. Over the past 30 years, the multicultural counseling literature has addressed cross-cultural communication and provided training material for counselors who practice with culturally different clients.

Culture has specific implications that are important to consider in the mental health arena. Cultural norms dictate acceptable and unacceptable forms of emotional expression and general conduct. Behaviors that fall outside those cultural norms are considered problematic, maladaptive, disturbed, or even deviant. The *Diagnostic and Statistical Manual of Mental Disorders,* 4th edition (*DSM-IV-TR*) is a primary tool used in the mental health field (including counseling, psychology, and psychiatry) to diagnose disorders and difficulties. The *DSM-IV-TR* cautions that when considering a clinical diagnosis, identified problem behaviors must lie outside those expected by the individual's cultural group in order to meet diagnostic criteria. In other words, the individual seeking counseling must be compared with his or her own racial or ethnic group rather than with another racial or ethnic minority group. This provision is designed to alert practitioners to subtle and obvious cultural differences in emotional and behavioral expression and thereby prevent practitioners from erroneously diagnosing as mental illness a behavior that is consistent with, appropriate within, and acceptable within the individual's cultural group.

Helping professionals who write in the area of multicultural counseling have done some tremendously important work to illuminate and normalize cultural differences. Multicultural specialists have also exposed inequities in the treatment of people of color by mental health professionals because of ignorance of cultural norms and institutionalized racism. Psychologists D. W. Sue and David Sue have emphasized the importance of cultural factors in the process of assessment, diagnosis, and treatment.

Multicultural counseling further recognizes the impact of culture, race, and oppression (such as racism and sexism) on the socioemotional development, psychological well-being, psychopathology, and psychotherapy of all people. These sociopolitical forces have traditionally been overlooked as major influences on individual development. Multicultural counseling makes these sociopolitical issues central to the work of counseling, particularly when working with members of the major racial and ethnic groups living in the United States. These groups include African Americans, Asian Americans and Pacific

Islanders, Native Americans and Alaska Natives, and Latinos. European Americans are also a major racial group. Historically (albeit erroneously), the European American cultural majority in the United States has been regarded as the standard and their developmental, psychological, and communication processes assumed to be universal.

Multicultural counseling recognizes that cultural differences themselves can cause emotional and interpersonal distress in individuals. For example, new immigrants often experience culture shock, which may be expressed as confusion about performing daily living tasks that were performed without difficulty in the country of origin (e.g., mailing letters at the post office); frustration about the limited ability to communicate; or depression resulting from separation from one's social network. Once again, multicultural counseling treats cultural differences as a very real cause of suffering and addresses them in counseling when necessary.

HISTORY OF MULTICULTURAL COUNSELING

The roots of psychology and psychotherapy were firmly established during the late 19th and 20th century in Europe. Although there were great philosophical differences among the early theorists of psychology and psychotherapy, their perspectives primarily reflected the experiences of educated men of European background. Examples include Sigmund Freud's psychoanalysis and Frederick Perls's gestalt therapy. Questions of culture, cultural differences, and cultural relativity of developmental processes were infrequently addressed during the early period in psychology and psychotherapy. Certainly, cultural differences were rarely addressed in a way that portrayed non-European cultures in a positive light.

There are at least two possible explanations for this inattention to culture. The first has to do with the general worldview held by educated and scientific minds of the time, which exemplified Eurocentrism (establishing European cultural expectations as the standard against which all other cultures are measured), racism, and oppression, all of which were institutionalized in the European academic, political, and social circles of the time. From this vantage point, culturally unique phenomena were often interpreted in pejorative terms. For example, an unfamiliar, culturally prescribed custom or ritual may have been described as primitive, underdeveloped, or savage.

The second explanation has been equally detrimental to the needs of multicultural populations. With views based on the more established hard sciences (biology, chemistry, and physics), early psychologists were invested in explaining human behavior through generalizable, universal patterns, if not laws. Thus, early psychologists and psychotherapists embraced the universal humanistic approach, which held that all human behavior and all human experiences have more commonalities than differences because of the underlying biological and physiological characteristics that make us all members of the same species.

European and European American psychological thought began to be challenged during the 1970s and 1980s in the United States. Frustrated and outraged by the unresponsiveness of the accepted psychotherapeutic practices of the time to the unique needs of racial and ethnic minorities in the United States, some psychologists began to criticize European and European American theories of personality development and the psychotherapeutic process. The arguments against blindly applying traditional approaches to work with minorities claimed such methods were not only ineffective but also unethical and potentially harmful to clients.

The lasting legacy of the mistreatment of racial and ethnic minorities in the professional psychological literature can still be felt. A supplement to the surgeon general's 1999 report, *Mental Health: Culture, Race, and Ethnicity,* affirmed that racial and ethnic minorities in the United States have less access to mental health services than their European American counterparts. Furthermore, the quality of care provided to minority groups is low. According to the report, these inequalities in mental health care are the result of our history of racism and discrimination, which had made racial minorities rightfully distrustful of treatment; deficiencies in cultural knowledge among mental health professionals; and a lack of competent bilingual services.

Juris G. Draguns, a multicultural psychologist, elucidates the potential outcomes of counseling encounters when cultural differences are overlooked. He asserts that clients whose cultural expectations are not met by counselors may feel frustrated and unheard, leave counseling prematurely, and feel distanced from counselors. According to Robert Carter, unexamined discrepancies in worldviews between clients and counselors will make the counselor's interventions unsuccessful. Furthermore, Draguns cautions that clients may even be emotionally, psychologically, or socially harmed when their needs are misinterpreted, misdiagnosed, and misaddressed.

In its practice, multicultural counseling attempts to rectify disparities in access to and quality of mental health services for racial and ethnic minority groups. Multicultural counseling strives to accomplish this goal by providing culturally relevant and responsive services that are delivered by culturally competent mental health professionals.

DIFFERENCES BETWEEN MULTICULTURAL AND EUROCENTRIC COUNSELING

Multicultural counseling can complement other Eurocentric theories of counseling (such as psychoanalysis and existentialist or person-centered approaches), yet it is distinctly different from them. Here we will examine the distinct features of multicultural counseling in comparison with Eurocentric counseling.

Multicultural counseling has a broad focus that takes into account the client's multiple social connections, such as family, school system, and workplace. Most Eurocentric counseling approaches, however, view the client in a narrow way, as an individual who is somehow disconnected from his or her social environment. This perspective is consistent with the individualistic European American worldview. An extension of this worldview is the conceptualization of problems as originating within the individual. Therefore, most Eurocentric theories have an *intrapersonal* focus and propose methods for change that almost exclusively require the individual to alter her or his own thoughts, feelings, and behaviors without effecting change in his or her larger social contexts. Finally, if the presenting problem is *intrapersonal,* counseling will likely focus on that single aspect of the client's identity. For example, a child who is in counseling for behavioral problems at school may be treated for anxiety, depression, attention-deficit/hyperactivity disorder, or any number of other problems without ever addressing his or her social position as a young person of color, a homeless person, or a recent immigrant with limited academic support at home.

Multicultural counseling does not assume that presenting problems originate exclusively within the individual. Rather, larger social forces are examined for their role in the client's current difficulties. Furthermore, the complexities of personal identity arising from simultaneous membership in multiple social groups (e.g., race, gender, social class) are acknowledged, along with the historical contexts of those memberships (e.g., racism, sexism, classism). Multicultural counseling includes in the work of therapy issues and concepts that are important to all cultural groups living in the United States, but particularly those that are salient to the major racial groups. These issues include ethnic and racial identity development, acculturation, and discrimination, areas that traditionally have been neglected by Eurocentric theories of psychotherapy and theories on the development of mental health problems.

In multicultural counseling, these concepts are explicitly addressed in the assessment of the client's presenting problem, diagnosis, treatment planning, and treatment delivery. In other words, the client's cultural background and membership in a particular cultural group play crucial roles in his or her overall sense of self and offer resources that may support treatment goals. Simultaneously, the client's social, economic, and political position in a predominantly European American society and culture may be the cause of his or her presenting problems or may be contributing to his or her personal difficulties. For example, a student of color at a predominantly European American university may seek counseling for anxiety and inability to concentrate. However, during the course of counseling, it may become apparent that the student began to experience anxiety only after signing up for a class in which the professor made disparaging remarks about the student's ethnic group. In this example, it would be unethical to treat the anxiety as originating within the student as a result of a physiological or hereditary predisposition. Instead, the racism experienced in the classroom would be the appropriate focus of treatment.

MODELS OF MULTICULTURAL COUNSELING

A multiculturally skilled counselor implicitly and explicitly takes into account not only the client's culture but also the cultural differences that exist between the client and the counselor. Helping professionals now realize that culture directly influences help-seeking behaviors, definitions of presenting problems by both counselors and clients, responsiveness to certain helping styles and approaches, and the overall client–counselor interactions. As Robert Carter points out, comparative cultural studies offer evidence that cultural views of mental health are so powerful that they can determine the expression, course, and outcome of mental illness.

The multicultural counselor is responsible for becoming knowledgeable about the client's culture rather than using the client as a cultural guide. However, the counselor needs to acknowledge that the client is the expert in the meaning of culture in his or her personal identity. Furthermore, the counselor has the responsibility to become aware of her or his own biases, stereotypes, prejudices, and privileges and the way those factors influence the therapeutic relationship. Finally, the counselor must undergo training and accumulate clinical experiences that will equip him or her with skills that are appropriate and effective for work with culturally different clients.

Multiculturally skilled counselors are able to manage several tasks related to culture in the counseling relationship. Multiculturally skilled counselors are able to identify their own culturally influenced expectations for clients' behaviors, communication styles, and other factors that are likely to influence counseling. They are familiar with their clients' cultures and can distinguish behaviors that are consistent with the client's cultural background without mislabeling them as problematic. Furthermore, multiculturally competent counselors are able to identify the influence of the client's culture on the therapeutic relationship and adjust their own counseling style so that it is culturally responsive and appropriate. For example, some Pacific Islander clients want personal knowledge of their counselor (e.g., family status or birthplace) before they feel comfortable in counseling. Eurocentric counseling theories typically limit this type of self-disclosure because it may take the focus of counseling away from the client. A multiculturally skilled counselor who is trained in Eurocentric approaches must determine for himself or herself the extent to which he or she is comfortable sharing personal information with the client for the benefit of the therapeutic relationship. Finally, multiculturally competent counselors are able to recognize when cultural similarities and differences may aid or impede the counseling relationship and when those concerns need to be directly addressed in counseling. This may be as simple as asking the client how he or she feels about working with a racially different counselor. Certainly, because race is an uncomfortable topic in U.S. society, clients may be reluctant to discuss their genuine feelings at the beginning of counseling. A culturally skilled counselor will recognize the need to revisit this issue throughout the counseling relationship.

A number of different methodologies have been suggested for multicultural counseling. One approach relies on cultural matching of clients and counselors. According to this method, clients are paired with culturally similar counselors in order to minimize culturally based misunderstandings. Research has shown that minority clients tend to prefer ethnically or racially similar counselors over dissimilar counselors. However, as Speight, Myers, Cox, and Highlen point out, taken to its logical conclusion, this approach has limited applicability. The problem arises because culture has many layers and facets: race, ethnicity, gender, sexual orientation, socioeconomic status, and physical ability, to name a few.

To illustrate the benefits and flaws of this method, let us look at an example: It may be plausible to match a male African American client with a male African American counselor. However, the likelihood of finding a match for a third-generation, upper-middle-class, Korean American single mother is far smaller. In their review of research on cultural matching, Donald Atkinson and Susana Lowe found that clients often rank similarities on identity dimensions other than race or ethnicity as more important. For example, a Latina client may be more interested in having a female counselor of a different ethnicity than an ethnically similar male counselor. Additionally, other multicultural psychologists affirm that being born into a cultural group does not automatically guarantee cultural competence with that or other groups. Effective multicultural counseling requires training and experience regardless of the counselor's cultural background.

Yet another possibility is to develop specific interventions that are tailored to distinct cultural groups. For example, strategies and techniques for counseling persons of African descent may be based on the unique social and political history and present-day realities of this racial group, as well as its unique cultural values. Speight, Myers, Cox, and Highlen, however, challenge this approach because it tends to overlook universal commonalities among cultures and individuals and sometimes appears to be a sort of a cookbook method, oversimplifying the cognitive, emotional, and social experiences of culture. Speight and her colleagues feel that multicultural counseling is more complex than accumulating facts about particular cultural groups. Another characteristic of this emic approach is the inclusion of traditional indigenous healers and practices in counseling. The potential benefit of such an approach is the large cultural overlap and congruence. Draguns, however, points out that traditional healing practices may not be relevant to individuals who have been removed from traditional social contexts.

A final approach combines the common-factors paradigm with the cultural-specificity and individual-uniqueness philosophies. In other words, this strategy relies on both etic and emic methodologies in multicultural counseling by recognizing the universal, culture-specific, and uniquely individual characteristics of our clients. An example of this approach is the multicultural counseling competencies model, which is based on the work of Sue, Arredondo, and Davis (originally published in 1992 and revised multiple times since then) and is the longest-standing model of multicultural counseling. This model proposes training in which counselors

- increase *awareness* of their own beliefs and attitudes;
- gain *knowledge* of their own and their clients' cultural heritage, as well as knowledge of how forms of oppression affect all people personally and professionally; and
- master *skills* that increase their effectiveness in counseling culturally diverse clients (these skills may include specialized training, advocacy, and supervision).

In its latest form, this model proposes 34 competencies along three dimensions that intersect personal and cultural factors. The first dimension, self-awareness, focuses on the counselor's attentiveness to his or her own cultural heritage and the way it influences personal values, expectations, and biases. The second dimension of multicultural competence requires increased understanding of the personal and collective experiences of the culturally different client. These experiences include social, historical, and political events, as well as cultural interpretations of reality and the human experience, commonly referred to as one's *worldview*. This dimension includes knowledge of racial and ethnic identity development; knowledge of the impact of race and ethnicity on the psychological, emotional, academic, and vocational development of individuals; and meaningful personal involvement with individuals and organizations representing the worldviews and experiences of culturally different persons. The third and final dimension offers guidelines and suggestions for developing culturally responsive interventions that fall outside

typical training in Eurocentric theories of counseling. Culturally responsive strategies may include the client's social support system in counseling, religious and spiritual practices, indigenous healers, and institutional advocacy on behalf of the client.

The model developed by D. W. Sue and his colleagues goes far in addressing the concerns that have accumulated over the past 30 years of multicultural counseling about the treatment of ethnic and racial minorities in the mental health system. It is complex and comprehensive and covers counselor training, client assessment, diagnosis, and treatment. The next step for this model is to establish its effectiveness in these areas through research.

—*Larisa Buhin*

See also Culture; Ethnicity; Multicultural Counseling Competencies; Race

FURTHER READING

American Psychological Association. (2003). Guidelines on multicultural education, training, research, practice, and organizational change for psychologists. *American Psychologist, 58,* 377–402.

Atkinson, D. R., Thompson, C. E., & Grant, S. K. (1993). A three-dimensional model for counseling racial/ethnic minorities. *Counseling Psychologist, 21,* 257–277.

Constantine, M. G. (2002). The intersection of race, ethnicity, gender, and social class in counseling: Examining selves in cultural contexts. *Journal of Multicultural Counseling and Development, 30,* 210–215.

Draguns, J. G. (1996). Humanly universal and culturally distinctive: Charting the course of cultural counseling. In P. B. Pedersen, J. G. Draguns, W. J. Lonner, & J. E. Trimble (Eds.), *Counseling across cultures* (4th ed., pp. 1–20). Thousand Oaks, CA: Sage.

Robinson, D. T., & Morris, J. R. (2000). Multicultural counseling: Historical context and current training considerations. *Western Journal of Black Studies, 24,* 239–253.

Speight, S. L., Myers, L. J., Cox, C. I., and Highlen, P. S. (1991). A redefinition of multicultural counseling. *Journal of Counseling and Development, 70,* 29–36.

Sue, D. W., & Sue, D. (2003). *Counseling the culturally different: Theory and practice* (4th ed.). New York: Wiley.

U.S. Department of Health and Human Services. (2001). *Mental health: Culture, race, and ethnicity* (Suppl. to *Mental health: A report of the surgeon general*). Rockville, MD: U.S. Department of Health and Human Services, Substance Abuse and Mental Health Services Administration, Center for Mental Health Services.

Vera, E. M., & Speight, S. L. (2003). Multicultural competence, social justice, and counseling psychology: Expanding our roles. *Counseling Psychologist, 31,* 253–272.

MULTICULTURAL COUNSELING COMPETENCIES

DEFINITION

In a broad sense, multicultural counseling competencies are skills that counselors and other mental health professionals possess and continually expand that enable them to work effectively with clients who are culturally different from themselves. The process of gaining multicultural competencies or becoming multiculturally competent involves specialized training and supervision, practice with diverse clients, meaningful personal relationships with individuals who are culturally different from oneself, and examination of one's own life experiences. This process is believed to be lifelong and ongoing, as our society is continually changing. Multicultural competence includes, but is not limited to, knowledge about the following:

- Various cultural groups that coexist in modern U.S. society, including their histories and present realities (this should also include knowledge of immigration patterns, acculturation, and biculturalism)
- Theories of identity development, such as racial and ethnic identity or sexual identity development
- The advantages and limitations of currently accepted forms of assessment, diagnosis, and treatment or intervention and their limited usefulness in working with culturally different clients
- The negative effects of inadequate care on the help-seeking behaviors of multicultural populations
- Alternative forms of assessment, diagnosis, and interventions that may be more suitable to the needs and cultural norms of diverse clients
- The matrix of sociopolitical and economic privilege and oppression (including White privilege, racism, discrimination, sexism, heterosexism, ablism, and ageism) that affects the lives of all individuals by dictating a hierarchy in which some groups are more valued and, consequently, have more power, affluence, and access to resources than others
- The limits of one's own area of expertise and the need to protect our clients' well-being by referring them to better-qualified professionals when necessary

When we refer to *culturally different* or *diverse* clients, we mean clients who are of a different race, ethnicity, gender, physical ability, or sexual orientation than the counselor. By *race* or *racial identity,* we mean self-selected membership or identification with one of the following racial groups in the United States: American Indian, Alaska Native, Native Hawaiian or other Pacific Islander, Asian American, African American, Latino or Hispanic American, Middle Eastern American, and European American. The terms *ethnicity* and *ethnic identity* typically refer to membership in a group that shares a country of origin as well as other nonbiological factors such as language, religion, and customs. Examples of ethnic identity designations would be Chinese American, Bosnian, and Nigerian.

Finally, multicultural counseling acknowledges that an aspect of membership in a particular group is a shared group culture. Culture comprises rules for social interaction, preferred modes of expression and communication among group members, beliefs, values, hierarchical structures, and so forth. Culture and group membership influence individuals' experiences of physical, interpersonal, and emotional realities or worldviews. Consequently, multicultural counseling recognizes that there is no one objective truth or perception of reality. Instead, multiculturally competent counselors strive to comprehend the worldviews of diverse clients through the individual client's cultural lens.

In a narrow sense, multicultural counseling competencies are a set of guidelines for providing effective counseling to culturally different clients. The multicultural counseling competencies model was developed during the early 1990s by Derald Wing Sue, Patricia Arredondo, and Roderick McDavis. In its latest form, the model conceptualizes 34 competencies along three dimensions. The first dimension, self-awareness, requires counselors to gain knowledge of their own cultural heritage (including race, ethnicity, and country of origin), values, expectations, and biases. The second dimension requires the counselor to become aware of the worldviews of culturally diverse clients. This dimension includes knowledge of racial and ethnic identity development; knowledge of the impact of race and ethnicity on the psychological, emotional, academic, and vocational development of individuals; and meaningful personal involvement with culturally different individuals. A culturally competent counselor strives to deepen his or her knowledge of other cultures beyond academic learning by making meaningful personal connections with individuals and organizations representing the worldviews and experiences of diverse cultures. The third and final dimension offers guidelines and suggestions for using culturally responsive interventions that fall outside typical training in Eurocentric theories of counseling. The Eurocentric theories that dominate mental health education emphasize individually focused talk therapies. This approach may not be effective with clients who come from diverse cultural traditions. Culturally responsive strategies, on the other hand, involve the client's extended social support systems in counseling, as well as indigenous healers, prevention, and institutional advocacy on behalf of the client.

In 2002, the American Psychological Association (APA) adopted the Guidelines on Multicultural Education, Training, Research, Practice, and Organizational Change for Psychologists, which are based on the work of Sue, Arredondo, and McDavis. The APA put forth six guidelines focusing on the recognition of cultural attitudes and beliefs of oneself and others, the application of multiculturalism in education, the conduct of culturally sensitive research, the application of culturally appropriate counseling interventions, and organizational change. The APA uses a narrow definition of multiculturalism, so the guidelines apply primarily to work with ethnic and racial minorities. The guidelines, which are less specific than the competencies proposed by Sue, Arredondo, and McDavis, offer an overview of current knowledge in the area of multicultural counseling and psychology and suggestions for training, education, research, and practice.

HISTORICAL CONTEXT

The multicultural movement, often referred to as the "fourth force" in counseling and psychotherapy, grew out of a recognition among mental health professionals that the mental health needs of cultural minority groups were not being met through the application of Eurocentric counseling theories (e.g., psychoanalysis, behaviorism, Gestalt, existentialism, person-centered therapy, and rational-emotive-behavioral therapy). One of the ways this failure is evident is the underutilization of mental health services by Asian Americans, African Americans, and Latinos. The multicultural literature has identified a number of reasons for the disparities in help-seeking behaviors between majority and minority cultural groups (inclusive of race, ethnicity, and sexual orientation).

Eurocentric theories of counseling, as artifacts of cultural embeddedness, do not adequately or accurately represent the realities of racial, ethnic, and other cultural minorities. This is partly the result of cultural differences that influence individuals' worldviews. Eurocentric theories largely represent the worldviews and life experiences of their authors, educated men of European descent. Some of the characteristics of this worldview include an individualist orientation (the individual is the unit of analysis), self-determination, personal achievement, and Judeo-Christian faith. From this perspective, many of the respected and popular theories of personality development and counseling are, at their core, focused on the individual as the agent of change. In comparison, many clients come from cultures that value the good of the family or the community more than the advancement of the individual. The individual focus of therapy and its brainchild, the process of individuation, do not fit such core cultural values and may directly clash with them.

Another reason that Eurocentric theories fail to represent diverse worldviews is that, for the most part, their creators either did not experience the oppressive forces at work in modern U.S. society or did not address them adequately in writing about personality and identity development. None of the major theories discuss the effects of racism, immigration, or ethnic identity on the development of personality and personal identity.

Eurocentric theories have limited usefulness in the lives and problems of culturally diverse clients. Some of the research on the effectiveness of psychotherapy with ethnic and racial minority clients indicates that as many as half of these clients do not return for counseling after the first session. This is a very serious problem—the implication is that the "helping profession" is not helping a significant portion of the U.S. population. The high drop-out rate of racial and ethnic minority clients may also be attributable to the fact that the majority of counselors and other mental health professionals are European American, as evidenced by the membership of professional organizations such as the APA. These counselors represent the worldview of the majority culture, which does not always align with the worldviews of minority cultures and sometimes denies, pathologizes, and suppresses minority cultures' realities. As members of the majority culture, European American helping professionals may become unwitting accomplices in an oppressive social structure, which contributed to their clients' difficulties in the first place.

Sue and Arredondo review three models that are frequently used in the psychological and psychotherapeutic literature to explain cultural differences. The first model attributes cultural differences to the evolutionary inferiority and pathology of non-European cultures. The second model inaccurately proposes a deficiency in racial and ethnic minority members' genetic makeup, which, in turn, is reflected in psychological differences between the European majority and racial and ethnic minority cultures. The third model suggests that minority groups do not have the right cultural conditions to achieve at the same level as their European counterparts. These approaches to cultural difference have been immensely detrimental to the well-being of cultural minority groups by influencing racist counseling and research practices, according to Sue and Arredondo.

Finally, a supplement to the surgeon general's 1999 report, *Mental Health: Culture, Race, and Ethnicity,* affirmed that racial and ethnic minorities in the United States have less access to mental health services than their European American counterparts. Furthermore, the quality of care provided to minority groups is low. According to the report, these inequalities in mental health care are the result of our history of racism and discrimination, which have made racial minorities rightfully distrustful of treatment; deficiencies in cultural knowledge among mental health professionals; and a lack of competent bilingual services.

All of these factors, as well as many that are beyond the scope of this discussion, have converged to create an environment in which the contributions and positive qualities of minority groups are routinely overlooked. In psychology and counseling, this environment translates into misunderstanding of strengths and problems, misdiagnosing culturally appropriate behaviors as mental illness, overpathologizing and further disenfranchising minority individuals and groups, and applying treatments and interventions that do not address real problems (e.g., racism, oppression, discrimination). The development of multicultural counseling competencies has been driven by all of these factors. But more than being a reaction to inequalities in treatment, multicultural counseling competencies aspire to recognize and value the strengths, accomplishments, and perspectives of all oppressed groups. Multicultural counseling competencies represent an effort by mental health professionals to provide culturally informed, sensitive, and responsive interventions that aim to benefit culturally different clients at the individual, family, and societal levels.

Example

To illustrate some of the concepts just presented, let us consider the case of a European American counselor, Mr. Janushkovsky. Mr. Janushkovsky may never have experienced racism or discrimination based on the color of his skin. For Mr. Janushkovsky, racism and discrimination are not necessarily a part of his daily reality. Coupled with this worldview, Mr. Janushkovsky has been trained in one of the Eurocentric theories that places the source of emotional and interpersonal problems within the individual rather than within his or her environment.

Mr. Janushkovsky is seeing a Chinese American student, Ms. Chen, for anxiety and academic difficulties in some of her classes. Ms. Chen is earning Cs and Bs in biology, chemistry, and physics. However, she is excelling in art history and drawing. Ms. Chen is being advised to pursue a career in medical research despite her interest in art. Ms. Chen's academic adviser, Mrs. Fonda, feels this is a good career path because "Asians are good at science." Certainly, Ms. Chen's university has a large number of Asian students majoring in the natural sciences, and Mr. Janushkovsky agrees that this would be a lucrative and prestigious career to pursue. Treatment focuses on teaching Ms. Chen relaxation techniques and provides a referral to a psychiatrist for antianxiety medication and a referral to a tutor. A month later, Ms. Chen is as anxious as before, although she is now showing symptoms of depression as well. What may have gone wrong in this counseling situation?

Clearly, Ms. Chen has suffered additionally from ineffective treatment because her primary concerns have been misdiagnosed. What led to this diagnosis? Although they may have had Ms. Chen's financial security in mind, both Mr. Janushkovsky and Mrs. Fonda allowed their biased views of Asian students to guide their professional behavior. Mr. Janushkovsky and Mrs. Fonda did not make up this particular stereotype on their own; they merely repeated and represented what society believes to be true about this particular racial group. Furthermore, because of his training, Mr. Janushkovsky did not consider the possibility that Ms. Chen's symptoms were the result of external factors, such as social pressure and oppression. Rather, he attributed them to qualities within Ms. Chen, a bias that is the result of his professional training.

A MODEL OF MULTICULTURAL COUNSELING COMPETENCIES

Psychologists Ponterotto, Fuertes, and Chen have identified multicultural counseling competencies as the longest-standing model of multicultural counseling. The multicultural counseling competencies model is based on the work of Sue, Arredondo, and McDavis, which was originally published in 1992 and has been revised many times since then. The model offers suggestions for counselor training as well as for intervening with culturally different clients. The model is organized around three dimensions: increasing *awareness,* understanding clients' worldviews (*knowledge*), and gaining intervention *skills* that adequately address the needs of culturally diverse clients. This model proposes training in which counselors

- increase *awareness* of their own worldviews, assumptions, beliefs, attitudes, and prejudices;
- gain *knowledge* of their clients' cultural heritage, as well as knowledge of how forms of oppression affect all people personally and professionally; and
- master *skills* that increase their effectiveness in counseling culturally diverse clients (for example, specialized training and supervision that are directly relevant to the cultural group with which the counselor is working).

Within each dimension, Sue, Arredondo, and McDavis propose specific strategies for moving toward multicultural competence and describe characteristics of multiculturally competent counselors. For example, on the awareness dimension, Sue and colleagues state that a multiculturally competent counselor is aware of cultural differences between himself or herself and his or her clients. Counselors who are members of the European American majority culture may be unaware of their own identity as racial beings in a multiracial society that does not value all of its members equally. It is essential that European American counselors become conversant in models of White racial identity development and explore the meanings and implications of their racial identity in counseling. Furthermore, a multiculturally competent counselor values and celebrates cultural differences. These differences may include time orientation (past, present, or future), people orientation (independence or interdependence), nature orientation (mastery or harmony), and individual activity in the world (doing/action or being).

On the second dimension—understanding culturally different worldviews—Sue and colleagues state that counselors should gain knowledge about their clients' cultural groups. This broad competency is further broken down into knowing about cultural norms and traditions, models of racial and ethnic identity development, effects of racial and ethnic status on dimensions of human development (e.g., personality, academic, vocational aspirations), and social inequities and forms of oppression that negatively affect cultural minority members.

On the third dimension, counselors are challenged to apply their knowledge of self, others, and society to a wide array of culturally appropriate interventions that reach beyond traditional one-on-one counseling. Examples include conducting counseling in the language preferred by the client (when this is impossible, a referral to another professional may be preferable), incorporating indigenous healing practitioners into the treatment plan, and intervening at a systemic or institutional level on behalf of the client, to name just a few.

If the counselor in our example, Mr. Janushkovsky, had been multiculturally competent, he would have been aware of his own bias toward Asian Americans and other cultural minority groups. He also would have recognized Mrs. Fonda's behaviors as prejudiced and oppressive. He then would have been able to conceptualize Ms. Chen's anxiety as a normal reaction to an oppressive situation and implement an appropriate and effective treatment plan. Mr. Janushkovsky also could have acted as an advocate for Ms. Chen by addressing bias in advising and counseling with Mrs. Fonda.

The model developed by Sue and colleagues goes far in addressing the concerns that have accumulated over the past 30 years of multicultural counseling about the treatment of ethnic and racial minorities in the mental health system. It is complex and comprehensive and covers counselor training, client assessment, diagnosis, and treatment. The next step for this model is to establish its effectiveness in all of these areas through scientific research.

MULTICULTURAL COUNSELING COMPETENCIES IN ASSESSMENT AND DIAGNOSIS

When conducting clinical assessment (initial intake interviews and personality, cognitive, and educational testing), multiculturally competent counselors are aware of potential problems with standardized tests and traditionally used assessment procedures. These include test development and interpretation, standardization norms, intake interview formats, and diagnostic criteria. Though a discussion of the problems with assessment and diagnosis is beyond the scope of this entry, we present here an abbreviated overview of the major issues pertaining to multicultural counseling competencies in assessment and diagnosis.

The potential pitfalls in assessment and diagnosis are similar to those discussed in other areas. Specifically, the preponderance of assessment instruments that are used today are based on a European American value system and normed (gathering and development of baseline data about expressions and prevalence of normal and abnormal cognitive, psychological, and behavioral processes) on a predominantly European American sample. Based on the assumptions that science and scientific findings transcend cultural differences and that all or most psychological constructs are universal, these instruments have been used to assess racial and ethnic minority populations. The problem with this practice lies in the assumptions themselves.

Scientists who explore and describe the lifestyles and cultural practices of different groups of people around the world, as well as scientists who conduct research on differences among cultural groups in the United States, have found that the assumptions of value-free and universal scientific process and findings may not be warranted. As a result of the growing awareness of cultural factors in mental health and well-being, a variety of culture-bound syndromes are now included in the *Diagnostic and Statistical Manual of Mental Disorders* published by the American Psychiatric Association. Culture-bound syndromes describe disorders that appear only in particular cultural groups. For example, *amok* is a condition that has been diagnosed exclusively in Malaysian individuals.

Research has shown that the use of assessment and diagnostic tools developed for one population (cultural group) with a different population often yields results that inadequately describe the nature of a construct or misrepresent the extent of a problem. Problems that stem from this practice and affect counseling with minority populations include the following:

- Culturally biased constructs that do not adequately represent the experiences of minority groups
- Test items that do not take into account cultural expressions of social, emotional, and behavioral functioning

- Inaccurate and often detrimental interpretations of test results based on norms that do not represent the cultural group in question
- Overpathologization (assigning more severe diagnoses based on counselor bias or ignorance of cultural differences) of members of racial and ethnic groups

To avoid the pitfalls of assessment instruments that may be culturally insensitive and inappropriate, multiculturally competent counselors are encouraged to expand their assessment protocols to include techniques and instruments that are consistent with clients' cultural backgrounds. For example, multiculturally competent assessment would take into account clients' worldviews, immigration status and generation, racial and ethnic identity development, and strengths and social support systems, as well as multiple sources of information (e.g., family members, schoolmates, or contacts at places of worship), and accurately interpret these data from the cultural perspective of the client rather than that of the counselor. As psychologist Lisa Suzuki and her colleagues point out, test developers are improving their procedures, which had led to more valid and reliable instruments. Finally, the guidelines of the APA encourage counselors to become familiar with a test's psychometric properties and apply caution and clinical judgment when using standardized instruments to assess members of minority groups.

MULTICULTURAL COUNSELING COMPETENCIES IN TREATMENT AND INTERVENTION

Multiculturally competent counseling recognizes that all individuals have a multitude of interconnected personal and social identities. Multiculturally competent counselors recognize that an individual's identity and well-being are influenced by his or her larger social, political, and historical contexts, which must be addressed in counseling. Multicultural counseling includes in the work of therapy issues and concepts that are important to all cultural groups living in the United States, but particularly those that are salient to members of minority cultural groups. These issues include ethnic and racial identity development, acculturation, oppression, racism, sexual identity development, and discrimination, to name a few. This viewpoint contrasts with Eurocentric counseling approaches, which tend to view the client as an individual who is disconnected from his or her social environment. Furthermore, this expanded and comprehensive view of the individual has implications for the way multiculturally competent counselors intervene with their clients.

Multiculturally competent mental health practitioners recognize that individual counseling based on European American values and beliefs may be ineffective with culturally different clients, not only because of the incompatibility of cultural beliefs but also because of the clients' presenting problems. In other words, the counselor and the client must agree on the definition of the problem, its sources, and possible means of ameliorating the issue. Eurocentric theories of psychological development, counseling, and therapy often describe psychological problems and treatment in overly restrictive ways. As a result, Eurocentric theories may overemphasize the role of the individual and underemphasize the role of the family and society in the etiology, maintenance, and resolution of psychological difficulties.

The idea that multiculturally competent clinicians are aware of the inadequacies of prevailing counseling theories is strongly related to the underlying tenets of multicultural counseling competencies, which state that one of the goals of multicultural counseling is the promotion of social justice for all individuals. Therefore, a multiculturally competent helping professional recognizes when his or her role as an individual counselor is insufficient to help clients achieve goals that are consistent with the idea of universal social justice. In such cases, multiculturally competent counselors can effectively act in a different capacity on behalf of the client. Psychologists Atkinson, Thompson, and Grant propose expanding the traditional counseling role to promote the well-being of counseling clients. They suggest that individual counselors may achieve this goal by adding the roles of adviser, advocate, and agent of social change when appropriate.

A client's cultural background and membership in a particular ethnic or racial group play crucial roles in his or her overall sense of self and offer resources that may support treatment goals. Simultaneously, a minority client's social, economic, and political position in a predominantly European American society and culture may be the cause of his or her presenting problems or may contribute to personal difficulties. These considerations are actively incorporated in counseling by culturally competent professionals. For many ethnic and racial minority clients, the individual

is not the appropriate level of intervention; rather, the appropriate level is the family or an equivalent social support system. Therefore, multiculturally competent counselors strive to include in counseling as many relevant members of the client's social network as the client believes will be helpful. Clients who belong to a cultural minority group may experience any number of problems that have been neglected in Eurocentric theories of human development and counseling. These presenting problems include normal developmental issues such as ethnic or racial identity development and sexual identity development. Presenting problems may also include events and obstacles that do not originate within individuals, such as acculturation stress resulting from recent immigration, employment discrimination, or unequal access to resources because of poverty or language barriers. These problems may be alleviated by individual counseling, but many mental health professionals argue that preventive and broader systemic interventions are better suited and more aligned with the goals of multicultural counseling and should be included prominently in the multicultural counseling competencies repertoire.

Example

To illustrate the concepts just described, let us consider the example of a multiculturally competent counselor working with a young lesbian college student who is struggling with her sexual identity. The counselor, Ms. Aisha, has taken several multicultural counseling classes in her training program; receives ongoing supervision during which she discusses topics that are relevant to the counseling of culturally different clients; and continues to explore her own cultural values, attitudes, and beliefs. Ms. Aisha is now faced with a number of practice issues that fall outside the traditionally and narrowly prescribed counselor role. Ms. Aisha should be familiar with lesbian sexual identity development and the coming out process, which have not historically been covered in counseling theories classes (counselor role). Ms. Aisha should also be familiar with the college or university services and resources for lesbian, gay, bisexual, and transgender (LGBT) students (adviser role), and she should be able to facilitate her client's connection with this support network (ally role). Additionally, Ms. Aisha should be an advocate for LGBT students on campus as well as other cultural minority groups and should make efforts to participate in events that raise awareness of LGBT issues (advocate and ally roles). Beyond her counseling relationship with this client, Ms. Aisha may choose to become involved with committee work at the organizational level to ensure that the college does not promote or condone policies that discriminate against LGBT students (agent for social change).

—*Larisa Buhin*

See also Acculturation; Ethnic and Racial Identity; Ethnicity; Multicultural Counseling; Race; Racial Identity Development; Racial Identity Models

FURTHER READING

American Psychological Association. (2003). Guidelines on multicultural education, training, research, practice, and organizational change for psychologists. *American Psychologist, 58,* 377–402.

Atkinson, D. R., Thompson, C. E., & Grant, S. K. (1993). A three-dimensional model for counseling racial/ethnic minorities. *Counseling Psychologist, 21,* 257–277.

Buckley, T. R., & Franklin-Jackson, D. C. (2004). Diagnosis in racial-cultural practice. In R. T. Carter (Ed.), *Handbook of racial-cultural psychology and counseling: Training and practice* (Vol. 2, pp. 286–296). Hoboken, NJ: Wiley.

Helms, J. E. (1995). An update of Helms's White and people of color racial identity models. In J. G. Ponterotto, J. M. Casas, L. A. Suzuki, & C. M. Alexander (Eds.), *Handbook of multicultural counseling* (pp. 181–191). Thousand Oaks, CA: Sage.

Katz, J. H. (1985). The sociopolitical nature of counseling. *Counseling Psychologist, 13,* 615–624.

Kluckhohn, F. R., & Strodtbeck, F. L. (1961). *Variations in values orientations.* Evanston, IL: Row, Patterson.

Ponterotto, J. G., Fuertes, J. N., & Chen, E. C. (2000). Models of multicultural counseling. In S. D. Brown & R. W. Lent (Eds.), *Handbook of counseling psychology* (3rd ed., pp. 639–669). Hoboken, NJ: Wiley.

Sue, D. W., Carter, R. T., Casas, J. M., Fouad, N. A., Ivey, A. E., Jensen, M., LaFromboise, T., Manese, J. E., Ponterotto, J. G., & Vazquez-Nutall, E. (1998). *Multicultural counseling competencies: Individual and organizational development.* Thousand Oaks, CA: Sage.

Suzuki, L. A., Kugler, J. F., & Aguiar, L. J. (2004). Assessment practices in racial-cultural psychology. In R. T. Carter (Ed.), *Handbook of racial-cultural psychology and counseling: Training and practice* (Vol. 2, pp. 297–315). Hoboken, NJ: Wiley.

U.S. Department of Health and Human Services. (2001). *Mental health: Culture, race, and ethnicity* (Suppl. to *Mental health: A report of the surgeon general*). Rockville, MD: U.S. Department of Health and Human Services, Substance Abuse and Mental Health Services Administration, Center for Mental Health Services.

Vera, E. M., & Speight, S. L. (2003). Multicultural competence, social justice, and counseling psychology: Expanding our roles. *Counseling Psychologist, 31,* 253–272.

MULTICULTURALISM

The term *multiculturalism* is constituted through the positioning of Anglophones of European descent as the founding people of the nation and all others as an ethnic mix of multicultural characters. This sets up a distinction between "us" and "them" whereby "them" are seen as less civilized or cultured than "us." Although multiculturalism was conceived as an alternative to assimilationist or integrationist ideology—often referred to as the *cultural melting pot*—its guise of celebrating different cultures overshadows the real critique of power relations that is inherent in the polarity of us and them. Multiculturalism can be defined as a stance that takes a position on the racial and ethnic diversity of the United States—a position that rejects assimilation and the melting pot image as an imposition of the dominant culture, preferring such metaphors as the *salad bowl* or the glorious *mosaic* in which each ethnic and racial element of the population maintains its distinctiveness.

During the 1970s and 1980s, the idea of multiculturalism provided a way of understanding complex issues of race, culture, and ethnicity in the context of the diverse communities living in the West. It allowed for a set of practices and behaviors and a particular set of words and vocabularies to explain how people live and react to others around them. Many of these ideas related to the acquisition of cross-cultural knowledge and competencies. However, very little effort was made in the theory and research to identify the social and political inequalities in the relationships between the dominant culture and the ethnic minority groups.

During the 1990s, newer formulations began to emerge under a new multicultural agenda to redress the imbalances resulting from multicultural policies in education, social work, and health care. These efforts took the form of antiracist projects aimed at specifically located and time-limited actions such as equal opportunity, political correctness, positive discrimination, and affirmative action. During the late 1990s and the 2000s, the concept of multiculturalism began to broaden to include race, culture, ethnicity, sexual orientation, gender, disability, religious affiliation, and socioeconomic class. However, this wider definition has led to confusion and conflict within the multicultural movement. For example, some proponents have argued for limiting multiculturalism to the racial and ethnic domains, whereas others want to see the inclusion of other disadvantaged groups, such as lesbian, gay, bisexual, and transgender individuals from both the European American and African American communities.

Bingham and colleagues suggest that building multicultural alliances necessitates improving one's ability to engage in difficult dialogues related to race, gender, disability, and sexual orientation. Often, groups feel excluded from the multicultural debate, find themselves in opposition to one another, and engage in a game of "who's more oppressed?" Although many oppressed or marginalized groups agree that monoculturalism expressed through European American culture represents a major barrier to working cooperatively, they have been less motivated and successful in understanding one another's concerns. Therefore, the concept of *diversity* has gained wider acceptance because it includes other disadvantaged communities, including those from the European American community.

The theory and practice of multiculturalism have always been problematic because they tend to express ethnic minority life experiences too simplistically or do not articulate a radical approach to cultural imperialism, racism, sexism, and economic oppression. The problematic nature of multicultural thinking, according to Apitzsch, is that it underestimates social forces that not only distinguish between cultures but also create distinctions, demarcations, coercion, and subordination that are disguised behind the label of culture or ethnicity. It is these social forces—underpinned by cultural imperialism, racism, sexism, hegemonic masculinity, and other projections—that individually and collectively interact to produce an environment in which ethnic minority individuals are denied and condemned.

Any new formulation of multiculturalism must seek to articulate a more critical idea of difference that empowers cultural traditions, facilitates economic development, respects ethnic customs, and supports nonracist values. Cornel West engages this notion in his essay "The New Cultural Politics of Difference," in which he argues that cultural differences are not simply oppositional in contesting the mainstream for inclusion. He maintains that cultural differences are distinct articulations produced to empower and enable social action for the expression of freedom, democracy, and individuality. Perhaps the greatest challenge to the location of a specific definition of multiculturalism is multiculturalism itself. The lack of a complex theory of multiculturalism is perhaps a testament to the fact that multiculturalism, as the term suggests, is a multiple articulation of varied, contradictory, and contested ideas and explanations for complex human behaviors, functions, rituals, and ceremonies. Therefore, any attempt to homogenize it into a singularly defined concept can only create confusion and reinforce the stereotypes that multiculturalism hopes to avoid in the first place.

If multiculturalism is related to the dynamic, reciprocal relationship between intrapsychic forces and environmental influences, then it should be part of the discourse of healing in whatever shape or form one conceives it to be. Reducing it to the margins or to the periphery of the therapeutic process is like leaving the client outside the clinical room while proposing to conduct therapy through the keyhole. But what are the ways in which psychologists can work effectively in a multicultural context?

It is imperative that psychologists examine the unconscious learned stereotypes and prejudices that they hold in relation to "the other." In other words, they must examine their own values and attitudes in relation to race, gender, sexual orientation, disability, and class. They must affirm their own uniqueness and diversity, which will translate into a positive appreciation of their clients' own qualities. Building an awareness of racist, homophobic, and sexist stereotyping in the media (and in society generally) and rejecting those stereotypes is key to building a skillful and competent base for working multiculturally. Finally, psychologists must work creatively and imaginatively, learn to recognize deep-seated negative thoughts, and use the charter of human rights as a guiding principle alongside ethics and professional practice guidelines to evoke healing in minority clients.

—*Roy Moodley*
—*Deone Curling*

See also Multiracial Individuals

FURTHER READING

Moodley, R. (1998a). Cultural returns to the subject: Traditional healing in counseling and therapy. *Changes: International Journal of Psychology and Psychotherapy, 16*, 45–56.

Moodley, R. (1998b). "I say what I like": Frank talk(ing) in counseling and psychotherapy. *British Journal of Guidance and Counseling, 26*, 495–508.

West, C. (2000). The new cultural politics of difference. In C. West (Ed.), *The Cornel West reader* (pp. 119–142). New York: Basic Civitas Books.

MULTICULTURAL PERSONALITY

The term *multicultural personality* was first coined by Professor Manuel Ramirez (University of Texas at Austin) to describe individuals who successfully negotiate and thrive in multiple cultures simultaneously. Ramirez conceptualized the multicultural personality in terms bicultural life-skills development. Specifically, he believed that immigrants to the United States who successfully synthesized components of their original-country worldview with the host-country worldview could develop broad multicultural coping and thinking styles that would facilitate their adjustment to and quality of life in the United States.

Since Ramirez's pioneering work on the multicultural personality, other researchers anchored in diverse psychology disciplines have expanded the construct. For example, working in the Netherlands in the field of organizational psychology, Professors Karen van der Zee and Jan Pieter van Oudenhoven examined the multicultural personality within the context of expatriates adapting to work and life in international contexts. Professor Joseph G. Ponterotto and colleagues in the United States addressed the multicultural personality as a positive indicator of enhanced quality of life for Americans living in an increasingly diverse society. These authors hypothesize that individuals who have multicultural personalities will adapt more effectively to a rapidly changing society and will exhibit higher levels of psychological and physical well-being.

The most comprehensive definition of the multicultural personality has been offered by Professors Joseph G. Ponterotto, Shawn O. Utsey, and Paul B. Pedersen, who noted that the multicultural personality is characterized by a cluster of affective, attitudinal, and behavioral components. These components include emotional stability and wide-reaching empathic ability; secure racial, ethnic, and other identities; and a spiritual essence and sense of connectedness to all persons. Additional components of the multicultural personality include a self-reflective stance, cognitive flexibility, sense of humor, and commitment to social activism in fighting racism and other forms of oppression.

In elaborating on the multicultural personality construct, Ponterotto and colleagues integrated work from multiple specialties within psychology. Specifically, the definition of the multicultural personality draws on theory and research on racial and ethnic identity development and coping with cultural diversity from the fields of counseling and developmental psychology; the "tolerant personality" from social psychology; an expansionist theory of gender roles and feminist identity development from feminist studies; the universal-diverse orientation from social and counseling psychology; African-centered mental health from Afrocentric psychology; and expatriate adjustment in international contexts from organizational and cross-cultural psychology.

Table 1 summarizes these theoretical models. The first column lists the model of focus, the second column extracts key characteristics of the model as they relate to the multicultural personality, and the third column highlights instruments that have been developed to operationalize and test the constructs.

RESEARCH SUPPORT FOR THE MULTICULTURAL PERSONALITY CONSTRUCT

Empirical research on the multicultural personality is limited because the construct is relatively new. At present, there is no all-inclusive instrument or test that measures every component of the multicultural personality. However, a good amount of empirical research has used validated research measures to examine the distinct theoretical components of the multicultural personality construct. By examining this research collectively, we can discern the importance of the broader definition of the multicultural personality presented earlier. A brief review of research on these models is presented in Table 1.

Generally speaking, adolescents and adults who score higher on measures of Black and White racial identity exhibit higher self-esteem, higher goal achievement, greater comfort examining their own emotional states, and more positive views of other racial and ethnic groups; for mental health professionals, they report greater multicultural counseling competence. Furthermore, women who scored within the higher stages of feminist identity development report higher self-esteem.

Adolescents and adults who score higher on a measure of the tolerant personality, which focuses on racial and gender attitudes, indicate higher levels of acceptance of gay men, greater acknowledgment of the reality of White privilege and institutional racism, and, for mental health professionals, higher levels of multicultural competence.

For the construct of universal-diverse orientation, adults who score higher on this construct exhibit higher levels of empathy, academic self-concept, coping skills, self-efficacy, and general multicultural tolerance.

Table 1   Components of the Multicultural Personality

Model	Description	Sample Research Instruments
Racial/ethnic identity theory (higher stages)	Connectedness to one's own racial/ethnic heritage; openness to people of other cultural groups; cognitively flexible; seeks opportunities to interact across cultures; aware of possible internalized racism and unearned privilege; commitment to social justice for all oppressed groups	Cross Racial Identity Scale Helms's Black and White Racial Identity Attitude Scales
Coping with cultural diversity (integration strategy; balanced biculturalism)	Balancing multiple roles; having bicultural and multicultural interaction and coping skills	Coping With Cultural Diversity Scale
Tolerant personality	Empathic skills with a broad spectrum of people; self-aware, introspective, and self-analytic; cognitively sophisticated; sense of humor	Quick Discrimination Index
Universal-diverse orientation	Appreciative of both similarities and differences between self and others; sense of connectedness and shared experience with all people	Miville-Guzman Universality-Diversity Scale
Expansionist theory of gender roles	Transcends multiple roles, thus enhancing social support and interpersonal anchoring; increased self-complexity; multiple roles promote similarity of experiences and enhanced empathy skills	Feminist Identity Composite Scale
African-centered values and mental health	Collectivist and spiritual essence to human interaction and self-growth	Africentrism Scale TRIOS Scale
Expatriate multicultural personality construct	Empathic, open-minded, emotionally stable, action oriented, adventurous, curious	Multicultural Personality Questionnaire

Source: Adapted with permission from J. G. Ponterotto, S. O. Utsey, and P. B. Pedersen, *Preventing Prejudice: A Guide for Counselors, Educators, and Parents.* Copyright © 2006 by SAGE Publications.

Finally, operationalizing the multicultural personality as conceived by Karen van der Zee and Jan Pieter van Oudenhoven and using the Multicultural Personality Questionnaire (probably the most comprehensive measure of the multicultural personality that is available), findings indicate that adults who score higher in one or more of the dispositions also score higher on measures of international career interest, multicultural activities (e.g., travel, cross-cultural friendships), life satisfaction, and psychological and physical well-being.

Research indicates that it is possible to isolate particular dispositions that may be conceived of as components of the multicultural personality construct. Furthermore, initial research studies in the United States and Europe provide empirical support for the psychological and physical health benefits gained by those who score higher in multicultural personality dispositions. However, research on this topic is still in its infancy, and additional research using both quantitative and qualitative methods is needed before we can fully understand the nature and mental health correlates of multicultural personality dispositions.

—*Joseph G. Ponterotto*

See also Multiculturalism; Race Psychology

FURTHER READING

Coleman, H. L. K. (1995). Strategies for coping with cultural diversity. *Counseling Psychologist, 23,* 722–740.

Miville, M. L., Gelso, C. J., Pannu, R., Liu, W., Touradji, P., Holloway, P., & Fuertes, J. N. (1999). Appreciating similarities and valuing differences: The Miville-Guzman Universality-Diversity Scale. *Journal of Counseling Psychology, 46,* 291–307.

Ponterotto, J. G., Costa, C. I., & Werner-Lin, A. (2002). Research perspectives in cross-cultural counseling. In

P. B. Pedersen, J. G. Draguns, W. J. Lonner, & J. E. Trimble (Eds.), *Counseling across cultures* (5th ed., pp. 395–420). Thousand Oaks, CA: Sage.

Ponterotto, J. G., Utsey, S. O., & Pedersen, P. B. (2006). *Preventing prejudice: A guide for counselors, educators, and parents* (2nd ed.). Thousand Oaks, CA: Sage.

Ramirez, M. (1999). *Multicultural psychotherapy: An approach to individual and cultural differences* (2nd ed.). New York: Pergamon.

van der Zee, K. I., & van Oudenhoven, J. P. (2000). The Multicultural Personality Questionnaire: A multidimensional instrument of multicultural effectiveness. *European Journal of Personality, 14*, 291–309.

MULTIRACIAL INDIVIDUALS

Multiracial individuals are those people living in the United States who claim two or more racial groups as part of their racial heritage. Racial groups may include African American, Asian, Caucasian/European American, American Indian, and Latino/a.

HISTORICAL CONSIDERATIONS

In 2000, for the first time in U.S. history, multiracial individuals were able to identify themselves as such in the U.S. Census. This event marked a substantial movement forward in recognizing the civil rights and social realities of multiracial people. The United States has a long history of racism and racial discrimination, and multiracial people have been affected by this history in a variety of ways. Historical examples include the use of the "One-Drop Rule" as a legal definition of racial heritage, as well as laws passed by state legislatures that made interracial marriages illegal for many generations. The One-Drop Rule was used as early as 1660 in laws that attempted to maintain or promote so-called racial purity among European immigrants. Based on the predominant belief that both "Negroes and Indians" were subhuman, the notion that a single drop of blood from an African American person would "contaminate" a person of European descent was codified into law by most states as the rule of hypodescent. The Supreme Court struck down laws prohibiting interracial marriage in 1967; the last antimiscegenation state law was repealed in 2001.

Thus, the 2000 U.S. Census marked a critical point at which multiracial people could finally begin to gain governmental legitimacy with respect to their rich and complex racial heritage. Indeed, according to the 2000 Census, nearly 7 million people—2.4% of the total U.S. population—checked more than one racial category.

Given the sociohistorical context described here, it is not surprising that there has been little research on the psychology and education of multiracial people. Only within the past two decades has most of the theory and research describing the unique experiences of multiracial people been proposed and conducted. With the publication of several book-length works, pioneering researchers have recently begun to present a variety of themes, methodologies, findings, and theories regarding multiracial people in a single forum.

MYTHS ABOUT MULTIRACIAL INDIVIDUALS

In light of the controversial and ambiguous sociohistorical context in which multiracial people have existed, a number of myths have been promoted about multiracial people.

- Myth: The stereotype of the "tragic mulatto" or the "marginal person" refers to the idea that multiracial people are destined to experience long-lasting social and psychological effects because they cannot identify with a clearly defined racial group. Reality: Much research in this area has found few psychological adjustment problems among this population.
- Myth: Multiracial individuals are forced to choose or identify with only one racial group. This refers to a related concept by which social groups have been defined along rigid racial lines in the United States because of the history of segregation and legalized discrimination. As a result, individuals who have a multiracial heritage are forced to choose one racial group over another, also leading to the denial of one's total heritage. Reality: Recent research indicates that the racial identities of multiracial people are fluid and dynamic and transcend racial group labels.
- Myth: Multiracial people do not like to discuss their racial identity. This myth refers to the notion that because of the social and psychological difficulty of growing up multiracial and denying part of one's heritage, multiracial people learn to avoid discussion of this

emotionally evocative topic. Reality: Most research on multiracial people has been qualitative in nature, involving narratives and personal stories of multiracial people to derive a variety of identity models.

PSYCHOSOCIAL ADJUSTMENT OF MULTIRACIAL INDIVIDUALS

A common myth about multiracial people is that because of their unique or multiracial heritage (and the presumed lack of a coherent or stable community), they are at risk of becoming confused and maladjusted. Thus, a primary area of research has focused on the psychological functioning of multiracial people. This research portrays multiracial people as generally well-functioning, although at some psychological risk. For example, several recent studies used a subsample of self-identified multiracial adolescents culled from the National Longitudinal Study of Adolescent Health. Results showed that biracial participants have higher rates of conduct problems, school problems, somatization, low self-worth, and counseling use. However, other studies have shown few or no differences, leading one researcher to comment on the resilience of multiracial individuals in the face of multiple stressors. Unfortunately, a major limitation of existing studies in this area is that racial identity (i.e., race as a psychological construct) has not been included as a variable; instead, most research uses a self-identified biracial label (i.e., race as a demographic label). Thus, little is known about the direct impact, both positive and negative, that being multiracial has on psychological functioning.

MULTIRACIAL BILL OF RIGHTS

Maria Root, a leading scholar in the field, proposed a "bill of rights" for multiracial people based on three primary themes: resistance, revolution, and change. *Resistance* refers to multiracial individuals' right to refuse to fragment, marginalize, or disconnect themselves from others. *Revolution* refers to the right to choose to cross racial boundaries and challenge the racial hierarchy and rigid social networks. *Change* is based on the right to build connections with others and develop a sense of wholeness in a racially fragmented social world. This bill of rights may be used as a framework to build educational and psychological interventions.

IMPLICATIONS FOR PROFESSIONAL PRACTICE

Because of their unique sociopolitical history in the United States, multiracial people are likely to face a number of stressors. Of primary concern is finding a community or social network that can provide meaningful support, particularly in the face of the overt racism that multiracial individuals face (i.e., the often-asked "what are you?" question). As Dr. Root notes in her bill of rights, multiracial people may come to define themselves in ways that are different from their parents, siblings, and peers. These self-definitions also may be multiple and fluid over time and context. Thus, finding support during this dynamic process of self-definition and adopting meaningful self-labels is critical to the development of a healthy biracial or multiracial identity.

Mental health professionals working with multiracial individuals need to be aware of the impact of multiple racial labels among their clients. For example, multiracial clients may exhibit cultural mistrust, which is typically evident in cross-racial dyads. Moreover, therapists and counselors who have been trained in traditional models of racial identity development and multicultural counseling may conceptualize their multiracial clients from a monoracial identity framework that does not provide a holistic understanding of clients' experiences. In other words, although mental health professionals may attempt to use racially and culturally sensitive frameworks in counseling, their interventions and conceptualizations may not be congruent with clients' public and private understanding of their own racial or cultural identity. Derald Wing Sue and David Sue suggest the following guidelines for practice with multiracial individuals:

- Become aware of one's own stereotypes and preconceptions about interracial marriages and multiracial people.
- Understand the history of multiracial people, such as the One-Drop Rule, issues of marginality, and ambiguity (the "what are you?" question).
- View multiracial people in holistic terms rather than as parts of a person.
- Help contextualize feelings of loneliness and marginality, should these be present, within a perspective of racial prejudice and social injustice.

- Emphasize the positive attributes and advantages of being multiracial.
- Incorporate family counseling, where possible, to help educate parents.

—Marie L. Miville

See also Biracial Identity; Racial Identity Development

FURTHER READING

Root, M. P. P. (1992). *Racially mixed people in America.* Newbury Park, CA: Sage.

Root, M. P. P. (1996). *The multiracial experience: Racial borders as the new frontier.* Thousand Oaks, CA: Sage.

Sue, D. W., & Sue, D. (2003). *Counseling the culturally diverse: Theory and practice* (4th ed.). New York: Wiley.

Wehrly, B., Kenney, K. R., & Kenney, M. W. (1999). *Counseling multiracial families.* Thousand Oaks, CA: Sage.

N

NATIONAL LATINA/O PSYCHOLOGICAL ASSOCIATION

The mission of the National Latina/o Psychology Association/Asociación Nacional de Psicología Latina (NLPA) is to generate and advance psychological knowledge and foster its effective application for the benefit of the Hispanic/Latino population. The NLPA mission includes the following goals:

- Generating and advancing psychological knowledge
- Fostering the effective application of psychological knowledge for the benefit of the Hispanic/Latino population
- Valuably contributing to the field of Latina/o psychology
- Promoting the educational and professional advancement of Latina/o psychologists
- Fostering communication with members of Latina/o communities at all levels for their mutual education
- Promoting an awareness and understanding of issues that Latina/o psychologists and mental health professionals might have, related to their educational and professional experiences

Organized in 1979 as the National Hispanic Psychology Association, the newly renamed National Latina/o Psychology Association has experienced a recent resurgence under the leadership of current president Patricia Arredondo of Arizona State University.

Since the time of the 2002 American Psychological Association Convention in Chicago, where a small group of dedicated individuals gathered to provide momentum to the evolution of the NLPA, the association has grown to include more than 450 professionals and students. Members are primarily of Latino heritage and from throughout the United States and other countries, including Guatemala, Japan, and Mexico.

Building on previous recent conferences in Chicana/o psychology (in Lansing, Michigan, in 1998) and in Latina/o psychology (in San Antonio, Texas, in 2000 and Providence, Rhode Island, in 2002), the NLPA recently held its inaugural conference in Scottsdale, Arizona, in 2004. The NLPA publishes a newsletter, *El Boetín* ("The Bulletin"), four times per year, has established a Web site at http://www.nlpa.ws and an e-journal (effective 2005), and hosts a list server for its members. In all of these venues, issues relevant to Latino psychology, including research, practice, and honors and awards of the membership, are highlighted.

—*Brian William McNeill*

See also American Psychological Association; Hispanic Americans

NATIVE AMERICANS

This entry focuses on peoples with ancestral ties to the native inhabitants of North American lands that are now known as the United States of America, Canada, and Mexico. These peoples represent numerous distinct nations and cultures. They are referred to by many names, including Native Americans, Alaska Natives (including the Inuit or Eskimos, Aleuts, and Arctic Indians), American Indians, Indigenous Peoples, People of the Sovereign Nations and Tribes, People of Turtle Island, in Canada as First Nations people, and in Mexico as *los indígenas.* The terms *Native Americans* and *American Indians and Alaska Natives* will be used to refer to the multitude of native groups. Although this entry is written with the utmost respect for those who are descendants of the first peoples to inhabit North America, it focuses primarily on groups who have ties to the North American lands of the United States.

DEMOGRAPHICS

In terms of establishing Native American identity, there is no universally accepted criterion. Tribal membership is determined by the tribe itself, and criteria vary across tribes. According to the U.S. government's Bureau of Indian Affairs, to be eligible for services through this organization, an individual must be a member of a state- or federally recognized tribe and must have at least one-half Indian blood of tribes native to the United States of America, or at least one-fourth Indian ancestry. Whether one has physical features, particularly facial ones, that are consistent with Native American physiognomy has both social and psychological implications; it can affect self-concept and acceptance by both Native and majority culture groups.

Population Statistics

As of the 2000 U.S. Census, there were 561 federally recognized tribes/nations in the United States, as well as others that are seeking such status and/or are recognized by states or other jurisdictions. Although the Native American population has been reduced by war and disease resulting from contact with Europeans, the population now is more than six times greater than its historic low of 248,000 in 1890, as detailed by the U.S. Department of Commerce. At present, Native Americans represent approximately 1% of the U.S. population. Those who identified themselves as being solely of Native ancestry numbered 2,475,956 in the 2000 U.S. Census. The number of Native Americans who also identified themselves as having both Native and other ethnic ancestry was more than 4 million. Furthermore, the Native American population tends to be young, with U.S. Census data indicating that about

45% are under the age of 25 and about 34% are under the age of 18, compared with 26% under the age of 18 in the total U.S. population.

Education

Level of educational attainment of course varies within Native American groups. Overall Native American educational achievement, however, is relatively low, similar to the rates for African Americans but higher than for Hispanics and lower than for Asians. According to U.S. Census data, approximately 71% of Native Americans have a high school degree or higher, as compared with 84% of Caucasians.

Location

American Indians and Alaska Natives live in virtually all geographic areas of the United States. Approximately three-fifths of Native Americans live in urban areas. United States Census data show that Native Americans reside in the West (43%), South (31%), Midwest (17%), and Northeast (9%). Approximately 25% to 33% of Native Americans live on reservations. Currently, there are about 275 Native American reservations, totaling 56.2 million acres, according to the Bureau of Indian Affairs.

Income and Employment

Although there are signs of expansion and improvement, the overall economic status of Native Americans is a concern. Poverty rates for Native Americans are high, involving 20% or more of their population, according to U.S. Census data. These numbers are similar to those for other groups (i.e., African Americans and Hispanics) but are considerably higher than the approximate 12% of the total population. Further, the mean income of Native Americans is approximately 62% of that of the general U.S. population. High rates of unemployment for Native Americans suggest lack of opportunity and other social restrictions, such as racism. According to 2000 Census data, American Indians and Alaska Natives have the highest unemployment rate of any ethnic group, at 7.6%, relative to the 5.8% for the general population and 2.9% for Whites. On reservations, where opportunities typically are much more restricted, unemployment is extremely high, depending on the area, with most estimates exceeding 50%.

GOVERNMENT AND TRIBAL DEVELOPMENT

Native Americans had highly evolved forms of self-government well before European contact. Typically, government involved high-ranking leaders such as a chief but also emphasized the role of council members and advisers. Indeed, so advanced was the Iroquois government that it was used as a conceptual framework for the U.S. Constitution. The Iroquois Confederacy, as it came to be known, was a unification of the Mohawk, Oneida, Onondaga, Cayuga, and Seneca, referred to as the Haudenosaunee, or "People of the Longhouse." The Tuscarora nation later joined this confederation. Similarly, the Creek, Chickasaw, Cherokee, Choctaw, and Seminole came to be known as the Five Civilized Tribes, given their elaborate systems of government, culture, and agrarian abilities.

Although some reservations are limited by geographic isolation and consequently fewer economic opportunities, some tribal governments have developed income streams in the gaming industry, tourism, ecotourism, and mineral/land usage rights. Several organizations aim to assist Native Americans' business development, including the National Center for American Indian Enterprise Development. Tourism helps sustain Native American heritage and traditions through economic independence. Native American people also are a growing force in fine arts and entertainment. Numerous all–Native American human resource agencies promote the entrepreneurial spirit of Native American people trained as educators, engineers, physicians, and businesspeople.

MILITARY SERVICE

Native Americans historically have maintained a strong presence in the U.S. armed forces. As detailed by Thomas Holm, the number of Native Americans in the military has greatly surpassed their proportion of the overall population since World War I. In World War I, Choctaw Indians, as well as members of other tribes, acted as code talkers, or soldiers who used their native language as secret code to communicate among troops. Members of the Navajo Nation also participated in military service as code talkers in World War II.

SELECTED HISTORY

Since the time of European contact, Native Americans have been exposed to discrimination, governmental oppression, diseases, enslavement, and even war. Throughout the 1800s, the U.S. government took increasingly extreme measures against Native American people. Among these measures were the 1830 Indian Removal Act and the 1835 Indian Policy, which were created to increase land open to European American settlement. The policies resulted in forcibly marching thousands of indigenous people away from their homelands in "trails of tears," to foreign environments west of the Mississippi River and reservation lands that often were inhospitable.

Eventually, further policies were initiated that increased the cost in land and life to Native Americans. With the Dawes Act of 1887, Native Americans experienced their most rapid land loss in U.S. history. On the surface, the Dawes Act initially appeared to be a gentler form of government, with Native American families being given an average of 160 acres, which they were to homestead and farm. The land was frequently poor and/or relatively foreign (i.e., removal/relocation involved transitioning Native Americans into markedly different ecological environments), however, as the most ideal lands were reserved for European American settlement. The Dawes Act also required Native Americans to state their blood quantum, or percentage of Indian blood, during a time of severe government oppression. Furthermore, registration names could not be traditionally Native. Although the Dawes Act purportedly was developed to assist Native Americans, it resulted in forced assimilation and active political oppression. Many Native American families were forced to sell their land to survive. Given that fact, and because of government cutbacks, land allocated to Native Americans under the Dawes Act was eventually reduced to about 50 million of the original 190 million acres. With the Miriam Report of 1928, a congressional collaboration with Native American leaders, the numerous abuses and vast corruption of the Dawes Act were revealed.

By the late 1800s, a mass genocide of indigenous people had occurred, reducing the Native American population through disease, famine, and war with non-Native explorers and settlers. The fewer than 200,000 Native Americans who remained met with another attempt at forced assimilation, in the form of government-mandated attendance of children at off-reservation boarding schools. From that time, well into the 1900s, Native American children were removed—sometimes forcibly—from their families, elders, and traditions. They were forced to adhere to majority-culture standards in terms of diet, clothing, sociability, and language, and suffered heinous abuses, such as beatings for speaking their native tongue. Such was the abhorrent treatment that the negative psychological effects have been transmitted cross-generationally, continuing in some cases to the present day.

In 1924, the Citizenship Act was passed, establishing Native Americans as U.S. citizens. The Indian Reorganization Act was passed in 1934, giving Native Americans the right of self-government, including the management of their own land on a tribal basis, and establishing some education and training programs. Sovereignty remained elusive, however, as government policy still controlled core aspects of Native American life, particularly in terms of ceremonial and religious practices. Thus, it was not until 1974 that the Indian Freedom of Religion Act was passed, finally allowing Native Americans access to their First Amendment rights, 50 years after they had been granted citizenship.

Societal pressures and changes not only have affected social functioning, including residential location and occupation, but also have resulted in the loss of Native American traditions. Language loss is a particularly pervasive and acute problem; many Native American languages are spoken almost solely by elders. Fewer than 9% of Native Americans speak their traditional language fluently today. At the time of European contact, there were an estimated 300 Native American languages in the present-day United States; only 175 of these presently are used. Over the last 10 years, the population on reservations and traditional Native lands has declined by 9%. Despite overall population growth, Native Americans have moved away from reservation and traditional lands in search of jobs and higher education. Nevertheless, the adaptability and resilience of Native American people demonstrate that they are capable not only of surviving cultural onslaught, but of thriving as unique and valued contributors to modern American culture, both their own and that of the larger society.

ACCULTURATION AND ETHNIC IDENTITY

Like many other indigenous peoples across the globe, Native Americans have had to adjust to the progressive societal incursions of Europeans and other cultural groups. Native American cultures remain rich in oral history; many traditions, ceremonies, and beliefs are passed on solely verbally. There are concerns that, as the number of Native speakers declines, knowledge of traditions will decline, as well. As a result, issues of ethnic identity become paramount. There is great cultural heterogeneity within the Native American population, with more than 500 separate and unique groups. Maintaining one's identity as a Native American can be personally important and a source of strength and spirituality. Personal identity can be associated with specific tribe or clan heritage, or with a more heterogeneous collection of various Native American traditions and spiritual ceremonies.

Acculturation is a process through which an individual from one culture incorporates the values and behaviors of another culture into his or her worldview. John Berry and other theorists have posited that acculturation is dynamic and progresses along multiple dimensions, with various possible outcomes, including assimilation, separation, integration, and marginalization.

With more Native Americans living in nontraditional environments than ever before, exposure to majority-culture mechanisms such as health care, financial, and educational institutions continues to grow. Thus, issues of acculturative orientation and one's ethnic identity are important factors in understanding Native Americans' utilization of these services.

A major focus for many Native Americans is continuing their clan and/or tribal spirit and "medicine" while living and working in majority-culture environments. For Native American heritages to survive the overwhelming influences of the majority culture takes great effort and dedication, particularly in passing oral traditions to the new generation. Avoiding *ethnic gloss,* as described by Joseph Trimble, and being considered part of a homogeneous group of Native Americans, demands public education. The adoption and co-opting of Native American ceremonies and symbols by majority-culture entities also threatens the integrity of personal, clan, and tribal identity. The work of Teresa LaFromboise on biculturalism (i.e., functioning effectively in both one's Native group and the majority culture) emphasizes the benefits of such an acculturative outcome, but also recognizes the effort and energy required to maintain it.

PSYCHOLOGICAL AND OTHER HEALTH CONSIDERATIONS

Native Americans are prone to certain health problems more than are other segments of the population.

For example, there are high rates of type 2 diabetes, heart disease, obesity, and alcoholism among Native Americans. The rate of type 2 diabetes is four times the national average for American Indian elders, affecting one in five. Consistent with the general population, however, heart disease is the leading cause of death for Native Americans. In comparison to that of other racial and ethnic groups, the life expectancy of Native Americans is appreciably lower. According to the work of Everett Rhoades, reasons for this discrepancy may include poverty, greater risk of interpersonal violence, increased abuse of substances, vehicular accidents, and greater rates of disease (e.g., diabetes).

In terms of mental health challenges, Native Americans most frequently experience substance abuse, anxiety, and depression, as described by Emily Sáez-Santiago and Guillermo Bernal. Some protective factors that may help maintain good mental health for Native Americans include a strong ethnic identity and involvement in cultural activities and traditions. For example, Tami De Coteau, Debra Hope, and Jessiline Anderson have suggested that participation in cultural activities and ceremonies may protect against depression, the experience of emotional distress, and stress for traditional Native Americans.

Further, the strong emphasis on the importance of family in this culture also may serve to protect Native Americans from psychological distress. The Native American family often includes members of the extended family and the community, including members of the tribe or group even though they might not be biologically related. The extended family and elders are highly respected, and the collective wisdom of the tribe is treasured. Individuals are expected to provide advice and counsel to tribe members and to reinforce the values of the culture. They are believed to be responsible for the decisions that they make; the correct decision is often the one that benefits the group or tribe, more than the self. This sense of community promotes a sense of interdependence and cooperation among individuals. Sharing is seen as honorable and respectful; it is considered important to share oneself, as well as material possessions, with others.

Though many protective mechanisms are evident in Native American cultures, there are several risk factors for mental health problems. Poverty and its resulting social conditions (e.g., poor access to health care) increase vulnerability to psychopathology. Tami De Coteau and colleagues found that the hardships of living on some reservations (likely related to lack of opportunity and isolation, among other factors), as well as a history of oppression and discrimination, can contribute to psychological distress.

There are a number of culturally related and/or culturally bound behaviors that may or may not be considered clinical syndromes. As with other aspects of understanding various Native American cultures, rather than applying to all groups, these behaviors appear to be specific to certain tribes, language groups, or regions. There is considerable doubt about some of these syndromes, as their purported existence is based on anecdotal accounts, and there may be errors in translation or errant labeling of normal behaviors as pathological from a Eurocentric perspective, among other issues. To fully understand psychopathology in an individual-specific or tribal-specific fashion, it is important to understand degree of acculturation and how the tribe and/or individual conceptualize psychological problems. Spero Manson and colleagues, for example, identified five different types of psychological disturbances among the Hopi that do not correspond well with accepted nosological categories in the majority culture.

Alternately, *windigo* has been extensively written about as a culture-bound syndrome of the northern Algonkian-speaking tribes. A windigo can be a monster with superhuman strength, the concept of which can be used to frighten children, either in a teasing way or to manage their behavior. The windigo also can be a person possessed of this monster's spirit, or someone with a psychotic reaction involving cannabalistic desires. Now largely discredited as a clinical syndrome, the genesis of the idea of windigo as a psychosis appears to be an anthropological accident.

Work by Joseph Trimble and colleagues suggests that there are four clusters of psychopathology found across many tribal groups: (1) soul loss (e.g., fainting, withdrawal, and preoccupation with death); (2) spirit intrusion (e.g., somatization related to the belief that one is ill because of spirit power); (3) taboo breaking (e.g., weight and sleep disturbances related to violation of social norms); and (4) ghost sickness (e.g., confusion and nightmares along with a preoccupation with death, which can be related to witchcraft). Ghost sickness also is a culturally bound syndrome listed in the *Diagnostic and Statistical Manual of Mental Disorders, Fourth Edition, Text Revised* (*DSM-IV-TR*). The other two *DSM* culture-bound syndromes listed for Native Americans are *pibloktoq*, a dissociative disorder found among the peoples of the Arctic involving withdrawal or irritability followed by wildly irrational behavior, and *amok,* a dissociative reaction involving aggression.

Anxiety

Native Americans not only experience anxiety and anxiety disorders as typically represented in the population; they also experience unique forms of culturally related anxiety. Anxiety, and its psychopathological forms in anxiety disorders, is underrecognized in these peoples. The few epidemiological data available, however, suggest anxiety is a common reason for seeking mental health services among Native Americans. Some empirical work is emerging in the area of anxiety and Native Americans. For example, Tami De Coteau and colleagues found that health problems and stressful life events were associated with higher anxiety in a Native American sample. J. Douglas McDonald, Thomas Jackson, and Arthur McDonald identified greater levels of generalized anxiety in Native American youth who left home to attend college, as compared with both Native Americans who pursued their education near home and non-Native students. Daniel McNeil and collaborators identified anxieties specific with Native Americans through the Native American Cultural Involvement and Detachment Anxiety Questionnaire, focusing on factors of social involvement with Native Americans and cultural knowledge, economic issues, and social involvement with the majority culture.

A culture-bound anxiety syndrome, *kayak-angst,* historically was found among the Inuit of west Greenland. The disorder appears to be a culturally specific variant of panic disorder, in that some individuals hunting seals while alone far from shore in a one-person kayak sometimes would have symptoms (e.g., unexpected and rapid onset of dizziness, trembling, and fear of death) consistent with panic attacks. These concerns would be relieved by returning to a safe place (e.g., land) or having help nearby in the form of safe persons (e.g., other hunters).

A form of intergenerational posttraumatic stress disorder also may be specific to Native Americans, given their unique cultural history. The abuses experienced historically by Native Americans, including boarding school experiences, may be transmitted across generations, leading to stress in current generations, who themselves face oppression and discrimination. The history of indigenous people in North America may, quite appropriately, lead to caution and even suspicion of governmental and other majority-culture institutions and those who, at least symbolically, represent them (e.g., majority-culture psychotherapists).

Depression

As a group, Native Americans face many stressors, such as the social onslaught of the majority culture, as well as racism, discrimination, and access to education and other services. Not surprisingly, the most common mental disorder among American Indians and Alaska Natives, for both children and adults, is depression. As noted by Traci Rieckmann and colleagues, however, the manifestation of depression in Native Americans may differ considerably from typical North American conceptualizations of the disorder, focusing more on somatic symptoms or a lack of balance or spiritual harmony.

A potentially grave consequence of depression in any population is the increased risk of suicide. With high rates of depression and substance abuse, suicidality among Native Americans is a considerable concern, particularly for adolescents. As reported by the U.S. Census, Native Americans ages 15 to 24 are two to four times as likely to attempt and complete suicide as are other adolescents.

Substance Abuse

Substance abuse has affected Native American culture in a significant manner. Specifically, alcoholism has been a severe problem for Native Americans since initial European contact. Increasing the risk for accidents, cirrhosis of the liver, suicide, and homicide, all primary causes of death for Native Americans, alcoholism has been called the "number one killer among American Indians" (French, 2004, p. 82). Additional consequences of alcoholism include fetal alcohol effects (FAE) and fetal alcohol syndrome (FAS), conditions that result from alcohol consumption during pregnancy. Of the various racial and ethnic groups within the United States, Native Americans are considered particularly at risk for FAE and FAS.

Ronald Vick and colleagues suggested that the recovery process for Native American individuals suffering from alcoholism may be aided by the sweat lodge, the Red Road, and the Recovery Medicine Wheel. The sweat lodge is a commonly used healing ceremony for the treatment of many illnesses, including alcoholism. The sweat lodge can represent spiritual and cultural identity for some Native Americans. Similarly, the Red Road is a holistic approach to the treatment of alcoholism in which prayer is used to provide healing to restore spiritual, physical, and emotional wellness. Finally, the Recovery Medicine Wheel is a 16-step program for sobriety, with four steps for each direction. A culturally important feature of this program is that individuals can begin at any point in the wheel and that because a circle never ends, neither does the medicine wheel, nor the healing process.

SPECIAL ISSUES IN PSYCHOLOGICAL TREATMENT

Awareness of unique issues related to mental health assessment and treatment for Native Americans is essential in providing the best services, as with other ethnic and cultural groups. Tribal-specific knowledge is important, as is avoiding accidental stereotyping, in the effort of being culturally sensitive. It may be appropriate for mental health treatment to be community-based (e.g., extended family) and to involve a medicine man or woman.

Cultural Competence

Special issues of concern for the clinician working with Native American clients may include extra effort required to build rapport and to establish a therapeutic alliance because of clients' and/or tribes' past experiences with the majority culture. Demonstration of cultural competence (e.g., avoiding making assumptions about individuals because of their racial or ethnic background, an awareness of one's own biases as a therapist, a willingness to learn about the client's culture) and respect for Native American culture aid the establishment of rapport.

It is important to learn about the culture of the client, including the specific traditions, beliefs, and spiritual practices of the client and/or his or her tribe, village, or other group. It is critical, however, not to overgeneralize and to be aware of individual differences. The presenting problems should be understood from a variety of perspectives, including a Native American worldview and degree of acculturation, and goals for treatment made congruent with the community culture. George Renfrey has suggested that a cognitive-behavioral therapeutic orientation may be particularly helpful in the treatment of Native American clients, stating that such an approach is in agreement with the unique preferences and mental health needs of Native Americans. Finally, psychological treatments that have been empirically supported in Native American populations should be considered, as in working with any group.

Cultural Factors in Treatment

A knowledge of culturally related factors and values that may affect the course of treatment, such as communication style and time orientation, will aid the progress of treatment. Certain nonverbal behaviors, for example, have been identified as characteristic of some Native Americans. In particular, Native Americans may avoid eye contact during a conversation out of respect, as described by Barbara Kawulich and William Curlette. A mild handshake may be used, because a firm handshake may be considered rude. Furthermore, Native Americans may feel more comfortable when allowed greater personal space than other societal norms indicate as appropriate. Consistent with a collectivist nature and extended-family orientation, it also is common for Native American clients to bring someone with them to therapy for support or to help them communicate.

Also, time orientation may be different for some Native Americans, as the focus is more on the present than on the past or on the future. An event often will be considered to begin with the arrival of individuals central to it. Furthermore, an unperturbed attitude and a stepwise approach to daily tasks are common.

Finally, several possible issues of concern in the clinical relationship with Native American clients include the way in which questions are posed. For example, Barbara Kawulich and William Curlette indicated that asking numerous detailed questions may be seen as rude by some clients. As such, they recommend that therapists provide Native American clients additional routes for communication, such as through storytelling techniques or the use of a third person to discuss emotions. Also, as some Native Americans may be quick to agree with the clinician but may not follow through with suggested interventions, it is important to assure that agreement on treatment goals and interventions has been reached between the client and the clinician. Furthermore, Geri Glover recommended that treatment may be more successful if relationships are developed with members of the community, to provide social support for clients.

CONCLUSIONS

Native Americans have endured social, racial, and economic oppression but have persevered despite these struggles. American Indians and Alaska Natives are part of a rich and diverse population that has realized many accomplishments. Historically, Native Americans have contributed to the development of both the government and cultures of the United States. It is important to acknowledge the uniqueness of Native Americans' cultures and experiences and to embrace the richness that this culture contributes to North America as a whole.

In examining the psychological research on American Indians and Alaska Natives, both the thriving and supportive nature of the Native American culture (e.g., protective factors such as extended-family orientation) and the unique challenges faced by its people (e.g., intergenerational trauma) are evident. Consistent with the current barriers (e.g., socioeconomic) and historical traumas impacting Native Americans, mental health problems, particularly depression, anxiety disorders, and substance abuse, are an unfortunate reality for far too many. Additional research, particularly concerning culturally related factors implicated in psychological health, is required to progress toward a better understanding of multicultural issues among American Indians and Alaska Natives.

—Renata K. Martins
—Rebecca K. Widoe
—Chebon A. Porter
—Daniel W. McNeil

See also Acculturation; Alaska Natives; Anxiety Disorders in Ethnic Minorities; Certificate of Degree of Indian Blood; Historical Trauma (Native Americans); Indian Health Service; Indigenous Treatments and Healers

FURTHER READING

American Psychological Association. (2000). *Diagnostic and statistical manual of mental disorders* (4th ed., text rev.). Washington, DC: Author.

Amering, M., & Katschnig, H. (1989). Panic attacks and culture-bound syndromes. *Psychiatria Fennica, Suppl.,* 91–95.

Barney, D. D. (2001). Risk and protective factors for depression and health outcomes in American Indian and Alaska Native adolescents. *Wicazo Sa Review, 16,* 135–150.

Berry, J. W. (2003). Conceptual approaches to acculturation. In K. M. Chun, P. Balls Organista, & G. Marin (Eds.), *Acculturation: Advances in theory, measurement, and applied research* (pp. 17–37). Washington, DC: American Psychological Association.

Choney, S. K., Berryhill-Paapke, E., & Robbins, R. R. (1995). The acculturation of American Indians: Developing frameworks for research and practice. In J. G. Ponterotto, J. M. Casas, L. A. Suzuki, & C. M. Alexander (Eds.), *Handbook of multicultural counseling* (pp. 73–92). Thousand Oaks, CA: Sage.

De Coteau, T. J., Hope, D. A., & Anderson, J. (2003). Anxiety, stress, and health in northern plains Native Americans. *Behavior Therapy, 34,* 365–380.

French, L. A. (1997). *Counseling American Indians.* Lanham, MD: University Press of America.

French, L. A. (2004). Alcohol and other drug addictions among Native Americans: The movement toward tribal-centric treatment programs. *Alcoholism Treatment Quarterly, 22,* 81–91.

Glover, G. (2001). Parenting in Native American families. In N. B. Webb & D. Lum (Eds.), *Culturally diverse parent–child and family relationships: A guide for social workers and other practitioners* (pp. 205–231). New York: Columbia University Press.

Gone, J. P. (2004). Mental health services for Native Americans in the 21st century United States. *Professional Psychology: Research and Practice, 35,* 10–18.

Holm, T. (1997). The militarization of Native America: Historical processes and cultural perception. *Social Science Journal, 34,* 461–475.

Kawulich, B. B., & Curlette, W. L. (1998). Life tasks and the Native American perspectives. *Journal of Individual Psychology, 54,* 359–367.

LaFromboise, T., Coleman, H. L. K., & Gerton, J. (1993). Psychological impact of biculturalism: Evidence and theory. *Psychological Bulletin, 114,* 395–412.

Manson, S. M., Shore, J. H., & Bloom, J. D. (1985). The depressive experience in American Indian communities: A challenge for psychiatric theory and diagnosis (pp. 331–368). In A. Kleinman & B. Good (Eds.), *Culture and depression: Studies in anthropology and cross-cultural psychiatry of affect and disorder.* Berkeley: University of California Press.

McDonald, J. D., Jackson, T. L., & McDonald, A. L. (1991). Perceived anxiety differences among reservation and non-reservation Native American and majority culture students. *Journal of Indigenous Studies, 2,* 71–79.

McNeil, D. W., Porter, C. A., Zvolensky, M. J., Chaney, J. M., & Kee, M. (2000). Assessment of culturally related anxiety in American Indians and Alaska Natives. *Behavior Therapy, 31,* 301–325.

Milbrodt, T. (2002). Breaking the cycle of alcohol problems among Native Americans: Culturally-sensitive treatment in the Lakota community. *Alcoholism Treatment Quarterly, 20,* 19–43.

Nebelkopf, E., & Phillips, M. (Eds.). (2004). *Healing and mental health for Native Americans: Speaking in red.* Walnut Creek, CA: Altamira Press.

Renfrey, G. S. (1992). Cognitive-behavior therapy and the Native American client. *Behavior Therapy, 23,* 321–340.

Rhoades, E. R. (2003). The health status of American Indian and Alaska Native males. *American Journal of Public Health, 93,* 774–778.

Rieckmann, T. R., Wadsworth, M. E., & Deyhle, D. (2004). Cultural identity, explanatory style, and depression in Navajo adolescents. *Cultural Diversity and Ethnic Minority Psychology, 10,* 365–382.

Trimble, J. E., & Dickson, R. (2005). Ethnic gloss. In C. B. Fisher & R. M. Lerner (Eds.), *Encyclopedia of developmental science: Vol. 1* (pp. 412–415). Thousand Oaks, CA: Sage.

Trimble, J. E., Manson, S. M., Dinges, N. G., & Medicine, B. (1984). Towards an understanding of American Indian concepts of mental health: Some reflections and directions (pp. 199–220). In P. Pederson, N. Sartorius, & A. Marsala (Eds.), *Mental health services: The cross cultural context.* Thousand Oaks, CA: Sage.

Vick, R. D., Smith, L. M., & Herrera, C. I. R. (1998). The healing circle: An alternative path to alcoholism recovery. *Counseling and Values, 42,* 133–141.

NEUROPSYCHOLOGY

Neuropsychology involves the study of the relationship between the brain and behavior. Neuropsychologists obtain specialized training in diagnosis and assessment and work with a variety of disorders that involve brain impairment. Although neuropsychologists traditionally have treated ethnic minority groups as part of their practice, neuropsychology has only recently begun to address the impact of culture on neuropsychological performance.

TRAINING

Neuropsychology originated as a subspecialty of clinical psychology, and thus the majority of neuropsychologists are clinical psychologists with specialized training in neuropsychology. A smaller portion of neuropsychologists are trained by neurologists. Training in neuropsychology involves extensive knowledge of clinical psychology including conceptualizing abnormal behavior, diagnosis, and psychological assessment. In addition, neuropsychologists are trained in neuroanatomy, neurochemistry, and neuropathology. Thus neuropsychologists tend to begin their training in graduate school, obtain extensive training at the internship level, and receive further specialized training at the postdoctoral level. There

have been calls by the specialty to require board certification to earn the label *neuropsychologist,* but that has not occurred to this point. Although neuropsychologists might receive training in working with culturally diverse populations as part of their general clinical training in graduate school, there is less emphasis on cultural issues in neuropsychology training at the internship and postdoctoral levels.

PRACTICE

Neuropsychologists predominantly perform cognitive assessments. Historically, the assessments were designed to determine the localization of the brain lesion, as imaging techniques were not available. Currently, neuropsychological assessment is used to determine the specific extent of impairment within the following cognitive domains: attention, memory, visuospatial functioning, psychomotor functioning, processing speed, language, and executive functioning (reasoning, judgment, organization, planning, and initiation). In addition, neuropsychologists provide recommendations based on their findings with respect to remediation, adaptation, and adjustment. Neuropsychologists work with individuals who are experiencing difficulties because of brain impairment caused by traumatic brain injury, brain tumors, brain infections, strokes, dementia, psychological disorders with known brain impairment (i.e., schizophrenia), and so on.

As with general psychological assessment, neuropsychological performance is influenced by culture. Factors such as ethnicity, gender, socioeconomic status, language, education, and acculturation status are beginning to be examined with respect to their influence on neuropsychological performance. Culture affects several factors related to assessment. Factors such as test-taking attitudes, motivation, and exposure to content can affect neuropsychological performance. In addition, neurobehavioral factors such as handedness and brain lateralization appear to be influenced by culture. These cultural factors would then affect neuropsychological performance. Thus, although cognitive performance may be universal with respect to most cognitive domains, culture may influence some aspects of neuropsychological performance.

Ethnicity has also been found to affect neuropsychological performance. Ethnic minorities are generally grouped into four major groups. Criticisms of this approach point to the heterogeneity within each of the four major groups. That said, studies have found differences in test patterns when comparing ethnic minority individuals to norms based on European Americans. For example, African Americans have been found to exhibit more impairment on measures of complex attention, language, verbal learning, and factual knowledge. Asian Americans may have more difficulty with language-based tasks, particularly if English is not their first language. Similarly, Latino Americans are more likely to perform similarly to European Americans when the assessment occurs in their dominant language. Although there is very little information available on neuropsychological performance with Native Americans, there have been indications of differences in brain lateralization, communication styles, and decision-making strategies that might influence neuropsychological performance. As noted earlier, factors such as language, acculturation, education, and socioeconomic status interact with ethnicity to influence the differential performance found for ethnic minority groups on neuropsychological test measures.

LANGUAGE

The majority of neuropsychological measures developed in the United States were developed and normed on native English-speaking populations. Using these measures with people for whom English is not their native language affects the validity of the scores based on their performance. Although some attempts have been made to translate these measures into different languages (e.g., Spanish), there are further criticisms of this approach. Some words may not translate accurately into another language, for example, or the language may have different meanings for similar words. There have also been attempts to use translators to conduct neuropsychological evaluations on nonnative English speakers, but this approach, too, is fraught with problems. For instance, it is unclear whether the translation is accurate, particularly when the translator is a family member. In addition, unless the translator is also a neuropsychologist, he or she may be unfamiliar with the concepts from the measures or unsure how to interpret the client's responses appropriately.

ACCULTURATION

Acculturation is defined as how much individuals from a different culture adopt the values, beliefs, and customs of the dominant culture in which they live. It is usually measured through such factors as length of time in the culture, language and food tastes, and knowledge of

cultural values. Recent attempts have been made to determine whether the neuropsychological deficits seen in ethnic minority groups might in part be explained by acculturation. The assumption is that those ethnic minority individuals who are more acculturated to the dominant American culture should have profiles that are more similar to the dominant culture. A few studies have been conducted with African Americans and neuropsychological performance. The researchers found that, indeed, when acculturation was controlled, many of the deficits (as compared with the norms for the measures) dropped out. Thus, researchers are now encouraging neuropsychologists to use an acculturation measure as part of the neuropsychological evaluation, as that might affect the interpretation of the test profile for ethnic minority individuals.

EDUCATION AND SOCIOECONOMIC STATUS

As with psychological assessment, neuropsychological assessment is influenced by both education and socioeconomic status. Numerous studies have found that individuals with higher levels of education exhibit higher levels of performance on neuropsychological measures. Therefore, norms have been developed that take education into account on many neuropsychological measures. Although norms based on education are important, they are inexact owing to the manner in which education is measured. Typically, education is measured by number of years in school. This measure doesn't take into account the quality of education. As several studies have documented, education interacts with socioeconomic status (SES). Individuals from higher-SES backgrounds are more likely to have a better-quality education. Individuals from ethnic minority groups are more likely to be from lower-SES backgrounds and thus receive inferior-quality education. This lower quality of education, too, could affect neuropsychological test performance, even when norms controlling for education are used.

As noted earlier, individuals from ethnic minority backgrounds are receiving neuropsychological evaluations to measure the extent and impact of brain impairment. As the majority of neuropsychological measures have been normed on native-English-speaking European Americans, the norms may not be appropriate for use with ethnic minority individuals, for the reasons noted earlier. Using these norms might lead to overpathologizing the ethnic minority individual, which could negatively affect the treatment recommendations and prognosis. Neuropsychologists need to be aware of the potential biases in using these measures and consider alternatives such as using an acculturation measure, using measures that were normed in the individual's native language, or at the very least viewing the results with caution.

—*Nina Alease Nabors*
—*Radhika Seghal*

FURTHER READING

Echemendia, R. J. (2004). Cultural diversity and neuropsychology: An uneasy relationship in a time of change. *Applied Neuropsychology, 11,* 1–3.

Ferraro, R. F. (2002). *Minority and cross-cultural aspects of neurosychological assessment.* Lisse, The Netherlands: Swets & Zeitlinger.

Fletcher-Janzen, E., Strickland, T. L., & Reynolds, C. R. (Eds.). (2000). *Handbook of cross-cultural neuropsychology.* New York: Kluwer-Academic/Plenum Press.

Nell, V. (2000). *Cross-cultural neuropsychological assessment: Theory and practice.* Mahwah, NJ: Erlbaum.

Pontón, M. O., & León-Carrión, J. (Eds.). (2001). *Neuropsychology and the Hispanic patient: A clinical handbook.* Mahwah, NJ: Erlbaum.

Wong, T. M., & Fujii, D. E. (2004). Neuropsychological assessment of Asian Americans: Demographic factors, cultural diversity, and practical guidelines. *Applied Neuropsychology, 11,* 23–36.

OFFICE OF ETHNIC
MINORITY AFFAIRS

Established in 1892, the American Psychological Association (APA) is the nation's largest professional and scientific association of psychologists. The Office of Ethnic Minority Affairs (OEMA) contributes to the APA's goal of advancing psychology as a science and a profession. In 2004, the APA had approximately 150,000 members; approximately 5,100 (5.8%) of its associates, members, and fellows and 10,000 (20%) of its student members identify themselves as persons of color. Psychologists of color now occupy 19 seats (11%) in the APA's highest governance body, the Council of Representatives. These and other successes of ethnic minority participation in the APA can be traced in part to the efforts of the OEMA.

Although race and ethnicity have been long-standing subjects of psychological research and discourse, the APA did not begin to examine racial and ethnic inequities within the profession until 1963, when its board of directors appointed an Ad Hoc Committee on Equality of Opportunity in Psychology. By 1978, concern had reached a point that prompted the APA and the National Institute of Mental Health to sponsor a conference of ethnic minority psychologists, "Expanding the Roles of Culturally Diverse People in the Profession of Psychology: The Dulles Conference." That conference opened up organizational space for the current structures for minority participation by recommending that the APA establish an office, governance board, and division on ethnic minority affairs. Consequently, in January 1979, the OEMA

was established. (The recommended board and division were established in 1980 and 1986, respectively.)

Initially, the OEMA was charged with the implementation of the Dulles conference recommendations, but this task was later expanded to its current mission: (1) increasing the scientific understanding of culture and ethnicity in psychology; (2) increasing minority participation in psychological education and training and within the APA; (3) promoting culturally sensitive models for the delivery of psychological services; (4) advocating the interests of ethnic minority psychologists and their communities within and outside the APA; and (5) providing staff support for APA governance groups focused on ethnic minority concerns.

To date, the OEMA has had five directors (Esteban Olmeda, 1979–1983; Lillian Comas-Díaz, 1984–1986; Christine I. Hall, 1987–1989; L. Philip Guzmán, 1990–1993; and Bertha G. Holliday, 1994–present), who have provided leadership for its major achievements: (1) developing a *Directory of Ethnic Minority Professionals in Psychology;* (2) securing the APA's adoption of guidelines for providers of psychological services to ethnic, linguistic, and culturally diverse populations; (3) launching the *Communiqué,* a semiannual news journal that provides a voice for ethnic minority issues in psychology; (4) organizing two conferences, "Ethnic Minorities: Issues and Concerns for Psychology Now and in the Future" (1992) and "Psychology and Racism" (1997); (5) administering the Diversity Project 2000 and Beyond, a summer institute for community college students of color; (6) administering the grant funds of the Committee on Ethnic Minority Recruitment, Retention, and Training in Psychology, which provide for innovative minority recruitment, retention, and training strategies; (7) administering the multimillion-dollar Minority Biomedical Research Talent in Psychology project, funded by the National Institute of General Medical Sciences, which operates at 14 postsecondary institutions and seeks to increase the participation of minorities in biomedical areas of psychology; (8) staffing the six-member APA delegation to the 2001 United Nations World Conference Against Racism in Durban, South Africa; and (9) establishing an initiative on psychology in minority-serving institutions, which includes a health disparities grant program for early career faculty at these institutions.

—Bertha G. Holliday

See also American Psychological Association; Council of National Psychological Associations for the Advancement of Ethnic Minority Interests

FURTHER READING

American Psychological Association, Office of Ethnic Minority Affairs. (2004, March). *Communiqué,* Special Section. Retrieved January 23, 2006, from http://www.apa .org/pi/oema/oema25thanniversary.pdf

Comas-Diaz, L. (1990). Ethnic minority mental health: Contributions and future directions of the American Psychological Association. In F. C. Serafica et al. (Eds.), *Mental health of ethnic minorities* (pp. 275–301). New York: Praeger.

Guthrie, R. (1976). *Even the rat was white: A historical view of psychology.* Boston: Allyn & Bacon.

Holliday, B. G., & Holmes, A. L. (2003). A tale of challenge and change: A history and chronology of ethnic minorities in psychology in the United States. In G. Bernal et al. (Eds.), *Handbook of racial and ethnic minority psychology* (pp. 15–64). Thousand Oaks, CA: Sage.

Richards, G. (1997). *Race, racism, and psychology: Towards a reflexive history.* New York: Routledge.

ORGANIZATIONAL DIVERSITY

Organizational diversity refers to processes and programs that raise awareness of diversity and enhance an organization's ability to leverage diversity. In contrast, affirmative action primarily concerns compliance with government guidelines regarding the inclusion of women and members of underrepresented ethnic groups in personnel decisions. Both value increasing representational diversity so that the workforce represents a consumer base or a geographic region. However, organizational diversity initiatives emphasize the global nature of the economy, involve broader efforts to increase the diversity competence of employees, and recognize the need to increase employees' abilities to work with others who are different from them in one way or another.

Much organizational diversity work is housed in human resource departments, and many of these efforts focus on race, ethnicity, and gender. However, leaders among diversity professionals define diversity as including a variety of demographic characteristics that have resulted in discrimination and bias. These include race, ethnicity, gender, age, sexual orientation, national origin, veteran status, disability status, and religious belief systems. In his book *Redefining Diversity*, Roosevelt Thomas expanded the definition even further to include any similarity or difference that can influence the workplace, such as differences between management and line workers. Lee Gardenswartz and Anita Rowe developed a four-layer model of diversity that provides a theoretical underpinning for effective organizational diversity interventions.

Employers on the forefront of these efforts invest in becoming "employers of choice" for underrepresented groups based on the assumption that an explicitly prodiversity environment will help them to be more productive and more competitive in attracting top talent. Media ventures such as DiversityInc.com periodically create lists recognizing the top companies for diversity.

To achieve these distinctions, organizations engage in practices that expand their diversity efforts well beyond affirmative action in personnel decisions while increasing the organization's effectiveness and profitability. Best practices include adopting diversity-sensitive policies; developing a mission statement that explicitly reflects a commitment to diversity; empowering a diversity officer as part of the leadership team; creating and funding affinity groups for employees; and creating diversity councils that provide diversity training, recommend diversity-sensitive policies, and enhance the working environment for all employees.

Much of the evidence for the effectiveness of diversity programs is anecdotal. Systematic empirical data, when collected, may be proprietary, and the paid consultants who complete much of this work have little motive to publish. However, there is a substantial literature on racial and gender discrimination in hiring practices, performance evaluation, and promotion.

Although gender discrimination in hiring and performance evaluation may have diminished in recent years, the effects of racial discrimination have not. In fact, European American men still tend to be overrepresented in higher-paying and more prestigious jobs. Research also demonstrates the adverse effects of prejudice on productivity and job satisfaction, as well as the economic benefits of a diverse workforce.

As yet, there is no license or professional credential for those wishing to provide consultation to organizations that are committed to increasing the extent to which their employees value diversity or improving employers' capacity to manage diversity. Psychologists with an interest and expertise in multicultural psychology have much to offer in this regard. Finally, additional research demonstrating the impact of best practices in organizational diversity and exploring aspects of diversity other than race and gender is sorely needed.

—*Michael R. Stevenson*

See also Affirmative Action

FURTHER READING

Gardenswartz, L., & Rowe, A. (1998). *Managing diversity: A complete desk reference and planning guide* (Rev. ed.). New York: McGraw-Hill.

Thomas, R. R. (1996). *Redefining diversity.* New York: American Management Association.

Whitley, B. E., Jr., & Kite, M. E. (2006). *The psychology of prejudice and discrimination.* Belmont, CA: Wadsworth.

P

PARENTING PRACTICES ACROSS FAMILIES OF COLOR

Nancy Darling and Lawrence Steinberg defined *parenting practices* as the means by which parents socialize their children. For example, parents may believe children should sit still and use good manners at the dinner table, but how parents accomplish this goal of teaching their children to have good manners varies. Some use physical punishment, others explain why good manners are important, and some may not intervene at all. The behaviors parents use to achieve their goal constitute parenting practices.

Much of the research that has examined parenting behavior has focused on *parenting style,* which refers to the emotional atmosphere created by parents. Diana Baumrind identified three parenting styles that are characteristic of how parents generally intervene with children across various situations. Parents who are consistently stern, lack warmth, and frequently use physical punishment are referred to as having an *authoritarian style.* Parents who are typically warm, reason with their children, yet set good limits are referred to as having an *authoritative style.* Parents who have a *permissive style* tend not to intervene and are extremely lenient with their children. Generally, an authoritative style is related to positive psychological and educational outcomes, whereas the other styles are related to negative outcomes. Researchers have attempted to identify relationships between parenting style and parents' ethnicity and race. However, understanding parenting behavior is complex, and attempts to correlate style with race and ethnicity has led to inaccurate characterizations of parents of various ethnic groups.

CULTURAL ECOLOGICAL INFLUENCES

The methods parents use to socialize their children result from multiple factors. John U. Ogbu suggested that generally, parents want to raise their children to be able to subsist, provide for themselves, and function successfully as adults. To do so, parents must equip their children with the necessary skills and knowledge. What parents consider to be the necessary skills and knowledge varies according to socioeconomic status, political and social contexts, and religious and cultural beliefs. Beliefs about parenting and the types of information necessary for survival are communicated from generation to generation, and in this way individuals become members of a group with shared views about important values, parenting practices, and ways to succeed in the environment. For children to be able to survive and flourish in their neighborhoods and communities, as well as navigate the majority culture, parents of color may adopt strategies that respond to the social and political environment and as a result use parenting practices different from those used by the majority culture.

Community Environment

Jay Fagan pointed out that low-income urban neighborhoods where a disproportionately high number of people of color reside tend to have poor school systems, few community agencies and facilities for recreation and support, and transient residents, all of which can lead to social isolation. There are elevated rates of unemployment, crime, incidences of violence, and teenage pregnancy in these neighborhoods, and people of color experience discrimination from the majority culture and have a history of oppression.

Such environmental factors demand that children learn a different set of skills than those used in middle-class neighborhoods. Many researchers have suggested that parents who live in impoverished neighborhoods may use harsh disciplinary strategies to keep their children safe in response to an environment that is fraught with danger. The use of harsh disciplinary strategies may be intentional, because parents may believe this approach is one way to prepare their children to live in dangerous surroundings and cope with racism and discrimination. In addition, dangerous impoverished neighborhoods increase the daily stress that parents experience, and numerous studies have found that parents who are feeling highly stressed are more likely to use harsh disciplinary strategies, including physical punishment.

Unique Cultural Beliefs

Individuals in various cultures have unique and distinct values, attitudes, and beliefs regarding child development, the role of parents, and the skills children need to learn so that they can respond to the demands of their environment and be successful in life. These cultural beliefs may influence the parenting practices that some ethnic parents use.

Cultural values are important influences because they shape the vision and hopes parents have for their children, and these visions and hopes vary from cultural group to cultural group and from person to person. For example, some parents may wish to foster cultural pride, or they may focus on helping their children develop a healthy racial identity. Religious instruction may be paramount for some groups, whereas others believe that it is critical to encourage their children to develop skills they perceive as necessary to survive within the majority culture, which may be hostile to minority and immigrant groups. How long-term outcomes are interpreted may also vary. For example, marrying and having children and a harmonious family life may be the measure of success for one group, but getting good grades in school, attending college, and obtaining a high-paying job may indicate success for another cultural group. The goals may differ within cultural groups depending on contextual factors such as socioeconomic status, level of acculturation, and personal characteristics of parents, such as educational level or marital status.

METHODOLOGICAL SHORTCOMINGS AND HOW RESEARCHERS HAVE RESPONDED

Numerous methodological concerns make it difficult to understand the differences in parenting practices among and within groups.

1. *The use of Western models, constructs, and psychological measures to examine practices of non-Western peoples.* Although Western constructs and psychological instruments used for studying parenting are highly developed, these tools may not be appropriate for use with non-Westerners. Sunita M. Stewart and Michael H. Bond suggested that instruments used to identify parenting practices may not be culturally sensitive when applied to groups other than European Americans because many of the measures were developed and normed on samples of U.S. mothers of young children. Researchers have responded to these concerns. Constructs in non-Western cultures that are useful for studying adjustment in non-Western cultures have been identified—for example, the notion of interpersonal harmony—and researchers have begun to examine the usefulness of some Western constructs in non-Western cultures. New measures are being developed or existing measures adapted so that they identify behaviors that are specific to the cultures being studied.

2. *Problems with comparison groups.* Many studies compared lower-income minority groups with middle-class European Americans, which may suggest that minority groups are deficient when they behave differently. Furthermore, early studies ignored the possibility that there may be within-group differences. Rather than consolidating people into large ethnic categories for the purposes of studying parental behavior, it is important to focus research on individual groups. Recent studies have used ethnic groups as comparison groups and examined within-group differences, resulting in a better understanding of similarities and differences in parenting practices of people of color.

3. *Marginalization of fathers in research studies.* Jay Fagan pointed out that most studies focused on mothers' parenting practices and involvement and ignored fathers' roles. Unfortunately, most current studies still focus primarily on mothers. This may be

because in many cultures, raising and educating the children is primarily the mother's responsibility.

4. *Variables were not controlled and external stressors have been ignored.* Acculturation, social class, and socioeconomic status (SES) frequently have not been controlled.

When these variables are not controlled, it is difficult to determine which, if any, parenting practices are preferred by various ethnic groups or if practices are a function of level of acculturation and low income.

Most studies have not considered that parenting practices may change over time as children move through stages of normal physical and emotional development, or as parents and families encounter difficulties in living, such as divorce, job loss, death, or catastrophic illness. More frequently, acculturation, SES, social class, psychological issues, and external stressors are considered in studies.

BELIEFS AND PRACTICES OF PARENTS OF COLOR

African Americans

According to Richard A. Bulcroft, Dianne C. Carmody, and Kris A. Bulcroft, traditional African values of patriarchy and communalism are reflected in the African American community's strong reliance on extended family members (kin) and family friends (nonkin) in the socialization of their children. Dependence on kin and nonkin and a strong allegiance to the African American community evolved as a way to cope with the slavery experience, the absence of parents, a risky or violent living environment, and discrimination from social agencies. These values may explain the tendency for many African American parents to be controlling of their young children but to grant greater independence and autonomy to their adolescent children, especially regarding personal issues such as their choice of hairstyle or clothing.

The belief that members of the community including peers will assume some responsibility for their children's socialization allows parents to lessen their control on their older adolescent children and let them have input into decision making. Where dating is concerned, parents retain control, perhaps in an effort to keep girls from becoming pregnant or sexually assaulted. The examination of parental control both within the home and outside the home suggests that African American families are highly structured, particularly when there are many children in the home and value is placed on fundamentalist religious beliefs. Such families tend to have rules to govern behavior in the home. Independence is granted to children as they grow older, so that older children have fewer rules to follow than their younger siblings. Although older adolescent boys typically must follow more rules for their behavior at home than do older adolescent girls, boys are likely to have later curfews and more independence outside the home than are girls.

A number of researchers, including Jennifer E. Lansford, Kirby Deater-Deckard, Kenneth A. Dodge, John Bates, and Gregory S. Pettit, have suggested that African Americans are more likely to use physical discipline, such as spanking, as a parenting strategy and less likely to view physical discipline as maltreatment than are European Americans. African Americans tend to believe that physical punishment is appropriate when it is used to teach right from wrong. For African American children, physical discipline may be effective when parents also express warmth and love to their children and are involved with their children's lives. Physical discipline is more likely to be used with younger children and during early adolescence and is seldom, if ever, used with older adolescents. Boys are more likely to be physically punished than are girls. The use of physical discipline increases when parents feel stressed or if parents perceive that their child's future is somehow jeopardized, such as when a child displays hostility or aggression.

Asian Americans

Fu-Mei Chen, Tom Luster, and Ruth Chao described how the teachings of Confucius influence some parenting practices. Confucian teachings identify and explain the outcomes parents should strive for when raising their children. Children raised by parents who hold traditional Japanese values are obligated to repay their parents for having given birth to them and for nurturing and socializing them. Repayment includes behaving appropriately, which in turn demonstrates respect toward the parents. Development of such behavior forms the foundation for future relationships. Similarly, Chinese parents who follow the teachings of Confucius believe that children should be obedient, respect their elders and their family, and accept family responsibilities. Both cultures value self-restraint as appropriate mature behavior.

Just as outcomes for children are identified, the roles parents must assume are described. For example, some Chinese parents accept that it is their responsibility to develop their children's character, teach the values of Confucius, and ensure that their children behave appropriately. Consequently, they assume a role that is akin to one of teacher, and discipline is considered to be an expression of love so that children learn appropriate behavior. These parents tend to be lenient and warm until children reach the "age of understanding," which occurs somewhere between the ages of 3 and 6, after which parents become more controlling.

In much of the earlier research, Chinese parents frequently were characterized as using an authoritarian parenting style. Recently, Chao suggested that the concept of parenting style may be inappropriate when studying Chinese parents, as well as other ethnic parents, because all the components of each parenting style may not exist or other combinations of behaviors may exist. Stewart and Bond also pointed out that using typologies to study parenting makes it difficult for researchers to identify whether the *combination* of behaviors results in certain outcomes or whether *particular* components of the type influence outcomes. Consequently, Chen and Luster reduced parenting styles to their components—that is, authoritative approaches were studied using the components of warmth/involvement, reasoning/induction, democratic participation, good-natured/easygoing, and authoritarian approaches were reduced to the components of verbal hostility, corporal punishment, nonreasoning/ punitive strategies, and directiveness. When Chinese mothers were studied using this approach, it was found that mothers used combinations of both approaches depending on their psychological well-being. Mothers who were depressed, felt hassled and stressed, and perceived their children to be emotional were more likely to scold, criticize, or use physical punishment even with young children, and as children grew older, mothers tended to be more demanding and directive, and to use physical punishment. Mothers who had more children also tended to be less warm and involved and were less likely to use reasoning with their children.

According to Hye-On Kim and Siegfried Hoppe-Graff, although South Korea has moved quickly to become a modern society, Korean culture is still a collectivist culture that relies heavily on the teachings of Confucius even though a type of fundamentalist Christianity has also been adopted by many Koreans. Values include respect for their elders, an understanding that adult children are expected to support their elderly parents both materially and emotionally, and an expectation that children must strive for academic and career success. Koreans traditionally value education for its intrinsic worth in addition to its use as a way to achieve success. Thus, parents communicate this value to their children, encourage them to study hard and do well in school, and have traditionally been involved in their children's education. When Koreans immigrate to the United States, they maintain this value even as they are influenced by and adapt to U.S. culture. Traditionally, mothers are responsible for raising their children, and fathers are responsible for providing materially for the family. Similar to Chinese mothers, Korean mothers may appear to be both warm and stern or even hostile at times as they discipline their children.

Latino Americans

Early studies of Latino American parents have characterized them as harsh, punitive, authoritarian, warm, nurturing, egalitarian, permissive, and authoritative. Several methodological problems may account for these contradictory results. In many studies, neither socioeconomic status nor level of acculturation were considered; consequently, it is difficult to interpret the results. Latino Americans continue to immigrate to the United States, whereas some families have spent many generations in the United States, so that there is a wide range of level of acculturation among Latino Americans. Further, the category *Latino American* is made up of vastly different groups of people from different geographic locations who have different sociopolitical histories and migration experiences. Numerous studies typically have grouped Latino Americans together, and as a result, less is known about the various parenting practices of different groups of Latino Americans. Recently, some researchers have begun to examine parenting practices of groups typically categorized as Latino American, although the majority of these studies focus on Mexican Americans.

Bulcroft and others have pointed out that although Latino Americans have differing histories, many share cultural values that may influence how they parent their children. These cultural values have their roots in Spanish culture and Catholicism, and these perspectives have been molded by various histories and immigration experiences, as well as by discrimination and Latino Americans' minority status.

Nevertheless, an emphasis on the notions of *famil-ismo, machismo,* and *marianismo* remain important in Latino families. *Familismo,* a strong sense of family loyalty and unity, is central to the Latino American culture, and family needs are typically placed above individual needs. Latino American families include kin and nonkin, and the extended family is extremely important and may assist in the socialization of children. Belief in *machismo* requires that men be respectful and generous and safeguard their wives, sisters, and mothers, as well as their children, and the idea of *marianismo* requires that women be nurturing and self-sacrificing. These notions are manifested in the parenting practices exhibited by mothers.

Maribel Vargas and Nancy A. Busch-Rossnagel compared the results of their study of Puerto Rican mothers with the results of a study of Mexican American mothers and found that both groups use didactic or teaching behaviors including directives, visual cues, and modeling when interacting with their infants and young children, and they frequently use disciplinary practices. However, Puerto Ricans may engage in these behaviors less frequently than Mexican Americans. In addition, mothers demonstrate warmth and affection through hugging and kissing as well as physical play.

Nancy E. Hill, Kevin R. Bush, and Mark W. Roosa found that low-income Mexican American mothers who were not highly acculturated to the United States used high levels of hostile control coupled with high levels of acceptance and warmth. This approach did not have an adverse effect on their children. Hill and others suggested that perhaps because of their cultural beliefs, these children tend to respond to these methods of discipline because they do not want to disappoint their parents by behaving poorly, and it is possible that the parenting practices exhibited by some Latino mothers closely resemble those used by some Chinese parents.

Pablo G. Cardona, Bonnie C. Nicholson, Robert A. Fox, and Pedro Solis-Camara conducted a number of studies, primarily of Mexican and Mexican American mothers. Their research suggests that Latino mothers tend to use physical punishment and invoke religious values to discipline their young children but keep their expectations for their children's behavior appropriate to the child's age. Further, Mexican Americans are more likely to spank, criticize, and threaten their children than are Anglos, but these behaviors are well within the range of normal behavior. Another study, this one conducted in Mexico, found that mothers of young children were likely to use more physical punishment as their children grew older. They had similar developmental expectations for the behavior of both boys and girls, and mothers who used more nurturing practices tended to use less physical punishment. Further, they found that when there were more children in the household, mothers had higher expectations and were more likely to discipline their children. Although various cultures have different understandings about what constitutes appropriate age-related behavior, the Mexican and Mexican American mothers in these studies held the same age-related expectations for behaviors as did Anglo mothers.

The value that Latino Americans place on chastity and virginity is apparent in the rules that parents set for their children; for example, according to Bulcroft and others, Latino American parents tend to set earlier curfews for boys and girls than do other ethnic groups, although boys are still given more autonomy and independence than are girls in the home. As girls grow older and prepare to marry and move out of the household, they are typically given later curfews than are boys.

Native American Indians

It is difficult to know and understand the parenting practices that are utilized by Native American Indians, because few empirical studies have been conducted. Language barriers, a distrust of the government and members of the majority culture, and a lack of professionals who are also tribe members generally impede research efforts.

The term *Native American Indians* refers to a diverse group of people who belong to more than 500 tribal nations, each with its own history and culture. Religious and cultural beliefs, rituals and ceremonies, family organization, and patterns of lineage—some are matrilineal and others are patrilineal—differ among the various groups. In addition, some of the beliefs of the majority culture, such as Christianity, have also been integrated into the belief systems of Native American Indians.

Native American Indians reside throughout the United States, although the majority reside in the southwestern states. Many live geographically isolated on rural reservations, although more than half live in urban areas. Over 150 languages are spoken by Native American Indians, and some individuals do not speak English.

Despite this great diversity among Native American Indians, some authors suggest that individuals who believe in traditional views also share similar views of child rearing. According to Fred Beauvais, generally, families rely on extended families and clans—that is, several families who share ancestry and live in close proximity—to share in child rearing. An emphasis on familism, with a respect for one another, elders, the tribe, *and children,* distinguishes their views from those of the parents belonging to other groups in the United States. Parents are responsible for providing for children's physical needs and often are forced to take jobs that are located far from the reservation, where there are few job opportunities. Traditionally, parents generally take a laissez-faire approach to raising their children, and other members in the extended family, such as aunts, uncles, and nonkin, serve as role models for appropriate behavior. Grandparents are likely to bear a great deal of the responsibility for raising children. Little direct instruction is used; generally there are few rules that children are required to follow, and physical discipline is generally avoided. Family members provide guidance so that children can learn to make appropriate decisions and choices, and children must bear the consequences of their behavior. The traditional goal of child rearing for these groups is to produce individuals who are self-reliant and who have a strong sense of obligation to and respect for their extended family, their tribe, nature, and the universe.

According to Fred Beauvais, when individuals living in tribal communities were not dependent on a wage-based economy, this approach to child rearing worked well; however, economic and governmental interference that disrupted the workings of the tribal community have also disrupted this approach to child rearing.

The boarding school system, instituted by the federal government and administered by the Bureau of Indian Affairs, was developed to strip Native Americans of their culture. Children were removed from their homes when they were very young and sent to distant boarding schools. These schools developed young adults who were disconnected from their culture. Also, teachers and support personnel harshly—often physically—disciplined children when they spoke their own language or attempted to participate in the dances, rituals, and ceremonies of their tribe. As a result, these children were not exposed to positive parenting models. Stripped of their culture and the opportunity to forge relationships with their parents, siblings, and extended family, when these children returned to their families, they were unable to fit in. Some authors speculate that these children, when they became parents, were uncertain about how to raise their own children. According to one study, conducted by Le Anne E. Silvey, some parents prohibited their children from learning about their ethnic and cultural background, believing that their children would have better life opportunities if they were able to assimilate. Their knowledge of parenting practices was limited to two approaches: should they rely on the kind of harsh physical discipline they had received in the boarding schools, or should they employ the traditional methods of child rearing? It is unclear what practices these parents have employed; however, one study concluded that Native American Indians were no more likely to use spanking than were other groups in the United States.

Currently, more children attend public schools administered by Native Americans on or near the reservations. Children in these schools study aspects of Native American Indian culture, and children are allowed to participate in their culture. However, the legacy of the boarding school system is still present, and children are likely to not experience a nurturing environment. Although some children attend boarding schools voluntarily, currently, the majority of children who are sent to boarding schools have behavioral or substance-abuse problems that have become too difficult for the tribal community.

—*Mary Kopala*

FURTHER READING

Baumrind, D. (1967). Child care practices anteceding three patterns of preschool behavior. *Genetic Psychology Monographs, 75,* 43–88.

Beauvais, F. (2000). Indian adolescence: Opportunity and challenge. In R. Montemayor, G. R. Adams, & T. P. Gullotta, *Adolescent diversity in ethnic, economic, and cultural contexts.* Thousand Oaks, CA: Sage.

Belsky, J. (1984). The determinants of parenting: A process model. *Child Development, 55,* 83–96.

Cardona, P. G., Nicholson, B. C., & Fox, R. A. (2000). Parenting among Hispanic and Anglo-American mothers with young children. *Journal of Social Psychology, 140,* 357–366.

Chao, R. K. (1994). Beyond parental control and authoritarian parenting style: Understanding Chinese parenting through the cultural notion of training. *Child Development, 65,* 1111–1120.

Chen, F. M., & Luster, T. (2002). Factors related to parenting practices in Taiwan. *Early Child Development and Care, 172,* 413–430.

Chen, X., Hastings, P. D., Rubin, K. H., Chen, H., Cen, G., & Stewart, S. L. (1998). Child-rearing attitudes and behavioral inhibition in Chinese and Canadian toddlers: A cross-cultural study. *Developmental Psychology, 34,* 677–686.

Darling, N., & Steinberg, L. (1993). Parenting style as context: An integrative model. *Psychological Bulletin, 113,* 487–496.

Fagan, J. (2002). African American and Puerto Rican American parenting styles, paternal involvement, and Head Start children's social competence. *Merrill-Palmer Quarterly, 46*(4), 592. Retrieved September 9, 2004, from http://www.questia.com

Furstenberg, F. F., Belzer, A., Davis, C., Levine, J. A., Morrow, K., & Washington, M. (1993). How families manage risk and opportunity in dangerous neighborhoods. In W. J. Wilson (Ed.), *Sociology and the public agenda* (pp. 231–238). Newbury Park, CA: Sage.

Hill, N. E., & Bush, K. R. (2001). Relationship between parenting environment and children's mental health among African American and European American mothers and children. *Journal of Marriage and the Family, 63,* 954–966.

Hill, N. E., Bush, K. R., & Roosa, M. W. (2003). Parenting and family socialization strategies and children's mental health: Low-income Mexican-American and Euro-American mothers and children. *Child Development, 74,* 189–204.

Jambunathan, S., Burts, D. C., & Pierce, S. (2000). Comparisons of parenting attitudes among five ethnic groups in the United States. *Journal of Comparative Family Studies, 31*(4), 395. Retrieved September 9, 2004, from http://www.questia.com

McLoyd, V. C., & Smith, J. (2002). Physical discipline and behavior problems in African American, European American, and Hispanic children: Emotional support as a moderator. *Journal of Marriage and the Family, 64,* 40–54.

Ogbu, J. (1981). Origins of human competence: A cultural-ecological perspective. *Child Development, 15,* 413–429.

Pena, D. C. (2000). Parent involvement: Influencing factors and implications. *The Journal of Educational Research, 94,* 42. Retrieved October 27, 2004, from http://www.questia.com

Silvey, L. A. E. (1999). Firstborn American Indian daughters: Struggles to reclaim cultural and self-identity. In H. P. McAdoo (Ed.), *Family ethnicity: Strength in diversity* (pp. 72–93). Thousand Oaks, CA: Sage.

Steinberg, L., Dornbusch, S. M., & Brown, B. B. (1992). Ethnic differences in adolescent achievement: An ecological perspective. *American Psychologist, 47,* 723–729.

Stewart, S. M., & Bond, M. H. (2002). A critical look at parenting research from the mainstream: Problems uncovered while adapting Western research to non-Western cultures. *British Journal of Developmental Psychology, 20,* 379–392.

Vega, W. A. (1990). Hispanic families in the 1980s: A decade of research. *Journal of Marriage and the Family, 52,* 1015–1024.

PERSONALITY DISORDERS

Personality disorders are a class of psychiatric disorder characterized by enduring patterns of maladaptive traits, which cause impairment or distress, are pervasive across contexts, and deviate markedly from the expectations of the individual's culture. This class of disorder was thought to differ from clinical syndromes (i.e., mood, anxiety, or psychotic disorders), which tend to be more episodic in nature and purportedly are more affected by biological versus psychosocial factors. The two primary domains of personality disorders are (1) interpersonal problems and (2) difficulties with identity and therefore are arguably more affected by sociocultural factors than are many other forms of psychopathology. Although biological factors certainly shape both personality and personality pathology, culture and other social factors are likely equally, if not more, important in this process. Cultural factors may play a role in the definition, classification, etiology, prevalence, and treatment of personality disorders.

The concept of personality disorder seems to have clinical utility, because the presence of a personality disorder often complicates treatment and tends to co-occur with clinical syndromes. Many people who suffer from depression, anxiety, an eating disorder, or psychosis also have co-occurring personality disorders. When personality disorder is present, clinical syndromes are likely to be more severe and chronic, and to have poorer course and outcome. Individuals with personality disorder, with or without coexisting clinical syndromes, typically are less responsive to conventional treatments such as psychotherapy or pharmacotherapy. Accordingly, the need for better understanding of etiology and related treatment interventions for personality disorder has been recognized.

Unfortunately, the study and assessment of personality disorders is plagued by a number of problems, including reliability of measurement, controversy over what sources to use during assessment (self, informant, or objective observer report), validity of a categorical versus a dimensional model, validity of existing psychiatric models, and the fact that most people diagnosed with one personality disorder will meet criteria for more than one personality disorder diagnosis. Assessing personality disorders requires more inference than does assessing other mental disorders and requires an understanding of the patient's culture. Clinicians must therefore be keenly aware of what cultural aspects they bring to their encounters with clients as well as carefully consider the meaning of a client's behavior within a cultural frame.

CURRENT DEFINITIONS OF PERSONALITY DISORDER

When discussing psychopathology, there are a few key domains that distinguish cultures. Cultures differ in terms of how people manifest their distress (physical, cognitive, emotional, and spiritual symptoms), the meaning of those symptoms, the cause ascribed to those symptoms, and what is considered appropriate treatment for those symptoms. In North American and Western European cultures, personality disorders are considered to be patterns of long-standing characteristics belonging to an individual, independent of physical illness or substance use, that cause significant functional impairment. In North America, personality disorders are defined by the American Psychiatric Association's *Diagnostic and Statistical Manual of Mental Disorders*.

Outside of these two dominant classification systems, there are a few maladaptive personality patterns described in other cultures, such as *empacho* (a Mexican and Cuban American pattern that has unique qualities as well as some of the characteristics of obsessive-compulsive personality disorder) and *piblokto* (an Eskimo pattern that has many of the features of borderline personality disorder and occurs primarily among females). Most other patterns that are described as culture-bound syndromes in the DSM-IV seem to describe acute reactions to various situations and therefore would be akin to clinical syndromes rather than to the chronic, rigid patterns characteristic of personality disorders.

According to the DSM-IV-TR, personality disorders are defined as enduring patterns of personality traits that are inflexible and pervasive across contexts. Each pattern is of long duration (with onset in adolescence or early adulthood), relatively stable, and maladaptive, and causes significant impairment in social, cognitive, or occupational functioning, or may cause substantial subjective distress. Personality disorders should not be diagnosed if a personality pattern can be directly linked to substance use (i.e., paranoia caused by ingestion of amphetamines), organic brain damage (i.e., personality change after head trauma), or a physical disease (i.e., the sequela

of Huntington's disease), or if it occurs only during episodes of other kinds of mental illness (i.e., symptoms of paranoid personality disorder occurring only during an outbreak of paranoid schizophrenia). Of most interest to this text is the rule that personality disorders must be a stable pattern of inner experience and behavior that substantially deviates from the expectations of the *individual's culture*. A careful diagnostician must make sure that all these conditions are met before deciding a person meets a particular criterion.

Under the official nomenclature of the American Psychiatric Association, found in the DSM-IV-TR, there are 10 personality disorders, which are grouped into three clusters based on their descriptive similarities. A perusal of all the criteria for personality disorders shows that the core features of personality disorder are chronic interpersonal difficulties and problems with identity and the self, two domains that are clearly shaped by aspects of culture.

Cluster A, also called the *odd/eccentric cluster*, includes paranoid, schizoid, and schizotypal personality disorders. Paranoid personality disorder is characterized by a marked distrust of others and unfounded beliefs that others are set on exploiting, deceiving, and harming the individual. Individuals with this pattern often believe others have betrayed them or will betray them, and such individuals often are unforgiving when a betrayal occurs. Schizoid personality disorder is characterized by a markedly restricted range of emotional responses and experience, as well as indifference to social relationships, pleasure, praise, or criticism. Those diagnosed with schizotypal personality disorder often have an eccentric appearance, hold eccentric beliefs (i.e., their thoughts can control the weather), and have odd ways of thinking, behaving, and relating to others.

Cluster B personality disorders are characterized by erratic, dramatic, and emotional behaviors. This cluster includes narcissistic, histrionic, borderline, and antisocial personality disorders. Narcissistic personality disorder is characterized by arrogance, an excessive need for admiration, pervasive envy, and interpersonal exploitation of others. In addition, there is a lack of empathy and ability to take the perspective of others, as well as disdain for others who are perceived as having low status. Those with histrionic personality disorder are described as shallow and compulsively attention-seeking with contextually inappropriate, exaggerated, rapidly shifting displays of emotion. These individuals are often easily influenced by others and lack a stable presentation of identity. Borderline personality disorder is characterized by rapid changes in emotion and impulsive behaviors (including self-harm behaviors), as well as a lack of a stable self-image. Those diagnosed with this disorder often have intense, unstable relationships and fear interpersonal abandonment. Those with a diagnosis of antisocial personality disorder, sometimes called *psychopaths* or *sociopaths,* refuse to abide by societal rules, use others for their own ends without remorse, and are often sensation-seeking, impulsive, and aggressive.

Cluster C consists of personality disorders that have anxious and fearful components: avoidant, dependent, obsessive-compulsive, and passive-aggressive (now a provisional diagnosis) personality disorders. Avoidant personality disorder is characterized by feelings of ineptness and inferiority, as well as severe social inhibition driven by fear of criticism, shame, or humiliation. Those diagnosed with dependent personality disorder often exhibit submissiveness, helplessness, and an extreme need for others to help them function in daily life. Obsessive-compulsive personality disorder is characterized by a preoccupation with orderliness, perfectionism, and mental and interpersonal control, at the expense of flexibility, openness, and efficiency. Finally, passive-aggressive personality disorder is characterized by passive resistance to fulfilling obligations, vacillation between defiance and contrition, and sensitivity to and criticism of authority.

The International Classification of Diseases-10 (ICD-10) has requirements nearly identical to those of the DSM-IV for the diagnosis of personality disorders, in terms of both inclusion criteria (i.e., of long duration and stable) and exclusion criteria (i.e., not related to substance use or a medical condition). However, the ICD-10 system goes beyond the inclusion that the behavior must markedly deviate from one's culture and instead suggests that it may be necessary to develop specific sets of criteria with regard to social standards and obligations when considering individuals from different cultures. An explicit manner for developing these criterion sets is not described. Except for some variations in naming, the personality disorders in the ICD-10 are quite similar to those of the DSM-IV, with two distinctions: (1) there is no specific personality disorder for narcissistic personality disorder, which instead is referred to as "other specific personality disorder"; and (2) schizotypal personality disorder is considered to be a mild variant of schizophrenia rather than a personality disorder.

HISTORY OF PERSONALITY DISORDERS

The cultural aspects of the diagnosis of personality disorder become apparent when one examines their changes through Western history. Maladaptive personality types have been described since early Greek times with Theophrastus's description of types of maladjusted character. Theories varied as to how such maladaptive personalities developed (i.e., imbalance among the various body humors, failure of religious practice, heredity), but from early Greek times through parts of the 19th century, these maladaptive personality types were often described as failures in moral character.

Over the years, various types of personality disorders have come and gone. In 1801, Philippe Pinel described a group of patients who suffered from *manie sans délire* (literally, "crazy without delirium"). People afflicted by such disturbances were a puzzle to clinicians, because their behavior did not fit the prototype of what was called lunacy, insanity, or craziness. Indeed, people with personality disorders may or may not experience distress, although their behavior frequently causes distress to or disturbs others.

In 19th-century America, psychiatric patients were sometimes described as having moral insanity, in terms such as *volitional old maid* and *vagabond.* In 1907, Emil Kraepelin described character disorders such as the *born criminal, cyclothymic disposition* (the unstable), *autistic temperament,* and the *morbid liar and swindler.* In 1923, Kurt Schneider described 10 personality types many of which were the forerunners to those listed in the DSM-II. These included types such as *hyperthymic, depressive, attention-seeking, weak-willed,* and *affectionless* personality. Given their history, there is no surprise that many clinicians refuse to give a personality disorder diagnosis because they fear stigmatizing their patients. However, not giving the diagnosis does not mean that a patient does not have maladaptive personality features that may be important to focus on in treatment, to communicate to the patient, or to communicate to other clinicians. What is important is to use this information in a way that directly or indirectly benefits the patient while minimizing the negative and stigmatizing effects in whatever way possible.

DEVELOPMENT OF PERSONALITY DISORDER

Most modern etiological theories of personality disorder propose that these patterns develop in response to biopsychosocial factors, although the theories differ in terms of the weight they ascribe to these component parts. Theories also differ in how they assign a factor to one of these broader domains (i.e., whether self-concept is a psychological factor or an interpersonally constructed social factor) and in their predictions about how these domains interact. Granted, these domains are largely of heuristic value, as we are all biological beings, and environment/culture shapes biology and psychology (and vice versa). For example, a child's inborn temperament may be seen as an asset or deficit depending on how it fits with those of the child's family. A child's temperament may in turn influence how he or she is parented and how well he or she succeeds in school or other social domains.

The biological factors usually mentioned in these theories are genetically inherited traits (i.e., harm avoidance, constraint, impulsivity), early temperament, neurotransmitter balance, gender, and intrauterine factors. The psychological factors usually included are coping strategies, emotionality, dominance, agreeableness, self-concept, motivational style, cognitive style, locus of control, flexibility, and more. The social factors that are often mentioned in etiological theories are parenting practices, intrafamily roles, expression of conflict, quality of early attachment, interpersonal style, socioeconomic status, or environmental stress. Social factors that are likely important but are not often studied in relation to personality disorders are social expectations, rate of social change, religious upbringing, educational systems, historical events affecting large groups or subgroups (i.e., political violence, social oppression), family traditions, environmental stability, the aspects of the environment in which the personality pattern is problematic (i.e., the occupational success of an individual whose interpersonal life is highly problematic), and how culture serves as a context that may encourage or discourage expression of a given characteristic.

A few examples of how cultural factors may play a role in the development of personality disorders may illustrate these ideas. One could imagine that having a childhood tendency toward emotional lability (wide fluctuations in affect) may have especially dire consequences on self-concept in some societies. For example, in parts of Chinese society, subtlety of affect is considered to be a prized characteristic, and lack of such subtlety reflects poorly on not only the individual but also the individual's family. Such a circumstance could result in a number of adaptive or maladaptive personality patterns (such as an avoidant pattern) depending on how close others react to the individual, what meaning is ascribed to such emotionality, whether that characteristic might be better tolerated in some occupational paths, or how helpful others are at teaching ways of coping with emotional lability. Likewise, an antisocial pattern may be more rewarded in cultures in which male dominance and success at all costs is prized. Indeed, many leaders who have risen to power have demonstrated such a pattern. Of interest is the fact that diagnosable antisocial personality disorder is almost never seen in the Hutterite communities in North America, a religious group that prizes humility, hard work, and community. Such an example provides anecdotal evidence that culture may affect the development of personality disorder.

CLASSIFICATION OF PERSONALITY DISORDER

As was reviewed in the section on the history of personality disorders, as cultures change or differ, their standards for what is considered insanity, sanity, normal, abnormal, typical, and atypical often change or differ. There are various schools of thought regarding how cultures and mental illness intersect. One school maintains that mental illness in general, and personality disorder specifically, is indistinguishable across cultures. Another school, the *generalist* position, emphasizes underlying similarity of mental illnesses across cultures (while granting that the outward presentation may be affected by culture). A third, the *relativist* school, emphasizes that culture significantly shapes the expression and development of psychopathology. Depending on which mental disorder or class of disorders one focuses on, researchers have shown evidence for all three of these positions. For instance, schizophrenia presents similarly across cultures although its course, treatment, and outcome vary significantly across cultures. Generalists might point to the evidence that the same five personality factors are common across cultures. Given that so much of the expression of personality disorder falls into the two domains of identity and interpersonal problems, one could argue that the relativist viewpoint may be more appropriate for this class of mental disorder.

Although many early doctors in European and North American societies created categorical systems for the description of personality disorder, Henrick Sjobring, a Swedish psychiatrist, developed a dimensional classification system, primarily used in Scandinavia, that is reminiscent of some modern generalist models of personality disorder. He proposed four dimensions akin to intellect, introversion versus extroversion, novelty-seeking versus novelty-avoiding, and reactive versus stable. The debate over whether personality disorders should be measured and classified dimensionally or categorically continues today. Dimensional proponents claim there are a limited number of universal dimensions that capture the personality pathology universe, whereas categorical proponents claim that categories are more congruent with existing diagnostic systems; are consistent with clinical decision making; and are easier to understand and communicate. Hybrid models may combine the best of both dimensional and categorical models. For example, dimensional models can be collapsed to categorical models, as exemplified by the Minnesota Multiphasic Personality Inventory-2 (MMPI-2), whose 10 dimensions are often communicated as categorical two-point code types.

Regardless of how personality disorders are measured, culture plays a role in how such personality patterns are interpreted. In more cohesive societies, people who might be described as having a personality disorder may be seen as vexatious individuals who have to be tolerated, whereas other societies may define such individuals as ill and needing treatment. Dependency is seen as less pathological in collectivist societies than in individualistic cultures. On the other hand, autonomous behaviors may be seen as less pathological in individualistic cultures than in collectivist ones.

ASSESSMENT OF PERSONALITY DISORDER

The DSM-IV recommends that clinicians take a patient's background, especially recent immigration, into account before deciding that he or she has a personality disorder. One criticism that has been made of the general category of personality disorder is that it is based on Western notions of egocentricity or individual uniqueness. One can question how applicable these diagnoses are to people from cultures with different definitions of personhood, such as in collectivistic societies. Furthermore, even within a culture, it can be difficult to define the limits of normality.

Of primary concern is the potential for a clinician's lack of familiarity with culturally sanctioned behavior to lead to pathologizing and misdiagnosis for a particular individual. Therefore, clinicians must consider each behavior in cultural context in addition to assessing all the aspects of a DSM-IV or ICD-10 diagnosis. Clinicians need to be exquisitely sensitive to people who are relatively new to a culture. This is important because new behaviors are generated during acculturation as the person enters a new culture and attempts to integrate his or her experiences. As a result, clinicians must consider how every behavior in question is understood from both an emic and an etic cultural perspective, so that behaviors are neither misjudged nor stereotyped. For example, the meaning of depersonalization (a sense of detachment or estrangement from one's self or body) in an Afro-Caribbean community may be markedly different from its meaning in New York City. This requires the clinician to know what is typical and atypical in the client's culture or cultural subgroup, keeping in mind that cultures are not often homogeneous entities. What is considered normative in Puerto Rico may not be in El Salvador, despite the fact that both groups are considered Hispanic. In other words, assessment must entail the meaning of a particular behavior in the client's original culture, a clear understanding of the biases and assumptions the clinician brings, and an understanding of how these interact within our modern Western psychiatric standard.

PREVALENCE

Establishing prevalence rates for personality disorders is difficult for a number of reasons. First, there is no gold-standard measure for diagnosing personality disorders, and different instruments and assessment methods yield varying prevalence rates. With that in mind, personality disorders are a prevalent form of mental disorder, although prevalence varies greatly by setting. In the general population, the proportion of individuals who suffer from personality disorders is estimated to be about 10%. About 27% of general medical patients are diagnosed with a personality disorder, and among psychiatric inpatient samples, the rate often exceeds 70%. Most of the studies of personality disorders either have not reported the ethnic makeup of their sample or have used primarily Western European and North American samples. When ethnic group is reported for a sample, studies have reported conflicting results regarding prevalence rates for personality disorders as a class as well as for specific personality disorders. Some studies show that personality disorders are more common in Caucasian samples; others show that certain ethnic groups are diagnosed with higher rates of personality disorders (or a specific personality disorder, or specific criteria), and other studies show no differences among various ethnic groups.

When ICD-10 and DSM-III-R personality disorder diagnoses were studied in North America, Europe, Africa, and Asia, most types were found in the 11 countries surveyed. The exceptions were that there were no avoidant diagnoses in India and no borderline diagnoses in Kenya. However, across all 11 countries, the most frequent diagnoses were borderline and avoidant, which replicates the prevalence finding in the United States. Granted, these are decidedly Western conceptions of personality disorder, but it should be noted that local clinicians were asked to judge the meaning of the behavior in the context of the culture and make judgments about chronicity, early onset, and functional impairment.

Many personality disorders are rarely studied. The bulk of the literature discusses borderline and antisocial personality disorders, and a small proportion of these report differences based on demographic variables. There are fairly reliable gender differences in the prevalence rates of some personality disorders. For example, the rate of women diagnosed with borderline personality disorder is four times that of men. The opposite pattern is found with antisocial personality disorder, and obsessive-compulsive personality disorder often has equal prevalence among men and women. When ethnicity is considered with gender, some studies suggest an interaction. One study found that borderline personality disorder had equal rates of occurrence among Hispanic men and women and that the rate of this disorder was greater for Hispanics than for either Caucasians or African Americans. The same study reported that African Americans had greater rates of schizotypal personality disorder than Hispanics or Caucasians. Other studies have shown that antisocial personality disorder is more prevalent among African Americans than among Caucasians and Hispanics, although others have suggested that these differences are attributable to socioeconomic status and not ethnicity.

If culture shapes personality, then one would expect prevalence differences between various groups. Socialization and cultural norms for affect and behavioral expression likely contribute to the gender differences in rates of some personality disorders. Some authors have suggested that antisocial and histrionic personality disorders are male and female counterparts of the same disorder in Western cultures. Perhaps the more interesting questions are what aspects of culture contribute to personality pathology, and do some cultures prime or protect their members from certain types of psychopathology? There has been a similar and particularly heated discussion regarding whether depression is somaticized (to mistakenly believe that an emotional pain is a physical symptom) in some cultures or whether in fact depression is *psychologized* (manifested as existential and cognitive) in other cultures. Somaticized depression actually occurs in more cultures and tends to occur in cultures where mental illness is particularly stigmatized.

TREATMENT OF PERSONALITY DISORDER

In many societies, having a personality disorder diagnosis is synonymous with being perceived as difficult, noxious, and untreatable. In fact, having such a diagnosis often precludes an individual from receiving treatment, owing to the prevalent belief that these patterns cannot be treated. Indeed, the bulk of the psychiatric literature shows that individuals with personality disorder diagnoses are less responsive to all kinds of treatment, are frequent users of medical services, and have difficulty in their relationships at work, at home, and with their health care professionals. Treating long-standing, rigid patterns with people who have trouble forming relationships is a challenge, but many recent studies have shown that at least some personality disorders are amenable to treatment and that these patterns may be less stable than once believed.

The American Psychological Association developed guidelines to assist clinicians in acquiring and applying multicultural skills to their work. These include developing awareness of one's own worldview and of the worldview of one's clients and coworkers. Such a perspective is meant to aid decision making about when culture-centered adaptations to assessment and treatment are needed. This perspective also entreats clinicians to help clients determine the source of identified problems including societal racism, prejudice, and acculturation. Clinicians are asked to consider the helping practices of other cultures and how these practices and their practitioners might be incorporated into the client's assessment and treatment, as well as to weigh the cultural appropriateness of interventions and methods clinicians use in their work.

In addition to these broad guidelines, there are a number that are more specific to the assessment and treatment of personality disorders. As reviewed, there are a number of behaviors, cognitive patterns, affective styles, and interpersonal ways that are normative in some cultures and yet could be misinterpreted as meeting a criterion for a DSM-IV or ICD-10 personality diagnosis. For example, distrust may be misinterpreted as paranoia. Distrust is sometimes appropriate (especially in totalitarian societies with secret police or when a client has been exposed to pervasive racism) and may be adaptive behavior in some cultures when dealing with individuals outside one's extended family. One could easily go through the list of personality disorder criteria and find instances when these descriptions of affect, behavior, and cognition are normative in some context, situation, or culture. Careful attention to the inclusion criteria (i.e., early onset, chronic, not normative in the client's culture or subcultural group) and exclusion criteria (i.e., not related to physical condition or substance) for personality disorders as a class will help the clinician avoid applying these diagnoses inappropriately. The next step is adoption of appropriate specific treatment strategies. Determining what is appropriate is no easy task, given that there is little formal evidence for adapting psychotherapeutic or pharmacological treatment to groups that have not been studied in clinical trials, which have largely been conducted with North Americans and Western Europeans. Treatment of personality disorder requires skillful exploration and handling of the client expectations of the therapist and therapy and how that interacts with a client's particular personality disorder and cultural background. For example, individuals from some cultures may expect the therapist to be an authority deserving deference, but with passive-aggressive personality disorder, such an expectation may create an unworkable tension. Treating personality disorders is difficult enough when a clinician speaks the same language and understands the broad cultural makeup of a client; when cultural differences are added to treatment, this mostly complicates efforts at successful treatment, although it may also present an opportunity to have a novel perspective unencumbered by assumptions about what clients bring to treatment.

CONCLUSION

Culture plays a role in the definition, classification, etiology, prevalence, and treatment of personality disorders. The role that culture plays can be seen in the changes that have occurred through history in terms of

what constitutes maladaptive personality as well as examining what is currently considered adaptive and maladaptive across cultures and subcultures. Culture, in all its various aspects, can play a protective or exacerbating role in the creation of particular personality patterns. This role is apparent when prevalence rates of personality disorder are examined across cultures and in the description of syndromes that resemble personality disorders that are specific to some cultures and not to others. Treatment of personality disorders is a challenge under any circumstances but would likely be even more so when the cultural assumptions of all involved parties remains unexamined and unexplored.

—*Tracey Leone Smith*

See also DSM-IV

FURTHER READING

Alarcón, R. D., & Foulks, E. F. (1995). Personality disorders and culture: Contemporary clinical views. *Cultural Diversity and Mental Health, 1,* 79-91.

Alarcón, R. D., Foulks, E. F., & Vakkur, M. (1998). *Personality disorders and culture: Clinical and conceptual interactions.* New York: Wiley.

American Psychiatric Association. (2000). *Diagnostic and statistical manual of mental disorders* (4th ed., text rev.). Washington, DC: Author.

Kendell, R. E. (2002). The distinction between personality disorder and mental illness. *British Journal of Psychiatry, 180,* 110–115.

Lewis-Fernandez, R., & Kleinman, A. (1994). Culture, personality, and psychopathology. *Journal of Abnormal Psychology, 103,* 67–71.

Loranger, A. W., Sartorius, N., Andreoli, A., Berger, P., Buchheim, P., Channabasavanna, S. M., et al. (1994). The International Personality Disorder Examination: The World Health Organization/Alcohol, Drug Abuse, and Mental Health Administration international pilot study of personality disorders. *Archives of General Psychiatry, 51,* 215–224.

Mombour, W., & Bronisch, T. (1998). The modern assessment of personality disorders: Part 1. Definition and typology of personality disorders. *Psychopathology, 31,* 274–280.

POSTTRAUMATIC STRESS DISORDER

A MAINSTREAM VIEW OF PTSD

Diagnostic Criteria. The syndrome that is currently called *posttraumatic stress disorder* (PTSD) has been recognized in some form since the beginning of recorded history. However, it was not until the 1980 publication of the third edition of the *Diagnostic and Statistical Manual of Mental Disorders* (DSM-III) that PTSD was officially codified in the psychiatric nomenclature. The current DSM-IV diagnostic criteria for PTSD stipulates that for more than one month following a traumatic event, a PTSD patient must report the following types of symptoms: (1) reexperiencing (e.g., intrusive memories, recurrent dreams, flashbacks, intense physiological or emotional responses when reminded of the trauma); (2) avoidance and/or numbing (e.g., effortful evasion of thoughts, feelings, people, or places that are reminiscent of the trauma; amnesia about the trauma; reduced interest in previously enjoyed activities; emotional detachment from others; reduced capacity for pleasure; or expectations of a truncated future); and (3) elevated arousal (e.g., insomnia, irritability, distractibility, hypervigilance, or hyperstartle).

However, DSM-IV also introduced some changes to the PTSD criteria that have implications for the diagnosis of PTSD in diverse ethnocultural groups. For example, DSM-IV changed the way that *trauma* is defined. In addition to the usual objective definition of trauma (i.e., experiencing, witnessing, or learning about an event involving serious injury, threat to physical integrity, and/or death), DSM-IV stipulates that the traumatic event must be accompanied by subjective emotions, such as intense fear, helplessness, and/or horror to qualify for the diagnosis of PTSD. Because there are known cultural variations in experiencing, expressing, and reporting emotions, it is conceivable that someone diagnosed with PTSD under previous criteria might not meet the current diagnostic criteria. For example, a trauma-exposed person from a culture that eschews the reporting of strong negative emotions (e.g., Chinese culture) may not meet current criteria. The DSM-IV also added a clinical significance requirement. To warrant a diagnosis of PTSD, the symptoms must cause distress or impairment in relationships, work, or other important domains of living. Because there is evidence that some cultural groups have a higher tolerance for or acceptance of psychiatric symptoms, this new criterion suggests that an individual with objectively observed PTSD symptoms that are not distressing or debilitating would not qualify for the PTSD diagnosis.

Associated Features/Comorbidities. There are also a number of symptoms and psychiatric disorders that commonly co-occur with PTSD but that are not considered part of the core diagnostic criteria. These include guilt, shame, depression, anxiety, relationship problems, social withdrawal, emotion dysregulation, impulsive behavior, dissociation, somatization, substance abuse, and personality changes. The assessment of PTSD in diverse groups is complicated by the fact that cultures vary in their sanctioning of these symptoms. For example, *dissociation* (i.e., disruptions in normally integrated aspects of consciousness) is a common part of religious practices among Native Americans and some Hispanic American subgroups. Thus, the presence of dissociation in these groups may or may not be related to PTSD.

General Epidemiology. The lifetime prevalence for PTSD among adults in the United States has been estimated at 8%. Prevalence rates are considerably higher for subgroups that have been exposed to particular types of trauma. For example, in individuals who have been exposed to combat, physical or sexual abuse, or refugee experiences, lifetime prevalence rates can be as high as 65%.

Factors Associated With PTSD. Because it is clear that most individuals who are exposed to trauma will not develop PTSD, a large body of research has been devoted to identifying variables that predict PTSD. Most of these variables have been assessed only after trauma exposure (posttrauma) rather than before trauma (pretrauma) or during trauma (peritrauma). Thus, it is unclear whether they are actually predictive of (or merely associated with) PTSD. Two meta-analyses have identified the following variables, listed in order from most to least strongly associated with PTSD: lower social support, greater *peritraumatic dissociation* (i.e., the tendency to experience time distortion, disrupted sense of reality, or other major disturbances of cognition or perception during a traumatic event), nontraumatic life stress, peritraumatic emotions (i.e., intense emotions occurring during the traumatic event), perceived life threat during the traumatic event, trauma severity, adverse childhood experiences other than abuse, lower intelligence, lower socioeconomic status, childhood abuse, female gender, family history of psychiatric disorder, previous adulthood trauma, history of pretrauma psychiatric difficulties, lower education, younger age, and ethnic minority status.

Three caveats are worth noting about these results. First, the meta-analyses did not include all important correlates of PTSD. For example, coping style was omitted even though the literature suggests that active (e.g., problem-solving) coping leads to better post-trauma outcomes than does passive (e.g., avoidance) coping. Second, although social support had the strongest relationship with PTSD, it is unclear whether lower social support acts as a risk factor for PTSD (e.g., having fewer friends makes one more susceptible to trauma) or is a consequence of having PTSD (e.g., people with PTSD symptoms have a hard time making friends). Thus, some have concluded that peritraumatic dissociation, which by definition occurs before the development of PTSD (i.e., during the trauma), may be the best predictor of PTSD in the literature. Finally, although ethnic minority status emerged as the weakest correlate of PTSD in the meta-analysis, in actuality, some studies reported a moderate positive relationship and others reported a moderate negative relationship between minority status and PTSD. Thus, it would be more accurate to say that sometimes minority status is associated with higher rates of PTSD and sometimes it is associated with lower rates of PTSD.

Treatment of PTSD. Posttraumatic stress disorder is most commonly treated with individual psychotherapy. Although a number of drug therapies have shown considerable promise for the treatment of PTSD, they will not be reviewed here. Among the psychotherapies, behavioral therapies (e.g., flooding, eye movement desensitization, and reprocessing) focus on both reducing the anxiety associated with reexperiencing symptoms and eliminating avoidant behaviors; cognitive therapies (e.g., stress inoculation training) focus on correcting distorted attributions, challenging negative or irrational thoughts, and teaching new coping skills; psychodynamic therapies (e.g., time-limited dynamic therapy) focus on regulating defenses, fostering insight, providing a safe context for remembering trauma, and helping the patient to integrate a sense of meaning regarding the trauma; and transpersonal therapies (e.g., Buddhist therapies, holotropic breathwork, shamanic counseling) focus on the role that spiritual factors play in healing trauma. Some of these approaches have shown evidence of efficacy in controlled and uncontrolled studies.

AN ETHNOCULTURAL PERSPECTIVE ON PTSD

The literature on PTSD in ethnic minorities is relatively small. The following section will review variation in PTSD prevalence and treatment recommendations for each of the four major ethnic minority groups in the United States: African Americans, Hispanic Americans, Asian and Pacific Island Americans, and Native Americans. The review will emphasize the results of studies using PTSD measures that have been normed on diverse ethnocultural groups and have shown adequate reliability and validity with these groups. Some of the better studies have translated instruments into the preferred language of the respondents and gathered qualitative supporting data. However, many studies are flawed in ways that weaken the conclusions that may be drawn from them (e.g., small and/or nonrepresentative samples, unstandardized measures, improper comparison groups, and/or failing to include Hispanic Americans, Asian Americans, or Native Americans in sufficient numbers to make statistical comparisons). Nonetheless, these studies make an important contribution to the understanding of ethnocultural variation in PTSD.

PTSD in African Americans

Prevalence Comparisons With Caucasians

Although many studies have reported no differences between African American and Caucasian people in rates of PTSD, a few studies, including the National Vietnam Veterans Readjustment Study (NVVRS), a large-scale, nationally representative study of Vietnam veterans, found that African American veterans had higher rates of PTSD than Caucasian veterans.

Explanations for Prevalence Disparities

Exposure. When African Americans have been found to have higher rates of PTSD than Caucasians, it has virtually always been because African Americans were exposed to more trauma than their Caucasian counterparts. African Americans have historically been exposed to more severe combat duty and atrocities than Caucasians. Several studies, including the NVVRS, have shown that statistically controlling for exposure eliminates or drastically reduces PTSD differences between African Americans and Caucasians.

Racism. A secondary contributor to elevated PTSD rates among African Americans is racism. Institutional racism has been a long-standing problem for African Americans that acts as a chronic stressor. Many studies of African Americans with PTSD, including military studies, have shown that African Americans report more racial discrimination than Caucasians and that racial discrimination is associated with higher PTSD rates.

Dissociation. Finally, a few studies have reported that African Americans have higher rates of dissociation than Caucasians. Because dissociation is an associated feature of PTSD, and because peritraumatic dissociation is one of the best predictors of PTSD, there is a question of whether elevated dissociation among African Americans accounts for elevated PTSD. The best evidence indicates that when elevated dissociation is observed in African Americans, it, too, is best explained by more severe trauma exposure.

Treatment Considerations for African American PTSD Patients

Assessment/Diagnosis. The assessment of PTSD in African American patients may be made more difficult by their emotionally blunted presentation (sometimes referred to as the *black mask*), which may be mistaken for PTSD avoidance/numbing symptoms, or their "healthy paranoia" of Caucasian therapists, which may be mistaken for hypervigilance symptoms. Cultural sensitivity and experience working with African American clients can help with differential diagnosis.

Service Utilization. Studies show that as compared with their Caucasian counterparts, African Americans make equal use of Veterans Administration (VA) services (including PTSD-specific clinics), civilian nonpsychiatrist physicians, inpatient hospitals, and clergy. On the other hand, African Americans use fewer non-VA mental health services and self-help groups, have lower participation rates in VA programs, and leave treatment earlier. Evidence suggests the lower African American participation rates may be related to the lack of available African American therapists. Pairing African American clinicians with African American patients leads to somewhat better participation.

Psychotherapy Outcome. Despite clinical lore that African Americans are less responsive to psychotherapy than are Caucasians, empirical evidence suggests

that they do equally well. This conclusion is based on several studies, including a multisite study of almost 5,000 veterans. There is also evidence that ethnic matching of therapist and patient can lead to somewhat better outcomes for African American PTSD patients.

Other Treatment Recommendations. The literature is also replete with as yet untested recommendations for treating African American PTSD patients based on extensive clinical experience. Many of these recommendations may be useful for working with other ethnic minority groups, and all of these recommendations may depend on the client's stage of ethnic identity development. First, because African Americans historically have been overmedicated, misdiagnosed, and underreferred to psychotherapy, it is especially important for the clinician to strive for accuracy in clinical decision making. Second, because PTSD patients are hyperaware of danger cues, African American PTSD patients may be especially mistrustful of clinical settings in which other African Americans are absent. Thus, clinicians should attempt to provide a racially heterogeneous setting. Third, because many African Americans are frequently denied services and treated with indifference or hostility, it is especially important that their psychotherapists not act in ways that can be construed as aloof or uncaring. In particular, therapists should maintain an empathically involved stance and avoid neutrality. Finally, non–African American therapists should monitor and manage their own discomfort with hearing about the African American client's daily struggles and experiences with institutional racism. Some therapists unconsciously respond to this discomfort by prescribing medications or by becoming overly active, interpretive, or didactic.

Summary

Apparent differences between African Americans and Caucasians in prevalence of PTSD are usually explained by differences in exposure. Although African Americans appear to underutilize treatment in a variety of settings, they also appear to benefit from it in proportions equal to Caucasians. There is suggestion that a variety of culturally sensitive approaches, including ethnic match, can enhance treatment effects for African Americans with PTSD.

PTSD in Hispanic Americans

Prevalence Comparisons With Non-Hispanic European Americans

Several large studies have reported that as compared with non-Hispanic European Americans, Hispanic Americans have higher PTSD rates. This has been true among combat veterans, police officers, survivors of Hurricane Andrew in Florida, and survivors of the September 11 attack in New York City. Unfortunately, ethnic differences in PTSD have not been examined in other regions targeted by the 9/11 attack (e.g., Pennsylvania and Washington, D.C.).

Explanations for Prevalence Disparities

Exposure. Unlike elevated rates of PTSD observed among African Americans, PTSD in Hispanic Americans has not been easily explained by differences in exposure. Many studies that report elevated PTSD among Hispanic Americans found no differences in exposure. Even in studies, such as the NVVRS, in which Hispanic Americans were more trauma exposed, controlling for exposure does not account for the elevated PTSD.

Reporting Bias. A commonly proposed, but rarely tested, alternative explanation is that Hispanic Americans overreport distress. This theory is not only inconsistent with the Hispanic culture's endorsement of stoic minimization of distress but also inconsistent with the results of a study examining this question directly, which found that Hispanic Americans with high PTSD symptoms were more likely to underreport, not overreport, distress.

Peritraumatic Dissociation. Because culture-bound dissociative syndromes have been widely reported in Latin America, and because peritraumatic dissociation (PD) is one of the best predictors of PTSD, studies have investigated whether elevated PD among Hispanic Americans accounts for differences in PTSD. One such study found that elevated PD among Hispanics was one of the most important variables accounting for PTSD differences between Hispanic and non-Hispanic European Americans.

Coping Style. Hispanic Americans have also been observed to be more likely to engage in wishful-thinking coping (e.g., responding to trauma with belief in

miracles, faith, or luck) and self-blame coping (e.g., criticizing or lecturing oneself). There is evidence that these coping styles, which are assumed to be tied to cultural Hispanic American fatalistic and religious beliefs, partially explain elevated PTSD among Hispanics.

Social Support. Social support may be particularly important to Hispanic individuals because of their greater cultural emphasis on collectivism. Studies show that Hispanic Americans have larger, denser social networks than do non-Hispanic European Americans; that Hispanic Americans with poor social relationships have more intense PTSD symptoms; and that lower social support partially explains the elevated PTSD rates among Hispanics.

Racism. Exposure to racism has also been linked to PTSD in Hispanic Americans. Several studies have shown that Hispanic Americans perceive and experience more racism than non-Hispanic European Americans but less than non-Hispanic African Americans. However, there is evidence that Hispanic Americans are more adversely affected by racism than African Americans, perhaps because they are less prepared for it by their families of origin.

Subgroup Differences. There are a number of subgroup differences among Hispanics that seem to be important in understanding their elevated risk for PTSD. For example, geographic origin is important. Caribbean Hispanics (e.g., Puerto Ricans) may be more vulnerable to PTSD than other Hispanic groups. A study of September 11 survivors in New York City found that Dominican and Puerto Rican Hispanics had more PTSD symptoms than other Hispanic subgroups. Level of acculturation also seems to be important. Studies found that less acculturated Hispanic American combat veterans and Hurricane Andrew survivors had the highest PTSD symptom levels, suggesting that less acculturated Hispanics may be at particularly high risk for PTSD. Finally, evidence suggests that Hispanic refugees are likely to have particularly high rates of PTSD.

Treatment Considerations for Hispanic American PTSD Patients

Assessment/Diagnosis. The assessment of PTSD in Hispanic American patients may be hindered by the fact that Hispanic Americans may use somatic complaints as idioms of distress rather than directly report emotional distress. This reporting style can make PTSD more difficult to detect.

Service Utilization. Like African Americans, Mexican American (but not Puerto Rican) veterans use fewer non-VA mental health services and self-help groups than their non-Hispanic European American counterparts. However, all Hispanic American groups were as likely as non-Hispanic European Americans to use services provided by nonpsychiatrist physicians, clergy, or the VA.

Psychotherapy Outcome. There are no well-designed studies in the literature focusing on differential psychotherapy outcome for Hispanic Americans with PTSD.

Other Treatment Recommendations. Treatment recommendations for Hispanics with PTSD are also not as well developed as recommendations for non-Hispanic African Americans. Of note are the recommendations that some Hispanic Americans may be particularly receptive to family therapy because of the importance of the family in Hispanic American culture. Some Hispanic Americans may also find transpersonal therapies to be consistent with their cultural and spiritual beliefs.

Summary

Cultural and social factors may play a major role in explaining the well-replicated finding of elevated PTSD among Hispanic Americans. Culturally sanctioned practices such as dissociation; faith-based, avoidant, and self-punitive coping; and depleted social resources and racial discrimination seem to leave Hispanic Americans more deeply affected by exposure to trauma. Further research needs to be done on effective psychotherapies for Hispanic Americans with PTSD.

PTSD in Asian and Pacific Island Americans

Prevalence Comparisons With European Americans

Asian Americans are an extremely heterogeneous group that includes Asian Indians, Cambodians, Chinese, Filipinos, Japanese, Koreans, Vietnamese,

and Pacific Islanders. Surprisingly, the literature comparing PTSD rates between Asian Americans and European Americans is extremely limited. One of the few cross-ethnic studies, the Hawaii Vietnam Veterans Project (HVVP), compared Japanese American and Native Hawaiian veterans with their NVVRS European American counterparts and found that Japanese American veterans had significantly lower PTSD rates and Native Hawaiians had significantly higher PTSD rates than European American veterans.

Prevalence Comparisons With Other Asian Subgroups

The findings of the HVVP study clearly indicate the importance of considering Asian subgroups. Southeast Asian refugees have been of particular interest to PTSD researchers because of their extensive premigration trauma histories, which typically included war, torture, murder of family members, political persecution, loss of personal possessions, separation from family, and incarceration. The evidence suggests that among Southeast Asians, Cambodian and Hmong refugees have some of the highest rates of PTSD, Laotian refugees usually have somewhat lower rates, and Vietnamese refugees usually have the lowest PTSD rates.

Explanations for Prevalence Disparities

Exposure. Differences in trauma exposure seem to be important in understanding both differences between Asian American groups and Caucasian Americans and differences among Asian American subgroups. Among Southeast Asian refugees, Cambodian refugees, who have the highest PTSD rates, experienced more trauma than Vietnamese and Laotian groups. Among veterans in the HVVP, Japanese American veterans not only had the lowest PTSD rate but also had the lowest exposure to combat among all ethnic groups. Native Hawaiian veterans, on the other hand, who had a much higher PTSD rate, served the longest in Vietnam and were more likely to have had multiple tours of duty. Interestingly, statistical adjustment for wartime exposure did not fully explain the lower rates of PTSD among Japanese American veterans, suggesting that other factors may be at play.

Reporting Bias/Emotion Display Rules. The finding of lower PTSD among Japanese American veterans may be an artifact of culture-related reporting style. Japanese typically report low rates of mental disorder, perhaps because Japanese culture associates mental disorder with shame and stigma. Furthermore, Japanese culture discourages public displays of strong emotions and encourages moderate expression of emotion. There is suggestion that some Asian groups, particularly Japanese, may find it more acceptable to express emotional distress in somatic terms. All of these factors could explain why Japanese Americans report low levels of PTSD.

Nontraumatic Life Stress. General life stress can exacerbate PTSD. Many of the Asian subgroups that have shown elevated PTSD are also exposed to disproportionately high life stress. Native Hawaiians face serious social problems (e.g., poverty and health problems) that may contribute to their management of traumatic stress. Southeast Asian refugees encounter significant postmigration acculturative stress.

Racism and Race-Related Stress. Asian Americans are often overlooked in discussions of racism. However, there is ample evidence that Asian American Vietnam veterans encountered considerable racism (verbal and physical assaults) and race-related stress (e.g., being mistaken for Vietnamese, marginalization) while in the military. One study found that after controlling for combat exposure, exposure to race-related stressors accounted for an additional 20% of the variance in PTSD symptoms.

Treatment Considerations for Asian American PTSD Patients

Assessment/Diagnosis. The assessment of PTSD in Asian Americans is complicated by a variety of factors, including their great subgroup diversity and cultural prohibitions against public displays of distress. Like Hispanic Americans, some Asian Americans have a cultural style of expressing emotional distress in somatic terms. Thus, it may be difficult to determine whether these Asian clients meet DSM-IV diagnostic criteria for PTSD.

Service Utilization and Psychotherapy Outcome. There are no well-designed studies focusing on service utilization or psychotherapy outcome for Asians with PTSD.

Other Treatment Recommendations. Given the heterogeneity among Asian subgroups, clinicians should be aware of the relative base rates of trauma exposure and PTSD within each subgroup. This would include an understanding of the military and refugee experiences that were typical of each subgroup. Clinicians should also be aware of their own tendency to view Asians as model minorities, which can lead to underdiagnosis of mental disorders. Finally, clinicians should consider incorporating Buddhist principles and other Eastern philosophies into treatment.

Summary

Attention to subgroups is particularly important in the consideration of PTSD in Asian and Pacific Island Americans. Cambodian and Hmong refugees appear to have particularly high rates of PTSD. Japanese Americans appear to have particularly low rates of PTSD. The most important conclusion from the literature, however, is that much more research needs to be done on all Asian subgroups. Particular attention should be given to the effects of treatment on Asians with PTSD.

PTSD in Native Americans

Prevalence Comparisons With Caucasians

The literature on PTSD in Native Americans is underdeveloped. One of the few cross-ethnic comparative studies in the literature, the American Indian Vietnam Veterans Project (AIVVP), compared Northern Plains and Southwest Native American tribes with their Caucasian NVVRS counterparts and found that the prevalence of PTSD was higher among Native American veterans.

Prevalence Within Native American Communities

Most of the Native American PTSD literature has focused on PTSD rates within Native American subgroups without making comparisons with other ethnic groups. The results of these studies have been inconsistent. Some studies report extremely low rates (e.g., 1.6%), whereas others report relatively high rates (e.g., 27%).

Explanations for Prevalence Disparities

Exposure. Like African American, Hispanic American, and Native Hawaiian Vietnam veterans, Native American Vietnam veterans were exposed to more combat, violence, atrocities, and deprivation than European American veterans. In one study, controlling for exposure variables fully explained the higher Native American PTSD rate.

Previous Trauma/Nontraumatic Life Stress. Although the effects of prior trauma on PTSD among Native Americans have not been formally studied, there is good reason to believe that prior trauma may play a contributing role in Native American PTSD rates. Native Americans have the highest infant mortality rate of any ethnic group in the United States, generations of forced relocation and genocide, disproportionately high poverty and suicide rates, and lower average life expectancy than their European American counterparts. All of these facts add up to the high likelihood that Native Americans will be exposed to traumatic and severe nontraumatic stress throughout their lifespan. These stresses are associated with higher risk for PTSD.

Reporting Bias. Given the high levels of stress and trauma exposure, it is surprising that some studies reported such low levels of PTSD. These low rates might stem from cultural stoicism and pride. For example, some Native Americans are reluctant to disclose distress, especially to outsiders, in face-to-face interviews. However, anecdotal and empirical evidence suggests that many Native Americans may more readily admit psychological effects of war trauma, perhaps because of long cultural traditions regarding the role of the warrior in society. There is also some evidence that Native Americans may give more valid responses on self-administered questionnaires than in face-to-face interviews.

Treatment Considerations for Native American PTSD Patients

Assessment/Diagnosis. In addition to the possible reporting bias described above, the assessment of PTSD in Native Americans may be complicated by the effects of generations of marginalization, discrimination, and genocide. For example, given that many Native Americans are among the last of their particular tribe and that they continue to suffer disproportionately high rates of loss, it is realistic that they might develop a sense of foreshortened future. Yet an uninformed clinician might view this symptom as a cognitive distortion caused by PTSD. A second

complication in the assessment of PTSD in these communities is dealing with the high prevalence of alcohol abuse and dependence, which may make PTSD harder to detect.

Service Utilization. There is evidence that, relative to European Americans, Native Americans with PTSD underutilize VA mental health services in favor of other professional and nonprofessional mental health services, especially traditional or alternative treatments.

Psychotherapy Outcome. There are no well-designed studies examining the effects of standard therapies on Native Americans with PTSD.

Other Treatment Recommendations. Experienced clinicians recommend incorporating traditional Native American healing practices with mainstream interventions. This might include consulting with spiritual leaders and performing healing ceremonies, which involve many members of the community and serve an important role in meaning-making, and sweat lodge purification rituals, in which spiritual insights, personal growth, and physical and emotional healing may take place. Transpersonal psychotherapies may be particularly well received by some Native American PTSD patients. However, before including such practices, it would be important to assess the patient's ethnic identity development to determine whether traditional approaches would be welcomed.

Summary

Like Asian Americans, Native Americans are seriously understudied with respect to PTSD. The available evidence shows that when exposed to more severe war trauma, Native Americans develop more severe PTSD. There is reason to believe that multigenerational trauma and current stresses in Native American communities would elevate Native Americans' general risk for PTSD. There is also reason to believe that underreporting of distress can be a concern in assessing PTSD in Native Americans. However, these ideas have not yet been formally demonstrated. Finally, there is evidence that Native Americans prefer alternative to mainstream treatments. It will be important to assess the efficacy of both types of treatments in these patients.

OVERALL SUMMARY

Posttraumatic stress disorder (PTSD) is a psychiatric condition that is triggered by exposure to severe trauma and, by definition, persists for more than one month. Overall, ethnic minority status has not been strongly associated with the development of PTSD. However, there is evidence that most minority groups have shown elevated risk for PTSD in some studies as compared with European Americans. A notable exception to this trend is Japanese Americans, who often show reduced rates of PTSD. When groups have shown elevated risk for PTSD, it has most commonly been explained by increased exposure to traumatic stress. However, Hispanic Americans appear to have an increased risk for PTSD that is not fully explained by greater exposure alone and appears to be tied to a variety of cultural and other factors. In general, Asians and Native Americans have been understudied relative to European Americans, African Americans, and Hispanic Americans. Although the literature on ethnocultural variations in the treatment of PTSD is also underdeveloped, so far it appears that ethnic minorities show equal benefit from psychotherapy. The major issue appears to be how to offer culturally sensitive treatment that is attractive to the particular group in question.

—*Nnamdi Pole*

FURTHER READING

Friedman, M. J., Schnurr, P. P., Sengupta, A., Holmes, T., & Ashcraft, M. (2004). The Hawaii Vietnam Veterans Project: Is minority status a risk factor for posttraumatic stress disorder? *Journal of Nervous and Mental Disease, 192,* 45–50.

Frueh, B. C., Brady, K. L., & de Arellano, M. A. (1998). Racial differences in combat-related PTSD: Empirical findings and conceptual issues. *Clinical Psychology Review, 18,* 287–305.

Marsella, A. J., Friedman, M. J., Gerrity, E. T., & Scurfield, R. M. (Eds.). (1996). *Ethnocultural aspects of posttraumatic stress disorder: Issues, research, and clinical applications.* Washington, DC: American Psychological Association.

Pole, N., Best, S. R., Metzler, T., & Marmar, C. R. (2005). Why are Hispanics at greater risk for PTSD? *Cultural Diversity and Ethnic Minority Psychology, 11*(2), 144–161.

Pole, N., Best, S. R., Weiss, D. S., Metzler, T., Liberman, A. M., Fagan, J., & Marmar, C. R. (2001). Effects of gender and ethnicity on duty-related posttraumatic stress symptoms among urban police. *The Journal of Nervous and Mental Disease, 189,* 442–448.

POVERTY

Social psychological explanations of poverty have traditionally been based on two divergent models: the dispositional and the situational. Both models differ in regard to the attributions they make about the causes of poverty and the type of interventions required for its amelioration. Although the situational perspective locates the cause primarily within the social and economic structure of the society, the dispositional model, which has been pervasive in its influence, attributes the causes of poverty to individual deficits and shortcomings.

THE DISPOSITIONAL MODEL OF POVERTY

The dispositional model of poverty assumes that the poor are of little value and thus deserving of their fate. The embracement of such beliefs results in poor people being stigmatized and subjected to various forms of class-based prejudice and discrimination.

The theoretical conceptualization under which the dispositional model of poverty has been expressed has taken a variety of forms. One such variation is the *culture of poverty thesis,* which proposes that poverty is transmitted across generations, resulting in poor people adopting values, beliefs, and behavioral practices that differ from those of the dominant group.

The culture of poverty perspective and the dispositional model from which it is derived are problematic in terms of offering viable solutions for the eradication of poverty. How a problem is conceptualized determines what is done about it. Effective interventions directed at eliminating poverty must transcend a person-blame orientation and address the situational forces responsible for creating and maintaining impoverished social conditions.

Barriers to Transcending the Dispositional View

The transcendence of the dispositional view is made difficult by two social psychological processes, one ideological and the other psychological. The first process is based on the ideology of individualism, the notion that people's station in life is based on their own doing. Such beliefs serve to justify and legitimate the prevailing class-based inequities as well as shift the responsibility for eliminating poverty from the existing structural constraints to the poor themselves.

The second process involves what is referred to as the *fundamental attribution error,* the tendency to underestimate the role of situational factors in shaping people's behavior, resulting in poverty being attributed to factors such as ability and motivation.

THE SITUATIONAL MODEL OF POVERTY

The transcendence of the dispositional perspective requires the development of a sociocultural consciousness, one that acknowledges the situational basis of poverty. A sociocultural consciousness, and the situational model from which it is derived, assumes that poverty is a product of social conditions and that its elimination is contingent on transforming such conditions. A prominent expression of this situational view is the conflict perspective, the origins of which are Marxian in nature. At the heart of this perspective is the notion of class conflict, which results from the unequal distribution of wealth and power. The solution to poverty, as advocated by proponents of conflict theory, is the redistribution of wealth.

MODELS OF POVERTY AND THEIR RELEVANCE FOR EXPLAINING THE DIFFERENTIAL RATES OF POVERTY AMONG RACIAL AND ETHNIC MINORITIES

When poverty is defined in absolute terms—that is, according to some fixed standard, usually the lack of money to purchase a minimum amount of food, shelter, and clothing—then disparities in the rates of poverty between European Americans and various racial and ethnic groups may be observed. For instance, although in the year 2000, 11% of European Americans fell below the poverty line, the rates for African Americans, Hispanic Americans, and Native Americans were 24%, 23%, and 26%, respectively. The explanations posited for the differential rates of poverty between European Americans and other ethnic groups are based on the model of poverty that one embraces. Whereas the dispositional model attributes the differential poverty rates among the various ethnic groups to factors such as personality or cultural or genetic deficiencies, the situational model attributes the differential rates of poverty to more sociostructural causes: institutional discrimination and increased immigration and population diversity, for example.

—*Edward Stephenson*

FURTHER READING

Hunt, M. O. (1996). The individual, society, or both? A comparison of Black, Latino, and White beliefs about the causes of poverty. *Social Forces, 75*(1), 293–322.

Kluegal, J. R., & Smith, E. R. (1986). *Beliefs about inequality: Americans' views of what is and what ought to be.* New York: Aldine de Gruyter.

Lewis, O. (1966). *The culture of poverty: Critique and counterproposals.* Chicago: University of Chicago Press.

POWERLESSNESS

Powerlessness is the perceived inability of a person, an institution, a society, or its constituent social, ethnic, or racial groups to effect change and influence salient outcomes. Orientations of this inability may evidence as internalized (as in sense of worth or shame), externalized (maintenance of a subordinate, aggressive role or status), or varying dimensions of both. To the extent that such orientations become a function of situational forces pertinent to a group's survival, particularly in multicultural and increasingly complex societies, or societies undergoing rapid change, they take on enormous implications for sociobehavioral health (e.g., delinquency, social withdrawal, etc.) and mental health (e.g., emotional disorders such as depression and anxiety). Individual risk factors integrate with macro-level influences to differentially influence aggregates of individuals (i.e., culture, race, class, gender, sexual orientation, and disability) to potentially convey outcomes to future offspring through intergenerational transfer mechanisms (culture). Powerlessness is derived from context inequality, rather than simple sociodemographic inequality, and reflects an external expression of individual and community-level struggles to meet the adverse effects of their environment.

The literature shows increasing attention to linkages to social and cultural processes that create risks for powerlessness, although reasons for powerlessness are not well understood. Some explanations explored that might account for an individual's feelings of relative powerlessness include disparities in social and political education (i.e., who one is, as defined by racism or stigma), social and economic structural conditions (e.g., poverty, rural or urban experience context, etc.) that contribute to low feelings of self-confidence, variations in intelligence, and differences in the political environment in which an individual lives. To the extent a person's reality and perceptions are structured by broad sociodemographic categories, powerlessness remediation entails promulgation of an informed sense of history to secure forms of restitution.

In recent years, there has been an increasing recognition that behaviors, as well as the environmental contexts in which they are exhibited, are important to the conceptualization of the health of marginalized individuals, particularly among racial and ethnic minorities. However, few studies have integrated into their conceptualization empirical explorations beyond the individual theoretical model to include the broader proximal social and psychological contexts by which many behaviors derive to convey subpopulation-level experiences. Given the implications of multicultural and minority group status, it is unquestionable that for large aggregates of individuals, race and ethnicity are not simple unitary constructs by which (1) the behaviors and outcomes of similarly ascribed individuals can be simply aggregated to (2) convey subpopulation-level experience. Understanding powerlessness must coincide with an appropriate understanding of "what is" urban, rural, racial, ethnic, and gender. If the desire is to identify the ready supply of social and psychological structures and mechanisms that continue to disparage and marginalize the lives of individuals, investigations must move beyond rhetoric and programmatic experimentation to provide active policy guidance on social, community, and cultural levels of experience. The intellectual discourse remains incomplete without a paradigmatic shift conceptually linking powerlessness to (1) sociopolitical issues in the exercise of power, oppression, and privilege and (2) analytic frameworks designed to empirically capture societal-level influences as differentiated, multi-factor higher-order mechanisms.

—Alvin L. Killough
—Christopher L. Edwards

FURTHER READING

Bruce, M. A., & Thornton, M. C. (2004, Summer). It's my world? Exploring Black and White perceptions of personal control. *Sociological Quarterly, 45*(3), 597–612.

Edwards, C. L., Feliu, M., & Johnson, S. (2003). Diversity and cultural competence: Part 1. The struggle for definition and meaning. *North Carolina Psychologist, 55*(5), 12–13.

Killough, A. L., Drewes, D., & Edwards, C. L. (2000). Underlying Construct Analysis (UCA): Where individual systems end and human systems begin. *Proceedings of the SouthEast SAS Users Group 8th Annual Conference,* 377–384.

PROJECTIVE TESTING

Despite controversy in the development and use of projective testing over the past 80 years, projective testing research and clinical application continue to take place at national and international levels. Historically, projective testing and techniques have been embedded within psychoanalytic-psychodynamic theory, whereby constructs of personality structures and processes can be observed via indirect information provided by individuals. Inherent within the psychoanalytic-psychodynamic framework is the premise of unconscious processes that are mitigated by conscious and unconscious defensive mechanisms. Accordingly, projective testing is a method in obtaining access to the complexities of personality structures and functioning as individuals project elements of their internal world and functioning onto stimuli that vary in degree of ambiguity (i.e., inkblots) and specificity in requests (i.e., telling a story).

Although projective testing was originally established with a European and European American worldview, cross-cultural, national/international, and multicultural research have taken place for over half a century, although such studies have been few in number. With the increasing diversification of the U.S. population and the growth in the global community where transnational and indigenous interpersonal contact occurs, a basic introduction to and understanding of the most commonly used projective tests with diverse populations is warranted. It is important to note that national standardized norms have not been developed for projective tests in various and specific multicultural communities in the United States.

RORSCHACH COMPREHENSIVE SYSTEM

The Rorschach inkblot test was developed by Hermann Rorschach in 1921 as a perceptual process task in identifying psychopathology; Rorschach is also credited for conducting early cultural-differences research on the inkblots. The use of the Rorschach in predominantly Anglo/European American samples has been hampered by the controversies linked to competing scoring systems, questions regarding validity and reliability, and clinical utility. With the development of the Comprehensive System, some psychometric concerns have subsided, with the Comprehensive System serving as an explanation for the Rorschach test's popularity—it was recently noted as the fourth most commonly used assessment tool following the Weschler intelligence test for adults and children and the Minnesota Multiphasic Personality Inventory I/II.

James Allen and Richard H. Dana provide an extensive critique and review of cross-cultural and multicultural research in the use of the Rorschach Comprehensive System. Specifically, Comprehensive System (CS) research has primarily occurred in international settings (i.e., Venezuela and Belgium), and less so with the multicultural populations within the United States. Relatedly, peer reviewed studies on the CS with African American, Latino American, and Native American/Alaska Native samples have been few in number.

THEMATIC APPERCEPTION TEST

The Thematic Apperception Test (TAT) was developed by Henry A. Murray and Christina D. Morgan in the 1930s and is one of the most frequently used personality assessment instruments in the United States and abroad. The TAT is built on the premise that individuals project the inner workings of thoughts, fantasies, emotions, and wishes on pictorial stimuli depicting intrapersonal and interpersonal situations. Persons create meaning out of the visual stimuli through a narrative process, revealing the ways in which they experience and make sense of the world, significant relationships, and themselves. Primary themes are identified across the stories, using a quantitative scoring need-press system that was largely psychodynamic in emphasis and predominantly Anglo/European American in worldview. Use of the TAT in cross-cultural settings began shortly after its publication. By the mid-1940s, anthropologists and others began altering the drawings on the original cards or designing new cards for use with specific cultures; however, the scoring of themes was still often rooted within an Anglo/European American worldview.

The contemporary use and application of the TAT as an assessment tool with multicultural populations has raised questions regarding the psychometrics of the TAT. To address this issue, Dana has put forward conceptualizations of valid etic-emic and emic approaches to use with culturally diverse groups. The etic-emic approach uses certain TAT cards believed to contain characters and settings that are familiar across cultures and are considered universal. Emic normative data of the established etics is then obtained in various cultures to support the importance of the universal

personality constructs in various national or cultural contexts. The emic approach refers to introduction of new, culture-specific TAT cards that reflect specific cultural settings and characters, and a corresponding scoring system. Examples of previous research done with the emic model include the Tell-Me-A-Story (TEMAS) test, developed by Giuseppe Costantino and Robert G. Malgady for use with Latino American, African American, and nonminority children 5 to 18 years of age in predominantly urban settings, the TAT thematic scoring of Navajo men's post–World War II experiences, and the development of an Asian American version of the TEMAS.

PROJECTIVE DRAWINGS

The Draw-a-Man Test, later referred to as the Draw-a-Person (DAP) test, was originally developed by Florence Goodenough in 1926 as a measure of cognitive abilities. The DAP has proved popular in multicultural contexts by virtue of the fact that it is essentially a nonverbal test, allowing for its use with non-English-speaking or nonverbal patients. In encouraging the appropriate use of the DAP, it is recommended that drawings be compared with culture-specific normative data sets and that clinicians possess a thorough knowledge and understanding of the culture to distinguish between cultural differences and differences arising from individual variation.

The development of the House-Tree-Person (HTP) test is largely attributed to John Buck and was founded on research demonstrating that tree drawings allowed for the projection of personality traits, and that house drawings often symbolize the self and basic life-family experiences. Most clinicians have used the HTP in an integrative manner, examining content and style of drawings as indicators of personality functioning.

The Kinetic Family Drawing (KFD) test asks individuals to depict their families engaged in some type of activity. Despite widespread use worldwide, there are few normative studies on this technique that take into account important variables such as cultural and developmental factors. Regarding use of the KFD in multicultural settings, it is essential to understand normal patterns of family behavior within the culture in question to be able to evaluate what is abnormal and how it may affect the child.

SUMMARY

During a period in which the U.S. population has become increasingly diversified, projective testing has been viewed as a viable and appropriate assessment method when applied in multicultural situations and communities. Projective tests are thought to have several advantages in working with multicultural populations. First, they are generally thought to contain less cultural bias, owing to the ambiguity of the test stimuli and the fact that the specific nature of the required performance is often unclear to the client. Second, test instructions are purposely very simple, minimal, and ambiguous. Perhaps the largest disadvantage of projective tests is the lack of statistical norms and reliable and valid scoring schemes for non-Western populations, potentially exposing these tests to cultural biases that may arise during the scoring of test results.

As an interim measure while culture-specific norms are being developed or the validity of universal measures is being established, researchers and clinicians may benefit from following an assessment-intervention model such as that put forward by Dana, which sets out a framework of questions to be asked by assessors in striving toward culturally competent assessment practices. But, as Dana and others have often stated, there is no substitute for immersion in the culture of communities of interest and language proficiency.

Future research and growth in projective testing could focus on culturally grounded and systematic research that addresses the complexities of a multicultural society and takes into consideration levels of acculturation, linguistic nuances, and experiences of overt and covert discrimination and racism.

—Gemma Dolorosa Skillman
—Jacob Pickard

See also Acculturation; Cross-Cultural Psychology; Emic Versus Etic Distinction; Ethnic and Racial Identity; Multicultural Personality

FURTHER READING

Allen, J., & Dana, R. H. (2004). Methodological issues in cross-cultural and multicultural Rorschach research. *Journal of Personality Assessment, 82,* 189–206.

Dana, R. H. (2000). *Handbook of cross-cultural and multicultural personality assessment.* Mahwah, NJ: Erlbaum.

Exner, J. E. (2003). *The Rorschach: A comprehensive system: Vol. 1. Basic foundations and principles of interpretation* (4th ed.). New York: Wiley.

Groth-Marnat, G. (1997). *Handbook of psychological assessment* (3rd ed.). New York: Wiley.

Handler, H. (1996). The clinical use of figure drawings. In C. S. Newmark (Ed.), *Major psychological assessment instruments* (pp. 206–293). Boston: Allyn & Bacon.

PSYCHOPHARMACOLOGY

One of the major treatment approaches in mental disorders is the use of psychoactive drug therapies, particularly in the more serious spectrum of disorders. The availability of a large range of modern psychopharmacological agents parallels the widespread and common use of these medications for a variety of conditions related to mental illness. There is now general consensus that the classes of drugs known as antipsychotics and antidepressants are both effective and beneficial in treating underlying symptoms of psychosis and depression, respectively. This applies equally to patients from diverse cultures and ethnicities. Although the exact mechanisms of action are not known, the current understanding is that neurobiological abnormalities are associated with illness states and that such drugs work by altering brain function and chemistry.

The dosing and effects of psychoactive medications are known to vary between individuals from different cultures. For example, Asian patients are found to require lower doses of medications than are Caucasian patients because they appear to be more drug-sensitive. Such ethnic variations in drug responses have increasingly been found in clinical experience, anecdotal reports, surveys, and systematic studies. The emerging field of ethnopsychopharmacology, which has gained recent recognition in the clinical and research arena, examines variability in pharmacological treatments and response across ethnicity, culture, and environment. The emphasis on the issues of culture and race in medication use highlights that treatment outcomes are influenced by both genetic and nongenetic factors, and observed differences found between population groups are caused by biological and environmental factors. There is growing evidence of genetic differences across various ethnic groups that affect both drug metabolism and effects. Consequently, different rates of metabolism for particular medications may result in either rapid or slow excretion of these drugs from the body. In general, Asian and African American subjects are more likely to metabolize certain psychiatric drugs more slowly than do Caucasian subjects. Hence, giving standard doses of medication to drug-sensitive individuals may cause excessive accumulation of the drug, leading to increased risk of side effects and subsequent nonadherence to treatment. Furthermore, environmental and dietary factors, including the use of herbal remedies, also play an important role in the metabolism of medicines for psychiatric conditions.

Despite the widespread use of psychiatric drugs across most cultures and countries globally, there remains a surprising lack of research in this area. Studies have shown that Asian patients receive a lower dose of antipsychotics or have a higher blood level of drugs than do Caucasians for a given dose, although the findings are not always consistent. In terms of antidepressants, comparative cross-ethnic research has shown mixed results, with some studies showing that Asians have slower metabolism of antidepressants than Caucasians, but other studies finding no differences. Moreover, cross-ethnic studies on the effect and use of newer medications are still limited. Comparative findings that are gradually emerging indicate that ethnic differences in medication effects reflect a close interaction among genetic, environmental, and cultural factors.

The principal biological process to eliminate drugs from the body is the metabolism of drugs. The metabolism of antidepressants and antipsychotics mostly involves the drug-metabolizing enzymes in the liver. Large individual and ethnic group variations are found in the activities of these liver enzymes, which can lead to differential drug levels and side effects. These enzymes' activities have been found to correlate with variations in the genetic makeup. These genetic differences show significant heterogeneity in various population groups. Other biological factors that affect drug processing and need to be considered in individualizing drug treatment include body mass, gender, age, pregnancy, and disease states.

The gene variants that control both the metabolism and actions of psychiatric drugs are among the most important biological determinants of interethnic and interindividual differences in drug metabolisms. Such genetic variability affects the metabolism of drug-metabolizing enzymes as well as drug targets and possibly intracellular mechanisms. The rapidly developing field of pharmacogenetics is defined as the study of variability in drug handling and drug response owing to genetic differences between individuals and populations. The genetic variations of drug-metabolizing enzymes that control the expression of metabolic activity result in several broad metabolic groups. These include normal or extensive metabolizers, who have normal to high metabolic activity, and poor metabolizers, who have low to absent metabolic activity. Intermediate metabolizers

also have impaired metabolic function, which is greater than that of poor metabolizers but less than that of normal metabolizers. Finally, ultrarapid metabolizers have extreme metabolic activity leading to rapid metabolism and excretion of drugs. Cross-culturally, there are differences in the frequency of metabolic groups across different racial groups. For example, Asian populations overall have a higher rate of individuals with low metabolic activity.

The expression of these genes is significantly modified by environmental variables, including diet, chemicals, pollutants, medications, and other substances. Dietary factors (such as smoking, caffeine, and alcohol) and herbal medications, especially those used in Eastern cultures, can either inhibit or induce the activity of liver enzymes. Thus variations in diet and lifestyle that are common to a given ethnic group or culture can influence drug metabolism and response. Apart from environmental factors, cultural attitudes toward drugs and the expectation of response may also affect drug response. These possibly play an important role in both placebo response and experience of side effects. Other cultural factors that could impinge on the effects of drugs experienced by patients with mental illness include the adherence to medication, the doctor–patient relationship, and illness behavior. Furthermore, prescribing biases of the clinician may often determine the type and the dosage of the medication during treatment initiation and maintenance, which may lead to differences in response.

Interindividual and interethnic differences in drug response have been found in clinical practice. For example, Asian subjects are shown to have greater therapeutic response to certain antihypertensive and antipsychotic drugs than Caucasian subjects have for the same amount of medication. The differences in psychiatric drug response reflect the richness in both biological and cultural processes affecting the clinical response to drug treatments. Although it is common in psychology and psychiatry to derive a formulation to understand the psychosocial uniqueness of each individual patient, the biological diversities among individuals are often neglected. There tends to be an underlying assumption that the biology of the recipients is more or less the same. Clearly, recent evidence of both individual and ethnic differences in pharmacological response indicates that this is not the case.

It is important to emphasize in this regard that such diversity in both biological and psychosocial variables is found not only between ethnic and cultural groups but also between individuals within an ethnic subgroup. Of note, group differences in genotype and drug response, although apparent across populations, may not apply to the individual patient because of variation within the group. Due to interindividual differences, stereotyped interpretations narrowly based on ethnic or racial categories should be avoided. Ethnicity alone cannot accurately specify individual metabolism or dosing of medications. However, ethnicity remains a useful and important clinical pointer in drug therapy, for considering the probability of high or low metabolic capacity.

In the modern era, there has been significant demographic shift, with increasing multicultural populations in both Western and non-Western societies. As a consequence, cultural psychiatry has grown internationally. With increasing pressure on health costs, there is a need to improve the cost-effectiveness of drug agents in treating mental disorders across all cultures. Despite the plethora of new drug developments in neuroscience, most clinical drug trials are conducted in predominantly Caucasian populations even though they are used frequently in non-Caucasian populations. There are doubts and unresolved questions on the appropriateness of extrapolating research data of clinical drug trials derived from one population to another. Both morbidity and mortality caused by medication side effects occurring in drug-sensitive individuals and populations remain significant health care issues.

To understand the complexity of cross-cultural determinants in psychopharmacology requires the consideration of multiple variables, including genetic, environmental, dietary, and sociocultural factors that play a role in therapeutic response. Furthermore, the relationships among these biological and sociocultural factors are not static or linear, as they are constantly being modified by the wider environmental context. For instance, an Asian subject who has inactive genes for drug-metabolizing enzymes may metabolize drugs poorly and experience severe drug side effects because of impaired drug metabolism. The subject may subsequently develop negative attitudes toward Western medications, become noncompliant, and drop out of treatment, leading to poor clinical outcome. Furthermore, the clinical effects of psychotropic agents, in terms of both therapeutic and adverse effects, are likely to be experienced differently as a result of cultural factors affecting illness expression.

—*Chee H. Ng*

FURTHER READING

Herrera, J. M., Lawson, W. B., & Sramek, J. J. (1999). *Crosscultural psychiatry*. New York: Wiley.

Lin, K. M., Anderson, D., & Poland, R. E. (1995). Ethnicity and psychopharmacology. *Psychiatric Clinic of North America, 18,* 635–647.

Lin, K. M., Poland, R. E., & Nakasaki, G. (Eds.). (1993). *Psychopharmacology and psychobiology of ethnicity*. Washington, DC: American Psychiatric Press.

Lin, K. M., & Smith M. W. (2000). Psychopharmacotherapy in the context of culture and ethnicity. In R. Ruiz (Ed.), *Ethnicity and psychopharmacology* (pp. 1–36). Washington, DC: American Psychiatric Press.

PUERTO RICAN AMERICANS

Puerto Rican Americans are the second-largest Hispanic group in the United States (following Mexican Americans); they constitute approximately 10% of the Hispanic population and 1% of the total population in the United States. In a legal sense, Puerto Ricans in the United States are migrants, American citizens coming from a U.S. territory. However, their experiences in the mainland resemble those of immigrant groups, because they come from a Hispanic sociocultural tradition and speak Spanish as their primary language. Because Puerto Ricans move frequently from the island to the mainland and back, to understand the mental health issues among Puerto Rican Americans it is necessary to be familiar with their experiences both in the island and on the mainland United States.

HISTORY AND POLITICAL STATUS

Cristóbal Colón landed in Puerto Rico (called Borikén by its inhabitants) in 1493 and claimed the island and its Taíno native population for Spain. By the 1800s, the Puerto Rican population, culture, and national identity had emerged as the product of a mix of ethnic and racial groups, including Spanish immigrants and their descendants, descendants of African slaves, people of mixed Taíno and Spanish heritage, and people of mixed African and Spanish heritage. In 1898, following the Spanish-American War, Puerto Rico became a U.S. territory, and in 1917 Puerto Ricans were granted American citizenship.

Politically, Puerto Rico is a commonwealth defined as a free state associated with the United States. Puerto Ricans have the right to elect their own democratic government and the ability to enact educational policy. However, important federal governance and economic institutions prevail on the island, including the currency and banking system, the military, immigration and naturalization services, and the postal system. Puerto Rico is neither a state nor an independent nation. Puerto Rico has two official languages, two flags, two national anthems, and two cultures. The blend of Spanish, Taíno, and African traditions that characterized the island's population in 1898 coexist today with the more immediate influence of the American economy and culture.

For the last few decades, one of the pressing political issues in Puerto Rico has been to resolve its political status by becoming either a state or an independent republic. Even though the power to decide on a change of status ultimately resides with the U.S. government, several referendums held on the island since the 1960s have shown that Puerto Ricans prefer to remain a commonwealth. The present status provides Puerto Ricans many of the advantages of American citizenship while allowing for the preservation of the Spanish language and of the Puerto Rican culture and national identity.

PUERTO RICAN MIGRATION TO THE UNITED STATES

The largest migration of Puerto Ricans to the United States occurred between 1945 and 1965, when large numbers of rural and poor Puerto Ricans relocated, primarily to New York City and to some areas of New Jersey, Connecticut, and Chicago, in search of better economic opportunities. Because of economic conditions in Puerto Rico and the United States, during the 1970s, large numbers of Puerto Ricans living in the United States returned to the island. In the 1980s, net migration again favored movement from the island to the mainland, where Puerto Ricans continued to disperse throughout the northeastern United States. More recently, Puerto Rican migration to the United States has included large numbers of professional and high-tech workers. Current census figures show that there are about the same number of Puerto Ricans living on the island (approximately 3,623,392) as there are in the mainland United States (approximately 3,406,178).

For decades, Puerto Ricans have been one of the most economically disadvantaged ethnic groups in the United States. They have a lower rate of labor force participation, a higher rate of unemployment, and a substantially higher poverty rate than do the European American (non-Hispanic) population and most other Hispanic groups. Based on data collected by the Census Bureau in 1999, the unemployment rate in the mainland among Puerto Ricans aged 16 years or older was 8.1%, compared with 3.4% for European Americans, 7% for Mexican Americans, and 5.8% for Cuban Americans. Close to 26% of Puerto Ricans lived below the poverty level, compared with less than 8% for European Americans, 24% for Mexican Americans, and 17% for Cuban Americans. Unlike other immigrant groups, Puerto Ricans of later generations have not showed substantial upward mobility. Several researchers have concluded that industrial restructuring in the northeastern United States that resulted in the loss of low-skilled jobs has been one of the major contributors to poverty among Puerto Rican immigrants.

CULTURAL VALUES

Puerto Rican Americans, like other Hispanic Americans, are described as placing more emphasis than European Americans on maintaining harmonious and interdependent relations with family and friends and less emphasis on individual autonomy. Values such as *familismo, personalismo, simpatía, machismo,* and *marianismo* have been used to describe Puerto Ricans' cultural orientation.

Familismo refers to the importance given to the family in one's life. Even though family is important for all cultural groups, it is believed that the emphasis given to family versus individual needs differs across groups. In contrast to predominant values in the Anglo-Saxon culture that emphasize the needs and rights of the individual, in most Latin cultures, including among Puerto Ricans, the needs and rights of the individual are tempered by those of the family. In Puerto Rican families, mutual dependency and family loyalty are stressed over individual rights. These values are evident in child-rearing practices in which parents emphasize nurturing their children more strongly than facilitating their children's autonomy (even though most parents do both). Similarly, in making life decisions, children and adults are expected to consider the impact of their decisions on the rest of the family as much as they consider their own needs and preferences. For Puerto Ricans, the meaning of family tends to be flexible; often people who are not blood relatives are considered part of the family.

Puerto Ricans are described as valuing *personalismo,* meaning that personal contact in most encounters is very important. The demarcation line between a professional and a personal relationship may not be as clear-cut as in the Anglo culture. Puerto Ricans are likely to bring small presents to their therapists and to invite them to family functions such as weddings and graduations. Puerto Ricans may not develop trust in their therapists until they have a sense that they know the therapist as a person. A related value is that of *simpatía,* which refers to the desire to maintain cordial relations. Puerto Ricans are more likely to ignore minor conflicts or disagreements than confront others with disagreeable information or a conflictive situation.

Historically, Puerto Ricans have subscribed to more traditional gender roles than Americans, even though this is an aspect of the culture that has experienced rapid change in recent years. Traditional gender roles for males have been labeled as *machismo,* a word that generally has negative connotations. In its more positive meaning, *machismo* implies that males are expected to be the dominant figures in public and primarily responsible for the well-being of the women and children in the family. *Marianismo,* on the other hand, refers to the expected role of women as mothers and wives. Women are compared to the Virgin Mary, in that they are expected to sacrifice themselves for the needs of their children, husbands, and other family members. Puerto Ricans living in the United States tend to subscribe to less traditional gender roles than Puerto Ricans living on the island.

Several studies have provided support for some of these differences in interpersonal orientation between Puerto Ricans and Caucasian Americans. A study conducted in 1997 presented vignettes depicting problematic interpersonal situations to English-speaking Puerto Ricans on the island and Caucasians in New York. In their responses to the vignettes, European Americans and Puerto Ricans primarily differed in two areas: the importance of maintaining harmonious relationships and the willingness to confront conflict directly. Consistent with the cultural value of personalismo, Puerto Ricans were more likely to defer to requests made by another person than to attend to their individual needs, such as managing their time efficiently and taking care of previous commitments. On the other hand, European Americans were more likely to take care of their own needs and to limit their time commitment to others. Consistent with the cultural values of simpatía, Puerto Ricans also tended to avoid dealing with conflict directly. For example, they preferred to tell a white lie than openly refuse to give information to a friendly stranger. In contrast, European Americans were more likely to face the conflict directly and deny the information to the stranger than to pretend not to have it.

In a series of studies, Robin Harwood and colleagues found that European American mothers differed from island and U.S. Puerto Rican mothers in their expressed long-term socialization goals for their children. Puerto Rican mothers emphasized goals that involved the development of proper demeanor and decency, whereas European American mothers emphasized the development of self-confident and independent behaviors. It is important to note that social-class differences were also observed in mothers' parenting values. Among both European Americans and Puerto Ricans, middle-class mothers were more likely to emphasize self-confidence and independence, whereas low-income mothers more strongly endorsed socialization goals in the areas of proper demeanor and decency. European American and island Puerto Rican middle-class mothers also differed in their expectations and preferences regarding their toddlers' behaviors. Island Puerto Rican mothers favored quiet, respectful, and attentive behaviors from their children in a doctor's waiting room, whereas European American mothers preferred more active, exploratory, self-expressive behaviors. In a videotaped normal feeding situation, most of the European American (81.3%) and very few of the Puerto Rican children (3.6%) primarily fed themselves. These findings indicate that, consistent with anecdotal descriptions, in interpersonal and child-rearing situations, Puerto Ricans tend to emphasize nurturing, harmonious, and close interpersonal relationships over individual autonomy and personal freedom.

ETHNIC IDENTITY

For the most part, Puerto Rican Americans, both migrants and those born in the United States, retain a strong sense of ethnic identity as Puerto Ricans (or *Boricuas,* as they often call themselves). However, when Puerto Rican immigrants, particularly those born or raised in New York City, returned to the island in the 1970s and 1980s, they were often referred to as *Newyoricans* or *Nuyoricans,* a label that implies a separate identity from island Puerto Ricans. Studies conducted in the 1990s indicated that college students who were residing in Puerto Rico but who had been raised in New York City differed from island Puerto Ricans in their definition of the Puerto Rican ethnic identity. For the islanders, the Puerto Rican identity was defined by the geographical boundaries of Puerto Rico, fluency in speaking Spanish, human relations based on expressed concerns for others, and traditional gender beliefs and behaviors. In contrast, the return migrants defined their ethnic identity in terms of their feelings of loyalty to their Puerto Rican ethnic background, regardless of their fluency in Spanish or other behaviors. Because Puerto Ricans from the United States tend to lack fluency in Spanish and to exhibit more assertive and liberal behaviors than is the norm on the island, in Puerto Rico they are considered Nuyoricans and not Puerto Ricans.

Migrant Puerto Ricans often face the painful reality of not fully belonging to either place; they are a minority group in the United States, and when they go to Puerto Rico they learn that on the island they are not considered fully Puerto Rican. Even though the term *Newyorican* originally was used in a negative way by island Puerto Ricans to differentiate themselves culturally from Puerto Rican migrants in the United States, Puerto Rican writers and artists in New York City adopted the label to capture their collective identity, which blends elements of the Puerto Rican culture and the American inner-city experience. During the mid-1970s, the Nuyorican Poets' Cafe was established in New York City to promote the work of Puerto Rican writers who wrote in English or in a blend of Spanish and English.

RACIAL IDENTITY

Race is primarily a social construct, and therefore cultural groups differ in how racial categories are defined. In the United States, race generally is defined in terms of a dichotomous White/non-White categorization, regardless of a person's appearance. In contrast, Puerto Ricans have a more fluid conception of race that considers a person's shade of skin color, facial features, and hair texture. Among Puerto Ricans, several terms are used to describe specific combinations of features. These include *trigueño* (light brown skin), *moreno* (dark brown skin), *indio* or *canela* (light brown skin with Caucasian features), or *jabao* (light skin color with Negroid facial features and/or hair texture). Island Puerto Ricans who move

to the United States, particularly those of darker skin color, are likely to encounter a more negative racial climate than they experienced on the island. Maybe because of these differences, Puerto Rican Americans prefer to identify themselves in terms of ethnic or national origin categories (e.g. Puerto Rican, Hispanic, Latino/a) rather than in terms of racial categories.

PREVALENCE OF MENTAL HEALTH DISORDERS

Results of epidemiological studies using the Diagnostic Interview Schedule (DIS) conducted during the 1980s in Puerto Rico and in five communities in the United States (New Haven, Baltimore, St. Louis, Durham, and Los Angeles) indicated that the prevalence rates of alcohol abuse and dependence, antisocial personality disorder, affective mood disorders, schizophrenic disorders, and generalized anxiety disorders were similar in both places. Level of cognitive impairment was higher in Puerto Rico than in the United States, whereas the prevalence rates of illicit drug use and drug abuse dependence symptoms were much lower in Puerto Rico than in the United States. In both countries, the prevalence of psychosexual, affective, and phobic disorders was higher in women than in men, whereas alcohol abuse and dependence were more prevalent in men. A comparison of data gathered with the DIS in Los Angeles and Puerto Rico revealed that when statistically controlling for demographic variables (age, gender, level of education, and number of people in the household), Puerto Ricans reported significantly more physical complaints and symptoms than European Americans and Mexican Americans born in the United States or in Mexico. Puerto Ricans in the United States also have reported higher levels of depression than European Americans and other ethnic minority groups (African Americans, Cuban Americans, and Mexican Americans). Among Puerto Rican Americans, depression levels are most severe among women and low-income or unemployed people. However, compared with African Americans, European Americans, and other Hispanic American groups in the United States, Puerto Rican Americans had the lowest suicide rates relative to their depression rates. Research findings suggest that, for the most part, the difficult economic situation of Puerto Ricans in the United States, and not cultural factors (e.g., acculturation, language proficiency), explains their higher levels of clinical depression and depressive symptoms.

Ataque de nervios is a culturally bound syndrome that is manifested in crying spells, anger, dizziness, nervousness, trembling, and heart palpitations. Approximately 16% of the general population in Puerto Rico report having experienced an ataque de nervios, making it the most common syndrome after generalized anxiety disorder (reported by 18% of the population). In Puerto Rico, these attacks were most prevalent among middle-aged, unemployed, low-income women who had experienced marital separation or divorce. In most cases, the onset of the attack was related to a traumatic event, such as the death of a loved one or a conflict with a spouse or child. Among Puerto Rican Americans attending primary care or mental health clinics in the United States, 26% to 75% reported having experienced an ataque de nervios. Both on the island and in the United States, Puerto Ricans who experience these attacks often report other psychological symptoms, such as depression, anxiety, anger, and panic episodes. Among Puerto Rican American women, the experience of ataque de nervios was not associated with sex-role traditionalism, level of acculturation to the United States, or perceived social support. Researchers have concluded that among Puerto Ricans, ataque de nervios seems to be a culturally sanctioned expression of anxiety, depression, and anger primarily among older, low-income women who experience traumatic situations.

FOLK HEALING TRADITIONS

In Puerto Rico, there are two main ethno-religious traditions, Spiritism and Santeria. Spiritism is based on the idea that God rules in a universe populated by a strong hierarchy of spirits and that the spirits of the dead remain connected with people on Earth. All people are believed to have spirits (or souls from the deceased) who guide and protect and, if need be, heal them. It is believed that Spiritist healers communicate with the spirits and the dead regarding their clients' problems in everyday living, such as health, family, relationships, and work. Healers report that they receive messages from the spirits to help them diagnose clients' problems, suggest herbal and ritual remedies, and reveal the future. The practice of Spiritism in Puerto Rico blends spiritual Amerindian traditions and the practice of Catholicism with the teachings of Allan Kardec, a Frenchman considered the father of modern Spiritism. Two books that codify the principles of Spiritism, *The Spirits Book* and *The Gospel*

According to Spiritism, are widely sold in Botánicas— shops that sell herbs and religious items in Puerto Rico and in Puerto Rican communities in the United States.

Santería is primarily based on African religious traditions brought to the Americas by African slaves. Because of the prevalence of Catholicism imposed by the Spaniards, Santería developed as an occult practice that blended Catholic and African imagery and traditions. Many Puerto Ricans believe and adhere to both spiritual traditions, Spiritism and Santería. A few studies have examined the extent to which Puerto Ricans consult Spiritist healers, the association of Spiritism to mental health disorders, and the expectations and outcomes for clients of mental health practitioners and Spiritist healers. Similar studies are lacking in relation to Santería.

In the epidemiological study conducted in Puerto Rico in the mid-1980s, 18% of the population reported having sought help from a Spiritist for an emotional problem. Those who had visited a Spiritist were more likely to be low-income, to work outside the home, to report symptoms of depression (although not be diagnosed with major depression), and to have visited mental health practitioners than those who reported never visiting Spiritists. Puerto Ricans, on the island and in the United States, visit Spiritists primarily to seek help for family-related problems, and they do not differ from Puerto Ricans who visit mental health clinics in terms of general psychological adjustment. In addition to the services they expect to receive from mental health providers, Puerto Ricans who visit healers expect to obtain spiritual guidance and advice about the future. Therefore, it is very likely that some Puerto Ricans who visit mental health clinics may simultaneously seek the guidance of Spiritists.

Many Puerto Ricans embrace the Spiritist tradition, even if they do not practice it or consult healers. In validating the Diagnostic Interview Schedule (DIS) for the Puerto Rican epidemiological study, researchers found that certain experiences of a religious and spiritual nature that were scored as indicators of schizophrenia on the DIS were not considered psychotic by experienced psychiatrists in Puerto Rico. These experiences, which included hearing or seeing dead relatives and having premonitions of future events, are considered a gift within the Spiritist tradition. In diagnosing Puerto Rican clients who report hearing voices or communicating with the dead, counselors and psychologists need to explore whether these experiences are within the normative realm of Spiritist beliefs or whether they express psychotic symptoms even within the Puerto Rican cultural tradition.

PSYCHOTHERAPY INTERVENTIONS

The few studies that have examined the effectiveness of psychological interventions with Puerto Ricans suggest that short-term behavioral and cognitive behavioral group and individual interventions lead to positive outcomes with Puerto Ricans in the United States and on the island. Also, semistructured group interventions that explicitly incorporated Puerto Rican cultural elements were modestly successful in reducing anxiety among young children who had exhibited disruptive behaviors in school.

Two studies conducted by Lillian Comas-Díaz and colleagues during the 1980s showed that short-term (five 1.5-hour sessions) behavioral and cognitive-behavioral group interventions were effective in reducing depression in Spanish-speaking Puerto Rican women in New York City. A 10-week group intervention designed to increase assertiveness among low-income Puerto Rican–born women participating in a job training program in the northeastern United States also showed positive results. However, in narrative evaluations, the women reported that family members often considered their assertive behaviors disrespectful and "too Americanized," suggesting that it might have been difficult for these women to retain and implement their newly acquired assertive behaviors in the long term.

Giuseppe Costantino and colleagues developed the cuento (storytelling) therapy intervention that explicitly incorporated cultural elements to work with Puerto Rican children and adolescents from low-income homes in New York City. One version of cuento therapy involved reading Puerto Rican folktales to small groups of children (aged 5 to 9) and their mothers, situating the stories either in Puerto Rico or in the multicultural inner-city environment of New York City, dramatizing the stories and discussing the adaptive and maladaptive consequences of the characters' actions. The cuento interventions were effective in reducing anxiety in the children; however, the children's disruptive behavior in class, their ability to delay gratification, and their self-concept were not changed by the intervention. A different application of storytelling to group therapy, implemented with older

Puerto Rican children and early adolescents (fourth to sixth grade), had participants in the group compose stories about familial and ethnic issues stimulated by pictures depicting Puerto Rican cultural elements (traditional foods, games) and Puerto Rican families and neighborhoods in American urban settings. Results showed that the 8-week intervention was effective in reducing anxiety in children of all grade levels and in improving the sixth graders' conduct in class as rated by the teacher.

Studies conducted in Puerto Rico also have yielded positive results for cognitive and behavioral interventions. Jeanette Roselló and Guillermo Bernal adapted cognitive-behavioral and interpersonal psychotherapy interventions developed on the United States for depressed adolescents in Puerto Rico. The adaptation primarily entailed integrating to therapy issues related to family dependence and ondependence that characterize parent–child relations on the island. Results of an outcome study conducted in the late 1990s showed that both cognitive-behavioral and interpersonal individual psychotherapy interventions were effective in reducing depression among Puerto Rican adolescents 13 to 17 years old. Eighty-two percent of the adolescents in the interpersonal psychotherapy intervention and 59% of those in the cognitive behavioral treatment had returned to normal functioning at the end of treatment. However, only adolescents who received interpersonal therapy showed higher gains in self-esteem and social adaptation than did the control group, which received no treatment. The authors speculated that interpersonal therapy may have resulted in stronger outcomes related to self-esteem and social adaptation because compared with cognitive therapy, interpersonal therapy has a greater degree of compatibility with the Puerto Rican values of personalismo (preference for personal contacts in social situations) and familismo (placing the interests of family over the interests of the individual). A short-term (three 2-hour sessions) structured learning group therapy was effective in teaching self-control to low-income fathers in Puerto Rico who had documented histories of physical child abuse. A brief relaxation training intervention (14 sessions of 22 minutes each) was effective in increasing relaxation levels and lowering depression among elderly people in Puerto Rico.

These findings suggest that with some adaptation, the therapeutic modalities that have proven effective in the United States seem to be applicable to Puerto

Rican populations on both the island and the mainland. However, broad generalizations about effective therapeutic interventions cannot be made, because there have been very few controlled studies of therapy outcome with Puerto Ricans.

—Consuelo Arbona

See also Cuento Therapy; Culture-Bound Syndromes; Hispanic Americans

FURTHER READING

Canino, G., Bird, H., Rubio-Stipec, M., & Bravo, M. (2000). The epidemiology of mental disorders in the adult population of Puerto Rico. *Revista Interamericana de Psicología/ Interamerican Journal of Psychology, 34,* 29–46.

Canino, G., & Canino, I. A. (1982). Culturally syntonic family therapy for migrant Puerto Ricans. *Hospital and Community Psychiatry, 33,* 299–303.

Costantino, G., Malgady, R. G., & Rogler, L. (1994). Storytelling through pictures: Culturally sensitive psychotherapy for Hispanic children and adolescents. *Journal of Clinical and Child Psychology, 23,* 13–30.

Cuadrado, M., & Lieberman, L. (2002). *Traditional family values and substance abuse: The Hispanic contribution to an alternative prevention and treatment approach.* New York: Kluwer Academic/Plenum.

Garcia-Preto, N. (1996). Puerto Rican families. In M. McGoldrick, J. Giordano, & J. K. Pearce (Eds.), *Ethnicity and family therapy* (pp. 183–199). New York: Guilford.

Harwood, R. L., Handwerker, W. P., Shoelmerich, A., & Leyendecker, B. (2001). Ethnic category labels, parental beliefs, and the contextualized individual: An exploration of the individualism-sociocentric debate. *Parenting Science and Practice, 1,* 217–236.

Harwood, R. L., Schoelmerich, A., Ventura-Cook, E., Schulze, P. A., & Wilson, S. P. (1996). Culture and class influences on Anglo and Puerto Rican mothers' beliefs regarding long-term socialization goals and child behavior. *Child Development, 67,* 2446–2461.

Ramos-McKay, J. M., Comas-Díaz, L., & Rivera, L. A. (1988). Puerto Ricans. In L. Comas-Díaz & E. E. Grifith (Eds.), *Clinical guidelines in cross-cultural mental health.* New York: Wiley.

Rodriguez-Cortés, C. (1990). Social practices of ethnic identity: A Puerto Rican psycho-cultural event. *Hispanic Journal of Behavioral Sciences, 12,* 380–396.

Roselló, J., & Bernal, G. (1999). The efficacy of cognitive-behavioral and interpersonal treatments for depression in Puerto Rican adolescents. *Journal of Consulting and Clinical Psychology, 67,* 724–745.

Zayas, L. H., Canino, I., & Suarez, Z. (2001). Parenting in mainland Puerto Rican families. In N. B. Webb & L. Doman (Eds.), *Culturally diverse parent–child and family relationships* (pp. 133–156). New York: Columbia University Press.

QUALITATIVE METHODS

Qualitative research is concerned with understanding human experience, interactions, and behavior patterns. It seeks to describe and interpret the *why* of human behavior and motivation. Qualitative approaches are well suited to explore the complexities of multicultural contexts and multicultural individuals. By its very nature, qualitative research recognizes the value and validity of personal experience and the existence of competing ways of understanding social realities. Rather than aiming to isolate and manipulate critical variables, qualitative research tries to interpret comprehensibly, and through language, the nature of the human condition; it incorporates the complexity of forces shaping cognition, affect, and behavior in a descriptive narrative.

Expanding psychology's research options requires that we review approaches that have taken root in related disciplines. Emerging research methodologies in social science are consistent with belief systems and epistemologies that favor interpretation over prediction; this pursuit is a search for meaning, rather than generalization.

Traditional (quantitative) psychological science, in contrast, suffers from predictable weaknesses when it attempts to study complex multicultural social systems, as well as diverse individuals enacting multiple roles, motivations, and identities. Quantitative social science reduces human phenomena to identifiable causative factors; this approach may lead to fragmented and incomplete understanding of human actions. When those methods are applied to diverse and multicultural populations, the obstacles to isolating causative factors may be insurmountable.

Traditional quantitative research approaches in the social sciences have been questioned in the past two decades as researchers have sought new ways of understanding. Those inquiry methods are grounded in the natural sciences and were uncritically adopted by psychologists. The current reexamination of research in the social sciences has been described as a crisis because it questions the very foundations of social science. Psychologists, however, have remained relatively unengaged in this debate. In fact, there is a contemporary effort to enshrine empiricist quantitative methods and establish standardized procedures for all psychological research.

As more social science researchers contend that quantitative approaches are poorly suited to be the main tool for understanding social interactions and human behavior, the emergence of alternative paradigms has gained momentum and academic recognition. This discourse is particularly relevant to multicultural research; it has shaped modern cultural anthropology and spawned the growth of ethnic, gender, cultural, and postcolonial studies. In psychology, new attention to qualitative research methods is driven by the need for alternative ways of understanding and interpreting human behavior.

To explore human experiences, and particularly when those experiences are informed by cultures and contexts unfamiliar to us, the subjective perspectives of participants in research are more than a curiosity. Those subjectivities must be acknowledged, addressed, and studied to access information relevant to the meaning of participants' behaviors. It may be argued that the ideological bases of the traditional quantitative research paradigm unwittingly become an obstacle to comprehending the complexity of human experience. By insisting on the necessity to minimize contextual influences, homogenize treatments, and investigate only key significant variables, researchers reduce experience to a narrow focus. Consequently, researchers are drawn to conclusions that reflect their own worldviews but neglect or remain uninformed about other perspectives on reality.

Multicultural research, to be valid, must seek to clarify how different cultures, statuses, contexts, and roles inform the subjective experience of subjects. Although this approach does not imply a challenge to the notion that there is a reality outside human experience independent of human perception, any knowledge we have of that reality is mediated by history, culture, and personal experience. In other words, we cannot pretend to understand human experience without taking into account the sociopolitical contextual nature of that experience. In seeking to understand research participants' experience and consciousness, we must expand our research modalities to include qualitative approaches, because those methods are more suitable to uncover the meanings of human behaviors.

Interpretivism suggests a way of knowing that springs from personal experience and maintains a relatively narrow locally situated focus. Individual narratives provide the best examples of the interpretivist approach. Bruner, in this vein, suggested that we learn from our encounters with the world, and that through these transactions we develop a sense of selfhood that gives meaning to our existence. The philosophical roots of interpretivism are in phenomenology, which may be described as the study of individual experience and ways of deriving meaning from those experiences. Interpretivist narratives seek to focus on and yield understanding. One may ask, given an array of options: Which intervention is better? From another perspective, one may ask: What happens when a particular intervention is implemented? The traditional quantitative-derived method offers ways to assess outcomes, appropriate for the first question. An interpretivist-informed approach would be better suited for gaining insight into the second question.

The following are common qualitative approaches:

ETHNOGRAPHY

Ethnographic approaches grow out of anthropology and require that researchers be immersed in the context under investigation. As in traditional field-based studies, the researcher becomes a participant-observer, capable of interpreting the overt and subtle manifestations of a culture. Although westerners seeking to understand cultures unfamiliar to them initially practiced this approach, current uses of this method are found in multiple contexts, including urban and technologically rich environments. As opposed to earlier ethnographies that implied observer objectivity, contemporary ethnography grapples with the position of the observer and the subjective interpretative frame imposed on the context.

PHENOMENOLOGY

Rooted in existential philosophy, phenomenology concerns itself with the essence of lived experience and may include biographical and autobiographical narratives, as well as observation and reflection. This method has been widely used to explore individual responses to the experience of particular events—for example, being a cancer patient or a victim of racism.

GROUNDED THEORY

First proposed by Glaser and Straus in the mid-1960s, grounded theory seeks to avoid the biasing effect of interpreting human interaction within a given setting from a preconceived theoretical frame. Instead, it provides a model for uncovering and interpreting the tacit rules that govern communications and organize a particular social context. Less concerned with generalization, this approach respects and recognizes the uniqueness and peculiarities of individuals and the traditions and patterns that evolve in subcultures and organizations.

CASE STUDY

Psychologists have used the case study since the early stages of the development of the discipline. Notably, Freud and his followers, and Piaget and Inhelder, used case studies as paths to describe and explore psychological processes. Because this approach—with the exception of quantitative single case studies—relies primarily on narrative description, it has fallen out of favor in psychological research. Perhaps paradoxically, it is still widely used in case presentation and in training psychologists for clinical work. Case study in current research often incorporates ethnography or phenomenology; the purpose remains to gain in-depth knowledge about an individual, a group of individuals, or other bounded fields of interest.

CRITICAL THEORY

Although not strictly a research method, critical theory has been essential in the formulation of several emerging disciplines, including ethnic, feminist, gender, and postcolonial studies. Critical theory is associated with the Frankfurt school of philosophy—a group of scholars whose work began between the world wars in Europe and continued in the United States. Best known among these scholars are Adorno and Marcuse. Critical theorists see research as a political act, because the purpose of investigations is to unmask beliefs, practices, and policies that impose limits on human freedom, justice, and democracy.

In this frame, the effect of research is not simply to elucidate a condition or context, but rather is the beginning of collective action for social change.

Qualitative researchers often employ a variety of approaches within a study, including quantitative methods—in such cases, the study may be described as *mixed method*. In a multicultural context, the various qualitative research approaches offer alternatives to reductionistic and contrived groupings and conceptualizations. They offer the hope of preserving and respecting the uniqueness, complexity, and integrity of individuals and groups being studied. These methods elevate subjects to the status of participants.

—*Alberto Bursztyn*

See also Ethnic Minority Research

FURTHER READING

Bernstein, R. J. (1983). *Beyond objectivism and relativism: Science, hermeneutics, and praxis.* Philadelphia: University of Pennsylvania Press.

Bruner, J. (1996). *The culture of education.* Cambridge, MA: Harvard University Press.

Ponterotto, J., Casas, J. M., Suzuki, L. A., & Alexander, C. M. (1995). *Handbook of multicultural counseling.* Thousand Oaks, CA: Sage.

Tolman, D. L., & Brydon-Miller, M. (2001). *From subjects to subjectivities: A handbook of interpretive and participatory methods.* New York: New York University Press.

Trueba, H. T. (1993). Cultural diversity and conflict: The role of educational anthropology in healing multicultural America. In P. Phelan & A. L. Davidson (Eds.), *Renegotiating cultural diversity in American schools* (pp. 195–215). New York: Teachers College Press.

Woolgar, S. (1996). Psychology, qualitative methods, and the ideas of science. In J. T. E. Richardson (Ed.), *Handbook of qualitative research for psychology and the social sciences* (pp. 11–24). Leicester, England: British Psychological Society Books.

R

RACE

The term *race* first appeared in the English language in 1508 to refer to a category or class of persons, without reference to anything biological. It was only in the late 18th century that the word *race* was invested with a physical connotation, and only in the early 19th century that specific theories of racial types began to emerge, most notably about populations outside Europe. Many of the ideas associated with genetics and racial differentiation during this period were founded on pseudo-scientific theories that are now discredited. But at the end of the century, eugenicists and social Darwinists were offering scientific justifications for genocide and imperialism through which Europeans projected many of their darkest impulses onto Africans.

In monographs, articles, and textbooks, the term *race* is often presented within quotation marks. This practice has created a double bind, on the one hand freeing race but also at the same time legitimizing it, thus giving it a reality and a theoretical background that does not exist. *Race,* like *culture* and *ethnicity,* has been problematized by ambiguous usage in various spaces and in different times. Social construction theorists have claimed that these concepts are products of specific histories and geopolitical experiences. Moodley suggested that sometimes they are used as empty signifiers covered in ideological meanings that promote particular self-interests but do nothing for African American and ethnic minority groups.

In the United States, the person who is most noted for thinking about race has been W. E. B. DuBois. DuBois argued that race was not scientific or biological but that it was a sociohistorical concept. However, scholars and researchers in psychology and other disciplines continue to use the notion of race to get at the truth about difference, meaning, genetics, and culture. Sometimes a reductionist and fixed view of race and racial difference becomes the basis for understanding the relationship with ethnic minority individuals and groups. As Karen Henwood and Ann Phoenix have pointed out, racial difference is neither fixed in stone nor merely illusionary, because it is the outcome of practices of (de)racialization, which position groups and subjects in more or less advantageous and discriminatory ways.

Race, racial difference, and the many forms of racism experienced by African American and other ethnic minority groups are not fixed categories, nor are they transhistorical, pointing to a time at which discrimination and domination originated. These ideas and ideologies are dynamic, forever changing in relation to the discursive social, economic, cultural, and political practices that operate at a given time. The most useful way to work with race is to explore the power relations that intersect between the personal and the social level to produce racism and misogyny. For psychologists who are critical or anxious about working with the ideas and ideologies of race and racial difference, understanding its social and cultural history will offer numerous possibilities of how problematic race can be when it is taken for granted and seen as biological.

—*Roy Moodley*
—*Deone Curling*

See also Ethnicity; Racial Identity Development; Racism and Discrimination

FURTHER READING

Alderman, G. (1985). Explaining racism. *Political Studies, 33,* 129–135.

Appiah, K. A. (1986). The uncompleted argument: Du Bois and the illusion of race. In H. L. Gates Jr. (Ed.), *"Race," writing, and difference* (pp. 21–37). Chicago: University of Chicago Press.

Brantlinger, P. (1985). Victorians and Africans: The genealogy of the myth of the dark continent. In Henry L. Gates Jr. (Ed.), *"Race," writing, and difference* (pp. 185–222). Chicago: University of Chicago Press.

Ferber, A. L. (1998). Constructing whiteness: The intersections of race and gender in US White supremacist discourse. *Ethnic and Racial Studies, 21,* 48–63.

RACE PSYCHOLOGY

From a historical perspective, *race psychology* in its broad meaning can be divided into four overlapping periods. At the beginning stood the association of race with certain aspects of the psyche or soul. Although so-called great thinkers provided prejudicial assessments of various ethnic groups (e.g., Aristotle) or attributed psychological qualities to certain cultures and types, such as the *noble savage* (e.g., J. -J. Rousseau), the systematic combination of psychological characteristics with race occurred in the 18th century, when humanity was classified into distinct groups.

RACE AND SOUL

Carolus Linnaeus combined in his human taxonomy varieties of humans (races) with psychological, natural, and social characteristics. He assigned the classical temperaments to four races: The *white Europeans* were defined as sanguine and governed by law; the *red Americans* as choleric and governed by custom; the *yellow Asians* as melancholic and governed by opinion; and the *black Africans* as phlegmatic and governed by the will of the master. The construction of psychological, aesthetic, moral, and natural competencies for various races was a common academic endeavor engaged in by scientists and philosophers such as Immanuel Kant, who described, for example, Africans as lazy.

THE BEGINNINGS OF RACE PSYCHOLOGY

The application of and the appeal to science introduced the second period of race psychology, when scientific observations were combined with the ideology of race. Johann Friedrich Blumenbach advanced the concept of the Caucasian based on his idea that European culture did not originate in Africa but was born in the Caucasus. Based on an analysis of skulls, he concluded that the prototype of the Caucasian could be recognized in the beautiful skull of a Georgian woman, with Georgia being located in the Caucasus. The term *Caucasian,* still used in empirical studies of psychology, has, however, no scientific meaning at all. In the second half of the 19th century, some European scholars suggested that the Caucasian variety divided into two branches, identified as Semites and Aryans. Both were associated with different psychological characteristics and formed the theoretical basis for German fascism and the race psychology of Hitler's regime. The second half of the 19th century also saw the association of mental ability and race. In the 1860s, John Langdon H. Down studied the structure and function of various organs in *idiots* and *imbeciles.* One group he observed was characterized by round faces, flattened skulls, extra folds of skin over the eyelids, protruding tongues, short limbs, and the retardation of motor and mental abilities. Down went on to classify this group on the basis of their resemblance to racial groups. He was convinced that the facial features and behavioral attributes of these individuals represented typical Mongols—hence his term *mongolism* for what is now called *Down syndrome* (trisomy 21). Pioneer of social psychology Gustav Le Bon combined intellectual ability, emotion, and volition with an ideology of race. Races were for him physiologically and psychologically distinct entities, and because all members of a race share an immutable race soul, races were conceived as different species. Eminent figures in the history of psychology participated in scientific racism and race psychology. Paul Broca was convinced that non-European races were inferior and used a variety of scientific tools to prove his preconceived conviction. Francis Galton showed contempt for Africans in his expeditions and writings. He argued that Europeans were by nature more intelligent than so-called primitive races and suggested the quantification of levels of racial intelligence. In the United States, pioneers of psychology such as Granville Stanley Hall, first president of the American Psychological Association, argued that "lower races" were in a state of adolescence, a claim that provided the rationale for segregation and the separate education of African Americans, First Nations people, and European Americans. From a theoretical point of view, the appropriation of Darwin's theory provided a tool for justifying colonialism because it was seen as the struggle between races. (Northern) Europeans were understood as the champions of evolution.

THE HEYDAY OF RACE PSYCHOLOGY

Empirical race psychology was most prominent during the first half of the 20th century. Race psychologists of that time used the accepted methods of the discipline and applied them to the empirical comparison of various races. An early example is the research that emerged from the Cambridge Torres Straits Expedition, the psychological results of which were published at the beginning of the 20th century and concerned mostly psychophysiological data on racial differences. Many race-psychological studies were used to demonstrate the inferiority of certain races and thus were part of the project of *scientific racism.* Among the other issues covered by race psychologists were immigration and the fear of the decline of national stock. Psychologists participated in empirically evidencing the inferiority of Southern and Eastern Europeans and African Americans. Based on a huge amount of empirical data, specifically the results of the Army Mental Tests, administered to 1.75 million recruits during World War I, it was concluded that there were inborn racial differences between European Americans and African Americans, and between various European races. Psychological studies played a significant role in the Immigration Restriction Act of 1924, which imposed quotas on so-called less intelligent ethnic groups from Europe. Leading American psychologists, including American Psychological Association president Robert M. Yerkes, who played a decisive role in the army testing, and Lewis Terman, who supported segregated education, participated in race psychology. Popular in race psychology was also the study of the mulatto hypothesis, which suggested that more European American blood in one's African American ancestry led to higher intelligence. Empirical psychological studies divided subjects into *dark children, medium-in-color children,* and *light-colored children;* or into *pure negroes, negroes three-fourths pure, mulattoes proper,* and *quadroons;* or into *pure Indian blood, three-quarters Indian blood, one-half Indian blood,* and *one-quarter Indian blood.* Most of the empirical studies executed during this period were unable to overcome prejudicial ideas and were grounded in the project of scientific racism. Empirical studies often found differences, but these differences, if they were real, did not speak for themselves and were interpreted in racist terms. They were understood as natural differences between races and seldom as cultural variations. Empirical studies were also unable to challenge the cultural meaning of psychological instruments, concepts, theories, and methods. The results of empirical race psychology were presented as scientific knowledge, and this situation continued to some extent into the second half of the 20th century. In particular, studies on differences between races in intelligence continue a racist legacy when differences are interpreted as representing essential racial divisions or when ideas of inferiority and superiority are invoked.

THE DECLINE OF RACE PSYCHOLOGY

After World War II and the international recognition that racism was an essential component of the atrocities committed in the name of racial superiority in Europe and Asia, empirical race psychology, which could not overcome its racist connotations, declined. In social psychology, the shift from race psychology to the study of prejudice was completed. Although not generally acknowledged in psychology, the move from understanding race as a natural and biological category to viewing it as a social and historical concept was also significant. This reconceptualization was partially inaugurated through the advancement of genetic analyses that showed that the variation *within* traditionally conceptualized races is much larger than between them. Empirical studies that include race as a variable are now often motivated by the idea that a sociohistorical concept of race should be taken into account when making generalizations in psychology. In fact, the concept of race has been abandoned in favor of the concept of ethnicity, and empirical differences are not interpreted as inborn and reflecting a natural hierarchy but as differences that must be understood in the context of the multicultural reality of North America. Empirical race psychology also demonstrates that scientific methods are not sufficient to prevent bias, prejudice, and racism. In fact, empirical methods were used to support racism. Race psychology has participated in epistemic violence, meaning that knowledge has been produced to shape negatively the lives, health, and opportunities of minorities. Challenges to the concept of race will emerge from studies of the human genome, which might lead to the transformation of race psychology into population psychology. However, a postcolonial psychology must move from conceptualizing race as a problem to understanding and identifying the problems that ethnic minorities encounter within a dominant sociocultural context.

—*Thomas Teo*

FURTHER READING

Bindmann, D. (2002). *Ape to Apollo: Aesthetics and the idea of race in the 18th century.* Ithaca, NY: Cornell University Press.

Jackson, J. P., & Weidman, N. M. (2004). *Race, racism, and science: Social impact and interaction.* Santa Barbara, CA: ABC-CLIO.

Richards, G. (1997). *"Race," racism and psychology: Towards a reflexive history.* London: Routledge.

Tucker, W. H. (1994). *The science and politics of racial research.* Urbana, IL: University of Illinois Press.

Winston, A. (Ed.). (2004). *Defining difference: Race and racism in the history of psychology.* Washington, DC: American Psychological Association.

RACIAL IDENTITY DEVELOPMENT

Researchers have long been intrigued by the processes by which young children transform nascent notions of race into mature identities in a racialized sociocultural context. Research on racial identity dates back more than 50 years and has produced findings that have influenced profound changes in social policy in the United States. Specifically, seminal studies by Kenneth and Mamie Clark were cited in support of the landmark 1954 U.S. Supreme Court decision *Brown v. Board of Education,* which concluded that segregated schools were not equal, resulting in the court order to desegregate public schools throughout the United States.

RACIAL IDENTITY DEVELOPMENT THEORIES

Below is a brief overview of theories explaining racial identity development. Within this literature, two overarching theoretical approaches have been used to conceptualize racial identity development. The first approach applies developmental theories to account for maturational changes in racial identity from early childhood through adolescence and includes work by Frances Aboud, Jean Phinney, and Stephen Quintana. This approach applies developmental principles discovered in other domains of children's functioning to

conceptualize children's understanding of race. For example, Aboud applied neo-Piagetian theories concerning children's understanding of their social world to explain the development of their understanding of their racial world.

The second approach, framing racial identity from a social identity perspective using Henri Tajfel's theory, suggests that racial identity is affected by many factors associated with the dynamics of social identification with a group. Research for the second approach includes seminal work by Kenneth and Mamie Clark and, more recently, by Robert Sellers. Social identity theory suggests that specific social dynamics occur when someone identifies with a group. For example, identification with a group leads to bias toward the in-group and against out-groups. Racial identity theorists have shown that the identification with a racial group, particularly when that racial group is stigmatized, is associated with the formation of particular attitudes toward the racial in-group and toward racial out-groups. Social identity theory describes the social and personal effects of belonging to a group, where *identity* is developed through membership in a group that is valuable to the individual. This theory also posits that identification with group membership can increase self-esteem and the sense of positive racial attitudes to an in-group. Social identity theory has been successfully applied to the study of racial identity and has been empirically supported for separate groups, including Hispanic Americans, Asian Americans, and African Americans.

Taken together, these two overarching theoretical approaches suggest that racial identity development is influenced by the maturation of cognitive and psychological processes internal to the child or adolescent and by the child or adolescent's context of complex sociocultural group dynamics. Most racial identity theories integrate both developmental and social identity perspectives but do so with different emphases. Quintana's model is used below to identify critical milestones in racial identity development.

Early Childhood

During preschool and early elementary grades, children's understanding of their social world is based on their observation of physical features. Consequently, children's understanding of race and ethnicity is based on their observation of the physical features associated with race, including skin color, facial features, and hair texture. Aboud has noted that very young children fail to understand that racial status is constant despite superficial changes in persons' appearance (e.g., clothing), which is analogous to Piaget's finding that young children lack object permanence. For example, physical appearances can mislead children about the constancy of substances when liquid is poured from a tall and narrow container to a short and wide container, giving the appearance that there is less liquid in the second container. Hence, young children can be misled by physical appearance of racial and social activity. To illustrate, during early childhood, children sometimes coin their own racial terms that are reflective of physical appearances, such as *brown* instead of *Black* to refer to African Americans.

Some of the most famous research on children's racial identity was performed in the late 1930s and through the 1940s by Kenneth and Mamie Clark, based on the tendency for young children to view race based on physical features. These researchers used dolls that differed in physical features, namely skin color, to explore the self-concept of African American children based on their preferences to play with either an African American or European American doll. These studies focused on the social identity of African American children when comparing themselves with a European American out-group. They found that African American children preferred same-race dolls at significantly lower rates than European American children did, suggesting to them that African American children had racial self-hatred. A conclusion drawn from these early doll preferences was that African American children internalized the negative stereotypes attributed to their racial group. These studies suggest that sociocultural messages about race influence preschool-aged children's social identity as early as 3 years of age. As mentioned above, these findings were used to support the famous U.S. Supreme Court argument that segregated schools negatively affected African American children's educational and psychological adjustment.

Subsequent research by Frances Aboud and Lawrence Hirschfeld has shown that early childhood, particularly for European American children, is marked by strong racial prejudices. Interestingly, this early racial prejudice does not seem to influence young children's actual social behavior or behavioral preferences for playmates. Rather, this early prejudice appears to reflect children's immature level of cognitive

development. That is, young children's cognitions are characterized by dualistic thinking in which groups of people are viewed either positively or negatively, so that if one group is positive, then a different group is assumed to be negative. This artifact of young children's cognitive functioning is believed to account, in part, for this early racial bias.

Middle Childhood

Quintana has suggested there is a reduction in young children's reliance on their observations of physical features to understand race across the early elementary school grades, when they rely increasingly on literal features to define their racial status. For example, during early childhood, children identify their racial status based on skin color or other physical features, but during middle childhood, children identify their own and others' racial status based on ancestry. Concomitant to this development, children acquire racial constancy, which is the understanding that their racial status remains constant despite superficial changes in appearance. Aboud also suggested that children during middle childhood develop a more flexible and less dualistic cognitive style in their appraisal of their own and other racial groups. That is, they can understand that there may be positive and negative characteristics associated with racial groups. The consequence of this cognitive development is that there is a reduction in the racial prejudice present in European American children earlier in childhood and these children develop a more complex understanding of their own and other racial groups.

During middle childhood, children emphasize cultural features (e.g., language, customs, or place of residence) to define ethnic and racial status. Martha Bernal and her colleagues have identified milestones associated with Mexican American children's ethnic identity based on their understanding of several cultural features, which includes knowledge about the cultural traditions of their ethnic or racial group and their racial feelings and preferences.

Preadolescence

Starting in the latter half of elementary school grades, youth gain a social perspective on their racial identity. It is at this age that youth are able to view themselves through the eyes of others. Whereas younger children tend to conceptualize their racial identity based primarily on either physical (e.g., skin color) or literal (e.g., ancestry) features, older youth supplement these perspectives with awareness of the implications of racial status for social interactions. Specifically, youth are aware that mundane social activities are influenced by racial identity and attitudes, and this awareness includes, for example, greater comprehension of the prevalence of racial prejudice and stereotyping. For example, youth are more able to understand that their teachers and peers, as well as police officers and other authorities, may manifest racial bias and discrimination.

The advance in youth's social cognitive skills associated with the increased ability to take a social perspective on their racial worlds corresponds to an important stage in William E. Cross Jr.'s racial identity model. Cross suggested African Americans first adopt, early in life, an unexamined racial identity and ideology that tends to minimize the role of racism in their own and other African Americans' lives and may involve a racial self-hatred and miseducation about racial issues. This racial identity appears similar to the racial self-hatred that was described in the early Clark and Clark research. At some point, African Americans are confronted with an encounter experience in which they are discriminated against by European Americans and begin to comprehend more fully how racism has influenced their lives. Although this encounter experience may not occur until later in adolescence or even adulthood, the social-cognitive ability to have a social perspective on racial identity provides a cognitive foundation for a transformative encounter experience. That is, the cognitive ability to see themselves through the eyes of others allows African American youth to understand how many European Americans view them in a prejudicial or discriminatory manner, which is an important component of Cross's description of the encounter experience.

Adolescence

Dramatic changes in racial identity development occur during adolescence, according to several theorists. Quintana described the milestone of adolescence as the development of an ethnic or racial group consciousness. This racial consciousness involves a merger between a personal and racial group identity, in which the sense of self is strongly connected to the adolescent's racial group. This advance in social-cognitive abilities is believed to set the stage for identity exploration, which is a critical stage in two theories of racial identity discussed in the following paragraphs.

Drawing on Erik Erikson and James Marcia's theories of ego identity development, Phinney proposed an analogous sequence for ethnic identity development. Marcia described the process of identity achievement as starting with either *identity diffusion,* in which the adolescent has only a vague sense of self, or *identity foreclosure,* in which the adolescent is committed to, without questioning, the self-identity he or she has had since childhood, which has been influenced largely by parents and family. At some point, many adolescents begin questioning their sense of self or identity and exploring alternative identities, which is considered *identity moratorium.* A successful resolution of an identity search or moratorium would result in *identity achievement* in which the adolescent had a strong commitment to a more authentic sense of self than experienced during identity foreclosure. Phinney applied these different kinds of identity status to ethnic identity development, in which adolescents moved from an unexamined commitment to an ethnic identity (ethnic identity foreclosure) or diffuse/weak sense of ethnic identity (ethnic identity diffusion) into an active search and exploration of their sense of ethnicity and race (ethnic identity search). Adolescents' commitment to an ethnic identity after a search was considered ethnic identity achievement.

Cross's racial identity development for African Americans follows a similar rhythm of development, from an unexamined racial identity (preencounter) through a crisis (encounter), through search and exploration of racial identity (immersion-emersion), to an achieved, integrated identity (identity internalization). To elaborate, a tenet of Cross's model is that ineffective early identities, denying the role of racism in African Americans' lives, are questioned and then reformulated as encounter experiences are integrated into their racial identity. As mentioned above, the preencounter stage involves unexamined racial attitudes in which the role of racism is minimized. The encounter stage of racial identity is a state of confusion when African Americans experience racialized oppression from European Americans. When individuals move out of the confusion of the encounter stage, they enter the immersion-emersion stage. In this stage there is a decrease in the amount of interactions with European Americans and an immersion or deep interest in African American culture. This immersion stage is when African Americans explore their racial identity in a more positive manner than during the preencounter stage. As individuals gain a deeper appreciation of being African American and forge a secure racial identity, they enter the final stage, internalization. This stage corresponds to a process by which African Americans gain a broader multicultural perspective in relation to other ethnic and racial groups. It is important to mention that Cross's model of racial identity development incorporates important aspects of the social identity approach. These aspects include the saliency of in-group experience from an out-group perspective, the subsequent affiliation with each group, and the emerging attitudes about the groups during the stages.

Subsequently, Cross's model became the framework for other models of racial identity development (e.g., Kim's model of Asian American identity development and Janet Helms's model of European American racial identity development). The stages in these models progress from an initial unexamined affiliation with majority European American culture, to a strong affiliation with minority-group cultures, followed by a broader acceptance of all ethnic or racial groups, transcending racial oppression. Additionally, these models include a conflict stage, which occurs directly as a response to experiences with and awareness of racial oppression. Cross has made several modifications to his original model, but he retained much of the rhythm of development described above.

A new direction in the research on racial identity has used a strictly social identity approach, which indicates the importance of individual differences within racial groups. The most apparent deviation from the stage model uses a social identity framework for conceptualizing racial identity. The Multidimensional Inventory of Black Identity (MIBI) of Robert Sellers, deriving from the broader multidimensional model of racial identity (MMRI), considers that individuals can identify with multiple salient group memberships (e.g., gender, age, occupation), with race being one, but not necessarily the most salient one. The MMRI also states that racial identity comprises both transient and stable characteristics and that these interact to influence behavior choice. It breaks away from other models in that it does not attribute certain attitudes and beliefs monolithically to an entire group. Rather, the MMRI allows individuals to determine how they identify and what meaning this identification represents to them. The MMRI also allows for different predictions based on the number and salience of different identities. If, for example, a person's central identity is African American, then it is likely that this person's behavior will conform more to racially based preferences (e.g., friendships) than will the behavior of another person for whom racial identity is less central, relative to other identities. This is important because there are no specific sets of behaviors that are enacted by one racial group, although it may be possible to predict some choices of behaviors and the meaning of those when one identity is more salient over the others.

A brief summary of the major models reviewed above is listed in Table 1. The table lists the relative emphasis given to developmental and social identity theories in each of these models.

EMPIRICAL EVALUATION OF RACIAL IDENTITY DEVELOPMENT

Important empirical evaluations of the theoretical models of racial identity development have involved some combination of developmental and social identity theories. Probably not surprisingly, research reveals strong support for the progressions of developmental models. Interestingly, research into these more developmentally based models tends to reveal less support for the influence of sociocultural influences on racial identity development. For example, Aboud's cognitive-development model of racial identity development and Quintana's ethnic perspective-taking models have shown strong connections to chronological age, as well as to other measures of cognitive development. These models have, however, shown less connection to sociocultural variables, such as level of acculturation. Quintana theorized that relatively little cultural stimulation may be needed to support movement across the racial identity models based on cognitive development, as long as the children had the requisite cognitive skills.

Conversely, the models that are based more on social identity theory reveal less of a developmental progression related to chronological age, but they are strongly connected to indices of the sociocultural factors. For example, identity exploration in Phinney's model has shown a weak, albeit significant, correlation with age and other measures of development. On the other hand, scores on Phinney's measures of identity affiliation have shown strong connections to adolescents' sociocultural backgrounds.

Table 1   Racial Identity Models

Author	Framework[a]	Tenet of Model
Clark & Clark	SI	Racism and other negative societal messages lead to the internalization of these messages and self-hatred
Aboud	D	Racial identity and cognitions determined by level of cognitive development
Quintana	D/SI	Understanding of racial identity influence by level of social-perspective-taking ability in sociocultural context
Phinney	SI/D	Ethnic and racial identity influenced by exploration and commitment
Cross	SI/D	Racism and oppression delineate a shift from a naive affiliation with European Americans to an immersion in African American culture, leading to an acceptance of all groups that transcends the experienced racism
Sellers	SI	Individuals are a combination of multiple group identities, some more salient than others according to the given environment

Source: Author. The table is reprinted with permission. Copyright © by Stephen M. Quintana.

[a]D = Developmental; SI = Social Identity.

Similarly, since the emergence of Cross's model, numerous quantitative studies have found support for his and other, related models of racial identity within the United States and throughout other parts of the world. This support indicates that the models account for important differences within racial groups. Conversely, the limitations indicate that the assumption of development across the stages has received, at best, weak support thus far in the literature. Moreover, racial identity stages may not represent a sequential and linear process for all individuals.

Researchers have mentioned several other limitations of the models of racial identity development, including lack of evidence supporting distinctiveness of the stages in Cross's and Helms's models, a reliance on understanding minority development in relation to outside groups, and a finding that the models do not adequately consider how other salient aspects of identity, such as physical disability or sexual orientation, interact with racial identity. Because of these limitations, more research should be done on racial identity development, given that some of these limitations may result from the lack of longitudinal research that has been done on these processes of racial identity.

FUTURE DIRECTIONS FOR RACIAL IDENTITY THEORY AND RESEARCH

The emergence of a social identity lens through which to examine racial identity development calls into question whether racial identity is a developmental process or a situation-specific set of identities. The theories and research do not delineate a clear answer; however, it may be helpful to understand that all the salient groups with which one identifies are learned through interactions with others and the messages received, as well as based on the development of cognitive and psychological processes. Therefore, there may be room for the convergence of these two approaches to conceptualizing racial identity. This is an exciting prospect because of some initial extensions of the theories using aspects of both the developmental and social identity theoretical approaches. These include Donald Atkinson and colleagues' model for minority identity development and Gushue's extension of Helms's model in family therapy and subsequent development of a nondominant culture identity development model.

Another avenue being explored by the current research on racial identity development is the study of a biracial identity development. Whether identifying as a member of two minority races, such as African American and Native American, or as from a majority and minority race, biracial individuals, particularly children, are presented with another set of factors. Racial identity development may be difficult for biracial children when their physical appearances differ substantially from that of their parents or if the children feel pressure to affiliate with one racial group over another. In addition, a biracial family may be contending with a history of oppression between or across the two or more races represented within the family.

With the significance society places on race, racial identity development cannot be ignored when working with any client in psychotherapy. Because everyone belongs to one or more racial groups and has had some interaction with other groups, it is important to determine the client's progression of racial identity development to understand his or her worldview and effect appropriate treatment and techniques.

—*Stephen M. Quintana*
—*Ruth Montero*

See also Race; Racism and Discrimination

FURTHER READING

Abrams, D., Rutland, A., & Cameron, L. (2003). The development of subjective group dynamics: Children's judgments of normative and deviant in-group and out-group individuals. *Child Development, 74,* 1840–1856.

Clark, K. B., & Clark, M. P. (1947). Racial identification and preference in Negro children. In T. M. Newcomb & E. L. Hartley (Eds.), *Readings in social psychology* (pp. 169–178). New York: Holt.

Cross, W. E., & Strauss, L. (1998). The everyday functions of African American identity. In J. K. Swim & C. Stangor (Eds.), *Prejudice: The target's perspective* (pp. 267–279). San Diego: Academic Press.

Erikson, E. (1968). *Identity: Youth and crisis.* New York: Norton.

Hirschfeld, L. A. (1994). The child's representation of human groups. *The Psychology of Learning and Motivation, 31,* 133–185.

Quintana, S. M. (1998). Children's developmental understanding of ethnicity and race. *Applied and Preventive Psychology, 7,* 27–45.

Roberts, R. E., Phinney, J. S., Masse, L. C., Chen, Y. R., Roberts, C. R., & Romero, A. (1999). The structure of ethnic identity of young adolescents from diverse ethnocultural groups. *Journal of Early Adolescence, 19,* 301–322.

Tajfel, H., & Turner, J. (1986). The social identity theory of intergroup behavior. In S. Worchel & W. Austin (Eds.), *Psychology of intergroup relations* (pp. 7–24). Chicago: Nelson-Hall.

RACIAL IDENTITY MODELS

A number of racial identity models have been proposed to explain how people develop racial identity. These models were originally developed to understand experiences of African Americans and then expanded to other racial groups in the United States. Many of them conceptualize racial identity development as a series of stages in which individuals change their attitudes and internalized images of their own racial group and other groups. Racial identity models are often used to aid counseling and research. Following are some of the major racial identity models.

CROSS'S NIGRESCENCE MODEL

This is a five-stage racial identity model for African Americans that describes a process of transformation from a negative attitude toward one's own race to a positive one, through racial identity exploration. This model is a basis for many racial identity models.

1. *Preencounter stage.* Individuals lack conscious awareness of what race means to them and idealize the dominant European American culture. They attempt to assimilate into European American culture and distance themselves from African American culture.

2. *Encounter.* Emotional events, such as experience of discrimination, force them to acknowledge the impact of race on their lives and to question their previous beliefs. Active exploration of racial identity begins.

3. *Immersion/Emersion.* They engage in intense immersion in African American culture and idealize it, while withdrawing from and holding anger and hostility toward European American culture. As their anger and hostility subside and a more balanced view toward African American culture develops, they emerge from the intense immersion.

4. *Internalization.* Secure and positive internalization of African American identity develops. They become capable of establishing relationships with European Americans while maintaining connections with African American culture.

5. *Internalization-Commitment.* Individuals put their attitudes and beliefs about race into action (e.g., political activities to confront racism).

ATKINSON, MORTEN, AND SUE'S RACIAL/CULTURAL IDENTITY DEVELOPMENT MODEL

This is a five-stage model for people of color, including Latino Americans, Asian Americans, and Native

Americans. It was developed based on Cross's model, and the stages portray changes in attitudes and beliefs regarding self, others of the same ethnic group, others of different ethnic minority groups, and the dominant group.

1. *Conformity.* Individuals prefer the dominant culture and have a negative attitude toward their own ethnic group and other ethnic minority groups.

2. *Dissonance.* They experience conflict between appreciating and depreciating attitudes for their own group, other ethnic minority groups, and the dominant group.

3. *Resistance and Immersion.* They attempt to learn more about their own group's culture and history and develop appreciation toward their group, while rejecting the dominant culture. Their attitudes toward other ethnic minority groups are conflicting.

4. *Introspection.* Individuals feel discomfort with their rigid views about groups from the previous stage. They start to feel more comfortable with their racial/cultural identity, and their attention focuses more on individual autonomy.

5. *Synergistic.* As a result of resolved conflicts from the previous stage, they experience a sense of accomplishment regarding their racial/cultural identity. Now they have appreciation toward self, their own group, and other ethnic minority groups, and a selective appreciation toward the dominant group.

HELMS'S PEOPLE OF COLOR RACIAL IDENTITY MODEL

This model was developed based on the above two models, and its structure and conceptualization are similar to them, with slightly different names for some of the statuses. It was developed for people of color and has been applied to many racial/ethnic groups.

1. *Conformity.* Individuals idealize European American culture and denigrate their own group. They are not aware of what race means to them.

2. *Dissonance.* They experience ambivalence and confusion regarding their own and society's definitions of race.

3. *Immersion/Emersion.* Individuals idealize and try to learn more about their own culture and denigrate European American culture.

4. *Internalization.* Individuals develop a positive racial identity, as well as balanced and objective views of European American culture.

5. *Integrative Awareness.* In addition to appreciation of their race, they are capable of integrating their racial identity with other aspects of self-identity. They also develop empathy for other oppressed groups.

HELMS'S WHITE RACIAL IDENTITY DEVELOPMENT MODEL

Although most racial identity models focus on people of color, this six-stage racial identity model was developed for European Americans. Through these stages, individuals' attitudes and behaviors toward their own and other racial groups change. To achieve a healthy racial identity, they need to abandon racism, understand what their race means to them, and internalize a positive view about their race.

1. *Contact.* Individuals are oblivious to the existence of racism and their race's privilege. Their attitudes and beliefs about people of color are based on external input (e.g., media, family).

2. *Disintegration.* Individuals experience guilt, shame, and anger as they become aware of their group's role in maintaining racism. To reduce this discomfort, they may deny the existence of racism, avoid contact with people of color, or try to change significant others' attitudes toward people of color.

3. *Reintegration.* They idealize their racial group and justify racism by claiming that racism exists because people of color are inferior. Their guilt and anger are redirected toward people of color.

4. *Pseudo-independent.* Individuals start to question their previously held racist views. Although they no longer hold the belief in European American superiority, they still apply this belief without being aware of it, performing actions such as trying to change people of color to eliminate racism. Their racial identity at this stage is neither negative nor positive.

5. *Immersion/Emersion.* To be more comfortable with and to redefine their racial identity, they actively explore their racial identity and seek information about their group's history and culture. They focus more on changing their own racial group to combat racism.

6. *Autonomy.* As a result of successful exploration, internalization of a positive and secure racial identity is achieved. Individuals engage in activities to confront racism and other types of oppression. Their view about race and culture is more balanced.

PHINNEY'S THREE-STAGE ETHNIC IDENTITY DEVELOPMENT MODEL

This is a three-stage ethnic identity model for adolescents from all ethnic groups, based on ego identity development models and other racial/ethnic identity models. These stages are differentiated based on presence and/or absence of exploration and achievement of ethnic identity.

1. *Unexamined Ethnic Identity.* This stage is characterized by a lack of exploration and search for ethnic identity. Individuals do not have any interest in ethnicity, or they accept views about their ethnic group that were provided by people around them (e.g., parents).

2. *Ethnic Identity Search.* This stage involves search and exploration of ethnic identity, and individuals in this stage try to understand what ethnicity means to them by participating in cultural events and learning the history of their ethnic group.

3. *Achieved Ethnic Identity.* As a result of a successful exploration, individuals resolve uncertainty about their ethnic identity and attain a clear understanding of what their ethnicity means to them.

RUIZ'S CHICANO/LATINO ETHNIC IDENTITY MODEL

Some ethnic identity models were developed for a specific ethnic group, and this is one of the examples. This model is tailored to the Chicano/Latino population, and

it provides clinical implications for therapists. Five stages describe ethnic identity conflicts and resolutions, as well as recommended interventions for each stage.

1. *Causal.* Sources of ethnic identity conflicts include parental messages, failure to identify with or rejection from one's ethnic group, and confusion or lack of familiarity with one's culture.

2. *Cognitive.* Faulty beliefs about ethnicity are held, such as associating ethnic group membership with poverty and prejudice and the belief that assimilation is the only way to succeed in life.

3. *Consequence.* Fragmentation of ethnic identity occurs. Ethnic identity conflicts are intensified, and the use of defense mechanisms to manage the conflicts increases.

4. *Working-Through.* Increased willingness to enter counseling or disclose concerns related to ethnicity because distress associated with ethnic conflicts cannot be handled well. Increase in ethnic consciousness, reintegration of fragmented ethnic identity, and a reconnection with ethnic community occur.

5. *Successful Resolution.* Greater acceptance of self, culture, and ethnicity; improvement in self-esteem; and a positive internalization of ethnic identity are achieved.

—*Shihoko Hijioka*

See also Ethnic Identity Development; Racial Identity Development

FURTHER READING

Atkinson, D. R., Morten, G., & Sue, D. W. (1993). *Counseling American minorities: A cross-cultural perspective* (4th ed.). Madison, WI: William C. Brown.

Cross, W. E. (1971). The Negro-to-Black conversion experience: Towards psychology of Black liberation. *Black World, 20,* 13–27.

Cross, W. E. (1995). The psychology of nigrescence: Revising the Cross model. In J. G. Ponterotto, J. M. Casas, L. A. Suzuki, & C. M. Alexander (Eds.), *Handbook of multicultural counseling* (pp. 93–122). Thousand Oaks, CA: Sage.

Helms, J. E. (1990). Toward a model of White racial identity development. In J. E. Helms (Ed.), *Black and White racial identity: Theory, research, and practice* (pp. 49–66). New York: Greenwood Press.

Helms, J. E. (1995). An update on Helms's White and people of color racial identity models. In J. G. Ponterotto, J. M. Casas, L. A. Suzuki, & C. M. Alexander (Eds.), *Handbook of multicultural counseling* (pp. 181–198). Thousand Oaks, CA: Sage.

Phinney, J. S. (1993). A three-stage model of ethnic identity development in adolescence. In M. E. Bernal & G. P. Knight (Eds.), *Ethnic identity: Formation and transmission among Hispanics and other minorities* (pp. 61–79). Albany: State University of New York Press.

Ruiz, A. S. (1990). Ethnic identity: Crisis and resolution. *Journal of Multicultural Counseling and Development, 18,* 29–40.

RACISM AND DISCRIMINATION

Racism can be defined as a system of oppression based on racial/ethnic group designations in which a pervasive ideology of racial superiority and inferiority provides the foundation for structural inequalities, intergroup conflict, discrimination, and prejudice. Racism, like all systems of oppression (e.g., sexism, classism, heterosexism/homophobia, ageism), is based on power asymmetries such that the dominant group is granted unearned privileges, such as respect and esteem, social validation and affirmation, opportunities and rewards, freedoms and safety, and greater access to valued societal resources.

Racial discrimination, prejudice, and stereotypes are the building blocks as well as the products of racism. *Stereotypes* are cognitive overgeneralizations, the labels associated with different groups. *Prejudice* is an attitude formed about a group of people without adequate evidence. When prejudgment is added to stereotypes, racial prejudice exists. *Racial discrimination* is differential treatment and behavior based on race. When action is added to racial prejudice, discriminatory behaviors are manifested. Racism is a systemic process. When power asymmetry is added to racial discrimination, the system of racism is operating.

Racial discrimination involves the expression of beliefs and attitudes rooted in racism. Discrimination includes major civil rights violations and illegal activities such as hate crimes, racial harassment, racial profiling, and job discrimination. Racial discrimination also includes everyday racism—day-to-day differential treatment such as a clerk or security employee following a member of a minority group around a department store with suspicion, a teacher calling on students of color less frequently, or the single racial/ethnic minority person in a group being marginalized or left out of a conversation. Discrimination can be intentional or unintentional, conscious or unconscious. The result of the behavior is racial discrimination, regardless of motivation, intentionality, or consciousness.

Racism and discrimination are manifested at multiple levels, including cultural, institutional, interpersonal, and individual. Racism and discrimination at the cultural level are reflected in the ideology of European American supremacy and can be seen in the cultural expressions and products of a society, such as art, literature, science, cinema, values, and standards of beauty and attractiveness. Racism and discrimination at the institutional level are expressed through the structures, policies, and practices of societal institutions such as the criminal justice, education, health care, political, and economic systems. Systematic disparities between racial/ethnic groups on outcomes reflect institutional racism. Racism and discrimination at the interpersonal level can be seen in interactions between individuals and relations between groups. Racism at the individual level is expressed in the beliefs, attitudes, and discriminatory behaviors of people.

RACISM AND THE FIELD OF PSYCHOLOGY

The ideology of racism has been embedded in psychological theory and research since its inception and continues to influence what is considered normal or abnormal, healthy or maladaptive, functional or dysfunctional. Within the field of psychology, racial difference studies on characteristics such as intelligence, aggression, alcohol use, and sexuality have contributed to the perpetuation of widespread beliefs in the superiority of European Americans, at worst, and European Americans as the normative standard, at best. Identifying healthy psychological functioning has historically been through the observation of the cognitive, affective, and behavioral status of heterosexual European American men. Differences from this norm have traditionally been viewed as indicating deviance or deficit.

Scientific racism is the use of research to demonstrate the innate inferiority or superiority of different racial groups and provide evidence to support racist ideology. Classification of human beings according to race is a creation of science, not of nature. However, scientific racism assumes biological determinism, that there are consistent and innate biological differences between racial groups. For nearly two centuries, attempts have been made by science to support racism through racial differences research. Psychological research has contributed to scientific racism and has been used to try to bring credibility to beliefs in the inferiority and deviance of targeted racial/ethnic groups, particularly African Americans, Native Americans, and Latino Americans.

Racial/ethnic minorities continue to be underrepresented in the field of psychology. Although there has been some progress in the number of psychotherapists and psychology professors of color, the field continues to have insufficient knowledge about the psychological functioning of or effective interventions relevant to racial/ethnic groups that are not European American. Furthermore, although knowledge is increasingly being accumulated through multicultural research, it is not effectively disseminated to current professionals, nor to students entering the field of psychology.

FORMS OF RACISM

In the psychological literature, the term *old-fashioned racism* is used to refer to explicit racial discrimination associated with the core beliefs about the inferiority and deviance of the targeted racial/ethnic group. It is associated with an endorsement of negative racial stereotypes, racial hostility, hatred, and strong advocacy for separation of the races. However, a solid body of research within social psychology suggests that contemporary manifestations of racism are more common than old-fashioned racism. These include symbolic racism, modern racism, and aversive racism.

Symbolic racism refers to racist beliefs that are socialized early in life but are acted out symbolically through a political issue, such as resistance to affirmative action or opposition to busing, rather than through direct advocacy for racial segregation. *Modern racism* also involves the displacement of racist beliefs onto abstract sociopolitical issues with a simultaneous lack of awareness of racist feelings.

Aversive racism is characterized by racial ambivalence that includes an aversion to outwardly expressed racist attitudes and a simultaneous discomfort with racial/ethnic minorities. It involves the embracing of egalitarian values, rejection of racial stereotypes, and a low frequency of overt discriminatory behaviors. However, there exists a great deal of anxiety and underlying negative feelings toward the target racial/ethnic

group that is expressed in subtle, indirect, and rationalizable ways. Unintentional discriminatory behaviors are expressed that benefit European Americans and disadvantage racial/ethnic minority groups, perpetuating the continuation of power asymmetries and social disparities. Symbolic and modern racism are associated with a conservative political orientation, and aversive racism is associated with a liberal political orientation.

Racism also has been examined in its relationship to psychopathology. Early studies attempted to identify a racist personality and focused on the study of the authoritarian personality as a characterological structure that included the devaluing of out-groups considered to be inferior. Racism also has been conceptualized as itself a diagnosable disease or disorder characterized by maladaptive defenses to manage anxiety. The anxiety is rooted in underlying guilt and shame regarding the existence of racism, as well as societal and individual silence and collusion. It is suggested that cognitive dissonance emerges from the national identity of "freedom and justice for all" existing alongside an awareness that interpersonal and institutional racism continue to perpetuate disparities and despair. Rationalization, minimization, projection, intellectualization, and denial operate to distort the reality of racism, which is too painful to confront, and create functional impairments in multiracial settings.

Among the most intense behavioral manifestations of racism are hate crimes and discriminatory violence. Physical attacks, verbal assaults, vandalism, harassment, and other hate-motivated acts of violence continue to be perpetrated against people of color and immigrant groups. Hate crimes against persons or property include words and/or actions that are intended to intimidate, humiliate, or do harm to members of a targeted group. Hate crimes reflect contempt and disdain for members of the group, with specific motivations of sending a message, teaching a lesson, or making an example of one or more individuals. Research suggests that racially motivated hate crimes are most often triggered by a sense of territorial threat; interracial marriage, dating, or sex; perceived cultural encroachment; or anti-immigration sentiments. Hate crimes create a social atmosphere characterized by a lack of safety and protection for members of targeted groups.

The phenomena of internalized racism and intragroup discrimination have received more theoretical than empirical attention in the psychological literature. In an attempt to protect themselves against racism, members of targeted racial/ethnic groups reject, put down, distance from, and exclude members of their own group while idealizing, seeking the approval of, and giving preferential treatment to European Americans. *Colorism* is a form of internalized racism in which darker-skinned members of a group are considered inferior and less attractive, and have less status, than lighter-skinned members of the group.

RACISM AND ITS TARGETS: UNDERSTANDING CONTEXTS AND EXPERIENCES OF RACISM

Racism and discrimination exist in multiple life domains, including education, employment, health care, housing, legal, leisure, commerce, media, finances, law enforcement, and interpersonal relationships. In the psychological context, racism and discrimination can be subjectively experienced as stress. *Racism-related stress* refers to the race-based transactions between people and their environments that emerge from the dynamics of racism and are perceived to tax individual and collective resources or threaten well-being. Sources of racism-related stress can be personal, vicarious, collective, or transgenerational.

Personal racism-related stress includes those experiences in which the individual is directly involved. These can be episodic events (e.g., being denied an apartment, being the victim of a hate crime), chronic conditions of living (e.g., toxic pollution reflecting environmental racism), or everyday racism experiences (e.g., microaggressions, such as being addressed with a racial epithet or being mistaken for a maid or bellboy in a hotel). *Vicarious* racism-related stress involves witnessing, observing, or hearing about others' experiences with racism and discrimination. *Collective* racism-related stress is the awareness of power asymmetries and systematic outcome disparities (e.g., health, employment) in which members of one's racial/ethnic group have less access to resources or more negative outcomes. *Transgenerational* racism-related stress includes the knowledge and ongoing vestiges of historical traumas (e.g., slavery, colonialism, internment, genocide) that have been passed down through generations.

Exposure to racism is related to a number of individual and contextual variables. These include specific racial/ethnic group membership, geographic location, gender, age, social class, sexual orientation, skin color, accent, generational status, and racial composition of the setting. For example, racism will be

experienced differently by a 25-year-old recently immigrated Pakistani man in New York City, a 70-year-old Japanese woman in a small California town, a 40-year-old Mexican American female attorney in suburban Chicago, and a 16-year-old African American boy in a predominantly European American high school in rural Connecticut.

A number of instruments were developed in the 1990s to assess racism and discrimination experiences. The most commonly used include the Index of Race-Related Stress, the Schedule of Racist Events, the Racism and Life Experience Scales, the Perceived Racism Scale, the Experience of Discrimination Questionnaire, and the Everyday Discrimination Scale. Overall, these instruments have very strong psychometric properties. They are most appropriate for research contexts. However, there are assessment, forensic, and psychotherapy applications, as well. Research using these instruments has found significant relationships between racism experiences and a number of psychological and health outcomes.

MULTIPLE EFFECTS OF RACISM AND DISCRIMINATION

Early studies conceptualized racism as leaving an inevitable mark of oppression on the psyche, leading to rage, low self-esteem, deviance, and psychopathology. Although attention to the damaging effects of racism was an important step, these early approaches reinforced a deficit-oriented perspective on the mental health of racism targets. The 1990s brought an increase in empirical studies on racism as a source of stress, and the resources and strengths that emerge in efforts to cope with living in the context of racism and discrimination.

The effects of racism and discrimination emerge in multiple areas of functioning. These include emotional, cognitive, and behavioral functioning, role performance, interpersonal relationships, identity, mental health, physical health, and spiritual well-being. The toll of the cumulative stress caused by episodic and chronic exposure to racism can last for years. However, strengths can also develop as part of the broader effects of racism and discrimination. Some of the most strongly supported effects of racism and discrimination on its targets are as follows:

Emotional. Emotional reactions to racism and discrimination can be immediate or long-term.

Immediate emotional reactions can include fear, anger, confusion, sadness, humiliation, and shame. Longer-term emotional styles can also develop in reaction to cumulative experiences of racism and discrimination. These include bitterness, hostility, numbness, irritability, apathy, pessimism, suspiciousness, and agitated hypervigilance. These emotional styles represent adaptations to living in the context of racism, and their ultimate function is protective. However, prolonged exposure to racism, for someone who may have existing psychological vulnerabilities and inadequate resources, can contribute to increased risk for psychopathology, violence, or self-destructive behaviors.

Coping Strategies and Styles. The effects of racism and discrimination can include the development of specific coping strategies, as well as general coping styles. *Racism-related coping strategies* are designed to manage the experience of racism and discrimination. These behavioral strategies can be grouped broadly according to their function, including changing the situation, changing oneself, soothing emotions, distancing or distraction, obtaining support, or collective social action. *Racism-related coping styles* develop over time and reflect a more general orientation to living in the context of racism and discrimination. Coping styles can include one or more of the following: activism (e.g., nationalistic, multicultural, antiracism), within-group affiliation, within-group rejection and European American assimilation, colorblind individualism, bicultural compartmentalization, protective isolation and avoidance, racism consciousness and vigilance, seeking European American approval, hostile separatism, and passive invisibility.

Racism-related coping fatigue can develop when significant psychic, emotional, and physiological energy is expended in attempts to manage racism. Reduced effort and less goal-directed behavior may result. Distancing behavior risks increased isolation and the exacerbation of negative effects. Apathy, depression, and decreased motivation present barriers to achievement and limit opportunities to develop both intragroup and intergroup supportive relationships.

A frequently misunderstood coping style is within-group affiliation. Targets of racism and discrimination may self-segregate with similar others as a defense against being rejected, misunderstood, or treated badly. This self-segregation can serve the adaptive function of affirming one's identity, humanity, worth, and place of belongingness in the larger context of racism and discrimination. This within-group connectedness and validation is sometimes wrongly assumed to go hand in hand with rejecting other racial groups, particularly European Americans.

Physical Health. Racism and discrimination can contribute to negative health outcomes. Much of the research on racism and physical health has focused on hypertension. Although social support may serve as a buffer, chronic exposure to racism has been associated with an increase in cardiovascular reactivity, with blood pressure remaining elevated even after the interaction has subsided. Knowledge of an incident or even imagining a racist situation seems to have the same adverse physiological consequences as experiencing it directly. Racism experiences have also been associated with increased cigarette smoking, obesity, and poor health care behaviors, increasing the risk for numerous negative health outcomes.

Mental Health Outcomes. More frequent and intense exposure to racism and discrimination increases risk for psychological distress. Studies have found experiences of racism to be related to depression, trauma-related symptoms, anxiety, relationship dysfunction, aggression, and substance abuse. These negative effects may be mediated by variables such as positive racial socialization, healthy racial identity, sociopolitical awareness, strong social support, sense of community connectedness, and access to racism-countering, affirming resources. These mediators can reduce feelings of marginality, mitigate against internalized racism, protect self-esteem, and provide alternative sources of validation.

Academic Role Functioning. Racism and discrimination can have negative effects on academic performance. Students of targeted racial/ethnic groups may have fewer visible role models of academic excellence, may internalize expectations of low achievement from school personnel, or may be tracked into non-college-bound programs of study. They also may not have the benefit of family members who can provide strong academic socialization (e.g., study tips, homework assistance). In addition, psychological reactions to stereotypes may interfere with academic performance. The phenomenon of *stereotype threat* suggests that when there is an awareness of expected low performance, actual performance may suffer.

When faced with situations in which a negative stereotype may potentially be confirmed, the subsequent increase in anxiety can contribute to the individual performing below his or her actual ability.

Identity and Self-Concept. Personal experience with racism and discrimination, or even witnessing public examples, can have a variety of effects on racial identity and self-concept. Racial identity can be compromised if one internalizes racism and develops negative beliefs about one's own racial group. Racial identity can be strengthened as a result of racism experiences when support, validation, and a broader sociopolitical understanding are present. Although retreating from racial identification may give an illusion of protection against racism and even facilitate the accomplishment of individual goals, self-hatred and internal turmoil can result. In addition, rejection of one's racial group can lead to collusion with the perpetuation of racism.

Resilience and Strengths. Racism and discrimination create adverse circumstances and have been connected to a number of negative outcomes. However, adversity provides opportunities to build strengths. Characteristics such as endurance, perseverance, passion, expressiveness, optimism, gratefulness, creativity, compassion, collectivism, spirituality, and faith can emerge. Racism and discrimination present contexts in which larger societal affirmation and encouragement may be minimal and social devaluation of one's group may be widespread. Positive psychological well-being in these contexts requires the development of inner strength and resilience in the face of ongoing negative messages about one's value and worth.

RACISM AND DISCRIMINATION IN MULTIPLE CONTEXTS

Efforts have been made to address the problem of racism and its effects across many contexts.

Racism in the Clinical Context

Racism and discrimination manifest in the clinical context in five primary ways: (1) unequal access to services, (2) clinical integration of racism experiences, (3) manifestations of the dynamics of racism within the therapeutic relationship, (4) assessment and treatment planning, and (5) use of interventions designed to provide protection and coping resources.

Unequal Access to Services. At the macrosystem level of analysis, there are systematic disparities in mental health services with respect to both quality and quantity. Racial/ethnic minority groups are less likely to receive (1) intervention at the optimal therapeutic level (e.g., number of sessions), (2) state-of-the-art psychotherapy techniques, (3) treatment from more experienced or highly trained therapists, and (4) treatment most appropriate for the presenting problem. In addition, racial/ethnic minority clients are likely to be overmedicated or inappropriately medicated and subject to waiting lists or unavailability of immediate services, and they may not receive treatment until a disorder is at more advanced stages and thus more difficult to treat. It is not clear, however, to what extent disparity in services is a function of socioeconomic status, race/ethnicity, or an interaction of both. Disentangling these factors is complex, because one of the larger societal impacts of racism is the disproportionate number of many racial/ethnic groups of color living in poverty or below the poverty line. Reducing the manifestations of racism at the macrosystem level can include advocating for sufficient quantity and quality of mental health services in culturally diverse communities, hiring experienced therapists with demonstrated expertise and effectiveness with culturally diverse groups, and encouraging supervision, consultation, and in-service training. Working to increase the presence of racial/ethnic minority psychologists and supervisors also can reduce incidents of racism and discrimination.

Clinical Integration. Clients from historically oppressed racial/ethnic groups have almost invariably been exposed to racism in one form or another (e.g., personal experience, vicarious experience, collective experience). A comprehensive understanding of a client's psychological world requires therapists to consider racism as a mental health risk factor. Overlooking the role of racism in case conceptualization risks missing critical elements of a client's life story and psychological functioning. Therapists should listen for and adequately assess a client's history of racism experiences, perceptions and attitudes about racism, and degree of internalized racism, as well the racism-related dynamics of current contexts and the styles and behavioral strategies that have been developed to cope with racism.

It is recommended that therapists be aware of their own discomfort with, minimization of, or avoidance of the topic of racism. Therapists should be cautious of interpreting the client's disclosure of racism experiences as avoidance of more important psychological issues or as a reflection of transference. A therapist's own agenda with respect to racism can also result in imposing interpretations of racism on clients. Misguided interpretations create empathic failures and risk damaging the therapeutic alliance by invalidating a client's life experience, decreasing trust and the client's sense of emotional safety, and silencing the client on an issue that may occupy a great deal of psychological space.

Dynamics of Racism in the Therapeutic Relationship. Interpersonal racism dynamics can emerge in the interaction between therapist and client. Awareness of racism-related countertransference is important and can be manifested in numerous ways. Therapists may relate to racial/ethnic minority clients in a condescending and patronizing manner or communicate disrespect, deviance, and inferiority. Therapists also may use the interracial therapy dyad as an opportunity to demonstrate that they are not racist. The need to have the client's approval, or the avoidance of any conflict with a racially different client, may indicate the therapist's underlying anxiety. Racial/ethnic minority therapists with a high degree of internalized racism may project their hostility and self-hate onto clients. Alternatively, when both client and therapist are members of racial/ethnic minority groups, there is a risk of overidentification, a need to rescue, protect, or join with the client in an us-against-them orientation.

Therapists also should be aware of racism-related transference phenomena. These include overcompliance and deferring to the therapist, behaviors that are intended to disprove racial stereotypes, and hostility toward the therapist. Racial/ethnic minority clients with high levels of internalized racism may seek to please a European American therapist and separate themselves from their own group. It is important for therapists to be cautious and resist accepting these manifestations of internalized racism. The therapeutic relationship can be damaged when a therapist takes a client's racial anger personally or reacts defensively.

Assessment and Diagnosis. In psychological assessment with diverse racial/ethnic groups, test construction, norming procedures, and the psychometric properties of the assessment tool are important considerations. Assessment instruments should be looked at carefully for their validity with the specific group and any indications of adverse impact. Caution in the interpretation of test scores, consideration of alternative explanations for behavior, and attention to base rate data and contextual variables can help reduce the impact of racism in the assessment process.

Diagnostic bias can be associated with racial attitudes and stereotypes. Clinicians may overpathologize racial/ethnic minority clients or interpret behavior as deviant when a client is not understood within a cultural context. Alternatively, clinicians may also underpathologize racial/ethnic minority clients and label a problem behavior as cultural in an attempt to *not* be perceived as racist. In both cases, the client is not receiving appropriate treatment. In addition, clinicians may associate a particular diagnosis with a particular racial/ethnic group and assign that diagnosis prematurely, frequently, and/or incorrectly (e.g., African Americans and paranoid schizophrenia).

Racism-Related Clinical Interventions. Therapists can facilitate the development of a strong racial identity through creating an evaluation of self that is not based on the norms of the majority, reframing racism experiences that are self-blaming, and modifying cognitive attributions that promote internalized racism. Clients also can be encouraged to find alternative sources of pride, identify with same-race role models, and seek affirming support systems. Within family therapy, parents can be assisted in positive racial socialization efforts that include preparing children to effectively cope with racism.

Additional Intervention Contexts

Racism-related interventions have application in many contexts outside psychotherapy. These include educational, employment, community, and health care contexts, as well as within the field of psychology.

In the educational context, explicit antibias curricula have been developed to try to counteract the subtle and pervasive racist ideology that contributes to the development of prejudice and discriminatory behavior in children. Multicultural curricula also have been developed so that knowledge acquired in school is less Eurocentric and more reflective of the contributions and perspectives of the diverse peoples of the world. These efforts extend from preschool through higher education. There are also efforts to create progressive schools that target a particular group (e.g., African

American boys) to enable specific needs to be met and to reduce the stigmatization and assumptions of inferiority that exist in traditional educational institutions.

Efforts to intervene with racism and discrimination in the employment context range from experiential diversity training to strategic organizational diversity initiatives, as well as diversity management and leadership seminars. Educational seminars on harassment and conflict resolution can also help reduce racism-related interactions in the workplace.

Within the community context, numerous interventions have been designed and implemented to improve race relations or resolve intergroup conflicts. There are also a growing number of rites-of-passage programs and other efforts that provide positive racial socialization, support racial identity, and minimize internalized racism. These interventions may buffer the potentially damaging effects of racism and discrimination.

In the health care context, efforts are being made in several areas. Professional training programs (e.g., medical residencies, nursing schools) are integrating various strategies to minimize bias and unintentional racism. There is increasing attention to issues of language access and health care interpretation so that target groups are not excluded from medical care. There are also early pipeline programs to support and facilitate youth of diverse racial backgrounds in entering a health care profession so that communities of color are not underserved or do not receive lower-quality health care.

Finally, there have been increasing efforts in the field of psychology to reduce the impact of racism and ethnocentrism in theory, research, practice, and training. For example, the development of the subfield of multicultural psychology has created a professional home for psychologists to generate, discuss, and publish theory and research relevant to diverse racial/ethnic groups that are free from the emphasis on comparative research with European Americans. Another important example is the advocacy and activism within the profession of psychology that led to an American Psychological Association resolution regarding multicultural competencies for the field. This resolution communicates the significance of recognizing and eliminating racial bias in the profession of psychology by providing guidelines for research, practice, training, and organizational development.

In addition, increasing attention has been given to diversity in the education and training of psychologists.

Multicultural courses that are experiential, knowledge-focused, and/or skills-oriented are offered in an increasing number of universities and professional schools of psychology. These courses aim to increase self-awareness, provide information, and improve professional practice so that racism and discrimination have a decreasing presence in psychology. Although racism and discrimination continue to exist in psychological theory, research, and practice, efforts such as these contribute to combating oppressive dynamics within the field and increasing the relevance and application of psychology for diverse racial/ethnic groups.

—*Shelly P. Harrell*
—*Gesenia Sloan-Pena*

See also Anti-Semitism; Critical Race Theory; Ethnocentrism; Eugenics; Institutional Racism; Internalized Racism; Measures of Racial Prejudice; Race; Tokenism/Psychology of Tokenism; White Privilege; Xenophobia

FURTHER READING

Jones, J. M. (1997). *Prejudice and racism* (2nd ed.). New York: McGraw-Hill.

Personal narratives on racism [special issue]. (1999). *Journal of Counseling and Development, 77*(1).

Rollock, D., & Gordon, E. W. (2000). Racism and mental health into the 21st century: Perspectives and parameters. *American Journal of Orthopsychiatry , 70*(1), 5–14.

RAPPORT

Therapy is based on the therapist developing a relationship with the client. *Rapport* has been described as an ideal version of this relationship between the therapist and client. The importance of the therapeutic relationship is accepted by most theoretical approaches. In some approaches, such as existential, person-centered, and Gestalt, the personal relationship is a crucial determinant of treatment outcomes, in contrast to other approaches, such as rational emotive behavior therapy, cognitive-behavior therapy, and behavior therapy, which, although they do not ignore the relationship, do not give it central importance. Developing this relationship requires honesty, sincerity, acceptance, understanding, and spontaneity. According to the literature, the relationship between the therapist and client is the key factor in client change, and the Rogerian core conditions of listening, reflecting, and clarification of feelings are fundamental to the development of a therapeutic relationship.

Rapport is characterized by openness, honesty, freedom for clients to be themselves, and a sense of comfort and acceptance. The development of this relationship can be influenced by many factors. One of these factors is the perception by the client of the therapist's association with an agency/organization that does not appear to have the client's best interests at heart. Another factor is the manner in which the client approaches therapy. If the client approaches therapy because she or he needs to talk about something and feels that talking to a therapist will be helpful, rapport will be easier to establish than when the client is unwilling to be in therapy but has been compelled to be there, such as in court-mandated therapy. Additional factors that affect the development of rapport are the client's initial impression of the therapist and the therapist's office, the therapist's response to the client challenging the therapist, and the extent to which the therapist is attuned to the client's feelings and able to communicate an understanding of the client in the initial session.

Historically, the use of microskills such as attending and listening, influencing, focusing, selective attention, and confrontation has been emphasized for the development of rapport between therapist and client. However, this expectation of the development of rapport through the use of these microskills is considered by many to be a European American concept and may not lead to rapport development with individuals who belong to minority cultures. There are several reasons for this.

Individuals from minority cultures may have different expectations of what the therapist can do for them and the goals of therapy. The client may define the therapist role very differently—as a medicine man, as a physician, and so forth—and the therapist needs to understand the client's definition in order to work with him or her.

Clients also may have different expectations from the initial therapeutic contact. Whereas European Americans may be comfortable with information collection being the focus of the first session to help the therapist in identifying and treating the problem, clients from diverse groups may view the same therapist as being technically and culturally incompetent. Thus, the therapist should not give the client the impression that a lot of information will be needed to understand the problem, and the presenting problem should be emphasized. The first session should focus on identifying the problem the client considers essential, providing concrete recommendations that will help the client problem solve, and establishing therapist credibility.

Another reason may be the emphasis placed on different components of the relationship. European Americans place an emphasis on equality in relationships, whereas other cultures place an equal or greater emphasis on respect and expect it to be given in relationships. There is large variance in the factors that determine respect across cultures. For example, in Arab cultures, age, occupation, family name and reputation, and social class/socioeconomic status all have an interactive effect on respect. In contrast, respect may reflect emotional dependence and dutifulness, such as in parent–child relationships, among Mexican families. A high value also may be placed on respect owing to the lack of respect shown to minority group members by the dominant culture historically.

The development of rapport is considered vital by psychologists working with individuals from different multicultural groups. It has been theorized that rapport development involves conceptual, behavioral, and cultural levels. At the conceptual level, the client and therapist need to have a perception of genuineness, naturalness, honesty, motivation, empathy, sensitivity, inquiring concerns, and trustworthiness. The behavioral level includes the client's perception of therapist competence and the therapist's perception of the client's competence and skill in following treatment plans.

At the cultural level, two hypotheses—cultural compatibility and the universalistic hypothesis—suggest differing ways to best establish rapport. The cultural compatibility hypothesis suggests that reducing racial and ethnic barriers between the client and the therapist to zero enhances assessment and treatment of multicultural groups. In contrast, the universalistic hypothesis suggests that, irrespective of client–therapist racial and ethnic differences or similarities, the therapist needs to engage in assessment and treatment strategies. Although the cultural compatibility hypothesis has not been substantiated by research, the universalistic hypothesis suggests that therapists also need to demonstrate an understanding of and competence in the skills needed to develop a therapeutic relationship with the client.

The importance of the first session in developing rapport cannot be emphasized enough. To that end, guidelines have been established for therapists' first session with clients from different minority groups and will be reviewed in the subsequent paragraphs. Although therapists should keep these guidelines in mind while conducting the first session, they also need to be mindful that there are more within-group differences than between-group differences. Assuming that all members of a specific group share similar values, beliefs, and contexts can lead a therapist to engage in monocultural practice and overlook the diversity that exists within each group. Thus, therapists should assess clients' identity and level of acculturation with the dominant culture. This will allow them to determine how mindful they need to be of cultural issues in session(s) and what strategies to utilize to build rapport with clients from different ethnic backgrounds.

It is recommended that therapists (irrespective of race or ethnicity) working with most African American clients should be prepared to discuss racial issues, explore clients' acculturation level, include the church in the process, avoid identification of the problem's origin, identify the problem(s) that will be addressed immediately, handle family secrets carefully, and screen carefully for depression and substance abuse.

For a therapist working with Hispanic clients, the first session usually should include an exploration of the client's acculturation level; emphasize *formalismo* over *personalismo;* explore, understand, and accept the client's explanations of the problems; interview the parents/partner alone (if needed); explore possibility of medication recommendations; and present a possible solution to the presenting problem.

In working with most Asian American clients, therapists, in the first session, should be prepared to demonstrate their expertise and authority while maintaining formality and a conversational distance. In addition, therapists should expect and accept a mental problem to be expressed in somatic terms and should not expect a discussion of emotional problems. An initial focus on somatic symptoms, followed by a focus on personal, family, and social problems, can facilitate the development of rapport. The therapist should also consider the first session a crisis, discuss alternative solutions before discussing hospitalization, provide concrete and tangible advice, and consider the client's physiological explanations of emotional problems. It is also believed that therapists can enhance the development of rapport with individuals from minority cultures by avoiding any identification with agencies that the client may perceive to be prejudicial. These include immigration services or entitlement agencies, among others.

Another factor to consider with clients whose first language is not English is that interpreters may be needed. Although referring clients to a clinician who is fluent in their language is preferable, it is not always an option. In those cases, it has been recommended that the therapist schedule a preassessment meeting with the interpreter to learn about the interpreter's background, as well as cultural, social, or political differences that can affect the therapy work and assist in establishing rapport. Family members should not be used as interpreters. Building rapport through an interpreter will be more difficult and may occur more slowly. As noted earlier, rapport is a necessary condition of psychotherapy and should be considered carefully when working with ethnic minority populations.

—*Radhika Seghal*
—*Nina Alease Nabors*

FURTHER READING

Arbuckle, D. S. (1975). *Counseling and psychotherapy: An existential-humanistic view* (3rd ed.). Boston: Allyn & Bacon.

Corey, G. (1996). *Theory and practice of counseling and psychotherapy* (5th ed.). Pacific Grove, CA: Brooks/Cole.

Gee, K. K., & Ishii, M. M. (1997). Assessment and treatment of schizophrenia among Asian Americans. In E. Lee (Ed.), *Working with Asian Americans: A guide for clinicians* (pp. 227–251). New York: Guilford.

Hays, P. A. (2001). *Addressing cultural complexities in practice: A framework for clinicians and counselors.* Washington, DC: American Psychological Association.

McGuiness, J. (2000). Therapeutic climate. In C. Feltham & I. Horton (Eds.), *Handbook of counseling and psychotherapy* (pp. 94–101). Thousand Oaks, CA: Sage.

Paniagua, F. A. (1998). *Assessing and treating culturally diverse clients: A practical guide* (2nd ed.). Thousand Oaks, CA: Sage.

Suzuki, L. A., McRae, M. B., & Short, E. L. (2001). The facets of cultural competence: Searching outside the box. *The Counseling Psychologist, 29*(6), 842–849.

REFUGEES

Recently the world has witnessed more than 60 nations in various states of war, genocide, and ethnic conflict, resulting in millions of people's lives being dramatically disrupted and physically displaced. The U.S. Committee for Refugees has estimated that there are 35 million refugees worldwide, 20 times more than there were 50 years ago. Refugee numbers are projected to continue rising.

Refugees are characterized by their involuntary forced migration, as contrasted with displaced persons, who freely choose to migrate and are thus classified as immigrants. Despite the growing numbers of refugees and a great need for receptive host countries, many nations are increasingly reluctant to open their doors for resettlement, as a result of governments more rigidly interpreting the 1951 United Nations Convention definition of refugee status. Reluctance by countries to accept refugees was further exacerbated by a post-9/11 mentality whereby international immigration policies have been more concerned with security than with humanitarian needs, which has driven politically conservative national policies and refugee quotas that resist resettling foreigners.

PSYCHOLOGICAL NEEDS

Meeting critical basic human needs for food, shelter, clothing, and medicine are essential first steps in caring for dislocated refugees. Once the basic survival needs are met, it is important to attend to short- and long-term psychological needs that relate to issues such as loss of family, friends, homes, communities, employment, and personal belongings; starvation; near death; rape and sexual abuse; physical and psychological violence; abuse; torture and injury; and witnessing of murder and violations of family, friends, and strangers in their home country or during their escape.

These experiences may cause serious mental health problems that can be further complicated during postmigration adjustment. As refugees attempt to navigate their adjustments to new life transitions and circumstances, they must come to terms with past trauma. The combination of premigration trauma with the barriers, severity, and complexity of postmigration resettlement has been found to result in serious psychological problems for some refugees.

To effectively provide mental health services to refugees, it is essential to address the refugee experience while giving attention to the broad spectrum, diversity, and differences in refugee cultures. This requires significant cross-cultural sensitivity and culturally relevant psychological interventions, requiring mental health professionals to be attuned to multicultural issues.

THE UNIQUE REFUGEE EXPERIENCE AND IMPLICATIONS FOR MENTAL HEALTH INTERVENTIONS

It has been clearly documented that the problem of forced displacement presents difficult, distinctive, and deep-rooted psychological problems that are specific to the refugee population. Premigration factors have been found to be a major predictor of psychological problems, such as culture shock and fatigue, acculturative stress, and the effects of political victimization and repression. Common features of these factors are the multiple losses of family, friends, and one's own culture, often accompanied by a psychological mourning for one's past life. Therefore, refugees may actually experience retraumatization during resettlement because of the combination of the pain, suffering, and sadness over the losses, transitions, and traumatic events of the past with the need to adapt to a new culture. Mental health professionals will need to address these multifaceted and complex issues, which comprise historical, social, political, cultural, psychological, and economic variables.

Culturally sensitive mental health interventions with refugees must be considered within a broader ecological context that constitutes the refugee experience. The relocation of refugees is further exacerbated by modern-day acts of terrorism, which present an added set of problems to the already existing trauma generally associated with forced migration. Thus refugee migration and relocation is a tumultuous process that is not only forced and involuntary without preparation or planning, but is most often devoid of personal decisions or choice about when to flee and where to go.

MENTAL HEALTH ISSUES

There are relationships between refugees' successful postmigration adjustment, premigration war experiences, and mental health. Several key issues have been found to affect refugee psychological well-being. One issue is survivor's guilt, whereby refugees who have successfully fled feel guilt and remorse about family and friends who did not escape, leading to idealizing of the past and an intense desire to return to their homeland.

A second major issue is the mastery of language. Studies have found correlations between language acquisition and positive psychological well-being. The inability to speak the language of the host country presents numerous barriers, for example to securing employment, job advancement, and access to further training and education. A third key issue relates to loss of social status; refugees may find themselves unemployed or underemployed and unable to transfer their skills to the resettlement country, leading to diminished socioeconomic status. Concurrently, they may have lost the social stature they had in their home country. Fourth, family relationships may be significantly altered, causing dramatic shifts in family roles and relationships. A fifth issue is culture shock, which is experienced when the refugee is resettled into a new location or country that differs dramatically from his or her homeland. A sixth issue is the psychological recoil effect, which relates to the witnessing of traumatic war events or terrorism that inflict psychological and physical harm on others.

MULTILEVEL MODEL OF PSYCHOTHERAPY AND SOCIAL JUSTICE

Given the uniqueness of the refugee experience, the multilevel model (MLM) of psychotherapy and social justice for refugees was developed. The MLM is a culturally sensitive model that takes into account the premigration, transition, and postmigration adjustment. The aim of the model is to help facilitate adaptation to a new culture and restimulate hope for the future. The model stresses that psychotherapists must have culturally sensitive skills in individual, family, and/or group psychotherapy, and knowledge and understanding of the refugee experience within a cultural, social, historical, and political context.

The MLM is a psychoeducational model that integrates cognitive, behavioral, and affective factors within the context of culture as a foundation for examining intrapersonal and interpersonal processes. The MLM includes five distinct yet interrelated levels that may be employed simultaneously and require using the refugees' conceptualization and expectations regarding healing and mental health.

Briefly, the five levels of the MLM are (1) *mental health education,* which provides clients with an education about expectations for psychotherapy and the role of the therapist; (2) *individual, group, and family counseling,* which incorporates traditional psychotherapy with culturally sensitive interventions that embrace the norms, belief systems, and healing practices of the client; (3) *cultural empowerment,* which assists refugee clients in gaining knowledge and mastering their environment; (4) *indigenous healing,* which takes into account the refugees' cultural conceptualization of mental health and healing and incorporates traditional Western methods with the refugees' indigenous cultural healing methods; and (5) *social justice/human rights,* which emphasizes equal access, fair treatment, and equal opportunities.

CONCLUSION

Refugees present a unique set of issues and challenges for mental health professionals. It is essential that there be a solid understanding of the refugee experience within a cross-cultural context, with a deep appreciation of how premigration and postmigration experiences interact with intrapsychic and interpersonal factors. The multilevel model of psychotherapy and social justice provides a culturally sensitive approach to mental health interventions that is unique to refugees and addresses the historical context and adaptation issues facing refugees.

—Fred Bemak

See also Immigrants

FURTHER READING

Bemak, F., & Chung, R. C. -Y. (2002). Counseling and psychotherapy with refugees. In P. B. Pedersen, J. G. Draguns, W. J. Lonner, & J. E. Trimble (Eds.), *Counseling across cultures* (5th ed., pp. 209–232). Thousand Oaks, CA: Sage.

Bemak, F., & Chung, R. C.-Y. (2002). Refugees and terrorism: Cultural innovations in clinical practice. In C. E. Stout (Ed.), *The psychology of terrorism: Vol. 2. Clinical aspects and responses.* Westport, CT: Praeger.

Bemak, F., Chung, C.-Y., & Pedersen, P. B. (2003). *Counseling refugees: A psychosocial approach to innovative multicultural counseling interventions.* Westport, CT: Greenwood Press.

RELIGION

Religion has almost as many meanings as writers on the subject. Traditionally, in Western culture the term *religion* refers to all aspects of our life in relation to the divine. However, the 20th century saw religion redefined, especially in academic circles. According to new definitions, *religion* refers to individual and corporate beliefs and practices dealing with our relationship with some ultimate being or reality and is distinguished from *spirituality,* which typically refers to the more experiential component of that relationship, or more broadly to one's core values or search for meaning. Some empirical work has begun to support the utility of this distinction, although in the United States it is most common for individuals to place importance on both.

GENERAL HISTORY AND DEVELOPMENT OF THE FIELD

Religion has been of interest to psychologists at least since the time of William James, whose classic work *The Varieties of Religious Experience* began a tradition of phenomenological work in the psychology of religion. The later work of Gordon Allport and Carl Jung provided a basis for personality and social psychologists to also examine religion, and since that time a rich empirical and theoretical literature has developed. However, two factors have limited our understanding of religion in a multicultural environment. First, the discipline of psychology has had an ambivalent relationship with religion. Most 20th-century philosophy of science in psychology was based on European positivism that saw religion as an impediment to be eliminated. Freud largely adopted this positivistic stance toward religion and pictured it as a primitive defense that had no place in a modern scientific world. Second, researchers have neglected the study of the relation between culture and religion. Psychology-of-religion researchers have mostly focused on Western versions of Christianity in European and North American Caucasian groups, and investigators in cross-cultural or multicultural psychology have seldom included religion as a meaningful variable in their studies.

Recently, interest in religion and its connection with culture has been growing. In most areas of the world, large majorities of the population adhere to some type of religion, although in some Western cultures, particularly in Europe, attachment to organized religion has been declining and interest shifting toward a smorgasbord type of individual spirituality. In global terms, the largest religions—Christianity, followed by Islam and varieties of Hinduism—have seen substantial growth in recent years. In the United States, the growth of conservative religion and of cultural groups traditionally committed to religion has challenged a therapeutic system unprepared to deal with religiously committed individuals, leading to a growing literature on handling religious and spiritual issues in counseling. Mounting scientific evidence that religion provides valuable coping strategies leading to enhanced resilience, well-being, and health has also increased general interest in religion within the fields of psychology, mental health, and medicine.

APPROACHES TO RELIGION AND CULTURE

A number of different positions have been taken on the relationship between religion and culture. One approach is to treat religion as a part of culture, as was done in classic anthropological work on religion. If we follow Geertz in defining culture as a symbolic conceptual system that helps form our knowledge and attitudes toward life, then religion can be seen as a subsystem of symbols residing within a larger cultural symbolic framework. In this view, a religion functions within a particular cultural context and cannot be understood outside of it. This postmodern-friendly perspective lies behind the work of scholars such as Steven Katz, who views religious experience as a phenomenon that is inseparable from the cultural context and religious tradition within which the individual lives. When this culture-centered view is applied to counseling, knowledge of religion becomes an expected part of the therapist's multicultural competency and is viewed as another aspect of the client's culture.

Another approach is to see religion as existing somewhat independent of culture. This has been the view followed by many transpersonal psychologists beginning in the 1960s, who saw religious practices and beliefs as something that could be studied without regard to the communal and cultural contexts within which the practices and beliefs normally function. Much research was done, for instance, on physiological and other effects of meditation procedures, and theorists such as Robert Foreman speculated on the universal nature of religious experience. Even modern transpersonal writers such as Ken Wilber, who acknowledge the importance of culture, continue to view spirituality and religion as tapping into levels of reality that are ultimately transcultural. In clinical work, spirituality is then thought of as a dimension of the patient's life somewhat separate from ethnicity or culture. This line of thought fits well with work on the neurobiological and evolutionary bases of religion.

Both of these traditional views have weaknesses. A culturally bound view of religion has difficulty dealing with the global nature of world religions and similarities in descriptions of religious experience in different cultures, whereas a strictly transcultural view cannot easily account for how a single religious tradition can take on quite different forms in various cultures. A modified interaction view, which approaches culture and religion as affecting each other in some ways but independent in others, seems most appropriate. Core characteristics of a religion are thus maintained across cultures, but interaction occurs through innovative adaptation, and religious experience is seen as an interaction of spiritual/religious, cultural, and even biological factors. The nature of this relationship probably differs in various contexts. For instance, the relation between religion and culture for Jewish men and women probably differs from that of many non-Jewish Western Europeans, given the closer identification of religion and ethnicity in Jewish culture.

SPECIFIC INTERACTIONS

The interaction between culture and religion is important in several ways. At the broadest level, religion can influence the basic worldview of the culture, as in the case of Hispanic Americans who are influenced by Catholic attitudes and practices even if they do not have a strong personal connection to religion. Culture also can have an impact on religious beliefs and practices, as, for example, in African American Christianity, which is often thought to have some unique features resulting from the influence of indigenous African culture and religious practices. Interactions also can occur in the case of identity development. For many groups, including African Americans, religion has formed one of the primary sources for ethnic identity, and culture in turn provides some of the materials for the construction of narratives that form the basis of religious identity. However, in a limited interaction model, we might also expect aspects of religious identity to develop independently from cultural identity.

It is difficult to make generalizations about the nature and importance of religious affiliation in specific U.S. cultural or ethnic groups. Reliable and recent statistics on types of religious participation for non–European American groups are almost nonexistent. It is also the case that there are significant variations between regions of the country and generational cohorts in the importance of religion and types of practices. However, it is clear that individuals coming from some ethnic and cultural groups (e.g., African Americans) attach more importance to religion and that certain types of religion will be more typical with particular groups (e.g., Catholicism among Hispanic

Americans), although there are many individual exceptions to these traditional patterns. Not surprisingly, individuals coming from groups that have a stronger religious orientation are likely to have a stronger connection between religion and various aspects of their life. For instance, the helpfulness of religion in the coping process has been demonstrated in a number of religious and cultural contexts but appears to be especially important in non–European American groups that have traditionally strong religious involvement.

Although religion in general is connected with better coping skills and life satisfaction, it is also associated with negative effects in certain situations. Research in the United States has identified some forms of fundamentalism and a utilitarian orientation to religion as connected with negative effects. Little is known about these factors in different cultural or religious traditions, although recent work has replicated U.S. research findings cross-culturally. Some recent studies have also explored the role of religion as a causative factor in violence, but given the strong pacific element in most religious traditions, this relationship is likely to be a complex one that includes a number of factors. Continued quantitative and qualitative research in the relation between culture and religion will help us better understand and utilize the resources of religion for the benefit of society and its members.

—*James M. Nelson*

See also Spirituality

FURTHER READING

Geertz, C. (1973). *The interpretation of cultures.* New York: Basic Books.
Pargament, K. (1997). *The psychology of religion and coping: Theory, research, practice.* New York: Guilford.
Spilka, B., Hood, R., Jr., Hunsberger, B., & Gorsuch, R. (2003). *The psychology of religion: An empirical approach* (3rd ed.). New York: Guilford.
Tarakeshwar, N., Stanton, J., & Pargament, K. (2003). Religion: An overlooked dimension in cross-cultural psychology. *Journal of Cross-Cultural Psychology, 34,* 377–394.

RELIGIOUS/SPIRITUAL BELIEFS: ESPIRITISMO

Espiritismo (spiritism) is a way of life that provides a profound understanding of the human soul, humanity's purpose, and spiritual evolution, helping establish important scientific principles of communication between the spiritual and physical worlds. It has opened new horizons for the study and interpretation of many psychic phenomena (i.e., channeling, clairsentience, clairvoyance, clairaudience, automatic writing, distant healing, mental telepathy) and has helped establish a scientific classification for *mediumship*. What was once explained as a magical phenomenon is now defined as the psychobiological predisposition inherent in those who under certain conditions are allowed to capture the thoughts of discarnate spirits, experience the astral plane, and establish contact with the spirit world.

Important principles found in the theory of relativity of quantum physics, and the newly developing fields of vibrational/energy medicine, as well as transpersonal psychology, support the concepts found at the core of Spiritist philosophy: the universal natural laws of reciprocity, cause and effect, karma, and reincarnation. In studying the organic and psychic phenomena of mediumship for more than a century, Brazil has led the world in establishing essential understanding of mediumistic healing principles that began with the teachings of Allan Kardec in 1858. His works have established essential principles for psychic healing and surgeries—innovative treatments that respond to patients' wider social, cultural, and cosmic realities.

Spiritist medical practitioners (individuals who are Spiritists and are also biomedical professionals) are convinced that physical and mental ailments that are not explained or successfully treated by conventional medicine can often be explained and treated with the intervention and assistance of the spirit realm. Within this new transcendental medicine, patients' symptoms of illness may be caused by accumulated negative energy, retribution for bad deeds, something neglected in this life or in a previous incarnation, or spells cast by others—all etiological elements that are beyond the diagnostic and treatment parameters of traditional biomedicine.

Drawing from a unique combination of spiritual and classical science, *espiritismo* uses both spiritual wisdom and material knowledge gained through a systematic study of illuminating spiritual and scientific texts. Its aim is to prepare individuals for more active roles as agents of change, working toward a society of universal order and progress, based on solidarity and selflessness. Individuals are encouraged to embark on a path of self-discovery by individual efforts of study, work, and activities of good works. The natural laws that regulate human behavior and guide the individual's free will, offered by the Spiritist explanation of the Gospels of Christ, are the patient's therapeutic modalities for everyday life that help redefine concepts of human imperfections, disease, and suffering. It is the fundamental moral concepts that have great potential to activate personal transformation and promote revolutionary ideas and critical thinking about individuals and their world, particularly where social, political, economic, health, and moral conditions are irrational. By redefining old habitual and destructive ways of thinking and encouraging a greater degree of personal responsibility, critical thinking, and discernment, *espiritismo* helps heal past emotional and physical wounds, gradually rebuilding the individual.

Aiming to contribute to the implantation of a new medical model throughout the world, and uniting professionals and their research efforts from all parts of the globe, Brazilian Spiritist physicians are working toward the development of the world's first integral model of health. They have formed important professional organizations, such as the National Congress of Spiritist Medical Doctors and the Medical-Spiritist Association, in their effort to construct a new generation of integrative health professionals working to create the world's first transcendental and humanistic model of medicine.

—*Sandra Nuñez*

See also Indigenous Treatments and Healers

FURTHER READING

Bragdon, E. (2004). *Kardec's Spiritism: A home for healing and spiritual evolution.* Woodstock, VT: Lightening Up Press.

Kardec, A. (2004). *Spiritist philosophy.* Philadelphia: Allan Kardec Educational Society.

RELIGIOUS/SPIRITUAL BELIEFS: FATALISMO

Research has shown that in the Latino American population, there is a notable discrepancy between the need for mental health services and the utilization of mental health services. When these services are actually sought, research has found a significantly higher tendency for Latinos to prematurely terminate treatment. These issues have become a growing concern in research and clinical practice as the population of Latinos in the Unites States continues to increase.

Many socioeconomic, psychotherapeutic, and cultural factors have been identified as possibly contributing to lack of utilization and premature termination. One of these factors is the notion of fatalism, or *fatalismo,* which is a part of Latino culture and is often linked to religious beliefs. *Fatalism* is the tendency to view life as controlled by divine will, with little or no control over the environment. Positive or negative life events may be attributed to simple good fortune or harmful wishes made by adversaries. Thus, Latinos who believe in fatalism and have a mental illness may view their difficulties as being a part of God's plan, as a curse, or as punishment for some previous misdeed or offense. When mental illness is viewed as out of their control, individuals may believe that they are incapable of changing their condition. As a result, Latinos are less likely to seek help from the mental health community for their psychological problems or may first look to the Church for help. When Latinos do seek therapy, a fatalistic view of life may be counterproductive, because most types of therapies encourage taking control of one's life to make change.

The degree to which Latino Americans adhere to fatalism varies greatly according to socioeconomic status and acculturation level. Studies have shown that individuals with higher socioeconomic status and greater level of acculturation tend to report less fatalistic views of life.

Many Latino immigrants reside in economically challenged areas and maintain strong cultural identities by preserving the language and cultural characteristics native to their countries of origin. This can make integrating the majority culture with their traditional culture a difficult and sometimes stressful process. Although acculturation difficulties, in addition to socioeconomic challenges, may place Latinos at risk for mental health problems, fatalism may hinder the utilization of mental health services.

It is important to note that a fatalistic orientation is not always maladaptive, particularly when combined with high levels of religiosity. Research has shown that, in less acculturated Latinos, individuals reporting high levels of fatalism in combination with high religiosity report less depression than do individuals with high levels of fatalism and low religiosity. In certain traumatic situations that are indeed out of a person's control, a fatalistic view can help absolve individuals of the blame or guilt they may initially place on themselves. In such instances, fatalism can facilitate therapy.

When working with Latino clients, it is important that clinicians explore how fatalistic beliefs affect both clients' mental health and their perceptions of the ability of therapy to help them. Because of the heterogeneity of the Latino population, it is important to recognize how different socioeconomic backgrounds and levels of acculturation influence fatalism in clients.

Such understanding may pave the way to bridging the gap between the need for mental health services and their utilization in the Latino population.

—*Joseph D. Hovey*
—*Lori R. Morales*

See also Hispanic Americans; Religion; Spirituality

FURTHER READING

Antshel, K. M. (2002). Integrating culture as a means of improving treatment adherence in the Latino population. *Psychology, Health, and Medicine, 7,* 435–449.

Kouyoumdjian, H., Zamboanga, B. L., & Hansen, D. J. (2003). Barriers to community mental health services for Latinos: Treatment considerations. *Clinical Psychology: Science and Practice, 10,* 394–422.

Neff, J. A., & Hoppe, S. K. (1993). Race/ethnicity, acculturation, and psychological distress: Fatalism and religiosity as cultural resources. *Journal of Community Psychology, 21,* 3–20.

RELIGIOUS/SPIRITUAL BELIEFS: MARIANISMO

Marianismo refers to the traditional idealized gender role and values associated in Latino cultures with being a woman. It is heavily influenced by Catholic religious doctrine and rooted in an emulation of the Virgin Mary by honoring and imitating both her virginal and maternal qualities. Within marianimso, qualities such as virginity, chastity, sexual naïveté, modesty, and self-sacrifice for the sake of one's partner's or children's needs are idealized. Furthermore, the belief that suffering is part of being a woman and part of the female identity is a part of marianista values.

Marianismo is significant in that it defines the female gender role within Latino cultures, including behavior that is acceptable and unacceptable for women, as well as shared values related to women. For example, according to traditional marianista values, premarital sexual activity, sexual knowledge, and placing one's own needs or desires above others are considered inappropriate qualities and behaviors for a woman. Given that marianismo promotes a particular set of values about what is acceptable female behavior, it influences normative beliefs about women, female sexual behavior, and the ways in which women care for themselves and others. Unlike machismo, the male gender role that, among other values, promotes proving virility through sexual relations and the belief that men's sexual urges are uncontrollable, marianismo promotes sexual purity and delaying sexual activity until marriage. Taken together, these two gender roles not only define normative behavior and values for interactions between men and women, but frequently uphold values for the two genders that are at odds with each other. For example, whereas men may be encouraged to engage in frequent sexual activities with multiple female partners, women may be encouraged to do the opposite—that is, to avoid sexual activity.

As noted previously, the association of self-sacrifice and suffering are central to the female gender role. These qualities mirror the life of the Virgin Mary, who sacrificed her own life to fulfill the will of God and suffered the loss of her only son. By this model, for a woman to suffer is considered virtuous and moral. Marianismo encompasses more than the physical suffering of pain; it is also a way of life. In the traditional conceptualization of marianismo, the equating of self-sacrifice and suffering with the feminine begins with the physical pain that women endure during childbirth. This linking of suffering with the feminine role is further extended to the notion that ideal women sacrifice their own needs and desires for the sake of their husbands' and children's happiness and they endure male partners' sexual infidelity (particularly as machismo defines male sexual urges as uncontrollable). For a woman to carry these burdens is considered a source of feminine nobility, respect, and even moral superiority. She is implicitly seen as fulfilling the idealized role of the Virgin Mary, suffering for her children and suffering for her sexuality.

Because marianismo, like all gender roles, is culturally bound and cultures change over time, it is important to consider marianismo as a dynamic construct. Traditional conceptualizations of marianismo emphasize women's submissiveness, sacrifice, and domesticity. However, there is a dearth of literature that discusses changing conceptualizations of marianismo and the Latina gender role in the context of developing cultures or the process of acculturation. Although these traditional values influence current views of gender roles, attending only to traditional conceptualizations ignores many Latinas' current evolving social and economic realities, which include education, careers, and increasing empowerment and independence. Holding only to traditional gender conceptualizations also reifies their existence at the cost of examining current trends in Latinas' lives.

—Mimi Doll

See also Machismo

FURTHER READING

Ehlers, T. B. (1991). Debunking marianismo: Economic vulnerability and survival strategies among Guatemalan wives. *Ethnology, 30*(1), 1–16.

Galanti, G. (2003). The Hispanic family and male–female relationships: An overview. *Journal of Transcultural Nursing, 14*(3), 180–185.

Melhuus, M. (1990). A shame to honour—A shame to suffer. *Ethnos, 55*(1–2), 5–25.

RELIGIOUS/SPIRITUAL BELIEFS: PERSONALISMO

The cultural script of *personalismo* states that relationships are valued in and of themselves and not as a means to another end. This means that many Latinos focus on the importance of personal relationships rather than institutional relationships. The focus on the interpersonal relationship means that having a positive connection with the clinical professional is of utmost importance. Hence, if a clinical professional leaves a setting and goes elsewhere, the individual or family may follow the clinical professional to the new setting. Similarly, if an individual or family has engaged in treatment with a clinical professional who leaves the clinic setting with no indication of where he or she is going, the individual or family may end treatment. One way a premature termination may be avoided is to have the clinical professional connect the individual or family to the new psychotherapist before leaving the clinic setting. This integrates personalismo into the transfer process, as the individual or family maintains a sense of relationship rather than feeling abandoned. Personalismo also relates to the physical space between the clinical professional and the family or individual. Latinos may prefer to have less interpersonal space between them and others in comparison to Anglo-Americans.

CONFLICTS WITH THE MENTAL HEALTH DELIVERY SYSTEM

It is important for clinical professionals to be aware of how to incorporate personalismo into the treatment process to avoid conflicts with the mental health delivery system. Physical space may be one such conflict, for instance, if the Latino patient perceives the clinical professional who maintains substantial interpersonal distance as unconcerned and unwelcoming. A second conflict relates to how personal greetings are extended. A formal greeting that maintains physical space, for example, may be viewed as insulting. Rather, the expectation for a greeting may be a kiss on the cheek.

A third conflict concerns the immediate focus on the patient's problem rather than beginning sessions with a discussion about the patient's life and family. An immediate focus on the problem may put the ability to cultivate the interpersonal relationship at risk. The individual may feel unheard and unimportant, and may ultimately leave the clinical session with a lack of *confianza* (trust) in the clinical professional. It is important that the clinical professional spend some time talking with the patient about his or her life in ways that are not necessarily connected to the problem.

A fourth conflict between the cultural script of personalismo and the mental health service delivery system is the adherence to strict timelines that often take the form of shorter clinic visits. It may not be until some time in the session has passed that the patient feels ready to openly share his or her emotions. Given that emotional expression may come at the end of the session, the patient may feel unappreciated and misunderstood if the clinical professional adheres to strict timelines and promptly ends the session.

Personalismo can be integrated into the treatment process in the following ways: (1) engage the individual rather than the individual's problem only; (2) be flexible with time; (3) be sensitive to cultural aspects of physical space; and (4) provide a connection to the next therapist during the transfer process.

—*Caroline S. Clauss-Ehlers*

See also Hispanic Americans; Religion; Spirituality

FURTHER READING

Antshel, K. M. (2002). Integrating culture as a means of improving treatment adherence in the Latino population. *Psychology, Health, and Medicine, 7*(4), 435–449.

Clauss, C. S. (1998). Language: The unspoken variable in psychotherapy practice. *Journal of Psychotherapy, 35*(2), 188–196.

Clauss-Ehlers, C. S. (2004). A framework for school-based mental health promotion with bicultural Latino children: Building on strengths to promote resilience. *International Journal of Mental Health Promotion, 6*(2), 26–33.

RELIGIOUS/SPIRITUAL BELIEFS: SANTERÍA

To the *Santeros* and to millions of practitioners, Santería is known simply as "the Religion." Santería originated in Nigeria, with the Yoruba people who were brought to the New World by slave traders centuries ago. With the Yoruba came their religion, known in Cuba as *Lucumí* and in Brazil as *Macumba* and *Candomblé*. The Cuban Lucumís (Yoruba people) were also deeply influenced by the iconolatry of their Spanish masters, and to hide their religious practice for fear of persecution, they identified their deities with Catholic saints. Thus, Santería represents the syncretism between two different beliefs, the rites of the Yoruba and the traditions of the Catholic Church.

The deities, *orishas,* oversee each person's life and rule over all forces of nature and interact with humankind as emissaries of God (Olodumare). The spiritual energy that makes up the universe and provides energy to all life and material things is Olorun, the source of *ashé*. Driven by energy and *ashé,* the orishas are protective guides that aid followers, providing direction for a better spiritual and material life. Communication between orishas and humankind occurs through prayer, ritual, divination, song, rhythms, and trance. To show respect and gratitude, *ebbo,* or offerings for worship, include food, fruits, candies, honey, tobacco, rum, and animal sacrifices including turtles, ducks, and goats.

The religion offers followers many orishas to consult for guidance, as each is known for a particular human trait with specific attributes. Although there are countless deities, the Seven African Powers most prominent include Obatala (peace and purity); Eleggua (messengers); Orula (divination); Chango (passion and enemies); Oggun (war and employment); Yemaya (maternity); and Oshun (love). The deities are also known by the forces of nature they rule over, and each is associated with a Catholic saint. For example, Yemayá lives and rules over the seas and lakes, as she is the symbol of maternity or the Mother of All, and she is syncretized with Our Lady of Regla.

Santería notes the various stages of spiritual development by granting members leveled positions. *Babalawos* are the highest priests (divine spiritual doctors), followed by *Santera/os,* priests of Santería.

The first step toward initiation is acquiring protective beads (necklaces, *elekes, collares*). The individual (usually a Santera/o) who initiates the new member serves as a guide and later becomes known as his or her *padrino* (godfather) or *madrina* (godmother), and the initiate becomes the Santera/o's *ahijada/o* (god-daughter/godson). The relationship between a Santera/o and the godchild is characterized by the godchild's respect, reverence, and obedience to the godparent and the godparent's protection and guidance of the godchild.

People consult Santera/os for various reasons, including physical illness, nervous conditions, and problems in life. The consultation, a *registro,* is similar to a visit with a psychotherapist, as the Santera/o listens, attempts to understand the problem, and identifies solutions. A *registro* may be conducted by the Santera/o through the *Diloggun,* or reading of the *caracoles* (seashells), through which the orishas speak to the Santera/o, telling him or her the problem and how to remedy it. The solution may be in the form of a ritual cleansing (*despojo*), a Catholic mass for the dead, or an animal sacrifice. In addition, most Santera/os are competent herbalists who can cure diseases.

Santería has migrated from the Caribbean to many other Latin American countries and thrives in the streets and barrios of New York, Chicago, and Los Angeles. Santería is the foundation to the Earth's wisdom; its principle of embracing nature creates an omnipresent existence of the religion in all entities and an influence on all human exchanges.

—*Brian McNeill*
—*Jeanett Castellanos*

See also Cuban Americans; Hispanic Americans

FURTHER READING

González-Whippler, M. (2001). *Santería: The Religion.* St. Paul, MN: Llewellyn.

S

SCHIZOPHRENIA

The diagnosis and treatment of schizophrenia is extremely complex. Schizophrenia is a disabling disease that often strikes patients in the prime of youth, between 18 and 25 years of age. Its cause is unknown, there is no available cure, and its treatment is problematic.

Historically, schizophrenia was known as dementia praecox. The term *dementia* indicates cognitive deficits, and the term *praecox* relates to the disorder's early onset. Emil Kraepelin (1856–1926), who coined this term, believed it was invariably a deteriorating condition. Later, Eugene Bleuler (1857–1939) used the term *schizophrenia* to describe this illness, referring to a schism or discrepancy in the cognitive, emotional, and behavioral aspects of the individual. There is a common misconception that schizophrenia means dual personality; however, this is not a correct definition.

Schizophrenia is more accurately defined as a problem orienting oneself to reality; sufferers experience hallucinations, both auditory and visual, and delusional thoughts. These delusions are known as *false beliefs*. When patients have false beliefs, they may perceive that they are being persecuted or controlled, and they may engage in bizarre behavior. For example, some patients believe that an electric current has been implanted their brain, causing them to have supernatural powers, or they may believe that someone is reading their mind or talking to them from the television. Obviously, these delusions cannot be substantiated.

The prevalence rate for schizophrenia in the United States is thought to be 1%. Prevalence rates for African Americans are difficult to document because schizophrenia may be overdiagnosed or misdiagnosed in African Americans. For example, blind studies have confirmed that the diagnosis of schizophrenia in African Americans is not always accurate, even when the psychiatrist is African American. The reasons relate to culture. The experience of racism has made many African Americans guarded, slow to trust, and suspicious. Sometimes this attitude is interpreted as paranoia, and schizophrenia is diagnosed. However, these feelings may only be the result of cultural attitudes or feelings developed within a family or within a community—this is *not* schizophrenia but perhaps a matter of self-preservation in the African American community.

Another cultural issue is auditory and visual hallucinations. Some African American individuals sincerely believe in spirits and hear them speak, or they may have religious experiences that are often interpreted as psychotic or schizophrenic in nature. This is also true in other cultures and religious groups, including some Asian and Hispanic cultures.

Although many clinicians have described the signs and symptoms of schizophrenia, others have postulated a psychodynamic or cultural genesis of the illness. For example, the *double-bind theory*, put forth by Gregory Bateson, relates to family interactions. Racism is a destructive institution that can wreck one's sense of adequacy and self-esteem: to be prevented from progressing or achieving because of one's skin color or culture is certainly hurtful and discouraging. Such negative perceptions and feelings of distress may pave the way for mental illness. This is not to say that every African American will develop schizophrenia; however, if one has a genetic predisposition for schizophrenia, there is certainly a greater risk of developing this illness given one's life circumstances.

As a result of the anger that is present for some in the African American community—an anger that has been well documented—many African Americans are consistently exposed to high emotional expression. This is another theory of cultural genesis. To hear rageful voices, to be addressed in rageful tones, to be "yelled at" by people of the majority culture is distressful, abusive, and hurtful. Living with high emotional expression is a stressor that could lead to mental illness. In addition, some African Americans live in dangerous urban environments, and violence in these neighborhoods may contribute with the emotional fears and anxiety that must be tolerated—high emotional expression at its most destructive level.

It is no longer accepted in the academic community that schizophrenia is caused by the dynamics of the family. Psychodynamic theories help us to understand the culture, family interactions, and other environmental stresses that are critical in determining the course of illness. Schizophrenia is now known to be a biological illness such as multiple sclerosis or Alzheimer's disease. But like these diseases, the causes of schizophrenia are not yet known, treatment does not provide a cure, and the course of the disease is variable. For reasons that are unknown, schizophrenia appears to shorten one's life span. Therefore, if one has a mental health disorder and other physical health concerns, this combination can be quite devastating and shorten one's life span considerably.

Another significant factor in the African American community is the matter of substance abuse. Use of methamphetamines, cocaine, marijuana, and other substances can lead to psychotic illnesses such as schizophrenia. However, there is a lack of awareness in the African American community as to the effects of illegal drugs on the health of the brain over time.

Often, African Americans with schizophrenia are not visible in the mental health system. The reason may be that there is greater acceptance and tolerance in the community for this condition and its associated behaviors. Often, African Americans do not even seek treatment. Those who are disabled or act differently—even those who may be actively hallucinating—are protected, given care, and generally spared hurt or ridicule. Thus, they receive no treatment and little

support from the wider community, yet they are accepted in their families and in their community.

One of the many reasons that some African Americans avoid the mental health system is that many African Americans have had negative experiences with the prescription of psychotropic medications, overmedication, misdiagnosis, and even stigmatization. It has been well documented that African American males have severe dystonic reactions to such antipsychotics as Haldol and Prolixin, which are used to treat psychotic symptoms. The older, traditional antipsychotics cause stiffness and muscle cramps, known collectively as extrapyramidal symptoms, and some can even result in tardive dyskinesia, a serious, long-term side effect that affects the control of movement. As a result, medication is frequently refused by those afflicted with schizophrenia. Because of the historical overuse of these medications, the African American community has a real, though distorted, view of all psychotropic medications, especially antipsychotics.

The new antipsychotic medications, generally referred to as the atypicals, are better tolerated and have fewer side effects. Mistrust of these medications, however, continues to be prevalent, not only in the African American community but among other ethnic groups as well.

Because discrimination and prejudice toward African Americans persist, responsive feelings such as anger, hurt, decreased trust, and feelings of inadequacy and low self-esteem are common. With the additional stigma of mental illness, some patients may assume they will face even more discrimination and prejudice. This can cause them to deny problems and avoid treatment—a serious concern because medications can and do work well. With proper medical and psychological treatment, there is hope for improvement and well-being. Although some patients do not receive significant benefits from treatments, efforts should be made to achieve a good treatment outcome. With the availability of new antipsychotic medications for the treatment of schizophrenia, it is hoped that resistance and denial in the African American community will lessen.

Advances in our knowledge and treatment of schizophrenia continue. But for many African Americans, it is difficult to access new treatments because of the reduced availability of services, cost, and cultural barriers of trust and denial. The availability of health insurance is very important, but good health insurance is often obtained by having a job and a higher socioeconomic status. Unemployment rates in the African American community are very high compared with the wider community, which may preclude access with health insurance and proper treatment.

In summary, the diagnosis and treatment of schizophrenia in the African American community involves significant therapeutic and cultural issues. It is a public and mental health issue that needs continued support and study.

—*M. DeVonne French*

FURTHER READING

American Psychiatric Association. (2000). *Diagnostic and statistical manual of mental disorders* (4th ed., text rev.). Washington, DC: Author.

SCHOLASTIC ASSESSMENT TEST

Near the turn of the 20th century, the College Entrance Examination Board (now referred to as the College Board) was formed to coordinate the admission testing requirements of selective colleges in the northeastern United States. In 1901, the College Board administered its first examination. Over a century later, standardized admissions tests in higher education have achieved unprecedented popularity.

The test that is currently used by the College Board is the Scholastic Assessment Test (SAT; formally called the Scholastic Aptitude Test), which was developed by the Educational Testing Service in Princeton, New Jersey. The SAT is widely used in the eastern and western United States. Similar tests, such as the American College Test (ACT), are primarily used in the midwestern United States.

The SAT is actually a testing program, not a single test. In its current form, this program includes the SAT I: Reasoning Test and the SAT II: Subject Tests (e.g., history, biology, chemistry). Because of its general use and wealth of research data, only the SAT I will be discussed here. Since 2001, the SAT I has consisted of three subtests: the Critical Reading Exam (commonly referred to as the SAT Verbal), the Mathematics Exam (commonly referred to as the SAT Math), and the Writing Exam. Scores on each of the subtests range from 200 to 800 with a mean of 500 ($SD = 100$). Scores on the SAT Verbal and SAT Math are commonly added together to form a single score ranging from 400 to 1600; however, these subtests are best characterized as testing separate attributes.

College entrance exams such as the SAT are important to the future of high school students in the United States. These test scores are one criterion—some would argue a *major* criterion—in college admissions decisions. Because test scores can have a great impact on the lives of students (including whether and where they will attend college), it seems reasonable to assume these tests are a good measure of academic achievement. However, for many students, especially students of color, these tests do not accurately reflect their academic achievement, creating a major barrier to access to higher education: not meeting the selection criteria for college admission.

Since the SAT was first implemented, researchers and educators have noted an ethnic disparity in SAT scores. Reports of average SAT scores by ethnicity have consistently found that European Americans generally score higher than people of color (including African Americans, Latino/a Americans, American Indians, and Asian Americans) on the SAT Verbal and, with only one exception (Asian Americans), on the SAT Math. The current consensus as to the etiology of the problem is that the differences in test scores among ethnic groups are primarily the result of unfair test bias.

Critics of standardized achievement tests (including the SAT) charge that differences in test results are not to the result of discrepancies in ability or achievement among groups (i.e., legitimate group discrimination). Instead, the noticeable statistical difference (i.e., bias) is more a function of how the test is presented, as well as the specific test content (i.e., content that is not relevant to the knowledge or skill being measured), which may be more familiar to some demographic groups (e.g., racial, cultural, or socioeconomic groups) than others. Much of the research examining the ethnic gap in SAT scores has focused on the importance of noncognitive variables such as self-esteem, coping with racism, preference for long-term goals, racial identity, and test preparation.

—*Jacob J. Levy*

See also Academic Achievement and Minority Individuals; Intelligence Tests

FURTHER READING

Sedlacek, W. E. (2004). *Beyond the big test: Noncognitive assessment in higher education*. San Francisco: Jossey-Bass.

SELF-DISCLOSURE

Self-disclosure is broadly defined as a therapist's communication of personal experiences, thoughts, and emotions to reveal personal aspects of himself or herself to a client. Specifically, it refers to the disclosure of one's professional background, such as training and practice, personal life circumstances, personal reactions, and feelings about the client, as well as the admission of mistakes made in therapy. Dating back to Sigmund Freud, who is credited with the discovery and study of psychoanalytic psychology, self-disclosure is seen by many therapists as a contamination of the therapeutic process. In contrast, feminists and multiculturalists advocate the appropriate use of therapist self-disclosure as an essential component of working with women and individuals from culturally diverse backgrounds. The conflict between the two camps has created an ethical dilemma for professionals despite findings that support the value of self-disclosure as a *technique* when working with women and culturally diverse individuals. Today, the debate continues among psychologists: Many believe that self-disclosure has no place in therapy, whereas others advocate its prudent use.

SELF-DISCLOSURE AS A THERAPEUTIC INTERVENTION

As the number of people of color in the United States continues to increase, there is no question that therapy practice guidelines have become a challenge for many psychologists. The Guidelines on Multicultural Education, Training, Research, Practice, and Organizational Change, published by the American Psychological Association, provide a launching pad from which psychologists can address the therapeutic needs of individuals from diverse backgrounds. These guidelines state that multiculturally competent psychologists should recognize that culturally specific therapy may require nontraditional interventions. Self-disclosure within the therapeutic relationship will be examined in this context.

A more significant concern than debating the appropriateness of self-disclosure in therapy is the responsibility to help students and clinicians identify their decision to self-disclose. Clarifying the rationale for self-disclosure makes its use in treatment an ethical matter. The most pertinent question that therapists need to ask themselves before self-disclosing is whether the decision is based on a desire to enhance the therapeutic relationship or on the therapists' own personal agenda.

An examination of the research on self-disclosure clearly indicates that its use in treatment must facilitate the client's therapeutic process. Therefore, what and when to self-disclose is more pertinent than whether self-disclosure has value in treatment. Self-disclosure is most effective when the therapist uses this technique to respond to concerns expressed by the client, thereby validating the client's experience. For example, in response to a client who is confused about whether an experience was racist or sexist, a therapist may appropriately disclose his or her own confusion about reading people's negative attitudes based on the therapist's own multiple identities. Within this context, the therapist's use of self-disclosure is based on the needs of the client, not those of the therapist. When it is restricted to issues that are introduced by the client, self-disclosure can help to reduce the client's level of distress and foster a perception that the therapist is friendly, open, and warm.

Feminist and multicultural therapists acknowledge the personal and authentic aspects of the therapeutic relationship. In contrast, traditional psychodynamic approaches to treatment focus more on the symbolic interactions in the therapeutic dyad. In this more traditional therapeutic relationship, the therapist may take the role of a "blank slate," portraying a neutral attitude onto which clients then project their transferential anxieties and fantasies. However, when working in a culturally sensitive way with clients from diverse backgrounds, such an approach can create distrust and distance between the client and therapist.

What is therapeutically appropriate for one client may not be appropriate for another. Therefore, it is necessary to assess each therapeutic interaction in a culturally specific manner. Ultimately, therapists have a responsibility to intervene in a culturally responsive manner that does not increase the risk of harm but instead enhances the therapeutic relationship. Some researchers have found that inappropriate self-disclosure is a "slippery slope" leading toward unethical relationships. Therefore, the unsophisticated therapist may face a dilemma as he or she attempts to balance the ethical mandate to protect the client and avoid harm with the theoretical implications of self-disclosure and the delivery of culturally relevant services. Nonetheless, the literature on self-disclosure provides evidence that its use is more facilitative than unwarranted, especially when working with women and multiculturally diverse individuals.

A more in-depth analysis of the literature on self-disclosure in therapy demonstrates that self-disclosure enhances the positive impact of treatment by increasing the number of disclosures by the client, facilitating client self-exploration and encouraging an atmosphere of honesty and understanding between client and therapist. Client–therapist understanding—or a lack thereof—is one of the most significant findings in the literature on the utilization of services among culturally diverse individuals. The underrepresentation of culturally diverse individuals in mental health treatment is thought to be a result of individuals' reluctance to seek services because of cultural misunderstandings or communication problems between themselves and the therapist or the service delivery agency. Specific directions for working in culturally responsive ways when delivering services to culturally diverse persons are also highlighted in the APA multicultural guidelines.

SELF-DISCLOSURE IN A MULTICULTURAL CONTEXT

All relationships between racially and ethnically diverse individuals and therapists need to be understood within a context of social relationships. An examination of race relations and sociopolitical history in the United States permits a more in-depth understanding of the need for therapists to assume a nontraditional stance in therapy to gain trust and credibility. It is not uncommon for multiculturally diverse individuals to mistrust therapy and European American therapists. For example, the mistreatment of American Indians by the U.S. government—which comprises a history of violence, attempted genocide, and a boarding school system, combined with current racial attitudes toward American Indians—provides a backdrop for American Indians' mistrust of non-Indian people. The African American experience includes a history of slavery and the persistence of institutionalized racism in all forms toward African Americans in today's society. One does not have to look very far to investigate the histories of all racial and ethnic groups in the United States for an extensive understanding of the oppression each has experienced and continues to experience. As a result of this oppression, many racially and ethnically diverse individuals have developed a mistrust of European American

culture, manifesting in therapy as an unwillingness to disclose experiences that may be invalidated by a culturally incompetent therapist who uses techniques such as the blank slate or intrapsychic interpretation. A culturally competent therapist builds a relationship that reinforces credibility, rapport, and trust by choosing an active stance that includes the use of appropriate self-disclosure. By incorporating a less traditional approach that includes self-disclosing personal experiences, limitations, and an understanding of collective experiences of culturally diverse individuals in the United States, culturally competent therapists inform their clients that they are not part of the untrustworthy establishment.

The need to assume a more nontraditional therapeutic role when working with racially and ethically diverse individuals is a daunting task for many therapists because it assumes the therapist is comfortable employing multiple roles in the therapeutic relationship and crossing boundaries (i.e., self-disclosure) that are dictated by traditional theories. These multiple roles may include advice giver, consultant, advocate, and community activist, in addition to the more traditional therapeutic role. The crossing of boundaries, which may include a willingness to self-disclose, and the ability to play multiple roles provide a foundation for connecting with multiculturally diverse clients in a nontraditional way in order to gain credibility and trust in the therapeutic relationship.

Collectivistic cultural groups—that is, those that value the group and family over the individual—prefer more active advice giving and personal relationships in therapy over the more traditional insight-oriented relationship. These groups include African Americans, Asian Americans, Latina/o Americans, American Indians, and those of Middle Eastern origin. For example, although Latina/o Americans value *familismo*, the primacy of the family over the individual, *personalismo*, the idea that the person is always more important than the task, is also an important value. Therefore, culturally responsive therapists working with Latina/o Americans intentionally build rapport and gain trust by assuming that the interventions they make in individual therapy will affect the client's family and thus inquire about them regularly, keeping the focus on interpersonal interaction in therapy, and valuing social expectations in therapy. For example, when a Latina brings her culturally responsive therapist food because he was able to squeeze her in at the last minute during his lunch hour, the therapist does not interpret this action but graciously accepts the food as his client's genuine gratitude that he values the therapeutic relationship over time constraints and traditional theoretical prohibitions against making exceptions and accommodations. In this situation, the self-disclosure may not be a verbal communication of an experience but a behavior as the therapist gratefully consumes the food during the session.

It is important to note that it is not safe to assume that any ethnic or racial group is homogeneous. Within-group variability is vast and must be taken into consideration when treating individuals from multiculturally diverse backgrounds. For example, researchers have found that class, education, and level of acculturation are significant moderating variables that make generalizations about groups difficult. This notwithstanding, self-disclosure in therapy has been found to be especially important in facilitating rapport and trust in working with women and culturally diverse individuals.

—*Miguel E. Gallardo*

FURTHER READING

Barrett, M. S., & Berman, J. S. (2001). Is psychotherapy more effective when therapists disclose information about themselves? *Journal of Consulting and Clinical Psychology, 69,* 597–603.

Hill, C. E., & Knox, S. (2002). Self-disclosure. *Psychotherapy: Theory, Research, Practice, Training, 38,* 413–417.

Kim, B. S. K., Hill, C. E., Gelso, C. J., Goates, M. K., Asay, P. A., & Harbin, J. M. (2003). Counselor self-disclosure, East Asian American client adherence to Asian cultural values, and counseling process. *Journal of Counseling Psychology, 50*(3), 324–332.

Peterson, Z. D. (2002). More than a mirror: The ethics of therapist self-disclosure. *Psychotherapy: Theory, Research, Practice, Training, 39*(1), 21–31.

SELF-ESTEEM

Self-esteem has been discussed in the psychology literature for more than half a century. It is associated with general psychological well-being, depression, hopelessness, anxiety, social isolation, and motivation. In addition, racial and ethnic differences with respect to self-esteem have been documented.

SELF-ESTEEM DEFINED

According to the most widely cited definition, proposed by Morris Rosenberg in 1965, self-esteem is an individual's overall appraisal of himself or herself. This appraisal is made by examining the totality of the individual and includes reflections on identity (who one is); life products (what one does); possessions (what one has); appearance (what one looks like); and associations and attachments (to whom one is connected). Within each characteristic, a number of tangible (e.g., physical appearance, financial assets) and intangible (e.g., reputation, power) qualities influence the appraisal. Individuals rate their experiences related to each characteristic by judging their actual behaviors and experiences to those of a self-determined ideal standard (e.g., mentor, God). If the summative evaluation is positive, one can be said to have high self-esteem. If the overall evaluation is negative, the person is regarded as having low self-esteem.

Although we would intuitively believe that having high self-esteem is the opposite of having low self-esteem, this is not the case. Persons with high self-esteem generally have a favorable opinion of themselves. On the other hand, those with low self-esteem typically *do not* have unfavorable views of themselves but rather seem to lack positive beliefs about themselves. If we consider this as a mathematical computation, a person would have a more negative (low) self-esteem if he or she perceived more negative (or neutral) values than positive ones.

SELF-ESTEEM ACROSS THE LIFE SPAN

Self-esteem begins at birth and ends at death. It is considered a trait that evolves continuously over time. Children generally have high levels of self-esteem as a consequence of highly positive (and often unrealistic) views of themselves. As they move into adolescence, self-esteem drops as teens experience anxiety about how they will be perceived by their peers and whether they will fit in. The move from adolescence to young adulthood and then to middle adulthood marks a slow rise in self-esteem as individuals experience successful life milestones (e.g., graduation, gainful employment, marriage). Self-esteem peaks in late midlife as individuals become more established in their work and personal lives and begin to see the accomplishments of their offspring (e.g., graduation, employment). People in their early 60s have the highest level of self-esteem. A more dramatic decline in self-esteem is seen during the 70s and 80s as people face losses in mental and physical skills and the death of loved ones (e.g., spouse, peers).

SELF-ESTEEM AND RACIAL AND ETHNIC MINORITIES

Racial and ethnic minority group members form self-esteem based on feelings of self-worth (personal self-esteem) and feelings about their membership in a particular racial or ethnic group (group self-esteem). Wade Nobels proposed a model for explaining the concept of self in African Americans; however, the model can easily be applied to all racial and ethnic minorities. The model postulates that the concept of self is a social process that comprises self-perceptions, internalized attitudes, and perceptions of one's racial or ethnic group. The latter is more complex than the exclusive consideration of feelings about one's own racial or ethnic group. Specifically, among African Americans (but arguably among other minorities as well), group identity includes attitudes about being a member of the African American (or other cultural group) community and feelings about being a member of the society at large. Therefore, members of racial and ethnic minority groups have dual identities and social positions that must be accounted for when evaluating personal worth and value. Group self-esteem is thus influenced by relatives, friends, cultural history (e.g., slavery, Civil Rights movement), and influential community agencies (e.g., African American church) for the community self. Other racial or ethnic group members, media, government agencies (e.g., police, court system), and corporations influence the society-at-large self.

Having a positive view of one's racial or ethnic group and identifying with and accepting this group as a positive reference is linked to positive self-esteem and positive mental health, whereas the rejection of one's racial or ethnic group is linked with social isolation and other maladaptive behaviors. Research studies have explored the association between race and self-esteem among children and adults. A relatively consistent finding is that self-esteem among African Americans is equal to or greater than that of Caucasians. A recent meta-analytic review examined whether this protective effect extends to other racial and ethnic minority groups. The researchers hypothesized that individuals from cultures that place a greater emphasis on collectivism (e.g., many Asian

cultures) rather than individualism (e.g., many North American and European cultures) exhibit lower levels of self-esteem. The analysis reviewed studies spanning four decades to examine race differences in self-esteem among African Americans, Asians, American Indians, Hispanic Americans, and Caucasians. The findings showed that African Americans scored higher than Caucasians on measures of self-esteem; however, Caucasians scored higher than other racial and ethnic minority group members (Hispanics, Asians, and American Indians).

Most research on improving self-esteem is based on work with children. The idea is that if a child is able to obtain high levels of self-esteem early in life, he or she will draw on that self-esteem as a resource throughout the life span. Three factors are associated with high self-esteem among children. First, parents and other caregivers should communicate a stance of unconditional positive regard with children in their care. Adults must communicate to children that although their behaviors or actions may be unacceptable, they are loved no matter what. Such a stance is often communicated within African American families and communities (and probably other racial and ethnic groups). African Americans are often forgiving of an individual's actions (even when they are legally or morally wrong) when the individual is a member of the community or regarded as a genuine or historical ally of the African American community (e.g., President Bill Clinton). This position is partly related to strong religious principles that advocate the forgiveness of sins and transgressions and allow God to sentence individuals for sins committed.

The second factor is the establishment of unambiguous and high standards. Parents and caregivers should develop and articulate a set of guidelines about how children are to behave and must expect the child to consistently follow this guidance. The development of clear and consistent rules and limits is characteristic of Asian American families. At a very young age, Asian American children are provided specific instruction on their role in their immediate family as well as their relationship to extended family and generations past. Youth often receive consistent messages at home that reinforce high standards of achievement, both academically and personally.

Finally, children with high self-esteem tend to experience freedom and latitude within the limits described previously. Parents and caregivers should provide praise for behaviors that are within the established rules and limits and express discontent when behaviors stray outside the established parameters. Pride and other positive acknowledgments contribute to children's positive self-appraisal. The expression of praise or other rewards for expected behavior is a practice that is not associated with any specific racial or ethnic minority group. Although the concept is not new to psychology, it is more difficult to get parents (or other adults, such as work supervisors) to engage in rewarding behaviors in addition to or instead of punishment or punitive actions. From the perspective of psychological and physical survival, which many racial and ethnic minorities face constantly, it may be more important to focus on impeding actions that limit survival (e.g., failing grades in school, illegal activities) than to concentrate on rewarding behaviors (e.g., good grades, legal behaviors) that may or may not enhance their existence.

—*Monica L. Baskin*

FURTHER READING

Bailey, J. A. (2003). The foundation of self-esteem. *Journal of the National Medical Association, 95*, 388–393.

Baumeister, R. F. (2005). Self-concept, self-esteem, and identity. In V. Derlega, B. Winstead, & W. Jones (Eds.), *Personality: Contemporary theory and research* (3rd ed., pp. 246–280). San Francisco: Wadsworth.

Coopersmith, S. (1967). *The antecedents of self-esteem.* San Francisco: W. H. Freeman.

Nobles, W. (1973). Psychological research and the Black self-concept: A critical review. *Journal of Social Issues, 29,* 11–31.

Porter, J., & Washington, R. (1993). Minority identity and self-esteem. *Annual Review of Sociology, 19,* 139–161.

Rosenberg, M. (1965). *Society and the adolescent self-image.* Princeton, NJ: Princeton University Press.

Twenge, J. M., & Crocker, J. (2002). Race and self-esteem: Meta-analysis comparing Whites, Blacks, Hispanics, Asians, and American Indians and comment on Gray-Little and Hafdahl. *Psychological Bulletin, 128*(3), 371–408.

SEXUAL ABUSE

Sexual abuse is a broad term that refers to any act of a sexual nature that is committed by one person (perpetrator) against another person (victim), either against their will or by use of force. Sexual abuse also refers to threats of acts of a sexual nature that a perpetrator makes against a victim. Sexual abuse typically is regarded as a means by which a perpetrator can assert power over a victim in order to demean or exploit the victim. Specific acts of sexual abuse may range from making obscene comments or suggestions to initiating unwanted touching to forcing sexual activity. Although these behaviors are thought to range along a continuum of severity, they are all serious because of potential adverse consequences to the victim.

The terms *sexual harassment*, *sexual imposition*, *sexual misconduct*, *domestic violence*, and *sexual assault* have all been used to describe the variety of sexually abusive behaviors on the continuum. At one end of the continuum is sexual or gendered attention that is directed at a person against his or her wishes or behaviors that is considered threatening or intimidating; this is often referred to as *sexual harassment*. At the other end of the continuum is sexual assault, a term that is often used interchangeably with the word *rape*. Broadly defined, rape refers to any penetration of the vagina or anus by a penis, tongue (mouth), fingers, or object, as well as any penetration of the mouth by a penis, that is perpetrated either against another person's will, by force, or without the consent of the victim. Any of these behaviors might occur in the context of an unfamiliar relationship or a close relationship or acquaintanceship; they could be perpetrated by a man or a woman and directed at a child or an adult.

What follows is an overview of sexual abuse, broadly defined, with a particular focus on minority populations in the United States. This review is divided into discussions of (1) the prevalence of sexual abuse, (2) general characteristics of sexual-abuse perpetrators, (3) the relationship between alcohol use and sexual abuse, (4) culturally specific factors that influence service utilization, and (5) culturally sensitive interventions for sexual abuse.

PREVALENCE OF SEXUAL ABUSE

Little is known about the relationship between sexual abuse and minority populations, particularly because of inconsistent findings from the few published studies examining such factors. Mary Koss, who conducted one of the most prominent research studies on prevalence rates, found that almost 54% of women reported some experience of sexual abuse and 15% reporting having been raped. In regard to minority populations, 40% of Native American women reported an experience of rape, followed by 16% of

Caucasian women, 12% of Hispanic women, 10% of African American women, and 7% of Asian women. In some studies, African American women were more likely to have reported an experience of rape than Caucasian women, but this finding was not substantiated in other studies.

The prevalence of childhood sexual abuse has also been examined. Between 10% and 60% of women experienced some form of sexual abuse as a child. Most research has downplayed the relationship between ethnic background and prevalence of childhood sexual abuse. However, some researchers have found that Hispanic and African American women are more likely to have been abused as children than Caucasian women. In addition, there are other reports that African American, Hispanic, and Caucasian women are more likely to have been abused as children than Asian women.

Perhaps one reason for the inconsistent findings in the literature is the inconsistent use of terminology. Researchers use a variety of terms to refer to sexually abusive behaviors, and many disagree on the definition of sexual abuse. For example, terms such as *sexual victimization*, *sexual assault*, and *rape* have all been used to refer to the same behavior across studies or to refer to quite different behaviors within studies.

The National Violence Against Women (NVAW) Survey is a recent, comprehensive large-scale examination of adult and childhood sexual abuse. Using the definition of rape outlined previously (i.e., sexually penetrative behavior perpetrated against a person's will, by force, or without consent), 17.6% of women and 3% of men reported that they had been the victim of attempted or completed rape in their lifetime. Comparing overall prevalence rates for Caucasians (17.7%) and non-Caucasians (19.8%), there is little difference in reported experiences of completed or attempted rape. There also is no difference between Caucasian men and non-Caucasian men regarding rape victimization. However, the use of the umbrella term *non-Caucasian* does little to illuminate the unique differences in the prevalence of rape among specific minority groups, and, in fact, it may conceal differences that exist among groups, thereby limiting the degree of assistance afforded to particular minority groups.

In fact, reducing the umbrella term *non-Caucasian* into more specific categories—African American, Asian and Pacific Islander, American Indian and Alaska Native, and mixed race—highlights significant differences. Compared to Caucasian women who had been raped (17.7%), about 34% of American Indian and Alaska Native women, 24.4% of mixed-race women, 8.8% of African American women, and 6.8% of Asian and Pacific Islander women reported that they had been raped.

These prevalence rates highlight the widespread victimization of adults by sexual abusers. In the NVAW survey, almost 10% of women and 1% of men reported having been raped since the age of 18. Among the women, 61.9% of rapes were perpetrated by a current or former intimate partner, 21.3% by an acquaintance, 16.7% by a stranger, and 6.5% by a relative. Similarly, data on both sexual and nonsexual victimization experiences among men revealed that a stranger—rather than a relative or an intimate partner—was the perpetrator in 50.4% of incidents. For women, an intimate, rather than a relative or stranger, was the perpetrator in 64% of incidents. Further, the majority of rapes against both male and female victims appear to be perpetrated by men. In fact, men were the perpetrators in close to 100% of cases against women and 70% of cases against men who had been raped since age 18.

Unfortunately, sexual abuse is not an experience that is isolated to adulthood. Sexual violence begins at an early age for many Americans, regardless of their ethnic background. Approximately 2% of men and 9% of women reported that they had been the victim of attempted or completed rape before age 18. Of those who reported an experience of sexual assault during their lifetime, 21.6% of the women and 48% of the men experienced their first rape before the age of 12. In addition, 32.4% of the women and 23% of the men experienced their first rape between ages 12 and 17. Most children and adolescents who were raped knew the perpetrator. Among women who were raped before age 18, 46.7% of the rapes were perpetrated by an acquaintance, 38.8% by a relative, 15% by a current or former intimate partner, and only 14.3% by a stranger. Among men who were raped before age 18, 44.2% of the rapes were perpetrated by an acquaintance, 30.5% by a relative, 6.5% by a current or former intimate partner, and 19.5% by a stranger. Furthermore, both male (89%) and female (99.2%) victims of childhood rape reported the perpetrator was male.

PERPETRATORS OF SEXUAL ABUSE

Our knowledge about the cultural variables that influence perpetrators of sexual abuse comes primarily from government crime statistics and research studies in which as yet undetected sexual offenders (such as college students) were surveyed anonymously. These sources of data have their limitations, particularly regarding cultural variables. Taken together, however, they are able to provide some culturally relevant information about the perpetrators of sexual abuse.

Crime statistics, such as the Uniform Crime Reports (UCR) collected by the Federal Bureau of Investigation, provide a window on the demographic breakdown of individuals who have been arrested for perpetrating sexually abusive behaviors. However, a limitation of the UCR data is that most sexual abusers are never apprehended for their crimes. Therefore, the UCR data cannot provide information about the vast majority of sexual abuse perpetrators. A second limitation of the UCR data is that it no longer provides arrest data on individuals of Latin American descent because of changes in the racial and ethnic classification system used by the U.S. Census Bureau. Despite these limitations, three important culturally relevant patterns emerge from the UCR data.

First, the ethnic breakdown of individuals arrested for sexually abusive behaviors is not proportional to the ethnic breakdown of the general U.S. population. In 2000, the Census Bureau classified 77% of Americans as Caucasian, 12.9% as African American, 4.2% as Asian, and 1.5% as American Indian or Alaska Native. These figures contrast with recent UCR statistics for individuals arrested for sexual offenses. Of the 20,127 arrests made for the completed or attempted rape of a female victim in 2002, 63.4% of those arrested were Caucasian, 43% were African American, 1.3% were Asian or Pacific Islander, and 1.2% were American Indian or Alaska Native. Furthermore, of the 67,761 arrests made for other kinds of sexual offenses (e.g., rape involving a male victim, exhibitionism), 74.3% of those arrested were Caucasian, 23.2% were African American, 1.3% were Asian or Pacific Islander, and 1% were Native American. This breakdown reflects a larger proportion of African American perpetrators and a smaller proportion of Asian perpetrators relative to their share of the population.

Second, regardless of ethnicity, most perpetrators arrested for sexual abuse are male. This is true for perpetrators of child sexual abuse as well as perpetrators of sexual abuse against adults. Even male victims of sexual abuse are more likely to be victimized by a male than by a female. Overall, males accounted for 98.6% of those arrested for completed or attempted rape and 91.7% of those arrested for other kinds of sexual offenses.

Third, sexual offenses tend to be intraracial rather than interracial. For example, 88% of attempted or completed rapes involve a perpetrator and victim of the same race. In addition, 80% of all sexual assaults that result in murder are intraracial. Overall, the data suggest that the most common sexual abuser is a male who offends a female of his own ethnic background.

Although statistics provide information on ethnic similarities and differences among sexual abuse perpetrators, they also provide an understanding as to how culture influences the commission of sexually abusive behavior. Recently, studies examined European American and Asian American male college students who perpetrated sexually abusive acts. When these groups are compared, ethnicity does not create a higher or lower risk for committing sexually abusive behavior. In fact, rates of sexually abusive behavior are similar between the two groups. Instead, the constructs that underlie ethnic differences between European Americans and Asian Americans, such as collectivism versus individualism, may be the primary predictors of sexually abusive behavior.

Generally, Asian cultures are collectivist in nature, whereas European American culture is individualist in nature. In collectivist cultures, the goals and concerns of the society are valued above those of the individual. Therefore, the risk that one will be perceived negatively by others is a significant concern. Negative perceptions shame not only the individual but also the family and the larger social group. Thus, the norms of society play an important role in an individual's behaviors. In individualist cultures, the goals and concerns of the individual are highly valued. Asserting one's personal identity and goals at the expense of society may be tolerated. The risk that one will be perceived negatively by others is not as much of a concern. Thus, personal goals and concerns play a large role in an individual's behavior.

Among European Americans, individual beliefs about rape and women are linked with sexually abusive behaviors, whereas collectivist concerns about the reaction of family and friends and the potential loss of face associated with apprehension for a sexual crime are not linked with sexually abusive behavior. Both collectivist and individualist variables were found to predict sexually abusive behaviors in Asian American college males. Among Asian Americans, concerns about loss of face and the reaction of family and friends, as well individual beliefs about rape and women, are important in predicting sexually abusive behavior.

Further research on culturally relevant constructs with sexual abusers from other ethnic minority groups is needed to better understand the role of culture in the commission of sexual abuse within and between groups. Ultimately, knowledge about culturally specific factors can be used to develop culturally specific treatments for preventing sexual abuse among individuals who are at risk or among identified sex offenders. Of course, knowing more about culturally relevant constructs may also help in developing culturally specific treatments for the victims of sexual abuse.

ALCOHOL, SEXUAL ABUSE, AND CULTURE

The relationship between alcohol use and sexual abuse has been consistently established in the research literature. Estimates of sexual abuse purport that a large majority of incidents involve alcohol consumption by the perpetrator, the victim, or both. Across a wide range of studies, 34% to 74% of perpetrators and 30% to 79% of victims reported having drunk alcohol at the time of sexual abuse. However, the statistical association between alcohol and sexual abuse does not explain their relationship. In general, most theoretical explanations of the alcohol–sexual abuse connection consider both person factors and situational factors.

Person factors refer to variables such as personality traits, long-term patterns of behavior, and attitudes. One person factor that appears to be important in explaining the alcohol–sexual abuse connection is an individual's pattern of alcohol use. Women who have been victims of sexual abuse are more likely to be heavy drinkers and to have experienced childhood sexual abuse. It may be that these women are more likely to drink alcohol in situations that may involve sexual activity as a means of coping with their ambivalent feelings about sex, thereby increasing their risk of being sexually assaulted. A perpetrator's tendency to abuse alcohol has also been linked to engagement in sexual abuse. Regular use of alcohol has emerged as one of the most important predictors of perpetrating one or more sexually assaultive behaviors. The frequency and intensity of drinking are also highly correlated with sexual abuse.

A second person factor that appears to be important in the alcohol–sexual abuse relationship is one's

attitude toward women's alcohol consumption. For example, intoxication may be seen as a "time out" from normal social rules and may excuse the sexual abuse of an intoxicated woman. Women who drink alcohol are frequently perceived as being more sexually available and promiscuous than women who do not drink alcohol.

In contrast to person factors, *situational factors* include characteristics of the immediate situation involving alcohol use and sexual abuse. Alcohol consumption may affect a man's (potential perpetrator's) perceptions of a woman's (potential victim's) cues, leading him to misperceive the woman as being more sexually encouraging than she really is. This narrowing effect on cognitive functioning—called alcohol myopia—has been consistently linked to sexual abuse.

Alcohol also may affect the likelihood of sexual abuse in other ways. For example, perpetrators may get drunk in order to justify their behavior, or they may try to get their victims drunk to facilitate sexually abusive behaviors. Alcohol myopia may lead perpetrators to focus on aggressive solutions to gaining sexual satisfaction, increasing the perpetrator's likelihood of behaving aggressively. For example, when intoxicated, a man might focus on his immediate sexual gratification, sense of entitlement, and anger instead of moral values, guilt, or the possibility of future punishment.

On the other hand, if a woman is intoxicated, she may be unable to effectively resist a perpetrator's aggressive response, further exacerbating his aggressive behavior. Women who reported drinking before they were sexually abused indicated that their intoxication had made them take risks that they normally would have avoided. For example, a woman may feel more comfortable accepting a ride home from a party with an unknown man, perhaps even allowing an intoxicated man to enter her residence. Although a victim's use of alcohol may increase the risk of sexual abuse, this does not imply the victim is to blame for the sexual abuse; rather, perpetrators are responsible for their own behaviors.

Culture presents another level of complexity in the alcohol–sexual abuse relationship. It is reasonable to suspect that the relationship between alcohol and sexual abuse differs across cultural groups because alcohol use varies significantly across cultural groups. Rates of alcohol use in the United States are highest among Caucasians (55%) and American Indians and Alaska Natives (45%) and lowest among African

Americans (40%) and Asians (37%), with Hispanic Americans (43%) in between. In addition to differences between cultural groups in rates of alcohol use, there also appear to be differences in the extent to which women from different cultural groups drink on dates. One study of college women found that 60% of African American women did not drink on dates, compared with 45% of Hispanic women, 41% of Asian women, and 24% of Caucasian women; these factors would suggest that the alcohol–sexual abuse connection is different across groups. On the other hand, the physical effects of alcohol have been found to be consistent across cultural groups; this would suggest that the alcohol–sexual abuse connection is similar across cultures. Research on the cultural impact of the alcohol–sexual abuse connection has been limited, but it has revealed some areas of similarity across cultural groups and some areas of difference.

Some research findings suggest that alcohol's impact on sexual abuse is similar across cultures. Data from a nationally representative survey of female rape victims found no differences in alcohol use involvement in sexual assault across cultural groups, although Caucasian victims were slightly more likely to report that the offender was under the influence of alcohol at the time of the offense than victims from other cultural groups. Another study found that college women who drank alcohol on dates or at social events were more likely to be victims of sexual assault than were women who did not use alcohol on these occasions, regardless of their cultural background.

On the other hand, some research findings suggest that culture moderates the relationship between alcohol and sexual abuse. One study found that Caucasian college women who had been sexually assaulted were significantly more likely to report that alcohol had been consumed by themselves and by the perpetrator before the assault than were African American college women who had been sexually assaulted. Future research should illuminate the extent to which culture influences the specific person and situational factors that link alcohol and sexual abuse.

CULTURE-SPECIFIC FACTORS THAT INFLUENCE SERVICE UTILIZATION

There are a variety of services available to sexual abuse victims, including law enforcement, psychotherapy, and violence shelters. One of the factors that influences the use of these resources is cultural norms; that is, some cultures have norms that facilitate help seeking, whereas some work in the opposite manner.

African Americans

Several factors have been identified that affect the service utilization rates of African American victims of sexual abuse. These include lack of economic resources, lack of availability of services, perceptions that resources are for the majority culture, reluctance to involve police or people from outside the community, fear of being disloyal to the African American community, racism, and stereotypes about race and violence. The African American culture maintains a tradition of relying on one's own resources and inner strength, which may discourage victims from disclosing information about abuse or seeking assistance. The extended family is also an important resource that may be more readily available than institutional resources such as shelters. In addition, reluctance to threaten family cohesion may lead some women to avoid seeking outside help. Finally, some African American women are likely to physically resist perpetrators, thereby increasing the severity of the abuse. An increase in physical resistance has been shown to decrease sympathetic responses from police and legal systems, thus decreasing the rate of reporting and seeking support from such entities among victims.

Hispanic Americans

For Hispanic victims of sexual abuse, a variety of factors have been identified that limit the utilization of services, such as language barriers, economic status, cultural norms regarding gender roles, and stress or limited social support among recent immigrants. Furthermore, religious values, such as the Catholic doctrine that limits familial separation through divorce, may dramatically influence a victim's decision making. Finally, the lack of culturally appropriate services for some Hispanic Americans, particularly the lack of bilingual services, may significantly reduce help-seeking behavior.

Asian Americans

Although Asian subcultures have diverse backgrounds, many of the Asian groups living in the United States share similar cultural values about the utilization of helping services. The value placed on the family unit is a strong inhibitor of service utilization. In addition, community and family disapproval of familial separation through divorce may be a significant factor. Other factors include reluctance to publicly discuss sexual issues, the importance of addressing problems within the family, and the stigma associated with emotional problems and mental illness. Furthermore, economic status, the ability to provide for children, comfort with the English language, immigration status, and fear of discrimination (a concern of all minority groups) may all significantly influence help-seeking behaviors.

Native Americans

There is generally a lack of research regarding Native American victims of sexual abuse. Therefore, our ability to identify the factors associated with service utilization is limited, especially for those individuals living in urban areas. However, some barriers have been identified that reflect the beliefs and living situations of many Native American victims. For example, many individuals are physically and socially isolated from other cultural groups. They may live in large, unpopulated stretches of land in small, cohesive groups in which access to treatment providers is limited. Victims may fear a lack of confidentiality when seeking treatment within the group or fear being considered disloyal for seeking assistance outside the group. In addition, the reduced privacy afforded by close-knit communities may exacerbate distress because of the stigma of sexual abuse. Finally, although some native healers are available, there is a general lack of Western services that are culturally relevant and financially suitable for this population.

CULTURALLY SENSITIVE INTERVENTIONS FOR SEXUAL ABUSE

Most research on sexual abuse has focused on characteristics of victims and perpetrators that may influence the risk of sexual abuse. However, much less research has been conducted on the cultural and psychosocial influences on sexual abuse. Clearly, there is a basic need for interventions that are culturally sensitive. That is, victims of sexual abuse, regardless of their background, need to feel connected with the treatment, validated, respected, understood, and supported. Researchers agree that all aspects of intervention must

be readily available to all sexual abuse victims. This includes providing interventions in the victim's language and associating with and maintaining links with community and religious leaders. Treatment providers must understand the issues that are relevant to the culture of the victim, including family dynamics, cultural norms, and the psychology of oppression.

There appear to be two broad and sometimes opposing viewpoints on the design of psychological interventions, such as interventions for the treatment of sexual abuse victims. The first camp believes that therapists and clients should be matched on a variety of demographic variables, such as gender, age, sexual orientation, and race or ethnicity. Proponents argue that such similarities facilitate trust and reduce victims' burden of explaining themselves, their backgrounds, and their unique psychosocial concerns. Furthermore, mismatching is believed to increase "ethnocultural disorientation," meaning that important verbal and nonverbal communication may be misinterpreted and thereby influence the content and process of the therapeutic relationship. Mismatching between the therapist and client may cause the intervention to focus on cultural differences rather than the actual experience or treatment of sexual abuse.

The second camp believes that therapists and clients do not need to be matched because a skilled clinician should be able to understand, empathize, and develop a warm, trusting therapeutic environment regardless of cultural differences between the therapist and the client. Proponents of this view see the differences between therapist and client as valuable dialogue for therapy, or conversely, that differences between client and therapist are irrelevant to the therapy process. Depending on the theoretical background and training of the therapist, the particular intrapsychic processes, learning histories, and irrational thoughts of clients may be seen as therapeutically relevant and important to treatment regardless of ethnic cultural origin.

A third perspective on the treatment of sexual abuse is to disregard fixed rules and to adopt a more individualized approach. For example, Gordon Paul believed that a research focus on the effectiveness of psychotherapy, broadly defined, is fundamentally meaningless. Rather, he believed that the only legitimate research question asks, what type of therapy, with what type of client, produces what kind of effect? Therefore, the minority client should choose a therapist with the individual characteristics that he or she deems critical for his or her own needs. As noted previously, there is much distinctiveness between individuals, and there is a tendency to overgeneralize cultural similarities within minority groups. Treatment providers should be aware of the minority status and affiliation of their clients, continually assess the adequacy of their communication styles and therapy methods, and be flexible enough to make adjustments as necessary. After all, sexual abuse victims should be treated as individuals regardless of their demographic categorization, including ethnic group and broad cultural background. Thus, in the shadow of Paul, perhaps the focus of treatment should be the type of therapy that is best suited for a particular minority person at a particular time.

—D. J. Angelone
—Damon Mitchell
—Richard Hirschman

See also Alcohol/Substance Use and Abuse; Child Abuse: Overview

FURTHER READING

Fontes, L. A. (1995). *Sexual abuse in nine North American cultures: Treatment and prevention.* Thousand Oaks, CA: Sage.

Kalof, L. (2000). Ethnic differences in female sexual victimization. *Sexuality and Culture: An Interdisciplinary Quarterly, 4,* 75–97.

Mitchell, D., Hirschman, R., Angelone, D. J., & Lilly, R. S. (2004). A laboratory analogue for the study of peer sexual harassment. *Psychology of Women Quarterly, 28,* 194–203.

Rennison, C. M. (2001). Criminal victimization 2000: Charges 1999–2000 with trends 1993–2000 (National Crime Victimization Survey, Rep. NCJ-187007). Washington, DC: U.S. Department of Justice.

Tjaden, P., & Thoennes, N. (2000). *Full report of the prevalence, incidence, and consequences of violence against women: Findings from the National Violence Against Women Survey.* Washington, DC: National Institute of Justice.

SEXUAL MINORITY STATUS IN PEOPLE OF COLOR

Being a member of an ethnic minority may come with the experience of bias and prejudice in everyday life. When ethnic minority status is combined with sexual minority status, the experience of bias and prejudice can be twofold. Having a lesbian, bisexual, or gay identity may put individuals further outside the mainstream society and at odds with the values of their own ethnic minority group.

For some ethnic minority groups, traditional values preclude the acceptance of homosexuality or bisexuality. This is especially true for families who are first- or second-generation immigrants to the United States. There is some speculation that ethnic minorities who are also sexual minorities face discrimination within the lesbian, gay, and bisexual (LGB) community. The following sections will focus on some of the specific issues that ethnic minorities face with regard to sexual minority status.

AFRICAN AMERICANS

The African American community is often described as close-knit and community based. Within this community, individuals may not feel comfortable disclosing their LGB status to other group members because they fear alienating themselves from their family and their community. This is an especially strong concern for African American males, who do not want to be seen as different from the rest of their peer group. In many ways, it is easier for female sexual minorities to come out in the African American community.

Recently, a trend among African American males has begun to come to light. Being on the "down-low" is a term that characterizes males who have sex with other males yet identify themselves as heterosexual. In this situation, the higher-status man usually takes the dominant sexual position and therefore maintains his feelings of masculinity and heterosexuality. This situation devalues the submissive partner and hides and shames the notion of homosexuality.

Studies have suggested that even when African Americans are comfortable telling their families about their sexual orientation, they may not disclose their status outside the family network. Supportive family ties may be in place, but individuals may still fear community disapproval. Therefore, African Americans are often less involved in LGB community organizations and activities.

Within the African American community, close church ties may strengthen the prejudice against homosexuality, which is considered a serious sin against God. Depending on their family's religious ties, individuals may not feel comfortable disclosing their sexual orientation to their family or community of church members.

ASIAN AMERICANS

Asian Americans also tend to have very close-knit, community-based groups of families. Individual needs are considered secondary to group needs, and therefore sexual minority status often does not fit within this community emphasis. The needs of the individual are not supposed to outweigh those of the group; being a sexual minority is quite often seen as yielding to an individual need or desire that is not compatible with community values. This is especially true for first- or second-generation members who resist assimilation to the majority American culture. When an individual in this community comes out as a member of a sexual minority, his or her actions may be seen as a reflection of his or her family's status within the community. This goes against the Asian principle of "saving face" and may alienate individuals from their cultural group.

Sexual minority individuals who are of Asian descent are even less likely to join LGB communities or activities outside of specialized Asian American LGB groups. They are also less likely to disclose their sexual orientation to family members or to others in their community.

LATINO/A AND HISPANIC AMERICANS

As part of another close-knit, family-oriented community, Latinos as and Hispanic American sexual minorities experience some of the same issues that African American sexual minorities encounter. This is especially true for male members of the community, who may have been raised in an environment that celebrates machismo, or the masculinity and dominance of men. For male sexual minorities, disclosure of their sexual orientation may mean the loss of respect from other males in their community, and they may be perceived as more feminine than masculine.

Studies suggest that Latinos/as and Hispanics tend to fall between European American and African American sexual minorities in their level of comfort with disclosing their sexual orientation to others and joining LGB communities and activities. Like African Americans, Latinos/as and Hispanics may feel comfortable telling their family members about their sexual orientation but not other people in their community. This ethnic group also has strong ties to Catholicism, which may strengthen the prejudice against homosexuality; the Catholic church condemns all sexual activity outside marriage.

NATIVE AMERICANS

Native Americans have a history of accepting sexual minority status among individuals, believing it to be a spiritual essence described as "two spirited." This term originally described the embodiment of both male and female qualities in one person. It now designates any sexual minority status in an individual. This term, which comes from the Northern Algonquin word *niizh manitoag*, was adopted in 1990 by a group of American Indian and Alaska Native tribes. Although sexual diversity has historically been accepted as a spiritual expression, this is not always the case in modern Native American tribes.

Studies of two-spirited LGB individuals in the Native American community found the rate of sexual and physical abuse among these individuals to be two times higher than among their heterosexual Native American counterparts. These individuals have also been found to abuse more alcohol and illegal drugs as a means of emotional escape.

Native American sexual minorities have been interviewed in several qualitative studies. These studies found that individuals try hard to maintain both their Native American identity and their sexual minority status, involving themselves in both Native American rituals and activities and LGB activities and groups.

MAJORITY PREJUDICE

In addition to rejection by their own families and ethnic groups, ethnic minorities who are also sexual minorities face prejudice from the European American LGB community. Historically, ethnic minorities have complained that the European American LGB community does not meet their needs or understand their cultural values. Predominantly European American LGB communities may place little value on families of origin because many individuals have been rejected by their families and formed new, unrelated families within the LGB community. This may be incomprehensible to ethnic minorities who still wish to maintain close ties with their families, even if that means not disclosing their sexual orientation.

As a result of differences experienced by ethnic minorities in the LGB community, many ethnic minorities have chosen to create their own LGB communities, exclusively for ethnic minority individuals. More and more of these groups are appearing on college campuses and in cities; they allow LGB individuals who are also ethnic minorities to gather together and discuss the additional stressors they experience as ethnic minorities.

Many of the statements made here are generalizations and may not capture the experience of every individual of multiple minority status. Individual experiences depend on family characteristics, environment (whether rural or urban), and many other factors. Indeed, there are more within-group differences among individuals of any minority group than there are differences between large minority groups. The concerns identified here are just a few of the issues discussed in the research on individuals who are both ethnic and sexual minorities.

—*Kimberlee M. Roy*

FURTHER READING

Balsam, K. F., Huang, B., Fieland, K., Simoni, J. A., & Walters, K. (2004). Culture, trauma, and wellness: A comparison of heterosexual and lesbian, gay, bisexual, and two-spirited Native Americans. *Cultural Diversity and Ethnic Minority Psychology, 10,* 287–301.

Rosario, M., Schrimshaw, E. W., & Hunter, J. (2004). Ethnic/racial differences in the coming-out process of lesbian, gay, and bisexual youths: A comparison of sexual identity development over time. *Cultural Diversity and Ethnic Minority Psychology, 10,* 215–228.

SOCIAL JUSTICE/ACTION

DEFINITION OF SOCIAL JUSTICE

Social justice is defined as the full and equal participation of all groups in a society that is mutually shaped to meet their needs. Social justice includes a vision of society in which the distribution of resources is equitable and all members are physically and psychologically safe and secure. Many definitions of social justice focus on equality. A core argument in the literature on social justice, however, is whether equal distribution of resources alone (i.e., resources, services, goods) constitutes justice. The focus on equal distribution has been criticized because this conceptualization ignores the *process* of social justice and the institutional context of the process. Specifically, critics argue that decision making, division of labor, and culture—all potential tools of oppression—are not accounted for in this conceptualization of social justice. For example,

goods could be distributed equally, but inequality could still exist because of certain groups' inability to access these goods.

Social justice is related to many pressing societal issues that psychologists are concerned with, including multiculturalism and oppression. *Multiculturalism* entails the study of diversity and how to bring diversity into research, training, and practice. Multiculturalism is closely linked to oppression, which occurs when an individual or group is dominated by others and thus experiences discrimination or exploitation. Alternatively, oppression also occurs when one group attempts to control another through institutionalized systems and policies. Because the oppression of many groups in society (e.g., women, the elderly, minorities, gay men, lesbian women) does not allow a large share of the population to participate fully in social life, social justice concerns a majority of the population. Some have argued that it is only by helping marginalized groups become aware of their oppression and embark on a plan of action (i.e., *conscientization*) that oppression can be countered.

HISTORY OF SOCIAL JUSTICE IN PSYCHOLOGY

The concept of social justice originated in ancient theology and philosophy. Since the days of Plato, justice has referred to a well-ordered society. Political philosophers such as John Locke and Jean-Jacques Rousseau conceptualized justice as related to liberty and equality. Locke's libertarian justice model outlined justice as equal opportunity for all, although he did not call for legislated equality. Rousseau later added to Locke's model, claiming that a system that allocates resources based on ability and achievement naturally leads to social inequities. Therefore, government should create laws that prevent social injustices but allow individual freedoms. Socialism, which is based on Marxist principles of enforced equality for all, is an extension of this theory in that government fully legislates equality, although at the expense of individual freedoms. Recently, a communitarian model has been proposed to better address aspects of social justice that lie beyond equal distribution. This model focuses on community empowerment and collective decision making.

Attention to social justice in psychology emerged from the field of community psychology. Community psychology evolved during the 1960s and challenged the traditional values of psychology, which focused primarily on the individual. Community psychology put forth ecological models that view social problems more systemically (i.e., as a result of the systems in which they exist). Community psychology called for psychologists to go out into the community and championed the collaboration of psychologists with community members. Central to all of these practices is the goal of social change. Much of this social change involves partnerships with oppressed groups.

In recent decades, the field of critical psychology has emerged, criticizing traditional psychology and its values as dictated by mainstream society. Critical psychology is based on Marxism and originally grew out of the students' movement of the 1960s. A central practice of mainstream psychology is to strengthen values and institutions that prevent people from living meaningful lives. For example, society encourages people to find meaning in advancing careers, watching television, or shopping, activities that make money for financial and commercial institutions but hinder efforts to bring people together for dialogue about community issues. Critical psychologists call for psychologists to no longer accept the status quo of mainstream psychology and instead be guided by a quest for social justice and human welfare. This quest involves psychologists closely examining their own socialization and applying this knowledge to counter oppression and inequality. This course of action calls for praxis, or reflection and action on the world in order to transform it.

Only recently has the call for social justice made its way into applied disciplines such as counseling and clinical psychology. In recent years some have argued that the field of counseling psychology is particularly well-suited for participation in this endeavor in light of its theoretical origins. Many authors have echoed this call to social justice, and the field has visibly increased its attention to the issue. The Fourth National Counseling Psychology Conference, held in 2001, embraced this theme, and several entire issues of national counseling psychology journals have been devoted to its deliberation. Several attempts have recently been made to outline examples of social justice–oriented training programs, social justice–guided research, and social justice–driven clinical practice.

CURRENT SOCIAL JUSTICE AGENDA

The goals and values of the current social justice agenda have been broadly defined as going beyond simple equal distribution. They include visible and meaningful participation in society's institutions, as well as sharing views on social life. In the field of counseling psychology, authors have drawn extensively from feminist and multicultural theory to define the principles underlying social justice. These include valuing ongoing self-examination, facilitating shared power, giving voice to the disenfranchised, raising consciousness about oppression, focusing on strengths, and helping to create interventions that are self-sustainable. Such principles, it is argued, help to transform social systems, ensure full and equal participation in society, and attend to equal access of resources.

In developing a social justice agenda, barriers and difficulties associated with the process have become clear. Not only does oppression come from external sources, but also it can be internalized within oppressed people. One example of internalized oppression is the construct of homonegativity. Internalized homonegativity is defined as a set of negative attitudes and affects toward homosexuality in other persons and toward homosexual features in oneself. Such oppression may begin externally but may result in psychological oppression of the individual by himself or herself, which is very difficult to counter with traditional psychotherapy. This suggests a need for expanded roles for psychologists, a willingness to become politically involved, and advocacy for the disenfranchised.

Ultimately, the goal for psychologists who are committed to social justice is to educate, create awareness, and incorporate social justice into their work and the world. Incorporating knowledge from multidisciplinary sources, whether they be philosophy, psychology, or other areas, is the best way to further the cause of social justice—a crucially important goal for our society today.

—Melissa Morgan
—Elizabeth Vera

FURTHER READING

Bell, L. A. (1997). Theoretical foundations for social justice education. In M. Adams, L. A. Bell, & P. Griffin (Eds.), *Teaching for diversity and social justice* (pp. 3–15). New York: Routledge.

Fox, D., & Prilleltensky, I. (1997). Introducing critical psychology: Values, assumptions, and the status quo. In D. Fox & I. Prilleltensky (Eds.), *Critical psychology: An introduction* (pp. 1–20). Thousand Oaks, CA: Sage.

Freire, P. (1990). *Pedagogy of the oppressed*. New York: Continuum.

Prilleltensky, I., & Nelson, G. (2002). *Doing psychology critically: Making a difference in diverse settings.* New York: Palgrave Macmillan.

Rawls, J. (1971). *A theory of justice.* Cambridge, MA: Harvard University Press.

Speight, S., & Vera, E. (2004). A social justice agenda: Ready or not? *Counseling Psychologist, 32*(1), 109–118.

SOCIETY FOR THE PSYCHOLOGICAL STUDY OF ETHNIC MINORITY ISSUES

The Society for the Psychological Study of Ethnic Minority Issues, Division 45 of the American Psychological Association (APA), is the major representative body for psychologists who conduct research on ethnic minority concerns and apply psychological knowledge and techniques to ethnic minority issues. The division's purpose is to advance psychology as a science and to promote public welfare through research, to apply research findings to address ethnic minority issues, and to encourage professional relationships among psychologists with these interests. It also represents ethnic minority concerns within the governance of the APA.

The mission of the Society for the Psychological Study of Ethnic Minority Issues reflects that of the APA. Specifically, the society serves as a means to promote the development of knowledge and understanding of ethnic minority psychology, the application of psychological principals specific to ethnic minorities, the consideration of how social concerns affect ethnic minority populations, and the incorporation of the importance of diversity in society. In the spirit of promoting diversity of the human experience, the society, through its policies and practices, attends to the concerns of ethnic minorities, with special sensitivity to gender, sexual orientation, physical ability, class, age, and religion. Ethnic minority groups that are represented in the society include American Indians and Alaska Natives, Asian Americans and Pacific Islanders, African Americans, Latino/as, and Hispanics living in the United States. Because it recognized that nomenclature changes over time, the society uses the terms *ethnic minority* and *people of color* interchangeably.

From its inception, the division has sponsored programs at the annual convention of the APA. Programs feature scientific papers, symposia, and poster sessions, during which the membership of the division and those interested in the application of psychological principles to ethnic minority issues can exchange ideas and disseminate research findings. Reflecting the diversity of interests within the division, topics cover a range of ideas related to ethnic minorities, such as psychosocial stress, HIV/AIDS, the development of self-identity, psychological assessment, substance abuse, and sexuality and sex roles. In addition to the annual APA convention, the division cosponsors a multicultural summit every two years.

The journal *Cultural Diversity and Ethnic Minority Psychology* is the peer-reviewed quarterly publication of Division 45. Membership includes a subscription to the journal and to the division newsletter, *Focus*, which is published two to three times per year. The *Focus* newsletter is designed to provide information about the activities of the division and its members, job notices, and updates on current events. The newsletter also publishes substantive articles on research findings and the application of psychological techniques to ethnic minority issues. In addition, it serves as a networking vehicle for its members.

Division 45 offers membership at the member, fellow, and associate levels, which are based on the requirements established for APA membership. Division 45 has two affiliate (non-APA member) categories: Professional affiliates are persons who are not members of the APA but who are professionals from disciplines bearing on the central interests of the division, and student affiliates are persons who support the mission of the division and are enrolled in an undergraduate or graduate program in psychology. All members and affiliates receive the division publications *Focus* and the quarterly journal *Cultural Diversity and Ethnic Minority Psychology*. Voting privileges are extended to all members, fellows, and five-year voting associates.

—*Eduardo Morales*

See also Council of National Psychological Associations for the Advancement of Ethnic Minority Interests; Office of Ethnic Minority Affairs, American Psychological Association

SOCIETY OF INDIAN PSYCHOLOGISTS

HISTORY

The Society of Indian Psychologists (SIP) in the only freestanding professional association for American

Indians and Alaska Natives who are psychologists or psychologists in training. The society emerged from two interest groups: one created during the late 1960s by Carolyn Attneave, the other founded in the early 1970s by Joe Trimble. Attneave formed a national network of Indian psychologists among people she had identified as having an American Indian background. Trimble formed an interest group of Indian psychologists when he was a student at Oklahoma City University. In 1973, Attneave changed the name of her network to the Society of Indian Psychologists. Trimble later integrated his group with the SIP. Since then, the SIP has grown to include more than 110 American Indian and Alaska Native psychologists. However, the number of American Indian and Alaska Native psychologists is unknown because many do not join the SIP or the American Psychological Association.

GOALS

Currently, the society's goals focus on improving the mental health of all American Indians and Alaska Natives, enhancing positive relationships among Native people, and promoting ideas to improve the quality of their lives. The organization serves as a support network for American Indian and Alaska Native psychologists through its listserv and an annual meeting; its goal is for members to assist one another in career development and to recruit more American Indians into the field of psychology. Finally, the society aspires to advance psychological services for all Native peoples of the Americas (see http://www.geoc ities.com/indianpsych/aboutsip.html).

MEMBERSHIP

Membership in the SIP is open to anyone of any career background who has an interest in the mental health concerns of American Indians and Alaska Natives. An annual SIP conference is held each June in Logan, Utah, under the auspices of the American Indian Students Program in the Department of Psychology at Utah State University. Officers—president, past president, president-elect, secretary, treasurer, and three graduate student liaisons—are elected at this meeting. In addition, the SIP offers a Web site and a listserv. The Web site offers information for students such as internship sites, graduate study programs, and scholarship information.

—*Diane Willis*

See also Bureau of Indian Affairs, Indian Health Service

FURTHER READING

Trimble, J. E. (2000). American Indian psychology. In A. E. Kazdin (Ed.), *Encyclopedia of psychology* (pp. 139–144). New York: Oxford University Press.

SOCIOECONOMIC STATUS

Measures of socioeconomic status (SES) purport to represent the relative distribution of prestige in a society. In many societies, SES is significantly associated with culture and ethnicity. For example, in the United States, European Americans have significantly higher per capita incomes and significantly lower poverty rates than all other major ethnic groups. Furthermore, these SES discrepancies play a causal role in many of the deficits in academic performance, mental health, and physical health that other U.S. ethnic groups show when compared with European Americans. The close association between ethnicity and SES, as well as the relationship between SES and important psychosocial variables, point to the importance for psychologists of understanding SES.

Failing to account for SES when working with cultural groups can limit the accuracy of psychological observations in two important ways. First, the effects of ethnicity and culture may be confounded with the effects of SES. When SES differences are reflected in the individuals involved in psychological research or applications and SES is not assessed, any significant association between SES and psychosocial variables may be erroneously attributed to culture or ethnicity. The second limitation is that failing to account for SES prevents the consideration of interactions with culture or ethnicity. When SES is not considered, it can be easy to mistakenly assume that the relationship between cultural group membership and a psychosocial variable remains the same across all levels of SES, or that the relation between SES and a dependent variable is the same in all cultures or ethnic groups. Both of these limitations are easily overcome by adequately conceptualizing and assessing SES. Accordingly, recommendations for the accurate conceptualization and measurement of SES are outlined here.

STRUCTURE OF SES

Unfortunately, the use of the term *socioeconomic status* in the psychological literature often connotes a unidimensional, homogeneous construct. For example, it is not uncommon for the psychological literature to claim that SES is associated with a given psychosocial outcome. However, the accumulated research evidence suggests that SES is a multidimensional construct with distinct but related components. The relation of any one component to an extraneous variable often differs both quantitatively and qualitatively from that of the other components. For example, existing research suggests that children's exposure to certain types of stress has a significant negative association with some components of SES (e.g., family assets and parental occupational status) but not with others (e.g., family income and parental education). Therefore, SES should not be conceptualized as a single indicator of societal prestige but as a collection of interrelated but independent components. Accordingly, greater accuracy is achieved by clearly referring to the relationship between a specific component (e.g., parental occupational status) and a given outcome whenever describing SES effects.

The components of SES are often categorized into three groups. The first group includes the financial resources available to any given individual (e.g., income). The second group represents the nonmaterial resources that an individual possesses, such as education. The final group incorporates an individual's social and interpersonal resources (e.g., social and family networks). However, certain important components of SES cannot be readily accommodated into this tripartite scheme. For example, occupational status—the culturally determined subjective value of an occupation—is an important component of SES that cannot be neatly incorporated into any of the three groups.

MEASUREMENT OF SES

Several existing measures of SES combine an individual's standing on a number of SES components into a composite estimation of relative social standing. Though seemingly convenient, these approaches hinder the useful interpretation of any relation between SES and psychosocial variables by obscuring the specific component (or components) through which social differences operate. For this reason, the use of composite SES scores in psychological research and applications with ethnic or cultural groups is strongly discouraged. Instead, the assessment of SES should focus on determining the resources available to an individual in each of the three categories (i.e., financial resources,

nonmaterial resources, and social and interpersonal resources) and obtaining some measure of occupational status. Furthermore, each of these components should be considered separately when analyzing or interpreting psychological data. The following paragraphs will provide some recommendations for measuring and interpreting psychological data that can be assigned to each of the three categories.

Financial resources are most often assessed through self-reported income over a fixed period of time (e.g., monthly, yearly). Several factors should be considered when deciding on a specific format for the assessment of income. First, the likelihood of obtaining accurate information increases when questions about income are presented in a multiple-choice format. The response categories offered to individuals should be determined by the expected range of income in the population represented. Second, measures of income should reflect the total amount of financial resources available to an individual. For this reason, reports of per capita household income are preferable to reports of individual income (e.g., when working with children or individuals living in households with multiple incomes). Per capita household income is calculated by dividing an individual's reported total household income by the number of individuals in the household. Finally, the accuracy of reporting may increase when questions about income and other financial resources are presented near the end of an interview or data-collection instrument.

Nonmaterial resources are most often assessed in adults through self-reported number of school years completed. For children and adolescents, the number of school years completed by the head of the household should be obtained. It should be noted that the head of the household is not always the child's mother or father. When children live with both their mother and father, it is preferable to obtain information about both parents.

The most important social and interpersonal resource that should be assessed is household structure. Common structural features include the number of individuals living in the household and the relationship of each individual to the person of interest (e.g., husband, daughter, friend). This information can be used to classify the individual into relevant categories (e.g., whether an individual is single or married, has children or not, is divorced, etc.). Categories should be determined by the purpose for which the information will be used. For example, although a category that differentiates between single-parent and two-parent households may be appropriate for research or applications with developing children, the same category may be less relevant in studies of cognitive processing in adults.

To obtain a measure of occupational status, information about an individual's occupation must first be acquired. This information can then be used to obtain prestige scores from any of the various status scales in existence. In work with children and adolescents, the usual practice is to assess the occupational status of the head of the household, realizing that in many cases, this may be someone other than the child's mother or father. When children live with both parents, it is preferable to obtain status ratings for both the mother's and the father's occupations. Although research suggests that most occupational status scales are highly correlated with each other, there are significant cultural differences in the distribution of prestige ratings. In other words, an occupation's prestige level may increase or decrease depending on the cultural group that is asked to evaluate it. Therefore, the applicability of specific scales to any given cultural group should be carefully considered.

The important SES differences among cultural groups in many societies and their role in perpetuating social inequalities point to the importance of incorporating SES into psychological theories and methods related to culture and ethnicity. The identification of SES effects and their disentanglement with those of culture will lead to a better understanding of the psychology of ethnic and cultural groups worldwide.

—*Ignacio David Acevedo-Polakovich*

FURTHER READING

Betancourt, H., & Lopez, S. R. (1993). The study of culture, ethnicity, and race in American psychology. *American Psychologist, 48*(6), 629–637.

Brady, S. S., & Mathews, K. A. (2002). The influence of socioeconomic status and ethnicity on adolescents' exposure to stressful life events. *Journal of Pediatric Psychology, 27*(7), 575–583.

Coleman, J. S. (1988). Social capital in the creation of human capital. *American Journal of Sociology, 94*(Suppl.), S95–S120.

Entwisle, D. R., & Astone, N. M. (1994). Some practical guidelines for measuring youth's race/ethnicity and socioeconomic status. *Child Development, 65*, 1521–1540.

Hauser, R. M. (1994). Measuring socioeconomic status in studies of child development. *Child Development, 65*, 1541–1545.

Liberatos, P., Link, B. G., & Kelsey, J. L. (1998). The measurement of social class in epidemiology. *Epidemiologic Reviews, 10*, 87–121.

SOMATIZATION

The term *somatization* is attributed to Wilhelm Stekel, who, in the early 20th century, defined it as a bodily disorder that is the expression of a psychic conflict. The psychosocial origins of somatic distress have been difficult to verify; therefore, contemporary theories view somatization as the tendency to experience and communicate psychological distress in the form of physical symptoms and to seek medical help for those physical symptoms.

MANIFESTATIONS OF SOMATIZATION

A patient presenting with somatization may complain of symptoms—often multiple symptoms—in any body part or organ system. Chest pain, abdominal pain, headache, and backache are by far the most common presenting complaints, along with fatigue. These physical symptoms may or may not involve detectable physiological dysfunction. Some are entirely subjective and may be viewed as culture-specific idioms of distress that are used to express emotional distress or conflict within particular social worlds. Culture-specific examples of somatization include the symptom clusters associated with *shenjing shuairuo* in China, *nervios* among Latinos in the United States and Latin America, and *koro* in Southeast Asia. Other symptoms appear to be manifestations of actual dysfunction in the affected body part or system, such as fibromyalgia, tension headache, and irritable bowel syndrome. In some cases, a demonstrable organic disease does exist, but the patient's complaints are judged to be grossly exaggerated.

NORMAL AND PATHOLOGICAL SOMATIZATION

Despite the common perception that somatization is more prevalent in certain cultural groups, cross-cultural research suggests that the tendency to experience and communicate psychological distress in the form of somatic symptoms is widespread in all cultures. About 80% of healthy individuals experience somatic symptoms in any given week. Somatization becomes a clinical problem, however, when an individual who is so predisposed attributes his or her bodily symptoms to physical illness and, as a result, seeks medical diagnosis and treatment. The condition is considered pathological when the patient persists in seeking medical evaluation and treatment in spite of repeated negative findings and reassurances that the symptoms have no physical basis. Among these patients, somatization may cause personal suffering and negatively affect family relationships. Somatization is an important matter of public health, a common cause of absenteeism, and a drain on limited medical resources. It has been estimated that one-fifth of all medical expenses are for patients who somatize or have hypochondriacal concerns. This has been described as medicine's unresolved problem.

THEORIES AND EMPIRICAL STUDIES ON SOMATIZATION

Somatization can be attributed to multiple causes. Empirical studies suggest that both genetic factors and environmental stresses contribute to somatization.

Somatization, Depression, and Anxiety

Studies have uncovered an association between somatization and depression: Depressed patients tend to have more somatic symptoms than nondepressed individuals, and somatizers tend to be more depressed than patients with physical disease. Somatization has also been described as masked depression. However, there is no conclusive evidence that somatization is a true depressive equivalent, meaning that it has the same etiology, course, and response to treatment.

Similarly, some writers have asserted that somatic sensations are the bodily manifestations of anxiety states. In a correlation study with neurotic patients, somatic symptoms were more strongly associated with anxiety than with depression. Across studies, there is a consistent relationship between emotional and somatic symptoms. Numerous drug studies have shown that somatic symptoms decrease in number and severity when the underlying anxiety or depressive disorder remits, suggesting that somatic symptoms are an integral part of these emotional states rather than a replacement.

Somatic Symptoms as Manifestations of Physiological Activity

Some authors regard somatization as a perception of physiological activity that is aggravated by emotions. Somatic symptoms have been associated with peripheral physiological changes in numerous studies. For example, contractions of the scalp muscles are associated with tension headaches. The electromyographic potential of painful muscles in other parts of the body are higher than those of control muscles. Some patients with low back pain have elevated electromyograph levels in paravertebral muscles, particularly when they are emotionally stressed.

Learned Responses and Selective Perception

Research has demonstrated that learning plays a substantial role in shaping bodily sensations. Children's symptoms often mirror symptoms that are present in other family members. Several retrospective studies suggest that adult somatization and hypochondriac attention to bodily sensations are associated with parental interest and attention to symptoms during the patient's childhood. Lower social class, education, and cultural factors also influence the extent to which emotional distress is expressed somatically. In non-Western cultures in particular, somatization is the normative mode of symptom presentation in treatment settings.

There is also evidence that selective perception can affect bodily sensations. With training, experimental subjects can learn to improve their perception of physical sensations. Selective attention to a part of one's body may improve a person's skill in perceiving sensations, which may contribute to an amplification, minimization, or denial of bodily sensation. Thus, some somatic symptoms are perceptions of actual physiological changes, not imagined.

Gain and Social Reinforcement

Among some individuals, somatization may have a self-serving component. For example, it may function as an attention-seeking device, an expression of a wish to assume the sick role, or an attempt to manipulate others. One study showed that patients who claim sickness benefits, pensions, or other disability compensation remain disabled longer than those who have no such insurance, even with diseases of similar severity. On the other hand, others point out that most somatizing individuals appear to genuinely suffer rather than profit from their symptoms.

Communication, Defense, and Conflict Resolution

Psychosomatic theories view somatization as a defense mechanism, much like repression, denial, or displacement. Somatizing patients are thought to preoccupy themselves with their physical state instead of dealing with an intolerable psychic conflict. However, these theories are difficult to test empirically.

PSYCHIATRIC CLASSIFICATION OF SOMATIZATION-RELATED DISORDERS

Somatization-related disorders are categorized as somatoform disorders in the *Diagnostic and Statistical Manual of Mental Disorders*, 4th edition, published by the American Psychiatric Association. Somatoform disorders are applied to individuals (1) who report physical complaints that cannot be attributed to organic pathology or pathophysiological mechanisms, or (2) in the case of organic pathology, whose physical complaints are grossly in excess of what would be expected from the physical findings. Somatoform disorders include somatization disorder, undifferentiated somatoform disorder, conversion disorder, pain disorder, hypochondriasis, body dysmorphic disorder, and the residual category of somatoform disorder not otherwise specified.

TREATMENT AND PROGNOSIS

Clinical studies suggest there is no single treatment method or strategy that is equally effective for all somatizing individuals. A large proportion of individuals recover with symptom treatment or reassurance by their physicians or through the use of psychiatric consultation. It is important to be sympathetic and accepting of the way somatizing patients interpret their symptoms and to recommend treatment that is compatible with the patient's cultural norms and illness beliefs. Psychotropic medications such as antidepressants and antianxiety medications, conventional psychotherapy, and complementary and alternative medical treatments have been used to successfully reduce symptom distress. However, some research suggests that significant functional impairment may remain as long as the underlying interpersonal conflicts or secondary gains associated with the patient's symptoms continue.

—*Albert Yeung*
—*Doris F. Chang*

See also Culture-Bound Syndromes: Koro; Culture-Bound Syndromes: Nervios; Culture-Bound Syndromes: Shenjing Shuairuo

FURTHER READING

American Psychiatric Association. (2000). *Diagnostic and statistical manual of mental disorders* (4th ed., text rev.). Washington, DC: Author.
Kellner, R. (1990). Somatization: Theories and research. *Journal of Nervous and Mental Disease, 3,* 150–160.
Kirmayer, R., & Robbins, J. M. (1991). *Current concepts of somatization: Research and clinical perspectives.* Washington, DC: American Psychiatric Press.
Lipowski, Z. J. (1988). Somatization: The concept and its clinical application. *American Journal of Psychiatry, 145,* 1358–1368.

SOUTHEAST ASIAN AMERICANS

Southeast Asian Americans comprise six Southeast Asian groups: Vietnamese, Cambodians, Laotians, Hmong, Chinese Vietnamese, and Mien. A majority of this population migrated to the United States during the Vietnam War. Since 1975, more than 1.5 million Southeast Asians have fled their homes and sought refuge in the United States. The mass exodus of the Southeast Asian population was prompted by political turmoil and genocide; as a result, they have become one of the fastest-growing ethnic groups in the United States. Southeast Asians have settled in every state in the United States, but they are especially concentrated in California, Texas, and Washington, D.C.

An overview of the psychosocial challenges encountered by this population will be provided. Because a majority of Southeast Asians arrived in the United States as refugees, it is important to address how refugee status has affected and continues to influence this population. This entry will provide a historical overview of Southeast Asians' premigration experience, a discussion of their postmigration challenges and current concerns, and a discussion of cultural considerations in working with this population.

HISTORICAL OVERVIEW

Because a large number of Southeast Asian Americans migrated to the United States as refugees, to fully understand this population, it is crucial to distinguish between refugees and immigrants. A key distinction is captured by the phrase *forced versus free*, which refers to involuntary versus voluntary migration. Refugees are forced to leave or displaced from their country of origin by events that are outside their control, such as war or genocide. Refugees, therefore, are distinguished from other migrants such as immigrants or sojourners by their involuntary and sudden departure. During the Vietnam War, Southeast Asians were ill-prepared for their sudden departure from their familiar world and faced uncertainty, confusion, high risk for their personal safety, and complete disruption of their normal lives. The chaos resulted in the loss of reference groups such as family, community, culture, and country, as well as the loss of personal identity.

Southeast Asians entered the United States in two waves, each wave having different demographic characteristics and experiences before and after migration. The first wave of Southeast Asians left Vietnam before the fall of Saigon in 1975 and entered the United States directly or through refugee camps. Because of their close association with the United States and the South Vietnamese forces, these refugees received assistance during the fall of Saigon from the American government, which hastily evacuated refugees by helicopter and sealift. This first wave of refugees, mainly Vietnamese, tended to be relatively well-educated and could speak some English.

The second wave of Southeast Asians, which entered the United States between 1978 and 1980, consisted of mainly Vietnamese, Laotians, Hmong, and Cambodians who had escaped their homes by sea or had made the hazardous journey through the jungle. Refugees from Vietnam left in small, overcrowded, and unseaworthy boats; they were known as "boat people." This group encountered brutal attacks by sea pirates, and many experienced severe violence, rape, or murder. Cambodians, Hmong, and Laotians escaped by land through the jungle, crossing minefields and avoiding ambushes by military soldiers. They encountered tropical diseases, death, hunger, starvation, and exhaustion. Further compounding the trauma, the second wave of refugees were forced to wait in overcrowded and unsanitary refugee camps in Thailand, the Philippines, and Hong Kong for months or even years before they were permanently resettled in the United States or elsewhere.

In contrast to the first wave, the refugees of the second wave tended to have less education and no prior English-language skills. Furthermore, many,

especially those from rural areas, had little or no exposure to Western culture before arriving in the United States. As a result of their means of escape and premigration experiences, the first wave of Southeast Asians adjusted more successfully than the second wave. The first wave of refugees, who managed to escape Vietnam before the fall of Saigon, were exposed to less premigration trauma, were better educated, and possessed more wealth and resources. As the political repression intensified in Cambodia, Vietnam, and Laos after 1975, many refugees of the second wave experienced human atrocities and genocide and were the victims of incarceration, torture, brutal beatings, violence, sexual abuse, rape, and starvation. Many also witnessed killings and torture or were forced to commit human atrocities themselves. For example, in Cambodia from 1975 to 1979, Pol Pot's Khmer Rouge government orchestrated mass genocide, violence, and atrocities against the Cambodian people. It is estimated that 1 million to 3 million of Cambodia's 7 million people died from execution, starvation, or illness, resulting in the virtual extermination of the Cambodian people and culture.

PSYCHOSOCIAL CHALLENGES

Two factors are associated with Southeast Asian Americans' psychosocial adjustment and adaptation in the United States: the degree of premigration trauma experienced before resettlement, and the level of difficulty in adjusting to the United States, a country that is significantly different from their home countries.

Impact of Premigration Trauma on Postmigration Psychosocial Adjustment

It is important to understand the premigration trauma experiences of Southeast Asian Americans, not only because of their impact on postmigration adjustment and adaptation but also because of their effect on subsequent generations (intergenerational trauma). Southeast Asians experienced premigration trauma in their home countries during the war, during the escape process, and in the refugee camps. The types of premigration trauma experienced by this population can be classified into four general categories: (1) deprivation (e.g., lack of food and shelter), (2) physical injury and torture, (3) incarceration and reeducation camps, and (4) killing and torture. The degree of premigration trauma experienced by this population influenced their postmigration adaptation and adjustment. For example, as a response to the severity of premigration trauma, some older Cambodian women display nonorganic or psychosomatic blindness. A significant relationship has been found between the number of years women were interned in refugee camps, the degree and level of traumatic events experienced, and subjective visual impairment.

One method of coping that Southeast Asians used to deal with traumatic experiences was to "act dumb." In order to survive, many Southeast Asians learned to comply with orders obediently, without question or complaint, because they knew that appearing smart, speaking up, or showing their true feelings would result in torture or execution. Therefore, they acted as if they were deaf, dumb, foolish, confused, or stupid. Refugees continued to use these deeply ingrained coping strategies in the United States. However, in U.S. culture, these skills and behaviors may appear aversive, antisocial, or even pathological. Another method that Southeast Asians used to cope with traumatic experiences was the "psychological recoil" effect. In order for Vietnamese Amerasians (children with American fathers and Vietnamese mothers) to survive in physically and psychologically dangerous environments, they developed strong defenses that resulted in emotional numbness to the painful environment. It was only when they were safe in the United States that the psychological effects of the trauma were displayed.

Postmigration Challenges

Premigration trauma may be exacerbated by the challenges of postmigration adaptation, especially the adjustment to a foreign country, such as the United States. Factors associated with successful adjustment depend on the phase of resettlement. The general pattern of resettlement during the first two years is to focus on basic needs such as housing and employment. During this period, refugees may experience a loss of control over decision making with regard to basic life issues. such as job opportunities and social networks. These difficulties may hinder refugees' enthusiasm for acculturation and create emotional and psychological problems as they confront the loss of their culture and identity. Tasks such as catching a bus, handling money, or going shopping—routine tasks in their home countries—may become ordeals during the process of acculturation. Thus, Southeast Asian Americans may undergo acculturative stress. This type of distress involves the many factors in adjusting to a foreign culture and changing one's identity, values, behaviors, cognitions, attitudes, and affectations.

Employment and English-Language Proficiency. Although this population has been in the United States for a long period of time, a high percentage remain dependent on welfare because of unemployment. Acquiring a job poses particular difficulties because the educational training and skills obtained in one's home country often are not transferable to resettlement countries. This may result in a dramatic change in socioeconomic status, causing some to take jobs for which they are overqualified and hence become underemployed. Research has found a tendency among refugee men to remain unemployed and dependent on welfare while they wait for a suitable position that matches their skills because taking any employment may result in downward mobility and loss of status. Although members of this group may have made remarkable progress in their adjustment, only a small percentage have regained their former socioeconomic status.

English-language proficiency plays an important role in adjustment, and it is a key factor in gainful employment. However, attendance at English as a second language (ESL) classes has been found to have a significant association with psychological distress. Learning English may prove challenging for those who are illiterate in their own language. In addition, it has been suggested that emotional and mental fatigue, as well as memory and concentration difficulties resulting from premigration trauma, may also inhibit ESL learning.

Changing Family Dynamics. Changes in family structure and dynamics may also occur. Because of the high rates of unemployment and underemployment among Southeast Asian men, it is often necessary for women to work to provide adequate financial family support. Although men may experience a downward turn in their socioeconomic status, women may experience upward mobility. By working outside the home and community and becoming exposed to American culture, women may begin to question their traditional cultural gender roles and seek more independence. Such shifts in roles and attitudes frequently cause marital conflict. The gender role changes brought by unemployment and underemployment may prompt men to assert their authority and control through spousal abuse.

Children and adolescents tend to acculturate faster than their parents, also contributing to changing roles and shifting family dynamics. Attending school provides exposure to non-Asian children and culture. Children are apt to learn the English language and American customs faster than their parents. This often shifts the family dynamic so that the children assume the role of language and cultural translator for their parents. Children frequently witness a transformation in their parents from competent, autonomous caretakers to depressed, overwhelmed, and dependent individuals. This may cause children to lose confidence in their parents as caregivers and providers, thus altering the traditional family structure dramatically. Furthermore, some children may feel shame and embarrassment because their parents lack English-language skills and may be perceived as dressing, behaving, and acting "funny" from an American viewpoint. They may also be embarrassed to speak publicly in their mother tongue with parents or family members because they fear their American peers will laugh at them.

Child-Rearing Practices. Child-rearing practices are another area of change within the family. Traditional disciplinary measures, such as corporal punishment, may be prohibited by U.S. laws. The use of traditional healing methods, such as coining, may also be problematic. The bruises left on the body by the coining practice may be misinterpreted as abuse. These issues present a serious dilemma for Southeast Asian American parents, who may already feel diminished in their status as parents and constricted in raising their children in ways that have been culturally acceptable for generations. Intergenerational conflict between parents and children may also occur regarding issues such as dating, marriage, curfew, and parental supervision. Many Southeast Asian American children face the difficult position of bridging two worlds: acculturating and adopting the customs and behaviors of their U.S. peer group while maintaining their role as a child in a traditional family. In their attempt to curtail a child's adoption of behaviors and values that are incongruent with traditional values and beliefs, some parents maintain a strict traditional upbringing. Despite this, many parents experience a loss of traditional authority and control as their children become more outspoken and challenge their authority and the "old culture."

School. Paralleling the home experience are difficulties faced in schools by many Southeast Asian American children and adolescents. They may experience racial prejudice and tension that are manifested in fighting, punching, mimicking, harassment, or robbery by non-Asian students. Furthermore, the norms regulating classroom and school behavior in the United States are different from those found in Southeast Asia. Although the acquisition of a new language is one of the most important factors in acculturation, this is highly complicated and symbolic of other facets of adjustment. In addition, children wishing to participate in extracurricular activities may have difficulty with parents who cannot understand "foreign activities" that do not emphasize studying. Many Southeast Asian American parents see educational success as a tool for upward mobility and do not understand the relevance of extracurricular activities. These issues, combined with the desire to belong and adjust, may generate both internalized and externalized tensions and conflicts for Southeast Asian children and adolescents. In addition, premigration trauma is compounded by parental stress and depression, setting the stage for high drop-out rates and low grade point averages. Parental psychological well-being has been shown to have a negative impact on children's psychosocial adjustment and academic achievement.

Racism. Southeast Asian Americans may also encounter discrimination and racism. The pains of the Vietnam War are still strong within the American psyche; therefore this group may encounter hostility and racism. Other ethnic groups in the United States may resent Southeast Asians because of the special assistance given to refugees, which may be perceived as services and resources that are being taken away from them. Vietnamese Amerasians who experienced rejection in Vietnam because of their biracial identity may experience the same type of discrimination in the United States, both in the Vietnamese community and in mainstream U.S. communities.

Gangs. There are approximately 25,000 Asian gang members in the United States. These gangs are reported to be especially dangerous because members grew up in war-torn countries and were victims or witnesses of atrocities. Members may join these gangs because of disappointment with life in the United States, difficulties in school and in the social arena, conflicts in the home, the desire for protection, or poverty and the intense desire to obtain money.

PSYCHOLOGICAL DISTRESS

It is not surprising to find that premigration trauma is a major predictor of psychological problems among this population. The major psychological problems exhibited by this group are posttraumatic stress disorder (PTSD), depression, somatization, and suicide. Studies have found that the onset of PTSD may be delayed many years after the initial trauma; however, premigration trauma tends to wane with time as other postmigration variables such as employment and housing assume more importance. Nevertheless, it has been clearly established that premigration trauma has a long-standing negative impact on mental health after resettlement.

Intergroup Differences

There are many intergroup differences in the level of psychological distress among Southeast Asian Americans. Cambodians, for example, tend to experience more psychological distress than do other groups, a finding that has been attributed to their experiences under Pol Pot's regime. Vietnamese and Chinese Vietnamese have been found to be the least distressed compared with other groups, a finding that is associated with higher levels of education, better English-language skills, financial assets upon arrival in the United States, and access to established Chinatown communities in the United States. Furthermore, the size of ethnic communities may be responsible for ethnic differences in depression among this population: Larger ethnic communities provide more social support, buffering stress and reducing depression. Gender differences in psychological distress have also been found: Women report a significantly higher level of psychological distress than their male counterparts.

At-Risk Groups

Within the Southeast Asian American population, specific subgroups have been identified as at risk for serious mental health problems. For example, older Southeast Asians may be at risk for psychological problems because they have encountered more difficulties in adjustment, such as downward social mobility, conflicts with children, changing family dynamics, difficulty learning English, and difficulty finding work. Those who are less proficient in English are at higher risk for depression because of the correlation between poor English proficiency and employment status.

Southeast Asian women are at high risk of developing serious psychological problems because of their premigration experiences of rape, sexual abuse, and violence. In the United States, women not only must cope with premigration trauma but also encounter significant challenges in postmigration adjustment. Although Southeast Asian women in general are at risk, Cambodian women in particular have a greater risk of developing serious mental health problems. For example, Cambodian refugee women report nearly nine times more trauma than other Southeast Asian American groups. In a community sample of 300 Cambodian women, 22% reported the death of a spouse and 53% reported the loss or death of other family members. In other studies, 95% of Cambodian women reported that they had been sexually abused or raped. Gender differences were also found in the predictors of psychological distress between and within Southeast Asian American groups.

Children and adolescents have also been identified as being at risk. Children and adolescents who arrived in the United States with the second wave of refugees report more difficulties in adjustment than do their first-wave counterparts. Vietnamese Amerasians and unaccompanied minors are specifically at risk because of their unique circumstances.

CULTURAL BELIEF SYSTEMS

Southeast Asian Americans exhibit distress through idioms of bodily complaints. They express psychological problems through somatic symptoms that have no apparent organic pathology, such as headaches, weakness, dizziness, abdominal pain, and fatigue. Mental illness in Asian cultures is highly stigmatized; therefore, the expression of neurasthenic symptoms is a culturally sanctioned method of expressing psychological distress that is consistent with their cultural belief system. Neurasthenia comprises predominantly somatic symptoms (e.g., headaches, weakness, pressure on the chest or head), as well as depression, anxiety, and psychosocial dysfunction. Although many Southeast Asian Americans exhibit distress through somatic channels, it is important to acknowledge that they are also capable of discussing their problems in psychological terms.

Cultural conceptualizations of mental health influence help-seeking behaviors and, therefore, treatment expectations and outcomes. For treatment to be effective, the psychotherapist must be aware of, acknowledge, and understand the client's cultural conceptualization of problems and employ culturally sensitive therapeutic interventions and skills. Those who arrived in the United States as refugees may be unfamiliar with Western mental health concepts because they had little or no exposure to Western mental health treatment in their home countries. Accordingly, when they seek help from Western psychotherapists, they expect a medical approach and quick symptom relief. Because they view mental illness as akin to physical disorders, they often request injections or medication.

Preferred Treatment Modalities

Many Southeast Asian Americans, especially those who migrated as refugees, reject Western practices and prefer traditional healing practices influenced by religious and cultural beliefs, such as possession, soul loss, and witchcraft. Rituals for exorcism, which are performed by shamans and Taoist priests in Vietnam and by Buddhist monks in Laos and Cambodia, consist of calling back the souls of individuals who are believed to be suffering from soul loss and asking local guardian gods for protection. Fortune-telling with cards and coins, the Chinese horoscope, and physiognomy (the reading of palms and facial features) are also popular methods of treatment. The Southeast Asian belief system is strongly influenced by Chinese medical practices. Vietnamese, Cambodians, and Hmong regularly use Chinese folk remedies, including herbal concoctions and poultices, forms of acupuncture, acupressure, and massage, and the dermabrasive practices of cupping, pinching, rubbing, and burning. Because mental illness is considered a disturbance of the internal vital energy, acupuncture is often used as a remedy for depression and psychosis. Vietnamese religious beliefs combine Buddhist, Taoist, and Confucian beliefs. Laotians strongly believe in animism (belief in the supernatural, gods, demons, and evil spirits) as an essential part of everyday life.

Furthermore, culture also influences the expression of grief and bereavement. Under Pol Pot, Cambodians were forbidden to perform the traditional mourning rituals that are fundamental to Buddhist beliefs. Any open display of grief was a sufficient pretext for death threats or even murder. Given the death and loss experienced by this population, it is critical that the psychotherapist take into account cultural styles of grief and bereavement and allow clients to display a cultural manifestation of bereavement.

Barriers to Mainstream Mental Health Services and Use of Traditional Methods

Studies have identified a serious need for mental health services in this population. Despite this great need, only a small percentage of Southeast Asians use mainstream mental health services or even services targeting Asian clients. The main reason for the low utilization of mainstream mental health services is that these services are not culturally responsive. When Southeast Asian Americans enter the mainstream mental health service system, the environment is foreign to them. Not only is there a language barrier between the client and psychotherapist; there are also cultural differences in both verbal (e.g., tone and volume of speaking) and nonverbal (e.g., eye contact and personal space) behaviors. For example, if the sole of the therapist's foot is facing the client or the therapist pats a child's head, these behaviors are considered extremely offensive. Poor accessibility may also be a hindrance to the utilization of mainstream mental health services.

Traditional beliefs and superstitions, such as a belief in the supernatural, are common barriers to mainstream mental health care. This population often relies on indigenous healers and folk medicine and rejects Western healing methods. One study found that many Southeast Asians report a preference for traditional healing methods, and their utilization of mainstream services in the United States is related to the unavailability of traditional methods. Often, they use both traditional and Western mainstream health care methods concurrently. In view of these cultural beliefs and preferences for traditional health care methods, it is crucial that psychotherapists work cooperatively with bilingual and bicultural mental health professionals, community leaders, elders, and traditional healers (e.g., spiritual leaders, monks, priests, herbalists, and shamans).

CULTURALLY RESPONSIVE TECHNIQUES

Many of the basic principles of effective psychotherapy with Asian Americans also apply to Southeast Asians—for example, avoiding premature termination by gaining both ascribed and achieved credibility with clients. Ascribed credibility is determined by the psychotherapist's status (e.g., age, education, and gender), whereas achieved credibility—that is, gaining the trust and confidence of the client—is determined by the psychotherapist's competency in the therapy sessions. Therefore, if the psychotherapist has a low ascribed credibility initially, he or she can acquire credibility by being culturally responsive. To achieve trust and credibility with this population, psychotherapists need to be aware of Southeast Asian clients' premigration history, postmigration adjustment challenges, cultural belief systems pertaining to health and mental health, and use of traditional and Western methods of health care.

There are a number of treatment strategies and interventions for working with this population, such as Kinzie's work with PTSD. The multilevel model of social justice, human rights, and psychotherapy incorporates partnership with indigenous healers, cultural empowerment, advocacy, and becoming a change agent. Cognitive- behavioral interventions have also been recognized as helpful. This approach may be effective with Southeast Asians because of its similarity to Buddhist beliefs. Other techniques that may be incorporated include storytelling, projective drawing, dream work, Gestalt, relaxation, role-playing, psychodrama, and group therapy.

The Southeast Asian American population is a diverse group. For treatment to be effective, psychotherapists must examine both intergroup and intragroup differences, as well as gender differences, with regard to premigration experiences, postmigration challenges, distress predictors, and level and degree of psychological distress. It is critical for psychotherapists to have an awareness, understanding, acceptance, and acknowledgment of cultural differences in the conceptualization of mental illness, expression of distress, help-seeking behavior, coping, and grieving and bereavement. Furthermore, it is necessary to understand and appreciate the strength and resiliency of this population.

—*Rita Chi-Ying Chung*

See also Immigrants

FURTHER READING

Bemak, F., & Chung, R. C. Y. (1998). Vietnamese Amerasians: Predictors of distress and self-destructive behavior. *Journal of Counseling and Development, 76,* 452–458.

Bemak, F., & Chung, R. C. Y. (1999). Vietnamese Amerasians: The relationship between biological father, psychological distress, and self-destructive behavior. *Journal of Community Psychosocial, 27,* 443–456.

Bemak, F., Chung, R. C. Y., & Pedersen, P. (2003). *Counseling refugees: A psychosocial approach to innovative multicultural interventions.* Westport, CT: Greenwood Press.

Chung, R. C. Y. (2001). Psychosocial adjustment of Cambodian refugee women: Implications for mental health counseling. *Journal of Mental Health Counseling, 23,* 115–126.

Chung, R. C. Y., & Bemak, F. (2002a). Revisiting the California Southeast Asian mental health needs assessment data: An examination of refugee ethnic and gender differences. *Journal of Counseling and Development, 80,* 111–119.

Chung, R. C. Y., & Bemak, F. (2002b). The relationship between culture and empathy. *Journal of Counseling and Development, 80,* 154–159.

Chung, R. C. Y., Chi, Y., Bemak, F., & Okazaki, S. (1997). Counseling Americans of Southeast Asian descent: The impact of the refugee experience. In C. C. Lee (Ed.), *Multicultural issues in counseling: New approaches to diversity* (2nd ed., pp. 207–231). Alexandria, VA: American Counseling Association.

Chung, R. C. Y., & Kagawa-Singer, M. (1993). Predictors of psychological distress among Southeast Asian refugees. *Social Science and Medicine, 36*(5), 631–639.

Chung, R. C. Y., & Okazaki, S. (1991). Counseling Americans of Southeast Asian descent: The impact of the refugee experience. In C. C. Lee & B. L. Richardson (Eds.), *Multicultural issues in counseling: New approaches to diversity* (pp. 107–126). Alexandria, VA: American Association for Counseling and Development.

Kinzie, J. D. (1985). Overview of clinical issues in the treatment of Southeast Asian refugees. In T. C. Owan (Ed.), *Southeast Asian mental health: Treatment, prevention, services, training, and research* (pp. 113–135). Rockville, MD: U.S. Department of Health and Human Services.

Mollica, R. F., Wyshak, G., & Lavelle, J. (1987). The psychosocial impact of war trauma and torture on Southeast Asian refugees. *American Journal of Psychiatry, 144*(12), 1567–1572.

SPIRITUALITY

SPIRITUALITY AND ETHNIC MINORITIES

Although the terms *religion* and *spirituality* are frequently used interchangeably, for many people they hold different meanings. Religion, which is often associated with an organized group, is defined as a specific set of beliefs and practices. Religion stipulates formalized behavioral patterns, practices, and expressions that provide a social identity. Spirituality is commonly defined as the animating forces of life, which are represented by such images as breath, wind, vigor, or courage, or the infusion or drawing out of spirit in one's life. Spirituality is also described as a capacity and tendency that is innate and unique to all persons. Thus, spirituality is more of a personal experience that can be obtained through different paths, both inside and outside formal religion.

Among ethnic minorities (African Americans, Latinos, Native Americans, and Asian Americans), spirituality is a recognized and celebrated aspect of the cultural experience. It serves as a means of understanding one's self, others, and the complexities of life, as well as a mechanism by which individuals prioritize the demands of their lives. Recently, several research studies have provided a better understanding of how spirituality manifests within different ethnic and linguistic minority groups. The following sections focus exclusively on the research on spirituality in four ethnic minority groups in the United States: African Americans, Latinos, Native Americans, and Asians.

SPIRITUALITY AND AFRICAN AMERICANS

Although the term *African American* is often used to refer to the Black population in general, this section focuses specifically on individuals who are descendants of slaves born in America. Among African Americans, spirituality is viewed as the propensity to make meaning through a sense of relation to dimensions that transcend the self in a way that empowers rather than devalues the individual. African American spirituality is a key source of strength and tenacity. It integrates individual and collective lives with all other realms of existence, including nature, humanity, the spirit world, and God's world. It is a key component of personality and culture, and it is correlated with positive mental health outcomes. Specifically, spirituality can help to negate hardships in the lives of African Americans, which are often precursors to poor mental health. Spirituality is also an important component of health locus of control (beliefs about what determines health) for African Americans. For example, African Americans are likely to view control over one's health as the result of a higher power (i.e., God). African Americans feel most spiritual in their

places of worship when they are praying, practicing psalms, and preaching. They believe these types of behavior help connect them to their higher power. Overall, African American spirituality is about the mutual preservation of the human life, body, and soul.

SPIRITUALITY AND LATINO AMERICANS

Conversely, Latinos tend to view spirituality as an attitude toward life that is interwoven with cultural, traditional, and personal elements. In the Latino community, spirituality greatly influences attitudes toward life, health, illness, and death. As a result, it is considered the primary method for coping with negative life events, such as the illness of a friend or family member. Spirituality is a communal (rather than an individual) process that develops from faith, devotion, and prayer, which are heavily rooted in Latinos' upbringing and in the Latino community. Spirituality is often learned in the parental home (i.e., from parents, grandparents, and other relatives) and through active participation in activities that are considered spiritual. For example, prayer and meditation are essential elements of Latino spirituality that individuals commonly learn in the parental home and through active participation. By watching and mimicking their parents' style of prayer and meditation, young Latinos develop their own sense of spiritual connectedness.

Although Latinos as a group share common characteristics such as language, an emphasis on family, and religion, there is significant variability within and between groups. For example, many Cuban Americans still practice *Santería*, an African-influenced religion that is often described as syncretic, as well as Haitian voodoo. Additionally, many Brazilians practice *Candomble*, a Yoruba-based religion that upholds a supreme God called *oludumare*. It has survived through the deliberate use of elements of the dominant cultural religious beliefs, particularly the association of the *orishas* (deities) with Catholic saints. Given the variety of religions practiced within Latino groups, it is common to find differences in spiritual practices and expressions of spirituality.

SPIRITUALITY AND NATIVE AMERICANS

There are hundreds of Native American tribes in the United States, and each tribe has its own set of spiritual values and beliefs. The origins of these beliefs, ceremonies, and rituals vary according to the tribe. For example, the basis of Lakota spirituality is the "seven sacred rites," whereas the sacred number of the Apache is four, and the Navajo use 24 chant complexes in their spiritual ceremonies. Despite clear differences in spirituality among the Native cultures, there are elements that are universal to all Native American groups. For example, for all Native Americans, spirituality is land based—that is, the underlying basis of spirituality is the relationship between human beings, the earth, and all of creation. Native Americans believe that everything is sacred and connected and that there is one single creator (*Kishelamakank*). For example, according to Native American beliefs, all human beings, animals, and land formations are endowed with spirit, and all are related because they derive from Kishelamakank. Native American ceremonies involve thanksgiving to the creator, to the animals, and to the land for the resources they provide. For example, Native Americans offer thanks to their hunted animals for giving their lives for the tribe's nourishment. Increasingly, the Native American church has begun to blend elements of traditional Native American spirituality with elements of Christianity, for example using peyote—a cactus with psychedelic properties—as a sacrament in religious rituals.

SPIRITUALITY AND ASIAN AMERICANS

Like other ethnic groups, the Asian American population is very diverse, as are their religions and practices of spirituality and faith. Currently, most of the data available on Asian Americans focuses primarily on religion. Although we have a basic understanding of how spirituality influences the lives of Asian Americans, very little is known about the specific presentation and manifestation of their spirituality. It can be said, however, that a common theme in Asian American spirituality is that spiritual beliefs help Asian Americans to adjust to life in the United States (i.e., the struggles of integration and adaptation to a new country) as well as other difficult personal and social transformations. Asian American spirituality is reported to help bond communities and has helped shape and give meaning to Asian Americans' lives.

CONCLUDING REMARKS

Spirituality is an important dimension that can be felt in most domains of individuals' lives, including professional as well as personal experiences. Additionally, spirituality is experienced in the physical, psychological, and social domains of individuals'

lives. For one individual, the positive effects of spirituality may be experienced only in one domain, whereas for another, the effects may be experienced in all domains. The impact of spirituality varies not only as a function of the individual but also as a function of the individual's cultural background. The beneficial effects of spirituality are felt by individuals across cultures and understood in different ways based on one's experiences.

—*Guerda Nicolas*
—*Diana Gonzalez-Eastep*
—*Angela DeSilva*

See also Indigenous Healers and Treatments; Religion

FURTHER READING

Gill, S. (1982). *Native American religions: An introduction.* Belmont, CA: Wadsworth.

Irwin, L. (2000). *Native American spirituality: A critical reader.* Lincoln: University of Nebraska Press.

Musgrave, C. F., Allen, C. E., & Allen, G. J. (2002). Spirituality and health for women of color. *American Journal of Public Health, 92*(4), 557–560.

Stolley, J. M., & Koenig, H. (1997). Religion/spirituality and health among elderly African Americans and Hispanics. *Journal of Psychosocial Nurse Mental Health Services, 35*(11), 32–38.

Williams, D. R., Griffith, E. E. H., Young, J. L., Collins, C., & Dodson, J. (1999). Structure and provision of services in Black churches in New Haven, Connecticut. *Cultural Diversity and Ethnic Minority Psychology, 5*, 118–133.

STRESS

A BRIEF HISTORY OF STRESS

To have a sound understanding of multicultural stress, the concept of stress from its beginnings to its current complex and multifaceted meanings must be examined. The application of stress to multicultural psychology moves the well-known concept of stress beyond its past and current meanings. Here, the intent is to present a Western positivistic view of stress and compare it with a multicultural view of stress. There are important and significant differences in conceptions of stress, such as the importance given to the individual versus the group; the importance of a person's cultural identity and self-concept; and the availability of resources for coping with stress. With regard to resources, it is necessary to consider the perspective of those who have and those who have not. This perspective considers a world of privilege and power, of subordination and domination, of powerlessness and disenfranchisement. Thus, from a multicultural perspective, stress cannot be viewed through current models and theories.

Walter Cannon was a pioneer in the study of stress whose research led to the development of the theory of homeostasis. Hans Selye described a stressor as a noxious agent and stress as a nonspecific reaction to a stressor. He first proposed the notion that stress exposure has a damaging effect on physical health. Selye's conception of general adaptation syndrome—a general, nonspecific physiological response to a stressor—provided an impetus for further research on stress. Other models of stress take into account concepts such as allostasis, the idea that maintaining homeostasis results in wear and tear on the bodily system, and allostatic load, the costs of the continued demands of maintaining homeostasis. Thomas Holmes and Richard Rahe introduced research that supported life changes as a source of stress. Later models specific to psychology and psychological stress incorporated appraisal and coping as part of the stress process.

Although there is a long tradition of separating the mind and the body—that is, the physical from the psychological—the division is not so clear. All physical stressors have a psychological component. Thus, much of the physical stress that individuals experience originates from psychological information and ideas. This needs to be kept in mind when we consider the topic of multicultural stress.

In psychology, cognition and emotions are considered essential parts of the stress process. At the psychological stress level, psychology focuses on individual persons and subgroups. It uses the concepts of stimulus—an event or stressor–stress appraisal that involves cognitively estimating the relative threat of stressors by weighing demands against available resources—and stress, a variable response or reaction that involves emotional, physiological, and behavioral coping responses to the appraised stressor.

Coping and appraisal are essential parts of the stress process. The selection of different types of coping mechanisms, such as emotion-focused, problem-focused, or avoidance coping, depends on the appraised nature of a situation and the likelihood of a solution. The coping response is situation specific: Coping that is effective in one situation may be counterproductive in another. For example, in preparing for a job interview, one can avoid the preparation and experience less stress, but this results in damaging consequences. Little can be done while

waiting for the results of the interview, so doing nothing and distancing oneself can be effective.

In psychology, the stress response is reciprocal. A stressor may have an effect on a person, but the person can also change the stressor. Persons do not simply respond or react; they are also agents who are capable of changing the environment. Individuals initiate coping responses depending on whether the stressor is perceived as a harm, threat, or challenge. For example, the death of a family member or being fired from one's job may be perceived as harmful; impending unemployment may be seen as a threat; and a job performance evaluation may be appraised as a challenge if the individual believes he or she can perform successfully.

POWER, PRIVILEGE, AND MULTICULTURAL STRESS

Although multicultural diversity may encompass persons with disabilities; gay, lesbian, bisexual, and transgender individuals; and others with a minority status because of language, culture, or religion, the topic is too large to be addressed here. Multicultural stress is presented as it relates and is applied to multicultural individuals from socioeconomic, gender, ethnic, and racial categories. Members of these groups are also referred to as *minorities* or *minority group members*. A minority position in American society, as the concept is used here, does not imply minority in a strict numerical sense. Rather, being a minority in America because of one's culture, ethnicity, or race means that a person is disenfranchised and disempowered.

In regard to multicultural stress, it is important to consider the impact of stress from a historical perspective and in light of the predominant political system on which this country and society were founded. Our country was founded by colonizers from western Europe who had a commercial goal in mind and who searched for religious freedom based on beliefs that valued achievement, hard work, the accumulation of material wealth, and prosperity. The drive to achieve economic power created wealth and prosperity for many, but at the same time, the majority remained in the lower working and social classes. The development of economic resources to uphold a strong nation required labor and a readily available and plentiful workforce. Our economy thus welcomed immigrants from abroad and from the Americas.

Although the current economic system proposes that anyone can become economically successful, many remain in lower socioeconomic classes. Thus, multicultural stress moves beyond the realm of the individual and his or her appraisal to individuals within a context that influences their ability to cope and deal with the environment itself. The stress process does not involve individual coping, but individual coping with an extra historical and social cultural stress load before the stressors that are commonly presented in the current stress literature can actually be dealt with. In order for the field of stress to move into the realm of multicultural stress, many other variables and factors need to be considered from a socioeconomic and historical perspective.

From a historical perspective, before *Brown v. Board of Education of Topeka*, before the Civil Rights movement, and before the Civil Rights Acts of the 1960s and other Supreme Court decisions that supported rights for the disadvantaged, psychological stress and coping models did not apply to ethnic and racial minority group members in the United States. A model that required the appraisal of a stressor and attention to needed resources for coping was meaningless because members of disenfranchised groups had limited freedom, limited rights, few privileges, little economic power, and even less social and personal respect—thus, no resources at all. For these groups, coping included submission, giving up, withdrawing, avoiding, denying, and internalizing oppression.

Therefore, for multicultural minority group members with identifiable ethnic and racial backgrounds, skin colors, and distinguishing phenotypic or physical features, stress is an especially important topic because it affects them in areas that do not affect members of mainstream society. Stress affects them at a universal level that includes the social and systemic meaning of stress, in addition to the individual perspective, which includes the subgroup and its cultural values and traditions.

Multicultural psychology focuses on the social structure and subgroups that the social system comprises, in addition to the state of mind of individual persons. Multicultural stress examines the impact of the environment using an ecological perspective. Communities, their inhabitants, and their cultural traditions are the focus of stress. Lack of education and meaningful employment, economic deprivation, and life in communities where the concentration of economic deprivation and disadvantages are high result in

poor mental health with increased distress, which is exhibited in poor physical and mental health.

Definitions of stress include coping resources as a significant factor in the stress process. The consequences of stress are situated in the sociocultural context of those who have and those who do not have. Individuals estimate the personal, psychological, economic, and systemic resources they have to deal with stressors. The availability of resources affects one's appraisals and coping responses significantly. Resources that are available to mainstream society may not be available to multicultural minority group members because of their disenfranchised status. Thus, for visibly identifiable ethnic and racial minority individuals, overriding factors that need to be considered include race, ethnicity, and the consequences of being identified as a disenfranchised group. Race and ethnicity have an impact on the lives and resources of people on a daily basis, in multiple situations and across the life span, as a result of a lack of privileges, prejudice, and oppression.

Environmental and sociocultural conditions that connect the social structure and culture to stress in disenfranchised and disempowered minority group members include a lack of education and resources; low income, unemployment, financial strain, and poverty; poor housing, crowding, high-crime neighborhoods, and violence; and alcoholism, suicide, and chronic mental disorders, such as depression and anxiety. Other sources of stress include immigration, the stress of acculturation and assimilation, social isolation, deprivation, and marginalization. All of these stressors are consequences of social distress, and they are most prevalent among people who have been marginalized in the social structure because of the dynamics of power, privilege, and oppression.

Multicultural stressors are chronic and cumulative, creating a much higher stress burden for those who have fewer coping resources. Environmental and sociocultural stressors increase the impact of negative life events. The consequences of these chronic stressors can result in damage, such as bad health. Research has established a link between psychosocial factors and the development or progression of chronic disease. Stressful life events appear to contribute to progression in chronic diseases such as diabetes, hypertension, and substance abuse and addiction. Research continues to support the existence of health disparities, adding to the burden of chronic stress. These chronic and acute life stressors contribute to more negative affective states and negative life events.

Although the literature has found links between factors that are more likely to be encountered by minorities, no attention has been given to racism, oppression, or discrimination. It is likely that if mainstream society links psychosocial factors to chronic disease, then minorities are likely to be even more susceptible to chronic disease as a result of these factors.

COVERT STRESSORS: STEREOTYPES AND AVERSIVE/REACTIVE RACISM

Multicultural individuals are exposed to a variety of stressors that stem from oppression and discrimination. Oppression leading to multicultural stress is readily apparent in overt behaviors and actions. For example, daily stressors include being stereotyped or treated with indifference. Multicultural minority group members are usually mistaken to be someone else who looks like them. They may be seen as maintenance or cleaning employees in business establishments or educational settings when they are, in fact, paying customers or members of the university faculty. Other behaviors include being profiled and stopped by law officers or government officials in the community, at airports, or in government buildings. Most essentially, though the ideal of democracy is the right to vote, many minorities are disenfranchised in terms of voting. Their voices in the political process are not heard. Such powerlessness can lead to chronic stress that compounds the effects of daily hassles and stressors.

Overt discriminatory and oppressive acts are still plentiful. However, they have also evolved to become more covert and subtle in today's society. The multicultural stress generated by prejudice and racism is made more stressful by the ambiguity of the expression of modern racism. In today's society, it is unlikely that most minority individuals will experience old-fashioned overt and clearly objective discrimination and racism. Overt acts still exist, but most expressions have gone underground, becoming complex, subtle, and so ambiguous that the effect is even more stressful. Not being able to prove racism can lead individuals to question their perceptions of reality. An act that is objective and overt can be coped with; however, ambiguity puts such processes out of the control of victims. Members of the dominant

group in our society have gradually accepted publicly expressed equalitarian views. However, these views conflict with feelings and attitudes that still express prejudice and racism toward minorities. In an attempt to act nonprejudicial and nonracist, they avoid overtly acting in such a manner; however, biased and prejudicial attitudes remain.

If a stereotyped individual who is proficient in a field he or she strongly identifies with becomes aware of the stereotype, this awareness can lead to distressful feelings that interfere with his or her performance. The individual tries to avoid the stereotype, but in the effort to do so, the stereotype interferes with optimal performance. Individuals who are not strongly identified with the topic or field will not underperform—they will perform as usual. Because they do not identify with the area, they do not have feelings that interfere with their performance. Thus, individuals become disidentified with certain topics or situations when it is likely that stereotypes about their identity will be brought out.

ACCULTURATION AND STRESS

Multicultural psychology addresses the problems of ethnic and racial minorities. Historically, problems have focused on race relations, and much of the cross-cultural research and literature have focused on African Americans and European Americans. The changing demographics of the United States call for a broader perspective. Asian and Hispanic immigration to the United States has increased significantly. The Hispanic population is now one of the largest ethnic minority groups in America. Population trends indicate this minority group will continue to grow, and when all current immigrant groups are combined, the percentage of European Americans will continue to decrease. All minority groups who immigrate to American need to adjust and socialize to the mainstream American culture. Acculturation, the process that occurs when two or more cultural groups interact, can be a source of significant stress for multicultural individuals.

Models of multicultural stress at the psychological level comprise an appraisal of resources and coping. This model is particularly relevant to acculturation, psychological stress, and coping. Persons who are acculturated to the majority culture are likely to view the environment as less threatening. Because of their acculturated status, they believe they have developed the necessary coping skills to deal with stressful situations. They may be more confident of successful outcomes. Persons who maintain a cultural identity that does not conform to the majority culture are likely to view the environment as less accepting, perhaps rejecting, and even threatening. When the environment is viewed as threatening, coping resources may be viewed as ineffective, and increased emotional arousal will lead to higher perceptions of psychological stress. Individuals who integrate and learn skills to function within two cultures may have appraisals that are different from those who are highly acculturated or separated from the majority culture. Acculturation theory posits that these individuals appraise the environment as less stressful than other acculturated individuals. However, this model of acculturative stress does not incorporate the significant influence of the dynamics of privileges, power, and dominance.

Power and unearned privileges contribute to the establishment and maintenance of institutional racism. The outcome of this disempowerment is that many ethnic and racial minority group members do not have access to education, economics, government, and politics. A lack of resources contributes to a weak resource base for coping with the stress of becoming acculturated to mainstream American society.

The process of acculturation is usually a matter of becoming socialized to the host culture. Although there are many ways of conceptualizing acculturation, in a host culture that has a clear intention to remain dominant, it is expected that the culture of origin will be discarded and the dominant culture will replace the individual's original cultural identity. When minority group members use their culture and its values, traditions, beliefs, and language to cope with acculturation resistance, they do not become socialized; instead, they are treated as unwanted because of a perception that they choose to remain unacculturated.

The process of acculturation is not a democratic process for many immigrants, especially those with a phenotype that differs from the western European (Caucasian) type. In most cases, acculturation does not occur within the principles of equality and freedom to pursue the ideal of the American dream. In fact, when a disempowered minority group attempts to socialize into a cultural group that has power and unearned privileges, the dominant culture may become a source of stress. Acculturation may be encouraged, but on a conditional basis. It is welcomed only if the minority group changes its behavior and identity to become similar to the dominant group. Because of differences such as skin color and physical features that cannot be changed, the expected changes are unrealistic or impossible. Oppression is the prevention and denial of who one is. The acculturation process is imbued with oppression, which results in a loss of culture and self-identity, low self-esteem, demoralization, and stress.

STIGMA AND IDENTITY

Although some people believe that bicultural individuals are fortunate because they have a cultural identity, many do not realize that some cultures, nationalities, races, or ethnicities have been stereotyped and stigmatized as inferior as part of the process of keeping these cultures subordinate.

Thus, minority group members may minimize or deny their cultural identity in order to be accepted. They may reject their cultural and ethnic identity as they strive to become acculturated and assimilated into mainstream society. Becoming acculturated is a task full of psychological stress. Members of the person's ethnic group may reject him or her because they feel they are being abandoned and that the individual is aligning him- or herself with an oppressive group. The host culture may not accept and may not welcome bicultural, bilingual, and visibly identifiable minority persons who have characteristics of a "foreign culture" and will forever be perceived as un-American. The ongoing struggle to develop an acceptable identity is a source of chronic stress in the daily lives of many bicultural Americans.

LANGUAGE AND COMMUNICATION STRESS

Verbal communication is considered extremely important in this age of information. The ability to communicate is essential in our modern society. Many bicultural individuals maintain their culture by speaking a language other than English. These individuals may be ridiculed for not speaking English or speaking English incorrectly. A lack of proficiency in English can be generalized to a person's overall ability and competence. Those who are not proficient in English may be spoken to in a loud voice or treated as if they are not capable. English proficiency is the foundation of functioning in social, economic, occupational, and educational realms; not being able to communicate is a source of stress for multicultural individuals.

LIFE SPAN MULTICULTURAL STRESS

Multicultural stress may occur at different developmental levels, but it is especially common among young children during their formative years. In the home environment, they may be exposed to the same chronic stressors that their parents experience. In some cases, the extreme conditions that parents live in reduce their coping abilities so that they are living in a survival mode. Supportive, nurturing, and other positive activities and interactions are reduced to a minimum at home. Things do not get better at school. For example, young children are ridiculed, excluded from activities, and labeled as slow learners, at risk, difficult to manage, and troublemakers. Minority adolescents and young adults have the highest rates of school dropout and unemployment. The prison population of multicultural young men is much greater than their numbers in colleges and universities. Health disparities lead to severe stress for older multicultural individuals who need medical services.

SUMMARY AND CONCLUSION

Multicultural stress is presented within models of mainstream stress research and theoretical models. However, this article proposes a new definition of stress that applies to multicultural ethnic and racial minority group members and to those who lack privileges and power in society. The intent is to look at multicultural stress from an individual perspective but also from a systemic, environmental, and ecological perspective. Multicultural stress comprises privilege, power, and disenfranchisement. Multicultural stress also involves an appraisal of stress and coping responses. Resources for coping are an important element. Those who are marginalized and disempowered tend to have fewer resources for coping with the demands of a competitive and rejecting environment.

Not all members of multicultural minority groups are at the whim of the dominant society or the victims of their culture, ethnicity, or race. Through their own agency, they are able to negotiate and change their cultural worlds and add to, reject, or change their culture to cope with external stressors. Although it may take extra resourcefulness and energy, many become good at coping with multicultural stressors. They are able to adapt and succeed in society and its institutions, becoming educated and gainfully employed and enjoying a good quality of life. However, even when they are successful, these individuals may continue to encounter multicultural stressors throughout their lives. Because of their culture, ethnicity, or race, multicultural individuals experience additional sources of stress as a result of their minority position in society. Successful coping is essential and needs to be a part of their daily experiences. Many multicultural individuals have been successful in the face of tremendous obstacles. The negative view of stress presented here is not entirely without hope—positive consequences have occurred and can continue in the future.

Disenfranchised minority group persons need to continue to develop effective coping strategies to solidify their personal, social, and economical resources.

Forms of oppression and racism continue to evolve with the changing political and cultural climate of our society. Multicultural individuals must become consumers of information that will help to deal with subtle and covert forms of oppressive dynamics of covert aversive and reactive racism. Our culture of helplessness must change to become one of optimism, and positive messages of encouragement must be heard and used to develop successful coping strategies that can lead to constructive change. Multicultural stress is likely to continue, but with positive information and knowledge, reciprocal changes can be initiated. Reciprocal positive change can be initiated as individual and group change affects the environment. The environment is then likely to reciprocate in kind.

—Jesse N. Valdez

FURTHER READING

Dovidio, J. F., & Gaertner, S. L. (Eds.). (1986). *Prejudice, discrimination, and racism.* Orlando, FL: Academic Press.

Hobfoll, S. E. (1998). *Stress, culture, and community: The psychology and philosophy of stress.* New York: Plenum Press.

Lazarus, R. S. (1993). From psychological stress to the emotions: A history of changing outlooks. *Annual Review of Psychology, 44,* 1–21.

Lovallo, W. R. (2005). *Stress and health: Biological and psychological interactions* (2nd ed.). Thousand Oaks, CA: Sage.

Mirowsky, J., & Ross, C. E. (2003). *Social causes of psychological distress* (2nd ed.). New York: Walter de Gruyter.

Swim, J. K., & Stangor, C. (Eds.). (1998). *Prejudice: The target's perspective.* San Diego: Academic Press.

SUICIDE

Suicide is a complex behavior involving many factors. Examining the cultural influences that contribute to rates of suicide among different ethnic groups can help us to better understand the risk and protective factors associated with suicide.

Several risk factors tend to be present across most ethnic groups. Regardless of ethnicity, females tend to have more suicide attempts but lower suicide completion rates than males. Individuals with certain psychiatric diagnoses, such as major depression, bipolar disorder, and substance abuse, tend to be at a higher risk for suicide. Higher suicide rates exist among those with easy access to firearms or poisons. Protective factors such as family closeness and high religiosity are also found across many groups, but they tend to play a larger role in certain cultures.

AFRICAN AMERICANS

Historically, the suicide rate for African Americans has been lower than the rate for European Americans. This pattern seems to be changing, however, with rates for African American males (especially adolescents) increasing faster than rates for European American males. African American females continue to have a very low suicide rate compared with members of other ethnic groups, although they attempt suicide at rates similar to European American females. Although the suicide rate for European American men increases with age, the rate for African American men decreases, with risk peaking at 25 to 34 years.

Risk factors for African Americans include poverty, racism and marginalization, age under 35, drug use, presence of a firearm in the home, and violent behavior. Protective factors include rural residence and educational attainment. African American culture may contribute to lower rates of suicide through its emphasis on religion and extended family. Religion can provide a source of support for individuals in need, and many churches condemn suicide as a sin. Extended family can provide a multigenerational environment of social support. Some researchers believe that older African Americans are less likely to commit suicide than older European Americans because they are more likely to be included in the family as useful and valued members.

LATIN AMERICANS

The Latin American population is so diverse that it is difficult to estimate suicide prevalence without looking at country of origin. In comparing Latino groups, Mexican Americans tend to have lower rates of suicide, whereas Cuban Americans and mainland Puerto Ricans have relatively higher rates. Compared with suicide rates in their countries of origin, suicide rates for Latin American people in the United States are significantly higher.

The stresses associated with migration and acculturation can increase the risk of suicide. For example, poverty, language barriers, discrimination and marginalization, and the unavailability or underutilization of mental health services may increase risk. The process of acculturation can erode protective factors from the native culture. For example, Mexican culture emphasizes the importance of extended family, which often serves to protect individual members from psychological distress by providing an extended support system, and the church, which may provide a more extended support network. Thus, Mexican Americans who become highly acculturated (usually the young) will have weak ties to these traditional supports and may display levels of suicide risk that are similar to the dominant culture.

ASIAN AMERICANS

Asian American suicide rates tend to be lower than those of European Americans and other ethnic groups. Suicide rates for Asian Americans are lowest during youth. Rates for both Chinese Americans and Japanese Americans tend to increase with age.

Eastern cultures tend to emphasize the interdependence of individuals within the community, especially within families. Extended families that include grandparents or great-grandparents provide guidance and support and serve as a protective factor against suicide. Some Asian American religious beliefs may also protect against suicide. Confucianism, for example, views suicide as disrespectful to the group one is a part of. In Buddhism, suicide is seen as selfish or overly passionate, and in Taoism, it may be seen as immoderate or unwise. Shintoism, which is widely practiced in Japan, is less forbidding of suicide. Most Asian American religions include a belief in some sort of life after death, making suicide less of an escape from one's problems.

Certain aspects of Asian culture may prevent distressed individuals from seeking help. Some decisions to commit suicide are based on a strong sense of family honor, and it may be considered preferable for one individual to die to protect the honor of the entire family. Elderly Asian Americans may feel neglected and disrespected when the traditional respect given to them is not afforded by their Americanized families. They may also blame themselves for their children's failure to provide for them, believing they must have been bad parents.

NATIVE AMERICANS

The Native American population currently consists of more than 500 tribes, which vary widely in their suicide rates. As a whole, Native American suicide rates are about one and a half to four times higher than the overall rate in the United States and about three to four times higher than the suicide rates of the other prominent ethnic groups. As a whole, the Native American population tends to be younger compared with other groups; the increased suicide risk of this population may reflect the higher risk in younger Native Americans. There are some indications that the suicide rate for Native Americans is decreasing.

A number of socioeconomic and cultural forces have contributed to high levels of poverty, substance abuse, depression, and other factors that increase the risk of suicide. Suicide rates in Native American tribes are positively correlated with stresses related to acculturation and negatively correlated with traditional integration. Many Native American cultures have been forced to deal with the loss of their native land and have been bombarded with Western education, missionaries, legislation, language, and child-rearing ideas. Native American tribes have become divided: Some individuals

want to preserve the traditional ways, whereas others prioritize different goals. Cultural conflict, seemingly hopeless environmental conditions, and a view of death as a natural part of the life cycle (with the possibility of reincarnation or life after death) may influence individuals in distress to consider suicide.

PROMOTING PROTECTIVE FACTORS

Clearly, cultural influences can play a role in suicide rates, and many of the cultural factors mentioned here act to protect members of these cultures from self-harm. Promoting such protective factors may decrease the risk of suicide.

—*Joseph D. Hovey*
—*Christine C. Larson*

FURTHER READING

Chance, S. E., Kaslow, N. J., Summerville, M. B., & Wood, K. (1998). Suicidal behaviors in African American individuals: Current status and future directions. *Cultural Diversity and Mental Health, 4*, 19–37.

Hovey, J. D. (2000). Acculturative stress, depression, and suicidal ideation in Mexican immigrants. *Cultural Diversity and Ethnic Minority Psychology, 6*, 134–151.

Ialongo, N., McCreary, B. K., Pearson, J. L., Koenig, A. L., Wagner, B. M., Schmidt, N. B., Poduska, J., & Kellam, S. G. (2002). Suicidal behavior among urban African American young adults. *Suicide and Life-Threatening Behavior, 32*, 256–271.

Novins, D. K., Beals, J., Roberts, R. E., & Manson, S. M. (1999). Factors associated with suicide ideation among American Indian adolescents: Does culture matter? *Suicide and Life-Threatening Behavior, 29*, 332–346.

Shiang, J. (2000). Considering cultural beliefs and behaviors in the study of suicide. In R. W. Maris, S. S. Canetto, J. L. McIntosh, & M. M. Silverman (Eds.), *Review of suicidology, 2000* (pp. 226–241). New York: Guilford Press.

T

TEACHING RACIAL IDENTITY

The phrase *teaching racial identity* is used in two distinctly different ways: (1) to describe ways parents and practitioners can facilitate the racial and ethnic socialization process, and (2) to teach about the concept of racial identity to students in graduate programs in teacher education, clinical and counseling psychology, and social work.

FACILITATING RACIAL IDENTITY DEVELOPMENT

Teaching racial identity is commonly referred to as *facilitating racial identity development*. A substantial body of literature addresses ways to promote positive racial identity development among individuals. Research has demonstrated relationships among the concepts of racial socialization, ethnic identity, perceptions of discrimination and racism, and acculturation. Facilitating racial identity is one part of the racial socialization process toward promoting positive racial identity development.

This topic has particular relevance to parents and teachers, because they play major roles in structuring children's daily experiences.

For many ethnic minorities, the development of a racial/ethnic identity becomes a central component of their overall identity formation process. *Teaching racial identity* (or *racial socialization*) describes the process of raising physically and emotionally healthy children through the development of a positive ethnic self-concept, an understanding of one's own and other

racial groups, and an awareness of one's status within and between ethnic groups, as well as in society as a whole.

A significant amount of research has shown that racial socialization processes are related to increased academic performance and motivation, self-efficacy, and racial identity development, as well as to decreased violence and drug abuse. The process of racial socialization occurs through both implicit teaching (e.g., modeling behavior) and explicit teaching (e.g., verbalizations, deliberate exposure to particular experiences and environments) regarding being a member of a racial minority group in the United States. Parents, as children's first teachers, play a major part in the teaching of racial identity, although schools and peers also serve as socializing agents. Parents' philosophies about and attitudes toward their own racial identity seem to influence the way in which they approach teaching racial identity to their children. Professionals working with ethnic families may consider examining parents' attitudes toward and methods of teaching racial identity.

FRAMEWORK FOR TEACHING RACIAL IDENTITY

The teaching of racial identity can be examined in terms of both frameworks of transmission and content of the message. Frameworks or a family's philosophy for approaching the teaching of racial identity can be categorized into three groups according to the degree to which teachings are Eurocentric versus culture-specific: (1) *mainstream*—valuing Eurocentric, middle-class culture and beliefs; (2) *minority*—communicating structural, institutional, and macroeconomic forces that affect minorities and their coping strategies; and (3) *cultural*—transmitting values specific to a culture (i.e., in terms of African Americans, spirituality, harmony, movement, verve, affect, communalism, expressive individualism, oral traditions, and social time perspective).

Examination of parents' socialization strategies through control of the community context in which their children develop has resulted in categorizing family frameworks as (1) race-conscious—actively seeking out same-race playmates and promoting involvement in cultural activities; (2) race-neutral—making no efforts to influence children's involvement with same- or other-race peers; (3) class-conscious—emphasizing the family's socioeconomic group as the major reference group; or (4) race-avoidant—distancing one's family from same-race individuals or entities.

The context in which socialization occurs has also been examined in terms of the degree to which culture-specific items are visible and/or available in the home (e.g., toys, artwork, religious figures, books, music, pictures, magazines, and clothing).

CONTENT OF RACIAL IDENTITY MESSAGES

The content of racial socialization messages has been examined in terms of broader categories based on themes that are represented. Four such categories include (1) racial identity—including racial pride, heritage, and familial and cultural history; (2) self-development—including the importance of academic achievement and effort; (3) racial barriers—including recognition of racism, prejudice, and the importance of fairness despite living in an antagonistic society; and (4) egalitarian views—such as justice, peace, and human rights.

Proactive and protective socialization methods have been identified as two factors involved in adaptive racial socialization. Proactive socialization promotes cultural empowerment, pride, spirituality, and appreciation of an extended family, whereas protective socialization promotes an awareness of societal racism. Other themes emphasized in teaching racial identity include self-esteem, self-respect, and living harmoniously with European Americans.

The teaching of racial identity by parents is done most often by mothers and may vary depending on the mother's age and education level, the ethnic- or biracial-identity status of the child or parent, and the gender of the child. The degree to which mothers

engage in teaching racial identity has been found to have an impact on children's social development. Children who experience moderate degrees of ethnic socialization have been found to display more warmth and positive communication compared with children who experience significantly higher or lower degrees of ethnic socialization. Moreover, among African Americans, males are more likely to receive messages regarding negative stereotypes, racism, and responding to discrimination and racism, and females are more likely to receive messages regarding racial pride and the importance of education.

Although parents are identified as the major socializing agents for children, parents are not the sole communicators of racial identity and indeed cannot teach children a healthy sense of racial pride if they themselves are not proud. Adaptive racial socialization can be promoted in other settings, such as schools, by encouraging same-race as well as cross-race peer relationships, providing opportunities for students to learn about their heritage, informing students about the accomplishments of members of their race, providing same-race role models, acknowledging different stages of racial identity, and encouraging positive racial identity development.

TEACHING ABOUT RACIAL IDENTITY

Teaching about the process and concept of racial identity often occurs in college-level courses that focus on the process of identity formation and racial socialization within the power dynamics of the U.S. macroculture. Topics of these courses typically include the exploration of cultural pluralism, racial and ethnic identity development, privilege and positionality in American society, self-concept, family socialization practices and values, influences of the peers, intergroup relations and intercultural communication, and current and historical perspectives on racism and discrimination in the United States. Many courses place particular focus on students' exploration of their own understanding and awareness of culture, race, and ethnicity. These courses are grounded in the philosophy and belief that individuals must clearly understand their own personal biases and level of privilege before reflecting on traits and characteristics of other groups.

Such courses are most effective when emphasis is placed on students' self-reflection regarding biases, racial and ethnic stereotypes, and how power, status, and privilege influence perceptions of others. These courses tend to be relatively small (5 to 25 students), and as a result of this size, the instructor creates activities in which students closely interact with one another in discussions and activities on difficult and sensitive topics that require active student engagement.

Students often take on the roles of both teachers and learners in the dynamic construction of the class, which facilitates a sense of community within the class. Many courses embrace a social-justice approach and have students collaborate on a service-learning project or social cause in the community to actualize the learning objectives. Courses structure learning activities so that students explore, discuss, and learn about the varied experiences of individuals while also discussing critical issues in people's understanding of race and ethnicity. Often, cultural simulations and interactive activities are used to create contrived situations of racism and discrimination so that the process of understanding the complexity of racial identity is apparent in a nonthreatening environment. Cultural simulations appear to be particularly effective tools for teaching European Americans about racial identity, racism, discrimination, and privilege, as many European Americans become defensive and "shut down" in traditional classroom discussions about the power dynamics of race, ethnicity, and culture in American society.

Historically, these courses have focused on teaching about specific features and traits of racial and ethnic groups; however, this emphasis often perpetuates stereotypes associated with racial and ethnic groups. Furthermore, this approach tends to neglect tremendous within-group diversity and often promotes dangerous generalizations.

—*W. David Wakefield*
—*April Z. Taylor*

See also Multicultural Counseling; Racial Identity Development

FURTHER READING

Derman-Sparks, L., & Brunson Phillips, C. (1997). *Teaching/ learning anti-racism: A developmental approach.* New York: Teachers College Press.

Locke, D. C. (1998). *Increasing multicultural understanding: A comprehensive model* (2nd ed.). Thousand Oaks, CA: Sage.

Rothenberg, P. S. (2002). *White privilege: Essential readings on the other side of racism.* New York: Worth.

Simulation Training Systems. (2005). *BaFáBaFá.* Del Mar, CA: Author. Retrieved May 9, 2005, from http://www .stsintl.com

Stevenson, H. C. (1994). Validation of the scale of racial socialization for African American Adolescents: Steps toward multidimensionality. *Journal of Black Psychology, 20,* 445–468.

Thornton, M. C. (1997). Strategies of racial socialization among Black parents: Mainstream, minority, and cultural messages. In R. J. Taylor, J. S. Jackson, & L. M. Chatters (Eds.), *Family life in Black America* (pp. 201–215). Thousand Oaks, CA: Sage.

Wakefield, W. D. (2005). Understanding privilege in American society. In E. Chen & G. Omatsu (Eds.), *Teaching about Asian Pacific Americans.* Walnut Creek, CA: Altamira Press.

TOKENISM/PSYCHOLOGY OF TOKENISM

In any social group, a category of people (e.g., women, people of color) may be underrepresented. When this discrepancy is extreme (less than 15% of the group), those individuals are considered to be token representatives of their group. If someone is the only group representative, she or he is defined as having solo status. Anyone can be a token or solo if underrepresented in a group, such as two men in a workplace of women. However, as a result of poor treatment from majority-group members, being a token or solo from a low-status group (e.g., racial minorities, women) is often associated with negative outcomes, such as increased depression and social withdrawal.

Visibility, contrast, and role encapsulation are three challenges faced by tokens. First, tokens are more visible. Because others pay a disproportionate amount of attention to them and are aware of their actions and behaviors, tokens may feel they are continually being scrutinized. Tokens may also be self-conscious about what they say and do because they are treated as representatives of their entire group (e.g., presuming one Latina's opinion reflects those of all Latinos/as). Further, tokens often feel pressure to work especially hard to have their achievements, rather than their group membership, recognized. Tokens may also be concerned that any poor performance will be interpreted as characteristic of their entire group's abilities. At the same time, tokens' performance may actually suffer because self-consciousness, impression management, and anxiety (caused by being the focus of majority-group members) are cognitive distractions that can interfere with their ability to focus on relevant information (e.g., recalling class lectures).

Second, majority-group members often contrast differences between themselves and tokens, creating artificial boundaries between the groups. These boundaries protect majority-group members who are unsure about the attitudes and beliefs of tokens, but also serve to isolate token individuals socially. Tokens may also isolate themselves because of poor treatment, or expectations of poor treatment, by majority-group members. Sometimes group boundaries are permeated, particularly when tokens are perceived to be exceptions to their group (e.g., being perceived as intelligent when other group members are perceived as dumb). However, although this can lead tokens to be included in the majority group, it may isolate them from their token group.

Finally, tokens undergo role encapsulation, or being forced to play a role based on stereotypes of their group. Tokens may be limited to stereotyped opportunities and roles (e.g., African Americans as athletes or janitors). When tokens fear confirming negative stereotypes about their group, they experience stereotype threat. Stereotype threat may interfere with performance in the stereotyped area (e.g., women performing poorly on a math test) because tokens fear they will be unfairly evaluated on the basis of the stereotype, not because they personally believe that the stereotype is true.

Although tokens may overcome these negative experiences and the mistaken beliefs of majority-group members, the process can be demanding. Therefore, reducing the difficulties associated with token or solo status requires there to be more diversity within any group so that no group is underrepresented, and that all groups attain equality in their social status.

—*Isis H. Settles*
—*NiCole T. Buchanan*

FURTHER READING

Kanter, R. M. (1977). *Men and women of the corporation.* New York: Basic Books.

Niemann, Y. F., & Dovidio, J. F. (1998). Relationship of solo status, academic rank, and perceived distinctiveness to job satisfaction of racial/ethnic minorities. *Journal of Applied Psychology, 83*(1), 55–71.

Steele, C. M. (1998). Stereotyping and its threat are real. *American Psychologist, 5*, 680–681.

TRANSLATION METHODS

As cross-cultural research has become mainstream and more of a necessity in our complex world, translation of measures into different languages has also become more necessary. It is often not possible or appropriate to provide translators for large numbers of research subjects, and instead researchers rely on translated versions of already established measures. And many of the most popular measures of psychological functioning have been developed in the United States, in English. Accurate translation of already established measures is essential for the comparison of responses of two different language or cultural groups. Accurate translation is also important for the standardized tests used by the educational system. There are four main established ways to translate measures for research: one-way or forward translation, double or back translation, translation by committee, and decentering.

One-way or forward translation is accomplished by having a bilingual individual translate the measure directly from the original language to the desired language. This is one of the easiest and most economical methods of measure translation. The problem with this method lies in its reliance on only one person to accurately translate both content and contextual meanings. Translation by one person can lead to a measure's contamination by personal beliefs and cultural context. This method also does not involve comparing the new version to the old version, but relies on the translation by one individual. Some researchers rely on forward translations of several individuals, but this approach still does not ensure accuracy of content in the translated version of the measure.

Double or back translation is accomplished by having a bilingual expert translate the measure into the new language and then having a second bilingual expert, with no knowledge of the original measure, translate the translation back into the original language. The original and the back-translated version are then compared for inconsistencies. This translation method relies on two experts and can be more accurate than forward translation. Opponents of this method point out that although this method can result in very literal translation, nuances of meaning can be lost. It is sometimes more important to convey the essential meanings and concepts of the original measure than to accomplish a very literal translation. This method is the preferred method of most researchers, however, as it allows for the use of two experts and provides a system of assessment of accuracy, while still being economical and not requiring a lot of time to complete.

Translation by committee is another method used to translate measures for use with other language groups or cultures. This method employs the help of several experts who work together to translate the measure to the new language, keeping context and culture in mind. The committee members work together to come up with the most accurate translation possible, keeping in mind the original purpose of the measure. This method is not often employed, because it is time-consuming and expensive. Also, problems can arise in committees when members of different subcultures each bring their own culture and idioms to the group. It is often necessary to consider the subculture of interest, as even within one language, local idioms can be very different and complicate accurate translation of ideas.

Another method of measure translation is decentering. Decentering involves simplifying and adjusting the original version of the measure as the translated measure is devised. In this way, both measures are adjusted, allowing for cultural and linguistic equivalence between the two versions. Guidelines for this type of translation include using short, simple phrases, employing active rather than passive voice, and avoiding metaphors and colloquialisms. Decentering involves creating an essentially new measure for the purpose of comparison between two cultural groups. The new version may lack the validity and reliability of the original measure but may be more useful in terms of the populations that are being studied. Decentering can also be time-consuming and involve several rounds of translation to provide the researcher with two accurate, comparable versions of a measure.

Regional variations in language must also be considered in the translation of measures. Although Spanish is the official language of both Spain and Mexico, Spanish and Mexican speakers do not use the same common words in their everyday speech. Similarly, among speakers of the English language from the British Isles and the United States, the essentials of the language are the same, yet basic, everyday language use can be quite different. The researcher must be aware of the cultural subset that a study is targeting and be careful to include bilingual experts from the right language and cultural group. If several cultural groups are to be included in a study, then several variations of a word may have to be included in the final translated version. Another solution is to add definitions of words and concepts within a measure. Every English word does not have a common translation into other languages. Some words may require explanation of their meaning instead of literal translation.

Another consideration in translation, in addition to whether the proper words are used, is the proper use of grammar in the translation. Measures written in one language and translated into another can include confusing double negatives, verb tenses that are not common, and other grammar problems. Literal translations can lead to problems in understanding what a question is asking the participant, and grammar must also be considered.

Perhaps the best translation method is to use a variety of methods in conjunction with one another. In this way, the researcher ensures development of the most accurate version possible of the measure and multiple experts agree that the measure is asking the questions that the researchers want the answers to. This approach requires dedication of time and resources but is the best way to ensure accuracy.

Translation is also an important issue in the area of education. The United States is a culturally and linguistically diverse country. Recent educational trends toward standardized testing and implementation of educational standards, combined with the ethnic diversity of the country, have led to the necessary translation of standardized tests into multiple languages. Several states have made efforts to provide translated versions of standardized tests to students whose first language is not English. Whether or not a standardized test is available often depends on state education laws and the number of non-English-speaking children who would be affected in a particular case. But whether or not a translated version of a test is appropriate for a student depends on many different factors, including the objective of the test. If the objective of a test is to test the level of acquired knowledge, then performance may depend on the language of instruction in that skill. If the test examines general knowledge, the language in which the child converses and reads most comfortably may be more appropriate.

Translation and choosing the method of translation used to most accurately convey meanings from one language to another is a complicated process. Researchers need to consider why they are translating the measure, the distinct subculture that may be answering the questions, and how much time and effort they can commit to the endeavor. Perhaps the most important part of translation of measures is having trusted experts involved in the process.

—*Kimberlee M. Roy*

See also Ethnic Research; Bilingualism

FURTHER READING

McGorry, S. Y. (2000). Measurement in a cross-cultural environment: Survey translation issues. *Qualitative Market Research: An International Journal, 3,* 74–81.

Stansfield, C. W. (2003). Test translation and adaptation in public education in the USA. *Language Testing, 20,* 189–207.

TRANSRACIAL ADOPTION

HISTORICAL BACKGROUND

Transracial adoption is defined as a form of adoption in which parents and children who are racially different from one another are legally conjoined as a family. Domestic transracial adoption typically occurs through private adoption, foster care, and interracial marriage with stepchildren, whereas international transracial adoption occurs when children are adopted from other countries and are considered racial and ethnic minorities in the adoptive country. In the United States, transracial adoptive parents are almost always racially White and of European descent, and adoptees are racial and ethnic minorities. As a result, adoptees and adoptive parents are inevitably confronted with an inherent racial discrepancy. Namely, transracial adoptees have access to certain privileges growing up in European American households, but these experiences are contradicted by their physical classification and treatment as racial minorities in society—a phenomenon referred to as the *transracial adoption paradox.*

Although the first documented incidences of domestic and international transracial adoptions occurred in approximately the same time period (the 1950s), they were propelled by different historical events. Domestic transracial adoption first occurred in an effort to assimilate Native Americans into mainstream European American society by removing children from reservations and placing them into European American families and institutions in the 1950s and 1960s. This effort was followed by the placement and adoption of African American children into European American homes in the 1960s and early 1970s. However, domestic transracial adoption was and still is a racially charged and controversial issue. In 1972, the National Association of Black Social Workers passed a resolution that called for the end of transracial adoption of African Americans. Similarly, 1978 brought passage of the Indian Child Welfare Act, which revised the placement procedures of Native American children.

International adoption began shortly after World War II with the adoption of war-orphaned Japanese and Greek children but became formalized after the Korean War in the 1950s. Until the 1990s, international adoption usually meant the adoption of children from South Korea. It is estimated that more than 150,000 Korean children have been adopted by American citizens since 1955 (equivalent to 10% of the present-day Korean American population). Today, annual international adoption rates in America have increased threefold from 7,093 in 1990 to 22,884 in 2004. These adoptions are predominantly made by European Americans who adopt from more than 40 countries worldwide, with China, Russia, Guatemala, and South Korea as the top sending countries. It is worth noting that international adoption increased in popularity as the availability of domestic adoption decreased, in part because of the preceding controversy over domestic transracial adoption.

The aforementioned paradox in which transracially adopted children experience many of the privileges associated with being raised in a European American adoptive family yet nevertheless are perceived and treated by society as racial and ethnic minorities has served as a conceptual springboard for most psychological studies on transracial adoption. In general, three types of research studies are associated with transracial adoption. Each of these study designs will be reviewed, followed by a brief summary of future research trends.

PSYCHOLOGICAL OUTCOME STUDIES

The most common type of adoption research is the psychological outcome study. Psychological outcome studies typically have compared adoptees and nonadoptees on measures of psychological adjustment. An underlying assumption of this line of research when applied to transracial adoptees is that racial and ethnic differences are not salient issues if transracial adoptees and same-race adoptees or nonadoptees do not differ in psychological adjustment. Early outcome studies found that adoptees, including transracial adoptees, exhibited more psychological problems and mental-health needs than nonadoptees, but these studies often were based on small clinical samples and biased by self-selection. Subsequent research on nonclinical and more representative samples suggests that the adjustment of adoptees, including domestic and international transracial adoptees, is comparable to that of nonadoptees, and adoptees are at only a slightly higher risk for emotional and behavioral problems. Moreover, the group differences between adoptees and nonadoptees tend to be small and often are mitigated by a variety of factors, such as age at adoption and adverse preadoption experiences (e.g., institutional deprivation). Other studies find no remarkable group differences between transracial adoptees and same-race adoptees or nonadoptees in levels of self-esteem and social adjustment. Thus, outcome studies seem to converge on the finding that transracial adoptees are not necessarily at greater risk for psychological problems. However, a persistent problem with outcome research is the failure to directly study or measure the racial and ethnic experiences of adoptees and how they relate to psychological adjustment.

RACIAL AND ETHNIC IDENTITY STUDIES

Although transracial adoptees may not differ dramatically from same-race adoptees and nonadoptees on adjustment measures, it is possible that they experience difficulties in their racial and ethnic identity development because of the transracial adoption paradox. Poor racial and ethnic identity development has been associated with lower well-being and greater psychological distress in nonadopted racial and ethnic minority populations. Consistent with this viewpoint, a number of descriptive studies have examined the racial and ethnic identity development of transracial adoptees. Early identity studies found that transracial adoptees reported lower racial and ethnic identity scores than same-race adoptees (usually European American adopted children of same-race adoptive parents). Additionally, transracial adoptees were more likely to identify with and to be highly acculturated to mainstream European American culture, although there is no research that connects this type of assimilation with well-being and adjustment. Recent studies suggest that transracial adoptees have mixed or varied feelings about their race and ethnicity. On the one hand, most transracial adoptees tend to report feeling proud of their racial and ethnic heritages; on the other hand, many transracial adoptees feel uncomfortable with their racial appearance, are distressed by experiences with racism and discrimination, and struggle to

come to terms with the loss of their birth family and culture. This racial and ethnic ambivalence has been found to be associated with lower well-being and greater distress; conversely, a positive racial and ethnic identity has been found to be associated with greater well-being and lower distress among transracial adoptees.

CULTURAL SOCIALIZATION STUDIES

Given the aforementioned racial and ethnic challenges that confront transracial adoptive families and the links between racial and ethnic identity and adjustment, there is emerging research on the cultural socialization experiences of adopted children. Cultural socialization within the family refers to the transmission and internalization of cultural values, beliefs, customs, and behaviors from parents to children. These cultural experiences, in turn, are believed to promote positive racial and ethnic identity development, to help prepare children to cope with racism and discrimination, and to encourage competent functioning in a diverse society. The extent to which parents acknowledge ethnic and racial differences within the family and engage in cultural socialization parenting practices, as well as the manner in which they engage in socialization, however, appears to vary quite a bit. In the past, transracial adoptive parents made little effort to teach their children about their birth culture and did not necessarily validate their children's unique racial and ethnic experiences. Instead, parents often encouraged assimilation as a means to be accepted into European American society, which was assumed to be adaptive for their adopted children. However, as adoptive parents have begun to recognize the paradox transracial adoptees face, today, an increasing number of transracial adoptive parents are exposing their children to their racial and ethnic heritage and openly discussing racial and ethnic issues.

The extent to which cultural socialization experiences contribute to racial and ethnic identity development and positive psychological adjustment is just now beginning to be understood. One study, for example, found that among 88 African American transracial adoptees, nearly half of all adoptive parents were likely to encourage biculturalism in the child's upbringing during childhood. However, adoptive parents were more likely to deny race and feel ambivalent about cultural socialization when the child reached adolescence. As expected, this de-emphasis of race by the parents corresponded with a decrease in the adoptees' ethnic identification as African Americans between childhood and adolescence. The researchers additionally found that those adoptees whose parents actively promoted their child's race had a more secure ethnic identity development and more positive psychological adjustment. Similar research findings have been made in recent studies of international transracial adoptees. A study of more than 200 Korean adolescent adoptees found that adoptees whose adoptive parents actively promoted their birth culture had more positive racial/ethnic identity development and, in turn, better psychological adjustment than those adoptees whose parents offered little encouragement.

FUTURE RESEARCH

Current research suggests that transracial adoptees are relatively psychologically well adjusted and exhibit variability in their racial and ethnic identity development. Moreover, emerging evidence supports the claim that adoptees whose adoptive parents facilitate the cultural understanding of their birth culture have higher racial/ethnic identity scores and, in turn, better adjustment. To strengthen the validity and interpretability of these results, improvement of the measurement of racial and ethnic experiences is needed. Past studies also have relied upon relatively small convenience samples of adoptive parents or adoptees rather than larger, more representative samples. To confirm that the experiences of transracial adoptees are unique, studies are necessary that compare transracial adoptees and same-race adoptees of the same racial/ethnic background or, minimally, with same-race non-adoptees. Last, research is required that examines the cultural socialization experiences of transracial adoptive families. Such research will shed light on ways in which adoptive parents and adoptees manage ethnic and racial differences throughout the life span and demonstrate resilience in the face of adversity.

—*Richard M. Lee*
—*Sueyoung Song*

FURTHER READING

Fanshel, D. (1972). *Far from the reservation: The transracial adoption of American Indian children.* Metuchen, NJ: Scarecrow Press.

Kirk, H. D. (1964). *Shared fate: A theory of adoption and mental health.* London: The Free Press.

Lee, R. M. (2003). The transracial adoption paradox: History, research, and counseling implications of cultural socialization. *The Counseling Psychologist, 31,* 711–744.

U

UNCLE TOM SYNDROME

Uncle Tom syndrome is the term used to describe a ritualized, accommodating, sycophantic style of behavior in African Americans toward Caucasians. The African American acts in a docile, nonassertive manner to appear nonthreatening to European Americans. The term traces its origins to the novel *Uncle Tom's Cabin,* written by Harriet Beecher Stowe in 1852. The book, originally a newspaper serial, was written as an attempt to convince readers of the evils of slavery. The book enjoyed considerable commercial success. In the first year it sold 300,000 copies and by 1856, 2 million copies. The book succeeded in its goal of raising the nation's consciousness about the evils of slavery.

There continues to be controversy over the book. In *Uncle Tom's Cabin,* Stowe attempted to humanize the slaves and show the cruelty of the slavery institution and slave owner. The lead villain, slave owner Simon Legree, is vicious in his beatings of the slave Uncle Tom. Stowe attempted to portray Uncle Tom as maintaining his humanity and dignity under inhumane conditions. Many modern-day reviewers, however, view the depiction of the Uncle Tom character as patronizing and offensive.

The term *Uncle Tom syndrome,* although derived from this book, has taken on specific cultural meaning beyond the original context. It has developed pejorative connotations, referring to a passive African American who seeks eagerly to appease Caucasians. This pejorative interpretation of the eager-to-please African American belies the importance of the adaptive survival intent of the attitudinal posture.

During slavery, the most dangerous act that a slave could do was to present a challenge or threat to the Caucasian slave owner. Any such overt threats were met with violence or death. The slave needed to develop a manner of interacting with the slave owner that would not threaten his or her safety. Two such ritualized accommodating styles that emerged out of this power dynamic were *playing it cool* and the Uncle Tom syndrome. *Playing it cool* is the practice of hiding one's feelings and presenting an impenetrable wall of seeming indifference. As stated, the Uncle Tom syndrome is another cross-racial interpersonal style in which the African American presents an agreeable, deferent, and placating attitude toward the slave owner. The Uncle Tom syndrome presents the least challenge to Caucasian authority.

Both of these ritualistic interpersonal styles continue in contemporary race relations. Although slavery is no longer legal, the power remains in the hands of Caucasians. European American power is perpetuated in economic, educational, and criminal-justice systems. In the current oppressive cultural milieu in which we live, it remains adaptive for African Americans to both hide their feelings and appease Caucasian authority figures. Uncle Tom syndrome is an intelligent survival strategy in a hostile world. Today, it may be just as important for African Americans to appease European American teachers, bosses, or judges to survive as it was to appease the Caucasian slave owner. These interpersonal styles are particularly relevant for African American men, who are seen by many

Caucasians as more threatening and hostile than African American women.

Recently, uses of the term and concept of the Uncle Tom syndrome have grown well beyond the United States' cross-racial context. This phrase is now used in an international context in which subjugated developing cultures display a similar attitude toward colonial authorities.

—*Paul E. Priester*

FURTHER READING

Grier, W. H., & Cobbs, M. P. (2000). *Black rage.* Eugene, OR: Wipf & Stock.

Hendrick, J. D. (1995). *Harriet Beecher Stowe: A life.* New York: Oxford University Press.

Stowe, H. B. (1983). *Uncle Tom's cabin.* New York: Bantam. (Original work published 1852)

VIETNAMESE AMERICANS

Vietnamese Americans represent one of the more recent refugee/immigrant populations in the United States. An introduction to Vietnamese Americans requires some familiarity with their historical and cultural backgrounds, to serve as contextual information for understanding their life experiences in America. This section on Vietnamese Americans briefly covers the following topics: Vietnamese American population, Vietnamese immigration to the United States, Vietnamese adaptation to American society, Vietnamese culture, Vietnamese American families, and mental health issues among Vietnamese Americans. Needless to say, this section does not represent an exhaustive description of Vietnamese Americans. Additional information can be obtained from resources listed at the end of this discussion.

VIETNAMESE AMERICAN POPULATION

Vietnamese Americans currently represent the fourth-largest Asian American population in the United States. According to the 2000 Census, there are approximately 1,122,528 people who identify themselves as Vietnamese alone and 1,223,736 people who identify themselves as Vietnamese alone or in combination with other ethnicities. The growth in the Vietnamese American population from 1990 to 2000 is 83% for Vietnamese alone and 99% for Vietnamese alone or in combination with other ethnicities. The two states that have the largest Vietnamese American populations are California, with 39.8% of all Vietnamese Americans, and Texas, with 12%. Orange County, California, is

home to the largest concentration of Vietnamese outside of Vietnam (233,573), with the neighborhood Little Saigon as its cultural and civic center.

VIETNAMESE IMMIGRATION TO THE UNITED STATES

Prior to 1975, there were few Vietnamese Americans in the United States. The end of the Vietnam War prompted several waves of refugees from Vietnam, the majority of whom eventually resettled in the United States.

The first wave of Vietnamese refugees, approximately 132,000 people, left Vietnam immediately following the fall of Saigon on April 30, 1975 (Saigon is now known as Ho Chi Minh City). The main reason for their flight from Vietnam was fear of persecution by the North Vietnamese communist government. These refugees included many high-ranking military officials, professional people who had worked with American personnel or companies in Vietnam, and individuals who were educated or had family ties in the United States. First-wave refugees were generally better educated, wealthier, and had more political connections with the U.S. government than refugees of subsequent waves.

The majority of first-wave refugees left Vietnam by cargo ships or air transportation dispatched by the U.S. military, which subsequently transferred them to military bases in the Philippines and Guam. From there, these refugees were transferred to resettlement centers located in different regions of the United States. They were then matched with voluntary agencies whose job was to coordinate the refugees' eventual resettlement. Vietnamese families that were officially matched with sponsors were flown to their resettlement destinations to start their new lives in America. Unlike the resettlement experiences of Cuban refugees in Florida, for instance, first-wave Vietnamese refugees were systematically dispersed throughout the country, an attempt by the federal government to discourage the formation of ethnic enclaves and to minimize the impact of Vietnamese refugee resettlement on any particular geographical area. Thus, many refugees found themselves in communities with little or no opportunities for contact with other Vietnamese refugees or other Asian Americans. Within a few years of the initial resettlement, however, a significant amount of secondary migration occurred, mainly to California and Texas, the two states that now have the largest Vietnamese populations.

The second wave of Vietnamese refugees (400,000) occurred between 1977 and 1982. As a result of political and societal changes in Vietnam, as well as renewed pressure by the Vietnamese government to expel ethnic Chinese, thousands of people fled to neighboring countries. Among the second-wave refugees were individuals associated with the former South Vietnamese government, and ethnic minorities of Vietnam. Second-wave refugees were also known as "the boat people" because many individuals escaped from Vietnam aboard small, overcrowded, and poorly equipped boats. As a result, many individuals lost their lives at sea or were victims of robbery, rape, or murder by Thai pirates. Those who escaped drowning, starvation, or victimization typically ended up in refugee camps in Thailand, Malaysia, Indonesia, Singapore, Hong Kong, or the Philippines, where they awaited permanent asylum in countries willing to accept them. The majority eventually were allowed to resettle in the United States. Following their arrival to the United States, second-wave refugees sought the aid and leadership of the established first-wave refugees through family sponsorship and/or mutual assistance associations.

In response to world outcry over the horrendous plight of the boat people, the Vietnamese government agreed to establish the Orderly Departure Program in 1979, enabling people to leave Vietnam legally for family reunion and humanitarian reasons. At the same time, the U.S. government also passed legislation to aid the refugees, which facilitated the departure of subsequent waves of immigrants from Vietnam. During the period from 1982 to 2000, the United States accepted approximately 531,000 Vietnamese individuals.

The different waves of Vietnamese refugees/immigrants and the nature of their migration to the United States highlight various aspects of diversity among Vietnamese Americans. For instance, Vietnamese Americans can include those who have been in the United States for at least three decades, as well as those who have just arrived. Knowledge of these pieces of historical information provides a crucial context for understanding the life experiences of Vietnamese Americans and their adaptation to American society.

VIETNAMESE ADAPTATION TO AMERICAN SOCIETY

Once safely resettled in the United States, Vietnamese refugees soon realized the challenges of adjusting to American life. Most experienced culture shock, although the degree partially depended on the characteristics of the refugees, including their socioeconomic status and the extent of exposure to American culture prior to leaving Vietnam. The challenges of adapting to American life ranged from simple matters, such as learning how to operate household appliances, grocery shopping, and using American money, to more complex matters, such as learning a new language, adopting culturally appropriate behaviors, and searching for employment. Many Vietnamese refugees, especially those who were resettled in colder regions and away from the coasts, also had to adjust to drastic changes in geography and climate. The systematic dispersion of Vietnamese refugees across the country and the lack of preexisting Vietnamese communities likely intensified the adjustment difficulties experienced by Vietnamese individuals and families. Indeed, within a few years of their initial entry into the United States, Vietnamese ethnic enclaves began to emerge, via secondary migration, perhaps as an effective coping reaction to the challenges of adjusting to American life. The ethnic enclaves established by first-wave refugees served as important support systems for subsequent waves of Vietnamese refugees and helped ease the difficulties associated with a new life in America.

The reception of Vietnamese refugees by communities across America was initially positive, which was partly motivated by guilt associated with American involvement in the Vietnam War, as well as genuine humanitarian concern for the refugees. The initial positive reception, however, was not without some negative sentiments among host communities, perhaps partly because of some Americans still feeling bitter about American defeat in Vietnam, native fears of losing jobs to immigrants, and/or misperceptions of Vietnamese refugees as communists. There was also resentment of Vietnamese refugees as welfare dependents. Unlike those of immigrant status, refugee status allowed Vietnamese individuals and families immediate access to federal assistance programs. Because of this and other previously mentioned factors, as well as the continuing influx of Vietnamese refugees, by 1979 the majority of Americans surveyed in various polls preferred that the Vietnamese be kept out of the United States. Although many host communities extended valuable assistance to Vietnamese refugees, these refugees also confronted considerable resistance and discrimination in their adjustment to American society. For example, Vietnamese fishermen in Texas were targets of prejudice and discrimination by the Ku Klux Klan, and Vietnamese Americans were victims of hate crimes.

The majority of Vietnamese refugees began their new life in America on public assistance and at the bottom of the socioeconomic ladder. However, immediately following resettlement, many refugees began searching for employment, with the main goal of attaining self-sufficiency. This was particularly important for Vietnamese men, as employment represents a core aspect of male identity and respectability. Vietnamese refugees accepted whatever work was available, and often this adaptability required accepting jobs inconsistent with the education and training they received in Vietnam. The level of underemployment was especially apparent among first-wave refugees, who were surprised to learn that their educational degrees and occupational skills were not automatically recognized by American employers. The underemployment of Vietnamese men often required many Vietnamese women to seek work outside the home. Although their jobs were typically of low status and pay, they made important contributions to family incomes and subsequent self-sufficiency.

Despite the difficult circumstances confronted by Vietnamese refugees—war-related stress, the traumatic exodus from their homeland, and a dramatic change in cultural context—they have made considerable economic progress in their adjustment to American society. For instance, one report showed that between 1975 and 1977, fewer than 5% of heads of Vietnamese refugee households were unemployed after 27 months in Houston, Texas. The census indicated that by 1990, the median household income of the Vietnamese was at $29,800, comparable to the average of $30,000 for all American households. It is important to note, however, that economic progress was uneven across different waves of Vietnamese refugees, with those from the first-wave cohort faring better than their counterparts of later waves. Yet, the overall continuing progress among Vietnamese refugees during the period between 1990 and 2000 is striking. As of 2000, the median household income among Vietnamese Americans was $46,929—a dramatic increase from 1990. Only 10.2% of Vietnamese were on public assistance, as compared with 25% in 1990, and 14.3% of Vietnamese families were below the poverty level, as compared with 24% in 1990. Progress was also evident in educational attainment; those with a high school degree or higher were at 62%, and those with a bachelor's degree or higher were at 19.5%. These and other statistics demonstrate the resiliency of Vietnamese refugees and their attainment of self-sufficiency in America. Equally important, anthropological evidence indicates a high degree of success by Vietnamese refugees in maintaining many aspects of Vietnamese culture, including the centrality of family and the Vietnamese language, while showing a willingness to integrate important aspects of American culture into their daily lives.

VIETNAMESE CULTURE

Historically, Vietnam has been greatly affected by foreign influences, mostly through invasion and colonialism, and the Vietnamese people themselves repeatedly fought for their national independence. Because of this history, Vietnamese people, including those living in the United States, have incorporated this sense of collective independence and perseverance as part of their Vietnamese culture and identity. Nonetheless, it must be recognized that Vietnamese culture was significantly influenced by the Chinese, who invaded Vietnam in 111 BCE and ruled it for more than 1,000 years. Thus, certain aspects of Vietnamese culture can be traced back to Chinese culture, especially those pertaining to Confucianism, Taoism, and Buddhism. Together, they emphasize concepts such as reincarnation, harmony among people and nature, filial piety, the idea that *life is suffering,* and patience. These three religions or philosophies underlie Vietnamese culture and influence the structure of the family and the behavior of the individual.

The family is the centerpiece of Vietnamese culture. The traditional Vietnamese family follows the extended multigenerational pattern, which commonly includes the father and mother, the father's parents, sons, the sons' wives and children, and any unmarried daughters. Other extended-family members who share the same family name or ancestors are also an important part of family life. The structure of the traditional family is patriarchal and patrilineal, such that age and sex determine one's role and authority within the family. The Vietnamese have an extensive language system of addressing one another according to their status, both within and outside the family. Individual behavior is much more driven by familialism than by the generic notion of collectivism. Within the traditional Vietnamese family, more emphasis is placed on family roles and obligations than on individual needs and desires. Individuals' social and public behaviors, positive or negative, reflect on the whole family. The concept *loss of face* refers to shame and embarrassment brought not only to the individual, but also to the family. Therefore, family members must do everything possible to preserve the family's face, or reputation.

At an early age, children learn from parents that a good son or daughter is a child who behaves according to the principles of filial piety, which require that children love, respect, and obey their parents. Children are discouraged from questioning parental authority or acting in discordance with parental wishes. Obligations to the family, especially obedience to the parents, do not end with coming of age or marriage. Filial piety also means financial support and care of one's parents in their old age. This obligation is most expected of the eldest son, although other children also are expected to provide additional support and care. Filial piety does not end with parental deaths, as it survives in the form of ancestral worship. Thus, ancestors are an important aspect of the traditional family life.

Adherence to gender roles is another important aspect of the traditional Vietnamese family. Like many other cultures, Vietnamese culture values the notion of male superiority, which is evident in both public and private spheres of Vietnamese social life. Within the traditional family, male members enjoy a higher status than their female counterparts. The highest status in the family is given to the father, whose authority is above other family members. Although it has been observed that Vietnamese women are given more opportunities and power than are other Asian

women, for instance, Chinese women, they clearly occupy a secondary place in the family. Although women, especially the mother, are treated with great respect, their prescribed female role is influenced by Confucian teachings, which expect them to obey their fathers when they are young, their husbands when they are married, and their eldest sons when they are widowed. The ideology of male superiority is expressed in traditional sayings, such as "A hundred girls aren't worth a single testicle." Thus, sons are much more valued than daughters in the traditional Vietnamese family. Female children typically are under stricter supervision and receive less education and fewer privileges than their male siblings. Parents rationalize their unequal investment in female children with the expectation that daughters will eventually leave to join another family.

It is important to note that certain aspects of filial piety, especially respect and obedience to authority, extend beyond the family and permeate Vietnamese culture. Knowledge of the traditional value system of the Vietnamese, whether within or outside the family, includes the recognition of respect as an essential aspect of Vietnamese culture. Nonetheless, the change in cultural context from Vietnam to the United States for Vietnamese refugees most likely entailed some significant changes in their traditional cultural values, especially those involving the traditional family.

VIETNAMESE AMERICAN FAMILIES

The change in cultural context has presented considerable challenges to the traditional Vietnamese family. These challenges are coupled with the fact that many Vietnamese refugees came to the United States with nonintact families. It is not uncommon to hear stories of a parent, a spouse, a sibling, or a child who was left behind in Vietnam or died during departure from Vietnam. Therefore, the traumatic nature of the exodus has had a major impact on the physical structure of many Vietnamese families. The traditional multigenerational pattern of kinship was often disrupted, leading to an incomplete system of family support and further intensifying the stress of adjusting to the American culture for many Vietnamese families.

Changes in the traditional family—especially in the dynamics of family relationships and hierarchy—and gender roles have been documented by social scientists. Relationships between family members have been altered in significant ways as a result of new cultural and economic demands, as well as differential adaptation of individual family members. The changes in family relationships are also caused in part by changes in gender roles. One aspect of American culture that many Vietnamese individuals came to realize is the relatively more equal status between males and females, both within the society in general and in the mainstream American family. Vietnamese men, who typically were the sole financial providers for their families in Vietnam, no longer are able to maintain that role in the United States as they find themselves underemployed or unemployed and on public assistance. The dramatic change in their social and occupational status serves to undermine male authority, especially of the father or husband, in Vietnamese families. This decrease in male authority is further affected by changes experienced by Vietnamese females. Life in the United States, for the first time, affords many Vietnamese women and girls new opportunities, especially in the areas of employment and education. These new opportunities help them develop a degree of independence and a separate identity from the prescribed traditional female roles and allow them to realize their potential occupational skills and educational talents. Although many Vietnamese women have adjusted well to these changes in their lives, there have been both positive and negative consequences. Many women experience a sense of accomplishment, especially the ability to contribute to their family's financial welfare in a way that goes beyond taking care of the household and children. On the other hand, they also feel overwhelmed by the changes in their roles, which entail work both outside and inside the home, because many Vietnamese men hesitate in taking on household responsibilities that were traditionally defined as women's work. Vietnamese men often feel threatened by the changes in their wives' status, which can create tension—sometimes leading to domestic violence—in spousal relations, as men perceive further erosion of their authority. Although divorce is highly stigmatized within Vietnamese American communities, this tension in the marital relationship perhaps partly explains the increase in divorce rates among Vietnamese Americans. Nonetheless, there is also evidence suggesting a level of adaptability of Vietnamese men and women to the changes in family and gender roles.

Another significant change in the traditional Vietnamese family centers on parent–child relationships. The acculturation processes typically differ between parents and children, and this difference can lead to intergenerational conflicts. The general pattern suggests that parents usually want to maintain core aspects of traditional Vietnamese values, whereas their children tend to adopt more mainstream American values and lifestyles. This differential pattern in adaptation is certainly influenced by differences in age and developmental stages of parents and children at the time of entry into the United States. Furthermore, parents and children are exposed to different socializing institutions (i.e., occupational/public assistance contexts for parents versus school/peer contexts for children) that involve varying cultural and behavioral demands. Within the school context, children learn from teachers and peers the importance of certain American values, such as individuality, assertiveness, and questioning of authority. Although incorporating these characteristics into their psychological and behavioral repertoire can facilitate educational success for children, the transfer of these characteristics into the Vietnamese family context can lead to intergenerational problems and upset the traditional roles of parents and children. Children may begin to challenge parental authority, and their parents may believe that they are not accorded the respect and obedience they deserve. The parents' traditionally prescribed dominant roles within the family may be further weakened by parents' need to rely on their children's more proficient English-language skills to cope with the challenges of daily life in America.

Changes in the parent–child relationships also may have different dynamics for sons and daughters. Sons, especially eldest sons, may question the traditional obligations of sharing the same household with their parents and providing financial support and care when their parents get old, whereas daughters may question traditional gender roles in which females receive fewer opportunities and privileges than do their male siblings. These and other factors may negatively affect the overall quality of parent–child relationships in Vietnamese American families.

Despite the disruption in the physical structure of the traditional Vietnamese family and the challenges to traditional family and gender roles, Vietnamese families generally have adjusted well to American life. For instance, many Vietnamese families have recreated the multigenerational extended-family pattern by incorporating distant relatives and friends in the active circle of close kinship. This rebuilding of kinship demonstrates the adaptability of Vietnamese families and facilitates a new network of support for family members in coping with other adjustment challenges. Although family members have become more and more adapted to changing family roles and relationships, there is also a desire to preserve important aspects of the traditional Vietnamese family. For example, a majority of Vietnamese youth in one survey strongly endorsed concepts of obedience and hard work as the most important values in their families. Another example is that although women appreciate the changes in gender roles, they also don't want those changes to undermine the authority of their husbands as well as their own authority as parents. These examples do not suggest that Vietnamese American families have overcome all the difficulties in their adjustment to American society or that they have successfully integrated values of both cultures, but they do show that changes often entail both positive and negative outcomes.

MENTAL HEALTH ISSUES AMONG VIETNAMESE AMERICANS

The term *refugee* may suggest possible exposure to trauma that consequently can influence the psychological adjustment of refugee individuals. Vietnamese refugees, especially those from the first and second waves, were faced with varying degrees of trauma, ranging from the sudden and chaotic nature of departure, to separation from or death of family members during flight, to being victims of horrific crimes by pirates. In thinking about these traumatic experiences, it is also important to consider the trauma relating to the lengthy Vietnam War itself. Prior to the forced exodus, many Vietnamese were also refugees within their own country as the war raged on and devastated many regions of Vietnam, forcing people to flee from their homes. Of course, experiences of trauma do not necessarily lead to mental health problems, because other variables—such as personal coping capacity and resources, family network and support, English-language proficiency, educational level, age, gender, and other important contextual and resettlement variables—may serve as important protective or risk factors in the development of mental health problems among Vietnamese refugees.

It has been observed that when mental health problems do begin to emerge among Vietnamese refugees, they usually occur within the initial period of 6 to 24 months after entrance into the United States. This suggests a delayed response to the refugee experience, such that only when individuals and families are safe and settled in their new environment and have time to reflect on the changes and losses do mental health problems begin to emerge. One of the challenges in identifying mental health problems involves their meaning to Vietnamese refugees. The term *mental health problem* as defined in the United States is a foreign concept to Vietnamese individuals, especially among recent arrivals. In Vietnam, if a person was viewed as having a mental health problem, it meant that he or she was "crazy" and should be confined in the home or isolated from society. Another challenge in identifying mental health problems is related to Vietnamese cultural concepts of familialism, life as suffering, and patience. Therefore, individuals and families often endure mental health suffering while keeping their problems to themselves or within the family. Despite these challenges, a number of basic mental health–related problems have been identified within Vietnamese American communities. Some examples include issues relating to traumatic experiences before and during their flight from Vietnam and of refugee camp conditions; anxiety and fear associated with resettlement; homesickness; loneliness and isolation, especially among the elderly; poverty and loss of social status; loss of cultural values; stress associated with role changes; intergenerational conflicts; and unrealistic expectations among many Vietnamese about how good life would be in the United States. These problems often are associated with psychosomatic manifestations and symptoms of depression, suicidal ideation, anxiety, posttraumatic stress disorder, alcohol abuse, and/or domestic violence. Although these symptoms are more prevalent among adults than among children or adolescents, and generally adults experience more difficulties than do children in their transition to a new culture, children also may suffer from adjustment problems. However, these problems frequently are associated with intergenerational conflicts, the challenges of navigating between their family culture and mainstream American culture, school adjustment, peer acceptance, and identity development. Some commonly reported symptoms among Vietnamese youth are depression, hopelessness, loneliness, anxiety, and low self-esteem.

In the provision of psychological services to Vietnamese individuals and families, it is recommended that mental health professionals have some general knowledge of Vietnamese cultural values (without resorting to stereotypes), historical events surrounding the Vietnam War and its aftermath, and potential cultural biases in Western perspectives of mental health problems and symptoms. Because many Vietnamese may be unfamiliar with psychological treatment, it is also recommended that mental health professionals orient them to the treatment process and be cognizant that clients may be uncomfortable disclosing personal information. In any treatment modality, a thorough assessment of clients' refugee/migration and resettlement history, their experiences and difficulties in the adjustment process, and their perspectives of current problems and what might be causing them is necessary. In addition, an assessment of acculturation is also essential in understanding the mental health status of the individual or family.

In thinking about mental health issues among Vietnamese Americans, both adults and children, it is important to keep in mind the demographic diversity of this population, as well as key contextual and environmental factors that may play significant roles in the manifestation of mental health problems. The length of time in American society also seems important in mental health status and other adjustment outcomes; the longer Vietnamese individuals and families have been in the United States, the better their psychological adjustment. Despite the myriad challenges and difficulties confronted by Vietnamese Americans—and certainly some of these experiences will be ongoing for many individuals and families—they have generally adjusted well to their new country, attesting to the strengths and resiliency of this refugee population.

—Khanh T. Dinh

See also Asian/Pacific Islanders

FURTHER READING

Dinh, K. T., Sarason, B. R., & Sarason, I. G. (1994). Parent–child relationships in Vietnamese immigrant families. *Journal of Family Psychology, 8,* 471–488.

Kibria, N. (1993). *Family tightrope: The changing lives of Vietnamese Americans.* Princeton, NJ: Princeton University Press.

Montero, D. (1979). *Vietnamese Americans: Patterns of resettlement and socioeconomic adaptation in the United States.* Boulder, CO: Westview Press.

Rumbaut, R. G. (1991). The agony of exile: A study of the migration and adaptation of Indochinese refugee adults and children. In F. L. Ahearn & J. L. Athley (Eds.), *Refugee children: Theory, research, and services* (pp. 53–91). Baltimore: Johns Hopkins University Press.

Rutledge, P. J. (1992). *The Vietnamese experience in America.* Bloomington: Indiana University Press.

Uba, L. (1994). *Asian Americans: Personality patterns, identity, and mental health.* New York: The Guilford Press.

Zhou, M., & Bankston, C. L. (1998). *Growing up American: How Vietnamese children adapt to life in the United States.* New York: Russell Sage Foundation.

WHITE PRIVILEGE

White privilege refers the largely unacknowledged and unearned advantages conferred on Caucasian people in the United States at the expense of people of color. White privilege benefits are socially, politically, and economically embedded at the systemic level and internalized at the psychological and interpersonal levels, particularly by Caucasian people (i.e., members of the dominant group). Therefore, Caucasians are resistant to efforts to recognize and ameliorate the causes and effects of the racial hierarchy that maintains these benefits.

At the systemic level, the advantages that Caucasian individuals enjoy include smaller class sizes in the elementary and secondary schools they attend, access to computer technology at home and at school, graduation from four-year colleges and universities, higher salaries, continued employment during economic downturns, access to home ownership and health insurance, and less stringent sentences for criminal offenses.

These manifestations of systemic White privilege are enabled and perpetuated at the psychological and interpersonal levels by the dominant and ethnocentric values of European Americans, conscious and unconscious beliefs in the superiority of Caucasian cultural norms over others, a sense of entitlement to resources, and the power to impose standards that continue to benefit Caucasian people and oppress people of color. Furthermore, the concept of White privilege includes not only a belief in the myth of meritocracy—that democratic choice and opportunity are equally available to all Americans regardless of race—but also an automatic tendency to be surprised by or discount evidence to the contrary. Most Caucasian Americans have been socialized to believe that their educational, financial, and social success is attributed solely to their own efforts and ability (i.e., merit); however, they fail to recognize the uneven playing field of advantage (i.e., their own White privilege) that they take for granted.

Peg McIntosh has identified many examples of the White privilege of daily experience that are outside the awareness of Caucasian people yet contrast perniciously with the daily microaggressions that are unavoidably experienced by people of color. Among these examples, McIntosh noted that Caucasian people take for granted the following advantages:

- They can arrange to be in the company of people of their own race most of the time.
- They can do well in a challenging situation without being called a credit to their race.
- They are never asked to speak for all the people of their racial group.
- They can usually go shopping alone without being followed or harassed by store clerks or security staff.
- If they should need to move, they can likely expect to be able to rent or purchase affordable and desirable housing.
- They can take a job with an affirmative action employer without having coworkers suspect that they got the job because of race.
- They are told about their heritage, which is deemed "civilization," and shown that people of their color made it what it is.
- They can be sure that their children will be given curricular materials that testify to the existence of their race.

From the humanistic, social justice, and multicultural competency perspectives, White privilege does harm to people of color. From an economic standpoint, White privilege limits the human capital resources available to U.S. society. White privilege has negative psychological consequences for Caucasian people by virtue of their collusion, intentional and conscious or not, in subordinating diverse others. White privilege likely reduces the ability of multicultural counseling professionals to accurately perceive or process cognitive information on racial oppression experienced by clients of color.

Therefore, Caucasian people need to raise their daily consciousness of White privilege and work to reconstruct their interpersonal and systemic power imbalances with people of color. Multicultural counseling professionals must develop a critical consciousness of their own experience with White privilege to practice ethically and effectively with clients of color.

—*Margo A. Jackson*

See also Ethnocentrism; Racism and Discrimination; White Racial Identity

FURTHER READING

Arredondo, P., Toporek, R., Brown, S. P., Jones, J., Locke, D. C., Sanchez, J., & Stadler, H. (1996). Operationalization of the multicultural competencies. *Journal of Multicultural Counseling and Development, 24,* 42–78.

Council of Economic Advisors. (1998). *Changing America: Indicators of social and economic well-being by race and Hispanic origin.* Washington, DC: Government Printing Office.

Gushue, G. V., & Carter, R. T. (2000). Remembering race: White racial identity attitude and two aspects of social memory. *Journal of Counseling Psychology, 47,* 199–210.

McIntosh, P. (1988). *White privilege and male privilege: A personal account of coming to see correspondences through work in women's studies* (Working Paper No. 189). Wellesley, MA: Wellesley College Center for Research on Women.

McIntosh, P. (1989, July/August). White privilege: Unpacking the invisible knapsack. *Peace and Freedom, 49,* 10–12.

McIntosh, P. (1998). White privilege: Unpacking the invisible knapsack. In M. McGoldrick (Ed.), *Re-visioning family therapy: Race, culture, and gender in clinical practice* (pp. 147–152). New York: Guilford Press.

National Center for Education Statistics. (2001). *The condition of education.* Washington, DC: U.S. Department of Education.

Neville, H. A., Worthington, R. L., & Spanierman, L. B. (2001). Race, power, and multicultural counseling psychology:

Understanding White privilege and color-blind racial attitudes. In J. G. Ponterotto, J. M. Casas, L. A. Suzuki, & C. M. Alexander (Eds.), *Handbook of multicultural counseling* (2nd ed., pp. 257–288). Thousand Oaks, CA: Sage.

Ridley, C. R., Mendoza, D. W., Kanitz, B. E., Angermeier, L., & Zenk, R. (1994). Cultural sensitivity in multicultural counseling: A perceptual schema model. *Journal of Counseling Psychology, 41,* 125–136.

Sue, D. W. (2003). *Overcoming our racism: The journey to liberation.* San Francisco: Jossey-Bass.

Sue, D. W., Carter, R. T., Casas, J. M., Fouad, N. A., Ivey, A. E., Jensen, M., LaFromboise, T., Manese, J. E., Ponterotto, J. G., & Vasquez-Nuttall, E. (1998). *Multicultural counseling competencies: Individual and organizational development.* Thousand Oaks, CA: Sage.

Sue, D. W., & Sue, D. (2003). *Counseling the culturally diverse: Theory and practice* (4th ed.). New York: Wiley.

Tatum, B. D. (1992). Talking about race, learning about racism: The application of racial identity development theory in the classroom. *Harvard Educational Review, 62,* 1–24.

Texeira, E. (2000, May 22). Justice is not color blind, studies find. *Los Angeles Times,* pp. B1, B8.

WHITE RACIAL IDENTITY

White racial identity theories are an influential framework for understanding individual psychological development in a racialized society. This framework comprises *White racial identity theory* and *White racial consciousness theory*. Issues such as White privilege, social power, and racial ideation are addressed by these theories, which provide a way to understand within-group variation in White racial identities and attitudes. These constructs have been used to determine how people structure racial information cognitively and behaviorally across a wide range of situations and settings, such as counseling dyads, multicultural competence, and sports consultation, and to further theory refinement with regard to the relationship with religious orientation and personality development.

To understand White racial identity theories, one must first have a brief understanding of their history and their association with Black racial identity theories. During the 1970s, to delineate within-group differences among racial groups, racial identity theories were constructed by William Cross and others, particularly those associated with Black racial identity research. Black racial identity models were initially stage models that described psychological responses to an oppressive society. These models, and others that followed, argued that African Americans have differing levels of commitment to the African American community and differing attitudes toward both their in-group and out-group members. These multistage models were advanced by Janet Helms and others who proposed their own racial identity models to include persons from a variety of racial and ethnic backgrounds. Their importance is underscored by the fact that researchers and clinicians can assess and measure within-group racial identity and racial attitudes instead of simplistically stating, for example, "African Americans differ from Caucasians on X variable." Thus, researchers and clinicians could begin to discuss how an individual's racial identity and attitudes differ from another individual's identity attitudes, although they are members of the same racial or ethnic group.

White racial identity models were formulated based on various Black racial identity models, with similar stages that Caucasians may progress through to achieve a nonracist identity. The Helms model is still the most widely considered White racial identity model in the literature. In essence, her model suggests that Caucasians are familiar with their Whiteness and move through a series of stages from being oblivious to racial issues to becoming comfortable with being Caucasian while simultaneously accepting other racial groups. Through the work of Wayne Rowe and colleagues, the White racial consciousness model has recently gained empirical attention as an alternative to White racial identity models. Given the prevalence of Helms's White racial identity model in the literature, an overview will be presented, followed by a description of the White racial consciousness model.

Helms argued that the primary developmental issue for Caucasians is the abandonment of entitlement, that is, understanding the benefits that are gained as a result of being Caucasian in a Caucasian-dominated society. The racial identity theory is premised on the notion that racial identity develops through a sequential process in which more mature ego differentiations occur as the individual matures. Ego status is reflected in dynamic information-processing strategies that people use to deal with racial information; it can be either dominant or nondominant. Observable manifestations of the ego status are called *schemata*. In other words, when racial information appears, the ego selects the dominant status in order to interpret the situation and allows certain information-processing strategies to be engaged; the person responds based on the content of the schemata.

According to Helms's six-stage White racial identity model, Caucasians begin to develop racial identity

in the *contact* status. In this status, Caucasians are oblivious to racism and enjoy the racial status quo. The *disintegration* status is reflected in racial anxiety and ambivalence. Persons in this status are confronted with moral dilemmas surrounding racial issues and must choose between maintaining the status quo or becoming involved with others from other racial and ethnic groups. The *reintegration* status is marked by idealization of the White race and denigration of other racial groups. Persons in this status are likely to color their attitudes based on selective perception. The *pseudo-independence* status is reflected in intellectualized acceptance of other racial groups; however, full acceptance is not attained. Individuals moving into the *immersion/emersion* status begin to consider ways that benefits have accrued to them as a result of being Caucasian. Additionally, there is an initial understanding of their role in a racist society and perhaps activism against racial oppression. Finally, the *autonomy* status includes those persons who possess a positive view of Caucasians but also understand the sociopolitical realities of other racial groups. They perceive the racial world from a more complex perspective and are likely to relinquish racial privileges. To assess these racial identity statuses, the White Racial Identity Attitudes Scale was developed.

During the 1990s, an alternative to the White racial identity model appeared in the racial identity literature. This model, called the White racial consciousness model, is premised on the notion that Caucasians in U.S. society do not typically consider their Whiteness an identity issue and instead possess various attitudes toward racial out-groups. The model differs from White racial identity theory both theoretically and empirically. The model comprises four attitude types that Caucasians have explored cognitively and are committed to: dominative, conflictive, reactive, and integrative. The *dominative* type describes Caucasians who hold attitudes that consider racial minority groups inferior and are strongly racist (e.g., "I believe that minority people are probably not as smart as Whites."). The *conflictive* type describes those who do not ordinarily support obvious discrimination but also do not support programs designed to fight discrimination (e.g., "Welfare programs are used too much by minorities."). *Reactive* attitudes are held by individuals who have almost militant views about the racism they perceive in American society (e.g., "It's impossible to get a fair deal if you are a minority person."). *Integrative* attitudes are represented as a more pragmatic view of racial and ethnic minority issues in that actions are based on the effect they are likely to have (e.g., "I would not mind it if a friend had an intimate relationship with a racial minority person."). The conflictive and reactive types share a concern for the construct of *racial justice*, whereas the dominative and integrative types are opposite ends of a bipolar construct called *racial acceptance*. White racial consciousness is measured using the Oklahoma Racial Attitudes Scale–Revised.

Regardless of which model is used, the field of racial identity theory has grown significantly over the past 10 years. White racial identity has considerable ramifications for a wide range of activities, such as counseling, business, research, government, and organizational activities. It is central to multicultural competence across these settings and domains. For example, recent studies have included identity to determine the conditions under which persons from different racial and ethnic backgrounds can work together effectively in therapy. Much of this ability depends on the identities or racial attitudes of the parties. Theoretically, racial identity and consciousness have significant implications for a host of everyday behaviors—for example, the way that politicians vote on issues that affect persons of color, hiring practices or advancement in business, and the interpretation of test results by psychologists. The field has developed to include instruments that are designed to assess identity and consciousness, but it has only recently begun to include empirically validated applications. Much more research needs to be conducted to determine the impact of identity and consciousness on daily decisions and behaviors. It is hoped that readers will critically assess the field and contribute their own ideas and studies to the scientific literature.

—*Mark M. Leach*

See also European Americans; Minority Status

FURTHER READING

Cross, W. E. (1995). The psychology of Nigrescence: Revising the Cross model. In J. G. Ponterotto, J. M. Casas, L. A. Suzuki, & C. M. Alexander (Eds.), *Handbook of multicultural counseling* (2nd ed., pp. 93–122). Thousand Oaks, CA: Sage.

Helms, J. E. (1995). Update on Helms's racial identity models. In J. G. Ponterotto, J. M. Casas, L. A. Suzuki, & C. M. Alexander (Eds.), *Handbook of multicultural counseling* (2nd ed., pp. 181–198). Thousand Oaks, CA: Sage.

LaFleur, N. K., Rowe, W., & Leach, M. M. (2002). Reconceptualizing White racial consciousness. *Journal of Multicultural Counseling and Development, 30,* 148–152.

Rowe, W., Behrens, J. T., & Leach, M. M. (1995). Racial/ethnic identity and racial consciousness: Looking back and looking forward. In J. G. Ponterotto, J. M. Casas, L. A. Suzuki, & C. M. Alexander (Eds.), *Handbook of multicultural counseling* (2nd ed., pp. 218–235). Thousand Oaks, CA: Sage.

WOMEN OF COLOR

The psychological literature on people of color has accumulated over the past 25 years as the field has recognized the importance of culture in the conceptualization of mental health. The American Psychological Association affirmed the importance of culture in its Guidelines on Multicultural Education, Training, Research, Practice, and Organizational Change for Psychologists, which suggest that future scholarship on people of color should continue to proliferate. The literature on women of color touches on issues ranging from behavioral norms and psychological disorders to the impact of stereotypes and discrimination. Several common themes emerge from this literature that cut across ethnic and racial boundaries, such as disparities in mental health problems, definitions of beauty, identity struggles, gender socialization, role overload, and combating sexism and racism. Because the majority of the psychological literature focuses on one of four ethnic or pan-ethnic groups, this chapter will summarize research involving women of color from four racial or ethnic groups: American Indians and Alaska Natives, Asian Americans and Pacific Islanders, African Americans, and Latina Americans.

AMERICAN INDIAN AND ALASKA NATIVE WOMEN

Limited information exists about American Indian and Alaska Native (AI/AN) women and the psychological issues they face. One major problem is access to this population. In 2003, the U.S. Census Bureau estimated there are approximately 4 million American Indians and Alaska Natives living in the United States, accounting for less than 2% of the U.S. population. Within these 4 million people, there are more than 550 federally recognized tribes, each with a distinct history, culture, and language. This makes it very hard to generalize findings from the few extant studies.

One of the biggest problems facing AI/AN women is that there are only approximately 101 AI/AN mental health providers available per 100,000 members of this ethnic group. This compares with 173 per 100,000 for Caucasians. The U.S. Department of Health and Human Services reports that there are no mental health outcome studies of American Indians and that the failure to conduct clinical research must be addressed.

Several areas of psychological research on AI/AN women align with the findings of the Indian Health Service, which reveal elevated rates of suicide, mortality, depression, and substance abuse in AI/AN women. The high mortality rate of AI/AN women has been one topic of research. Reasons for elevated mortality rates include violence, alcoholism, treatable and preventable diseases (such as diabetes and tuberculosis), and suicide. In addition to higher mortality rates, AI/AN women appear to have higher rates of alcohol use and disorders, anxiety disorders, and anxiety and depression comorbidity compared with other samples of non-AI/AN women in primary care settings.

Depression in AI/AN women is a second research area. According to statistics published by the Indian Health Service, depression affects approximately 75% of AI/AN women seeking services. There are many reasons for the high prevalence of depression in the AI/AN population, including spiritual illness and shame, subjective feelings of rejection and discrimination, inability to acquire upward mobility in American society, guilt stemming from collective and personal denial of one's heritage, and the substantially greater number of personal losses that Native Americans suffer, such as accidental deaths of relatives or friends. Depression is also closely linked to the prevalence of physical and sexual abuse and high rates of suicide within this population.

Given their elevated rates of depression, it is not surprising that suicide attempts are more common among AI/AN women than among their Caucasian counterparts. The abuse of alcohol has been found to be highly related to suicide attempts in this population. For example, researchers investigated the relationship between alcohol use before suicide among American Indians in New Mexico from 1980 to 1998 and found that alcohol was detected in 69% of all suicides compared with 44.3% of the overall population.

Abuse is another area of research on AI/AN women. Native American women experience the highest rates of violent victimization of any race in the United States. Results from studies and surveys over the past several years have consistently found that females report a history of sexual abuse almost twice that of males. This is likely an underrepresentation because, as in other cultures, incestuous relationships are seldom reported because of victims' loyalty to offenders through clan and extended family. Exposure to violence is also linked to a variety of mental health problems. In one study, 87% of women reported some form of physical or sexual abuse in their lifetime, 50% reported a history of depression, and nearly one-third had attempted suicide. It has also been found that younger AI/AN women are more likely to become pregnant when they are the victims of domestic violence. Finally, exposure to violence also is related to increased vulnerability to sexually transmitted diseases, including HIV. Hobfall et al. found that AI/AN women who had been physically or emotionally abused as children were five times more likely to contract a sexually transmitted disease during their lifetime than women who had experienced only marginal or no physical or emotional abuse.

Systemic issues may exacerbate many of the problems discussed here. For example, AI/AN women frequently face racism, sexism, unemployment, and a lack of formal education. According to the *Trends in Indian Health* report, 65.3% of American Indians graduate from high school, compared with 75.2% of the total U.S. population. Only 8.9% have a bachelor's degree or higher, compared with 20.3% for the total population, and females face unemployment of 13.4%, compared with only 6.2% for the total population.

In addition, AI/AN women who live in urban areas (approximately 50% of the population) face other risks. The literature is mixed when it comes to assessing the general well-being of AI/AN women who live in urban versus rural areas. Some argue that urban residence protects against suicide ideation and substance abuse, whereas others assert that it adds to these problems. One study discussed a "triangle of risk" for urban American Indian women whereby sexual trauma, injection drug use, and HIV sexual risk behaviors were higher for urban AI/AN women. These results revealed that 91% of urban AI/AN women had engaged in at least one lifetime HIV sexual or drug risk behavior, including 19% who had had sex with an injection user and 7% who had traded sex for drugs. Another study looked at stressors facing urban AI/AN working mothers that had a negative impact on their psychological well-being. For example, a more highly educated American Indian woman may enjoy greater economic opportunity, but this may come at the expense of acculturating to the majority culture, which can contribute to a significant source of identity conflict and bicultural stress.

Although the majority of the literature on AI/AN women focuses on psychological problems rather than psychological resources and strengths, there is increasing attention to the needs of these women. As a population, AI/AN women would greatly benefit from additional research, which would allow the field to provide more culturally competent services to these women.

ASIAN AMERICAN AND PACIFIC ISLANDER WOMEN

Asian American and Pacific Islander (AA/PI) women residing in the United States are a highly diverse group, encompassing individuals who vary in their ethnicity, cultural background, socioeconomic status, acculturation, education, marital status, and generation. The term *Asian* refers to the people of China, Japan, Korea, India, Southeast Asia, and Asia, and to Pacific Islanders, which include the people of Micronesia, Melanesia, Polynesia, and the U.S. Hawaiian Islands. These groups speak more than 100 different languages and dialects.

There are several common stereotypes of AA/PI women in mainstream culture, and these images have psychological ramifications. Stereotypes depict AA/PI women as exotic and hypersexual (e.g., a "dragon lady"); as childlike, fragile, and innocent (e.g., "China dolls" and "Asian Thumbelinas"); or as asexual, smart, and industrious laborers. It is important to recognize these stereotypes as racist and sexist and to recognize the identity crises that AA/PI women may face when they internalize such stereotypes.

Family issues are an important area of research for AA/PI women. As a group, AA/PI women have the highest rate of interracial marriage. Researchers propose that this population's light skin color, higher socioeconomic status, higher degree of acculturation, higher education, occupational attainment, higher income, proximity to different racial groups, and small numbers contribute to the high rates. Research on gender role conflicts in the family is also found in the literature. For various reasons, AA/PI women have had to become the heads of households,

make unilateral decisions, discipline the children, and acculturate to American ways of life. Because traditional Asian cultures dictate that the male makes most of the family decisions, conflicts can arise in families and between spouses.

Identity is another topic of psychological research on AA/PI women. Identity is a careful balance in which gender, race, culture, class, and the psychological aspects of the self must be integrated. Some of the literature has examined extreme identity conflicts in AA/PI women, such as the desire to physically alter one's appearance to conform to American standards of beauty. For example, some researchers have examined AA/PI women's attempts to change their racial features with eye surgery, nose reconstruction, and breast implants. Such extreme decisions are believed to be a function of racist and sexist beliefs that are projected onto AA/PI women by comparing them to European standards. One aspect of identity that has been ignored in the literature is sexual orientation. Lesbianism and bisexuality are taboo topics in many AA/PI cultures, making research on these women challenging.

Sexuality is another emerging area of psychological research for AA/PI women. Although Asian cultures tend to hold sexually conservative views, this is an issue that greatly affects women because of its connection to abuse and the general health of women. Research has indicated that AA/PI women engage in unsafe sex at rates similar to those of women of other cultures and races; this opens the door to many health concerns, such as sexually transmitted diseases and HIV/AIDS.

Violence is another taboo yet relevant concern for AA/PI women. The tendency among Asian Americans to protect the name of the family makes it difficult to report sexual abuse and domestic violence. Traditional Asian values of close family ties, harmony, and order may not discourage physical and verbal abuse in one's home—in fact, these values may only support the minimization and secrecy of such problems.

All of the topics discussed thus far relate to the general well-being of AA/PI women. Despite the apparent need for mental health interventions in this population, there is a serious problem of underutilization. The stigma and shame that is associated with seeking mental health services appears to be the reason why AA/PI women do not seek services until their problems become overwhelming. Language and cultural barriers also exist. For example, of the mental health care professionals practicing during the late

1990s, there were only approximately 70 Asian American providers for every 100,000 Asian Americans in the United States. To help bridge the gaps—which exist in both the research and practice relating to Asian Americans—there must a proactive commitment to recruiting and training AA/PI psychologists and to supporting research that expands the concept of mental health for these women.

AFRICAN AMERICAN WOMEN

As the descendants of a history of slavery and oppression, African American women, like other women of color, must overcome many barriers in their daily lives. Having survived the legacy of slavery, which made women pieces of property, African American women must forge their own identities in spite of prevalent stereotypes and exposure to external and internal racism. Fortunately, many African American women have the assistance of a strong kinship network that helps to buffer the effects of racism and strengthen their cultural pride. The field of psychology can help by articulating the barriers and coping mechanisms related to the mental health concerns of African American women.

According to the 2000 U.S. Census, 36 million people (12.9% of the population) identify themselves as being of African descent. Despite their representation as one of the largest ethnic minority groups in the United States, racism is a large part of the African American experience, and sexism is an additional burden for African American women. The nexus of racism and sexism is often reflected in stereotypes of African American women, which threaten their psychological well-being. One such stereotype is that African American women are impulsive, sexually promiscuous, morally loose, strong, aggressive, and lacking in emotional control in comparison to their Caucasian counterparts. These stereotypes often lead African American women to internalize racism, resulting in identity conflicts.

Mainstream culture exacerbates these identity conflicts by valuing physical features that are associated with Whiteness, a value that has permeated African American culture. Often, African American women whose features are most Caucasian are valued and appreciated above others in the family and community. Although it may be beneficial to be considered attractive by mainstream society, these women still experience difficulties within the African American community, which may view them as not "Black" enough. For many, judging oneself against any external standard results in a sense of inadequacy and internalized oppression, which can have serious psychological effects. Although other ethnic groups manifest eating disorders as one such psychological effect, African American women appear to be at less risk than other ethnic women of developing an eating disorder. There is a need for research that examines the consequences of stereotypes and internalized racism on the identity of African American women.

African American women's role in society and the family has also been a topic of psychological research. African American women are often expected to contribute to the family out of financial necessity. This contribution has not been limited to traditional female professions. African American women have been expected to work in all forms of manual labor. Often, African American women also continue to serve as heads of their households. This has been a source of conflict in some African American families, where men may feel emasculated by the woman's ability to find a job while they cannot. Ironically, blame is sometimes placed on the woman for occupying the traditional "man's place" instead of focusing on the larger systemic issues that create unemployment and underemployment for African American men.

Despite the fact that African American women are better represented in the workplace than men in some instances, they must deal with racism and doubts about their abilities, which may lead women to question their success in the workplace. African American women may be led to believe they gained their positions only because of affirmative action, causing them to develop what is known as *imposter syndrome.*

As for other women of color, the underutilization of psychological services is an issue for African American women. Often, women in this community have difficulty seeking psychological help because they are used to serving in a caretaking role (i.e., the "Superwoman" syndrome). They also may be reluctant to take time for themselves when it could be used to care for others. Admitting that they may need someone to address their needs may invoke a sense of disloyalty to the family. Therefore, psychologists must find ways to make their services more available and attractive to those in the African American community who might need them.

In terms of future research on African American women, it is important to look specifically at African

American cultural values involving family and religion to gain insight into the strengths of African American women. For example, some recent research has found that spirituality and a psychological sense of community are related to low-income African American women's ability to cope with adversity. Additionally, examining vocational successes—despite racism and the imposter syndrome—might serve as an indication of how resiliency develops among African American women. Healthy body image also seems to be a strength for African American women, and understanding their lower risk for eating disorders is another important area for future research. In conclusion, African American women have much to teach psychologists about persistence and coping with oppression, and the field must do more to support the psychological and physical health of African American women.

LATINA AMERICANS

Latina American women find themselves navigating between two cultures—their ancestors' place of origin and their current home, the United States. When we speak about Latina Americans as a group, it is important to remember that this population comprises many ethnic and national backgrounds. The term *Latina American* itself may be a point of contention; may women of Latin American descent prefer nationalistic labels (e.g., Cuban, Mexican). In 1978, the Office of Management and Budget imposed the umbrella term *Hispanic* to describe people of Latin American descent. For many, however, Hispanic is an unacceptable identifier because it is an imposed label. In this brief discussion, the term *Latina American* will be used to describe women of Latin American descent who are living in the United States.

Many Latina Americans were born in the United States, whereas others, either independently or with their families, made the choice to start a new life in a new country. According to the U.S. Census Bureau, in 2003, there were 37.4 million people of Latin American descent in the United States, representing 13.3% of the total population. Because they belong to several minority groups (women and people of color), Latina Americans have special considerations that may have an effect on their mental health. Immigrant status may lead Latina Americans to feel different and experience feelings of alienation and isolation from their mainstream American counterparts. Those living in the United States illegally must live with the fear

and anxiety of being discovered and deported. Often employed in low-status work, Latina Americans must endure the stress of negotiating a society that benefits from their labor yet views their existence as unwanted.

Family is the stronghold that binds Latinas and provides a sense of connection and identification with one's culture. Family influences affect the gender roles, religion, language, education, and career aspirations of Latina Americans. It is not unusual to find that the head of the household is a dominant male in many Latino American families. Though this is true for some families, it is not true for all, but gender role conflicts can be present for Latina Americans within their families where such traditions exist.

Placing the family's well-being over one's own individual achievement may be viewed as a lack of assertiveness or as a sense of collectivism, depending on one's view or bias. Even for Latina Americans who have challenged this expectation and have entered the workforce out of economic need or for their own fulfillment, vocational obligations become an extension of their responsibilities to the family, which can result in role overload. Seeking formal education may also put Latina Americans in direct conflict with cultural values. In such circumstances, the Latina American may be accused of being a "sellout" or a *vendida* for attempting to be too White and for elevating education above family obligations. This is a difficult path for Latina Americans, as the label *vendida* can be conveniently extended to all areas of her life: her choice of language, style, television show preferences, and romantic relationships.

Latina Americans are vulnerable to gender role expectations that may be unrealistic. One's reputation must remain pristine in all areas of life because it not only reflects on the woman but also on the family as a whole. This seems to place Latina Americans in the position of walking a fine line between Madonna and whore. That is, the stereotypes that are often applied to this population portray Latinas as saintly or unrealistically perfect (i.e., like the Madonna) or as amoral and hypersexual (i.e., a whore). Because they are influenced greatly by the Catholic church, many families do value a woman's virginity and naïveté. Female sexuality is a taboo subject that is moderated by religious beliefs and social mores.

Latina American lesbians face even greater barriers because of traditional family gender role stereotypes that value marriage and children for daughters. For many Latina Americans who come out of the closet, disapproval or even expulsion from the family and community may result. This can be exacerbated for Latina American lesbians who are immigrants. As an immigrant, a mourning process may be involved for the loss not only of the home country but also of a level of comfort that surrounds her with family.

As is the case for other women of color, Latina Americans face barriers to receiving psychological services, such as monolingual service providers, cultural stigmas on taking private matters outside the family, and alternative, supernatural conceptualizations of mental health. The ability to create accessible psychological services for Latina Americans and other women of color is intimately tied to increasing our knowledge of the psychological needs of this group.

Although research on the psychology of Latina Americans is beginning to reveal important findings, additional questions are emerging. In particular, it would be beneficial to test the relationships between stereotypes and identity development, feminist consciousness and gender roles, and phenotype and stigmatization within the Latino American community. For psychologists, research that centers on counselor expectations and comparisons of Latina Americans with women of other ethnic groups might help to develop more culturally competent treatments.

There is a great deal of good that psychologists can do in the Latino American community in general and with Latinas specifically. One key to addressing the needs of Latinas is to have a stronger knowledge base on which to design interventions.

CONCLUSION

This entry has provided an overview of many important issues that are relevant to the lives of women of color. However, it should be clear that many questions have yet to be answered. Women of color represent an important population for psychologists, and the need for increased attention from researchers is highly warranted. As the psychological scholarship on women of color continues to develop, the ability to offer culturally competent care will increase.

—*Elizabeth M. Vera*
—*Veronica Vasquez*
—*Rebecca Corona*

FURTHER READING

Anderson, K. (1996). *Changing woman: A history of racial ethnic women in modern America.* New York: Oxford University Press.

Bohn, D. K. (2003). Lifetime physical and sexual abuse, substance abuse, depression, and suicide attempts among Native American women. *Issues in Mental Health Nursing, 24,* 333–352.

Comas-Diaz, L., & Greene, B. (Eds.). (1994). *Women of color: Integrating ethnic and gender identities in psychotherapy.* New York: Guilford Press.

Niemann, Y. F. (2004). Stereotypes of Chicanas and Chicanos: Impact on family functioning, individual expectations, goals, and behavior. In R. J. Velasquez, L. M. Arellano, & B. W. McNeill (Eds.), *The handbook of Chicana/o psychology and mental health* (pp. 61–82). Mahwah, NJ: Lawrence Erlbaum.

Pinderhughes, E. (1989). *Understanding race, ethnicity, and power: The key to efficacy in clinical practice.* New York: Free Press.

Root, M. P. P. (1998). Women. In L. C. Lee & N. W. S. Zane (Eds.), *Handbook of Asian American psychology* (pp. 211–231). Thousand Oaks, CA: Sage.

WORLDVIEWS

Worldviews shape the philosophies of a culture and guide a society's institutional policies. In turn, the broadly conceived philosophies of these entities influence individuals and groups and give meaning to individual life experiences. Although one's worldview affects individual life experiences, the societal and cultural practices that evolve from social, moral, religious, educational, economic, and political customs are shared with other members in an individual's reference group. A worldview is an unspoken but inevitable outcome of the socialization process, yet it is all but invisible: A worldview is a set of conceptual lenses through which to view the surrounding environment without "seeing" itself.

FRAMEWORKS

A useful philosophical framework that can be applied to define the concept of worldview is *root metaphor theory.* This theory suggests that personal and social constructions of the world can be organized into four fundamental categories: formism, mechanism, contextualism, and organicism. *Formism* is informed by trait and type models and by theories and psychiatric diagnostic practices that are based on medical model classification schema. *Mechanism* is influenced by the notion of strict psychic determinism, which is prominent in Freud's dynamic principle and in learning theories based on the analysis of stimuli, responses, and consequences. *Contextualism* is defined by relationships within contexts: Observers are a part of the phenomena they observe, and knowledge cannot be separated from the perspective and vision of those who define the content of what is known. *Organicism* views the world in terms of complex patterns or constellations that rely on holistic, patterned, and systemic thinking rather than on single elements or linear relationships.

CULTURAL AND SOCIOPOLITICAL IMPLICATIONS

Notions of culture are often interchangeable with the meanings given to worldview. However, the differences between culture and worldview are rooted in what is and is not observable; culture is readily apparent and observable, whereas a worldview is indirectly conveyed through cognition and value orientation. Some observers of culture believe that cultural differences exist because of the variability in worldviews; others suggest that a relationship exists between worldview and culture, but culture is not determined by worldview. The latter explanation is influenced by two cognitive theories: *locus of control* and *locus of responsibility.* According to these theories, worldview is not defined by culture alone but is influenced by the interplay between the interpretation given to culture and the construction of worldview. In this recursive interaction, the locus of control may be an *internal* locus of control, which encourages the individual to take personal responsibility in constructing an optimal worldview, or an *external* locus of control, which places responsibility on tradition or fate rather than individual action and determination.

Worldview may be strongly correlated with sociopolitical history. For example, the worldviews of racial minority populations are often influenced by the dominant population, which defines a minority group by a set of denigrating values while believing that it possesses idealized values. These dichotomous and stereotyped attributions lead to worldviews that affect the social, political, and economic aspects of people's lives.

VALUE ORIENTATIONS

Values and their specific orientations are reflected in the worldview of a culture and mirror the variations that occur in cultural value orientations. The noted anthropologist Clyde Kluckhohn considered value orientations to be generalized and organized conceptions of

several dimensions: *time,* the temporal focus of human life; *activity,* the preferred pattern of action in interpersonal relations; *relational orientation,* the preferred way of relating in groups; *humans-nature orientation,* the way people relate to the natural or the supernatural environment; and the *basic nature of humans,* the attitudes held about the innate good or evil in human behavior. In addition to Kluckhohn's dimensions, a wide variety of other dimensions have been proposed: power distance, uncertainty avoidance, individualism–collectivism, and masculinity–femininity.

The comparison of value orientations provides a useful way of contrasting differences between worldviews. For example, if the worldviews of the African, Hispanic, Native American, Asian, and U.S. cultures were considered along the dimension of time, the U.S. culture would consider time to be the future, Hispanics would consider time to be the present, and Native Americans, Asians, and Africans would conceive of time as the past, a reflection of their homage to ancestors. For the dimension of activity, the worldview of the U.S. culture focuses on doing rather than being, as does the Hispanic culture, whereas African, Asian, and Native populations focus on being-in-becoming. Relational dimensions of the U.S. worldview are individualistic, whereas in African, Asian, Native American, and some Hispanic cultures, collectivism is a prominent relational factor. In the relationship of humans to nature, the worldview of the U.S. culture promotes domination over nature rather than subjugation to it, whereas the worldviews of Hispanic cultures emphasize harmony with it, as do the worldviews of African, Asian, and Native cultures. In Asian, African, and Native cultures, the worldview of the intrinsic nature of humans is basically good, whereas in Hispanic cultures, human nature is flawed, and in U.S. culture, human nature is a mix of neutral, good, and flawed. The dimensions expressed in worldviews are so embedded that members of a culture may not be aware of the influence of their value orientations.

CLINICAL APPLICATIONS AND WORLDVIEW

The worldviews of clients and clinicians affect every aspect of clinical application, from engaging clients at the initial stage of treatment, progressing through the treatment process, assessing clients and their presenting issues, and selecting a specific treatment modality. Even before the first encounter, the worldviews of clinicians and clients have already shaped their expectations of treatment and attitudes about the other participant. Skin color, language usage, and dialects are immediate and visible manifestations of assumed differences in worldviews. Other factors, such as the meaning of mental health, familiarity with mental health services, notions about symptom relief, and expectations about the clinician's role, are also affected by worldview. If clinicians develop treatment plans and goals that are consistent with their own worldview but do not adapt them to their clients' worldviews, treatment interventions may be irrelevant, blocked, and even discontinued.

—*MaryAnna Domokos-Cheng Ham*

FURTHER READING

Ibrahim, F. A., Roysircar-Sodowsky, G., & Ohnishi, H. (2000). Worldview: Recent developments and needed directions. In J. G. Ponterotto, J. M. Casas, L. A. Suzuki, & C. M. Alexander (Eds.), *Handbook of multicultural counseling* (2nd ed., pp. 425–456). Thousand Oaks, CA: Sage.

Kluckhohn, F. R., & Strodtbeck, F. L. (1961). *Variations in value orientations*. Evanston, IL: Row, Peterson.

Lyddon, W. J. (1989). Root metaphor theory: A philosophical framework for counseling and psychotherapy. *Journal of Counseling and Development, 67,* 442–448.

Roysircar-Sodowsky, G., & Johnson, P. (1993). Worldviews: Culturally learned assumptions and values. In P. Pedersen & J. C. Carey (Eds.), *Multicultural counseling in schools: A practical handbook* (pp. 59–79). Boston: Allyn & Bacon.

XENOPHOBIA

The word *xenophobia* comes from the Greek words *xénos* ("stranger" or "guest") and *phóbos* ("fear"), which, when combined, mean "fear of strangers." The word was first used in a novel by Anatole France in 1901 and first appeared in a French dictionary in 1906. Several years later, it began appearing in English-language dictionaries.

The word *xenophobia* is widely used by the mass media and by political actors and has entered everyday language. It is not a word commonly used by psychologists, who prefer more theoretically defined concepts, such as *stereotypes, prejudice,* and *ethnocentrism.*

In social psychology, xenophobia is normally interpreted as a logical extension of ethnocentrism. *Ethnocentrism* was originally coined by William Graham Sumner and denotes a process that simultaneously produces in-group solidarity and out-group hostility as a result of the human striving for belonging, for "we-ness." The *us* is defined against *them.* Like ethnocentrism, xenophobia is characterized by a belief that it is natural for people to live among others of their own kind and have a corresponding hostility toward people of another kind. However, this hostility need not be activated until strangers come too close to the in-group (in geographical space or in social space) and are believed to threaten the identity (beliefs, practices, mores, and traditional values) or the material interests of the in-group. Strangers at a distance will not meet with the same hostility or be as feared. The ambiguous etymological meaning of *xenophobia,* fear of strangers or guests, is thus very apt: it is strangers as unwanted *guests* that are being feared or met with hostility.

Yet, in social science, as in everyday speech, *xenophobia* has increasingly come to mean *hatred* of strangers rather than fear of strangers. Simultaneously, social scientists have increasingly used the concept of xenophobia to denote hatred of immigrants or other ethnic minorities, rather than of strangers. This is an unfortunate development. The strength of the concept of xenophobia is in its broader definition, which includes more than racism and ethnic prejudice. As shown by Norbert Elias and John L. Scotson's study of the small English city "Winston Parva," xenophobia may be highly manifest also when members of two opposing groups belong to the same race, ethnicity, religion, and social class. In the case of Winston Parva, one group happened to have lived in the city longer (they were the *established*) than the other (the *newcomers*). The established defined themselves against the newcomers and did not want to mingle with the newcomers, whose badness and impurity the established feared would infect them. Xenophobia may thus result from either a real or a perceived threat to the identity or interests of an individual or an in-group to which one belongs, posed by someone belonging to an out-group or by the out-group as a whole.

Therefore, one may argue that xenophobia (understood as fear of strangers—or as hostile skepticism toward strangers—as unwanted guests) is a relatively basic and mostly unconscious phenomenon. Xeno-phobia thus understood is not something that has to be learned during the course of one's life or that emerged at some point in history, but rather is something that one has to learn how to become free of.

—Jens Rydgren

See also Anti-Semitism; Racism and Discrimination

FURTHER READING

Elias, N., & Scotson, J. L. (1994). *The established and the outsiders: A sociological enquiry into community problems.* London: Sage.

Rydgren, J. (2004). The logic of xenophobia. *Rationality and Society, 16*(2), 123–148.

Sumner, W. G. (1906). *Folkways.* New York: Ginn.

Index

Southeast Asian Americans, 437–443
  at-risk groups within, 441
  barriers to mainstream treatment, traditional methods and, 442
  child-rearing practices and, 440
  culturally sensitive psychotherapy and, 443
  cultural values/belief systems and, 441–442
  education and, 440
  employment, English-language proficiency and, 439
  family dynamics, changes in, 439–440
  gang activity and, 440–441
  historical overview of, 438
  intergroup differences and, 441
  mental health services and, 441–442
  postmigration challenges, 439–441
  premigration trauma, postmigration psychosocial adjustment and, 438–439
  psychological distress and, 441
  psychosocial challenges of, 438–441
  racism and, 440
  treatment modality preferences and, 442
  See also Asian/Pacific Islander Americans (APIAs)
Speight, S., 313, 316
Spiritism, 377–378, 408–409
Spirituality, 407, 443–445
  African Americans and, 444
  Asian Americans and, 445
  ethnic minorities and, 443–444
  Hispanic Americans and, 444
  impact of, 445
  Native Americans and, 444–445
  See also Religion
Spitzer, R., 162, 163
Stake theory, 188
Standardized tests, 1
  learning potential assessment and, 2
  translation and, 457
  See also Education; Scholastic Aptitude Test (SAT)
Stanford-Binet test, 207, 261–262
Steinberg, L., 347
Steketee, G., 47
Stereotype threat phenomenon, 399–400, 448
Stereotyping:
  covert stressor of, 448
  dozens and, 157–158
  ethnic identity development and, 179
  racial stereotyping, 2, 22
  social attributions and, 62–63
  See also Racism and discrimination
Sterilization, 208
Stewart, N. A., 28
Stewart, S. M., 348
Stigma, 24, 26, 61, 449
Stowe, H. B., 461
Strauss, A. L., 382
Stress, 445–450
  acculturative stress, 6, 7, 18, 152, 448–449
  covert stressors, stereotypes/racism and, 448
  cultural identity, stigma and, 449
  history of, 445–446

  institutional racism and, 449
  language/communication stress, 449
  life span multicultural stress, 449–450
  life stress perspective, 93
  power/privilege, multicultural stress and, 446–448, 450
  race-related stress, 398
  See also Coping mechanisms; Psychological distress
Substance Abuse and Mental Health Services Administration, 38
Substance abuse. *See* Alcohol/substance use and abuse
Subtle and Blatant Prejudice Scales, 293
Sue, D., 47, 179, 209, 312, 313, 329
Sue, D. W., 47, 51, 179, 209, 311, 312, 313, 317, 318, 320, 321, 329, 393
Sue, S., 51
Suicide, 450–452
  African Americans and, 451
  Alaska Natives and, 32, 33
  alcohol/substance use and abuse and, 39
  Asian Americans and, 451–452
  Filipino Americans and, 220
  Hispanic Americans and, 451
  historical trauma and, 232
  Native Americans and, 452
  protective factors, promotion of, 452
  suicidal ideation and, 18
Suinn-Lew Asian Self-Identity Acculturation Scale (SL-ASIA), 9, 13, 17, 183
Sukra prameha syndrome, 49
Sumner, F. C., 27
Sumner, W. G., 204, 267, 483
Support. *See* Social support
Susto syndrome, 48, 134, 144–145
Szapocznik, J., 184, 228, 230
Szasz, T. S., 158

Tai Chi, 101
Taifel, H., 187, 266, 388
Taijin-kyofu-sho (TKS) syndrome, 50, 55–56, 145–146
Taking the attitude of the other (TAO), 275–276
Teaching racial identity, 453–455
  framework for, 453–454
  process/concept of racial identity and, 454–455
  racial identity development, facilitation of, 453
  racial identity messages, content of, 454
Tell-Me-A-Story (TEMAS) test, 370
Temporary Aid for Needy Families (TANF), 241
Terman, L. M., 207, 387
Thematic Apperception Test (TAT), 370
Thomas, C. W., 185
Thomas, R. R., 344
Thompson, C. E., 323
Three-Stage Ethnic Identity Development Model, 395
Ting-Toomey, S., 107
Title VII, 171
Title IX, 168
Toarmino, D., 47
Tokenism/psychology of tokenism, 455–456
Torres Straits Expedition, 387
Torrey, E. F., 250